W9-BVT-971

Caribbean Sea

ATLANTIC OCEAN

CENTRAL AMERICA

Gulf of Panama

Galápagos Islands (Ecuador)

PACIFIC OCEAN

VENEZUELA **GUYANA**

SURINAME **FRENCH GUIANA (France)**

COLOMBIA

ECUADOR

PERU

BRAZIL

BOLIVIA

PARAGUAY

CHILE

ARGENTINA

URUGUAY

ATLANTIC OCEAN

Orinoco R.
Negro R.
Amazon R.
Madeira R.
Tapajós R.
Xingu R.
Tocantins R.
São Francisco R.
Paraguay R.
Paraná R.
Río de la Plata

Maracaibo
Santa Marta
Barranquilla
Cartagena
Coro
Barquisimeto
Caracas
Barcelona
Cumaná
Maturín
Maracay
Valencia
Mérida
Barinas
Cúcuta
Bucaramanga
San Cristóbal
Ciudad Guayana
Ciudad Bolívar
Georgetown
Paramaribo
Medellín
Manizales
Pereira
Tunja
Villavicencio
Bogotá
Cali
Neiva
Pasto
Florencia
Boa Vista
Macapá
Esmeraldas
Quito
Ibarra
Portoviejo
Ambato
Riobamba
Guayaquil
Cuenca
Machala
Loja
Iquitos
Manaus
Santarém
Belém
São Luís
Piura
Cajamarca
Chiclayo
Pucallpa
Fortaleza
Teresina
Natal
João Pessoa
Trujillo
Huánuco
Rio Branco
Porto Velho
Chimbote
Cerro de Pasco
Recife
Maceió
Lima
Huancayo
Cusco
Aracaju
Ayacucho
Ica
Trinidad
Cuiabá
Brasília
Salvador
Juliaca
La Paz
Goiânia
Arequipa
Cochabamba
Santa Cruz
Tacna
Oruro
Sucre
Uberlândia
Belo Horizonte
Arica
Potosí
Campo Grande
Iquique
Tarija
Pedro Juan Caballero
Vitória
Antofagasta
San Salvador de Jujuy
Salta
Asunción
Campinas
Rio de Janeiro
São Paulo
San Miguel de Tucumán
Ciudad del Este
Santos
Niterói
Copiapó
Resistencia
Posadas
Encarnación
Curitiba
Catamarca
Santiago del Estero
Corrientes
Florianópolis
La Serena
La Rioja
Córdoba
Santa Fe
Rivera
Porto Alegre
San Juan
Mendoza
Salto
Paysandú
Valparaíso
Rosario
Santiago
San Luis
Buenos Aires
Montevideo
Talca
Rancagua
Concepción
Chillán
Bahía Blanca
Mar del Plata
Temuco
Neuquén
Puerto Montt
Comodoro Rivadavia

Falkland Islands (Islas Malvinas) (U.K.)

Strait of Magellan
Punta Arenas
Ushuaia

South America

Elevation in Feet
15,000
10,000
5,000
2,000
1,000
0
Below sea level

Major Cities
⊛ Capital city
■ Over 5,000,000
● 1,000,000–5,000,000
▪ 500,000–999,999
● 250,000–499,999
• 100,000–249,999
○ Less than 100,000

0   250   500 mi.
0   250   500 km

ENCYCLOPEDIA OF

LATIN AMERICAN HISTORY AND CULTURE

EDITORIAL BOARD

ENCYCLOPEDIA OF

LATIN AMERICAN HISTORY AND CULTURE

SECOND EDITION

Volume 1

A–B

Jay Kinsbruner

EDITOR IN CHIEF

Erick D. Langer

SENIOR EDITOR

CHARLES SCRIBNER'S SONS
A part of Gale, Cengage Learning

Detroit • New York • San Francisco • New Haven, Conn • Waterville, Maine • London

Encyclopedia of Latin American History and Culture

Jay Kinsbruner, Editor in Chief
Erick D. Langer, Senior Editor

For product information and technology assistance, contact us at
Gale Customer Support, 1-800-877-4253.
For permission to use material from this text or product,
submit all requests online at **www.cengage.com/permissions.**
Further permissions questions can be emailed to
permissionrequest@cengage.com

While every effort has been made to ensure the reliability of the information presented in this publication, Gale, a part of Cengage Learning, does not guarantee the accuracy of the data contained herein. Gale accepts no payment for listing; and inclusion in the publication of any organization, agency, institution, publication, service, or individual does not imply endorsement of the editors or publisher. Errors brought to the attention of the publisher and verified to the satisfaction of the publisher will be corrected in future editions.

Library of Congress Cataloging-in-Publication Data

Encyclopedia of Latin American history and culture / Jay Kinsbruner, editor in chief; Erick D. Langer, senior editor. -- 2nd ed.
    p. cm. --
Includes bibliographical references and index.
    ISBN 978-0-684-31270-5 (set) -- ISBN 978-0-684-31441-9 (vol. 1) -- ISBN 978-0-684-31442-6 (vol. 2) -- ISBN 978-0-684-31443-3 (vol. 3) -- ISBN 978-0-684-31444-0 (vol. 4) -- ISBN 978-0-684-31445-7 (vol. 5) -- ISBN 978-0-684-31598-0 (vol. 6)
    1. Latin America--Encyclopedias. I. Kinsbruner, Jay.

F1406.E53 2008
980.003--dc22   2008003461

Gale
27500 Drake Rd.
Farmington Hills, MI, 48331-3535

978-0-684-31270-5 (set)   0-684-31270-0 (set)
978-0-684-31441-9 (vol. 1)   0-684-31441-X (vol. 1)
978-0-684-31442-6 (vol. 2)   0-684-31442-8 (vol. 2)
978-0-684-31443-3 (vol. 3)   0-684-31443-6 (vol. 3)
978-0-684-31444-0 (vol. 4)   0-684-31444-4 (vol. 4)
978-0-684-31445-7 (vol. 5)   0-684-31445-2 (vol. 5)
978-0-684-31598-0 (vol. 6)   0-684-31598-X (vol. 6)

This title is also available as an e-book.
ISBN-13: 978-0-684-31590-4 ISBN-10: 0-684-31590-4
Contact your Gale, a part of Cengage Learning, sales representative for ordering information.

Printed in the United States of America
1 2 3 4 5 6 7 12 11 10 09 08

IN MEMORIAM

This work is dedicated to the memory of Jay Kinsbruner, Editor in Chief, who passed away on October 6, 2007, just as the encyclopedia was entering its final phase of production.

Jay was a tireless worker who cared deeply about the study of Latin America. Jay's thoughtful leadership served as an inspiration to his colleagues. His hard-driving work ethic, which kept him at his desk well into his illness, had far-reaching momentum as members of the Editorial Board and project staff labored to keep pace.

No one can single-handedly produce a multi-volume reference work, especially one that attempts to profile such a large subject by way of so many individual entries. However Jay, more than any other person, is responsible for transforming a colossus of words and ideas into a focused, authoritative encyclopedia. Jay was a true professional, and he will be missed.

EDITORIAL AND PRODUCTION STAFF

Project Editor
Scot Peacock

Art Editor
Jennifer Wisinski

Editorial Support
Angela Allen, Deirdre Blanchfield, Shawn Corridor, Douglas Dentino, Angela
Doolin, Jason Everett, Alan Hedblad, John McCoy, Mark Mikula, Jenai Mynatt,
Rebecca Parks, Carol Schwartz, Andrew Specht, Jennifer Stock, Ken
Wachsberger

Editorial Assistants
Andrea Fritsch, Lauren Grace, Carly Kaloustian, Darcy Thompson

Copyeditors
Anne Davidson, Jessica Hornik Evans, John Krol, Michael Levine, Mary Russell,
Linda Sanders, Drew Silver

Researchers
Emily Berquist, Jennifer Bookbinder, Byron Crites, Daniela Garreton, Meredith
Glueck, Sean Goforth, Amanda Gray, Monica Hernandez, James McBride, Kelly
McDonough, Joshua Nadel, Jana Nelson, Naomi Wood, Jackie Zahn

Proofreaders
Carol Holmes, Melodie Monahan, Kathleen Wilson

Captions
Sheryl Ciccarelli, Meredith Glueck

Translations
Comms Multilingual

Cartography
Mapping Specialists

Custom Graphics
GGS Information Services, Pre-PressPMG

Indexer
Katharyn Dunham

Technical Support
Mark Drouillard, Mark Springer

Page Design
Pamela A. E. Galbreath

Imaging
Lezlie Light

Permissions
Dean Dauphinais, Kelly Quin, Jhanay Williams

Manufacturing
Wendy Blurton

Editorial Director
John Fitzpatrick

Publisher
Jay Flynn

CONTENTS

INTRODUCTION

This, the second edition of the *Encyclopedia of Latin American History and Culture*, is a monumental work and represents the best of scholarship on Latin America. Based on the landmark first edition published in 1996, the second edition incorporates new material in substantial ways. It includes 568 new entries, expanding the total number of articles to 5824. One hundred and fifty-five articles have been replaced and 403 were substantially revised. More than 4,000 bibliographies were updated and 537 entries were partially revised and had bibliographic updates. Of the 3322 biographies, 366 are new and the rest have been revised, replaced, or updated. Debuting in this edition are eight new "Mega Essays," authored by renowned specialists and treating such important themes as "Democracy," "Economic Development," "Hispanics in the United States," and "Race and Ethnicity" in articles of up to 10,000 words.

This edition has been careful to include Spanish and Portuguese-language sources as much as possible, since the vast bulk of knowledge about the region is produced by Latin Americans themselves. It also includes many more Latin American authors—about a quarter of the total new contributors—many of whom initially wrote their entries in their respective languages.

Other new features are an extensive chronology that is useful in placing events, processes, and people into their appropriate temporal contexts; a thematic outline of subjects with a separate table of biographical subjects by profession; maps for all Latin American countries; a new and revitalized selection of photos and illustrations; and six full-color photo essays presented as an insert in each volume.

The Encyclopedia has retained the best characteristics of the first edition, written under the editorship of Barbara Tenenbaum and her team of editors and contributors. They deserve credit for conceiving this massive work and bringing it to fruition more than ten years ago. It immediately became the standard of reference for the field and marked a turning point for Latin American scholarship in terms of encyclopedic scope and level of detail. For this reason, we have remained inclusive of all periods, going from prehistoric times to the present. Cultural issues continue to occupy an important place. Biographies of important personages remain the single largest category (with more than 3300 entries). The

Portuguese empire and Brazil are treated equally and the non-Spanish-speaking Caribbean countries are also included.

This edition strives to set a new, even higher, standard. Extensive updating was necessary because the fields of Latin American history and culture have changed considerably. Initially, plans were made to produce a supplement. However, it quickly became clear that too much needed to be updated and instead a new edition was planned. Latin America as a subject of study has exploded since the last edition of the Encyclopedia. New research areas have opened up and we understand old and new processes much better. A partial list of these new areas includes the following: New finds have revolutionized the field of Latin American archaeology, especially for the Andes and the Amazon. Atlantic history has enriched our analysis of colonial economic and cultural processes. The new institutional economic history has been instrumental in understanding economic development in Latin America. The field of nineteenth-century political history has been revitalized by focusing on the construction of the nation-states and the role of subalterns in this process. The postmodern twist to culture and identity has stimulated much debate. The study of gender has broadened our understanding of women and the relationship between the sexes. The recognition that indigenous peoples have played an active role in recent Latin American history has led to research on ethnic movements and a reconsideration of their roles farther into the past. These are among the many new topics that have led to a greater comprehension of the region.

Also, Latin America has changed considerably since the mid-1990s. Electoral democracy has been more firmly established in the hemisphere. Mexico is no longer a one-party state. Leftist leaders have taken power through elections in Brazil, Bolivia, Ecuador, Venezuela, and Nicaragua. Some leaders, such as Hugo Chávez of Venezuela, have tried to make common cause against the United States. Latin American literature, music, and cinema have become mainstream and are known throughout the world. In many countries, indigenous movements have emerged and have had a significant impact on local and national levels. Economic growth has returned to the region, though economic disparities between the rich and the poor, with few exceptions, remain as stark as before. Trade zones have increased in importance, including NAFTA, Mercosur, and ALBA. Emigration from Latin America has accelerated. Although the United States remains the largest recipient country, the European Union and Canada have also absorbed large number of Latin Americans. Be that as it may, in the United States "Hispanics" have become the largest minority, overtaking African Americans. Entries to reflect these facts have been incorporated into this edition.

Encyclopedias are meant to pull together a body of knowledge that will stand the test of time and can serve as references for many years to come. Nevertheless, encyclopedias also reflect current events and, certainly, current perspectives on history and the present. This encyclopedia is no different. In this case, however, the editors have consciously addressed the tension between current interpretations and historical "facts." This has led to the inclusion of "Mega Essays." They are lengthy essays that summarize the state of knowledge in particular fields and contextualize the entries contained in the Encyclopedia. They include highly respected scholars such as John Coatsworth and José Moya. The authors also provide their own interpretation of their field and so these treatises are also original contributions to the scholarly literature, though written for a broad audience. These entries are (in no particular order): "Race and Ethnicity," "Migration and Migrations," "Democracy," "Hispanics in the United States," "Economic Development," "Hemispheric Affairs," "Nationhood and the Imagination," and "Globalization." Written by foremost experts in their respective fields, they create a narrative, pulling together the disparate articles into coherent sets of knowledge. They are intended for the reader who wants to get a good overview of larger issues. These essays are an important supplement to the joys of leafing through a work such as this and picking out interesting entries to read.

This edition also is different because it incorporates even more cultural content than in the pathbreaking first one. There are nearly 600 photographs, tables, charts, maps, and other images, including six full-color photo essays on the regions and cultures and arts of Latin America. A great number of the new biographies are on authors, musicians, and cultural figures. Given the increasing worldwide importance of Latin American culture, this is very appropriate.

On a personal note, Jay Kinsbruner should have written this Introduction. Jay was the Editor in Chief of the Encyclopedia from 2006 onward. Unfortunately, he was diagnosed with cancer. Jay continued to work on the Encyclopedia despite his illness and forged ahead between his medical treatment and increasing weakness. He passed away on October 6, 2007. I began working on the Encyclopedia in September 2007 when Jay felt too ill to continue to work on the Encyclopedia. My hope was that my job would be temporary and that Jay would take over at the end and see his work in published form. It was not to be.

Although I was only involved during the last months of this project and only because of tragic circumstances, it was a pleasure to work with so many colleagues and with the staff at Cengage. My thanks to Barbara Tenenbaum, who encouraged me to take on the project and gave me great advice, as did Georgette Magassy Dorn. In particular, I want to thank the Associate Editors, who worked very hard to write scopes for articles, add to the original list of entries, find authors to write them, and check the accuracy of the entries. They include (in alphabetical order) Patrick Barr-Melej, Matthew Childs, Jorge Chinea, Catherine Conaghan, Barbara Driscoll de Alvarado, Romana Falcón, Andrew J. Kirkendall, Mary Roldán, and Thomas Ward. In addition, Andrew J. Kirkendall and Thomas Ward supervised graduate students who helped with updating bibliographies. I also want to thank especially my graduate students at the Georgetown Center for Latin American Studies, who came through in heroic fashion at the end to put to bed most of the last updates and articles. Byron Crites, Meredith Glueck, and Sean Goforth merit special mention as "clean-up hitters" who at the very end went far beyond the call of duty to get the last articles written and produced fine work. Others who have worked on the Encyclopedia in different capacities include Anthony Maingot, Marco Pamplona, Ed Shaw, and Hilda Sábato.

The staff at Cengage was crucial to this endeavor. John Fitzpatrick invited me to join this project and Scot Peacock, the Project Editor, was a maestro in moving things along and making sure that all entries were finished in time. Many thanks to Jennifer Wisinski, the Art Editor, who oversaw the selection of hundreds of images and graphics, including the full-color inserts.

The copyediting staff, which consisted of Anne Davidson, Jessica Hornik Evans, John Krol, Michael Levine, Mary Russell, Linda Sanders, and Drew Silver, turned entries around in record time with great efficiency and amazing accuracy.

Comms Multilingual did an excellent job in translating Spanish and Portuguese entries into English.

But most of all, this work is a monument to Jay Kinsbruner, who I'm sure would be proud of this important intellectual undertaking that he so ably led almost to the end.

ERICK D. LANGER
SENIOR EDITOR

USING THE ENCYCLOPEDIA

This Encyclopedia contains more than 5800 separate articles. Most topics appear in English alphabetical order, according to the letter-by-letter system. Certain subjects are clustered together in composite entries, which may comprise several regions, periods, or genres. For example, the "Slavery" and "Mining" entries contain separate articles for Brazil and Spanish America. "Art" embraces separately signed essays on pre-Columbian, colonial, nineteenth-century, and modern art, as well as folk art.

National topics are frequently clustered by country, under one or more of the following subheadings:

Constitutions
Organizations
Political Parties (including former revolutionary movements that have entered the political system)
Revolutionary Movements
Wars and Revolutions

Note that an event with a distinctive name will be found under that term, whereas a generic name will appear under the appropriate country. Thus, the Chibata Revolt appears under *C* and the Pastry War under *P*, but the Revolution of 1964 appears under "Brazil, Revolutions."

Measurements appear in the English system according to United States usage. Following are approximate metric equivalents for the most common units:

1 foot = 30 centimeters
1 mile = 1.6 kilometers
1 acre = 0.4 hectares
1 square mile = 2.6 square kilometers
1 pound = 0.45 kilograms
1 gallon = 3.8 liters

Topic entries (numbering more than 2500) are classified by general theme in an appendix located in volume 6. Also included in volume 6 is a separate listing of biographical entries (numbering more than 3,300), classified according to sex and general field(s) of activity.

Cross references, which appear as "See also" references at the end of each essay, call attention to articles of relevance. For full cross-referencing consult the index in volume 6.

LIST OF CONTRIBUTORS

MARIA ISABEL ABREU
Georgetown University

ESTHER ACEVEDO
Dirección de Estudios Históricos
Instituto Nacional de
Antropología e Historia (México)

**ELISABETH ACHA
KUTSCHER**
Faculty of Social Sciences
Pontificia Universidad Católica
del Perú

WILLIAM ACREE
Assistant Professor, Department of
Spanish and Portuguese
San Diego State University

VÍCTOR ACUÑA
Department of History
Universidad de Costa Rica

FRANCIS ADAMS
Associate Professor, Department of
Political Science
Old Dominion University

R. E. W. ADAMS
University of Texas at San
Antonio

MICHAEL ADAMSON
Department of History

California State University,
Sacramento

GEORGE M. ADDY
Brigham Young University

JEREMY ADELMAN
Department of History
Princeton University

JORGE AGUILAR MORA
University of Maryland at College
Park

ADOLFO AGUILAR ZINSER
Diputado Federal, PRD México

RICHARD E. AHLBORN
Smithsonian Institution

SÉRGIO ALCIDES
Researcher, Cátedra Jaime
Cortesão
Universidade de São Paulo

ROBERT J. ALEXANDER
Department of Economics
Rutgers, The State University of
New Jersey

JUDITH ALLEN
Madison, Wisconsin

LEAH ALLEN
Candidate for MA in Latin
American Studies, Edmund A.
Walsh School of Foreign Service
Georgetown University

**MARÍA DEL CARMEN
ALMODOVAR**
Universidad de Havana

PAULA ALONSO
Departamento de Humanidades
Universidad de San Andrés

CARLOS ALTAMIRANO
Director del Centro de Estudios e
Investigaciones
Universidad Nacional de
Quilmes, Argentina

JANAÍNA AMADO
Universidade de Brasília

CHARLES D. AMERINGER
Department of History
Pennsylvania State University

LAURA M. AMRHEIN
Assistant Professor of Art History,
Department of Art
University of Arkansas at Little
Rock

DANNY J. ANDERSON
Department of Spanish & Portuguese
University of Kansas

ROBERT ANDERSON
Associate Professor of Portuguese
Winston–Salem State University

THOMAS P. ANDERSON

ANTHONY P. ANDREWS
Division of Social Sciences
New College of the University of
South Florida

NORWOOD ANDREWS, JR.
Department of Classical and
Modern Languages and Literatures
Texas Tech University

PATRICIA ANDREWS

KENNETH J. ANDRIEN
Department of History
Ohio State University

ALEJANDRO ANREUS
Jersey City Museum

**CORINNE ANTEZANA-
PERNET**
Department of History
University of California, Irvine

PAULINE ANTROBUS
External Relations Department
University of Essex

NANCY APPELBAUM
Associate Professor, Department of
History
State University of New York at
Binghamton

ORLANDO R. ARAGONA

ROCIO ARANDA-ALVARADO
Curator
Jersey City Museum

LUIS O. ARATA
Professor, Department of Modern
Languages
Quinnipiac University

JOSEPH L. ARBENA
Professor Emeritus, Department of
History
Clemson University

CHRISTON ARCHER
Department of History
University of Calgary

ARTURO ARIAS
San Francisco State University

CHARLES W. ARNADE
Department of Government and
International Affairs
University of South Florida

LINDA ARNOLD
Department of History
Virginia Polytechnic Institute

ASTRID ARRARAS
Princeton University

G. POPE ATKINS
Institute of Latin American Studies
University of Texas at Austin

KENNETH ATWOOD
Department of Modern Foreign
Languages & Literatures
University of Tennessee, Knoxville

PATRICIA AUFDERHEIDE
Center for Social Media
The American University

SUZANNE AUSTIN
Professor, Department of History
University of Delaware

JO ANN FAGOT AVIEL
International Relations
Department
San Francisco State University

FELIPE AVILA
Mexican Historian, Researcher of
the Instituto de Investigaciones
Históricas
Universidad Nacional Autónoma
de México (UNAM)

MIRIAM AYRES
New York University

CARMEN LUCIA AZEVEDO
Owner and Publisher
Reminiscências Pesquisa e
Produção Cultural, São Paulo,
Brasil

ANA MARIELLA BACIGALUPO
Associate Professor of Anthropology
State University of New York
(SUNY), Buffalo

KAREN S. BACKSTEIN
Independent Scholar

MARÍA BADÍAS
Georgetown University

JAMES A. BAER
Department of Social Science
Northern Virginia Community
College

**ALEXANDRA BAHARONA DE
BRITO**
Senior Associate and Researcher
Institute of Strategic and
International Studies, Lisbon

JOAN BAK
University of Richmond

GEORGE BAKER, III
Mexico Energy Intelligence
Oakland, California

PETER BAKEWELL
Department of History
Emory University

DANIEL BALDERSTON
Professor and Collegiate Fellow,
Department of Spanish and
Portuguese
University of Iowa

ANDREW K. BALKANSKY
Associate Professor, Department of
Anthropology
Southern Illinois University

CLARA BARGELLINI
*Instituto de Investigaciones
Esteticas
Universidad Nacional Autonoma
de México*

B. J. BARICKMAN
*Department of History
University of Arizona*

RODERICK BARMAN
*Professor Emeritus, Department of
History
University of British Columbia*

MONICA BARNES
Cornell University

ALWYN BARR
*Department of History
Texas Tech University*

ROBERT R. BARR
*Department of Political Science
and International Affairs
University of Mary Washington*

JOSÉ PEDRO BARRÁN
*Universidad de la República
Oriental del Uruguay*

PATRICK BARR-MELEJ
*Associate Professor, Department of
History
Ohio University*

JOEL BARROMI
*Ministry of Foreign Affairs
Israel*

SERGIO BARROSO
*IREME Music Studio
Canada*

JORGE BARRUETO
*Assistant Professor of Spanish,
Department of Language and Letters
Walsh University*

MIRIAM BASILIO
*Institute of Fine Arts
New York University*

RUDY BAUSS
*Department of History, Austin
Community College in Austin, Texas,
Palo Alto Community College in
San Antonio, Texas, and Temple
College in Taylor, Texas*

PETER M. BEATTIE
*Department of History
Michigan State University*

MARC BECKER
*Associate Professor, History
Truman State University*

WILLIAM BEEZLEY
*Department of History
University of Arizona*

BRIAN C. BELANGER
Saint Anselm College

ANDREA BELL
*Professor, Spanish and Latin
American Studies, Department of
Modern Languages and Literatures
Hamline University*

JOHN PATRICK BELL
*Indiana University
Purdue University at Fort Wayne*

SHANNON BELLAMY
Tulane University

CLAUDIA BENAGLIO
Independent Scholar

ADÁN BENAVIDES, JR.
University of Texas at Austin

RAÚL BENAVIDES
University of Texas at Austin

CARMEN BENITO-VESSELS
*Department of Spanish and
Portuguese
University of Maryland at College
Park*

THOMAS BENJAMIN
Department of History

Central Michigan University

ELIZABETH BENSON
*Institute of Andean Studies
Berkeley, California*

GUY BENSUSAN
Northern Arizona University

RODRIGO BENTES
MONTEIRO
*Professor of Modern History,
History Department
Fluminense Federal University,
Rio de Janeiro, Brazil*

FRANCES F. BERDAN
*Department of Anthropology
California State University, San
Bernadino*

MARY BERG
*Resident Scholar, Women's Studies
Research Center
Brandeis University*

SUSAN BERGLUND
*Universidad Central de
Venezuela*

KATY BERGLUND-
SCHLESINGER
*Center for Latin American
Studies
Georgetown University*

EMILIE BERGMANN
University of California, Berkeley

LEOPOLDO M. BERNUCCI
*Professor, The Russell F. and Jean
H. Fiddyment Chair in Latin
American Studies
University of California, Davis*

EMILY BERQUIST
*Assistant Professor, Colonial Latin
America, Department of History
California State University, Long
Beach*

CHARLES R. BERRY
Wright State University

SUSAN K. BESSE
Department of History
City College of the City University
of New York

MELISSA H. BIRCH
University of Virginia

ELBA D. BIRMINGHAM-POKORNY
Southern Arkansas University

DIANA BIRRICHAGA
Faculty of Humanities
Independent University of the
State of Mexico

JOSIAH BLACKMORE
Department of Spanish and
Portuguese
University of Toronto

CHARLES BLAKE
Professor of Political Science
James Madison University

COLE BLASIER
Georgetown University

DAVID BLOCK
Curator of Latin American
Collections, Kroch Library
Cornell University

DON BOHNING
Retired Latin America Editor
Miami Herald

O. NIGEL BOLLAND
Charles A. Dana Professor of
Sociology and Caribbean Studies,
Emeritus, Department of Sociology
and Colgate University

PHILIPPE BONNICHON
University of Paris–Sorbonne

DAIN BORGES
University of California, San
Diego

DARIO BORIM, JR.
Associate Professor and Chair,
Department of Portuguese
University of Massachusetts,
Dartmouth

VIRGINIA M. BOUVIER
University of Maryland at College
Park

CHRISTOPHER T. BOWEN
Department of History
Tulane University

KRISTINA BOYLAN
Institute of Technology
State University of New York
(SUNY)

ERIC BRAHM
Assistant Professor, Department of
Political Science
University of Nevada, Las Vegas

ETHRIAM CASH BRAMMER
Assistant Director, Center for
Chicano–Boricua Studies
Wayne State University

ROSEMARY BRANA-SHUTE
Department of History
College of Charleston and
University of Charleston

JEFFREY T. BRANNON
University of Texas at El Paso

MARISABEL BRÁS

HERBERT BRAUN
Department of History
University of Virginia

TAMARA BRAY
Associate Professor, Department of
Anthropology
Wayne State University

WALTER V. BREM, JR.
Bancroft Library
University of California, Berkeley

JAMES BRENNAN
Georgetown University

EDWARD BRETT
La Roche College

JOHN BRITTON
Department of History
Francis Marion University

LOLITA GUTIÉRREZ BROCKINGTON
North Carolina Central
University

JONATHAN BROWN
Associate Director, Lozano Long
Institute of Latin American
Studies
University of Texas at Austin

KENDALL W. BROWN
Professor, Department of History
Brigham Young University

LARISSA BROWN

RICHMOND F. BROWN
Department of History
University of South Alabama

MICHAEL J. BROYLES
Department of History
University of Western Ontario

MAURICE P. BRUNGARDT
Department of History
Loyola University, New Orleans

SAMUEL BRUNK
Professor, Department of History
University of Nebraska–Lincoln

STEPHEN B. BRUSH
University of California, Davis

PABLO BUCHBINDER
Doctor Historia, Professor adjunto en la Facultad de Ciencias Sociales Universidad de Buenos Aires

JURGEN BUCHENAU
Professor of History and Director of Latin American Studies University of North Carolina at Charlotte

HILARY BURGER
Harvard University

RICHARD L. BURGER
Peabody Museum Yale University

WINFIELD J. BURGGRAAFF
Department of History University of Missouri–Columbia

MARCUS B. BURKE
Hispanic Society of America

MICHAEL E. BURKE
Villanova University

LOUISE M. BURKHART
Anthropology Department State University of New York at Albany

MARK A. BURKHOLDER
Department of History University of Missouri–St. Louis

SUZANNE HILES BURKHOLDER
University of Missouri–St. Louis

E. BRADFORD BURNS
University of California, Los Angeles

JO-MARIE BURT
Associate Professor of Government and Politics, Department of Public and International Affairs George Mason University

AMY TURNER BUSHNELL
College of Charleston

DAVID BUSHNELL
Professor of History Emeritus University of Florida

KIM D. BUTLER
Department of Africana Studies Rutgers University

WES SCHWEMMER CADY
Department of History and Philosophy University of Southwestern Louisiana

GERARDO CAETANO
Universidad de la República Montevideo Centro Latinoamericano de Economía Humana

LARA CAHILL
PhD Candidate, Department of English University of Miami

BRUCE CALDER
University of Illinois at Chicago

JULIO CALVO PÉREZ
Catedrático de Lingüística General, Departamento Teoría de los Lenguajes y Ciencias de la University of Valencia (Spain)

ROSARIO CAMBRIA
Department of Foreign Languages and Literatures Baldwin–Wallace College

MAXWELL CAMERON
Professor, Department of Political Science University of British Columbia

RODERIC AI CAMP
Professor of the Pacific Rim, Department of Government Claremont McKenna College

MÁRCIA ELISA DE CAMPOS GRAF
Universidade Federal do Paraná

ADRIANA MICHÉLE CAMPOS JOHNSON
Assistant Professor, Department of Comparative Literature University of California–Irvine

JAMES CANE
Assistant Professor, Department of History University of Oklahoma

JOSEPH (SETH) MOORER CANTEY, JR.
MA Student, Center for Latin American Studies Georgetown University

ALEX CANTOR
Georgetown University

ERNESTO CAPELLO
Assistant Professor, Department of History University of Vermont

DEBORAH CAPLOW
Lecturer, Interdisciplinary Arts and Sciences University of Washington, Bothell

THOMAS GEORGE CARACAS GARCIA
Department of Music Miami University of Ohio

DAVID CAREY, JR.
Tulane University

JUAN C. CARLOS GALDO
Assistant Professor, Department of Hispanic Studies Texas A&M University

JOHN B. CARLSON
Center for Archaeoastronomy University of Maryland at College Park

GLEN E. CARMAN
Associate Professor, Department of Modern Languages
DePaul University

THOMAS CAROTHERS
Vice President for Studies
Carnegie Endowment for International Peace

CHARLES CARRERAS
Ramapo College of New Jersey

JULIO CARRION
Associate Professor of Political Science and International Relations
University of Delaware

JUAN MANUEL CASAL
Professor, Department of History
Universidad de Montevideo

THOMAS E. CASE
Department of Spanish and Portuguese
San Diego State University

SUZANNE CASOLARO
Center for Latin American Studies
Georgetown University

QUETZIL E. CASTANEDA
Founding Director, OSEA (The Open School of Ethnography and Anthropology)
Visiting Professor and Research Associate, Indiana University

JORGE CASTAÑEDA
Global Distinguished Professor of Politics and Latin American Studies
Center for Latin American and Caribbean Studies, New York University

ELENA CASTEDO
Accent Media

FERNANDO CASTRO
Instituto de Investigaciones Filosóficas
Universidad de Lima

PEDRO CASTRO
McKenna Professor of the Pacific Rim, Government Department
Claremont McKenna College

SUEANN CAULFIELD
Department of History
University of Michigan

CÉSAR N. CAVIEDES
Department of Geography
University of Florida

ADELA CEDILLO
Facultad de Filosofía y Letras
Universidad Nacional Autó de México

ELENA AZUCENA CEJA CAMARGO
Facultad de Filosofía y Letras, Posgrado de Historia
Universidad Nacional Autónoma de México

MIGUEL CENTELLAS
Visiting Assistant Professor of Latin American Politics, Department of Political Science
Dickinson College

RODOLFO CERDAS CRUZ
Departamento De História, Universidad de Costa Rica
San Pedro, Costa Rica

JOSÉ CERNA-BAZÁN
Department of Spanish and Portuguese
University of Texas at Austin

MARIO CERUTTI
Facultad de Filosofía y Letras
Universidad Autónoma de Nuevo León

BILLY JAYNES CHANDLER
Department of History
Texas A&M University–Kingsville

EUGENIO CHANG-RODRÍGUEZ
Queens College and Graduate School
City University of New York

RAQUEL CHANG-RODRÍGUEZ
City College
City University of New York

ARLEN F. CHASE
Department of Sociology and Anthropology
University of Central Florida

FRANCIE CHASSEN-LÓPEZ
Department of History
University of Kentucky

JOHN CHASTEEN
Department of History
University of North Carolina at Chapel Hill

KAREN L. MOHR CHÁVEZ
Department of Sociology, Anthropology, and Social Work
Central Michigan University

YOLANDA CHAVEZ-CAPPELLINI
Assistant Professor, Department of Foreign Languages
State University of New York at New Paltz

JANET M. CHERNELA
Department of Sociology and Anthropology
Florida International University

BRIDGET CHESTERTON
Assistant Professor, Department of History and Social Studies Education
SUNY Buffalo State College

JACK CHILD
Department of Languages &
Foreign Studies
The American University

MATTHEW CHILDS
Associate Professor, History
Florida State University

OSWALDO CHINCHILLA
MAZARIEGOS
Curador, Museo Popol Vuh
Universidad Francisco Marroquín

JORGE CHINEA
Associate Professor of History &
Director, Center for Chicano–
Boricua Studies
Wayne State University

MARGARET CHOWNING
University of California, Berkeley

DYLAN J. CLARK
PhD Candidate, Department of
Anthropology
Harvard University

MARY A. CLARK
Department of Political Science
Tulane University

SUSAN E. CLARK

ROBERT H. CLAXTON
Department of History
West Georgia College

LAWRENCE A. CLAYTON
Department of History
University of Alabama

WAYNE M. CLEGERN
Department of History
Colorado State University

CARROL F. COATES
Department of Romance
Languages and Literatures
State University of New York at
Binghamton

JOHN COATSWORTH
Professor, Department of History
and School of International and
Public Affairs
Columbia University

ELIZABETH A. COBBS
University of San Diego

JAMES D. COCHRANE
Tulane University

DON COERVER
Department of History
Texas Christian University

JOHN COHASSEY

ISAAC COHEN
Economic Commission on Latin
America and the Caribbean

THOMAS M. COHEN
Associate Professor of History,
Oliveira Lima Library
Catholic University of America

WILLIAM S. COKER
Department of History
University of West Florida

SIMON COLLIER
Department of History
Vanderbilt University

FRANCISCO COLOM
GONZÁLEZ
Research Scientist, Spanish
National Research Council (CSIC)
Centre for Human and Social
Sciences

CATHERINE CONAGHAN
Department of Political Studies
Queen's University, Canada

ROSINA CONDE
Professor, Creative Writing Academy
Mexico City Autonomous University

ANDREW CONNELL
Assistant Professor of Music

James Madison University School
of Music

CARYN C. CONNELLY
Assistant Professor of Spanish,
Department of Literature and
Language
Northern Kentucky University

MICHAEL L. CONNIFF
Global Studies
San José State University

ROBERT EDGAR CONRAD
Center for Latin American Studies
University of Pittsburgh

ANNABELLE CONROY
Department of Political Science
University of Central Florida

CHRISTEL K. CONVERSE

ANITA G. COOK
Catholic University of America

NOBLE DAVID COOK
Florida International University

JERRY W. COONEY
Professor Emeritus of History,
Department of History
University of Louisville

R. DOUGLAS COPE
Department of History
Brown University

EMILIO CORAL
Visiting Researcher, Centro de
Estudios Históricos
El Colegio de México

IRINA CÓRDOBA
Centro de Estudios Históricos
El Colegio de México

WILFREDO CORRAL
Chair, Foreign Languages
Sacramento State University

JAVIER CORRALES
Department of Political Science
Amherst College

SOFÌA CORREA

LUIS CORREA-DÍAZ
Department of Modern Languages
Catholic University of America

ROCÍO CORTÉS
Department of Foreign Languages
and Literatures
University of Wisconsin–Oshkosh

AMALIA CORTINA ARAVENA
Universidad de Buenos Aires

ROLANDO COSTA PICAZO
Universidad de Buenos Aires

MICHAEL P. COSTELOE
Hispanic and Latin American
Studies
University of Bristol

BRIAN E. COUTTS
Professor and Head, Department
of Library Public Services
Western Kentucky University,
Bowling Green

EDITH COUTURIER
National Endowment for the
Humanities

MARGARET E. CRAHAN
Department of History, Hunter
College
City University of New York

RAYMOND CRAIB, III
Associate Professor, Department of
History
Cornell University

WINIFRED CREAMER
Presidential Research Professor,
Department of Anthropology
Northern Illinois University

A. CAROLINA CASTILLO CRIMM
Department of History
Sam Houston State University

JOSEPH T. CRISCENTI
Emeritus
Boston College

BYRON CRITES
Department of History
The University of Texas at Austin

JOHN CROCITTI
Department of History
University of Miami

LARRY N. CROOK
Department of Music
University of Florida

RAÚL CUCALÓN
U.S. Army Defense Language
Institute

LIGHT TOWNSEND CUMMINS
Department of History
Austin College

ROGER CUNNIFF
Department of History
San Diego State University

NICHOLAS P. CUSHNER
State University of New York
Empire State College

ANN CYPHERS
Senior Research Scientist
Instituto de Investigaciones
Antropológicas and Institution
Universidad Nacional Autónoma de
México

GLORIA DA CUNHA
Professor of Spanish, Department
of Modern Languages
Morehouse College

GERARDO DAMONTE
Department of Social Sciences

Universidad Nacional Mayor de
San Marcos

JUAN JOSÉ DANERI
Department of Foreign Languages
and Literatures
East Carolina University

MARY L. DANIEL
Department of History
University of Wisconsin–Madison

RAMON E. DAUBON
United States Agency for
International Development

WILLIAM DAVIDSON
Department of Geography/
Anthropology
Louisiana State University

JERRY DAVILA
Associate Professor, Department of
History
University of North Carolina at
Charlotte

DARIÉN DAVIS
Department of History
Middlebury College

SONNY DAVIS
Department of History
Western State College of Colorado

SANTIAGO DAYDÍ-TOLSON
Department of Spanish and
Portuguese
University of Wisconsin–
Milwaukee

GABRIELLA DE BEER
Department of Romance Languages
City College of the City University
of New York

RENÉ DE LA PEDRAJA
Department of History
Canisius College

JESÚS F. DE LA TEJA
Southwest Texas State University

CARLOS DE LA TORRE
Professor of Political Studies
FLACSO–Ecuador

WARREN DEAN
New York University

SUSAN DEANS-SMITH
Department of History
University of Texas at Austin

WARREN DEBOER
Department of Anthropology,
Queens College
City University of New York

ALLAN FIGUEROA DECK, S.J.
Department of History
Loyola Marymount University

MIRIAM DECOSTA-WILLIS
University of Maryland,
Baltimore County

SUSAN DEEDS
Department of History
Northern Arizona University

ALICIA DEL AGUILA
PERALTA
Social Sciences Department
San Marcos University

GUSTAVO DEL ÁNGEL
Professor, División de Economía
Centro de Investigación y
Docencia Económicas (México)

ANGELA B. DELLEPIANE
City College and Graduate Center
City University of New York

JOSEPHINE DELORENZO

HELEN DELPAR
Professor Emerita of History
University of Alabama

ROBERTA M. DELSON
United States Merchant Marine
Academy

ARTHUR DEMAREST
Vanderbilt University

MILAGROS DENIS
Visiting Assistant Professor,
Department of African and Puerto
Rican/Latino Studies
Hunter College

WATSON DENIS
Political Adviser, Association of
the Caribbean States
Centre de Recherches Historiques
et Sociologiques, Universite d'Etat
d'Haïti

DAVID DENSLOW
Department of Economics
University of Florida

SANDRA MCGEE DEUTSCH
Department of History
University of Texas at El Paso

JOSEPH DI BONA
Program in Education
Duke University

ROBERTO DI STEFANO
Dottore di Ricerca in Storia Religiosa
Instituto de Historia Argentina y
Americana "Dr. Emilio Ravignani,"
Universidad de Buenos Aires

TODD A. DIACON
Department of History
University of Tennessee, Knoxville

ELAINE CRISTINA DIAS
Postdoctoral researcher, School of
Architecture and Urbanism
Universidade de São Paulo

JESÚS DÍAZ CABALLERO
Department of History
University of Pittsburgh

JOHN P. DICKENSON
Department of Geography
University of Liverpool

BERNADETTE DICKERSON
Department of Rhetoric,
Communications, and Journalism
Oakland University

RICHARD DIEHL
University of Alabama

THOMAS DODD
United States Embassy
Montevideo, Uruguay

DALISIA MARTINS DOLES
Universidade Federal de Goiás

RONALD DOLKART
Department of History
California State University,
Bakersfield

CHRISTOPHER B. DONNAN
Department of Anthropology
University of California, Los
Angeles

WILLIAM DONOVAN
Department of History
Loyola College

GEORGETTE MAGASSY
DORN
Chief, Hispanic Division
Library of Congress

PAUL J. DOSAL
University of South Florida

MICHAEL DOUDOROFF
University of Kansas

JAMES DOW
Department of Sociology and
Anthropology
Oakland University

PAUL W. DRAKE
University of California, San
Diego

BARBARA DRISCOLL DE ALVARADO
Visiting Assistant Professor, History Department
Assumption College

JOHN DUDLEY
Department of History
Tulane University

JOHN DUGAS
Associate Professor of Political Science
Kalamazoo College

JOHN W. F. DULLES
University of Texas at Austin

FRANCISCO DURAND
Professor of Political Science and Sociology, University of Texas at San Antonio
Pontificia Universidad Catolica del Peru

FRANCIS A. DUTRA
Professor of History
University of California, Santa Barbara

DANIEL DWYER
Siena College Friary

JORDANA DYM
Associate Professor, Department of History
Skidmore College

MARSHALL EAKIN
Department of History
Vanderbilt University

PETER G. EARLE
Department of History
University of Pennsylvania

COLLEEN EBACHER
Associate Professor of Spanish, Department of Foreign Languages
Towson University

ROLAND H. EBEL
Department of Political Science
Tulane University

MUNRO S. EDMONSON
Tulane University

MARTHA EGAN

EVERETT EGGINTON
School of Education
University of Louisville

JOHN ELIAS
Adult Education
Fordham University

STEVE ELLNER
Professor, History and Political Science
Anzoátegui Campus of the Universidad de Oriente, Venezuela

DAVID ELTIS
W. E. B. Du Bois Institute, Harvard University
Queen's University, Ontario

CHARLOTTE EMMERICH
Setor de Linguistica
Universidade Federal do Rio de Janeiro

FROYLÁN ENCISO
Research Assistant
El Colegio de México

J. LYNNE ENGLAND
Lecturer, Behavioral Sciences Department
Utah Valley University

NORA C. ENGLAND
Department of Anthropology
University of Iowa

IRIS H. W. ENGSTRAND
Department of History
University of San Diego

EVAN C. ENGWALL
University of Illinois at Urbana–Champaign

ARTHUR J. ENNIS, O.S.A.
Augustinian Historical Institute
Villanova University

J. A. EPPLE
Department of Romance Languages
University of Oregon

EDWARD EPSTEIN
Professor, Department of Political Science
University of Utah

CARMEN ESCALANTE

JOSÉ ESCORCIA
Universidad de Cali

ENRIQUE ESQUEDA

ANGEL ESTEBAN
Professor, Department of Spanish and Latin American Literature
University of Granada (Spain)

MARK EVERINGHAM
Associate Professor of Political Science
University of Wisconsin–Green Bay

JUDITH EWELL
Newton Professor of History Emerita
College of William and Mary

MARK FALCOFF
American Enterprise Institute for Public Policy Research

TAMARA L. FALICOV
Department of Theatre and Film and Center for Latin American Studies
University of Kansas

MINDI J. FARBER DE ANDA
Energetics, Inc.
Washington, D.C.

JOHN ALAN FARMER
Museum of Contemporary Art
Los Angeles

LINDA FARTHING
Independent scholar

ROBERT FELDMAN
The Field Museum
Chicago

MAYRA FELICIANO
University of South Carolina

KARIN FENN
MA Candidate, Latin American
Studies, School of Foreign Service
Georgetown University

MANUEL FERNÁNDEZ
University of Southern California

MARTA FERNÁNDEZ
WHIGHAM
Universidad Nacional de
Asunción, Paraguay

ELIZABETH FERRER
The Americas Society
New York

THOMAS FIEHRER
The Plantation Society
New Orleans

ALISON FIELDS
Doctoral Candidate, American
Studies
University of New Mexico

VICTOR FIGUEROA
Assistant Professor, Department of
Romance Languages and
Literatures
Wayne State University

CARLOS FILGUEIRA
Centro de Informaciones e
Estudios de Uruguay
Universidad de la República,
Montevideo

FERNANDO FILGUEIRA
Department of Sociology
Northwestern University

HENRY FINCH
Department of Economic and
Social History
University of Liverpool

FEDERICO FINCHELSTEIN
Assistant Professor of History,
Historical Studies
The New School

KENNETH V. FINNEY
North Carolina Wesleyan College

JOHN R. FISHER
University of Liverpool

MICHAEL FLEET
Department of Political Science
Marquette University

SARA FLEMING
University of Pittsburgh

JUSTO MIGUEL FLORES
Licenciado, Centro de Estudios
Históricos
El Colegio de México

ALBERTO FLÓREZ
MALAGÓN
Associate Professor, History
Department
University of Ottawa

NANCY M. FLOWERS
Hunter College
City University of New York

HEIDY P. FOGEL
Yale University

CARMENZA OLAYA
FONSTAD
Bunker Hill Community College

FRANCISCO FOOT
HARDMAN
Professor of Brazilian History and
Culture, Instituto de Estudos da
Linguagem
Universidade Estadual de
Campinas

MERLIN H. FORSTER
Department of Spanish and
Portuguese
Brigham Young University

DAVID WILLIAM FOSTER
Regents' Professor of Spanish and
Women and Gender Studies,
School of International Letters
and Cultures
Arizona State University

JACQUELINE FOWKS
Associate Professor of Journalism,
Facultad de Ciencias y Artes de la
Comunicación
Pontificia Universidad Católica
del Perú

WILLIAM R. FOWLER
Department of Anthropology
Vanderbilt University

HEATHER FOWLER-
SALAMINI
Department of History
Bradley University

JENNIFER FOX
University of Texas at Austin

PERLA ORQUÍDEA
FRAGOSO LUGO
Postgraduate student of Social
Anthropology
Centro de Investigación y Estudios
Superiores en Antropología Social,
D.F.

MARTHA PALEY
FRANCESCATO
George Mason University

ROSS H. FRANK
Associate Professor, Department of Ethnic Studies
University of California, San Diego

ANA FREGA
Professor and Director, Departamento de Historia del Uruguay
Universidad de la República, Facultad de Humanidades y Ciencias de la Educación

JUDY BIEBER FREITAS
Department of History
University of New Mexico

JOHN D. FRENCH
Department of History
Duke University

WILLIAM FRENCH
Department of History
University of British Columbia

MAX PAUL FRIEDMAN
Associate Professor, Department of History
American University

HUGO FRÜHLING
Professor, Public Affairs Institute, and Director of the Center for the Study of Citizen Security
University of Chile

MICHAEL FRY
Department of History
Fort Lewis College

PETER FURST
University Museum
University of Pennsylvania

JUAN CARLOS GALEANO
Department of Modern Languages
Florida State University

MIRIAM JUDITH GALLEGOS GÓMORA
Sección de Arqueología

Instituto Nacional de Antropología e Historia

EZEQUIEL GALLO
Universidad Torcuato di Tella

KLAUS GALLO
Associate Professor
Universidad Torcuato di Tella, Argentina

EDUARDO A. GAMARRA
Department of Political Science
Florida International University

PAUL GANSTER
Institute for Regional Studies of the Californias
San Diego State University

DAVID GARCIA
Assistant Professor, Department of Music
University of North Carolina at Chapel Hill

MARIA CRISTINA GARCIA
Professor, Department of History
Cornell University

PETER GARCIA
Visiting Professor, Ethnomusicology and Folklore
Department of Chicana and Chicano Studies
University of California, Santa Barbara

CARLOS GARCÍA BLAYA
Licenciado
Comisión Nacional de Actividades Espaciales

RODRIGO DE J. GARCÍA ESTRADA
Professor, History Department
Universidad de Antioquia, Medellín

MAGDALENA GARCÍA PINTO
Department of Romance Languages
University of Missouri–Columbia

MERCEDES GARCÍA SARAVÍ
Prof. de Literatura Latinoamericana, Departamento de Letras
Universidad Nacional de Misiones

IÑIGO GARCIA-BRYCE
Associate Professor, Department of History
New Mexico State University

ISMAEL GARCÍA-COLÓN
Assistant Professor of Anthropology
College of Staten Island, CUNY

LAURA GARCÍA-MORENO
Department of Spanish
Georgetown University

LEONARDO GARCÍA-PABÓN
Professor of Spanish, Department of Romance Languages
University of Oregon

ROBERTO GARGARELLA
CONICET, Argentina
Chr. Michelsen Institute, Norway

LYDIA M. GARNER
Department of History
Southwest Texas State University

PAUL GARNER
Department of Hispanic Studies
University of Wales

RICHARD L. GARNER
Pennsylvania State University

THOMAS GAROFALO
Georgetown University

VIRGINIA GARRARD-BURNETT
Institute of Latin American Studies
University of Texas at Austin

MARTA GARSD
Lincoln University College, Buenos Aires
Supreme Court of Justice, Republic of Argentina

JANINE GASCO
Institute of Archaeology
University of California, Los Angeles

ALBERT GASTMANN
Emeritus
Trinity College

MIGUEL A. GATTI
Catholic University of America

DAVID GEGGUS
Professor, History Department
University of Florida

DICK GERDES
Department of Modern and Classical Languages
The University of New Mexico

JOAN GERO
Department of Anthropology
University of South Carolina

PAULA S. GIBBS
Department of History
Tulane University

HANNAH GILL
Assistant Director, The Institute of Latin American Studies
University of North Carolina at Chapel Hill

STEVEN S. GILLICK
Gonzaga University

JOHN GLEDSON
Department of Hispanic Studies
University of Liverpool

THOMAS F. GLICK
Department of History
Boston University

MEREDITH GLUECK
Doctoral Candidate, Department of History
University of Texas at Austin

HORACIO GNEMMI
Facultad de Arquitectura, Urbanismo y Diseño
Universidad Nacional de Córdoba

TED GOERTZEL
Professor of Sociology
Rutgers University at Camden

ALVIN GOFFIN
Instructor, Department of History
University of Central Florida

SEAN H. GOFORTH
Graduate Student, School of Foreign Service
Georgetown University

CEDOMIL GOIC
Director, Centro de Estudios de Literatura Chilena, Facultad de Letras
Pontificia Universidad Catolica de Chile

MICHAEL GOLD-BISS
Professor of National Security Affairs, Center for Hemispheric Defense Studies
National Defense University

CHARLES GOLDEN
Department of Anthropology
Brandeis University

SHIFRA M. GOLDMAN
Latin American Center
University of California, Los Angeles

ELIANA MARIA REA GOLDSCHMIDT

MIGUEL GOMES
Professor, Department of Modern & Classical Languages
University of Connecticut–Storrs

GALE GOODWIN GOMEZ
Professor, Department of Anthropology
Rhode Island College

LUIS A. GONZALEZ
Librarian for Latin American Studies, Herman B. Wells Library
Indiana University

ANN GONZÁLEZ
University of North Carolina at Charlotte

JORGE H. GONZÁLEZ

FERNANDO GONZÁLEZ DAVISON
Instituto de Investigaciones Políticas y Sociales
Universidad de San Carlos de Guatemala

SILVIA GONZALEZ MARIN
Instituto de Investigaciones Bibliográficas
Universidad Nacional Autonoma de Mexico

LOUIS W. GOODMAN
The American University

PAUL B. GOODWIN, JR.
Department of History
University of Connecticut

PAUL GOOTENBERG
State University of New York at Stony Brook

DAVID B. GRACY, II
Graduate School of Library and Information
University of Texas at Austin

LAURA GRAHAM
Associate Professor, Department of Anthropology
University of Iowa

SANDRA LAUDERDALE
GRAHAM
Department of History
University of Texas at Austin

LANCE R. GRAHN
Department of History
Marquette University

LUIS FERNANDO
GRANADOS
Georgetown University

ANGELA GRANUM
MA Candidate, Latin American
Studies
Georgetown University

ROGER GRAVIL
Department of Historical Studies
University of Natal, South Africa

AMANDA GRAY
Graduate Student, Latin
American Studies, Edmund A.
Walsh School of Foreign Service
Georgetown University

JAMES GREEN
Department of History
Brown University

MICHAEL R. GREEN
Texas State Archives

STANLEY GREEN
Department of History
Laredo State University

ANNE GREENE

GERALD MICHAEL
GREENFIELD
University of Wisconsin–Parkside

KAREN M. GREINER

KENNETH J. GRIEB
Interdisciplinary Center
University of Wisconsin

TERENCE GRIEDER
Department of Art
University of Texas at Austin

ERWIN P. GRIESHABER
Department of History
Mankato State University

JO ANN GRIFFIN

WILLIAM J. GRIFFITH
Emeritus
University of Kansas

JUAN CARLOS GRIJALVA
Assistant Professor of Spanish,
Department of Modern and
Classical Languages and Cultures
Assumption College

RICHARD GRISWOLD DEL
CASTILLO
Professor Emeritus, Chicana and
Chicano Studies Department
San Diego State University

PETER GUARDINO
Department of History
Indiana University

LOWELL GUDMUNDSON
Department of Latin American
Studies
Mount Holyoke College

VIRGINIA GUEDEA
Instituto de Investigaciones
Históricas
Universidad Nacional Autónoma
de México

TONATIUH GUILLEN LOPEZ
Estudios Politicos
El Colegio de la Frontera Norte

HORACIO GUTIÉRREZ
Professor of Latin American
History, Department of History
Universidade de São Paulo, Brazil

MAGDALENA GUTIÉRREZ
University of Illinois – Chicago

LAURA GUTIERREZ-WITT
Retired Director, Benson Latin
American Collection
University of Texas at Austin

DONNA J. GUY
Department of History
University of Arizona

DAVID T. HABERLY
University of Virginia

JUNE E. HAHNER
State University of New York at
Albany

CHARLES HALE
Department of History
University of Iowa

PAULA HALPERIN
PhD Candidate, Department of
History
University of Maryland, College
Park

MICHAEL T. HAMERLY
Professor Emeritus, University of
Guam
Special Project Librarian, John
Carter Brown Library, Brown
University

HUGH M. HAMILL
Department of History
University of Connecticut

BRIAN HAMNETT
Department of History
University of Essex

HOWARD HANDELMAN
Professor Emeritus, Department of
Political Science
University of Wisconsin–
Milwaukee

MICHAEL HANDELSMAN
Modern Foreign Languages and
Literatures
University of Tennessee, Knoxville

CARL A. HANSON
Maddux Library
Trinity University

JOHN MASON HART
Department of History
University of Houston

STEPHEN HART
Department of Spanish and Latin
American Studies
University College London

ROBERT HASKETT
Department of History
University of Oregon

TIMOTHY P. HAWKINS
Department of History
Tulane University

EVELYN J. HAWTHORNE
Howard University

ROBERT A. HAYES
Department of History
Texas Tech University

JAMES HAYES-BOHANAN
Department of Geography
Bridgewater State College

SAMUEL K. HEATH
Director, Meadows Museum,
Owen Arts Center
Southern Methodist University

J. LEÓN HELGUERA
Vanderbilt University

MARY W. HELMS
University of North Carolina,
Greensboro

JOHN HEMMING
Director and Secretary, Royal
Geographical Society
Royal Society of London

JAMES D. HENDERSON
Department of Politics

University of South Carolina–
Coastal Carolina College

PETER V. N. HENDERSON
Department of History
Winona State University

CRAIG HENDRICKS
Department of History
Long Beach City College

RICK HENDRICKS
The Vargas Project
University of New Mexico

JACQUELINE HERMANN
History Department
Universidade Federal do Rio de
Janeiro

MARK HERNANDEZ
Assistant Professor of Latin
American and U.S. Latino
Literatures and Cultures,
Department of Romance
Languages, Olin Tufts University

JOSÉ MANUEL HERNÁNDEZ
Georgetown University

OMAR HERNÁNDEZ
University of Texas at Austin

MONICA HERNANDEZ
QUIJANO
MA Latin American Studies,
School of Foreign Service
Georgetown University

MARÍA HERRERA-SOBEK
University of California, Irvine

DAVID J. HESS
Department of Composition and
Writing
Colgate University

FREDERIC HICKS
Department of Anthropology
University of Louisville

KATHLEEN JOAN HIGGINS
Department of History
University of Iowa

DAVID HIGGS
Department of History
University of Toronto

TRAVIS SCOTT HIGH
Student, Latin American Studies
Georgetown University

ROBERT M. HILL, II
Division of Behavioral and
Cultural Sciences
University of Texas, San Antonio

STEPHEN E. HILL

ROBERT HIMMERICH Y
VALENCIA
University of New Mexico

EMILY HIND
Assistant Professor of Spanish,
Department of Modern and
Classical Languages
University of Wyoming

PERCY HINTZEN
Professor, African American Studies
University of California, Berkeley

STEVEN J. HIRSCH
Department of History
George Washington University

KENNETH HIRTH
Professor of Anthropology
Pennsylvania State University

LOUISA S. HOBERMAN
University of Texas at Austin

PAUL E. HOFFMAN
Department of History
Louisiana State University

THOMAS H. HOLLOWAY
Director, Hemispheric Institute on
the Americas
University of California, Davis

SHEILA HOOKER
Wixom Public Library

ROY HORA
Associate Professor, Centro de Estudios e Investigaciones Universidad de Quilmes/CONICET

JOE HORAN
Doctoral Student, Department of History Florida State University

JOEL HOROWITZ
Department of History Saint Bonaventure University

EVELYN HU-DEHART
Professor of History and Ethnic Studies, Center for the Study of Race and Ethnicity in America Brown University

KATHERINE CLARK HUDGENS
Museum and Schools Information Exchange Washington, D.C.

MAGGIE K. HUMMEL
Center for Latin American Studies, Edmund A. Walsh School of Foreign Service Georgetown University

REGINA IGEL
University of Maryland at College Park

CRISTINA IGLESIA
Professor of Nineteenth Century Argentinian Literature, Literature Department Facultad de Filosofía y Letras, University of Buenos Aires

FIDEL IGLESIAS
University of Florida

FE IGLESIAS GARCÍA
Instituto de Historia, Havana Cuba

RICHARD H. IMMERMAN
Department of History Temple University

MARÍA INÉS DE TORRES

ESTELA IRIZARRY
Georgetown University

ESTELLE JACKSON

K. DAVID JACKSON
Department of Spanish and Portuguese Yale University

ROBERT H. JACKSON
Department of History Texas Southern University

HECTOR JAIMES
Associate Professor of Latin American Literature and Culture North Carolina State University

IVAN JAKSIC
Department of History Stanford University

DILMUS D. JAMES
Department of Economics and Finance University of Texas at El Paso

MICHAEL L. JAMES
Rutgers, The State University of New Jersey

LAURA JARNAGIN
Colorado School of Mines

SHELLY JARRETT BROMBERG
University of Texas at Austin

DAVID L. JICKLING
Centro de Investigaciones Regionales de Mesoamérica (CIRMA)

OLGA JIMÉNEZ DE WAGENHEIM
Rutgers, The State University of New Jersey, Newark

H. B. JOHNSON
University of Virginia

LYMAN L. JOHNSON
University of North Carolina at Charlotte

KEVIN JOHNSTON
Pennsylvania State University

JANICE L. W. JOLLY
Bureau of Mines United State Department of the Interior

KRISTINE L. JONES
Pontífica Universidad Catóolica Madre y Maestra, Santo Domingo

GILBERT M. JOSEPH
Department of History Yale University

CAROLYN JOSTOCK

CLAIRE JOYSMITH
Professor, CISAN Universidad Nacional Autónoma de México (UNAM)

JOHN JUSTESON
Professor, Department of Anthropology University at Albany

GLORIA ELISABETH KAISER
Iniciativa Cultural Austro–Brasileira

KAREN KAMPWIRTH
Knox College

DEBORAH KANTER
Department of History Albion College

WILFREDO KAPSOLI-
ESCUDERO
Department of Humanities
Universidad Ricardo Palma

MARY KARASCH
Department of History
Oakland University

THOMAS L. KARNES
Arizona State University

NANCY KASON POULSON
Professor of Spanish and Latin
American Studies, Linguistics and
Comparative Literature
Florida Atlantic University

WILLIAM H. KATRA
Department of Foreign Languages
University of Wisconsin–La Crosse

ILONA KATZEW
Institute of Fine Arts
New York University

DOUGLAS R. KEBERLEIN
Tulane University

PETER KELLER
Director
Bowers Museum of Cultural Art,
Santa Ana

BILL KELLEY, JR.
Managing Director and Editorial
Advisor
www.LatinArt.com

SUSAN KELLOGG
Department of History
University of Houston

CHARLES KENNEY
Associate Professor, Political
Science Department
University of Oklahoma

JACQUELYN BRIGGS KENT
State University of New York at
Cortland

MARY KENT
Graphic Artist/Photographer
Digital Domain, Florida

JOHN L. KESSELL
University of New Mexico

JOHN E. KICZA
Department of History
Washington State University

JAMES PATRICK KIERNAN
Organization of American States

THOMAS W. KILLION
National Museum of Natural
History
Smithsonian Institution

A. DOUGLAS KINCAID
Latin American and Caribbean
Center
Florida International University

NICOLE R. KING
University of Maryland at College
Park

JAY KINSBRUNER
Professor Emeritus of History,
Queens College
City University of New York

KENNETH F. KIPLE
Department of History
Bowling Green State University

ANDREW J. KIRKENDALL
Department of History
Texas A&M University

CLAYTON KIRKING
Chief, Art Information Resources
Art and Architecture Collection,
New York Public Library

WADE A. KIT
Department of History
Wake Forest University

ROGER A. KITTLESON
Northwestern University

NORMA KLAHN
Department of Literature
University of California, Santa Cruz

JEFFREY KLAIBER, S.J.
Facultad de Historia
Pontificia Universidad Católica
del Perú

PETER KLARÉN
Department of History
George Washington University

IGNACIO KLICH
University of Westminster

VIVIANA KLUGER
Universidad de Buenos Aires,
Argentina
Universidad de Ciencias
Empresariales y Sociales,
Argentina

ALAN KNIGHT
Latin American Centre, Saint
Anthony College
Oxford University

ROBERT J. KNOWLTON
Emeritus
University of Wisconsin–Stevens
Point

JERRY KNUDSON
Temple University

EDMOND KONRAD
Department of History
Tulane University

SOPHIA KOUTSOYANNIS
PhD Candidate in History
York University, Toronto

JEFF KARL KOWALSKI
School of Art
Northern Illinois University

EFRAIN KRISTAL
Professor, Department of
Comparative Literature
UCLA

DIRK KRUIJT
Professor of Development Studies,
Department of Cultural
Anthropology, Faculty of Social
and Behavioral Utrecht
University, The Netherlands

MATT KRYSTAL
Department of Anthropology
Tulane University

ALLAN J. KUETHE
Texas Tech University

GARY G. KUHN
Department of History
University of Wisconsin—La
Crosse

MONICA E. KUPFER
Universidad de Panamá

ELIZABETH KUZNESOF
Center of Latin American Studies
University of Kansas

SARA LADRÓN DE GUEVARA
Director of the Museo de
Antropología de Xalapa
University of Veracruz

DAVID LAFRANCE
Department of History
Oregon State University

CARL HENRIK LANGEBAEK R.
Departmento de Antropologia
Universidad de los Andes,
Colombia

ERICK D. LANGER
Department of History
Georgetown University

LESTER LANGLEY
Research Professor Emeritus,
Department of History
University of Georgia

ALCIDES LANZA
Schulich School of Music
McGill University

PEDRO LASARTE
Associate Professor of Spanish,
Department of Romance Studies
Boston University

GEORGE LAU
University Lecturer, Sainsbury
Research Unit
University of East Anglia, U.K.

GEORGE M. LAUDERBAUGH
Troy State University, Alabama

MARY LOU LECOMPTE
Department of Kinesiology and
Health Education
University of Texas at Austin

JOHN LENT
Editor
International Journal of Comic
Art

THOMAS M. LEONARD
Department of History
University of North Florida

JEFFREY LESSER
Department of History
Connecticut College

MARIA LETÍCIA CORREA
Doutora em História Pela
Universidade Federal Fluminense
(UFF)
Professora No Departamento De
História Da Universidade Do
Estado Do Rio De Janeiro (UERJ)

ROBERT M. LEVINE
Department of History
University of Miami

LINDA LEWIN
Department of History
University of California, Berkeley

DANIEL K. LEWIS
Chair, History Department
California State Polytechnic
University

PAUL H. LEWIS
Department of Political Science
Tulane University

STEPHEN E. LEWIS
Associate Professor, History
California State University, Chico

VAUGHAN LEWIS
Professor of the International
Relations of the Caribbean, St.
Augustine Campus
University of the West Indies,
Trinidad and Tobago

HE LI
Department of Political Science
Merrimack College

DOUGLAS COLE LIBBY
Universidade Federal de Minais
Gerais

MYRON LICHTBLAU
Department of Foreign Languages
Syracuse University

MICHAEL D. LIND

RICHARD LINDLEY
Austin Community College

HÉCTOR LINDO-FUENTES
Fordham University

JUDITH LISANSKY
World Bank

PEGGY K. LISS
Washington, D.C.

SHELDON B. LISS
University of Akron

KATHRYN LITHERLAND
Department of History, University
of Maryland
Managing Editor, Hispanic
American Historical Review

TODD LITTLE-SIEBOLD
Department of History
Lewis and Clark College

MIRTA ZAIDA LOBATO
Facultad de Filosofía y Letras
Universidad de Buenos Aires

EULALIA MARIA LAHMEYER LOBO

JAMES LOCKHART
Department of History
University of California at Los Angeles

WILLIAM LOFSTROM
United States Department of State

RUSS LOHSE
Assistant Professor, Department of History
University of Southern Indiana

JOHN V. LOMBARDI
Department of History and Chancellor
University of Massachusetts, Amherst

MARY LUCIANA LOMBARDI
Institute for Historical Study
San Francisco and Santa Cruz

FRANCISCO LOMELI
Chair of Spanish and Portuguese, Spanish and Portuguese Department
University of California–Santa Barbara

GAYLE WAGGONER LOPES
United States Department of State

MARIA ANGÉLICA LOPES
Department of Spanish, Italian, and Portuguese
University of South Carolina

KIMBERLE LOPEZ
Associate Professor Department of Spanish and Portuguese
University of New Mexico

FERNANDO LÓPEZ D'ALESSANDRO
Instituto de Estudios Sociales, Montevideo

BRIAN LORDAN
Washington, D.C.

JOSEPH LOVE
Professor Emeritus, History
University of Illinois, Urbana–Champaign

W. GEORGE LOVELL
Department of Geography
Queen's University, Ontario

BRIAN LOVEMAN
Professor of Political Science
San Diego State University

SARAH M. LOWE
Graduate School and University Center
City University of New York

AURORA LOYO

JOSÉ ANTONIO LUCERO
Assistant Professor, Jackson School of International Studies
University of Washington

CATHERINE LUGAR

WILLIAM LUIS
Department of Spanish and Portuguese
Vanderbilt University

LESLEY R. LUSTER

STACY LUTSCH
PhD student, Department of Spanish and Portuguese
University of Kansas

CHRISTOPHER H. LUTZ
Plumsock Mesoamerican Studies
Centro de Investigaciones Regionales de Mesoamérica

JOHN LYNCH
Institute of Latin American Studies
University of London

EUGENE LYON
Center for Historic Research
Flagler College

PATRICIA J. LYON
Institute of Andean Studies
University of California, Berkeley

NEILL MACAULAY
Emeritus
University of Florida

DAVID MACIEL
Department of History
University of New Mexico

COLIN MACLACHLAN
Department of History
Tulane University

MURDO J. MACLEOD
Department of History
University of Florida

RICHARD S. MACNEISH
Andover Foundation for Archaeological Research

LORI MADDEN
Shippensburg University

MARIA ELISA MADER
Professora de História da América do Departamento de História da Pontifícia
Universidade Católica do Rio de Janeiro

RUSSELL MAGNAGHI
History Department
Northern Michigan University

AARON PAINE MAHR
University of New Mexico

ANTHONY P. MAINGOT
Professor Emeritus of Sociology
Florida International University

SCOTT MAINWARING
*Helen Kellogg Institute for
International Studies
University of Notre Dame*

CARLOS MALAMUD
*Professor of Latin American
History, Department of
Contemporary History
Universidad Nacional de
Educación a Distancia (UNED),
Madrid, Spain*

**HAMILTON BOTELHO
MALHANO**
*Museu Nacional
Universdiade Federal do Rio de
Janeiro*

PEDRO MALIGO
Michigan State University

TIA MALKIN-FONTECCHIO
*Assistant Professor, Department of
History
West Chester University of
Pennsylvania*

WILLIAM MALTBY
*Department of History
University of Missouri–Saint Louis*

MARKOS J. MAMALAKIS
*Professor of Economics Emeritus
University of Wisconsin–
Milwaukee*

PATRICK J. MANEY
Tulane University

ALBERTO MANRIQUE

ANDREA MANTELL-SEIDELL
*Associate Professor of Dance and
Director
Intercultural Dance and Music
Institute/Latin American and
Caribbean Center, Florida
International University*

JOSÉ MARÍA MANTERO
*Department of Modern Languages
Xavier University*

VALERIA MANZANO
*History Department
Indiana University at
Bloomington*

LUIGI MANZETTI
*Department of Political Science
Southern Methodist University*

LILLIAN MANZOR
*Latin American Studies Program
University of Miami*

GABRIEL MARCELLA
*Professor of Third World Studies,
Department of National Security
and Strategy
United States Army War College*

LISA MARIĆ BRANKO
Chemonics International

CARLOS MARICHAL
*Centro de Estudios Históricos
El Colegio de México*

ROBERTO MÁRQUEZ
*William R. Kenan, Jr. Professor of
Latin American Studies
Mount Holyoke College*

CHERYL ENGLISH MARTIN
*Department of History
University of Texas at El Paso*

OSCAR J. MARTÍNEZ
*Regents' Professor, History
Department
University of Arizona*

**LUIS MARTÍNEZ-
FERNÁNDEZ**
*Department of History
University of Central Florida*

**TERESITA MARTÍNEZ-
VERGNE**
*Department of History
Macalester College*

HEITOR MARTINS

WILSON MARTINS
New York University

JOHN D. MARTZ
*Department of Political Science
Pennsylvania State University*

DANIEL M. MASTERSON
*Department of History
U.S. Naval Academy*

SUSAN N. MASUOKA
*Fowler Museum of Cultural
History
University of California, Los Angeles*

RAY MATHENY
*Department of Anthropology
Brigham Young University*

W. MICHAEL MATHES
*Emeritus
University of San Francisco*

ILMAR MATTOS
Pontificia Universidade Catolica

KENNETH R. MAXWELL
*Council on Foreign Relations,
New York*

**JUDITH M. MAXWELL
IXQ'ANIL**
*Department of Anthropology
Tulane University*

RACHEL A. MAY
*Interdisciplinary Arts and
Sciences
University of Washington,
Tacoma*

ROBERT E. MAY
*Department of History
Purdue University*

ALINNE BETANIA MAZE
*Latin American Studies, Edmund
A. Walsh School of Foreign Service
Georgetown University*

RICHARD A. MAZZARA
Oakland University

TOMÉ N. MBUIA-JOÃO
Voice of America, Washington, D.C.

JAMES MCBRIDE
Center for Latin American Studies
Georgetown University

ROBERT MCCAA
Minnesota Population Center
University of Minnesota

FRANK D. MCCANN, JR.
University of New Hampshire

WILLIAM MCCARTHY
University of North Carolina at Wilmington

CYNTHIA MCCLINTOCK
Department of Political Science
George Washington University

STUART MCCOOK
Department of History
University of Guelph

JENNIFER MCCOY
Director, The Latin American Program
The Carter Center

DAVID MCCREERY
Department of History
Georgia State University

ARCHIE P. MCDONALD
Stephen F. Austin State University

KEITH MCDUFFIE
Department of Hispanic Languages and Literatures
University of Pittsburgh

GORDON F. MCEWAN
Department of Sociology/ Anthropology
Wagner College

ANTHONY MCFARLANE
School of Comparative American Studies
University of Warwick

CHRIS MCGOWAN
Billboard Magazine

SUE DAWN MCGRADY
Tulane University

JILL LESLIE MCKEEVER-FURST
Moore College of Art and Design

MARIANA MCLOUGHLIN
MA Candidate, Latin American Studies, School of Foreign Service
Georgetown University

JOHN MCNEILL
Department of History
Georgetown University

DONALD MCVICKER
Professor of Anthropology
North Central College, Illinois

TERESA MEADE
Department of History
Union College

CAREN A. MEGHREBLIAN
Art Institute of Seattle

JOSÉ CARLOS SEBE BOM MEIHY
Universidade de São Paulo

ANDRÉS MEJÍA ACOSTA
Fellow, Institute of Development Studies
University of Sussex

MARISELLE MELÉNDEZ
Associate Professor of Colonial Spanish American Literatures and Cultures
University of Illinois

WILBUR E. MENERAY
Howard Tilton Memorial Library
Tulane University

M. NOEL MENEZES, R.S.M
Saint John Bosco Convent, Guyana

DANUSIA L. MESON
Department of Languages and Foreign Studies
The American University

DANIEL MESQUITA PEREIRA
Doutor em História pela Puc–Rio
Professor Adjunto do Departamento de Comunicação Social da Puc–Rio

ALIDA C. METCALF
Department of History
Trinity University

JOAN E. MEZNAR
Department of History
University of South Carolina

EDUARDO MÍGUEZ
History Department
Universidad Nacional del Centro de la Provincia de Buenos Aires

JERALD MILANICH
Florida Museum of Natural History

MARY JO MILES

FRANCESCA MILLER
Washington Center
University of California, Davis

GARY M. MILLER
Central Michigan University

HUBERT J. MILLER
Department of History and Philosophy
University of Texas–Pan American

JOSEPH C. MILLER
Department of History
University of Virginia

MARY ELLEN MILLER
Department of Art History
Yale University

GIOVANNA MINARDI
Investigadora de Literatura
hispanoamericana, Facultad de
Filosofia y Letras
Universidad de Palermo, Italia

CHRISTOPHER MITCHELL
Department of Politics
New York University

MICHAEL MITCHELL
Department of Political Science
Arizona State University

SMITH DOUGLAS MONSON
Center of Latin American
Studies, Edmund Walsh School of
Foreign Service
Georgetown University

VERONICA MONTECINOS
Professor of Sociology
The Pennsylvania State University

JOHN M. MONTEIRO
Department of Anthropology
Universidade Estadual de Campinas

TOMMIE SUE
MONTGOMERY
University of Miami

MARILYN M. MOORS
Professor Emerita of Anthropology
Montgomery College

WALTRAUD QUEISER
MORALES
Department of Political Science
University of Central Florida

DAVID MORA-MARIN
University of North Carolina at
Chapel Hill

ELENA MOREIRA
Fashion and Beauty Editor
Cosmopolitan Argentina

TERRELL A. MORGAN
Associate Professor of Hispanic
Linguistics, Department of
Spanish and Portuguese
Ohio State University

ZACHARY MORGAN
Assistant Professor, Department of
History
Boston College

CRAIG MORRIS
Department of Anthropology
American Museum of Natural
History

JOSE MOYA
Professor of History, Director of the
Forum on Migration
Barnard College

BARBARA MUJICA
Professor of Spanish, Department
of Spanish and Portuguese
Georgetown University

JOSEPH E. MULLIGAN
Society of Jesus, Nicaragua

PATRICIA A. MULVEY
Bluefield State College

GERALDO MUNCK
School of International Relations
University of Southern California

MARTIN MUNRO
Department of Liberal Arts
University of the West Indies, St
Augustine, Trinidad and Tobago

CHRISTOPHER LANCE
MURCHISON
Department of History
University of Miami

JOSEPH M. MURPHY
Department of Theology
Georgetown University

EDMUNDO MURRAY
Latin American Studies
University of Zurich

PAMELA MURRAY
Associate Professor, History
Department
University of Alabama at
Birmingham

JORGE MYERS
Universidad Nacional de Quilmes

ROBERT MYERS
Yale University

CAROLE A. MYSCOFSKI
Department of Religion
Illinois Wesleyan University

SILVIA NAGY
Department of Modern Languages
Catholic University of America

GUILLERMO NÁÑEZ
FALCÓN
Latin American Library
Tulane University

NANCY PRISCILLA SMITH
NARO
Universidade Federal Fluminense

MARYSA NAVARRO
Dartmouth College

JOYCE E. NAYLON
Tulane University

ROBERT A. NAYLOR
Fairleigh Dickinson University

MURIEL NAZZARI
Department of History
Indiana University

JEFFREY NEEDELL
Department of History
University of Florida

ANA JANAINA PRINCE
NELSON
Center for Latin American
Studies, School of Foreign Service
Georgetown University

BEN A. NELSON
Department of Anthropology
State University of New York at
Buffalo

GUILHERME NEVES

LÚCIA M. BASTOS P. NEVES
Universidade do Estado do Rio de
Janeiro

WALTER A. NEVES
Full Professor, Laboratory for
Human Evolutionary Studies,
Department of Genetics and
Evolutionary Biology
Instituto de Biociências,
Universidade de São Paulo, Brasil

RONALD C. NEWTON
Department of History
Simon Fraser University

WESLEY PHILLIPS NEWTON
Auburn University

H. B. NICHOLSON
Department of Anthropology
University of California, Los
Angeles

R. ANDREW NICKSON
Reader in Latin American
Studies, International
Development Department
University of Birmingham,
England

THOMAS NIEHAUS
University of the South

ANA LUIZA NOBRE
Department of Arts and Design
Catholic University of Rio de
Janeiro

XAVIER NOGUEZ
Centro de Estudios Históricos
El Colegio Mexiquense,
Zinacantepec, Estado de México

MARCOS NOVARO
Assistant Professor, Political
Science Department
Universidad de Buenos Aires

SUSANA NUCCETELLI
Associate Professor, Department of
Philosophy
Saint Cloud State University

FREDERICK M. NUNN
Professor Emeritus
Portland State University

ROBERT W. O'CONNELL
Astronomy Department
University of Virginia

ALAN O'CONNOR
Cultural Studies Program
Trent University

LESLIE S. OFFUTT
Vassar College

RAFAEL OLEA FRANCO
El Colegio de México

AMY A. OLIVER
Department of Language and
Foreign Service
The American University

WILLIAM I. OLIVER
Department of Dramatic Arts
University of California, Berkeley

OTTO OLIVERA
Emeritus
Tulane University

MATTHEW O'MEAGHER
Department of History
Duke University

REBECCA J. OROZCO
Izabal Archaeological Project,
Guatemala

LUIS ORTEGA
Professor, Departamento de
Historia
Universidad de Santiago de Chile

CARL OSTHAUS
Department of History
Oakland University

OKEZI TIFFANI OTOVO
Doctoral Candidate, Department
of History
Georgetown University

THOMAS O. OTT
University of North Alabama

KENNETH N. OWENS
Department of History
California State University,
Sacramento

BRIAN OWENSBY
Corcoran Department of History
University of Virginia

AUGUSTO OYUELA-
CAYCEDO
Assistant Professor, Department of
Anthropology
University of Florida

JOSÉ EMILIO PACHECO
University of Maryland at College
Park

LUIS PALACÍN
Universidade Federal de Goiás

VICENTE PALERMO
Instituto de Investigaciones Gino
Germani
Universidad de Buenos Aires

JOEL W. PALKA
Associate Professor, Anthropology
and Latin American and Latino
Studies
University of Illinois, Chicago

COLIN A. PALMER
Graduate School and University
Center
City University of New York

DAVID SCOTT PALMER
*International Relations and
Political Science
Boston University*

ELÍAS JOSE PALTI
*UNQ (Universidad Nacional de
Quilmes) Professor Titular,
Programa de Historia Intelectual
CONICET (Comisión Nacional
de Investigaciones científicas,
Educativas y Tecnológicas)*

EUL-SOO PANG
Colorado School of Mines

LAURA JARNAGIN PANG
*Associate Professor, Division of
Liberal Arts and International Studies
Colorado School of Mines*

JOSE R. PANTOJA REYES

ROBERT L. PAQUETTE
Hamilton College

ROBERTO PAREJA
*PhD
Universidad Nur, Santa Cruz de
la Sierra*

JAMES WILLIAM PARK
San Diego Community College

DAVID S. PARKER
*Department of History
Queen's University, Ontario*

ROBERT L. PARKER
*School of Music
University of Miami*

LEE A. PARSONS
Jay K. Kislack Foundation

GRETE PASCH
*Universidad Francisco
Marroquín, Guatemala*

ROBERT PASTOR
*Professor, School of International
Service
The American University*

MIGUEL PASTRANA FLORES
*Instituto de Investigaciones
Históricas
Universidad Nacional Autónoma
de México*

SUZANNE PASZTOR
*Department of History
University of Wisconsin–La Crosse*

DAPHNE PATAI
*Department of Spanish and
Portuguese
University of Massachusetts*

ROBERT W. PATCH
*Department of History
University of California,
Riverside*

BLAKE D. PATTRIDGE
Tulane University

ANNE PAUL
*Institute of Andean Studies
University of California, Berkeley*

GUSTAVO PAZ
*Assistant Professor, Department of
History
University of Buenos Aires,
Argentina*

JULYAN G. PEARD
San Francisco State University

DEBORAH M. PEARSALL
*American Archeology Division
University of Missouri – Columbia*

**OSCAR G. PELÁEZ
ALMENGOR**
*Universidad de San Carlos de
Guatemala*

VINCENT PELOSO
*Department of History
Howard University*

JUAN MANUEL PÉREZ
*Hispanic Division
Library of Congress*

JOSÉ PÉREZ DE ARCE
*Museo Chileno de Arte
Precolombino*

**JOSÉ ANTONIO PÉREZ
GOLLÁN**
*Museo Etnográfico
Universidad de Buenos Aires*

LAURA PÉREZ ROSALES
*Dept. de Historia
Universidad Iberoamerica*

CHARLES A. PERRONE
*Professor of Portuguese and Luso–
Brazilian Literature and
Culture, Department of Romance
Languages and University of
Florida*

**VERÓNICA PESANTES-
VALLEJO**
University of Chicago

INEKE PHAF
*University of Maryland at College
Park*

WILLIAM D. PHILLIPS, JR.
*Department of History
University of Minnesota–Twin
Cities*

RONN F. PINEO
*Professor, History Department
Towson University*

ANTONIA PI-SUÑER
*Full Professor, Facultad de
Filosofía y Letras
Universidad Nacional Autónoma
de México*

KATHRYN PLUMMER
*Master Candidate, Center for
Latin American Studies
Georgetown University*

JANET M. PLZAK

JUAN POBLETE
*Associate Professor, Literature
Department
Provost, Kresge College, University
of California, Santa Cruz*

GUIDO A. PODESTÁ
University of Wisconsin–Madison

JOHN POHL
*Fowler Museum of Cultural History
University of California, Los Angeles*

MICHAEL A. POLL

MICHAEL A. POLUSHIN
*Department of History
University of Southern Mississippi*

CHERYL POMEROY

STAFFORD POOLE, C.M.
Vincentian Studies Institute

MARION POPENOE HATCH
*Director, Center for
Archaeological and
Anthropological Research
Department of Archaeology,
Universidad del Valle de Guatemala*

ROLAND E. POPPINO
*Department of History
University of California, Davis*

SUYAPA G. PORTILLO
VILLEDA
*PhD Candidate, History
Cornell University*

EDUARDO POSADA CARBO
*Research Associate, Latin
American Centre
St Antony's College, Oxford*

MICHAEL POWELSON
*Department of History
California State University–
Northridge and California State
University–Channel Islands*

SHELIA POZORSKI
*University of Texas–Pan
American*

ANA REBECA PRADA
*Department of Spanish and
Portuguese
University of Maryland at College
Park*

ESTHER J. PRESSEL
*Department of Anthropology
Colorado State University*

MARIE D. PRICE
George Washington University

CARLOS ALBERTO PRIMO
BRAGA
The Johns Hopkins University

SUSAN CANTY QUINLAN
*Department of Romance
Languages
University of Georgia*

ELOISE QUIÑONES KEBER
*Graduate School and University
Center
City University of New York*

ANA PATRICIA QUINTANA
MEZA
Universidad Ricardo Palma

INÉS QUINTERO
*Universidad Central de
Venezuela*

JACINTO QUIRARTE
*Department of History
University of Texas at San
Antonio*

ALFONSO W. QUIROZ
*Baruch College and Graduate School
City University of New York*

W. DIRK RAAT
*Department of History
State University of New York at
Fredonia*

JOSÉ RABASA
*Department of Romance
Languages
University of Michigan*

KAREN RACINE
*Associate Professor of History
University of Guelph*

CYNTHIA RADDING
University of New Mexico

MELVIN B. RAHMING
*Professor of English
Morehouse College*

SUSAN E. RAMÍREZ
*Department of History
DePaul University*

DONALD RAMOS
Cleveland State University

MARÍA DEL ROSARIO
RAMOS GONZÁLEZ
Johns Hopkins University

CARMEN RAMOS-
ESCANDÓN
Occidental College

LAURA R. RANDALL
*Professor Emerita, Department of
Economics
Hunter College of the City
University of New York*

JOANNE RAPPAPORT
*Department of Spanish and
Portuguese
Georgetown University*

JANE M. RAUSCH
*Department of History
University of Massachusetts at
Amherst*

LUIS REBAZA-SORALUZ
University of London

VERA BLINN REBER
Department of History and Philosophy
Shippensburg University

CARLOS REBORATTI
Licenciado
CONICET – University of Buenos Aires, School of Agriculture

RICHARD REED
Professor, Department of Sociology and Anthropology
Trinity University

SAMUEL O. REGALADO
Department of History
California State University, Stanislaus

CHRIS REID
Principal Lecturer in Economics, Department of Economics
University of Portsmouth, United Kingdom

F. KENT REILLY, III
Department of Anthropology
Southwest Texas State University

JOÃO JOSÉ REIS
Universidade Federal da Bahia

RICHARD D. REITSMA
Visiting Assistant Professor of Spanish and Latin American Studies
Gettysburg College

GUSTAVO REMEDI
Trinity College

JOSÉ LUIS RÉNIQUE
Lehman College and the Graduate Center
City University of New York

JULIA BECKER RICHARDS
Universidad Rafael Landívar de Guatemala

DOUGLAS RICHMOND
Department of History
University of Texas at Arlington

MÓNICA RICKETTS
Department of History
Harvard University

ROBERT B. RIDINGER
Chair, Electronic Information Resources Management
Northern Illinois University

EUGENE RIDINGS
Santa Cruz, California

EDWARD A. RIEDINGER
Ohio State University

FERNANDO RIOS
Visiting Assistant Professor Department of Music, Vassar College

JOEL RIPPINGER
Marmion Abbey
Aurora, Illinois

ALFREDO RIQUELME
Pontificia Universidad Católica de Chile

JONATHAN RITTER
Assistant Professor of Ethnomusicology, Department of Music
University of California, Riverside

ROCÍO RIVADENEYRA
Assistant Professor, Department of Psychology
Illinois State University

CLAUDIA RIVAS JIMENEZ
PhD Candidate, Department of History
Florida State University

CRISTIÁN ROA-DE-LA-CARRERA
Associate Professor, Department of Spanish and Latin American and Latino Studies
University of Illinois at Chicago

JAMES W. ROBB
Romance Languages
George Washington University

MARTHA BARTON ROBERTSON
Latin American Library
Tulane University

EUGENIA J. ROBINSON
Middle American Research Institute
Tulane University

FERNANDO ROCCHI
Director del Posgrado en Historia, Universidad Torcuato DiTella
Director académico Máster en Periodismo La Nación, Universidad Torcuato DiTella

BÉLGICA RODRÍGUEZ
Art Museum of the Americas

CELSO RODRÍGUEZ
Department of Cultural Affairs
Organization of American States

LEOPOLDO F. RODRÍGUEZ
Pan American Books
Organization of American States

LINDA A. RODRÍGUEZ
Latin American Center
University of California, Los Angeles

MARIO RODRÍGUEZ
University of Southern California

JAIME E. RODRÍGUEZ O.
Department of History
University of California, Irvine

V. DANIEL ROGERS
*Department Chair, Modern
Languages and Literatures
Wabash College*

**MATTHIAS RÖHRIG
ASSUNÇÃO**
*Department of History
University of Essex*

LAURA ROJAS
*Research Assistant, Centro de
Estudios Históricos
El Colegio de México*

LADY ROJAS-BENAVENTE
*Associate Professor, Classics,
Modern Languages and
Linguistics
Concordia University*

DENISE ROLLEMBERG
*Doutora em História, Professora
de História Contemporânea
Universidade Federal Fluminense*

EDUARDO ROMANO
*Professor Asociado Consulto,
Departamento de Letras
Instituto de Literatura Argentina*

LUIS ALBERTO ROMERO
*Consejo Nacional de
Investigaciones Científicas,
Escuela de Politica y Gobierno
Universidad Nacional de San
Martin*

PABLO ROMO
*PhD Candidate in Human
Rights
Coordinador del Observatorio de
la Conflictividad Social en México*

CHARLES E. RONAN, S.J.
Loyola University, Chicago

**ANNA CURTENIUS
ROOSEVELT**
*Professor, Department of
Anthropology
University of Illinois, Chicago*

J. MONTGOMERY ROPER
*Associate Professor of Anthropology
Grinnell College*

STEVE C. ROPP
*Professor, Department of Political
Science
University of Wyoming*

KEITH ROSENN
*School of Law
University of Miami*

JOSHUA M. ROSENTHAL
*Assistant Professor, Department of
History and Non–Western
Cultures
Western Connecticut State
University*

KATHLEEN ROSS
*Department of Romance Studies
Duke University*

IDA ELY RUBIN
The Americas Foundation

MARÍA HELENA RUEDA
*Department of Spanish and
Portuguese
Smith College*

MARK RUHL
*Glenn and Mary Todd Professor of
Political Science
Dickinson College*

RUBÉN RUIZ GUERRA
*Centro de Investigaciones Sobre
America Latina y el Caribe
Universidad Nacional Autónoma
de México*

A. J. R. RUSSELL-WOOD
*Department of History
The Johns Hopkins University*

HILDA SABATO
*History
Universidad de Buenos Aires,
Argentina*

GEORGINA SABAT-RIVERS

JAMES SCHOFIELD SAEGER
*Department of History
Lehigh University*

SYLVIA SAÍTTA
*Universidad de Buenos Aires—
Conicet*

ELIZABETH SALAS
University of Washington

**JORGE MARIO SALAZAR
MORA**
*Escuela de Historia
Universidad de Costa Rica*

MARIA A. SALGADO
*Department of Romance
Languages
University of North Carolina at
Chapel Hill*

SUSANA SALGADO
Library of Congress

RICHARD V. SALISBURY
*Department of History
Western Kentucky University*

FRANK SALOMON
*Department of Anthropology
University of Wisconsin – Madison*

LINDA K. SALVUCCI
*Department of History
Trinity University*

BALBINA SAMANIEGO
University of Salamanca

**CONSUELO NOVAIS
SAMPAIO**
Universidade Federal da Bahia

KATHRYN SAMPECK
*Visiting Assistant Professor, Stone
Center for Latin American
Studies
Tulane University*

JEFFREY D. SAMUELS
Goucher College

JOSEPH P. SÁNCHEZ
Spanish Colonial Research Center
University of New Mexico

DANIEL H. SANDWEISS
Department of Anthropology
Carnegie Museum

JAVIER SANJINÉS C.
Associate Professor, Department of
Romance Language and
Literatures
University of Michigan

CRISTINA SANTOS
Department of Modern
Languages, Literatures and
Cultures
Brock University

WILLIAM SATER
Professor Emeritus of History
California State University, Long
Beach

GEORGE SCHADE
Department of Spanish
University of Texas at Austin

ROBERT SCHEINA
Industrial College of the Armed
Forces

GABRIELA SCHIAVONI
Anthropologist, National Council
for Science and Technology
National University of Missions
(Argentina)

GUILLERMO
SCHMIDHUBER
Department of Modern Languages
University of Louisville

BETTINA SCHMIDT
School of Theology and Religious
Studies
Bangor University, United
Kingdom

GREGORY SCHMIDT
Professor and Chair, Department
of Political Science
University of Texas at El Paso

CYNTHIA SCHMIDT-CRUZ
Department of Foreign Languages
and Literatures
University of Delaware

ERIC SCHNITER
Master of Science, Department of
Anthropology
University of California, Santa
Barbara

KAI P. SCHOENHALS
Department of History
Kenyon College

DIETER SCHONEBOHM
Universidad de la República
Instituto Goethe, Montevideo,
Uruguay

MONICA SCHULER
Wayne State University

KIRSTEN C. SCHULTZ
New York University

JOHN F. SCHWALLER
President
State University of New York at
Potsdam

STUART SCHWARTZ
Department of History
Yale University

CARL E. SCHWARZ

REBECCA J. SCOTT
Department of History
University of Michigan

DARIO SCUKA
Institute for International
Affairs, Ltd.

DANIEL J. SEGEL

CATALINA SEGOVIA-CASE
University of San Diego

PHILIPPE L. SEILER
Department of History
Tulane University

DAN SEINFELD
MS, Department of Anthropology
Florida State University

MARTHA L. SEMPOWSKI
Research Division
Rochester Museum and Science
Center

STANLEY F. SHADLE
Division of Humanities
College Misericordia

RUTH SHADY SOLIS
Archaeologist
Head of the Special Caral–Supe
Archeological Project

EDWARD L. SHAW
Independent scholar

DAVID M. K. SHEININ
Department of History
Trent University

CARA SHELLY
Oakland University

WILLIAM L. SHERMAN
University of Nebraska–Lincoln

IZUMI SHIMADA
Southern Illinois University

CARL SHIRLEY
Department of Spanish Italian
and Portuguese
University of South Carolina

ALEX SHOUMATOFF

NICOLAS SHUMWAY
University of Texas at Austin

PETER SIAVELIS
Associate Professor
Wake Forest University

EDUARDO SILVA
Fundação Casa De Rui Barbosa,
Ministério da Cultura
Rio de Janeiro

MARIA BEATRIZ NIZZA DA
SILVA
Departamento de Ciências
Históricas
Universidade Portucalense
Infante D. Henrique

SERGIO SILVA-CASTAÑEDA
PhD Candidate, History
Department
Harvard University

HAROLD DANA SIMS
Department of History
University of Pittsburgh

WILLIAM SKUBAN
Department of History
University of California, Davis

RICHARD W. SLATTA
Professor of History
North Carolina State University

ANDREW SLUYTER
Department of Geography
University of Texas at Austin

ROBERT SMALE
Assistant Professor, Department of
History
University of Missouri–Columbia

RUSSELL SMITH
School of Business
Washburn University

WILLIAM J. SMOLE
Emeritus, Department of
Anthropology
University of Pittsburgh

SUSAN M. SOCOLOW
Department of History
Emory University

DOUGLAS O. SOFER
Assistant Professor, Department of
History, Division of Humanities
Maryville College, Maryville,
Tennessee

ETEL SOLINGEN
Department of Politics and Society
University of California, Irvine

REYNALDO SORDO CEDEÑO
Departamento Académico de
Estudios Generales
Instituto Tecnológico Autónomo de
México

SAÚL SOSNOWSKI
Department of Spanish and
Portuguese
University of Maryland at College
Park

DAVID SOWELL
Professor of History and
International Studies
Juniata College

HOBART A. SPALDING
Brooklyn College and Graduate
School
City University of New York

D. M. SPEARS
Department of History
Tulane University

JEREMY STAHL
Department of History
Middle Tennessee State University

DIANE STANLEY
Centro de Investigaciones
Regionales de Mesoamérica

E. JEFFREY STANN
American Association for the
Advancement of Science

CHARLES L. STANSIFER
Department of History
University of Kansas

ANTHONY STANTON
Centro de Estudios Lingüísticos y
Literarios
Colegio de México

CYNTHIA STEELE
Department of Romance
Languages and Literature
University of Washington

JUDITH GLUCK STEINBERG
Museum of American Folk Art

NANCY LEYS STEPAN
Department of History
Columbia University

IRWIN STERN
Columbia University

D. F. STEVENS
Drexel University

O. CARLOS STOETZER
Emeritus
Fordham University

RICHARD J. STOLLER
Coordinator of Selection and
International Programs, Schreyer
Honors College
Pennsylvania State University

K. LYNN STONER
Department of History
Arizona State University

KAREN E. STOTHERT
Department of Sociology and
Anthropology
Trinity University

JOSEPH STRAUBHAAR
Brigham Young University

GEORGE B. STUART
National Geographic Society

ANA ROSA SUAREZ
Dirección de Investigación
Instituto Mora Mexico

MANUEL SUÁREZ-MIER
Banco de México

J. DAVID SUÁREZ-TORRES
Georgetown University

JAIME SUCHLICKI
Graduate School of International
Studies
University of Miami

WILLIAM SUMMERHILL
Department of History
University of California, Los
Angeles

ALLAN S. R. SUMNALL
Tulane University

JOHN C. SUPER
Department of History
West Virginia University

JOAN E. SUPPLEE
History Department
Baylor University

JUAN SURIANO

JANE EDDY SWEZEY
Centro de Investigaciones
Regionales de Mesoamérica

PETER A. SZOK
Tulane University

LEWIS A. TAMBS
Department of History
Arizona State University

REGINA TAPIA
Postgraduate Student, Centro de
Estudios Históricos
El Colegio de México

ARTURO TARACENA
ARRIOLA
Universidad de Costa Rica

MYRIAM TARRAGÓ
Facultad de Filosofía y Letras
Universidad de Buenos Aires

WINIFRED TATE
Assistant Professor, Department of
Anthropology
Colby College

CHARLES TATUM
Department of Spanish and
Portuguese
University of Arizona

CÉSAR TCACH
Director of the Master's Program
in Political Parties, and Academic
Coordinator of the Doctorate in
Latin American Centro de
Estudios Avanzados de La
Universidad Nacional de Cordoba

FERNANDO TEIXEIRA DA
SILVA
Departamento de História
Cidade Universitária Zeferino
Vaz

BARBARA A. TENENBAUM
Hispanic Division
Library of Congress

JOHN JAY TEPASKE
Department of History
Duke University

MARCELA TERNAVASIO
CONICET (Consejo de
Investigaciones Científicas y
Técnicas) y Facultad de
Humanidades y Artes
Universidad Nacional de Rosario

HEATHER THIESSEN-REILY
Professor of History
Western State College of Colorado

JACK RAY THOMAS
Department of History
Bowling Green State University

GUY P. C. THOMSON
Department of Comparative
American Studies
University of Warwick

IAN THOMSON
Writer

JOHN THORNTON
Millersville University

ANDY THORPE
Reader in Development Economics
University of Portsmouth, United
Kingdom

MARK THURNER
Department of History
University of Florida

DALE W. TOMICH
State University of New York at
Binghamton

STEVEN TOPIK
Department of History
University of California, Irvine

JUAN CARLOS TORCHIA
ESTRADA
Organization of American States

VALENTINA TORRES
SEPTIEN
Director of Graduate Studies
Universidad Iberoamericana,
Ciudad de México

JOSÉ DE TORRES WILSON
University of Pittsburgh

SILVIO TORRES-SAILLANT
Dominican Studies Center

CAMILLA TOWNSEND
Colgate University

RAUL TREJO
Instituto de Investigaciones
Sociales de la Universidad
Nacional Autónoma de México

Ciudad de la Investigación en Humanidades, Circuito Mario de la Cueva, Ciudad Universitaria, Coyoacán

MICHEL-ROLPH TROUILLOT
Department of Anthropology
The Johns Hopkins University

BRETT TROYAN
Assistant Professor, History Department
State University of New York at Cortland

BRIAN TURNER
Professor, Political Science
Randolph–Macon College

CHRISTINA TURNER
Guarani in Bilingual Paraguay, School of World Studies
Virginia Commonwealth University

SOLVEIG A. TURPIN
Research Scientist, Institute of Latin American Studies
University of Texas at Austin

MARK UNGAR
Associate Professor of Political Science, Brooklyn College and Criminal Justice, Graduate Center
City University of New York

JAVIER URCID
Department of Anthropology
Brandeis University

LIDIO VALDEZ
Adjunct Professor, Archaeology Department
University of Calgary

FERNANDO VALE CASTRO
Doutor em História
Universidade Católica do Rio de Janeiro

ROBERTO VALERO
George Washington University

LUIZ FERNANDO VALLIM LOPES
Assistant Director, Latin American Music Center
Indiana University

MARK J. VAN AKEN
Department of History
California State University, Hayward

NANCY E. VAN DEUSEN
Department of History
University of Illinois at Urbana–Champaign

CHARLENE VAN DIJK
MA Candidate, Center for Latin American Studies, Edmund A. Walsh School of Foreign Service
Georgetown University

ERIC VAN YOUNG
Department of History
University of California, San Diego

PAUL J. VANDERWOOD
Department of History
San Diego State University

CLARET VARGAS
Independent Scholar, Romance Languages and Literatures
Harvard University

MARY KAY VAUGHAN
University of Illinois at Chicago

ADRIÁN VELÁZQUEZ CASTRO
Archaeologist of the Templo Mayor Museum
Museo del Templo Mayor, Instituto Nacional de Antropologia e Historia

LILIA VENEGAS AGUILERA
Dirección de Estudios Históricos
Instituto Nacional de Antropología e Historia

HUGO VERANI
Department of Spanish and Classics
University of California, Davis

JOHN W. VERANO
Department of Anthropology
Tulane University

GUSTAVO A. VERDESIO
Associate Professor, Department of Romance Languages and Literatures and Program in American Culture
University of Michigan

GARY M. VESSELS
Portuguese Department
Georgetown University

ANDREA VICENTE
Doctoral Student, Department of History
Michigan State University

ROSÂNGELA MARIA VIEIRA
Department of Modern Languages and Literatures
Howard University

CAROLYN E. VIEIRA-MARTINEZ

VÍCTOR VILLAVICENCIO
Facultad de Filosofía y Letras
Universidad Nacional Autónoma de México

KHRISTAAN VILLELA
Thaw Art History Center
College of Santa Fe

JON S. VINCENT
Department of Spanish and Portuguese
University of Kansas

STUART F. VOSS
Department of History
State University of New York at Plattsburgh

CHRISTINE J. WADE
Dept. of Political Science
Washington College

MARIA LUISE WAGNER
Department of History
Georgetown University

JOHN WALDRON
University of California, Irvine

KATHY WALDRON
Department of Spanish and
Portuguese
University of California, Irvine

CHARLES F. WALKER
Department of History
University of California, Davis

JEANNE C. WALLACE
Department of Spanish
Rutgers, The State University of
New Jersey

BOB J. WALTER
Professor, Department of
Geography
Ohio University

RICHARD J. WALTER
Professor, Department of History
Washington University, St. Louis

PETER M. WARD
Lyndon B. Johnson School of Public
Affairs
University of Texas at Austin

THOMAS WARD
Professor of Spanish, Modern
Languages and Literatures
Loyola College

MAUREEN WARNER-LEWIS
National Humanities Center
University of the West Indies,
Jamaica–Mona Campus

J. BENEDICT WARREN
University of Maryland

RICHARD WARREN
St. Joseph's University

MARK WASSERMAN
Department of History
Rutgers, The State University of
New Jersey

MAIDA WATSON
Professor, Department of Modern
Languages
Florida International University

DAVID J. WEBER
Department of History
Southern Methodist University

STEPHEN WEBRE
Department of History
Louisiana Tech University

ROBERT S. WEDDLE

BARBARA WEINSTEIN
Department of History
State University of New York at
Stony Brook

MARTIN WEINSTEIN
William Paterson College of New
Jersey

W. MICHAEL WEIS
Illinois Wesleyan University

CLIFF WELCH
Associate Professor of History
Grand Valley State University

JOHN H. WELCH
Lehman Brothers, Inc.

ALLEN WELLS
Department of History
Bowdoin College

THOMAS L. WHIGHAM
Professor of History
University of Georgia

DAVID E. WHISNANT
University of North Carolina at
Chapel Hill

JOSEPH W. WHITECOTTON
Department of Anthropology
University of Oklahoma

NEIL L. WHITEHEAD
Professor of Anthropology &
Religious Studies
University of Wisconsin–Madison

IÊDA SIQUEIRA WIARDA
Hispanic Division
Library of Congress

ANN M. WIGHTMAN
Department of History
Wesleyan University

ROBERT WILCOX
Department of History and
Geography
Northern Kentucky University

S. JEFFREY K. WILKERSON
The Institute for Cultural Ecology
of the Tropics

J. ROSS WILKINSON

W. MARVIN WILL
Political Science Department
The University of Tulsa

ADRIANA WILLIAMS

AKILAH EMILY WILLIAMS
Professor, Professional Writing
and Liberal Arts Department,
Savannah College of Art and
Design
SCAD–Atlanta

RAYMOND LESLIE
WILLIAMS
Department of Spanish and
Portuguese
University of Colorado at Boulder

EILEEN M. WILLINGHAM
Assistant Professor, Spanish &
Portuguese
University of Iowa

ELIZABETH WILLINGHAM
Baylor University

LARMAN C. WILSON
School of International Service
The American University

JOHN J. WINBERRY
Professor Emeritus of Geography
University of South Carolina

CAROL WISE
Associate Professor, School of
International Relations
University of Southern California

WALTER R. T. WITSCHEY
Professor of Anthropology and
Science Education
Cook–Cole College of Arts and
Sciences, Longwood University

FLAVIO WOLF DE AGUIAR
Brazilian Literature Professor
University of São Paulo

JOEL WOLFE
Department of History
Rice University

JOSEPH R. WOLIN
Columbia University

ANDREW WOOD
Associate Professor of History
University of Tulsa

JAMES WOOD
Associate Professor, Department of
History
North Carolina A&T University

STEPHANIE WOOD
Center for the Study of Women in
Society
University of Oregon

LAURA L. WOODWARD
Department of History
Centro de Investigaciones
Regionales de Mesoamérica

RALPH LEE WOODWARD, JR.
Joe & Teresa Long Professor of
Social Science
Tarleton State University

GEORGE WOODYARD
Professor Emeritus, Department of
Spanish and Portuguese
University of Kansas

THOMAS C. WRIGHT
Professor of History
University of Nevada, Las Vegas

WINTHROP R. WRIGHT
Department of History
University of Maryland

LAWRENCE A. YATES

JORDAN M. YOUNG
Pace University

REYNALDO YUNUEN
ORTEGA
Centro de Estudios
Internacionales
El Colegio de México

PATRICIO ENRIQUE
ZAMORANO
Center for Latin American
Studies
Georgetown University

JAMES A. ZEIDLER
Senior Research Scientist, Center
for Environmental Management
of Military Lands
Colorado State University

ANTONIO ZEPEDA

ERIC ZOLOV
Associate Professor
Franklin & Marshall College

ANN L. ZULAWSKI
Department of History
Smith College

ABADÍA MÉNDEZ, MIGUEL (1867–
1947). Miguel Abadía Méndez (*b*. 5 June 1867; *d*.
15 May 1947), Colombian president (1926–1930).
Born in La Vega de los Padres (now Piedras),
Tolima, Abadía was sent to Bogotá for his education.
He attended various private schools and received his
doctorate in law in 1889 from the Colegio del
Rosario. He became a publicist for Conservative
Party ideals and was editor of several Bogotá newspapers. He also taught history and law. Abadía's
energy, dedication, and deserved reputation for probity won him election to several congresses. An
expert in constitutional law, he served as minister in
the cabinets of several Conservative regimes before
becoming president in 1926. During his presidency,
the last of the "Conservative Hegemony," there was
further irresponsible borrowing abroad to support
the country's infrastructure. The economic downturn at the end of the 1920s brought increasingly
violent confrontations with newly organizing labor
in the petroleum fields (Santander) and the bloody
repression of the banana workers' strike (Magdalena,
November–December 1928). These episodes in turn
provoked further civil unrest, including popular and
student demonstrations and deaths (8–9 June 1929)
in Bogotá. As a result, Abadía was forced to fire his war
minister and others, and the Conservative Party fragmented. His political life was over. He died at La
Unión, Cundinamarca, after five years of severe mental
illness.

See also **Colombia, Political Parties: Overview;
Colombia, Political Parties: Conservative Party.**

BIBLIOGRAPHY

Terrence B. Horgan, "The Liberals Come to Power in
Colombia, *por Debajo de la Ruana:* A Study of the
Enrique Olaya Herrera Administration, 1930–1934"
(Ph.D. diss., Vanderbilt University, 1983), pp. 18–56.

Ignacio Arizmendi Posada, *Presidentes de Colombia, 1810–
1990* (1989), pp. 225–227.

Additional Bibliography

Hernández García, José Angel. *La Guerra civil Española y
Colombia: Influencia del principal conflicto entreguerras
en Colombia.* Chía, Cundinamarca, Colombia: Universidad de La Sabana; Bogotá: Editorial Carrera 7a, 2006.

Sáenz Rovner, Eduardo. *La ofensiva empresarial: Industriales,
políticos, y violencia en los años 40 en Colombia.* Bogotá:
Grupo de Investigación Conflicto Social y Violencia,
Centro de Estudios Sociales-CES, Facultad de Ciencias
Humanas, Universidad Nacional de Colombia: Grupo
TM, 2007.

Silva, Renán. *República liberal, intelectuales y cultura popular.* Medellín: Carreta Editores, 2005.

J. LEÓN HELGUERA

ABAD Y QUEIPO, MANUEL (1751–
1825). Manuel Abad y Queipo (*b*. 26 August 1751;
d. 15 September 1825), bishop of Michoacán (1810–
1814) and acute social commentator on late colonial
Mexico. The illegitimate son of a noble Asturian
family, Abad y Queipo was born in Santa María de
Villarpedre, Asturias, Spain. He studied at the University of Salamanca for ten years before immigrating
to the Americas, where he received a doctorate in
canon law from the University of Guadalajara in

1805. He served in Michoacán from 1784 to 1814, rising through the ecclesiastical hierarchy to become acting bishop (unconfirmed by captive King Ferdinand VII) in 1810. An exemplification of the enlightened clergyman, Abad y Queipo strove to improve local economic conditions, in one instance by promoting the production of raw silk. He also advocated social reforms, such as the abolition of tribute, and he criticized many Bourbon policies, notably the Intendancy System and the sequestration of pious funds.

Abad y Queipo, however, always favored reform within the imperial system. In 1810, when the rebellion led by his old friend Miguel Hidalgo y Costilla broke out, he excommunicated the insurgent leader and unceasingly preached the social and economic evils of civil war. Nonetheless, he was suspected of harboring dangerously liberal views, and the restored Ferdinand VII recalled him to Spain in 1814. Abad y Queipo was finally confirmed as bishop of Michoacán but was never allowed to return to Mexico. In 1822 he resigned his hard-won bishopric to become bishop of Tor-tose. He also served in the provisional junta of 1820, which rekindled Ferdinand's doubts about the cleric's political loyalty; this led in 1824 to his arrest and imprisonment in the monastery of Sisla, where he died.

See also **Michoacán.**

BIBLIOGRAPHY

Lillian Estelle Fisher, *Champion of Reform: Manuel Abad y Queipo* (1955).

Hugh M. Hamill, Jr., *The Hidalgo Revolt: Prelude to Mexican Independence* (1966).

Nancy M. Farriss, *Crown and Clergy in Colonial Mexico: The Crisis of Ecclesiastical Privilege* (1968).

Additional Bibliography

Luna, Pablo F. "Sociedad, reforma y propiedad: El liberalismo de Manuel Abad y Queipo, fines del siglo XVIII-comienzos del siglo XIX." *Secuencia* 52 (January–April 2002): 153-179.

Ortíz Escamilla, Juan. "Morelos y Abad y Queipo: Enfrentamiento político, 1812-1814." In *El nacimiento de México*, edited by Patricia Galeana de Valadés. Mexico: Archivo General de la Nación, Fondo de Cultura Económica, 1999.

R. DOUGLAS COPE

ABAJ TAKALIK. *See* **Takalik Abaj.**

ABALOS, JOSÉ DE. José de Abalos, intendant of the province of Venezuela (1776–1783). Born in La Mancha, Spain, Abalos was chief official of accounting and of general administration on the island of Cuba and chief accountant in the province of Venezuela. When the intendancy of Venezuela was created by royal decree on 8 December 1776, he was appointed to the office of intendant by order of King Charles III.

By order of the crown, Abalos developed a program of instruction for the workings of the intendancy, which can be considered the first organic law for the administration of finance in Venezuela. While serving as intendant, he promoted numerous initiatives for the economic and commercial benefit of the province. He was inflexible in the collection of taxes; intervened in and confronted the Compañía Guipuzcoana; offered credits to landowners; stimulated the diversification of crops; reactivated the mining industry; fought contraband; and established the state monopoly on playing cards, spirits, and tobacco. By the time of his retirement from the post in 1783, Abalos had brought about important advances in the reorganization of the royal finances and in the recuperation of the economy of the province of Venezuela.

See also **Cuba: The Colonial Era (1492-1898); Intendancy System; Venezuela: The Colonial Era.**

BIBLIOGRAPHY

For Abalos's influence on the colonial Venezuelan economy, see Eduardo Arcila Farías, *Economía colonial de Venezuela* (1946). See also P. Michael Mc Kinley, *Pre-revolutionary Caracas: Politics, Economy, and Society, 1777–1811* (1985); María Teresa Zubiri Marín, "José Abalos, primer intendente de Venezuela, 1777–1783," *Boletín Americanista* (Barcelona) 30, no. 38 (1988): 287–297.

Additional Bibliography

Lucena Giraldo, Manuel, José de Abalos, and Pedro Pablo Abarca de Bolea. *Premoniciones de la independencia de Iberoamérica: Las reflexiones de José de Abalos y el conde de Aranda sobre la situación de la América española a finales del siglo XVIII.* Madrid: Fundación Mapfre Tavera, 2003.

INÉS QUINTERO

ABASCAL Y SOUZA, JOSÉ FERNANDO (1743–1821).

José Fernando Abascal y Souza (*b*. 3 June 1743; *d*. 31 July 1821), viceroy of Peru (1806–1816). A native of Oviedo in northern Spain, Abascal pursued a military career and first visited America in 1767 as a junior officer assigned to the garrison of Puerto Rico. Following service in Spain, he returned to the empire with the 1776 expedition to the Río de la Plata, which captured the outpost of Sacramento on the eastern bank of the river from the Portuguese and established a new viceroyalty governed from Buenos Aires. After further service in Santo Domingo and Havana, he went to Guadalajara (Mexico) in 1799 as president of the *audiencia* (tribunal of justice). Appointed viceroy of the Río de la Plata, Abascal was transferred to Peru before he was able to take up his position in Buenos Aires; wartime complications delayed his arrival in Lima until 1806.

Abascal's fame derives primarily from his firmness in repressing conspiracies against continued Spanish rule in Peru during the period 1809–1810 (at a time when his counterparts in other viceregal capitals were meekly acquiescing to the demands of creole revolutionaries), and in raising expeditionary forces to put down the early independence movements in Chile, Ecuador, and Upper Peru (Bolivia). A firm royalist and absolutist, he obstructed the implementation in Peru of the Spanish Constitution of Cádiz, promulgated in 1812. Although disturbed in 1814–1815 by a serious insurrection in Cuzco, Peru remained a bastion of royalism when Abascal retired to the peninsula in 1816.

See also **Peru: From Conquest through Independence.**

BIBLIOGRAPHY

Vicente Rodríguez Casado and Guillermo Lohmann Villena, eds., *Memoria de gobierno del virrey Abascal* (1947).

Timothy E. Anna, *The Fall of the Royal Government in Peru* (1979).

Additional Bibliography

Hamnett, Brian. *La política contrarrevolucionaria del Virrey Abascal: Peru, 1806-1816.* Lima: IEP, 2000.

Peralta Ruiz, Víctor. *En defensa de la autoridad: política y cultura bajo el gobierno del virrey Abascal: Perú, 1806-1816.* Madrid: Consejo Superior de Investigaciones Científicas, Instituto de Historia, 2002.

JOHN R. FISHER

ABASOLO, MARIANO (c. 1783–1816).

Mariano Abasolo (*b*. ca. 1783; *d*. 14 April 1816), Mexican insurgent leader. A native of Dolores, in 1795 Abasolo entered the regiment of the Queen's Provincial Dragoons at San Miguel el Grande. He joined Miguel Hidalgo in Dolores when the priest led an uprising against the colonial regime in September 1810. Abasolo became a colonel in the insurgent forces and eventually rose to the rank of field marshal. On 28 September 1810 he besieged Guanajuato and demanded its surrender, but he did not participate in the sack of the city. After the insurgents' defeat at Calderón Bridge in January 1811, he fled north with Hidalgo. He refused to remain in command of the troops when the principal insurgent leaders decided to continue to the United States. Captured at Acatita de Baján on 21 March 1811, Abasolo was taken to Chihuahua, where during his trial he denied all responsibility for the insurrection. Because of his denials and his wife's efforts he was condemned to perpetual exile rather than to death. He died in the fortress of Santa Catalina in Cádiz, Spain.

See also **Allende, Ignacio.**

BIBLIOGRAPHY

José María Miquel I Vergés, *Diccionario de insurgentes* (1969), pp. 2–3.

Hugh M. Hamill, Jr., *The Hidalgo Revolt*, 2d ed. (1970).

Lucas Alamán, *Historia de Méjico*, vol. 1 (1985).

Carlos María De Bustamante, *Cuadro histórico de la Revolución Mexicana*, vol. 1 (1985).

Additional Bibliography

La independencia de México: Galeana "El Pípila," Jiménez, Villalongín y Abasolo. Mexico: Magesterio, 1969.

VIRGINIA GUEDEA

ABBAD Y LASIERRA, ÍÑIGO (1745–1813).

Íñigo Abbad y Lasierra (*b*. 17 April 1745; *d*. 24 October 1813), author of the first history of

Puerto Rico, *Historia geográfica, civil y natural de la Isla de San Juan Bautista de Puerto Rico* (1788). Born in Lérida, Spain, Abbad was educated at the monastery of Santa María la Real in Nájera, Spain. A Benedictine, he went to Puerto Rico in 1772 as confessor to the bishop Manuel Jiménez Pérez. He died in Valencia, Spain.

In the nineteenth century, Abbad's history underwent two editions, in 1831 and 1866. The latter edition, corrected and annotated by the Puerto Rican scholar José Julián Acosta, is still considered a valuable source of information. In 1959, the University of Puerto Rico reissued Abbad's work with an introduction by the historian Isabel Gutiérrez del Arroyo. *Historia geográfica, civil y natural de la isla de San Juan Bautista de Puerto Rico* was republished in 2002 jointly by Editorial Doce Calles (Madrid) and Centro de Investigaciones Históricos (Puerto Rico). Also recently republished by Miraguano Ediciones (Madrid) was *Diario del viaje a América.*

See also **Acosta, José de.**

BIBLIOGRAPHY

Information on Abbad can be found in Kenneth R. Farr, *Historical Dictionary of Puerto Rico and the U.S. Virgin Islands* (1973); Esther M. Melón De Díaz, *Puerto Rico: Figuras, apuntes históricos, símbolos nacionales* (1975); and Adolfo De Hostos, *Diccionario histórico bibliográfico comentado de Puerto Rico* (1976).

OLGA JIMÉNEZ DE WAGENHEIM

ABC COUNTRIES.

The ABC countries are Argentina, Brazil, and Chile. The name was in use during the period preceding World War I.

Following the settlement of boundary disputes between Argentina and Chile, these nations, along with Brazil, as the region's dominant economic and cultural powers, sought to establish a political alliance to mediate regional and hemispheric disputes. This effort was solidified with the so-called ABC Treaty of 1915, which followed the successful arbitration of a conflict between the United States and Mexico.

The ABC countries further advanced their role in inter-American diplomacy by mediating disputes between Colombia and Peru and, unsuccessfully, between Paraguay and Bolivia. The coalition dissolved in 1917 as a result of Brazil's entry into the Allied effort against Germany. While the direct results of the ABC Treaty were short-lived, the alliance among its three nations demonstrated their international aspirations as well as the potential for inter-American diplomacy.

During the mid 1970s, the links between the governments of the three countries had a sinister profile. The right-wing military dictatorships of Argentina, Brazil and Chile, among other countries, joined together under the national security doctrine paradigm in the Operation Condor (officially established in 1975), with the purpose of eliminating the "leftist subversion" by means of coordination of state-led terrorism and intelligence operations.

The spirit of the age changed meaningfully with the return to democracy during the 1980s. In 1985 presidents Sarney of Brazil and Alfonsin of Argentina issued the Declaracion de Iguazu, and in 1988 signed the Tratado de Integracion, Cooperacion y Desarrollo (integration, cooperation, and development treaty). In 1991 Argentina and Brazil, with Paraguay and Uruguay, signed the Asunción Treaty, which gave birth to Mercosur (the Southern Common Market), and in 1996 Chile entered the union as an associate member. After a long period of political instability in the region, the political and economic bonds among the three ABC countries had been strengthened, and treaties established to reinforce the mechanisms of cooperation on regional security and democracy.

See also **Alfonsín, Raúl Ricardo; Mercosur; Sarney, José.**

BIBLIOGRAPHY

Bouzas, Roberto and Hernán Soltz. "Institutions and Regional Integration: The Case of Mercosur." *NetAmericas*, 2001. Available from http://netamericas.net/Researchpapers/Documents/Bouzas/Bouzas1.pdf.

Dozer, Donald M. *Latin America: An Interpretive History*, rev. ed. Tempe: Center for Latin American Studies, Arizona State University, 1979.

JOHN DUDLEY
VICENTE PALERMO

ABENTE Y LAGO, VICTORINO (1846–1935).

Victorino Abente y Lago (*b.* 2 June 1846; *d.* 22 December 1935), Paraguayan poet. Abente published his first poems in his native town of Murguía, in the province of La Coruña, Spain. He went to Asunción in 1869, where he saw firsthand the sacking of the capital during the War of the Triple Alliance. Profoundly shaken by the devastation and ruin, he began to write poems reflecting human solidarity in the face of total destruction while harboring a deep faith in man's ability to recover and rebuild. Having developed a fondness for its land and people, he decided to remain in Paraguay and become a citizen. Abente was the first poet on record to sing of the Paraguayan woman in "Kygua Verá" (Lustrous Comb) and of her role in Paraguayan history in "La sibila paraguaya." He published most of his poems in Asunción dailies.

See also **War of the Triple Alliance.**

BIBLIOGRAPHY

Hugo Rodríguez-Alcalá, *Historia de La literatura paraguaya* (1971), pp. 34–35.

Victorino Abente, *Antología poéticas* (1984).

CATALINA SEGOVIA-CASE

ABERTURA.

ABERTURA. *Abertura,* the policy of political liberalization or "opening" to democracy in Brazil initiated by the government of General João Batista Figueiredo in 1979. With *abertura,* the military regime planned to implement democratic reform under the careful supervision of state political strategists in order to provide a more permanent means of support for the national security state. The forces of liberalization unleashed by the Figueiredo government, however, soon swept the military regime out of power.

The first stage in the *abertura* process was the passage of the Amnesty Act of 1979. This law revoked the imprisonment and banishment orders for persons convicted of political crimes by past regimes. Later that year, the Party Reform Bill allowed the creation of numerous opposition parties—a measure meant to divide the government's opponents. Nevertheless, it established the most open political system that Brazil had seen in over a decade.

Another major step in the *abertura* process occurred in November 1980 when Congress passed an executive-proposed constitutional amendment that reintroduced the direct election of state governors and all federal senators. Threatened by the progress of the *abertura,* military hard-liners initiated a series of bombings to thwart the liberalization process. Although it spread fear, the campaign of violence did not halt the decline of the hard-liners' influence.

The power of the National Renovation Alliance (ARENA), the regime's party, also began to wane. Opposition groups made key gains in the 1982 elections, and opponents of the military government organized a campaign for direct presidential elections (*diretas*) that gained vast popular support but fell short of securing the two-thirds' majority of senators needed to amend the Constitution. The end of the military regime came on 15 January 1985, when a majority of government party members joined forces with the opposition to elect Tancredo Neves, Brazil's first civilian president since 1964.

See also **Brazil, Amnesty Act (1979); Brazil, Political Parties: National Renovating Alliance (ARENA).**

BIBLIOGRAPHY

Maria Helena Alves, *State and Opposition in Military Brazil* (1985).

Thomas Skidmore, *The Politics of Military Rule in Brazil, 1964–1985* (1988).

Alfred Stepan, *Rethinking Military Politics* (1988).

Additional Bibliography

Farcau, Bruce W. *The Transition to Democracy in Latin America: The Role of the Military.* Westport: Praeger, 1996.

Hagopian, Francis, and Scott Mainwaring. *The Third Wave of Democratization in Latin America: Advances and Setbacks.* New York: Cambridge University Press, 2005.

Kingstone, Peter R., and Timothy J. Power. *Democratic Brazil: Actors, Institutions, and Processes.* Pittsburgh: University of Pittsburgh Press, 2000.

Maciel, David. *A argamassa da ordem: Da ditadura militar à nova república (1974-1985).* São Paulo: Xamã, 2004.

Rossiaud, Jean, Ilse Scherer-Warren, and Paulo Evaristo Arns. *A democratização inacabável: As memórias do futuro.* Petrópolis: Editora Vozes, 2000.

Whitehead, Laurence, *Democratization: Theory and Experience.* Oxford: Oxford University Press, 2002.

MICHAEL POLL

ABIPÓN PEOPLE. The Abipón people were a branch of the Guaycuruan linguistic family who lived in nonsedentary bands between the Río Salado and the Río Pilcomayo in northeastern Argentina. Before the arrival of the Spaniards, the Abipones hunted wild game and harvested vegetable foods, such as carob bean, coconuts, and dates. By 1600, the Abipones had abandoned their previous seasonally-mobile lifestyle of hunting, gathering, and small-scale farming; they captured thousands of cattle and horses from the Spaniards, and within a few generations had transitioned into a nomadic horse-based society. The language, today considered by linguists to be extinct, resembled those of the Mocoví and Toba peoples, each differing from the others much as the Romance languages of Europe do. The societies of these three nations also shared similar cultural characteristics. In the 1750s the Abipones comprised three bands: the Riïkahés, of the plains of the southern Chaco; the Nakaiketergehés, a woodland people; and the Yaaukanigás, once a separate riverine people whose original identity was lost after a conquest. The Abipones were immortalized in the famous *Historia de Abiponibus equestri, bellicosaque Paraguariae natione* (1784) by Martin Dobrizhoffer, a Jesuit missionary and gifted ethnologist who served with the Abipones in the 1750s and 1760s and wrote his work of comparative anthropology in exile in Vienna.

Like the Mocoví, mounted Abipones raided the encroaching Spanish farms, ranches, missions, and interprovincial commerce. In peacetime they traded with merchants and rural peoples of the upper Río de la Plata region. After 1640, in response to an increased Spanish military presence that sought to impose colonial authority, contact between the Abipones and the Spanish became increasingly violent. Around 1750, the changing Chaco ecology, the increase in violence between and among Spaniards and native peoples, the decimation of the native population due to disease, and the loss of access to cattle because of new practices of corrals and guards for livestock caused the Abipones, who numbered about 5,000, to join Catholic missions. The first Riïkahé group settled in the San Jerónimo mission of Santa Fe in 1748. Jesuits also helped Abipones establish three more missions, and a fifth Abipón mission was founded after the expulsion of the Jesuits. When independence destroyed the missions, Abipones, many of whom were sedentary cultivators and herders, settled down between the Río Salado and Río Bermejo west of the Río Paraná, but quite a few Abipón men joined the armies of José Gervasio Artigas and later fought under other leaders in post-Independence Platine conflicts. In the 1850s, Italian Franciscans founded new missions for the Abipones in Santa Fe. After these missions were secularized in 1912, the Abipones slowly lost their tribal identity as they joined rural and urban lower classes of the provinces of Santa Fe, Chaco, and Formosa in Argentina.

See also **Artigas, José Gervasio; Indigenous Peoples; Missions: Jesuit Missions (Reducciones); Mocoví.**

BIBLIOGRAPHY

Martin Dobrizhoffer, *An Account of the Abipones: An Equestrian People of Paraguay,* 3 vols., translated by Sara Coleridge (1822; repr. in 1 vol., 1970).

Alfred Métraux, "Ethnography of the Chaco," in *Handbook of South American Indians,* vol. 1, edited by Julian H. Steward (1946), pp. 197–300.

James Schofield Saeger, "Another View of the Mission as a Frontier Institution: The Guaycuruan Reductions of Santa Fe, 1743–1810," in *Hispanic American Historical Review* 65, no. 3 (1985): 493–517.

Additional Bibliography

Lucaioli, Carina Paula. *Los grupos abipones hacia mediados del siglo XVIII.* Buenos Aires: Sociedad Argentina de Antropología, 2005.

JAMES SCHOFIELD SAEGER

ABOLITION OF SLAVERY. *See* **Slavery: Abolition; Slave Trade, Abolition of: Brazil; Slave Trade, Abolition of: Spanish America.**

ABRANCHES, GIRALDO JOSÉ DE. *See* **Inquisition: Brazil.**

ABREU, DIEGO DE (?–1553). Diego de Abreu (*d.* 1553), conquistador and early settler. Abreu was born in Seville, Spain, and came to the Río de la Plata with the expedition of Pedro de Mendoza in 1536. After the original settlement of

Santa María del Buen Aire was abandoned, and after Mendoza's death earlier that year, Juan de Salazar y Ezpinosa founded Asunción in 1537. When Alvar Núñez Cabeza de Vaca, the second *adelantado* of the Río de la Plata, and the settlers of Asunción came into open conflict over how the settlement should be run, Abreu supported Nuñez. He later protested the naming of Domingo Martínez de Irala as governor and was sent to prison. He escaped, and led a group of loyalists against Martínez. When Martínez left Asunción on an exploratory trip in 1547, Abreu demanded that his successor, Francisco de Mendoza, surrender command. Abreu had Mendoza imprisoned and executed. When Martínez returned in 1549, Abreu abandoned the governorship he had assumed by force and fled inland. He wrote a detailed report of these disputes in 1548. Abreu never returned to Asunción and died in an Indian hamlet.

See also **Cabeza de Vaca, Alvar Núñez; Conquistadores; Irala, Domingo Martínez de; Mendoza, Pedro de.**

BIBLIOGRAPHY

Ricardo Levene, *A History of Argentina* (1963).

Additional Bibliography

Koebel, W. H. *Argentina: Past and Present.* Koebel Press, 2007.

NICHOLAS P. CUSHNER

ABRIL, XAVIER (1905–1990).

Xavier Abril (*b.* 1905; *d.* 1990), Peruvian poet and critic. A leading member of Peru's avant-garde movement from the mid-1920s, Abril helped introduce surrealism and other modernist movements in Peru and Latin America, particularly with his contributions, both poetry and criticism, to *Amauta,* the leading cultural journal of the period.

His early poetry, usually ascribed to surrealism, is collected in *Hollywood* (1931) and *Difícil trabajo: Antología 1926–1930* (1935). In these books of verses and short prose, oneiric images of natural elements and human anatomy present a self in the process of fragmentation, and a desire for reintegration.

Abril's literary criticism includes studies of the work of Stéphane Mallarmé and the Peruvian poet José María Eguren; he is best known for his works on the poetry of César Vallejo: *Vallejo: Ensayo de aproximación crítica* (1958), *César Vallejo o la teoría poética* (1962), and *Exégesis trílcica* (1980).

Abril's focus on literary criticism, particularly his writings on Mallarmé, seems to coincide with a shift in his poetry to a more controlled use of imagery. Another factor in this change is the influence of Spanish medieval and Golden Age poets, which is reflected in his use of more conventional poetic forms, including traditional meters. Although this shift is apparent in his third collection, *Descubrimiento del alba* (1937), it is the determining element of his later poetry, which is marked by abstract symbolism.

See also **Vallejo, César.**

BIBLIOGRAPHY

Luis Monguió, *La poesía postmodernista peruana* (1954), pp. 158–160; *Creación & Crítica* no. 9–10 (1971).

Washington Delgado, "La calle, la locura, el hogar y el mundo," in *Dominical (El Comercio),* 3 February 1980: 12.

Ricardo González-Vigil, *Poesía Peruana: Antología general,* vol. 3, *De Vallejo a nuestros días* (1984), pp. 65–67 and 471–472.

James Higgins, *A History of Peruvian Literature* (1987), p. 170.

Additional Bibliography

Lauer, Mirko. *Antología de la poesía vanguardista peruana.* Lima: Ediciones El Virrey, 2001.

JOSÉ CERNA-BAZÁN

ACÁ CARAYÁ CAVALRY.

Acá Carayá Cavalry, a famed escort regiment of the Paraguayan army. Established by Francisco Solano López in the period just prior to the War of the Triple Alliance (1864–1870), the Acá Carayá saw service in that conflict as a presidential guard unit and, later, as a shock force against the Brazilians. The regiment was distinguished by colorful uniforms and metal helmets adorned with the tails of howler monkeys (from which the unit earned its Guaraní appellation, meaning "monkey heads"). The Acá Carayá saw renewed service during the Chaco War (1932–1935) with Bolivia. The regiment remains a featured attraction of military parades during Independence Day and other national holidays in Paraguay.

See also **Chaco War; War of the Triple Alliance.**

BIBLIOGRAPHY

Leandro Aponte B., *Hombres, armas y batallas* (1971).

Charles Kolinski, *Historical Dictionary of Paraguay* (1973), p. 2.

Additional Bibliography

Bethell, Leslie. *The Paraguayan War (1864-1870)*. London: Institute of Latin American Studies, 1996.

Leuchars, Chris. *To the Bitter End: Paraguay and the War of the Triple Alliance*. Westport: Greenwood Press, 2002.

Marco, Miguel Angel de. *La guerra del Paraguay*. Buenos Aires: Planeta, 1995.

Whigham, Thomas. *The Paraguayan War*. Lincoln: University of Nebraska Press, 2002.

THOMAS L. WHIGHAM

ACADEMIA DE LA LENGUA Y CULTURA GUARANÍ.

Academia de la Lengua y Cultura Guaraní, Paraguay's leading institution dedicated to the study and promotion of the national Indian language, Guaraní. Founded in 1949 by ethno-botanist Guillermo Tell Bertoni, the Academia draws its inspiration from an earlier institution, the Sociedad de Cultura Guaraní (founded in 1920). The goals of the current institution include organizing classes in Guaraní, supporting literary efforts in that language, hosting regular sessions of the international Congreso de la Lengua Tupí-Guaraní, and helping to formulate government policy toward language use, especially insofar as education and the standardization of orthography are concerned.

Academia members have included such poets, playwrights, artists, and linguists as Marcos Morínigo, Branislava Susnik, Pablo Alborno, and Grazziella Corvalán. Though their work tends to be read only by specialists at present, the growing popular acceptance of the value of the Guaraní tongue can be little doubted. This is seen, for example, in the number of television programs and theater presentations in Guaraní. The Paraguayan government has also responded to these developments, albeit in a haphazard fashion, by publishing some of its official documents in Guaraní in addition to Spanish. The philosophy faculty of the National University of Asunción offers a degree in Guaraní, and it is now a required subject in the nation's secondary schools. In the twenty-first century, over 90 percent of the population could speak Guaraní. Also, people frequently use a mixture of Spanish and Guaraní, called Jopara.

See also **Guarani Indians.**

BIBLIOGRAPHY

Charles J. Kolinski, *Historical Dictionary of Paraguay* (1973), p. 2.

Tadeo Zarratea and Feliciano Acosta, *Avañe'e* (1981).

Additional Bibliography

Gómez, Gérard. *El plurilingüismo paraguayo, un fenómeno que enlaza y separa: Evolución de la lengua guaraní y proceso de jerarquización lingüística*. Asunción: Servilibro, 2006.

Horst, René Harder. *The Stroessner Regime and Indigenous Resistance in Paraguay*. Gainesville: University Press of Florida, 2007.

Meliá, Bartomeu. *La Lengua guaraní del Paraguay: Historia, sociedad y literatura*. Madrid: Editorial MAPFRE, 1992.

MARTA FERNÁNDEZ WHIGHAM

ACADEMIA DE SAN CARLOS.

Academia de San Carlos, the first art academy in the New World and the principal Mexican artistic institution of the nineteenth century. Through the Academia de San Carlos, formally opened in 1785, the Bourbon administration implanted academic neoclassicism and dealt a definitive blow to the guild system of artistic production in New Spain. Teachers and materials, particularly an important collection of plaster casts of classical works, were sent from Spain. Closed between 1821 and 1824, the academy functioned fully again only after 1843, when it was reorganized. There were European teachers, annual exhibitions, scholarships to send the best students to Europe, and new plaster casts. In addition, a permanent collection of both Mexican and foreign paintings was formed. Under various names (Academia Imperial, Escuela Nacional de Bellas Artes, Academia Nacional de Bellas Artes) the academy continued; it promoted art with nationalist themes and, in the early twentieth century, assimilated artistic renewal. A student strike in 1911–1913 and an experiment in painting outdoors (*escuelas al aire libre*) accompanied the entry of the academy into the modernist movement. In 1929, with Diego Rivera as director, the academy became part of the Universidad Nacional Autónoma de México with the name of Escuela Nacional de Artes Plásticas. As such, it continues today.

See also **Art: The Nineteenth Century; Rivera, Diego; Universities: The Modern Era.**

BIBLIOGRAPHY

Justino Fernández, *El arte del siglo XIX en México* (1967).

Jean Charlot, *Mexican Art and the Academy of San Carlos, 1785–1915* (1962).

Additional Bibliography

Bailey, Gauvin A. *Art of Colonial Latin America.* New York: Phaidon, 2005.

Carrera, Magali M. *Imagining Identity in New Spain: Race, Lineage, and the Colonial Body in Portraiture and Casta Paintings.* Austin: University of Texas Press, 2003.

Cañizares-Esguerra, Jorge. *Nature, Empire, and Nation: Explorations of the History of Science in the Iberian World.* Stanford: Stanford University Press, 2007.

CLARA BARGELLINI

to the colonial authorities on 13 September 1810, leading to the arrest of several conspirators. Hoping to prevent his wife from notifying the rest of the conspirators, Domínguez, as a magistrate, locked her in their house. But Doña Josefa managed to alert Allende, and he in turn told Hidalgo what had happened. Consequently, Hidalgo launched the uprising on 16 September 1810.

See also **Abasolo, Mariano; Aldama y González, Juan de; Allende, Ignacio; Domínguez, Miguel; Hidalgo y Costilla, Miguel; Ortiz de Domínguez, Josefa.**

BIBLIOGRAPHY

Hugh M. Hamill, Jr., *The Hidalgo Revolt*, 2d ed. (1970).

Lucas Alamán, *Historia de Méjico*, vol. 1. (1985).

Carlos María De Bustamante, *Cuadro histórico de la Revolución Mexicana*, vol. 1 (1985).

Additional Bibliography

Archer, Christon I., ed. *The Birth of Modern Mexico, 1780-1824.* Wilmington, DE: Scholarly Resources Inc., 2003.

Ibarra Palafox, Francisco A. *Miguel Hidalgo: Entre la libertad y la tradición.* México, D.F.: Porrúa: Facultad de Derecho, U.N.A.M., 2003.

Rodríguez O, Jaime E., ed. *The Origins of Mexican National Politics, 1808-1847.* Wilmington: SR Books, 1997.

VIRGINIA GUEDEA

ACADEMIA LITERARIA DE QUERÉTARO.

Academia Literaria de Querétaro, a group of persons discontented with the colonial regime that formed in the city of Querétaro, Mexico. It included Corregidor Miguel Domínguez and his wife, Josefa Ortiz De Domínguez; military men such as Ignacio Allende, Juan Aldama, and Mariano Abasolo; clergymen; lawyers; and others, such as the brothers Epigmenio and Emeterio González. At the invitation of Allende, Miguel Hidalgo, curate of Dolores, attended on various occasions. Several members of the group met secretly to conspire against the colonial regime and to plan a popular uprising to apprehend peninsular Spaniards and confiscate their wealth to finance the movement.

The conspirators, who sought to obtain the support of military units, gathered arms and ammunition. They proposed to establish an emperor and some dependent kingdoms. The plot was denounced

ACADEMIAS.

Academias, series of ongoing literary and scientific meetings in eighteenth-century Brazil. The first academy was created in 1724 and was called Academia Brasílica dos Esquecidos (Brazilian Academy of the Forgotten). Begun under the patronage of Viceroy Vasco Fernandes César da Meneses, it lasted until 1725. The historian Sebastião Rocha Pita and other notables in Bahian society belonged to this academy.

Until the end of the eighteenth century, almost thirty academies existed in colonial Brazil. After the 1772 reform of the University of Coimbra, where the Brazilian elite studied, these meetings became more scientific and less literary, but in either case the Brazilian academies were not so firmly established as their European counterparts. In Brazil scholars met in various towns and cities of the captaincies and wrote memoirs and proposed subjects for discussions, but their activity remained sporadic. For instance, when the count of Valadares assumed the government of the captaincy of Minas Gerais, an academy meeting took place 4 Septem-ber 1768. Cláudio Manuel da Costa (1729–1789) read a poetic work he had written especially for the event.

A more organized academy was the Academia Brasílica dos Renascidos (Brazilian Academy of the Reborn), founded in Bahia in 1759, which lasted only six months. In 1772 the viceroy, the Marqués of Lavradio (ca. 1729–1790), supported in Rio de Janeiro an "assembly or academy" whose purpose was to study the three realms of nature. It was composed of medical doctors, surgeons, botanists, chemists, and some amateurs (*curiosos*). However, the most important contribution by Brazilian-born scientists and scholars to the study of natural history and agriculture was due not to the local academies but to the well-established Royal Academy of Sciences in Lisbon.

See also **Brazilian Academy of Letters.**

BIBLIOGRAPHY

João Lúcio Azevedo, *Novas Espanáforas: Estudos de história e literatura* (1932).

José Aderaldo Castelo, ed., *O movimento academicista no Brasil, 1641–1820* (1969–1978).

Massaud Moisés, *História da literatura brasileira*, vol. 1, *Origens, barroco, arcadismo* (1983).

Additional Bibliography

Silva, Joaquim Norberto de Souza e and Roberto Acízelo Quelha de Souza. *História da literatura brasileira e outros ensaios*. Rio de Janeiro: Zé Mario Editor: Ministerio da Cultura, Fundação Biblioteca Nacional, Departamento Nacional do Livro, 2002.

Stegagno Picchio, Luciana. *História da literatura brasileira*. Rio de Janeiro: Lacerda/Nova Aguilar, 2004.

MARIA BEATRIZ NIZZA DA SILVA

ACAPULCO. Acapulco de Juaréz, a port city of over one million inhabitants (2005) has long been recognized as having the finest natural harbor on Mexico's Pacific coast. Its great harbor notwithstanding, Acapulco's role in the nation's economic geography has been defined more by its isolation from the central plateau by the rugged mountains of the state of Guerrero. The area was settled by the Spaniards in the 1530s as a site primarily for building ships to explore the Pacific coast. The first ships, built in 1532, traded and explored south to Peru and north to the Colorado River. Acapulco played an important role during the colonial period as New Spain's major Pacific port, and in 1565 the first Manila Galleon entered its protected bay. The annual galleons from the Philippines carried silks, jades, ivory, perfumes, and incense from the Orient, products that were traded for silver in Peru and Mexico, and ultimately reached to Spain.

Because of its hot and oppressive climate, however, Acapulco remained a small settlement despite its importance. At the beginning of the nineteenth century, it had only about 4,000 permanent inhabitants, a large proportion of whom were blacks or mulattoes. The city's population rose as high as 9,000 to 12,500, however, during the annual two-week *feria*, referred to by the nineteenth-century German explorer Alexander von Humboldt as "the most renowned fair of the world." The *feria*, associated with the arrival and departure of the galleon, drew large numbers of merchants southward along the "China Road" to the port.

Acapulco was described as a squalid place, but it was protected by Castle San Diego, built in 1616, and, after 1776, by Fort San Diego. With the end of the Manila galleon in 1815 and the subsequent independence of Mexico, Acapulco settled into relative obscurity as its mule trail fell into disuse. With no railroad across the mountains that separate Acapulco from the interior, the port lost its domination of commerce to Manzanillo, which was farther north along the coast and was the terminus of a rail line to Guadalajara and Mexico City.

Acapulco, however, was destined for a very different role. In 1927 an automobile road to the city was opened, and the first resort hotel was built on the beach in 1938. Miguel Alemán, as president of Mexico, promoted the further development of tourism in Acapulco with the completion of a paved four-lane highway in 1955. Acapulco rapidly developed into a major resort area. In the 1990s completion of the road known as the Ruta del Sol (Route of the Sun), connecting Mexico City to Acapulco, improved accessibility further still. The city's unchecked growth, however, has created problems with water and sewage, severe pollution of the bay, and a general deterioration of the ecology. Overcrowding has cau-sed a

Acapulco's beaches littered with garbage after heavy rains, 2006. Continued development of tourism and the rapid growth of settlements along the coast have taken its toll on Acapulco's environment. © JESUS TRIGO/EPA/CORBIS

housing shortage and resulted in a sprawl of squatter settlements up the mountain slopes surrounding the bay. In 1997 Hurricane Pauline made landfall, destroying many of these homes and inundating the city with torrential rain and mudslides. Since this disaster, the government has invested money to rebuild infrastructure and improve city services. Municipal, state, and federal funding in 2003 went toward cleaning up the bay. New resorts continue to open along the Pacific and Caribbean coasts of Mexico, but Acapulco, with its dry winter and multiracial population, has remained a popular destination for both Mexican and foreign tourists.

See also **Tourism.**

BIBLIOGRAPHY

William L. Schurz, *The Manila Galleon* (1939), esp. pp. 371–384.

James Cerutti, "The Two Acapulcos," in *National Geographic* 126 (December 1964): 848–878.

Additional Bibliography

Alvarez Ponce de León, Griselda. *México, turismo y cultura.* Mexico: Editorial Diana, 2001.

Berger, Dina. *The Development of Mexico's Tourism Industry: Pyramids by Day, Martinis by Night.* New York: Palgrave Macmillan, 2006.

Cárdenas, Alejandra. *Hechicería, saber y trasgresión: Afromestizas ante la Inquisición: Acapulco, 1621–1622.* Mexico: Candy, 1997.

Clancy, Michael. *Exporting Paradise: Tourism and Development in Mexico.* New York: Pergamon, 2001.

Sales Colín, Ostwald. *El movimiento portuario de Acapulco: El protagonismo de Nueva España en la relación con Filipinas, 1587–1648.* Mexico: Plaza y Valdés Editores, 2000.

JOHN J. WINBERRY

ACARAY RIVER. Acaray River, affluent stream in eastern Paraguay that after a 108-mile course, joins the Paraná River 6 miles upstream of the mouth of the Iguaçú River. In 1968 a hydroelectric plant was built, with the assistance of Italian engineers, near the settlement of Hernandarias. The 45,000-kilowatt output feeds the capital city of Asunción, and secondary lines supply border towns in Brazil and northeastern Argentina. Expansion in 1976 enlarged production to 240,000 kilowatts.

See also Energy.

BIBLIOGRAPHY

Hugo G. Ferreira, *Geografía del Paraguay* (1975).

Additional Bibliography

Prebenna, David. *Planet Earth: Macmillan World Atlas.* Germany: Wiley, 1996.

César N. Caviedes

ACEVAL, BENJAMÍN (1845–1902). A

Paraguayan educator and diplomat, Benjamín Aceval is commonly associated with the Gran Chaco border negotiations of the 1870s and 1880s, but was also largely responsible for the recovery of his country's educational system in the wake of the disastrous War of the Triple Alliance (1864–1870). A native asunceño (resident of Asunción, Paraguay's capital), he received his early education at the Colegio de Monserrat in Córdoba, Argentina, before going on to complete legal studies in Buenos Aires in 1873. He accompanied the stream of expatriates returning to Paraguay during the Brazilian occupation, and upon arrival in his native city took up journalism, becoming the editor of the liberal newspaper *La Reforma*. For a short time, he headed the Justice and Education ministries before heading the negotiating team sent to Washington in 1875 to argue the Paraguayan side of the Chaco border dispute with Argentina. Aceval's careful delineation of claims, backed up by an impressive command of archival documentation, placed him in sharp contrast with his Argentine counterparts, and when President Rutherford B. Hayes announced his arbitral decision, it was in no small measure due to Aceval's labors that the Paraguayan position was upheld.

Returning to Asunción, Aceval gave up diplomacy for a time and dedicated himself wholeheartedly to public education, which had fallen into terrible disrepair since the end of the war. He helped establish the Colegio Nacional in the capital, with a branch in Villarrica. In 1878 he turned down the foreign minister's portfolio in order to continue as director of the Colegio, which he administered for eight years and saw grow into an institution of considerable importance in just a short time.

While the Chaco difficulties with Argentina had been resolved, those with Bolivia had just started, and the government continued to call on Aceval as an adviser on the matter. In February 1887 he signed the Aceval-Tamayo treaty, which, though it failed to resolve the land dispute, nonetheless kept the peace with Bolivia for the better part of a generation. Throughout this time he worked as a professor of law at the Facultad de Derecho and was sometimes rector of the university. He died in Asunción.

See also Chaco Region; Paraguay: The Nineteenth Century; War of the Triple Alliance.

BIBLIOGRAPHY

Zubizarreta, Carlos. *Cien vidas paraguayas.* Asunción: Araverá, 1985.

Thomas L. Whigham

ACEVEDO DÍAZ, EDUARDO INÉS

(1851–1921). Eduardo Inés Acevedo Díaz (*b.* 1851; *d.* 18 June 1921), Uruguayan journalist and novelist, born in Montevideo. Connected from early on with his country's National (or Blanco) Party, Acevedo Díaz took up arms on three occasions between 1870 and 1897 to participate in revolutionary movements. As a journalist, he wrote tough polemics concerning party struggles in such periodicals as *La Democracia, La Razón,* and *El Nacional*. Due to his political militancy, he was imprisoned and exiled on several occasions, and it was during his exile in Argentina between 1876 and 1895 that he wrote his most representative works, the historical novels *Brenda* (1886), *Ismael* (1888), *Nativa* (1890) and his famous *Soledad* (1894), a series that would be completed in 1914 by *Lanza y sable*.

Acevedo Díaz is considered to be the first Uruguayan novelist as well as the founder of the historical novel in Uruguay. His entire work can be seen as an investigation into the origin of nationality, yet his effort occurred in the framework of the modernizing process carried out by the ruling class between 1870 and 1920. This process entailed the formation of a modern state, which required for its legitimacy the building of a nationalist sentiment in order to lend cohesion to the community. The work of Acevedo Díaz, like that of his contemporary Juan Zorrilla De San Martín (*La leyenda Patria* [1879] and *Tabaré* [1888]), were significant contributions to this effort.

See also **Literature: Spanish America; Uruguay, Political Parties: Blanco Party; Zorrilla de San Martín, Juan.**

BIBLIOGRAPHY

Alberto Zum Felde, *Proceso intelectual del Uruguay,* vol. 1 (1930).

Eduardo Acevedo Díaz, *La vida de batalla de Eduardo Acevedo Díaz* (1941).

Walter Rela, *Eduardo Acevedo Díaz* (1967).

Emir Rodríguez Monegal, *Vínculo de sangre* (1968).

Arturo Sergio Visca, "Eduardo Acevedo Díaz," in *Diccionario de literatura Uruguaya,* vol. 1 (1989).

Additional Bibliography

Deus, Sergio. *Eduardo Acevedo Díaz: El caudillo olvidado* Montevideo, Uruguay: Acali Editorial, 1978.

Lasplaces, Alberto. *Eduardo Acevedo Diaz/por Alberto Lasplaces.* Montevideo, Uruguay: C. García, 1931.

Rodríguez Monegal, Emir. *Vínculo de sangre; crítica.* Montevideo, Uruguay: Editorial Alfa, 1968.

MARÍA INÉS DE TORRES

ACEVEDO HERNÁNDEZ, ANTONIO

(1886–1962). Antonio Acevedo Hernández (*b.*1886; *d.* 21 September 1962), one of the founders of modern Chilean theater and the originator of social theater. His first plays date back to 1913–1914, a period in Chile marked by the influence of European theater and the Spanish *comedia*. His primary preoccupation as a dramatist was to define the creative options of an autochthonous theater that could express the social problems and existential dilemmas of the marginated strata—campesino sectors and lower-class urban settlements—of a society in the process of capitalist modernization.

A man of humble origins, Acevedo Hernández was forced to make a living moving from place to place working various jobs, such as farmhand, manual laborer, office worker, and free-lance journalist. This rich and diverse living experience became the main thematic source for his dramas and *comedias*. He wrote approximately thirty plays that include a variety of forms ranging from *sainetes* and *comedias* to political and social theater, and even biblical dramas. Durán Cerda provides a useful classification of Acevedo Hernández's plays. His most important works are *Arbol viejo* (1930; The Old Tree), which presents the dramatic conflict between the ancestral wisdom of the campesino's world and the changing values fostered by urban society, and *Chañarcillo* (1933), an epic drama of miners' struggles for social justice in nineteenth-century Chile. In his autobiography *Memorias de un autor teatral* (1982; Memories of a Playwright), Acevedo Hern-ández describes his literary formation through an intimate account of the conflicts and challenges he was forced to confront in order to stage his works. He died in Santiago.

See also **Theater.**

BIBLIOGRAPHY

Julio Durán Cerda, *Panorama del teatro chileno, 1842–1959* (1959), pp. 56–62.

Juan Villegas, "Teatro chileno y afianzamiento de los sectores medios," in *Ideologies and Literature* 4, no. 17 (1983): 306–318.

Additional Bibliography

Pereira Poza, Sergio. *Dramaturgia social de Antonio Acevedo Hernández.* Santiago de Chile: Editorial Universidad de Santiago, 2003.

J. A. EPPLE

ACHÁ, JOSÉ MARÍA (1810–1868). José

María Achá (*b.* 8 July 1810; *d.* 29 January 1868), president of Bolivia (14 January 1861–28 December 1864). After coming to power via a coup, Achá shared power in a three-man junta from 14 January until 4 May after which he became constitutional president.

Achá's presidency was marked by intense internal political agitation. His chief of police of La Paz, Plácido Yáñez, was responsible for Bolivia's worst political massacre on 23 October 1861. Yáñez arrested and then executed more than seventy political opponents, among whom was former president Jorge Córdova. Yáñez was later lynched by a mob. Known as the "Massacre de Yáñez," this episode detracted from Achá's positive accomplishments in the areas of economic and administrative reforms. Achá's administration also faced Chile's first attempts at expansion on the Bolivian coast, actions that eventually precipitated the War of the Pacific (1879–1884), the conflict in which Bolivia lost its coastal area.

Achá's political career, which included an unsuccessful attempt to overthrow the government of Manuel Isidoro Belzú (1850), was ended by a military coup led by Mariano Melgarejo.

See also **Córdova, Jorge; War of the Pacific.**

BIBLIOGRAPHY

Julio Arguedas Díaz, *Los generales de Bolivia* (1929).

Moisés Alcázar, *Sangre en la historia* (1956).

Alcides Arguedas, *La dictatura y la anarquía*, in *Obras completas*, vol. 2 (1959).

CHARLES W. ARNADE

ACHÉ. The Aché (Guayakí) are foragers of the subtropical forests of eastern Paraguay. Although their language is affiliated with that of the larger Guarani population, the Aché have lived almost exclusively from hunting, fishing, and gathering in nomadic bands, eschewing the semi-permanent communities and shifting cultivation of other indigenous people of the area.

In addition, the Aché are notable for their relatively small stature and light skin, with a propensity for male baldness rare in indigenous populations.

Two scenarios have been advanced to explain the presence of this distinct population amid the larger Guarani population: The Aché could be a remnant of the Ge people, who inhabited the region before the Guarani arrived. Or they might have been a Guarani group who chose foraging over slash and burn cultivation, isolated themselves, and over time diverged in biology and culture.

Through most of the twentieth century the Aché avoided contact with European and other indigenous groups, eluding the few hunters and loggers who entered the region. Beginning in the 1960s, however, expanding cattle ranches and commmercial agriculture greatly reduced the forests, destroying the game on which the Aché depended. Their population, never large, was reduced to less than 350 people. Hunger forced the last of the nomadic Aché from the forest in 1978. In the early twenty-first century, the Aché have a modicum of protection on mission stations and government reservations. With political assistance the Aché are gaining control of their lives, and with medical care their population, according to Paraguay's census of indigenous populations, has grown to more than 1,200 people.

As one of the last foraging groups to leave the forests of lowland Latin America, the Aché are important to understanding human behavioral ecology. Anthropologists have analyzed their foraging strategies, population demography, and life history, exploring factors such as marriage and menopause that affected evolution in humanity's long foraging past.

See also **Guarani Indians; Paraguay: The Nineteenth Century; Paraguay: The Twentieth Century.**

BIBLIOGRAPHY

Clastres, Pierre. *Chronicle of the Guayaki Indians.* New York: Zone Books, 1998.

Hill, Kim, and A. Magdalena Hurtado. *Ache Life History: The Ecology and Demography of a Foraging People.* New York: Aldine de Gruyter Press, 1995.

Maybury-Lewis, David, and James Howe. *The Indian Peoples of Paraguay: Their Plight and Prospects.* Cambridge, MA: Cultural Survival, 1980.

RICHARD K. REED

ACONCAGUA. Aconcagua, at 22,834 feet, the highest mountain of the Western Hemisphere. It is located in the Andes of western Argentina at 33 degrees south latitude. The Aconcagua River springs at its foot and flows in an 84-mile course into the Pacific Ocean. Considered the beginning of historical Central Chile, the well-irrigated valley was settled by Indians and Spaniards. Wine, fruits, tobacco, flax, and vegetables are grown for domestic consumption and export. Major centers in the valley are San Felipe, Los Andes, and Quillota. Not far from the river's mouth, in Chile, are the sister cities of Valparaíso and Viña Del Mar, both of which are connected with Mendoza (Argentina) by an electric railway and a paved road.

See also **Argentina, Geography.**

BIBLIOGRAPHY

César N. Caviedes, *Geomorfología del Cuaternario del valle del Aconcagua, Chile Central* (1972).

Additional Bibliography

Aldunate del Solar, Carlos, and Luis Cornejo B. *In the Footsteps of the Inka in Chile*. Santiago: Museo Chileno de Arte Precolombino, 2001.

                                    CÉSAR N. CAVIEDES

ACORDADA. Acordada, an enforcement and judicial agency established in New Spain provisionally in 1710 and officially in 1722. Staffed by a salaried captain-judge and a small group of subordinates, it drew its unsalaried agents from landholders, merchants, and their retainers who concentrated on property crimes, notably banditry. Initially operating in rural areas, it extended its jurisdiction to cities in 1756. In 1772 the Juzgado de Bebidas Prohibidas, charged with suppression of illegal intoxicants, came under its supervision. The organization maintained its own prison and sentenced offenders with little interference. It was extinguished by the Constitution of 1812's prohibition of independent judicial organizations.

See also **Banditry; Judicial Systems: Spanish America.**

BIBLIOGRAPHY

Alicia Bazán Alarcón, "El Real Tribunal de la Acordada y la Delincuencia en la Nueva España," *Historia Mexicana* 13, no. 3 (1964): 317–345.

Colin M. Mac Lachlan, *Criminal Justice in Eighteenth Century Mexico: A Study of the Tribunal of the Acordada* (1974).

Additional Bibliography

Barrios, Feliciano, ed. *El gobierno de un mundo: Virreinatos y audiencias en la América hispánica*. Cuenca, Ecuador: Ediciones de la Universidad de Castilla-La Mancha: Fundación Rafael del Pino, 2004.

                                 COLIN M. MACLACHLAN

ACORDADA, REVOLT OF. Revolt of Acordada, an insurgency following the Mexican election of 1828. After a heated campaign in which the function of the church, the status of Spaniards, mass politics, and secret societies played an important role, the moderate Yorkino (York Rite Mason) Manuel Gómez Pedraza won the presidential election of 1828. But on the night of 30 November, several hundred officers and men barricaded themselves in the building of the Acordada in Mexico City, demanding that the elections be annulled and all Spaniards expelled from the country. Fighting between government forces and the rebels erupted on 2 December. The following day the defeated presidential candidate General Vicente Guerrero joined the insurgents. On 4 December, president-elect Gómez Pedraza resigned and fled the country rather than precipitate a bloody civil war. Nevertheless, mass demonstrations continued in the capital, ultimately resulting in a riot that destroyed the Parián, the city's principal market.

See also **Gómez Pedraza, Manuel; Guerrero, Vicente; Parián.**

BIBLIOGRAPHY

Romeo R. Flores Caballero, *Counterrevolution: The Role of the Spaniards in the Independence of Mexico, 1804–38,* translated by Jaime E. Rodríguez O. (1974), esp. pp. 116–120.

Michael P. Costeloe, *La Primera República Federal de México, 1824–1835* (1975), esp. pp. 198–206.

Lorenzo De Zavala, *Ensayo histórico de las revoluciones de México desde 1808–hasta 1830*, vol. 2 (1985), esp. pp. 77–111.

Additional Bibliography

Hale, Charles C. *The Transformation of Liberalism in Late Nineteenth-Century Mexico*. Princeton: Princeton University Press, 1989.

Rodríguez O, Jaime E., ed. *The Divine Charter: Constitutionalism and Liberalism in Nineteenth-Century Mexico*. Lanham, MD: Rowman & Littlefield, 2005.

Thomson, Guy P.C. *Patriotism, Politics, and Popular Liberalism in Nineteenth-Century Mexico: Juan Francisco Lucas and the Puebla Sierra*. Wilmington, DE: Scholarly Resources, 1999.

Wasserman, Mark. *Everyday Life and Politics in Nineteenth-Century Mexico: Men, Women, and War*. Albuquerque: University of New Mexico Press, 2000.

                                 JAIME E. RODRÍGUEZ O.

ACOSTA, CECILIO (1818–1881).

A writer, journalist, historian, and politician, Cecilio Acosta (January 2, 1818–August 7, 1881) was one of the most influential public intellectuals in nineteenth-century Venezuela. Born to a poor family, he moved to Caracas as one of the students to whom opportunities were opened as a consequence of Venezuelan independence. After receiving a classical education at the Seminario Tridentino de Santa Rosa as a planned prelude to joining the priesthood, he abandoned his religious studies and enrolled at Universidad Central de Venezuela. There he received his law degree in 1848 and was later employed as a lecturer. Acosta's writings on politics and society appeared in the most important Caracas newspapers, including *La Época* and *El Federal*, which earned him a reputation as one of the key figures in the social and political debates between the Conservative and Liberal parties. In 1856 he published his best-known essay on education, titled *Cosas sabidas y cosas para saberse*. In his later years he maintained correspondence with the most important intellectuals in Latin America and Spain, even earning praise and homage from the Cuban writer José Martí. Acosta died in complete poverty in 1881, but he has been honored in the twentieth century: his body was moved to the National Pantheon in 1937, and in 1982 the Fundación La Casa de Bello published his *Obras completas*.

See also **Journalism; Martí y Pérez, José Julián.**

BIBLIOGRAPHY

Acosta, Cecilio. *Obras Completas*, 2 vols. Caracas: Fundación Casa de Bello, 1982.

Herrera, José Rafael. *La filosofía de Cecilio Acosta*. Caracas: Universidad Central de Venezuela, Ediciones de la Biblioteca, 2000.

Milani, Domingo, et al. *Vigencia de Cecilio Acosta*. Maracaibo, Venezuela: Universidad Católica Cecilio Acosta, 2002.

MATTHEW CHILDS

ACOSTA, JOSÉ DE (1540–1600).

José de Acosta (*b.* September or October 1540; *d.* 15 February 1600), Spanish Jesuit historian. Born in Medina del Campo, Acosta joined the Jesuit order while young and went to Peru in 1571. He lived there for fourteen years, and in Mexico City for one, before returning to his native Spain in 1587. His *Historia natural y moral de las Indias* (A Natural and Moral History of the Indies) was published in Seville in 1590. Widely read by educated Spaniards and quickly translated into most important European languages as well, Acosta's *Historia* enjoyed immediate success. Like other similar texts, the *Historia* places the entire American continent within a universal and providential Christian framework, implying a divine role for Spain as a conquering power. Many features of the natural American world, as well as indigenous religions, cultures, and governments, are described in great detail, making Acosta's work an invaluable source of information. It is considered by literary scholars and historians to be an elegantly written, classic example of sixteenth-century New World historiography.

Duke University Press published a new translation of *Historia* with an introduction by Walter Mignolo in 2002.

See also **Literature: Spanish America.**

BIBLIOGRAPHY

A complete English translation by Frances López-Morillas of Acosta's *Historia natural*, with notes and introduction by Walter Mignolo, is presently in preparation. The best Spanish edition is José De Acosta, *Historia natural y moral de las Indias*, edited by Edmundo O'Gorman (1962). For a study of Acosta's ethnological method see Anthony Pagden, *The Fall of Natural Man: The American Indian and the Origins of Comparative Ethnology* (1982), pp. 146–200.

Additional Bibliography

Burgaleta, Claudio M. *José de Acosta, S.J., 1540-1600: His Life and Thought*. Chicago: Jesuit Way, 1999.

Hovde, James Marc. "God's Order and Worldly Action: José de Acosta, Ignatius Loyola, and Augustine." Ph.D. diss., University of San Diego, 2003.

Shepherd, Gregory J. *An Exposition of José de Acosta's Historia natural y moral de las Indias, 1590: The Emergence of an Anthropological Vision of Colonial Latin America*. Lewiston, NY: Edwin Mellen Press, 2002.

KATHLEEN ROSS

ACOSTA, TOMÁS (1744–1821).

Tomás Acosta (*b.* 1744; *d.* 1821), governor of Costa Rica from 1797 to 1810. Born in Cuba, Tomás Acosta is considered one of the most beloved and capable of

Costa Rica's colonial governors. As early as 1805, he exposed the harmful effects of the tobacco monopoly on Costa Rica's economy and instituted policies designed to diversify agricultural production. Under the general aegis of the Bourbon Reforms, Acosta removed some of the taxes from coffee production and greatly increased the growth of that important crop. His administration contributed to a growing sense of nationality among Costa Ricans in the pre-Independence era. Acosta, though a Spanish colonial official, was popular enough among Americans to have been considered as the intendant for Costa Rican economic affairs in 1812. He died in Cartago.

See also **Bourbon Reforms.**

BIBLIOGRAPHY

Ligia María Estrada Molina, *La Costa Rica de don Tomás de Acosta* (1965).

Ralph Lee Woodward, J r., *Central America: A Nation Divided* (1985).

Theodore S. Creedman, *Historical Dictionary of Costa Rica*, 2nd ed. (1991).

KAREN RACINE

ACOSTA GARCÍA, JULIO (1872–1954).

Julio Acosta García (*b.* 23 May 1872; *d.* 6 July 1954), president of Costa Rica (1920–1924). As a nephew of Braulio Carrillo (president 1834–1841) and a descendant of the conquistador Juan Vázquez de Coronado, Acosta was well positioned for public life. He held many posts in the Costa Rican government, including delegate to the Constitutional Congress of 1902–1906, governor of his home province of Alajuela (1907), and consul to El Salvador (1912–1915) before winning the presidency in 1920. Acosta, a Liberal, served as Costa Rica's delegate to the Central American Unionist Party. He engaged troops in a border conflict with Panama. After his term he received many national and international awards and was the chief of Costa Rica's delegation to the United Nations organizational meetings in San Francisco in 1945.

See also **Costa Rica, Constitutions.**

BIBLIOGRAPHY

Academia De Geografía E Historia De Costa Rica, *Homenaje al lic. Don Julio Acosta García* (1972).

Carlos Meléndez Ch., *Historia de Costa Rica* (1979).

Harold H. Bonilla, *Los presidentes* (1979).

Additional Bibliography

Oconitrillo García, Eduardo. *Julio Acosta: el hombre de la providencia.* San Jóse: Editorial Costa Rica, 1991.

KAREN RACINE

ACOSTA LEÓN, ÁNGEL (1932–1964).

Ángel Acosta León (*b.* 1932; *d.* 1964), Cuban painter. Born in Havana, Acosta León attended the famous San Alejandro school of painting and sculpture on a scholarship. He worked at odd jobs, including train conductor, to support himself while pursuing a career in the arts. In 1958 and 1959 he won prizes at expositions in Havana and received another award in 1959 from the National Salon. In 1960 Acosta León won a poster contest sponsored by the new National Institute of Industry and Tourism, and his oil painting *Carruaje* earned him a prize at the Second Pan-American Biennial in Mexico. Images of wheels and modern technology dominate Acosta's paintings; his major works are *Cafetera, Carro,* and *El circo* (all 1959), and *Carruaje* (1960).

See also **Art: The Twentieth Century.**

BIBLIOGRAPHY

Government of Cuba, *Pintores cubanos* (1962).

Adelaida De Juan, *Pintura cubana: Temas y variaciones* (1978).

Additional Bibliography

García Montiel, Emilio. "Angel Acosta León." *Art Nexus* 47 (January–March, 2003): 78–83.

KAREN RACINE

ACOSTA ÑU, BATTLE OF.

Battle of Acosta Ñu, one of the final engagements of the War of the Triple Alliance, fought on 16 August 1869. In the hill country some 45 miles east of Asunción, the retreating Paraguayan army of Francisco Solano López left behind a rear-guard force of some 4,500 teenage boys, women, and old men, having ordered them to slow the advance of 20,000

Brazilian troops under the conde d'Eu. Purportedly wearing false beards in order to frighten their opponents, the boys put up a stiff and bloody resistance, but were overwhelmed by enemy cavalry. The battle, which Brazilian historians call "Campo Grande," has taken on the character of a national epic in Paraguay. Its immediate consequences, however, were minimal, as the Brazilians were soon able to resume their pursuit of López, who was eventually killed by Brazilian forces in March 1870.

See also **Campo Grande; López, Francisco Solano; War of the Triple Alliance.**

BIBLIOGRAPHY

Charles Kolinski, *Independence or Death! The Story of the Paraguayan War* (1965).

Leandro Aponte B., *Hombres, armas y batallas* (1971).

Additional Bibliography

Bethell, Leslie. *The Paraguayan War (1864-1870)*. London: Institute of Latin American Studies, 1996.

Leuchars, Chris. *To the Bitter End: Paraguay and the War of the Triple Alliance*. Westport: Greenwood Press, 2002.

Marco, Miguel Angel de. *La Guerra del Paraguay*. Buenos Aires: Planeta, 1995.

Whigham, Thomas. *The Paraguayan War*. Lincoln: University of Nebraska Press, 2002.

THOMAS L. WHIGHAM

ACQUIRED IMMUNE DEFICIENCY SYNDROME (AIDS).

Diagnoses of acquired immune deficiency syndrome and the human immunodeficiency virus that causes it (hereto jointly referred to as HIV/AIDS) began surfacing in Latin America and the Caribbean in the 1970s. The first case was in the Caribbean, and larger countries such as Brazil and Mexico followed in the early 1980s. In 2005 the prevalence rate was 0.57 percent, an increase from previous years. Though the HIV/AIDS epidemic in the region has not reached the same proportions as those seen in sub-Saharan Africa, it continues to be a significant public-health problem throughout the region. One challenge has been the difficulty of collecting accurate data; this results in a high degree of underestimation. Outdated surveillance mechanisms, varying country stand-

ards, and limited testing access contribute to the underreporting of HIV/AIDS cases in Latin America and the Caribbean (UNAIDS 2006; World Bank 2001).

Several demographic groups that are categorized as having a higher risk for HIV/AIDS are used as indicators of the intensity of the epidemic in a country. They include men who have sex with men, sexually transmitted infection patients, and commercial sex workers. The epidemic is generally concentrated in these high-risk groups in Latin America, with some exceptions (García Abreu 2003). In Latin America the first and third groups are particularly important to understanding the disease's evolution.

Prevalence of HIV, total percentage of population ages 15–49

Country name	2003	2005
Latin America & Caribbean	0.533371908	0.56589
Antigua and Barbuda	—	—
Argentina	0.57	0.61
Aruba	—	—
Bahamas, The	2.884	3.274
Barbados	1.568	1.548
Belize	2.09	2.49
Bolivia	0.132	0.134
Brazil	0.504	0.539
Cayman Islands	—	—
Chile	0.262	0.285
Colombia	0.535	0.608
Costa Rica	0.261	0.288
Cuba	0.091	0.091
Dominica	—	—
Dominican Republic	1.168	1.114
Ecuador	0.278	0.287
El Salvador	0.914	0.921
Grenada	—	—
Guatemala	0.864	0.9
Guyana	2.44	2.448
Haiti	3.81	3.811
Honduras	1.504	1.536
Jamaica	1.509	1.527
Mexico	0.274	0.284
Netherlands Antilles	—	—
Nicaragua	0.208	0.243
Panama	0.86	0.894
Paraguay	0.353	0.376
Peru	0.53	0.566
Puerto Rico	—	—
St. Kitts and Nevis	—	—
St. Lucia	—	—
St. Vincent and the Grenadines	—	—
Suriname	1.718	1.936
Trinidad and Tobago	2.565	2.643
Uruguay	0.425	0.49
Venezuela, RB	0.649	0.721
Virgin Islands (U.S.)	—	—

SOURCE: World Bank World Development Indicators.

Table 1

HIV-positive Mexicans protest outside the Institute of Social Security, 2000, demanding that the public health system provide to HIV patients the drugs needed to prevent the virus from developing into AIDS. © REUTERS/CORBIS

Both men who have sex with men and the clients of commercial sex workers often maintain relationships with other women, spreading the infection when they contract it, and contributing to the rise in the number of women with HIV/AIDS in the region (UNAIDS 2006). Though the majority of infections in the region are in males, the recent trend of feminization of the HIV/AIDS epidemic in Latin America is apparent. The male-to-female ratio has been decreasing, and the infection rate has been increasing in pregnant women and children (García Abreu 2003; World Bank 2001).

SUBREGIONAL VARIATION
Central American countries have some of the highest infection rates in the Spanish-speaking Americas; the three countries with the highest rates are Honduras, Guatemala, and Panama. In contrast, Nicaragua has comparatively low infection rates. In Honduras, the country with the highest infection rate, the preva-

lence rate among Garífunas living on the Caribbean coast is six times higher than the national average. Central America is one of the few regions where the disease is transmitted almost exclusively through heterosexual intercourse, with the exception of Costa Rica, where men who have sex with men have the highest infection rates. Additionally, the epidemic in Central America is highly concentrated in urban areas (García Abreu 2003).

In Mexico the prevalence of HIV/AIDS has leveled off. Traditionally, the primary means of transmission was sex between men, but Mexico has seen an increasing number of women being infected. Additionally, there has been an increase in the number of rural infections in Mexico, due in part to migration patterns (García Abreu 2003).

New cases of HIV/AIDS have leveled off in Brazil, although the percentage of the population living with HIV/AIDS has continued to rise due to a government program providing affordable antiretroviral medicine, which has decreased the death rate of HIV/AIDS patients. Brazil is unique in the breath of the epidemic's impact; the disease is transmitted through a variety of means. HIV/AIDS is concentrated in the southeast, with the highest rates in Rio de Janeiro and São Paulo, but it is beginning to spread to the northeast (García Abreu 2003). There has also been an increase in the number of Brazilian women affected by HIV/AIDS (UNAIDS 2006).

Data reporting for the Andean region is particularly bad, contributing to underreporting and a lack of understanding about the nature of the epidemic in this area. Sex between men is a significant mode of transmission, with heterosexual intercourse contributing in certain areas, such as the Atlantic Coast of Colombia, parts of Peru, and Bolivia. Evidence also suggests that high levels of risky sexual behavior (measured by the prevalence of other sexually transmitted infections) are contributing to the spread of the disease in the region (García Abreu 2003).

In the Southern Cone, injection drug use has been the most significant factor in the transmission of HIV/AIDS, especially in Argentina and Uruguay. In Paraguay, transmission is most often via heterosexual sex or sex between men. Argentina also had a high rate of infection among pregnant women, especially in urban areas (García Abreu 2003).

The Caribbean has the worst HIV/AIDS epidemic in the world outside of sub-Saharan Africa, and Haiti is the country with the highest prevalence outside of sub-Saharan Africa. Transmission is most often through heterosexual sex, followed closely by sex between men. Since the 1990s there has been a significant increase in the number of women infected compared to the number of men, representing the most extreme manifestation of the overarching regional trend (World Bank 2001). Commercial sex workers in the Caribbean have extremely high rates of infection, some above 20 percent (UNAIDS 2006).

TREATMENT AND PREVENTION

Most of the prevention measures implemented in Latin America involve mass-media campaigns and education. Some campaigns—mostly those in Brazil, Mexico, and Central America—have been broadly based to reach the general public. Most education and public-outreach efforts do not place significant emphasis on consistent and proper condom usage, though Brazil's and Costa Rica's are major exceptions (García Abreu 2003). In addition, in addressing the HIV/AIDS epidemic, Latin American and Caribbean nations have not targeted their preventative measures at high-risk groups with high incidences of infection (García Abreu 2003; UNAIDS 2006).

Brazil and Costa Rica lead the region in providing antiretroviral therapy to afflicted patients, and some other Latin American nations are close behind. The United Nations estimated that 73 percent of Latin Americans in need of treatment were receiving it in 2005. However, poorer countries in Central America, the Caribbean, and the Andes have a harder time providing treatment to their citizens. Caribbean nations fare the worst, with less than one in four of those in need of antiretroviral therapy receiving treatment (UNAIDS 2006).

See also **Diseases; Public Health.**

BIBLIOGRAPHY

García Abreu, Anabela; Isabel Noguer; and Karen Cowgil. *HIV/AIDS in Latin American Countries: The Challenges Ahead.* Washington, DC: World Bank, 2003.

Smallman, Shawn C. *The AIDS Pandemic in Latin America.* Chapel Hill: University of North Carolina Press, 2007.

UNAIDS. *Report on the Global AIDS Epidemic 2006.* Geneva, Switzerland: Author, 2006. Available from http://www.unaids.org/en/HIV_data/2006GlobalReport/default.asp.

World Bank. *HIV/AIDS in the Caribbean: Issues and Options.* Washington, DC: Author, 2001.

World Bank. *World Development Indicators 2007.* Washington, DC: Author, 2007. Available from http://web.world bank.org/WBSITE/EXTERNAL/DATASTATISTICS/0,,contentMDK:21298138~pagePK:64133150~piPK:64133175~theSitePK:239419,00.html.

ANGELA M. GRANUM

ACRE. Acre, a Brazilian state sharing borders with Peru, Bolivia, and Amazonas. Although Brazil gave the little-known equatorial rain forest area to Bolivia in a treaty enacted in 1867, it was Brazilian, not Bolivian, *seringueiros* (rubber gatherers) who flooded into the area during the rubber boom. When Bolivia tried to establish its dominance over this 59,000-square-mile territory in 1899, Acreanos revolted and continued to rebel until 1902, when Bolivia and Brazil sent in troops. After a brief period of tension, Brazil's minister of foreign affairs, Barão do Rio Branco (1845–1912), skillfully negotiated a settlement giving Brazil the rubber-rich territory of Acre. Called the Treaty of Petrópolis, it was signed 17 November 1903. Although first attached to the state of Amazonas, Acre was converted into a federal territory in 1943 and became a state in 1962.

Most of Acre's residents worked gathering rubber from the forests and mingled with the 6,600 (as of 1988) people of pre-Columbian origin who lived there. In the 1970s, speculators and cattle ranchers infiltrated Acre via newly constructed roads, such as BR 364, BR 317, and the Transamazon Highway, which were part of the government's Operation Amazonia (1965) program. At the end of 1988, Acre was still the least populated (417,000 people) and developed state in Brazil. It had gained international notoriety, however, as a battleground between rubber workers and large landowners who clashed over control of the land.

See also **Mendes Filho, Francisco "Chico" Alves; Rio Branco, Barão do; Seringueiros; Transamazon Highway.**

BIBLIOGRAPHY

Chico Mendes, with additional material by Tony Gross, *Fight for the Forest: Chico Mendes in His Own Words*, 1989.

Andrew Revkin, *The Burning Season* (1990).

Susanna Hecht and Alexander Cockburn, *The Fate of the Forest: Developers, Destroyers, and Defenders of the Amazon* (1990).

Additional Bibliography

Barham, Brad, and O. T. Coomes. *Prosperity's Promise: The Amazon Rubber Boom and Distorted Economic Development*. Boulder: Westview Press, 1996.

O'Dwyer, Eliane Cantarino. *Seringueiros da Amazônia: Dramas sociais e o olhar antropológico*. Niterói, RJ: Editora da Universidade Federal Fluminense, 1998.

Stanfield, Michael Edward. *Red Rubber, Bleeding Trees: Violence, Slavery, and Empire in Northwest Amazonia, 1850-1933*. Albuquerque: University of New Mexico Press, 1998.

CAROLYN JOSTOCK

ACUERDO. Acuerdo (*real acuerdo*), the regularly scheduled meeting of the judges of a tribunal (audiencia) with its president and crown attorney (*fiscal*) or attorneys to discuss matters of political administration. Exclusively at this meeting was correspondence from the king to be opened and read. When treasury officials were added to the group, the *acuerdo* was called a *junta de hacienda*. The decisions reached at an *acuerdo* were termed *autos acordados* and had the force of law. Through the *acuerdo*, the *audiencia* exercised its political authority. The legislative and administrative authority that emanated from the *acuerdo* gave the American *audiencias* significantly greater power than was exercised by their peninsular counterparts. Since the decisions were issued jointly by the region's chief executive and its *audiencia*, moreover, they carried considerable weight. The chief executive of the *audiencia* district was responsible for implementing the *acuerdo*'s decisions.

See also **Audiencia.**

BIBLIOGRAPHY

Recopilación de leyes de los reynos de las Indias, 4 vols. (1681; repr. 1973), *libro* II, *título* XV, *leyes* xxiii, xxvi, xxvii, xxviii, xxx.

Clarence H. Haring, *The Spanish Empire in America* (1947), p. 134.

John H. Parry, *The Audiencia of New Galicia in the Sixteenth Century* (1948), pp. 8, 137–138.

Additional Bibliography

Sanciñena Asurmendi, Teresa. *La audiencia en México en el reinado de Carlos III*. México: Universidad Nacional Autónoma de México, 1999.

MARK A. BURKHOLDER

ADAMS, GRANTLEY HERBERT (1898–1971). Grantley Herbert Adams (April 28, 1898–November 28, 1971) served as the first premier of Barbados and as the prime minister of the West Indies Federation. Adams was born to a middle-class family and returned from England as a barrister and soon entered politics. Given that Adams was faced with the most racially exclusive and politically entrenched white plantocracy of the British West Indies, his political victories were nothing short of monumental. His political philosophy was that of the British Labour Party, Fabian democratic socialism; his initial political vehicles were the Barbados Workers' Union (BWU) and the Barbados Labour Party (BLP). He was first elected to the House of Assembly in 1934. He agitated for universal adult suffrage, instituted in 1950, and full ministerial government, granted in 1954. In 1957 he became the first and only prime minister of the ill-fated West Indies Federation. After the demise of the federation in 1962 he returned to Barbadian politics as leader of the opposition as his island was led to full independence under Errol Barrow, leader of the Demo-cratic Labour Party (DLP). When he resigned from the BLP in 1970, his son, J. M. G. (Tom) Adams succeeded him as president of the party and be-came prime minister in 1976. Grantley Herbert Adams is honored in Barbados for his dedica-tion to social justice and for his probity and fair-mindedness.

See also **Barbados; West Indies Federation.**

ANTHONY P. MAINGOT

ADAMS–ONÍS TREATY (1819).

Adams–Onís Treaty (1819), an agreement between Spain and the United States ceding the Floridas to the latter. Also known as the Transcontinental Treaty and the Tratado de Cesión, the document was signed on 22 February 1819 by U.S. secretary of state John Quincy Adams and veteran Spanish minister to the United States Luis de Onís y Gonzáles. The key provisions of the treaty ceded all territories held by the Spanish crown in the West and East Floridas to the United States and established a "transcontinental" boundary west of the Mississippi River that allowed the United States direct access to the Pacific Ocean. The line went north from the Sabine River; west along the Red River and Arkansas River, well above Santa Fe; then north and due west at 42 latitude, into the Oregon territory claimed by both the United States and Great Britain. Spain wanted the United States to relinquish claims to Texas, which it did in Article 3. Spain also wanted the United States to withhold recognition of any Spanish American provinces that might revolt; however, such a proviso was not part of

the final draft. The United States did agree to cancel up to $5 million in claims against Spanish citizens in Florida.

The U.S. Senate unanimously ratified the treaty on 24 February 1819, but the Spanish Council of State advised Ferdinand VII to send Francisco Vives to Washington to try to negotiate better terms. Nevertheless, the original version was finally approved by the U.S. Senate on 22 February 1821, and Mexico inherited Texas from Spain, "as delimited by the Transcontinental Treaty."

Negotiations between Adams and Onís were protracted, influenced strongly by a variety of considerations, including the invasion of the Florida territory by the U.S. general Andrew Jackson (1819), the intervention of the French minister Hyde de Neuville in discussions, and British-U.S. boundary disputes in the Northwest. Adams viewed the Pacific boundary as a major triumph for the United States; the historian Samuel Flagg Bemis asserts that "even without Texas the Transcontinental Treaty with Spain was the greatest diplomatic victory won by any single individual in the history of the United States."

See also **Boundary Disputes: Overview; United States-Latin American Relations.**

BIBLIOGRAPHY

Philip Coolidge Brooks, *Diplomacy and the Borderlands: The Adams-Onís Treaty of 1819* (1939), which contains the text of the treaty.

Samuel Flagg Bemis, *John Quincy Adams and the Foundations of American Foreign Policy* (1949) and *John Quincy Adams and the Union* (1965).

Elena Sánchez-Fabrés Mirat, *Situación histórica de las Floridas en la segunda mitad del siglo XVIII (1783–1819): Los problemas de una región de frontera* (1977), pp. 289–316.

LINDA K. SALVUCCI

ADDITIONAL ACT OF 1834.

Additional Act of 1834, amendment to the Brazilian Constitution of 1824 that decentralized the system of government. The act created legislative provincial assemblies, elected regency, and abolished the Council of State. It gave provincial assemblies power to indict provincial presidents and magistrates; jurisdiction over civil, judicial, and ecclesiastical organizations; control of taxation, revenue, public education, public works, and police force; ability to create and abolish positions; and permission to contract loans. The autonomy given to provinces weakened the central government, fueled centrifugal forces, and nearly caused the dissolution of the state. Its interpretation in 1840 abolished the most decentralizing provisions and permitted political, administrative, and judicial recentralization.

See also **Brazil: 1808–1889; Brazil, Constitutions.**

BIBLIOGRAPHY

Roderick J. Barman, *Brazil, the Forging of a Nation, 1798–1852* (1988), pp. 160–216.

Additional Bibliography

Jancsó, István. *Brasil: formação do estado e da nação.* São Paulo: Editora Hucitec, 2003.

Needell, Jeffrey D. *The Party of Order: The Conservatives, the State, and Slavery in the Brazilian Monarchy, 1831–1871.* Stanford, CA: Stanford University Press, 2006.

LYDIA M. GARNER

ADELANTADO. Adelantado, title often given to the leader of an expedition of conquest in medieval Castile and in the New World. The term *adelantado* was employed in medieval Castile for the military and political governor of a frontier province. The title was later used in the conquest and colonization of the Canary Islands and continued to be used in the conquest and colonization of the New World. Typically, an *adelantado* held the military title of captain-general and served as governor and chief magistrate over the men in the expedition. When a conquest was successful, the *adelantado* took over governance of the native population. In his contract (*capitulación*) with the crown, an *adelantado* normally received land for himself and the rights to assign land to his followers, to oversee the collection of revenues, and to administer justice. Sometimes he could assign native labor as well. The era of the *adelantados* came to an end as the crown sought to end the disruption and instability resulting from conquest and to establish tighter control over the New World. To accomplish this, the crown created audiencias and, beginning in 1535, sent out viceroys with substantial authority. Many *adelantados,* however, had been granted extensive landholdings and had access to native labor. Although their formal political power was restricted by royal bureaucrats, they and their immediate heirs remained important members of the emerging colonial aristocracy. Although men titled *adelantados* were still leading conquests on the frontiers of the colonial world in the late sixteenth century, the era of the *adelantado* had ended by the 1570s.

See also **Audiencia; Conquistadores; Viceroyalty, Viceroy.**

BIBLIOGRAPHY

Clarence H. Haring, *The Spanish Empire in America* (1947), pp. 22–25.

Lyle N. McAlister, *Spain and Portugal in the New World, 1492–1700* (1984), pp. 35, 63–64, 91, 97, 99, 137, 184, 312.

Additional Bibliography

Elizondo, Carlos. *El escorpión de oro: Luces y sombras en la extraordinaria vida de Hernán Cortés.* México, D.F.: EDAMEX, 1996.

Grunberg, Bernard. "The Origins of the Conquistadores of Mexico City." *Hispanic American Historical Review* 74:2 (May 1994): 259–283.

López de Gómara, Francisco, and Silvia L. Cuesy. *Historia de la conquista de México.* México, D.F.: Editorial Océano de México, 2003.

MARK A. BURKHOLDER

ADELANTADO OF THE SOUTH SEA. Adelantado of the South Sea, Vasco Núñez de Balboa (1475–1519), Spanish explorer who claimed the Pacific Ocean for the Spanish crown. An enterprising youth, Balboa had sailed for the Caribbean in 1500 to trade in pearls. After several business failures, he fled to Darién, Panama, where the Spanish attempted to establish permanent settlements. Balboa got along well with the natives of the region and emerged as the natural leader of his Spanish colleagues. In 1513, while searching for a wealthy tribe, he sighted the Pacific Ocean and descended to its shores to claim it for Spain. In reward, he was named governor of Darién and Adelantado of the South Sea. In 1519, however, Pedro Arias de Ávila (Pedrarias), representing jealous rivals, replaced Balboa as governor and had him beheaded.

See also Ávila, Pedro Arias de; Balboa, Vasco Núñez de; Darién.

BIBLIOGRAPHY

Kathleen Romoli, *Balboa of Darién: Discoverer of the Pacific* (1953).

Charles L. G. Anderson, *Life and Letters of Vasco Núñez de Balboa* (1941; repr. 1970).

Frederick W. Turner, "Visions of the Pacific," in *Southwest Review* 70 (1985): 336–349.

Additional Bibliography

García Rodríguez, Ariadna. "Vasco Núñez de Balboa y geopsiquis de una nación." *Revista Iberoamericana.* 67:196 (July–September 2001): 461–473.

MICHAEL L. CONNIFF

ADEM CHAHÍN, JOSÉ (1921–1991).

José Adem Chahín (*b.* 27 October 1921; *d.* February 1991), leading Mexican mathematician. A native of Tuxpan, Veracruz, Adem received his early education in his birthplace. He studied mathematics at the National University of Mexico from 1941 to 1945, after which he did graduate work at the Mathematics Institute (1946–1948). He traveled to the United States to complete a doctorate at Princeton University (1952). A researcher and educator, Adem taught at the National School of Engineering and Sciences and the National University, becoming a full-time researcher at the Mathematics Institute (1954–1961). His works on algebra have appeared in English. He directed the mathematics department at the National Polytechnic Institute from 1961 to 1973. He was a member of the National College, and received Mexico's National Prize in Sciences (1967). A book of interviews was published under his name in 1984: *Imagen y obra escogida* (Mexico City: UNAM, 1984).

See also **Mexico: Since 1910.**

BIBLIOGRAPHY

Jesús Silva Herzog, *Biografías de amigos y conocidos* (1980).

RODERIC AI CAMP

ADEM CHAHÍN, JULIÁN (1924–).

Julián Adem Chahín (*b.* 8 January 1924), leading Mexican geophysicist and specialist in atmospheric sciences. Adem obtained an engineering degree from the National University (1948) and his doctorate in applied mathematics from Brown University (1953), after which he completed advanced studies in atmospheric sciences in Stockholm (1955–1956). After serving as a full-time researcher at the Geophysics Institute, he became its director and then founded the Center for Atmospheric Sciences. Invited to be a member of the prestigious National College, Adem received Mexico's National Prize in Sciences (1976). Adem founded the journal *Atmósfera* in 1988 and served as editor until 2002. Brother of mathematician José Adem Chahín, he is known for his discovery of a long-range predictive thermodynamic model.

See also **Adem Chahín, José; Science.**

BIBLIOGRAPHY

Colegio Nacional, Memoria, vol. 8 (1974).

Additional Bibliography

Adem Chahín, Julián, and Rosa Campos de la Rosa. *Bibliografía de Julián Adem.* Mexico: El Colegio Nacional, 1997.

RODERIC AI CAMP

ADMIRABLE CAMPAIGN.

Admirable Campaign, a series of military engagements in the Venezuelan War of Independence. With operations in New Granada finished, Simón Bolívar solicited the support of the government there for an invasion of Venezuelan territory to renew the fight for independence. The campaign began in New Granada on 14 May 1813 and ended in Caracas on 6 August of the same year. After crossing the summits of the Andes, he arrived in Mérida and from there continued to Trujillo, where he made his famous War to the Death speech on 15 June. He continued eastward, defeating his adversaries along the way, until the royal army capitulated in the city of La Victoria, not far from Caracas. The success, organization, and speed of the campaign allowed the republican forces to regain control of western Venezuela.

See also **Bolívar, Simón; Venezuela: The Colonial Era.**

BIBLIOGRAPHY

Lino Iribarren Celis, *La Campaña Admirable* (1963), and Universidad De Los Andes, *1813–1963: Mérida, Venezuela. Revista "Libertador" commemoration del Sesquicentenario de la Campaña Admirable* (1963).

Additional Bibliography

Lynch, John. *Simón Bolívar: A Life*. New Haven, CT: Yale University Press, 2006.

Mendizábal, Francisco Javier de. *Guerra de la América del Sur, 1809-1824*. Buenos Aires: Academia Nacional de la Historia, 1997.

INÉS QUINTERO

ADONIAS FILHO. *See* **Aguiar, Adonias.**

AFRANCESADO.

The term *afrancesado* ("the Frenchified") was applied to Spaniards who collaborated with the regime of Joseph Bonaparte during the War of Independence (1808–1814). In 1808 Napoleon lured Charles IV and his son, Ferdinand VII, into exile in France and placed his brother, Joseph, on the Spanish throne. The *afrancesados* were constitutional monarchists—though not wedded to one particular dynasty—who advocated moderate social and political reforms. Some preferred French domination of Spain to repression or dismemberment and considered Joseph's regime a lesser evil. Others hoped that the Napoleonic system and the enlightened Constitution of Bayonne (1808) would generate reform from above. Some historians have portrayed the *afrancesados* as misguided and confused conformists. Perhaps the best known *afrancesado* in Spain was the *costumbrista* (folklore) author Mariano José de Larra (1809–1837), who influenced prominent Latin American figures such as the Argentines Domingo Faustino Sarmiento and Juan Bautista Alberdi and the Peruvian Manuel González Prada.

Although some commentators view Latin American independence as a homegrown enterprise, others see the long arm of the Enlightenment as igniting the spark. Certainly prominent Latin Americans who were in exile in Europe, such as the Venezuelan revolutionary Francisco de Miranda, came into contact with French thought. The first *afrancesados* in the New World were perhaps the readers of Enlightenment philosopher Jean-Jacques Rousseau's *Social Contract* (1762), which circulated widely in South America after being translated into Spanish in 1810. After this initial thrust, other prominent *pensadores*, such as Sarmiento and the Argentine poet and novelist José Mármol, aligned themselves politically, economically, and intellectually with the French as a way to combat the dictatorship of Juan Manuel de Rosas. Chateaubriand, the founder of Romanticism in French literature, became a model for prominent novelists such as the Cuban Gertrudis Gómez de Avellaneda and the Colombian Jorge Isaacs, whose famous protagonist in his novel *María* wishes to read Chateaubriand's novella *Atala*.

After midcentury the doctrine of positivism as elaborated by the French philosopher Auguste Comte made inroads in various countries and especially in Argentina, Peru, and Brazil. In Peru it was embraced, in some cases tentatively, by the novelist Mercedes Cabello de Carbonera, who wrote a tract on Comte's philosophy and whose novel *Blanca Sol* censures the exorbitant French influence on *criolla* society, and by the poet-essayist Manuel González Prada, who eventually abandoned it in favor of French anarchism. In Brazil, Comte's ideas became the basis for the 1891 constitution, and the positivist phrase "order and progress" became a permanent feature of the Brazilian flag. In Peru, French ideas served to revamp the educational system.

See also **Alberdi, Juan Bautista; Bonaparte, Joseph; Enlightenment, The; Gómez de Avellaneda y Arteaga, Gertrudis; González Prada, Manuel; Isaacs, Jorge; Mármol, José Pedro Crisólogo; Miranda, Francisco de; Positivism; Sarmiento, Domingo Faustino; Wars of Independence, South America.**

BIBLIOGRAPHY

Artola, Miguel. *Los afrancesados*. Madrid: Alianza, 1989.

Carr, Raymond. *Spain, 1808–1975*, 2nd edition. Oxford: Clarendon Press, 1982. See especially pp. 110–115.

Davis, Harold Eugene. *Latin American Thought: A Historical Introduction*. Baton Rouge: Louisiana State University Press, 1972. See especially pp. 31–62 & 97–134.

Hale, Charles. "Political and social ideas in Latin America," *The Cambridge History of Latin America*. Vol. 4, edited by Leslie Bethell. Cambridge/New York: Cambridge University Press, 1986, See especially pp. 382–391.

Mercader Riba, Joan. *José Bonaparte, rey de España, 1808–1813*. 2 vols. Madrid: Consejo Superior de Investigaciones Científicas, Instituto Jerónimo Zurita, Escuela de Historia Moderna, 1971–1983.

SUZANNE HILES BURKHOLDER
THOMAS WARD

AFRICA, CUBAN INTERVENTION IN. *See* Cuban Intervention in Africa.

AFRICA, PORTUGUESE. Portuguese contacts in Africa began with the earliest navigation beyond Cape Bojador in 1434. An early period of raiding was replaced after 1456 by more peaceful contacts with the African states of the coast. Factories were established at Arguin Island in 1448 and at Elmina (São Jorge de Mina) in 1482, and colonies were established on the uninhabited offshore islands of Cape Verde (1462) and São Tomé (1472). In 1498 the Portuguese reached Mozambique, where they encountered already well established centers of trade with ties to Arab communities. After the successful rounding of the Cape of Good Hope in 1488 the Portuguese established posts at Sofala in 1505, Kilwa, and Mombasa.

The diplomatic efforts of Portuguese navigators and the later settlers of the offshore islands resulted in substantial influence on the adjacent coastline. Portugal established close relations with the African kingdoms of Jolof, Kongo, and Benin in the late fifteenth century. In Kongo especially these contacts resulted in the adoption of Christianity and literacy in Portuguese. The small Nigerian kingdom of Warri became Christian in 1580, and several small states in Sierra Leone also converted in the early seventeenth century.

Under King Sebastian, Portugal sought to develop a colonial presence on the coast, especially in areas where trade and diplomacy had been most successful. In the 1570s Portuguese forces established a colony in Angola and extended its control inland about 60 miles by 1620; at the same time Portuguese forces conducted a less successful series of operations in what would eventually become Mozambique against the kingdom of the Mwene Mutapa. The colonists of the Cape Verde Islands also sought to establish control on various posts along the coast of modern Guinea-Bissau, although these did not result in any significant territorial gains. After 1620 there were no more initiatives of this sort, although gains made by local initiative extended Angola slightly. In Mozambique local settlers managed to secure land grants from local rulers, which they registered as property of the Portuguese crown and received back as *prazos* (feudal estates), although in many ways they were more like independent petty rulers than Portuguese subjects.

A much more serious attempt to extend Portuguese control in Africa began in the 1850s and continued through the period of the "scramble for Africa," roughly from 1880 to 1920. The nuclei of the colonization were long-established groups of settlers or subjects in Angola, Mozambique, and the mainland across from the Cape Verde Islands, which became Guinea. These local settlers, the Afro-Portuguese, were a combination of mestizos and culturally Lusitanized Africans who owned land or held lower offices in the colony. Afro-Portuguese often pioneered the expansion, but metropolitan interests took over the resulting expanded colony in the late nineteenth century. As a result the holders of the Mozambican *prazos* had to be conquered by metropolitan armies, while the Angolan Afro-Portuguese protested in their press what became a significant loss of rights.

Portuguese colonial policy focused on making Angola a center for Portuguese colonization, and the central highlands region in particular received thousands of colonists. There was less colonization in Mozambique, which was given over to large concession companies or to supplying contracted labor for South African mines. In Guinea concessions obtained what little profit Portugal received from the small colony.

Officially, Portugal had a "civilizing mission" in Africa, and its policy stressed assimilation, whereby Africans would be granted the rights of Portuguese when they had absorbed Portuguese language and customs. However, the government provided little

Portuguese soldiers in Angola, 1961. This troop of sharpshooters was among those sent to Angola in 1961 in an attempt to put down a rebellion by anticolonial guerrillas. AP IMAGES

in the way of educational opportunities to make the assimilation policy effective. Most educational and social services were provided by underfinanced Catholic Church missions or foreign missionaries, who were often subject to persecution.

After 1926 the New State dictatorship sought to tie the colonies more closely to the needs of Portugal, envisioning the metropole and its colonies as a cooperative zone, but one that worked to the benefit of the Portuguese of the metropole and colonies. These trends became more effective after the Second World War, when a wave of settlers and foreign capital flooded into the colonies. By the 1950s a number of African dissident groups had developed, sometimes in alliance with local groups of Afro-Portuguese. Government repression led to revolt, and by 1965 there were strong anticolonial guerrilla movements in all three colonies. In 1974 a revolution in Portugal, provoked in large part by the military demands of the antiguerrilla activities in the colonies, overthrew the dictatorship and set

in motion the process that resulted in the granting of independence to all the African colonies in 1974–1975.

Since African independence there has been increased contact between Lusophone Africa and Brazil that demonstrates the similarities between the African and Brazilian religions, as well as the African cultural identities that have survived in Brazil in varying degrees of purity. Most recently, the Portuguese presence in Africa received press coverage in the United States because Teresa Heinz, the wife of the Democratic Party's 2004 presidential candidate John Kerry, was born to Portuguese parents in Mozambique.

See also **Angola; Cape Verde Islands; Portuguese Empire; São Tomé.**

BIBLIOGRAPHY

Additional Bibliography

Alexandre, Valentim. *Origens do colonialismo português moderno (1822–1891)*. Lisbon: Sá da Costa Editora, 1979.

Almeida, Pedro Ramos de. *História do colonialismo português em Africa: Cronologia*. Lisbon: Editorial Estampa, 1979.

Axelson, Eric. *Portugal and the Scramble for Africa, 1875–1891*. Johannesburg: Witwatersrand University Press, 1967.

Birmingham, David. *Portugal and Africa*. New York: St. Martin's Press, 1999.

Boxer, C. R. *Four Centuries of Portuguese Expansion, 1415–1825: A Succinct Survey*. Berkeley: University of California Press, 1969.

Cann, John P. *Counterinsurgency in Africa: The Portuguese Way of War, 1961–1974*. Westport, CT: Greenwood Press, 1997.

Duffy, James. *Portuguese Africa*. Cambridge, MA: Harvard University Press, 1959.

Lloyd-Jones, Stewart, and António Costa Pinto. *The Last Empire: Thirty Years of Portuguese Decolonization*. Portland, OR: Intellect, 2003.

Macqueen, Norrie. *The Decolonization of Portuguese Africa: Metropolitan Revolution and the Dissolution of Empire*. London: Longman, 1997.

Russell-Wood, A. J. R. *A World on the Move: The Portuguese in Africa, Asia, and America, 1415–1808*. New York: St. Martin's Press, 1993.

Sweet, James H. *Recreating Africa Culture, Kinship, and Religion in the African-Portuguese World, 1441–1770*. Chapel Hill: University of North Carolina Press, 2003.

JOHN THORNTON

AFRICAN-BRAZILIAN CULTURAL AND POLITICAL ORGANIZATIONS.

During the colonial era religious brotherhoods were created with the assistance of Catholic clergy. These brotherhoods, often open to slaves as well as free persons, provided more than simply religious education to members, offering a range of financial and medical services for people of color that were unavailable elsewhere. They also made loans, offered insurance, and guaranteed their members proper burials. One of their most important functions was providing assistance in buying the freedom (*carta de alforria*) of those members who were slaves. Religious brotherhoods flourished in the late seventeenth and eighteenth centuries. Some, like Our Lady of the Rosary (Nossa Senhora do Rosário), had branches throughout the Portuguese territories in Africa, the Atlantic islands, the New World, and Portugal. Among the largest were the brotherhoods of the Rosary, Santa Ephigenia, and São Benedicto.

These brotherhoods continue to be active in Brazil today.

The African population of Brazil was concentrated in the North and Northeast during most of the slave era, but in the nineteenth century the slave trade flourished in southeastern Brazil to provide labor for the coffee plantations. The prospect of abolition prompted plantation owners to search for replacements for their slave labor. By the time of abolition in 1888, a government-sponsored program of European immigration had flooded both the rural and urban labor markets with new workers. Many Afro-Brazilians sought opportunities in the growing industrial cities, only to confront housing, employment, and other forms of racial discrimination. In São Paulo, where blacks were a small minority of the population, Afro-Brazilians formed a number of social and recreational clubs out of which eventually emerged a national movement for racial equality.

The Afro-Brazilian social clubs of São Paulo created between 1900 and 1920 used membership dues to finance small newspapers for the dissemination of club news. By the early 1920s a black press was active in the capital of São Paulo. Newspapers such as *Clarim da Alvorada* and *Progresso* began to advocate racial equality and circulate political ideas, including information from the Chicago *Defender* and Marcus Garvey's *Negro World*.

In 1926 the Centro Civico Palmares in São Paulo became the first Afro-Brazilian organization to develop a platform of advocacy for integration and equality for Afro-Brazilians, beginning with its efforts to integrate the police force of São Paulo. Increased racial consciousness and activism in São Paulo eventually led to the creation of the Frente Negra Brasileira in 1931, the first national Afro-Brazilian advocacy organization. It identified and fought instances of racial discrimination in São Paulo and more than twenty branch cities across Brazil. The Frente combined its activism with vocational training, basic elementary education, voter registration, and artistic and recreational activities. It was forcibly closed by President Getúlio Vargas in 1937 when he banned all political parties under the Estado Novo regime.

Although Afro-Brazilian political activity was curtailed after 1937, cultural organizations continued to flourish. In southern Brazil, small Carnival associations known as *cordões de samba* soon evolved into the larger *escolas de samba*. These predominantly black social organizations quickly spread across the nation, eventually popularizing Carnival in mainstream Brazilian culture. In the Northeast, Filhos de Gandhi (Sons of Gandhi), founded in the 1940s, began a new era of Afro-Brazilian group participation in Bahia's Carnival after many decades of discrimination against African themes and musical forms. They utilized the *afoxé* rhythms of the Ijexá Afro-Brazilian religion in contrast to the European themes and music popular during the 1930s. These cultural pioneers led the way for previously marginalized Afro-Brazilian Carnival traditions to become an integral part of the national culture.

After World War II the black press of São Paulo began publishing a new generation of journals. Journals such as *Senzala* and *Alvorada* reflected a broader awareness of the conditions of other black communities around the world, particularly those in the United States. Also during the 1940s, Abdias do Nascimento introduced theater as a new forum for the discussion of racial issues with the creation of the Teatro Experimental do Negro (Black Experimental Theater).

The military coup of 1964 silenced many black journals, which were considered potential threats to national security. However, the liberation struggles in the Portuguese African colonies of Mozambique and Angola awakened a new international consciousness among Afro-Brazilian youth. Though radical blacks were persecuted by the government, an underground black consciousness movement grew throughout the 1970s and culminated in the creation of the Uni-fied Black Movement (Movimento Negro Unificado— MNU). The MNU approved its charter on 20 November 1978, a date chosen to commemorate the anniversary of the murder of Zumbi, the last ruler of Palmares, a state founded by escaped slaves that flourished during the seventeenth century. Previously, most annual Afro-Brazilian celebrations had focused on 13 May, the anniversary of the abolition of slavery. The MNU argued that true abolition had not yet occurred, and established 20 November as the National Day of Black Consciousness. Zumbi became a symbol of the black consciousness movement, which for two years included every Afro-Brazilian organization in the country. Lélia Gonzalez, a Brazilian anthropologist and one of the founders of the MNU, also helped develop the Afro-Brazilian

women's movement. In the 1980s Gonzalez criticized the feminist movement in Brazil for ignoring the ways in which race affected Afro-Brazilian females. Consequently, Gonzalez founded and worked with several groups focusing on black women's issues.

In the years following the creation of the MNU there was a resurgence in Afro-Brazilian cultural organizations. In the Northeast, Ile Aiye pioneered a new type of Carnival group known as the *bloco afro*. Each of these *blocos* chose themes in African and Afro-Brazilian history for their Carnival music and costumes, and some restricted membership to blacks only. Afro-Brazilian cultural traditions such as Capoeira, a martial arts form of Angolan origin, moved from obscurity to public awareness when schools were established in major cities.

Simultaneously, Afro-Brazilians formed organizations to address social and economic problems. Community leaders such as Benedita da Silva in Rio de Janeiro created a movement to improve conditions in the urban Favelas (slums), heavily populated by blacks. Other organizations emerged to promote awareness of racial discrimination, a problem often obscured by the government's promotion of Brazil as a racial democracy. Some, like the Institute for the Study of Black Culture (IPCN), publicized cases of overt discrimination, while others concentrated on the study of social and economic issues and their impact on the black community. Benedita da Silva became the first black woman to serve in the national Congress, and spearheaded efforts to ensure greater Afro-Brazilian participation in politics. Local women's groups in Salvador, Brazil, also increased their presence in the 1990s, pushing for affirmative action and campaigning for black women who were running for local offices. Today, the black consciousness movement incorporates social, cultural, political, and economic strategies to improve conditions for Afro-Brazilians.

See also **African-Latin American Religions: Brazil; Brazil, Revolutions: Revolution of 1964; Brotherhoods; Carnival; Palmares; Race and Ethnicity; Silva, Benedita da; Slavery: Brazil; Zumbi.**

BIBLIOGRAPHY

Florestan Fernandes, *The Negro in Brazilian Society*, translated by Jacqueline D. Skiles, A. Brunel, and Arthur Rothwell (1969).

Anani Dzidzienyo, *The Position of Blacks in Brazilian Society* (1971).

Michael Mitchell, "Racial Consciousness and the Political Attitudes and Behavior of Blacks in São Paulo, Brazil" (Ph.D. diss., Indiana University, 1977).

A. J. R. Russell-Wood, *The Black Man in Slavery and Freedom in Colonial Brazil* (1982).

Clóvis Moura, *Brasil: Raízes do protesto negro* (1983).

Pierre-Michel Fontaine, ed., *Race, Class, and Power in Brazil* (1985).

George Reid Andrews, *Blacks and Whites in São Paulo, Brazil, 1888–1988* (1991).

Kim D. Butler, "Up from Slavery: Afro-Brazilian Activism in São Paulo, 1888–1938," in *Americas* 49, no. 2 (1992): 179–206.

Additional Bibliography

Caldwell, Kia Lilly. *Negras in Brazil: Re-envisioning Black Women, Citizenship, and the Politics of Identity.* New Brunswick, NJ: Rutgers University Press, 2007.

Covin, David. "The Role of Culture in Brazil's Unified Black Movement, Bahia in 1992." *Journal of Black Studies* 27, no.1 (1996): 39–55.

Jones-De Oliveira, Kimberly F. "The Politics of Culture or the Politics of Race: Afro-Brazilian Mobilization, 1920–1964." *Journal of Third World Studies* 20, no. 1 (2003): 103–120.

Romo, Anadelia A. "Rethinking Race and Culture in Brazil's First Afro-Brazilian Congress of 1934." *Journal of Latin America Studies* 39, no. 1 (2007): 31–54.

Sheriff, Robin E. *Dreaming Equality: Color, Race, and Racism in Urban Brazil.* New Brunswick, NJ: Rutgers University Press, 2001.

Soares, Carlos Eugênio Líbano. *A negregada instituição: Os capoeiras na Corte Imperial, 1850–1890.* Rio de Janeiro: Access Editora, 1999.

KIM D. BUTLER

AFRICAN–BRAZILIAN EMIGRATION TO AFRICA. African–Brazilian Emigration to Africa, a "return" of approximately 4,000 freed persons to Africa during the course of the nineteenth century. Although some émigrés were Brazilian-born, most had been taken as slaves from the Yoruba- and Fon-speaking areas of present-day Benin, Togo, and southwestern Nigeria during a period of widespread civil and religious warfare. Portuguese colonial law provided Brazilian slaves the opportunity to purchase their own freedom. Many Africans in Brazil participated in organized savings societies with the hope of returning to their homeland as free persons. The majority of émigrés left from Bahia, a province engaged in direct trade with the African coast in tobacco and slaves, while a smaller number left from Rio de Janeiro. Large-scale emigration began after 1835 in the wake of an attempted rebellion led by African Muslims in Bahia's capital. Backlash against Africans prompted hundreds to risk their meager savings and even their lives in the transatlantic voyage.

Most émigrés were unable to return to their original homelands, instead forging new communities in the coastal cities of Ouidah and Grand Popo, where they became known as the "Bresiliens." Because the local populations had been long established in subsistence and commercial agriculture, the returnees carved their niche in skilled trades and commerce. From the 1830s through the 1850s, several Bresilien families accumulated substantial fortunes in the illicit slave trade. They traded to Europeans in exchange for Bahian rum and tobacco, diversifying after the end of slavery to trade in palm products and other local goods. Returnees also engaged in skilled occupations such as carpentry, masonry, boat building, and barbering. Some gained positions of prominence in society and politics. Less successful were those who settled in Lagos. They found themselves in competition with resident European traders and Yoruba freed persons released from the British protectorate of Sierra Leone. They did not speak English, they were Catholic rather than Protestant, and they rarely had the necessary capital to establish commercial enterprises. The Brazilians in Lagos became artisans, using the skills they had acquired as slaves. Some Central Africans returned to small communities in Benguela, Luanda, and the Cabinda coast.

See also **Angola; Bahia; Slavery: Brazil.**

BIBLIOGRAPHY

J. Michael Turner, "Les Bresiliens: The Impact of Former Brazilian Slaves upon Dahomey," (Ph.D. diss., Boston University, 1975).

Manuela Carneiro Da Cunha, *Negros, estrangeiros: Os escravos libertos e sua volta a Africa* (1985).

Mary C. Karasch, *Slave Life in Rio de Janeiro, 1808–1850* (1987).

Pierre Verger, *Fluxo e refluxo do trafico de escravos entre o Golfo do Benin e a Bahia de Todos os Santos dos seculos XVII a XIX*, 3d ed. (1987).

KIM D. BUTLER

AFRICAN BRAZILIANS, COLOR TERMINOLOGY.

Color is one of the crucial social variables of Brazil and constitutes one of the unique characteristics of Latin American culture. Like the terms "race" and "ethnicity," skin color is an imperfect concept used to identify people in Latin America. It is but one of the characteristics used. Other physical traits, such as hair and facial features like the shape of the nose, are also employed. In addition, an identification determined by physical appearance can be modified by such social variables as wealth and education.

Color terms utilized in Brazil describe the almost infinite shadings that result from race mixing among Indians, Europeans, and Africans, and among the mixtures themselves. During the colonial period, racist perceptions and medical notions combined to create multiple hierarchies. One was based on the idea that pure races were better than mixed races inasmuch as the latter, it was believed, contained the worst characteristics of the parents. The other, and more common, hierarchy was based on social usage that placed whites at the top of the social hierarchy and blacks or Indians at the bottom and arranged other groups by the degree to which they appeared white. "Purity of blood," which was used to describe whites of demonstrable European ancestry, was essential for entry into the highest stratum of society.

Race mixing is not unique to Latin America. But whereas other societies, such as that of the United States, have acknowledged a comparatively limited range of racially mixed groups, Latin American societies have historically recognized many differences. The result has been a plethora of racial identities, many of them conveying negative images. Over the years, hundreds of racial terms have been used in Brazil, but the most common have included *branco,* white; *branco da terra,* white of the land, a person whose whiteness was recognized only in a specific area; *moreno,* a light-skinned mulatto; pardo or *mulato,* referring originally to the offspring of one white and one black parent; *mestiço,* Mameluco, or Caboclo, an Indian-white mixture; *cafuzo,* a black and Indian mixture; *crioulo,* a Brazilian-born black; *negro* or *prêto,* a dark-skinned or African-born black; and *indigo,* Indian. Often the same term is applied to different groups in different parts of Brazil. *Cabra,* for example, was used to describe a very light-skinned mulatto, or a mixture of Indian, black, and white, or of Indian and black.

The existence of such a range of identified color groups is complemented by several other crucial characteristics. First is the mutability of such labels. Because part of the label is socially and culturally defined, a person's identity can change over time. Second, the existence of such fine gradations prevents an objective definition of such labels. While during the colonial period efforts were made to describe and define each possible combination, in reality this process was a failure. Instead, the labeling is often done by the observer on the basis of the relationship of the personal characteristics of the observer and the observed. The result is the imprecise definition of groups. This ambiguity has served effectively to prevent political organizing around racial identification.

Such ambiguity does not mean the absence of prejudice. Rather, it points to color-conscious societies in which the phenotypical appearance and culture of individuals is extremely important. Thus the differences among people make it difficult to redress social injustices.

BIBLIOGRAPHY

Charles Wagley, "On the Concept of Social Race in the Americas," in *Contemporary Cultures and Societies of Latin America*, edited by Dwight B. Heath and Richard N. Adams (1965), pp. 531–545.

Marvin Harris, "Referential Ambiguity in the Calculus of Brazilian Racial Identity," in *Southwestern Journal of Anthropology* 26 (Spring 1970): 1–14.

Robert M. Levine, *Race and Ethnic Relations in Latin America and the Caribbean: An Historical Dictionary and Bibliography* (1980).

Thomas M. Stephens, *Dictionary of Latin American Racial and Ethnic Terminology* (1989).

Additional Bibliography

Appelbaum, Nancy P., Anne S. Macpherson, and Karin Alejandra Rosemblatt, eds. *Race and Nation in Modern Latin America*. Chapel Hill: University of North Carolina Press, 2003.

Hanchard, Michael George. *Racial Politics in Contemporary Brazil.* Durham, NC: Duke University Press, 1999.

Stephens, Thomas M. *Dictionary of Latin American Racial and Ethnic Terminology.* Gainesville: University of Florida Press, 1989.

DONALD RAMOS

AFRICAN-LATIN AMERICAN RELATIONS.

Africa's relationship with Latin America dates to the earliest days of European expansion in the Atlantic world. It was European, particularly, Portuguese, attempts to expand the slave trade to the West African coast during the fifteenth century that led to the shipbuilding and navigational innovations that enabled Europeans to cross the Atlantic. Because African slavery already existed in Europe, both free and enslaved Africans accompanied the earliest European voyages of exploration and conquest, including the Cortez and Pizarro expeditions.

The widespread introduction of African slaves to the Americas followed the Portuguese success at transferring plantation techniques to Brazil from islands off the West African coast. The technologies of sugar monoculture and refining, along with the use of coerced labor, soon spread to other European colonies. In total, between eight and ten million African slaves were brought to the Americas from the sixteenth through the mid-nineteenth centuries. Their presence was heaviest in the Caribbean, the most intensely exploited parts of Brazil, and the coasts of Mexico, Venezuela, Colombia, Ecuador, and Peru.

The slave trade marked Latin America culturally and demographically, cementing means of production and social organization based on the inequitable participation of peoples of African descent. In Africa the trade caused political instability and the drain of productive labor. The exchange changed food culture, especially by introducing manioc and corn to Africa, and introducing sugar, rice, and open-range cattle ranching to the Americas. In the nineteenth century, a contraband slave trade sustained direct contact between Africa and Parts of Latin America, particularly Cuba, Puerto Rico and Brazil, where slavery was still practiced until the last decades of the nineteenth century. Slave ships also carried African goods—particularly religious artifacts—to Latin American markets and carried some former slaves to Africa, especially from Brazil. These created neighborhoods of merchants, and their descendants continued to consider themselves ethnically Brazilian. Brazilian districts survive in Ghana, Nigeria, Togo, and Benin. Ironically, the suppression of the slave trade during the nineteenth century spurred the formal European colonization of Africa and closed African societies to external trade, virtually ending contact between Africa and Latin America.

RELATIONS IN THE POSTCOLONIAL ERA

African decolonization changed this equation. African nationalism in the aftermath of World War II addressed not only the struggle to be rid of colonial masters but also sought *liberation*—the breaking of webs of dependency and exploitation. This conception coincided with the rise of developmentalism in Latin America, which aimed as well to liberate these countries from economic dependency. Whereas the coincidence of these goals brought Africa and Latin America back to each other's attention, in practice they proved unreachable. African countries succumbed to neocolonial economic relations with their former colonial rulers. Latin American countries failed to reconcile the more radical implications of developmentalism with their conservative social structures.

Still, the decolonization of Africa reshaped the Atlantic. Brazil, revolutionary Cuba, and to a lesser extent Mexico and Argentina, sought to develop ties with new African states. The most ambitious of these initiatives was that of Brazil, which opened embassies in Ghana, Senegal, Nigeria, Zaire, South Africa, Kenya, and Ethiopia during the 1960s. For Latin Americans, the multiplication of states in the developing world seemed to increase their leverage with the developed world. This was the focus of the 1955 Bandung Conference of Asian and African states, which led in 1961 to the creation of the Non-Aligned Movement, an alliance of countries seeking autonomy from the United States and the Soviet Union. Latin American countries participated in this movement to varying degrees. Brazil sent observers. Fidel Castro led the movement during part of the 1970s.

Since 1960, African-Latin American relations have been focused on four areas: 1) generating coalitions within international organizations; 2) forming producer's associations able to improve market conditions for such commodities as coffee and cacao; 3) direct trade; 4) political alliances in favor of specific foreign policy goals.

An example of these relationships can be found in the case of Brazil, the Latin American country with the most extensive involvement in Africa. Through the influence of foreign ministers Mario Gibson Barboza (1969–1974) and Antonio Azeredo da Silveira (1974–1979), Brazil built coalitions with African cacao- and coffee-producing countries and gained support for its candidates for positions at the United Nations and other international organizations. It imported Nigerian oil and exported cars and trucks as well as consumer goods particularly suited to African markets (such as refrigerators that ran on propane and could be used in areas without electricity, promoted by soccer star Pelé). It succumbed to African pressure to support the decolonization of Portuguese Africa in 1974–1975 and to oppose South African apartheid.

A dramatic moment in Latin America's relationship with Africa was the deployment in 1975 of Cuban troops to the former Portuguese colony Angola. Eventually, 45,000 Cuban soldiers were sent to help the Marxist Angolan government fight an invasion by South Africa, and they remained until 1991. The Cubans fought South African soldiers on Angolan soil, eroding the white South African regime's confidence in its ability to sustain apartheid militarily, especially as white families became increasingly reluctant to enlist their sons.

While Cuban involvement in Angola was conducted initially without the knowledge of the Soviet Union, which reluctantly backed its ally, in 1977 it was the Soviet Union that compelled Cuba to take part in Ethiopia's war with Somalia. Cuba's legacies in Africa were the preservation of Angolan autonomy, the destabilization of Ethiopia, and an extensive program of deploying doctors and teachers to different countries. It was the only one of the warring factions in Angola that left behind maps of its landmines.

The Cuban commander in Angola and Ethiopia, General Arnaldo Ochoa, was the figure most visibly identified with that country's military successes. He was executed in 1996 on drug smuggling charges, though some argued that he was really executed because he rivaled Castro in popularity. Castro visited Africa in 1977, and Brazilian President General João Baptista Figueiredo did so in 1983. Brazilian president Luiz Inácio "Lula" da Silva made four trips that included seventeen countries between 2003 and 2005, reigniting Brazilian efforts to forge a united front among developing countries on world trade, the manufacture of generic drugs for diseases such as HIV, and debt relief.

See also **Cuba: Cuba Since 1959; Slave Trade.**

BIBLIOGRAPHY

Boxer, Charles Ralph. *The Portuguese Seaborne Empire: 1415–1825.* New York: Alfred A. Knopf, 1969.

Chilcote, Ronald H., ed. *Protest and Resistance in Angola and Brazil: Comparative Studies.* Berkeley: University of California Press, 1972.

Curtin, Philip D. *Atlantic Slave Trade: A Census.* Madison: University of Wisconsin Press, 1969.

Eltis, David. *The Rise of African Slavery in the Americas.* Cambridge, U.K., and New York: Cambridge University Press, 1999.

Gleijeses, Piero. *Conflicting Missions: Havana, Washington and Africa, 1959–1976.* Chapel Hill: University of North Carolina Press, 2002.

Klein, Herbert S. *African Slavery in Latin America and the Caribbean.* New York: Oxford University Press, 1986.

Miller, Joseph C. *Way of Death: Merchant Capitalism and the Angolan Slave Trade, 1730–1830.* Madison: University of Wisconsin Press, 1988.

Moreno Fraginals, Manuel, ed. *Africa in Latin America: Essays on History, Culture and Socialization.* Teaneck, NJ: Holmes & Meier, 1984.

Rodrigues, José Honório. *Brazil and Africa.* Berkeley: University of California Press, 1965.

Spitzer, Leo. *Lives in Between: Assimilation and Marginality in Austria, Brazil ,West Africa, 1780–1945.* Cambridge, U.K., and New York: Cambridge University Press, 1990.

Sweet, James. *Recreating Africa: Culture, Kinship and Religion in the African-Portuguese World, 1441–1770.* Chapel Hill: University of North Carolina Press, 2006.

Thornton, John. *Africa and Africans in the Making of the Atlantic World, 1400–1800.* Cambridge, U.K., and New York: Cambridge University Press, 1992.

JERRY DÁVILA

AFRICAN–LATIN AMERICAN RELIGIONS

This entry includes the following articles:
OVERVIEW
BRAZIL

OVERVIEW

Between 1492 and 1870, at least 10 million Africans, representing hundreds of ethnic groups, were carried as slaves to the islands of the Caribbean and the Atlantic coasts of South, Central, and North America. Many thousands more were taken after the close of legal slavery or induced to emigrate as indentured servants. Despite the harshness of life both in slavery and after emancipation, they were more or less able to reconstruct a cultural identity on the basis of the elements of the African cultures that they carried with them and the social environments in which they found themselves.

Among the many cultural skills that Africans brought to the Americas were patterns of spiritual beliefs and practices that varied with each ethnic group. Some of the slaves were trained priests and priestesses of African spirits who carried with them powers of enchantment and healing. Thrown into the maelstrom of Atlantic slave societies, they found these skills to be valuable in meeting the challenges of plantation and urban life. In most cases the specific ethnic context of the beliefs and practices was lost, but in others sufficient numbers of Africans from the same region were able to reconstitute themselves as "nations" within the multiethnic societies to which they were taken. Through these nations, or communities, African beliefs and practices were preserved and developed in dialogue with the non-African traditions in their milieu.

The most influential African peoples in Latin America came from the coastal and forest zones of western Africa. Particularly notable were the Ashanti and Fanti peoples of present-day Ghana and Côte d'Ivoire (Ivory Coast); the Ewe- and Fon-speaking peoples of present-day Togo and Benin; the Hausa, Yoruba, and Ibo peoples of present-day Nigeria; and the many interrelated peoples of the former Kongo kingdom of present-day Zaire and Angola. Depending upon the conditions that members of each group encountered in the Americas, they were able to preserve more or less complex patterns of their spiritual beliefs and practices. Factors such as racial and ethnic demographics, agricultural and mercantile systems, and opportunities for manumission or escape all influenced the transplantation of African religions in the Americas.

Perhaps the most significant factor in the development of these traditions was the established European religion of a particular region. In the Roman Catholic colonies of Spain, Portugal, and France, slaves were baptized as a matter of law, and in some regions, particularly urban areas, the Catholic Church actively supported slave rights and manumission. The Catholic Church also accepted a wide variety of ethnic ceremonials as legitimate supplements to the orthodox sacraments. The Protestant chur-ches of the British and Dutch colonies, by contrast, did not legislate the baptism of slaves and lacked the political power to influence their legal or social status. Slaves and free blacks came to accept Christianity through nonconforming Baptist and Methodist churches, which emphasized local leadership, biblical foundations, and personal conversion.

The social and religious factors stemming from these European religious traditions were crucial in determining the ways in which the African religions developed in their particular milieus. While there are many exceptions, as a broad general rule, Africans and their descendants in Catholic regions developed religious institutions alternative and parallel to Christianity, such as Candomblé in Brazil, vodun (vodou, voodoo) in Haiti, or Santería in Cuba. In the Protestant regions, however, they created alternative forms of Protestant Christianity, such as Revival in Jamaica or the Spiritual Baptists of Trinidad. This dialogue of religious elements either by juxtaposition in Catholic regions or reinterpretation in Protestant regions has been the primary focus of researchers who see in African-derived traditions models for understanding culture change. More recently, researchers have looked to the traditions for light on issues of the multiple meanings of symbols and the coexistence of plural identities.

In the Latin American world, African religious traditions have been particularly influential in areas of intensive eighteenth- and nineteenth-century sugar production. The African-derived traditions of Haiti, northeastern Brazil, and Cuba have shaped the national cultures of those countries, and their emigrants have established the traditions in other Latin-

and English-speaking countries. Perhaps the most famous of the traditions, Haitian vodou, owes its reputation to the role of devotees in the slave revolt that overthrew the French colonial authorities of Saint Domingue and established the "black republic" of Haiti in the midst of slaveholding colonies and the newly independent United States. Tales of voodoo barbarism were revived during Haiti's occupation by U.S. Marines in the twentieth century and continue to serve to discredit black spirituality in that country and elsewhere. Vodou means simply "spirit" in the Fon language of enslaved Dahomeans brought to Haiti in the eighteenth century, and the tradition centers on cultivating the spirits' protection and inspiration in meeting the harsh challenges of the lives of the Haitian poor.

In Brazil, particularly the Northeastern city of Salvador da Bahia, the African-derived traditions are called *Candomblé*. Due to Brazil's relative proximity to Africa, a thriving reciprocal trade brought not only slaves but free Africans to Bahia. In the late eighteenth and early nineteenth centuries, they established a number of houses of worship based on the African traditions of the houses' founders. The prestige of these early houses formed the model for the veneration of African spirits throughout Brazil. While the old Bahian houses pride themselves on the purity of their African liturgies, others have wedded elements of their practices to European and Amerindian ideas, thus creating thousands of variants known collectively as Umbanda. It is largely through Umbanda's popularization of *Candomblé* that African spirits known as *orishas* (Orixás) are popular throughout the country. The festival of Iemanjá, the maternal spirit of the oceans, is attended by hundreds of thousands on the beaches of Rio de Janeiro and millions of others throughout the country.

Africans in Cuba, like those in Brazil and to a lesser extent in Haiti, were able to maintain ethnic identities through religious organizations. The most widespread tradition is often called *Santería,* a name deriving from the correspondences developed between the spirits of the Yoruba people and the Catholic saints. Kongo practices form the basis of another tradition, known alternately as *Palo* or *Mayombe.* The secret religious societies of the Efik and Ejaham peoples have been transplanted to Cuba, where they are known as *Abakua.* While these traditions never achieved the approval of the wider society, their influence in festivals and popular music brought elements of their spiritualities to every sector of the Cuban population.

The traditions of Haiti, Brazil, and Cuba are only the best-known of African-Hispanic traditions. All the countries of the Atlantic littoral have produced more or less developed spiritualities that have their origin in Africa. The Haitian, Brazilian, and Cuban traditions have become most important because they have been studied by scholars and because emigrants have carried these traditions to other countries, where they often act as models for a renewed African consciousness. Haitians have taken vodou to the Dominican Republic and the United States; Brazilians have established *Candomblé* houses in Argentina; and Cubans have taken *Santería* to the United States, Puerto Rico, Mexico, Venezuela, and Colombia.

See also **Catholic Church: The Colonial Period; Lwa; Orixás; Protestantism; Rastafarians; Santería; Slavery: Spanish America; Syncretism; Vodun, Voodoo, Vaudun.**

BIBLIOGRAPHY

An extraordinary bibliography with nearly 6,000 entries may be found in John Gray, comp, *Ashé: Traditional Religion and Healing in Sub-Saharan Africa and the Diaspora, a Classified International Bibliography* (1989).

Other important studies include Melville J. Herskovits, *The New World Negro: Selected Papers in Afroamerican Studies* (1966); Roger Bastide, *African Civilisations in the New World,* translated by Peter Green (1972); Angelina Pollak Eltz, *Cultos afroamericanos* (1972); Leonard E. Barrett, *Soul-Force: African Heritage in Afro-American Religion* (1974); George Eaton Simpson, *Black Religions in the New World* (1978); Robert Farris Thompson, *Flash of the Spirit: African and Afro-American Art and Philosophy* (1983); Kortright Davis and Elias Farajajé-Jones, eds., *African Creative Expressions of the Divine* (1991); Joseph M. Murphy, *Working the Spirit: Ceremonies of the African Diaspora* (1994).

Additional Bibliography

Cros Sandoval, Mercedes. *Worldview, the Orichas, and Santería: Africa to Cuba and Beyond.* Gainesville: University Press of Florida, 2006.

Daniel, Yvonne. *Dancing Wisdom: Embodied Knowledge in Haitian Vodou, Cuban Yoruba, and Bahian Candomblé.* Urbana: University of Illinois Press, 2005.

Fernández Olmos, Margarite, and Lizabeth Paravisini-Gebert. *Creole Religions of the Caribbean: An Introduction from Vodou and Santería to Obeah and Espiritismo.* New York: New York University Press, 2003.

Greenfield, Sidney M., and A. F. Droogers, eds. *Reinventing Religions: Syncretism and Transformation in Africa and the Americas.* Lanham: Rowman & Littlefield, 2001.

Sweet, James H. *Recreating Africa: Culture, Kinship, and Religion in the African-Portuguese World, 1441-1770.* Chapel Hill: University of North Carolina Press, 2003.

JOSEPH M. MURPHY

BRAZIL

A culturally diverse population, Brazilians also practice a variety of different faiths, several of which are rooted in the history of African slaves brought to work on Brazilian sugar plantations beginning in the sixteenth century. West African Yoruba and Dahomean peoples retained impressive segments of their religious beliefs and practices through syncretization with Catholic cultural elements. Bastide notes that on the special Catholic saints' days that were observed by plantation owners, Africans secretly celebrated their own deities. An example is the Yoruba deity Ogum, god of iron and patron of blacksmiths forging iron weapons and farm tools. In some regions of Brazil, Africans clandestinely worshipped Ogum under the guise of celebrating St. George, who was depicted in paintings, lithographs, and figurines on a white horse while slaying a dragon with a long iron sword. Cultural Syncretism proceeded along two lines. First, the Yoruba *orixás* (deities) and Catholic saints were both structural intermediaries between a high and remote Olorun (God) and ordinary people on earth. Second, cultural items such as the iron weapons linking Ogum and St. George brought together *orixá* and saint. Over time the link between iron farm tools and Ogum weakened in Brazil in that the slaves had no concern for the profitability of the master's plantation. The iron weapons retained as cultural elements, however, would serve as important symbols in the ongoing war, both real and psychological, between master and slave.

Yoruba beliefs and practices comprise a common cultural pattern running through most African Brazilian religions. However, each African Brazilian religion has been differentially shaped by the larger Brazilian milieu, which also included Central African religious traditions, indigenous shamanistic beliefs and practices, and a type of spiritualism known as Kardecismo. Furthermore, worshippers were not restricted to persons of African descent, and membership generally reflects the ethnic composition of a particular locale. African Brazilians dominate Candomblé in Salvador, Bahia, while in the southern

The festival of Iemanja, the Candomblé goddess of the sea, Salvador, Brazil, 1985. This festival, held every year on February 2nd in Salvador, has its roots in the Yoruba culture of West Africa. © STEPHANIE MAZE/CORBIS

cities of São Paulo and Pôrto Alegre, European Brazilians comprise 50 percent of the members in the Umbanda religion.

CANDOMBLÉ

During the latter part of the slave era and after emancipation in 1888, African Brazilians more openly practiced Candomblé in urban religious centers. Two Yoruba-influenced religions emerged: Candomblé in Salvador and Xangô in Recife. A closely related Dahomean-influenced religion known as Tambor Das Minas developed in São Luís.

Each religious center is led by a *mãe de santo* (mother of saint) or a *pai de santo* (father of saint). According to Wafer, their initiates are divided into two categories: those who go into trance and are possessed by deities, and those who do not. Of the latter, the males are called *ogãs* and the females are known as *equedes;* they work in special supporting roles that, in part, help provide financing and labor for the religious center and its celebrations in exchange for ritual protection and opportunities to dance along with the deities.

A religious center recognizes each deity during its annual cycle of celebrations. While dancing to polyrhythmic drumming and Yoruba songs and words in the more conservative religious centers, spirit mediums known as "horses" are possessed by the various deities in all practices of Candomblé. An important part of each celebration is feeding the honored deity as well as those who come to observe and enjoy the beautifully costumed deities and their dancing. After the main part of the celebration, the deities take their leave, and the "horses" are possessed by childlike spirits known as *erê.* Although spirits of the dead are an important part of many African Brazilian religions, it is rare that Candomblé in its more conservative form has anything to do with them. Instead, *eguns* (spirits of dead ancestors) are dealt with in the cult of Egum.

BATUQUE

The Batuque religion in Belém is an independent religious system, which Leacock and Leacock say deserves recognition in its own right. Although African origins are present, Batuque has been "Brazilianized" far more than Candomblé. An early form of Batuque was brought to Belém at the time of the Amazon rubber boom (1890–1913). It probably included cultural elements from the Dahomean influence in São Luís, generalized Yoruba religious traits, folk Catholicism, Brazilian and Iberian folklore and history, and indigenous Brazilian shamanic traits from the Pajelança of Pará and the Catimbó cult of northeastern Brazil.

Members of Batuque refer to the supernatural beings that possess them as *encantados.* They include a variety of spirits of the dead as well as deities, but not Catholic saints. Saints are said to live in the sky, while the *encantados* live in *encantarias* deep in the forest; under rivers, lakes, and the sea; and even in underground cities directly beneath human cities.

UMBANDA

Umbanda is another highly Brazilianized religion with Central and West African, pre-Columbian indigenous, folk Catholic, and spiritist origins. It is practiced primarily in southern Brazil, especially in Rio de Janeiro, São Paulo, and Pôrto Alegre. It is also found in nearly all major urban areas.

Umbanda apparently evolved out of Macumba in the 1920s. According to Bastide, Macumba was in part an outgrowth of the introduction of Yoruba deities into the earlier Central African Bantu cult known as Cabula. Congolese and Angolan religious traditions were present in Macumba and later in Umbanda, as, for example, in the use of the name Zambi for the high god, instead of the Yoruba name Olorun. Also, Central African beliefs in possession by spirits of the dead were retained in Macumba. This helped set the scene for the diffusion of Kardecist spiritist beliefs related to spirits of the dead, supernatural fluids, and "passes" to remove evil fluids from sick and troubled individuals. The new sociocultural mélange became Umbanda. According to Karasch, the frequent changes in symbols, beliefs, and rituals in Umbanda as it spread throughout Brazil was part of the flexibility that characterized Central African religions brought by slaves to southern Brazil.

Brown, in describing the "whitening" of Umbanda, notes that many early leaders of Umbanda were middle-class professionals, mostly European Brazilians. They were unhappy with the "highly evolved" Kardecist spirits who gave long-winded lectures on doctrine. They enjoyed the curing rituals of the African and Indian spirits in Umbanda but did not care for animal sacrifices, drinking, and the drumming and dancing often associated with what they regarded as the more primitive forms of Umbanda rituals. These "low" features were dropped from Pure Umbanda. During the 1950s some African Brazilians reacted to Umbanda Pura by decrying the de-Africanization of Umbanda. Differences in religious beliefs and practices to some extent reflected different social and racial sectors. Today these divisions within Umbanda maintain a relatively peaceful coexistence.

See also **Candomblé; Music: Popular Music and Dance; Syncretism; Umbanda.**

BIBLIOGRAPHY

Octavio Da Costa Eduardo, *The Negro in Northern Brazil* (1948).

Seth and Ruth Leacock, *Spirits of the Deep: A Study of an Afro-Brazilian Cult* (1972).

Esther Pressel, "Umbanda in São Paulo: Religious Innovation in a Developing Society," in *Religion, Altered*

States of Consciousness, and Social Change, edited by Erika Bourguignon (1973).

Roger Bastide, *The African Religions of Brazil* (1978).

Mary Karasch, "Central African Religious Tradition in Rio de Janeiro," in *Journal of Latin American Lore* 5 (1979): 233–253.

Chester E. Gabriel, *Communications of the Spirits: Umbanda, Regional Cults in Manaus, and the Dynamics of Mediumistic Trance* (1980).

Patricia B. Lerch, "An Explanation for the Predominance of Women in the Umbanda Cults of Pôrto Alegre, Brazil," in *Urban Anthropology* 11 (1982): 237–261.

Diana Degroat Brown, *Umbanda: Religion and Politics in Urban Brazil* (1986).

Jam Wafer, *The Taste of Blood: Spirit Possession in Brazilian Candomblé* (1991).

Júlio Braga, *Ancestralidade afro-brasileira: O culto de Babá Egum* (1992).

Additional Bibliography

Caroso, Carlos, and Jeferson Afonso Bacelar. *Faces da tradição afro-brasileira: Religiosidade, sincretismo, anti-sincretismo, reafricanização, práticas terapêuticas, etnobotânica e comida.* Rio de Janeiro: Pallas: CNPq; Salvador: CEAO, 1998.

Kiddy, Elizabeth W. *Blacks of the Rosary: Memory and History in Minas Gerais, Brazil.* University Park: Pennsylvania State University Press, 2005.

Parés, Luis Nicolau. *A formação do candomblé: História e ritual da nação jeje na Bahia.* Campinas: Editora Unicamp, 2006.

Selka, Stephen. *Religion and the Politics of Ethnic Identity in Bahia, Brazil.* Gainesville: University of Florida Press, 2007.

Silva, Vagner Gonçalves da. *O antropólogo e sua magia: Trabalho de campo e texto etnográfico nas pesquisas antropológicas sobre religiões afro-brasileiras.* São Paulo: Edusp, 2000.

Sweet, James H. *Recreating Africa: Culture, Kinship, and Religion in the African-Portuguese World, 1441-1770.* Chapel Hill: University of North Carolina Press, 2003.

Voeks, Robert A. *Sacred Leaves of Candomblé: African Magic, Medicine, and Religion in Brazil.* Austin: University of Texas Press, 1997.

ESTHER J. PRESSEL

AFRICANS IN HISPANIC AMERICA.

People of African descent live in all of the former Spanish colonies in the Americas. With few exceptions, they are the descendants of African slaves who were first brought to the Americas in 1502. African slavery finally ended in Spanish America in 1886, when Cuba became the last society to abolish it. A century later, the legacy of slavery remains apparent in all of the former slave-holding societies. Individuals who claim African ancestry are struggling everywhere for self-definition and a secure place in the lands of their birth.

Although blacks are a part of the human landscape everywhere, it is difficult to determine their demographic distribution. This is due to the fact that census data in most societies do not include the population's "racial" or ethnic heritages. The process of miscegenation, in addition, has occurred to such an extent that it complicates the task of "racial" identification. Some persons, reflecting a variety of complex historical and psychological factors, will not readily acknowledge that they are of African descent. These difficulties notwithstanding, one may cautiously divide the former Spanish possessions into three groups in accordance with the presumed size of their populations of African descent.

The first group consists of those societies where Afro-Latinos comprise one-third or more of the population. This is especially the case in the three Caribbean islands—Cuba, the Dominican Republic, and Puerto Rico. As much as 80 percent of the population of the Dominican Republic may be of African descent. Between one-third and two-fifths of Puerto Rico's population can claim African ancestry. In 1981 the Cuban census showed that 34 percent of the population was of African ancestry, a figure widely acknowledged by specialists as low. Taken together, the population of these three polyglot societies is approximately 18 million, of which 8 to 10 million may be of African descent. It should not be difficult to understand why this is the case. These islands, particularly Cuba, had been the recipients of sizable numbers of African slaves between the sixteenth and nineteenth centuries. With the exception of Panama, none of the societies of Central and South America falls into the first group. Many of the Afro-Panamanians are descendants of immigrants from the British Caribbean who came to help construct the Panama Canal and the railroad during the late nineteenth and early twentieth centuries.

Afro-Cuban women pray at the altar of the Virgin of Regla, Havana, Cuba, 2004. The patron saint of Havana's harbor, Cuba's Virgin of Regla, a black virgin holding a white child, is closely associated with Iemanja, the West African Yoruba goddess of the sea. © CLAUDIA DAUT/REUTERS/CORBIS

The second category of former Spanish colonies consists of those with African-derived populations of between 5 and 30 percent. These include Nicaragua, Costa Rica, Honduras, Venezuela, Ecuador, and Colombia. Although most of these people are descendants of the African slaves who worked in those societies, a fairly high percentage of the Afro-Venezuelans and Afro–Costa Ricans are immigrants from the West Indies and their progeny.

The third group comprises societies where less than 5 percent of the population is of African descent. In Argentina, Chile, Bolivia, Uruguay, and Paraguay, the presence of blacks is negligible. They comprise a slightly higher proportion of the population in Mexico, Peru, Guatemala, and El Salvador.

It is important to underscore this demographic variation because there is a rough correlation bet-

ween the size of the black population and its impact on the larger society. In addition, politicians in societies with large black populations, such as those in the Caribbean, cannot ignore their presence and are compelled to treat them as significant interest groups. Consequently, blacks in those societies are able to influence the political culture to a far greater extent than are their counterparts who constitute a smaller share of the body politic elsewhere. Nevertheless, in countries such as Colombia and Ecuador, the peoples of African descent have wielded some degree of power in those areas and regions where their number is not inconsequential. These areas include the Esmeraldas district in Ecuador, and Buenaventura on the Pacific coast of Colombia.

Afro-Latin Americans do not constitute a monolithic group. They possess, for example, phenotypes ranging from very black at one extreme to Caucasoid at the other. There are class divisions, religious differences, and distinctions between those who are native to a particular society and those of foreign birth. Some individuals, regardless of the country in which they reside, will deny the African part of their heritage because of its association with slavery and the unhealthy impact that racism has had on their personhood. These persons have internalized a societal zeitgeist that ascribes a lesser human worth to those who share an African ancestry. Consequently, they are likely to define themselves in national terms such as "Cuban," "Mexican," or "Peruvian," and to eschew any "racial" identification. There is, of course, no incompatibility in simultaneously acknowledging a national as well as a "racial" or "ethnic" origin. The seeming rejection of one's "racial" heritage reflects the continuing salience and pernicious effects of a racist ideology that has never disappeared from the Spanish American landscape.

Racial prejudice, however, has never operated with the same overt and unrelenting malevolence in Spanish America as it has in the United States, and racial segregation never became official policy anywhere. Nevertheless, immigration laws were overtly racist in Spanish America until the 1950s, and institutional barriers to equality and social justice were omnipresent. Hispanic societies are not color blind: Undeniable systemic obstacles prevent the advancement of Afro-Latinos everywhere, and social prejudice directed at them remains an inescapable fact of life. Some observers maintain that the Spanish American variant of racism has had a more damaging impact on its victims than its more virulently expressed counterpart in the United States. One American noted in 1963, after a visit to Puerto Rico, "the Latin American system knows more about how to discriminate against the Negroes and make them like it than North Americans."

Under the circumstances, any assessment of the Afro-Latino condition must be made in the context of a racial zeitgeist that limits their possibilities and, in varying degrees, debases them as persons. Scholars have often noted that the adage "money whitens" is used in popular discourse in some societies and have mistakenly concluded that this indicates that an individual's position in society is largely a function of economic circumstances and not of "racial" heritage. The racism that under-

scores this adage, however, is obvious because it suggests that whiteness represents the societal standard. The depiction of Afro-Latinos in textbooks, comics, literature, and in private and public discourse is frequently negative, thereby demonstrating the pervasiveness of a racism that refuses to die.

The complex interplay of race and class in Spanish America has resulted in a disproportionate share of blacks occupying the lowest ranks of the social order. Poverty almost always wears a black face, or at least a brown one. This is the consequence of the survival of the structural and racial barriers to the advancement of blacks and Indians, who traditionally have been excluded from the elite groups. Cuba probably represents an exception to this pattern. The revolution effected fundamental changes in the country's social, economic, and political systems, as a result of which Afro-Cubans experienced an improvement in their condition. The Castro regime also tackled, with some success, the problem of institutional racism. The prejudice that undergirds and legitimizes social relations in Cuba, however, has been far more resistant to change. In addition, Afro-Cubans are less likely than Caucasians to be appointed to positions of real power in the government.

Despite the enormity of the problems they confront, Afro-Latinos have struggled to create a livable space for themselves. There are examples of individuals who have held and continue to hold elective office, usually at the local level, in the Dominican Republic, Puerto Rico, Colombia, Venezuela, and elsewhere. Others have acquired a fair amount of real estate in Costa Rica, the Dominican Republic, and the coastal areas of Ecuador, Colombia, Venezuela, and Peru. In Central America, Afro-American populations have begun to organize for better rights. Also, governments in Brazil, Colombia, Nicaragua, and Honduras now officially recognize the land rights of some maroon communities. Afro-Latinos, however, are still more likely to be found in service positions everywhere or to be unemployed. Although the professions have never been legally closed to them, at least in recent years, few persons have had the resources to acquire the requisite training. Contemporary Cuba stands alone in providing free education to those with the necessary aptitude, regardless of "racial" ancestry. However, Afro-Latin American organizations are trying to change this dynamic.

In 2001 Brazil began to implement affirmative action policies for government agencies and university admissions.

If the impact of Afro-Latinos on the political systems in which they live is not significant in most societies, the same cannot be said of their cultural influence. Linguists readily acknowledge the continuing impact of African languages on the vocabulary of Spanish and the ways in which it is spoken in societies, such as those of the Caribbean, that imported large numbers of slaves. African musical instruments, such as the marimba and the drum, still enjoy wide appeal. Similarly, musical styles, dance, culinary tastes, and art forms reflect, in varying degrees of vigor, African influences.

The problems that Afro-Latinos confront are similar, in many respects, to those that bedevil other peoples of African descent in the diaspora. Overwhelmingly poor, largely excluded from positions of political power, and invariably the victims of a systemic racism, hope is a luxury for many of them. Some still cling to vestiges of an African past; others welcome integration into the body politic. Those who constitute insignificant minorities in many countries face the prospect of being absorbed by the larger groups. In time, their more numerous counterparts in other societies may see the barriers to their progress weaken, if not disappear entirely.

See also **Race and Ethnicity; Slavery: Spanish America; Slave Trade.**

BIBLIOGRAPHY

Franklin Knight, *The African Dimension in Latin American Societies* (1974).

Robert Brent Toplin, ed., *Slavery and Race Relations in Latin America* (1974).

Leslie B. Rout, Jr., *The African Experience in Spanish America, 1502 to the Present Day* (1976).

Reid Andrews, *The Afro-Argentines of Buenos Aires, 1880–1900* (1980).

Richard Graham, ed., *The Idea of Race in Latin America, 1870–1940* (1990).

Winthrop R. Wright, *Café con Leche: Race, Class, and National Image in Venezuela* (1990).

Michael L. Conniff and Thomas J. Davis, *Africans in the Americas: A History of the Black Diaspora* (1994).

Additional Bibliography

Andrews, George Reid. *Afro-Latin America, 1800–2000.* Oxford and New York: Oxford University Press, 2004.

Ares Queija, Berta, and Alessandro Stella, eds. *Negros, mulatos, zambaigos: Derroteros africanos en los mundos ibéricos.* Seville, Spain: Escuela de Estudios Hispano-Americanos, Consejo Superior de Investigaciones Científicas, 2000.

Davis, Darién J. *Beyond Slavery: The Multilayered Legacy of Africans in Latin America and the Caribbean.* Lanham, MD: Rowman and Littlefield, 2007.

Landers, Jane, and Barry Robinson, eds. *Slaves, Subjects, and Subversives: Blacks in Colonial Latin America.* Albuquerque: University of New Mexico Press, 2006.

Naro, Nancy Priscilla, ed. *Blacks, Coloureds and National Identity in Nineteenth-century Latin America.* London: Institute of Latin American Studies, 2003.

Velázquez Gutiérrez, María Elisa, and Ethel Correa Duró, eds. *Poblaciones y culturas de origen africano en México.* Mexico: Instituto Nacional de Antropología e Historia, 2005.

COLIN A. PALMER

AGACE INDIANS. *See* **Payaguá Indians.**

AGIOTISTA. Agiotista, derogatory term used in nineteenth-century Mexico to describe those who made short-term loans to governments at very high rates of interest, usually assessed monthly rather than yearly, and often paid directly from tariff collections at the ports. The practice began in 1827 when Mexican treasuries, unable to borrow from abroad, started to rely on merchants for enough cash to meet a portion of their payrolls. Given their low creditworthiness, Mexican governments accepted loans whose face values were comprised of virtually worthless debt paper as well as cash. When tax collections shrank, *agiotistas* also received debt paper, forcing many into bankruptcy. It would appear that the practice ended in 1867 with the restored republic, but it is equally likely that it assumed different forms until banking achieved a firm foothold at the end of the nineteenth century.

BIBLIOGRAPHY

Ciro F. S. Cardoso, ed., *Formación y desarrollo de la burguesía en México: Siglo XIX* (1978).

Barbara A. Tenenbaum, *México en le época de los agiotistas, 1821–1857* (1985) and "'Neither a Borrower nor a Lender Be': Financial Constraints and the Treaty of Guadalupe Hidalgo," in *The Mexican and Mexican American Experience in the Nineteenth Century*, edited by Jaime E. Rodríguez O. (1989).

Additional Bibliography

Serrano Ortega, José Antonio, and Luis Jáuregui, eds. *Hacienda y política: Las finanzas públicas y los grupos de poder en la primera República Federal Mexicana.* Zamora: El Colegio de Michoacán; Mexico, D.F.: Instituto Mora, 1998.

BARBARA A. TENENBAUM

AGRAMONTE Y LOYNAZ, IGNACIO

(1841–1873). Ignacio Agramonte y Loynaz (*b.* 23 December 1841; *d.* 11 May 1873), Cuban general. Agramonte is known to Cubans as a man of irreproachable behavior in both his public and his private lives. His gallantry as a cavalry commander is legendary. Few Cuban military feats against Spanish forces are better known than the daring rescue of his friend, Colonel Julio Sanguily, from the Spanish column that had captured him.

Agramonte, born in Camagüey, in central Cuba, was a distinguished lawyer and cattle farmer who became one of the insurgent leaders in his region when the Ten Years' War (1868–1878) broke out. He espoused the radical liberal ideas that were supported by many Camagüeyans but were in opposition to the conservative views of the head of the revolt, Carlos Manuel de Céspedes. When the vicissitudes of war forced Céspedes to come to terms with the Camagüeyans, they hastily drafted a constitution for the insurgent provisional government. Agramonte was one of the two authors of this constitution, which was a solemn manifestation of Camagüeyan liberalism.

Agramonte's relationship with Céspedes, who had been proclaimed president of free Cuba, continued to be marred by serious conflicts, some of them of a personal nature. But the two men succeeded in burying their differences, and Céspedes finally put Agramonte in command of the insurgent forces in Camagüey, where he developed into an exceptional military leader, quickly becoming the soul of the rebellion. After Agramonte was

killed by a stray bullet while deploying his troops, his body fell into the hands of the Spaniards, who took it to the city of Camagüey, where they put it on display. Later the body was cremated, and Agramonte's ashes were scattered to the wind.

See also **Céspedes, Carlos Manuel de (the Elder); Cuba, Political Movements, Nineteenth Century; Ten Years' War.**

BIBLIOGRAPHY

There are no English sources available on Agramonte. See Carlos Márquez Sterling, *Ignacio Agramonte, el Bayardo de la revolución cubana* (1936); and Juan J. E. Casasús, *Vida militar de Agramonte* (1981).

Additional Bibliography

Sterling, Carlos Márquez. *Ignacio Agramonte, el bayardo de la revolución.* Miami: Editorial Cubana, 1995. A new edition of Sterling's 1936 work.

JOSÉ M. HERNÁNDEZ

AGRARIAN REFORM.

From the Spanish conquests in the fifteenth and sixteenth centuries to the early twenty-first century, both government and private institutions have instituted agrarian reform programs in Latin America. The extent to which calls for agrarian reform have been voiced over the past five hundred years is perhaps the best evidence of the failure, with a few notable exceptions, of most efforts at such reform. While land pressures in Latin America have been no greater than in other regions of the world, the fact that such a large proportion of the population still derives all or part of its subsistence from the land has pushed the issue to the forefront throughout the region. It is for this reason that throughout the history of Latin America, various political movements have called for agrarian reform.

COLONIAL PERIOD

The first efforts at agrarian reform were carried out almost as soon as the Spanish established their empire in the New World. The first land grabs of the Spanish conquistadors in the Caribbean led to the extinction of the indigenous population and the monopolization of land by the conquistadors. This in turn resulted in the emergence of both *latifundia* (the concentration of large tracts of land in the hands of a few Spanish landlords) and *minifundia* (the division of the remaining lands among peasants into parcels not large enough to provide subsistence for a peasant family). This land crisis led the Spanish crown to introduce land reform. The New Laws of 1542 abolished the *encomienda*, recognized the autonomy of the Indian community, and prohibited Spaniards from occupying the Indian lands or living in Indian villages. Encroachments on Indian lands, however, continued throughout the colonial period, and in the eighteenth century the Bourbon Reforms sought once again to enforce limited agrarian reform. In Brazil, the Portuguese crown grants, *sesmarias*, were extended to a few privileged settlers who dominated the good coastal lands for sugar production. As in Spanish America, colonial Brazil set the pattern of latifundia for the few and minifundia for the many.

INDEPENDENCE

After independence from Spain, most Latin American governments embraced classical liberal notions of agrarian reform, which argued that Indians and Latino peasants would be better off if they owned their own individual parcels of land and were free to partition and sell according to the dictates of the free market. Under this formula, lands traditionally controlled by the corporate Indian community were often divided up and sold, which only intensified the earlier trend of land concentration. During the latter half of the nineteenth century land was concentrated in this way throughout Latin America as the region embraced capitalist market relations. In Mexico, for example, both Benito Juárez and Porfirio Díaz oversaw and approved of the concentration of land by both the Mexican upper class and foreign investors.

To varying degrees this model was followed in other Latin American countries. In Brazil the government ceased granting lands in *sesmarias* in the mid-nineteenth century and sought instead to sell lands through the General Bureau of Public Lands, established in 1854, which resulted in further concentration of land-ownership. Land concentration resulted in landlessness and rural unemployment for many Latin American peasants, which in turn led to political unrest. The Mexican Revolution of 1910 was in part a response to the free-market policies so cherished by Porfirio Díaz and his *científicos*.

TWENTIETH CENTURY

The combination of monopolistic control of huge tracts of land and foreign ownership of the mineral resources of Mexico mobilized millions to demand a nationalist strategy for land distribution. In the wake of the Mexican Revolution, agrarian reform was written into the Constitution of 1917. Encompassed in the *ejido* program, the Mexican government sought to redistribute lands to the small- and medium-size farmers. At its peak, during the presidency of Lázaro Cárdenas (1934–1940), substantial redistribution of land was carried out, so that the proportion of landless peasants went down from 68 percent of the rural population in 1930 to 36 percent in 1940. After 1940, however, landlessness among rural dwellers steadily increased in Mexico at the same time that land became concentrated into the hands of private large landowners. Technological advances only widened the gap between large landowners and *ejidatarios*, since the former had more capital to purchase advanced machinery, seeds, and fertilizer.

In Brazil, which had no agrarian reform comparable to Mexico's *ejido* program, pressures on land were released by expansion westward into Brazil's vast interior. Brazilian strongman Getúlio Vargas (1930–1945, 1950–1954) encouraged westward expansion, since only 4 percent of Brazil's land was under cultivation as late as 1945. The opening up of western land helped reduce land concentration somewhat and vastly increased the number of farms.

Other Latin American countries experienced similar opposition to the concentration of land in the hands of the wealthy and landlessness among the rural poor. In Central America, elite control of arable land caused widespread unrest. In Guatemala, for example, the government of Jacobo Arbenz passed the Agrarian Reform Law (Decree 900) in 1952 allowing for the redistribution of over 600,000 hectares of land to over 100,000 Guatemalan families. The law was perceived by the United States to be a plot to expropriate lands owned by the U.S.-based United Fruit Company. Thus the United States planned and carried out the coup of 1954, in which the elected president Arbenz was overthrown and replaced by a Guatemalan leader acceptable to the United States, Colonel Carlos Castillo Armas.

In El Salvador, where by the early 1990s virtually all of the prime farmland was controlled by the elites and where over 70 percent of the peasants had no land at all, decades of conflict between peasants and large landowners over land control and distribution continued into the early 2000s. The *matanza* (slaughter) of the 1930s, in which an estimated thirty thousand Salvadoran peasants were killed, was due largely to struggles between peasants and the elite over the land. In the 1980s further conflicts over land resulted in the estimated deaths of over 70,000, most of them peasants and small farmers. And while a truce was reached in 1992, the pressures on land promised to give rise to even more fighting.

In 1961 Brazilian president João Goulart called for the expropriation of all large and medium landholdings adjacent to highways, rail lines, and public projects as a beginning to agrarian reform. This was perhaps one reason that Brazilian elites and the military backed his overthrow in 1964 to be replaced by a military dictatorship.

Because efforts to legislate agrarian reform have proved unsuccessful in Latin America, agrarian reform has usually been forced through by revolutionary upheavals, as was the case in Mexico. In the Bolivian Revolution of 1952, peasants mobilized and expropriated farmlands while workers seized control of the mines. In both Cuba and Nicaragua, agrarian reform was achieved only after prolonged revolutionary struggles. In Peru, a left-leaning military dictatorship that came to power in 1968 oversaw the breakup of farmland controlled by Peru's traditional landed elites. Yet while agrarian reform in Peru resulted in the diminished power of the traditional landed oligarchies, it did not benefit the majority of the peasant class. Despite promises, Peru's peasants still lack access to arable lands in the twenty-first century. This has had two negative consequences: malnourishment, which plagues over 10 percent of Peru's population (and an even greater part of its peasant population); and landlessness. The lack of serious agrarian reform gave revolutionary organizations such as the Shining Path a base of support among many of Peru's peasants in the 1980s. As a result of government repression (over thirty thousand died in Peru's civil war), the Shining Path was finally defeated, but many of the issues that drove Peruvians to join the Shining Path remain unresolved.

In Brazil, pressures on land led to open conflict in the countryside, and the 1994 Workers Party candidate for president, Luis Inácio "Lula" da Silva, called for broad land redistribution. Despite Lula's election in 2004, however, land reform has largely been stalled, and Brazil's landless peasants number over 5 million in 2007. Thus, calls for land redistribution continue to have strong support among Brazil's poor.

In Mexico, efforts to end the *ejido* program written into the 1917 Constitution were one stated reason for a guerrilla uprising in the southern state of Chiapas on January 1, 1994. As of 2007 Zapatista guerrillas still held isolated positions in Chiapas in hopes of pressuring the government to institute agrarian reform. Despite this rebellion, the Mexican government has repudiated Article 27 of the Mexican Constitution and has ceased all land redistribution to poor Mexican farmers and campesinos.

In two Latin American countries, however, agrarian reform advanced further than elsewhere. In the wake of both the Cuban and Nicaraguan revolutions, radical land reform was carried out with mixed results. In Cuba the large sugar and tobacco fincas were taken over by the revolutionary Cuban government, while only the smallest landholdings were left in the hands of individual owners. Programs of education, health, and housing transformed the Cuban countryside, and Fidel Castro's regime still enjoyed considerable support among Cuba's rural workers into the twenty-first century. Cuba's state-run agricultural industries, however, have been noted for their waste and inefficiency in both production and distribution. This is especially true of the sugar industry, where between 1990 and 2005 Cuba has seen a steady decline in sugar output. Part of this is due to stated government policies to phase out Cuba's reliance on sugar production.

To stimulate the agricultural sector, the Castro government periodically allows for independent farming and market sales of goods produced by private farmers. In the past this policy has resulted in more efficient production and better distribution of agricultural commodities, but the downside for the Cuban government is that independent farmers and merchants who accumulate land and capital are considered a threat to the Cuban government's state-run economy. With the collapse of Soviet aid beginning in the mid-1980s and the severe economic crisis of the early 1990s, the Cuban government was forced to allow independent small farming and the spread of farmers' markets, both of which could strengthen the small business class in Cuba, which in turn could represent a threat to Castro's rule. More recently, urban gardens have sprouted in the towns and cities of Cuba as a way to alleviate chronic food shortages. Thus, despite the most radical agrarian reform of any Latin American nation, Cuba's agricultural sector has declined considerably since the revolution in 1959.

In Nicaragua, after the revolution of 1979 the Sandinistas expropriated lands owned by the Somoza family and its supporters. These lands were converted into collective farms, as were much of Nicaragua's previously uncultivated lands. This program aroused resentments among Nicaraguan peasants, who supported the revolution in hopes of receiving their own parcels of land. In response to a growing guerrilla movement (the Contras) in the countryside, the Sandinistas enacted one of the most comprehensive land reforms in Latin America. Beginning in the mid-1980s collectivization was deemphasized and peasants were granted individual tracts of land. To prevent latifundization the Sandinista government denied landholders the right to sell or divide up their land, thereby ensuring that land given to peasants would not later be sold off to large landowners. With the defeat of the Sandinistas in the 1990 elections, however, efforts were revived to return expropriated lands to their former owners. Despite its political popularity, Sandinista land reform was unable to revive Nicaragua's agricultural sector. A ten-year civil war and a vigorous embargo by the United States ensured that Nicaragua's economy, including its agricultural industry, would stagnate throughout the 1980s. While land redistribution won the support of many peasants, it also angered urban dwellers, who suffered through constant scarcity of basic goods. After the elections of 1990, the conservative-dominated Nicaraguan legislature voted to turn back virtually all of the land reforms enacted by the Sandinistas during their rule.

See also **Agriculture.**

BIBLIOGRAPHY

De Janvry, Alain. *The Agrarian Question and Reformism in Latin America.* Baltimore, MD: Johns Hopkins University Press, 1981.

Enriquez, Laura. *Harvesting Change: Labor and Agrarian Reform in Nicaragua, 1979–1990.* Chapel Hill: University of North Carolina Press, 1991.

Frank, Andrew G. *Capitalism and Underdevelopment in Latin America: Historical Studies of Chile and Brazil.* Rev. ed. Harmondsworth, U.K.: Penguin, 1971.

Furtado, Celso. *Economic Development of Latin America: A Survey from Colonial Times to the Cuban Revolution.* Translated by Suzette Macedo. Cambridge, U.K.: Cambridge University Press, 1970.

Stavenhagen, Rodolfo. *Social Classes in Agrarian Societies.* Translated by Judy Adler Hellman. Garden City, NY: Anchor Press, 1975.

MICHAEL POWELSON

AGREGADO. Agregado, a term referring to a wide variety of dependent individuals or, literally, "retainers." In Brazil's colonial period *agregados* could be freed slaves, free servants, or poor relatives who resided with a host family of slaveowners or peasants. For peasants, *agregados* usually worked as servants or extra laborers; for slaveowners, *agregados* typically were dependent kin or the families of freed slaves. In the nineteenth century, *agregados* came to denote the following that supported a wealthy landowner in local elections. Such *agregados* received favors, such as land, in return for votes. This patron-client bond maintained the hegemony of the landowners after Brazilian independence.

BIBLIOGRAPHY

Eni De Mesquita, "O papel do agregado na região de Itú—1780–1830," *Coleção Museu Paulista* 6 (1977): 13–121.

Richard Graham, *Patronage and Politics in Nineteenth-Century Brazil* (1990).

Additional Bibliography

Goldman, Marcio, and Moacir Palmeira. *Antropologia, voto e representação política.* Rio de Janeiro: Contra Capa, 1996.

ALIDA C. METCALF

AGRESTE. Agreste, a term associated with northeastern Brazil, designating a transitional zone between the coastal *zona da mata* and the interior backlands (Sertão). Rainfall is one aspect of this intermediary position: The *agreste* receives an annual average of 30 to 43 inches — considerably more than the arid and semi–arid *sertão* but less than the humid *zona da mata*. The *agreste* first emerged during the later nineteenth century as an area characterized by polyculture and a large number of independent small holders. This zone traditionally has served as a refuge during times of drought and as a commercial intermediary between the backlands and the coast.

BIBLIOGRAPHY

Kempton Evans Webb, *The Changing Face of Northeast Brazil* (1974).

Manuel Correia De Andrade, *The Land and People of Northeast Brazil*, translated by Dennis V. Johnson (1980).

GERALD MICHAEL GREENFIELD

Incan agriculture. Incan men use footplows while women sow corn, a staple of the Mesoamerican diet. As illustrated in *El primer nueva cronica y buen gobierno* (1583–1615) by Felipe Guaman Poma de Ayala. THE GRANGER COLLECTION, NEW YORK

AGRICULTURE.

Latin America's variety of habitats—from polar to tropical climates, deserts to rain forests, highly fertile plains to shallow-soil high-altitude slopes and valleys—has given rise to diverse styles of agriculture. Highly developed at the time of the European invasions, they varied greatly in productivity, technology, and type of land tenure. Lack of easy transport kept long-distance trade limited to commodities of high value. Staple agricultural production thus needed to supply most required commodities within circumscribed regions of exchange.

PRE-COLUMBIAN FOUNDATIONS

Indigenous American civilizations accomplished the domestication of what would become major staple food and industrial crops relatively early: squash by 8000 BCE, the common bean by 5500 BCE, maize by c. 5000 BCE, yam and manioc in the fifth millenium BCE, quinoa—the protein-rich high-altitude Andean grain—by c. 3000 BCE, potato and cotton by ca. 2000 BCE, and cocoa no later than 200 CE. Contradicting older notions of an "agricultural revolution" in the Americas, recent scholarship has shown that the transition from foraging to sedentary farming proceeded gradually. Sedentary agricultural villages depending overwhelmingly on domesticated crops for their sustenance became widespread in highland Mesoamerica and the Andes, and along parts of the Gulf and Pacific coasts of Peru, only during the second millennium BCE. They appeared towards the middle or end of the first millennium in the Greater Antilles, the Yucatan peninsula, and parts of the lower Amazon River Valley, around Santarem. In parts of the Southern Cone, Amazon and Orinoco basins, northern Mexico, lower Central America and coastal areas around the north and east of South America, people continued to rely primarily on foraging or fishing until the European invasions. Central Andean llamas and alpacas were the only large mammals in the Americas domesticated (around 1000 BCE) before the European invasions, providing meat, wool, leather, and furs as well as serving as pack animals for transport.

Agricultural technologies changed with population densities, social complexity, and structures of rule; at times new crops and technologies (e.g., the introduction of irrigation on the Peruvian coast) preceded changes in social and political structures. Semitropical and tropical lowland agriculturalists used swidden, or slash-and-burn, methods to create fields for farming, for instance *milpa*-style production among lowland Maya: clearing of forests through extended family labor, planting of maize and complementary crops for three to five years, abandonment of the original clearing, and starting the process again with a new clearing, a production process with high productivity adequate for regions of low population density. With greater population densities, lowland cultures raised staple crop productivity through ridged fields (*camellones*), swamp drainage, and, in the Greater Antilles, mounds (*conucos*). With increasing population densities and state control of labor, highland cultures guarded against irregular seasonal rainfalls through a variety of irrigation and water control systems (dams, canals, ridged fields, terraces). *Chinampas*—fields along lakeshores built through drainage canals and continuous addition of lake sediments and decomposing algae as topsoil—were developed in the Valley of Mexico during the late pre-Columbian era (c. 1350 CE). The most productive agricultural complex in the Americas, it allowed continuous planting with three crops per year. Pre-Columbian tools for fieldwork and processing were mostly made from wood or stone, except in the Andean region, where digging sticks (*chaki taqllas*) had narrow blade tips made from copper alloys; iron tools were unknown.

Economic specialization, allowing increased regional and long-distance trade, grew in importance where socially stratified state structures became prominent, from around 200 BCE, especially in Mesoamerica (Teotihuacan, the Maya city-states) and the central Andes (the Mochica and Tiwanaku) until reaching their highest level in the Aztec and Inca empires during the last century before the European invasions. Specialized craft production of agricultural, livestock, or fishery-derived goods included spinning and weaving, net-making, tanning, papermaking, charcoal production, alcohol production (Mexican *pulque*, made from the maguey plant; Andean *chicha*, a fermented maize beverage), and drying of fish, meat (Andean *charki*), and potatoes (Andean *chuñu*). The most elaborate craft production was carried out on an industrial scale in enclosed workshops controlled by lords and associated with objects central for ritual and prestige—the spinning of fine cloth in the Andes, feather-working in Mesoamerica.

Systems of distribution and redistribution ranged from reciprocal exchange to trade by specialists. Communities of farmers exchanged goods and labor with neighboring communities, with their lords, and at times with distant producers of special products they lacked themselves. Such networks of exchange served both to supply scarce goods and to reinforce longstanding hierarchical or horizontal relationships. Lords redistributed food and other surplus agricultural commodities from alcohol to cloth at ceremonial occasions or during periods of food shortages, both to buttress their claims to authority and as a measure of social control; the most celebrated case of such redistribution concerns the Inca polity that maintained massive supplies of staple foods and other commodities in thousands of small storage towers dispersed in regional administrative centers throughout its vast territories. In Mesoamerica markets (*tianguis*) and state-privileged merchants (*pochteca*) developed gradually from the beginning of the Common Era. Even staple goods may have been exchanged through such markets among people living in different climatic zones. It has long been thought that in the Andes exchange was largely carried out among producers of the same ethnic group connecting different vertically arranged production zones, from the coast to the frigid *altiplano*. Evidence is mounting, however, that in the northern regions of the Inca territories specialized autonomous traders also connected producers of different ethnic origins. Long-distance trade was everywhere limited to high-value items usually linked to ceremonial functions of lords. Such privileged high-value networks of exchange could stretch over hundreds and at times even thousands of kilometers. For example, the Buriticá chiefdom (in the Cauca-Patía depression of Colombia) traded gold, emeralds, fish, salt, textiles and slaves throughout northern South America and Central America. While much of the long-distance trade relied on human carriers (such as the hereditary *tlamemes* in the Aztec empire), large dugouts and coastal rafts (which became very elaborate along the South American Pacific coast by the late post-Classic period) introduced economies of scale to long-distance trade; canoes could carry forty times as much as a human porter, and the large ocean-going Inkaic rafts even more. Specialized drivers of llama caravans facilitated the integration of large-scale late post-classical political economies in the central Andes and provided an impetus for the 25,000-kilometer Inca road system, not matched until the twentieth century. In areas of high population density, barter or market exchange of agricultural commodities was thus growing during the last centuries before the European invasions.

Access to resources, from croplands and pastures to water, fisheries, salt deposits, and mines during the early phases of agriculture was mediated through kinship and local lords, and during the Classic and post-Classic eras increasingly through regional chiefs and paramount lords or states, depending on the complexity of social and political organization. In kin-based communities as the Andean *ayllu* and those of the Tupis along the coast of Brazil, access to resources depended on gender-stratified participation in common labor tasks, from clearing fields for planting, to maintaining drainage and irrigation canals, and keeping the tidal area mangrove forests well irrigated for the staple shellfish colonies. While the right to cultivate croplands may have passed within the same family from generation to generation, such lands would belong to the entire kin group, and be subject to redistribution. The community set aside specified land and labor resources for the lord, in exchange for his services to the community. In the Aztec realms some of the land belonged directly to lords and nobles, and they worked it directly, as their own private estates. Farming communities received usage rights to land from the lords. In the Inca empire land held quasi-privately close to the capital of Cuzco by lineages of the royal family were just beginning to appear at the moment of Pizarro's invasion. But the state held some of the most fertile lands—such as the Cochabamba valley (in present-day Bolivia)—for the production of staple crops through corvée labor (*mitimaes*) drawn from far-flung ethnic groups. Thus by the late post-Classical period land tenure regimes had become highly diversified in the Americas, although the great majority of farmers continued to work the land in kin-based communities. In regions with complex state structures, by the late Classic period farming communities had become accustomed to paying tribute to their paramount lords or kings, either in the form of commodities or of labor.

INVASION AND COLONIALISM, 1500–1750

The European invasions and colonization of the Americas after 1492 initially affected agriculture through five principal processes: (1) the devastating collapse of indigenous populations; (2) the introduction of new crops and types of livestock; (3) the introduction of new agricultural tools and technologies; (4) the opening of new markets for agricultural and livestock products; and (5) new legal and regulatory frameworks for land tenure and labor. While in some areas of Latin America the transformation of agriculture was swift, in many regions it occurred more gradually or only centuries after the initial European invasion.

The unprecedented demographic catastrophe that affected most areas in the Americas after coming into contact with Europeans—it is estimated that as much as 90 percent of indigenous populations were wiped out by disease or violence in core regions such as central Mexico, parts of the Andes, and coastal regions elsewhere within 100 years of invasion and conquest—necessarily had a massive impact on colonial agriculture. Production of food crops by indigenous farmers declined, and much land previously farmed was abandoned, focusing production on the most fertile plots. In some regions intensively farmed before 1492 this allowed recovery of soil fertility and regrowth of forest. A recent environmental history suggests that Latin America was more heavily forested in 1800 than in 1500, not unlike parts of Western Europe during the century after the onset of bubonic plague around 1350.

American landscapes were transformed by the Mediterranean biota the Iberians brought with them. One historian ascribes the success of the colonial enterprise to the ecological similarity of the early core regions of Iberian colonization to their Mediterranean homelands; these regions were thus well suited to produce the range of food crops and livestock species to which the Iberians were accustomed. The Spaniards flourished in the Mexican highlands and the central Andes because these regi-ons were perfect for planting wheat, olive trees, and vineyards, and offered virgin grasslands for cattle, horses and donkeys, and goats and sheep. The tropical coast of Brazil became a successful colony for the Portuguese because the region had the perfect climate and soils for planting sugar cane, which the Portuguese had previously brought to the Atlantic islands. The most drastic environmental changes resulted from European livestock species that multiplied exponentially in favorable American habitats. Horses and especially cattle counted in the millions a few decades after being introduced into virgin grasslands in northern Mexico, the *llanos* of the Orinoco River (Venezuela) and the fertile pampas of the River Plate (Argentina, Uruguay and Paraguay), and many herds turned feral. At a minimum intense grazing changed the configuration of grasses in these regions, and at worst overgrazing led to growing soil erosion and aridity. In the core settlement zones livestock seriously threatened the crop production of indigenous farmers; in Cuba and Hispaniola large herds of feral pigs dug up the Arawaks' root crops (like manioc), contributing to the deadly combination of malnutrition and epidemics that virtually wiped out the islands' native populations within fifty years after Columbus's arrival. In central Mexico sheep herds destroyed maize fields of indigenous farming communities. Nevertheless, indigenous farmers more readily adapted to the husbandry of European animals than to planting European food crops, especially wheat.

The introduction of iron tools, especially iron-tipped ploughs, hoes as well as machetes, increased per capita productivity of Latin American agriculture during the sixteenth and seventeenth centuries. So did the adoption of draft and transport animals. In the Andes llamas were replaced by mules as a major form of transport only after the mid-seventeenth century, and in southern Mesoamerica—especially Guatemala and Chiapas—porters continued to be used as cheap corvée labor for transporting agricultural and other commodities for much of the colonial period. But the increasing use of mules in most of Latin America lowered transport costs and allowed longer distance marketing for staple crops. European processing technologies such as water- or animal-driven mills for grains, presses for sugarcane, distilleries for alcohol, and large looms for weaving cotton and wool thread, began the industrialization of rural enterprises. But they required such large outlays of capital that only the wealthiest Spanish or Portuguese landholders could afford them, thus contributing to a widening stratification of farm incomes. While Iberians introduced some new irrigation technologies (such as the animal-driven *noria*, a kind of water pump), regions with complex pre-Columbian civilizations saw a deterioration of irrigation systems at least until the eighteenth century (in some areas until 1900). Overall the early effect of European colonization on agricultural productivity was mixed and regionally varied. The concentration on the most fertile croplands, the introduction of iron farm tools and draft and transport animals all tended to increase per capita productivity. However, per hectare productivity may have declined, especially in the production of food crops for local consumption in the regions most densely populated during the pre-Hispanic period, as European grains produced lower hectare yields than American staples such as maize and potatoes. Indigenous farmers also faced damages to crops from roaming livestock herds, and some highly productive fields were abandoned due to the decay of pre-Columbian irrigation systems.

The Iberians explored and settled the Americas with the hope of new trade routes and opportunities for commercializing high-value commodities. Due to exorbitant transatlantic transport costs, the range of American agricultural products that could be profitably marketed in Europe, Africa or, after 1700, Anglo-America remained limited until late in the colonial period. It included New World products such as timber (from the Caribbean coast of Central America and Brazil), dyestuffs (indigo and cochineal from southern Mexico and Central America), cocoa (from Central America and later Ecuador and Venezuela), tobacco (from Cuba, Mexico and Brazil), and some spices and herbs. But by far the most important agricultural product sold in Europe was sugar. Between the 1540s and 1690s, it was the driving force for the settlement of the coastal territories making up most of Brazil until that time. Brazil became the first modern plantation colony thriving on sugar exports and transforming colonial society through the massive and sustained importation of enslaved Africans, more than three million between the early sixteenth century and the abolition of the transatlantic slave trade in the 1850s. The number of sugar mills in Brazil rose from sixty in 1570 to 350 in 1629, and production from 6,000 tons annually in 1580 to as much 22,000 tons during the 1620s, most of which was exported to Europe. Thereafter Brazilian production stagnated until the late eighteenth century, due to the twenty-five-year Dutch occupation of the northeastern captaincy of Pernambuco (1630–1654), and the establishment of more efficient sugar plantations in the Dutch, French, and British Caribbean during the second half of the seventeenth century. Before the late colonial era, the bulk of Spanish American sugar production—from Michoacán in

Mexico, to the Cauca valley in Colo-mbia, the coast of Peru and Tucumán in Argentina—was marketed regionally within the Americas, unable to compete with Brazilian or non-Spanish Caribbean sugar in European markets because of lower productivity and higher labor and transportation costs.

Most food crops and livestock products produced in Latin America were marketed locally or regionally before the late colonial period. Due to declining transportation costs and high regional prices driven by the Mexican and Andean silver export complexes, the core regions of the Spanish empire sustained increasing long-distance trade even in staple foods. This fostered a degree of regional specialization in commercial crops and livestock products. In Spanish South America, an integrated regional "Andean space" grew around the skyrocketing demand for agricultural crafts and industrial goods in the central silver mining and processing city of Potosí (Bolivia), the largest city in the Western hemisphere for a few decades in the early seventeenth century (140,000 people during the 1620s, despite the 4000-meter altitude). Córdoba (central Argentina) supplied mules, Chile's central valley and the Cochabamba Valley (Bolivia) wheat, Paraguay *yerba mate* (herbal tea), the valleys around Cuzco (Peru) maize and sugar, Arequipa (Peru) wine and brandy, Piura (northern Peruvian coast) tallow and goatskins, Quito (Ecuador) woolen cloth. Similar flows existed between central and western Mexico (the agricultural and craft production zones between Puebla and Guadalajara) and the northern mining centers of Zacatecas and San Luis Potosí. Major administrative and commercial cities, from the viceregal capitals of Lima and Mexico City on down, also provided markets that drew supplies at times from hundreds of kilometers away. But smaller provincial towns distant from commercial arteries had a smaller food supply area, and many staple commodities in more isolated regions were traded only locally. Most farmers—from squatter on a few hectares to plantation owners—sought to diminish monetary expenditures for inputs and household consumption by producing a broad range of crops and livestock products. But from the early colonial period most farmers also sought to produce a marketable surplus in at least one crop or livestock product for commercial profit or to defray unavoidable monetary expenses, including crown and church taxes and fees. This was true also for the majority of indigenous

farmers. Part of their farm surpluses were extracted through colonial administrative fiat, mostly in the form of crops or labor; first through the *encomienda* system (in which payment to Spaniards was a duty of vassalage the Spanish king), later as *tributo* (the semiannual head tax levied on adult indigenous men) or for the *reparto de bienes* (the forced distribution of goods in a commercial scheme instituted in predominantly indigenous provinces by the *corregidores*, the highest provincial-level crown officers). The incorporation of indigenous farmers into self-regulating markets was a drawn-out process, not fully completed until the early 2000s, proceeding at different rates in different places depending on the social position of the farmers, on the region, and on the specific commodities. Indigenous farmers also maintained some of the pre-Hispanic long-distance barter networks between communities outside the control of Hispanicized traders.

As the supply of commodities and labor directly from indigenous communities diminished as a result of the population collapse, and colonists recognized the commercial opportunities for agriculture in the American colonies, Spanish and Portuguese settlers gradually developed their own farms based on royal land grants, de facto appropriations of indigenous lands, judicial settlements (*composiciónes*), and notarized sales contracts. By the late sixteenth century this gave rise to the *hacienda* (*fazenda* in Brazil), the Latin American manorial estate that would prove to be—through multiple transformations—one of the most durable rural institutions. In many parts of Latin America it reached its apex only during the early twentieth century and entered terminal crisis during the mid-twentieth century. The defining feature of the hacienda was that it had a resident labor force and a settlement nucleus, at times with its own chapel. More than a large farm, it was a social unit over whose workers the owner exercised considerable informal, at time quasi-legal power. Haciendas varied tremendously in size, type of labor force, product mix, capital investment, and commercialization of goods. The largest haciendas, such as some of the livestock ranches in northern Mexico, or the *sertão* (semi-arid grasslands) of northeastern Brazil, could encompass several hundred thousand hectares with more than 500 resident laborers and their families, while on the smallest estates of fifty to one hundred hectares the owner might work alongside two or three labor tenants (sharecroppers) or slaves, sowing and harvesting grains, tobacco, or tubers.

In lowland areas such as the coast of Brazil, the Caribbean, the Gulf coast of Mexico, the Caribbean coast of Colombia and Venezuela, and the Pacific coast of Peru and Ecuador, the majority of estates came to rely on African slave labor. Slaves often constituted their single largest capital investment. Focusing on commercial products as sugar, tobacco, cocoa, and wine, such haciendas—like the analogous Anglo-American plantations—were more highly capitalized than the average cereal- or livestock-producing hacienda in the Mesoamerican and Andean highlands. For their labor force these relied predominantly on labor tenants (called *peones acasillados, colonos, yanaconas,* or *inquilinos* in different areas), tenants, and day laborers from adjacent communities and villages of independent farmers, as well as corvée laborers drafted by local authorities. In the large haciendas of either type, complex social hierarchies developed, between skilled and unskilled, permanent and temporary workers, slave and free. Even most of the highly capitalized haciendas, such as sugar plantations, dedicated only a minor share of their land to their commercial crops, with the rest used for food production, livestock pastures, and woodlands. In contrast to Caribbean slave plantations, Brazil's sugar *engenhos* (fazendas with their own sugar mills) often provided provisioning grounds for their slaves, akin to the garden plots granted to labor tenants on highland haciendas.

Given cyclical harvest crises, most haciendas—except for the most efficiently managed slave plantations—generated relatively low long-term average revenues (perhaps about 5 percent of the value of movable and immovable property). Startup capital and cash to weather crises was transferred from family fortunes generated in mining or commerce, as members of Latin America's colonial creole elite sought to buttress their social power and standing by becoming large landholders. Various organizations of the Catholic Church provided long-term loans to the more powerful hacendado families. By the late colonial period the Church had become the largest landholder in many parts of Latin America.

The majority of Latin America's rural population during the colonial era lived and worked outside of manorial estates or plantations. Especially in areas with rapidly growing mestizo populations, there developed a fluid sector of independent small and middling farmers and ranchers, such as the wheat-growing *rancheros* of Mexico's *bajío* (around León), the grain farmers of Antioquia (Colombia), and Brazil's *lavradores de cana* (cane farmers without a sugar mill) and *casave* (cassava or manioc) farmers. Some of them aspired to become hacendados themselves while others only managed to eke out a poor livelihood for their family. Many small farmers depended on powerful hacendados or sugar planters to process their crops and on local traders for small cash advances before the harvest.

From the late sixteenth century both the Spanish and Portuguese crowns established protective policies for the indigenous populations of their American colonies, often honored in the breach. In order to sustain an indigenous labor force and base of taxation, the crown sought to protect communal lands from neighboring Iberian and mestizo landholders. Indigenous communities adopted some aspects of European farming, property relations, and cultural-political structures while insisting on their autonomy and their land, often through court battles and at times through rebellions. While regular land redistribution schemes continued in many highland communities from central Mexico to the Andes, internal social differentiation increased. More affluent indigenous farmers began to own their own land alongside their redistribution plots, and in some regions *caciques* (indigenous headmen) acquired large landholdings and operated them as haciendas. Communal farmers focused on producing such traditional foodstuffs as maize, cassava, potatoes, and livestock products, garnering lower prices in urban markets than European foodstuffs and transatlantic trade goods such as sugar. Where necessary for the production of transatlantic trade goods, such as cochineal in Oaxaca, local crown authorities administered prices and payment schedules.

THE TRANSITION PERIOD, 1750–1850

The late colonial and early post-independence eras of Latin America witnessed varying and at times countervailing trends in agriculture. Some regions that had been marginal during the earlier colonial era saw sustained growth of agricultural production and trade, while others could not sustain their growth through the era of Napoleonic wars. The period saw rapid shifts in access to overseas markets and transport costs due to foreign wars, revolutions and wars of independence, and changing regulatory frameworks. Government policies on property and labor shifted slowly for most of this transition century until undergoing massive liberal reforms during the third quarter of the nineteenth century.

Transatlantic trade with the Iberian peninsula more than doubled between the early 1770s and mid-1790s, and agricultural goods, especially from the east coast of Latin America (from the River Plate in the south to Cuba in the north), contributed with growing exports of leather, sugar, tobacco, cocoa, indigo, cochineal, and cotton. Decreasing transatlantic transport costs, thanks to larger and faster ships, heightened demand in Western Europe (e.g., for dyestuffs and cotton for the burgeoning textile industry). Direct legal access to more ports by foreign shipping (as in Buenos Aires) and increased supply of slave labor for sugar production (as in Cuba after the brief 1762 British occupation of Havana) all fueled this growth of exports.

Agricultural production for domestic consumption had also grown significantly in many areas of Spanish America for much of the eighteenth century, in tandem with sustained population increases, growing urban populations, and peak silver output in the last quarter of the century. In Mexico demand outpaced food production between the 1760s and 1780s, leading to hunger crises during the 1780s. Several regions saw Malthusian cycles: growing production allowing population growth until a ceiling was reached and mortality rates rose sharply through harvest failures and disease, which in turn lowered food prices and allowed populations to rise again. The growth of agricultural production during the eighteenth century was the result of increasing acreage under the plow (at times diminishing livestock herds or pushing them further from population centers, as in Chile), and some measures of internal colonization such as irrigation and swamp drainage were undertaken. But there is little evidence for widespread productivity increases in agriculture during this era. Spanish and Portuguese policies favored mineral production while increasing sales taxes for agricultural and crafts production. Insufficient improvements of roads may also have been a bottleneck for many agricultural regions. The establishment of a Spanish royal monopoly on the production and sale of tobacco products in various regions during the 1760s and 1770s significantly raised public revenues and at least in Mexico created an important factory sector, but at the same time inhibited the growth of tobacco production.

Prices for food crops and livestock products increased again during the era of the revolutions of independence (1810–1825) in many parts of Latin America, due to disruption of supplies and scarcity of transport animals. Unable to repay at times substantial mortgages on their land, contracted over decades with the Church, many hacendados were forced to sell their estates. In highland regions of Mesoamerica and the Andes small farmers, including those in indigenous communities, weathered these crises better, and entered a phase of relative stability—with diminished conflicts with neighboring haciendas—until about mid-century.

The independence of mainland Latin America by 1825 led to direct trading relationships with the major powers of Western Europe and the United States, but for the majority of the new republics did not lead to a transformation or growth of their agricultural sector. Commodity prices remained low from the mid-1820s through the late 1840s, and labor regimes and other agrarian institutions as well as farm productivity did not change substantially. Exceptions to this rule were Argentina and Uruguay, whose exports of livestock products, begun during the last decades of the eighteenth century, continued to grow: dried meat for slave populations in Brazil and the United States, and, after independence, sheep wool exports to the U.K. and the United States. This rapid growth transformed the landscape of the humid pampas around Buenos Aires, first with a change from grain fields to livestock pastures, and from 1831, the rapid expansion of livestock estancias into territory previously held by the autonomous groups of indigenous people. Another exception concerned the early exportation of coffee from Brazil, Venezuela, and Costa Rica during the decades after independence, produced on farms of widely different sizes and labor regimes: from slave-based large *fazendas* in Rio de Janeiro province to small farms controlled by highly capitalized coffee processors and traders in Costa Rica's central valley.

Beginning in the 1790s both Brazil and Cuba were rapidly expanding their sugar production and exports, benefiting economically from the Haitian revolution of 1791 that eliminated the largest sugar producer of the late eighteenth century. The spectacular growth of sugar production in Brazil faltered after mid-century, due to higher prices for slaves in the coffee-growing region than in the northeast sugar zone (a circumstance that led to the establishment of an internal slave trade) and the failure of *engenho* owners to invest in more productive processing technology, a trend reversed only in the last third of the nineteenth century. Cuba was able to sustain an even more spectacular increase of sugar production, based on massive slave imports during the first half of the nineteenth century, additional sources of imported regimented labor thereafter (Chinese "coolies"), and heavy investment in transport and cane processing technology first by Spanish, and after mid-century, U.S., capital. At the cost of environmental degradation (cutting the forests as fuel for the mills) and increasing social polarization, Cuba became the largest world producer of sugar by the 1840s.

Reforms of the property and labor regimes established during the sixteenth and seventeenth centuries proceeded haltingly before the mid-nineteenth century. Spain's Bourbon reformers began to weaken the protective policies for indigenous communities since about 1730. Aiming to achieve a more "rational" land tenure regime and under pressure from Hispanicized landholders to open fertile lands close to markets, colonial administrators no longer recognized the historical titles of indigenous communities in Mesoamerica and the Andes. Instead they calculated land requirements per family in the redistribution lands, and sold off "excess lands" to Hispanicized farmers (communal lands were legally considered crown lands held by indigenous farmers in usufruct). At least in the Andes, this was one of the contributing factors to a rising tide of rural rebellions between 1730 and 1780, and the policy was curtailed as politically destabilizing thereafter.

During the 1820s, the early years after independence, some Spanish American republics passed laws disestablishing communal landholdings. But such laws remained without major effect before the second half of the nineteenth century, because pressure on indigenous land was then low, and states in Mesoamerica and the Andes found ethnic communal organizations still indispensable for fiscal and administrative purposes. In contrast to some of the era's European liberal agrarian reform laws, the Latin American laws never touched the property and judicial structures of the manorial estate, and, with minor exceptions, began regulating private rural labor regimes only after mid-century. Colonial corvée labor systems (*mita*, *repartimiento*) were outlawed, but often kept functioning informally on the local level.

INDUSTRIALIZED AGRICULTURE AND THE EXPORT TRADE, 1850–1980

Latin American agriculture underwent more profound changes between the late nineteenth and late twentieth centuries than at any time since the European invasions. The motors of that change were growth and migration of populations, the transport "revolution," productivity gains and increasing capital investments, and rapidly shifting agrarian policies and regulatory frameworks regarding property, labor, and trade. The end result of these processes was the diminution of agriculture as a share of GNP and of the proportion of the economically active population devoted to it, and simultaneously a widening gap between capital-intensive and traditional farms and between income levels in the countryside and in the cities.

Latin America's population grew from around thirty million in 1850 to 469 million in 1995, the result of both natural population growth and immigration. Growth peaked in most countries during the 1960s, at over 2 percent annually for the entire region (in some countries, such as Costa Rica, as high as 3.5 percent). It declined to around 1.5 percent by 2000 (ranging from 0.4 percent in Cuba to 2.8 percent in Bolivia). Parallel to overall population growth, Latin Americans began to migrate at an accelerating clip, both between rural areas and from the countryside to the city (aside from several waves of emigration abroad). By the late twentieth century the ratio between Latin America's rural and urban population was just about reversed from a century earlier: from roughly 80:20 in the 1870s to 30:70 by the 1980s (and 25:75 in 2007). Yet the absolute number of people living in the countryside has continued to grow in the region as a whole, although there are now some rural districts and entire provinces whose population has begun to decline in absolute terms. While capital-intensive agriculture initially was overwhelmingly geared towards export

Processing coffee beans, Brazil, c. 19th century. Brazil became the world's primary producer of coffee in the late nineteenth century. © UNDERWOOD & UNDERWOOD/CORBIS

markets, the growth of ever larger urban markets slowly broadened productivity gains and capital investment also in domestic-use agriculture (DUA).

The transport revolution—the introduction of steamships and railroads—of the second half of the nineteenth century allowed a growing range of Latin American crops and livestock products to be profitably marketed overseas. Freight rates between Latin America and the U.K. declined by roughly 50 percent between 1860 and 1900. As late as 1865, transporting wool by llama from a hacienda in the Peruvian altiplano for 300 kilometers to the Pacific port of Islay could take longer than the steamship voyage from Islay to Liverpool; after the completion of the railroad line from Mollendo to the northern altiplano in 1876, it took three days to

convey the wool from hacienda to port. Specialized transportation technologies such as the United Fruit Company's steamers with cooled cargo compartments for bananas, and the steamers that took chilled beef from Buenos Aires to London, were vital for satisfying the increased demand for Latin American agricultural products in Europe and the United States. The growth of trucking and road construction since the 1920s further lowered transport costs for rural producers by extending the network of modern transport into many localities where the railroad had never reached; the truck also facilitated rural—urban travel for people and thus provided the means for rapidly rising rates of migration after 1950.

In aggregate quantitative terms, the growth of export volumes between the 1850s and World War

I was impressive in Latin America. Yet growth varied greatly from country to country and region to region, and its impact on economic development has been highly controversial. Per capita export values grew fourfold for all of Latin America between 1850 and 1912, and, except for three Andean nations and Mexico (with strong mining sectors rivaling or surpassing agro-exports), this was mostly due to crops and livestock products. In Argentina per capita export earnings increased more than sixfold between 1850 and 1912, and export agriculture—principally cereals and meat—literally transformed the nation, by drawing more than three million immigrants, fostering the growth of major cities as commercial entrepots and processing points for agricultural products, building Latin America's largest railroad network, and bringing the land under intense cultivation or fencing it for improved livestock raising. For countries like Mexico and Honduras, growth of agricultural exports had less positive impacts. Links to other sectors of the economy were minimal in some export regions—such as the henequen (rope fiber) production in Yucatan or the coastal banana zone around San Pedro de Zulas. In many agricultural export complexes productivity increases were greatest in processing—e.g. Cuba's modern sugar *centrales* (refineries), or Costa Rica's *beneficios* (hulling and drying facilities) for coffee beans, and less impressive in field operations.

Many agro-export complexes were destructive to their environment: use of fertilizers remained low, soils eroded, and in some areas—as on São Paulo's coffee frontier—farms relocated after some years, clearing forested virgin lands for new coffee groves, and leaving the exhausted lands for less intensive uses, such as livestock pasture. This began to be reversed in some regions after 1930, when agricultural extension services proliferated, and fertilizers were used more widely. Still, some Latin American commercial agricultural complexes have remained highly destructive throughout the twentieth century, such as the cotton growing areas along the Pacific coast of Guatemala during the 1950s and 1960s through the use of dangerous herbicides and insecticides, or the expanding cattle ranching and soybean farming industries in the Amazon basin since the 1970s through the cutting down of the rainforest.

Capital for investment in agro-export complexes came from traditional national sources (trade and mining), from foreign export merchants and from a fledgling banking system that often favored short-term crop loans over long-term loans for industrial investment. From the 1860s, foreign capital flowed into some strategic agro-export sectors: U.S. corporate investment in Cuban sugar and most Caribbean banana complexes, European immigrants' investments in coffee fincas in Central America and Peru's large north coast sugar plantations. But in contrast to other primary resources, such as petroleum and minerals, the major part of modernizing crop and livestock production for export remained under the control of Latin American entrepreneurs.

Domestic-use agriculture experienced much less capital investment before 1930, and thus productivity grew minimally if at all in this sector. Increased production was achieved mostly through colonization projects, often involving violent expropriation of lands previously claimed by indigenous ethnic groups such as the Yaqui in Sonora, Mexico, or the Mapuche in southern Chile. Highland cereal and livestock haciendas in the old core regions of the Spanish Empire (central and southern Mexico, Guatemala, and the central Andes) also grew rapidly at the expense of indigenous communities. The indigenous peoples of Latin America probably lost more land to large landholders and individual *ranchero* family farmers between 1850 and 1950 than during the entire colonial period. In any case, the increase in production of staple crops through increased acreage was insufficient to guarantee adequate food supplies for Latin America's bourgeoning urban population after the 1880s; many countries became net importers of food crops.

The transition from peonage and slavery to wage labor in agriculture was slow in most areas, often not completed before the mid-twentieth century. It depended on the availability of ample pools of labor—achieved only after major increases in the population of land-poor or landless rural dwellers and growing migrant labor streams—or, in rare instances, on relatively flat rural social hierarchies. In the central valley of Costa Rica or the fertile pampas of Argentina, both without strong traditions of servile labor, wage labor became the norm as early as the mid-nineteenth century. After the abolition of slavery in Brazil (1888), Cuba (1886), and Peru (1854), the expanding agro-export complexes turned to semi-servile forms of labor as Chinese indentured servants (coolies) and, in Brazil's coffee regions, the complex *colono* system, combining elements of wage labor, sharecropping, and peonage. In some regions with scarce labor supply the boom of agricultural exports before World War I prompted large landholders or merchants to employ coercive labor regimes: the slave-like conditions of Maya recruited for Yucatan's henequen plantations, or the brutal regime forcing members of indigenous groups to work as rubber tappers in the Amazon region of Peru. Migrant labor streams (organized by labor contractors) often mimicked older hierarchical power structures based on race or class: highland indigenous peoples brought to sugar haciendas in Peru (*enganche*) and coffee fincas in Guatemala (*mandamiento*), or the migrations of blacks from the West Indies to sugar and banana plantations in Cuba and Central America. In large landholdings focused on DUA, peonage and sharecropping expanded with the haciendas between 1860 and 1930, although such systems increasingly came to reflect labor market conditions. Except perhaps in the Southern Cone and in Costa Rica, Latin America's real agricultural wages improved only modestly before World War II, and even declined in a few regions.

In most of the countries for which data is available, productivity in the agricultural sector grew much faster between the 1930s or 1940s and the 1970s than during the height of the first agro-export boom. The major reasons for this were the declining rate of growth of the economically active population in agriculture (in Argentina, Chile, and Venezuela the rate was actually negative) and the extension of significant capital investments to DUA, which still employed more labor and occupied more land than the export sector. Many family and multi-family farms became mechanized during these decades, began to use fertilizers on a regular basis, and adopted more productive hybrid seeds (the "green revolution") and disease-resistant livestock strains (the cebu cattle in lowland Colombia and parts of the Amazon). Massive state-sponsored dam projects made irrigation available to arid or semi-arid agricultural zones, especially in northern Mexico, northeastern Brazil, the Oriente of Bolivia and Chaco of Paraguay, and some parts of the Andes. As a result of both productivity increases and the extension of acreage through colonization, agricultural production in Latin America doubled between 1930 and 1980.

The liberal reforms carried out in most Latin American nations between the 1850s and 1880s cleared away many of the colonial legacies of rural labor and property regimes. Laws sought to disestablish corporate landholding (primarily by indigenous communities and the Catholic Church) with the aim of creating a free land market and securely titled private property. The Church ceased to be a significant owner of rural property in most regions after the early twentieth century. Old and new large landholders benefited from the often fraudulent sales of Church or communal lands. But in many areas of the Andes and Mesoamerica indigenous traditions of working and administering lands communally adapted to the new legal frameworks and survived. Slavery was abolished in Peru and Venezuela during the 1850s and in Cuba and Brazil in the 1880s. The liberal laws also abolished the indigenous head tax (successor of colonial tribute), tithes on agricultural crops, and unpaid labor services. But forced labor drafts for public purposes (road building, cleaning irrigation ditches) continued locally in many regions through the early twentieth century. While new civil codes modeled on the Code Napoleon sought to guarantee property titles for all citizens, in fact they often furnished legal tools to swindle poor farmers out of their land. In spite of its declared universalist intentions, in fact much of the liberal legislation favored powerful large landholders.

Changing ideological currents, growing state capacities and resources, and the perceived threat of heightened social tensions, led most Latin American governments to implement increasingly interventionist policies for the agricultural sector during the first three quarters of the twentieth century, but especially between the 1930s and 1970s. They were principally aimed at making agricultural production more efficient and productive, incorporating small farmers and landless rural workers—viewed as the most backward members of society—into national development (through improved income levels, education, and public health measures in the countryside), and undermining the power of traditional large landholder elites. In some cases such policies constituted a wholesale reversal of liberal land policies of the later nineteenth century, once again guaranteeing the right of indigenous communities to collective property (as in the famous article 27 of Mexico's revolutionary constitution of 1917, and Peru's constitution of 1920). Agricultural extension services and credit banks were established in the 1930s and 1940s. Between the 1950s and 1970s, governments launched regional development plans for impoverished regions, most famously the Superintendência para o Desenvolvimento do Nordeste (Superintendency for the Development of the Northeast, or SUDENE) for northeastern Brazil, and created production, marketing, and service cooperatives that organized machine pooling and crop storage. State agricultural agencies became powerful bureaucracies. Latin American governments' expenditures for agriculture grew at 8 percent annually in real terms between 1950 and 1980 (in Bolivia it grew by more than 1000 percent during that period). At the same time, however, price controls for staple foods—aimed at demobilizing burgeoning urban populations—and preferential exchange rates favoring targeted industrial growth sectors at times discouraged investments in agriculture, as occurred in Peron's Argentina during the early 1950s.

The land reforms carried out in the majority of Latin American republics between the 1910s and 1980s, and especially between 1950 and 1975, were the most spectacular form of state intervention in the agrarian sector. While they shared the goals of making rural incomes less unequal and breaking the power of the large landholding elites, they varied in terms of specific measures, their radicalism, and their long-term effects. Mexico's land reform—perhaps the core issue for rank and file followers of the 1910 revolution—began in 1915 and reached its apex between 1935 and 1940. It distributed some sixty-five million acres of land from former haciendas and public lands to small farmers and farm workers. The distributed land was organized in *ejidos* (agrarian communities holding inalienable title to the land) in which the beneficiaries mostly worked their lands individually; during the 1930s some collective *ejidos* were created on large commercial farms. Between the 1930s and 1960s the reform improved the livelihoods of millions of Mexican farmers and served as a major prop for the political stability of the regime of the ruling party, the PRI, while not blocking the development of capital-intensive private farms.

The land reforms of Bolivia (1953), Guatemala (1952, reversed by the 1954 CIA coup), Ecuador (1964–76) and Chile (1964–73) also benefited individual smallholders. But the reforms in Cuba (1961), Peru (1969–75) and Nicaragua (1981–90) created state-controlled cooperatives or outright state farms. The percentage of farmers receiving land was as high as 75 percent in Bolivia and as low as 5 to 10 percent in Costa Rica and Ecuador. The successful reforms did make distribution of land somewhat less uneven and raised income standards, especially for relatively affluent small and middling farmers. Nearly everywhere there was a still growing strata of poor small farmers and landless rural people who benefited least. They had least access to capital and improved farming techniques, and demand for year-round farm labor declined sharply due to mechanization, while the need for seasonal laborers increased. The notion that land reforms reduced agricultural productivity only held for a few cases (as in Peru). In Chile productivity grew faster during the entire land reform period than it had in the preceding decades except for 1972 and 1973, refuting one of the major justifications of the Pinochet regime's reversal of the policy.

By 1980 Latin America's agriculture had been thoroughly transformed. Most large landholdings had become highly productive commercial farms producing an ever-growing range of goods both for the export and domestic markets. Mid-sized family farms, employing mostly seasonal labor, had also become highly productive. At the same time the number of impoverished farmers with too little land and no access to credit or technology had also grown. Many of them now had to supplement farm incomes through seasonal labor in the commercial farm sector or in cities.

GLOBALIZATION AND CHANGE SINCE 1980

During the past twenty-five years Latin American agriculture has become involved in another cycle of globalization that has exacerbated some of the trends already noticeable in the 1960s and 1970s. Globalization was enabled by cheaper and faster transport and communication technologies (widely accessible jet air travel and air freight, containerized ocean transport, electronic media and communications). But the shift by most Latin American governments away from interventionist economic and social policies towards neoliberalism—begun in Pinochet's Chile during the mid-1970s and adopted elsewhere in the region between 1985 and the early 1990s—has intensified the impact of global economic forces on the region's agricultural sector. The "Washington Consensus," as economists call neoliberalism since 1989 in reference to policy prescriptions by the International Monetary Fund (IMF), World Bank, and the U.S. Treasury Department, prescribes, among other measures, fiscal discipline, liberalized trade and investment policies, and privatization of state enterprises. The push by the U.S. government and Latin American exporters for free trade agreements in the Americas (NAFTA, covering Canada, the United States, and Mexico, 1994; CAFTA for several Central Ameri-can and Caribbean nations, 2005; bilateral treaties between the United States, and Chile, Colombia, and Peru between 2002 and 2007) followed from the neoliberal prescriptions. These agreements have created growing markets for agricultural ex-ports from Latin America, but have also hurt the poor farmers producing food crops by cheaper imports of grains, corn, rice, vegetable oils, and other foodstuffs from the United States.

Land reforms were rolled back in countries from Mexico to Chile through parcelization of ejidos and cooperatives, and the auction and sale of land in the reformed sector to private commercial farmers. This rollback also created more *minifundistas*, as some cooperative or collective farms were split up into *parcelas* on which poor *parceleros* eked out a living. While state credit agencies for small farmers were closed or curtailed in several nations, governments focused their rural expenditures on infrastructure and technology for the agricultural export sector. Prodded by the World Bank and other international agencies, Latin American governments undertook efforts to create secure property titles for farmland, usually benefiting owners of mid-sized and large farms.

During the crisis-ridden 1980s and early 1990s, even while prices and net barter terms of trade for most agricultural commodities declined, Latin American agro-exports grew, albeit at a slower pace than during the preceding three decades. Productivity gains in agriculture also leveled off, at least through the mid-1990s. Besides growing exports of traditional staples such as coffee, sugar, meat, and grain, globalized infrastructure and transportation technologies have now created international markets for a broad range of commodities from fruits and vegetables to wine, shrimp, salmon, timber, and processed coca leaves (cocaine). This trend has accelerated since 2000, as many agricultural commodity prices have risen due to rapidly growing demand, especially from Asia. By 2006, Brazil had

become the largest exporter of soybeans and orange juice, and Chile led the world in salmon exports. Still, the share of the economically active population employed in agriculture, livestock raising, forestry and fisheries has continued to decline, along with growing urbanization. Yet the neoliberal emphasis on resource extraction as motor of the economy has reversed the long-term decline of agriculture's share of the GDP, which rose from 10.1 to 10.9 percent during the 1980s, with larger gains probable since 2000. The new export crops have also significantly contributed to a decrease in the commodity concentration of the leading two exports (including non-agricultural commodities) in each of the Latin American nations from an average of 57.5 percent in 1950 to 28.3 percent in 1995. At the same time, the new emphasis on agro-exports has made agricultural production and farm incomes more volatile once again.

While much of the new investments in export agriculture came from Latin American corporations and wealthy families in the cities, international corporations became prominent in the export of tropical fruits, seafood and wine. In 2004, wealthy farmers from Illinois invested in soybean production in cleared Amazon forest lands in the Brazilian state of Tocantins, where lower land and labor costs allowed them to produce more cheaply than at home. The world's largest pork producer, from Virginia, built a 50,000-head hog farm in the western Brazilian state of Mato Grosso, planning to export pork chops to China once the trans-Andean highway to the Peruvian Pacific port of Ilo is completed.

The new emphasis on agricultural exports has mostly benefited modern commercial farms. The minifundistas producing traditional staple crops as maize, beans, potatoes, and manioc, whose number is still growing, have seen their incomes stagnate or decline. By the mid-1990s, after more than a decade of rapid growth of new agro-exports, 55 percent of Chile's rural households lived in extreme poverty. Unemployment and underemployment increased throughout Latin America during the 1980s and early 1990s, and has only declined slightly since then. More than two-thirds of the extremely poor people in Latin America live in the countryside. The income gap between owners of highly productive commercial farms and the owners of unimproved minifundios has remained huge. Many small farmers are now semiproletarianized, increasingly relying on supplemental wage income. Environmental costs of agro-exports have grown through the depletion and pollution of water resources, uncontrolled logging, and soil erosion.

Unions of small farmers and farm workers have grown since the 1960s, and have gained in militancy (after a lull during the 1980s) since the 1990s. Some, as the Ejercito Zapatista de Liberación Nacional (Zapatista National Liberation Army) in Chiapas state, Mexico, have aimed their campaign against the effects on their livelihoods of globalization, which has decreased prices for their crops. Brazil's Movimento dos Trabalhadores Rurais Sem Terra (the Movement of Landless Rural Workers, MST) has become the largest social movement in Latin America, advancing its demand for farmland both through militant invasions of large landholdings and through well-organized protests, lobbying, and negotiations with the political authorities.

The rise of left-wing governments in Latin America since the late 1990s has its major cause in the broad public frustration about the social costs of the region's globalized economies and neoliberal policies, especially apparent in the rural sector. Brazil's President Lula da Silva implemented a program ("zero hunger") to guarantee minimum income to the poor; Venezuela's president Hugo Chávez has begun an agrarian reform project and made significant investments in public health and education, and Argentina's former president Nestor Kirchner reintroduced price controls. Yet most of these left-of-center governments have maintained fiscal austerity and relied heavily on commercial export agriculture to grow their economies. Whether any of their policies will result in diminishing the extreme inequality in Latin America's agricultural sector remained unclear in the early 2000s.

See also **Agrarian Reform; Brazil, Economic Miracle (1968–1974); Economic Commission for Latin America and the Caribbean (ECLAC); Economic Development; Fazenda, Fazendeiro; Food and Cookery; Hacienda; Indigenous Peoples; International Monetary Fund (IMF); Livestock; Mita; Neoliberalism; Peons; Plantations; Repartimiento; Slavery: Brazil; Slavery: Indian Slavery and Forced Labor; Slavery: Spanish America; World Bank.**

BIBLIOGRAPHY

Barraclough, Solon L. *Agrarian Structure in Latin America*. Lexington, MA: D.C. Heath, 1973.

Bauer, Arnold J. *Goods, Power, History: Latin America's Material Culture*. Cambridge: Cambridge University Press, 2001.

Bulmer-Thomas, Victor. *The Economic History of Latin America since Independence*. Cambridge, U.K.: Cambridge University Press, 1994.

Cortes Conde, Roberto, and Shane Hunt, eds. *The Latin American Economies: Growth and the Export Sector*. New York: Holmes and Meier, 1985.

Crosby, Alfred W. *The Colombian Exchange: Biological and Cultural Consequences of 1492*. Westport, CT: Greenwood Press, 1972.

Dean, Warren. *Brazil and the Struggle for Rubber: A Study in Environmental History*. Cambridge, U.K.: Cambridge University Press, 1987.

De Janvry, Alain. *The Agrarian Question and Reformism in Latin America*. Baltimore, MD: Johns Hopkins University Press, 1981.

Diaz Alejandro, Carlos F. *Essays on the Economic History of Argentina*. New Haven, CT: Yale University Press, 1970.

Duncan, Kenneth, and Ian Rutledge, eds. *Land and Labour in Latin America: Essays on the Development of Agrarian Capitalism in the Nineteenth and Twentieth Centuries*. Cambridge, U.K.: Cambridge University Press, 1977.

Edelman, Marc. *The Logic of the Latifundio: The Large Estates of Northwest Costa Rica since the Late Nineteenth Century*. Stanford, CA: Stanford University Press, 1992.

Foweraker, Joe. *The Struggle for Land: A Political Economy of the Pioneer Frontier in Brazil from 1930 to the Present Day*. Cambridge, U.K.: Cambridge University Press.

Furtado, Celso. *The Economic Growth of Brazil*. Berkeley: University of California Press, 1963.

Grindle, Merrilee. *State and Countryside: Development Policy and Agrarian Politics in Latin America*. Baltimore, MD: Johns Hopkins University Press, 1986.

Johnson, Lyman, and Enrique Tandeter, eds. *Essays on the Price History of Eighteenth-Century Latin America*. Albuquerque: University of New Mexico Press, 1990.

Kaerger, Karl. *Agricultura y colonización en México en 1900*. Transl. P. Lewin and G. Dohrmann. Mexico, 1986.

Kalmanovitz, Salomón, and Enrique López Enciso. *La agricultura colombiana en el siglo XX*. Bogotá: Fondo de Cultura Económica, 2006.

Kay, Cristobal. *El sistema señorial europeo y la hacienda latinoamericana*. Mexico City: Ed. Era, 1980.

Kepner, Charles, and J. Soothill. *The Banana Empire: A Case Study in Economic Imperialism*. New York: Vanguard, 1936.

Konetzke, Richard, ed. *Colección de documentos para la formación de Hispanoamérica, 1493–1810.* 3 vols. Madrid, 1953–1962.

Larson, Brooke. *Colonialism and Agrarian Transformation in Bolivia.* Princeton, NJ: Princeton University Press, 1988.

Lewis, Oscar. *Life in a Mexican Village.* Urbana: University of Illinois Press, 1951.

Long, Norman, and Bryan Roberts. *Agrarian Structure of Latin America, 1930–1990.* Institute of Latin American Studies, University of Texas, Austin, 1992. Texas Papers on Latin America, No. 92-02.

Melville, Elinor G. K. *A Plague of Sheep: Environmental Consequences of the Conquest in Mexico.* Cambridge, U.K.: Cambridge University Press, 1994.

Miller, Shawn W. *An Environmental History of Latin America.* Cambridge, U.K.: Cambridge University Press, 2007.

Moreno Fraginals. Mauel. *El ingenio.* Havana, 1964.

Murra, John. *Formaciones económicas y políticas del mundo andino.* Lima: IEP, 1975.

Schwartz, Stuart. *Sugar Plantations in the Formation of Brazilian Society: Bahia, 1550–1835.* New York: Cambridge University Press, 1985.

Steen, Harold K., and Richard P. Tucker, eds. *Changing Tropical Forests: Historical Perspectives on Today's Challenges in Central and South America.* Durham, NC: Forest History Society, 1992.

Stein, Stanley. *Vassouras: A Brazilian Coffee County, 1850–1900.* Cambridge, MA: Harvard University Press, 1957.

Thiesenhusen, William C. *Broken Promises: Agrarian Reform and the Latin American Campesino.* Boulder, CO: Westview Press, 1995.

NILS JACOBSEN

AGUARDIENTE DE PISCO. Aguardiente de Pisco, a grape brandy distilled in several Pacific Coast valleys of Andean South America. Made from grapes of quality too poor for wine, the brandy was developed by seventeenth-century planters. Distillation resulted in a clear brandy with a sweetish flavor and strong aftertaste, which, along with its alcohol content, made it a popular beverage for festive occasions. It combined well with fruits, and lime quickly became the favorite. Historians are uncertain why the brandy was labeled *pisco.* Local legend holds that Pisco Valley (Peru) landowners turned to distillation of grapes for brandy because

they failed at making wine, thus giving *aguardiente de Pisco* a lead for brand recognition. For a time wine and brandy were both made in the Pisco region, but after Chilean wines captured foreign markets in the early nineteenth century, vineyard owners turned solely to brandy. Thereafter distilling *aguardiente de Pisco* moved to the upriver Pisco plantations, where cotton cultivation did not prevail. Shipped on muleback in teardrop-shaped clay casks, corked at the spherical end, it soon reached markets throughout Peru. Many travelers remarked favorably on the drink, and numerous popular legends arose regarding the proper way to imbibe it and its aftereffects. *Pisco* has become an item in the tourist trade and the foreign market only to the degree that the *"pisco* sour," a frothy blend of *pisco,* egg white, lime juice, and salt, has achieved popularity as an exotic drink.

BIBLIOGRAPHY

Nicholas P. Cushner, *Lord of the Land: Sugar, Wine, and Jesuit Estates of Coastal Peru, 1600–1767* (1980), pp. 126–128.

Vincent Peloso, "Succulence and Sustenance: Region, Class, and Diet in Nineteenth-Century Peru," in *Food, Politics, and Society in Latin America,* edited by John C. Super and Thomas C. Wright (1985), pp. 45–64.

Additional Bibliography

Brown, Kendall W. *Bourbons and Brandy: Imperial Reform in Eighteenth-Century Arequipa.* Albuquerque: University of New Mexico Press, 1986.

Gutiérrez, Gonzalo. *El pisco: apuntes para la defensa internacional de la denominación de origen peruana.* Lima: Fondo Editorial del Congreso del Perú, 2003.

Rice, Prudence M. "Wine and Brandy Production in Colonial Peru: A Historical and Archaeological Investigation (in Research Note)." *Journal of Interdisciplinary History,* Vol. 27, No. 3. (Winter, 1997): 455-479.

VINCENT PELOSO

AGUASCALIENTES, CONVENTION OF. The Convention of Aguascalientes was one of the central events of the Mexican Revolution. It was the first and most representative revolutionary assembly during a period in which the Mexican revolutionary process was on the ascent and at its most radical. At this time the three factions that defeated the Victoriano Huerta regime—the Constitutionalists, Villistas (followers of Francisco Villa), and Zapatistas (followers of Emiliano Zapata)—decided to assemble a group of military representatives in order to elect a national government and define a program of reforms that would have the support of all of the revolutionary factions.

The convention had three different phases. The first and most representative phase brought together military delegates from the three main factions between August and October 1914. Held in the city of Aguascalientes, the convention declared itself sovereign, debated the platform for the government, and decided that none of the three leaders—Venustiano Carranza, Villa, and Zapata—should hold power. Carranza did not recognize the convention, however, and decided to fight it, which led to a split between the Villistas and Zapatistas on one side and the Constitutionalists headed by Carranza on the other. Carranza was soon joined by the brilliant military leader Álvaro Obregon. Unable to resolve the differences between the military leaders and incapable of establishing unity among the revolutionaries, the convention was divided, and a bloody civil war erupted between the Villista-Zapatista alliance and the Constitutionalists.

The second phase of the convention took place between November 1914 and June 1915. In this phase the Villa-Zapata alliance was able to occupy the capital of the country, name a government headed by Eulalio Gutiérrez, and prepare to confront Carranza. During this period the destiny of the convention, and that of the Mexican Revolution, was decided militarily in the great battles of el Bajío, where Álvaro Obregón defeated Francisco Villa. Villa's defeat became the defeat of the convention, which had to abandon Mexico City and deal with the dissolution of the Villa-Zapata alliance. Nevertheless this was the most fertile period of the convention in political and ideological terms because while the armies were confronting each other on the battlefield, the revolution's most radical program for social, economic, and political reforms was debated and passed inside the assembly. During this time the convention established a parliamentary system and passed a land distribution law and radical labor reforms.

The third phase of the convention lasted from June 1915 until its formal dissolution in 1916.

During this period the convention was exclusively a Zapatista assembly, in which the delegates from the south were able to set forth a clean political proposal for the organization of the national state and to pass radical laws on education, justice, employment, and land. These could not be enforced, however, because Zapata's troops were on the run and would soon be defeated by the Constitutionalists. In spite of its political and military defeat, however, the convention was very significant in that it left a political legacy that was taken up, at least in part, by the new Mexican Constituent Congress in 1917.

See also **Carranza, Venustiano; Mexico, Constitutions: Constitution of 1917; Mexico, Wars and Revolutions: Mexican Revolution; Villa, Francisco "Pancho"; Zapata, Emiliano.**

BIBLIOGRAPHY

Amaya, Luis Fernando C. *La Soberana Convención Revolucionaria, 1914–1916.* México: Trillas, 1975.

Avila Espinosa, Felipe Arturo. *El pensamiento económico, político y social de la Convención de Aguascalientes.* México: Instituto de Cultura de Aguascalientes—INEHRM, 1991.

Quirk, Robert E. *The Mexican Revolution 1914–1915: The Convention of Aguascalientes.* Bloomington: Indiana University Press, 1960.

FELIPE AVILA

AGUAYO, MARQUÉS DE (c. 1677–1734).

Marqués de Aguayo (marqués de San Miguel de Aguayo y Santa Olalla; *b.* ca. 1677; *d.* 9 March 1734), rancher, military governor of Coa-huila and Texas. Born in Spain to a landed family of Aragon, Aguayo married Ignacia Xaviera Echeverz Subiza y Valdés, heiress to the marquisate of San Miguel de Aguayo, through whom he acquired his title. In 1712 the couple moved to Coahuila, where Aguayo took over the administration of the family estates, increasing holdings by over 3 million acres by the time of his death.

Aguayo served as governor of Coahuila and Texas from 1719 to 1722. In 1716 he had provided livestock to the Domingo Ramón expedition, which established the permanent occupation of Texas. Three years later, in response to a French attack on the Spanish in east Texas, Aguayo offered to mount an expedition to drive the French out. Receiving a viceregal commission to raise five hundred men, he proceeded in 1720 to San Antonio and then to Los Adaes (present-day Robeline, Louisiana), where he restored the abandoned presidio and missions. He also founded Presidio de los Texas, near present-day Nacogdoches, and Presidio Bahía del Espíritu Santo (now Goliad, Texas). Soon after his return to Coahuila, Aguayo resigned the governorship, citing poor health. Philip V rewarded Aguayo for his services in Texas by naming him field marshal in 1724.

See also **Texas.**

BIBLIOGRAPHY

Eleanor Claire Buckley, "The Aguayo Expedition into Texas and Louisiana, 1719–1722," in *The Quarterly of the Texas State Historical Association* 15, no. 1 (July 1911): 1–65.

Vito Alessio Robles, *Coahuila y Texas en la época colonial,* 2d ed. (1978).

Charles H. Harris III, *A Mexican Family Empire: The Latifundio of the Sánchez Navarros, 1765–1867* (1975).

Additional Bibliography

Santos, Richard G. *Aguayo Expedition into Texas, 1721: An Annotated Translation of the Five Versions of the Diary Kept by Br. Juan Antonio de la Peña.* Austin: Jenkins Pub. Co., 1981.

JESÚS F. DE LA TEJA

AGUAYO, SERGIO (1947–). Born in La Ribera de Guadalupe, Jalisco, Mexico, on September 10, 1947, Sergio Aguayo Quezada is a prominent Mexican scholar who has actively promoted human rights and democracy. He obtained his Ph.D. degree from the Johns Hopkins University School of Advanced International Studies. Professor at El Colegio de México since 1977, he is a prolific writer on national security, democracy, human rights, U.S.–Mexico relations, and refugees. He also writes a widely-read weekly column that is carried in nearly twenty newspapers throughout Mexico. He has received several awards and has participated in organizations such as the Mexican Academy of Human Rights and Civic Alliance. In 2004 he became president of the board of Fundar, an independent center doing applied research on democracy.

See also **Democracy; Human Rights.**

BIBLIOGRAPHY

Primary Works

1968: Los archivos de la violencia. México, D.F.: Grijalbo-Reforma, 1998.

El panteón de los mitos: Estados Unidos y el nacionalismo mexicano. México, D.F.: Grijalbo–El Colegio de México, 1998. Translated by Julian Brody as *Myths and [Mis]-Perceptions: Changing U.S. Elite Visions of Mexico.* San Diego and México: Center for U.S.-Mexican Studies (UCSD)/Centro de Estudios Internacionales, El Colegio de México, 1998.

La charola: Una historia de los servicios de inteligencia en México. México, D.F.: Grijalbo, 2001.

El almanaque del Distrito Federal. México, D.F.: Hechos Confiables, 2002.

México en cifras. México, D.F.: Grijalbo, 2002.

Diagnóstico sobre la situación de los derechos humanos en México. México, D.F.: Oficina del Alto Comisionado de las Naciones Unidas para los Derechos Humanos en México, 2003.

México a la mano. México, D.F.: Grijalbo, 2003.

El pequeño almanaque mexicano. México, D.F.: Hechos Confiables-Grijalbo, 2004.

Secondary Sources

Padgett, Tim. "Sergio Aguayo." *Time International* 150, no. 26 (December 29, 1997): 54.

TONATIUH GUILLEN LOPEZ

AGÜERO ROCHA, FERNANDO (1918–). Fernando Agüero Rocha (*b.* 1918), Nicaraguan Conservative Party leader (1960–1972). Agüero assumed the leadership of a revived Conservative Party in 1960. The party's platform not only was anti-Somoza but also favored a "democratic revolution." Agüero stressed the need for economic and social reforms to prevent a Communist takeover in response to Somoza's entrenchment. In early 1963 he announced that the Conservative Party would boycott the forthcoming elections because the Somozas controlled the election machinery. True to Agüero's accusations, René Schick Gutiérrez, the Somoza's handpicked successor, won the presidency.

In the presidential election of 1967, Anastasio Somoza Debayle was a candidate himself. The opposition, consisting of Conservatives, Independent Liberals, and Christian Democrats, formed the National Opposition Union (UNO), and coalesced behind their candidate Agüero. Somoza won by a three-to-one margin, prompting Agüero to charge Somoza with election fraud, claiming that ballot boxes were seized from Granada (an opposition center) and that intimidation at the polls and violation of voting secrecy were commonplace.

The unrest and scandal stemming from Somoza's election led to elaborate plans for his cession of the presidency without relinquishing his power. In 1971, the Kupia-Kumi Pact, arranged between Liberals and Conservatives, provided that Somoza would step down in favor of a three-man junta, comprised of two Liberals and one Conservative. Agüero joined the junta, calling the pact a "national solution," although he still opposed Somoza. The junta, commonly referred to as "The Three Little Pigs," split the opposition. Somoza controlled the junta and the National Guard; thus, the junta wielded no real authority. This lack of power was seen clearly in the aftermath of the 1972 earthquake, when Somoza appointed himself head of a national emergency council with special powers.

Agüero opposed Somoza's rule by decree, so Somoza removed him from the junta. By this time, Agüero had lost the popular backing of students and had been removed as Conservative Party leader anyway. In addition, Agüero's cooperation with Somoza resulted in the alienation and disillusionment of younger Conservatives and others, thereby splintering the Conservatives.

See also **Nicaragua**.

BIBLIOGRAPHY

Bernard Diederich, *Somoza and the Legacy of U.S. Involvement in Central America* (1982).

Walter La Feber, *Inevitable Revolutions: The United States in Central America* (1984), esp. p. 163.

John A. Booth, *The End and the Beginning: The Nicaraguan Revolution*, 2d ed. (1985).

Additional Bibliography

Gambone, Michael D. *Capturing the Revolution: The United States, Central America, and Nicaragua, 1961-1972*. Westport, CT: Praeger, 2001.

Soto, Lilly. *Nicaragua, el desarrollo histórico de los partidos políticos en la década del 60 (1960-1969)*. Managua: L. Soto Vásquez, 1998.

SHANNON BELLAMY

AGÜEYBANA II

(?–1511). Agüeybana II (*d.* 1511), nephew of Agüeybana I and next in line to rule the political confederacy of Boriquén (Puerto Rico) when the Spaniards took over the island in 1508. Agüeybana was of the Taino culture. Given in *encomienda* to the settler Cristóbal de Sotomayor, Agüeybana II led a revolt against the Spaniards in 1511. He succeeded in destroying their settlement and killing Sotomayor, but also lost his own life in the struggle to defeat the Spaniards.

BIBLIOGRAPHY

Information on Agüeybana II appears in most history books on Puerto Rico as well as in Cesario Rosa Nieves and Esther Melón, *Biografías Puertorriqueñas: Perfil histórico de un pueblo* (1970).

Additional Bibliography

Cabrera, Gilberto R. *Puerto Rico y su historia íntima 1500: Tomo I (siglos XVI, XVII, XVIII)*. San Juan, P.R.: G.R. Cabrera, 1997.

OLGA JIMÉNEZ DE WAGENHEIM

AGUIAR, ADONIAS

(1915–1990). Adonias Aguiar (Adonias Filho; Aguiar Filho; Adonias; *b.* 27 November 1915; *d.* 4 August 1990), Brazilian novelist. Set largely in the author's native state of Bahia, Adonias Filho's fiction blends the social themes of the regionalist novel of the 1930s and early 1940s with the existential and metaphysical concerns of the psychological novel that began to emerge at the same time. Such works as *Memórias de Lázaro* (1952), *Corpo vivo* (1962), and *O forte* (1965) juxtapose multiple levels of time and space in a dense, poetic, elliptical style, creating a dreamy atmosphere in which human beings fulfill their frequently tragic destinies.

See also **Literature: Brazil**.

BIBLIOGRAPHY

Thomas Deveny, "Narrative Techniques in Adonias Filho's *Memórias de Lázaro*," in *Hispania* 63, no. 2 (1980): 321–327.

Fred P. Ellison, "The Schizophrenic Narrator and the Myth of Renewal in *Memórias de Lázaro*," in *From Linguistics to Literature: Romance Studies Offered to Francis M. Rogers* (1981).

Additional Bibliography

Araújo, Vera Lúcia Romariz Correia de. *Palavra de deuses, memória de homens: Diálogo de culturas na ficção de Adonias Filho*. Maceió: EDUFAL, 1999.

Paranhos, Maria da Conceição. *Adonias Filho: Representação épica da forma dramática*. Salvador: Fundação Casa de Jorge Amado, 1990.

RANDAL JOHNSON

AGUILAR, JERÓNIMO DE (c. 1490–1531).

Jerónimo de Aguilar (*b.* ca. 1490; *d.* 1531), colonist and translator. Born in Écija, Spain, Aguilar was aboard a ship proceeding from Darién to Santo Domingo in 1511. When it struck shoals off Jamaica, he was among twenty men who escaped in a longboat that drifted to the east coast of the Yucatán Peninsula. The local cacique soon sacrificed thirteen of the men, but seven, including Aguilar, escaped into the territory of another ruler, who maintained them as servants. When Hernán Cortés's expedition arrived in 1519, Aguilar was one of only two Spaniards still surviving; the other chose to remain among the Mayas. Aguilar, fluent in Spanish and Maya, proved invaluable as a translator for Cortés. Unable to speak Nahuatl, the language of the Aztecs, he teamed up with Cortés's mistress Doña Marina (Malinche), who spoke Nahuatl and Maya, to translate from Nahuatl to Spanish once the expedition reached the Aztec Empire. Rewarded with an encomienda after the Conquest, Aguilar died without marrying.

See also **Cortés, Hernán.**

BIBLIOGRAPHY

Robert Himmerich y Valencia, *The Encomenderos of New Spain, 1521–1555* (1991).

Hugh Thomas, *The Conquest of Mexico* (1993).

Additional Bibliography

Butterfield, Marvin Ellis. *Jerónimo de Aguilar, Conquistador.* Tuscaloosa: University of Alabama Press, 1969.

JOHN E. KICZA

AGUILAR, MARTÍN DE (?–1603).

Martín de Aguilar (*d.* January 1603), Spanish mariner, explorer of the Californias. Aguilar began his career of exploration as a sailor on the expedition of Sebastián Vizcaíno in the Gulf of California (June–November 1596). Subsequently he was an ensign on Vizcaíno's voyage that charted the coast of the Californias in 1602–1603. Next he served on the frigate *Tres Reyes,* the crew of which explored, made soundings, and obtained provisions along the coast to Monterey. From 17 December 1602 to 3 January 1603 he provisioned the *Tres Reyes,* which sailed north from Monterey. Separated from the flagship *San Diego* north of Point Reyes on 5 January, the *Santo Tomás* was forced beyond Cabo Blanco, Oregon. Aguilar discovered a large, raging river thought to be the Strait of Anián.

Aguilar and his pilot, Antonio Flores, died at sea; the pilot's aide, Esteban López, returned to Navidad, Jalisco, on 28 February 1603. The torrential river, first named the Santa Inés, was subsequently named the Martín de Aguilar (and was also known as the Antón Flores).

See also **Explorers and Exploration: Spanish America.**

BIBLIOGRAPHY

W. Michael Mathes, ed., *Californiana I: Documentos para la historia de la demarcación comercial de California, 1583–1632* (1965); and *Vizcaíno and Spanish Expansion in the Pacific Ocean, 1580–1630* (1968).

Additional Bibliography

Rodríguez Sala de Gómezgil, María Luisa. "Sebastián Vizcaíno y Fray Antonio de la Ascensión: Una nueva etapa en el reconocimiento de las Californias novohispanas; estudio socio-histórico." *Estudios Fronterizos,* 35–36 (Jan.–Dec 1995), pp. 9–41.

W. MICHAEL MATHES

AGUILAR, ROSARIO FIALLOS DE (1938–).

Rosario Fiallos de Aguilar (*b.* 29 January 1938), Nicaraguan novelist. Born in León, Nicaragua,

Aguilar has lived her entire life in the same city except for her studies in the United States (1955–1956) and a brief period in Costa Rica during the turmoil of the Sandinista revolution. Her first novel, *Primavera sonámbula* (1964), is the story of a young woman tottering between sanity and insanity. *Aquel mar sin fondo ni playa* (1974) tells the haunting story of a stepmother's guilt and her rejection of a severely retarded child. *Siete relatos sobre el amor y la guerra* (1986) is a collection of stories linked thematically by the Sandinista fight to oust the dictatorship of Anastasio Somoza. Her 1992 novel, *La niña blanca y los pájaros sin pies*, re-creates the lost female voices of the Spanish conquest of Central America. While Aguilar denies she is a feminist writer, her novels all center around women, maternity, and the consequences of rejecting motherhood, the Latin American social imperative for women. In 1999, Aguilar became the first woman to be admitted as *miembro de número* to the Academia Nicaragüense de la Lengua. She won the VI Premio Internacional de Literatura Latinoamericana y del Caribe Gabriela Mistral for her novel *La Promesante* in 2001. The Latin American literary critic Raymond Souza called her "one of the best-kept secrets in contemporary Spanish American fiction."

BIBLIOGRAPHY

Aguilar's fiction is treated at length by Raymond D. Souza in *La historia en la novela hispanoamericana moderna* (1988) and "Novel and Context in Costa Rica and Nicaragua," *Romance Quarterly* 33, no. 4 (1986): 453–462. See also the interview of Edward W. Hood with Aguilar, "Una conversación con Rosario Aguilar," in *South Eastern Latin Americanist* 37, no. 2 (1993): 15–21.

Additional Bibliography

Barbas-Rhoden, Laura. *Writing Women in Central America: Gender and the Fictionalization of History.* Athens, OH: Ohio University Press, 2003.

González, Ann. "Find More Like This 'Las mujeres de mi país': An Introduction to the Feminist Fiction of Rosario Aguilar." *Revista/Review Interamericana* 23.1-2 (Spring Summer 1993): 63-72.

Palacios, Nidia. *Voces femeninas en la narrativa de Rosario Aguilar.* Managua: Editorial Ciencias Sociales, 1998.

ANN GONZÁLEZ

AGUILAR VARGAS, CÁNDIDO (1888–1960).

Cándido Aguilar Vargas (*b.* 12 February 1888; *d.* 19 March 1960), Mexican revolutionary, Constitutional, Convention leader, and politician. From modest origins in rural Veracruz, Aguilar signed the first revolutionary program in Veracruz, the Plan of San Ricardo, in 1910. A supporter of Francisco Madero, he became a Constitutionalist in 1913 and was governor of his home state from 1914 to 1917. He was a deputy to the Constitutional Convention of 1917, of which he was elected first vice president, a position he used to publicize progressive issues. He served as secretary of foreign relations under Venustiano Carranza (1918), to whom he remained loyal until 1920. Aguilar went into exile in the early 1920s, after the rebellion led by Adolfo De La Huerta, but returned to political activity as a federal deputy and senator in the 1930s and 1940s. He was expelled from the Mexican Revolutionary Party in 1944 for exposing corruption. He retired from the army as a division general. He spent his last years in self-imposed exile in El Salvador and Cuba and died in Mexico.

See also **Mexico, Constitutions: Constitution of 1917.**

BIBLIOGRAPHY

Miguel A. Peral, *Diccionario biográfico mexicano* (1944), pp. 5–6.

Roderic A. Camp, *Mexican Political Biographies, 1884–1934* (1991), pp. 1–2.

Additional Bibliography

Corzo Ramírez, Ricardo, José g. González Sierra, and David Skerritt Gardner. *Nunca un desleal: Cándido Aguilar, 1889-1960.* Veracruz: Colegio de México; Centro de Estudios Históricos, 1986.

RODERIC AI CAMP

AGUILERA MALTA, DEMETRIO

(1909–1981). Demetrio Aguilera Malta (*b.* 24 May 1909; *d.* 29 December 1981), Ecuadorian novelist and playwright. Hailing from the Andes mountains and the coast, respectively, Jorge Icaza (1906–1979) and Aguilera Malta are the two best-known Ecuadorian fiction writers. The latter's fiction spans several decades, beginning with *Don Goyo* (1933) and ending forty years later with *El secuestro del general* (1973). Early on, Aguilera Malta copublished a set of short stories, *Los que se van* (1931), that focused on problems of economic and ethnic exploitation of the coastal lower classes.

His other novels take up many themes, among them, problems of economic development, the Cuban Revolution, the travels of Vasco de Balboa, and indigenous beliefs and customs. An intriguing, well-crafted novel, *Siete lunas y siete serpientes* (1970) adeptly meshes legend, witchcraft, and modern superstition with the machinations of a local, lustful political boss bent on governing with an iron hand. In this work Aguilera Malta blends magic and realism to make an ironic commentary on Ecuadorian politics. In *El secuestro del general*, Aguilera Malta uses wordplay and irony to capture the way in which the power of language can sway and subjugate people to the absolute power of dictators. Language, myth, legend, fantasy, and concepts of power are the basic ingredients of the fictional worlds of Aguilera Malta.

See also **Icaza Coronel, Jorge.**

BIBLIOGRAPHY

Gerardo Luzuriaga, *Del realismo al expresionismo: El teatro de Aguilera Malta* (1971).

Antonio Fama, *Realismo mágico en la narrativa de Aguilera-Malta* (1977).

Clementine Christos Rabassa, *Demetrio Aguilera-Malta and Social Justice* (1980).

Additional Bibliography

Troya, María Soledad. *Don Goyo: el héroe cholo de Demetrio Aguilera Malta*. Quito: Casa de la Cultura Ecuatoriana "Benjamín Carrión," Fondo Editorial, 1997.

Wishnia, Kenneth J.A. *Twentieth-Century Ecuadorian Narrative: New Readings in the Context of the Americas*. Lewisburg, PA: Bucknell University Press, 1999.

DICK GERDES

AGUIRRE, ATANASIO (1801–1875).

A statesman and legislator, Atanasio Aguirre was acting president of Uruguay during the period 1864–1865. Born May 2, 1801, he began his career in 1825 as an official in the army commissariat and became the director of military procurement in 1833. When Fructuoso Rivera toppled constitutional president Manuel Oribe in 1838, Aguirre resigned his post and eventually joined the latter during the 1843–1851 siege of Montevideo. He was the Blanco representative in the constitutional government inaugurated in 1852, but was ousted one year later when Colorado strongman Venancio Flores seized power. With the return of constitutional rule, Aguirre again entered government, first as an elected representative in 1858 and then as a senator in 1861. As a consequence of Flores's 1863 invasion of Uruguay, which set off the series of events that eventually involved Uruguay in the Paraguayan War, the national legislature found it impossible to organize regular presidential elections at the end of President Bernardo Berro's term. Aguirre, who at that point was president of the senate, was chosen interim president of the republic in March 1864.

Aguirre's efforts as president were focused on resisting the invaders, who enjoyed overt assistance from Argentina and less evident support from Brazil. In May, a Brazilian plenipotentiary demanded that Aguirre's government give immediate satisfaction for numerous claims made by Brazilian residents in Uruguay. Aguirre rejected the claims, whereupon Brazilian troops entered Uruguay and linked up with those of Flores, giving the latter indisputable military supremacy. In an indignant reaction, Aguirre ordered the public burning of the treaties signed in 1851 by Uruguay and Brazil, which had recognized Brazilian rights over long disputed border territories and had established a virtual Brazilian tutelage over Uruguayan finances. This gesture earned him praise from succeeding generations of Uruguayans. Aguirre's term ended in February 1865 and his successor, Tomás Villalba, capitulated to Flores. Under Spanish protection, Aguirre fled to Argentina, only returning to Uruguay in 1867. He dedicated his last years to private life, and died September 28, 1875.

See also **Uruguay, Political Parties: Blanco Party; Flores, Venancio; Oribe, Manuel; Rivera, Fructuoso; Uruguay, Political Parties: Colorado Party.**

BIBLIOGRAPHY

Casal, Juan Manuel. "Uruguay and the Paraguayan War: The Military Dimension." In *I Die with My Country: Perspectives on the Paraguayan War*, edited by Hendrik Kraay and Thomas L. Whigham. Lincoln and London: University of Nebraska Press, 2004.

Fernández Saldaña, José M. *Diccionario Uruguayo de Biografías, 1810–1940*. Montevideo: Amerindia, 1945.

JUAN MANUEL CASAL

AGUIRRE, JUAN FRANCISCO DE

(1758–1811). A Spanish naval officer, Aguirre is principally known in the early twenty-first century for a multivolume diary and official report of his observations along the Paraná and Paraguay rivers during the 1780s and 1790s. He was born August 17, 1758, into an aristocratic Navarese family in Donamaria, just outside of Pamplona, during the reign of Carlos III, a Bourbon monarch whose distinct interest in administrative reform brought many changes in the empire. Aguirre was destined to play a role in these changes. He entered the Real Compañía de Guardia Marinas in his teens, and served in the navy for some time before coming to the Río de la Plata in 1777. By the time his vessel, the *Santísima Trinidad*, reached Platine waters, the king had already confirmed his rank as *teniente de navío*, and the young officer could look forward to a distinguished career in the royal service.

Aguirre owed his presence in South America to the negotiations behind the signing of the Treaty of San Ildefonso between Spain and Portugal. This agreement, which attempted to define the boundaries between Brazil and the Spanish colonies, required border commissioners to scout and delineate the territories involved and submit their findings to higher authorities in Madrid and Lisbon. The viceroy of La Plata, Juan José de Vértiz y Salcedo, decided to divide the responsibilities of the Spanish commissioners, sending Félix de Azara and a large party of aides overland through the Argentine Mesopotamia (the provinces that lie between the Paraná and Uruguay rivers—Entre Rios, Corrientes, and Misiones) and into Paraguay. Aguirre, for his part, received orders to sail slowly up the Paraná past Santa Fe and Corrientes before entering the Paraguay River, taking hydrographic readings as he went, and studying the various communities and people he encountered, especially the Indians. In fulfilling this task, Aguirre left Buenos Aires in late December 1783. He reached Asunción four months later and was there welcomed by Governor Pedro Melo de Portugal, who put the entire provincial government at the lieutenant's disposal. Aguirre's stay in Paraguay lasted a full twelve years, during which time he incessantly wrote and rewrote his *Diário*, always adding more details and nuances to an already sophisticated account. At that particular juncture, Paraguay was undergoing an economic boom thanks to the growing trade in yerba maté, the green tea that commanded an impressive market in Buenos Aires and elsewhere in the southern reaches of the continent. Aguirre took all this in. He often traveled far afield from Asunción on horseback in order to assemble the most up-to-date information. His 1791 description of yerba operations in Caati, for example, is the only extensive analysis of Paraguayan tea extraction produced during the colonial period. To some extent, Aguirre's work paralleled that of Azara, but whereas the latter was especially enthralled with the flora and fauna of the country, the people and the economy interested Aguirre more and he wrote with great sensitivity in those areas.

After years of extensive labor, in which he received no help from either Madrid or his Portuguese counterparts, Aguirre finally requested leave to return to Spain in 1797. His health had been broken in the tropics long since, and though he was promoted to *capitán de navío* in 1805, he saw little active service thereafter. He died on February 17, 1811, at the time of the Peninsular War, evidently in French captivity. As for his long study of Paraguay, it received almost no attention during his lifetime and was published in its entirety only in the early 1950s.

See also **Río de la Plata; Paraná River; Azara, Félix de; San Ildefonso, Treaty of (1777); Vértiz y Salcedo, Juan José de; Yerba Mate; Yerba Mate Industry.**

BIBLIOGRAPHY

Aguirre, Juan Francisco de. "Diário del capitán de fragata de la Real Armada ..." *Revista de la Biblioteca Nacional de Buenos Aires* 17–20 (1949–1951).

Brezzo, Liliana M. "Las exploraciones y los escritos del capitán de navío Juan Francisco de Aguirre en el Paraguay." *Historia Paraguaya* 43 (2005): 481–536.

Zubizarreta, Carlos. *Cien vidas paraguayas.* Asunción: Aravera, 1985.

THOMAS L. WHIGHAM

AGUIRRE, JULIÁN (1868–1924). Julián
Aguirre (*b.* 28 January 1868; *d.* 13 August 1924), Argentine composer and pianist. Born in Buenos Aires, Aguirre spent his formative years in Spain. At

fourteen, he enrolled in the Madrid Royal Conservatory, where he studied composition with Emilio Arrieta, piano with Pedro Beck, harmony with José María Aranguren, and fugue with Cató. He was awarded first prize in piano, harmony, and counterpoint. In Madrid the celebrated Spanish composer Isaac Albéniz heard his music and predicted a brilliant career for the young musician. Aguirre returned to Argentina in 1886 and made a name for himself by giving concerts around the country. He spent a year in Rosario studying and experimenting with folk music before settling in Buenos Aires, where he played an important role in the artistic and musical life of the city. His early works drew their inspiration from European styles and forms, but from 1889 on, when he joined with Alberto Williams and others to create a distinctive nationalist style, his compositions for voice and piano—especially the *tristes* for piano—are based on the folk tunes, rhythms, and harmonies of his native Argentina.

Considered one of the best Argentine composers of his generation, Aguirre was also active in the field of music education, holding administrative and academic positions (professor of harmony) at Williams Conservatory. He founded the music department of the Athenaeum of Buenos Aires (1892) and the Argentine School of Music (1916). He wrote more than sixty piano pieces, two of which, the popular *Huella* and *Gato,* were orchestrated and performed by Ernest Ansermet in 1930. The remarkable *Rapsodia criolla* for violin and piano is a seminal work in the development of an Argentine nationalist style. Aguirre's output of nearly a hundred works includes chamber pieces, voice and piano works, and numerous songs and choral works, many for children. He died in Buenos Aires.

See also **Music: Art Music.**

BIBLIOGRAPHY

J. F. Giacobbe, *Julián Aguirre* (1945).

Rodolfo Arizaga, *Enciclopedia de la música argentina* (1971).

Gérard Béhague, *Music in Latin America* (1979); *New Grove Dictionary of Music and Musicians,* vol. 1 (1980).

Additional Bibliography

García Muñoz, Carmen. *Julián Aguirre.* Buenos Aires: Ministerio de Cultura y Educación, 1970.

SUSANA SALGADO

AGUIRRE, LOPE DE (1518–1561).

Lope de Aguirre (*b.* 1518; *d.* 27 October 1561), self-proclaimed rebel leader of ill-fated descent of the Amazon River. Few sixteenth-century Spanish explorers have secured the notoriety of Lope de Aguirre. He was a soldier from Oñate, in the province of Guipuzcoa, Spain, who joined the Pedro de Ursúa expedition to the Amazon. Aguirre was one of the instigators of a plot to assassinate Ursúa, and at first supported Fernando de Guzmán to replace the slain Ursúa. As the group traveled against great odds downstream, discipline disintegrated, Indian carriers were abandoned, and an increasing number of men were killed in brawls. Aguirre captained Guzmán's militia, heading fifty Basque harquebusiers. Paranoid and filled with delusions of grandeur, he cowed followers and massacred Guzmán and all others suspected of disloyalty.

Challenging the authority of king and church, Aguirre argued that the land belonged to the conquerors. His unrealistic goal was to descend the Amazon, sail northwestward until he could attack Spanish authorities in Peru frontally, then assume the land's administration. Shortly after he reached the Venezuelan coast, however, royal supporters surrounded his encampment. He killed his own daughter to prevent her capture. His was one of the bloodiest and most controversial expeditions of the Age of Discovery.

See also **Explorers and Exploration: Brazil; Ursúa, Pedro de.**

BIBLIOGRAPHY

José Antonio Del Busto Duthurburu, *Historia general del Perú,* vol. 2, *Descubrimiento y conquista* (1978).

John Hemming, *Red Gold: The Conquest of the Brazilians* (1978).

Additional Bibliography

Lacarta, Manuel. *Lope de Aguirre: el loco del Amazonas.* Madrid: Alderabán Ediciones, 1998.

NOBLE DAVID COOK

AGUIRRE, NATANIEL (1843–1888).

Nataniel Aguirre (*b.* 10 October 1843; *d.* 11 September 1888), Bolivian writer and politician. Born in

Cochabamba, Aguirre was an important political figure during the period of the War of the Pacific (1879). He was a firm believer in liberal ideas and a great defender of federalism. But Aguirre's importance comes from his literary work. He is the author of plays, short stories, and a historical novel, *Juan de la Rosa: Memorias del último soldado de la Independencia* (1885), which is his most important work and is considered the national novel of Bolivia. He also wrote historical books and diverse political treatises.

Juan de la Rosa is the story of the uprising of Cochabamba between 1810 and 1812, at the beginning of the War of Independence. Its narrator and protagonist is a twelve-year-old boy who participates in the events leading to the emergence of nationalism in the future Republic of Bolivia. In this novel, Aguirre endorses the main ideas of liberalism and tries to blend them with the vital force of the mestizo (mixed-blooded) population, which is portrayed as the protagonist of these early battles.

See also **War of the Pacific.**

BIBLIOGRAPHY

Porfirio Díaz Machicao, *Nataniel Aguirre* (1945).

Walter Navia Romero, *Interpretación y análisis de "Juan de la Rosa"* (1966).

José Roberto Arze, Prologue to *Nataniel Aguirre,* 2d ed., by Eufronio Viscarra (1969).

Alba María Paz Soldán, "Una articulación simbólica de lo nacional: *Juan de la Rosa* de Nataniel Aguirre" (Ph.D. diss., University of Pittsburgh, 1986).

Additional Bibliography

Mariaca, Guillermo. *Nación y narración en Bolivia: Juan de la Rosa y la historia.* La Paz, Bolivia: Facultad de Humanidades y Ciencias de la Educación, UMSA, 1997.

LEONARDO GARCÍA PABÓN

AGUIRRE CERDA, PEDRO (1879–1941).

Pedro Aguirre Cerda (*b.* 6 February 1879; *d.* 25 November 1941), president of Chile (1938–1941). Born to a modest family in Pocuro, a village in Aconcagua Province, Aguirre Cerda graduated from the University of Chile with degrees in pedagogy and law. A member of the Radical Party, he served in the Chamber of Deputies from 1915 to 1921 and in the Senate from 1921 to 1924. He also held ministries in the administrations of Juan Luis Sanfuentes and Arturo Alessandri Palma. He was elected president in 1938 as the candidate of the Popular Front, a coalition of the Radical, Socialist, Communist, and Democratic parties and the Chilean Labor Confederation, narrowly defeating Conservative candidate Gustavo Ross. Rightist strength in Congress and Aguirre Cerda himself, who had parlayed law and politics into a personal fortune, assured that Chile's first government of the working and middle classes would not pursue radical objectives. Aguirre Cerda had originally opposed the Popular Front concept, which originated in Moscow as an anti-Fascist strategy; Chile's was the only Popular Front government elected in Latin America.

As president, Aguirre Cerda vetoed the efforts of his Marxist allies to unionize agricultural workers, thus preserving the overrepresentation of landowners in Congress. He faced the rebuilding of the south-central provinces in the wake of the devastating 1939 earthquake centered in Chillán. Among his major achievements were the founding of the Chilean Development Corporation (CORFO), the state agency charged with fostering industrialization, establishing the minimum wage for urban workers, reforming education, and recognizing Chilean territorial claims in Antarctica. A genuinely popular president, Aguirre Cerda died unexpectedly after less than three years in office.

See also **Chile, Organizations: Development Corporation (CORFO); Chile, Political Parties: Radical Party.**

BIBLIOGRAPHY

John Reese Stevenson, *The Chilean Popular Front* (1942).

Alberto Cabero, *Recuerdos de don Pedro Aguirre Cerda,* 2d ed. (1948).

Alberto Baltra Cortés, *Pedro Aguirre Cerda* (1960).

Additional Bibliography

Palma Zúñiga, Luis. *Pedro Aguirre Cerda, maestro, estadista, gobernante.* Santiago: Editorial Andrés Bello, 1963.

Quezada Vergara, Abraham. *Pedro Aguirre Cerda, o, La trayectoria de un ideal educativo.* Santiago: Universidad de Chile, Facultad Ciencias Económicas y Administrativas, Editorial de Economía y Administración, 1991.

THOMAS C. WRIGHT

AGUIRRE Y SALINAS, OSMÍN (1889–
1977). Osmín Aguirre y Salinas (*b.* 1889; *d.* 1977),
president of El Salvador (1944–1945). A career
military officer, Osmín Aguirre y Salinas was a member of the junior officers' clique which deposed
President Arturo Araújo in December 1931, establishing military control of El Salvador. During the
regime of General Maximiliano Hernández Martínez he was governor of the departments of Cuzcatlán, La Paz, and Usulután and chief of staff of the
National Police, rising to the rank of colonel.

His brief tenure as president was part of the
tumultuous era that followed the overthrow of Hernández Martínez. Fearing the fragmentation of the
nation, an army coup removed Hernández Martínez's successor, the defense minister, General Andrés I. Menéndez, from the presidency in October
1944, installing Aguirre y Salinas. The Salvadoran
Supreme Court declared his tenure unconstitutional,
and the United States, which considered his regime
profascist, withheld recognition.

Aguirre y Salinas maintained power despite protests, conducting elections during January 1945
installed the official candidate, General Salvador Castañeda Castro. Aguirre y Salinas's career ended
when he led an unsuccessful coup against his handpicked successor.

BIBLIOGRAPHY

Additional Bibliography

Parkman, Patricia. *Insurrección no violenta en El Salvador:
La caída de Maximiliano Hernández Martínez.* San
Salvador: Dirección de Publicaciones e Impresos,
Consejo Nacional para la Cultura y el Arte, 2003.

KENNETH J. GRIEB

AGUSTÍN, JOSÉ (1944–). José Agustín
(*b.* 19 August 1944), Mexican novelist born José
Agustín Ramírez Gómez. In his novel *La tumba,* a
youth-centered narrative rejecting middle-class morality and the clichés of nationalism, and celebrating
pleasure and self-exploration, Agustín uses street
slang to create a lively, ironic narrative voice. With
its publication in 1964, Agustín (together with
Gustavo Sainz) founded the literary movement
known as "La Onda." In what is perhaps his best

novel to date, *Se está haciendo tarde (final en laguna)*
(1973), Agustín engages in a self-critique of the
potential narcissism and alienation of such individualistic quests. In *Ciudades desiertas* (1982), based on
his experiences in the University of Iowa's International Writing Program, the author advocates a
return to the family and monogamy and to Mexican
national culture, while lampooning the sterility of life
in the United States. This reconciliation is extended
to the family in *Cerca del fuego* (1986), in which the
author attempts to fuse anti-imperialist and Jungian
discourses.

As the preeminent enfant terrible of his generation, Agustín has maintained an irreverent, independent leftist stance (from his participation in the
Cuban literacy campaign to his attacks on Mexican
literary mafias and censorship). His three volume
history of contemporary Mexico, *Tragicomedia mexicana 1: La vida en México de 1940 a 1970* (1990),
*Tragicomedia mexicana 2: La vida en Mexico de 1970
a 1982* (1992), and *Tragicomedia mexicana 3: La
Vida en mexico de 1982 a 1994* (1998), reflects this
position.

BIBLIOGRAPHY

Margo Glantz, "La onda diez años después: ¿Epitafio o
revalorización?" in her *Repeticiones: Ensayos sobre literatura mexicana* (1979), pp. 115–129.

June C. D. Carter and Donald L. Schmidt, *José Agustín:
Onda and Beyond* (1986).

Cynthia Steele, "Apocalypse and Patricide: *Cerca del fuego*
(1986), by José Agustín," in her *Politics, Gender, and
the Mexican Novel, 1968–1988: Beyond the Pyramid*
(1992), pp. 110–142.

Additional Bibliography

Calvillo, Ana Luisa. *José Agustín: Una biografía de perfil.*
México, D.F.: Blanco y Negro Editores, 1998.

Kim Lee, Joong. *Cultura y sociedad de México en la obra de
José Agustín.* Guadalajara, Jalisco, México: Universidad
de Guadalajara, 2000.

CYNTHIA STEELE

AGUSTINI, DELMIRA (1886–1914).
Delmira Agustini (*b.* 24 October 1886; *d.* 7 July
1914), Uruguayan poet. Born in Montevideo,
Agustini was a member of the Uruguayan group
of writers of 1900—together with Julio Herrera y

Reissig, María Eugenia Vaz Ferreira, Alberto Zum Felde, and Angel Falco—and an innovative voice in Spanish American poetry. During her short life she published *El libro blanco (Frágil)* (1907), *Cantos de la mañana* (1910), and *Los cálices vacíos* (The Empty Chalices, 1913). The *Obras completas,* published posthumously in 1924, includes unpublished poems possibly belonging to a projected volume titled *Los astros del abismo* (The Stars of the Abyss), which included a group of poems titled "El rosario de Eros." Her early poetry, published in literary magazines, was very well received and showed the influence of *Modernismo.* In her later collections, she developed a more personal style and a voice that departs steadily from the canonical modernist poetics to which she subscribed. The language and imagery of her poetry was acclaimed for its erotic nature, an important foundational feature in Spanish American feminine poetics.

Agustini lived with her parents in Montevideo and spent long periods in Buenos Aires. Although she was well known in the cultural and social life of Montevideo, she was not an active member of the intellectual groups of her epoch. In 1913 she married Enrique Job Reyes, a common man with no intellectual interests, with whom she had had a long and formal relationship. She left him after a short period and returned to her parental household for comfort.

There are several unexplained mysteries regarding Agustini's short life. She was killed by her former husband, who then killed himself. This tragic event brought to Agustini's biography considerable sensationalism, which has colored the critical studies of most literary historians. It is fair to say that her life and her poetry are characterized by contradictory features that deserve much attention. A new translation of Agustini's work was published in 2003 as *Selected Poetry of Delmira Agustini: Poetics of Eros.*

See also **Reissig, Julio Herrera y.**

BIBLIOGRAPHY

Emir Rodríguez Monegal, *Sexo y poesía en el 900 uruguayo* (1929).

Clara Silva, *Genio y figura de Delmira Agustini* (1968).

Doris T. Stephens, *Delmira Agustini and the Quest for Transcendence* (1975).

Luzmaría Jiménez Faro, *Delmira Agustini: Manantial de la brasa* (1991).

Additional Bibliography

Escaja, Tina. *Delmira Agustini y el modernismo: nuevas propuestas de género.* Rosario, Argentina: Beatriz Viterbo, 2000.

Varas, Patricia. *Las mascaras de Delmira Agustini.* Montevideo: Vintén Editor, 2002.

MAGDALENA GARCÍA PINTO

AHUIZOTE, EL. *El Ahuizote* (The Barb) was a weekly satirical humor publication in Mexico that ran from 1874 to 1876, created in express opposition to President Sebastián Lerdo de Tejada. It was founded by Vicente Riva Palacio, an exceptional writer and humorist, together with the talented cartoonist José María Villasana. Political cartoons engraved and lithographed by Villasana and Jesús T. Alamilla; editorials written by Juan N. Mira-fuentes; and satirical texts, couplets, and songs by Riva Palacio filled its pages. Originally planning to call the newspaper *El Nahual* (a mythological person who can take on animal forms), Riva Palacio and Villasana chose instead *El Ahuizote*, which had a more confrontational connotation in the popular mind as something troublesome and irritating that brings bad luck—a perfect title for an opposition newspaper.

See also **Journalism in Mexico; Riva Palacio, Vicente.**

BIBLIOGRAPHY

Barajas Durán, Rafael (el Fisgón). *El país de "El Ahuizote": La caricatura mexicana de oposición durante el gobierno de Sebastián Lerdo de Tejada (1872–1876).* Mexico City: Fondo de Cultura Económica/Tezontle, 2005.

Ortiz Monasterio, José. *Patria, tu ronca voz me repetía: Vicente Riva Palacio y Guerrero.* Mexico City: Universidad Nacional Autónoma de México-Instituto Mora, 1999.

REGINA TAPIA

AIDS. *See* **Acquired Immune Deficiency Syndrome (AIDS); Diseases.**

AIZENBERG, ROBERTO (1928–1998).

Roberto Aizenberg (*b.* 22 August 1928), Argentine painter and printmaker. Born in Villa Federal, province of Entre Ríos, Aizenberg studied architecture at the University of Buenos Aires, receiving a degree in 1954. He later studied painting with Juan Battle Planas. Aizenberg achieved a level of maturity quite early in life. His images relate to the subjective world of the unconscious and continue the surrealistic tradition exemplified in Argentina by Battle Planas. He received the Palanza Prize (Buenos Aires, 1967) and the Cassandra Foundation Award (Chicago, 1970). From 1977 to 1981, he lived in Paris, later moving to Milan for one year and then back to Argentina. In 1985–1986, and again in 1993, he taught painting at Buenos Aires' Escuela Nacional de Bellas Artes. He died in Buenos Aires on February 16, 1998.

See also **Art: The Twentieth Century.**

BIBLIOGRAPHY

Vicente Gesualdo, Aldo Viglione, and Rodolfo Santos, *Diccionario de artistas plásticos en la Argentina* (1988).

Additional Bibliography

Aizenberg, Roberto, and Marcelo E. Pacheco. *El caso Roberto Aizenberg: Obras 1950–1994.* Buenos Aires: Centro Cultural Recoleta, 2001.

Day, Holliday T., and Hollister Sturges. *Art of the Fantastic: Latin America, 1920–1987.* Indianapolis, IN: Indianapolis Museum of Art, 1987.

AMALIA CORTINA ARAVENA

ALAGOAS.

Alagoas, a state in northeastern Brazil, encompasses 11,031 square miles. It has a population of 2.8 million (2000 estimate), composed primarily of people of mixed racial descent. The capital is Maceió. Along the coast, the climate is hot and humid; in the interior, hot and dry. To the west is Paulo Alfonso Falls, once regarded as one of the world's great waterfalls but now used for hydroelectric power so that little water passes over it except during the rainy season. Industrialization is proceeding slowly. The state remains primarily an agricultural region, where cotton, sugar, rice, tobacco, beans, and other crops are raised. Industries revolve around these products, textile manufacturing and sugar refining being the most important. As in much of the region, the state has attempted to parlay the beauty of its beaches into major tourist attractions since the 1980s.

Originally part of the captaincy of Pernambuco, the area that is present-day Alagoas was occupied by the Dutch in the early 1600s. Sugar cultivation employing enslaved Africans dominated as it did in other places on the northeast coast. Its forests and rugged interior offered havens to *quilombos* (communities of runaway slaves), among the most notable of which was Palmares. As Portuguese-Dutch conflicts disrupted plantations, Palmares burgeoned to the point of developing its own sophisticated governing structure and even maintaining a standing army. Palmares resisted both the Dutch and the Portuguese until concerted Portuguese efforts finally destroyed the community in 1694.

Alagoas became an independent captaincy in 1817, a province of the Brazilian Empire in 1823, and a state of the republic in 1889. Its most prominent native sons include the writer Graciliano Ramos and President Fernando Collor de Mello (1990–1992), whose family dominates the state's mass media and who was governor of the state (like his father before him) prior to becoming president.

See also **Brazil: Since 1889; Brazil: Geography.**

BIBLIOGRAPHY

Conti, Mario Sergio. *Notícias do Planalto: A Imprensa e Fernando Collor.* São Paulo: Companhia das Letras, 1999.

Diégues Júnior, Manuel. *O Banguê nas Alagoas: Traços do Sistema Econômico do Engenho de Açucar na Vida e na Cultura Regional.* Rio de Janeiro: Instituto do Açucar e do Álcool, 1949.

Moreira Alves, Márcio. *Teotônio, Guerreiro da Paz.* Petrópolis: Vozes, 1984.

Ramos, Graciliano. *Viventes das Alagoas (Quadros e Costumes do Nordeste).* São Paulo Livraria Martins, 1962.

CARA SHELLY

ALAKALUF.

Alakaluf (also spelled Alcaluf, Alacalufe; Kaweshkar or Kaweshrar in recent usage), maritime inhabitants of the fjords, archipelagos, and canals in the Chilean region south of the peninsula of Taitao approaching the Strait of Magellan. The Alakaluf are related linguistically to the Yámana (Yaghanes). Scholars dispute their origins; some claim Paleolithic roots; others argue that Alakaluf are descendants of peoples arriving in 6000–5000 (the Archaic period).

Early European explorers referred to these groups as Fuegians. Alakaluf bands maintained traditional subsistence patterns of hunting, gathering, and fishing by canoe until the mid-nineteenth century, when European colonization of the region and contact with whalers hastened their demise through disease and assimilation. The lack of economic opportunities contributed to the near extinction of this group, which had been primarily occupied with fishing and artisan work. According to the 1996 census, twelve Alakaluf lived in the small community of Puerto Edén on the east coast of Wellington Island in Chile, sixty-four resided in Puerto Arenas, and another twelve in Puerto Natales. The 1993 passage of the *Ley Indígena* (19.253) in Chile, and resulting programs favoring indigenous rights, has been influential in the current organization of the Alakaluf people. In the first decade of the twenty-first century, 101 Alakaluf were registered with the Chilean Corporación Nacional de Desarrollo Indígena (CONADI).

See also **Indigenous Peoples.**

BIBLIOGRAPHY

Junius Bird. "Antiquity and Migrations of the Early Inhabitants of Patagonia," in *Geographical Review* 28 (April 1938): 250–275.

Richard Shutler, Jr., ed. *South America: Early Man in the New World* (1983): 137–146.

Museo Chileno De Arte Precolombino. *Hombres del sur: Aonikenk, Selknam, Yámana, Kaweshkar* (1987).

Osvaldo Silva G. *Culturas y pueblos de Chile prehispano* (1990), p. 17.

Additional Bibliography

Emperaire, Joseph. *Los nomades del mar.* Translated by Luis Oyarzún. Santiago: LOM Ediciones, 2002.

KRISTINE L. JONES

ALAMÁN, LUCAS (1792–1853). Lucas Alamán (*b.* 18 October 1792; *d.* 2 June 1853), Mexican statesman and historian. Born in Guan-

ajuato, Alamán studied in Mexico City at the School of Mines. In January 1814 he traveled to Europe, where he observed politics in the Cortes in Spain and in other nations, met leading officials and men of science and learning, and studied mining and foreign languages. He returned to Mexico in 1820, beginning his political career in 1821 when he was elected deputy to the Cortes from Guanajuato. Alamán played an active role in the Spanish parliament, proposing programs to restore the mining industry as well as a project for home rule for the New World, taking Canada as its model.

In 1822, upon learning that Mexico had declared its independence, Alamán traveled to London, where he organized the Compañía Unida de Minas (United Mining Company), arriving in Mexico in March 1823. He served as minister of interior and exterior relations during the periods 1823–1825, 1830–1832, and 1853. Initially, he distinguished himself as a liberal and a strong critic of the Vatican for failing to recognize his nation's independence. As a result of the increasing radicalization of politics in the later 1820s, however, he became a conservative and a supporter of the church as the one institution that could help maintain order.

During his term as minister of the interior from 1830 to 1832, Alamán gained notoriety as an authoritarian but also as a strong fiscal conservative. He devoted much of his effort to rebuilding the nation's economy, particularly the mining and the textile industries. He founded the Banco de Avío, the hemisphere's first development bank, and served as director of the ministry of industry from 1842 to 1846. He also reorganized the Archivo General de la Nación and founded the Museo de Antigüedades e Historia Nacional.

In his later years, Alamán became a champion of conservatism and advocated the return to monarchy. He is best known for his writings, particularly his *Disertaciones sobre la historia de la República Méjicana...*, 3 vols. (1844–1849), and his *Historia de Méjico desde los primeros movimientos que prepararon su independencia en el año 1808, hasta la época presente*, 5 vols. (1849–1852), a magisterial work that remains the best and most distinguished account of the epoch.

See also **Mexico: 1810-1910.**

BIBLIOGRAPHY

Moisés González Navarro, *El pensamiento político de Lucas Alamán* (1952).

Charles Hale, *Mexican Liberalism in the Age of Mora, 1821–1853* (1968), esp. pp. 11–38.

Jaime E. Rodríguez O., *The Emergence of Spanish America: Vicente Rocafuerte and Spanish Americanism, 1808–1832* (1975), esp. pp. 167–178, 179–228, and "The Origins of the 1832 Revolt," in Jaime E. Rodríguez O., *Patterns of Contention in Mexican History* (1992).

José C. Valadés, *Alamán: Estadista e historiador* (1977).

Additional Bibliography

Cuevas Landero, Elisa Guadalupe. *La paradoja nación revolución en el pensamiento político de Lucas Alamán*. México, D.F.: Universidad Nacional Autónoma de México, 1995.

Méndez Reyes, Salvador. *El hispanoamericanismo de Lucas Alamán, 1823-1853*. Toluca, Estado de México: Universidad Autónoma del Estado de México, 1996.

Morán Leyva, Paola. *Lucas Alamán*. México: Planeta DeAgostini, 2002.

JAIME E. RODRÍGUEZ O.

ALAMBERT, ZULEIKA (1924–).

Zuleika Alambert (*b.* 1924), Brazilian Communist Party leader and feminist activist. Born in the port city of Santos, Alambert joined the Brazilian Communist Party (PCB) during the political ferment that accompanied the end of World War II and the Estado Nôvo. She was elected to São Paulo's state legislature for the PCB at the age of twenty-four. When the party was banned in 1947 she went underground until 1954.

Alambert served as a member of the overwhelmingly male-dominated central committee of the Moscow-line PCB. Several years after the establishment of a military dictatorship in Brazil in 1964, she went into exile in Chile. Following Salvador Allende's overthrow in 1973, she left Chile for France, where she participated in the organization of the European Committee of Brazilian Women. Returning to Brazil after almost ten years in political exile abroad, she, like some other female activists, encountered difficulties in channeling gender-specific claims through male-dominated political party organizations. She left the PCB and in 1986 published a theoretical criticism of Communist understandings of the "woman question." She served as president of São Paulo's State Council on the Status of Women, and then as special adviser to subsequent council presidents. In 2004 Alambert published a collection of articles entitled *A mulher na história–a história da mulher.*

See also **Brazil, Political Parties: Brazilian Communist Party (PCB).**

BIBLIOGRAPHY

Zuleika Alambert, "Zuleika Alambert, Dezembro de 1978," in *Memórias das Mulheres do Exílio,* edited by Albertina de Oliveira Costa, Maria Teresa Porciuncula Moraes, Norma Marzola, and Valentina da Rocha Lima (1980), pp. 48–68.

Additional Bibliography

Blay, Eva Alternam. "Um caminho ainda em construção: A igualdade de oportunidades para as mulheres." *Revista da USP* 49 (março/abril/maio 2001): 82-97.

French, John D. with Mary Lynn Pederson. "Women and Working-Class Mobilization in Postwar São Paulo, 1945-1948." *Latin American Research Review*, Vol. 24, No. 3 (1989): 99-125.

JUNE E. HAHNER

ALAMO, BATTLE OF THE.

Battle of the Alamo. On 6 March 1836, Mexican troops under General Antonio López de Santa Anna, stormed the Alamo, on the edge of San Antonio, Texas, killing or executing all of its defenders (over 180 men) and taking heavy casualties. The battle ended a thirteen-day siege of the former Franciscan mission, which had served most recently as a barracks and fortification for soldiers from the Flying Company of Alamo de Parras (1801–1825).

For Santa Anna, it had seemed essential to take the Alamo quickly, so that he could march deeper into Texas and quash an insurrection—one of several provincial rebellions against his centralized dictatorship. The defenders of the Alamo, commanded jointly by Lieutenant Colonel William Barret Travis and James Bowie, believed that significant reinforcements would come to their aid and they could defend the site. Their miscalculation and the disaster that followed helped rally Texans, who defeated Santa Anna at the decisive battle of San Jacinto on 21 April 1836 amid cries of "Remember the Alamo."

Of little military significance, the battle for the Alamo has remained important for its symbolic dimensions. Wartime propaganda and Texas enthusiasts turned the Alamo's Anglo-American defenders, including David ("Davy") Crockett, into heroic martyrs, celebrated in prose, poetry, and cinema, and the battle site itself into a national shrine. At least seven Texas Mexicans also fought to the death alongside the Anglos, but memory of their role was obliterated by the anti-Mexican passions of the battle's aftermath and largely forgotten until Mexican Americans began to become a prominent political and intellectual force in American life in the 1970s. Discovered by a Mexican coin collector in 1955, the diary of José Enrique de la Peña, a soldier in Santa Anna's army, generated controversy because it stated that Davy Crockett survived the battle and was executed afterward. While scholars still debate the diary's authenticity, the polemic surrounding the diary has led to studies on the relationship among culture, politics, and the memory of the Alamo.

See also **Santa Anna, Antonio López de.**

BIBLIOGRAPHY

Few scholars have examined this battle, but there are many popular accounts, most of the older ones highly romantic. Jeff Long, *Duel of Eagles: The Mexican and U.S. Fight for the Alamo* (1990), offers a sprightly and unrelentingly unsentimental view and a guidance to sources. For the mythic Alamo, see Susan Prendergast Schoelwer, *Alamo Images: Changing Perceptions of a Texas Experience* (1985), a smart, handsomely illustrated work. For the often overlooked Mexican side, including Santa Anna's self-defense and criticism by his officers, see Carlos E. Castañeda, ed. and trans., *The Mexican Side of the Texas Revolution* (1928).

Additional Bibliography

Crisp, James E. *Sleuthing the Alamo: Davy Crockett's Last Stand and Other Mysteries of the Texas Revolution.* New York: Oxford University Press, 2005.

Flores, Richard R. *Remembering the Alamo: Memory, Modernity, and the Master Symbol.* Austin: University of Texas Press, 2002.

Hardin, Stephen L. *Texian Iliad: A Military History of the Texas Revolution, 1835–1836.* Austin: University of Texas Press, 1994.

DAVID J. WEBER

ALARCÓN, MARTÍN DE (c. 1691–c. 1721). Martín, de Alarcón (flourished 1691–1721), governor of Coahuila (1705–1708) and governor of Coahuila and Texas (1716–1719). Alarcón's expedition, in 1718 and 1719, to aid Spaniards on the Neches River in east Texas and monitor the French who entered Texas from Louisiana, led to the founding of the Mission San Antonio de Valero (the Alamo) and a *villa* (a Spanish town) at present-day San Antonio. These institutions became the nucleus of Spanish influence in the province of Texas. Before his service in northern New Spain, Alarcón was a soldier of fortune in Oran; he also served in the Spanish navy and was a sergeant major in the Guadalajara militia of New Spain (1691) and an *alcalde mayor* (a local appointed magistrate) and captain of Jacona and Zamora (Michoacán).

See also **Texas.**

BIBLIOGRAPHY

Fritz Leo Hoffmann provides the most thorough information about Alarcón; see especially the introduction to his translation of Fray Francisco Céliz, *Diary of the Alarcón Expedition into Texas, 1718–1719* (1935), pp. 18–27, and "Alarcón, Martin de," in *The Handbook of Texas,* vol. 1 (1952), p. 24. Also: Oakah L. Jones, Jr., *Los Paisanos: Spanish Settlers on the Northern Frontier of New Spain* (1979), pp. 41–42.

Additional Bibliography

Foster, William C. *Spanish Expeditions into Texas, 1689-1768.* Austin: University of Texas Press, 1995.

ADÁN BENAVIDES JR.

ALASKA.   *See* **Pacific Northwest.**

ALBÁN, LAUREANO (1942–). Laureano Albán (*b.* 9 January 1942), Costa Rican poet. Born in Santa Cruz de Turrialba, Costa Rica, Albán is best known for the poetry he wrote after leaving Costa Rica for Spain in 1978. That is especially true of *Herencia del otoño* (1980; *Autumn's Legacy,* 1982) winner of Spain's coveted Adonais Prize for poetry and the Costa Rican Prize for literature. *El viaje interminable* (1983; *The Endless Voyage,* 1984) was awarded the First Prize of Hispanic

Culture by the Ministry of Spanish Culture. Albán's dedication to poetry began at fifteen when he and the Costa Rican poet Jorge Debravo formed the Turrialba group. In the 1960s he created the Costa Rican Writers Circle, published his first book of poems, *Poemas en cruz* (1962), and went on to establish the transcendentalist literary movement with his wife, the poet Julieta Dobles, and two younger Costa Rican poets, Ronald Bonilla and Carlos Francisco Monge. His English translator, Frederick Fornoff, describes his view of poetry as "a vehicle through which the poet carries his audience beyond the limited, circumstantial nature of human experience to the world of transcendent intuition that is universally confirmable through and only through poetry." Alban's work has been translated into French and Hebrew as well as English. He published *Infinita memoria de América* in 1991 and *Los nocturnos de Julieta* the following year. In 1995 Alban published *Encyclopedia of Wonders (Enciclopedia de maravillas)*, an encyclopedia on the history of literature written in poetry.

See also **Literature: Spanish America.**

BIBLIOGRAPHY

Arnoldo Mora Rodríguez, "La poesía religiosa de Laureano Albán," in *Káñina* 9, no. 1 (1985): 81–86.

Frederick Fornoff, "La poética de ausencia en Laureano Albán," and Amparo Amoros, "Una metafísica del mito originario: La poesía de Laureano Albán," in *Iberoamericana* 53 (1987): 138–139, 331–361.

Juan Manuel Marcos, "La poesía de Laureano Albán" in *Hispanofila* 32, no. 94 (1988): 69–77.

Additional Bibliography

Debravo, Jorge, and Erick Gil Salas. *Poesía turrialbena, 1960-1999: Antología*. San José, Costa Rica: Editorial Universidad Estatal a Distancia, 2000.

ANN GONZÁLEZ

ALBERDI, JUAN BAUTISTA (1810–1884). Juan Bautista Alberdi (*b*. 29 August 1810; *d*. 19 June 1884), Argentine diplomat, political philosopher, and constitution maker. Perhaps Alberdi's most salient trait was that he did not fit the usual image of the Latin American nation builder. He was a sullen and somewhat timid man who spent most of his adult life away from his native land and who was devoid of eloquence and leadership qualities. Yet because he had a powerful mind and an acute sense of reality, Alberdi was able to influence his contemporaries to such an extent that he is rightly considered one of modern Argentina's founding fathers. The constitution of 1853 is essentially a reflection of his political creed, and it was his ideas that largely prevailed when the process of national unification culminated in 1880 and the country began to transform itself into one of the wealthiest and most dynamic in Latin America. At this time, too, Argentina was on the way to becoming the most Europeanized nation in the region as a result of an uninterrupted flood of immigration. This was a key development with which the name Alberdi is inextricably associated.

HISTORICAL SETTING

This remarkable statesman was born the same year that the Argentine independence movement began. At that time the total area of the new nation (more than a million square miles) was populated by fewer than 400,000 people. For this reason, and because the population centers were isolated and remote from one another, Argentines referred to their land as the "desert." Long little-regarded by Spain, it had developed along a pattern of disunity. Originally it had been settled from different and unrelated points in the neighboring territories, and it had been further divided by the political and economic systems imposed by the metropolis. As a consequence, Argentina had grown up as a polarized colony. On the one hand, there was the port city of Buenos Aires, which after its opening to transatlantic trade late in the eighteenth century, was economically and culturally oriented toward Europe. On the other, there were the cities of the interior, which had remained satellites of other colonial economies such as that of present-day Bolivia. This cleavage reflected not only conflicting interests, but also diverse social arrangements and lifestyles.

By setting up a "national" government in 1810 without first consulting the provinces, the porteños (people of the port city of Buenos Aires) further complicated the situation and so paved the way for the period of internal strife and anarchy that followed. Buenos Aires wanted unity, but only if the provinces accepted its supremacy. The provincial caudillos, for their part, rejected centralization under *porteño* rule, favoring instead local autonomy under a loose federal system. Total disintegration might have been Argentina's fate had it not been for the rise of a strong man, Juan Manuel de Rosas, who governed with an iron hand between 1829 and 1852. He paid lip service to federalism, because in that way he would not have to share the income generated by the Buenos Aires customhouse with the provinces. But Rosas exercised authority over the country as a whole, more so than anyone before him. He also symbolized the traditionalist, nativist reaction that set in against the liberal and "exotic" ideas of Bernardino Rivadavia, who had attempted to modernize the country during the previous decade.

EARLY YEARS

Alberdi arrived in Buenos Aires from his native Tucumán in 1824. He was a weak, poor youngster who had lost both parents. But he had family connections and had been awarded a scholarship to study in the College of Moral Sciences of the University of Buenos Aires, recently founded by Rivadavia. Young Alberdi's ambition was to become a lawyer.

Alberdi indulged in too much outside reading, however, and for this reason was a poor student; it took him a long time to achieve his professional goal. But the delay gave him the opportunity to witness the emergence of Rosas, develop personal contacts with him and other caudillos, and most importantly, join the "generation of 1837," a group of intellectuals largely born after 1810. These young men were strongly influenced by romanticism, the new literary and political movement that Esteban Echeverría had introduced from France in 1830. They formed a literary salon in June 1837, at one of whose meetings Alberdi read his first important paper, an attempt to interpret Argentine reality in terms of romantic ideology. On this occasion he also dismissed Rivadavia as doctrinaire and proclaimed that Rosas's power was legitimate.

Nevertheless, when Rosas's dictatorship tightened shortly afterward, the salon had to go underground (under the name "May Association"), and its members later had to seek refuge in Montevideo, Uruguay. Here Alberdi was finally able to obtain his law degree and begin a profitable practice. Having turned against the dictator like most of his colleagues, he became involved in the literary warfare that the exiles waged for the liberation of their

country. In addition, he supported the military campaign of the Uruguayan anti-Rosas faction and its French allies. But these activities led nowhere, and he felt increasingly disappointed. When a victorious pro-Rosas Uruguayan army laid siege to Montevideo in 1843, he realized that he had no taste for the life of a soldier. Alberdi left for Europe, where he met Argentina's most illustrious exile, General José de San Martín, the hero of national independence. Upon returning to the Americas, Alberdi chose Chile as his haven, settling there in April 1844.

ALBERDI AND NATIONAL ORGANIZATION

By this time Alberdi was a man of note among Argentine exiles. His articles and pamphlets were well known, and his analyses and political opinions were widely commented upon and discussed. He had the opportunity to put them to work when, in 1852, a coalition led by provincial caudillo Justo José Urquiza ousted Rosas and called a convention to draw up a new constitution. Alberdi wrote a book especially for the occasion, commonly called *Bases,* which rapidly turned into the most influential of its time. It was the convention delegates' chief source of information on constitutional matters.

Unsurprisingly, therefore, the new constitution, promulgated on 25 May 1853, largely followed Alberdi's recommendations. Seeking to reconcile Argentina's warring factions, it provided for a federal system of government similar to that of the United States, but it also included significant adaptations to Argentina's peculiar needs. According to Alberdi, Argentina had to set aside "its ridiculous and disgraceful mania for the heroic" and move forward along the path of material progress. It had to promote the advance of learning and instruction in general, build railroads and navigable canals, attract foreign capital, and encourage and facilitate the colonization of the lands of the national domain. Above all, there was Alberdi's most celebrated aphorism, "to govern is to populate." Argentina had to promote immigration (especially of hardworking Anglo-Saxons) in order to transform the "desert" into a source of wealth and abundance. All of this required writing into the constitution the fundamental principles of economic liberalism, which the delegates did, including a remarkable bill of rights guaranteeing liberty, equality, the right to work and trade, and the civil rights of aliens.

NATIONAL UNIFICATION

Another feature of the constitution was the stipulation that Buenos Aires should be the capital of the republic and that the income from customs was to belong to the nation. This was unacceptable to Buenos Aires, and as a result Argentina now split into two separate states: the city of Buenos Aires and its province and the inland Argentine Confederation. Urquiza remained as head of the latter, and Alberdi broke with his own Buenos Aires associates—including Domingo F. Sarmiento and Bartolomé Mitre—in order to serve him through a diplomatic mission to Europe, to which he went without setting his foot in the territory of the confederation. He spent seven years as a diplomat and a writer, defending the integrity of Argentina against Mitre's policies. To him, *mitrismo* was *rosismo* in disguise, just as Rosas's dictatorship had simply been a prolongation of colonial practices.

In 1861 Mitre's forces defeated the Confederation at Pavón; Alberdi lost his position the following year. But although he remained in Europe, Alberdi did not retire to private life; rather, he continued to write about Argentine problems, albeit not always accurately, as was the case with the Paraguayan War (1865–1870). The criticisms that he directed against the Buenos Aires government on this occasion showed that he was not well informed; furthermore, he was dubbed a traitor to the fatherland. Because of this, and because he had to contemplate how his enemies rose to power while he aged perceptibly in exile, he lived through bitter days. This is clearly reflected in his writings, wherein he began to justify his actions with an eye on posterity.

By the late 1870s, however, things began to change in the distant fatherland. There was an upsurge of provincial opposition to *porteño* domination, and a native of Tucumán, Nicolás Avellaneda, was elected president. Alberdi's followers thought that the time was ripe for his political comeback and elected him to congress. He arrived in Buenos Aires in 1879. By this time, however, he was a tired man of sixty-nine who could not even read his own speeches. Therefore, he could not give a good account of himself. But he was able to witness the triumph of his ideas about national unification, for it was during his Buenos Aires sojourn that the port city finally became part of the Argentine federal republic as its capital, as the 1853 constitution had called for.

LAST YEARS

Defeat did not silence Alberdi's critics, who fiercely opposed the diplomatic appointment that the Argentine government proposed to bestow upon him in 1881. It was obvious that his compatriots would never give him the wide recognition that he deserved. Disillusioned and disappointed, Alberdi expatriated himself, living again in France. He died there three years later, surrounded by a few friends. He had never married.

In 1889, by popular request, his remains were brought back to Buenos Aires, where they were buried in an impressive ceremony. The most prominent representatives of the local and national government were not present.

See also **Argentina, Constitutions; War of the Triple Alliance.**

BIBLIOGRAPHY

On Alberdi's ideas, see José Luis Romero, *A History of Argentine Political Thought* (1963). On Alberdi himself, most of the literature is in Spanish. The best biographical study is Jorge M. Mayer, *Alberdi y su tiempo* (1963). For a scholarly edition of Alberdi's most important work, see Mayer's edition of *Las "Bases" de Alberdi* (1969).

Additional Bibliography

Herrero, Alejandro. *La política en tiempo de guerra: La cultural política francesa en el pensamiento de Alberdi (1837-1852)*. Remedios de Escalada, Pcia. de Buenos Aires: Ediciones de la UNLA, 2006.

López Gottig, Ricardo. *Los fundadores de la república: Juan Bautista Alberti, Nicolás Avellaneda, Esteban Echeverría, Bartolomé Mitre, Guillermo Rawson, Domingo F. Sarmiento*. Buenos Aires: Grito Sagrado Editorial: Fundación Friedrich A. von Hayek, 2006.

Terán, Oscar. *Las palabras ausentes: Para leer los escritos póstumos de Alberdi*. Buenos Aires: Fondo de Cultura Económica, 2004.

JOSÉ M. HERNÁNDEZ

ALBERNI, PEDRO DE (1745–1802).

Pedro de Alberni (*b.* 1745; *d.* 11 March 1802), Spanish soldier and explorer. Alberni, a native of Tortosa, Catalonia, joined the Barcelona-based Catalonian Volunteers in 1767. Following the Sonora Expedition of 1767–1771 in Mexico, he served in Jalisco and Nayarit, where he married Juana Vélez of Tepic. In 1782, Alberni was promoted to captain of the First Company of Catalonian Volunteers. Between 1789 and 1793 he commanded his unit on several expeditions to the Pacific Northwest. He established a Spanish base for the expeditions at Nootka Sound on Vancouver Island. As troop commander, Alberni assigned Catalonian Volunteers to assist in the mapping of the Spanish claim to the coast of Alaska and the Pacific Northwest prior to the Nootka Sound Convention that led to Spain's loss of the area. He made friends with the Nootka Indians and compiled a small dictionary of 633 words in their language and their Spanish equivalents. While military commander of California, Alberni died at Monterey and was buried at Mission Carmel. Port Alberni on Vancouver Island is named for him.

See also **Catalonian Volunteers.**

BIBLIOGRAPHY

Joseph P. Sánchez, *Spanish Bluecoats: The Catalonian Volunteers in Northwestern New Spain, 1767–1810* (1990).

Additional Bibliography

Higueras, Dolores. "Pedro Alberni y los voluntarios de Cataluña en Nutka 1790-1792." In *Nootka: regreso a una historia olvidada*, edited by Mercedes Palau de Iglesias. Madrid: Ministerio de Asuntos Exeriores de España, Dirección General de Relaciones Culturales y Científicas, 1998.

Soler Vidal, Josep. *California, la aventura catalana del noroeste*. Mexico City: Libros de Umbral, 2001.

JOSEPH P. SÁNCHEZ

ALBERRO, FRANCISCO DE.

Francisco de Alberro, governor and commander in chief of the province of Venezuela (1677–1682). Alberro was appointed to both posts by the royal decree of 11 August 1675 after he gave 28,000 pesos to meet the needs of the monarchy. This marked the beginning of a series of appointments that were made in exchange for monetary gifts to help meet the colonial administration's economic needs. While in office he enforced the royal decree abolishing the use of Indians as personal servants. He also promoted wall-building and fortification projects in the cities of La Guaira and Caracas, both undertaken simultaneously after the French pirate François Grammont's attack on the port of La Guaira in June 1680.

At the end of Alberro's term, his successor, Diego de Melo Maldonado, convoked a trial of residence, as was the custom. In voluminous records Alberro is accused of abuse of power, illegal money collecting, unwarranted seizures, and carelessness and negligence in the performance of his duties.

BIBLIOGRAPHY

On colonial administration, see José Gil Fortoul, *Historia constitutional de Venezuela*, vol. 1, 4 (1954), and Guillermo Morón, *Historia de Venezuela*, vol. 1 (1971).

Additional Bibliography

Rosas González, Otilia. *El tributo indígena en la provincia de Venezuela*. Caracas: Historiadores, S.C., 1998.

INÉS QUINTERO

ALBERTO, JOÃO (1897–1955). João Alberto (*b.* 16 June 1897; *d.* 26 January 1955), prominent Brazilian political figure. As a young artillery officer, Alberto participated in the Prestes Column that traversed Brazil's interior during much of the 1920s. Alberto eventually broke with Prestes, joining the Revolution of 1930 that brought Getúlio Vargas to power. Appointed federal intervenor in São Paulo by Vargas in 1930, Alberto served less than a year in the post. In 1932 he was appointed chief of police in the Federal District, where he created the special police to repress groups and individuals opposed to Vargas. Alberto was elected to the National Constituent Assembly the following year as a representative from Pernambuco, affiliated with the Social Democratic Party (PSD). In 1935 Alberto entered the diplomatic service, discharging various duties in Europe and the Americas until 1942. With Brazil's entry in World War II, Alberto led the Coordenação da Mobilização Econômica, a newly created superministry tasked with wartime economic planning and industrial-policy formulation. Following the progressive weakening of Vargas's Estado Novo in 1944, Alberto once again led the Federal District police forces, until Vargas was removed from power in 1945. Vargas's return to the presidency in 1951 occasioned Alberto's return to government service in various positions, most prominently as the Brazilian representative to the General Agreement on Tariffs and Trade.

See also **Brazil, Revolutions: Revolution of 1930; Prestes Column.**

BIBLIOGRAPHY

Thomas E. Skidmore, *Politics in Brazil, 1930–1964* (1967).

Israel Beloch and Alzira Alves De Abreu, eds., *Dicionário histórico-biográfico brasileiro, 1930–1983* (1984).

WILLIAM SUMMERHILL

ALBIZU CAMPOS, PEDRO (c. 1891–1965). Pedro Albizu Campos (*b.* ca. 12 September 1891; *d.* 21 April 1965), president of the Puerto Rico Nationalist Party in the 1930s and figurative head of the island's struggle for independence. Albizu Campos was born in Ponce, the illegitimate son of a black mother and a white Spanish father. He excelled in his studies as a young man, obtaining a scholarship to attend college in the United States. While at Harvard, he was drafted to serve in the U.S. army, in which he was placed in a segregated regiment. He returned to Harvard Law School after the war and obtained his degree in 1923.

Back on the island that year, Albizu became active in the Nationalist Party, founded in 1922. In the final years of the decade, he traveled to several Latin American and Caribbean countries, advocating the cause of Puerto Rican independence before government leaders and thus internationalizing "the colonial question." Upon his return, he took over a divided movement that weakly opposed the U.S. presence on the island, began to criticize the nature of existing relations between Puerto Rico and the United States, and committed himself to end U.S. colonial domination through the use of force. Under Albizu's leadership (he was elected president in 1930), the Nationalist Party of the 1930s was pro-Hispanic, militant, and violent. Its membership reached nearly 12,000.

The activities of the Cadets of the Republic, the paramilitary arm of the Nationalist Party, led to frequent clashes with government authorities. In 1936 chief of police Francis Riggs was shot to death, and shortly thereafter two nationalist supporters were seized and killed by police. Albizu and seven others were arrested in connection with the assassination and accused of conspiring to overthrow the government of the United States. The court sentenced Albizu to imprisonment in a federal penitentiary, where he remained until 1947.

In a climate of economic uncertainty following the Depression and political persecution promoted by U.S. colonial authorities, violent confrontations continued in the late 1930s. The "Ponce Massacre" gained the most notoriety, as twenty-one persons, including two policemen, were killed in what had been planned as a peaceful march. The commotion arose when Nationalists, shortly after Albizu's conviction, decided to hold a parade in Ponce, despite the last-minute revocation of their permit to march. The demonstrators apparently carried no arms, although a shot provoked the police into firing at the crowd. An American Civil Liberties Union investigation concluded that the ensuing violence was the result of extremist agitation and lack of police restraint.

Albizu returned to the political scene as Puerto Rico debated the benefits of permanent association with the United States, following the approval of Public Law 600, the precursor to local self-government. In 1950 from the mountain town of Jayuya he was involved in the declaration of independence. In a simultaneous move, police headquarters and the Puerto Rican governor's residence were attacked, as was Blair House, the temporary home of the U.S. president in Washington. Albizu was again arrested and found guilty of attempted murder, illegal use of arms, and subversion. Governor Luis Muñoz Marín granted him conditional freedom in 1953.

In 1954 three young nationalists fired their guns at U.S. representatives while the House was in session, wounding six people. Again, Albizu was jailed, until declining health required his transfer to a hospital in 1964. Governor Muñoz pardoned him on 15 November 1964; he died shortly thereafter. Although many have rejected Albizu's glorification of violence to achieve the lofty ideal of independence, his unequivocal actions and fiery rhetoric have inspired nationalists of all persuasions for many decades.

See also **Puerto Rico, Political Parties: Overview.**

BIBLIOGRAPHY

Fernando Picó, *Historia general de Puerto Rico* (1988).

Luis A. Ferrao, "Pedro Albizu Campos, el Partido Nacionalista y el catolicismo, 1930–1939," in *Homines* 13, no. 2 (1989) and 14, no. 1 (1990): 224–247.

Carlos Rodríguez-Fraticelli, "Pedro Albizu Campos: Strategies of Struggles and Strategic Struggles," in *Centro de Estudios Puertorriqueños Bulletin* 4, no. 1 (1991–1992): 24–33.

Ruth Vassallo and José Antonio Torres Martinó, *Pedro Albizu Campos: Reflexiones sobre su vida y su obra* (1991).

Marisa Rosado, *Las llamas de la aurora: Acercamiento a una biografía de Pedro Albizu Campos* (1992).

Additional Bibliography

Ferrao, Luis Angel. *Pedro Albizu Campos y el nacionalismo puertorriqueño*. San Juan: Editorial Cultural, 1990.

Gutiérrez del Arroyo, Isabel. *Pedro Albizu Campos o la agonía moral: el mensaje ético de Pedro Albizu Campos*. San Juan: Editorial Causa Común, 2000.

TERESITA MARTÍNEZ-VERGNE

ALBUQUERQUE. Albuquerque, city of 448,607 inhabitants and metropolitan region of 712,000 (2000) at the foot of the Sandia Mountains in the Middle Rio Grande Valley of central New Mexico. Francisco Cuervo y Valdés, then governor of New Mexico, founded Albuquerque in the spring of 1706, naming the new *villa* for Francisco Fernández de la Cueva Enríquez, duke of Alburquerque, then viceroy of New Spain. (The extra *r* in the city's original spelling gradually disappeared with the arrival of Anglo settlers in the mid-nineteenth century.) The first settlers were 35 families, totaling 252 people, from the capital of Santa Fe about 60 miles to the north. In 1752 the population was 476, and it had reached only 763 by 1776.

Like the other *villas* in New Mexico, Albuquerque was a farming and ranching settlement on the far northern frontier of the Spanish Empire. Their distance from the viceregal administration and culture in Mexico City obliged them to forge a tightly knit, self-sufficient traditional culture, elements of which grace the New Mexican cultural landscape to this day. Following the Mexican-American War (1846–1848), the city became a part of the United States and began to establish commercial relations with the eastern United States. The arrival of the Atchison, Topeka, and Santa Fe Railway (which bypassed the rival city of Santa Fe) in 1880 solidified Albuquerque's position as the most important Borderlands city of the region. Between 1890 and 1900, the population nearly doubled, reaching 6,326.

See also **New Mexico.**

BIBLIOGRAPHY

Richard E. Greenleaf, "The Founding of Albuquerque, 1706: An Historical-Legal Problem," in *New Mexico Historical Review* 39, no. 1 (1964): 1–15.

Oakah L. Jones, Jr., *Los Paisanos: Spanish Settlements on the Northern Frontier of New Spain* (1979), esp. pp. 109–167.

Marc Simmons, *Albuquerque: A Narrative History* (1982).

Additional Bibliography

Casado Fuente, Ovidio. *Don Francisco Cuerbo y Valdés, gobernador de Nuevo México, fundador de la ciudad de Albuquerque*. Oviedo: Principado de Asturias, Instituto de Estudios Asturianos del C.S.I.C., 1983.

Cutter, Donald C. *España en Nuevo México*. Trans. Andrea Cutter. Madrid: Editorial MAPFRE, 1992.

Montgomery, Charles H. *Spanish Redemption: Heritage, Power and Loss on New Mexico's Upper Rio Grande*. Berkeley: University of California Press, 2002.

Reséndez, Andrés. *Changing National Identities at the Frontier: Texas and New Mexico, 1800–1850*. New York: Cambridge University Press, 2005.

Simmons, Marc. *Hispanic Albuquerque, 1706–1846*. Albuquerque: University of New Mexico Press, 2003.

J. DAVID DRESSING

ALBUQUERQUE, ANTÔNIO FRANCISCO DE PAULA (1797–1863). Antônio Francisco de Paula Albuquerque (*b.* 1797; *d.* 1863), Brazilian imperial statesman, senator, and Liberal politician. Albuquerque was educated in Germany and began his career in the military, serving in Mozambique, in Macao, and in the 1824 revolt in Pernambuco. He retired with the rank of lieutenant colonel in 1832. Albuquerque represented his home state, Pernambuco, in both the Chamber of Deputies and the Senate. He ran unsuccessfully for regent in 1835 and 1838. Albuquerque served in eight different cabinets: as minister of the treasury in 1830, 1831, 1832, 1846, and 1852; as minister of the empire, in 1832 and 1839; as minister of justice in 1839; as minister of war in 1844; and as minister of the navy in 1840, 1844, and 1846. He was appointed counselor of the state in 1850 and was awarded the title of viscount.

See also **Brazil: 1808-1889.**

BIBLIOGRAPHY

Miguel Archanjo Galvão, *Relação dos cidadãos que tomaram parte no governo do Brasil no periodo de março de 1808 a 15 de novembro de 1889* (1894), pp. 15–27; *Nôvo dicionário de história do Brasil* (1971), p. 37.

Roderick J. Barman, *Brazil: The Forging of a Nation, 1798–1852* (1988), pp. 180–181, 198–199.

Additional Bibliography

Barman, Roderick. *Citizen Emperor: Pedro II and the Making of Brazil, 1825-1891.* Stanford, CA: Stanford University Press, 1999.

Beattie, Peter M. *The Human Tradition in Modern Brazil.* Wilmington, DE: SR Books, 2004.

Schultz, Kirsten. *Tropical Versailles: Empire, Monarchy, and the Portuguese Royal Court in Rio de Janeiro, 1808-1821.* New York: Routledge, 2001.

JUDY BIEBER FREITAS

ALBUQUERQUE, MATIAS DE (1595–1647).

Matias de Albuquerque (*b.* 1595; *d.* June 1647), governor and *capitão-mor* of Pernambuco (1620–1626), thirteenth governor-general of Brazil (1624–1627), superintendent of war in Pernambuco and inspector and military engineer for the captaincies of the north (1629–1635). Born in Lisbon and baptized in the church of Loreto, Albuquerque was the younger son of Jorge de Albuquerque Coelho, third lord-proprietor of Pernambuco, and his second wife, Dona Ana, daughter of Dom Alvaro Coutinho, commander of Almourol. Later in life he changed his baptismal name, Paulo, to Matias in honor of his guardian, his father's first cousin, Matias de Albuquerque, viceroy of India (1591–1597), who was himself childless and named Matias as his heir. In 1604, after a papal dispensation was obtained because he was underage, young Albuquerque received a knighthood in the Order of Christ. In 1619, having served three years in North Africa, the Mediterranean, and the Straits of Gib-

raltar at his own expense, he was summoned to Madrid.

In March of 1620 Albuquerque was named governor and *capitão-mor* of his brother's (Duarte de Albuquerque Coelho) captaincy of Pernambuco, Brazil, and arrived there the following day. Three urgent problems awaited him in his new post. The first was the restoration of donatarial authority after almost a half-century of absenteeism on the part of the second, third, and fourth lords-proprietor of Pernambuco and after the last four governors-general had resided in his family's captaincy instead of in Bahia, the Brazilian capital. Second, there was the need to supply men, foodstuffs, and materials for the expanding Portuguese presence in northern and northeastern Brazil. Last, old defenses had to be rebuilt and new ones erected, and the local militias had to be trained to protect Pernambuco from threats of a Dutch attack. When the Dutch West India Company seized Bahia along with the governor-general, Diogo de Mendonça Furtado, in 1624, Albuquerque was named thirteenth governor-general of Brazil. From Pernambuco he helped wage war against the Dutch until the joint Spanish-Portuguese armada of 1625 succeeded in recapturing the Brazilian capital in May of that year. As governor-general, he continued to coordinate efforts to supply Bahia, put down Indian revolts in the interior of the northeast, and prevent Dutch reinforcements from establishing themselves in Baía de Traição in the neighboring captaincy of Paraíba.

On 18 June 1627, Albuquerque departed from Pernambuco for Portugal. During the next two years, while he was in that kingdom and in Spain, he penned a number of important memorials to the crown on such varied topics as navigation in the Atlantic and Brazil's fortifications, sugar industry, and lack of coinage. Because of reports of plans of another Dutch attack on Portuguese America, Albuquerque was sent back to Brazil in 1629, arriving there on 18 October. This time, he was given a new post, free from the control of the governor-general—that of superintendent of war in Pernambuco and inspector and military engineer for the captaincies of the north. Four months later, on 15 February 1630, the Dutch West India Company's force of approximately sixty-seven ships and 7,000 men attacked Pernambuco. By 3 March they had control of the towns of Olinda and Recife and the adjoining island of Antônio Vaz. Albuquerque rallied his outmanned and outgunned forces, and for the next two years, from his strategically located headquarters at the Arraial do Bom Jesus three miles away from both Olinda and Recife, he kept the Dutch, who were superior in numbers, hemmed in and unable to profit from the captaincy's rich sugar plantations. He was attempting to follow the successful policy that had enabled the Portuguese to recover Bahia from the Dutch in 1625.

But this time no Spanish-Portuguese armada arrived to challenge Dutch control of the sea. With the desertion by April 1632 of several important Brazilian soldiers and the arrival of substantial reinforcements from Europe, the Dutch soon expanded up and down the coast of Pernambuco and other captaincies to the north. The Portuguese fought back, but to little avail. By the end of 1634, the Dutch controlled the coast from Rio Grande do Norte to the Cape of Santo Agostinho, and a great number of Portuguese settlers had made peace with them. In 1635, Porto Calvo, the Arraial do Bom Jesus, and Fort Nazaré were captured, and much of the surrounding rich sugar land was in Dutch hands. Albuquerque and over 7,000 Portuguese settlers, their families, and slaves were forced to retreat to the southernmost part of the captaincy to what is now the state of Alagoas. In late 1635, Dom Luis de Rojas y Borgia, a former governor of Panama, landed with 2,500 soldiers in Alagoas, replacing Albuquerque as head of the forces fighting the Dutch. Albuquerque continued by land to Bahia before returning to Portugal in 1636. Blamed for the loss of Pernambuco, he was imprisoned in the Portuguese border town of Castelo da Vide. In late 1640, his place of incarceration was moved to Lisbon's Castelo de São Jorge. Soon after the acclamation of the Duke of Bragança as King João IV on 1 December 1640, Albuquerque was freed.

He pledged his loyalty to Portugal's new monarch and, because of his military background, was made a member of the newly established Council of War and given the post of *mestre de campo general* (commander in chief) of the army that was being raised to defend the Alentejo. In that province he continued to train the Portuguese troops and help with the fortifications. He was also active in the early fighting and was given the post of commander of the troops (*governador das armas*) in the Alentejo, the

first of three times he held that position. However, Albuquerque was soon imprisoned again, suspected of treason because his brother, the fourth lord-proprietor of Pernambuco, had been in Madrid when the Portuguese revolution began and remained there and because Albuquerque was a close relative of several of those involved in the conspiracy of 1641 against King João IV. Eventually his innocence was established, and he was restored to full honors and made a member of the Council of State. On 26 May 1644, he led Portuguese troops to victory at the battle of Montijo in Spanish Extremadura—the first significant Portuguese victory in a war that lasted almost thirty years, until peace was finally signed in 1668. Soon after his victory, Albuquerque was named the first count of Alegrete. At about that time, he married Dona Catarina Barbara de Noronha, sister of the future first count of Vila Verde. They had no children. Albuquerque retired from active duty late in 1646 and died the following year.

See also **Pernambuco.**

BIBLIOGRAPHY

Helio Vianna's pioneering *Matias de Albuquerque* (1944) has been updated by Francis A. Dutra, *Matias de Albuquerque: Capitão-mor de Pernambuco e Governador-Geral do Brasil* (1976). Details of the struggle between donatarial authority and centralized government are found in Francis A. Dutra, "Centralization vs. Donatarial Privilege: Pernambuco, 1602–1630," in *Colonial Roots of Modern Brazil*, edited by Dauril Alden (1973). Defense problems are discussed in Francis A. Dutra, "Matias de Albuquerque and the Defense of Northeastern Brazil, 1620–1626," in *Studia* 36 (1973): 117–166. A valuable contemporary account of Portuguese America during Albuquerque's first tour of duty in Brazil is Franciscan Frei Vicente Do Salvador, *História do Brasil 1500–1627*, 5th ed. (1965). The Dutch campaigns of the 1630s are described by Albuquerque's brother, an eyewitness and fourth lord-proprietor of Pernambuco, Duarte De Albuquerque Coelho, *Memorias Diarias de la Guerra del Brasil por discurso de nueve años empeçando desde el de M.D.C. XXX* (1654). Also useful for understanding Brazil during this time period is Ambrósio Fernandes Brandão's classic account, *Diálogos das Grandezas do Brazil* (1618). There is a second edition of this title edited by José Antônio Gonsalves De Mello (1966); a good English translation is titled *Dialogues of the Great Things of Brazil*, translated and annotated by Frederick Holden Hall, William F. Harrison, and Dorothy Winters Welker (1987).

FRANCIS A. DUTRA

ALCABALAS. Alcabalas (sales taxes), first imposed in Spain in 1342, in Mexico in 1574, and later in the sixteenth century in other areas of the Spanish Indies. Initially all goods were taxed at 2 percent of their sale price, but in 1632 another 2 percent was added for the empire-wide Union of Arms. In 1635 the tax was increased in Mexico by still another 2 percent in order to finance the Spanish Main fleet (Armada de Barlovento). Although the rate fluctuated periodically in times of financial exigency and was widely differentiated after 1775, 6 percent prevailed in most areas of the Spanish Empire at the end of the colonial period. Certain items were exempt from the sales tax, including arms, dowries, booty, medicine, paintings, books, corn, and grain; clerics, Indians, and certain regions of the Indies were also exempt.

Until the beginning of the eighteenth century, *alcabala* collection was in semiprivate or private hands, normally those of the cities or the merchant guild (Consulado), whose officials periodically contracted with viceregal authorities on the amounts to be paid to the royal treasury for collection rights. In Peru in 1724 and Mexico in 1764, however, royal treasury officials began collecting sales taxes directly. By 1800 *alcabalas* generated close to 600,000 pesos annually in Peru and 2.5 million in Mexico.

See also **Public Sector and Taxation.**

BIBLIOGRAPHY

Recopilación de leyes de los reynos de las Indias, 4 vols. (1681; repr. 1973); libro VIII, título XIII.

Fabian De Fonseca and Carlos De Urrutia, *Historia general de Real Hacienda*, vol. 2 (1849).

Additional Bibliography

Grosso, Juan Carlos, and Juan Carlos Garavaglia. *La región de Puebla y la economía novohispana: Las alcabalas en la Nueva España, 1776–1821*. Puebla, Mexico: Benemérita Universidad Autónoma de Puebla, 1996.

JOHN JAY TEPASKE

ALCALDE. Alcalde, a local magistrate. *Alcaldes ordinarios* were municipal magistrates normally elected each January 1 for a one-year term by the town council (Cabildo or Ayuntamiento). Cities had two *alcaldes;* small towns normally had one. Although elected by a *cabildo*, *alcaldes* usually were not also *regidores* of the council.

Alcaldes were men of substance in the community. While many were native to the town, outsiders who married into prominent families could become *alcaldes*. Early *alcaldes* were routinely *encomenderos* or their relatives, but later *hacendados*, other property owners, and eventually merchants served.

Alcaldes exercised first-instance jurisdiction in civil and criminal cases within the municipality's boundaries, but they could not issue sentences of death or mutilation. Appeals from their decisions were heard by an *alcalde mayor* or *corregidor*, or by the audiencia within whose jurisdiction the town lay. Despite their judicial responsibilities, *alcaldes* were not required to have formal training in jurisprudence. In some cases *alcaldes* fulfilled non-judicial responsibilities assigned by the *cabildo*. In others, indigenous *alcaldes* were name by the *corregidor* to dilute the political power of *curacas*, ethnic leaders.

See also **Audiencia.**

BIBLIOGRAPHY

Clarence H. Haring, *The Spanish Empire in America* (1947).

Additional Bibliography

Dym, Irene, and Christophe Belaubre, eds. *Politics, Economy, and Society in Bourbon Central America, 1759–1821*. Boulder: University Press of Colorado, 2007.

Río, Ignacio del. *La aplicación regional de las reformas borbónicas en Nueva España: Sonora y Sinaloa, 1768–1787*. México: Universidad Nacional Autónoma de México, Instituto de Investigaciones Históricas, 1994.

Taylor, William B. *Magistrates of the Sacred: Priests and Parishioners in Eighteenth-Century Mexico*. Stanford, CA: Stanford University Press, 1996.

MARK A. BURKHOLDER

ALCALDE MAYOR. Alcalde mayor, the chief administrator of a territorial unit known as an *alcaldía mayor*. *Alcaldías mayores* were provincial units of varying size and significance. The term was used most frequently in New Spain, where there were about two hundred of these units in the 1780s. In Peru similar provincial units were termed *corregimientos.*

The *alcalde mayor* had judicial, administrative, military, and legislative authority. Judicial appeals from his decisions were heard by an *audiencia.*

Alcaldes mayores usually were appointed for terms of three to five years. Originally the viceroys named most *alcaldes,* but in 1677 the crown started selling appointments, thereby greatly reducing the viceroys' patronage. The sales, moreover, resulted in the *alcaldes mayores* placing even more pressure on the native populations of their districts in order to recoup their investment and make a profit. Working closely with wholesale merchants, they routinely required the natives to purchase animals and merchandise from them (*repartimiento de mercancías* or *bienes*) at inflated prices, and in some cases they forced the natives to sell their produce to them at below market prices.

The abuses of the *alcaldes mayores* and their lieutenants led to their replacement in most parts of the empire by intendants in the late eighteenth century.

See also **New Spain, Viceroyalty of.**

BIBLIOGRAPHY

Clarence H. Haring, *The Spanish Empire in America* (1947).

Peter Gerhard, *A Guide to the Historical Geography of New Spain* (1972).

Additional Bibliography

Baskes, Jeremy. *Indians, Merchants, and Markets: A Reinterpretation of the Repartimiento and Spanish-Indian Economic Relations in Colonial Oaxaca, 1750–1821.* Stanford, CA: Stanford University Press, 2000.

Dym, Irene, and Christophe Belaubre, eds. *Politics, Economy, and Society in Bourbon Central America, 1759–1821.* Boulder: University Press of Colorado, 2007.

Río, Ignacio del. *La aplicación regional de las reformas borbónicas en Nueva España: Sonora y Sinaloa, 1768–1787.* México: Universidad Nacional Autónoma de México, Instituto de Investigaciones Históricas, 1994.

Taylor, William B. *Magistrates of the Sacred: Priests and Parishioners in Eighteenth-century Mexico.* Stanford, CA: Stanford University Press, 1996.

MARK A. BURKHOLDER

ALCARAZ, JOSÉ ANTONIO

(1938–2001). José Antonio Alcaraz (*b.* 5 December 1938), Mexican composer. Alcaraz studied at the National Conservatory in Mexico and then pursued postgraduate studies at the Schola Cantorum in Paris, the summer courses for new music in Darmstadt, and the Opera Center in London. With his interest in music theater and mixed media, Alcaraz has composed some very significant works, including the aleatoric opera *Arbre d'or à deux têtes* for voice, piano, and toy instrument; an evening of theater music entitled *Qué es lo que faze aqueste gran roido, sol de mi antojo* (1983); and a series of profane madrigals for voice and piano. *De Telémaco* for soprano, flute, and piano (1985); *Toccata* for piano (1957); *Otra hora de junio,* a two-voice madrigal (1988); *D'un inconnu* for violin and voice (1973); and *Cuanta consagración para tan poca primavera* (1981) and *Aubepine* (1984) for four mezzo-sopranos. His ballet *Homenaje a Lorca* (1963) received a prize from the University of the Theater of the Nations in Paris.

Alcaraz wrote *Hablar de música* (1982), *Suave teatro* (1984), and *Al sonoro rugir del telón* (1988). He founded the Micrópera de Mexico and the Opera de Cámara of the National Institute of Fine Arts (INBA). He published *Reflexiones sobre el nacionalismo musical mexicano* in 1991 and *Carlos Chávez, un constanta renacer* in 1996. He was appointed as a research scholar at the Carlos Chávez National Center for Musical Research, Documentation, and Information. He died in Mexico City in October 2001.

See also **Music: Art Music.**

BIBLIOGRAPHY

Pauta (1982), p. 123; *X Foro internacional de música nueva* (1988), pp. 15, 44–45; *XIV Foro internacional de música nueva* (1992), p. 128.

Additional Bibliography

Estrada, Julio, ed. *La música de México.* 2 vols. Mexico City: Instituto de Investigaciones Estéticas, Universidad Nacional Autónoma de México, 1984–1988.

ALCIDES LANZA

ALCOHOLIC BEVERAGES. Long before

the Conquest, peoples of the Americas produced and consumed fermented beverages. These drinks became integral to the fabric of life, and withstood efforts to eliminate or replace them after the arrival of the Europeans. Some are still consumed today.

TRADITIONAL BEVERAGES

Chicha is a generic name for beverages made from grains or fruits. *Chicha* can be nonalcoholic, such as *chicha de quinoa,* which is simply a quinoa broth. But it is the fermented beverage that has had the most influence on Latin American history. Plantains, algarroba, palms, berries, cassava, sweet potatoes, and maize have been commonly used. The *chicha* from the Andean region is best known. To produce it, maize kernels were moistened, a diastase (often the saliva of women who chewed the kernels) and water added, and then the mixture was cooked.

(*Masato,* or the common manioc beer of the Amazon region, was made in essentially the same way.) Malting (letting grains germinate after soaking), akin to the European method of beer making, was another method of fermentation. The alcoholic content of *chicha* varied from 2 to 12 percent, depending on the type of maize and the fermentation process. Twentieth-century Peruvian cookbooks present standard recipes for some of the more traditional *chichas.*

Pulque was the Nahuatl *octli,* the "honey water" common to the cultures of central Mexico. Pulque was also a ritual drink, associated with certain gods and ceremonial practices. As with *chicha,* the process of pulque production was simple. The stem of the maguey plant was cut, allowing the juice (*aguamiel*) to collect in the cavity of the plant. Traditionally this

Quechua women drinking chicha, Urcos, Peru, c. 2003. "Chicha," a drink usually made of fermented corn, has been part of the Incan and Peruvian diet since ancient times. © ROBERT VAN DER HILST/CORBIS

was extracted from the plant with a long tube, and placed in wooden or leather containers. The addition of already prepared pulque initiated the fermentation process, which could last from a week to a month. Variants of pulque (*pulque curado*) might include nuts, fruits, and herbs as sweeteners and flavorings. Frances Calderón De La Barca, perhaps Mexico's most famous nineteenth-century observer, wrote: "It is said to be the most wholesome drink in the world, and remarkably agreeable when one has overcome the first shock occasioned by its rancid odor." With distillation (a process introduced after 1492), the juice of the maguey also produced mescal and tequila, beverages that became increasingly popular in the nineteenth and twentieth centuries. In the twenty-first century, tequila enjoys worldwide acclaim.

Chicha and pulque survived the Conquest and competition from imported beverages. They were admirably suited to the geography and culture of the Andes and Mexico. Ingredients were readily available and production was simple. This popularity was also due to their ceremonial use, as offerings to the gods to insure good harvests and to provide strength during battle. They were believed to have a range of magical and relating qualities that insured the continuation of the community and the culture. They were also valued for medicinal purposes, useful in combating infection and disease. The nutritional quality of *chicha* and pulque has been disputed since the sixteenth century, but modern nutritional analysis has demonstrated that both could, depending on ingredients used and the manner of preparation, contain significant amounts of protein, thiamine, riboflavin, niacin, vitamin C, calcium, and iron, in addition to other nutrients.

BEER

Europeans introduced their own beer—made from barley—soon after the Conquest, receiving licenses to manufacture it in Mexico as early as 1544. Despite early protection from the crown and efforts to limit consumption of Indian beverages, European beers made slow inroads in Latin America until the late nineteenth century, when a new wave of European immigration prompted changes in alcoholic consumption patterns. Regions receiving the largest numbers of immigrants experienced the most profound changes, but throughout Latin America, even those areas with dense indigenous populations, beer gradually became more popular. In Mexico in the twentieth century, the local and regional characteristics of beer have given way to uniform taste and quality as the three giant producers, La Cervecería Cuauhtémoc, Cervecería Moctezuma, and Cervecería Modelo, have dominated the industry. In Brazil, where beer has almost achieved the status of a national drink, the same process of centralization of production and distribution has occurred with the giant breweries of Brahma, Antártica, and Kaiser.

WINE

Wine was the staple drink of the Spanish diet in the sixteenth century, and the preference for wine was carried to the New World. Despite the centrality of wine in the Iberian diet, however, it did not become the universal drink of Latin America. In Mexico, the production of wine had a sporadic history, as mercantilist legislation attempted to prevent its production. Disruptions in trade and the need for wine for religious and medicinal purposes led to occasional permission to grow grapes for wine, but it was not until the late nineteenth century that the industry developed in earnest. And it was only after World War II that Mexico developed a wine industry comparable to that of Peru, Chile, and Argentina. Peru, the center of Spanish civilization in South America, supported a flourishing wine industry in its coastal valleys. It hoped to maintain a monopoly of production and supply, but distribution problems led to the development of vineyards in other countries. Eventually, Chile, Argentina, and southern Brazil emerged as important producers. Wine, especially among the immigrant populations of the late nineteenth and early twentieth centuries, became common in the diet. Since the 1960s, wine production both for domestic consumption and for export has increased. Chile became an important wine exporter in the mid 1990s, followed by Argentina in the early twenty-first century. Chile has a climate and soil suitable for both red and white wine varieties, and its area devoted to cultivation has doubled. Since 2003 the volume of Argentine wine exports has increased twofold, and its value has tripled. Argentina is the fifth largest wine producer in the world, and is known for its trademark Malbec.

CONSUMPTION AND ITS CONTROL

The introduction of distilled beverages had a profound impact on drinking habits in Latin America.

High-alcohol spirits were substituted for low-alcohol traditional beverages and the more expensive European wines and beers. References to drinking habits from the sixteenth to the twentieth centuries suggest widespread indulgence, at least compared with what was deemed socially acceptable. Grape brandy, first imported from Spain, then produced at the successful vineyards established in Peru, Chile, Argentina, and Mexico, provided spirits for increasingly enthusiastic consumers. It did not, however, equal the popularity of *aguardiente,* known generally as *cachaça* or *aguardente* in Brazil, a spirit made from distilling the juice of sugarcane. The addition of citrus and other flavorings to the beverage helped create variety. Sugar, wherever it was grown in Latin America, was the basis for alcohol production. In the case of the Caribbean, sugar—and its products of molasses and rum—became one of the foundations of trade patterns linking New England, Europe, West Africa, and Latin America. The Spanish islands (and Venezuela) soon became known for light, dry rums, while the English islands produced heavier, darker rums.

Drinks made from these spirits have entered the global cocktail lexicon, and taken their place among martinis and manhattans as popular beverages. Two of the most favored are daiquiris, a drink of Caribbean origin, made from rum, fruit juice, and sugar, and margaritas, made from tequila, lemon or lime juice, sugar, and salt. A rival in taste if not in popularity is the pisco sour, a Peruvian concoction of pisco (a grape brandy), citrus juice, and sugar. Brazilian cocktails have not yet achieved the international reputation of margaritas, daiquiris, and pisco sours, but caipirinhas and batidas, made from Aguardiente, fruit juice, and sugar, are worthy contenders.

Widespread use (and concern about abuse) of alcoholic beverages in colonial society led to attempts to regulate their production, distribution, and consumption. As early as 1529, the Spanish crown considered banning the production of pulque, the prelude to a succession of laws that sought to limit or ban certain types of alcoholic beverages. In some cases the crown's economic motive was clear; in other cases it was hidden behind laments over the moral decay of society. By the eighteenth century, cane brandy had come under as much attack as the local beverages of *chicha* and pulque. It was the "demon rum" of the colonies that was blamed for

most social problems. Excessive drinking disrupted family life, slowed economic production, and caused a range of medical problems. Indians and mestizos drank the most, but Spaniards as well consumed excessive amounts of cheap cane brandy.

In Mexico, *chinquirito,* a type of cane brandy, was widely consumed, though it was only one of a dozen or so "prohibited beverages." Extremists argued that high mortality rates in the Indian population were largely due to excessive consumption of *chinquirito.* Compared with this noxious drink, some officials thought that the traditional pulque was "innocent, healthful, medicinal, and necessary." Produced in small stills throughout central Mexico, *chinquirito* prompted a century-long effort to curtail its production, distribution, and consumption. The trade in *chinquirito* had reached a level that negatively affected the wine and brandy producers of Andalusia. As fewer wines and spirits were transported across the Atlantic, taxes shrank and the maritime capacity of Spain was reduced.

At stake in the regulatory effort was control over a vast economic activity. In Mexico City alone there were over 1,500 shops, known by many different names, selling alcoholic beverages. The potential for taxing and licensing income was substantial. One eighteenth-century solution was to centralize control through the awarding of monopolies for production and distribution. Here the administrative history of spirits finds comparison with that of tobacco, meat, and other colonial products. In Colombia, this included the regulation of anise, which was the most popular local flavoring for *aguardiente.* As with other monopolistic efforts, success was often elusive. The availability of ingredients and the simple, inexpensive technology required for production undermined the most thorough legislation. Moreover, because local taverns provided income and were important public spaces for Latin America's nonelites, Mexicans resisted colonial officials' attempts at regulation.

The political explanation for the control of alcoholic beverages invariably pointed to the social and health problems related to drinking, even though medical thought continued to argue in the late eighteenth century that alcohol was important for health, especially in hot regions. One important issue, from the sixteenth through the twentieth

Harvesting agave bulbs for tequila, Mexico, 1996.
Juice of the agave plant forms the basis of several alcoholic
beverages, including tequila, which is popular not only in
Mexico but throughout the world. © DANNY LEHMAN/CORBIS

century, was excessive drinking among Indians,
blacks, and *castas*.

Alcoholic consumption among Indians before
the Conquest was associated with religious ceremonies; the availability and distribution of alcoholic beverages was controlled by politics and custom. After the Conquest, drinking became more
widespread, leading to accusations by Europeans
that drunkenness was extensive among Indians.
By the late eighteenth century, there were carefully
articulated theories explaining Indian susceptibility
to alcohol due to natural temperament, though
consumption was at times regulated in Indian communities by social and religious customs that curtailed widespread alcoholic abuse.

The concern over Indian drinking intensified in
the late nineteenth and early twentieth centuries.

From Mexico to Bolivia, Indian drinking was equated with character and genetic weaknesses. Alcoholism among Indians was referred to as a grave national
problem, and began to call forth the efforts of political
reformers and educators. It was said to weaken countries economically, physically, and morally. More progressive interpretations, evident by the end of the
nineteenth century, saw Indian alcoholism as another
attempt by ruling groups to enslave the Indian. Education promised hope for eradicating alcoholism, and
the new schools of revolutionary Mexico in the 1920s
initiated campaigns to combat drinking, emphasizing
the detrimental effects of excessive pulque consumption. When this did not work, reformers considered
enacting plans similar to the Volstead Act, which
ushered in prohibition in the United States. Nevertheless, consumption of fermented and distilled beverages continued, often to an extent that troubled the
national conscience.

Employers throughout the Americas in the late
nineteenth and early twentieth centuries were concerned about alcohol and drinking. For them,
drinking was an obstacle to securing a dependable
labor force: Workers failed to show up to their posts
on Mondays, instead taking the day off in what
became known as the *San Lunes* holiday, or they
left their posts early at the end of the week to drink.
The physical and psychological dependency on *chicha* and pulque, as well as on the new beverages
introduced after 1492 has been singled out as the
cause of everything from crime to malnutrition.

Pre-Conquest alcoholic beverages retained their
cultural significance into the twentieth century.
Methods of preparation and rituals of consumption
remained intact following the introduction of European beers and wines, though cheap, distilled beverages, especially cane brandy, have provided a popular
alternative to the traditional beverages since the early
sixteenth century.

See also **Aguardiente de Pisco; Cuisines; Wine Industry.**

BIBLIOGRAPHY

Introductions to the history of pulque and *chicha* can be
found in Oswaldo Gonçalvez De Lima, *El maguey y el
pulque en los códices mexicanos* (1956); Mario C.
Vázquez, "La chicha en los paises andinos," *América
Indígena* 27 (1967): 265–282; A. Paredes, "Social
Control of Drinking Among the Aztec Indians of
Meso-America," in *Journal of Studies on Alcohol* 36,
no. 9 (1975): 1139–1153; and C. Morris, "Maize

Beer in the Economics, Politics, and Religion of the Inca Empire," in *Fermented Food Beverages in Nutrition,* edited by Clifford F. Gastineau, William J. Darby, and Thomas B. Turner (1979), pp. 21–35. Gilma Lucia Mora De Tovar provides a thorough institutional history of cane brandy in *Aguardiente y conflictos sociales en la Nueva Granada durante el siglo XVIII* (1988). For comparisons with Mexico, see Gilma Lucia Mora De Tovar, *El aguardiente de cana en México, 1724–1810* (1974). The social history of drinking is presented in William B. Taylor, *Drinking, Homicide, and Rebellion in Colonial Mexican Villages* (1979); Michael C. Scardaville, "Alcohol Abuse and Tavern Reform in Late Colonial Mexico City," in *The Hispanic American Historical Review* 60, no. 4 (1980): 643–671; and John C. Super, *Food, Conquest, and Colonization in Sixteenth-Century Spanish America* (1988).

Additional Bibliography

Chalhoub, Sidney. *Trabalho, lar e botequim: O cotidiano dos trabalhadores no Rio de Janeiro da belle époque.* 2nd Edition. Campinas, Brazil: Editora da Unicamp, 2001.

Curto, José C. *Enslaving Spirits: The Portuguese-Brazilian Alcohol Trade at Luanda and Its Hinterland, c. 1550–1830.* Boston: Brill, 2004.

Godoy, Augusto, Teófilo Herrera, and Miguel Ulloa. *Más allá del pulque y el tepache: Las bebidas alcohólicas no destiladas indígenas de México.* México: Universidad Nacional Autónoma de México, Instituto de Investigaciones Antropológicas, 2003.

Llano Restrepo, María Clara, and Marcela Campuzano Cifuentes. *La chicha, una bebida fermentada a través de la historia.* Bogotá: Instituto Colombiano de Antropología, 1994.

Moncaut, Carlos Antonio. *Pulperias, esquinas y almacenes de la campana bonaerense: Historia y tradición.* City Bell, Argentina: Editorial El Aljibe, 1999–2000.

Orlove, Benjamin, and Ella Schmidt. "Swallowing Their Pride: Indigenous and Industrial Beer in Peru and Bolivia (in Symposium on Food and Cuisine)." *Theory and Society* 24, no. 2 (April 1995): 271–298.

Pardo, Oriana, and José Luis Pizarro T. *La chicha en el Chile precolombino.* Santiago: Editorial Mare Nostrum, 2005.

Ramírez Rancaño, Mario. *Ignacio Torres Adalid y la industria pulquera.* México, D.F.: Universidad Nacional Autónoma de México, 2000.

Rodríguez Ostria, Gustavo, and Humberto Solares Serrano. *Sociedad oligárquica, chicha y cultura popular: Ensayo histórico sobre la identidad regional.* Cochabamba, Bolivia: Editorial Serrano, 1990.

Venâncio, Renato Pinto, Henrique Carneiro, and Andréa Lisly Gonçalves. *Alcohol e drogas na história do Brasil.* São Paulo: Alameda, 2005.

Viqueira Albán, Juan Pedro. *Propriety and Permissiveness in Bourbon Mexico.* Translated by Sonya Lipsett-Rivera and Sergio Rivera Ayala. Wilmington, DE: Scholarly Resources, 1999.

JOHN C. SUPER

ALCORIZA, LUIS (1920–1992). Luis Alcoriza (*b.* 1920; *d.* 1992), Mexican film director. Born in Badajoz, Spain, into a theatrical family, Alcoriza performed in various plays as a child. After the fall of the Spanish Republic in 1939, the Alcoriza family immigrated to Mexico, where Luis continued his acting career in films in the 1940s. He also worked as a screenwriter for director Luis Buñuel on the acclaimed films *El gran calavera* (1949), *Los olvidados* (1950), *El bruto* (1952), and *El ángel exterminador* (1962). He made his directorial debut in 1960 with the film *Los jóvenes.* Throughout the 1960s, Alcoriza directed a number of noted pictures, which constitute the most important film productions of the era: they include *Tlayucan* (1961), *Tiburoneros* (1962), *La puerta* (1968), and *Mecánica nacional* (1971), for which he received the Mexican film academy award, the Ariel, for best director. Other Alcoriza films include *Las fuerzas vivas* (1979) and *Lo que importa es vivir* (1987).

See also **Buñuel, Luis.**

BIBLIOGRAPHY

Luis Reyes De La Maza, *El cine sonoro en México* (1973).

E. Bradford Burns, *Latin American Cinema: Film and History* (1975).

Carl J. Mora, *Mexican Cinema: Reflections of a Society: 1896–1980* (1982).

John King, *Magical Reels: A History of Cinema in Latin America* (1990).

DAVID MACIEL

ALCORTA, DIEGO (1801–1842). Diego Alcorta (*b.* November 1801; *d.* 7 January 1842), Argentine philosopher, physician, and politician. Born in Buenos Aires and educated there at the Colegio de la Unión del Sur and the University (1823–1827), Alcorta was more successful as an educator than as a politician. He was a founder of the Sociedad Elemental de Medicina in 1824 and became one of the pioneering surgeons of the Hospital de Hombres in 1828, a year after completing his medical studies. Also named principal professor of philosophy at the university that year, he dominated the philosophy department for fourteen years. An entire generation of writers and intellectuals had their first brush with European liberal writings under Alcorta's tutelage. His favorite texts came from the French Enlightenment, a reflection of the vogue for rationalism and utilitarianism in Buenos Aires in the 1820s. Among his students were Juan Bautista Alberdi, Juan María Gutiérrez, José Mármol, Felix Frías, and Vincente Fidel López, the shining lights of the Generation of 1837. As a deputy in the Chamber of Representatives, Alcorta voted in 1832 against the reinstatement of the caudillo Juan Manuel de Rosas as governor of Buenos Aires. In 1833 he became vice rector of the University of Buenos Aires, but was ousted by Rosas supporters a year later. This did not prevent him from helping to write a blueprint constitution, which was dismissed in the emerging caudillo order as too liberal. Alcorta died in Buenos Aires.

See also **Colegio Nacional de Buenos Aires.**

BIBLIOGRAPHY

Carlos I. Salas, *Apuntes biográficos del Dr. Diego Alcorta* (1889).

Juan Maria Gutiérrez, *Origen y dessarrollo de la enseñanza pública superior en Buenos Aires* (1915).

JEREMY ADELMAN

ALDAMA Y GONZÁLEZ, IGNACIO DE

(?–1811). Ignacio de Aldama y González (*d.* 19 June 1811), Mexican insurgent leader. A lawyer who engaged in commerce, Aldama became magistrate of his native San Miguel el Grande. His brother Juan had joined Miguel Hidalgo, who launched an armed rebellion against the colonial regime on 16 September 1810. When Hidalgo reached San Miguel at the end of that month, Aldama signed an accord recognizing the authority of the insurgent leader. He subsequently joined the insurgent forces, eventually attaining the rank of field marshal. In February 1811, when Hidalgo and other insurgent leaders decided to retreat to

the United States in search of aid, Aldama was sent, in the company of Friar Juan Salazar, as ambassador to Washington. Both men were captured in San Antonio Béjar, along with 100 bars of silver. Taken to Monclova, Aldama was tried and condemned to death. After submitting a disavowal of his actions, he was shot.

See also **Allende, Ignacio.**

BIBLIOGRAPHY

José María Miquel I Vergés, *Diccionario de insurgentes* (1969), 15–16.

Hugh M. Hamill, Jr., *The Hidalgo Revolt*, 2d ed. (1970).

Lucas Alamán, *Historia de Méjico*, vol. 1 (1985).

Carlos María De Bustamante, *Cuadro histórico de la Revolución Mexicana*, vol. 1 (1985).

VIRGINIA GUEDEA

ALDAMA Y GONZÁLEZ, JUAN DE

(1774–1811). Juan de Aldama y González (*b.* 3 January 1774; *d.* 26 June 1811), Mexican independence leader and corevolutionary of Father Miguel Hidalgo. A Mexican creole *hacendado* anxious for recognition and social improvement, Aldama joined the Regimiento de Dragones Provinciales de la Reina, based in San Miguel el Grande, during the 1795 reorganization of the army of New Spain. Beginning service as a lieutenant, he had been promoted to the rank of militia captain by 1808. Involved in the Querétaro conspiracy (1810), Aldama traveled to the town of Dolores to inform Father Hidalgo and Captain Ignacio Allende that the plot had been exposed. He was present during the first moments of the Hidalgo revolt, when prisoners were liberated from the Dolores jail and the district subdelegate was arrested.

From the beginning, Aldama attempted to maintain moderation among the rebels and opposed excesses such as property destruction and violence against Spaniards. Following the rebel capture of Guanajuato and the occupation of Valladolid, Morelia, he was promoted to lieutenant general. After the rebel defeat at Puente de Calderón (17 January 1811), Aldama retreated north with other principal rebel leaders. He was captured on 21 March 1811 and tried by royalist court-martial at Chihuahua. Despite his claims that he was a minor participant, Aldama was condemned to death and executed by firing squad.

See also **Mexico, Wars and Revolutions: War of Independence.**

BIBLIOGRAPHY

Lucas Alamán, *Historia de México desde los primeros movimientos que prepararon su independencia en el año de 1808 hasta la época presente,* 5 vols. (1849–1852; repr. 1942).

Hugh M. Hamill, *The Hidalgo Revolt: Prelude to Mexican Independence* (1966).

Brian R. Hamnett, *Roots of Insurgency: Mexican Regions, 1750–1824* (1986).

Additional Bibliography

Márquez Terrazas, Zacarías. *Proceso que se le instruyó a don Juan de Aldama en Chihuahua el mes de mayo de 1811.* Chihuahua: Gobierno del Estado de Chihuahua, 2000.

CHRISTON I. ARCHER

ALDANA, JOSÉ MARIA (1758–1810). José Maria Aldana (*b.* 1758; *d.* 7 February 1810), Mexican composer and violinist. Aldana began violin lessons while a choirboy at the cathedral in Mexico City. In 1775 he joined the cathedral orchestra but relinquished that post in 1788 when his duties as violinist at Mexico City's Coliseo theater, begun two years earlier, conflicted. In 1790 he was named the Coliseo's orchestra director, a position he held concurrently, after 1808, with leadership of the Mexico City choir school. Compositions such as his vesper psalms for the Office of the Dead and other sacred and secular works (*Boleras nuevas; Minuet de variaciones*) place Aldana among the best native composers of his day.

See also **Music: Art Music.**

BIBLIOGRAPHY

Robert Stevenson, *Music in Mexico: A Historical Survey* (1952).

ROBERT L. PARKER

ALDEIAS. Aldeias, Indian village settlements also known as *reduções. Aldeias* were Indian villages organized as missions by the regular clergy or colonial governors of Brazil. They were self-sufficient economic units that included the mission proper and the agricultural fields surrounding it. These mission villages stretched along the coast from the Amazon to the interior of southern and central Brazil. In Spanish America they were known as *reducciones.* Defeated Indians were often gathered into segregated fortified missions to facilitate conversion, pacification, and civilization. White merchants were not allowed into the *aldeias* without a special license. The missionaries tried to protect the Indians from mistreatment and enslavement by the white settlers, who disdained manual labor.

The most successful *aldeias* were established after 1549 by the Jesuits in Brazil. Since the Jesuits were few in number, the creation of permanent villages facilitated mass conversion. A handful of missionaries usually gathered scattered tribes into an *aldeia,* with a church, school, dormitory, kitchen, and warehouse, usually leaving one or two brothers behind to preside over these Christian settlements. To facilitate conversion of the entire tribe, evangelization usually aimed at converting the *caciques* (chiefs) and shamans first. The missionaries mastered the Tupi language, writing a dictionary, grammar, and catechism. The protection and gifts, as well as the religious ritual and music, offered by the Jesuit missionaries attracted the Indians. By 1655 the Jesuit Order was given complete control over all the Indian *aldeias* in Brazil.

Because of the threat of disease and enslavement, the missions were isolated from white settlements. For over two hundred years the Jesuits fought against Indian enslavement with the support of the crown. This resulted in white rebellion and Jesuit expulsions in 1662 and 1684. By the mid-seventeenth century the Jesuits had to compromise with the white settlers' desire for Indian labor by allowing a contract labor system for up to six months. The Jesuits began to arm their mission villages to protect the Indians from the slave-hunting expeditions (*bandeiras*) from São Paulo. In 1759 the Jesuit order was expelled from Brazil by order of the marquis of Pombal. With the expulsion of the Jesuits, the larger *aldeias* fell under the control of the

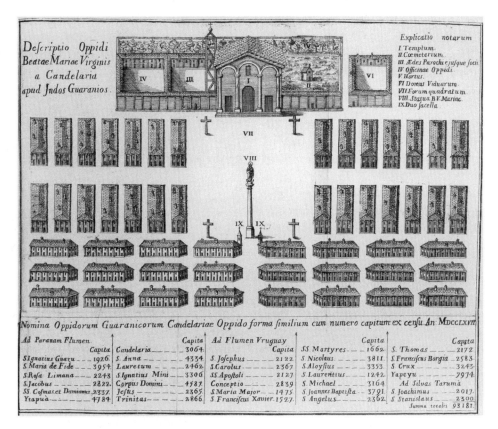

An aldeias, or Jesuit mission, in Paraguay, engraving from *De Vita et Moribus Tredecim Virorum Paraguaycorum* by Joseph Manuel Peramas, 1793 by Spanish School (18th century) (b/w photo). BIBLIOTHEQUE LES FONTAINES, CHANTILLY, FRANCE/ ARCHIVES CHARMET/ THE BRIDGEMAN ART LIBRARY

secular clergy, who incorporated the missions into the parish system; others were placed under secular directors until they were all disbanded by the end of the century.

Life was regimented in the *aldeias;* the ringing of bells summoned the Indians to pray, hear mass, study, and work in the fields. The Indians were often forced to accept Christianity and to perform manual labor for the missionaries. The congregation of the Indian tribes often facilitated the spread of diseases, such as smallpox and measles, which decimated whole tribes. Nonetheless, the *aldeias* provided a safe haven for many small tribes and helped to ensure Portuguese settlement and control of Brazil.

BIBLIOGRAPHY

John Hemming, *Red Gold: The Conquest of the Brazilian Indians, 1500–1760* (1978).

E. Bradford Burns, *A History of Brazil,* 2d ed. (1980).

John Hemming, *Amazon Frontier* (1987).

Additional Bibliography

Almeida, Maria Regina Celestino de. *Metamorfoses indígenas: Identidade e cultura nas aldeias coloniais do Rio de Janeiro.* Rio de Janeiro: Presidencia da República, Arquivo Nacional, 2003.

Fausto, Boris. *A Concise History of Brazil.* New York: Cambridge University Press, 1999.

Flores, Moacyr. *Reduções jesuíticas dos guaranis.* Porto Alegre: EDIPUCRS, 1997.

Pompa, Cristina. *Religião como tradução: Missionários, Tupi e Tapuia no Brasil colonial.* Bauru: EDUSC; São Paulo: ANPOCS, 2003.

PATRICIA MULVEY

ALEGRE, FRANCISCO JAVIER (1729–1788).

Francisco Javier Alegre (*b.* 12 November 1729; *d.* 16 August 1788), historian of the Jesuits in New Spain, Latinist, and literary critic. A Jesuit priest and teacher born in Veracruz of Spanish parents, Alegre is best known for his *Historia de la Provincia de la Compañía de Jesús de Nueva España*. In this four-volume work, Alegre chronicles the history of Jesuit missionary activity in New Spain from their arrival in 1572 to shortly before the suppression of the order in 1767. Alegre was known to be a brilliant teacher and writer with broad interests. He wrote several poetic works as well as a prodigious multivolume treatise on theology, *Institutionum theologicarum*, published posthumously in 1789. After the Jesuits of New Spain were banished to the Papal States in 1767, Alegre, along with several of his colleagues, lived the rest of his life in Italy and made a living as a tutor and librarian. One of the more original works of this period is his *Arte poético del Mon. Boileau*, a translation and extensive commentary on Nicolas Boileau's *L'art poétique*, published posthumously by Joaquín García Icazbalceta in 1889. This is an early instance of literary criticism from a decidedly Latin American perspective.

See also **Jesuits.**

BIBLIOGRAPHY

See Ernest J. Burrus and Feliz Zubillaga's critical edition of Alegre's *Historia de la Provincia de la Compañía de Jesús* (1956), esp. pp. 1–32 for a bio-bibliography. Allan Figueroa Deck studies Alegre as a precocious literary critic in *Francisco Javier Alegre: A Study in Mexican Literary Criticism* (1976).

Additional Bibliography

Abad, Diego de. *Francisco Javier Alegre y Diego José Abad: humanistas gemelos.* Edited by Julio Pimentel Alvarez. Mexico City: Universidad Nacional de México, 1990.

ALLAN FIGUEROA DECK

ALEGRÍA, CIRO (1909–1967).

Ciro Alegría (*b.* November 1909; *d.* February 1967), Peruvian novelist, essayist, and politician. A relative of the Argentine novelist Benito Lynch, in his youth, Alegría had as his first-grade teacher the *mestizo* César Vallejo, one of the most important Latin American poets of the twentieth century. Alegría lived for some time on his paternal grandfather's estate in Marcabal Grande, where he familiarized himself with the indigenous culture, camping with the natives at the edge of the jungle and listening to their tales.

Alegría was active in the American Popular Revolutionary Alliance (Alianza Popular Revolucionaria Americana—APRA), for which he was imprisoned in 1932–1933. Forced into exile from 1934 to 1960, he returned to Peru and was elected to the Peruvian Chamber of Deputies in 1963. While in exile Alegría lived and wrote in Santiago, Chile, winning prizes for his first three novels: *La serpiente de oro* (1935; The Golden Serpent), *Los perros hambrientos* (1938; The Hungry Dogs), and *El mundo es ancho y ajeno* (1941; Broad and Alien Is the World), which was honored by its American publisher Farrar and Rinehart. It subsequently was translated into twelve languages. In the 1940s Alegría lived in the United States, where he taught at several universities.

Revealing his concern for the marginalized members of Peruvian society, particularly the indigenous population, Alegría's novels demonstrate considerable artistic merit and are of great testimonial value. According to Mario Vargas Llosa, *Broad and Alien Is the World* is "the point of departure for modern Peruvian narrative literature and its author [is] our first classic novelist." Alegría cared little about novelistic structure and form, but was able to re-create with great skill the experiences and dialogue of indigenous peoples, achieving at his best considerable lyrical intensity.

See also **Literature: Spanish America; Peru, Political Parties: Peruvian Aprista Party (PAP/APRA).**

BIBLIOGRAPHY

Angel Flores, *The Literature of Spanish America* (1966–1969), vol. 4, pp. 245–258.

Emir Rodríguez Monegal, *Narradores de esta América* (1969), pp. 166–174.

Eileen Early, *Joy in Exile: Ciro Alegría's Narrative Art* (1980).

Additional Bibliography

Apaza, Felipe. *Alegría.* Trujillo, Perú: Algo te identifica, Editora Gráfica Real, 2001.

Poeta Movima (Nicomedes Suárez-Araúz). *Literary Amazonia: Modern Writing by Amazonian Authors.* Gainesville: University of Florida Press, 2004.

Varona, Dora. *La sombra del condor: biografía ilustrada de Ciro Alegría.* Lima: Diselpesa, 1993.

KEITH MCDUFFIE

ALEGRÍA, CLARIBEL (1924–).

Claribel Alegría (*b.* 1924), Salvadoran writer. An outstanding poet, Alegría pioneered feminism as well as the modernization of the Central American novel with her masterpiece, *Cenizas de Izalco* (Ashes of Izalco, 1965). Her middle-period works have been recognized for their testimonial writing about Salvadoran women. After the death of her husband, she has dedicated considerable time to writing poetry.

Although she was born in Nicaragua, Alegría was taken to El Salvador at age one. She was only seven when the *matanza* (massacre) of 1932—in which dictator Maximiliano Hernández Martínez assassinated 30,000 peasants in the space of a month—took place. She swore that one day she would write down everything she had witnessed. She studied at George Washington University in Washington, D.C., during the late 1940s and became one of the first Central American women to obtain a university degree. While in Washington she married Darwin Flakoll, with whom she wrote *Cenizas de Izalco,* which initiated a shift from poetry to narrative as the basic Central American literary form. Flakoll also translated this work in 1989. In the 1950s they moved to the small town of Deyá on the island of Majorca, Spain. They lived next to the English poet Robert Graves, and shared an expatriate life with well-known artists and writers. In 1980 Alegría moved to Nicaragua, where she worked on behalf of the Salvadoran people. She also cowrote with Flakoll her testimonial narrative about women, *No me agarrarán viva: La mujer salvadoreña en la lucha* (1983), translated by Amanda Hopkinson as *They Won't Take Me Alive: Salvadoran Women in the Struggle for National Liberation* (1984). Although roughly contemporaneous with the Latin American Boom authors, she has not received the critical attention they have in the English-speaking world.

Besides *Cenizas,* her books include *Sobrevivo* (1978), winner of the Casa de las Américas Award; *Álbum familiar* (1984), translated by Amanda Hopkinson as *Family Album* (1991); *Pueblo de Dios y de mandinga* (1985); *Luisa en el país de la realidad* (1987), translated by Flakoll as *Luisa in Realityland* (1987); *Umbrales* (1996); *Sorrow* (1999); and a tribute to Flakoll who died in 1995, *Soltando Amarras,* translated as *Casting Off* (2003). Alegria was awarded the Neustadt International Prize for Literature in 2006. Curbstone Press in Willimantic, Connecticut has been the steward and publisher of her works in the United States

See also **Literature: Spanish America.**

BIBLIOGRAPHY

María B. De Membreno, *Literatura de El Salvador* (1959).

Manlio Argueta, *Poesía de El Salvador* (1983).

José Coronel Urtecho, *Líneas para un boceto de Claribel Alegría* (1987).

Sandra Boschetto and Marcia McGowan, eds., *Claribel Alegría: An Anthology of Critical Essays* (1994).

Additional Bibliography

Barbas-Rhoden, Laura. *Writing Women in Central America: Gender and the Fictionalization of History.* Athens: Ohio University Press, 2003.

Craft, Linda J. *Novels of Testimony and Resistance from Central America.* Gainesville: University Press of Florida, 1997.

Velásquez, Antonio. *Las novelas de Claribel Alegría: Historia, sociedad y (re)visión de la estética literaria centroamericana.* New York: P. Lang, 2002.

ARTURO ARIAS

ALEGRÍA, FERNANDO (1918–2005).

Fernando Alegría (*b.* 26 September 1918; *d.* 29 October 2005), Chilean writer and scholar. Born and raised in Santiago, Chile, he moved to the United States in 1940. His creative works (fifteen novels and four volumes of short stories) have centered primarily on the historical reality of his native country, but have also focused on the relationships and divergences between the Latin American and North American cultures. He began his academic career as professor of Latin American literature at the University of California, Berkeley (1947–1967), and later taught at Stanford University, where in 1990 he was awarded an endowed chair in the humanities.

Three thematic concerns dominate Alegría's narrative work. The first is the literary representation of the founding fathers of Chile's social history, found in the biographical novels *Recabarren* (1938), *Lautaro, joven libertador de Arauco* (1943; Lautaro, a Young Liberator, 1944), and *Allende*

(1989). The second distinctive theme is the reevaluation of the historical and cultural experience of the Generation of 1938, developed in *Mañana los guerreros* (1964; Tomorrow the Warriors) and the autobiographical novel *Una especie de memoria* (1983; A Type of Memoir). Finally, he wrote a trilogy focusing on the picaresque misadventures of Chileans who come to work in the United States where they are later forced to confront their true identities vis-à-vis the contradictions of American society: *Caballo de copas* (1957; *My Horse González*, 1964), *Amerika* (1970; *The Funhouse*, 1986), and *La rebelión de los placeres* (1990; The Rebellion of the Placeres).

See also **Literature: Spanish America.**

BIBLIOGRAPHY

Juan Armando Epple, *Para una fundación imaginaria de Chile. La literatura de Fernando Alegría* (1987).

Nicolás Kanellos, ed., *Biographical Dictionary of Hispanic Literature in the United States* (1989), pp. 6–13.

Helmy Giacomán, ed., *Homenaje a Fernando Alegría* (1972).

Additional Bibliography

Epple, Juan Armando. *Actas de Palo Alto: La obra literaria de Fernando Alegría.* Santiago de Chile: Mosquito Editores, 2000.

Guerra-Cunningham, Lucía. "Historia y memoria en la narrativa Fernando Alegría." *Revista Chilena de Literatura*, 48 (Apr 1996): 23-38.

J. A. EPPLE

ALEIJADINHO (c. 1738–1814). Aleijadinho (Antônio Francisco Lisbôa; *b.* ca. 1738; *d.* 18 November 1814), Brazilian architect and sculptor. Born in the provincial capital of Villa Rica do Ouro Prêto, Aleijadinho was a product of colonial Brazil, where the baroque and rococo art and architecture of Minas Gerais was a vehicle of nativist expression; here Saint Michael the Archangel appeared in a profusion of feathers, and a dark-skinned Virgin Mary was portrayed as a *mestizo*. Contributing to this nativism was Antônio Francisco Lisbôa, known as Aleijadinho (the Little Cripple), whose prolific and distinctive work as an architect, sculptor, and decorator of Mineiro churches is emblematic of the era.

Church of São Francisco de Assis, 1766–1796 by Aleijadinho (Antonio Francisco Lisboa; 1738–1814) (photo), one of Aleijadinho's most important works. **OURO PRETO, MINAS GERAIS, BRAZIL/ PAUL MAEYAERT/ THE BRIDGEMAN ART LIBRARY**

Aleijadinho was the son of Manuel Francisco Lisbôa and a slave named Isabel; he had two full siblings. The year Aleijadinho was born, his father married another woman, by whom he had four legitimate children. Although his father recognized Antônio Francisco as his son, gave him his name, and brought him into his profession of builder and artisan, little documentation illuminates their relationship. His father may have learned his craft from family members in Portugal, because his brother, Antônio Francisco Pombal, was also an architect who built Mineiro churches; on their mother's side they were presumably related to the celebrated Portuguese architect João Antunes. In addition to working under his father's direction, Aleijadinho was taught design by the painter João Gomes Baptista.

Aleijadinho executed his first pieces in wood and stone at age fourteen and worked steadily at his craft until close to his death in Ouro Prêto at the age of seventy-six. He made effective use of

Brazil's native soapstone, which is relatively easy to carve when freshly cut. He often worked in conjunction with the painters Francisco Xavier Carneiro and Manoel da Costa Ataíde.

The church was the center of Mineiro social life and Aleijadinho's main patron. Eighteenth-century Portuguese church architecture was influenced by that of Bavaria and Austria, in part due to the cultural interchange resulting from the marriages of King João V (reigned 1707–1750) and the Marquês of Pombal to Austrian princesses. The Austrian-Bavarian influence is apparent in the churches of Minas, particularly those designed and decorated by Aleijadinho. Although Aleijadinho never left Brazil, printed engravings gave him a familiarity with European forms.

While Aleijadinho's body of work is immense, and he is known to have contributed to many projects as a subcontractor, his documented work is concentrated in Ouro Prêto, Sabará, São João del Rei, and Congonhos do Campo. His most important works are the churches of São Francisco in Ouro Prêto and São João de Rei, Nossa Senhora do Carmo in Sabará, and Bom Jesus de Matosinhos in Congonhos. This last church is a pilgrimage site graced by Aleijadinho's magnum opus, sixty-six wooden life-size figures that comprise an incomplete set of the stations of the cross (1796–1799) and twelve remarkable soapstone statues of the Old Testament prophets (1800–1805), arranged in a dramatic, ballet-like way on the entry terrace.

Much of this work was done under the handicap of a debilitating and painful disease that has been variously described as leprosy, syphilis, or a viral influenza contracted in 1777. It caused scarring, crippling, progressive loss of movement, and disfigurement, and gained for him the name by which he is best known, O Aleijadinho—little cripple. He lost his toes, his hands atrophied and shriveled, and he had to be carried to his work sites, where curtains shielded him from casual viewers. He executed the Congonhos prophets with chisel and mallet strapped to the stumps of his gnarled hands.

Details of Aleijadinho's life are provided by his mid-nineteenth-century biographer, Rodrigo José Ferreira Brêtas, who obtained information from Aleijadinho's daughter-in-law, Joana Francisca Lopes, in whose home the artist spent his last days. Among the known facts of Aleijadinho's personal life is that he had a son with a slave named Ana; Manuel Francisco Lisbôa was born circa 1775 and followed his father's profession.

More than a dozen Mineiro towns and Rio de Janeiro claim to possess statues, retables, pulpits, altars, doorways, windows, fountains, and buildings attributed to Aleijadinho. Some of the many items ascribed to him may have been done by his assistants and students. His most distinctive works are undoubtedly his sculptures, which Aleijadinho infused with his own suffering. Art historian Pál Kelemen wrote, "Aleijadinho carried Brazilian Rococo to its fullest flowering.... A rare human story lives in his masterpieces; his gift was genius."

See also **Architecture: Architecture to 1900.**

BIBLIOGRAPHY

No modern definitive biography of Aleijadinho exists. Researchers should begin with Rodrigo José Ferreira Brêtas, *Antônio Francisco Lisbôa—O Aleijadinho*, in *Revista do Arquivo Público Mineiro*, vol. 1 (1896): 163–174. The premier work by a great authority on Baroque art is Germain Bazin, *Aleijadinho et la sculpture baroque au Brésil* (1963). For the Latin American context see Pál Kelemen, *Baroque and Rococo in Latin America* (1967). A brief study that tackles some of the questions of authenticity of attributed works and has an abbreviated version of Brêtas is Sylvio De Vasconcellos, *Vida e obra de Antônio Francisco Lisbôa, O Aleijadinho* (1979). In a similar vein are Delson Gonçalves Ferreira, *O Aleijadinho* (1981); Fernando Jorge, *O Aleijadinho: sua vida, sua obra, seu génio*, 6th rev. ed. (1984); and Myriam A. Ribeiro De Oliveira, *Aleijadinho: Passos e Profetas* (1985). For an excellent photo essay on his magnum opus, see Hans Mann and Graciela Mann, *The Twelve Prophets of Aleijadinho* (1967). For Aleijadinho's place in Mineiro culture see the classic by Alceu Amoroso Lima, *Voz de Minas*, 2d rev. ed. (1946). Those seeking fuller listings of sources should consult the fine bibliographies by James E. Hogan (Librarian, College of the Holy Cross), "Antônio Francisco Lisbôa: 'O Aleijadinho': An Annotated Bibliography," in *Latin American Research Review* 9, no. 2 (1974): 83–94; and "The Contemporaries of Antônio Francisco Lisbôa: An Annotated Bibliography," in ibid., 138–45.

Additional Bibliography

Ferreira, Delson Goncalves. *O Aleijadinho*. Belo Horizonte: Rona Editora, 2001.

Jardim, Marcio. *O Aleijadinho: uma sintese histórica*. Belo Horizonte: Stellarum, 1995.

Straumann, Patrick, and Ferrante Ferranti. *L'Aleijadinho: Le lépreux constructeur de cathédrales. Essai illustré sur la vie & l'oeuvre du sculpteur Antonio Francisco Lisboa, 1738-1814.* Paris: Chandeigne, 2005.

FRANK D. MCCANN JR.

ALEM, LEANDRO N.

ALEM, LEANDRO N. (1842–1896). Leandro N. Alem was one of the founders of Argentina's Radical Civic Union Party (Unión Cívica Radical). He served as the party's president and was its principal leader from its founding until his own tragic death.

Alem was born on 11 March 1842, in Buenos Aires. His father, Antonio Alén, was a member of Argentina's Mazorca secret police during the dictatorship of Juan Manuel de Rosas (1835–1852) and was sentenced to death and hanged in a public square. His death brought public contempt on the family and deprived it of a regular income. Leandro, who was eleven years old when his father was executed, changed his last name to Alem. He left his law studies several times for service in the army (at Cepeda in 1859, at Pavón in 1861, and in the Paraguayan War in 1865) and finally earned his law degree in 1869.

Alem began his political career in the Autonomist Party and was elected deputy to the provincial legislature of Buenos Aires in 1872 and reelected two years later. Alem's most prominent roles prior to his founding of the Radical Civic Union Party were as founding member of the Republican Party in 1878 and as fervent opponent of the federalization of Buenos Aires in 1880. The Republican Party had split off from the Autonomist Party in opposition to the policy of conciliation of President Nicolás Avellaneda (1874–1880). After an initial success that took Alem to the legislature in 1878, the party dissolved when it was defeated in the elections for governor of the province of Buenos Aires that same year. In 1880, after the National Congress approved the law to federalize Buenos Aires and when the provincial legislature was debating it, Alem led the small minority that opposed federalization, giving one of the most passionate speeches of his political career in defense of the federal system.

After federalization was approved, Alem resigned from his party and withdrew from public life for almost a decade. He returned to politics in late 1889 when opposition began to form against President Miguel Juárez Celman (1886–1890). During the presidency of Julio A. Roca (1880–1886) and then during the subsequent presidency of Juárez, the National Autonomist Party was in government and dominated national politics. Except for brief participation in the presidential elections 1886, the opposition parties in Buenos Aires (the Mitrista, Autonomist, and Catholic parties) abstained from participating in elections during that decade, arguing that suffrage was not guaranteed. Rival political careers and struggles for leadership made it difficult for these groups to form a united front of opposition to the political dominance of the National Autonomist Party. The economic crisis that began in 1889 and intensified the following year and the involvement of younger generations of political leaders made it possible for the older politicians of Buenos Aires (Bartolomé Mitre, Aristóbulo del Valle, Bernardo de Irigoyen, Alem, and others) to work together temporarily. At the end of 1889, these leaders agreed to form a group called the Civic Union, a smoke screen for organizing a revolution to overthrow Juárez. The revolution took place in July 1890, and although the government withstood it, Juárez resigned in early August.

Alem was elected president of the Civic Union Party and entrusted with the political organization of the revolution. Juárez's resignation prompted internal divisions within the party concerning which strategy to follow. The Mitre faction chose to make an electoral pact with the National Autonomous Party for the presidential elections of 1892, while Alem, along with Bernardo de Irigoyen, led the faction that decided to form a party in opposition to the government and called it the Radical Civic Union. The party's initial stages were strongly marked by Alem's leadership, and under his guidance the party withstood strong opposition from the administration that emerged in after Juárez's resignation and which deployed an arsenal of resources against it. The Radical Civic Union Party ran candidates in national elections in the city and province of Buenos Aires and obtained a minority of representatives in the National Congress. Within Congress, the Radical representatives attempted to improve the electoral process and, above all, pushed for economic liberalism and free trade as opposed to the national government's preferred policy of industrial protection. But what most characterized the party was its public defense of the revolution in the pages of its principal newspaper, *El Argentino*, and the implementation of its ideas through a series of uprisings that kept the national government on edge. *El Argentino* joined together into a single voice traditional ideas of the political parties of Buenos Aires. The Radicals accused the government of monopolizing power, doing away with the representative system, eliminating political life, distorting the political traditions forged over the two preceding decades, interfering with the federal system by centralizing power in the hands of the national executive, and having thereby violated the national constitution. In their eyes, this situation legitimized revolutionary action to restore the nation's institutions.

The Radicals' principal revolutions took place during 1893 in the provinces of Santa Fe, San Luis, Buenos Aires, Corrientes, and Tucumán. Revolutionary defeats and electoral successes in the city and province of Buenos Aires triggered a series of disputes within the party between those who wanted to continue the revolutionary route and those who preferred to concentrate on competing within the context of elections. At the height of the dispute, Alem committed suicide on 1 July 1896. His followers were left confused, and the party, unsettled by internal pressures, dissolved and was later revived in the first decade of the twentieth century under the leadership of Alem's nephew, Hipólito Irigoyen. Alem's personality, courage, moral dictums, and suicide made him a legendary figure in Argentine politics.

See also **Argentina, Political Parties: Radical Party (UCR); Irigoyen, Bernardo de; Irigoyen, Hipólito.**

BIBLIOGRAPHY

Aguirre, Gisela. *Leandro N. Alem.* Buenos Aires: Planeta, 1999.

Peralta, Wilfrido R. *Historia de la Unión Cívica Radical: Su origen, su vida, sus hombres: Estudio político 1890 y 1916.* Buenos Aires: G. Pesce, 1917.

PAULA ALONSO

ALEMÁN VALDÉS, MIGUEL (1900–1983).

Miguel Alemán Valdés (*b.* 29 September 1900; *d.* 27 September 1983), president of Mexico (1946–1952). Alemán represents a notable political generation in twentieth-century Mexico. He was the first civilian to hold the presidency for a full term after a series of revolutionary generals, a feat that marked the beginning of the dominance of the professional politician in Mexico. His administration is remembered for the young, college-educated politicians appointed to his cabinet; for corruption in high office; for an emphasis on state-supported industrialization; for the reform of the government-controlled party, the Institutional Revolutionary Party (Partido Revolucionario Institucional—PRI); for the decline in the number of military officers in political office; for additions to the National University; and for increased ties between politicians and business elites. Alemán produced one of the two most influential political groups in contemporary politics (the Alemanistas), one that influenced decision making through the 1970s.

Alemán was born in the small rural community of Sayula, Veracruz, on Mexico's east coast, the son of a farmer who became a general during the Mexican Revolution (1910–1920). He studied in various towns before moving to Mexico City to enroll at the National Preparatory School. Alemán continued his studies at the National Autonomous University, where he received his law degree in 1928. Although he initially practiced law, specializing in labor disputes, he soon entered the political arena.

Alemán's first post was as an adviser to the Secretary of Agriculture and Livestock (1928–1930); he subsequently was appointed a judge of the Superior Court of the Federal District from 1930 to 1934. At the age of thirty-four, he represented his home state in the Senate, and two years later he achieved national recognition by winning election as governor of Veracruz (1936–1939). Before completing his term of office, Alemán was appointed head of General Manuel Ávila Camacho's presidential campaign in 1939. Following Ávila Camacho's successful bid for the presidency, Alemán was named minister of internal affairs (1940–1945), a position that he used to set his career on a course toward the presidency in 1946.

After leaving government, Alemán directed Mexico's tourism agency from 1961 until his death. He became a major figure in business circles, developing holdings in print and electronic media, including Televisa, Mexico's largest television network. The president's son, Miguel Alemán Velasco, has continued to be an important figure in Mexican television.

See also **Mexico, Political Parties: Institutional Revolutionary Party (PRI).**

BIBLIOGRAPHY

George S. Wise, *El México de Alemán* (1952).

Miguel Alemán, *Miguel Alemán contesta* (1975).

Luis Medina, *Civilismo y modernización del autoritarismo, historia de la Revolución mexicana* (1979).

Additional Bibliography

Krauze, Enrique. *El sexenio de Miguel Alemán.* Mexico City: Clio, 1999.

Martínez, María Antonia. *El despegue constructivo de la revolución: Sociedad y política en el alemanismo.* México: Miguel Angel Porrúa, 2004.

RODERIC AI CAMP

ALENCAR, JOSÉ MARTINIANO DE

(1829–1877). José Martiniano de Alencar (*b.* 1 May 1829; *d.* 12 December 1877), Brazilian writer, playwright, poet, and statesman. He was born in Messajana, state of Ceará, in northern Brazil. In 1850 he graduated from law school and founded the academic journal *Ensaios Literários,* of which he was the editor. Between 1851 and 1855, Alencar contributed to *Ensaios Literários* and other academic journals and also worked as a journalist on several daily newspapers. Most of his political career occurred between 1859 and 1877.

Alencar is considered to be one of the founders of Brazilian narrative writing. He cultivated Indianist and urban novels and introduced some of the most significant techniques observed in the Latin American narrative. As a romantic writer and an artist, he sought to underscore nationalistic themes and undermine Eurocentric aesthetics, which were so prevalent at the time. Before Alencar, Brazilian letters were characterized by Gongoristic classicism, which also dominated Portuguese literature. In all of his work, Alencar demonstrated an acute concern for language and the establishment of a true Brazilian linguistic expression, one devoid of all Portuguese influence.

Some of his most significant works are *O marquês de Paraná* (1856), an autobiographical piece; *O guarani* (1857), an interpretation of Brazilian colonial history in which he depicts the relationship between native Brazilians and the Portuguese colonizers; *O demônio familiar* (1857), a two-act comedy; *A noite de São João* (1857), a musical comedy, with music by Elias Lobo; *As asas de um anjo* (1860), a comedy in one prologue, four acts, and one epilogue. His novel *Lucíola* was first published in Paris in 1862. *As minas de prata* (1862, 1865–1866) is another historical novel.

The novel *Iracema* (1865), subtitled by Alencar "the myth of Ceará," is considered to be his chief work. Its leitmotiv is the beauty of Brazil. It is seen as the most nationalistic of his books, a work that has merited translations in several languages and is acclaimed as one of the world's most important classics of romantic literature. Alencar's narrative displays the Portuguese language as it was spoken in the Americas, with its own dynamic linguistic expressions, and with creative images and symbols that capture in great detail the unique beauty of Brazil. It is a romantic love story between an Indian princess, Iracema, and the white Martim; from their love is born Moacyr, whose name means "the son of pain." Iracema is also considered to be the first heroine of the Brazilian novel, for her death is depicted in the narrative as the sacrifice of her love for Martim. Alencar died in Rio de Janeiro.

See also **Literature: Brazil.**

BIBLIOGRAPHY

Claude Hulet, *Brazilian Literature,* vol. 1 (1974).

Academia Cearense De Letras, *Alencar 100 anos depois* (1977).

Assis Brasil, *O livro de ouro da literatura brasileira* (1980).

Renata Mautner Wasserman, "Re-Inventing the New World; Cooper and Alencar," in *Comparative Literature* 36 (1984): 130–152.

María Tai Wolff, "Rereading José de Alencar: the Case of *A Pata da Gazela,*" in *Hispania* 71 (December 1988): 812–819.

Laura Lynn Franklin, "Indianism in *Atala* of Chateaubriand and *Iracema* of José de Alencar: A Reappraisal" (Ph.D. diss., George Washington University, 1989).

Gustavo Pérez Firmat, *Do the Americas Have a Common Literature?* (1990), esp. p. 394.

Additional Bibliography

Rodrigues, Antonio Edmilson Martins. *José de Alencar: O poeta armado do século XIX.* Rio de Janeiro: Editora FGV, 2001.

ROSÂNGELA MARIA VIEIRA

ALESSANDRI PALMA, ARTURO (1868–1950).

Arturo Alessandri Palma (*b.* 20 December 1868; *d.* 24 August 1950), president of Chile (1920–1925 and 1932–1938). Educated at the University of Chile as a lawyer, he entered politics as a candidate of the Liberal Party (PL). A bombastic orator and tireless campaigner, he served in the Chamber of Deputies, in the Senate, and as a cabinet minister. Running on a reformist ticket, he was elected president in 1920. Alessandri had the bad luck to become president when Chile was suffering from a massive economic dislocation caused by the postwar collapse of the nitrate market.

Alessandri hoped to introduce numerous economic and social reforms, but his political opposition refused to pass his legislative program. Caught between widespread social unrest and an entrenched parliamentary opposition, Alessandri's reforms languished. The president found an unexpected ally in disaffected field-grade army officers who, distressed by their own wretched economic situation and the nation's suffering, intimidated the legislature into passing the reform package.

While initially pleased with his newfound support, Alessandri discovered that the officer corps was demanding that the legislature resign. Aware that he could not control them, Alessandri quit in January 1925, and a conservative military junta began to rule. When it became clear that the junta would attempt to elect a conservative to the presidency, junior army officers seized power and requested Alessandri to return. Upon doing so in March, Alessandri, ruling under the newly written Constitution of 1925, managed to pass certain reformist legislation. He resigned a second time in October, when he realized that he could not

control the minister of war, Carlos Ibáñez Del Campo, who would seize power in 1927.

Alessandri went into exile, joining the various plots to overthrow Ibáñez. After the dictator's fall, in 1931, Alessandri returned to Chile, where he unsuccessfully ran against Juan Esteban Montero Rodríguez for the presidency. In 1932, following the collapse of the Montero administration and the Socialist Republic, Alessandri became president for a second term.

Due to widespread unrest and the collapse of the economy, Alessandri's second term of office was only slightly less turbulent than his first administration. He nonetheless managed to govern the nation, stimulating the economy by encouraging the creation of national industries and supporting the construction of public and private housing. His brutal suppression of an abortive Nazi coup in 1938 alienated many people, contributing to the defeat of Gustavo Ross Santa María, Alessandri's candidate for the presidency.

An energetic and dynamic individual, Alessandri remained active in Chile's political life, serving as president of the Senate. A forceful leader, he may best be remembered as the man who appealed to the lower classes and who, using the powers provided by the 1925 Constitution, restored order to Chile and led it out of the Great Depression.

See also **Chile, Political Parties: Liberal Party; Chile, Constitutions.**

BIBLIOGRAPHY

Ricardo Donoso Novoa, *Alessandri, agitador y demoledor. Cincuenta años de historia política de Chile,* 2 vols. (1952–1954).

Arturo Alessandri Palma, *Recuerdos de gobierno,* 3 vols. (1967).

Robert J. Alexander, *Arturo Alessandri. A Biography,* 2 vols. (1977).

Paul W. Drake, *Socialism and Populism in Chile, 1932–1952* (1978).

Bill Albert, *South America and the First World War: The Impact of the War on Brazil, Argentina, Peru, and Chile* (1988), pp. 286–287, 311–312.

Additional Bibliography

Pinto Vallejos, Julio, and Verónica Valdivia Ortiz de Zárate. *Revolución proletaria o querida chusma?: Socialismo y*

Alessandrismo en la pugna por la politización pampina (1911-1932). Santiago: LOM Ediciones, 2001.

WILLIAM F. SATER

Stallings, Barbara. *Class Conflict and Economic Development in Chile, 1958–1973*. Stanford, CA: Stanford University Press, 1978.

WILLIAM SATER

ALESSANDRI RODRÍGUEZ, JORGE

(1896–1986). Jorge Alessandri Rodríguez (May 19, 1896–August 31, 1986) was a prominent Chilean businessman who served as a congressman, senator, and government minister before following in the footsteps of his father, Arturo Alessandri, and becoming president of Chile (1958–1964). His attempts to modernize the Chilean economy, including initiating an agrarian reform program, faltered, as did his attempts to end inflation caused by low copper prices and excessive demand for imports. He sought the presidency again in 1970 only to lose to Salvador Allende—whom he had barely defeated in 1958—in a three-way election. A strong anti-Marxist, he had opposed the Unidad Popular (UP, Popular Unity) government, which supported Allende, particularly in its attempt to seize control of the manufacture of newsprint.

Following his 1973 coup, General Augusto Pinochet selected Alessandri to serve as head of the Council of State. Alessandri ran afoul of Pinochet when he opposed the latter's desire to rule as a dictator and to use piecemeal measures to replace the old 1925 constitution. Believing that a return to constitutional rule was more democratic and would improve Chile's international image, Alessandri called for either revising the existing 1925 constitution or, failing that, writing a new constitution, which a national plebiscite would approve. Anxious to remain in power, Pinochet rejected Alessandri's proposition, which would have limited the junta to a single five-year term and mandated elections to seat a new congress and to select a new president. When Pinochet refused to accept his suggestions, the incorruptible Alessandri resigned his position on the Council of State.

See also **Chile: The Twentieth Century.**

BIBLIOGRAPHY

Collier, Simon, and William F. Sater. *A History of Chile, 1808–2002*, 2nd edition. New York: Cambridge University Press, 2004.

ALEXANDER, EDWARD PORTER

(1835–1910). Edward Porter Alexander (*b.* 26 May 1835; *d.* 28 April 1910), American diplomat. Following distinguished service as a Confederate artillery and engineering officer during the Civil War, Alexander successfully adapted to civilian life in business, railroading, and rice planting in Georgia and southern California. In 1897 President Grover Cleveland appointed him as arbitrator of the Costa Rica–Nicaragua boundary dispute under the terms of the Convention of San Salvador (27 March 1896). Alexander spent three years in Central America, mostly in San Juan del Norte (Greytown), Nicaragua, and rendered several decisions leading to a temporary agreement between the two states in 1900. Alexander's role in this affair reflected the rising U.S. presence in the diplomatic affairs of the isthmus.

See also **United States-Latin American Relations.**

BIBLIOGRAPHY

Douglas Southall Freeman, "Edward Porter Alexander," in *Dictionary of American Biography* (1928), vol. 1, pp. 164–166.

Ralph Lee Woodward, Jr., "Las impresiones de un general de las fuerzas confederadas sobre Centroamérica en los años finales del siglo XIX," in *Anuario de estudios centroamericanos* 4 (1979): 39–66.

RALPH LEE WOODWARD JR.

ALEXANDER VI, POPE (1431–1503).

Pope Alexander VI (*b.* 1 January 1431; *d.* 31 October 1503), pope (1492–1503). The Spaniard Rodrigo de Borja, the future Alexander VI, is notorious for his immorality and corruption. He fathered four illegitimate children and bribed other cardinals to elect him pope. As a protégé of King Ferdinand II of Aragon, Alexander issued a number of papal bulls sanctioning Spain's conquest and colonization of the New World. The papal bull of 1493 fixed the demarcation line of the future American empire along a circle which passed 100 leagues (3 nautical miles) west of the Cape Verde Islands and set the stage for the Treaty of Tordesillas (1494). Alexander also confirmed the new Spanish territories as a papal fief held by the crown (1493), granted the crown all tithes levied in the New World (1501), and charged the monarchs with christianizing the native populations. The responsibility for conversion was linked to Alexander's conferring upon Ferdinand and Isabella the title "the Catholic kings" (*los reyes católicos*) (1494).

See also **Catholic Church: The Colonial Period.**

BIBLIOGRAPHY

John H. Elliott, *Imperial Spain, 1469–1716* (1963), esp. pp. 52–100.

John H. Parry, *The Age of Reconnaissance* (1963).

Additional Bibliography

Chamberlin, Eric Russell. *The Bad Popes.* Gloucestershire: Sutton, 2003. Originally published in New York by Dial Press, 1969.

SUZANNE HILES BURKHOLDER

ALEXIS, JACQUES STÉPHEN (1922–
1961). Jacques Stéphen Alexis (*b.* 22 April 1922; *d.* April 1961), Haitian novelist, story writer, essayist, and physician. Son of historian, novelist, playwright, and diplomat Stéphen Alexis, Jacques Stéphen was born in Gonaïves during the American occupation of Haiti. Successor to the Marxist nationalism of Jacques Roumain, he eventually emerged to become the compelling exponent of his own lyrically infused, proletarian-identified vision of a uniquely Haitian "marvelous realism." Initially educated at the College Stanislas in Paris and the Institution Saint-Louis de Gonzague in Port-au-Prince, Alexis took an early, active part in Haitian avant-garde cultural and political life. A member of the Communist Party at sixteen, he later also wrote regularly, as Jacques la Colère, for the radical journal *La Ruche*. With René Depestre and other members of its editorial staff, he directly contributed to the success of the Revolution of 1946, which brought down the government of Élie Lescot. While pursuing his medical studies in Paris, Alexis moved in radical, left-wing, surrealist,

existentialist, and Antillean négritude circles. Thereafter, he traveled through Europe, the Middle East, Russia, and China. Returning to Haiti in 1954, Alexis published *Compère général soleil* (1955), the novel that established his reputation as one of his country's most important writers of fiction. *Les Arbres musiciens* (1957), *L'espace d'un cillement* (1959), and *Romancero aux étoiles* (1960), a collection of short stories, followed in quick succession to confirm that original assessment.

Representing a formal and thematic convergence between literary realism, Afro-Antillean cultural nationalism, Marxist anticolonialism, and a universalizing art that "is indissolubly linked to the myth, the symbol, the stylized, the heraldic, even the hieratic," Alexis's fiction strives for "a new balance . . . born of singularity and antithesis" (J. S. Alexis, "Of the Marvelous Realism of the Haitians," *Présence Africaine* [English edition], nos. 8–10 [1956]: 265). Extending the legacy of Jacques Roumain, it enlarges the settings, formal daring, thematic range, and visionary reach of the Haitian peasant and working-class novel. His influence among contemporary writers continues to be felt near the end of the twentieth century and is particularly evident in René Depestre's *Le mât de cocagne* (1979) and Pierre Clitandre's *Cathédrale du mois d'aout* (1982).

Radical opposition to the François Duvalier regime forced Alexis to leave Haiti clandestinely in 1960. Attempting to land secretly at Mole Saint Nicholas a year later as part of a small guerrilla group, Alexis was apprehended, imprisoned, and finally stoned to death by his captors. In addition to published novels, stories, and essays bearing witness to his passionate devotion to Haiti's common folk and a historical materialist critique of essentialist versions of négritude, he left behind two unpublished works in progress, *L'Eglantine* and *L'étoile absinthe*.

See also **Lescot, Élie; Négritude.**

BIBLIOGRAPHY

Europe: Revue Mensuelle 49, no. 501 (January 1971), is largely devoted to an assessment of Alexis and the literature of Haiti. See also J. Michael Dash, *Jacques Stéphen Alexis* (1975), and David Nicholls, *From Dessalines to Duvalier: Race, Colour, and National Independence in Haiti* (1979).

Additional Bibliography

Boadas, Aura Marina. *Lo barroco en la obra de Jacques Stephen Alexis.* Caracas: Centro de Estudios Latinoamericanos Rómulo Gallegos, 1992.

Jonassaint, Jean. *Des romans de tradition haïtienne: sur un récit tragique.* Paris: L'Hartmann, and Montreal: CIDIHCA, 2002.

Mudimbe-boyi, M. Elisabeth. *L'oeuvre romanesque de Jacques-Stephen Alexis: une écriture poétique, un engagement politique.* Montreal: Humanitas nouvelle optique, 1992.

Sarner, Eric. *La Passe du vent: une histoire haïtienne.* Paris: Editions Payot & Rivages, 1994. This work has been translated into Spanish and published as *El paso de viento: una historia haitiana.* Translated by Tatiana Sule Fernández. Mexico: Fondo de Cultura Económica, 1999.

ROBERTO MÁRQUEZ

ALFARO, RICARDO JOAQUÍN (1882–1971).

Ricardo Joaquín Alfaro (*b.* 20 August 1882; *d.* 23 February 1971), a Panamanian statesman who served as minister to the United States (1922–1930; 1933–1936), foreign minister (1946), and provisional president (1931–1932). A tireless advocate of Panamanian rights in the Canal Zone, Alfaro negotiated the Hull–Alfaro Treaty (1936) and served as an adviser during the treaty negotiations with the United States in 1947. He also protested the continued U.S. occupation of defense sites after World War II until the U.S. withdrawal in 1948. Alfaro presided over the 1932 presidential campaign with fairness and honesty, a rarity in Panamanian politics. Subsequently, he served as a member of the International Court of Justice at The Hague (1959–1964).

See also **Hull-Alfaro Treaty (1936).**

BIBLIOGRAPHY

Ricardo J. Alfaro, *Medio siglo de relaciones entre Panamá y los Estados Unidos,* new ed. (1959).

Walter La Feber, *The Panama Canal: The Crisis in Historical Perspective* (1978).

Michael Conniff, *Panama and the United States* (1991).

Additional Bibliography

Rivera Forero, Franklin. *Ricardo J. Alfaro, vida diplomática.* Panamá: Editorial Universitaria "Carlos Manuel Gasteazoro," 1999.

THOMAS M. LEONARD

ALFARO DELGADO, JOSÉ ELOY

(1842–1912). José Eloy Alfaro Delgado (*b.* 25 June 1842; *d.* 28 January 1912), president of Ecuador (interim 1896–1897, constitutional 1897–1901, interim 1906–1907, constitutional 1907–1911). Born in Montecristi, Manabí, Alfaro began his political career as a partisan of General José María Urvina, leading revolts in 1865 and 1871 against the conservative regime of Gabriel García Moreno (1869–1875). When the movements failed, he fled to Panama, where he developed a successful business and married. He subsequently used his wealth to finance liberal publications and insurrections against conservative governments in Ecuador and to support liberal causes throughout Latin America. By 1895, when he returned to Ecuador to lead the liberal forces, Alfaro had an international reputation as a revolutionary. With the support of wealthy coastal exporting interests, Alfaro's forces defeated the government troops. Alfaro convened a constituent assembly that wrote a new liberal constitution and elected him president. The liberals would retain power for the next three decades.

Despite a commitment to liberal principles, including the creation of a secular, activist state, Alfaro's political style was authoritarian and personalist. Until his death in 1912, he sought to maintain power by any means and was a principal cause of the political turmoil that characterized Ecuador in this period. He failed in his effort to prevent the inauguration of his successor Leonidas Plaza in 1901, but managed to oust Lizardo García, who took office in 1905. As in 1896, Alfaro convened the 1906 constituent assembly to legitimize his usurpation of power.

During Alfaro's second constitutional term, the Quito and Guayaquil Railroad was inaugurated, and real property held in *mort-main* by religious orders was nationalized. These accomplishments were partly eclipsed by Alfaro's harsh repression of political opponents and lack of respect for civil liberties.

Failing to prevent the inauguration of Emilio Estrada as his successor on 31 August 1911, Alfaro once again fled to Panama. However, when Estrada's untimely death in December 1911 unleashed a civil war, he returned from Panama to participate in the unsuccessful insurrection against the government. The public damned Alfaro and his supporters as unprincipled opportunists willing to destroy the nation to gain their ends and demanded that the rebels be punished. Alfaro was taken to Quito for trial. A mob burst into the prison and murdered the prisoners, including Eloy Alfaro.

See also **Ecuador, Constitutions; Ecuador, Revolutions: Revolution of 1895.**

BIBLIOGRAPHY

Luis Robalino Dávila, *Orígines de Ecuador de hoy,* vol. 7, pts. 1–2 (1969).

Linda Alexander Rodríguez, *The Search for Public Policy: Regional Politics and Government Finances in Ecuador, 1830–1940* (1985), esp. pp. 46–49.

Frank Macdonald Spindler, *Nineteenth Century Ecuador* (1987), esp. pp. 147–210.

Additional Bibliography

Espinales Tejena, Vicente. *Eloy Alfaro y la cultura.* Quito: Casa de la Cultura Ecuatoriana "Benjamín Carrión," 1995.

Santos Rodríguez, José. *Eloy Alfaro: Su personalidad multifacética y la revolución liberal.* Guayaquil: Universidad de Guayaquil, 1995.

LINDA ALEXANDER RODRÍGUEZ

ALFARO SIQUEIROS, DAVID (1896–1974). David Alfaro Siqueiros (*b.* 29 December 1896; *d.* 6 January 1974), Mexican artist. Muralist, painter, printmaker, theoretician, labor organizer, soldier, and Communist Party leader, Siqueiros not only produced a sizable and influential body of political-artistic theory but was the most technically innovative of the *tres grandes,* the Big Three of the Mexican School, begun in 1922 with Diego Rivera and José Clemente Orozco. After returning in 1922 from studies in Europe, Siqueiros, along with Rivera and Xavier Guerrero, organized the Syndicate of Technical Workers, Painters, and Sculptors and began to publish the artist newspaper *El Machete* (1924).

David Alfaro Siqueiros in front of one of his best known works, the multi-paneled mural *March of Humanity,* 1965. OLLIE STACKMAN/TIME LIFE PICTURES/GETTY IMAGES

In the search for materials and methods that could be used for outdoor murals that would be legible to spectators in transit, Siqueiros was the first artist, from 1932 on, to employ industrial synthetic paints (Duco or pyroxilyn, vinylite, etc.), an electric projector to transfer images onto the wall, and a spray gun (with stencils) to paint murals. He also used surfaces such as damp cement, masonite, and plywood, as well as more traditional grounds. He invented polyangular perspective, often on curved walls, to activate filmically a static surface. He also used blowups of documentary photographs as contemporary visual sources and *esculto-pintura* (sculptural painting). His painting style was dramatic and exuberant, even baroque, with simplified solid images thrusting forward, illusionistic destruc-tions and re-creations of space (floors, walls, and ceilings), and the building up of surfaces with granular materials.

Far from being merely a formalist innovator, Siqueiros employed these means to strengthen and make more powerful his political content, an approach he called *pintura dialéctico-subversiva* (dialectic-subversive painting). He championed monumental rather than easel painting, street murals, collective artistic teams, a scientific and psychological knowledge of artistic tools and forms, multiple and portable paintings rather than unique ones. He wrote to Anita Brenner, explaining that "what we seek is not only technique and style in art that sympathizes with revolution, but an art that itself is revolutionary."

See also **Art: The Twentieth Century; Orozco, José Clemente; Rivera, Diego.**

BIBLIOGRAPHY

Bernard S. Myers, *Mexican Painting in Our Time* (1956).

Raquel Tibol, *Siqueiros: Introductor de realidades* (1961), and *David Alfaro Siqueiros* (1969).

Mario De Micheli, *Siqueiros* (1968).

Orlando S. Suárez, *Inventario del muralismo mexicano* (1972).

Additional Bibliography

Folgarait, Leonard. *Mural Painting and Social Revolution in Mexico, 1920-1940: Art of the New Order.* Cambridge: Cambridge University Press, 1998.

Rochfort, Desmond. "The Sickle, the Serpent, and the Soil: History, Revolution, Nationhood, and Modernity in the Murals of Diego Rivera, José Clemente Orozco, and David Alfaro Siqueiros." In Mary Kay Vaughn and Stephen E. Lewis, editors, *The Eagle and the Virgin: Nation and Cultural Revolution in Mexico, 1920-1940.* Durham: Duke University Press, 2006.

Rochfort, Desmond. *Mexican Muralists: Orozco, Rivera, and Siqueiros.* London: Laurence King, 1993. Published in Spanish as *Pintura mural mexicana: Orozco, Rivera, Siqueiros* by Editorial Limusa, 1993.

SHIFRA M. GOLDMAN

ALFONSÍN, RAÚL RICARDO (1926–).

Raúl Ricardo Alfonsín (*b.* 13 March 1926), president of Argentina (1983–1989). The son of a local storekeeper, Alfonsín was raised in Chascomús, Buenos Aires Province. His maternal great-grandfather was an Irishman named Richard Foulkes, who married Mary Ford, daughter of a family of Falkland Islands kelpers. Staggeringly different from most British residents of South America, Don Ricardo became a passionate Argentine patriot fighting alongside the famous Radical leader Hipólito Irigoyen in the abortive revolution of 1905. With such family traditions, Alfonsín grew up fiercely opposed to electoral fraud, dictatorship, and corporatism. But it was only after Ricardo Balbín's death in September 1981 that he attained power in the Radical Party by winning the presidency (his first government post) in October 1983. The Radicals, who normally polled about 25 percent, got 51.7 percent, while the Peronists, with 40 percent, suffered their lowest vote and first ever defeat. The Alfonsín government introduced heterodox economic shock treatment, dubbed the Austral Plan, organized the first human rights trials in Latin America, and withstood three military uprisings. Defeat came in the shape of a civilian challenge. The Peronist Carlos Saúl Menem captured 47 percent in the May 1989 election, reducing Alfonsín to an opposition figure once again.

In 1994 Alfonsín and Menem signed the *Pacto de Olivos*, a set of documents that formed the foundation for that year's constitutional reform and allowed Menem to be reelected. Alfonsín stepped down as leader of the Radical Party in 1995.

See also **Argentina, Political Parties: Radical Party (UCR).**

BIBLIOGRAPHY

Pablo Giussani, *Los días de Alfonsín* (1986).

Jimmy Burns, *The Land That Lost Its Heroes: The Falklands, the Post-War, and Alfonsín* (1987).

Additional Bibliography

Acuña, Marcelo Luis. *Alfonsín y el poder económico: El fracaso de la concertación y los pactos corporativos entre 1983 y 1989.* Buenos Aires: Corregidor, 1995.

McAdam, Andrew, Víktor Sukup, and Claudio Oscar Katiz. *Raúl Alfonsín: La democracia a pesar de todo.* Buenos Aires: Corregidor, 1999.

Melo, Artemio Luis. *El gobierno de Alfonsín: La instauración democrática argentina (1983-1989).* Rosario, Argentina: Homo Sapiens Ediciones, 1995.

ROGER GRAVIL

ALGARROBO. Algarrobo, a hearty South American tree that grows in desert and semi-arid regions of mountains, plains, the Gran Chaco (lowland region in the Rio de la Plata Basin), at the edges of mountainous rainforests, and in pampean woodlands in Brazil, Argentina, Bolivia, and Paraguay. Various species exist: *Prosopis alba, Prosopis alba* of the panta variety, *Prosopis nigra, Prosopis chilensis,* and *Prosopis hassleri.* The algarrobo measures between 5 and 20 meters (16 and 65 feet), with a diameter of 10 meters (33 feet), and will normally flower and produce pods in September. The Spanish named this tree after the algarrobo (carob tree). In Guaraní, the algarrobo is called *ibopé* or *igopé*; in Quechua, it is *yaná tacú.* Many societies refer to the algarrobo simply as "the tree." Since very ancient times it has been a source of construction material, fuel, ingredients for food and drink, and forage for animals. A flour made from its legumes (carob beans) is used to make a kind of cake (*el patay*) known for its high nutritional value and long preservation. The same legumes are used to prepare a fermented beverage called *aloja.* The algarrobo's wood is very strong and can be polished to a beautiful luster. Modern-day usage has concocted a new mixed drink rivaling the *pisco sour* as Peru's national cocktail. This drink, called *algarrobina,* is made blending carob-tree syrup with *pisco,* along with other ingredients.

See also **Aguardiente de Pisco; Pisco.**

BIBLIOGRAPHY

H. L. D'Antoni and O. T. Solbrig, "Algarrobos in South American Cultures, Past and Present," in *Mesquite, Its Biology in Two Desert Ecosystems,* edited by B. B. Simpson (1977).

JOSÉ ANTONIO PÉREZ GOLIÁN

ALGUACIL MAYOR. Alguacil mayor, the chief constable of an audiencia or sheriff of a municipality. By the late sixteenth century he purchased the position for life, was able to bequeath it to an heir upon payment of the requisite tax, and received a portion of the fines he imposed. His responsibilities included executing court orders, arresting suspects, and maintaining public order. Since he could name assistants throughout the *audiencia* district, he enjoyed substantial patronage. The position could be very lucrative, but initially it was expensive; in 1611 a purchaser of the post in New Spain paid 115,000 pesos for it.

The *alguacil mayor* of a municipality also bought his post and held it for life. The responsibilities and patronage were similar to those of the *audiencia* counterpart but on a municipal scale. In addition, the *alguacil mayor* was usually entitled to participate in the city council's deliberations.

See also **Alcalde Mayor.**

BIBLIOGRAPHY

Clarence H. Haring, *The Spanish Empire in America* (1947).

John H. Parry, *The Sale of Public Office in the Spanish Indies Under the Hapsburgs* (1953).

Additional Bibliography

Alfaro Ramírez, Gustavo Rafael. "¿Quién encarceló el alguacil mayor de Puebla?: La vida, los negocios y el poder de don Pedro de Mendoza y Escalante, 1695–1740." *Estudios de Historia Novohispana.* 17 (1997): 31–62.

MARK A. BURKHOLDER

ALHÓNDIGA. The alhóndiga was the public granary in Spanish colonial towns. The term continued in use during the national period in many places. One of the most famous was the Alhóndiga of Guanajuato, Mexico, a massive, fortress-like structure erected in 1798–1809 by Intendant Juan Antonio Riaño to store sufficient grain to supply the city for a year. When Riaño received word that the rebel forces of Father Miguel Hidalgo were approaching the city, he ordered the granary prepared for a lengthy siege. Gathering coin, silver bars, and other valuables, the royalists became the target not only for the rebel forces but also for the plebeians of the city. On September 28, 1810, Riaño was killed in the first assault; the rebels overwhelmed the defenses, sacked the building, and massacred about 300 European Spaniards, creoles, and royalist militiamen. In 1811, following the executions of the rebel leaders Hidalgo, Ignacio Allende, Juan Aldama, and Mariano Jiménez, their heads were placed on display in iron cages on the corners of the Alhóndiga, where they remained until Mexican independence in 1821.

See also **Aldama y González, Juan de; Allende, Ignacio; Hidalgo y Costilla, Miguel; Riaño y Bárcena, Juan Antonio.**

BIBLIOGRAPHY

Alamán, Lucas. *Historia de Méjico desde los primeros movimientos que prepararon su independencia en el año de 1808, hasta la época presente,* 5 vols. Mexico City: Editorial Jus, 1942 (1849–1852).

Bustamante, Carlos María de. *Cuadro histórico de la Revolución Mexicana, inciada el 15 de septiembre de 1810 por el c. Miguel Hidalgo y Costilla, cura del pueblo de Dolores en el obispado de Michoacán.* 3 vols. Mexico City: Edicions de la Comisión Nacional para la Celebración del Sesquicentenario de la Proclamación de la Independencia Nacional y del Cincuentenario de la Revolución Mexicana, 1961.

Hamill, Hugh M. *The Hidalgo Revolt: Prelude to Mexican Independence.* Gainesville: University of Florida Press, 1966.

CHRISTON I. ARCHER

ALIANZA CÍVICA.

ALIANZA CÍVICA. Alianza Cívica is a Mexican nongovernmental (NGO) electoral organization organized shortly before the Mexican presidential election in April 1994. Seven organizations with experience in election observations combined their efforts to create an honest electoral setting by involving some twenty thousand volunteers, including large numbers of foreign visitors, in observing the electoral process. It has observed all of the federal elections between 1994 and 2003, and many local elections. Alianza Cívica played a major role in improving the electoral process and legitimizing Mexican elections, thus contributing significantly to the democratic transformation in Mexico. Most political analysts also attribute many improvements in the functions and tasks of the Federal Electoral Institute (IFE) to past Alianza Cívica criticisms and suggestions.

Alianza Cívica has also published numerous reports on media bias in past elections, as well as problems with vote buying in the 2000 presidential election. It continues to pursue civic education programs to better inform potential voters, and has concentrated significantly on educating voters about their federal representatives, as well as about congressional functions. It has encouraged increased citizen participation in making their demands heard before congress and in monitoring campaigns for members of congress from each district. It also maintains affiliates in each of the thirty-two administrative divisions of Mexico. It frequently organizes citizen conferences, similar to those of the League of Women Voters in the United States, designed to educate and inform voters about leading public policy issues. Alianza Cívica is one of the NGOs held in the highest regard by Mexicans.

See also **Mexico: Since 1910.**

BIBLIOGRAPHY

Alianza Cívica Internet site. Available from www.alianzacivica.org.mx.

Olvera, Alberto. "Civil Society in Mexico at Century's End." In *Dilemmas of Political Change in Mexico,* edited by Kevin J. Middlebrook. London: Institute of Latin American Studies, 2004.

Regadas Robles Gil, Rafael. "La Alianza Cívica/Observación 94." Available from http://www.vinculando.org/sociedadcivil.mx.

RODERIC AI CAMP

ALLENDE, IGNACIO (1769–1811).

ALLENDE, IGNACIO (1769–1811). Ignacio Allende (*b.* 25 January 1769; *d.* 26 June 1811), Mexican independence leader and corevolutionary of Father Miguel Hidalgo. Born to a wealthy landowning family, Allende joined the militia of San Miguel el Grande as a lieutenant and was promoted in 1797 to captain. He participated in the meetings of creole societies that plotted for Mexican independence, favoring independence under King Ferdinand VII or some other member of the Spanish royal family. When the regime discovered the Querétaro conspiracy in September 1810, Allende went to the town of Dolores to assist Father Miguel Hidalgo, who later named him captain-general of the American armies.

Many historians point to Allende's military background, but it should be remembered that he was a militia officer who had not commanded significant forces. A creole, he experienced difficulties with a rebellion that exploded rapidly into a mass movement dominated by Indians and mestizos. During and after the bloody occupation of Guanajuato, Allende attempted to restore order and to halt atrocities against Spaniards, uncontrolled pillaging, and other excesses. At Valladolid, Morelia, he ordered his troops to use force against insurgent looters. On many occasions, he opposed Hidalgo's apparent willingness to sanction violence as a means to attract supporters to the revolutionary cause.

After the battle of Monte de las Cruces (30 October 1810), Hidalgo rejected Allende's belief that the capital should be occupied, and the insurgents began the peripatetic wanderings that led to the occupation of Guadalajara. Even before the disastrous rebel defeat at Aculco (7 November 1810), many Indians and mestizos abandoned the rebel army. Allende was present in Guanajuato, but he did not play a major role in the battle of 25 November 1810 that resulted in the second major rebel defeat. Following the royalist victory at the battle of Puente de Calderón on 17 January 1811, the insurgent chiefs replaced Hidalgo, naming Allende supreme commander. Retreating to the north, Allende decided to regroup the insurgent forces in the United States. However, on 21 March 1811, the senior rebel commanders were surprised by treachery and captured north of Saltillo. Allende was taken prisoner, tried by court-martial at Chihuahua, and executed by firing squad.

See also **Hidalgo y Costilla, Miguel; Mexico, Wars and Revolutions: War of Independence.**

BIBLIOGRAPHY

Lucas Alamán, *Historia de México desde los primeros movimientos que prepararon su independencia en el año de 1808 hasta la época presente*, 5 vols. (1849–1852; repr. 1942).

Carlos María de Bustamante, *Cuadro histórico de la Revolución Mexicana*, 3 vols. (1961).

Hugh M. Hamill, *The Hidalgo Revolt: Prelude to Mexican Independence* (1966).

John Tutino, *From Insurrection to Revolution in Mexico: Social Bases of Agrarian Violence, 1750–1940* (1986).

Additional Bibliography

Rodríguez Frausto, Jesús. *Ignacio Allende y Unzaga, generalísimo de América.* Guanajuato: Universidad de Guanajuato, 1969.

CHRISTON I. ARCHER

ALLENDE, ISABEL (1942–).

Isabel Allende (*b.* 2 August 1942), Chilean novelist, born in Peru, where her father was a member of the diplomatic corps. After her parents separated, she was brought up in an old labyrinthine house surrounded by stories that eventually influenced her first novel, *La casa de los espíritus* (1982; *The House of the Spirits,* 1985), a work that brought Isabel Allende immediate international recognition. The novel is a melodramatic account of a patriarchal family saga whose story runs parallel to Chile's history in the twentieth century. Translated into several languages, it achieved remarkable success throughout the Western world.

From 1967 to 1974, Allende worked as a journalist for *Paula,* a woman's magazine in her native Santiago. In 1973 her uncle, Chilean president Salvador Allende, was assassinated by the Chilean military during a coup d'état that ousted his Socialist government. In 1975, fearing for her life, Isabel left Chile and went into exile. She settled with her family in Caracas, Venezuela, where she continued to practice journalism.

In *The House of the Spirits* she highlights the independent nature of the female characters, whose lives become increasingly entangled in the political process of their country, assumed to be Chile but never actually named. Her second novel, *De amor y de sombra* (1984; *Of Love and Shadows,* 1987), centers around a historical event, the discovery of the remains of a group of victims of a massacre by the military regime in a mine at Los Riscos, Chile. The novel can be interpreted as a denunciation of the military regime that ousted President Allende's government. Beginning with her third novel, *Eva*

Luna (1987; *Eva Luna,* 1988), Allende's attention shifts from Chile's contemporary reality to a broader setting, where storytelling from a female viewpoint becomes the focus of her fiction. In 1989, after moving to California, she published *Los cuentos de Eva Luna* (*The Stories of Eva Luna,* 1991), tales told by the title character of her previous novel. Later works include *El plan infinito* (1991; *The Infinite Plan,* 1993) *Paula* (1994, trans. 1995); *Aphrodite* (1997); *Hija de la fortuna* (*Daughter of Fortune,* 1999); *Mi país inventado* (*My Invented Country,* 2003); and *Inés del alma mia* (*Inés of My Soul,* 2006). In 1994 she was awarded the Orden al Mérito Gabriela Mistral by the Chilean government.

See also **Allende Gossens, Salvador; Literature: Spanish America.**

BIBLIOGRAPHY

Marcelo Coddou, *Los libros tienen sus propios espíritus* (1987), and *Para leer a Isabel Allende* (1988).

Magdalena García Pinto, *Women Writers of Latin America* (1991).

Additional Bibliography

Correas de Zapata, Celia. *Isabel Allende: Vida y espíritus.* Barcelona: Plaza & Janés Editores, 1998.

Feal, Rosemary Geisdorfer, and Yvette E. Miller. *Isabel Allende Today: An Anthology of Essays.* Pittsburgh, PA: Latin American Literary Review Press, 2002.

Levine, Linda Gould. *Isabel Allende.* New York: Twayne Publishers, 2002.

MAGDALENA GARCÍA PINTO

ALLENDE GOSSENS, SALVADOR

(1908–1973). Salvador Allende Gossens served as president of Chile from 1970 to 1973. Born in Valparaíso on July 26, 1908, to an upper-middle-class family, Allende studied in the public schools and graduated from the University of Chile with a medical degree in 1932. He was an active Mason throughout his adult life. Allende was attracted to socialist doctrine during his youth. He participated in university politics and in 1933 was a founding member of the Socialist Party. He was elected to the Chamber of Deputies in 1937 and served as minister of health (1939–1942) in the Popular Front government of Pedro Aguirre Cerda. His

long career in the senate began in 1945 and continued until 1969. As a senator he gained a reputation as an expert in parliamentary procedure and rose to the presidency of the senate (1965–1969). Allende held various offices in the Socialist Party, serving twice as secretary-general.

Allende ran for the presidency of Chile four times. In 1952 he garnered only 5.4 percent of the vote. In 1958 and 1964 he ran as the candidate of the Popular Action Front (FRAP), founded in 1956 to unite the Communist, Socialist, and smaller leftist parties. With coalition support, Allende received 28.9 percent of the vote in 1958, losing to Jorge Alessandri Rodríguez by only 33,500 of 1,236,000 votes cast. The leftward movement of Chilean politics in the wake of the Cuban Revolution (1959) raised expectations of an Allende victory in the 1964 presidential election. To prevent that possibility, the rightist Conservative and Liberal parties broke their alliance with the Radical Party and threw their support to reformist Christian Democrat Eduardo Frei. After an intense campaign featuring Central Intelligence Agency (CIA) financing and scare tactics equating Allende with Fidel Castro, Frei won with 55.6 percent of the vote to Allende's 38.6. Throughout the Frei administration, Allende was the most visible spokesman of the opposition Left and an advocate of more vigorous reform.

The 1970 presidential election offered Chileans clear choices. The Right reorganized as the National Party in reaction to Frei's reforms and selected former president Jorge Alessandri as its candidate. The Christian Democrats ran Radomiro Tomic of the party's left-center bloc. Allende was the candidate of Popular Unity (UP, or Unidad Popular), a new coalition of the Socialists and Communists and four non-Marxist parties, including the historic Radical Party. Allende won a close race, receiving 36.5 percent of the vote to Alessandri's 35.2 and Tomic's 28.0. After two months of U.S.-orchestrated attempts to block congressional ratification of the popular election and to foster a military coup, Salvador Allende took office on November 3, 1970.

Allende's election fixed the world's attention on Chile, which would provide the laboratory for testing the question: Is there a peaceful road to socialism? Allende had promised to move Chile rapidly toward socialism through the acceleration of agrarian reform and extensive nationalization in key economic sectors. His first year in office was highly successful in meeting those goals and in building popular support. Thereafter, mounting problems began to plague his government, compounding the difficulties imposed by opposition control of congress and the judiciary. By the end of 1971 accelerating inflation, the exhaustion of foreign currency reserves, and disinvestment in the private sector had weakened the economy. Meanwhile, the Christian Democrats and the National Party formalized an anti-UP alliance, the Nixon administration stepped up its destabilization campaign, and critical divisions within the UP and Allende's own Socialist Party began to surface.

Although the pace of reform rose dramatically under the UP, popular expectations rose faster, resulting in widespread extralegal worker occupations of haciendas and factories. Torn between his legal obligations and his commitment to the *pueblo,* Allende vacillated on the wave of takeovers; he lost crucial middle-class support by appearing soft on the rule of law. The opposition struck a major blow in an October 1972 "bosses' strike." Called by the *gremio* (guild) movement, a broad coalition of business and professional groups, the strike paralyzed the economy, revealed the government's vulnerability, and forced Allende to bring military officers into his cabinet. From this point forward, confrontation escalated and much of the opposition embraced the goal of overthrowing the government.

Despite the growing polarization and the rise of violence, Allende achieved an impressive record of reform. Under his administration, the traditional rural estate virtually ceased to exist, the state took control of the "commanding heights" of the economy, and progress was made in income redistribution. The final test of UP popularity was the March 1973 congressional election. The UP received 44 percent of the vote, down from the 49.7 percent it had won in the April 1971 municipal elections but still 7.5 points above the 1970 presidential vote tally. Nonetheless, the UP's failure to achieve a congressional majority and the opposition's failure to attain the two-thirds majority necessary to impeach the president signaled three and a half more years of conflict before the next scheduled presidential election in 1976. A

second *gremio* strike took place in July and August 1973. With the country in chaos and the government near collapse, the military staged a coup on September 11. Salvador Allende, *compañero presidente* to Chile's poor, committed suicide in the Moneda Palace while it was under military attack. The overthrow and death of Allende marked the end of the transition to socialism and the beginning of the Pinochet dictatorship (1973–1990).

Allende was buried following a private ceremony in a small Viña del Mar cemetery; visits to his grave were prohibited for several years. The military dictatorship initially demonized Allende as justification for the coup and its mission of eradicating the Chilean left. Through its absolute control of publishing, the media, and school curricula, the regime subsequently attempted to erase Allende from the collective memory. However, when mass protests erupted in 1982, the figure of Allende reemerged as a symbol of democracy in the struggle to end the dictatorship.

Since the return of elected government in 1990, Allende's figure has been rehabilitated. On September 4, 1990, exactly twenty years after his election as president, Allende was given the public funeral he had been denied in 1973. Following mass in the Santiago cathedral, Allende's remains were buried in Santiago's venerable Cementerio General, where all but one of Chile's dead presidents repose. In 2000, Allende's Socialist Party returned to the presidential palace with the election of Ricardo Lagos; the same year, Allende became only the third president to be honored with a statue in the Plaza de la Constitución, adjacent to the Moneda Palace. In 2003, the thirtieth anniversary of the coup and Allende's death, his daughter Isabel Allende Bussi assumed the presidency of the Chamber of Deputies and Allende was commemorated in multiple ceremonies, including the naming of streets and plazas around the country. While Chileans remain deeply divided over their recent past, the figure of Salvador Allende has assumed its rightful place in national history.

See also **Chile, Political Parties: Popular Unity; Chile, Political Parties: Popular Action Front; Chile: The Twentieth Century; United States-Latin American Relations.**

BIBLIOGRAPHY

Allende Gossens, Salvador. *Chile's Road to Socialism*, edited by Joan Garcés, trans. J. Darling. Harmondsworth, U.K.: Penguin, 1973.

Bitar, Sergio. *Chile: Experiment in Democracy*, trans. Sam Sherman. Philadelphia: Institute for the Study of Human Issues, 1986.

De Vylder, Stefan. *Allende's Chile: The Political Economy of the Rise and Fall of the Unidad Popular*. New York: Cambridge University Press, 1976.

Garcés, Joan. *Allende y la experiencia chilena: Las armas de la política*. Barcelona: Ariel, 1976.

González Pino, Miguel, and Arturo Fontaine Talavera, eds. *Los mil días de Allende*. 2 vols. Santiago de Chile: Centro de Estudios Públicos, 1997.

Jorquera, Carlos. *El chicho Allende*. Santiago de Chile: Ediciones Bat, 1990.

Puccio, Osvaldo. *Un cuarto de siglo con Allende: Recuerdos de su secretario privado*. Santiago de Chile: Editorial Emisión, 1985.

Sigmund, Paul E. *The Overthrow of Allende and the Politics of Chile, 1964–1976*. Pittsburgh, PA: University of Pittsburgh Press, 1977.

Veneros, Diana. *Allende: Un ensayo psicobiográfico*. Santiago de Chile: Editorial Sudamericana, 2003.

THOMAS C. WRIGHT

ALLENDE-SARÓN, PEDRO HUMBERTO (1885–1959).

Pedro Humberto Allende-Sarón (*b.* 29 June 1885; *d.* 17 August 1959), Chilean composer. Allende was born in Santiago and studied composition at the National Conservatory in Santiago (1899–1908). He studied piano and violin, the latter under the guidance of Aurelio Silva. Early in his career he taught violin and general musical subjects in secondary schools and later taught composition and harmony at the National Conservatory. He was a key figure in revitalizing the music education system in Chile, both at the primary and secondary school levels. After a trip to Europe in 1910–1911, Allende was elected to the Chilean Folklore Society. In recognition for his research and compositional efforts, as well as for his contribution to music education, in 1945 he received the Premio Nacional de Arte, becoming the first composer to be so honored.

Allende was the first important figure to promote Chilean musical nationalism by integrating in his works the songs and dances of the Araucanian and Mapuche Indians as well as mestizo folk music, which he orchestrated in a lavish French impressionist style. He wrote *Paisaje chileno* for chorus and orchestra (1913); *Escenas campesinas chilenas* (1913–1914), a symphonic suite; *La voz de las calles* (1919–1920), a symphonic poem; *Tonadas de carácter popular chileno*, for piano (1918–1922); *Concerto sinfónico* for cello and orchestra (1915); *Luna de la media noche* for soprano and orchestra (1937); Violin Concerto (1940); and *La Cenicienta* (Cinderella, 1948), a chamber opera for children.

Allende's writings include *Metodología original para la enseñanza del canto escolar* (1922); *Conferencias sobre la música* (1918); "La música popular chilena" in *Art populaire*, from the First International Congress of Popular Art, Prague (1928); and "Chilean Folk Music," in the *Bulletin of the Pan American Union* (September 1931).

See also **Music: Art Music.**

BIBLIOGRAPHY

John Vinton, ed., *Dictionary of Contemporary Music* (1974), pp. 7–8.

Gérard Béhague, *Music in Latin America: An Introduction* (1979); p. 179; *New Grove Dictionary of Music and Musicians* (1980).

Additional Bibliography

Allende-Blin, Juan. "Pedro Humberto Allende Saron. Algunos aspectos característicos de su obra." *Revista musical chilena* 56 (January 2002): 77–80.

ALCIDES LANZA

ALLIANCE FOR PROGRESS.

Alliance for Progress was a policy inaugurated in 1961 by President John F. Kennedy as a ten-year $20 billion cooperative effort to bring political stability and representative government to Latin America. Events in the late 1950s brought the United States to the realization that within Latin America the economic, social, and political disparities that divided the region's peoples served as breeding grounds for revolution. Building off of smaller-scale, U.S.-funded social investments in Latin America that had begun in the late 1940s, the United States designed development programs that climaxed with the Alliance for Progress Charter. All members of the Organization of American States, except Cuba, signed the charter at Punta del Este, Uruguay, on 17 August 1961. The Alliance hoped to bring political stability and representative government to Latin America through economic reform by providing funds to improve the infrastructure for industrialization (such as roads and dams) and by collaborating in private investment projects. Economic and social justice was encouraged by changing the inequitable tax systems and by providing for schools and health care facilities. The policies were formulated within the context of the cold war because both the U.S. and Latin American leadership feared that Communist-inspired Fidelismo would spread from Cuba to other parts of the hemisphere. The Alliance sought to deter the Communist appeal by supporting social reform and economic growth that would create political stability.

Under the Alliance for Progress, Latin American armed forces placed a new emphasis on counterinsurgency, which included civic action programs, such as literacy training, teaching of technical skills, opening new land, building schools and highways, improving sanitation and health facilities, and other projects useful to civilians. Alliance programs have been criticized for buying supplies primarily from U.S. companies, which limited the impact of foreign development aid. Indeed, 90 percent of all commodity expenditures went to U.S. businesses. Also, the Alliance never spent enough money to make a major impact. The United States opened many health clinics throughout Latin America, but their impact was limited by the very large population growth during the period. The Alliance also shifted emphasis from defense against offshore incursions to internal security. Enthusiasm for the Alliance quickly waned. By 1963 military governments had come to power in several Latin American countries, diminishing the hope for democracy, and in some countries the military lost interest in the civic action programs, using counterinsurgency training only to suppress political opposition.

In the United States, President Lyndon B. Johnson was less committed than Kennedy to democratic reform and favored private over public investment.

Plagued by the war in Vietnam, the costs of the Great Society, and civil violence at home, and reassured by the apparent inability of Fidel Castro to encourage revolution elsewhere, the United States gave less attention to Latin America in the late 1960s. When Richard M. Nixon assumed the presidency in 1969, he noted that the Alliance was a concept with great promise that had not achieved its economic and social objectives, and when Congress terminated it in 1972, the Agency for International Development (AID), which had administered most of the Alliance programs, agreed. Despite the problems associated with the Alliance, AID continued to fund social, education, and development programs throughout Latin America into the early 2000s.

See also **Agency for International Development (AID).**

BIBLIOGRAPHY

Hernando Agudelo Villa, *La revolución del desarrollo: Orígen y evolución de la Alianza para el Progreso* (1966).

William D. Rogers, *The Twilight Struggle: The Alliance for Progress and the Politics of Development in Latin America* (1967).

Jerome Levinson and Juan De Onis, *The Alliance That Lost Its Way: A Critical Report on the Alliance for Progress* (1970).

Arthur M. Schlesinger, Jr., "The Alliance for Progress: A Retrospective," in *Latin America: The Search for a New International Role*, edited by Ronald G. Hellman and H. Jon Rosenbaum (1975).

Additional Bibliography

Gambone, Michael D. *Capturing the Revolution: The United States, Central America, and Nicaragua, 1961–1972.* Westport, CT: Praeger, 2001.

Lleras Camargo, Alberto, and Otto Morales Benítez. *Reflexiones sobre la historia, el poder y la vida internacional.* Bogotá: Ediciones Uniandes, Tercer Mundo, 1994.

Rabe, Stephen G. *The Most Dangerous Area in the World: John F. Kennedy Confronts Communist Revolution in Latin America.* Chapel Hill: University of North Carolina Press, 1999.

Taffet, Jeffrey F. *Foreign Aid as Foreign Policy: The Alliance for Progress in Latin America.* New York: Routledge, 2007.

THOMAS M. LEONARD

ALMAFUERTE

ALMAFUERTE (1854–1917). Almafuerte (*b.* 13 May 1854; *d.* 28 February 1917), pseudonym of Pedro Bonifacio Palacios, Argentine poet and journalist. Born in San Justo in Buenos Aires province, Almafuerte was self-taught. Raised by an aunt in Buenos Aires, he remained in the capital, living in poverty and solitude.

Almafuerte cultivated an extravagant persona that bespoke his commitment to exemplifying attributes and values of a mystical, unsettled, and contradictory self-identity that transcended established middle-class conventions. To be sure, during this period Buenos Aires remained relatively sedate alongside its European models. Yet, Almafuerte was able to project a complex, idiosyncratic persona that gave him a unique status among the writers of the period as something of a prophet concerning the impact on the solitary individual of the multiple tensions of a society undergoing vertiginous modernization. In this sense, Almafuerte may be read as an antiphony to the vast sociopolitical undertaking of the Generation of 1880, who sought to impose a liberal hegemony on Argentine society.

In the worldly and often aggressively profane (or, at least, decidedly materialistic) context of the Generation of 1880, Almafuerte aligned himself with a traditional, humanitarian Christian sentiment that is reflected in titles like *Evangélicas* (1915), *Cristianas y Jesús, El drama del Calvario, Cantar de cantares, Lamentaciones* (1906), and *El misionero* (1905) and in the didactic, sermonizing tone of many of his compositions. Yet, despite this sort of catechistic focus, the structure of his poetry frequently reflects the innovative exercises of the more urbane and sensual modernists.

See also **Journalism.**

BIBLIOGRAPHY

Romualdo Brughetti, *Viva de Almafuerte, el combatiente perpetuo* (1954).

Enrique Lavié, *Almafuerte* (1962).

Marta Morello-Frosch, "Almafuerte: Ética y estética a contrapelo de la historia," in *Cuadernos hispanoamericanos* 296 (1975): 420–427.

Damián Ferrer, *Perfil de Almafuerte* (1980).

Additional Bibliography

Molina, Gerardo. *Almafuerte y otros estudios literarios.* Canelones, Uruguay: Biblioteca Nacional y Americana, 2005.

Saxe, Facundo. "Vinculaciones entre el 'cierre' del '80, el ciclo de La bolsa y La sombra de la patria de Almafuerte," and Dellarciprete, Rubén. "La locura en el contexto social y lterario de fin del siglo XIX: El loco, un relato de Almafuerte." In María Minellono, editor, *Las tensiones de los opuestos: libros y autores de la literatura argentina del '80.* Buenos Aires: Nuevohacer, Grupo Editor Latinoamericano, 2004.

DAVID WILLIAM FOSTER

ALMAGRO, DIEGO DE

ALMAGRO, DIEGO DE (c. 1475–1538). Diego de Almagro (*b.* ca. 1475; *d.* 8 July 1538), conqueror of Peru and Chile. Almagro, illegitimate son of Juan de Montenegro and Elvira Gutiérrez, was born in Almagro, in New Castile. His first years were economically and socially difficult ones, and in 1514 he left for the Indies in search of fortune. He participated with some distinction in minor discoveries in Castilla del Oro and became a close associate of Francisco Pizarro, another dynamic social-misfit soldier of fortune. With some financial assistance from cleric Hernando de Luque, who may have been representing a silent partner, the two men began making plans to explore South America's west coast, widely believed to be the seat of an empire of great riches.

Pizarro set sail southward from the Isthmus of Panama in the first expedition of 1524; Almagro, responsible for maintaining supplies, followed behind, covering much the same route and suffering hardships similar to those of the Pizarro group. In an encounter with the *cacique* (chief) of Las Piedras, Almagro lost an eye at Pueblo Quemado. On the second expedition (1526), which was jointly planned with Pizarro, neither the leaders nor their men got along well. When Almagro returned to the isthmus for more troops and supplies, he inadvertently carried notice of the discontent. When the governor of Panama got wind of the situation, he recalled both men. In the meantime, Pizarro was able to secure enough evidence of wealth to convince the official that a third and more massive attempt was warranted.

At this juncture Pizarro returned to Spain and procured an agreement with the crown that made him chief commander of the expedition, leaving Luque as bishop of Tumbes. Almagro, who received relatively minor offices in the north, remained on the isthmus ill, perhaps with syphillis, as Pizarro started the third expedition near the end of 1530. By the time Almagro and his men were able to reach Pizarro at Cajamarca, the Inca ruler Atahualpa had already been captured and much of the wealth allocated to Pizarro's men. Almagro did secure appointment as the chief commander of New Toledo, about 520 miles south of Pizarro's New Castile, and marched into Cuzco (Peru) on 15 November 1533.

Convinced that vast cities and wealth lay to the south, and perhaps encouraged by the duplicitous Pizarrists who wanted to be rid of him, he organized an expedition and marched southward on 3 July 1535. The group passed Lake Titicaca, crossed with great hardship and loss of life through frigid Andean passes, and entered Chile at Copiapó. The expeditionary force marched as far south as the Maule River in south-central Chile, but found no indication of the expected treasures. Instead, the Europeans were attacked by fierce Indian fighters who had eluded Inca rule.

Almagro and his men gave up and returned to Peru via the desert coastal route. The soldiers passed through what became Arequipa and marched into Cuzco on 8 April 1537, shortly after Pizarro supporters had broken the siege led by Manco Inca. Almagro and his men occupied Cuzco, believing it to be within the jurisdiction of New Toledo. Almagro, to ensure his control, imprisoned Francisco's brothers, Hernando and Gonzalo Pizarro, while Friar Francisco de Bobadilla, a suspected Pizarrist, began negotiations to effect a peaceful settlement of the territorial dispute. Gonzalo Pizarro escaped jail, and Almagro freed Hernando on the condition that he return to Spain. Hernando, however, fielded a Pizarrist army that met and defeated Almagro on 6 April 1538 at Salinas, near Cuzco. Fearing an uprising of Almagro's supporters, Hernando Pizarro ordered him executed in his cell. He was buried in Cuzco's Mercedarian church.

Almagro's illegitimate mestizo son, Diego de Almagro the Younger, born in Panama in 1520 (his mother was Ana Martínez, a native of the isthmus),

would later head a movement to overthrow Pizarrist domination of Peru. After the assassination of Francisco Pizarro in Lima on 26 June 1541, he governed Peru briefly, but fell to the king's forces, led by Governor Cristóval Vaca de Castro, on 16 September 1542 in the battle of Chupas, near Huamanga. He was captured and executed in Cuzco. Only twenty-two years old when he died, he was buried alongside his father in the Mercedarian church.

See also **Conquistadores; Pizarro, Francisco.**

BIBLIOGRAPHY

Rolando Mellafe and N. Meza Villalobos, *Diego de Almagro* (1954).

José Antonio Del Busto Duthurburu, *Diego de Almagro* (1964).

Additional Bibliography

Ballesteros Gaibrois, Manuel. *Diego de Almagro.* Madrid: Historia 16: Quorum, 1987.

Larraín Valdés, Gerardo. *Diego de Almagro: Biografía.* Santiago: Editorial Luxemburgo, 1996.

NOBLE DAVID COOK

ALMAZÁN, JUAN ANDRÉU

ALMAZÁN, JUAN ANDRÉU (1891–1965). Juan Andréu Almazán (*b.* 12 May 1891; *d.* 9 October 1965), Mexican politician. Almazán, a general, was an important figure during and immediately following the Mexican Revolution (1910–1920). Noted for his candidacy in the Mexican presidential election of 1940, Almazán represented the Revolutionary Party of National Unification (Partido Revolucionario de Unificación Nacional—PRUN) in opposition to the government candidate, General Manuel Ávila Camacho, who was chosen to succeed President Lázaro Cárdenas. The campaign generated considerable electoral violence, and some observers expected Almazán to lead a rebellion against the government after losing. Instead he went into exile in Panama, Cuba, and the United States. He returned to Mexico in 1947, and was a businessman until his death in Mexico City.

See also **Mexico, Political Parties: National Revolutionary Party (PNR).**

BIBLIOGRAPHY

James W. Wilkie, *México visto en el siglo XX* (1969).

Albert L. Michaels, *The Mexican Election of 1940* (1971).

Roderic A. Camp, *Mexican Political Biographies, 1935–1981* (1982), p. 16.

Additional Bibliography

Langston, Joy. "Breaking Out Is Hard to Do: Exit, Voice, and Loyalty in Mexico's One-Party Hegemonic Regime." *Latin American Politics and Society* 44 (Autumn 2002): 71-88.

Moguel, Josefina. *Juan Andreu Almazán.* Mexico City: Planeta DeAgostini, 2003.

Mora García, Carlos. *Almazanismo y Salinismo, 1940-1988: Dos expresiones políticas del liberalismo revolucionario mexicano.* Mexico City: Cactus, 2001.

                                        RODERIC AI CAMP

ALMEIDA, JOSÉ AMÉRICO DE (1887–1980).

José Américo de Almeida (*b.* 10 January 1887; *d.* 10 March 1980), a leading Brazilian social novelist of the 1930s. Almeida was an important figure in both Northeastern and national Brazilian politics until his death. A strong supporter of Getúlio Vargas's 1930 revolution and a minister in Vargas's government, his own presidential candidacy was thwarted by Vargas's coup in 1937. Later he served as governor of his home state of Paraíba. These and other episodes of his political life were described in his memoirs *Ocasos de sangue* (1954).

Influenced by positivism and Euclides da Cunha's *Os sertões,* Almeida wrote *A Paraíba e seus problemas* (1923), which documents his sociopolitical concerns about his state and region. Although he wrote three novels with similar economic and social themes and the same poetic style, *A bagaceira* (1928; *Trash,* 1978) is recognized as his most important work. A pioneering regionalist work within the nationalist ideology of Brazilian modernism, *A bagaceira* is primarily a literary exemplification of beliefs and ideas he expressed in *A Paraíba e seus problemas.* In this poetic novel replete with regionalist expressions, he describes the effects of the periodic droughts on the people of the Northeast and, specifically, the conflict between the *sertanejos* (frontiersmen) and the *brejeiros* (marshmen). Today, however, the novel is considered more of a monument of that period than a vibrant work of literature.

See also **Literature: Brazil; Vargas, Getúlio Dornelles.**

BIBLIOGRAPHY

R. L. Scott-Buccleuch, "Translator's Foreword," in *Trash* (1978).

Additional Bibliography

Castro, Angela Maria Bezerra de. *Re-leitura de A bagaceira: Uma aprendizagem de desaprender.* Rio de Janeiro: J. Olympio Editora, 1987.

Pereira, Joacil. *José Américo de Almeida: A saga de uma vida.* João Pessoa: Instituto Nacional do Livro, 1987.

                                        IRWIN STERN

ALMEIDA, LUIS DE. *See* **Lavradio, Marquês do.**

ALMEIDA, MANUEL ANTÔNIO DE (1831–1861).

Manuel Antônio de Almeida (*b.* 17 November 1831; *d.* 28 November 1861), Brazilian novelist. Almeida is famous for a single text, the novel *Memórias de um sargento de milícias,* which was serialized in 1853 and published in two volumes in 1854–1855. It was rediscovered, after 1922, by the modernists, who celebrated it for its detailed and quite realistic descriptions of urban life in Rio de Janeiro in the years just before independence in 1822—descriptions that include a broader range of social types than any other Brazilian novel of its time—and for its entertaining and highly unsentimental vision of life. Some critics endeavored to classify Almeida's *Memórias* as an early example of the realist novel in Brazil, but clearly its literary roots can be traced to such eighteenth-century British works as Henry Fielding's *Tom Jones.* It has also been suggested that the nineteenth-century Brazilian novel would have developed along quite different lines had Almeida not died in a shipwreck in 1861, but there is no evidence that he produced any prose fiction between 1853 and his death.

See also **Literature: Brazil.**

BIBLIOGRAPHY

Memoirs of a Militia Sergeant, translated by Linton L. Barrett (1959).

Antônio Cândido, "Dialética da malandragem," in *Revista do Instituto de Estudos Brasileiros* 8 (1970): 67–89.

John M. Parker, "The Nature of Realism in *Memórias de um sargento de milícias,*" in *Bulletin of Hispanic Studies* 48 (1971): 128–150.

Additional Bibliography

Guimarães, Reginaldo. *O folclore na ficção brasileira: Roteiro das Memórias de um sargento de milícias.* Rio de Janeiro: Livraria Editora Cátedra, 1977.

DAVID T. HABERLY

ALMEIDA JÚNIOR, JOSÉ FERRAZ DE

ALMEIDA JÚNIOR, JOSÉ FERRAZ DE (1850–1899). José Ferraz de Almeida Júnior (*b.* 8 May 1850; *d.* 13 November 1899), Brazilian painter best known for his *caipira* paintings. Born in Itú, São Paulo, Almeida Júnior enrolled in the Imperial Academy of Fine Arts in 1869. A disciple of Vítor Meireles, Almeida Júnior specialized in drawing and historical painting. Between 1871 and 1874 he won seven student painting awards. In 1874 he obtained the gold medal in historical painting, entitling him to compete for the academy's European travel award competition. Although he declined, he did accept a monthly stipend to travel in Europe offered by the emperor, Pedro II, who took an active interest in supporting talented young artists.

In Paris he studied with French academic artists and entered several Salon exhibitions. When he returned to Rio in 1882, he organized an exhibition to show the eight paintings he had completed while in Europe. They included religious paintings, figure studies, genre paintings, and a new category, *caipira* painting. His *O Derrubador brasileiro,* the first in a series of *caipira* paintings, expanded the narrow thematic options then available to historical and genre painters. It remained faithful to the traditional academic aesthetic canons but depicted a scene in the daily life of the common people from the interior of the state of São Paulo. These paintings helped bring into focus the important historical role of the Brazilian backwoodsmen. His other *caipira* compositions include *Caipiras negaceando,* *Caipira picando fumo, Pescando, Amolação interrompida,* and *Caipira pitando.*

See also **Meireles de Lima, Vitor.**

BIBLIOGRAPHY

Gastão Pereira Da Silva, *Almeida Júnior: Sua vida e sua obra* (1946).

Marcos Antônio Marcondes, *Almeida Júnior: Vida e obras* (1980).

Additional Bibliography

Coli Júnior, Jorge Sidney. "A violência e o caipira." *Estudos Históricos* 30 (2002): 23-31.

Mello Júnior, Donato. "O pintor Almeida Júnior e o imperador d. Pedro II." *Revista do Instituto Histórico e Geográfico Brasileiro* 337 (October-December 1982): 185-192.

CAREN A. MEGHREBLIAN

ALMOJARIFAZGO

ALMOJARIFAZGO. Almojarifazgo, a tax, of Arab origin, on the maritime trade of Andalusia. The *almojarifazgo* was charged on Seville's trade with America from 1543, constituting thereafter the principal duty on imperial commerce until its abolition in 1778. Initially levied at 2.5 percent on exports and 5 percent on imports, its rates were equalized at 5 percent in 1566 and thereafter varied, as did the practice of granting exemptions for particular products or regions. It was also charged on most intercolonial as well as transatlantic trade. The issue of determining the values of commodities in order to calculate the *almojarifazgo* was never resolved satisfactorily, and its collection thus provided much scope for fraud.

See also **Fleet System: Colonial Spanish America.**

BIBLIOGRAPHY

Clarence H. Haring, *The Spanish Empire in America* (1947), esp. pp. 261–263.

Ismael Sánchez-Bella, *La Organización financiera de las Indias, siglo XVI* (1968), esp. pp. 238–247.

Additional Bibliography

Acosta Rodríguez, Antonio, Adolfo Luis González Rodríguez, and Enriqueta Vila Vilar. *La Casa de la Contratación y la navegación entre España y las Indias.* Sevilla, Spain: Universidad de Sevilla, 2003.

Martínez Shaw, Carlos, and José María Oliva Melgar. *Sistema atlántico español: Siglos XVII–XIX.* Madrid: Marcial Pons Historia, 2005.

Romano, Ruggiero. *Mecanismo y elementos del sistema económico colonial americano, siglos XVI–XVIII.* México: El Colegio de México, Fideicomiso Historia de las Américas, 2004.

JOHN R. FISHER

ALMONTE, JUAN NEPOMUCENO

(1803–1869). Juan Nepomuceno Almonte (*b.* 1803; *d.* 1869), regent of Mexico's Second Empire (1863–1864). The illegitimate child of José María Morelos y Pavón—a leader of Mexico's independence movement—Almonte was awarded the rank of brigadier general before the age of thirteen by the Congress of Chilpancingo. In 1815 he was part of the commission sent by Morelos to the United States, the first of many diplomatic posts he would hold. After serving as part of a commission to establish the border between Mexico and the United States (1834), Almonte fought against the rebellion in Texas at the battles of the Alamo and San Jacinto, where he was captured. Freed in 1836, Almonte served as minister of war (1839–1841) before returning to the United States as ambassador in 1842.

When the United States admitted Texas as a state, Almonte returned to Mexico to support the war effort. Originally a federalist, he became a conservative and a monarchist. He served as Mexico's minister to London and later to Paris. After the republican forces won the War of the Reform (1858–1861), Almonte openly sought European intervention to establish a monarchy in Mexico. He returned to Mexico with the support of the French army in 1862 and was selected as one of the executive triumvirate of the Council of Notables and later regent. Emperor Maximilian gave Almonte various honors, including a cabinet post, before naming him as the Mexican Empire's representative to Napoleon III (1866). On the fall of the Second Empire, Almonte remained in Paris, where he died.

See also **San Jacinto, Battle of; Napoleon III; French Intervention (Mexico).**

BIBLIOGRAPHY

Alberto María Carreño Escudero, *Jefes del ejército mexicano en 1847* (1914).

Alfred Jackson Hanna and Kathryn Abbey Hanna, *Napoleon III and Mexico: American Triumph over Monarchy* (1971); *Diccionario Porrúa de historia, biografía y geografía de México,* 5th ed. (1986).

Additional Bibliography

Almonte, Juan, Jack Jackson, and John Wheat. *Almonte's Texas: Juan N. Almonte's 1834 Inspection, Secret Report and Role in the 1836 Campaign.* Austin: Texas State Historical Association, Center for the Study of Texas History, University of Texas at Austin, 2003.

Gutiérrez Ibarra, Celia. *Cómo México perdió Texas: Análisis y transcripción del Informe secreto (1834) de Juan Nepomuceno Almonte.* Mexico City: Instituto Nacional de Antropología e Historia, 1987.

D. F. STEVENS

ALOMÍA ROBLES, DANIEL (1871–1942).

Daniel Alomía Robles (*b.* 3 January 1871; *d.* 17 July 1942), Peruvian ethnomusicologist and composer. Born in Huánuco, Alomía Robles was sent as a child to Lima to study solfège with Cruz Panizo and piano with Claudio Rebagliati. From 1892 to 1894 he studied medicine in San Fernando. While doing research on the Campas Indians, he was encouraged by a Franciscan friar to study aboriginal music. He eventually dedicated more than twenty years of his life to the subject. His research took him to remote regions of Ecuador and Bolivia, where he collected and classified folk materials. In 1910 he gave a celebrated lecture on Andean melodies at the University of San Marcos in Lima. Alomía Robles's wife, the pianist Sebastiana Godoy, assisted in the harmonization of native music. Although he became a noted composer, he is best known for his research on Indian music. He died in Lima.

See also **Music: Popular Music and Dance.**

BIBLIOGRAPHY

Rodolfo Holzmann, "Catálogo de las obras de Daniel Alomía Robles," in *Boletín Biblioteca Universidad Mayor de San Marcos* 13 (1943).

Gérard Béhague, *Music in Latin America* (1979); *New Grove Dictionary of Music and Musicians,* vol. 1 (1980).

Additional Bibliography

Bolaños, César, José Quesada, Enrique Iturriaga, Juan Carlos Estenssoro, Enrique Pinilla, and Raúl Romero. *La música en el Perú.* Lima: Patronato Popular y Porvenir, 1985.

Robles Godoy, Armando. *La obra folclórica y musical de Daniel Alomía Robles.* Lima: Consejo Nacional de Ciencia y Tecnología, 1990.

Varallanos, José. *El cóndor pasa: vida y obra de Daniel Alomía Robles, musico, compositor y folklorista peruano, biografía, glosario, texto del drama, documentario, partituras.* Lima: Talleres Gráficos, 1988.

SUSANA SALGADO

ALONSO, AMADO (1896–1952). Amado Alonso (*b.* 13 September 1896; *d.* 26 May 1952), Argentine writer and literary critic. Born in Lerín, Navarra, Spain, Alonso directed the Institute of Philology at the University of Buenos Aires from 1927 to 1946, a position that allowed him to exercise considerable influence on the introduction of European formalism and stylistics into Argentina, and from there into Latin American literary and linguistic scholarship. In 1938 Alonso, along with Pedro Henríquez Ureña, published *Gramática castellana,* one of the classic structuralist analyses of the Spanish language. The *Gramática,* designed to be used in secondary-school courses, had numerous reprintings in subsequent decades. Alonso authored many important studies on Iberian and Latin American literature, including early studies on Jorge Luis Borges. His most important text, however, remains *Poesía y estilo de Pablo Neruda* (1940), probably the first full-length monograph on a Latin American poet to be written from the point of view of formalist stylistics, in addition to being one of the earliest studies on the Chilean poet. In 1945, Alonso translated into Spanish Ferdinand de Saussure's *Curso de lingüística general* (1945), one of the founding texts of modern linguistics. Whether writing specifically about poetry or exploring the poetic dimension of prose, Alonso exemplified the importance accorded by the literary criticism of the period to the questions of the specific qualities of literariness.

See also **Borges, Jorge Luis.**

BIBLIOGRAPHY

Diego Catálan Menéndez Pidal, *La escuela lingüística española y su concepción del lenguaje* (1955).

Emilio Carilla, *Estudios de literatura argentina, siglo XX,* 2d ed. (1968), pp. 163–172.

Laurence Samuel Johnson, "The Literary Criticism of Amado Alonso and His Principal Disciples" (Ph.D. diss., Columbia University, 1970).

Additional Bibliography

Gómez Alonso, Juan Carlos. *La estilística de Amado Alonso como una teoría del lenguaje literario.* Murcia: Universidad de Murcia, 2002.

Quiroga Torrealba, Luis. *Tres lingüistas de América: Andrés Bello, Angel Rosenblat, Amado Alonso.* Caracas: Fondo Editorial de la Universidad Pedagógica Experimental Libertador, 2003.

DAVID WILLIAM FOSTER

ALONSO, MANUEL A. (1822–1899). Manuel A. Alonso (*b.* 6 October 1822; *d.* 4 November 1899), Puerto Rican essayist, story writer, and poet. Son of a Spanish captain posted in Caguas, Alonso received his early education there. He went on to study medicine in Barcelona, Spain. Returning as a doctor in 1849, he assumed his place in colonial Puerto Rican society as one of the group of moderate liberal reformers that identified an authentic national purpose with the ascendency of the island's progressive white creole elite. As a writer, he was the first to give effective literary expression to its programmatic outlook and its defense of the existence of a distinctly Puerto Rican nationality. While studying in the Catalán metropolis, he joined other Puerto Rican students in compiling, contributing to, publishing, and sending home the *Aquinaldo puertorriqueño* (1843, 1846; Puerto Rican Christmas Carol), the *Album puertorriqueño* (1844; Puerto Rican Album), and *El cancionero de Borinquén* (1846; Puerto Rican Songbook) now generally regarded as the catalytic events promoting a self-consciously Puerto Rican literature.

After 1849, Alonso quickly emerged as the island's signal *costumbrista,* its preeminent writer on local idiosyncrasy, particularly peasant folkways, creole custom, lore, and traditions. Published in 1849, and in an expanded two-volume edition in 1882–1883, Alonso's signature collection of lyric vignettes and ethnographic prose sketches, *El jíbaro,* gave the titular metaphor of the independent rural mestizo peasant symbolic currency as the emblematic representation of the popular ethos and the recalcitrant obstacle to the creole elite's presumptively more enlightened, entrepreneurial notions of national progress. Impressively synthesizing the colonial, ethnic, and interclass drama of a historically evolved local culture during a crucial period of transition, *El jíbaro* established Alonso as the key figure of a nascent insular tradition of short narrative, literary criticism, and the essay of cultural commentary. After later visits to Spain (1858–1861 and 1866–1871), Alonso returned to Puerto Rico, serving in his later years as editor of the liberal reformist periodical *El agente* and as medical director of the Asilo de Beneficencia.

See also **Creole.**

BIBLIOGRAPHY

Modesto Rivera y Rivera, *Concepto y expresión del costumbrismo en Manuel A. Pacheco (El Gíbaro)* (1952), and *Manuel A. Alonso: Su vida y su obra* (1966).

Josefina Rivera De Álvarez, *Diccionario de literatura puertorriqueña*, vol. 1 (1970), pp. 49–52.

Additional Bibliography

Díaz, Luis Felipe. "Ironía e ideología en el discurso del siglo XIX: Alonso, Tapia y Rivera, Hostos y Zeno Gandía." *Revista de Estudios Hispánicos (Puerto Rico)* 29 (2002): 49–69.

Faría Cancel, Edith. "Manuel A. Alonso, al margen de un clásico: Algunos recuerdos y bocetos autobiográficos." *Revista de Estudios Hispánicos (Puerto Rico)* 29 (2002): 15–23.

ROBERTO MÁRQUEZ

ALONSO, MARIANO ROQUE (1792–1853).

Mariano Roque Alonso (*b.* 1792?; *d.* 1853), Paraguayan consul (1841–1844) and military figure. Alonso emerged during the hectic months following the September 1840 death of José Gaspar Rodríguez de Francia, Paraguay's first authoritarian dictator and leader of the country since 1814. Francia had left no formal provision for a successor, and when he died, power devolved to the four chiefs of the Asunción barracks, who proved to be ineffectual and corrupt administrators. In January 1841, they were replaced by a triumvirate headed by a sergeant and two former alcaldes of the city. This regime was itself displaced within a month by Alonso, then a junior officer with many years of service but with little real authority or talent. Evidently feeling himself inadequate to the task of governing, he made a fateful decision to appoint as his secretary Carlos Antonio López, a noted attorney from the interior. Alonso needed the latter's help in organizing a national congress that would create and legitimize a new government. When the congress met in March 1841, however, Alonso played the role of subordinate to López, and agreed to join with him in a two-man consular regime authorized by the congress. After the consuls took office, Alonso in effect abdicated his position, preferring to return to the barracks and the company of rustic soldiers like himself. He made sure that his military colleagues refrained from further interference in politics. This show of support brought him many rewards from López, who continued to favor him with a substantial annual pension after the consulate was replaced by a presidential regime in 1844.

In his later years, Alonso lived quietly on his cattle ranch in the interior, where he died in 1853.

See also **López, Carlos Antonio.**

BIBLIOGRAPHY

Charles J. Kolinski, *Historical Dictionary of Paraguay* (1975), p. 217.

John Hoyt Williams, *The Rise and Fall of the Paraguayan Republic, 1800–1870* (1979), pp. 103–105.

THOMAS L. WHIGHAM

ALONSO, RAÚL (1924–1993).

Raúl Alonso (*b.* 24 January 1924; *d.* 31 July 1993), Argentine painter and printmaker. Born in Buenos Aires, the son of the distinguished Spanish artist Juan Carlos Alonso, Raúl was self-taught. In 1958 he traveled to Europe and settled in Paris for a while. He exhibited around the world. He was invited to the Universal Exhibition in Brussels and to the Ibero-American Biennials in Mexico City, São Paulo, Valparaíso, Cali, and Punta del Este. In 1991 he had a show at the Hammer Gallery in New York. He received several awards, including the honor prize at the National Salon (Buenos Aires, 1975). He illustrated several books, among them *The Ten Commandments, Amatoria,* and *Borradores.* Alonso's paintings combine nature and imagination, appealing not only to the mind but also to the emotions of the viewer.

See also **Art: The Twentieth Century.**

BIBLIOGRAPHY

Vicente Gesualdo, Aldo Biglione, and Rodolfo Santos, *Diccionario de artistas plásticos en la Argentina* (1988).

Additional Bibliography

Gutiérrez Zaldívar, Ignacio. *Raul Alonso.* Buenos Aires: Zurbarán, 2003.

AMALIA CORTINA ARAVENA

ALOU, FELIPE ROJAS (1935–). Major league baseball player and manager Felipe Alou was born in 1935 in Bajos de Haina, Dominican Republic. Aside from his professional accomplishments, he has also served as a leading voice on behalf of Latin American players who, like him, faced discrimination and difficulties in adapting to U.S. culture.

Alou was the eldest of five children, two others of whom also played in the big leagues. He grew up in poverty and his day-to-day survival seemed more meaningful than baseball. Though he had hoped for a career in medicine, his ability at baseball ignited a special hunger by which he could both escape his environs and also sustain his family. He signed with the New York Giants in 1955 and was assigned to their minor league system.

In 1958, Alou arrived in the big leagues with the Giants (who by then had moved to San Francisco). A good glove man, he played both infield and outfield and, in 1961, hit 25 home runs, drove in 98, and batted for a .316 average. His brothers Mateo (Matty) and Jesus joined the club in 1960 and 1963, respectively, and in a 1963 game all three played the outfield, a major league first for brothers.

Alou spent the next six seasons with the Braves; in 1966 he hit 31 home runs and finished the season with a .327 batting average, second in the National League to his brother Matty, who took the crown. He finished his playing career in1974. From 1976 to the beginning of the 1992 season, Alou coached and managed in the Montreal Expos' minor league system.

In 1992 the Montreal Expos hired Alou to manage their club and he showed a gift for developing young talent. In 1994 he was named National League Manager of the Year. After being dismissed by the Expos in 2001, he was signed by the San Francisco Giants to manage their club starting with the 2003 season. In his first year, he took the team to a 100–61 won-loss record and the National League West title. Alou managed the Giants through the 2006 whereupon the club replaced him with Bruce Bochey and reassigned the legendary Dominican to a special assignments position with the organization. By then he had compiled a lifetime managing record of 1033 wins to 1021 losses.

Felipe Alou's 1967 autobiography, with Herm Weiskopf, remains one of the more insightful portraits of the trauma Latinos faced in the United States in the 1950s. His 1963 article in *Sport* magazine regarding the problems and concerns of Latin American ballplayers is an important statement.

See also **Sports.**

BIBLIOGRAPHY

Alou, Felipe, with Arnold Hano. "Latin American Ballplayers Need a Bill of Rights." *Sport* 37 (November 1963), 76–79.

Alou, Felipe, with Herm Weiskopf. *Felipe Alou: My Life and Baseball.* Waco, TX: Word Books, 1967.

Zirin, Dave. "Si Se Puede: Felipe Alou Stands Up to Bigotry." *Edge of Sports*, August 8, 2005. Available from http://edgeofsports.com/2005-08-08-147/index.html.

SAMUEL O. REGALADO

ALPACA. *See* **Llama.**

ALSINA, ADOLFO (1829–1877). Adolfo Alsina (b. 14 January 1829; d. 29 December 1877), Argentine politician. Alsina was born in Buenos Aires, the only son of Valentín Alsina and Antonia Maza. He received his early education in Buenos Aires and Montevideo, and a law degree from the University of Buenos Aires in 1854. After the battle of Caseros, he wrote articles attacking the commander, Justo José de Urquiza, and plotted his assassination. As a member of the Liberal Party, to which his father belonged, he helped defend Buenos Aires when it was besieged by Urquiza. He subsequently fought at the battle of Cepeda, was one of the *porteño* (Buenos Aires) deputies denied admission to the congress that met in Paraná, and participated in the battle of Pavón.

In 1862 Alsina was elected deputy to the national congress. During an internal party dispute over a proposal to federalize the city of Buenos Aires, he and his followers broke with the Liberal Party to form the Autonomista Party. The party, which consisted of important *estancieros*, Federal Party intellectuals, José Hernández, and Leandro Alem, had little support outside the province of Buenos Aires. In 1866 Alsina became governor of Buenos Aires, with Nicolás Avellaneda as his minister of government. Among the accomplishments of his administration was the separation of the office of justice of the peace from that of the military commandant.

In 1867, Alsina was Domingo Sarmiento's running mate in the latter's successful bid for the presidency. His relations with Sarmiento were never harmonious, but he did support Sarmiento's decision in 1870 to punish Ricardo López Jordán for the assassination of Urquiza. He again was a candidate for the presidency in 1874, and in the congressional elections of that year he won in Córdoba and La Rioja but not in Buenos Aires, which his partisans controlled, because Sarmiento sent national troops to supervise the elections. Lacking support, Alsina withdrew his candidacy and endorsed the man Sarmiento had selected as his successor, Avellaneda, and his own supporter, Mariano Acosta, for the vice presidency.

President Avellaneda appointed Alsina his minister of war and the navy. Alsina was responsible for the suppression of the Revolution of 1874, a pro-Bartolomé Mitre movement, and for the campaign that built a new frontier line of forts from Carhué to Laguna del Monte and to Trenque Lauquén. He hoped to minimize Indian resistance to the advance by incorporating some tribes into the national guard, but as a precaution he supplied the national army with revolvers and telegraph lines. In 1877 he furthered the policy of "conciliation" by persuading Mitre to stop his partisans from starting a revolution; he was planning another advance of the frontier line when he died in Buenos Aires.

See also **Sarmiento, Domingo Faustino; Argentina, Political Parties: National Autonomist Party.**

BIBLIOGRAPHY

Jacinto R. Yaben, "Alsina, A.," in *Biografías argentinas y sudamericanas,* vol. 1 (1938), pp. 118–122.

Ysabel F. Rennie, *The Argentine Republic* (1945), pp. 111, 115, 120–125, 139.

José Luis Romero, *A History of Argentine Political Thought,* translated by Thomas F. McGann (1963).

Vicente Osvaldo Cutolo, "Alcina, A." in *Nuevo diccionario biográfico argentino, 1750–1930,* vol. 1 (1968), pp. 100–101.

Ricardo Levene et al., "Historia de las presidencias: 1862–1898," in Academia Nacional de la Historia, *Historia argentina contemporánea, 1862–1930,* vol. 1 (1965), sec. 1, pp. 257–263.

Additional Bibliography

Gamboni, Olga Dina. *Adolfo Alsina, gobernador de la Provincia de Buenos Aires y conquistador del desierto.* La Plata: María Amalia Gamboni, 1994.

Hora, Roy. *The Landowners of the Argentine Pampas: A Social and Political History, 1860-1945.* Oxford: Oxford University Press, 2001.

Martínez, Carlos M. *Alsina y Alem: porteñismo y milicias.* Buenos Aires: Ediciones Culturales Argentinas, 1990.

JOSEPH T. CRISCENTI

ALSINA, VALENTÍN (1802–1869). Valentín Alsina (*b.* 16 December 1802; *d.* 6 September 1869), Argentine politician. Alsina was born in Buenos Aires, the son of Juan de Alsina and María Pastora Ruano. He studied at the University of Córdoba, where Gregorio Funes was one of his teachers, and received his law degree in Buenos Aires. From 1824 to 1827 he contributed articles to *El Nacional* and *El Mensajero Argentino* and was undersecretary of foreign affairs in the government of Bernardino Rivadavia. Alsina supported General Juan Lavalle's revolution of 1 December 1828, and briefly served in his government. In 1829 he was the director of the public library in Buenos Aires. He was persecuted by Buenos Aires Governor Juan Manuel de Rosas and was kept a prisoner aboard the lighter *Sarandí* until Colonel Enrique Sinclair, a relative, and Dr. Manuel Vicente Maza, his father-in-law, arranged for his escape to Colonia in 1835. His wife, Antonia Maza, and their small child, Adolfo, fled from Buenos Aires with the help of Sinclair's friend Ricardo Haines, an Englishman. The family was reunited in Montevideo, where Alsina became a member of the Argentine Commission, which had as its aim the overthrow of Rosas. The commission sent his brother, Juan José Alsina, to represent it; he was later replaced by his relative, Governor Pedro Ferré of Corrientes. Unlike many members of the commission, Valentín Alsina never believed that Lavalle and his Ejército Libertador would overthrow Rosas.

In 1843 Alsina participated in the defense of Montevideo, then besieged by Manuel Oribe, by enrolling in the Argentine Legion. His function was to contribute anti-Rosas articles to the local newspapers *El Moderador, El Nacional, El Grito Argentino,* and especially to *El Comercio del Plata.* In 1843 he wrote his famous "Notes" to the first edition of Sarmiento's *Civilización i barbarie* (1845), in which he maintains that terror first appeared in Buenos Aires with Rosas.

In 1852 Alsina was appointed minister of government by Vicente López y Planes, governor of Buenos Aires. As minister he restored to their rightful owners the properties Rosas had confiscated. He represented the extreme wing of the Unitarian Party, opposing national organization and the Acuerdo de San Nicolás because representation in congress would be based on population. Elected governor of Buenos Aires Province 30 October 1852, Alsina made Bartolomé Mitre his minister of the interior, annulled the land grants Rosas had made to the veterans of the Indian campaigns and civil wars, organized an invasion of Entre Ríos, and appointed Hilario Lagos and Cayetano Laprida to the departmental posts of military commandant. When Lagos and Laprida revolted on 1 December 1852, he resigned as governor.

In 1853 Alsina was president of the Court of Justice, and in 1854 he was twice elected senator but did not serve. From 1855 to May 1856 he was minister of government and foreign affairs in the administration of Pastor Obligado. In 1857 he was again elected governor of Buenos Aires Province, approved the return to Buenos Aires of Rivadavia's remains, and evidently became involved in a plot to assassinate the military commander Justo José de Urquiza. The legislature forced Alsina to resign after the provincial forces were defeated by the confederation armies at the battle of Cepeda. Three days later Buenos Aires and the Argentine Confederation signed the Pact of San José de Flores (11 November 1859), which was mediated by Francisco Solano López, whereby Buenos Aires agreed to join the confederation after a provincial convention examined the Constitution of 1853. Alsina participated in that convention.

In 1862, after the battle of Pavón, he was elected a senator of the national Congress that met in Buenos Aires and refused the presidency of the Supreme Court. That year he was entrusted with the task of writing the provincial rural code that became law in 1865. As the temporary president of the senate, he proclaimed the election of Bartolomé Mitre and Marcos Paz as president and vice president in 1862, and of Domingo Sarmiento and of his son Adolfo Alsina as president and vice president in 1867. He died in Buenos Aires.

See also **Argentina, Movements: Unitarists; Argentine Confederation.**

BIBLIOGRAPHY

Estanislao S. Zeballos, "Apuntes biográficos del doctor Valentín Alsina," in *Revista de derecho, historia y letras* 10 (1901): 171–175.

Adolfo Saldías, *La evolución republicana* (1903).

Ramón J. Cárcano, *De Caseros al 11 de septiembre (1851–1852)* (1918).

Ysabel F. Rennie, *The Argentine Republic* (1945), pp. 80, 84, 86–87, 89–90, 103.

Harold F. Peterson, *Argentina and the United States, 1810–1960* (1964).

Jacinto R. Yaben, *Biografías argentinas y sudamericanas,* vol. 1 (1968), pp. 125–129.

Vicente Osvaldo Cutolo, *Nuevo diccionario biográfico argentino, 1750–1930,* vol. 1 (1969), pp. 104–106.

Joseph F. Cuscinti, ed., *Sarmiento and His Argentina* (1993).

Tulio Halperín-Donghi et al., eds., *Sarmiento: Author of a Nation* (1994).

Additional Bibliography

Cernadas de Bulnes, Mabel Nelida. *Valentín Alsina: Periodista, jurista y hombre de gobierno.* Bahía Blanca: Utopía Ediciones: Universidad Nacional del Sur, Departamento de Humanidades, 1996.

JOSEPH T. CRISCENTI

ALSOGARAY, ÁLVARO (1913–2005).

An Argentine economist, politician, and military man, Álvaro Alsogaray was born on June 23, 1913, in Esperanza, in the province of Santa Fe. He studied at the Military College and received a degree in engineering. After serving as minister of industry for the military dictatorship that overthrew Juan Domingo Perón in 1955, was called on by President Arturo Frondizi (1958–1962), who was under intense pressure from the military, to be his minister of economy. He was replaced when Frondizi was forced to resign, but returned to head the ministry during the José María Guido administration (1962–1963). He is remembered for the phrase "We have to get through the winter," justifying the orthodox adjustment policies he prescribed for overcoming the country's economic crisis at that time, and is the emblematic figure of Argentine orthodox liberalism.

In 1966, after supporting the military coup, he was named ambassador to the United States, and he remained there until 1968. In 1982 he founded the Union of the Democratic Center (UCD) and ran as a presidential candidate for the liberal right. Between 1983 and 1999, he served in the national chamber of deputies and was an adviser to the executive during the presidency of Peronist Carlos Saúl Menem (1989–1999). During this period, he fiercely defended the process of privatizing state enterprises. He died on April 1, 2005.

See also **Argentina: The Twentieth Century; Frondizi, Arturo; Guido, José María; Menem, Carlos Saúl; Perón, Juan Domingo.**

BIBLIOGRAPHY

Cavarozzi, Marcelo. *Autoritarismo y Democracia, 1955– 1996. La transición del estado al mercado en La Argentina.* Buenos Aires: Ariel, 1997.

Potash, Robert A: *El ejército y la política en Argentina 1962–1973,* Vol. 2: *De la caída de Frondizi a la restauración Peronista.* Buenos Aires, Sudamericana, 1994.

VICENTE PALERMO

writer. Born in Tixtla, Guerrero, Altamirano learned Spanish and studied at the Instituto Literario de Toluca, a school for the education of indigenous scholars. Journalist, bureaucrat, statesman, and diplomat, Altamirano supported liberal causes in Mexico during the years of the Reform, the French Intervention, and thereafter. He founded the review *El Renacimiento* (The Renaissance), which lasted for one year (1869), in order to advocate and foment a national literary culture. His series of articles, *Revistas literarias de México* (Literary Reviews of Mexico [1868–1883]), constitutes the first serious attempt to produce a systematic history of Mexican literature since Independence. In his criticism, he viewed the novel as the ideal genre for educating readers and establishing a national literary culture. His narrative production includes a collection of novellas, *Cuentos de invierno* (Winter Tales [1880]); and three novels, *Clemencia* (1869), *La navidad en las montañas* (Christmas in the Mountains [1871]), and *El Zarco* (written between 1886 and 1888, published posthumously in 1901). After years of public service as a teacher in Mexico and as a consul in Spain and France, Altamirano died in San Remo, Italy.

See also **Literature: Spanish America.**

BIBLIOGRAPHY

Chris N. Nacci, *Ignacio Manuel Altamirano* (1970).

Ledda Arguedas, "Ignacio Manuel Altamirano," in *Historia de la Literatura Hispanoamericana,* vol. 2, *Del neoclasicismo al modernismo,* edited by Luis Íñigo Madrigal (1987) pp. 193–201.

Additional Bibliography

Chávez Guerrero, Herminio. *Ignacio Manuel Altamirano: Biografía.* Chilpancingo, Guerrero: Instituto Guerrerense de la Cultura, 1985.

Sierra, Catalina, and Cristina Barros. *Ignacio Manuel Altamirano.* Mexico City: Consejo Nacional para la Cultura y las Artes, 1993.

Wright-Rios, Edward N. "Indian Saints and Nation-States: Ignacio Manuel Altamirano's Landscapes and Legends." *Mexican Studies/Estudios Mexicanos* 20 (Winter 2004): 47–68.

DANNY J. ANDERSON

ALTAMIRANO, IGNACIO MANUEL

(1834–1893). Ignacio Manuel Altamirano (*b.* 13 November 1834; *d.* 13 February 1893), Mexican

ALTAR DE SACRIFICIOS.

Altar de Sacrificios, a modest Formative and Classic-Period Maya site at the strategic junction of the Usamacinta and La

Pasión rivers on the modern Mexico-Guatemala border in the department of Petén, Guatemala. It is readily linked to the larger Yaxchilán, downstream, and to Seibal, upriver on La Pasión. Though relatively small, this ceremonial center was from 455 CE the region's capital city due to its control over commercial water routes between Petén's central highlands and lowlands. Ceramic evidence (the Xe Ceramic Complex, about 900–700 BCE) shows that Altar was occupied quite early. A 12-foot-high platform facing a plaza has been dated to the Middle Formative Period and demonstrates the early construction of civic-ceremonial architecture. Dated stone monuments at Altar begin with Stela 10, 9.1.0. 0.0. (455 CE) and close with Stela 22, 10.1.0.0.0 (849 CE).

In addition to its early occupation, the site is noteworthy for providing ceramic evidence, as does nearby Seibal, of occupation by foreigners (Putun or Mexicanized Mayas) moving up the Usamacinta and La Pasión rivers during the Terminal Classic Period. Scholars also suggest that inhabitants developed a new artistic style synthesized from classic forms, independent of foreign influences.

A tomb excavated beneath Structure A-III at Altar provides evidence for several additional lines of thought regarding both political relationships and other factors involved in the Classic Maya collapse. The fully extended elite internment included the Altar Vase, which illustrates a funeral rite dated to 754 CE. The scenes show ritual dancing and sacrifice ceremonies by six individuals, including, apparently, ruling elite from three other sites. The vase also shows a young woman committing ritual suicide (by cutting her throat with a flint knife). A similar (or the actual) knife was recovered near the vase itself. The skeletal material from Altar dated to the Late Classic Period also indicates increasing nutritional deficiencies near the time of the Classic Maya collapse.

See also **Maya, The.**

BIBLIOGRAPHY

Ledyard A. Smith, *Excavations at Altar de Sacrificios: Architecture, Settlement, Burials, and Caches* (1972).

Gordon R. Willey, *The Artifacts of Altar de Sacrificios* (1972).

Richard E. W. Adams, "Maya Collapse: Transformation in the Ceramic Sequence at Altar de Sacrificios," in *The Classic Maya Collapse,* edited by T. P. Culbert (1973), pp. 21–34.

Additional Bibliography

Demarest, Arthur. *Ancient Maya: The Rise and Fall of a Rainforest Civilization.* Cambridge and New York: Cambridge University Press, 2004.

Lucero, Lisa J. *Water and Ritual: The Rise and Fall of Classic Maya Rulers.* Austin: University of Texas Press, 2006.

Pring, Duncan. *The Protoclassic in the Maya Lowlands.* Oxford: John and Erica Hedges, dist. Hadrian Books, 2000.

WALTER R. T. WITSCHEY

ALTEPETL. Altepetl, a term derived from *in atl, in tepetl* ("the water, the mountain") denoting the provincial unit, or regional state, of pre-Hispanic Nahua society. By definition, each *altepetl* had a ruler, land base, marketplace, and temple dedicated to a patron deity. The *altepetl* was subdivided into smaller districts (groups of four, six, and eight were common) known as Calpulli or Tlaxilacalli, which enjoyed political representation and gave tribute services by means of a rotational system. After the Spanish invasion, institutions such as the encomienda and parish were based directly on the *altepetl,* known later as a pueblo, which generally continued to be governed by indigenous elites.

See also **Nahuas.**

BIBLIOGRAPHY

Excellent discussions of *altepetl* structure before and after the Conquest can be found in James Lockhart, *The Nahuas After the Conquest: A Social and Cultural History of the Indians of Central Mexico, Sixteenth through Eighteenth Centuries* (1992), and James Lockhart, Frances Berdan, and Arthur J. O. Anderson, trans. and ed., *The Tlaxcalan Actas: A Compendium of the Records of the Cabildo of Tlaxcala (1545–1627)* (1986). Though he barely mentions the term *altepetl,* Charles Gibson's monumental study *The Aztecs Under Spanish Rule: A History of the Indians of the Valley of Mexico, 1519–1810* (1964) provides an invaluable study of the evolution of the indigenous corporate entity.

Additional Bibliography

Fernández Christlieb, Federico, and Angel Julián García Zambrano. *Territorialidad y paisaje en el altepetl del siglo XVI.* Mexico: Fondo de Cultura Económica, 2006.

Reyes García, Cayetano. *El Altépetl, origen y desarrollo: Construcción de la identidad regional náhuatl.* México: El Colegio de Michoacán, 2000.

ROBERT HASKETT

ALTIPLANO. Altiplano, the largest plateau in the Andes mountains. This historically important region lies in contemporary southern Peru and Bolivia. Starting in the region of Lake Titicaca, the altiplano extends southward in an opening between two branches of the southern Andes, at an average altitude of about 12,500 feet. Most of the area is Bolivian national territory and includes the cities of La Paz, Oruro, and Potosí. The altiplano contains important agriculture lands, pasturage, and mineral deposits and, according to Herbert Klein, was the site of "the domestication of the staple products of Andean civilization," particularly the potato, and of "the American cameloids: the llama, alpaca, and vicuña."

The altiplano was home to a number of indigenous societies, most notably the Aymara, who were incorporated into the Inca empire in the fifteenth century. Under Spanish rule, the altiplano's indigenous peoples were forced into settlements that were subject to heavy tribute and labor obligations to the colonial state, in particular labor for the *mita de minas* for the silver mines at Potosí, the most profitable mining area in the sixteenth-century empire. The altiplano communities resisted these demands, most overtly in a series of eighteenth-century uprisings. Although silver production declined in the late colonial period, the altiplano remained an important economic zone, particularly after the rise of tin mining in the late nineteenth and early twentieth centuries. The altiplano's mining unions and agricultural communities have played major roles in contemporary Bolivian politics.

See also **Silver Industry.**

BIBLIOGRAPHY

Herbert S. Klein, *Bolivia: The Evolution of a Multi-Ethnic Society* (1982) especially pp. 3–26.

Additional Bibliography

Bergman, Roland W. *Tierras del altiplano y economía campesina: Agricultura en los limítes más altos de Los Andes del Sur del Perú.* Cuzco, Perú: Centro de Estudios Regionales Andinos "Bartolomé de las Casas," 2000.

Bleiwas, Donald I. and Christiansen, Robert G. *Geology and Mineral Resources of the Altiplano and Cordillera Occidental, Bolivia.* Denver, CO: Survey, 1992.

Brownman, David L. "Titicaca Basin Archaeolinguistics: Uru, Pukina and Aymara." *World Archaeology* 26, no. 2 (October 1994): 235-251.

Del Pozo-Vergnes, Ethel. *De la hacienda a la mundialización: Sociedad, pastores y cambios en el altiplano peruano.* Lima: Instituto de estudios peruanos, 2004.

McFarren, Peter. *Ayllu: El altiplano boliviano.* La Paz, Bolivia: Editorial los Amigos del Libro, 1984.

ANN M. WIGHTMAN

ALTUN HA. The Mayan site of Altun Ha is notable for its unusually high population density, abundant material wealth, and remarkable and diverse architecture, especially in light of the site's moderate size and its location in a swampy, desolate area in north-central Belize, approximately 50 kilometers north of Belize City and 10 kilometers inland from the Caribbean shore. The first archaeological reconnaissance was conducted by A. H. Anderson and W. R. Bullard in the early 1960s. A seven-year program beginning in 1963 of intensive excavations, mapping, and artifact analysis was sponsored by the Royal Ontario Museum and directed by David Pendergast. This thorough archaeological investigation has revealed a long and complex development that is distinct within Maya prehistory.

Occupation of Altun Ha began approximately 200 BCE (Late Preclassic) and persisted until about 925 CE (Late Classic). An Early Classic post-interment tomb offering included Teotihuacán-style (Miccaotli phase) ceramic vessels and green Pachuca obsidian eccentric lithics. Another Early Classic offering at Altun Ha included a claw-shaped bead of tumbaga (gold-copper alloy) from the Coclé culture of central Panama. Slightly later finds include a four-kilogram jade head of Kinich Ahau and an engraved jade plaque with a Mayan long-count date of 584 CE. During its maximum florescence, the site core of Altun Ha measured approximately one square kilometer and included fifteen large monumental structures set around two adjoining plazas. The urban settlement surrounding the site core covered about five square kilometers and was nearly twice as dense as Tikal. Altun Ha had long-distance relationships with the inland and southern Maya area, central Mexico, and lower Central America that may have been based in part on commerce in marine materials. Isotopic ratios present in human bone from Altun Ha demonstrate a stronger maritime diet than at any other Maya site and a reduced consumption of corn after the Early Classic.

A complete or partial hiatus in occupation occurred from 900 to 1000 CE. In contrast to most Maya sites to the west, Altun Ha witnessed a resurgence during the Late Postclassic Ueyeb phase, 1225–1500 CE. The community of Rockstone Pond is currently located adjacent to the ancient ruins. Considerable effort has been made to restore Altun Ha as a national monument and to foster economic development through tourism.

See also **Archaeology; Goldwork, Pre-Columbian; Maya, The; Teotihuacán; Tikal.**

BIBLIOGRAPHY

Hammond, Norman. "The Prehistory of Belize." *Journal of Field Archaeology* 9, no. 3 (1982): 349–362.

Pendergast, David M. *Excavations at Altun Ha, Belize, 1964-1970*, 3 vols. Toronto: Royal Ontario Museum, 1979–1990.

White, Christine D., David M. Pendergast, Fred J. Longstaffe, and Kimberley R. Law. "Social Complexity and Food Systems at Altun Ha, Belize: The Isotopic Evidence." *Latin American Antiquity* 12, no. 4 (2001): 371–393.

KATHRYN SAMPECK

ALURISTA

(1947–). Widely recognized as the chief poet of the Chicano movement, Alurista (the pen name of Alberto Baltazar Urista Heredia) was born on August 8, 1947, in Mexico City. He lived in the border town of Tijuana until his teens, when he immigrated to San Diego, California. He became a leading voice in 1968 by promoting the southwestern United States as the mythic homeland of the Aztecs, known as Aztlán. Alurista made pivotal contributions to Chicano poetics: He revolutionized bilingual or Spanglish expression as a legitimate form of literature; he recovered an indigenous sensibility and mythology, mainly Nahuatl from the Aztecs, and gave them a new place in Chicano poetry; he promoted the term *Chicano* as a new ethnic identity for peoples of Mexican descent in the United States; and he produced highly experimental poetry and a novel in a new kind of American literary voice.

Alurista has distinguished himself as a political activist and cultural warrior, a spokesman for ethnic politics, and a poet of an original oeuvre that encompasses barrio aesthetics, indigenous themes, clever wordplay, and virtuosity in linguistic slang and calligraphic expression. His constant innovations and flair made him a key poet from the 1960s through the 1980s. He developed cultural nationalism to a higher level among Chicanos, but his legacy lies in his ability to spearhead a new poetics of Spanglish.

See also **Hispanics in the United States; Literature: Spanish America.**

BIBLIOGRAPHY

Primary Works

Floricanto en Aztlán. Los Angeles: University of California Chicano Studies Center, 1971.

Timespace Huracán: Poems, 1972–75. Albuquerque, NM: Pajarito Publications, 1976.

A'nque: Collected Poems 1976–79. San Diego, CA: Maize Press, 1979.

Spik in Glyph? Houston, TX: Arte Público Press, 1981.

As Our Barrio Turns ... Who the Yoke B On? San Diego, CA: Calaca Press, 2000.

Secondary Sources

Keller, Gary. "Alurista, Poeta-Antropólogo, and the Recuperation of the Chicano Identity." In *Return: Poems Collected and New*, pp. xi–xlix. Ypsilanti, MI: Bilingual Press/Editorial Bilingue, 1972.

Lomeli, Francisco A. "Alurista (1947–)". In *Latino and Latina Writers*, ed. Alan West-Durán, pp. 101–116. New York: Charles Scribner's Sons, 2004.

Ybarra-Frausto, Tomás. "Alurista's Poetics: The Oral, the Bilingual, the Precolumbian." In *Modern Chicano Writers*, ed. Joseph Sommers and Tomás Ybarra-Frausto, pp. 117–132. Englewood Cliffs, NJ: Prentice-Hall, 1979.

FRANCISCO A. LOMELÍ

ALVA IXTLILXOCHITL, FERNANDO

(c. 1578–1650). Fernando de Alva Ixtlilxochitl was a historian of noble Amerindian descent from Texcoco, Mexico, whose work challenges the traditional dichotomy between conquered and conqueror. Prominent examples of the "Amerindian chronicle," Alva Ixtlilxochitl's numerous accounts narrate the history of his hometown from ancient times to the early sixteenth century, and portray the Aculhua (Chichimecs) from Texcoco as a great pre-Christian nation, whose evolution towards monotheism turned the 1519 Spanish invasion into a joyful encounter with the revealed Christian god.

Alva Ixtlilxochitl's most polished work, *Historia de la nación chichimeca* (History of the Chichimec Nation, c. 1625) narrates the history of Texcoco from its foundation to the Spanish conquest. Aculhuas are depicted as a nation experiencing a steady cultural development before contact with Europeans. They become sedentary, adopting prestigious cultural practices from other nations, such as Nahuatl language and customs from Toltec groups. An alleged parallel evolution towards monotheism occurs, embodied in the famous Texcocan king Nezahualcoyotl, a double of the biblical King David. This identification implies that Texcocans are equivalent to the Jewish people of the Old Testament. Thus, the Spanish conquest becomes the last step in this nation's development towards Christianity and civilization. The *Historia* creates a distinction between the "barbarous Mexicas" from Tenochtitlan and the nearly Christian Aculhuas, from which local Amerindian authorities and the author himself could benefit politically and economically in their relations with the Spanish colonial administration.

While it is true that Alva Ixtlilxochitl distorts the history of Texcoco, his works offer a wealth of information about a notable Mesoamerican group. Furthermore, these distortions may prove to be essential in determining how Amerindian intellectuals negotiated their place in colonial society. Alva Ixtlilxochitl's work is part of the emergence of historical accounts by non-European authors in New Spain after 1570, including Alvarado Tezozomoc, Chimalpahin, and Muñoz Camargo. Incorporating these authors' narratives into an understanding of Amerindian cultures is historically responsible, and also relevant to current discussions about Amerindian peoples' historical rights to land and within globalization processes.

See also **Alvarado Tezozomoc, Hernando; Chimalpahin; Muñoz Camargo, Diego.**

BIBLIOGRAPHY

Adorno, Rolena. "Arms, Letters, and the Native Historian in Early Colonial Mexico." In *Rediscovering Colonial Writing*, edited by René Jara and Nicholas Spadaccini. Minneapolis, MN: Hispanic Issues, 1989.

Adorno, Rolena. "The Indigenous Ethnographer: The 'Indio Ladino' as Historian and Cultural Mediation." In *Implicit Understandings: Observing, Reporting, and Reflecting on the Encounters Between Europeans and Other Peoples in the Early Modern Era*, edited by Stuart B. Schwartz. Cambridge, U.K.: Cambridge University Press, 1994.

Alva Ixtlilxochitl, Fernando de. *Obras históricas.* 2 vols. Edited by Edmundo O'Gorman. Mexico D.F.: Universidad Autónoma de México, 1975–1977.

Velazco, Salvador. *Visiones de Anáhuac. Reconstrucciones historiográficas y etnicidades emergentes en el México colonial: Fernando de Alva Ixtlilxóchitl, Diego Muñoz Camargo y Hernando Alvarado Tezozómoc.* Guadalajara, Mexico: Universidad de Guadalajara, 2003.

JUAN JOSÉ DANERI

ALVARADO, ANTONIO (1938–).

Antonio Alvarado (*b.* 1938), Panamanian abstract painter. Although he studied under the figurative painter Alberto Dutary (*b.* 1932), Alvarado's early works showed a keen awareness of international trends such as abstract expressionism. A UNESCO grant in 1969 allowed him to travel to Japan, where he was influenced by oriental art, Zen, and Buddhism.

In his drawings, serigraphs, and bright acrylic paintings, Alvarado experiments with reducing art to its essential forms, and his work ranges from precise, hard-edge paintings like *Homenaje a Varèse* (1972) to such strong gestural compositions as *Buda No. 120* (1981). In the 1970s, he held the position of director of the Department of Visual Arts of Panama's Instituto Nacional de Cultura.

See also **Art: The Twentieth Century.**

BIBLIOGRAPHY

Gilbert Chase, *Contemporary Art in Latin America* (1970).

Damián Boyón, *Artistas contemporáneos de América Latina* (1981).

Additional Bibliography

Salón las Perlas. *Expo-trayectorias: décadas 1950-1960-1970-1980: 12 grandes de la pintura Panameña: Antonio Alvarado, et al.: Salón las Perlas, Panamá, 28 agosto, 1984.* Panamá: Club Unión de Panama, 1984.

MONICA E. KUPFER

ALVARADO, LISANDRO (1858–1929).

Lisandro Alvarado (*b*. 19 September 1858; *d*. 10 April 1929), Venezuelan ethnologist, linguist, naturalist, and historian. At the age of twenty, Alvarado traveled to Caracas to study medicine at the University of Caracas; where he came in contact with the positivist and evolutionist ideas that were in vogue in Latin America in the latter part of the nineteenth century. The tenets of these schools of thought would serve as a guide to his diverse intellectual activities. Alvarado conducted investigations in the areas of ethnography, linguistics, and history and studied ancient and modern cultures, traveling throughout the country as part of his research. He was proficient in several languages and was one of the first Venezuelans to study the indigenous customs and languages of the country's aboriginal groups. Alvarado was a regular member of the academies of medicine, language, and history. His major works include: *Sobre las guerras civiles del país* (1894) and *Glosario de voces indígenas de Venezuela* (1921).

See also **Positivism.**

BIBLIOGRAPHY

Pascual Venegas Filardo, *Lisandro Alvarado (1858–1929)* (1973).

Pedro Grases, *Obras completas,* 7 vols. (Caracas, 1953–1958), *La obra lexicográfica de Lisandro Alvarado* (Caracas, 1981).

Cesia Ziona Hirshbein, *Historia y literatura en Lisandro Alvarado* (Caracas, 1981).

Additional Bibliography

Pérez Hernández, Francisco Javier. "Testimonios de lexicógrafos: un texto inédito del padre Barnola sobre los glosarios de Lisandro Alvarado." *Montalbán* 32 (1999): 357-372.

INÉS QUINTERO

ALVARADO, MARÍA JESÚS (1878–1971).

María Jesús Alvarado Rivera, born in Chincha, Peru, on May 27, 1878, was a sociologist, modernist educator, and feminist writer. In 1912 she published *El Feminismo,* the first revolutionary essay of the twentieth century in Peru. In 1914 she formed Evolución Femenina, an association for women's progress, with a defiant political stance that demanded changes in society: education for women, access to jobs and professions, civil rights equal to those of men, and, as she put it in *El Feminismo,* "the political rights to participate directly in the nation's destiny." In her novel *Nuevas Cumbres* (1923), Alvarado envisions a utopia of men and women living as equals.

Alvarado founded the Moral and Labor School-Workshop, the three pillars of which were culture, work, and citizenship, to prepare poor young prostitutes for the labor market. Her commitment to women and abandoned children and her solidarity with the indigenous people and workers of Peru made her the target of dictator Augusto B. Leguía. Deported by the regime to Argentina in 1924, she lived in exile there until 1937.

Alvarado founded the Ollantay Academy of Dramatic Art, which staged several of her plays: *Ante los hijos, El matrimonio ultramoderno, El puñal del abuelo* and *El imperativo de la sangre* (1938), and *El tesoro de la Isla* and *Mártir Olaya* (1939). In her novels *La Perricholi: Novela histórica dramatizada en treinta jornadas* (1946) and *Amor y Gloria: El romance de Manuela Sáenz y el Libertador Simón Bolívar* (1952), she fashioned historical figures into literary characters. She died in Lima in 1971.

See also **Feminism and Feminist Organizations; Leguía, Augusto Bernardino; Peru: Peru Since Independence.**

BIBLIOGRAPHY

Chaney, Elsa M. "Significado de la Obra de María Jesús Alvarado Rivera." *Cuadernos Culturales* 2 (1988): 1–16.

Mannarelli, María Emma. *Limpias y modernas: Género, higiene y cultura en la Lima del novecientos.* Lima: Ediciones Flora Tristán, 1999.

LADY ROJAS-BENAVENTE

ALVARADO, SALVADOR (1880–1924).

Salvador Alvarado (*b.* 1880; *d.* June 1924), military leader of the Mexican Revolution and social reformer. Alvarado, the son of a printer, was born in northwest Mexico. After opposing the Porfiriato in the anarcho-syndicalist Mexican Liberal Party (Partido Liberal Mexicano—PLM) and participating in the brutally suppressed workers' strike at Cananea in 1906, he transferred his allegiance in 1909 to the more moderate, broader-based movement of Francisco I. Madero. His organizational and tactical skills elevated him rapidly in the military hierarchy during the revolutionary campaigns against Porfirio Díaz and Victoriano Huerta. In 1914, Madero's successor, the Constitutionalist leader Venustiano Carranza, promoted him to division general. Then, following a brief stint as military commandant of the Federal District, he became Carranza's proconsul for the conquest and administration of the state of Yucatán.

Subduing a powerful regional oligarchy with his 7,000-man army in March 1915, Alvarado immediately attempted to make Yucatán a model of what the Mexican Revolution could accomplish, to transform the region into a social laboratory. His three-year governorship (1915–1918) was characterized by an effective blend of populist reform and authoritarian military rule. Buoyed by a swell in henequen revenues generated by World War I, Alvarado established more than a thousand new schools, the majority of them in remote, previously untouched hamlets and hacienda communities. He enforced an earlier, moribund decree "freeing" the debt peons who worked in slavelike conditions on the henequen estates and attempted to redress labor abuses through state-run tribunals. Under Alvarado's aegis, Mexico's first feminist congresses were convened, and special feminist leagues were organized. Alvarado was also responsible for the creation of a small but powerful urban labor movement, based in Mérida, the state's capital, and in Progreso, its principal port. In 1916, seeking to institutionalize his regional movement, Alvarado incorporated the workers and campesinos into a nascent state party, the Socialist Workers' Party (Partido Socialista Obrero). Its name was changed a year later to the Socialist Party of Yucatán (Partido Socialista de Yucatán). Many now regard it as a forerunner of Mexico's present-day corporatist edifice, the Institutional Revolutionary Party (Partido Revolucionario Institucional—PRI).

Carranza removed Alvarado as governor in 1918; although Alvarado harbored presidential aspirations, he never regained the renown he had known as Yucatán's revolutionary caudillo. In 1924, with fellow Sonoran Adolfo De La Huerta and an important segment of the Mexican army, he rebelled against Carranza's successor, Alvaro Obregón Salido, and was killed by Obregonistas in El Hormiguero, Chiapas, in June 1924.

See also **Mexico, Wars and Revolutions: Mexican Revolution.**

BIBLIOGRAPHY

Francisco J. Paoli Bolio, *Yucatán y los orígenes del nuevo estado mexicano: Gobierno de Salvador Alvarado, 1915–1918* (1984).

Gilbert M. Joseph, *Revolution from Without: Yucatán, Mexico, and the United States, 1880–1924*, rev. ed. (1988).

Additional Bibliography

Chacón, Ramón D. "Salvador Alvarado and the Agrarian Reform in Yucatán, 1915-1918: Federal Obstruction of Regional Social Change." In *Land, Labor & Capital in Modern Yucatán: Essays in Regional History and Political Economy*, Jeffrey Brannon and Gil Joseph, editors. Tuscaloosa: University of Alabama Press, 1991.

Fallaw, Ben W. "Dry Law, Wet Politics: Drinking and Prohibition in Post-Revolutionary Yucatán, 1915–1935." *Latin American Research Review* 37 (2002): 37–64.

Herrera y Cairo, Othón. *Salvador Alvarado: Vida y obra.* Sinaloa[?]: Gobierno del Estado de Sinaloa, 2004.

GILBERT M. JOSEPH

ALVARADO TEZOZOMOC, DON HERNANDO (c. 1525–c. 1610).

This historian from Mexico-Tenochtitlan, commonly known as Tezozomoc, wrote two narratives on pre-conquest Mexico. His works, published during the nineteenth and twentieth centuries, are important sources on the history of Tenochtitlan, the most important center of the so-called Aztec Empire. Tezozomoc was a grandson of Motecuzoma Xocoyotl, *tlatoani* (ruler) of

Tenochtitlan (*c.* 1502–1520), and son of don Diego de Alvarado Huanitzin, tlatoani of Ecatepec (1520–1539) and later governor of Tenochtitlan (1539–1542). He served as a *nahuatlato*, or Nahuatl interpreter, under the viceroy don Gaspar de Zúñiga y Acevedo (1595–1603). Although no sources exist that document Tezozomoc's formal education, his scholarly knowledge is patent in his *Cronica Mexicana* (c. 1598), written in Spanish. Composed of 112 chapters—two are lost—this narrative, in the format of a European chronicle, focuses on the rise and fall of Tenochtitlan. It creates a hybrid genre in which alphabetic writing is used to transcribe oral and pictographic ancient accounts. An ambivalent discourse of admiration and abjection emerges, as a result of narrating native practices that at times conflict with Christian principles.

A second narrative attributed to Tezozomoc is the so-called *Cronica Mexicayotl* (1609), written in Nahuatl, in a preconquest format known as annals. This format, distinct from the European format of same name, was used mainly by native historians and focused on chronological events of quotidian as well as of remarkable character. The *Cronica Mexicayotl* contains an imperial history of the Mexica Empire and a genealogical history of its rulers. In the introduction Tezozomoc expresses his role as keeper and transmitter of the ancient Mexica word, a privilege the Mexica wise men granted him because of his lineage. The earliest manuscript of the *Cronica Mexicayotl* is a holograph also signed by the indigenous historian from Chalco-Amaquemecan, don Domingo de San Antón Muñón Chimalpahin Cuauhtlehuanitzin, known as Chimalpahin.

Manuscripts of the narratives by Tezozomoc and his native and *mestizo* (Spanish-Indian) contemporaries were donated to the Mexican *criollo* (American-born Spanish) erudite Carlos de Sigüenza y Góngora and later served as a source for criollo intellectuals in their production of a Mexican historiography during the eighteenth and nineteenth centuries. These texts are important sources for critical investigations in different areas of research, from linguistics to the social sciences, cultural studies, and postcolonial studies. Written after the conquest under an alien political and ideological hegemony, these narratives provide insight into the processes of meaning-making and representation.

See also **Colonialism; Tenochtitlán; Aztecs; Alva Ixtlilxochitl, Fernando; Chimalpahin; Muñoz Camargo, Diego; Sigüenza y Góngora, Carlos de.**

BIBLIOGRAPHY

Garibay, Miguel Angel. *Historia de la literatura náhuatl.* 2 vols. México: Porrúa, 1954.

Lockhart, James. *The Nahuas after the Conquest.* Stanford, CA: Stanford University Press, 1992.

Editions of Works by Alvarado Tezozomoc

Crónica mexicana. Edited by Manuel Orozco y Berra. 4th edition. Mexico City: Porrúa, [1878] 1987.

Crónica mexicana. Edited by Mario Mariscal. 2nd edition. Mexico City: Universidad Nacional Autónoma de México, [1943] 1994.

Crónica mexicana. Edited by Gonzalo Díaz Migoyo and Germán Vázquez. Las Rozas, Madrid: Dastin, 2001.

Crónica mexicayotl. Translated by Adrián León. Mexico City: Universidad Nacional Autónoma de México, [1949], 1975, 1998.

Cronica mexicayotl: Codex Chimalpahin. Vol. 1. Translated by Susan Schroeder and J. O Anderson. Norman and London: University of Oklahoma Press, 1997.

ROCÍO CORTÉS

ALVARADO XICOTENCATL, LEONOR (1524–1583).

Leonor Alvarado Xicotencatl (*b.* 22 March 1524; *d.* 1583), the first prominent *ladina* (child of Spanish and Indian parents) born in Guatemala.

Daughter of the conquistador Pedro de Alvarado and of Luisa de Xicotencatl, a Tlascalteca Indian princess, doña Leonor was born at Utatlán, the capital of the Quiché, and was brought up by her godparents. Alvarado arranged her marriage to his friend and chief lieutenant, Pedro de Portocarrero, about 1541. She escaped death when a mudslide resulting from a flood and earthquake covered the capital at Almolonga and killed her stepmother, doña Beatríz de la Cueva, in 1541.

After the death of Portocarrero in 1547, doña Leonor married Francisco de la Cueva, the brother of her stepmother. From this marriage were born the children who were Pedro de Alvarado's descendants in Guatemala. Her second husband died in 1576, and doña Leonor died seven years later, at the age of fifty-nine. Her remains were buried in the Cathedral at Santiago (now Antigua Guatemala), beside those of her father and her stepmother.

See also **Cueva de Alvarado, Beatriz de la.**

BIBLIOGRAPHY

José Milla, *La hija del adelantado,* 4th ed. (1936), a novel.

Adrian Recinos, *Doña Leonor de Alvarado, y otros estudios* (1958).

Additional Bibliography

Vega, Carlos B. *Conquistadoras: Mujeres heroicas en la conquista de América.* Jefferson, NC: McFarland & Co., 2003.

DAVID L. JICKLING

ALVARADO Y MESÍA, PEDRO DE

(1485?–1541?). Pedro de Alvarado y Mesía (*b.* 1485?; *d.* 29 June 1541?), a leader in the Spanish conquests of Mexico, Central America, and Ecuador. Born in Badajoz to a family of the minor nobility, Alvarado came to the Americas around 1510. He was a member of the Juan de Grijalva expedition to the Gulf coast of Mexico, and then accompanied Hernán Cortés as his chief lieutenant on his conquest of central Mexico (1519–1521). He was in charge of the garrison in Tenochtitlán (Mexico City) and by instituting a massacre during the Toxcatl holiday sparked the events that led up to the disastrous Spanish withdrawal from the city (the Noche Triste) and played an outstanding role in the final siege and Spanish victory.

Known to the native peoples as "Tonatiuh" (the Sun), Alvarado was sent south by Cortés in 1523 with an army of 429 Spaniards and some 20,000 Tlaxcalans and other Indian allies. He wreaked havoc on various Maya settlements as he led the Spanish conquests of Soconusco, Guatemala, and El Salvador, and pushed into Honduras, where he met conquistador groups coming from Nicaragua. His two letters of *relación* to Hernán Cortés are the only extant and immediate eyewitness accounts of the campaign. In all these events he showed his customary bravery, impetuousness, and cruelty.

After the Conquest he ruthlessly suppressed a major Cakchiquel revolt, and founded the first two Spanish capitals, Almolonga and Ciudad Vieja. (The latter was destroyed in 1541 by an avalanche of water and mud that killed his second wife shortly after he himself had died.) He seized the best *encomiendas* and slave *cuadrillas* for himself, his five brothers, and other relatives and associates. Many of his indigenous slaves were put to work on gold panning or shipbuilding. At one time he allegedly owned 1,500 branded native slaves who worked in the gold fields.

Alvarado dominated much of Central America for about seventeen years (1524–1541). His life after he became governor of Guatemala was marked by ambition and restlessness. His frequent absences and predatory return visits were disruptive. Each new expedition deprived the region of Spaniards, native auxiliaries, and supplies.

Leaving his brother Jorge in charge, Alvarado returned to Spain via Mexico in 1526–1527 to defend himself against charges of wrongdoing. While there, he married Francisca de la Cueva, a member of the high nobility, won his case, and was named governor and captain-general of Guatemala. His new wife died in Veracruz (1528) during the return journey to Guatemala.

Alvarado immediately began to plan an expedition to the South Seas but was diverted from it by news of the wealth won in Peru by Francisco Pizarro and Diego de Almagro. Against royal orders, he set off for Quito in 1534, again leaving Jorge as lieutenant governor. This time he took some 500 Spaniards and 2,000 native auxiliaries with him. Penetrating inland, Alvarado met Almagro. Potential conflict turned to negotiations when Alvarado realized that his men were tired, and that some of them were being induced to change sides. He finally agreed to turn over most of his men, ships, and equipment in return for 100,000 gold pesos. After his return to Guatemala (1535) he complained to the crown about Almagro's conduct, and his anger was increased by the discovery that some of the payment he had received consisted of adulterated and even falsified coinage.

Again facing accusations, this time from Mexico, Alvarado boldly set off from the coast of Honduras to plead his case in Spain (1536). There, on 22 October 1538, Charles V absolved him of all blame, and reappointed him as governor of Guatemala for seven more years. Charles also obtained a papal dispensation so that Alvarado could marry Beatríz de la Cueva, his deceased wife's sister.

Alvarado had been absent for over three years when he returned to Santiago de Guatemala in 1539. On his way from the coast he took over the governorship of Honduras from Francisco de Montejo and moved its main city inland to Gracias a Dios. In Guatemala he vigorously set about finding places for the large entourage that he and his new wife had brought from Spain. He also began to build ships and to collect men and supplies for yet another voyage of discovery to the Spice Islands.

He sailed with the new expedition in 1540, leaving Francisco de la Cueva in charge. This time he took 850 Spaniards and many auxiliaries with him. The fleet stopped for supplies at a port in Jalisco, where Alvarado met Viceroy Antonio de Mendoza, made a series of agreements with him, and joined in the suppression of a native revolt in Nueva Galicia. In late June 1541, during a skirmish, he was crushed to death by a falling horse.

See also **Conquistadores.**

BIBLIOGRAPHY

William R. Sherman, "A Conqueror's Wealth: Notes on the Estate of don Pedro de Alvarado," in *The Americas* 26 (1969): 199–213.

Adrián Recinos, *Pedro de Alvarado, Conquistador de México y Guatemala*, 2d ed. (1986).

Additional Bibliography

Flint, Richard, and Shirley Cushing Flint. *Documents of the Coronado Expedition, 1539-1542: "They Were Not Familiar with His Majesty, nor Did They Wish to Be His Subjects."* Dallas: Southern Methodist University Press, 2005.

Jaramillo, Mario. *Perfiles de conquista: La aventura de España en América.* Bogota, Colombia: Universidad Sergio Arboleda, Fondo de Publicaciones, 2003.

MURDO J. MACLEOD

ÁLVAREZ, JUAN (1790–1867). Juan Álvarez (*b.* 27 January 1790; *d.* 21 August 1867), president of Mexico (1855–1856). The orphaned son of a landowner in Santa María de la Concepción Atoyac in coastal Guerrero State, Álvarez joined the insurgent army of José María Morelos y Pavón in 1810. After independence Álvarez commanded militia forces in Guerrero and participated in several federalist revolts of the 1820s and 1830s. He is best known for his strong relationship with Guerrero's peasantry. During widespread peasant revolts in the 1840s he mediated land claims and reduced taxes. He simultaneously recruited the peasant rebels for federalist movements and the war against the United States. His efforts and political connections led to the creation in 1849 of the state of Guerrero, of which he was the first governor. In 1854–1855 Álvarez led the Revolution of Ayutla against the conservative government of Antonio López de Santa Anna. This movement began the period of the Reform. Álvarez retired to Guerrero after a brief stint as president from October 1855 to September 1856. He remained politically active and supported the Liberal governments of Benito Juárez against both the Conservatives and Maximilian's empire. He died at his hacienda on the Guerrero coast.

Álvarez was most important as a champion of the incorporation of Mexico's peasant masses into the polity of the young nation-state. Advocating universal male suffrage and municipal autonomy, he utilized the fundamental similarities between the peasant tradition of annual elections for village office and the basic tenets of popular sovereignty common to nineteenth-century political ideologies in Mexico and elsewhere. In promoting this model of state formation, Álvarez differed from both conservatives and many prominent liberals.

See also **Mexico, Wars and Revolutions: The Reform.**

BIBLIOGRAPHY

Clyde G. Bushnell, "The Military and Political Career of Juan Álvarez, 1790–1867" (Ph.D. diss. University of Texas, 1958).

Daniel Muñoz y Pérez, *El general don Juan Álvarez* (1959).

Fernando Díaz Díaz, *Caudillos y caciques: Antonio López de Santa Anna y Juan Álvarez* (1972).

Additional Bibliography

Arzola Nájera, Tomás. *La herencia de Juan Alvarez: El Estado Libre y Soberano de Guerrero.* Acapulco: Editorial Sagitario, 1997.

McGowan, Gerald L. *La separación del sur, o, Cómo Juan Alvarez creó su estado.* Toluca: Colegio Mexiquense, 2004.

Salazar Adame, Jaime, Rafael Rubí Alarcón, and María Teresa Pavía Miller. *Juan Alvarez Hurtado: Cuatro ensayos.* México: Gobierno del Estado de Guerrero; Asociación de Historiadores de Guerrero; M.A. Porrúa Grupo Editorial, 1999.

PETER GUARDINO

ALVAREZ, JULIA (1950–). The Dominican American writer Julia Alvarez was born in New York City, returning shortly thereafter to the Dominican Republic, where she spent her early childhood. In 1960 her family immigrated to the United States, fleeing the dictatorship of Rafael Leónidas Trujillo Molina and the threat caused by her father's involvement in antiregime activities. She was raised in New York.

Going against the grain of her Latino upbringing and its cultural expectations for women, Alvarez attended college and went on to pursue a career in writing. She received her B.A. summa cum laude from Middlebury College in 1971, and received her M.F.A. from Syracuse University in 1975. She taught English and creative writing in schools and universities while also holding various positions as a visiting writer. She became a professor in the English Department at Middlebury College in 1988, and was granted tenure in 1991. In 1998 she gave up her tenure to focus on writing, but she retains a position at the college as a writer-in-residence and adviser to Latino students.

Alvarez's work is greatly influenced by her own experiences as a Dominican exile and a "hyphenated American." She frames her alienation and assimilation as a cultural and linguistic predicament that is quite common among ethnic Americans. Such themes figure prominently in her semiautobiographical essays and poetry. In her books for young readers she translates bicultural and bilingual experiences into stories that help young Hispanic Americans understand their history, culture, and new language.

Alvarez earned acclaim in the early 1990s with her first two novels, *How the García Girls Lost Their Accents* (1991), which follows a Dominican family adjusting to their new life in the United States between the 1960s and 1980s, and *In the Time of the Butterflies* (1994), a fictionalized first-person account of the real-life Mirabal sisters, Dominican underground leaders who were brutally murdered by Trujillo's secret police. The metafictional and historiographic aspects of these novels are characteristic of her methodology; in the novels she has written since, she also imagines the perspectives and situations surrounding important Latin American historical and cultural events. All of her work is published in both English and Spanish editions.

Though Alvarez makes her home in Vermont, she and her husband have also established themselves in the Dominican Republic. Their *finca*, Alta Gracia, produces specialty coffees using organic sustainable farming methods and houses a school on site to promote literacy in the community.

See also **Dominican Revolt (1965); Dominicans; Feminism and Feminist Organizations; Hispanics in the United States; Trujillo Molina, Rafael Leónidas; Women.**

BIBLIOGRAPHY

Primary Works: Novels

How the García Girls Lost Their Accents. Chapel Hill, NC: Algonquin, 1991.

In the Time of the Butterflies. Chapel Hill, NC: Algonquin, 1994.

¡Yo!. Chapel Hill, NC: Algonquin, 1997.

In the Name of Salomé. Chapel Hill, NC: Algonquin, 2000.

A Cafecito Story. White River Junction, VT: Chelsea Green, 2001.

Saving the World. Chapel Hill, NC: Shannon Ravenel, 2006.

Primary Works: Nonfiction

Once Upon a Quinceañera: Coming of Age in the U.S.A. New York: Viking, 2007.

Primary Works: Poetry

The Other Side/El Otro Lado. New York: Dutton, 1995.

Homecoming: New and Collected Poems. New York: Plume, 1996.

The Woman I Kept to Myself. Chapel Hill, NC: Algonquin, 2004.

Primary Works: Essays

Something to Declare. Chapel Hill, NC: Algonquin, 1998.

Primary Works: For Young Readers

The Secret Footprints. New York: Knopf, 2000.

How Tía Lola Came to Visit. New York: Knopf, 2001.

Before We Were Free. New York: Knopf, 2002.

Finding Miracles. New York: Knopf, 2004.

A Gift of Gracias: The Legend of Altagracia. New York: Knopf, 2005.

Secondary Works

Di Pietro, Giovani. *La dominicanidad de Julia Alvarez.* San Juan: Editora Imago Mundi; Santo Domingo: Librería La Trinitaria, 2002.

Johnson, Kelli Lyon. *Julia Alvarez: Writing a New Place on the Map.* Albuquerque: University of New Mexico Press, 2005.

Sirias, Silvio. *Julia Alvarez: A Critical Companion.* Westport, CT: Greenwood Press, 2001.

LARA B. CAHILL

ÁLVAREZ, LUIS HÉCTOR (1919–).

The Mexican politician and opposition party leader Luis Héctor Álvarez was born on October 25, 1919, in Ciudad Camargo, Chihuahua. Álvarez received part of his education in El Paso, Texas, and took an engineering degree from MIT. A businessman, he was first employed in the textile industry, after which he became director of the Río Bravo Industrial Company (1957). He joined the National Action Party (PAN) in the early 1950s, having been active in numerous civic and business associations in Ciudad Juárez, including serving as director of the chamber of commerce. He served on the party's National Executive Committee. Selected by the PAN as its presidential candidate, he opposed Adolfo López Mateos in the 1958 presidential election.

Although he remained out of the national political limelight for many years, he won election as mayor of Chihuahua in 1983. He received national media attention in 1986 for engaging in a forty-one-day hunger strike in protest against voter fraud by the Institutional Revolutionary Party. He is credited with inspiring a resurgence of activism and support for his party in Chihuahua.

Upon completion of his term as mayor, he served as president of the PAN from 1987 to 1993. Under his leadership PAN ran the most successful presidential campaign in its history in 1988, with Manuel Clouthier as its candidate. As a leading contributor to the democratic opening in Mexican politics, Álvarez served as a senator from 1994 to 2000. His colleagues appointed him as president of the congressional peace commission to the Zapatistas in 1997. As of 2006 he continued to serve ex officio on his party's National Executive Committee.

See also **Mexico, Political Parties: National Action Party (PAN); Mexico: Since 1910.**

BIBLIOGRAPHY

Mizrahi, Yemile. *From Martyrdom to Power: The Partido Acción Nacional in Mexico.* Notre Dame, IN: University of Notre Dame Press, 2003.

Shirk, David A. *Mexico's New Politics: The PAN and Democratic Change.* Boulder, CO: Lynne Rienner, 2005.

RODERIC AI CAMP

ÁLVAREZ, MANUEL (1794–1856). Manuel Álvarez (*b.* 1794; *d.* 5 July 1856), fur trapper, merchant, and government official in New Mexico. The life of Álvarez, a native of Abelgas, Spain, exemplifies the tremendous opportunities that existed in New Mexico during the first half of the nineteenth century for an enterprising and well-connected immigrant.

In 1818 Álvarez immigrated to Mexico; in 1823 he moved to Cuba after Mexican independence unleashed anti-Spanish sentiment. There he obtained a U.S. passport and sailed to New York, planning to work his way back to Mexico. By 1824, Álvarez had joined a trading group in Saint Louis and had reached New Mexico, where he became friends with Charles Bent. There he opened a store to sell goods imported from Missouri.

The contacts and commercial ties that Álvarez built during the 1820s enabled him to take up fur trapping in 1829, when Mexican authorities expelled all Spanish residents from the country. By 1831, Álvarez worked for the American Fur Company as the leader of a team of forty fur trappers hunting in an area that is now part of

Yellowstone National Park. Álvarez managed his store in Santa Fe from a distance until 1834, when he returned there, his Spanish origin no longer a problem.

While claiming Mexican citizenship, Álvarez used his U.S. passport to gain an appointment as U.S. consul for Mexico, based in Santa Fe. Forced loans that American merchants made to the New Mexican officials during the 1837 revolt in Taos and Río Arriba, and losses to Americans resulting from the Texan expedition against Santa Fe in 1841, prompted American claims for reimbursement. Even though he never received complete confirmation of his post, Álvarez represented these petitions to the New Mexican governor and Mexican officials. His success in this role came from his relationship with Governor Manuel Armijo, based in part on the information that Álvarez and Bent provided about Apache and Texan movements of concern to New Mexico.

Upon the U.S. declaration of war against Mexico in 1846, the Americans sent "spies" to speak to Álvarez. He appears to have provided reports about affairs in New Mexico and advice on how to proceed with its occupation. Álvarez met with Governor Armijo and probably contributed to his decision not to oppose Colonel Stephen Watts Kearny and his force when it arrived to occupy Santa Fe. Although his friend Charles Bent served as interim governor of New Mexico until his murder during the 1847 revolt against the Americans, Álvarez received no post in the administration.

In the wake of the military government imposed on New Mexico after the revolt of 1847, Álvarez began to use his political skills in defense of the Spanish-Mexican population of the territory. He came to lead a political party, arguing against the propensity of military rule to ignore the civil rights of the population and advocating immediate statehood for New Mexico in order to bring back civilian rule. After a brief stint as editor of one of the early New Mexican newspapers in order to gain support for the statehood faction, Álvarez won the post of lieutenant governor alongside Congressman William Messervy in the election of 1850. Because Messervy had to spend most of his time in Washington, D.C., lobbying for statehood, running the state fell to Álvarez. Opposition from the army and the territorial party hampered the new government's ability to function. Soon after, the Compromise of 1850, admitting California to the Union as a free state and organizing New Mexico and Arizona into a single territory, made the position of the Statehood faction untenable.

Álvarez was never again involved as prominently in the affairs of the territory, and withdrew to his commercial ventures during the last years of his life. His ambition, and his service as an advocate for various American and Spanish-Mexican constituencies, wove him into the fabric of the critical events of New Mexican history bridging the Mexican and American periods. He died in Santa Fe.

See also **New Mexico.**

BIBLIOGRAPHY

Howard Roberts Lamar, *The Far Southwest, 1846–1912: A Territorial History* (1966).

David J. Weber, *The Taos Trappers: The Fur Trade in the Far Southwest, 1540–1846* (1971).

Janet Lecompte, *Rebellion in Rio Arriba, 1837* (1985).

Thomas E. Chávez, *Manuel Álvarez, 1794–1856: A Southwestern Biography* (1990).

ROSS H. FRANK

ÁLVAREZ ARMELLINO, GREGORIO CONRADO

(1925–). Gregorio Conrado Álvarez Armellino (*b.* 26 November 1925), Uruguayan military leader and president (1981–1985). Álvarez played an important role from 1973 to 1985, when the armed forces governed the country. The press, including that of the Left, had already popularized the figure of "Goyo" Álvarez, a commanding officer with a nationalist orientation and sympathies toward the leftist militarism of Peruvian General Juan Velasco Alvarado. Álvarez was appointed president by the military regime in 1981. He became one of the elements most opposed to the move toward democracy in Uruguay. After the election of Julio María Sanguinetti to the presidency, the political parties refused to accept the transfer of power directly from General Álvarez. The president of the Supreme Court of Justice had to intervene as a transitional leader in order for the restoration of democracy to be completed.

See also **Sanguinetti, Julio María; Velasco Alvarado, Juan.**

BIBLIOGRAPHY

Angel Cocchi, *Nuestros partidos,* vol. 2 (1984).

Martin Weinstein, *Uruguay: Democracy at the Crossroads* (1988).

JOSÉ DE TORRES WILSON

Maiz-Peña, Magdalena. "Cuerpo fotográfico, subjetividad(es) y representación visual: Lola Alvarez Bravo y Frida Kahlo." *Studies in Latin American Popular Culture* 22 (2003): 193–206.

ELIZABETH FERRER

ÁLVAREZ BRAVO, LOLA (1907–1993).

Lola Álvarez Bravo (*b.* 3 April 1907; *d.* 31 July 1993), Mexican photographer. A pioneering modernist photographer, Álvarez Bravo's career spanned six decades. Born in Lagos de Moreno, Jalisco, she studied photography in the 1920s under the tutelage of Manuel Álvarez Bravo, to whom she was married from 1925 to 1949. While some of her early imagery bears relation to his, by the 1930s she had developed a distinct pictorial language that evinces her deep interest in the cinema as well as her empathy for the Mexican people. Her oeuvre includes photographs documenting everyday urban and rural life; these compositions often emphasize the ironic, humorous, or poetic aspects of mundane events. Other bodies of work include landscapes, still lifes, portraits of Mexican artists and intellectuals, and innovative photomontages. Álvarez Bravo was active as a teacher, documentary photographer for governmental agencies, exhibition curator, and director of the prestigious Galería de Arte Contemporáneo in Mexico City (1951–1958), which mounted important exhibitions featuring the artists of the Mexican School. She died in Mexico City.

See also **Photography: The Twentieth Century.**

BIBLIOGRAPHY

The most comprehensive study is Centro Cultural/Arte Contemporáneo, *Lola Álvarez Bravo, fotografías selectas 1934–1985* (1992). See also Lola Álvarez Bravo, *Recuento fotográfico* (1982), which contains conversations with the artist and extensive illustrations; Olivier Debroise, *Lola Álvarez Bravo, reencuentros* (1989); *Lola Álvarez Bravo, the Frida Kahlo Photographs* (1991); and Elizabeth Ferrer, "Lola Álvarez Bravo: A Modernist in Mexican Photography," in *History of Photography* 18, no. 3 (1994): 211–218.

Additional Bibliography

Ferrer, Elizabeth. *Lola Alvarez Bravo.* New York: Aperture and London: Thames & Hudson, 2006.

ÁLVAREZ BRAVO, MANUEL (1912–

2002). Manuel Álvarez Bravo (*b.* 4 February 1912; *d.* 19 October, 2002), Mexican photographer. Álvarez Bravo grew up in Mexico City in a family closely associated with the local artistic scene. In his youth, he associated with well-known photographers and painters, such as Diego Rivera. Self-taught in the art of photography, Álvarez has practiced the profession since 1923. In the 1930s, he began to capture on film the works of the Mexican muralists and other scenes of Mexican cultural life. Soon after his first exhibition, in 1932, his photographs were discovered by the international art community. Probably his most famous photograph, *Obrero en huelga, asesinado* (Striking worker, assassinated, 1934), depicts the body of a dead worker, covered in blood. This famous image tackles the politics of the time, but many of his photographs explore the nuances and contradictions of daily life in Mexico. While Álvarez Bravo picked up on nationalistic themes coming out of the Mexican Revolution, he did not present stereotypical images of Mexican culture. For instance, he photographed peasants, but the images reflected individualism rather than the standard themes of oppression and poverty. Álvarez Bravo has exhibited his work in museums and galleries all over the world. He was awarded the National Prize for Art in 1975, and has been the recipient of numerous other national and international awards for photography. He is a member of the Mexican Academy of Arts.

Álvarez Bravo uses black and white film; his themes are creativity and beauty, and he is known for his portraits of famous as well as common people, and urban and rural scenes of a changing Mexico. He is one of the most renowned Latin American photographers.

See also **Art: The Twentieth Century; Photography: 1900–1990; Rivera, Diego.**

BIBLIOGRAPHY

Luis Reyes De La Maza, *El cine sonoro en México* (1973).

E. Bradford Burns, *Latin American Cinema: Film and History* (1975).

Carl J. Mora, *Mexican Cinema: Reflections of a Society: 1896–1980* (1982).

John King, *Magical Reels: A History of Cinema in Latin America* (1990).

Additional Bibliography

Debroise, Olivier. *Mexican Suite: A History of Photography in Mexico.* Translated by Stella de Sá Rego. Austin: University of Texas Press, 2001.

García Krinsky, Emma Cecilia, Rosa Casanova, and Claudia Canales. *Imaginarios y fotografía en México: 1839–1970.* Barcelona, Spain: Lunweg, 2005.

Kismaric, Susan. *Manuel Álvarez Bravo.* New York: Museum of Modern Art, 1997.

DAVID MACIEL

ÁLVAREZ DE PINEDA, ALONSO (?–1520).

Alonso Álvarez de Pineda (*d.* 1520), sailor. Little is known about Álvarez de Pineda, except that he was captain-general of the first European expedition to navigate systematically the entire coastline of the Gulf of Mexico from the Florida Keys to the Yucatán Peninsula. The voyage resulted in a hand-drawn map showing the peninsula of Florida as part of the mainland, not an island, as had been believed. The voyage also located the mouth of the Mississippi River (Río del Espíritu Santo), with its great discharge of fresh water.

Made in 1519, the voyage was sponsored by the governor of Jamaica, Francisco de Garay, who sought knowledge of the lands between those Juan Ponce de León had reached in 1513 (west of the Florida Peninsula) and the region west of Cuba (Yucatán and Central America). He also hoped to find a passage to the "South Sea" (the Pacific Ocean), discovered by Vasco Núñez de Balboa. Álvarez de Pineda was most likely slain by Huastec warriers upon whose land he had encroached on the shore of the Pánuco river.

See also **Explorers and Exploration: Spanish America.**

BIBLIOGRAPHY

An early (ca. late 1530s) navigational guide that must have incorporated Álvarez de Pineda's information is Paulino Castañeda, Mariano Cuesta, and Pilar Hernández, *Transcripción, estudio y notas del "Espejo de navegantes" de Alonso Chaves* (1983). See also Robert S. Weddle, *Spanish Sea: The Gulf of Mexico in North American Discovery, 1500–1685* (1985), esp. pp. 95–108.

JERALD T. MILANICH

ÁLVAREZ GARDEAZÁBAL, GUSTAVO (1945–).

Gustavo Álvarez Gardeazábal (*b.* 31 October 1945), Colombian writer. A native of Tuluá, Valle, he studied chemical engineering at Medellín's Universidad Pontificia. About 1963 he published parts of his first novel, *Piedra pintada* (1965), and was expelled from the university. Álvarez returned to Valle and continued to write fiction. The "Violencia" in Valle remained a major theme of his work, but after 1977 his novels reflected other currents as well, including opposition to the Gran Cauca elite. Álvarez taught at the Universidad del Valle (Cali) and was elected in 1978 to the municipal councils of Cali and of Tuluá. Recognized as Valle's major writer, he was a Guggenheim fellow in 1984–1985 and has won numerous other awards. His novels include *La tara del papa* (1971); *Cóndores no entierran todos los días* (1972); *Dabeiba* (1973); *El bazar de los idiotas* (1974); *El titiritero* (1977); *Los míos* (1981); *Los sordos ya no hablan* (1991); *Prisionero de la esperanza* (2000); and *Comandante Paraíso* (2002). He was elected Governor of Valle del Cauca in 1997. In 1999 he was accused of corruption and sentenced to six and a half years in prison, although his supporters doubted the fairness or legality of the proceedings against him. Alvarez himself referred to his case as "orchestrated by the presidential campaign of Horacio Serpa and the U.S. Embassy."

See also **Literature: Spanish America.**

BIBLIOGRAPHY

Raymond L. Williams, comp., *Aproximaciones a Gustavo Álvarez Gardeazábal* (1977).

Raymond L. Williams, *The Colombian Novel, 1844–1987* (1991).

David C. Foster, *Handbook of Latin American Literature,* 2d ed. (1992), p. 210.

Additional Bibliography

González Rodas, Pablo. *Colombia: Novela y violencia.* Manizales, Colombia: Secretaria de Cultura de Caldas, 2003.

Tittler, Jonathan. *El verbo y el mando: Vida y milagros de Gustavo Alvarez Gardeazábal.* Tuluá, Colombia: Unidade Central del Valle/Collección CantaRana, 2005.

Zambrano, Jaime. *La violencia en Colombia: La ficción de Alvarez Gardeazábal y el discurso histórico.* New York: P. Lang, 1997.

J. León Helguera

ALVAREZ MARTÍNEZ, GUSTAVO

(1937–1989). Gustavo Alvarez Martínez (*b.* 12 December 1937; *d.* 26 January 1989), Honduran general, chief of the armed forces. When Honduras resumed a civilian government in January 1982 with the election of Roberto Suazo Córdova to the presidency, the military coalesced under the leadership of Colonel Alvarez Martínez, appointed by the national assembly as commander in chief of the armed forces. Leading the armed forces as a "third party" of hard-liners in the Honduran political spectrum, Alvarez Martínez centralized and modernized the command structure, a feat that earned him a promotion from colonel to brigadier general. Then, with President Suazo Córdova, he forged a united front that stressed military subordination to the constitution as well as an alliance between the armed forces and the Liberal Party of Honduras. However, fellow officers, annoyed by his "high-handedness," ousted Alvarez Martínez and split decisively with Suazo in 1984. Five years later, the general was assassinated in Tegucigalpa by six men, an act for which the Popular Liberation Front claimed responsibility.

See also **Honderas.**

BIBLIOGRAPHY

James A. Morris, *Honduras: Caudillo Politics and Military Rulers* (1984).

James Dunkerley, *Power in the Isthmus: A Political History of Modern Central America* (1988).

Additional Bibliography

Centro de Documentación de Honduras. *Militarismo en Honduras: el reinado de Gustavo Alvarez, 1982-1984.* Tegucigalpa: Centro de Documentación de Honduras, 1985.

Ronfeldt, David F., Konrad Kellen, and Richard Millett. *U.S. Involvement in Central America: Three Views from Honduras.* Santa Monica: RAND, 1989.

Ruhl, J. Mark. "Redefining Civil-Military Relations in Honduras." *Journal of Interamerican Studies and World Affairs* 38 (Spring, 1996): 33-66.

Jeffrey D. Samuels

ÁLVAREZ PONCE DE LEÓN, GRISELDA

(1913–). Born in Guadalajara on April 5, 1913, Griselda Álvarez is considered one of the foremost feminist poets in México. She is both a politician and a poet. In 1979 she became the first female governor of the state of Colima. As an accomplished poet, capable of creating an unmatched verbal sensuality, Álvarez owes her fame to the rich, erotic lyrics that have characterized much of her work. In her introduction to *10 mujeres en la poesía Mexicana del siglo XX*, Álvarez points out that women long for the right to have an active sexuality, and this satisfaction can be found within a woman's soul, where she is "unpredictable like the cyclones" (p. 10).

See also **Feminism and Feminist Organizations; Literature: Spanish America.**

BIBLIOGRAPHY

Primary Works

Cementerio de Pájaros. México: Cuadernos Americanos, 1956.

Anatomía superficial. México: Fondo de Cultura Económica, 1967.

Estación sin nombre. Barcelona: Ediciones Marte, 1972.

Editor. *10 mujeres en la poesia mexicana del siglo XX.* México: Colección Metropolitana, 1973.

Desierta compañia. Colima, México: Universidad de Colima, 1980.

Secondary Works

Manca, Valeria. *El Cuerpo del deseo: Poesía erótica femenina en el México actual.* México, D.F.: Universidad Autonoma Metropolitana, 1989.

Jiménez Faro, Luzmaría. *Breviario de los sentidos: Poesia erótica escrita por mujeres.* Madrid: Torremozas, 2003.

Ocampo Aurora M., and Ernesto Prado Velázquez. *Diccionario de escritores mexicanos.* México: UNAM, 1967.

Rodríguez, Victoria Elizabeth. *Women's Participation in Mexican Political Life.* Boulder, CO: Westview Press, 1998.

JORGE J. BARRUETO

ALVEAR, CARLOS MARÍA DE (1789–1852).

Carlos María de Alvear (*b.* 25 October 1789; *d.* 2 November 1852), Argentine soldier and politician. Alvear, born in Misiones, was the son of a Spanish naval officer and a creole mother. After service in the Peninsular War he returned to Buenos Aires in 1812 with José de San Martín and other patriots to play a leading role in the military and political organization of independence. As president of the Assembly of the Year XIII (1813), he influenced its policy in the direction of liberal reform. The capture of Montevideo from the Spanish in 1814 strengthened Alvear's military base, and he was appointed supreme director of the United Provinces of the Río de la Plata to restore stability to the revolutionary government. His tendency toward dictatorship and centralism caused his overthrow and exile after less than four months in office (April 1815).

Alvear subsequently changed political direction and joined forces with the Littoral caudillos in an attempt to overthrow the Buenos Aires government and establish a federal system. But the caudillos' success at Cepeda (1820) failed to secure him the governorship he desired. He was recalled to office by Bernardino Rivadavia and, while minister of war, fought a successful military campaign against Brazil at Ituazingó early in 1827. He retired to private life until Juan Manuel de Rosas appointed him minister to the United States in 1838. He died in New York.

See also **Rivadavia, Bernardino.**

BIBLIOGRAPHY

Thomas B. Davis, Jr., *Carlos de Alvear: Man of Revolution* (1955).

Tulio Halperín Donghi, *Politics, Economics, and Society in Argentina in the Revolutionary Period* (1975).

Additional Bibliography

Ocampo, Emilio. "Alvear, ¿traidor?: En defensa de un hombre público." *Todo es Historia* 443 (June 2004): 62–76.

Ocampo, Emilio. *Alvear en la guerra con el imperio del Brasil.* Buenos Aires: Claridad, 2003.

Pinedo, Enrique. *Los relegados.* Buenos Aires: Corregidor, 2000.

JOHN LYNCH

ALVEAR, MARCELO TORCUATO DE (1868–1942).

Marcelo Torcuato de Alvear (*b.* 4 October 1868; *d.* 23 March 1942), Argentine political leader and president (1922–1928). Born into a prominent landed Buenos Aires family, Alvear became involved in the political reform activities of Leandro Alem and the Radical Civic Union (UCR) as a law student at the University of Buenos Aires. Alvear supported the UCR's 1893 uprising, but in the wake of its failure and the UCR's declining fortunes, he undertook a self-imposed exile in Europe and was not present at the time of the Radicals' 1905 rebellion. Despite this, Alvear maintained close contacts with Hipólito Irigoyen and other prominent Radicals and was elected to congress in 1912.

As Irigoyen's ambassador to France (1916–1920), Alvear had his first serious differences with the Radical leader, specifically in his opposition to Argentina's neutrality in World War I. Alarmed by labor protests and the oligarchy's increasing hostility to his government, Irigoyen chose Alvear as his successor, seeing his aristocratic credentials as an asset and his lack of a solid base within the party as leaving him open to manipulation. As president, Alvear tried to solve the problem of the national debt, a legacy, in large part, of Irigoyen's patronage practices.

During Alvear's presidency, Irigoyen's rivals within the UCR organized a separate party, the Antipersonalist Radical Civic Union, though Alvear himself was not a promoter of the *antipersonalista* movement. After the 1930 coup, he was forced into exile in Brazil but returned to assume control of the party, supporting its policy of electoral abstention until 1935 and then serving as the leader of the Radicals' loyal opposition to the nondemocratic governments of the period, losing as the 1937 Radicals' presidential candidate in an election characterized by widespread fraud.

See also **Argentina, Political Parties: Radical Party (UCR).**

BIBLIOGRAPHY

Félix Luna, *Alvear* (1974).

David Rock, *Politics in Argentina, 1890–1930: The Rise and Fall of Radicalism* (1975).

Luis A. Alen Lascano, *Yrigoyenismo y antipersonalismo* (1986).

Additional Bibliography

Aguirre, Gisela. *Marcelo T. de Alvear.* Buenos Aires: Planeta, 2001.

Cattaruzza, Alejandro. *Marcelo T. de Alvear: el compromiso y la distancia.* Buenos Aires: Fondo de Cultura Económica, 1997.

JAMES P. BRENNAN

ALVES, FRANCISCO (1889–1952). Francisco Alves (Francisco de Morais Alves; *b.* 19 August 1889; *d.* 27 September 1952), Brazilian singer and songwriter. Alves was born in Rio de Janeiro and raised in the Saúde district of São Paulo. He began his musical career in 1918 as a singer in the João de Deus-Martins Chaves Circus. The following year, Alves made his first recording with an interpretation of "Pé de anjo" (Angel's Foot) and "Fala, meu louro" (Speak, My Parrot), both by Sinhô. He continued singing and recording while driving a taxi and occasionally performing in the circus or musical theater. In 1927 Alves began recording at the Odeon, where he took the stage name Chico Viola. Subsequently, he became a great success performing in Carnival celebrations, with the sambas "A Malandragem" (Gypsy Life) in 1928, "Amor de malandro" (A Scoundrel's Love) in 1930, "Se você jurar" (If You Promise) in 1931, and "Sofrer é da vida" (Life Is about Suffering) in 1932. At the Odeon, Alves made the first electronically produced record in Brazil with his interpretation of Duque's "Albertina" and "Passarinho do má" (Bad Little Bird) in 1927. In 1952 Alves was killed in an automobile accident; his funeral was attended by thousands. Known as the *rei da voz* (king of voice), Alves recorded the most 78 rpm LPs of any Brazilian singer: almost 500 records.

See also **Music: Popular Music and Dance.**

BIBLIOGRAPHY

Marcos Antônio Marcondes, ed., *Enciclopédia da música brasileira: Erudita folclórica popular* (1977).

Additional Bibliography

Cardoso Júnior, Abel. *Francisco Alves: As mil canções do Rei da Voz.* Paraná: Revivendo, 1998.

McCann, Bryan. *Hello, Hello Brazil: Popular Music in the Making of Modern Brazil.* Durham: Duke University Press, 2004.

Rangel, Patrícia. *Francisco Alves: Chico viola no tempo do rei da voz.* Rio de Janeiro, 2000.

LISA MARIC

ALVES BRANCO, MANUEL (1797–1855). Manuel Alves Branco, second viscount of Caravelas and poet, was among the most respected of the Empire of Brazil's liberal statesmen. A graduate of the University of Coimbra, Portugal (1823), Branco entered politics by 1830. A Bahian deputy (1830–1837), then a senator (1837–1855), he emerged during the crises between the abdication of the emperor Pedro I in 1831 and the installation of Pedro II in 1840. His reputation as a liberal derived from his work on the reform *Code of Criminal Procedure* (1832), his decentralism, and his championship of the reformist wing of the *moderados* (Regency liberals). Branco was a key minister for the embattled reformist regent, Diogo Antônio Feijó (1835–1837), during the dramatic rightward parliamentary shift against liberal reforms and in the context of revolts, secession, and diminishing state authority associated with them. However, with the triumph of the reactionary (later, Conservative) party of 1837, Branco refused to succeed Feijó and, after the early enthronement (1840) at the age of fourteen of Pedro III, left partisanship, confining himself to serving the emperor as a minister. Appointed to the Council of State in 1842, Branco also became the first cabinet minister to occupy the new position of prime minister, in 1847. Both appointments recognized his political skills, his loyalty to the monarch, and his achievements as a financial reformer.

See also **Brazil: 1808–1889; Brazil: Constitutions; Brazil: The Empire (Second); Brazil: Liberal Movements; Brazil: The Regency; Feijó, Diogo Antônio.**

BIBLIOGRAPHY

Barman, Roderick J. *Brazil: The Forging of a Nation: 1798–1852.* Stanford, CA: Stanford University Press, 1988.

Flory, Thomas. *Judge and Jury in Imperial Brazil, 1808–1871: Social Control and Political Stability in the New State.* Austin: University of Texas Press, 1981.

Lyra, Tavares de. *Instituições políticas do Império.* Brasília: Senado Federal, 1979.

Needell, Jeffrey D. *The Party of Order: The Conservatives, the State, and Slavery in the Brazilian Monarchy, 1831–1871.* Stanford, CA: Stanford Univ. Press, 2006.

Sacramento Blake, Augusto Victorino Alves. *Diccionario bibliographico brazileiro.* 7 vols. Rio de Janeiro: Nacional, 1893–1902.

JEFFREY D. NEEDELL

ALVES BRANCO TARIFF.

Alves Branco Tariff (1844), Brazil's first post-Independence tariff reform. Named for the finance minister of the time, the tariff raised import duties from an across-the-board rate of 15 percent ad valorem to 20 percent for cotton textiles and 30 percent for most other goods. Duties for a few agricultural products such as tobacco, tea, and hemp were set at 40 to 60 percent. The tariff was enacted after negotiations to renew the Anglo-Brazilian commercial treaty of 1827 became entangled in diplomatic disputes over Brazil's failure to halt the slave trade and Britain's refusal to lower duties on Brazilian sugar and coffee. Sometimes described as protectionist, the tariff was chiefly a fiscal measure intended to increase government revenues, which came overwhelmingly from customs receipts. Falling short of the more consistently protectionist proposals made in 1843 by a parliamentary commission, it had scarcely any adverse effects on British trade with Brazil. More important for the development of domestic industry was an 1846 decree eliminating all taxes on imported machinery.

As a result of both the 1844 increase in tariffs and the general growth in foreign trade, government revenues nearly doubled between 1845 and 1855. An even more liberal tariff schedule superseded the Alves Branco tariff in 1857.

See also **Slave Trade, Abolition of: Brazil.**

BIBLIOGRAPHY

Nícia Vilela Luz, *A luta pela industrialização do Brasil* (1961).

Leslie Bethell, *The Abolition of the Brazilian Slave Trade: Britian, Brazil, and the Slave Trade Question, 1807–1869* (1970).

Additional Bibliography

Rivière, Peter. *Absent-Minded Imperialism: Britain and the Expansion of Empire in Nineteenth-Century Brazil.* London: Tauris Academic Studies, 1995.

B. J. BARICKMAN

ÁLZAGA, MARTÍN DE (1757–1812).

Martín de Álzaga (*b.* 1757; *d.* 11 July 1812), Argentine merchant and political figure. A Basque of humble origins, Álzaga probably arrived in Buenos Aires in 1769. After serving a ten-year clerkship with the prominent merchant Gaspar de Santa Coloma, Álzaga launched his own mercantile career in 1780, becoming a successful merchant, a leading figure in the local *cabildo* (town council), and a spokesman for those merchants who worked to preserve the Spanish monopoly trade. Dismayed by the liberal trade policies enacted by Viceroy Santiago de Liniers y Bremond, and convinced that Liniers was an agent of the hated French, Álzaga and his followers attempted a royalist coup d'état on 1 January 1809, which was defeated by an increasingly radicalized militia led by Cornelio de Saavedra.

After independence in 1810, Álzaga continued to represent the concerns of Spanish loyalists. In July 1812 he again led a coup against a creole government that he viewed as inimical to the interests of Spain. No more successful than three years earlier, Álzaga and his followers were arrested by the government, now under the leadership of Bernardino Rivadavia, and were executed.

See also **Rivadavia, Bernardino.**

BIBLIOGRAPHY

Enrique Udaondo, *Diccionario biográfico colonial argentino* (1945), pp. 65–67.

Enrique Williams Álzaga, *Dos revoluciones* (1963) and *Martín de Álzaga en la reconquista y en la defensa de Buenos Aires, 1806–1807* (1971).

Additional Bibliography

Lozier Almazán, Bernardo P. *Martín de Alzaga: Historia de una trágica ambición*. Buenos Aires: Ediciones Ciudad Argentina, 1998.

SUSAN M. SOCOLOW

ALZATE Y RAMÍREZ, JOSÉ ANTONIO DE

ALZATE Y RAMÍREZ, JOSÉ ANTONIO DE (1737–1799). José Antonio de Alzate y Ramírez (*b.* 21 November 1737; *d.* 2 February 1799), prominent figure in the Mexican Enlightenment. Born in Ozumba (modern state of Mexico), Alzate studied at the Colegio de San Ildefonso, where he received a bachelor's degree in theology in 1756, the same year he took holy orders. From an early age, Alzate was also deeply drawn to secular studies, including mathematics, physics, astronomy, and the natural sciences; his wide-ranging interests earned him the sobriquet the "Pliny of Mexico." Alzate carried out his own research, such as conducting astronomical observations to determine the latitude of Mexico City. However, he made his greatest scientific contribution as an author and editor, promoting new scientific knowledge and the worldview of the Enlightenment through a series of publications, culminating in the *Gazeta de literatura de México* (1788–1795). Though sometimes marred by polemics, this journal informed readers of the latest scientific advances in both Europe—Alzate had become a member of the Royal Academy of Sciences in Paris in 1771—and the Americas. Alzate translated foreign materials and himself contributed numerous articles in which he described Mexico's rich natural and human resources and pointed out the practical benefits of new scientific methods for Mexican economic development.

See also **Enlightenment, The.**

BIBLIOGRAPHY

Clement Motten, *Mexican Silver and the Enlightenment* (1950).

Bernabé Navarro B., *Cultura mexicana moderna en el siglo xviii* (1964).

Elías Trabulse, *El círculo roto: Estudios históricos sobre la ciencia en México* (1982).

Additional Bibliography

Aceves Pastrana, Patricia, editor. *Periodismo científico en el siglo XVIII: José Antonio de Alzate y Ramírez*. Mexico City: Universidad Autónoma Metropolitana, Unidad Xochimilco, Sociedad Química de México, 2001.

Aguila, Yves. "Estrategias del discurso científico criollo: Espejo y Alzate." *Jahrbuch für Geschichte von Staat, Wirtschaft und Gesellschaft Lateinamerikas* 34 (1997): 245–257.

Codding, Mitchell A. "Perfecting the Geography of New Spain: Alzate and the Cartographic Legacy of Sigüenza y Góngora." *Colonial Latin American Review* 3 (1994): 185–219.

Saladino García, Alberto. *El sabio: José Antonio Alzate Ramírez de Santillana*. Toluca: Universidad Autónoma del Estado de México, 2001.

Saladino García, Alberto. *Dos científicos de la Ilustración hispanoamericana: J.A. Alzate y F.J. de Caldas*. México: Centro Coordinador y Difusor de Estudios Latinoamericanos, Universidad Nacional Autónoma de México, 1990.

R. DOUGLAS COPE

AMADO, JORGE

AMADO, JORGE (1912–2001). Jorge Amado (*b.* 10 August 1912, *d.* 6 August 2001), perhaps the most widely known and most popular of all Brazilian novelists. A major figure of the generation that developed the social "novel of the Northeast" in the 1930s, Amado wrote for more than six decades, completing more than twenty novels. His work has been translated into at least thirty languages and has inspired many films, television series, and even popular songs. A recipient of numerous international awards, Amado was elected to the Brazilian Academy of Letters in 1961.

From the 1930s until the 1950s Amado was both a political activist and a writer. He was a member of the Aliança Nacional Libertadora (1935) and the Brazilian Communist Party, of which he was an elected federal congressman during its brief period of legality (1945–1947). Because of his political activities, he spent several periods in exile. The trilogy *Os subterrâneos da liberdade* (1954) re-creates, in novelistic form, the political struggles against Getúlio Vargas's authoritarian Estado Novo in the 1930s and 1940s.

Amado's literary production ranges from novels marked by social protest and denunciation, especially during his "proletarian" phase of the 1930s—for example, *Cacau* (1933), *Suor* (1934; *Slums*, 1938), *Jubiabá* (1934; *Jubiabá*, 1984)—to those notable for the colorful, humorous, and often picaresque chronicles of the political customs and sexual mores of Brazilian society; these latter often have memorable female protagonists, for example, *Dona Flor e seus dois maridos* (1966; *Dona Flor and Her Two Husbands*, 1969), *Tereza Batista, cansada de guerra* (1972; *Tereza Batista, Home From the Wars*, 1975), and *Tieta do Agreste, pastora de cabras* (1977; *Tieta the Goat Girl*, 1979). Many critics have pointed to *Gabriela, cravo e canela* (1958; *Gabriela, Clove and Cinnamon*, 1962) as the dividing line between Amado's politically engaged narratives and his more exuberant, picturesque, populist tales that exalt the freedom to live and love outside the confines of bourgeois morality. The short *A morte e a morte de Quincas Berro d'Água* (1959) ingeniously and satirically contrasts bourgeois and "popular" culture and values.

Amado's novels and his occasional short narratives typically deal with different aspects of his home state, focusing primarily on the city of Salvador or the cacao region of southern Bahia. Novels such as *Terras do sem-fim* (1943; *The Violent Land*, 1945), *São Jorge dos Ilhéus* (1944), and *Tocaia Grande: A face obscura* (1984) re-create struggles for control of rich cacao lands, combining political intrigue and intertwined love affairs.

Those works set in Salvador often focus on the life and culture of the city's predominantly black lower classes, frequently portrayed as living in a sort of harmonious primitive communism (*Capitães de areia*, 1937) and spiritually sustained by the values of the Afro-Brazilian religion Candomblé. Amado's praise of miscegenation and Afro-Brazilian culture reaches its high point in *Tenda dos milagres* (1969; *Tent of Miracles*, 1971).

Amado's idealization of the lower classes has drawn harsh criticism from those who see him as exploiting, rather than celebrating, their culture. But his defenders argue that his insistent focus on the poor, even if vitiated by the use of "exotic local color," made him an eloquent spokesman for the downtrodden and the oppressed in Brazilian society.

See also **Literature: Brazil.**

BIBLIOGRAPHY

Maria Luisa Nunes, "The Preservation of African Culture in Brazilian Literature: The Novels of Jorge Amado," in *Luso-Brazilian Review* 10, no. 1 (Summer 1973): 86–101.

Walnice Galvão, "Amado: Respeitoso, respeitável," in her *Gatos de outro saco: Ensaios críticos* (1976), pp. 13–22.

Fred P. Ellison, "Jorge Amado," in his *Brazil's New Novel: Four Northeastern Masters* (1979), pp. 81–108.

Alfredo Wagner Berno De Almeida, *Jorge Amado: Política e literatura* (1979).

Bobby J. Chamberlain, "Salvadore, Bahia, and the Passion According to Jorge Amado," in *The City in the Latin American Novel*, edited by Bobby J. Chamberlain (1980).

Additional Bibliography

Brower, Keith H., Earl E. Fitz, and Enrique E. Martinez-Vidal. *Jorge Amado: New Critical Essays*. New York: Routledge, 2001.

Duarte, Eduardo de Assis. *Jorge Amado: Romance em tempo de utopia*. Rio de Janeiro: Editora Record, 1996.

Gattai, Zélia. *Memorial do amor*. Rio de Janeiro: Editora Record, 2004.

RANDAL JOHNSON

AMADOR, MANUEL E. (1869–1952).

Manuel E. Amador (*b.* 25 March 1869; *d.* 1952), one of Panama's first modern artists, creator of the national flag (1903). Amador occupied the public posts of minister of finance (1903–1904) and consul in Hamburg, Germany (1904–1908) and in New York City, where he lived from 1908 to 1925. Later, he worked as an auditor in Panama's Contraloría General (1926–1940).

Amador produced most of his oeuvre between 1910 and 1914, and after 1940. His style of vigorous drawing, gestural brush strokes, and somber colors reflected the lessons of German expressionism and the American artist Robert Henri (1865–1929). He painted landscapes and still lifes, but his main subject was the human figure, as exemplified by *Cabeza de Estudio* (1910) and *Rabbi* (1948). The University of Panama holds an important collection of his drawings, watercolors, and prints.

See also **Art: The Twentieth Century.**

BIBLIOGRAPHY

Rodrigo Miró, *Manuel E. Amador: un espíritu sin fronteras* (1966) and "Lewis, Amador, Ivaldi," in *Revista Lotería,* no. 219 (May 1974): 72–80.

Additional Bibliography

Cedeño Cenci, Diógenes. *Tres estudios sobre la cultura nacional.* Panama: Universidad de Panamá, 1993.

MONICA E. KUPFER

AMADOR GUERRERO, MANUEL

(1833–1909). Manuel Amador Guerrero (*b.* 30 June 1833; *d.* 2 May 1909), physician and politician, first president of Panama (1904–1908). Born in Turbaco, Colombia, Amador Guerrero was a member of a distinguished Colombian family. In 1855 he began studying medicine and became a successful physician. Beginning his political career as a Conservative, he was named president of the department of Panama in 1867, but a revolution prevented him from assuming the post. After a year in exile, he returned to become chief physician of the Panama Railroad. In 1903 he traveled to the United States to secure support for the independence movement. (French engineer Philippe Jean Bunau-Varilla arranged for financial and military support for the cause in return for an appointment as ambassador to the United States.) The price Amador paid for support was the unfavorable Hay–Bunau-Varilla Treaty of 1903, which dominated U.S.-Panamanian relations for years to come. Amador became the first president of the independent republic of Panama in 1904 and immediately embarked on a vigorous public-works program. His term ended a year before his death.

See also **Hay-Bunau-Varilla Treaty (1903).**

BIBLIOGRAPHY

Manual María Alba C., *Cronología de los gobernantes de Panamá, 1510–1967* (1967), pp. 249–254.

David G. Mc Cullough, *The Path Between the Seas: The Creation of the Panama Canal, 1870–1914* (1977), pp. 341–402.

Eduardo Lemaitre, *Panamá y su separación de Colombia* (1980), pp. 480–558.

SARA FLEMING

AMAPÁ.

Amapá, a Brazilian state that once guarded the Amazon delta against foreign invasion via the Atlantic Ocean. The seventeenth-century Portuguese showed no interest in this strategic area on the northern seaboard until France occupied land adjacent to it. In 1637, the future Amapá became Costa do Cabo Norte, the first captaincy that was clearly west of the line drawn by the Tordesillas Treaty of 1494. Sixty years later, the French invaded Costa do Cabo Norte, but Portugal forced their withdrawal. After the Portuguese dissolved Costa do Cabo Norte in the mid-eighteenth century, the French once again encroached on the area between the Amazon and Oyapock rivers. The ongoing border conflicts with France were not resolved until the twentieth century, when Brazil and France turned to an impartial arbitrator, Walther Hauser, president of Switzerland. Hauser awarded Amapá to Brazil on 1 December 1900, after which it became part of the state of Pará. The federal government detached the area in 1943 and created the territory of Amapá (54,161 sq mi). On 1 January 1990, Amapá became a state.

Since it is in Amazonia, rubber gathering was and still is important in Amapá. The Bethlehem Steel Company has mined and exported most of the magnesium, which was discovered in 1945. Prospectors have extracted alluvial gold from the rivers in Amapá since the 1970s, and other residents have farmed, mined coal, and cut timber. By 1990, over half of its 252,000 inhabitants resided near the capital city, Macapá, which rests on the equator.

See also **Amazon Region; Amazon River.**

BIBLIOGRAPHY

Leslie Bethell, ed., *Colonial Brazil* (1987).

David Cleary, *Anatomy of the Amazon Gold Rush* (1990).

Susanna Hecht and Alexander Cockburn, *The Fate of the Forest: Developers, Destroyers, and Defenders of the Amazon* (1990).

Additional Bibliography

Andersen, Lykke E. *The Dynamics of Deforestation and Economic Growth in the Brazilian Amazon.* Cambridge, U.K.: Press Syndicate of the University of Cambridge, 2002.

Barham, Brad, and O. T. Coomes. *Prosperity's Promise: The Amazon Rubber Boom and Distorted Economic Development*. Boulder, CO: Westview Press, 1996.

O'Dwyer, Eliane Cantarino. *Seringueiros da Amazônia: Dramas sociais e o olhar antropológico*. Niterói, RJ, Brazil: Editora da Universidade Federal Fluminense, 1998.

CAROLYN JOSTOCK

AMAPALA, TREATIES OF (1895, 1907).

The first of these agreements was signed in Amapala, Honduras, on 20 June 1895 and created a confederation known as the "República Mayor de Centro América," which was later changed to "Los Estados Unidos de Centro América." Within three years this union was defunct due to a revolution begun in El Salvador. The official dissolution of the first treaty took place on 30 November 1898. In 1907, the second Treaty of Amapala ended a conflict between Honduras and Nicaragua, and reflected the tone of the Marblehead Pact of July 1906. The latter had recognized the interests of the United States in the region and had created the Central American Court of Justice. The court had its first test the following summer, when Nicaragua complained that Guatemala and El Salvador had instigated a revolutionary movement in Honduras. The ensuing conference ended hostilities, complied with the court's orders, and fueled hopes that a new spirit of peaceful coexistence would replace the characteristic interventionism of nineteenth-century Central America.

See also **Central American Court of Justice; El Salvador; Honduras; Nicaragua.**

BIBLIOGRAPHY

Michael Rheta Martin, *Encyclopedia of Latin American History;* revised edition by L. Robert Hughes (1968).

Thomas L. Karnes, *The Failure of Union*, rev. ed. (1976).

Nicaragua: Ministerio De Relaciones Exteriores, *Documentos oficiales referentes a la guerra entre Nicaragua y Honduras de 1907, y la participación de El Salvador* (1907).

JEFFREY D. SAMUELS

AMARAL, ANTÔNIO JOSÉ AZEVEDO DO (1881–1942).

Antônio José Azevedo do Amaral (*b.* 1881, *d.* 1942), Brazilian journalist. Born in Rio de Janeiro, Amaral earned a degree from Rio's Faculdade de Medicina in 1903, but he soon established himself in Carioca journalism, writing for *Jornal do Commércio, a Notícia*, and *Correio da Manhã*. Expelled from England for his pro-German reporting in 1916, he returned to Brazil. After becoming the editor of the *Correio da Manhã*, he went on to edit *O País* and founded *Rio-Jornal* (1918) with João do Rio and *O Dia* (1921) with Virgílio de Melo Franco. A translator of the corporativist Mihail Manoilesco, Amaral is most noted for the rightist nationalism of his own essays, which made him an influential spokesman for the nationalist authoritarianism and statist industrialization of the Estado Nôvo era.

See also **Salgado, Plinio; Vargas, Getúlio Dornelles; Viana, Francisco José de Oliveira.**

BIBLIOGRAPHY

Azevedo Amaral's works include *Ensaios brasileiros* (1930), *O Brasil na crise atual* (1934), *A aventura política do Brasil* (1935), and *O estado autoritário e a realidade nacional* (1938). Other helpful sources are A. Guerreiro Ramos, *A crise do poder no Brasil* (1961).

Aspásia B. Alcântara, "A teoria política de Azevedo Amaral," in *Revista DADOS 2/3* (1967).

Jarbas Medeiros, *Ideologia autoritária no Brasil, 1930–1945* (1978).

Bolivar Lamounier, "Introdução," to Azevedo Amaral, *O estado autoritário e a realidade nacional*, 2d ed. (1981).

Additional Bibliography

Freitas, Marcos Cezar de. *Da micro-historia áhistoria das ideias*. São Paulo: Cortez Editora, 1999.

Piva, Luiz Guilherme. *Ladrilhadores e semeadores: A modernizacao brasileira no pensamento político de Oliveira Vianna, Sérgio Buarque de Holanda, Azevedo Amaral e Nestor Duarte (1920-1940)*. Sao Paulo: Departamento de Ciencia Poliítica da USP, 2000.

Souza, Francisco Martins de. *Raízes teóricas do corporativismo brasileiro*. Rio de Janeiro: Tempo Brasileiro, 1999.

JEFFREY D. NEEDELL

AMARAL, TARSILA DO (1886–1973).

Tarsila do Amaral (*b.* 1 September 1886; *d.* 17 January 1973), Paulista artist and salon leader whose paintings, sculpture, drawings, engravings, and illustrations helped to define, inspire, and stimulate the Brazilian modernist movement, especially the *Pau Brasil* (Brazilwood) and *Antropófagia* (Cannibals) avant-garde submovements. Her works are known for their cubist forms, Brazilian colors and themes. *A negra, a caipirinha, Abaporu, Floresta, Antropófagia,* and other works were shown at galleries and museums in Paris, London, Argentina, Chile, and Brazil from 1922 until 1970. Amaral also wrote poems and articles and illustrated books and periodicals. Other writers and composers dedicated works to her, and she was the subject of a film, books, articles, and interviews.

Amaral grew up on the family *fazenda* and attended *colégios* in Santana, São Paulo, and Barcelona. After her 1906 marriage to André Teixeira Pinto, she settled in São Paulo, where she studied sculpture with Zadig and Mantovani, and design and painting with Pedro Alexandrino and Georg Fischer Elpons. In Paris in the early 1920s Amaral attended the Académie Julian and studied at the studios of Émile Renard, Pedro Alexandrino, André Lhote, Albert Gleizes, and Fernand Léger.

She joined the "Grupo dos Cinco" (with Anita Malfatti, Mário de Andrade, Oswaldo de Andrade, and Menotti del Picchia) in 1922. With other Brazilians, including Lucília Guimarães Villa-Lobos, Heitor Villa-Lobos, Victor Brecheret, and Emiliano Di Calvalcanti, Amaral traveled annually between Europe and Brazil until 1928. In 1930 she briefly became diretora-conservadora of the Pinacoteca do Estado (State Painting Museum) in São Paulo. In 1931 she exhibited at the Moscow Museum of Modern Western Art, which bought one of her works (*O pescador*). Recognized by retrospective exhibits in Rio (1933, 1969), São Paulo (1950–1951, 1969), and Belo Horizonte (1970), Amaral's work is widely reflected in the literature on Latin American art and culture.

See also **Art: The Twentieth Century.**

BIBLIOGRAPHY

Marta Rossetti Batista, *Brasil. Vol. 1, Tempo Modernista—1917/29: Documentacão* (1972).

Aracy A. Amaral, *Tarsila—Sua Obra e Seu Tempo,* 2 vols. (1975).

Mary Lombardi, "Women in the Modern Art Movement in Brazil: Salon Leaders, Artists, and Musicians, 1917–1930" (Ph.D. diss., University of California at Los Angeles, 1977).

Additional Bibliography

Amaral, Aracy A., compiler. *Correspondência Mario de Andrade & Tarsila do Amaral.* São Paulo: Instituto de Estudos Brasileiros, Editora da Universidade de São Paulo, 1999.

Damian, Carol. "Tarsila do Amaral: Art and Environmental Concerns of a Brazilian Modernist." *Woman's Art Journal* 20 (Spring, 1999): 3–7.

Gotlib, Nádia Battella. *Tarsila do Amaral: A modernista.* São Paulo: Editora SENAC, 1998.

Justino, Maria José. *O banquete canibal: A modernidade em Tarsila do Amaral (1886-1973) = The Cannibal Feast: Modernity in Tarsila do Amaral.* Paraná: Editora UFPR, 2002.

Miceli, Sergio. *Nacional estrangeiro: História social e cultural do modernismo artístico em São Paulo.* São Paulo: Companhia das Letras, 2003.

MARY LUCIANA LOMBARDI

AMARANTH.

Amaranth (*amaranto* in Spanish and Portuguese), an annual herb with tiny seeds (genus: *Amaranthus;* family: Amaranthaceae) that includes fifty to sixty species, the most nutritious of which are the grain amaranths. Three species utilized in the Americas are *A. hypochondriacus* in northwestern and central Mexico, *A. cruentus* in southern Mexico and Central America, and *A. caudatus* in the Andes. Growing from 1 to 10 feet tall, with broad, colorful leaves, the plant bears up to half a million seeds on each seed head. The leaves, eaten like spinach, are high in protein, rich in vitamins and iron, and are also used to produce natural dyes to color foods and beverages. The grain is a complete-protein food source, containing all nine essential amino acids and has a pleasant, nutty flavor that is enhanced with toasting. Once toasted, boiled, or milled, the seeds may be eaten in cereals, baked as flour in breads, popped like popcorn, and made into candies. The Mexicans mix honey or molasses and popped amaranth into a popular sweet they call *alegría* (happiness), which is commonly found throughout the country in both large and small markets.

Domesticated in the Americas, pale-seeded amaranth dates from 4000 BCE in Tehuacán, Puebla. Archaeologists have also located amaranth in 2,000-year-old tombs in northwestern Argentina. Before 1500 CE the core regions of amaranth cultivation were in Central Mexico, Peru, and northwestern Argentina. Additional pockets were in Ecuador, Guatemala, southern and northwestern Mexico, and the North American southwest. By 1519 amaranth was a major food crop subject to tribute in the Aztec Empire. Each year the Aztecs filled eighteen granaries with the ivory-white seeds (*huauhtli* in Náhuatl). They utilized the plant as a toasted grain, for greens, and as a drink. They also popped it. Although an important part of the Aztec diet, amaranth was banned by the Spanish because of its ritual use. In the early sixteenth century, the Aztecs celebrated a feast in honor of their patron deity, Huitzilopochtli, whose statue made of amaranth dough they paraded through the streets of Tenochtitlán. Returning to the temple, the priests broke the statue into pieces, consecrated it as the bones and flesh of Huitzilopochtli, and distributed the pieces in a "communion" ceremony. Other deities were also represented by amaranth dough, while the Tepanecs and Tarascans used it to form images of birds and animals.

In spite of Spanish prohibitions, indigenous peoples of Mexico and Guatemala continued to plant amaranth and to make statues with the dough. Over time it was even assimilated into Christian rituals, being used to make rosaries. Farmers in the Andean highlands of Peru, Bolivia, and northwestern Argentina also cultivated amaranth, and the colonial Spanish recorded that red and white amaranth seeds (*bledos*) were very commonly used to make candies by the local people. Due to its antiquity in the Andes, it is known by various names: *kiwicha, achis, achita, ckoito, coyo,* or *coimi* in Peru; and *coimi, cuime, millmi,* or *quinua millmi* in Bolivia. Daniel K. Early notes that amaranth is making a comeback in Peru and Mexico as a subsistence and commercial crop cultivated primarily by indigenous peoples following traditional techniques.

See also **Spices and Herbs.**

BIBLIOGRAPHY

Jonathan D. Sauer, "The Grain Amaranths: A Survey of Their History and Classification," in *Annals of the Missouri Botanical Garden* 37, no. 4 (1950): 561–632, and "Grain Amaranths," in *Evolution of Crop Plants*, edited by N. W. Simmonds (1976), pp. 4–7.

John N. Cole, *Amaranth from the Past for the Future* (1979).

Daniel K. Early, "The Renaissance of Amaranth," in *Chilies to Chocolate: Food the Americas Gave the World*, edited by Nelson Foster and Linda S. Cordell (1992), pp. 15–33.

MARY KARASCH

AMAR Y BORBÓN, ANTONIO (1742–1826).

Antonio Amar y Borbón (*b.* March 1742; *d.* 26 April 1826), viceroy of New Granada (1803–1810). Amar y Borbón had a distinguished career in Spanish military service before becoming viceroy of New Granada in 1803. A conscientious ruler, he was generally well liked during the first part of his administration. After 1808, however, he faced creole demands for the establishment of American juntas to assume rule during the captivity in France of King Ferdinand VII. When such a junta was created in Quito (1809), he was unable to suppress it, in part because he had to deal with the same demands in Bogotá. He first sought to head off the junta movement there, while the viceroy of Peru saw to Quito. But as conditions in Spain deteriorated further with further French advances, a junta was formed in Bogotá on 20 July 1810. Largely as a figurehead, the viceroy was made a member and then deposed five days later. Expelled from the colony, he returned to Spain and remained there until his death.

See also **New Granada, Viceroyalty of.**

BIBLIOGRAPHY

Robert L. Gilmore, "The Imperial Crisis, Rebellion and the Viceroy: Nueva Granada in 1809," in *Hispanic American Historical Review* 40 (Feb. 1960): 1–24.

Mario Herrán Baquero, *El virrey don Antonio Amar y Borbón* (1988).

Carmen Pumar Martínez, "La narración perdida de Amar y Borbón sobre los sucesos de julio de 1810: Una historia diferente," in *Boletín de historia y antigüedades* 76, no. 766 (1989): 689–704.

Additional Bibliography

Pumar Martínez, Carmen. *Don Antonio Amar y Borbón, último virrey del Nuevo Reino de Granada.* Borja: Centro de Estudios Borjanos, Institución Fernando el Católico, 1991.

DAVID BUSHNELL

AMAT Y JUNIENT, MANUEL DE

(1704–1782). Manuel de Amat y Junient (*b.* 1704; *d.* 1782), viceroy of Peru (1761–1776). Born in Varacisas into a noble Catalan family, Amat pursued a military career in Europe and North Africa until becoming captain-general of Chile in 1755. In Santiago he promoted higher education and public order, but his efforts to subdue the Araucanian Indians were unsuccessful.

As viceroy of Peru, Amat oversaw with ruthless efficiency the expulsion of the Jesuits in 1767, and, superficially at least, undertook a major overhaul of defenses, fortifying ports and organizing militia companies throughout the provinces. Although public revenues expanded considerably in this period, Amat's vice-regency was pervaded by corruption, according to his many critics, including Antonio de Ulloa (1716–1795), who served under him as governor of Huancavelica, in south-central Peru. Following his return to Barcelona in 1777, the aged bachelor married a young Catalán, leaving for both her and posterity the splendid Palacio de la Virreina, now a museum.

See also **Peru: From the Conquest Through Independence.**

BIBLIOGRAPHY

Vicente Rodríguez Casado and F. Pérez Embid, eds., *Memoria de gobierno del virrey Amat* (1947).

José Cruces Pozo, "Cualidades militares del virrey Amat," in *Anuario de Estudios Americanos* 9 (1952): 327–345.

Leon G. Campbell, *The Military and Society in Colonial Peru, 1750–1810* (1978), esp. pp. 21–68.

Additional Bibliography

Aragón, Ilana Lucía, and Carlos Pardo-Figueroa Thays, editors. *El virrey Amat y su tiempo.* Lima: Pontificia Universidad Católica del Perú, Instituto Riva-Agüero, 2004.

Marks, Patricia H. "Confronting a Mercantile Elite: Bourbon Reformers and the Merchants of Lima, 1765-1796." *The Americas* 60 (April 2004): 519–558.

JOHN R. FISHER

AMAUTA.

Amauta, a Quechua word designating an ancient adviser to the Inca nobility; a wise and noble man, interpreter of the firmament and religious issues, keeper of knowledge. In modern Peru, during the Indianist (*indigenista*) revival of the 1910s and 1920s, the word became a symbol for the group of radical intellectuals, politicians, and artists headed by socialist José Carlos Mariátegui, founder of the journal *Amauta*. This journal was published in thirty-two issues between September 1926 and September 1930. Contributions by the most important Peruvian progressive figures of the time, including Víctor Raúl Haya De La Torre (until his political break with Mariátegui in 1928), José Sabogal, Jorge Basadre, and Martín Adán, as well as by foreign intellectuals, made *Amauta* a major source for analysis of Peruvian national problems with an international perspective.

See also **Indigenismo.**

BIBLIOGRAPHY

Jesús Chavarría, *José Carlos Mariátegui and the Rise of Modern Peru, 1890–1930* (1979).

Additional Bibliography

Veres, Luis. *Periodismo y literatura de vanguardia en América Latina: El caso peruano* (2003).

ALFONSO W. QUIROZ

AMAZONAS.

Amazonas, Brazil's largest state. Occupying some 602,000 square miles in the heart of the vast tropical Amazon Region, Amazonas is entirely lowlands, much of it flooded for months at a time and most of it covered with tropical rain forest. The main physical features are the Negro and Solimões rivers, which flow together to create the Amazon River.

When the region was first explored by Europeans in the 1540s, it was densely populated by native peoples. Gradually the native population declined, due mostly to diseases new to the area. By the 1630s, when Portuguese military expeditions established a permanent presence there, the natives were already disappearing. In 1669 the Portuguese built a small fort near the confluence of the Negro and Solimões/Amazon rivers, focus of a settlement called São José do Rio Negro, that gradually grew into the modern city of Manaus. By the 1730s, the Portuguese had mostly dislodged the Spanish from the central Amazon. These territorial gains were legalized in the Treaty of Madrid of 1750 (confirmed in the 1777 Treaty of San Ildefonso).

For most of the colonial era, the Portuguese administered the central Amazon from Belém and São Luís, Maranhão. In 1755, however, the region was designated the captaincy of São José do Rio Negro in order to promote economic exploitation. In the ensuing years, merchants and adventurers in São José mounted great Indian slaving expeditions. The town also became the gathering point for animals and plant materials destined for export.

Amazonas became a separate province in 1850 (and a state after 1891). São José was designated a city and gained its modern name shortly afterward. From then on, Manaus was the center of a boom in natural rubber exports, stimulated by Charles Goodyear's development in 1839 of the vulcanization process for hardening rubber. The boom peaked in the early years of the twentieth century, when incredible profits accumulated in the hands of local merchants. Before the bubble burst, city fathers erected a sumptuous opera house to show off their wealth. Manaus then went into decline, but the federal government began to promote and aid the city in the 1960s. Today Manaus has more than a million inhabitants, a busy deep-water port, a free-trade zone, and a great variety of exports.

Because it is still 98 percent rainforest, Amazonas has been at the center of debates about deforestation and environmental protection. In 2007 Eduardo Braga, the governor of Amazonas, signed Brazil's first climate change law, which offered to pay farmers who avoid deforestation.

See also **Amazon Region.**

BIBLIOGRAPHY

Artur Reis, *Estado do Amazonas* (1978).

Leo A. Despres, *Manaus* (1991).

Additional Bibliography

Andersen, Lykke E., Clive W. J. Granger, Eustáquio J. Reis, et al. *The Dynamics of Deforestation and Economic Growth in the Brazilian Amazon.* Cambridge, U.K.: Cambridge University Press, 2002.

Barham, Brad, and O. T. Coomes. *Prosperity's Promise: The Amazon Rubber Boom and Distorted Economic Development.* Boulder, CO: Westview Press, 1996.

Pontes Filho, Raimundo P. *Estudos de história do Amazonas.* Manaus, Brazil: Valer Editora, 2000.

MICHAEL L. CONNIFF

AMAZON BASIN, ARCHAEOLOGY.

Archaeology Amazon Basin. The archaeology of the Colombian Amazon Basin is concentrated in the Caquetá River in the region of Araracuara and La Pedrera and in the Amazon River in the region close to the city of Leticia, Colombia. The research done in these areas has focused on the identification of pottery traditions and on the study of the early human adaptations to the forest environment. The first studies defined the existence of an early pottery tradition related to the Barrancoid ceramics (2000 BCE), whose occurrence may be the result of migrations from the central or lower Amazon. The pottery is characterized by simple forms with incised decoration. A second pottery tradition is characterized by an elaborate polychrome pottery whose origin is presumed to be at the mouth of the Amazon River (Marajoara complex) or in the northern Andes.

The studies geared toward the understanding of human adaptations to the tropical forest of the Amazon are focused on the existence of soils arising from intentional human enrichment (anthropic soils). However, the origin of these rich organic soils sometimes called *terra preta* is in debate. Most of the existing evidence indicates that *terra preta* soils are formed by natural processes related to fires, flooding, and other factors that affect the soil's chemical composition. The objective of the research conducted in this area is to understand if the Amazon Basin sustained large-scale societies in the past.

See also **Precontact History: Amazonia.**

BIBLIOGRAPHY

For a more descriptive review of the archaeology of the Amazon Basin, see Leonor Herrera, "Amazonía colombiana," in Alvaro Botiva Contreras, et al., *Colombia prehispánica* (1989). For a detailed study on the Araracuara region, see Santiago Mora C. et al., *Cultivars, Anthropic Soils and Stability* (1991). A good review of the archaeological problem surrounding the debate on ancient productivity of *terra preta* soils and population density is presented in Thomas P. Myers, "Agricultural Limitations of the Amazon in Theory and Practice," in *World Archaeology* 24, no. 1 (1992): 82–97.

Additional Bibliography

Nimuendajú, Curt. *In Pursuit of a Past Amazon: Archaeological Researches in the Brazilian Guyana and in the Amazon Region.* Göteborg, Sweden: Världskulturmuseet, 2004.

Reynolds, Jan. *Amazon Basin: Vanishing Cultures.* San Diego: Harcourt Brace & Co., 1993.

AUGUSTO OYUELA-CAYCEDO

AMAZON PACT (1978).

The Treaty for Amazon Cooperation provides a framework for collaboration on economic development, conservation, and use of natural resources among the countries of Amazonia. Signed on 3 July 1978 by Bolivia, Brazil, Colombia, Ecuador, Guyana, Peru, Suriname, and Venezuela, the pact was designed to curtail foreign influence by giving member nations the exclusive responsibility for the development of the Amazon region. The member countries could not sustain the isolationist purpose of the pact, however, because their development projects required substantial external financing. In 1989, facing a virtual boycott on foreign lending until environmental standards for Amazonian projects were improved, the pact members created permanent committees on natural resources and the environment. These committees have taken the initiative in developing projects that meet the environmental demands of international financiers. The current collaboration among the member states under the Amazon Pact has laid the groundwork for more ambitious regional projects, including economic integration.

See also **Economic Development.**

BIBLIOGRAPHY

Maria Elena Medina, "Treaty for Amazonian Cooperation: General Analysis," in *Land, People, and Planning in Contemporary Amazonia*, edited by F. Barbira-Scazzocchio (1980), pp. 58–71.

Michael J. Eden, *Ecology and Land Management in Amazonia* (1990).

Juan De Onís, *The Green Cathedral: Sustainable Development of Amazonia* (1992).

MICHAEL A. POLL

AMAZON REGION.

The Amazon region is the area in South America formed by the Amazon River basin. It measures about 2.3 million square miles (6 million sq. km.) and covers parts of Brazil (more than half of its total area), Bolivia, Peru, Ecuador, Colombia, Venezuela, Guiana, Suriname, and French Guyana.

ENVIRONMENT

The region is the richest ecosystem in the world. It contains about 20 percent of the total available fresh water on earth and includes the Amazon, known as the River Sea: the worlds largest river in terms of water volume and drain basin, as well as some 1,000 tributaries. About 10 percent of the world's living species, many of them yet to be studied, can be found in the region. Its magnificent rain forests cover both the vast and unflooded uplands (*tierras firmes* in Spanish; *terras firmes* in Portuguese) and the inundated and swampy lands near its major rivers (in Spanish, *várzeas;* in Portuguese, *igapós*).

The Amazon offers an amazing diversity of natural products, many with economic value, including cacao, coca, guaraná, manioc, nuts, palm hearts, plants used as medicines or in the composition of medicines, rubber, spices, tropical fruits, oils, and different kinds of wood. The region is also rich in minerals. Its soil, however, is poor; only 6 to 7 percent of it is appropriate for conventional agricultural production.

COLONIAL HISTORY

When the conquistadores arrived in the Amazon region, the area was inhabited by Indians. The many indigenous groups had distinct and sometimes sophisticated cultures, living along the rivers, trading with one another, and sustaining themselves by hunting, fishing, and gathering in the forest. Great civilizations had once flourished at Santarém and on Marajó Island. The first white man reported to have entered the region was the Spaniard Vicente Yañez Pinzón. The Tordesillas Treaty, signed in Europe in

Amazon women warriors. Spanish explorer Francisco de Orellana's account of being attacked by Amazonian women like those of the Greek myth fed the fantastical images Europeans had of this region. THE GRANGER COLLECTION, NEW YORK

1494, granted control of the Amazon region to Spain, but the area was also of interest to Portugal, Holland, England, and France, all of which were eager to exploit its riches.

Indeed, the region fired the imagination of Europe, for many Europeans believed that El Dorado, a mythical kingdom full of precious metals, was hidden in the Amazon, and some actually organized expeditions to search for it. The name of the Amazon River and its surrounding region was also derived from a myth: In 1541 the Spanish explorer Francisco de Orellana, the first European to descend the river from the Andes to the Atlantic, reported that he had been attacked by women warriors much like the Amazons of the Greek myth. Since then, the word *Amazon* has designated both the region and its major river.

The English, Dutch, and French penetrated the Amazon from the north, establishing a few trading posts that assured them sites for their future colonies of British, Dutch, and French Guiana. After the slave trade was introduced in this region, its rain forests frequently served as a refuge for fugitive black slaves. The Spanish entered the Amazon from the Andes, the Portuguese from the Atlantic. Both counted on the work of Catholic missionaries. These missionaries, especially Jesuits, Capuchins, Franciscans, and Dominicans, gathered the Indians in places where they could be Christianized and used to extract products of commercial value, such as spices and medicines, to be exported to Europe. Indian labor was also exploited by the *encomenderos*, who had authorization from the Spanish Crown to do so.

Spain and Portugal, aiming to maintain control over an area coveted by other European nations, established outposts, sent out settlers and military personnel, and constructed forts around which towns grew up. In 1750, by the terms of the Treaty of Madrid, which was based on the *uti possidetis* principle (whoever had it, possessed it), Spain ceded to Portugal the eastern part of the Amazon region from the Atlantic to the junction of the Madeira River. In 1759 the marquis of Pombal, minister of King José I of Portugal, expelled the Jesuits from the area and made an abortive attempt to develop commercial agriculture under state control, via the General Company of Pará and Marahão.

Since the beginning of the eighteenth century the Amazon region has been regularly visited by European scientific expeditions. In 1736 the expedition of the French mathematician Charles-Marie de la Condamine identified local species such as rubber, quinine, and curare. He also measured depths, falls, and speeds of the Amazon River. Condamine's expedition was followed by expeditions led by the Prussian scientist Alexander von Humboldt (1799–1804), the Austrians Johann Baptist von Spix and Carl Friedrich von Martius (1817–1820), and the Swiss Louis Agassiz (1865), among others.

Despite visits by missionaries, adventurers, *encomenderos*, armies, and scientists, and the efforts of a few settlers, the Amazon region remained basically an Indian territory until modern times. Most of it was still unknown, unexplored, and untouched by white people when Spain and Portugal withdrew from South America at the beginning of the nineteenth century.

NATIONAL HISTORY

Settlement of the Amazon region by nonnatives progressed slowly until the last decades of the nineteenth century, when a rubber boom prompted substantial changes in the area. Rubber had been in great demand since 1839, when Charles Goodyear (1800–1860) discovered how to stabilize and vulcanize it, thereby making it commercially useful. The richest *Hevea* trees on earth were in the Amazon region, especially in the area where Brazilian and Bolivian territory meet. Large numbers of migrants moved to the region to work as rubber tappers. They extracted the liquid from the rubber trees, transformed it into huge balls of rubber, and sold them to local trading posts. At these posts they bought, at exorbitant prices, the products they needed to live. The rubber was then transported to the trading houses at the Brazilian ports of Belém and Manaus, where it was exported.

Rubber was responsible for creating the local millionaires—the rubber barons—during a time of frenetic activity and luxury. The magnificent Manaus Opera House remains a symbol of those days. But the lust for rubber also caused a serious border dispute between Bolivia and Brazil. Moreover, it attracted foreign capital to the area, especially to trade houses and to charter companies such as the Bolivian Syndicate. Foreign capital was also applied to the construction of railroads, such as the Madeira-Mamoré Railway (finished in 1912) linking Brazil and Bolivia.

From the beginning of the twentieth century, however, Amazon rubber faced—and lost out to—competition from the Malayan plantations. By the 1910s the Amazon rubber boom was finished, leaving few lasting benefits for the region. From then on, the activity was carried on only by the descendants of the earlier migrants, poor rubber-tappers reduced to debt peonage. The only exception was the attempt made by the automobile magnate Henry Ford (1863–1947), who planted rubber trees between 1927 and 1945 across 2.5 million acres he owned in Pará, Brazil. Ford's failure—due to lack of knowledge about local conditions and to diseases among the plants—helped to perpetuate the legend that the Amazon destroys those who attempt its conquest. Indeed, in 1967 Daniel Keith Ludwig (1897–1992) started the Jari Project, a huge agroindustrial complex in Pará, but after taking large losses, in 1981he gave up and sold the enterprise to a Brazilian conglomerate.

CONTEMPORARY HISTORY

In the second half of the twentieth century the Amazon region saw the most dramatic transformation of its entire history. Its population increased to unprecedented levels due to massive migration. The original Indian population, however, dropped dramatically due to diseases, conflicts with the settlers and ranchers, and disorganization of their way of life. From an original 2 to 5 million in 1500, the Amazon Indian population is estimated to have shrunk to 150,000 to 200,000 people.

Recent migrations to the Amazon have been the result of socioeconomic changes in other regions, such as the increase of land and income concentration and urban poverty. Migrations also have been stimulated by the Brazilian federal government, which launched programs to attract homesteaders and formulated policies of tax exemptions and subsidies to attract companies and businesses. Brazil has been the only country in the region to carry on an explicit state policy aimed at integrating the Amazon into the national economy.

The Amazon has been crossed by an extensive network of roads and highways, such as the pioneer Marginal Forest Highway (1948) linking Santa Cruz, Bolivia, to Caracas, Venezuela, and the four highways that unite different parts of the Amazon with Brazil's capital, Brasília. These highways serve as economic axes: A great number of cities, towns, and hamlets have sprung up beside them, transforming the once-rural Amazon population into an increasingly, and in the case of Brazil, predominantly, urban population.

Various economic activities currently occupy the region. Agroforestry has proven to be productive and not environmentally damaging. Agriculture, carried on mainly by homesteaders, has been frustrated by the inadequacy of soil and ignorance about local conditions. The traditional Indian crop of coca, recently associated with the international traffic of drugs, has penetrated into the forests of Colombia, Bolivia, and Peru. It has produced local fortunes, but has also increased social tensions. Cattle ranching, developed mainly on large estates, increased dramatically during the 1970s in the Brazilian Amazon in response to federal incentives. This activity, together with wood cutting, has been responsible for high rates of deforestation. State and private exploration of the rich Amazon mineral reserves, especially gold, manganese, cassiterite, iron, and copper, has been intense since the 1960s.

The environmental consequences of the recent large-scale occupation of the Amazon has made exploitation of the region an international issue, bringing together actors with sometimes conflicting interests, including entrepreneurs, environmental groups, government and nongovernment organizations, *fazendeiros*, homesteaders, Indians, land speculators, missionaries, national and transnational corporations, peasants, politicians, professionals, traders, and wage laborers. Despite greater environmental activism, in the 1990s and the early twenty-first century Brazil began to open its economy to international trade and competition, which accelerated the environmental changes in the Amazon. Brazil's renewed emphasis on agricultural and mineral exports has led to more land usage and rain forest destruction. In the past, wanting to encourage greater development, the Brazilian government had been reluctant to make major policy changes to protect the Amazon. Whereas international groups have argued that the protection of the Amazon is good for the world environment, Brazilian politicians often have countered that developed countries need to focus on their own environmental management rather than burdening developing nations. But recent environmental catastrophes have caused national policy makers to rethink this position. A major drought in the Amazon in 2005 led to large fires, the destruction of crops, and harm to the regional economy. Also, scientists have linked Brazil's overall agricultural productivity to changing rainfall patterns in the Amazon. However, the size of the Amazon and the limited resources of the government will make environmental protection in this region difficult. The main challenge for the future of the Amazon will continue to be creating a balance between economic progress, social justice, and ecological preservation.

See also **Environmental Movements; Explorers and Exploration: Brazil; Forests.**

BIBLIOGRAPHY

Aragón, Luis E., and Luc J. A. Mougeot. *Migrações internas na Amazônia.* Belém, Brazil: Universidade Federal do Pará, 1986.

Arrarás, Astrid, Joseph S. Tulchin, and Heather A. Golding. *Environment and Security in the Amazon Basin.* Washington, DC: Woodrow Wilson International Center for Scholars Latin American Program, 2002.

Barbosa, Luiz C. *The Brazilian Amazon Rainforest Global Ecopolitics, Development, and Democracy.* Lanham, MD: University Press of America, 2000.

Becker, Bertha. *Geopolítica da Amazônia.* Rio de Janeiro, Zahar, 1982.

Branford, Sue, and Oriel Glock. *The Last Frontier—Fighting over Land in the Amazon.* London: Zed Books, 1985.

Bunker, Stephen G. *Underdeveloping the Amazon: Extraction, Unequal Exchange, and the Failure of the Modern State.* Chicago: University of Chicago Press, 1985.

Dean, Warren. *Brazil and the Struggle for Rubber.* New York: Cambridge University Press, 1987.

De Souza Martins, José. *Caminhada no chão da noite.* São Paulo: Hucitec, 1989.

Hecht, Susanna, and Alexander Cockburn. *The Fate of the Forest.* New York: Verso, 1990.

Hemming, John H. *Amazon Frontier: The Defeat of the Brazilian Indians.* Cambridge, MA: Harvard University Press, 1987.

Mora, Carlos, and Carlos E. Aramburu. *Desarrollo Amazónico: Una perspectiva latinoamericana.* Lima: Centro de Investigación y Promoción, 1986.

Prance, Ghillean T., and Thomas E. Lovejoy, eds. *Amazonia.* Oxford, U.K.: Pergamon Press, 1985.

Rivas, Alexandre, and Carlos Edwar de Carvalho Freitas. *Amazônia-uma perspectiva interdisciplinar.* Manaus, Brazil: Editora da Universidade do Amazonas, 2002.

Schmink, Marianne, and Charles H. Wood. *Frontier Expansion in Amazonia.* Gainesville: University of Florida Press, 1984.

Smith, Anthony. *Explorers of the Amazon.* London: Viking, 1990.

JANAÍNA AMADO

AMAZON RIVER. Amazon River, the world's largest river. The Amazon is 3,900 miles long (exceeded only by the Nile), discharges an average 7 million cubic feet per second, and drains more than 2.5 million square miles. It arises in Peru, drops down the eastern slopes of the Andes, and then flows east through Brazil to the Atlantic Ocean. Its depth varies from 66 to 660 feet within Brazil, and its width ranges up to 7 miles (near where it is joined by the Xingu River). Throughout much of its lowlands plain, the Amazon is actually a labyrinth of waters, fed and interconnected by some 11,000 large and small tributaries. A northwestern tributary, the Rio Negro, is joined to the Orinoco basin by the swampy Casiquiaré Canal.

The lowlands basin is bounded to the north by the Guiana Highlands and to the south by the Brazilian Highlands. Thus the river and its tributaries are forced into a narrow course for their last several hundred miles before reaching the sea. This creates a daily tidal bore (the *pororoca*) up to 16 feet high, which makes navigation hazardous.

Due to the enormous size of the Amazon, the first Europeans in the region called it the River Sea. Today, Brazilians call it the Amazonas only to its junction with the Rio Negro; above there it is known as the Solimões. Spanish Americans refer to the section west of Iquitos as the Marañón. The lowlands constitute the world's largest rain forest, renowned for its incredibly rich biological diversity.

Because the drainage lies in the Northern and Southern hemispheres, the Amazon experiences two rainy seasons, in February and July. The floodwaters rise as much as 50 feet over dry-season levels. The main course of the river, fed by Andean tributaries, carries vast quantities of silt and organic matter. For this reason, the natives called it white water. The Negro, however, drains lowlands, is relatively free of silt, and picks up a dark, acidic character from mangrove roots along its course. Its waters were called black by the people who originally lived along its banks. When they meet near Manaus, the white and black waters swirl and intermingle for nearly 30 miles before blending.

In 1500 and 1501, explorers Vicente Yáñez Pinzón and Amerigo Vespucci sailed across the Amazon's mouth, which straddles both the equator and the Tordesillas Line. At that time an estimated 2.4 million natives lived in the basin.

The Spanish government claimed the river, based on the Treaty of Tordesillas. This claim was reinforced by the first exploration, carried out by a Spaniard. In 1541–1542, Francisco de Orellana took command of an expedition organized by Gonzalo Pizarro and sailed down the Amazon, claiming it for Spain. Because the South Atlantic lay within Portugal's sphere, however, the Portuguese gradually gained jurisdiction. Spain annexed Portugal in 1580, so the matter seemed moot.

In 1637–1639 the Portuguese captain Pedro Teixeira, with secret orders to secure the area for his government, led an expedition up the Amazon. When Portugal declared its independence from Spain in 1640, the Amazon remained under its control.

View of the Amazon River with a hotel in the foreground, Amazonas, Brazil. Linked to thousands of tributaries, the Amazon, the world's longest river, extends in all directions. © YANN ARTHUS-BERTRAND/CORBIS

In 1750 Spain and Portugal signed the Treaty of Madrid, which recognized Portugal's effective occupation of the southern Amazon basin. It designated the Paraguay, Guaporé, Mamoré, and Madeira rivers as an international boundary. Over the next century and a half, Portugal (and later Brazil) managed to annex more territory in the northern and western Amazon basin.

See also **Brazil, Geography.**

BIBLIOGRAPHY

Hilgard O'Reilly Sternberg, *The Amazon River of Brazil* (1975).

John Hemming, *Red Gold* (1978) and *Amazon Frontier* (1987).

Gordon MacCreagh, *White Waters and Black* (1985).

Roger D. Stone, *Dreams of Amazonia* (1985).

Anthony Smith, *Explorers of the Amazon* (1990).

Additional Bibliography

Becker, Bertha. "Una visión de la región amazónica sin extremismos." *Revista Pesquisa* 102 (2004).

Brack Egg, Antonio. *Amazonía: Desarrollo y sostenibilidad.* Lima: Mimeo, 1996.

Davis, Wade. "El río: Exploraciones y descubrimientos en la selva amazónica." *Revista Luna Azul* 22 (January–June 2006): 639–642.

London, Mark. *The Last Forest: The Amazon in the Age of Globalization.* New York: Random House, 2007.

Olarte Zapata, Dora María. *Luz de América: Comunidad y biodiversidad Amazónia.* Jakarta, Indonesia: Centro Internacional para la Investigación Forestal, 2003.

Santos, Fernando. *Globalización y cambio en la Amazonía indígena.* Quito: Abya-Yala, 1996.

MICHAEL L. CONNIFF

AMBROGI, ARTURO (1875–1936). Arturo Ambrogi (*b.* 19 October 1875; *d.* 8 November 1936), Salvadoran writer. Born in San Salvador, the son of an Italian-born Salvadoran army general, Ambrogi edited several literary reviews in San Salvador in the 1890s before traveling widely in South America, where he was much influenced by intellectuals in Chile and Uruguay, particularly by Rubén Darío in Buenos Aires. He became one of the leading Salvadoran modernist and impressionist writers of the early twentieth century, especially with his lyrical *Manchas, máscaras y sensaciones* (1901) and *Sensaciones crepusculares* (1904), *El libro del trópico* (1907), *El tiempo que pasa* (1913), and *Sensaciones del Japón y de la China* (1915). His frequent travels throughout the world are strongly reflected in his work, which also contains much folklore.

See also **Literature: Spanish America.**

BIBLIOGRAPHY

Arturo Ambrogi, *Marginales de la vida* (1912).

José Gómez Campos, *Semblanzas salvadoreñas* (1930).

Luis Gallegos Valdés, *Panorama de la literatura salvadoreña del período precolombino a 1980* (1987), esp. pp. 115–130.

Additional Bibliography

Barraza Arriola, Marco Antonio. *Antología de escritores del istmo centroamericano.* San Tecla: Clásicos Roxsil, 1999.

RALPH LEE WOODWARD JR.

AMEGHINO, FLORENTINO (1854–1911).

Florentino Ameghino (*b*. 18 September 1854; *d*. 6 August 1911), Argentine geologist and paleontologist. The son of Italian immigrants, Ameghino was born at Luján in Buenos Aires Province. As a boy he was an avid collector of bones and fossils, and he continued this avocation while working as a schoolteacher and storekeeper. He never received formal scientific training, but his reputation as a man of learning spread, especially after he traveled to Paris in 1878 with part of his collection. He ultimately published almost two hundred articles and monographs, corresponded with foreign specialists, and served as museum director in La Plata and Buenos Aires. Ameghino won greatest notoriety for his hypothesis that humankind originated in and spread from South America. This was not generally accepted, yet he is recognized as a tireless investigator and a pioneer of Argentine science.

See also **Science.**

BIBLIOGRAPHY

José Balbini, *Historia de la ciencia argentina* (1949), pp. 92–98.

José Gabriel, *El loco de los huesos* (1940).

Additional Bibliography

D'Auria, Rafael. *Ameghino a la luz de la verdad.* Córdoba: Biffignandi Ediciones, 1982.

González, Alberto Rex. "Florentino Ameghino: Destino y vocación." *Todo Es Historia*, 31 (May 1997): 16–18.

Podgorny, Irina. "De la santidad laica del científico Florentino Ameghino y el espectáculo de la ciencia en la Argentina moderna." *Entrepasados* 6 (1997): 37–61.

DAVID BUSHNELL

AMÉLIA, EMPRESS (1812–1873).

Empress Amélia (Amélia Augusta de Leuchtenberg; *b*. July 1812; *d*. January 1873), empress consort of Brazil (1829–1831). Milan-born daughter of Eugène de Beauharnais, Napoleon's stepson, and the Bavarian duchess of Leuchtenberg, Amélia became the second wife of Emperor Pedro I of Brazil in 1829. A young woman of rare beauty and sensitivity, Amélia appeared in Rio de Janeiro at a critical time for the Brazilian monarchy—a time of recrimination over the loss of Uruguay, governmental deadlock, financial crisis, nativist ferment, and growing public dissatisfaction with the emperor.

Amélia's arrival in Rio was predicated on the banishment of Pedro's mistress, the marchioness of Santos, which cleared the way for the emperor's reconciliation with José Bonifácio de Andrada E Silva, a bitter foe of the marchioness. Empress Amélia joined Andrade in advising Pedro to appoint a new cabinet headed by the marquis of Barbacena, who had been her escort from Bavaria to Brazil. The Barbacena ministry smoothed the emperor's relations with parliament and probably prolonged his reign. Pedro's dismissal of Barbacena a year later set off the chain of events that led to the abdication and exile of Pedro and Amélia in April 1831.

From Brazil they went to Paris, where Amélia bore the former emperor a daughter, Maria Amélia, and served as guardian of his eldest daughter,

Maria da Glória, when Pedro left for Portugal to secure the Portuguese throne for Maria da Glória. Amélia rejoined Pedro in Lisbon in September 1833, a year before his death. She devoted most of the rest of her life to charity work in Portugal.

See also **Maria II of Portugal (Maria da Gloria); Pedro I of Brazil.**

BIBLIOGRAPHY

Maria Junqueira Schmidt, *A segunda imperatriz do Brasil* (1927).

Ligia Lemos Tôrres, *Imperatríz dona Amélia* (1947).

Additional Bibliography

Barreira, Lauro. *A imperatriz desterrada*. Rio de Janeiro: Editora Cia Brasileira de Artes Gráficas, 1979.

NEILL MACAULAY

AMENÁBAR, JUAN (1922–1999). Juan Amenábar (*b.* 22 June 1922, *d.* 3 February 1999), Chilean composer. Born in Santiago, Amenábar was introduced to music by his father, a cellist and member of the Bach Society. At age thirteen he entered the Catholic Conservatory, where he studied harmony with Lucila Césped and choral techniques with Luis Vilches. In 1940 he enrolled at the University of Chile to study civil engineering. He attended the composition classes of Jorge Urrutia Blondel from 1948 to 1952 at the National Conservatory of Santiago. Amenábar joined the National Society of Composers (1953) and while chief of the music programs at Radio Chilena (1953–1956) he promoted contemporary Chilean composers and started to experiment with electronic music. From 1954 to 1957 he organized the concerts of the music department at the Catholic University in Santiago, where he founded the experimental sound workshop. His *Los peces* (1957), a study on the Fibonacci series, was the first tape composition made in Latin America. In 1958 he took electronic music courses given by Werner Meyer-Eppler at the University of Bonn. Upon his return to Chile, he worked with José Vicente Asuar in the creation of an electronic music studio at the University of Chile.

Amenábar taught composition and served as president of the National Association of Composers.

In addition to electronic music, he wrote religious choral music, incidental music for theater and films, chamber music, and piano and organ pieces. He also wrote and published musicological essays about new musical techniques, music for movies, folk music, and more.

See also **Music: Art Music.**

BIBLIOGRAPHY

John Vinton, ed., *Dictionary of Contemporary Music* (1974); *New Grove Dictionary of Music and Musicians,* vol. 1 (1980).

Gérard Béhague, *Music in Latin America* (1979); *Composers of the Americas,* vol. 17 (1971), p. 15.

Additional Bibliography

Dal Farra, Ricardo. "Something Lost, Something Hidden, Something Found: Electroacoustic Music by Latin American Composers." *Organised Sound* 11 (2006): 131-142.

SUSANA SALGADO

AMERICA. The term "America" first appeared in 1507 when Martin Waldseemüller designed a map depicting the New World from the European perspective. These new lands were named after Amerigo Vespucci (1451–1512), an Italian explorer who had suggested that the New World was not in East India.

The western hemisphere is divided into North and South America. However, there are also other important divisions such as Central America and the Caribbean. "Spanish America" is a term used to designate all the Spanish-speaking countries while "Latin America" is a term used to encompass all of Central and South America, including the Portuguese-speaking Brazil. In the English-speaking world, "America" is colloquially used to refer to the United States, and "American" is the adjective used for a citizen of that country.

The colonial period left imprints on the newly formed continental region that can still be seen today. For example, territorial disputes between the United Kingdom and Guatemala delayed the independence of Belize until 1981; Guyana, which became independent in 1966, has pending territorial disputes with Venezuela and Suriname. Suriname itself became independent in 1975 and French Guiana—which borders Suriname—is a territory of

A drawing of Amerigo Vespucci and the lands bearing his name. JAMES WHITMORE/TIME LIFE PICTURES/GETTY
IMAGES

France. The same colonial dependency can be seen in the Caribbean region, where one can still find overseas territories of France, the United Kingdom and the Netherlands. Cuba and Puerto Rico were the last two colonies to become independent from Spain in 1898, after the Spanish-American War. It was that same year that the United States established a naval base at Guantanamo Bay, Cuba, and annexed Puerto Rico as an unincorporated territory. Brazil, the most populous country in Latin America, constitutes a major political and economic force in the region, but because of linguistic (the language of Brazil is Portuguese) and cultural barriers between it and the bordering nations, it is not completely integrated with its neighbors.

The cultural, historical, ethnic, and economic heterogeneity of North and South America has generated an equally vast and heterogeneous array

of academic studies in many disciplines, including American studies, gender studies, Latino/Chicano studies, Latin American studies, cultural studies, postcolonial studies, and subaltern studies, along with studies of visual culture. Applying multidisciplinary and transdisciplinary methodologies, which in some cases attempt to narrow the gap between the social sciences and the humanities, cultural studies typically means the study of culture in all its broad social manifestations, as distinct from art and literary culture, sometimes referred to as high culture. Current debates in cultural studies revolve around issues of globalization, postmodernity, nationalism, cultural diversity, migration, social integration, and the political remapping of the region.

See also **Cartography: Overview; Colonialism; Vespucci, Amerigo.**

BIBLIOGRAPHY

Cañizares-Esguerra, Jorge. *How to Write the History of the New World: Histories, Epistemologies, and Identities in the Eighteenth-Century Atlantic World.* Stanford, CA: Stanford University Press, 2001.

Haines, Michael R., and Richard H. Stechel. *A Population History of North America.* Cambridge, U.K.: Cambridge University Press, 2000.

Hart, Stephen M., and Richard Young. *Contemporary Latin American Cultural Studies.* London: Arnold, 2003.

Mignolo, Walter D. *The Idea of Latin America.* Malden, MA: Blackwell Publishing, 2005.

Moraña, Mabel, Ed. *Nuevas perspectivas desde/sobre América Latina: El desafío de los estudios culturales.* Santiago de Chile: Editorial Cuarto Propio/Instituto Internacional de Literatura Iberoamericana, 2000.

O'Gorman, Edmundo. *The Invention of America: An Inquiry into the Historical Nature of the New World and the Meaning of Its History.* Bloomington: Indiana University Press, 1961.

Sarto, Ana, and Alicia Ríos. *The Latin American Cultural Studies Reader.* Durham, NC: Duke University Press, 2004.

HÉCTOR JAIMES

AMERICAN ATLANTIC AND PACIFIC SHIP CANAL COMPANY.

American Atlantic and Pacific Ship Canal Company, a North American firm owned by Cornelius Vanderbilt and associates that successfully negotiated an exclusive canal concession with Nicaragua on 27 August 1849. Assisted by Ephraim George Squier, representative for the United States government, the company agreed to build, at its own expense, a canal across the Nicaraguan isthmus open to vessels of all nations and to provide support services of rail and carriage lines. Debate over canal privileges and Nicaraguan rights of sovereignty and property heightened tensions between British and North American interests in the region, and resulted in the passage of the Clayton–Bulwer Treaty in 1850. Plans for eventual construction were thwarted by both inadequate financing and geographical barriers.

See also **Clayton-Bulwer Treaty.**

BIBLIOGRAPHY

Gerstle Mack, *The Land Divided, History of the Panama Canal and Other Isthmian Canal Projects* (1944), esp. 184–185, 188–190.

David I. Folkman, Jr., *The Nicaragua Route* (1972), esp. 18, 33, 35–37.

Additional Bibliography

Gobat, Michel. *Confronting the American Dream: Nicaragua under U.S. Imperial Rule.* Durham: Duke University Press, 2005.

Herrera, René. *Relaciones internacionales y poder político en Nicaragua.* México, D.F.: Colegio de México, 1992.

D. M. SPEARS

AMERICANOS. *See* **Confederates in Brazil and Mexico.**

AMERICAN REVOLUTION, INFLUENCE OF.

The American Revolution influenced Latin America because it was the first modern movement of anticolonialism. Drawing its ideology from the Enlightenment, it manifested a deep faith in the ability of people to advance their rights.

As the Seven Years' War ended (1763), the balance of power shifted in England's favor at the expense of the French and Spanish Bourbons, thus setting the scene for the period (1775–1825) that Herbert Eugene Bolton has called "the greater American Revolution," during which most European powers lost their colonies. Americans shared a keen resentment of Europeans for their obsession with the balancing of power, which often coincided with the loss of American lives and money. President George Washington underscored this dislike for European entanglements in his Farewell Address.

From the mid-1760s, England expected its colonists to participate in and help pay for the defense buildup. When the colonists resisted, the North American struggle for independence began; Spanish Americans likewise complained of increased levies and resorted to insurrection. In 1781, José de Abalos, a Spanish official in Venezuela, noted the "vehement desire for independence" among South Americans influenced by the success of the North Americans. A. R. J. Turgot warned the Bourbons in 1776 that the American Revolution stood for anticolonialism in the New World—a fact that Spain could no longer ignore.

Turgot's message registered in Spain, where Charles III (1759–1788) introduced governmental reforms to produce greater defense revenues. "Free" trade conducted through Spain (1778) and the adoption of the Intendancy System also were meant to stop British threats. The opening of new ports and the formation of merchant guilds overseas attracted American capital for regional economic development. The Bourbons also sponsored measures favoring laissez-faire, among which were the publication of the *Informe de la ley agraria* (Agrarian Report) of 1795 and the 1807 recommendation to study political economy in the universities, using Adam Smith's *Wealth of Nations* as a text. Documenting conclusions from varied sources, the Agrarian Report cited figures from the United States—a convincing example of what a free economy could contribute to national prosperity. It also underscored economic "federalism" by stressing the advantage of regional production rather than Bourbon centralization. Although the Portuguese-Brazilian context differed, the Marquês de Pombal's reforms had the same effect: Regional economies under the Brazilian elites expected to align themselves with Europeans, as long as the relationship was one of equality.

To provide this equality, the Iberians promoted "federative" monarchies in accord with the regional economic structures. This type of commonwealth relationship, however, failed in practice through lack of trust between Europeans and Americans. Through this monarchical reform, however, Latin Americans were exposed to two models: the republican United States and the Iberian constitutional projects. They preferred the hemispheric model because of its remarkable success by 1808.

The Spanish world was fascinated with events in North America from the outset, and the contacts were many. Spain was well aware of the possibility of furthering anticolonialism among its subjects. Thus, the choice was made not to resort to censorship; instead, Spanish subjects were permitted to read freely about the American Revolution in books and periodicals. Spanish Americans thus were able to study the debates that were held in Philadelphia, the minutes of sessions in England (Parliament) and America, and the list of grievances. In short, Latin Americans were fully exposed to the American

Revolution and the subsequent establishment of the prosperous United States republic.

Francisco de Miranda, having served as a Spanish officer in the American Revolution, subsequently witnessed the young nation's transition from war to peace (1783–1784). He recorded his impressions in a diary and gained the close friendship of the nation's key leaders. From 1785 until his return to his native Venezuela in 1810, Miranda tried to secure England's help for his projects to emancipate Venezuela. His greatest contribution was the propaganda sent from London—bundles of documents and letters that specified revolutionary procedures as well as the type of government that should be emulated: that of the United States of America.

The most influential writer for Miranda on behalf of Britain's assistance with Latin America's emancipation, and especially as an advocate of the American model, was the pseudonymous William Burke, who reflected the ideas of two great English reformers: James Mill and Jeremy Bentham, Miranda's close friends. From 1810 to 1812 James Mill was the principal organizer of Burke's editorials in Venezuela. These writings offered an excellent analysis of the American Revolution and the successful growth of the United States from 1787 to 1810. Among other things, they provided a review of Alexander Hamilton's financial program; the first full version of "Western Hemisphere idea," the promotion of inter-Americanism; and an account of the development of a Spanish American political unit (March 1811) that would join with the United States in guiding the destiny of the Americas.

See also **Democracy; Enlightenment, The.**

BIBLIOGRAPHY

William Spence Robertson, *The Life of Miranda*, 2 vols. (1929).

Charles Carroll Griffin, *The United States and the Disruption of the Spanish Empire, 1810–1822* (1937).

Harry Bernstein, *Origins of Inter-American Interest, 1700–1812* (1945).

José De Onís, *The United States as Seen by Spanish American Writers, 1775–1890* (1952).

Arthur Preston Whitaker, *The Western Hemisphere Idea: Its Rise and Decline* (1954).

Mario Rodríguez, "The Impact of the American Revolution on the Spanish- and Portuguese-Speaking World," in

The Impact of the American Revolution Abroad, edited by Richard B. Morris (1976), pp. 100–125; *La revolución americana de 1776 y el mundo hispánico: Ensayos y documentos* (1976); "The First Venezuelan Republic and the North American Model," in *Revista interamericana de bibliografía* 37, no. 1 (1987): 3–17; and *"William Burke" and Francisco de Miranda: The World and the Deed in Spanish America's Emancipation* (1994). For Portuguese America, see Kenneth R. Maxwell, *Conflicts and Conspiracies: Brazil and Portugal, 1750–1780* (1973) and "The Generation of the 1790s and the Idea of Luso-Brazilian Empire," in *Colonial Roots of Modern Brazil,* edited by Dauril Alden (1973), pp. 107–144.

See also E. Bradford Burns, "The Intellectuals as Agents of Change and the Independence of Brazil," pp. 211–246; Emilia Viotti Da Costa, "The Politics of Emancipation of Brazil," pp. 43–48; and A. J. R. Russell-Wood, "Preconditions and Precipitants of the Independence Movement in Portuguese America," pp. 3–40; all in *From Colony to Nation,* edited by A. J. R. Russell-Wood (1975).

Additional Bibliography

Brading, D. A. *The First America: The Spanish Monarchy, Creole Patriots, and the Liberal State, 1492–1867.* Cambridge: Cambridge University Press, 1991.

Lewis, James E. *The American Union and the Problem of Neighborhood: The United States and the Collapse of the Spanish Empire, 1783–1829.* Chapel Hill: University of North Carolina Press, 1998.

MARIO RODRÍGUEZ

AMERICAS, THE. The scholarly journal *The Americas: A Quarterly Review of Inter-American Cultural History* was founded in 1944, with the first issue appearing in July of that year. Founded under the auspices of the Academy of American Franciscan History (AAFH), it was intended to provide a forum for "authoritative contributions by outstanding scholars of all the Americas," to create "deeper understanding, mutual respect and amity among all institutions of learning." The journal has focused largely on issues dealing with Latin America, in the broadest sense of the term, including the borderlands (the largely Hispanic areas on the U.S. side of the U.S.-Mexico border) and French-speaking Canada. The overwhelming majority of articles appear in English, with a few exceptions. Although sponsored by the AAFH and housed at the Catholic University of America, the journal has never been uniquely dedicated to issues of church history, but rather deals with cultural history in general. In addition to articles, the journal publishes scholarly book reviews, historical documents, and "Inter-American Notes," traditionally an important venue for professional announcements. In the more than sixty years of its existence it has had ten editors. Of these, in the first forty-five years, all were Franciscans, with Fr. Antonine Tibesar, OFM (1909–1992), having served the longest, a total of twenty years. Since 1988 none of the editors has been a Franciscan, but lay persons and leading scholars of Latin American history serving five-year terms. In 1998 Judith Ewell became its first woman editor, and the first woman to edit a major scholarly journal dealing with Latin America. The journal boasts a very thorough editorial review process. Nearly all submissions are read by the editorial board (the editor and associate and assistant editors) before outside referees are sought. Their comments are then scrutinized by the board before it reaches a final decision. The editors call upon professionals in the field to evaluate submitted articles and provide book reviews, particularly those in two groups of outside editors, the area editors and senior editors. The journal participates in Project MUSE for its recent issues, and JSTOR for earlier issues. The Conference of Latin American History awards an annual Tibesar Prize for the best article published in the journal during the previous year.

See also **Franciscans.**

BIBLIOGRAPHY

The Americas: A Quarterly Review of Inter-American Cultural History. Available from http://www.drexel.edu/coas/theamericas/.

JOHN F. SCHWALLER

AMERICO DE FIGUEREIDO E MELO, PEDRO (1843–1905). Pedro Americo de Figuereido e Melo (*b.* 29 April 1843; *d.* 7 October 1905), Brazilian painter. Americo's artistic career began at a young age. At the age of nine he was chosen to accompany the naturalist Louis-Jacques Brunet on a scientific mission through Northeastern

Brazil. Soon after his return from the expedition, he moved to Rio, and in 1855 enrolled in the Imperial Academy of Fine Arts. By 1858 his artistic capabilities had captured the attention of the Emperor Pedro II, who personally awarded him a European travel stipend. In Europe, Americo studied painting with such masters as Ingres and Horace Vernet. But his interests and talents extended beyond the fine arts. He wrote a criticism of Ernest Renan's *Life of Jesus,* for which he received a commendation from Pope Pius IX, and obtained a doctorate from the University of Brussels in natural science and applied physics. When he returned to Brazil in 1864, he wrote a novel entitled *Holocausto.* The same year he won the competition for professor of figure drawing at the academy.

Although Americo lived a good part of his adult life in Europe, he nevertheless left an important artistic legacy in Brazil. Alongside Vítor Meireles, Americo was instrumental in producing visual images that official institutions of the Second Empire sponsored and prized. His artistic repertory includes religious and allegorical compositions as well as court portraits and historical paintings. His most important historical paintings include two military paintings depicting battles from the War of the Triple Alliance, the 1872 *Batalha de Campo Grande* and the 1879 *Batalha do Avaí,* and his 1888 homage to Brazilian independence, *Grito do Ipiranga.*

See also **Art: The Nineteenth Century.**

BIBLIOGRAPHY

Arte no Brasil, vol. 1 (1979), pp. 543–550.

Donato Mello Júnior, *Pedro Americo de Figuereido e Melo, 1843–1905* (1983).

Caren Meghreblian, "Art, Politics, and Historical Perception in Imperial Brazil, 1854–1884" (Ph.D. diss., UCLA, 1990).

Additional Bibliography

Rosemberg, Liana Ruth Bergstein. *Pedro Américo e o olhar oitocentista.* Rio de Janerio: Produções Barroso Editoriais, 2002.

CAREN A. MEGHREBLIAN

AMÉZAGA, JUAN JOSÉ DE (1881–1956).

Juan José de Amézaga (*b.* 28 January 1881; *d.* 21 August 1956), president of Uruguay (1943–1947). Amézaga was born in Montevideo.

After receiving his law degree in 1905, he was a professor of philosophy, director of the Labor Office, twice a representative for the department of Durazno, minister of industry, ambassador to Argentina (1916), adviser on secondary education, president of the State Insurance Bank (1918), and attorney for the Central Railroad of Uruguay. Amézaga was elected president as Uruguay emerged from a decade of institutional changes initiated in 1933 by President Gabriel Terra's coup d'état and culminating with the coup of his successor, General Alfredo Baldomir, in 1942. Greatly influenced by international trends, Baldomir guaranteed free elections and a restoration of democracy. From that new electoral process, the Colorado Party and Amézaga emerged triumphant by promoting Batllismo, the ideology based on the political, economic, and social ideas of the former president, José Batlle y Ordóñez. With its exports of meat and wool, Uruguay prospered economically during World War II. Amézaga's election guaranteed that Uruguay would be aligned with the Allied cause during the war.

Amézaga was the author of numerous legal texts, including *Enseñanza del derecho civil* (1908) and *Un capítulo de historia internacional* (1942).

See also **Uruguay, Political Parties: Colorado Party.**

BIBLIOGRAPHY

Arturo Scarone, *Uruguayos contemporáneos* (1937).

Benjamin Nahum et al., *Crisis política y recuperación económica, 1930–1950* (1984).

Juan Carlos Pedemonte, *Los presidentes del Uruguay* (1984).

JOSÉ DE TORRES WILSON

AMORIM, ENRIQUE (1900–1960).

One of the most important Uruguayan writers of the twentieth century, Enrique Amorim was born July 25, 1900, in Salto, where he settled and composed most of his poetry, short stories, and novels. Amorim spent much of his childhood in the Uruguayan countryside, which infuses his writing. He attended high school in Buenos Aires, where he first experimented with poetry and later taught literature. His compatriot and fellow author Horacio Quiroga encouraged him to contribute to *Caras y Caretas*, the most popular Rioplatense magazine of the first half of the twentieth century. He opposed the *golpe de estado* (coup d'etat) led by Gabriel Terra in 1933, and voiced his opposition to the 1940s government of Juan Domingo Perón in Argentina.

Amorim traveled often to Montevideo and Buenos Aires, and he made several trips to Europe. His best-known work is the novel *La Carreta* (1932), though it is only part of a large body of writing consisting of short story collections, including *Amorim* (1923); the novel *El paisano Aguilar* (1934); and works of nonfiction and drama. In addition, Amorim wrote screenplays and worked on documentary film projects. He died on July 28, 1960. His residence, Las Nubes, is a memorial that visitors to Salto can still see in the early twenty-first century.

See also **Uruguay: The Twentieth Century; Literature: Spanish America; Perón, Juan Domingo; Quiroga, Horacio; Terra, Gabriel.**

BIBLIOGRAPHY

Amorim, Enrique. *El paisano Aguilar* [1934]. Montevideo: Editores Asociados, 1989.

Amorim, Enrique. *La carreta* [1932]. Colección de Clásicos Uruguayos, vol. 172. Montevideo: Archivo General de la Nación, Centro de Difusión del Libro, 2004.

Miranda Buranelli, Alvaro, and Carlos Nodar Freire, eds. *Enrique Amorim*. Montevideo: Editores Asociados, 1990.

Mose, K. E. A. *Enrique Amorim: The Passion of a Uruguayan*. New York: Plaza Mayor, 1972.

WILLIAM G. ACREE JR.

AMORIM, PEDRO (1958–). Brazilian *choro* musician Pedro Amorim made his debut in the band Nó em Pingo D'Água as a bandolimist (a *bandolim* is a Brazilian mandolin), replacing original member Marco de Pinna. He was influenced by legendary musician Jacób do Bandolim, one of the founding members of the choro movement in Brazil, although he does note a difference in the musical education of contemporary *chorões* (choro musicians): "Choro musicians are more informed about other types of music, they know how to read music.... And this brought about an enrichment of the genre" (Livingston-Isenhour, p. 153). He later formed the choro group O Trio with fellow chorões Maurício Carrilho on guitar and Paulo Sérgio Santos on clarinet. In 1993 they recorded their first album together, *O Trio*, which was released in Europe to critical acclaim and won a 1994 Sharp Award for best instrumental album.

In 1998 Amorim collaborated on the album *Os Bambas do Bandolim* with other popular choro musicians, and in 2001 was a participant in the national choro panel at the renowned Centro Cultural Banco do Brasil (Bank of Brazil Cultural Center) in Rio de Janeiro. He has worked with many noteworthy Brazilian musicians of other musical genres, including Chico Buarque and Beth Carvalho. He has also recorded a solo album, *Pedro Amorim Toca Luperce Miranda* (1995).

See also **Choro, Chorinho; MPB: Música Popular Brasileira; Music: Popular Music and Dance; Musical Instruments.**

BIBLIOGRAPHY

Livingston-Isenhour, Tamara Elena, and Thomas George Caracas Garcia. *Choro: A Social History of a Brazilian Popular Music*. Bloomington: Indiana University Press, 2005.

McCann, Bryan. *Hello, Hello Brazil: Popular Music in the Making of Modern Brazil*. Durham, NC: Duke University Press, 2004.

STACY LUTSCH

AMPARO, WRIT OF. Writ of Amparo, constitutional action that originated in Mexico and since has been adopted by several other Latin American nations. As authorized by Articles 103 and 107 of the Mexican Constitution of 1917, presently in force, the *amparo* (literally, protection) permits any private individual or group to seek federal judicial relief from a broad range of official abuses of rights guaranteed by Articles 1–29 of the Constitution, Mexico's Bill of Rights.

The writ was first established under the leadership of Manuel Crescencio Rejón by the Yucatán Constitution of 1841, by federal statute in the Reforms Act of 1847 (spearheaded by Mariano

Otero), and constitutionally by the liberal Federal Constitution of 1857. The *amparo* bears the influence of U.S. legal practice, especially judicial review, the Bill of Rights, and the Anglo-American writ of habeas corpus, as revealed to Latin America at large through translations of De Tocqueville's *Democracy in America* (1855). It also derives from Spanish sources, including ancient *fueros* (special privileges) and the procedures of the royal courts of Castile and Aragon and various special tribunals of colonial Spanish America, and from the French judicial appeal of *cassation*, the Constitutional Senate of 1799, and the Declaration of the Rights of Man. The *amparo* is thus of hybrid origin.

In Mexico, the writ has become the sole judicial instrument for correcting constitutional violations by legislators, executive officials, and judges, both federal and local. According to the eminent jurist-scholar Héctor Fix Zamudio, the remedy now has at least five major constitutional control functions and procedural forms. It is used as an emergency procedure to protect fundamental human rights such as life, liberty, and physical safety (usually while the petitioner is under confinement by local police or courts) and is brought first to the federal district courts as with the Anglo-American habeas corpus, federal removal, prohibition, and injunction procedures. It is also employed as an appeal to finalize—that is, review and reverse—mistaken interpretations of federal or state codes by lower courts or any administrative tribunal. Known as the judicial, cassation, or direct *amparo*, it is comparable to the U.S. writ of *certiorari* or, more so, the French *cassation*. Constituting some 80 percent of all Mexican *amparo* cases, it is brought directly to one of the four chambers of the federal Supreme Court (criminal, administrative, civil, or labor) or, if a case of lesser importance, to one of the Collegiate Circuit Courts. In addition, Mexicans use the *amparo* as a remedy against abuses by executive agencies and bureaucrats. This administrative, or indirect, *amparo* is first brought to federal district courts; as such it is comparable to the Anglo-American petitions for injunction, declaratory judgment, and mandamus. Appeals may then be taken directly to the Supreme Court when the issue is of "transcending national importance" (giving the High Court *certiorari*-like discretion to hear the case). *Amparo* has been used as a method to challenge unconstitutional (per Article 27) official confiscations of the land and water rights of small individual, communal village, and *ejido* farmers.

In these agrarian *amparos*, formal procedural requirements may be waived for petitioners. Finally, as the only vehicle that can challenge the validity of a legislative statute, the constitutionality *amparo* (*amparo contra leyes*) approaches United States–style judicial review. But this last use of the procedure is limited in effect, rarely successful, and procedurally cumbersome; for example, only the full 21-member Supreme Court can issue a negative declaration, which applies only to the parties-litigant (*inter partes*), not broadly, or *erga omnes*. As with all *amparo* decisions, however, five consecutive judgments of the court do bind all state and federal courts and administrative tribunals as precedent (*jurisprudencia*).

The *amparo* is used across the socioeconomic spectrum in Mexico, as evidenced by the crushing amount of caseloads in the federal courts with *amparo* jurisdiction. It now serves, with certain limits on its application to major government policies, as the principal guardian of the national legal order, from edicts of the president to the smallest *municipio*. In various forms, the writ has been adopted constitutionally by Argentina, Bolivia, Chile, Costa Rica, Ecuador, El Salvador, Guatemala, Honduras, Nicaragua, Paraguay, and Venezuela.

See also **Judicial Systems: Spanish America.**

BIBLIOGRAPHY

Richard D. Baker, *Judicial Review in Mexico: A Study of the Amparo Suit* (1971), is the only book on the *amparo* in English, but is dated in several important respects. A seminal counterpart in Spanish is Ignacio Burgoa, *El juicio de amparo*, 24th ed. (1988). Comprehensive articles in English include: Héctor Fix Zamudio, "A Brief Introduction to the Mexican Writ of *Amparo*," in *California Western International Law Journal* 9, no. 2 (1979), and "The Writ of *Amparo* in Latin America," in *Lawyer of the Americas* 13, no. 3 (1981).

Carl E. Schwarz, "Judges Under the Shadow: Judicial Independence in the United States and Mexico," in *California Western International Law Journal* 3, no. 2 (1973), and "Rights and Remedies in the Federal Trial Courts of Mexico and the United States," in *Hastings Constitutional Law Quarterly* 4 (1977).

Additional Bibliography

Gudiño Pelayo, José de Jesús. *Introducción al amparo mexicano*. México, D.F.: Noriega Editores, 1999.

James, T.M. *Law and Revolution in Mexico: A Constitutional History of Mexico's Amparo Court and Revolutionary Social Reform, 1861–1934.* Ph.D. diss., University of Chicago, 1999.

CARL E. SCHWARZ

AMPÍES, JUAN DE (?–1533). Juan de Ampíes (*d.* 8 February 1533), Spanish conquistador. Ampíes played an important role in the process whereby Spain established itself in the New World. In 1511 he became the first royal factor on the island of Hispaniola. An advocate of a peaceful Conquest, he defended the the original inhabitants of the Los Gigantes Islands (today Curaçao, Aruba, and Bonaire) and was partly responsible for their being declared *indios guaitiaos* (friendly Indians). When the Cumaná peoples who inhabited the coastal region of northeastern Venezuela put to death the missionaries who had come to evangelize the area, Ampíes opposed the use of retaliatory measures against them. When the first peaceful colonizing activities were undertaken with conquered peoples considered to be friendly—activities that were consistent with the doctrines promoted by Fray Bartolomé de Las Casas—Ampíes was assigned in 1520 to populate Los Gigantes with a group of Caquetío Indians. He later established contact with the inhabitants of the South American mainland and was able to gain their confidence.

In 1526 Ampíes bought some slaves on Hispaniola and then freed them making use of a commercial expedition to return them to their homelands. This gesture led to the organization of an expedition under the leadership of his son, whose object was to create a permanent settlement on the mainland. The result was the founding of Coro on 26 July 1527. Because of an agreement with the House of Welser banking firm, however, Ampíes had to abandon the settlement of Coro in 1528 and limit his authority and jurisdiction to the island territories.

See also **Conquistadores.**

BIBLIOGRAPHY

See the translation by Jeannette Johnson Varner of the classic eighteenth-Century work by José Oviedo y Baños, first historian of the province of Venezuela, titled *The Conquest and Settlement of Venezuela* (1987). More specific is Demetrio Ramos Pérez, *La fundación de*

Venezuela: Ampíes y Coro, una singularidad histórica (1978).

Additional Bibliography

Mira Caballos, Esteban. "La primera utopía americana: Las reducciones de indios de los jerónimos en La Española, 1517-1519." *Jahrbuch für Geschichte Lateinamerikas* 39 (2002): 9-35.

INÉS QUINTERO

AMPUDIA Y GRIMAREST, PEDRO DE (1805–1868). Pedro de Ampudia y Grimarest (*b.* 1805; *d.* 1868), Mexican military officer and minister of war (1859–1860). Born in Havana, Cuba, Ampudia arrived in Mexico in 1821 as a lieutenant in the retinue of the last viceroy of New Spain, Juan O'Donojú. He joined the Army of the Three Guarantees and supported the Plan of Iguala for Mexican autonomy and independence. Ampudia fought against the Spanish holding the fort of San Juan de Ulúa in the harbor of Veracruz, and later against the rebels in Texas. He served as governor of the state of Tabasco (1843–1844). During the war with the United States (1846–1848), Ampudia directed the defense of Monterrey and fought under General Antonio López de Santa Anna at the battle of Angostura. Ampudia also served during the war as governor of the state of Nuevo León, and he held that office again during several months in 1854. Elected to the Constituent Congress of 1856–1857, Ampudia fought on the republican side during the War of the Reform; during the Second Empire, he served Maximilian.

See also **Mexico, Wars and Revolutions: Mexican-American War; Mexico, Wars and Revolutions: The Reform.**

BIBLIOGRAPHY

Alberto María Carreño Escudero, *Jefes del ejército mexicano en 1847* (1914).

Charles L. Dufour, *The Mexican War: A Compact History, 1846–1848* (1968); *Diccionario Porrúa de historia, biografía y geografía de México,* 5th ed. (1986).

D. F. STEVENS

AMUNÁTEGUI ALDUNATE, MIGUEL LUIS (1828–1888).

Miguel Luis Amunátegui Aldunate (*b.* 11 January 1828; *d.* 22 January 1888), Chilean historian and public figure. Born and educated in Santiago, and one of the numerous disciples of Andrés Bello, Amunátegui was a brilliant member of a brilliant Chilean generation. A devoted Liberal, he was eight times elected to the Chamber of Deputies and also served in the cabinet during the presidencies of José Joaquín Pérez, Aníbal Pinto, and (briefly) José Manuel Balmaceda. In 1875 he was offered the chance to become the official candidate for the presidency. The government's control over elections would have ensured his triumph, but he declined.

Among the great nineteenth-century Chilean historians, Amunátegui can be ranked as second only to Diego Barros Arana. His chief works were *La reconquista española* (1851), *La dictadura de O'Higgins* (1853), *Los precursores de la independencia de Chile* (3 vols., 1870–1872), and *La crónica de 1810* (3 vols., 1876). His numerous other writings cover a range from philology to the Chilean frontier dispute with Argentina. His two-part work on the latter theme, *Títulos de la República de Chile a la soberanía y dominio de la extremidad austral del continente americano* (1853, 1855), was the first to give coherent shape to Chile's territorial claims.

See also **Chile: The Nineteenth Century.**

BIBLIOGRAPHY

Munizaga Aguirre, Roberto. *Los hermanos Amunátegui, don Claudio Matte.* Santiago: Instituto de Chile, Academia de Ciencias Sociales Políticas y Morales, 1983.

SIMON COLLIER

ANÁHUAC.

Anáhuac, a term from the Nahuatl *atl* (water) and *nahuac* (near) that usually refers to Mexico City (once surrounded by large lagoons) and, by extension, to the Valley of Mexico, the central highlands, and the Mexican nation, particularly in conjunction with the region's pre-Hispanic heritage. Originally, however, a reference to the water's proximity might also have implied the seacoast, warm lowlands inhabited by the Aztecs' trading partners. Alonso de Molina, in his classic Nahuatl dictionary, defines the modified term *anauacayotl* as "things that are brought from neighboring lands." Anáhuac was also the destination of the legendary ruler-god Quetzalcoatl when he left Tula, heading east.

See also **Aztecs; Nahuas.**

BIBLIOGRAPHY

Nigel Davies, *The Aztecs: A History* (1973), pp. 12, 333.

Alonso De Molina, *Vocabulario en lengua castellana y mexicana y mexicana y castellana,* 4th ed. (1977), pt. II, p. 6.

Additional Bibliography

Reyes, Alfonso. *Visión de Anáhuac.* In *Obras completas,* vol. 2. México: Fondo de Cultura Economica, 1976, pp. 8–34.

Ward, Thomas. "Expanding Ethnicity in Sixteenth-Century Anahuac: Ideologies of Ethnicity and Gender in the Nation-Building Process." *MLN* 116.2 (March 2001): 419-452.

STEPHANIE WOOD

ANARCHISM AND ANARCHOSYNDICALISM.

Anarchism and anarchosyndicalism—ideologies that sought to replace existing political orders with a collective society based upon the needs of workers—were the most important currents to influence the labor movement from its origins to 1930. Early anarchists writing on various facets of Latin American societies were Rafael Barrett, Manuel González Prada, Ricardo Flores Magón, and Florencio Sánchez. Anarchists also undertook much of the early organizing and propaganda and acted as individuals. Anarchosyndicalism, which replaced anarchism as the most widely held position among workers, reached its maximum influence in the early twentieth century. By the 1930s, however, both ideologies lost ground, although a few adherents still existed. The appeal of anarchism, in particular, stemmed partly from the fact that small firms or artisanal shops dominated most manufacturing sectors. Pressured by the emergence of modern larger production units, artisans looked for ways to survive and better their lives. Later, anarchosyndicalism proved attractive as a means to combat the emerging capitalist economy that threatened to marginalize artisans and subordinate workers to industrial discipline with low wages. Countries where large groups of southern European immigrants lived tended to have stronger anarchist and anarchosyndicalist movements because many new arrivals (some fleeing persecution at home) carried these ideologies with them. Vibrant organizations that espoused one of these doctrines first emerged in Argentina, southern Brazil, and Uruguay.

Anarchism took both a collective and an individualistic form. It gathered strength in Mexico's highly artisanal economy after 1860. Before 1900, immigrant members of the First International, based in Europe, founded short-lived sections in several large Latin American cities. By 1900, however, anarchism in some forms had appeared almost everywhere in Latin America. Anarchists differed concerning which strategies and tactics to pursue. Many saw trade unions as inherently reformist and chose to work through small affinity groups to win workers and others to the cause. Anarchists agreed that they should build a revolutionary movement to destroy the state and create a new society, but they often disagreed upon its shape. Independent artisans tended to favor a society composed of small producers, each governing a particular area of production. Occasionally anarchists joined unions just to recruit people. Some workers practiced "propaganda by the deed" and perpetrated individualist acts, such as the killing of Buenos Aires's police chief in 1909 for his role in the massacre of workers on May Day that year. Proletarian violence in the face of bourgeois violence, anarchists argued, justified such deeds.

Anarchosyndicalism played an even larger role in Latin America, but differences emerged among its followers. Its main objective was to adapt anarchist principles to the conditions of an emerging industrial capitalism. It spread rapidly, and after 1900 organizations pledged to it formed wherever a labor movement existed. Both a revolutionary and proletarian doctrine, anarchosyndicalism attempted to overcome the ineffectiveness of anarchist practice. Although theory and practice varied considerably over space and time, direct action formed one central feature. Workers relied on strikes, sabotage, or boycotts rather than gains through the institutions of the capitalist state. The proletariat was not to participate in political parties because voting just legitimized the system. Anarchosyndicalists undertook to

destroy the state, not to control or reform it. Trade unions could act as vehicles of struggle and as the nucleus of the new society, which some envisioned as a free association of free producers gathered into unions that would govern through a large federation. Even union organization created controversy. Some saw unions as minorities of militants and argued against enrolling everyone regardless of whether or not they identified as working class or saw employers as the enemy. Others warned that union bureaucracies weakened revolutionary militancy, and they opposed paid officials, permanent staff, or strike funds. In general, anarchosyndicalists turned to organizing on an industrial rather than craft basis (anarchists generally favored the latter). These groups would join local, provincial, national, regional, and eventually international federations. National groupings formed in several countries, and continental conferences met, uniting workers in given trades and in these federations. All persuasions of anarchists maintained extensive international contacts. Members of the U.S. anarchosyndicalist Industrial Workers of the World, for example, founded branches in Chile after 1910.

Anarchosyndicalists sought to destroy the state through the revolutionary general strike, which either became an armed confrontation of the masses against the forces of repression representing capital or else took place peacefully when all workers dropped their tools and walked away from their jobs. In theory they discredited strikes for limited objectives, but in practice supported them because they believed that understanding came through struggle. In reality, most anarchosyndicalist unions negotiated with the state, although some did not. Both anarchists and anarchosyndicalists published newspapers, edited books, and ran cultural programs for workers and their families, offering an alternative lifestyle. The strongest anarchosyndicalist organizations emerged in Argentina and Brazil, but they also exercised influence over workers and the labor movement through at least the 1920s in Chile, Cuba, Mexico, Peru, Uruguay, and elsewhere. The widespread failure of revolutionary general strikes eventually led workers to follow less radical strategies and seek limited gains.

The appearance of Communist parties after 1917 and the growing strength of syndicalism doomed both anarchist currents either to disappear as an important force or else to play a decidedly secondary role. The last great movements in which anarchosyndicalists played a leading part occurred around World War I. The defeats suffered in the São Paulo (1917) and Montevideo (1919) general strikes, for example, helped discredit anarchosyndicalism, as did the severe repression after the Semana Trágica (1919) in Argentina. Nevertheless, in the 1920s anarchosyndicalist unions still proved influential in Bolivia and Ecuador, in the broad social movement that overthrew the Cuban dictator Gerardo Machado in 1933 and in rural strikes in the Argentine Chaco and Patagonia. After 1930 anarchism and anarchosyndicalism declined as significant forces. There remained, however, individual workers and specific unions that still espoused each of them. Gradual economic development doomed these doctrines, which once spoke to the needs of workers and artisans caught in the initial stages of capitalist development.

See also **Baralt, Rafael María; Flores Magón, Ricardo; González Prada, Manuel; Sánchez, Florencio.**

BIBLIOGRAPHY

General overviews of the early period of the Latin American labor movement are found in Hobart A. Spalding, *Organized Labor in Latin America* (1977), chaps. 1 and 2, and Michael Hall and Hobart A. Spalding, "The Urban Working Class and Early Latin American Labour Movements, 1880–1930," in *The Cambridge History of Latin America*, vol. 4, edited by Leslie Bethell (1986), reprinted as "Urban Labor Movements" in *Latin America: Economy and Society, 1870–1930*, edited by Leslie Bethell (1989) (see especially the bibliography, which surveys the field). Among the leading country studies of anarchism and anarchosyndicalism are John W. F. Dulles, *Anarchists and Communists in Brazil, 1900–1935* (1973); Angel Quintero Rivera, *Workers' Struggle in Puerto Rico: A Documentary History* (1976); Guillermo Lora, *A History of the Bolivian Labour Movement, 1848–1971*, translated by Christine Whitehead, edited and abridged by Laurence Whitehead (1977); John M. Hart, *Anarchism and the Mexican Working Class, 1860–1931* (1978); Jacov Oved, *El anarquismo y el movimiento obrero en Argentina* (1978); Peter Blanchard, *The Origins of the Peruvian Labor Movement, 1883–1919* (1982); and Peter De Shazo, *Urban Workers and Labor Unions in Chile, 1902–1927* (1983).

Additional Bibliography

Alves, Paulo. *Anarquismo e anarcosindicalismo: Teoria e prática no movimento operário brasileiro, 1906–1922*. Curitiba, Brazil: Aos Quatro Ventos, 2002.

Benyo, Javier. *La alianza obrera Spartacus: Anarquismo, vanguardia obrera e institucionalización del movimiento sindical en la década de 1930*. Buenos Aires: Libros de Anarres, 2005.

Rama, Carlos M., and Angel J. Cappelletti, eds. *El Anarquismo en América Latina*. Caracas: Biblioteca Ayacucho, 1990.

Robles Gómez, Jorge, and Luís Ángel Gómez. *De la autonomía al corporativismo: Memoria cronológica del movimiento obrero en México, 1900–1980*. Mexico City: El Atajo Ediciones, 1995.

Shaffer, Kirwin R. *Anarchism and Countercultural Politics in Early Twentieth-Century Cuba*. Gainesville: University Press of Florida, 2005.

Suriano, Juan. *Anarquistas: Cultura y política libertaria en Buenos Aires, 1890–1910*. Buenos Aires: Manantial, 2001.

Toledo, Edilene. *Anarquismo e sindicalismo revolucionário: Trabalhadores e militantes em São Paulo na Primeira República*. São Paulo: Editora Fundação Perseu Abramo, 2004.

Ward, Thomas. *La anarquía inmanentista de Manuel González Prada*. Lima: Universidad Ricardo Palma/Editorial Horizonte, 2001.

HOBART A. SPALDING

ANAYA, PEDRO MARÍA DE

ANAYA, PEDRO MARÍA DE (1794–1854). Pedro María de Anaya (*b.* 1794; *d.* 21 March 1854), president of Mexico (1847, 1847–1848). A career military officer, Anaya served as deputy in the Mexican Congress (1829–1830) and as a senator (1844–1845). He was appointed minister of war in 1845 by President José Joaquín de Herrera. He was substitute president for Antonio López de Santa Anna from 2 April 1847 to 20 May 1847 and later that year was elected interim president, serving from 13 November 1847 until 8 January 1848. As defender of the convent of Churubusco on the southern outskirts of Mexico City during the war with the United States, Anaya was forced to surrender by U.S. General David E. Twiggs. When Twiggs occupied Churubusco and asked him where the munitions were, Anaya answered, "Si hubiera parque, no estarían ustedes aquí" ("If we had any munitions, you would not be here"). Anaya served as minister of war in 1848 and again in 1852, and was governor of the Federal District in 1849. He was serving as director general of the post office at his death in Mexico City.

See also **Mexico: 1810–1910.**

BIBLIOGRAPHY

Alberto María Carreño Escudero, *Jefes del ejército mexicano en 1847* (1914).

Charles L. Dufour, *The Mexican War: A Compact History, 1846–1848* (1968).

José María Miguel I Vergés, *Diccionario de insurgentes* (1969); *Diccionario Porrúa de historia, biografía y geografía de México,* 5th ed. (1986).

Additional Bibliography

Rivera Marín, Guadalupe, and Juan Manuel Menes Llaguno. *Si hubiera parque!*. Mexico City: Instituto Nacional de Estudios Históricos de la Revolución Mexicana, 1993.

D. F. STEVENS

ANAYA, RUDOLFO (1937–). One of the fathers of Chicano literature, the novelist, short story writer, and poet Rudolfo Alfonso Anaya was born on October 30, 1937, in Pastura, New Mexico. He received BA and MA degrees in English from the University of New Mexico (1963, 1968), where he began teaching in 1974 and retired as professor emeritus in 1993. Like many Chicano authors, he encountered difficulties finding a publisher for his first novel, owing mainly to his use of both Spanish and English. Yet when *Bless Me, Ultima* was finally published in 1972, it was awarded the Premio Quinto Sol and became a classic of Chicano literature. Partly autobiographical, set in 1940s New Mexico, this coming-of-age story depicts Mexican-American rural Southwest experience. It was translated into Spanish by Alicia Smithers as *Bendíceme, Última,* published by Warner Books in 1994.

Anaya is also known for the novels *Heart of Aztlán* (1976), *Tortuga* (1979), and *Alburquerque* (1992; spelled with an extra *r* as in the original Spanish), as well as the Sonny Baca mysteries; and his short story collection *The Silence of the Llano* (1982), among other writings. He is the recipient of many awards, including two NEA fellowships (1979, 1980), the Before Columbus American Book Award (1980), the PEN-Center West Award for Fiction (1992); the National Medal of the Arts (2002), and the Luis Leal Award for Distinction in Chicano/Latino Literature (2004). Anaya's manuscript collection is located at Zimmerman Library, University of New Mexico.

See also **Hispanics in the United States; Literature: Spanish America.**

BIBLIOGRAPHY

Poetry

The Adventures of Juan Chicaspatas. Houston, TX: Arte Publico Press, 1985.

Elegy on the Death of Cesar Chavez. El Paso, TX: Cinco Puntos Press, 2000.

Collections

As editor. *Voces: An Anthology of Nuevo Mexicano Writers*. Albuquerque: University of New Mexico Press, 1987. A collection of poetry.

The Anaya Reader. New York: Warner Books, 1995.

Children's Books

Mayás Children: The Legend of La Llorona. Illustrations by Maria Baca. Berkeley, CA: Tonatiuh-Quinto Sol, 1984.

Farolitos for Abuelo. New York: Hyperion, 1998.

The Santero's Miracle: A Bilingual Story, illus. Amy Córdova; Spanish trans. Enrique Lamadrid. Albuquerque: University of New Mexico Press, 2004.

CLAIRE JOYSMITH

ANCASH. Ancash, Peruvian department northeast of Lima known as Huaylas before 1839, when it was renamed Ancash (Quechuan for "blue"). The capital city of Huaraz (population 50,000 in 1990) stands at 10,000 feet above sea level. The department's highland region features the impressive Callejón de Huaylas, a canyon formed by the river Santa and flanked by the White and Black ranges of the Peruvian Andes. This region has been struck by devastating earthquakes and subsequent landslides, especially in 1941, 1962, and 1970. In the latter, approximately 70,000 people died, including most of the inhabitants of the cities of Yungay and Ranrahirca, who were buried by an avalanche from the northwest side of the Huascarán, the highest mountain of the Peruvian Andes.

Tourist sites include the towns of Caraz, Carhuáz, and the pre-Inca center of Chavín. The major industrial city is the port of Chimbote (1990 population 325,000), powered by the Santa hydroelectric complex.

See also **Earthquakes.**

BIBLIOGRAPHY

Félix Alvarez-Brun, *Ancash: Una historia regional peruana* (1970).

Anthony Oliver-Smith, *The Martyred City: Death and Rebirth in the Andes* (1986).

Additional Bibliography

Salinas Sánchez, Alejandro. *Parroco y señor: gamonalismo en Macate (Ancash), 1853–1893.* Lima: Seminario de Historia Rural Andina, Universidad Nacional Mayor de San Marcos, 2005.

Thurner, Mark. *From Two Republics to One Divided: Contradictions of Postcolonial Nation-making in Andean Peru.* Durham, NC: Duke University Press, 1997.

Varón Gabai, Rafael. *Curacas y encomenderos acomodamiento nativo en Huaraz, siglos XVI y XVII.* Lima: P.L. Villanueva, 1980.

ALFONSO W. QUIROZ

ANCHIETA, JOSÉ DE (1534–1597).

José de Anchieta (*b.* 19 March 1534; *d.* 6 September 1597), Jesuit missionary. An early Jesuit missionary known as the "Apostle of Brazil," José de Anchieta was skillful in teaching and evangelizing the native Indians. Of Spanish origin, he was born in Tenerife, in the Canary Islands, and studied at the University of Coimbra, where he entered the Society of Jesus as a brother in 1551. In 1553 he arrived in Brazil, where he taught at the Jesuit College of São Paulo. He was an accomplished writer and linguist. A master of Latin grammar and prose, he was one of the first missionaries to learn the Tupi language of the Indians well enough to write a Tupi grammar to augment the Jesuit missionary endeavors in Brazil. He served as the secretary to Manuel da Nóbrega, the leader of the first group of Jesuit missionaries in Brazil. He was responsible for the founding in Brazil of the Jesuit educational system based on the *ratio studiorum*, which emphasized classes in

Latin, grammar, philosophy, mathematics, cosmography, and astronomy. In 1577 he made solemn profession as a priest in the Jesuit order.

While Manuel da Nóbrega was working in northern Brazil, Anchieta concentrated his efforts on founding *aldeias,* or fortified missions, in the southern captaincies of São Vicente, Rio de Janeiro, and Espírito Santo. He founded a third regular college in 1554 in São Paulo, where he was a zealous teacher. He also composed a great number of hymns, sacred songs, plays, and a poem in praise to Our Lady. In 1563 he worked with Manuel da Nóbrega in a pacification mission among the Tamoios, who were allied with the French and attacking settlements in Santos and São Vicente. After serving as a teacher and missionary, he was appointed Jesuit provincial of southern Brazil from 1578 to 1587.

A saintly and dynamic missionary, Anchieta spent forty-four years laboring in South America, despite a painful back injury which often incapacitated him. His letters and sermons give glowing accounts of the natural beauty of Brazil and are an excellent chronicle of early Brazilian history. Various miracles were attributed to him and he is called the "miracle worker" of Brazil.

See also **Missions: Jesuit Missions (Reducciones).**

BIBLIOGRAPHY

Serafim S. Leite, *História da Companhia de Jesus no Brasil,* vol. 2 (1938).

Charles R. Boxer, *Salvador de Sa and the Struggle for Brazil and Angola (1602–1686)* (1952).

Serafim S. Leite, *Novas paginas da história do Brasil* (1965).

Helio Vianna, *História do Brasil colonial* (1975).

John Hemming, *Red Gold: The Conquest of the Brazilian Indians* (1978).

Additional Bibliography

Massimi, Marina, Miguel Mahfoud, Paulo José Carvalho da Silva, and Silvia H. S. Avancini. *Navegadores, colonos, missionarios na Terra de Santa Cruz.* São Paulo: Edições Loyola, 1997.

PATRICIA MULVEY

ANCHORENA, TOMÁS MANUEL DE

(1773–1847). Tomás de Anchorena (November 29, 1873–April 29, 1847), an important figure in

Argentina's political struggles after independence, was a consistent promoter of a republican program with Catholic and conservative leanings and incorporating a degree of xenophobia. The son of a Basque merchant who amassed a significant fortune, Anchorena studied at the Real Colegio de San Carlos in Buenos Aires and earned a doctorate in law from the Universidad de Charcas in 1807. He began his public life as an alderman on the town council of Buenos Aires in the last years of Spanish rule, but with the May Revolution of 1810 he joined the supporters of the break with Spain. He was a deputy in the Congress of 1816 that declared independence; in that occasion, he made a well-known speech in favor of federal republicanism and against the proposals of monarchy.

An enemy of the Directorate and later of Bernardino Rivadavia's centralizing project, Anchorena was a distinguished member of the Buenos Aires faction of the Federalists in the 1820s. During the first administration of Juan Manuel de Rosas (1829–1832), he served as minister of foreign affairs. In 1832, in broken health, he retired from political life but continued to exercise influence over Governor Rosas, his cousin, until his (Anchorena's) death in 1847.

See also **Argentina: The Nineteenth Century; Argentina, Federalist Pacts (1831, 1852); Rosas, Juan Manuel de.**

BIBLIOGRAPHY

Hora, Roy. "Patrones de inversión y negocios en Buenos Aires en la primera mitad del siglo XIX: *La trayectoria de Tomás Manuel de Anchorena*." *História Económica & História de Empresas* 8, no. 1 (January–June 2005).

Irazusta, Julio. *Tomás de Anchorena: Prócer de la Revolución, la independencia y la federación, 1784–1847.* Buenos Aires: Editorial La Voz del Plata, 1950.

Poensgen, Ruprecht. *Die Familie Anchorena, 1750–1875: Handel und Viehwirtschaft am Rio de la Plata zwischen Vizekönigreich und Republik.* Cologne, Germany: Böhlau, 1998.

ROY HORA

ANCÓN, TREATY OF (1883).

Treaty of Ancón (1883), an agreement between Chile and Peru ending Peru's participation in the War of the Pacific. The treaty ceded Tarapacá to Chile, allowing Santiago to occupy the provinces of Tacna and Arica for a period of ten years. Santiago annexed Tarapacá subject to outstanding claims of foreign creditors. The agreement also called for a plebiscite to take place in 1893 in the two provinces; the winner could retain the two provinces, and the loser would receive $10 million in silver pesos.

Because it did not specify the procedures under which the plebiscite should occur, the treaty failed to settle the issue of the ownership of Tacna and Arica. Santiago successfully resisted attempts by the Pan-American movement and the United States to settle this boundary issue until, in 1929, it signed an agreement with Lima. In return for retaining control of Arica, Chile constructed some port facilities in Tacna, paid Lima $6 million, and returned Tacna to Peruvian control. Thus, the Ancón agreement, while ending the formal state of war, did not completely resolve the territorial disputes arising from the 1879 war.

See also **War of the Pacific.**

BIBLIOGRAPHY

William J. Dennis. *Tacna and Arica: An Account of the Chile-Peru Boundary Dispute and of the Arbitrations by the United States.* Hamden: Archon Books, 1967.

Robert N. Burr. *By Reason or Force: Chile and the Balancing of Power in South America, 1830–1905.* Berkeley: University of California Press, 1965. 160–164.

WILLIAM F. SATER

ANDAGOYA, PASCUAL DE (1495–1548).

Pascual de Andagoya (*b.* 1495; *d.* 1548), early Spanish explorer and chronicler of the Conquest. Andagoya arrived in the Caribbean in 1514 with Pedrarias Davila (Pedro Arias de Ávila), and in 1521 he became governor of Panama. The following year he led a group to explore to the south. Andagoya sailed down the Pacific coast to the San Juan River of southern Colombia, where, suffering from an injury and virtually out of supplies, he turned back. Andagoya returned with tales of great riches to the south. Inspired by these tales, Francisco Pizarro utilized the information uncovered by Andagoya in subsequent forays south. In

1537 Andagoya became governor of the Pacific coast region of Colombia. However, his rival Sebastián de Belalcázar brought charges against him, believing that Andagoya had encroached on his domain. Andagoya was jailed and sent to Spain. According to some accounts, he died in Cuzco, Peru, in 1548; others maintain that he never returned to the New World.

As an explorer Andagoya enjoyed a special reputation for his humane regard for the natives. He is most remembered for his lively account of the deeds of conquest, *Narrative of the Proceedings of Pedrarias Davila in the Provinces of Tierra Firme or Castilla del Oro, and of the Discovery of the South Sea and the Coasts of Peru and Nicaragua* (translated by Sir Clements Markham, 2d ed. 1978).

See also **Balboa, Vasco Núñez de.**

BIBLIOGRAPHY

Beyond Andagoya's own writings, the early Spanish exploration, conquest, and settlement of Panama and Colombia are covered in Carl Ortwin Sauer, *The Early Spanish Main* (1969). Two classic works capture much of the flavor of the times: Sir Clements Markham, *The Conquest of New Granada* (1912); and Frederick Alexander Kirkpatrick, *The Spanish Conquistadores* (1934).

Additional Bibliography

Andagoya, Pascual de. *Relación y documentos,* edited by Adrian Blázquez. Madrid: Historia 16, 1986.

RONN F. PINEO

ANDEAN PACT. The Cartagena agreement of May 1969 established the Grupo Andino or Andean Common Market. The pact sought to integrate the economies of Colombia, Ecuador, Peru, Bolivia, and Chile. Venezuela joined in 1973, and Chile withdrew in 1976. The primary objective of the Andean Pact was to promote regional industrialization. To this end, it adopted several innovative strategies: the elimination of internal constraints on trade, the formation of a common external tariff, the development of sectoral programs, and the strict regulation of foreign investment.

Initially the Andean Group's efforts at cooperation produced substantial increases in regional trade and industrial growth. By the 1980s, however, these positive trends were reversed. The policy of substituting local industrial products for imports was costly. Internal economic inequalities were intensified. Owing to the fragility of Andean economies and the international economic crisis, regional trade declined. Andean economic integration also suffered setbacks due to conflicts of national interest over tariffs, a boundary war between Ecuador and Peru, and failures to enforce Pact policies. Venezuela decided in 2006 to withdraw from the Group, citing dissatisfaction with the bilateral free trade agreements (FTAs) that Colombia and Peru signed with the United States. Despite making some progress in achieving economic unity, as of 2007 the Andean Pact had yet to overcome structural problems and deep-seated regional conflicts.

See also **Economic Integration.**

BIBLIOGRAPHY

Roger W. Fontaine. *The Andean Pact: A Political Analysis.* Beverley Hills, CA: Sage Publications, 1977.

Lynn Krieger Mytelka. *Regional Development in a Global Economy: The Multinational Corporation, Technology, and Andean Integration.* New Haven, CT: Yale University Press, 1979.

Ciro Angarita and Peter Coffey. *Europe and the Andean Countries: A Comparison of Economic Policies and Institutions.* London: Pinter Publishers, 1988.

Additional Bibliography

Ocampo, José Antonio, and Pilar Esguerra. "The Andean Group and Latin American Integration." In *Economic Integration in the Western Hemisphere,* edited by Roberto Bouzas and Jaime Ros. Notre Dame, IN: University of Notre Dame Press, 1994.

STEVEN J. HIRSCH
ALFONSO W. QUIROZ

ANDERSON IMBERT, ENRIQUE (1910–2000). Enrique Anderson Imbert, whom the noted Argentine novelist Julio Cortázar considered one of the most important short story writers of Latin America, was the first major Argentine writer of his era to cultivate the fantastic. He was also one of the leading critics of his generation, an essayist, a literary historian, and an influential teacher. Born on February 12, 1910, in Córdoba, he studied philology and philosophy at the University of Buenos

Aires with Pedro Henríquez Ureña and Alejandro Korn. He taught at the University of Cuyo (Mendoza) in 1940 and at the University of Tucumán (1941–1947). Having established an early reputation as a literary critic writing for the Buenos Aires daily *La Vanguardia* through 1930, Anderson Imbert published his first novel *Vigilia* (1934), which was awarded the Buenos Aires Municipal Prize for Literature, and in 1937 *La flecha en el aire*. He wrote articles for major journals such as *Sur*. In 1947 Anderson went to the United States on a Guggenheim fellowship and taught at the University of Michigan until 1965, returning briefly to Argentina in 1955 to teach at the universities of Buenos Aires and La Plata. From 1954 to 1956 he published his best-selling and influential *Historia de la literatura hispanoamericana* (A history of Spanish-American literature). From 1965 to 1980 he was the John Eliot Norton Professor of Poetry at Harvard University.

After his retirement from Harvard, Anderson Imbert divided his time between Argentina and the United States, writing fiction, lecturing, and serving as president of the Argentine Academy of Letters. His major works of fiction include *El grimorio* (1961), *El gato Cheshire* (1965), *La locura juega al ajedrez* (1971), and *Evocación de sombras en la ciudad geométrica* (1989). He died in Buenos Aires on December 6, 2000.

See also **Cortázar, Julio; Literature: Spanish America.**

BIBLIOGRAPHY

Anderson Imbert, Enrique. *Woven on the Loom of Time: Stories.* Translated by Carleton Vail and Pamela Edwards-Mondragón. Austin: University of Texas Press, 1990.

Giacomán, Helmy F., ed. *Homenaje a Enrique Anderson Imbert: Variaciones, interpretaciones en torno a su obra.* Madrid: Anaya, 1974.

Hall, Nancy Abraham, and Lanin Gyurko, eds. *Studies in Honor of Enrique Anderson Imbert.* Newark, DE: Juan de la Cuesta Hispanic Monographs, 2003.

Liggera, Rubén Américo. *De espejos, fantasmas y esqueletos: Ensayos sobre la obra literaria de Enrique Anderson Imbert.* Buenos Aires: RundiNuskín, 1990.

GEORGETTE MAGASSY DORN

ago) when the South American continental plate overrode and submerged under the Pacific the Nazca and Cocos plates. The rising of the mountains still continues, as evidenced by constant earthquakes and volcanic eruptions. The intrusion of rising magma into ancient marine sediments explains the abundance of limestone and metallic ores (gold, silver, copper, iron, and tin) that are the foundation of the national economies of countries such as Bolivia, Peru, Chile, Colombia and Venezuela. Frequent volcanic activity adds calcium, sodium and potassium to the soil, rendering it very fertile, but it also means that many settlements in the mountains and their forelands have been devastated. There is almost no city along the Andes that has not been either destroyed or severely damaged by earthquakes.

The Andes are a sequence of parallel ranges that converge in "knots" (*nudos*) and enclose high basins (*altiplanos* or *cuencas*). These high basins have a great cultural significance for South America because in them developed prehispanic cultures such as the Muisca-Chibcha (Colombia), Caras and Quitu (Ecuador), Huari and Inca (Peru), Chiripá and Tiwanaku (Bolivia), and Atacameño (northern Chile). The Andes are also the realm in which the cultivation of potato, maize, and quinoa, and the domestication of llamas (descended from wild guanacos), occurred. The highest peak in the Andes, Mount Aconcagua in Argentina (6,958 meters), is the tallest mountain in the Americas and the western hemisphere.

See also **Earthquakes; Llama.**

BIBLIOGRAPHY

Lamb, Simon. *Devil in the Mountain: A Search for the Origin of the Andes.* Princeton, NJ: Princeton University Press, 2004.

Veblen, T., K. R. Young, and A. R. Orme, eds. *The Physical Geography of South America.* New York: Oxford University Press, 2007.

CÉSAR N. CAVIEDES

ANDES. The Andes, also known as Cordillera de los Andes, is an 8,000-kilometer mountain chain stretching from the Caribbean island of Trinidad to Cape Horn. The mountain system started to rise during the Cretaceous period (130 million years

ANDRADA, ANTÔNIO CARLOS RIBEIRO DE AND MARTIM FRANCISCO RIBEIRO DE. Antônio Carlos Ribeiro de Andrada and Martim Francisco Ribeiro de Andrada, Brazilian statesmen and younger brothers of José

Bonifácio de Andrada. Children of a merchant of Santos, they all graduated from Coimbra University and entered government service. All three were self-assured, quarrelsome, unscrupulous, and vindictive when crossed, confusing personal and family advancement with the public interest.

Antônio Carlos (*b.* 1 November 1773; *d.* 5 December 1845), then a royal judge, gave support to the 1817 revolt in Pernambuco, suffering three years' imprisonment. Elected from São Paulo to the Lisbon Cortes in 1821, he took the lead in asserting Brazil's rights. Martim Francisco (*b.* 27 June 1775; *d.* 23 February 1844) served as minister of finance in the cabinet headed by José Bonifácio from 1822 to 1823. The three brothers sat in the Constituent Assembly and, following the dismissal of José Bonifácio and Martim Francisco as ministers, launched a campaign of opposition to Pedro I that contributed to the violent dissolution of the Constituent Assembly in November 1823. Deported to France, the brothers did not return from exile until 1829. After the abdication of Pedro I in 1831, the brothers tried by various means, legal and illegal, to secure control of power. They were involved in the abortive coup of April 1832 and in the Caramurú movement for Pedro I's restoration. In 1834 and again in 1838 Antônio Carlos unsuccessfully sought election as regent. He and Martim Francisco played a leading part in securing the premature declaration of Pedro II's majority in July 1840. The two brothers dominated the first cabinet appointed by the emperor, but their ambition and highhandedness brought about their dismissal from office in February 1841. Antônio Carlos, the most energetic and domineering of the three brothers, became a leader of the new Liberal Party, securing election to the Senate prior to his death.

See also **Brazil: The Colonial Era, 1500-1808; Brazil: 1808-1889.**

BIBLIOGRAPHY

Barman, Roderick. *Citizen Emperor: Pedro II and the Making of Brazil, 1825–1891.* Stanford: Stanford University Press, 1999.

Beattie, Peter M. *The Human Tradition in Modern Brazil.* Wilmington, DE: SR Books, 2004.

Schultz, Kirsten. *Tropical Versailles: Empire, Monarchy, and the Portuguese Royal Court in Rio de Janeiro, 1808–1821.* New York: Routledge, 2001.

RODERICK J. BARMAN

ANDRADA, JOSÉ BONIFÁCIO DE

(1763–1838). José Bonifácio de Andrada (*b.* 13 June 1763; *d.* 6 April 1838), statesman and geologist, known in Brazil as the patriarch of independence. A native of Santos, São Paulo, and the eldest of the Andrada Brothers, José Bonifácio settled in Portugal after graduating in 1788 from Coimbra University. In 1790 the Portuguese government sent him on a mission to study scientific topics in northern Europe. During a decade's absence, he established himself as an expert on minerals and mining. In 1801 he was appointed to several government posts in Portugal. The multiplicity of his new responsibilities and his impatient, imperious character reduced his effectiveness as a bureaucrat. Following the French invasion of Portugal in 1807, he did not accompany the government to Brazil but played a notable role in organizing resistance. His subsequent career in Portugal was stultifying. In 1819 he finally secured permission to retire to Santos, still drawing most of his salary.

The revolution that began in Pôrto in 1820 drew José Bonifácio to the center of Brazilian politics. He played a key role in the provisional government of São Paulo and publicly advocated the continuance of the kingdom of Brazil created in 1815. When the prince regent, Dom Pedro, decided in January 1822 to defy the Cortes and to stay in Rio, José Bonifácio was the logical choice to serve as the prince's chief minister and adviser. José Bonifácio's self-confidence, energy, and determination were indispensable during the next year and a half in establishing the prince's authority within Brazil. The flow of events forced José Bonifácio, not originally an advocate of political independence, to accept that outcome in September 1822. He preserved for the new emperor Pedro I the traditional powers of the Portuguese monarchy.

José Bonifácio's very successes undercut his position. As the new nation-state was consolidated, so his talents became less indispensable and his domineering character less tolerable. Intrigues at court achieved his dismissal as minister in July 1823. José Bonifácio and his brothers, as members of the Constituent Assembly, sitting at Rio since May, went into opposition, denouncing the Portuguese-born faction at court and thereby attacking the emperor himself. The outcome was the violent dissolution of the assembly in November 1823 and the exiling to France of the Andrada brothers until 1829.

On his return, José Bonifácio again became a favored advisor of Pedro I. When the emperor abdicated on 7 April 1831, he named José Bonifácio to be his son's guardian (*tutor*). Although the new regime refused at first to recognize this nomination, the legislature voted in June to make José Bonifácio guardian. His handling of his position was not successful. Pedro II and his sisters did not flourish physically or psychologically. José Bonifácio used his position for political purposes, being involved in plots to overthrow the regime. The government forcibly removed him as guardian in December 1833. José Bonifácio spent his remaining years in quiet retirement on Paquetá Island, Rio de Janeiro.

See also **Brazil, Independence Movements.**

BIBLIOGRAPHY

Octavio Tarquino De Sousa, *História dos fundadores do império*, vol. 1, *José Bonifácio* (Rio de Janeiro, 1957).

Additional Bibliography

Barretto, Vincente. *Ideologia e política no pensamento de José Bonifácio de Andrada e Silva*. Rio de Janeiro: Zahar Editores, 1977.

Viotti da Costa, Emilia. "José Bonifáciode Andrada e Silva: A Brazilian Founding Father." In *The Brazilian Empire: Myths and Histories*. Chapel Hill and London: University of North Carolina Press, 2000.

RODERICK J. BARMAN

ANDRADE, CARLOS DRUMMOND DE (1902–1987).

Carlos Drummond de Andrade (*b.* 31 October 1902; *d.* 17 August 1987), considered Brazil's most important twentieth-century poet. Drummond (or "The Master," as he is best known) was an active poet and writer through several literary generations—from modernism through concretism—and influenced many contemporary Brazilian poets. Born in Minas Gerais and intimately associated with that state in his poetry, Drummond spent most of his life in Rio de Janeiro where, like many other Brazilian writers, he earned his living as a bureaucrat—in the education ministry— and a journalist. He contributed poetry to major

literary reviews and translated many of the classic writers of French and Spanish literature. He also wrote hundreds of *crônicas* (journalistic sketches) about daily life that reveal a genuine, kind soul.

Drummond was not an original member of the group that "founded" Brazilian modernism in São Paulo in 1922. Nevertheless, under their influence, he, along with other contemporary young *mineiro* (that is, of Minas Gerais) writers (e.g., Emílio Moura [1901–1971]), founded *A Revista*, the leading literary review of *mineiro* modernism in 1925. It was not until his 1928 collaboration on Oswald de Andrade's journal *Revista de Antropófagia* (Review of cannibalism) that he attained national acclaim. His poem "No meio do caminho" (In the middle of the road) established the characteristics he pursued in all his poetry: a rejection of traditional forms and structures; a conversational tone and a highly colloquial language reflecting actual Brazilian speech; and an interest in everyday affairs of life, often from a satirical point of view.

Collections of poems published in the 1930s and early 1940s reflected contemporary political upheavals. He debated leftist ideologies and antibourgeois sentiments in *A rosa do povo* (1945), but the volume ends on a note of a search from within for resolution of these dilemmas. Later collections would turn to his sense of isolation from his small-town roots and a growing displeasure with big-city life. *A vida passada a limpo* (1959) reviews his perennial interests within a new light. Here, the elegy on the destruction of Rio's Hotel Avenida assumes several levels of symbolic meaning: society's change, the "endurance" of a work of art (be it one of architecture or poetry), and the role of the artist. Among his other important collections are *Lição das coisas* (1962), which includes experimental concretist verse, and *As impurezas do branco* (1973), which examines modern technology.

Drummond was a friend of the American poet Elizabeth Bishop, who spent some twenty years in Brazil. His reputation in the United States was a consequence of her translations of his works, often published in the *New Yorker*, and also of later translations by Mark Strand, among others. Drummond's influence on modern Brazilian poetry has been immense.

See also **Literature: Brazil.**

BIBLIOGRAPHY

Collected translations include: *The Minus Sign,* translated by Virginia de Araújo (1981), and *Travelling in the Family,* translated by Thomas Colchie et al. (1986). Irwin Stern, "A Poet for All Brazilians," in *Review* 32 (1984): 16–17, offers a brief critique. Frederick G. Williams and Sergio Pachá, eds., *Carlos Drummond de Andrade and His Generation* (1986) and *The Unquiet Self: Self and Society in the Poetry of Carlos Drummond de Andrade* are the major studies in English.

Additional Bibliography

Cançado, José Maria. *Os sapatos de Orfeu: Biografía de Carlos Drummond de Andrade.* São Paulo: Scritta Editorial, 1993.

                                                   IRWIN STERN

ANDRADE, GOMES FREIRE DE

(1688–1763). Gomes Freire de Andrade (*b.* 11 July 1688; *d.* 1 January 1763), governor and captain-general of southern and western Brazil. A member of a distinguished family whose roots trace back in Galicia before 711, the year of the Moorish invasion, and in Portugal since the fourteenth century. For centuries the Freire de Andrades contributed senior officials to Portugal's army, navy, church, and civil service. Andrade, named after an uncle who served as governor of Maranhão during the Beckman Revolt, was born in Jeromenha, situated between Vila Viçosa and Badajóz. He attended the University of Coimbra and became fluent in French and Spanish. Along with his father, he served in the War of the Spanish Succession, after which he retained an appointment in a cavalry unit stationed in the capital. In 1733 he was appointed governor and captain-general of the captaincy of Rio de Janeiro, a post he retained until his death. It was the first of many administrative units for which he became responsible. By 1748 he governed all of western and southern Brazil, including Minas Gerais, Goiás, Mato Grosso, São Paulo, Santa Catarina, and Rio Grande do Sul. Among his notable responsibilities were the settlement of coastal Rio Grande do Sul, the definition of Brazil's southern boundary in accordance with the Treaty of Madrid (1750), commander of

Portuguese forces in Rio Grande do Sul during the Guaraní War (1752–1756), and the expulsion of the Jesuits (1760) from lands under his jurisdiction. Andrade never married; he died in Rio de Janeiro after an extended illness.

See also **Brazil: The Colonial Era, 1500–1808.**

BIBLIOGRAPHY

Charles R. Boxer, *The Golden Age of Brazil, 1695–1750: Growing Pains of a Colonial Society* (1962).

Robert Allan White, "Gomes Freire de Andrade: Life and Times of a Brazilian Colonial Governor, 1688–1763" (Ph.D. diss., University of Texas, 1972).

Additional Bibliography

Reagan, Mary Agneta. "The Role Played by Gomes Freire de Andrade in the Expulsion of the Jesuits from the Portuguese Empire." Ph.D. diss., Catholic University of America, 1978.

                                                   DAURIL ALDEN

ANDRADE, JORGE

(1922–1988). Jorge Andrade (*b.* 1922; *d.* 1988), Brazilian playwright. In his theater Jorge Andrade was the sensitive historian and understanding judge of a fast-disappearing society. He became in every sense the first completely successful modern Brazilian playwright, doing for São Paulo what the novelists and dramatists of the Northeast and Érico Veríssimo in the South have been accomplishing for their regions, for Brazil, and for the world since the 1930s.

A moratória (1954), a play in three acts with two sets, demonstrates the dramatist's great maturity. The subject is essentially a continuation of that of *O telescópio* (1951), both chronologically and thematically, but reflects the considerable development of the author as a person and artist. Here, the slow, painful, and somehow inconclusive passage from one era to another is emphasized more sharply. Simultaneous use of two sets, one the *fazenda* in 1919, the other a city apartment in 1932, requires superior technical skills as well as literary sophistication for full realization and appreciation.

Employing carefully selected situations, emotions, and language, which appear simple and natural without naturalistic triviality, the author solves the age-old problems of classical tragedy with Flaubertian precision. The entire, balanced action turns on the past and its influence on the present through the use of graphic reminiscences that join the two times and places for the author and spectator, whereas the characters must rely on memory alone. With a view of both the past (1919) and the fictional present (1932), we in the actual present are afforded unique historic and dramatic perspective. Transitions from hope to despair on one level, underscored ironically or fatalistically on the other, grip the audience emotionally.

Having vindicated through its ancestors a society whose demise he had begun to record, Jorge Andrade now turned to another class of that society, the tenant farmers. *A vereda da salvação* (published 1957; produced 1964) has as its point of departure a tragic example of religious fanaticism in Minas Gerais, the details and analyses of which the playwright studied most carefully. During a long period of revision, Andrade reconsidered the events, the criticism of his work, and his own meditations on the human condition. More than ever, the new *Vereda da salvação* is neither *mineiro* nor *paulista,* but Brazilian and universal. In fact, it has enjoyed long successful runs in Poland.

The collection *Marta, a árvore e o relógio* (1970) is a very interesting anthology from several points of view. Not only does it contain two new plays, but it also presents Jorge Andrade's major works in a historico-fictional chronology, rather than in the chronology of their writing, to create his full cycle of São Paulo. Thus, the newest play, *As confrarias,* is the first in the collection, and *O sumidouro,* long in progress and the second newest, is the last. The other eight are inserted between these two in more or less fictional order and not in the order in which they were written. The title is comprised of symbols that recur throughout the series of plays.

Having in every way explored everything possible in the world of coffee barons and São Paulo and having realized that censorship made it virtually impossible to stage anything serious on current matters in Brazil, Jorge Andrade turned to television after 1970. When he did create another play, *Milagre na cela* (1977), which dealt with political oppression and torture, his public could receive it only in published form.

See also **Literature: Brazil.**

BIBLIOGRAPHY

Leon F. Lyday and George Woodyard, *Dramatists in Revolt: The New Latin American Theater* (1976), pp. 206–220.

Additional Bibliography

Guidarini, Mário. *Jorge Andrade na contramão da história.* Florianópolis: Editora da UFSC, 1992.

RICHARD A. MAZZARA

ANDRADE, MÁRIO DE (1893–1945).

Mário de Andrade (*b.* 9 October 1893; *d.* 25 February 1945), Brazilian writer. Mário Raul Moraes de Andrade was a man of multiple talents and immensely varied activities. From a relatively modest background, especially compared with his modernist counterparts, he was born in São Paulo and, after graduating from the Ginásio Nossa Senhora do Carmo, studied music and piano at the Conservatorio Dramático e Musical in São Paulo, and was professor of piano. Widely acknowledged as the leading figure—or "pope"—of the Brazilian modernist movement of the 1920s, he was arguably Brazil's most important and versatile literary personage during the first half of the century. He was involved in almost all of the literary, artistic, and cultural movements of the period. He wrote novels, short stories, and poetry; he was a literary, art, and music critic and theorist; he was also a musicologist, a folklorist, and an ethnographer. As director of São Paulo's Department of Culture from 1935 to 1938, he fostered many activities that promoted the development of modern social science in Brazil.

One of the governing concepts of Andrade's cultural and artistic activity, along with his insistence on freedom of artistic expression and experimentation, is what has variously been called his "sense of commitment" or his "quasi-apostolic consciousness." Especially important in this regard is his extensive research into the specific characteristics of Brazilian speech and popular culture, research intended to help forge a more authentic cultural identity. Andrade conceived of nationalism as the first step in a process of self-discovery that would eventually contribute to universal cultural values, to the extent that it was authentic and faithful to itself. His ultimate goal was the integration of Brazilian culture into universal culture, not the closure implied by the more xenophobic currents of nationalism that also found expression within the Brazilian modernist movement. Andrade recognized the difficulty of creating an authentic national culture in a country permeated by European values and standards. He expressed this theme as early as 1922 in the poem "Inspiração," which opens the collection *Paulicéia desvairada* (*Hallucinated City*), when he wrote: "São Paulo! comoção de minha vida... / Galicismo a berrar nos desertos da América!" (São Paulo! tumult of my life... / Gallicism crying in the wilderness of America!). In "O trovador" in the same volume, he wrote, "Sou um tupi tangendo um alaúde!" ("I am a Tupi Indian strumming a lute!").

Andrade's artistic answer to this dilemma was to use popular forms of expression structurally—not merely ornamentally—in elite cultural forms. He began by systematizing errors committed in everyday speech as a means of capturing an authentically national social and psychological character through language itself. By bringing those errors into educated speech and writing, he hoped to help in the formation of a Brazilian literary language. His interest in popular culture as a means of understanding Brazil evolved into the systematic study of Brazilian folklore and the re-creation of popular forms on an erudite level. Knowing and incorporating the foundations of Brazilian popular thought, he felt he could help lead Brazil to self-knowledge and contribute to its passage from nationalism to a universal level in the higher arts. The 1928 novel *Macunaíma*, which David Haberly has described as both an etiological myth of national creation and an eschatological myth of national destruction, represents the artistic culmination of Mário de Andrade's research in Brazilian folklore and popular forms of expression.

See also **Modernism: Brazil.**

BIBLIOGRAPHY

Thomas R. Hart, "The Literary Criticism of Mário de Andrade," in *The Disciplines of Criticism: Essays in Literary Theory, Interpretation, and History,* edited by Peter Demetz (1968), pp. 265–288.

Haroldo De Campos, *Morfologia do Macunaíma* (1973).

Joan Dassin, *Política e poesia em Mário de Andrade* (1978).

Randal Johnson, "Cinema Novo and Cannibalism: *Macunaíma*" and "*Lesson of Love*," in *Brazilian Cinema,* edited by Randal Johnson and Robert Stam (1982), pp. 178–190, 208–215.

David T. Haberly, *Three Sad Races: Racial Identity and National Consciousness in Brazilian Literature* (1983), pp. 123–160.

João Luiz Lafetá, *Figuação de intimidade: Imagens na poesia de Mário de Andrade* (1986).

Additional Bibliography

Hühne, Leda Miranda. *A estética aberta de Mário de Andrade.* Rio de Janeiro: UAPE, 2002.

Rosenberg, Fernando J. *The Avant-garde and Geopolitics in Latin America.* Pittsburgh: University of Pittsburgh Press, 2006.

RANDAL JOHNSON

ANDRADE, OLEGARIO VICTOR

(1839–1882). The Argentine poet, journalist, and politician Olegario Andrade was born March 6, 1839, in Alegrete, Rio Grande do Sul, during his parents' exile in Brazil during the dictatorship of Juan Manuel de Rosas. The family returned to Entre Ríos province in 1845 and after his parents died he became a ward of Justo José Urquiza, who later served as president of the Argentine Confederation (1854–1869). Andrade married the Uruguayan poet Eloísa González. He began writing poetry in high school in Concepción, Uruguay, and became a politician and journalist during the turbulent years of nation-building, writing for newspapers such *Reforma Pacífica, Pueblo Entrerriano,* and *Porvenir.* He served as deputy in the legislature of Santa Fe province (1859) and was secretary to president Santiago Derqui. Once he moved to Buenos Aires he became an opponent of President Bartolomé Mitre and, after 1865, of the War of the Triple Alliance against Paraguay. An influential romantic and epic poet of nineteenth century Argentina, especially the generation of 1880, with Eugenio Cambaceres, Eduardo Wilde, Miguel Cané, and Rafael Obligado, he wrote his best poetry during the years 1876–1881, in the collections *El nido de condores* and *El arpa perdida.* His complete works can be found in his *Obras poéticas*, published in 1915. He died in Buenos Aires October 30, 1882 and is buried in its famed Recoleta Cemetery.

See also **Cambaceres, Eugenio; Cané, Miguel; Derqui, Santiago; Mitre, Bartolomé; Rio Grande do Sul; Rosas, Juan Manuel de; Urquiza, Justo José de; War of the Triple Alliance; Wilde, Eduardo.**

BIBLIOGRAPHY

Andrade, Olegario Victor. *Obras poéticas.* Buenos Aires: La Cultura argentina, 1923.

Tiscornia, Eleuterio F. *Vida de Andrade.* Buenos Aires: Academia Argentina de Letras, 1943.

Salduna, Horacio. *Lucio V. Mansilla y la historia de Entre Ríos: Una olvidada polémica con Olegario Víctor Andrade, 1877.* Buenos Aires: Editorial Dunken, 2003.

Vazquez Cey, Arturo. *La poesía de Olegario Andrade y su época.* Buenos Aires: Coni, 1929.

GEORGETTE MAGASSY DORN

ANDRADE, OSWALD DE (1890–1954).

Oswald de Andrade (*b.* 11 January 1890; *d.* 22 October 1954), Brazilian writer and intellectual. As a theoretician of Brazil's social and aesthetic modernization, Andrade was a leading contributor to the Brazilian modernist movement in the arts and culture, initiated formally by the Modern Art Week held in February 1922 in São Paulo, which he helped to plan. His principal modernist contributions are the "Manifesto da poesia pau Brasil" (1924; Brazilwood Manifesto), whose ideas inspired the cubistic geometrism and "constructive innocence" of Tarsila do Amaral's canvases of the mid-1920s—and the "Manifesto antropófago" (1928; Cannibal Manifesto), which led to the founding of a national vanguardist movement whose model of "devouring assimilation" of foreign influence under the totem of the cannibal tribes who devoured Europeans was summarized in the aphorism "Tupy or not Tupy, that is the question." The *Antropofagia* movement—again paralleled in the plastic arts by Amaral's paintings—created a paradoxical telluric and vanguardist model for resolving the dialectic between national and foreign cultural influences.

Andrade's early years reflect the transition from Brazil's belle époque aesthetic to modernism. A graduate of São Bento Seminary and the Largo de São Francisco Law School, Andrade began his literary career as a journalist and contributor to fin-de-siècle and premodernist magazines (*O Pirralho, Papel e Tinta*), in which he introduced Italo-Paulista dialect. With Guilherme de Almeida he wrote two plays in French in 1916. His premodernist life is fictionalized in *A trilogia do exílio,* later published as *Os condenados,* and in the collective diary *O perfeito cozinheiro das almas deste mundo.* During the 1920s he spent much of his time in Paris with Amaral and her circle. Influenced by cubism and the poetic prose of Blaise Cendrars, his early modernist work includes two "inventions" combining fragmented poetry with prose, *Memórias sentimentais de João Miramar* (1924) and *Serafim Ponte Grande* (1933); the poetry collection *Pau Brasil* (1925); and the two manifestos.

Andrade also wrote expressionistic drama (*O homem e o cavallo; O rei da Vela; A morta*), followed by the social mural novels in the series *Marco-Zero.* His works after 1945 include poetry ("Cântico dos cânticos para flauta e violão") and essays on literature, culture, and philosophy addressing utopian themes. In the 1960s his work began to receive critical reevaluation, culminating in the current recognition of his texts as foundations of Brazil's literary and intellectual modernity.

See also **Modernism, Brazil.**

BIBLIOGRAPHY

Oswald de Andrade is included in the UNESCO Archives Series on Latin American writers (to appear in Portuguese and English). Introductions to his life and works may be found in Haroldo De Campo, ed., *Oswald de Andrade: Trechos escolhidos* (1967); K. David Jackson, "Rediscovering the Rediscoverers," in *Texas Quarterly* 19, no. 3 (Autumn 1976): 162–173; Jorge Schwartz, ed., *Oswald de Andrade* (1982); and Maria Augusta Fonseca, *Oswald de Andrade* (*1890–1954*): *Biografia* (1990).

Additional Bibliography

Jackson, K. David, ed. *One Hundred Years of Invention: Oswald de Andrade and the Modern Tradition in Latin American Literature.* Austin, TX: Department of Spanish and Portuguese, Abaporu Press, 1992.

Schwartz, Jorge. *Vanguardia e cosmopolitismo en la década del veinte: Oliverio Girondo y Oswald de Andrade.* Rosario, Argentina: B. Viterbo Editora, 1993.

K. DAVID JACKSON

ANDRADE, ROBERTO (1850–1938).

Roberto Andrade (October 26, 1850–October 31, 1938), intellectual and political activist, is most famous for committing an act of murder. Along with fellow conspirators Manuel Cornejo Astorga, Abelardo Moncayo, Manuel Polanco, Gregorio Campuzano, and Faustino Rayo, Andrade participated in the assassination of Ecuadorian leader Gabriel García Moreno, on August 6, 1875, in the Ecuadorian capital of Quito. After Rayo struck García Moreno across the head with a machete, Moncayo, Cornejo, and Andrade shot the fallen president at close range.

The assassination grew out of broader liberal disaffection with the conservative García Moreno dictatorship (1860–1875). Particularly influential was author and liberal critic Juan Montalvo, who actively encouraged violent opposition to García Moreno. The youthful Andrade was profoundly affected by Montalvo's writings, especially his *La dictadura perpetua* (The perpetual dictatorship). After the assassination Montalvo reportedly proclaimed, "my pen killed him."

Fleeing prosecution, Andrade spent more than two decades in self imposed exile. When he returned in 1894 he was arrested, tried, and convicted, but was released after the successful 1895 liberal revolt. He devoted much of his subsequent career to writing, serving as a deeply partisan advocate for liberal causes. Andrade produced a multi-volume *Historia del Ecuador*, which was published in Guayaquil in the 1930s in sixty-two pamphlets, or *entregas*. The more than two thousand pages of prose consisted exclusively of vituperative attacks on García Moreno and paeans to all things liberal. The work has no value as a study of history. As one reviewer, Richard Pattee, writing in the *Hispanic American Historical Review* in 1938 put it, Andrade's *Historia del Ecuador* was "a distorted history, marred by unbelievable reliance on flimsy evidence; gross manipulation of the facts, and often the most unreasonable conclusions.... The cause of historical scholarship," Pattee said, "[was] injured" by its publication (pp. 90-91).

See also **García Moreno, Gabriel; Montalvo, Juan.**

BIBLIOGRAPHY

Pattee, Richard. Review of Roberto Andrade, *Historia del Ecuador*, in *Hispanic American Historical Review* 18:1 (February 1938): 90–91.

Spindler, Frank MacDonald. *Nineteenth Century Ecuador: An Historical Introduction.* Fairfax, VA: George Mason University Press, 1987.

RONN PINEO

ANDREONI, JOÃO ANTÔNIO (1649–1716).

João Antônio Andreoni (pseud. of André João Antonil; *b.* 1649; *d.* March 13, 1716), Jesuit administrator and author of a seminal study of the economic roots of early eighteenth-century Brazil, *Cultura e opulência do Brasil por suas drogas e minas* (1711). Born in Tuscany and educated in law at the University of Perugia, he entered the Society of Jesus on May 20, 1667 and came to Bahia, Brazil, in 1681. There, after serving as secretary to Antônio Vieira, he became Vieira's rival and leader among German- and Italian-born Jesuits serving in Brazil. A proficient Latinist and a keen administrator, he held a succession of posts in the Society of Jesus, from minister of novices to rector of the college at Bahia, and served both as provincial Visitor and as provincial. Unlike Vieira, he sided with the settlers in their efforts to obtain Indian labor and, again unlike Vieira, he was anti-Semitic. But he is best known for his unique and outstanding treatise concerning the sources of Brazil's wealth—sugar, tobacco, gold, and cattle. He died in Bahia.

See also **Jesuits.**

BIBLIOGRAPHY

Serafim Leite, *História da companhia de Jesús no Brasil,* 10 vols. (Rio de Janeiro, 1938–1950).

Andrée Mansuy, ed., *Cultura e opulência do Brasil por suas drogas e minas* (Paris, 1965).

Additional Bibliography

Donizete Ambires, Juarez. "Os Jesuítas e a Administração dos Índios por Particulares em São Paulo no Século XVII." M.A. thesis, University of São Paulo, 2000.

Lima da Silva, Wilton Carlos. *As terras inventadas:discurso e natureza em Jean de Léry, André João Antonil e Richard Francis Burton.* São Paulo: Editora UNESP, 2003.

DAURIL ALDEN

ANDRESOTE.

Andresote (Andrés López Del Rosario), the *zambo* leader of the rebellion in Venezuela against the Compañía Guipuzcoana of Caracas in 1730–1733. Andresote dealt in contraband in the region of Yaracuy, mocking the controls which the Compañía Guipuzcoana sought to place on the commerce of the province of Venezuela. To protect his interests, the director general of the *compañía* ordered his arrest. Andresote and his followers clashed violently with the authorities and representatives of the *compañía* in their effort to continue their contraband operations with the island of Curaçao. Troops were sent from Caracas to put down Andresote's group, but when they failed to accomplish this in 1732, the commander in chief of Venezuela vowed to combat him personally. Andresote fled in 1733 to Curaçao, where he died a short while later.

See also **Venezuela: The Colonial Era.**

BIBLIOGRAPHY

Tulio Febres Cordero, *La Rebelión de Andresote (Valles del Yaracuy, 1730–1733)* (Caracas, 1952), and Carlos Felice Cardot, *La Rebelión de Andresote (Volles de Yaracuy, 1730–1733)* (1957).

Additional Bibliography

Castillo Lara, Lucas Guillermo. "La odisea peregrinante a Calabozo de los sublevados de Andresote." *Boletín de la Academia Nacional de la Historia (Venezuela)* 58:232 (Oct.–Dec. 1975): 731–749.

INÉS QUINTERO

ANDREVE, GUILLERMO (1879–1940).

Guillermo Andreve (*b.* 1879; *d.* 1940), Panamanian journalist, intellectual, and politician. Andreve was one of the most influential liberal leaders in Panama in the early twentieth century. He held many government positions. He was a member of the National Assembly, secretary of public education, secretary of government and justice, and an ambassador in Latin America and Europe. Andreve wrote on many subjects, and his writings are an important source for the study of Panamanian politics in the 1920s. In his writings Andreve dwells on the inadequacies of the laissez-faire structure created by nineteenth-century liberalism and advocates a more interventionist state for Panama.

See also **Panama.**

BIBLIOGRAPHY

"Escritos de Andreve," in *Revista lotería,* nos. 282–284 (August–October 1979).

Jorge Conte Porras, *Diccionario biográfico ilustrado de Panamá,* 2d ed. (1986).

Additional Bibliography

Andreve, Guillermo. *Una punta del velo.* 2nd ed. Panama: Asamblea Legislativa, 2001.

JUAN MANUEL PÉREZ

ANDUEZA PALACIO, RAIMUNDO

(1843–1900). Raimundo Andueza Palacio (*b.* February 1843; *d.* 17 August 1900), president of Venezuela (1890–1892). Andueza began his political and military activity after the Federal War (1859–1863) as aide-de-camp and secretary to the president of the Republic, Marshal Juan Crisóstomo Falcón (1863–1868). Having ties with the Liberal Party, he carried out important, and sometimes divisive, public duties during the administrations of Antonio Guzmán Blanco (1870–1877) and Francisco Linares Alcántara (1877–1878). After a brief period of exile, Andueza returned to Venezuela and became one of the political leaders of the Partido Liberalismo Amarillo (Yellow Liberalism Party).

With the end of the hegemony of Guzmán's policies during the administration of Dr. Juan Pablo Rojas Paúl (1888–1890), the Federal Council elected Andueza president for the 1890–1892 term. In an atmosphere of conflict between militarists and those favoring civilian rule, he declared himself a defender of the trend toward civilian rule and appointed a cabinet composed primarily of civilians. His administration is seen as having been blessed by a period of economic boom. Andueza saw the completion of various public projects begun before his regime and fostered a politics of clientele, with the object of creating a broad base of support that would allow him to remain in power. From within the state legislatures, he promoted a constitutional reform that included, among many other amendments, the lengthening of the presidential term from two to four years. Congress refused to launch this constitutional reform immediately, but the president declared that the new statute was in effect. The immediate result was the beginning of the Legalist Revolution led by General Joaquín Crespo, who put an end to Andueza's term of office. When Crespo died in 1898, Andueza returned from exile and again took up political activity, becoming minister of foreign affairs under General Cipriano Castro, who became president in 1900.

See also **Venezuela, Political Parties: Liberal Party.**

BIBLIOGRAPHY

Manuel Alfredo Rodríguez, *Andueza Palacio y la crisis del liberalismo venezolano* (1960), and Ramón J. Velásquez, *La caída del liberalismo amarillo: Tiempo y drama de Antonio Paredes* (1977).

Additional Bibliography

Pineda, Victor. "Raimundo Andueza Palacio: el caso del continuismo político venezolano en el siglo XIX," *Boletín de la Academia Nacional de Historia (Venezuela)* 84: 335 (July–Sept., 2001), pp. 48–66.

INÉS QUINTERO

ANGEL, ALBALUCÍA (1939–). Albalucía Angel (*b.* 7 September 1939), Colombian novelist. Angel is one of Colombia's most important writers since Gabriel García Márquez. Following an independent narrative style, she has produced four distinct novels. *Los girasoles en invierno* (1970) is an experiment in radical feminism, and *Dos veces Alicia* (1972) plays on the Lewis Carroll text of *Alice in Wonderland*. The later novels delve into deeper issues of Colombian history and cultural values. *Estaba la pájara pinta sentada en el verde limón* (1975), her most significant novel, deals with the period of Colombian history known as La Violencia (1948–1956) and intriguingly reconstructs the era through two parallel but opposing perspectives: on the one hand, the unseen violence perpetrated by a young female adolescent who is not allowed to leave her house, and on the other, the quoted firsthand descriptions of actual grotesque political killings as reported in journals and books.

Misiá Señora (1982) looks at the relationship of a daughter, mother, and grandmother. Through erotic imagery, soliloquy, and monologue, the novel captures what was once the ideal of femininity, which encompassed sensuality, decency, courage, inner strength, and a feeling of fulfillment. The four novels show not only the author's search for innovation through language and theme and creativeness in her early period but also her successful later efforts to transform the literary act into a profound social and cultural commentary on her native land.

Other works include the poetry collection *Cantos y encantamiento de la lluvia* (2004) and the publication of "Out of Silence," a lecture given in 1998 at the Inter-American Development Bank Cultural Center.

See also **Literature: Spanish America.**

BIBLIOGRAPHY

Dick Gerdes, "*Estaba la pájara pinta sentada en el verde limón*: Novela testimonial/documental de 'La Violencia' en Colombia," *Revista de Estudios Colombianos* 2 (1987): 14–19; *Manual de literatura colombiana*, vol. 2 (1988).

Additional Bibliography

Lindsay, Claire. *Locating Latin American Women Writers: Cristina Peri Rossi, Rosario Ferré, Albalucía Angel, and Isabel Allende.* New York: Peter Lang, 2003.

Taylor, Claire. *Bodies and Texts: Configurations of Identity in the Works of Griselda Gambaro, Albalucía Angel, and Laura Esquivel.* Leeds: Maney Pub. for the Modern Humanities Research Association, 2003.

DICK GERDES

ÁNGELES, FELIPE (1869–1919). Felipe Ángeles (*b.* 13 June 1869; *d.* 26 November 1919), Mexican revolutionary. A well-educated career soldier, Ángeles was in France when the revolution broke out in 1910. He returned to Mexico in 1912. Sharing Francisco Madero's liberalism, Ángeles soon became one of the new president's closest confidants within the military. Ángeles was arrested because of this association after the February 1913 coup that brought Victoriano Huerta to power, but he was soon able to join the Constitutionalists in their fight against the Huerta regime. Within this camp he quickly found his most important revolutionary role as Pancho Villa's close advisor and played a large part in the fighting that would eventually lead to Huerta's downfall. In 1914 Ángeles helped bring the Villistas and the Zapatistas together in an alliance against the followers of Venustiano Carranza. But after Villa lost the big battles of Celaya and León de las Aldamas in 1915—often ignoring the tactical advice of Ángeles in the process—Ángeles fled the country in exile to the United States. Always ambitious, he tried to rejoin the revolutionary struggle by leading a small band of soldiers across the border into Chihuahua. In 1919, he was captured there and executed by forces loyal to Carranza.

See also **Mexico, Wars and Revolutions: Mexican Revolution; Villa, Francisco "Pancho."**

BIBLIOGRAPHY

Federico Cervantes, *Felipe Angeles y la revolución de 1913. Biografía (1869–1919)*, 2d ed. (1943).

Alvaro Matute, ed., *Documentos relativos al General Felipe Angeles* (1982).

Alan Knight, *The Mexican Revolution*, 2 vols. (1986).

Additional Bibliography

Guilpain Peuliard, Odile. *Felipe Ángeles y los destinos de la Revolución Mexicana*. Mexico City: Fondo de Cultura Económica, 1991.

Katz, Friedrich. *The Life and Times of Pancho Villa*. Stanford: Stanford University Press, 1998.

SAMUEL BRUNK

ANGEL FALLS. Angel Falls, the highest waterfall in the world at 3,212 feet, is located in the Guyana highlands of Bolívar state, Venezuela. It drops from a high, mesa-type mountain, Auyan Tepuy (Devil's Mountain), into the Carrao River below. Angel Falls is in the Canaima National Park, the largest national park in the world, totaling 3 million hectares (larger than Belgium).

The indigenous people of the area, the Pemon, call the waterfall *Parekupa-meru*. It is likely that the Venezuelan explorer Ernesto Sánchez La Cruz was the first nonindigenous person to see the falls in 1910, but he did not publicize his find. In 1935 James Crawford "Jimmie" Angel (1899–1956), a U.S.-born gold prospector and former Canadian Air Force pilot, flew by the falls, and on 9 October 1937, he returned with his wife and one or two others. He landed the plane on top of the mountain, where it became stuck; Angel and his companions took eleven days to hike down the mountain and back to the nearest mission. The falls were named after Angel, who became a hero for discovering this natural wonder. His airplane was recovered in 1970 and put on display in the city of Maracay, in north central Venezuela.

Commercial flight has made Angel Falls one of the top tourist attractions of Venezuela. Tourists fly to Ciudad Bolívar and beyond, and then either take helicopter tours or hike to the falls. In 1994 the Canaima National Park was declared a World Heritage Site by UNESCO.

See also **Tourism.**

BIBLIOGRAPHY

Stalcup, Ann. "Exploring the Angel Falls Region of Venezuela." *Faces: People, Places, and Cultures* 20, no. 5 (January 2004): 30–35.

ERICK D. LANGER

ANGELIS, PEDRO DE (1784–1859). Pedro de Angelis (*b*. 29 June 1784; *d*. 10 February 1859), essayist and scholar. Bernardino Rivadavia, former president of Argentina (1826–1827), persuaded Angelis, an Italian intellectual living in Paris, to take up residence in Buenos Aires and help develop the cultural life of the new nation. Angelis arrived in 1827 and became co-editor of Rivadavia's official paper, *La crónica política y literaria de Buenos Aires*. He also founded the Ateneo (an intellectual society) and edited the *Gaceta mercantil*. In 1828 Angelis edited the Latin text *Cornelli Nepotis ... vitae excellentium imperatorum* for the university.

He attained prestige in the Argentine literary world and served Rivadavia's cause as well as that of Juan Manuel Ortiz de Rosas. During the second Rosas dictatorship (1835–1852), Angelis became fascinated with history and began collecting original historical documents, many of which he included in his six-volume work *Colección de obras y documentos relativos a la historia antigua y moderna de las provincias del Río de la Plata. Ilustrada con notas y discertaciones* (1836–1837). He served as head of the government printing office and was head archivist. In 1852 Angelis sold his collection of over twenty-seven hundred books and twelve hundred manuscripts to the government of Brazil, where today they can be consulted in the National

Library (in Rio de Janeiro) under *Colección de Angelis.*

See also **Literature: Spanish America.**

BIBLIOGRAPHY

Ricardo Caillet-Bois, Rafael Alberto Arrieta, and Domingo Buoncore, eds., *Historia de la literatura argentina,* vol. 6 (1960), pp. 27–32. Elías Díaz Milano, *Vida y obra de Pedro de Angelis* (1968).

Additional Bibliography

Sabor, Josefa Emilia. *Pedro de Angelis y los orígenes de la bibliografía argentina: Ensayo bio-bibliográfico.* Buenos Aires: Ediciones Solar, 1995.

NICHOLAS P. CUSHNER

ÂNGELO, IVAN (1936–).

Ivan Ângelo (*b.* 1936), Brazilian novelist, short story writer, and journalist. Born in Minas Gerais, Ângelo began his literary career in 1956 in Belo Horizonte, Minas Gerais, as an editor of the literary journal *Complemento.* Three years later he published a collection of short stories, *Homem sofrendo no quarto,* for which he was honored with the Prêmio Belo Horizonte. In 1966 he moved to São Paulo and began a career with the newspaper *Jornal da Tarde,* becoming editor in chief in 1984. Ângelo's very successful and highly political novel *A festa* (1976) details, in a fragmented style, life in Brazil under military rule in the early 1970s. *A Casa de vidro: Cinco histórias do Brasil* (1979) is a critical investigation of Brazilian society. A collection of dynamic short stories, *A face horrível* (1986), reveals the author's commitment to facing the social issues affecting the country. His novel *Pode me beijar se quiser* won the 1999 prize of the Paulista Art Critics Association.

See also **Literature: Brazil.**

BIBLIOGRAPHY

Emir Rodríguez Monegal, "Writing Fiction Under the Censor's Eye," in *World Literature Today,* 53 (Winter 1979): 19–22.

Candace Slater, "A Triple Vision of Brazil," in *Review: Latin American Literature and Art,* 32 (January–May 1984): 13–15.

Robert E. Di Antonio, "The Confluence of Mythic, Historical, and Narrative Impulses in Ivan Angelo's *A Festa,*" in *International Fiction Review,* 14 (Winter 1987): 18–22.

Nelson H. Vieira, "Ivan Angelo," in *Dictionary of Brazilian Literature,* edited by Irwin Stern (1988); pp. 29–30.

Additional Bibliography

Sternberg, Ricardo da Silveira Lobo. "Celebrating the Celebration." *Revista Canadiense de Estudios Hispánicos,* 26: 1-2 (Fall-Winter 2001-2002): 241-253.

GARY M. VESSELS

ANGOLA.

Angola, former Portuguese colony and independent country in west central Africa since 1975. Angola was one of Brazil's major trading partners before 1850 and homeland of many enslaved Africans imported into Latin America. The meanings of "Angola" have changed over time. "Ngola" first referred to the ruler of Ndongo, then to the hinterland of Luanda, and finally to the region from Cape Lopez to Benguela in southern Angola. Africans identified as "Angolans" in Latin America generally came from the Portuguese-controlled central region of Angola, in particular the capital Luanda and the Kwanza River valley, and the region between and to the east of Kasanje. Major populations include the Kongo of northern Angola, the Mbundu in the center, the Lunda-Chokwe to the east, and the Ovimbundu and Ngangela in southern Angola.

See also **Africa, Portuguese; Slavery: Brazil; Slavery: Spanish America; Slave Trade.**

BIBLIOGRAPHY

Philip D. Curtin, *The Atlantic Slave Trade* (1969).

Mary C. Karasch, *Slave Life in Rio de Janeiro, 1808–1850* (1987).

Joseph C. Miller, *Way of Death* (1988).

Additional Bibliography

Birmingham, David. *Empire in Africa: Angola and Its Neighbors.* Athens: Ohio University Press, 2006.

Rodrigues, Jaime. *De costa a costa: Escravos, marinheiros e intermediários do tráfico negreiro de Angola ao Rio de Janeiro, 1780-1860.* São Paulo: Companhia das Letras, 2005.

MARY KARASCH

ANGOSTURA, CONGRESS OF.

Congress of Angostura, convoked by Simón Bolívar in order to place the patriot regime in Venezuela on a formal legal footing. At the opening session, held at the Orinoco River port of Angostura (today Ciudad Bolívar), on 15 February 1819, Bolívar delivered a major address in which he warned against imitation of Anglo-American institutions and called for a new constitution featuring a hereditary Senate and a "moral power" with special responsibility for education and morals. The Congress failed to act on these two suggestions but did produce a Venezuelan constitution and confirmed Bolívar as supreme commander.

The Congress had token representation of New Granadans, in line with Bolívar's strong commitment to union with the neighboring colonies. In December 1819, following the patriots' victory at Boyacá, the Congress formally proclaimed the union of all the former Viceroyalty of New Granada as the Republic of [Gran] Colombia. The Congress dissolved on 19 July 1820.

See also **Bolívar, Simón.**

BIBLIOGRAPHY

Vicente Lecuna, comp. and Harold A. Bierck, Jr., ed., *Selected Writings of Simón Bolívar*, 2 vols. (1951), vol. 1, pp. 173–197, for Bolívar's address.

Gerhard Masur, *Simon Bolivar*, rev. ed. (1969), chap. 19.

Additional Bibliography

Lynch, John. *Simón Bolívar: A Life*. New Haven, CT: Yale University Press, 2006.

Mendizábal, Francisco Javier de. *Guerra de la América del Sur, 1809–1824*. Buenos Aires: Academia Nacional de la Historia, 1997.

DAVID BUSHNELL

ANGUILLA.

Anguilla, the northernmost of the Leeward Islands in the Caribbean. Settled by the British in 1650, the small, 35-square-mile island successfully repelled attacks by Carib Indians in 1656, a contingent of Irishmen in 1688, and French marauders in 1745 and 1796. From the seventeenth to the nineteenth century, Anguilla attempted to develop a plantation economy, but failed because of inadequate rainfall. Remnants of the invasion forces and the subsequent introduction of slaves are seen in the ethnic mixture of the population. The estimated seventy-five hundred inhabitants are predominantly of African descent, with some European, especially Irish, blood.

In 1825, Anguilla became more closely linked politically to neighboring Saint Kitts, in whose House of Assembly an Anguilla representative was seated. In 1871 Anguilla, along with Saint Kitts, became part of the Leeward Island Federation. Dominated historically by Saint Kitts, Anguilla petitioned unsuccessfully for direct rule from Britain. No political change occurred, however, until 1967, when Saint Kitts, Nevis, and Anguilla were granted self-government as an associated state of the United Kingdom. Anguilla seized the opportunity to launch a final offensive for separation from Saint Kitts. Attempts at mediation failed, and in 1969, British security forces invaded. In 1980, Anguilla successfully separated from the associated state, becoming a British dependent territory. In 1982, a new constitution, providing for self-government, was approved.

See also **Caribbean Sea, Commonwealth States.**

BIBLIOGRAPHY

Central Office of Information for the Government of Anguilla, *Anguilla: The Basic Facts* (1979).

Colville L. Petty, *Anguilla: Where There's a Will There's a Way* (1984).

Additional Bibliography

Dyde, Brian. *Out of the Crowded Vagueness: A History of the Islands of St. Kitts, Nevis and Anguilla*. Oxford: Macmillan Caribbean, 2005.

D. M. SPEARS

ANHANGUERA. *See* **Bandeiras.**

ANÍSIO, CHICO. *See* **Chico Anísio.**

ANNALS OF THE CAKCHIQUELS.

Annals of the Cakchiquels, also called the *Memorial of Sololá*, are an account of Kaqchikel (Maya) history from their immigration to Guatemala through the Spanish invasion and up to the seventeenth century, compiled by two members of the Xajil royal lineage, Francisco Hernández Arana and Francisco Díaz. Written in Kaqchikel and later translated into French, Spanish, and English, the *Annals* are assumed to have been written during the sixteenth century. The portion narrating pre-Columbian Kaqchikel history is thought to have been passed along orally for centuries before being recorded in its written form.

The *Annals* chronicle the Spanish arrival, the accompanying wars, pestilence, social and economic disruption, and finally community restructuring, as told from the indigenous perspective. An important aspect of the *Annals* is the detailed list of indigenous lineage, births and deaths, land purchases, and church activities.

The pre–invasion part of the document is linguistically and culturally "pure," eschewing loanwords and recording practices out of favor with the Spanish church and civil laws. Although the *Annals* evince less accommodation than the K'iche' (Quiché) *Popol Vuh*, it may be argued that the emphasis on lineage status and politics, in both the pre–invasion and post–invasion sections, is partially a response to Spanish policy of awarding cacique privileges: tribute and work levies, as well as land titles.

See also **Chilam Balam; Kaqchikel; Maya, The; Mayan Epigraphy; Popol Vuh.**

BIBLIOGRAPHY

Daniel G. Brinton, trans., *The Annals of the Cakchikels* (1885, repr. 1969).

Robert M. Carmack, *Quichean Civilization: The Ethnohistoric, Ethnographic, and Archaeological Sources* (1973), 47–50.

Additional Bibliography

Contreras R., J. Daniel, and Jorge Luján Muñoz. *El Memorial de Sololá y los inicios de la colonización Española en Guatemala*. Guatemala: Academia de Geografía e Historia de Guatemala, 2004.

Recinos, Adrián. *Memorial de Sololá: Anales de los cakchiqueles*. Mexico: Fondo de Cultura Económica, 1950.

JUDITH M. MAXWELL IXQ'ANIL

ANTARCTICA.   In contrast to most North Americans who tend to think of Antarctica as a remote and isolated continent, many Latin Americans, especially those in the Southern Cone, view Antarctica as relatively close and linked to the South American mainland through geology, geopolitics, and history. The tip of the Antarctic Peninsula is only about 600 miles from Tierra del Fuego, and two South American nations, Argentina and Chile, have made formal claims of sovereignty to portions of Antarctica. Furthermore, the 1947 Rio Treaty (Inter-American Treaty of Reciprocal Assistance) defines the security zone of the Americas as extending to the South Pole and includes the sectors claimed by Argentina and Chile. Thus, there is reason to speak of a "South American quadrant" of Antarctica extending from the Greenwich Meridian (0 longitude) to 90 west longitude.

No human being had seen Antarctica until early in the nineteenth century, when, within a few short years, British, Russian, and U.S. sailors reported discovering it. There is also a suggestion (unfortunately without documentation) that sealers operating out of Buenos Aires might have seen Antarctica as early as 1817.

During the so-called heroic period of Antarctic exploration in the early twentieth century, the southern nations of Latin America supported expeditions from Europe and the United States by providing them with supplies and assisting in rescue efforts when necessary. Two noteworthy efforts were the Argentine rescue of a Swedish expedition in 1903 and that of Sir Ernest Shackleton's crew by the Chileans a decade later.

By the late 1940s seven nations had made sovereignty claims to Antarctica, three of which (Argentina, Chile, and Great Britain) overlapped in the South American Antarctic quadrant. The nationalistic regime of Juan Domingo Perón in Argentina stressed the linkage between the Argentine Antarctic claim and the effort to recover Las Malvinas (Falkland Islands). Tensions between Great Britain and Chile were exacerbated to the point that there were numerous diplomatic protests and at least one shooting incident.

To defuse Antarctic tensions, a group of twelve nations proposed a program of scientific cooperation (the International Geophysical Year, 1957–1958), and out of this effort grew the Antarctic Treaty

Antartica, view from the Eduardo Frei air base in Chile, 2004. Antartica's increased popularity as a destination for tourists has led enviromentalists to become concerned about the impact on the continent's delicate ecosystem. VICTOR ROJAS/AFP/ GETTY IMAGES

(signed 1959; in force since 1961), which ensures that a demilitarized Antarctica is preserved for scientific study. The treaty does not permit new or expanded sovereignty claims, but does not require nations with preexisting claims to abandon them.

More than forty nations have signed the Antarctic Treaty, and almost half of these maintain permanent or temporary scientific stations on the ice. These include Argentina, Chile, Brazil, Uruguay, Peru, and Ecuador; Colombia and Cuba have also signed the treaty and have sent personnel to Antarctic bases of other countries.

Tensions over international competition for Antarctic resources, especially mineral deposits, were eased in October 1991 at a special meeting in Madrid, when the treaty members signed a "Protocol on Environmental Protection." The protocol confirms that Antarctica should be a special natural reserve dedicated to peace and science; a key provision bans mining activity in Antarctica for at least fifty years.

In September of 2004, the Buenos Aires–based *Antarctic Treaty Secretariat* was formally established by the Antarctic Treaty Consultative Meeting (ATCM) to oversee international involvement in Antarctica, and to support the annual ATCM and CEP (Committee for Environmental Protection) meetings.

See also **Rio Treaty (1947).**

BIBLIOGRAPHY

Peter J. Beck, *The International Politics of Antarctica* (1986).

Jack Child, *Antarctica and South American Geopolitics: Frozen Lebensraum* (1988); translated as *Geopolítica del Cono Sur y la Antártida* (1990).

Carlos J. Moneta, ed., *La Antártida en el sistema internacional del futuro* (1988).

M. J. Peterson, *Managing the Frozen South: The Origin and Evolution of the Antarctic Treaty System* (1988).

Philip J. Quigg, *A Pole Apart* (1983).

Deborah Shapley, *The Seventh Continent: Antarctica in a Resource Age* (1985).

Reader's Digest, *Antarctica*, 2d ed. (1990).

Additional Bibliography

Antarctic Treaty Secretariat, http://www.ats.aq/.

JACK CHILD

ANTARCTIC FRANCE. *See* **French Colonization in Brazil.**

ANTEQUERA. *See* **Oaxaca (City).**

ANTEQUERA Y CASTRO, JOSÉ DE

(1693–1731). José de Antequera y Castro (*b.* 1693; *d.* 5 July 1731), governor of Paraguay (1721–1725) and leader of an anti-Jesuit uprising. In 1724 Antequera led Paraguayan forces into battle against a Jesuit-trained Guaraní militia from the missions who sought to remove him from office. Born in Panama, Antequera was the son of a Spanish bureaucrat. Educated first by Jesuits, he earned his licentiate in arts and doctorate in law in Charcas and Lima and went to Spain to seek employment. He became a member of the Order of Alcántara and secured an appointment for several years as protector of the Indians for the Audiencia of Charcas, where his father had once been a judge (*oidor*). As acting prosecutor (*fiscal*) in 1720, he took sides in a feud between Paraguayans and Jesuits that reached the *audiencia*. He undertook a judicial review of an unpopular governor, Diego de los Reyes y Balmaceda, an ally of the Jesuits, and simultaneously got the *audiencia* to name him next governor of Paraguay, a common but technically illegal combination, although the viceroy confirmed the appointment.

After Antequera arrived in Paraguay in 1721, he removed Reyes from office, took a Paraguayan mistress, and befriended an opponent of the Jesuits, José de Ávalos y Mendoza. In retaliation, the Jesuits had the viceroy reinstate Reyes, although he never again served. In 1722 the Jesuits helped Reyes flee to Corrientes, infuriating Paraguayans and from there threatening Antequera. The latter insisted that the Jesuits accept him as governor. Antequera argued that the dispute was a matter of justice, not government, and that the *audiencia*, not the viceroy, had jurisdiction. The *audiencia* agreed until 1724, when an aggressive viceroy, José de Armendáriz, challenged the Charcas judges. He ordered an army of mission Guaranis led by Baltasar García Ros, lieutenant governor of Buenos

Aires, to depose Antequera, but 3,000 Paraguayans with Antequera destroyed the smaller Guaraní force in August 1724 at the Tebicuary River. They then expelled the Jesuits from Asunción.

Antequera's victory made his position untenable. The viceroy, the Jesuits, officials in Buenos Aires, and the new bishop of Paraguay, José de Palos, opposed him. His former colleagues in Charcas cut him adrift, and in 1725 he fled to Córdoba, where Franciscans sheltered him, and then moved to Charcas. He was apprehended and sent to Lima. From 1726 to 1731, he was jailed at the viceregal court, where he prepared his defense. Renewed rebellion in Paraguay in 1730 caused the viceroy to demand that the Audiencia of Lima find Antequera guilty of heresy and treason, and the judges complied. They ordered his execution and that of his principal lieutenant, Juan de Mena. The sentence was so unpopular that it provoked a riot in Lima, and the viceroy's troops shot Antequera on his way to the gallows. Four decades after Antequera's death, King Charles III, who had expelled Antequera's Jesuit enemies from Spain in 1767, posthumously exonerated Antequera. In Asunción, Antequera's legacies were the spirit of rebellion and José Cañete, his natural son and father of the noted jurist Pedro Vicente Cañete. Antequera's memory is honored by streets named for him in Asunción and Lima.

See also **Jesuits; Paraguay: The Colonial Period.**

BIBLIOGRAPHY

Colección general de documentos que contiene los sucesos tocantes á la segunda época de las conmociones de los Regulares de la Companía en el Paraguay y señaladamente la persecución que hicieron a don Josef de Antequera y Castro (1769).

James Schofield Saeger, "Origins of the Rebellion of Paraguay," in *Hispanic American Historical Review* 52, no. 2 (1972): 215–229, and "Institutional Rivalries, Jurisdictional Disputes, and Vested Interests in the Viceroyalty of Peru: José de Antequera and the Rebellion of Paraguay," in *The Americas: A Quarterly Review of Inter-American Cultural History* 32, no. 1 (1975): 99–116.

Adalberto López, *The Revolt of the Comuneros, 1721–1735: A Study in the Colonial History of Paraguay* (1976).

Additional Bibliography

Barba, Enrique M. "El fin de Antequera: su justificación," *Investigaciones y Ensayos,* 29 (July-Dec. 1980), pp. 15–26.

Romero, Roberto A. *La revolución comunera del Paraguay: su doctrina política.* Asunción: Impr. Leguizamón, 1995.

JAMES SCHOFIELD SAEGER

ANTHROPOLOGY. Latin American scholars began the anthropological enterprise aiming to identify, describe, and understand the multiple cultures and ethnic groups that populate the region. Hegemonic in their approach until the 1970s, theories of cultural assimilation or acculturation assumed that "static" indigenous societies would eventually be subjugated by dynamic modernizing forces, adopting dominant cultures to the detriment of their autonomy and particular ethnic characters. Therefore, early anthropological research was mainly concerned with documenting indigenous cultural heritages such as language, ritual, and myth, and/or supporting indigenous people through the inexorable acculturation process. In regions with relatively small and isolated indigenous populations, detailed ethnologies of still-living indigenous ethnic cultures dominated the discipline for decades. Darcy Ribeiro's original work in Brazil, which added a critical political dimension to comparative descriptions of indigenous peoples, advanced the research agenda for later ethnological studies on indigenous communities in Amazonia, Patagonia, and elsewhere in remote areas.

In countries with large native populations, intellectual debates on possible indigenous contribution to and incorporation into national cultural projects informed anthropological developments. In Mexico, most studies followed official discourses of cultural assimilation toward the constitution of an imagined *mestizo* (mixed-heritage) national character; Guillermo Bonfil's work on indigenous resistance against state cultural impositions is a relevant exception. In the Andes, the first decades of systematic anthropological work saw both applied research projects intended to foster indigenous modernization and impressive ethnographic studies on enduring indigenous cosmologies and social structures. At the same time, a branch of political economy studies started to give valuable insights on campesino communities' political organizations and systems of production.

As national assimilative projects reached their limits, critical indigenous voices began to populate the anthropological literature. José María Arguedas's pioneer work manifests indigenous agency in shaping the processes of cultural transformation, informing a decade-long debate about ethnicity and *mestizaje* (mixed ancestry) in the Andes. Similarly, Rigoberta Menchu's testimony on terror and political consciousness in Guatemala stimulated important indigenous literary production as well as a controversy about the epistemology of testimonies. The work of the *Taller de Historia Oral Andina* (Andes oral history workshop) in Bolivia is a good recent example of this branch of indigenous literary anthropology.

Moreover, the issues of massive indigenous rural-to-urban migrations and continuous transformations of urban popular cultures and rituals have brought anthropological inquiry to the cities. Roberto Damatta's work on the symbolic constitution of an alternative national discourse in Brazilian carnivals is a fascinating early piece, whereas Néstor García Canclini's excellent research on hybrid cultures and urban social landscapes well represent recent urban anthropology studies.

Since the 1970s anthropological literature has focused on the politics of identity in light of the emergence of social movements and the cultural processes of globalization. Research on the indigenous uprising in Chiapas, Mexico, nationwide revolts in Ecuador, or electoral gains in Bolivia analyzes the construction of indigenous political narratives and national alternatives. Likewise, studies on indigenous and grassroots mobilizations in the southern cone, Central America, and Colombia examine the increasing political and cultural visibility of historically marginalized social groups. Xavier Albo's work on Aymara's political representations, Minor Sinclair's compilation on social movements in Central America, and *The Journal of Latin American Anthropology*'s issues on Mayan and Argentinean indigenous movements are significant examples of studies that connect local, national, and global power spheres.

Moreover, significant developments, drawing mostly on post-theories such as postmodern, post-colonial, and subaltern studies, have decentered the meanings of race, class, ethnicity, and gender in postulating the coexistence of contested and multiple identities. Arturo Escobar's work is a good start on ethnic discursive reconstitution and empowerment, whereas Marisol de la Cadena's research on ethnicity and gender has produced an interesting assessment of power-related constructions of identities. Finally, later developments on collective memory and spatial dimensions have contributed to the unfinished anthropological quest for understanding and grasping Latin America's extraordinary cultural diversity and political complexity.

See also **Arguedas, José María; García Canclini, Néstor; Menchú Tum, Rigoberta; Ribeiro, Darcy; Sociology.**

BIBLIOGRAPHY

Albó, Xavier. *Pueblos indios en la política.* La Paz: Plural Editores/CIPCA, 2002.

Alvarez, Sonia E., Evelina Dagnino, and Arturo Escobar, eds. *Cultures of Politics/Politics of Cultures: Re-Visioning Latin American Social Movements.* Boulder, CO: Westview Press, 1998.

Arguedas, José María. *Indios Mestizos y Señores.* Lima: Editorial Horizonte, 1985.

Bonfil Batalla, Guillermo. *México Profundo: Reclaiming a Civilization.* Austin: University of Texas Press, 1996.

Cadena, Marisol de la. *Indigenous Mestizos: The Politics of Race and Culture in Cuzco, Peru, 1919–1991.* Durham, NC: Duke University Press, 2000.

García Canclini, Néstor. *La antropología urbana en México.* México, D.F.: Conaculta, UAM, FCE, 2005

García Canclini, Néstor. *Hybrid Cultures: Strategies for Entering and Leaving Modernity.* Minneapolis: University of Minnesota Press, 1995.

Matta, Roberto da. *Carnivals, Rogues, and Heroes: An Interpretation of the Brazilian Dilemma.* Notre Dame, IN: University of Notre Dame Press, 1991.

Menchú, Rigoberta, and Elisabeth Burgos-Debray. *I, Rigoberta Menchú: An Indian Woman in Guatemala.* London and New York: Verso, 1984.

Ribeiro, Darcy. *Os índios e a civilização: A integração das populações indígenas no Brasil moderno.* 4th ed. Vol. 5. Petrópolis, Brasil: Vozes, 1982.

Rivera Cusicanqui, Silvia, and Taller de Historia Oral Andina. *La mujer andina en la historia.* La Paz: Ediciones del THOA, 1990.

Sinclair, Minor. *The New Politics of Survival: Grassroots Movements in Central America.* New York: Monthly Review Press, 1995.

GERARDO DAMONTE

ANTICLERICALISM. Anticlericalism was both a widespread attitude and a deeply ingrained sentiment among Latin America's intellectual and political elites who viewed organized religion, especially the Roman Catholic Church, as a threat to the state and an obstacle to social change. Although anticlericalism reached its zenith in the nineteenth century, it had its roots in the eighteenth and perdured as a powerful force well into the twentieth. It was an attitude shared by both conservatives and liberals, although not always for the same reasons.

Conservative anticlericalism was rooted in the struggle of the enlightened Catholic monarchs of Europe and their liberal advisers to reform the church and to subordinate it to the crown's interests. Charles III, influenced by the count of Aranda, Pedro Rodríguez de Campomanes, and others, represented the apogee of regalism, the Spanish form of Gallicanism. Both doctrines claimed that the king had the right to exercise temporal authority over the church, including the power to name bishops and collect tithes. The marquis de Pombal, with the full approval of the Portuguese crown, led the way by expelling the Jesuits from both Portugal and Brazil in 1759. These governing elites believed that in order for their nations to be great once again, they must modernize themselves. To do so would involve, most of all, reforming the church, which in Spain, Portugal, and the New World had come to resemble the church as it had been on the eve of the Reformation. The eighteenth-century church in the Hispanic-Lusitanian world had acquired enormous properties held in mortmain; monasteries and convents were overpopulated; and a tradition-laden clergy was a source of frequent scandal. Many of the reform measures that the newly independent states in Hispanic America enacted to limit the number of the clergy or to reduce church wealth were in fact modeled on earlier Bourbon Reforms.

The regalist tradition, fashioned in Spain and Portugal, resurfaced in one way or another in every one of the new republics. Simón Bolívar, although not unfriendly to the church, sought to impose restraints and controls on it. But other leaders, such as José Gaspar Rodríguez de Francia in Paraguay and Guzmán Blanco in Venezuela, subjected the church to harsh scrutiny and did not hesitate to expel or even to execute priests, confiscate church property, and curtail clerical influence in every way possible. Even where conservatives considered the church an ally, they nonetheless viewed with suspicion any independent activity on its part. They resented any outside influence on the church, which meant especially the pope. In Brazil, relations between Dom Pedro II and the church, with the exception of a clash with the bishops (1873–1875), were in general rather harmonious, and the church survived the monarchy relatively unscathed.

Liberals shared with the conservatives the belief that the church should be subordinate to the aims of the newly independent states. In this sense most Latin American liberals were essentially regalists in their treatment of the church. But unlike the conservatives, they also wanted a more open, democratic society based on law. For this reason they, like liberals in Europe, considered the church, with its landed estates, special privileges, and extraordinary influence in society as the primary obstacle in the way of implanting republican ideals and bringing about social change. The liberals were influenced by the criticism the philosophers of the Enlightenment had leveled at organized religion, by the example of Protestant Europe and America, and by certain liberal doctrines within Catholicism itself that called for church reform. In particular, the ideas of the Gallicanist Abbé de Pradt and other European thinkers who proposed the creation of a national church freed from the tutelage of Rome, were well received by Bolívar, Bernardino Rivadavia in Argentina, and certain liberals in Peru.

Liberal anticlericalism mirrored the same phenomenon in Europe, but given Latin America's slower development, it arrived in the New World in smaller dosages and in differentiated phases. In general, three distinct phases can be discerned: an incipient but rather tepid anticlericalism at the time of Independence; a more aggressive mid-century anticlericalism, which coincided with the rise of liberal capitalism; and in the latter part of the century a more socially minded and openly antireligious anticlericalism, which reflected the influence of positivism.

In general, most liberals at the time of Independence were neither antireligious nor desirous of destroying the church. Rather, they sought to control it, reform it, and place it at the service of the new republics. Many of the first liberals were priests who supported the reforms. Singled out for reform from the beginning, however, were the religious orders. The liberals, not unlike the Protestant reformers, viewed religious life as an aberration in the history of Christianity. Also, given the fact that there were far more Spanish missionaries among the religious than among the secular clergy before Independence, the former were more readily associated in the public mind with the colonial past. Early on in Mexico, Peru, Gran Colombia, and Argentina, liberals enacted laws that severely limited the number of religious and that placed them under the control of the local bishops. The Jesuits in particular were the *bête noire* of the liberals, who had the newly returned Society of Jesus expelled from many of their countries.

As the century wore on, in Europe liberal hostility toward the church increased, and the church in turn, especially during the pontificate of Pius IX (1846–1878), assumed a more defiant attitude toward liberalism. In Latin America a second generation of liberals, determined to bring about social reform and influenced by utilitarian philosophies, became considerably more outspoken in its criticism of the church. In Chile, Francisco Bilbao, essayist and politician, equated Catholicism with absolutism. In Peru, Francisco de Paula González Vigil was excommunicated for championing the cause of freeing both the church and governments from the influence of the Roman Curia.

By mid-century, liberal minorities in Peru, Colombia, and Mexico had declared open war on the church's wealth, properties, and privileges, especially the ecclesiastical fuero. In Mexico the church decried the Reform Laws of Benito Juárez and welcomed Maximilian's rule. Liberalism in Mexico in particular made control of the church a cornerstone of its reformist thrust. The strong anticlerical articles in the Constitution of 1917 reflected the liberals' perception of the church as both a conservative and an antinationalist force. In a similar way, in Ecuador toward the end of the century José Eloy Alfaro Delgado swept aside all of the church's privileges, which had been created in Gabriel García Moreno's time, and opened the door to Protestant missionaries.

Finally, in the latter part of the nineteenth century, anticlericalism entered a third phase by assuming the mantle of positivism and scientific progress. Intellectuals such as Manuel González Prada in Peru went beyond denouncing church privileges; they attacked religion itself. González Prada, like other pro-Indian advocates, singled out clerical influence on the indigenous population as one of the principal reasons for Latin America's backwardness. In universities and avant-garde circles, intellectuals accused the clergy of maintaining women, children, and the lower classes in ignorance by appealing to their emotions and catering to their superstitions.

The greatest number of anticlerical laws in Latin America were enacted in the decade of 1880–1890. These laws called for obligatory civil marriage, the end of clerical control of the civil registry, the secularization of cemeteries, the end of the church's monopoly over public charities, and in some cases the laicization of education. Separation of church and state, unrestricted tolerance for non-Catholics, and the right to divorce were measures that only gained acceptance in most countries in the twentieth century.

Anticlericalism was an attitude most prevalent among the emerging capitalistically oriented middle and upper classes, usually centered in the capital and port cities. These classes were especially receptive to innovative and radical ideas from Europe. Masonic lodges in particular became the nerve centers of hostility toward the church. Anticlericalism, by way of contrast, was much less observable among the traditional upper-class families of the rural interior or the urban lower middle classes, for whom Catholicism was perceived as a source of stability. In general, anticlericalism was not a common attitude among the lower classes, least of all the Indians and blacks.

As a psychological phenomenon, anticlericalism can be explained in part as an expression of the liberals' frustration over the survival of the colonial mentality and its tenacious hold over the majority of Latin Americans long after Independence, and the subsequent lack of social progress that resulted from that influence. For many liberals and social reformers, hostility toward the church became the principal mode of rejecting that colonial past. Anticlericalism was also primarily a masculine attitude. Most women, even the wives of leading liberals, continued to practice their religion as in colonial times. Insofar as liberalism stood for freedom and the use of reason, Catholicism symbolized passive submission to authority and dogma.

In time classical liberalism was superseded by reform ideologies and thinkers with a more subtle and sophisticated view of religion and social change, and anticlericalism began fading away. Most important, since the Second Vatican Council, the church has undergone a historic reform and renewal, relieving some of the old sources of antagonism.

See also **Catholic Church: The Colonial Period; Catholic Church: The Modern Period; Francia, José Gaspar Rodríguez de; González Prada, Manuel; Liberalism; Masonic Orders; Mexico, Wars and Revolutions: The Reform.**

BIBLIOGRAPHY

On regalism in Bourbon Spain see Richard Herr, *The Eighteenth-Century Revolution in Spain* (1958) and John Lynch, *Bourbon Spain, 1700–1808* (1989). An overview of church-state conflicts can be found in J. Lloyd Mecham, *Church and State in Latin America: A History of Politico-Ecclesiastical Relations,* 2d ed. (1966). To understand the intellectual background of anticlericalism see Leopoldo Zea, *The Latin American Mind,* translated by James H. Abbot and Lowell Dunham (1963). On González Prada and other Peruvian anticlerics see Jeffrey Klaiber, *Religion and Revolution in Peru, 1824–1976* (1977). On anticlericalism in Mexico see Robert E. Quirk, *The Mexican Revolution and the Catholic Church, 1910–1929* (1973).

Additional Bibliography

Butler, Matthew. *Faith and Impiety in Revolutionary Mexico.* New York: Palgrave Macmillan, 2007.

Chasteen, John C., and James A. Wood, eds, *Problems in Modern Latin American History: Sources and Interpretations: Completely Revised and Updated.* Wilmington: SR Books, 2004.

Hamnett, Brian R. *Juárez.* New York: Longman, 1994.

JEFFREY KLAIBER S.J.

ANTIGUA. Antigua, largest of a three-island unit in the Leeward Islands that, along with Barbuda and Redonda, comprises the independent state of Antigua and Barbuda.

Although the island was sighted during Columbus's second voyage to the Caribbean in 1493, geography and a lack of natural resources, including a limited supply of fresh water, conspired to deter sustained, permanent settlement by both the indigenous peoples of the region, the Arawaks and the Caribs, and the conquering Spanish. Unguarded and unexploited for over a century, Antigua was seized by an English expedition in 1632. Initially populated by small-scale subsistence and tobacco farmers, the island became a producer of sugarcane in the 1660s, a change that, with the subsequent introduction of African slaves, completely transformed the nature of the colony. By 1700 Antigua had developed into a traditional plantation society comprised of large estates, a small European planter class, and large numbers of slave laborers.

Full integration into the British mercantile system as a sugar producer provided Antigua with a secure, stable market into the nineteenth century. By the 1830s, however, as abolition and free trade became imperial policy, this flourishing dependence had begun to collapse. Acceptance of crown colony status in 1868 by the island elites preserved the basic features of colonial life, though growing numbers of bankrupt sugar estates and newly formed free villages of ex-slaves heralded the eventual stagnation of plantation society.

As the old planter and bureaucratic elite declined in numbers and influence in the early decades of the twentieth century, Antigua's long-oppressed lower classes began to mobilize. Inspired by the labor movements and pan-Africanist ideology that swept through the Caribbean in the years following World War I, local blacks formed the Antigua Trades and Labor Union (ATLU) in 1939 to promote political, economic, and social reforms. In the years that followed, as Britain began its long process of decolonization, the ATLU and its political wing, the Antigua Labor Party (ALP), under the leadership of Vere Bird, came to dominate island politics.

Having guided Antigua to independence in 1981, Bird became its first prime minister and

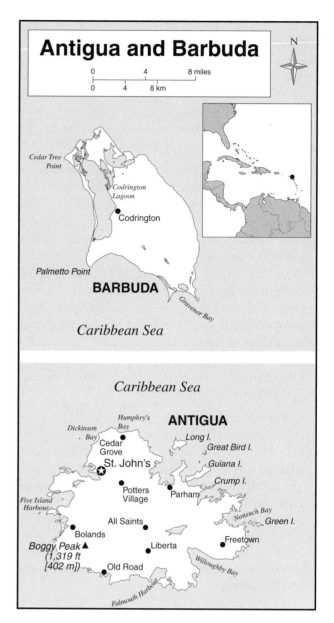

proceeded to set up a personalist regime based on extensive corruption and nepotism, before passing power to his son, Vere Jr., in 1994. Vere Jr. has also been accused of corruption and engaging in bribery and questionable offshore banking dealings. In the 2004 elections, Bird and his ALP government were handily defeated by Baldwin Spencer of the United Progressive Party (UPP), which took control of 12 of the 17 legislative seats, thus ending the long-standing Bird family's grip over island politics. In the early 2000s, the ALP has been severely weakened from internal factionalism, and Vere Jr. faces criminal charges for corruption during his presidency.

Antigua and Barbuda

Population:	69,481 (2007 est.)
Area:	Antigua 108 sq. mi; Barbuda 62 sq. mi
Official language:	English
Languages:	Local dialects
National currency:	East Caribbean dollar
Principal religions:	Anglican 25.7%; Seventh Day Adventist 12.3%; Pentecostal 10.6%; Moravian 10.5%; Roman Catholic 10.4%; Methodist 7.9%; Baptist 4.9%; Church of God 4.5%; other Christian 5.4%; other 2%; none or unspecified 5.8%
Ethnicity:	Black 91%; mixed 4.4%; white 1.7%; other 2.9%
Capital:	Saint John's
Annual rainfall:	Averages 46 in
Economy:	*GDP per capita:* US$10,900 (2005)

With nearly total elimination of agro-exports from its economy, Antigua is in the early 2000s heavily reliant upon U.S. capital and tourism. Antigua is involved in a trade dispute with the United States over its ban on online gambling, which is Antigua's second largest employer. Despite the WTO repeatedly siding with Antigua, the United States has made no changes.

See also **Barbuda; Bird, Vere Cornwall; Leeward Islands.**

BIBLIOGRAPHY

Henry Paget, *Peripheral Capitalism and Underdevelopment in Antigua* (1985).

Franklin W. Knight, *The Caribbean: The Genesis of a Fragmented Nationalism,* 2d ed. (1990).

Robert Coram, *Caribbean Time Bomb: The United States' Complicity in the Corruption of Antigua* (1993).

Additional Bibliography

"New Prime Minister (Antigua & Barbuda)." *Caribbean Update,* May 1, 2004.

Rivlin, Gary. "Gambling Dispute with a Tiny Country Puts U.S. in a Bind." *New York Times,* August 23, 2007.

TIMOTHY P. HAWKINS

ANTIGUA (LA ANTIGUA GUATE-MALA). The appellation came into being several years after devastating earthquakes in July and December of 1773 forced Spanish crown officials, over church and local opposition, to move the capital of Spanish Central America from Antigua, then known as Santiago de Guatemala, to the present site of Guatemala City.

Capital of the *audiencia* of Guatemala from 1541 to 1773 (for all but several short periods) and the most important city of the region, Antigua was conceived out of natural disaster. Santiago en Almolonga, its predecessor, was founded in 1527 on the lower northern slopes of the dormant Agua volcano. As the first permanent capital of Guatemala it lasted but fourteen years. In early September 1541, after three days of heavy rain, a mudslide exploded down the steep slopes of Agua, largely destroying the settlement's Spanish core.

Within months of the destruction of the old city (known as Ciudad Vieja), and after much debate, local authorities decided on a location in the Panchoy Valley, about 3 miles north of Santiago en Almolonga. By late 1541, the city's *cabildo* (city council) had begun to supervise laying out the new city.

All of the Indian slaves and many *naborias* (dependent servants) held by the city's Spanish *vecinos* (citizens) were freed in 1549–1550 by order of the *audiencia* president, Alonso López De Cerrato, as part of his efforts to enforce the New Laws, promulgated by Spain in 1542. Angry at losing their labor force to emancipation, Santiago's Spanish *vecinos* were further incensed when the religious orders persuaded large numbers of these freedmen and their families to establish barrios in the shelter of their monasteries, on the perimeter of the Spanish city.

Thus, within a decade of its founding, Santiago had a Spanish core abutted on three sides by Indian communities. It was a microcosm of the Spanish ideal

View of Antigua, Guatemala, 2005. UNESCO designated Antigua a World Heritage Site in 1979 due to its monuments and numerous colonial-era ruins. © KEITH DANNEMILLER/CORBIS

of "two republics," whereby Spaniards and Indians lived and worked beside each other while maintaining separate statuses and social identities. However, because the Indians, highly vulnerable to Old World diseases, began to decline drastically and were seen as incapable of hard labor, small numbers of African slaves were introduced into Spanish Central America before 1550. Confined at first to rural mines and sugar plantations, black, and later mulatto, slaves were brought to Santiago's Spanish households.

Due to the shortage of Spanish women, the Spanish community absorbed a number of Indian women. It also admitted some *casta* (mixed) offspring, especially legitimate children of both sexes and illegitimate mestizas (female offspring of Indian–Spanish unions). Mestizos not taken into the Spanish community either retained the *casta* status or entered the Indian group.

By the 1560s and 1570s, free *castas,* free blacks, and even poor Spaniards began to spill into the Indian barrios adjoining the Spanish city. Such intrusions led to Indian displacement, Indian–*casta* unions, and an increased likelihood of either Indian Hispanization or flight to rural areas to escape both tribute payment and the onerous labor obligations associated with Indian tributary status. These factors, combined with the impact of epidemic disease, resulted in the decline of Indian tributary populations and barrio self-rule.

Santiago in the late seventeenth and eighteenth centuries was a large urban center of over 30,000 inhabitants. It had a large multiethnic artisan population and served as a center for both the distribution of imported trade goods and the collection and sale of Indian tribute items for crown and individual *encomenderos* (recipients of Indian tribute). Santiago also served as an entrepôt for the export trade in cacao, hides, tobacco, and indigo.

Antigua has enjoyed a varied existence since its destruction in 1773. During the late eighteenth century (and later), its colonial ruins served as a source of architectural details (doors, grills, etc.) for the buildings of the new capital and elsewhere;

its crumbling walls, as a source of saltpeter for making gunpowder. In the early nineteenth century, Antigua was one of Guatemala's main centers of cochineal production. By the 1850s, the city and its fertile surrounding lands began to be intensively devoted to coffee production.

Despite the post-1773 dismemberment of Antigua's colonial architectural heritage and the important role of coffee cultivation, the city in recent decades has been recognized by regional and international bodies as a cultural monument worthy of preservation. The United Nations Educational, Scientific and Cultural Organization (UNESCO) designated Antigua a World Heritage Site in 1979. Set amid spectacular natural surroundings, its numerous colonial ruins, public buildings, and houses rebuilt in the colonial style have made Antigua a tourist center and a magnet for a sizable resident foreign community. The 2002 census reported 19,938 residents in the city of Antigua and 41,097 in the broader municipal.

See also **Earthquakes.**

BIBLIOGRAPHY

Important and accessible studies on Antigua's architectural history are Sidney David Markman, *Colonial Architecture of Antigua Guatemala* (1967).

Verle L. Annis, *The Architecture of Antigua Guatemala, 1543–1773* (1968). Antigua's social and population histories are analyzed in Christopher H. Lutz, *Santiago de Guatemala, 1541–1773: City, Caste, and the Colonial Experience* (1994). Important aspects of the city's sixteenth- and seventeenth-century socioeconomic and political elite history are covered in Pilar Sanchiz Ochoa, *Los hidalgos de Guatemala: Realidad y apariencia en un sistema de valores* (1976).

Stephen A. Webre, "The Social and Economic Bases of Cabildo Membership in Seventeenth Century Santiago de Guatemala," (Ph.D. diss., Tulane University, 1980). The destruction and move of the capital city are described in María Cristina Zilbermann De Luján, *Aspectos socioeconómicos del traslado de la Ciudad de Guatemala (1773–1783)* (1987). Manuel Rubio Sánchez, *Monografía de la ciudad de Antigua Guatemala* (1989), is one of the few studies to adequately consider the city's history after the 1773 earthquake and the move of the capital to what is now Guatemala City.

Additional Bibliography

Alvarez P., Rafael V. *Terremotos en Antigua: Secuencias y secuelas.* Guatemala: s.n., Centro Editorial Vile, 2001.

Little, Walter E. *Mayas in the Marketplace: Tourism, Globalization, and Cultural Identity.* Austin: University of Texas Press, 2004.

Santos Pérez, J. Manuel. *Élites, poder local y régimen colonial: El cabildo y los regidores de Santiago de Guatemala, 1700-1787.* South Woodstock: Plumsock Mesoamerican Studies, 1999.

CHRISTOPHER H. LUTZ

ANTILLES. *See* **Caribbean Antilles.**

ANTIOQUIA. Antioquia, a department in northwestern Colombia comprising an area of 24,600 square miles. In 1985, the department had a population of 3,828,000, concentrated in the temperate valleys of the Central and Western Cordilleras. The capital of Antioquia is Medellín, the second largest city in Colombia. Named after the Syrian city of Antioch, the department has played a leading role in the economic development of Colombia, and its people, known as *paisas,* are sometimes said to constitute a "race" different from that of other Colombians.

Little is known about Antioquia's indigenous population, which may have numbered as many as 600,000 at the time of the arrival of the first Spaniards under Jorge de Robledo, who founded Santa Fé de Antioquia in 1541. Early settlers were lured by reports of gold in the area, especially the lode at Buriticá and the placers of the Nechí and Cauca rivers. Gold mining, sustained by the labor of African slaves, remained a mainstay of the local economy throughout the colonial period, eventually being supplemented by commerce, stock raising, and agriculture. The region experienced considerable economic growth in the late eighteenth century, a development that some historians attribute to reforms introduced by Juan Antonio Mon y Velarde, a judge of the Bogotá audiencia (high court), who conducted a visita (official investigation) of Antioquia from 1782 to 1785.

Between the eighteenth and twentieth centuries, Antioqueño colonizers established many new settlements to the south and southwest of the original province. This process of expansion is prominent in the myth of Antioqueño distinctiveness, although colonization was probably not as egalitarian as was once believed. Part of the territory colonized by the Antioqueños was detached from the department to form the new department of Caldas in 1905. Its capital, Manizales, was founded by Antioqueños in 1848.

In the twentieth century, Antioquia and Caldas became major coffee producers, accounting for 36 percent of Colombia's total output by 1914 and 47 percent by the late 1950s. Antioquia also became Colombia's principal industrial center with the establishment of large factories producing textiles, apparel, and other consumer goods. The department's economic growth was spurred by improved transportation, notably completion of a railroad in 1929 linking Medellín with the Magdalena River at Puerto Berrío and extensive road construction afterward.

Numerous explanations have arisen to account for the entrepreneurial skills of the Antioqueños as well as their propensity to colonize. Some have attributed these qualities to the Basque ancestry of early settlers in the region. Others have stressed habits derived from their experience in mining or have argued that gold mining and associated commerce generated the capital necessary for investment in industry. By the late twentieth century, however, Antioquia's economic primacy had diminished as other regions industrialized.

See also **Colombia: From the Conquest Through Independence.**

BIBLIOGRAPHY

James J. Parsons, *Antioqueño Colonization in Western Colombia*, rev. ed. (1968).

Keith H. Christie, "Antioqueño Colonization in Western Colombia: A Reappraisal," in *Hispanic American Historical Review* 58 (1978):260–283.

Jaime Sierra García, *Cronología de Antioquia* (1982).

Ann Twinam, *Miners, Merchants, and Farmers in Colonial Colombia* (1982).

Additional Bibliography

Botero Herrera, Fernando. *Estado, nación y provincia de Antioquia: Guerras civiles e invención de la región 1829–1863.* Medellín, Colombia: Hombre Nuevo Editores, 2003.

Londoño-Vega, Patricia. *Religion, Culture, and Society in Colombia: Medellín and Antioquia, 1850–1930.* Oxford: Clarendon Press, 2002.

HELEN DELPAR

ANTOFAGASTA. The Antofagasta is the largest region of continental Chile (50,578 square miles, population as of 2001 493,984). Its capital is the port of Antofagasta (2001 population 296,905), the "metropole of the North." Most of Antofagasta's territory was incorporated into Bolivia when that country was created in 1825. It was then sparsely inhabited by silver and copper miners, with settlements found only in the river oases, where Indian tribes belonging to the Atacameño culture pursued agricultural and pastoral activities. In the War of the Pacific (1879–1884) Chilean troops occupied the coastal fringe and pushed the Bolivian army back toward the interior. In 1904 Bolivia relinquished its rights to the area, thus opening the way for migrants from Chile's Norte Chico.

Under Chilean control the region developed into a thriving mining center with nitrate mines (*salitreras*) and huge copper mines at Chuquicamata, La Exótica, La Escondida, and Mantos Blancos. Industrial fisheries in Tocopilla, Mejillones, Antofagasta, and Taltal are other mainstays of the regional economy. In this desert environment the population is concentrated in urban centers. Antofagasta is the main administrative hub, with two universities, the northern bases of the Chilean naval and air forces, and a nationally known soccer team. It is also the terminus of the railroad from Oruro in Bolivia and Salta in Argentina. The second largest city is Calama (2001 population 128,400), also a bustling mining center with a well-known soccer team. Of lesser importance are the industrial fishing ports of Tocopilla, Mejillones, and Taltal, which are also shipping terminals for copper and other mining products.

See also **Mining: Modern; Nitrate Industry; War of the Pacific.**

BIBLIOGRAPHY

"Región del Bíobío." In *Geografía de Chile*, vol. 9. Santiago de Chile: Instituto Geográfico Militar, 1986.

CÉSAR N. CAVIEDES

ANTONIL, ANDRÉ JOÃO. *See* Andreoni, João Antônio.

ANTÔNIO CONSELHEIRO. *See* Conselheiro, Antônio.

ANTUÑANO, ESTEVAN DE (1792–1847).

Estevan de Antuñano (*b.* 1792; *d.* 1847), Mexican industrialist. One of Mexico's first modern industrialists, Antuñano was born in Veracruz into a Spanish immigrant family. He was educated in Spain and in England, where he became familiar with industrial production. In the 1830s he led the modernization of the textile industry in Puebla, setting up Mexico's first mechanized spinning factory, La Constancia Mexicana, which produced cotton yarn on Arkwright spindles powered by the waters of the Río Atoyac. By the early 1840s, he owned four such factories in Puebla.

An enlightened entrepreneur, Antuñano recognized that the mechanization of spinning deprived women and children of employment and tried to alleviate the problem by turning La Constancia into a model experiment in the employment of family labor. He provided both housing and health care for his workers. Unfortunately, wages were low and people worked eleven to sixteen hours daily.

A vigorous propagandist, who authored over sixty pamphlets, Antuñano had a vision of national development. He wanted to see the traditional manufacturing center of Puebla wrest control of northern Mexican markets, then dependent on contraband. Trade with the north would revitalize Mexico's central cities and agricultural districts. Silver exports would bring in foreign exchange. His vision floundered on the realities of the scarcity of raw cotton and currency, the persistence of contraband, and national disintegration. Antuñano died of natural causes during the U.S. Army's occupation of the city of Puebla. A French merchant, to whom he owed money, acquired most of his properties.

See also **Textile Industry: The Colonial Era.**

BIBLIOGRAPHY

Miguel A. Quintana, *Estevan de Antuñano*, 2 vols. (1957).

Jan Bazant, "Industria algodonera poblana de 1803–1843 en números," in *Historia Mexicana* 14 (July-September 1964): 131–143.

Guy P. C. Thomson, *Puebla de los Angeles: Industry and Society in a Mexican City, 1700–1850* (1989).

Additional Bibliography

Illades, Carlos. *Estudios sobre el artesanado urbano en el siglo XIX*. Mexico City: Universidad Autónoma Metropolitana, Unidad Iztapalapa 2001.

Sanchez, Evelyne. "L'indépendance économique du Mexique: le parcours de l'entrepreneur Estevan de Antuñano (1792-1847)." Ph.D. dissertation, University of Toulouse, 2002.

MARY KAY VAUGHAN

ANTÚNEZ, NEMESIO (1918–1993).

Nemesio Antúnez (*b.* 1918; *d.* 19 May 1993), Chilean artist, whose work is characterized by optical and psychological effects achieved by means of perspective distortions and geometric configurations. Antúnez's work has been classified as surrealist, due to the unusual effects resulting from his manipulation of space. He studied architecture at Catholic University in his native Santiago from 1937 to 1943 and at Columbia University in New York City in 1945. A fellowship enabled him to study with Stanley W. Hayter of Atelier 17 in New York in 1947. In 1950 he followed Hayter to Paris. After returning to Chile in 1953, he organized *Taller 99*, an artists' collective. In the late 1950s his work anticipated op art effects, with an emphasis on expression. He executed a mural, *Heart of the Andes*, at the United Nations (1966). A characteristic presentation of space in Antúnez's painting consists of rectangular boxes telescoping out of one another as though suspended in a void. Seemingly transparent planes and figures are used to create the illusion of endless expanses of space. Minuscule anthropomorphic figures often populate these spatial configurations (e.g., *New York, New York 10008,* 1967). His work consolidates the heritage of geometric art and surrealism, two strong movements in the art of Latin America.

Antúnez held several administrative posts, including director of the Museum of Contemporary Art, University of Chile, Santiago (1961–1964), cultural attaché at the Chilean embassy, New York City (1964–1969); director, National Museum of Fine Arts, Santiago (1969–1973).

See also **Art: The Twentieth Century.**

BIBLIOGRAPHY

Lowery S. Sims, "New York Dada and New World Surrealism," in Luis Cancel et al., *The Latin American Spirit: Art and Artists in the United States, 1920–1970* (1988), pp. 174–175.

Additional Bibliography

Palmer Trias, Montserrat. *N. Antúnez.* Santiago de Chile: Ediciones ARQ, Escuela de Arquitectura, Pontificia Universidad Católica de Chile, 1997.

Verdugo, Patricia. *Conversaciones con Nemesio Antúnez.* Santiago de Chile: Ediciones ChileAmérica, 1995.

MARTA GARSD

ANZA, JUAN BAUTISTA DE (1736–1788).

Juan Bautista de Anza (*b.* 1736; *d.* 19 December 1788), military officer, governor of New Mexico (1778–1788). One of the most effective instruments of the Bourbon Reforms on the northern frontier of New Spain, Anza was born at the presidio of Fronteras (Sonora), where his father, a member of the landowning-military-merchant elite, served as commander. While captain at Tubac (present-day southern Arizona), young Anza led an exploring party overland to southern California in 1774, and in 1775–1776, by the same route, he escorted the colonists who founded San Francisco. Appointed governor in 1777, Anza rode personally with the combined Hispano-Indian force that defeated Cuerno Verde, the Comanches' leading war chief, in New Mexico in 1779. His diplomacy resulted in treaties and alliances, first with the Comanches in 1786, and then with the Utes, Jicarilla Apaches, and Navajos. A generation of relative peace ensued, with steady growth of the Hispanic population and unprecedented territorial expansion. Anza died in Arizpe (Sonora).

See also **Bourbon Reforms.**

BIBLIOGRAPHY

Herbert E. Bolton, *Outpost of Empire* (1931), and Alfred B. Thomas, *Forgotten Frontiers: A Study of the Spanish Indian Policy of Don Juan Bautista de Anza, Governor of New Mexico, 1777–1787* (1932).

Additional Bibliography

Garate, Donald T. *Juan Bautista de Anza: Basque Explorer in the New World.* Reno: University of Nevada Press, 2003.

JOHN L. KESSELL

ANZALDÚA, GLORIA (1942–2004).

The renowned Chicana cultural theorist, poet, and writer Gloria Evanjelina Anzaldúa was born on 24 September 1942, in the Rio Grande Valley of South Texas, a seventh-generation *tejana.* She received her B.A. and M.A. degrees from the University of Texas, Austin. Her groundbreaking multigenre *Borderlands/La Frontera: The New Mestiza* (1987) was selected as one of the 100 best books of the twentieth century by the *Hungry Mind Review* and *Utne Reader;* it contains her celebrated quote, "The U.S.–Mexican border *es una herida abierta* where the Third World grates against the first and bleeds" (p. 3). Editor of the multicultural anthologies *This Bridge Called My Back: Writings by Radical Women of Color* (with Cherríe Moraga, 1981) and *Making Face, Making Soul/Haciendo Caras: Creative and Critical Perspectives by Women of Color* (1990), Anzaldúa redefined lesbian/queer identities and developed an inclusionary feminist movement.

Anzaldua died on May 15, 2004. Among her honors are awards from the Before Columbus Foundation (1986) and the National Endowment for the Arts (1991). In 2007 the Society for the Study of Gloria Anzaldúa was established at the University of Texas, San Antonio; the Anzaldúa archive is housed at the Nettie Lee Benson Latin American Collection at the University of Texas, Austin.

See also **Homosexuality and Bisexuality in Literature; Literature: Spanish America.**

BIBLIOGRAPHY

Works by Anzaldúa

Interviews/Entrevistas, ed. AnaLouise Keating. New York: Routledge, 2000.

As editor, with AnaLouise Keating. *This Bridge We Call Home: Radical Visions for Transformation.* New York: Routledge, 2002.

"Let Us Be the Healing of the Wound: The Coyolxauhqui Imperative—La Sombra y El Sueño." In *One Wound for Another/Una herida por otra: Testimonios de Latin@s in the U.S. through Cyberspace (11 de septiembre de 2001–11 de marzo de 2002)*, edited by Claire Joysmith and Clara Lomas. Mexico City: Centro de Investigaciones Sobre América del Norte, Universidad Nacional Autónoma de México, together with the Colorado College and Whittier College, 2005.

Children's Books by Anzaldúa

Friends from the Other Side/Amigos del Otro Lado. Illustrated by Consuelo Méndez. San Francisco: Children's Book Press, 1993.

Prietita and the Ghost Woman/Prietita y La Llorona. Illustrated by Cristina Gonzalez. San Francisco: Children's Book Press, 1995.

Secondary Works

Alarcón, Norma. "Anzaldúa's Frontera: Inscribing Gynetics." In *Chicana Feminisms: A Critical Reader*, edited by Gabriela F. Arredondo et al. Durham, NC: Duke University Press, 2003.

Joysmith, Claire. "Ya se me quitó la vergüenza y la cobardía: Una plática con Gloria Anzaldúa." *Debate Feminista* 4 no. 8 (September 1993).

Keating, AnaLouise, ed. *Entre Mundos/Among Worlds: New Perspectives on Gloria E. Anzaldúa*. New York: Palgrave Macmillan, 2005.

CLAIRE JOYSMITH

ANZOÁTEGUI, JOSÉ ANTONIO

(1789–1819). José Antonio Anzoátegui (*b.* 14 November 1789; *d.* 15 November 1819), officer in the Venezuelan Emancipating Army. Anzoátegui was on the pro-independence side from the beginning of the independence movement in 1810. In his birthplace of Barcelona, Venezuela, he stood out as a leader of the Sociedad Patriotica de Caracas who was in favor of emancipation. Anzoátegui took part in the Guiana campaign of 1812, and when the First Republic fell, he was imprisoned in the vaults of La Guaira.

Anzoátegui returned to war in 1813 and fought in numerous battles. He helped Simón Bolívar take the city of Bogotá in 1814; participated in the two Los Cayos expeditions financed by Alexandre Pétion, president of Haiti; was present at the taking of Angostura in 1817, in the Los Llanos campaign of 1818, and in the campaign for the liberation of New Granada in 1819. Bolívar placed him in charge of operations in Santa Marta and Maracaibo, but his death prevented him from carrying out his mission. For his military actions, he was decorated with the Order of the Liberators of Venezuela and the Boyacá Cross.

See also **Venezuela: The Colonial Era.**

BIBLIOGRAPHY

Esteban Chalbaud-Cardona, *Anzoátegui (general de infantería)* (1941).

Fabio Lozano y Lozano, *Anzoátegui: Visiones de la Guerra de Independencia* (1963).

Carlos Sánchez Espejo, *Vida útil y gloriosa* (1970).

Additional Bibliography

Franco Brizuela, Jovito. *Anzoátegui (general bolivariano).* Caracas: Academia Nacional de la Historia, 1994.

Quintero, José Gilberto. "Vida de un titan," *Boletín de la Academia Nacional de Historia (Venezuela)* 72: 228 (Oct.–Dec. 1989), pp. 85–93.

INÉS QUINTERO

APACHES. The Apaches are twelve linguistically related tribes that occupied an extensive territory (known as *Apachería*) from the Colorado River to the Rio Grande, and from northern canyons in present-day Arizona and New Mexico extending south a thousand miles into present-day Mexico. They combined hunting and gathering with small-scale agriculture. Initially attracted to the material benefits of the Spanish missions, they subsequently rejected the regulation of their lives and the attempt to suppress their traditional religion and its practice. They launched a general rebellion in 1677, initiating a century of hostility that halted the extension of the northern frontier of the Viceroyalty of New Spain. The Bourbon crown's expansion of presidio garrisons and initiation of subsistence rations in the 1770s brought generally peaceful relations into the 1820s, with a substantial growth in the Hispanic population south of Apache-dominated areas.

The gradual dissolution of the presidio garrisons for want of material support, and the attempt by state officials in the early 1830s to force the Apaches to become sedentary workers in order to receive subsistence rations, led to a renewal of the periodic, devastating Apache raids. The frontier countryside was slowly depopulated. Though U.S. annexation after 1848 carried with it the promise of controlling Apache incursions, for nearly three decades the United States limited itself to protecting the settlements on its side of the border. In 1873 Colonel Ronald Mackenzie led 400 U.S. soldiers in an extermination campaign against the Lipan Apache; survivors were deported to the Mescalero Apache Reservation in the Sacramento Mountains of New Mexico, established in that same year. Only in the 1880s, when the U.S. and Mexican governments reached an agreement on mutual border crossing were the Apache raids ended, with the remnants of the tribes permanently restricted to reservations. The Apaches are known to be among the last indigenous peoples to accept colonial domination. Chief Geronimo (1829–1909), of the Chiricahua Apache, was one of the more famous Apache warriors, battling and evading both the Mexican and U.S. troops for more than twenty-five years, finally surrendering in Arizona in 1886.

As of the 2000 U.S. Census, many of the 66,800 people who make up the ten tribes of the Apaches still reside in reservations in Arizona, New Mexico, and Oklahoma. Reservation life, marked by poverty and limited economic opportunities, continues to be a challenge for the Apache; for example, in the late 1990s over 50 percent of the San Carlos Apache were unemployed. However, in the late twentieth century many of the reservations initiated casino operations, tourism, and timber and agricultural businesses that have improved the standard of living on the reservations. The resort and casino run by the Mescalero Apaches attracts visitors year-round. Many Apaches are nationally and internationally respected artists, writers, and scholars, such as the poet Jose L. Garza (Coahuilateca and Apache), the historian Veronica E. Velarde Tiller (Jicarilla Apache), and the sculptor Allen Houser (Chiricahua Apache).

See also **Indigenous Peoples.**

BIBLIOGRAPHY

John Upton Terrell, *Apache Chronicle* (1972).

John L. Kessell, *Friars, Soldiers, and Reformers: Hispanic Arizona and the Sonora Mission Frontier 1767–1856* (1976).

David J. Weber, *The Mexican Frontier, 1821–1846: The American Southwest Under Mexico* (1982).

Francisco R. Almada, *Diccionario de historia, geografía y biografía de sonorenses* (1983), pp. 56–63.

Additional Bibliography

León García, Ricardo, and Carlos González Herrera. *Civilizar o exterminar: Tarahumaras y Apaches en Chihuahua, siglo XIX.* Tlalpan, Mexico: CIESA, INI, 2000.

Thrapp, Dan L. *The Conquest of Apacheria.* Norman: University of Oklahoma Press, 1967.

Stuart F. Voss

APALACHEE.

The Apalachee are a native people whose name was given to a Spanish mission province in northwest Florida and mistakenly given to the Appalachian Mountains. The Apalachee, associated with the late pre-Columbian Fort Walton archaeological culture, inhabited the region from the Aucilla River west to the Ochlockonee River. Throughout their history the Apalachee were farmers governed by a paramount chief and a hierarchy of village chiefs and officials. At the time of the first European contact (the Pánfilo de Nárvaez expedition in 1528), they numbered about fifty thousand. Hernando de Soto's army wintered at the Apalachee town of Anhaica for five months in 1539–1540. The resulting introduction of diseases and military conflict had a severe impact.

Beginning in 1633 Spanish Franciscan priests established missions in Apalachee. Nine to fifteen missions, most with several satellite villages, functioned throughout the remainder of the seventeenth century. When English raiders from the Carolinas, aided by native allies, destroyed the missions in 1703–1704, the Apalachee population, which by 1675 had stabilized at about eight thousand, was shattered. Survivors were enslaved or fled west toward Alabama, Texas, and Louisiana. To escape persecution by Anglo-American immigrants, the Apalachee migrated into Louisiana's Kisatchie Hills. Although the small band of Apalachee had left ancestral lands, in the hills they were able to maintain some of their traditional ways.

In the twenty-first century the Talamali Apalachee chief, Gilmer Bennett, serves the three hundred registered Apalachee from the tribal office in Libuse, Louisiana, although tribal members regularly return to ancestral lands in Tallahassee, Florida. The main concern of Chief Bennett's administration has been obtaining federal recognition of the tribe.

See also **Indigenous Peoples; Missions: Spanish America.**

BIBLIOGRAPHY

Mark F. Boyd, Hale G. Smith, and John W. Griffin, *Here They Once Stood: The Tragic End of the Apalachee Missions* (1951).

John H. Hann, *Apalachee: The Land Between the Rivers* (1988).

Charles R. Ewen, "Anhaica: Discovery of Hernando de Soto's 1539–1540 Winter Camp," in *First Encounters: Spanish Explorations in the Caribbean and the United States, 1492–1570,* edited by Jerald T. Milanich and Susan Milbrath (1989).

Additional Bibliography

Figuero y Del Campo, Cristóbal. *Misiones franciscanas en la Florida: Reseña histórica.* Madrid: Comisión Episcopal del V Centenario, 1992.

Lee, Dayna Bowker. *The Talimali Band of Apalachee.* Louisiana Regional Folklife Program, 2007. Available from http://www.nsula.edu/regionalfolklife/apalachee/before1763.html.

JERALD T. MILANICH

APARICIO, LUIS (1934–). Luis Aparicio, born Luis Ernesto Aparicio Montiel, was a baseball player who became the model for durability and stellar play as a major league shortstop. A native of Maracaibo, Venezuela, Aparicio came from a baseball family: His father was a legendary shortstop and owned a professional club.

Rising through the ranks of Venezuelan baseball, Aparicio was signed by the Chicago White Sox, and he made his major league debut with that team in 1956. That year he led the American League in stolen bases and was named the major league Rookie of the Year. He was the American League stolen base leader for his first nine consecutive seasons (1956–1964). In his career he won nine Gold Glove trophies and played in ten All-Star games. He concluded his career in 1973, having played 2,581 games at shortstop, which at that time then ranked him first on the all-time list at that position. He also ended his career

as the all-time shortstop leader in assists, double plays, putouts, and chances. In 1984 Aparicio was inducted into the Baseball Hall of Fame.

See also **Sports.**

BIBLIOGRAPHY

Bjarkman, Peter C. *Baseball with a Latin Beat: A History of the Latin American Game.* Jefferson, NC: McFarland, 1994.

Regalado, Samuel O. *Viva Baseball! Latin Major Leaguers and Their Special Hunger.* Urbana: University of Illinois Press, 1998.

Wendel, Tim. *The New Face of Baseball: The One-Hundred-Year Rise and Triumph of Latinos in America's Favorite Sport.* New York: Rayo, 2003.

SAMUEL O. REGALADO

APOLINAR (1928–). Apolinar (Pablo Livinalli Santaella; *b.* 23 July 1928), Venezuelan artist. Although born in the small town of Guatire, Apolinar has spent his life in Petare, near Caracas. His preference for religious themes derives from years spent in a Catholic boarding school. He became an artist in 1965, when he produced his first painting, *The Bolivarian Neighborhood.* Since then his works have combined a primitive style with religious intimacy. In 1967 three of his paintings were included in the First Retrospective of Twentieth-Century Venezuelan Primitive Art, at the Musical Circle Gallery in Caracas. In the early 1970s he began a series of very imaginative books, the *Biblioteca de Apolinar,* which were first exhibited in 1972. The artistic and thematic complexity of these books gained him immediate recognition and inclusion in the 1977 Creadores al Margen show at the Museum of Contemporary Art in Caracas.

See also **Art: The Twentieth Century.**

BIBLIOGRAPHY

Dawn Ades, *Art in Latin America* (1989), pp. 297, 338.

BÉLGICA RODRÍGUEZ

APONTE-LEDÉE, RAFAEL (1938–). Rafael Aponte-Ledée (*b.* 15 October 1938), Puerto Rican composer. Born in Guayama, Puerto Rico, where he was educated, Aponte-Ledée left Puerto Rico in 1957 to study with Cristóbal Halffter at the

Madrid Conservatory. He remained in Madrid until 1964, when he left to begin studies with Alberto Ginastera and Gerardo Gandini at the Torcuato di Tella Institute in Buenos Aires. After returning to Puerto Rico in 1965, Aponte-Ledée moved to the forefront of the new music movements of the 1960s. In San Juan he cofounded the Fluxus group (1967) with Francis Schwartz. He also spent several years teaching music composition and theory at the University of Puerto Rico (1968–1973) and at the Puerto Rico Conservatory (from 1968).

Aponte-Ledée's works include *Tema y 6 diferencias* for piano (1963); elegies for strings (1965, 1967); *Presagio de pájaros muertos* (1966); *Impulsos...in memoriam Julia de Burgos* for orchestra (1967); *La ventana abierta* (two versions; 1968, 1969); *SSSSS²* (1971); and *El palacio en sombras* for orchestra (1977). He also published a biography of the Puerto Rican singer Fatty (1902-1941) in 1996.

See also **Gandini, Gerardo; Ginastera, Alberto Evaristo.**

BIBLIOGRAPHY

Isabel Aretz, *América latina en su música* (1977).

Gérard Béhague, *Music in Latin America* (1979).

Additional Bibliography

Thompson, Donald. "Film Music and Community Development in Rural Puerto Rico: The DIVEDCO Program (1948-91)." *Latin American Music Review,* 26:1 (Spring/Summer 2005): 102-114.

SARA FLEMING

APPLEYARD, JOSÉ LUIS (1927–).

José Luis Appleyard (*b.* 1927), Paraguayan poet. Born in Asunción, Appleyard studied law. He also taught literature and history at the Ateneo Paraguayo (Atheneum of Paraguay) and at the National University. He belongs to the poetry group that calls itself Academia Universitaria del Paraguay. Appleyard was awarded the First Prize in Poetry in 1943 and the Municipal Poetry Prize of Asunción in 1961. He is an aesthetic and nostalgic poet, with an oeuvre firmly rooted in the Paraguayan land and culture. In *Los monólogos* (1973) and *La voz que nos hablamos* (1983) he explores the "third language of Paraguay," the mixture of Spanish and Guaraní. Among Appleyard's lyrical works are *Tomando de la mano* (1981), *El labio y la palabra* (1982), *Solamente los*

años (1983), and *Las palabras secretas* (1988). Other works by Appleyard are *Entonces era siempre* (1946); *El sauce permanece* (1947); *Imágenes sin tierra* (1964); and *Antología poética* (1996).

See also **Literature: Spanish America.**

BIBLIOGRAPHY

Diccionario de autores iberoamericanos (1982).

Additional Bibliography

Delgado, Susy. *25 nombres capitales de la literatura paraguaya.* Asunción, Paraguay: Servilibro, 2005.

WILLIAM H. KATRA

APRA/APRISMO. *See* **Peru, Political Parties: Peruvian Aprista Party (PAP/APRA).**

APURÍMAC.

Apurímac, a major river draining the southern Peruvian Highlands into the Amazon basin. The Apurímac is one of the principal headwater tributaries of the Amazon River and forms a nearly impassable natural boundary. In Inca times the river was spanned by a rope suspension bridge made famous in modern times by the American writer Thorton Wilder in the novel *The Bridge of San Luis Rey.* The Incas held the river to be sacred and its name, Apurímac, can be translated from Quechua as "Great Oracle" or "Revered Speaker."

See also **Amazon River.**

BIBLIOGRAPHY

Burr Cartwright Brundage, *The Empire of the Inca* (1963) and *The Lords of Cuzco: A History and Description of the Inca People in Their Final Days* (1967).

Additional Bibliography

Benavides Estrada, Juan Augusto. *Atlas del Perú.* Lima: Editorial Escuela Nueva, 1995.

Contreras Ivarcena, Eduardo. *La violencia política en Apurimac: Su impacto social y económico.* Cusco: Centro de Estudios Regionales Andinos "Bartolomé de las casas," 1991.

Giddgings, Calvin J. *Demon River Apurimac: The First Navigation of Upper Amazon Canyons.* Utah: University of Utah Press, 1996.

GORDON F. MCEWAN

ARAB-LATIN AMERICAN RELATIONS.

The first links between Latin America and the Middle East were made through immigration. Arab immigration began in the mid-nineteenth century and intensified after World War I. According to Omar el Hamedi, president of the Congress of Arab Peoples, some 15 million Latin Americans are of Arab descent. Former president Carlos Saúl Menem of Argentina, the Mexican actress Salma Hayek, and the Mexican billionaire Carlos Slim are prominent examples of Arab assimilation into Latin American society. Arab immigrants called for the extension of diplomatic recognition to the newly independent Syrian and Lebanese states after 1945. However, there was little diplomatic interaction between Latin America and the Middle East until the 1960s, when, after helping to found the Organization of Petroleum Exporting Countries (OPEC), Venezuela worked closely with Arab oil exporters, and Cuba's new revolutionary government attempted to solidify contacts with the more radical Arab governments and groups. In the 1970s some Arab countries launched a diplomatic offensive in Latin America as elsewhere in an effort to line up support against Israel in the United Nations (UN), and many Latin American nations began to identify with the third world movement. Economic relations increased after the rise in oil prices in 1973–1974 as nations such as Brazil and Argentina realized they could offset trade deficits with Arab oil producers by increasing their exports to them and sought to attract investment. The Sandinista victory in Nicaragua in 1979 brought increased relations with Arab nations and Iran, and the breaking of relations with Israel.

CULTURAL RELATIONS

Since 1974 annual Arab–Pan-American congresses have been attended by officials from Arab countries as well as by Latin Americans of Arab descent. The first congress established an Arab–Pan-American Federation of Arab Communities in Latin America. Committees of friendship with Arab countries, such as the Arab-Uruguayan Friendship Association, exist in a number of Latin American countries as do joint cultural institutions. Arab countries have encouraged the furthering of Arab studies at universities, and cultural exchange programs have

been developed in cooperation with the Arab League and the Organization of American States (OAS). The Arab League publishes Spanish- and Portuguese-language journals and has financed the publication of translated Arab books. Saudi King Faisal donated $100,000 for the construction of the first mosque in Buenos Aires.

POLITICAL RELATIONS

Egypt, Lebanon, Algeria, Iraq, Syria, and Libya are, in decreasing order of importance, the Arab countries most heavily represented in Latin America. The Palestine Liberation Organization is represented in seven countries and the Western Saharan Polisario in three. The Arab League has four missions—in Brasilia, Buenos Aires, Santiago, and Mexico City. Egypt, Morocco, and Saudi Arabia have observer status in the OAS. Since the Iranian revolution, Iran has sought to expand its relations in Latin America. Brazil and Venezuela have had the longest diplomatic representation in the largest number of countries of the Middle East, with Argentina, Mexico, and Cuba also having extensive diplomatic representation in the region.

Membership in the Group of Seventy-Seven and the Nonaligned Movement and in the UN provides opportunities for gaining mutual support on issues of importance. Representatives of the 115 developing nations that are members of the Group of Seventy-Seven assemble to coordinate policies prior to major UN meetings. Latin American nations with membership in the Nonaligned Movement have taken the most consistently pro-Arab stance. In 1975 Arab nations succeeded in obtaining the support of Brazil, Mexico, Cuba, Grenada, and Guyana for a UN resolution condemning Zionism. This was repealed in 1991, with Cuba the only Latin American nation voting in opposition. During the 1970s, Augusto Pinochet's Chile and the military regime in Argentina sought to prevent the Arab world from supporting international condemnation of their human rights record. Argentina succeeded in obtaining support against Britain for its stance on the Malvinas (Falkland Islands) from all the Arab nations with the exception of Oman. During its conflict with the United States, Nicaragua was able to obtain Arab support for resolutions in the UN and for winning a seat on the Security Council in 1982.

The United States has expressed concern about Islamic radicalism in Latin America. In 1992, in what was the largest attack ever on an Israeli diplomatic post, Islamic Jihad bombed the Israeli embassy in Buenos Aires. The United States suspects that Islamic radicals have established an enclave in the border region between Argentina, Paraguay, and Brazil. Many proponents of tighter security along the U.S.-Mexico border have expressed concern over the possibility that Islamic radicals and terrorists could sneak into the United States.

MILITARY RELATIONS

Cubans have been involved in training Palestinian guerrillas and in combat operations in the Middle East. Cuban military personnel were sent to Syria and the Republic of Southern Yemen and assisted pro-Marxist guerrillas in Oman as well as Eritrean separatists until Cuba transferred its support to the Marxist government in Ethiopia. Some Sandinistas trained in Palestinian camps and participated in operations in both the Middle East and Europe. Later, Palestinians as well as Libyans worked with the Nicaraguan armed forces in training in the use of Soviet-bloc weapons. Libya and Algeria supplied tanks and other arms. Saudi Arabia in turn funded the purchase of light arms and planes for use against the Sandinista government.

Chile sold both Iran and Iraq cluster bombs during the Iran-Iraq war. Iraq provided missiles to Argentina in the Malvinas war and helped to fund development of a medium-range guided missile. However, during the Gulf War, Argentina sent two warships, the only Latin American nation to participate in the coalition against Saddam Hussein. Brazil, the world's sixth largest arms exporter, sells one-third of its weapons to the Middle East. Although Brazil's largest customer, in 1989 Iraq defaulted on weapons bills and after the invasion of Kuwait, Brazil agreed to honor the UN embargo.

ECONOMIC RELATIONS

Until the Iran-Iraq war disrupted supplies, Brazil imported half of its oil from Iraq, financed largely through arms sales. Braspreto, the overseas subsidiary of the state oil company, has drilling concessions in Saudi Arabia, Libya, Egypt, Iraq, and Algeria. After the UN embargo on Iraq, Iran replaced that country as Brazil's leading foreign supplier of crude oil and became an important market for Brazilian manufactures and technology. Argentina has not depended as much as Brazil on oil imports from the Arab world, but has succeeded in selling agricultural as well as industrial products there, with Egypt, Saudi Arabia, and Iran being the largest customers. Argentine scientists have assisted Iranian nuclear research since 1976. The Libyan Arab Foreign Bank joined with Argentine capitalists to form a Libyan Argentine Investment Bank and with a variety of other sources to form the Arab Latin American Bank with headquarters in Lima. Iran helped Peru finance the Trans-Andean pipeline and with Venezuela established a jointly owned maritime oil transportation company.

There have been frequent diplomatic exchanges to promote trade between the two regions. Since the breakup of the Soviet Union, this has been especially important for Cuba because of the long-standing U.S. embargo. In the 1990s and early twenty–first century Venezuela pushed OPEC to lower oil production to help bolster oil prices. In 2005 the Brazilian government hosted a summit to promote greater economic relations between the Middle East and Latin America.

See also **Nicaragua, Sandinista National Liberation Front (FSLN).**

BIBLIOGRAPHY

Roger W. Fontaine and James D. Theberge, eds., *Latin America's New Internationalism: The End of Hemispheric Isolation* (1976), esp. pp. 172–196.

Edward S. Milenky, "Latin America: New World or Third World in International Affairs?" in *Europa-Archiv* (1977).

Edy Kaufman, Yoram Shapira, and Joel Barromi, *Israel–Latin American Relations* (1979).

Fehmy Saddy, ed., *Arab–Latin American Relations: Energy, Trade, and Investment* (1983); "Arab League takes closer look at region; Syro-Lebanese & Palestinian immigration no longer ignored," *Latin America Weekly Report*, 23 April 1987.

Damian J. Fernández, *Cuba's Foreign Policy in the Middle East* (1988).

Damian J. Fernández, ed., *Central America and the Middle East: The Internationalization of the Crises* (1990).

Joann Fagot Aviel, "Arab-Iranian Relations with Nicaragua," in *Review of Latin American Studies* 3, no. 2 (1991).

Additional Bibliography

Agar Corbinos, Lorenzo, and Raymundo Kabchi. *El mundo árabe y América Latina*. Madrid: Ediciones UNESCO, 1997.

Klich, Ignacio, and Jeff Lesser, eds. *Arab and Jewish Immigrants in Latin America: Images and Realities*. London and Portland, OR: F. Cass, 1998.

Ramírez, Ma. Dolores, María M. Caballero, and Pablo Beneito. *Raíces mediterráneas en Latinoamérica: Cultura árabe, cultura italiana*. Sevilla, Spain: Mergablum, 2001.

Roberts, Lois J. *The Lebanese Immigrants in Ecuador: A History of Emerging Leadership*. Boulder, CO: Westview Press, 2000.

Velcamp, Theresa Alfaro. "Immigrant Positioning in Twentieth-Century Mexico: Middle Easterners, Foreign Citizens and Multiculturalism." *Hispanic American Historical Review* 86, no. 1 (2006): 901–911.

JoAnn Fagot Aviel

ARACAJU. Aracaju is the capital and only significant city in the small state of Sergipe in northeastern Brazil. With a population of about 470,000 (2000 estimate), Aracaju is a port city and regional economic center located on the Rio Sergipe approximately six miles from the coast. Its name derives from the cashew nut trees that abound in the area. Unlike other northeastern capitals established in the colonial era, Aracaju was not founded until 1855. Its creation as a new capital to replace São Cristóvão with its inadequate port was expected to further local economic development. Its grid pattern is unusual among Brazilian cities.

Aracaju's population surpassed that of all other cities in the state by the 1890s, and the relative concentration of the state's population there continued to increase with the building of railroad lines during World War I. Agricultural products such as hides, cotton, and sugar historically dominated the commerce of the port; local industry has centered on the processing of these and other agricultural products. The state's first textile plant was established there in 1884; in the early decades of the twentieth century, the city exported a significant percentage of its textiles to other Brazilian states, including Rio de Janeiro, Rio

Grande do Sul, and Pernambuco. The state's production of sugar and cotton declined in the 1940s due to competition from southern states. Migration from the countryside to the city began to grow significantly in the following decades, particularly after the 1960s. In 1970 Petrobrás, the national oil company, established a regional office there, and offshore oil drilling has expanded considerably since the late 1970s. There have been some efforts made to create an infrastructure for tourism, although the city lags behind other northeastern coastal cities in this area.

See also **Brazil: Brazil Since 1889; Petrobrás.**

BIBLIOGRAPHY

Andrade, Rosane P. *Aracaju, Sergipe*. São Paulo: Editora Rios, 1986.

Cabral, Mário. *Roteiro de Aracaju*, 2nd edition. Aracaju: Livraria Regina Limitada, 1955.

Diniz, José Alexandre Felizola. *O Subsistema Urbano Regional de Aracaju*. Recife: SUDENE, 1987.

Graça, Tereza Cristina Cerqueira da. *Pés de Anjo e Letreiros de Neon: Ginasianos no Aracaju dos Anos Dourados*. Aracaju: Universidade Federal de Sergipe, 2002.

Ibge-Sudene. *Aracaju e sua Região*. Rio de Janeiro: Instituto Brasileiro de Geografia, 1971.

Ribeiro, Neuza Maria Góis. *Transformações do Espaço Urbano: O Caso de Aracaju*. Recife: Editora Massangana, 1989.

Silva, Nilton Pedro da, and Dean Lee Hansen. *Economia Regional e Outros Ensaios*. Aracaju: Universidade Federal de Sergipe, 2001.

Cara Shelly

ARADA, BATTLE OF. Battle of Arada (February 2, 1851). José Francisco Barrundia, Doroteo Vasconcelos, José Dolores Nufio, and other Central American liberals sought to oust Guatemalan caudillo Rafael Carrera, but Guatemalan troops resisted the raids of their National Army in 1850. After Barrundia was elected president of the Representación Nacional at Chinandega, Nicaragua, on January 9, 1851, the group plotted a new invasion, even though the Chinandega Diet refused to sanction it. They entered Guatemala on January 22, 1851 with the intention of taking Guatemala City. Skillfully outmaneuvering his enemy, Carrera routed them at San José la Arada, south of Chiquimula, in the most stunning victory of his military career. Remnants of the National Army straggled into Honduras and El Salvador, pursued by Carrera, who carried out a deliberate campaign of reprisal until the Salvadoran government came to terms on August 17, 1853.

His victory at Arada brought Carrera enormous prestige and assured his return to the Guatemalan presidency and establishment of an authoritarian dictatorship. Arada ended the efforts of Barrundia and the middle-state liberals to reorganize the federation and destroyed Salvadoran pretensions of leadership of a new federation.

See also **Barrundia, José Francisco.**

BIBLIOGRAPHY

Pedro Zamora Castellanos, *Vida militar de Centro América* (1924).

José N. Rodríguez, *Estudios de historia militar de Centro-América* (1930), pp. 218–223.

Manuel Rubio Sánchez, *El Mariscal de campo José Clara Lorenzana* (1987), pp. 47–71.

Ralph Lee Woodward, Jr., *Rafael Carrera and the Emergence of the Republic of Guatemala* (1992).

Additional Bibliography

Gudmundson, Lowell, and Héctor Lindo-Fuentes. *Central America, 1821–1871: Liberalism before Liberal Reform.* Tuscaloosa: University of Alabama Press, 1995.

Leiva Vivas, Rafael. *La unión centroamericana: Utopía, lirismo y desafío.* Tegucigalpa, Guatemala: ENAG (Empresa Nacional Artes Gráficas), 2004.

RALPH LEE WOODWARD JR.

ARAGON. Aragon, northeastern region and former kingdom of Spain united with Castile through the marriage of Ferdinand II and Isabella I.

The states of Catalonia, Aragon, and Valencia composed the crown of Aragon, which in the thirteenth and fourteenth centuries acquired a commercial empire in the Mediterranean. Aragonese prosperity was eclipsed in the fifteenth century by plague, civil war, and a financial crisis which led to a decline in trade and industry. Although the marriage of the "Catholic kings" (1469) united the crowns of Castile and Aragon, the three Aragonese states retained separate courts (*cortes*) and distinct feudal privileges (fueros), which limited the Castilian monarch's ability to raise armies and taxes. However, this unification, alongside the defeat of the Moors, gave the kingdom the necessary stability to look to overseas commerce. Consequently, Ferdinand and Isabella funded Christopher Columbus's expedition to find a new trade route to the Indies. This project ultimately led to Europe's invasion of the New World.

When the Aragonese sensed an infringement on their traditional liberties by the Spanish crown, they characteristically rebelled (1591–1592, 1640–1652). In the War of the Spanish Succession (1701–1714) Aragon supported the Archduke Charles of Austria, and consequently Philip V abolished its political privileges (1716) as punishment for supporting his rival claimant to the Spanish throne.

See also **Castile.**

BIBLIOGRAPHY

Gerald Brenan, *The Spanish Labyrinth* (1943), esp. pp. 87–130.

John H. Elliott, *Imperial Spain, 1469–1716* (1963), esp. pp. 17–43, 273–280, 317–353.

Raymond Carr, *Spain 1808–1975,* 2d ed. (1982), esp. pp. 1–78.

Henry Kamen, *Spain, 1469–1714: A Society of Conflict* (1983, 2d ed. 1991) esp. pp. 9–15, 139–144, 235–240.

Additional Bibliography

Cawsey, Suzanne F. *Kingship and Propaganda: Royal Eloquence and the Crown of Aragon, C. 1200–1450.* Oxford: Clarendon Press, 2002.

López Pérez, María Dolores. *La corona de Aragón y el Magreb en el siglo XIV, 1331–1410.* Barcelona: Consejo Superior de Investigaciones Científicas, 1995.

SUZANNE HILES BURKHOLDER

ARAGUAIA RIVER. Araguaia River, a waterway that rises southwest of Goiás in Brazil and flows northward, forming the natural border between the states of Goiás and Mato Grosso and Tocantins and Pará, and covering a distance of 1,366 miles. It joins the Tocantins River at Bico do Papagaio. Midway through its course, the Araguaia separates into two branches that enclose the island of Bananal, the largest fluvial island in the world. Its basin covers 150,000 square miles. Without a firm riverbed, the Araguaia is long and shallow and includes many lakes with broad, white-sand beaches. During the summer, it floods well beyond its banks. Navigation is difficult, and until recently human habitation along the river has been scarce.

During the seventeenth century, explorations and raids out of São Paulo and Belém reached as far as the Araguaia in search of Indians from the various tribes in the region: Caiapó, Javaé, Carajá, Chambioá, Crixá, Xavánte, and Apinagé. The mining industry in Goiás and Mato Grosso during the eighteenth century did not contribute to the growth of the area's population. In the nineteenth century, the government of Goiás tried to encourage the formation of settlements in order to make navigation to the Pará possible. To this end military detachments were established at Leopoldina (today Aruaña), São José, and Santa Maria (today Araguacema), but the effort was not successful. It was not until the 1960s that true habitation of the valley occurred, aided by new means of communication as well as farming and ranching projects. Owing to the Araguaia's abundance of fish and to its beaches, tourism has developed into a growing industry.

On 26 October 1999 a federal court in Cuiabá suspended the licensing process of the Tocantins-Araguaia Hidrovia, an industrial waterway for transporting cargo, finding that its construction along the Tocantis and Araguaia Rivers would have benefited only agribusiness corporations and shipping and construction companies. However, the construction of small dams along the river has affected aquatic life and wetlands and resulted in increased catastrophic floods, principally affecting riverbank dwellers and indigenous communities.

See also **Brazil, Geography.**

BIBLIOGRAPHY

Dalísia Elisabeth Martins Doles, *As comunicações fluviais pelo Tocantins e Araguaia no século XIX* (1973).

Couto De Magalhães, *Viagem ao Araguaia*, 7th ed. (1975).

Additional Bibliography

Almeida, R. *Araguaia-Tocantins: Fios de uma História camponesa*. Brasilia: Fórum Carajás, 2006.

Borges, Durval. *Rio Araguaia, corpo e alma*. São Paulo: Editorial Universidad de São Paulo, 1987.

De Mirada, Lima. *O Dia–A–Dia no Araguaia*. Goiânia, Brasil: Gráfica e Editora Lider, 1989.

Esterci, Neide. *Conflito no Araguaia: Peões e posseiros contra a grande empresa*. Petrópolis, Brasil: Vozes, 1987.

Gómez, Desider Kremling. "Brasil: Los bosques amazónicos, situación actual y perspectivas." In *Amazonía: Selva y Bosques diez años después de Río,* Edited by Censat-Agua Viva. Colombia, Brasil: Censat-Agua Viva, 2002.

LUIS PALACÍN

ARAMAYO FAMILY. Aramayo family, a wealthy silver and tin dynasty of the nineteenth- and twentieth-century Bolivian oligarchy. The first members in the New World were a Spanish silver miner, Diego Ortiz de Aramayo, from Navarre, and a Chichas landowner, Francisco Ortiz de Aramayo. Francisco's son, Isidoro Ortiz de Aramayo, was the father of José Avelino, born on 25 September 1809 in Moraya, a small town in the province of Sud Chichas. A mining industrialist, writer, and public servant, José Avelino founded the tin dynasty. A self-made man and a mining innovator, he bought silver mines in Potosí and, with European associates, began mechanizing Bolivian silver mining. As a writer and national deputy, he opposed the crude military despotism of Manuel Isidoro Belzu, Mariano Melgarejo, and Agustín Morales. At his death in Paris on 1 May 1882, he reportedly left more debts than riches to his descendants.

On 23 June 1846, José's son Félix Avelino was born in Paris. In the family tradition he became a mining industrialist, writer, and noted diplomat. In 1901, while serving as Bolivia's ambassador to London, he gave an Anglo-American company, the Bolivian Syndicate of New York, concessionary rights to the rubber-rich Acre region to prevent further Brazilian encroachments. War ensued, however, and Bolivia ceded the territory to Brazil in the 1903 Treaty of Petrópolis. As part of Félix Avelino's modernization of the family tin and bismuth mines, he incorporated the Aramayo, Francke Company in London in 1906. Before his death in 1929, he passed control to his son Carlos Víctor, who internationalized family holdings by founding the Compagnie Aramayo des Mines de Bolivie in Geneva in 1916.

Carlos Víctor was born in Paris on 7 October 1889, and died there in April 1981. One of Bolivia's three tin barons (with Simón Patiño and Mauricio Hochschild), he epitomized the Aramayo dynasty's zenith. Critics charged that the family's wealth, second in the country, benefited neither the state nor the mine workers. Although their share of national tin output averaged only 7 percent, the Aramayos exerted enormous political influence. Carlos Víctor bankrolled the Republican Party and owned La Paz's reactionary newspaper, *La Razón*. He successfully plotted with Hochschild and Patiño against reformist governments of the 1930s and 1940s, but failed to prevent revolution and expropriation in 1952.

See also **Tin Industry.**

BIBLIOGRAPHY

Ernesto O. Rück, *Centenario de Aramayo* (1909).

Adolfo Costa Du Rels, *Félix Avelino Aramayo y su época, 1846–1929* (1942).

David Fox, *The Bolivian Tin Mining Industry* (1967).

Alfonso Crespo, *Los Aramayo de Chichas, tres generaciones de mineros bolivianos* (1981).

Additional Bibliography

Albarracín Millán, Juan. *El poder financiero de la gran minería boliviana.* La Paz, Bolivia: Ediciones AKA-PANA, 1995.

Arce, Roberto. *Desarrollo económico e histórico de la minería en Bolivia.* La Paz, Bolivia: Plural Editores, 2003.

WALTRAUD QUEISER MORALES

ARAMBURU, PEDRO EUGENIO

(1905–1970). An Argentine politician and military man, Pedro Eugenio Aramburu was de facto president of the nation from 1955 to 1958 and was assassinated by the Montoneros guerrilla organization in 1970. He studied at the Colegio Militar de la Nación, was director of the School of War and headed the Revolución Libertadora (Freedom Revolution) that toppled President Juan Domingo Perón on 21 September 1955. A representative of the liberal segment of the army, that same year he replaced General Eduardo Lonardi (who had a policy of conciliation towards the Peronists) and assumed the Argentine presidency.

The proscription of Peronism began during his administration, and labor unions were taken over. It was even prohibited to mention the name of Perón, who came to be called the "fugitive tyrant." In economic affairs Aramburu implemented the Prebisch Plan, an attempt to modernize the economy by stimulating investment and freezing workers' wages, and under his tenure Argentina joined the International Monetary Fund. As president, Aramburu authorized the execution of legalist military members who rose against the de facto government in June 1956.

In 1958, with Peronism proscribed, Aramburu called for elections and retired from military activity. In the presidential elections of 1963 he stood as a candidate for the Union of the Argentine People Party, but was defeated by the Radical Civic Union Party's ticket of Arturo Umberto Illia and Carlos H. Perette (1915–1992). In 1970 he made some moves aimed at reconciliation with Peronism and national pacification, but he was kidnapped on May 29 of that year in the first armed action of the Peronist guerrilla movement, the Montoneros. His captors gave him a "revolutionary trial" and executed him on June 1. The act was a heavy blow to the military dictatorship and divided public opinion. Four years later, his killers gave a detailed account of the assassination in *La Causa Peronista* magazine.

See also **Montoneros; Perón, Juan Domingo; Prebisch, Raúl.**

BIBLIOGRAPHY

Fraga, Rosendo. *Aramburu: la biografía.* Buenos Aires: Javier Vergara, 2005.

Gillespie, Richard. *Montoneros: Soldados de Perón.* Buenos Aires: Grijalbo, 1987.

Potash, Robert. *El ejército y la política en Argentina.* Buenos Aires: Emecé, 1971.

Romero, Luis Alberto. *Breve historia contemporánea de la Argentina*, 2nd edition. Buenos Aires: Fondo de Cultura Económica, 2001.

VICENTE PALERMO

ARANA, FELIPE DE (1786–1865).

Felipe de Arana (*b*. 23 August 1786; *d*. 11 July 1865), Argentine landowner and official. Born in Buenos Aires to a merchant family, Arana took a law degree in Chile, then returned to Buenos Aires to participate in the revolution of May 1810. He was president of the House of Representatives in 1828 during the first government of Juan Manuel de Rosas and was appointed minister of foreign affairs when Rosas returned to office in 1835. His policy was nationalist in tendency, and he negotiated treaties (1840 and 1850) that ended French intervention in the Río de la Plata. But Arana had few ideas of his own, and on domestic as well as foreign policy was little more than a mouthpiece of Rosas. During the terror of 1840–1842 he was deputy governor of Buenos Aires.

See also **Argentina: The Nineteenth Century.**

BIBLIOGRAPHY

H. S. Ferns, *Britain and Argentina in the Nineteenth Century* (1960).

Ernesto H. Celesia, *Rosas: Aportes para su historia*, 2d ed., 2 vols. (1968–1969).

JOHN LYNCH

ARANA, FRANCISCO J. (1905–1949).

Francisco J. Arana (*b.* 1905; *d.* 18 July 1949), chief of the armed forces of Guatemala (1945–1949). A leader of the October revolution of 1944, Arana became a member of a three-man revolutionary junta that supervised the transition to the democratic and reformist government of Juan José Arévalo in March 1945. As Arévalo's chief of the armed forces, he suppressed a number of attempted coups by right-wing landowners and reactionary officers. Entertaining presidential ambitions of his own, he eventually courted the right-wing opposition to the revolution by promising to curb the growing influence of communism. The other presidential aspirant, Colonel Jacobo Arbenz Guzmán, another hero of the 1944 revolution, pursued a left-wing agenda with the support of leftist labor unions. Political rivalry between Arana and Arbenz intensified in the summer of 1949. Arana was allegedly plotting the takeover of the government when he was shot resisting arrest by partisans of Arbenz. The suppression of the revolt that followed Arana's assassination cleared the way for Arbenz's election in 1950.

See also **Arbenz Guzmán, Jacobo; Arévalo Bermejo, Juan José.**

BIBLIOGRAPHY

Piero Gleijeses, *Shattered Hope: The Guatemalan Revolution and the United States, 1944–1954* (1991).

Richard H. Immerman, *The CIA in Guatemala: The Foreign Policy of Intervention* (1982).

Additional Bibliography

Aguilar de León, Juan de Dios. *El asesinato del coronel Francisco Javier Arana en el Puente de la Gloria, el 18 de julio de 1949.* Guatemala, 1995.

Gleijeses, Piero. "The Death of Francisco Arana: A Turning Point in the Guatemalan Revolution," *Journal of Latin American Studies* 22: 3 (October 1990), pp. 537–552.

PAUL J. DOSAL

ARANA, JULIO CÉSAR (1864–1952).

Julio César Arana (*b.* 1864; *d.* 1952), a Peruvian businessman who exploited rubber and other jungle products in the Putumayo River lowlands of northeastern Peru. By 1903, after some twenty years of work, he had set up the largest natural rubber-gathering business of the era. He controlled Amazon lands totaling 25 million acres, importing men from the British Caribbean colonies as overseers and workers and using members of local tribes as actual rubber gatherers. The company demanded that the workers meet daily quotas. Many were beaten, and some were murdered if they did not comply. News of enslavement and terror in the rubber camps eventually reached human rights groups. An international scandal developed after British diplomat Roger Casement witnessed the abuses in 1910 and reported that the native population had been reduced by four-fifths. Pressure from the United States and England in 1910 led the Peruvian government to force Arana to stop the worst abuses, and his power declined as the natural rubber boom ended.

See also **Rubber Industry.**

BIBLIOGRAPHY

Fredrick B. Pike, *The Modern History of Peru* (1967), p. 194.

Thomas M. Davies, Jr., *Indian Integration in Peru: A Half Century of Experience, 1900–1948* (1974).

Additional Bibliography

Aguirre, Carlos. *The Criminals of Lima and Their Worlds: The Prison Experience, 1850-1935.* Durham, NC: Duke University Press, 2005.

Klarén, Peter F. *Peru: Society and Nationhood in the Andes.* New York: Oxford University Press, 2000.

Mallon, Florencia E. *Peasant and Nation: The Making of Postcolonial Mexico and Peru.* Berkeley: University of California Press, 1995.

VINCENT PELOSO

ARANA OSORIO, CARLOS (1918–2003).

Carlos Arana Osorio (*b.* 17 July 1918, *d.* 6 December 2003), president of Guatemala (1970–1974). Born in Barbareña, Santa Rosa, Arana pursued a military career. Graduating from the Escuela Politécnica in 1939, he rose rapidly as a military officer, achieving the rank of lieutenant colonel in 1952. During the presidency of Julio César Méndez Montenegro (1966–1970), he directed a counterinsurgency campaign that earned him the title "Butcher of Zacapa." Allegedly head of the Mano Blanca (White Hand), a right-wing terrorist organization, he was implicated in the plot to delegitimize the left by kidnapping archbishop Mario Casariego in 1968.

In 1970 Arana was elected president in a campaign marked by violence and fraud. His presidency was characterized by repression and economic nationalism. State planning produced marked increases in public investment and economic growth. After leaving office he remained politically influential through the CAN (Central Auténtica Nacional), until a few years before his death in 2003.

See also **Guatemala.**

BIBLIOGRAPHY

George Black, *Garrison Guatemala* (1984).

Michael McClintock, *The American Connection,* Vol. 2, *State Terror and Popular Resistance in Guatemala* (1985).

James Dunkerley, *Power in the Isthmus: A Political History of Modern Central America* (1988).

Additional Bibliography

Schirmer, Jennifer G. *The Guatemalan Military Project: A Violence Called Democracy.* Philadelphia: University of Pennsylvania Press, 1998.

Sichar Moreno, Gonzalo. *Guatemala, contrainsurgencia o contra el pueblo?: Crónica de una guerra no declarada y una paz firmada: Historia de los partidos políticos guatemaltecos.* Madrid: H+H, 1998.

ROLAND H. EBEL

ARANGO, DÉBORA (1907–2005).

Débora Arango (*b.* 11 November 1907, *d.* 5 December 2005), Colombian artist. Born in Medellín, Arango studied with Eladio Vélez in the Medellín Institute of Fine Arts, from 1933 to 1935, first displaying her works in 1937. Her bold and expressive use of color and contrast, often of exaggerated human forms, inspired heated debate over the morality of herself and her work, especially from the Roman Catholic Church in Bogotá. Indeed, Arango's innovative and vibrant oil and watercolor paintings of provocative nudes shocked many sectors of Colombian society in the 1940s.

Arango then turned to social criticism, often from a feminist perspective, focusing upon such themes as prostitutes and popular culture. Her work of the late 1940s and 1950s, which retained its highly political and anticlerical character, much in the style of the caricaturist Ricardo Rendón (1894–1931), placed her in the vanguard of Colombian abstract art. In the 1950s, Arango traveled to England and Paris, where she added ceramics to her repertoire. She became professor at the Institute of Fine Arts in 1959.

See also **Art: The Twentieth Century.**

BIBLIOGRAPHY

Santiago Londoño, "Paganismo, denuncia y sátira en Débora Arango," in *Boletín Cultural y Bibliográfico* 22, no. 4 (1985): 2–16.

Additional Bibliography

Londono Vélez, Santiago, and Débora Arango Pérez. *Débora Arango: Vida de pintora.* Bogota: Ministerio de Cultura, República de Colombia, 1997.

Viveros, M., et al. *De mujeres, hombres y otras ficciones: Género y sexualidad en América Latina.* Bogota, Colombia: T/M Editores, 2006.

DAVID SOWELL

ARANGO Y PARREÑO, FRANCISCO DE (1765–1837).

Francisco de Arango y Parreño (*b.* 22 May 1765; *d.* 21 March 1837), Cuban statesman, economist, and sugar planter. Educated in Cuba and Spain, Arango y Parreño graduated with a degree in law and spent his life in public service, including representing the city of Havana to the court in Spain and as one of two representatives from the island to the Cortes of Cádiz. In 1792 he wrote the *Discourse on the Agriculture in Havana and Ways of Developing It* that called for development of the sugar industry, utilizing massive slave labor, a position he modified after the Haitian Revolution. He returned to Cuba and, with the cooperation of Governor Luis de las Casas, shifted the focus of the island's economy to development of sugar. He also co-owned one of the five largest plantations on the island. He served as director of the Economic Society in 1795 but believed its function less important than that of the *consulado,* of which he was also a member. He contributed articles to the *Papel Periódico* favoring government intervention to develop the sugar industry and hinder the Spanish monopolies. His writings and his defense of Cuba in Spain helped form the liberal Cuban mind of the period. The major effect of his policies on the island, however, was the growth of the sugar industry, and its benefit to those who are now referred to as the "sugarocracy."

See also **Cuban American Sugar Company; Sugar Industry.**

BIBLIOGRAPHY

Arango's life and work are examined in detail in Ramiro Guerra y Sánchez, et al., eds., *A History of the Cuban Nation,* vol. 3, translated by Raoul L. Washington (1958).

Manuel Moreno Fraginals, *The Sugarmill: The Socioeconomic Complex of Sugar in Cuba 1760–1860,* translated by Cedric Belfrage (1976).

W. W. Pierson, Jr., "Francisco de Arango y Parreño," in *Hispanic American Historical Review* 16 (November 1936): 451–478.

Additional Bibliography

Monal, Isabel, and Olivia Miranda Francisco. *Pensamiento cubano, siglo XIX* vol. 1. Havana: Editorial de Ciencias Sociales, 2002.

Morillo-Alicea, Javier. "The Wealth of Empire: Francisco Arango y Parreño, Political Economy, and the Second Slavery in Cuba." In *Interpreting Spanish Colonialism: Empires, Nations, and Legends,* edited by Christopher Schmidt-Nowara and John M. Nieto-Phillips. Albuquerque: University of New Mexico Press, 2005.

JACQUELYN BRIGGS KENT

ARANHA, OSWALDO (1894–1960).

Oswaldo Aranha (*b.* 15 February 1894; *d.* 27 January 1960), Brazilian politician and diplomat. Aranha was part of the clique from Rio Grande do Sul that came to national prominence after the Revolution of 1930. A close friend of Getúlio Vargas, Aranha was one of the architects of the Revolution of 1930. He served successively as minister of justice and minister of finance in the provisional government (1930–1934) and helped Vargas establish national authority by turning the blame for Brazil's economic crises away from the elite classes. From 1934 to 1937 Aranha served as Brazilian ambassador to the United States and became convinced that Brazil should ally itself with the United States, not with Germany. In 1938 he became foreign minister and moved Brazil into a clear pro-Allied role first as a supplier of raw materials, and later as a supplier of troops who fought in Italy.

Although often identified as a "liberal" member of the Estado Novo, Aranha viewed race, ethnicity, and class as determinants of intelligence and success, and he shaped Brazil's immigration laws to attract urban professionals at the expense of rural laborers. From 1947 to 1948 Aranha served as president of the General Assembly of the United Nations, where he increased Brazil's international presence and is best known for presiding over the partition of Palestine. In 1953 Aranha was appointed minister of finance in the democratically elected Vargas government. Aranha withdrew from public life following the suicide of Vargas in 1954 but remained an active member of the Partida Trabalhista Brasileiro until his death.

See also **Brazil, Revolutions: Revolution of 1930.**

BIBLIOGRAPHY

Frank McCann, *The Brazilian–American Alliance, 1937–1945* (1973).

Stanley Hilton, *Brazil and the Great Powers, 1930–1939; The Politics of Trade Rivalry* (1975).

Boris Fausto, *A revolução de 1930* (1986).

Additional Bibliography

Corrêa do Lago, Luiz A. *Oswaldo Aranha, o Rio Grande e a Revolução de 1930: Um político gaucho na República Velha.* Rio de Janeiro: Editora Nova Fronteira, 1995.

This work uses family records not open to other researchers.

Hilton, Stanley E. *Oswaldo Aranha: uma biografia*. Rio de Janeiro: Editora Objetiva, 1994.

JEFFREY LESSER

ARAU, ALFONSO

ARAU, ALFONSO (1932–). A Mexican actor and director, Alfonso Arau emerged in the early 1990s as one of the most successful filmmakers in Latin America. Born on January 11, 1932, he studied acting and dancing and, later, pantomime in Paris. Arau created a dance team with Sergio Corona and hosted a television program in Havana. As an actor he appeared in numerous films in Mexico and, later, Hollywood. As a director his films include *Picking Up the Pieces* (2000), *To Catch a Falling Star* (2000), *Un paseo por las nubes* (*A Walk in the Clouds*, 1995), *Chido guan* (*Tacos de oro*, 1984), *Mojado Power* (1979), *Caribe, estrella y águila* (1976), *Calzonzin inspector* (1974), and *El águila descalza* (1971). This Mexican filmmaker reached the pinnacle of art-house idolatry when he adapted a best-selling novel about the mystical aspects of gourmet cooking, written by his then wife, Laura Esquivel. *Cómo agua para chocolate* (*Like Water for Chocolate*, 1992), whose script was also written by Esquivel, was met with worldwide acclaim and became the highest-grossing foreign-language film up to that time in the United States.

See also **Cinema: From the Silent Film to 1990; Cinema: Since 1990.**

BIBLIOGRAPHY

Ciuk, Perla. *Diccionario de directores del cine mexicano*. Mexico: Consejo Nacional para la Cultura y las Artes (CONACULTA) y Cineteca Nacional, 2000.

JUAN CARLOS GRIJALVA

ARAUCANA, LA.

ARAUCANA, LA. *La Araucana*, Spanish epic poem in thirty-seven cantos and three parts (Part 1, 1569; Part 2, 1578; Part 3, 1589), written by Alonso de Ercilla y Zúñiga (1533–1594). Its stanzas (in ottava rima) narrate the warfare between the invading Spaniards and the Araucanians of southern Chile from the arrival of the conquistador Pedro de Valdivia to the years 1557–1558, at which point Ercilla was a soldier in Chile. The poem follows the course of events very closely, though with a number of imaginative flourishes. By 1632 no less than eighteen editions of the epic had appeared, a tribute to its widespread popularity. *La Araucana* was praised by Cervantes in *Don Quixote* and was admired by Voltaire. It was the first book to bring Chile to the attention of Europe, and in Chile itself it is regarded as a national classic.

While *La Araucana* offers some sympathetic portraits of the Native American population and criticisms of Spanish actions, the text ultimately reaffirms Spain's colonial project. Moreover, this epic also highlights tensions between Europe empires. Reaction to imperial competition from Portugal caused Ercilla to increasingly praise and advertise Spanish culture in Part 2.

The sixth stanza of Canto 1, beginning "*Chile fértil provincia y señalada / En la región antártica famosa*" (Chile, fertile province / located in the famous southern region) can be recited by most educated Chileans. The classic modern study of the poem is a five-volume work (1910–1918) by Chilean scholar José Toribio Medina.

See also **Ercilla y Zúñiga, Alonso de; Literature: Spanish America; Mapuche.**

BIBLIOGRAPHY

F. Rand Morton, *Notes on the History of a Literary Genre: The Renaissance Epic in Spain and America*. Ph.D. dissertation. Harvard University, 1958.

Alonso de Ercilla y Zúñiga, *La Araucana*, edited by Olivo Lazzarín Dante (1977).

Additional Bibliography

Ercilla y Zúñiga, Alonso de. *La Araucana*. Madrid: Ediciones Cátedra, 2003.

Davis, Elizabeth B. *Myth and Identity in the Epic of Imperial Spain*. Columbia: University of Missouri, 2000.

Mejías-López, William. "La relación ideológica de Alonso de Ercilla con Francisco de Vitoria y fray Bartolomé de las Casas." *Revista Iberoamericana* 61 (170-171) (Jan-June 1995): 197-217.

Nicolopulos, James. *The Poetics of Empire in the Indies: Prophecy and Imitation in La Araucana and Os lusíadas*. University Park: Pennsylvania State University Press, 2000.

SIMON COLLIER

ARAUCANIANS. Araucanians (*Araucano* in Spanish), historical term used to refer to indigenous peoples in the southern cone exclusive of Tierra del Fuego and Patagonia. The etymology of the word "Araucanian" is unclear, but it was used in the earliest Spanish observations of the native inhabitants in southern Chile (see, for example, Pedro de Valdivia's letters and chronicles and Alonso de Ercilla y Zúñiga's epic poem *La Araucana*). Some believe the word derives from the terms used by the Inca (*Aucas* or *Promaucas,* from the Quechua *purem,* "wild enemy," and *auka,* "rebel") to refer to the southern peoples they were unable to conquer. The term *Araucano* (sometimes *Auca*) was used by colonial and military officials in documents and literature to refer to native inhabitants encountered in the southern colonial frontier (Chile and Argentina). Scholars continue to use the term, although there is growing preference for *Mapuche* (*mapu,* meaning "land," and *che,* "people," in Mapundungun), the name used by the people to refer to themselves.

The Araucanian world in the sixteenth century encompassed the valleys and coasts, and transcordilleran highlands of the southern Andes, ranging south of the Bío-Bío River to the northern regions of Chiloe along the western slopes of the cordillera and extending into the eastern precordillera to the headwaters of the Río Chubut and Río Colorado.

A common language encoded shared cultural understandings about social organization and religious beliefs and linked the Araucanians. An exogamous kinship system allowed the expansion of Araucanian family groups, which were loosely organized according to specific territorial claims. Each individual kin group, though related to other groups by shared linguistic and ceremonial forms, retained autonomy. The autonomous decision-making power of each kin leader was maintained over the centuries, even though at different times the Araucanians joined together to form bands, tribes, and even confederations in their attempts to maintain cultural and political independence.

The Araucanians resisted the incursion of the Inca in the mid-fifteenth and early sixteenth century, and their experience prepared the Araucanians to resist the Spaniards as well. While it is possible that earlier contacts between individual Araucanians and Spanish explorers may have gone unrecorded, the first sustained encounter began with the arrival of Pedro de Valdivia and the founding of Concepción in 1550 near the Bío-Bío River. There followed over three centuries of warfare and resistance to Spanish conquest on the part of the Araucanians.

Araucanian experience in maintaining a defensive frontier against Inca and Spanish forces in the fifteenth and sixteenth centuries also prepared them militarily and technically to expand their activities into the south and to the east in the late eighteenth and nineteenth centuries. In this process, the exogamous nature of Araucanian social relations facilitated the incorporation of neighboring peoples, including the linguistically and culturally related Pehuenches (fifteenth–seventeenth centuries) and later the more distantly linked Pampas (also called Puelche) and Tehuelches (eighteenth–nineteenth centuries), bands of the Gününa kёna linguistic family which had roamed the pampas and southern Patagonian steppes for millennia.

When Araucanians and Pehuenches from the cordillera began to send hunting and raiding parties (Malones) into the pampas east of the cordillera (late seventeenth–eighteenth centuries), they came into conflict with the Creole ranching interests there. When competition with Chilean colonists for control of fertile land in southern Chile accelerated in the early nineteenth century, increasing numbers of Araucanians moved from the eastern cordilleran highlands and precordillera to settle in permanent encampments in the Argentine pampas. In this epoch, the Araucanians enjoyed a cultural and economic renaissance, expanding their material and ceremonial base through raids and alliances to coalesce into powerful intertribal confederations.

Traditionally, the Araucanians have been treated as interesting but marginal forces in the historiography of both Chile and Argentina. Because primary archival sources tend to be located either in Chile or in Argentina, knowledge of the Araucanian world prior to their ultimate military conquest in the late nineteenth century tends to be colored by nationalistic concerns. The story of Araucanian military resistance to Spanish conquest was recast by creole independence leaders in the nineteenth century as emblematic of a Chilean nationalism. Public statuary in Santiago immortalized as a national hero Lautaro, the Araucanian warrior held responsible for Valdivia's capture and death in 1553, at the same time that government policies of "pacification" eroded Mapuche lives and property in the south. On the other side of the cordillera, the Araucanians traditionally have been viewed as invading hordes who plagued the expansion of the southern Argentine frontier in the eighteenth and nineteenth centuries, although in Argentina, too, the Araucanians on occasion have been cast as symbols of independence and nationalism, as exemplified by the first Montoneros in the early nineteenth century.

More recent analytical approaches to Araucanian history, which have led to a reassessment of the role of the Araucanians, tend to view them as significant actors who participated in fundamental ways in the history of both Chile and Argentina.

See also **Anthropology; Indigenous Peoples; Valdivia, Pedro de.**

BIBLIOGRAPHY

Julian H. Steward, ed., *Handbook of South American Indians,* vol. 2 (1946), pp. 687–766.

Louis Faron, *The Hawks of the Sun: Mapuche Morality and Its Ritual Attributes* (1964).

Bernardo Berdichewsky, "Araucanians," in *Encyclopedia of Indians of the Americas,* vol. 2 (1974).

Patricia J. Lyon, ed., *Native South Americans* (1974), pp. 327–342.

José Bengoa, *Historia del Pueblo Mapuche: Siglos XIX y XX* (1985).

Judith Ewell and William Beezeley, eds., *The Human Tradition in Latin America: The Nineteenth Century* (1989), pp. 175–187.

Leonardo León Solis, *Maloqueros y Conchavadores en Araucanía y las Pampas, 1700–1800* (1990).

Additional Bibliography

Ercilla y Zúñiga, Alonso de, and Isaías Lerner. *La Araucana.* Letras hispánicas, 359. Madrid: Cátedra, [1569, 1578 & 1589] 1998.

Mallon, Florencia E. *Courage Tastes of Blood: The Mapuche Community of Nicolás Ailío and the Chilean State, 1906–2001.* Radical perspectives. Durham, NC: Duke University Press, 2005.

KRISTINE L. JONES

ARAUJO, ARTURO (1878–1967). Arturo Araujo (*b.* 1878; *d.* 1 December 1967), president of El Salvador (1 March–2 December 1931). Arturo Araujo's presidential campaign and brief presidency revealed fundamental changes that had occurred in Salvadoran politics by 1930. Himself a member of the landowning oligarchy, Araujo was educated as an engineer in England and returned to El Salvador with pro-union sentiments and admiration for the British Labour Party. In June 1918, Araujo was the keynote speaker at the First Workers' Congress, held in the western town of Armenia, where he received the title of Benefactor of the Working Classes in General for his efforts on their behalf. The next year, Araujo made an unsuccessful bid for the presidency, then attempted to come to power through an invasion from Honduras in 1922. When Pío Romero Bosque declined to name his successor in the elections of 1930, Araujo and the Partido Laborista won with a platform based on Alberto Masferrer's nine-point *mínimum vital* program. He guaranteed adequate food, clothing, housing, education, and work for all Salvadorans and held out the promise of agrarian reform to the dispossessed rural population. However, government corruption and the Great Depression prevented the fulfillment of these campaign planks, and Araujo was overthrown in a coup engineered by his vice-president, General Maximiliano Hernández Martínez. Araujo's failed experiment with labor-based appeal resulted in fifty years of direct military rule in El Salvador and the elite's deep distrust of popular politics.

See also **El Salvador.**

BIBLIOGRAPHY

Julio Contreras Castro, *De cómo fue traicionado el presidente ingeniero Arturo Araujo por Maximiliano Hernández Martínez* (1944).

Thomas P. Anderson, *Matanza: El Salvador's Communist Revolt of 1932* (1971).

Rafael Guidos Véjar, *El ascenso del militarismo en El Salvador* (1980).

Additional Bibliography

Walter, Knut, and Phillip J. Williams. *Militarization and Demilitarization in El Salvador's Transition to Democracy.* Pittsburgh: University of Pittsburgh Press, 1997.

KAREN RACINE

ARAUJO, JUAN DE (1646–1712).

Juan de Araujo (*b.* 1646; *d.* 1712), Spanish composer active in Peru and Bolivia. Araújo was born in Villafranca de los Barros, Extremadura. He studied music in Lima, first with his father, and later at the University of San Marcos. It is possible that Torrejón y Velasco may have been Araujo's music teacher during the 1660s. For a while Araujo worked as choirmaster in churches in Panama, but around 1672 he was back in Lima, where he was ordained a priest and designated choirmaster of the cathedral of Lima, where he served until 1676. After spending some time in the area of Cuzco, in Peru, he traveled to Bolivia, where in 1680 he was appointed chapelmaster of the cathedral of La Plata, a position he retained until his death. In La Plata (now Sucre), one of the most influential and wealthy cities of the Viceroyalty of Peru, Araujo substantially expanded the musical library of the cathedral with Spanish and European religious music. He also formed several important boy choirs and during some celebrations conducted works for ten voices. He composed a number of pieces, including several religious works: a Passion, two Magnificats, three Lamentations, a Salve Regina, as well as religious hymns and other choral works, most of them now in the archives of the Sucre Cathedral and the seminary of San Antonio Abad in Cuzco. In more than 106 *villancicos* and *jácaras*, Araujo displayed a vivid wit in his adept utilization of the polychoral technique. The texts of the *villancicos* are taken from Spanish baroque poetry, usually accompanied by a harp. The collection of *villancicos* is now preserved at the Archives of the Musical Section of the Museo Histórico Nacional of Montevideo, Uruguay.

See also **Music: Art Music.**

BIBLIOGRAPHY

Robert Stevenson, *The Music of Peru* (1960).

Lauro Ayestarán, "El barroco musical hispano-Americano, los manuscritos de la iglesia de San Felipe Neri (Sucre, Bolivia), existentes en el Museo Histórico Nacional del Uruguay," in *Yearbook of the Interamerican Institute of Musical Research, Tulane University,* vol. 1 (1965); *New Grove Dictionary of Music and Musicians,* vol. 1 (1980).

Additional Bibliography

Houmard, Charles James. "A Historical and Musical Analysis of the Villancico Los Coflades de la Eztleya by Juan de Araujo." D.M.A. diss., University of Texas at Austin, 1999.

Susana Salgado

ARAÚJO LIMA, MARQUIS OF OLINDA, PEDRO DE (1793–1870).

Born on December 22, 1793, Araújo Lima was one of the most influential and dynamic political leaders responsible for political consolidation of the Brazilian empire. A graduate in canon law from the University of Coimbra, he began his public life in 1821, when he was elected as a member of the Cortes (the Portuguese Assembly) in Lisbon. After Independence he participated in the Brazilian Constituent Assembly in 1823. During the First Reign, Araújo Lima was briefly minister of the empire; he was also a member of the General Assembly of the empire, serving a series of terms from 1826 to 1837, before being elected senator from Pernambuco. While Dom Pedro II was still too young to become king, during the Regency period he participated in the conservative resistance that mounted an opposition to Father Diogo Antônio Feijó's governance, replacing him as the empire's last regent, from 1837 to 1840. He was also chairman of the Chamber of Deputies, minister, president of the Council of Ministers during the Second Reign, and a member of the Council of State by 1841 and for some years thereafter.

In his early days he participated in the intense parliamentary debates of the Portuguese and Brazilian constituents and encountered, throughout his trips to Europe, staunch English parliamentarians as well as the unconstitutional actions of Charles X of France. As regent he faced revolts in Bahia, Maranhão, and Rio Grande do Sul. He strongly supported proposals for centralization such as the Interpretation of the Amendment Act (1840) and the Reform of the Criminal Procedure Code (1841), bills inspired by monarchical conservatives who sought to curtail the privileges of the provincial assemblies and return control of political, administrative, and judicial power to a central authority. During his administration important initiatives were undertaken, such as the creation of the Colégio Dom Pedro II, the Brazilian Institute of Geography and History, and the Imperial Public Archives, as well as the reorganization of the Imperial Army. Araújo Lima's government represented the end of the liberal period of political and administrative decentralization. He contributed to the restoration of the monarchy's prestige and was part of the group that led the conservative reaction, defending a strong, centralized government as an antidote to disorder and chaos. As such he was among those responsible for consolidating the Brazilian empire by strengthening the monarchy and preserving both the slavocrat order and territorial unity.

Because he disagreed with the guidelines imposed by the Conservative Party through the Saquarema trinity (the given nickname of the three important politicians [Paolino Jose, Jose Rodrigues Torres, and Eusébio de Queirós]) especially on issues related to foreign affairs in the Rio de la Plata region, he gradually distanced himself from his former party colleagues. In 1858 he accepted the emperor's invitation to organize the ministry, pledging to continue the policy of reconciliation among the parties. Thereafter he drew closer to the liberals and became one of the founders of the Progressive Party, a new party formed by moderate conservatives and liberal politicians. In 1854 he received the title of Marquis of Olinda. His political, institutional, and administrative knowledge of imperial life and great talent for political negotiation made him one of the most powerful and influential political figures of the Second Reign. He died on June 7, 1870.

See also **Brazil: 1808-1889; Feijó, Diogo Antônio; Pedro II of Brazil.**

BIBLIOGRAPHY

Cascudo, Luis da Câmara. *O Marquez de Olinda e seu tempo (1793–1870)*. São Paulo: Companhia Editora Nacional, 1938.

Mattos, Ilmar Rohloff de. *O tempo Saquarema*. São Paulo: Editora Hucitec, 1987.

Nabuco, Joaquim. *Um estadista do Império*. 5th ed. Rio de Janeiro: Topbooks, 1997.

MARIA ELISA MÄDER

ARAWAKS. *See* **Caribs.**

ARBENZ GUZMÁN, JACOBO (1913–1971). Jacobo Arbenz Guzmán (*b.* 14 September 1913; *d.* 27 January 1971), president of Guatemala (1951–1954). Born in Quezaltenango to a Swiss immigrant father and a Guatemalan mother, Arbenz completed his military education in 1935 at the Escuela Politécnica, where he excelled in athletics. In 1939 he married the daughter of a wealthy Salvadoran planter, María Cristina Vilanova, who was alleged to have Communist sympathies.

Arbenz participated in the movement to overthrow President Jorge Ubico in July 1944, going into exile when he became disillusioned with Ubico's successor, General Federico Ponce Vaides. He joined the October Revolution against Ponce and became a member of the triumvirate that conducted the elections of December 1944, which brought Juan José Arévalo to power.

Named minister of defense by President Arévalo, Arbenz began to maneuver to succeed him. He also used his position to obtain the necessary bank loans to enable him to become a wealthy landowner. Faced with formidable political opposition from armed forces chief Major Francisco Javier Arana, Arbenz conspired with Arévalo to have him assassinated while investigating an illegal arms cache on 18 July 1949. This provoked a military uprising that was put down when Arbenz distributed arms to students and workers. Now the undisputed head of the Revolution and backed by a coalition made up of the military, many peasants, the trade unions, government employees, and a number of centrist and left-wing parties (named the Unidad Nacional), he was overwhelmingly elected president in November 1950.

Although perceived in the United States as either Communist or under Communist influence, the Arbenz regime can best be understood as populist and nationalist. Arbenz's economic policies were directed toward creating a modern capitalist nation. In his inaugural address, President Arbenz stated that his economic policies would stress private initiative, but with Guatemalan capital in the hands of Guatemalans. To achieve that end, he adopted the proposals of the World Bank to begin construction of an Atlantic port and highway to compete with the port and railroad owned by the United Fruit

Company; he also built a hydroelectric plant to compete with the U.S.-owned power plant.

Arbenz's populism was reflected in his support for the newly formed National Confederation of Guatemalan Campesinos (CNCG)—which gradually came under Communist influence—and its campaign to increase agricultural wages. Most important was the enactment of the famous Decree 900, the agrarian reform law that was designed to expand domestic purchasing power and put unused land under cultivation. Under the law, idle land on holdings above 223 acres could be expropriated and distributed to peasants for lifetime usufruct. Owners were to be compensated through twenty-five-year bonds for an amount equal to their self-declared tax valuation for 1952 and paid for by the peasants at a rate of 3 to 5 percent of their annual production. Under the program some one hundred thousand peasants received 1.5 million acres, for which the government issued over $8 million in bonds.

The United Fruit Company, which had only 15 percent of its land under cultivation, was particularly hard hit: 400,000 of its more than 550,000 acres were expropriated for $1,185,115—the amount of its own valuation for tax purposes. The company declared that the property was worth at least $16 million.

The agrarian reform law, the perceived radicalization of the peasantry by the now Communist-led CNCG, and the growing influence of a small cadre of Communists such as José Manuel Fortuny, Carlos Manuel Pellecer, and Víctor Manuel Gutiérrez, galvanized both upper- and middle-class opposition, even from many of the individuals and groups that had originally supported the Revolution. Intense lobbying by the United Fruit Company and the fear that Guatemala might become a Communist "bridgehead" in the Americas galvanized the Eisenhower administration into making common cause with the opposition, now led by the exiled Colonel Carlos Castillo Armas and General Miguel Ydígoras Fuentes. When a shipment of arms from Czechoslovakia arrived in Guatemala in May 1954, the CIA helped Castillo Armas invade from Honduras. Abandoned by the army, Arbenz resigned the presidency on 27 June. U.S. Ambassador John Puerifoy dictated a settlement that resulted in Castillo Armas assuming the presidency on 8 July. Arbenz went into exile,

living in Cuba, Uruguay, France, Switzerland, and finally Mexico, where he died.

See also **United Fruit Company.**

BIBLIOGRAPHY

James Dunkerly, *Power in the Isthmus: A Political History of Modern Central America* (1988).

Manuel Galich, *¿Por qué lucha Guatemala? Arévalo y Arbenz: Dos hombres contra un imperio* (1956).

Piero Gleijes, *Shattered Hope: The Guatemalan Revolution and the United States* (1991).

Jim Handy, "Resurgent Democracy and the Guatemalan Military," in *Journal of Latin American Studies* 18 (1986): 383–408.

Richard H. Immerman, *The CIA in Guatemala: The Foreign Policy of Intervention* (1982).

Stephen C. Schlesinger and Stephen Kinzer, *Bitter Fruit: The Untold Story of the American Coup in Guatemala* (1982, 1983).

Ronald M. Schneider, *Communism in Guatemala, 1944–1954* (1958).

Additional Bibliography

Cullather, Nick, and Piero Gleijeses. *Secret History: The CIA's Classified Account of Its Operations in Guatemala, 1952–1954.* Stanford, CA: Stanford University Press, 1999.

ROLAND H. EBEL

ARBITRISTAS. Arbitristas, a diverse group of seventeenth-century peninsular and Creole innovators who propounded ideas aimed at the reform of the political, social, and economic life of Spain and the Indies. They included some serious economic and political thinkers, inventors of useless gadgets, and even a few charlatans (e.g., alchemists).

These *arbitristas,* who usually shared a common faith in empiricism, compiled detailed information on each problem before devising a solution, however impractical. They had no common ideology or program and most often attempted to repair existing institutions. Given the hierarchical political system in the Spanish Empire during the seventeenth century, they looked to the existing political leadership to sponsor their projects. In Spain, the *arbitristas* tended to flock around the chief minister of King Philip IV, the Conde-Duque de

Olivares. *Arbitristas* in the Indies usually sought the patronage of the viceroy and turned their attention to pressing colonial problems: American Indian relations, the output of precious metals, corruption, fiscal innovations, and moral rejuvenation.

See also **Olivares, Conde-Duque de.**

BIBLIOGRAPHY

An excellent survey of the *arbitristas* in Spain is J. H. Elliott, "Self-perception and Decline in Early Modern Spain," *Past and Present* 74 (1977): 41–61. For the *arbitristas* in the Indies see Fred Bronner, "Peruvian *Arbitristas* Under Viceroy Chinchón, 1629–1639," *Scripta Hierosolymitana* 26 (1974): 34–77.

Additional Bibliography

Perdices Blas, Luis. *La economía política de la decadencia de Castilla en el siglo XVII: Investigaciones de los arbitristas sobre la naturaleza y causas de la riqueza de las naciones.* Madrid: Síntesis, 1996.

KENNETH J. ANDRIEN

ARBOLEDA, CARLOS (1929–). Carlos Arboleda (*b.* 1929), Panamanian sculptor and painter. Arboleda studied at the San Marcos Academy in Florence, Italy (1949–1954), and at the Real Academia de Bellas Artes in Barcelona, Spain (1955–1960). Upon his return to Panama, he became professor of sculpture at the Escuela Nacional de Artes Plásticas (1961–1964). He was the founder of and a teacher at the Casa de la Escultura, later renamed Centro de Arte y Cultura (1964–1990).

Although his early works included neoclassical nudes in marble, like *Serenidad* (1950), Arboleda also worked in wood, stone, ceramics, and metal, developing a less academic, more symbolic mature style. His talent is most outstanding in sculptures with indigenous themes such as *Piel Adentro*.

See also **Art: The Twentieth Century.**

BIBLIOGRAPHY

M. Kupfer, *Encuentro de Escultura* (1987).

Rosa Martínez De Lahidalga, *Carlos Arboleda, pintor y escultor panameño* (1974).

MONICA E. KUPFER

ARBOLEDA, JULIO (1817–1862). Julio Arboleda (*b.* 9 June 1817; *d.* 12 November 1862), Colombian poet, politician, and presidential claimant (17 August–12 November 1862). Born to a family of aristocrats in Timbiquí, Cauca, he studied at Stoneyhurst College in England (1831–1834) and the University of Popayán (1837–1838). He lost part of his wealth while serving in the War of the Supremes (1839–1841). A gifted orator and an elegant essayist, Arboleda served as congressman (1844–1846). He opposed President José Hilario López in the press, was jailed, and led a revolt against López (1851). Fleeing to Peru, he remained in exile there until November 1853, when he was elected to the senate. Back in Bogotá, in 1854 he escaped from the dictator José María Melo, against whom he had campaigned. Elected president designate (stand-in) in 1857, 1858, 1859, and 1860, Arboleda won the presidency (1860) for the 1861–1865 term but was not sworn in. During the Liberal revolution led by his uncle, Tomás Cipriano de Mosquera, he fought at Santa Marta (November–December 1860), moved his forces across Panama, and reached Pasto in May 1861. A year of bitter civil warfare that wracked southern Colombia ensued. Arboleda routed an invading Ecuadorian army (July 1862), and was killed at Berruecos (Narino) four months later. Although Arboleda was celebrated for his literary genius, his greatest work, the epic poem *Gonzalo de Oyón,* survives only in fragments.

See also **Mosquera, Tomás Cipriano de.**

BIBLIOGRAPHY

Daniel Zarama, *Don Julio Arboleda en el sur de Colombia* (1917).

Carlos Arturo Caparriso, *Arboleda* (n.d.).

J. León Helguera and Alberto Lee López, "La exportación de esclavos en la Nueva Granada," in *Archivos* (Bogotá), 1, no. 2 (1967): 447–459.

Gerardo Andrade González, *Prosa de Julio Arboleda: Jurídica, política, heterodoxa y literaria* (1984).

Additional Bibliography

Arboleda, Julio. *Obra lírica y poemas desconocidos,* edited by Héctor H. Orjuela. Colombia: [n.d.], 2004.

J. León Helguera

ARCE, ANICETO (1824–1906).

Aniceto Arce (*b.* 17 April 1824; *d.* 14 August 1906), president of Bolivia (1888–1892). Born in Tarija to an important merchant family, Arce was the largest shareholder of the Huanchaca Company, the most prosperous silver mining company in late-nineteenth-century Bolivia. He became one of the leaders of the Conservative (or Constitutionalist) Party and one of the most effective presidents of Bolivia during the period of hegemony of the Conservative oligarchy (1884–1899). He helped capitalize the Huanchaca Company through close association with the sources of Chilean capital. During the War of the Pacific (1879–1884), Arce favored a peace treaty with Chile, but he was exiled. His competition with Gregorio Pacheco in the 1884 elections, in which both candidates tried to outspend the other, signaled a new oligarchical electoral style. When Arce became president in 1888, he sponsored the building of a rail network that tied the Bolivian silver mines to the Pacific coast. He also improved the road system, reformed the military, and fostered the exploration of the Chaco frontier. According to a controversial biography by Ramiro Condarco Morales, Arce attempted to reform the hacienda labor system and bring Bolivia into the industrial age rather than, as other authors asserted, exploit the country for his personal profit. He died in Sucre.

See also **Bolivia, Political Parties: Constitutionalist Party.**

BIBLIOGRAPHY

The most recent and sympathetic biography is Ramiro Condarco Morales, *Aniceto Arce* (1985). See also Alipio Valencia Vega, *Aniceto Arce* (1982). An excellent history of the Huanchaca Company and Arce's role in silver mining is Antonio Mitre, *Los patriarcas de la plata: Estructura socioeconómica de la minería boliviana an el siglo XIX* (1981). Herbert S. Klein, *Bolivia: The Evolution of a Multi-Ethnic Society* (1982) deals with many facets of Arce's life and influence.

Additional Bibliography

Condarco Morales, Ramiro. *Aniceto Arce: Artífice de la extensión de la revolución industrial en Bolivia*, 2nd ed. La Paz, Bolivia: Fondo Editorial de los Diputados, 2002.

ERICK D. LANGER

ARCE, MANUEL JOSÉ (1787–1847).

Manuel José Arce (*b.* 1 January 1787; *d.* 14 December 1847), the first constitutionally elected president of the United Provinces of Central America. Born in San Salvador to a creole family, he studied at the University of San Carlos in Guatemala but did not graduate. Much influenced by Doctor Pedro Molina and Father José Matías Delgado, Arce participated in the Salvadoran insurgencies of 5 November 1811 and 24 January 1814, the latter of which resulted in his imprisonment until 1818. He led the Salvadoran forces who opposed Central American annexation to Agustín de Iturbide's Mexican Empire until his defeat at San Salvador by General Vicente Filísola on 7 February 1823, when he went into exile in the United States.

After Central American independence from Mexico (1 July 1823), Arce returned in February 1824 to join the governing junta of the new republic, serving briefly as provisional president. After a heated electoral campaign in 1825, the federal congress elected him Central American president over José Cecilio del Valle by a vote of 22 to 5 (even though del Valle had won a plurality of 41–34 in the electoral college, only one vote short of the required majority). Arce's deals with conservative legislators cost him support among his liberal supporters, and his attempts to strengthen the Central American federation by interventions in the state governments led to the civil war of 1827–1829. Frustrated and disillusioned, he turned over power to his conservative vice president, Mariano Beltranena, on 14 February 1828. When Francisco Morazán triumphed in the war, Arce went into exile in Mexico, where he wrote his memoirs, a valuable historical source for the 1820s.

Arce attempted to return to power in 1832, but, defeated at Escuintla by federal forces under the command of General Nicolás Raoul, he retreated to Soconusco, where he engaged in agriculture for several years. In 1843 he returned to El Salvador but soon was forced to flee to Honduras. In 1844 he appeared again in Guatemala, where he raised a force with the intention of ousting General Francisco Malespín from power in El Salvador. Malespín dealt him another military defeat in May of that year, preventing Arce's return to his native land until after Malespín's death in 1846. Arce died a year later, impoverished, in San Salvador.

See also **Central America, United Provinces of.**

BIBLIOGRAPHY

See Ramón A. Salazar, *Manuel José Arce* (1899), and Manuel José Arce, *Memoria del General Manuel José Arce* (1830, several subsequent editions), Arce's memoir. A useful short sketch is Víctor Jerez, "El General D. Manuel José Arce," in *San Salvador y sus hombres* (1967), pp. 53–57; also useful is Rolando Velásquez, *Carácter, fisonomía y acciones de don Manuel José Arce* (1948). Philip Flemion, "States' Rights and Partisan Politics: Manuel José Arce and the Struggle for Central American Union," in *Hispanic American Historical Review* 53, no. 4 (1973): 600–618, provides a detailed examination of the intrigue surrounding Arce's presidency. His "Manuel José Arce and the Formation of the Federal Republic of Central America" (Ph.D. diss., University of Florida, 1969) contains a more extensive account of his career.

Additional Bibliography

Meléndez Chaverri, Carlos. *Don Manuel José Arce: Una vida al servicio de la libertad*. San Salvador: Editorial Delgado, 2000.

RALPH LEE WOODWARD JR.

ARCE CASTAÑO, BAYARDO (1949–).

Bayardo Arce Castaño (*b*. 21 March 1949), Nicaraguan leader and member of the Sandinista National Directorate. Arce was born in Managua. His father's career as a journalist led him to become a reporter for *La Prensa* while a student at the National Autonomous University in León. He came into contact with the Sandinista National Liberation Front through his work at the newspaper and joined the Student Revolutionary Front in 1969. Arce was responsible for rural logistical support in the northern highlands from 1974 to 1976. He belonged to the Prolonged Popular War faction of the Sandinistas. Tomás Borge chose Arce to be his representative on the unified Sandinista National Directorate in March 1979.

After the fall of Anastasio Somoza in 1979, Arce became head of the Sandinista political commission. He greatly influenced the September 1979 meeting of the Sandinista leadership that set forth its short-term strategies in the "Seventy-Two-Hour Document." In May 1980 he became president of the Council of State. As a leading radical theorist, Arce gave a speech in 1984 rejecting the need for elections and endorsing a one-party state. He organized the Sandinista presidential campaigns in 1984 and 1990. In 1993 Arce became president of the editorial council of the newspaper *Barricada*. After the Sandinistas won the presidential election in 2006, Arce was named presidential advisor on economic and financial affairs.

See also **Nicaragua, Sandinista National Liberation Front (FSLN).**

BIBLIOGRAPHY

Gabriele Invernizzi et al., *Sandinistas: Entrevistas a Humberto Ortega Saavedra, Jaime Wheelock Román y Bayardo Arce Castaño* (1986).

Dennis Gilbert, *Sandinistas: The Party and the Revolution* (1988).

Additional Bibliography

Aguirre Solís, Danilo. *Historia, institucionalidad democrática y libertad de prensa en Nicaragua*. Managua: Fondo Editorial CIRA, 2001.

MARK EVERINGHAM

ARCHAEOASTRONOMY. *See* Astronomy.

ARCHAEOLOGY.

The European discovery of the existence of the American continents begun by the voyages of Christopher Columbus in the 1490s set up the conditions for a massively disruptive collision between two very different worlds of cultural and technological development. Despite achievements ranging from huge cities to the invention of unique writing and recording systems, the civilizations of Mexico and Central and South America were unable to withstand the combined impacts of more advanced technology and unfamiliar diseases or to mount effective military resistance to occupation and colonization.

The presence of ruins of many types posed questions almost immediately as to where the peoples of these lands had originated, how they had adapted to a huge variety of challenging environmental conditions, and what their histories had been. Answers have been sought through archaeological investigations ranging from surveys to long-term excavation and conservation projects. Over four centuries, a certain mystique has attached to the ancient Americas in the public mind, creating a global readership receptive to news of ongoing fieldwork and discoveries revealing the complexities of the hemisphere's past.

THE IDEA OF ARCHAEOLOGY
IN LATIN AMERICA

When the conquistadores encountered the high cultures of the region, societies whose ancestry lay in a progression of invention and adaptation to environments as diverse as the jungles of Guatemala, the altiplano of Peru, and the Valley of Mexico, their mystification gave rise to the idea of archaeology in Latin America. The clash of cultures in the early sixteenth century was accompanied by the almost total destruction of written native histories and chronicles as well as the deaths of oral historians as a result of introduced diseases. Thus no more than fragmentary answers can be found to questions as to the origins and growth of the native American civilizations. Much of the surviving information comes from ethnographic accounts, compiled by friars such as Bernardino de Sahagún, and from histories written by eyewitnesses such as Bernal Díaz del Castillo and by descendants of the native ruling classes who had been educated in reading hieroglyphic writing systems and the cycles of the calendar, such as Pedro de Cieza de León, known as "El Inca."

Advocates for the treatment of the conquered peoples as human beings, such as Bartolomé de Las Casas, also wrote histories. In the eighteenth and early nineteenth centuries speculation on the age and possible relationships of the New World to the recorded and mythological pasts of the Old ranged from the Lost Tribes of Israel to survivors of Atlantis. Yet even at this time scholars of Latin America had begun to attempt an objective assessment of their past, excavating at major sites such as Teotihuacán and beginning to gather the surviving manuscripts and artifacts that would form the core of the first national museum collections in Peru and Mexico during the 1820s.

Latin American archaeology in the modern scientific sense had its beginnings in the 1840s, when the findings of the American John Lloyd Stephens and the British Frederick Catherwood exploded into print as *Incidents of Travel in Central America,* *Chiapas and Yucatan* (1841) and *Incidents of Travel in Yucatan* (1843), discussing and illustrating the ancient cities of Uxmal, Copan, and Palenque. The discovery of the ruins of Tikal in 1848 spurred further investigations by a highly varied cadre of outsiders, ranging from the American diplomat Ephraim Squier's visits to the major sites of Peru and Bolivia in the 1860s to photographic documentation produced by the French archaeologist Désiré Charnay (1828–1915). In the later nineteenth century the archaeological heritage of each nation began to be recognized as worth protecting. For example, the Mexican congress in 1880 passed an act to stop Charnay from exporting the results of his excavations.

Lord Pacal, c. 650, from Temple of the Inscriptions, Palenque, Mexico. Considered one of the most significant ruins of the Mayan world, Palenque flourished under the reign of Lord Pacal during the seventh century. SCALA/ART RESOURCE, NY

By the 1890s excavations were under way across Latin America, if not always under well-controlled conditions. Pottery types and stratigraphy were the first analytic tools used to attempt to construct an accurate picture of cultural succession, as in the work of the German archaeologist Max Uhle (1856–1944) on the Nasca and Moche areas of the Peruvian coast and his model of a sequence of six cultures progressing from fishermen to the fully developed Inca civilization.

The new methodology was adopted by Latin American archaeologists first in Argentina and later in Mexico, where the establishment of the Escuela Internacional de Arqueología y Etnología on January 20, 1911, laid the foundation for training future generations of excavators, among them Alfonso Caso. Stratigraphy, however, yielded only very broad divisions of cultural development, overlooking or minimizing individual local or regional phases. In 1917 Manuel Gamio's excavations beneath the lava beds of the Pedregal at the site of Cuicuilco revealed the first of what would come to be known as the Formative era cultures in the Valley of Mexico. Foreign involvement in the region continued for four decades, beginning in 1914 under the auspices of the Carnegie Institution of Washington, D.C, led by the Mayanist scholar Sylvanus G. Morley (1883–1948), with attention centered on the complex world of Mesoamerica's interacting civilizations.

MESOAMERICA

Mesoamerican research in the 1920s and 1930s addressed the questions of deciphering the glyphic writing systems and their origin and determining the developmental sequence of the interwoven civilizations in the highlands and tropical forests. Excavations at sites as varied as Zacatenco in the Valley of Mexico, the Mayan sites of Uaxactún and Kaminaljuyú, and the Zapotec ceremonial center of Monte Albán yielded data supporting general agreement on common features of regional cultural evolution. The question of the ancestral Olmec and their relationship to Mayan prehistory was partially resolved with the 1938 discovery of a stela at Tres Zapotes bearing a date earlier than any then known at a Maya site. Both the American archaeologist Matthew Stirling (1896–1975) and his Mexican colleague Miguel Covarrubias endorsed the concept of an Olmec core region in Veracruz and Tabasco preceding the known Formative phase of Maya culture. Subsequent radiocarbon testing of specimens from San Lorenzo and La Venta verified this model, although debate continues on the exact relationship of the two civilizations.

By the 1950s the predominance of North Americans as field investigators had begun to shift to joint projects with their Latin American host nation counterparts, allowing for increased funding. Their ambitious projects were often aimed at the stabilization and reconstruction of major sites with a view toward making them tourist destinations. Although such efforts had long-term preservation value, fewer resources were consequently available for more focused research on topics relating to more abstract cultural features, such as vanished political systems or economic structures. Attitudes toward foreign involvement in excavations (whether as administrators or field workers) began to shift during the 1960s to a more nationally oriented mindset. The discovery of the ruins of the Templo Mayor in Mexico City in 1978 as part of the construction of a mass transit system brought this disparity to public attention.

The decipherment of the Mayan glyphic writing system was a major project from the 1950s through the 1980s, with various approaches taken. The idea of Mayan society as led by priests whose city centers were unoccupied except at specific seasons (popularized by Morley and Eric Thompson) ignored the many depictions of warfare on both stelae and in the spectacular murals of Bonampak, known since 1946. The first major breakthrough in Mayan hieroglyphic linguistics was made in 1952, when the Russian scholar Yuri Knorozov (1922–1999) demonstrated that the glyphs were a mixture of phonetic as well as pictographic characters, followed in 1958 with the identification of name glyphs for specific sites. The discovery of a royal tomb at Palenque in 1959 by the Mexican archaeologist Alberto Ruiz further challenged the picture of Mayan society by offering instead an image of city-states led by kings engaged in dynastic wars. A sequence of rulers based on the glyphic signatures was first worked out in 1960 by the Russian-American Mayanist scholar Tatiana Proskouriakoff (1909–1985) for the Guatemalan site of Piedras Negras, followed by 1964 for similar king lists for Quirigua and Yaxchilán. The founding of the Corpus of Maya Hieroglyphic Writing project in 1967 laid the groundwork for further unifying the investigation of written Maya. The next three decades saw an extension of decipherment to retrieve details of individual reigns and an expansion of settlement, economic, and agricultural land use studies, a development that revised sharply upward the potential populations of centers such as Tikal into the tens of thousands and forced a reevaluation of Preclassic era accomplishments. The increase in textual data also allowed for the study of sociopolitical structures and the roles played by social elites and ideologies in the shaping of Mesoamerican cultures. An unusual new focus of field survey and excavation emerged in the late 1980s centering on the use of caves as centers of ritual activity and portals to the underworld. The 1976 discovery of the settlement of Cerén in El Salvador preserved under volcanic ash allowed for a detailed reconstruction of daily life and represents the expansion of archaeological work into areas outside the traditional core regions. In May 1993 the Declaration of Copán was signed by the governments of the five nations with significant Maya archaeological sites, committing resources to ecological conservation and the management of cultural resources.

The currently employed chronology of pre-Columbian Mesoamerica is as follows:

2000–900 BCE: Early Formative/Preclassic
900–400 BCE: Middle Formative/Preclassic
400 BCE–200 CE: Late Formative/Preclassic
250–900: Classic
900–1200: Early Postclassic
1200–1519: Late Postclassic

SOUTH AMERICA

The principal regions of archaeological investigation and interest in South America prior to the twentieth century were Peru and adjacent areas of Bolivia, Ecuador, and Chile, which had been part of the Inca empire until its conquest by Francisco Pizarro in the 1530s. The massive ruins of Inca and pre-Inca architecture (whether freestanding such as the fortress of Sacsahuaman and Tiwanaku's Gateway

Ruins of the Incan city of Machu Picchu, near Cuzco, Peru, late 20th century. ALISON WRIGHT/CORBIS

of the Sun, or integrated into colonial Spanish buildings, the fate of Cuzco's Temple of the Sun) maintained a sense of the past as a visible presence for the Andean peoples in a fashion similar to the pyramids of Teotihuacán in Mexico. Hiram Bingham's 1911 discovery of the ruins of Machu Picchu in the Urubamba Valley was followed after World War I by excavations focused on determining the origins of Andean culture and showing that New World high civilization had its beginning in Peru rather than in Mexico. Julio Tello advanced the theory of a tropical forest culture moving into the mountains and later to the coast, based on his fieldwork at Chavín de Huántar, while his colleague Rafael Larco Hoyle saw Peruvian civilization arising on the coast and moving into the highlands, an argument rooted in work at the north coastal site of Cupisnique.

Beginning in the 1920s, research goals shifted from defining origins to establishing accurate cultural sequences for the central Andes through concentrated excavations at major sites of occupation. This concept was expanded in 1946 with the Viru Valley Project, which used one manageable, well-defined area as a model of the interplay of land use and culture, and yielded the most detailed sequence yet known anywhere in the Andes. Similar work continued in both the highlands and on the coast, centering attention on the origins and growth of public structures and regional cultural development. Emilio Estrada's 1956 discovery of the coastal site of Valdivia subsequently yielded pottery dating to 3000 BCE, pushing back the dating of ceramics in Peru by a millennium. The 1960s saw major Peruvian campaigns by Japanese archaeologists testing the viability of Julio Tello's theory of the Chavín past, and the adoption by Peru's own archaeologists of a focus on ethnobotany, manifested in the international Ayacucho Archaeological-Botanical Project. The University of San Marcos renewed work at Chavín de Huántar, while regional work shifted emphasis to tracing stylistic variations over time (an example being the chronological sequence for the Ica Valley) and combining field data with ethnohistorical sources for Cuzco and the Incan province of Huánuco. The 1970s saw a renewal of large-scale investigations at sites as varied as Huari in the Central Highlands and the coastal metropolis of Chan Chan, exploring the development of urbanism and continuing the regional focus with work in the Moche Valley.

Debate over the origins of the Chavín tradition was augmented by findings documenting the

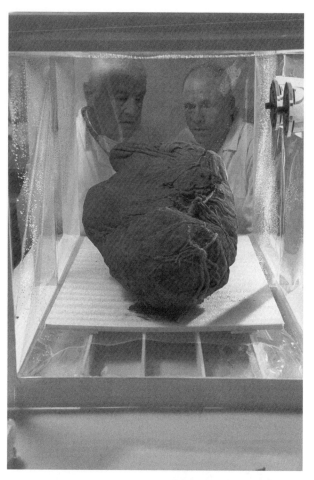

Archaeologists study mummy, Ica, Peru. Bodies from the Paracas, Nazca, and Ica cultures, some naturally mummified by the dry climate, have been found throughout southern Peru. IRA BLOCK/NATIONAL GEOGRAPHIC IMAGE COLLECTION

existence of a tradition of monumental architecture on the coast and the verification of a highland ceremonial complex, both predating the appearance of ceramics. International public attention focused on Peruvian archaeology, with the finding of a lavish Moche burial at the coastal site of Sipán in 1987, and the almost perfectly preserved frozen body of a young woman at the peak of Mount Ampato in 1995. The widely scattered collections of *khipu*, the knotted cords used as recording systems by the Inca, began to be united and analyzed by computer according to physical features and components in the Khipu Database Project in 1996, incorporating then-recent finds from the northern Peruvian site of Chachapoyas.

The picture of Peru as the early center of cultural development for the continent shifted as further

Uncovering ancient settlements in the heart of Mexico City. A Mexican archaeologist examines human remains, estimated to date to 300 to 700 BCE found in Chapultepec Park, 2005. © DANIEL AGUILAR/REUTERS/CORBIS

fieldwork was carried out in adjacent regions. Coastal cultures from Ecuador to Chile were understood to serve as sources for maritime materials traded from sites such as Valdivia into the highlands; further insight into the roles of the cultures of northwest South America and the Amazon basin began to develop. The 1961 discovery in northern Colombia of Puerto Hormiga (with ceramics of the same age as those on the Peruvian coast) was followed by similar work in lowland Ecuador and Donald Lathrap's research on the Ucayali River in the upper Amazon Basin. Lathrap advanced the idea that the richly varied Amazon environment had been capable of supporting complex societies, regarding the early ceramic sites outside Peru as supporting Tello's idea of an ancient tropical culture ancestral to much later development.

Away from the more intensively worked areas of the Andes and the western coast, archaeology developed along other lines. The vast landscape of Brazil, with field survey data organized by state, posed special problems for fieldwork because of a climate inimical to the preservation of artifacts made of materials other than stone, pottery, or shell. An early classification offered in 1937 by the Argentine archaeologist Antonio Serrano split the shell middens (known locally as *sambaquis*) into two groups by associated fauna, and Joao Angyone Costa's *Introducao a arqueologia brasileira* appeared in 1934 and was updated in 1938, when Anibal Mattos's *Prehistoria brasileira* was published. The archaeology of the Amazon basin before the end of the 1940s was based primarily on analysis of museum collections from Marajo and Santarem, a situation altered by the fieldwork of Betty Meggers at a group of sites in the mouth of the Amazon in 1948. The next thirty years witnessed the transformation of Brazilian archaeology from hobby to science, the revival and expansion of professional associations and opportunities for training, and the inauguration of long-term projects such as the five-year Programa Nacional de Pesquisas Arquelogicas (a partnership of the Smithsonian Institution and the Conselho Nacional de Pesquisas). This project surveyed the Atlantic coast of Brazil from the Amazon delta to the Uruguayan border, an effort yielding more than fifteen hundred sites ranging in age from pre-ceramic to colonial in date. The foundation of the Instituto de Arqueologia Brasileira by Ondemar Dias in 1961 provided for popular education and involvement in field excavations and laid the groundwork for the formation of the Sociedade de Arqueologia Brasileira in 1980.

South American archaeological chronology is as follows:

?–2500 BCE: Preceramic
2500–1800 BCE: Late Preceramic
1800–900 BCE: Initial Period
900 BCE–1 CE: Early Horizon (Chavín)
1–600 CE: Early Intermediate
600–1000: Middle Horizon
1000–1476: Late Intermediate
1476–1532: Late Horizon (Inca)

Somewhat overshadowed by the spectacular nature of the ruins of pre-Columbian civilizations, archaeology of historical period sites had nevertheless begun to emerge as a distinct area of research in South America during the later 1960s, particularly in Argentina, Brazil, and Uruguay, although investigations of sites such as the eighteenth-century hostel at Pajatambo had begun in Peru by the 1970s. The types of sites examined ranged from Carlos Magono Guimaraes's work on maroon settlements in Minas Gerais, Kern's Jesuit Missions studies in southern Brazil (unique, as the sites were considered both Guarani and European communities), and Daniel Schávelzon's work on the past of Buenos Aires.

The Caribbean. Caribbean archaeology has likewise focused fieldwork on a mixture of historic period sites (often associated with some aspect of slavery) and investigations on the indigenous populations of the islands and their legacies since the initial settlement around 3100 BCE. The foundation of the International Association for Caribbean Archaeology in 1961 created a professional forum for discussion on needed research priorities and current excavations with its conferences.

ARCHAELOGICAL QUESTIONS: THE 1990S
Major questions for Latin American archaeologists during the 1990s addressed developments occurring over a substantial portion of the continent,

such as the domestication of the llama and alpaca in the Andes, the development and symbolic uses of metallurgy and the artifacts it produced, a reevaluation of the prehistory of the Amazon basin, and consideration of the unique processes that resulted in Latin American urbanism in cities as varied as Cuzco, Mayapan, and Tikal. Research in Brazil turned its attention to the antiquity of human presence in South America, the interplay of ecology and the prehistoric cultures of Brazil, and a return to the study of rock art, long a uniquely successful focus of fieldwork, publication, and classification within the country's scientific establishment. An ongoing regional problem for Latin American archaeology in general is the dissemination of theoretical proposals and important discoveries on the prehistory of the hemisphere outside the network of local or regional scientific publications and conferences; many of the models for the population of the Americas are dominated by arguments put forward by the North American archaeological community that either minimize Latin American work or do not integrate its results into their framework at all. In the tradition begun by Ignacio Bernal, the history of regional archaeology has continued to be written in works such as Mario Orellana Rodríguez's *Historia de la arqueologia en Chile, 1842–1990* (1996) and Rafael Cobos's *Sintesis de la arqueologia de El Salvador, 1850–1991* (1994), allowing significant research to receive the recognition it deserves. Efforts continue at the national and international levels to stem the trade in looted artifacts from Latin American sites. However, this effort collides with economic realities of the past, as resources are commonly exploited by "subsistence digging," a practice likely to continue until underlying factors of poverty and development are addressed.

See also **Bernal y García Pimentel, Ignacio; Caso y Andrade, Alfonso; Catherwood, Frederick; Cerén; Chan Chan; Chavín de Huántar; Cieza de León, Pedro de; Covarrubias, Miguel; Cuicuilco; Cupisnique Culture; Cuzco; Díaz del Castillo, Bernal; Gamio Martínez, Manuel; Guarani Indians; Huánuco; Huari; Incas, The; Kaminaljuyú; Knorosov, Yuri; Las Casas, Bartolomé de; Machu Picchu; Maya, The; Mayapan; Moche; Monte Albán; Nasca; Olmecs; Piedras Negras, Guatemala; Puerto Hormiga; Quirigua; Sacsahuaman; Sahagún, Bernardino de; Sipán; Squier, Ephraim George; Stephens, John Lloyd; Tello, Julio César; Templo Mayor; Teotihuacán; Thompson, Eric; Tikal; Tiwanaku; Uaxactún; Valdivia Culture; Yaxchilán; Zapotecs.**

BIBLIOGRAPHY

Bernal, Ignacio. *Historia de la arqueología en México*. México: Editorial Porrúa, 1979.

Brady, James Edward, and Keith M. Prufer, eds. *In the Maw of the Earth Monster: Mesoamerican Ritual Cave Use*. Austin: University of Texas Press, 2005.

Burger, Richard L. "An Overview of Peruvian Archaeology (1976–1986)." *Annual Review of Anthropology* 18 (1989): 37–69.

Cobos, Rafael. *Síntesis de la arqueología de El Salvador, 1850–1991*. San Salvador: Dirección General de Publicaciones e Impresos, 1994.

Farnsworth, Paul, ed. *Island Lives: Historical Archaeologies of the Caribbean*. Tuscaloosa: University of Alabama Press, 2001.

Fash, William L. "Changing Perspectives on Maya Civilization." *Annual Review of Anthropology* 23 (1994): 181–208.

Funari, Pedro Paulo A. "Archaeology, History, and Historical Archaeology in South America." *International Journal of Historical Archaeology* 1, no. 3 (1997): 189–206.

Haviser, Jay B., ed. *African Sites Archaeology in the Caribbean*. Princeton, NJ: Markus Wiener Publishers, 1999.

King, Jaime Litvak. "Mesoamerica: Events and Processes, the Last Fifty Years." *American Antiquity* 50, no. 2 (1985): 374–382.

Matsuda, D. "The Ethics of Archaeology, Subsistence Digging, and Artifact Looting in Latin America: Point Muted Counterpoint." *International Journal of Cultural Property* 7, no. 1 (1998): 87–97.

Orellana Rodríguez, Mario. *Historia de la arqueología en Chile, 1842–1990*. Santiago, Chile: Bravo y Allende Editores, 1996.

Politis, Gustavo G., and Benjamin Alberti, eds. *Archaeology in Latin America*. London and New York: Routledge, 1999.

Schávelzon, Daniel. *The Historical Archaeology of Buenos Aires: A City at the End of the World*, trans. Alex Lomonaco. New York: Kluwer, 1999.

Scheinsohn, Vivian. "Hunter-Gatherer Archaeology in South America." *Annual Review of Anthropology* 32 (2003): 339–361.

Stahl, Peter W., ed. *Archaeology in the Lowland American Tropics: Current Analytical Methods and Recent Applications*. Cambridge, U.K., and New York: Cambridge University Press, 1995.

Stanish, Charles. "The Origin of State Societies in South America." *Annual Review of Anthropology* 30 (2001): 41–64.

ROBERT B. RIDINGER

ARCHILA, ANDRÉS (1913–2002).

Andrés Archila (*b.* 24 December 1913, *d.* 2 March 2002), Guatemalan violinist and musical conductor. Archila was the son of Andrés Archila Tejada, director of a well-known marimba band. Recognized as a prodigy and violin virtuoso, Archila studied at the Santa Cecilia Academy in Rome. After returning to Guatemala in 1944, he promoted the organization of the National Symphony Orchestra, of which he was conductor until 1959, when he moved to the United States. For more than twenty-five years he was third violin in the National Symphony Orchestra as well as associate director of the Washington Symphonic Orchestra in Washington, D.C. He also founded and played first violin in the Pan American Union String Quartet.

See also **Music: Art Music.**

BIBLIOGRAPHY

José A. Mobil, *Historia del arte guatemalteco*, 9th ed. (1988), p. 353; *Crónica* (Guatemala), 15 June 1990, p. 81.

Carlos C. Haeussler Yela, *Diccionario general de Guatemala*, vol. 1 (1983), p. 88.

RALPH LEE WOODWARD JR.

ARCHITECTURE

This entry includes the following articles:
ARCHITECTURE TO 1900
MODERN ARCHITECTURE

ARCHITECTURE TO 1900

The European discovery of America presented Spain and Portugal with an unprecedented opportunity to introduce new ideas, customs, objects, architecture, and cities there. Iberian occupation of the territory was tied directly to the process of converting the Indians to Christianity that began with the discovery itself, and the church as an institution made the biggest initial contribution to the new American architecture.

European conquest did not proceed evenly throughout the vast American territory. For a half century following Columbus's voyages, European settlement was centered in the Caribbean, where

Temple of the Masks, Yucatán, Mexico, c. 8th century. Mayan building on the Temple of the Masks began in the eighth century and continued for several hundred years. Also known as *Codz Poop,* the pre-Columbian temple features decorative masks in honor of the rain god *Chaac* stretching across its façade. © ATLANTIDE PHOTOTRAVEL/CORBIS

the Spanish imposed architectural styles with features ranging from Gothic to Renaissance to Mudejar. The architecture that resulted was characterized by a varying synthesis of native and imported influences that depended on the experience, education, and cultural background of its designers and artisans.

Forts developed into complexes that blended medieval and Renaissance plans, as exemplified by El Morro in Puerto Rico, built at the end of the sixteenth century. With the founding of Havana in 1514, the center of Spanish activity began to shift away from Santo Domingo. Havana's fortified nature influenced its life and development, but the need for military severity blended with a certain local architectural flair to define Havana's individuality, a process of adaptation to local conditions repeated for other cities in the New World. For example, when the Cathedral of Santo Domingo was completed in 1541, it used a Gothic floor plan, but without its

accompanying solidity and horizontality, and contained a plateresque main portico featuring carving in plaster and stone, all of which exemplified spontaneous local adaptations.

The religious orders established their presence not only in the quality and quantity of their buildings, but also through their labors in the organization of new settlements and the consolidation of existing ones. As in the Caribbean, a synthesis of European theories and practices developed, with architectural works of marked Gothic influence in the sixteenth century and pronounced Renaissance influence in the seventeenth. It was during the sixteenth century that the great Mexican cathedrals were constructed. The Cathedral of Mexico City was begun in 1563, but not completed until 1813. Modifications of its original plan resulted in a church with the central nave higher than the two lateral ones and with a cupola and two towers at the front. It is a building of great proportions, in which the characteristic synthesis of many architectural styles from the plateresque to the neoclassic is meticulously expressed.

In addition to the more than 200 traditional churches and convents constructed in less than a century, New World circumstances often led Spaniards to build fortified convents and open chapels. The former were solid and introverted buildings with battlements that created the image of a spiritual fortress and made them seem even more alien when set against the backdrop of the countryside. The open chapel, which had European roots, was particularly popular in Mexico. It combined the Spanish impulse toward conversion with the indigenous reverence for nature by placing altar and fountain in a limited space.

Functionally, churches and convents alluded directly to known European styles. Nonetheless, the preponderance of indigenous craftsmen and laborers involved in their construction often influenced their stylistic outcome. This is most evident in changes made to the portals of the churches. Because of the value that indigenous peoples attached to exterior space, and the ways they used it, the portal became a representative, symbolic, and instructional element of great importance, incorporating native themes and styles of workmanship and decorative representation.

In South America, the Conquest and expansion proceeded slightly after that of Mexico. The numerous cloisters built in the city of Quito, Ecuador, founded in 1534, were of imposing proportions and had grandiose and ingenious solutions, in which once again Indian craftsmanship provided silent witness to his presence.

Although the Spanish and Portuguese effort to build new cities did not meet strong opposition, they were created by combining European architectural thought with the environmental and human factors specific to each site. That mixture was demonstrated in the city of Puebla de los Angeles in Mexico, founded in 1532, which established an ordered, urban plan.

The 1573 Planning Ordinances of Philip II introduced urban planning criteria that both capitalized on acquired experience and sought to standardize future settlements. Although Renaissance thought inspired the plans for the new cities, their appearance differed greatly from that of ideal European cities, approximating more nearly the criteria and proposals of the Roman architect Vitruvius

in his treatise on city planning, *De architectura*, favored by architects of the Italian Renaissance. Three principal elements characterized the grid layout of the new American cities/administrative centers: the street, the blocks of buildings, and the plaza. That link of spatial structure and administrative function led to the emergence of new urban traits such as the possibility of growth within the same grid and a formal link to the surrounding territory. This allowed for a gradual urban expansion into the surrounding rural space.

The central point of reference in Spanish American cities was the plaza, which helped to integrate their political and religious functions. The straight lines of the streets defined the characteristic image of the urban landscape, and the importance of buildings was gauged by their proximity to the plaza. To the general plan proposed by the ordinances were added all the modifications and variations that practicality, experience, and necessity demanded.

This process continued until the eighteenth century, but the founding of major cities—many of which were to become capitals, such as Mexico City, Caracas, Bogotá, Lima, and La Paz—took place in the sixteenth century. Those that followed continued with the original policies and adopted the same regular plan. Also, previously established centers grew and developed in the eighteenth century. The only exception to the planning style of the ordinances was that of the Jesuits in their Guaraní Indian missions. Yet there were also irregular and superimposed cities that demonstrated the synthesis of two cultures, with the indigenous providing a basis for the Spanish. Cuzco, Peru, is an example of new architectural language expressed amid the huge, severe walls of the Incas, thus signifying the confrontation between two opposing conceptions of the world.

In contrast to the Spanish, early Brazilian urban settlements were largely shaped by Portuguese policies of focusing on strategic coastal sites. São Salvador da Bahia de Todos os Santos (commonly called Bahia), founded in 1549, marked the beginning of a period of city building. Institutions defining an ordered style did exist here, but they were without the marked rationality of the Renaissance-Spanish style, and allowed planners and designers more creative freedom. The Portuguese selected a suitable and convenient site to build the humble fortified port of

Bahia, which thanks to its Afro-Brazilian population would develop a colorful syncretic aspect unlike any other city in Spanish America.

THE BAROQUE

From 1650 until the latter eighteenth century, Latin America adopted an architectural style with a manner and language that, despite regional variations, demonstrates numerous stylistic commonalities. During this period, the church modified European baroque to capitalize on previous architectural experiences and create new vistas, while at the same time buildings established a more harmonious relationship with the city. Each region introduced its own original variants. Since the Conquest, the Mexican indigenous population had appropriated and mastered interior space and produced a body of professionals that included few Europeans. Mexican buildings exhibited a riotous expanse of color often supplemented by extravagant polychrome plasterwork, the mingling of curved and straight forms, and highly original tilework. Portals acquired more richness and volume, and in many cases their ornamentation dominated the entire church facade. During this period, the Mexicans developed the *estípite,* a pilaster shaped like a truncated upside-down pyramid. The use of this ornament became characteristic of a new style, churrigueresque, often termed "estípite baroque." The Jesuit church of San Martín Tepotzotlán demonstrates the combination of a more Europeanized intricately carved white facade that leads into a graceful tower with a completely decorated and sensuous interior. El Sagrario in Mexico City, Santa Prisca in Taxco, and Santo Domingo and San Francisco Acatepec in Puebla are a few more examples of the baroque during this period.

The Andean baroque, by contrast, began in Cuzco during the period 1651–1669 with the construction of the Cathedral and La Compañía church. It was followed in Lima from 1657 to 1675 with the construction of the new Church of San Francisco. Cuzco regained its architectural authority under the leadership of Bishop Manuel de Mollinedo (1673–1700), and its style predominated in more than fifty churches from Belén and San Pedro in Cuzco itself to the church in the town of Asillo near Lake Titicaca. Finally, the baroque reached its apogee in Lima from 1700 to 1740 with the Torre Tagle Palace and the churches of San Agustín and La Merced.

In Brazil, religious architecture evolved energetically in the seventeenth and eighteenth centuries, especially in Bahia, where churches had a sole nave, usually with a wooden roof. Although the styles continued to be European, the valuable decorative elements reflected the exuberance of the population. These buildings were notable for the large interiors designed to accommodate the entire community, and combined with a sense of sculpture, they brought a new element to the urban landscape.

After 1750, Minas Gerais was the center of Brazilian development. In the last decades of the century, Aleijadinho (Antônio Francisco Lisboa) made his unique contribution. Aleijadinho brought sculpture nearer to architecture with such force and mastery that his work became a style unto itself. The facade of the church of São Francisco de Assis, designed in 1774, and built in Ouro Prêto, is testimony to the management of space and other changes that Aleijadinho brought to architecture. In this church the oval towers recede, yet they remain visually and materially integrated by an undulating cornice that traverses the entire facade. Sculpture plays an important role in linking the facade with the interior using the altarpiece, the pulpit, and the ceiling of painted wood to provide a distinctive spatial and optical effect.

Architecture in Paraguay and the region of the Guaraní Indians followed a different course, shaped by the availability of abundant supplies of wood. The site chosen for each church with its perimetrical gallery, and the spatial value of the plaza as atrium and cemetery, endowed the building with multiple meanings, as demonstrated by the eighteenth-century San Roque Church in Yaguarón. The use of a gallery, created in response to the demands of the climate, replaced the idea of the facade.

The Jesuit mission settlements in Argentina, Brazil, Paraguay, and Bolivia, infused with the charisma and spirit of the Order, developed a sense of coherence and spatial balance unique in urban America. A small group of priests and a significant number of indigenous people joined forces to contribute their respective visions and versions of reality. The architecture—from simple sheds to elaborate churches—consciously grew out of indigenous communal life, combining simplicity with dignity. Skilled woodworking resulted in balanced buildings of marked horizontality in which technological solutions were readily seen, clearly distinguishing them from buildings that made use of alternative solutions. Their buildings were simple, but not lacking in such details as pulpits and Solomonic columns. Their refined painted murals lent them an artistic value not ordinarily apparent from the pronounced rationalism of the structure.

The Cathedral of Córdoba, Argentina, begun at the end of the seventeenth century, represents an important moment in the history of architecture in that country and in all of America. Of great volume and harmonious proportions, the Cathedral always tends toward the horizontal, its cupola and the two towers of the facade adding character to the solid and stony presence. Exterior ornamentation is concentrated on the cupola and the towers, which are rendered with special grace and ingenuity. The serene and static interior space was "altered" with overwrought ornamentation added in the nineteenth century.

THE ARCHITECTURE OF INDEPENDENCE

Spanish professors introduced the neoclassical style to Latin America at the Academia De San Carlos, created in Mexico in 1785. In the beginning, the introduction of neoclassicism represented a decision and aspiration to follow similar trends in Europe, and it confronted its followers with a style that many did not hesitate to refer to as consolidated archaisms. The period signified, above all, the beginning of the end of the baroque style. The novelty and freshness of neoclassicism suited the spirit of independence that was spreading throughout Latin America. In Mexico City, for example, many buildings dating from as early as the sixteenth century were torn down by government decree to make way for the more simplified style. European architects led the way almost everywhere, from Manuel Tolsá in Mexico City (the School of Mines), Domingo de Petrés in Bogotá (the Cathedral), Joaquín Toesca in Santiago (La Moneda Palace and the Cathedral), and Próspero Catelin in Buenos Aires (the Cathedral).

Following Independence, many Latin American nations suffered crises of organization and identification. Italy, France, England, and the United States variously contributed ideas, capital, and immigrants, each of which left a pronounced stamp on regional development. Neoclassicism may have replaced the baroque, but as in Europe, it was followed by the neo-Gothic. In the Americas, both neoclassicism and the neo-Gothic lacked the ideological content they possessed in their European environments, and relied on their merely symbolic aspects. It was not until after 1870, however, that changes initiated decades earlier began to affect the urban landscape.

As in Europe, academic posture was confronted by a romantic one, and functional traditionalism also found its niche. During the late nineteenth century, there was a notable increase in the quality and quantity of new architectural themes and forms of expression which were displayed in the many theaters, libraries, government buildings, railroad stations, prisons, and exhibition centers constructed at that time. Construction activity was not equal in all Latin American countries; Argentina boasts many important works during this period, not only in Buenos Aires, but in La Plata and Córdoba as well. The Teatro Colón and the Congressional Palace, built between 1892 and 1906 in Buenos Aires, testify to this notable period of architectural history.

The new cities founded in the nineteenth century covered a wide range of styles, but almost all were affected by high levels of European immigration. In Argentina, an important pole of attraction, towns grew around railroads and agricultural communities. Out of sheer practicality, the grid layout was widely adopted, and immigrant artisans and laborers often added varied interpretations and combinations. La Plata, founded in 1882 as the capital of the province of Buenos Aires, is a typical example. The traditional grid was superimposed, with an irregular web of plazas at major points of intersection. A monumental axis crosses the city, and public buildings serve as points of attraction, interest, and reference. The structure of this city is completed by the green in the streets and in the great park at the foot of the axis. The city had a large European population, whose architectural influence is evident in the neo-Gothic cathedral and in the neoclassic Museum of Natural Sciences.

Haussmann's Paris served as a model for numerous urban reconstructions complete with new buildings. Mexico City, Lima, Havana, Asunción, Bahia, and Buenos Aires, among others, acquired during the second half of the nineteenth and the beginning of the twentieth centuries boulevards, promenades,

Calle San Martin in Buenos Aires, Argentina, c. 1890. Combined with a rejection of Spanish tastes after achieving independence, waves of immigrants from Italy in the nineteenth century influenced the architecture of major urban centers in Argentina. © HULTON-DEUTSCH COLLECTION/CORBIS

and parks, along with infrastructural works and the first low-income housing projects, such as those built in Buenos Aires in 1885.

By the beginning of the twentieth century, the modernist spirit had arrived in the art world, which began to feel the rejection of academe in architecture. The alternative to academe was art nouveau, whose diffusion in Latin America was not widespread. In countries where it found a home, such as Brazil, Mexico, and Argentina, only its formal features were preserved, and in some cases only its decorative elements.

The Nationalist Restoration movement, which had few concrete results, was nonetheless important as the first attempt to create an American architecture with its own theoretical corpus. It also implied the need for the study and valuation of an architectural heritage. Argentina provided much theoretical substance for this movement, and interesting and representative works were created in Peru. Carlos Noel, Angel Guido, Juan Kronfuss, Alejandro Christophersen, and Pablo Hary are some of the names associated with the Nationalist Restoration movement.

The third anti-academe alternative that arose during the first three decades of the twentieth century was that of art deco, whose geometrization and simplification, along with the use of reinforced concrete, opened the way to modern architecture.

See also **Academia de San Carlos; Aleijadinho; Art: The Colonial Era; Art: The Nineteenth Century; Teatro Colón.**

BIBLIOGRAPHY

Leopoldo Castedo, *A History of Latin American Art and Architecture from Pre-Columbian Times to the Present* (1969).

Jorge Hardoy et al., *Colóquios sobre urbanización en América desde su origen a nuestros días,* 4 vols. (1970–1978).

Graziano Gasparini, *América, barroco y arquitectura* (1972).

Javier Aguilera Roja and Luis J. Moreno Rexach, *Urbanismo español en América* (1973).

Damián Bayón, *Sociedad y arquitectura colonial sudamericana* (1974).

Marcello Carmagnani, *América latina de 1880 a nuestros días* (1975).

Michael Ragon, *Historia mundial de la arquitectura y el urbanismo modernos*, vol. 1 (1979).

Additional Bibliography

Arbeláez Camacho, Carlos. *De arquitectura e historia*. Medellín: Universidad Pontificia Bolivariana, 1968.

Bottineau, Yves. *Living Architecture: Iberian-American Baroque*. London: Macdonald & Co., 1971.

Buschiazzo, Mario José. *Historia de la arquitectura colonial en Iberoamérica*. Buenos Aires: Emece? Editores, 1961.

Donahue-Wallace, Kelly. *Art and Architecture of Viceregal Latin America: 1521–1821*. Albuquerque: University of New Mexico Press, 2008.

Gutiérrez, Ramón. *Arquitectura colonial: Teoría y praxis*. Resistencia, Argentina: Instituto Argentino de Investigaciones en la Historia de la Arquitectura y Urbanismo, 1980.

Kubler, George. *The Art and Architecture of Ancient America: The Mexican, Maya, and Andean Peoples*. Harmondsworth, England; New York: Penguin Books, 1984.

Robertson, Donald, *Pre-Columbian Architecture*. New York: G. Braziller, 1963.

Telesca de Abbondio, Ana María. *Arquitectura Colonial*. Buenos Aires: Centro Editor de América Latina, 1977.

HORACIO GNEMMI

MODERN ARCHITECTURE

Through the nineteenth century and into the early twentieth century, neoclassical architecture predominated in much of Spanish America. In Europe, modernist architecture began to develop after the Industrial Revolution. This new style, with its focus on economy and practicality, found a receptive audience in Spanish American countries, even though their industrialization occurred later. In particular, the Swiss architect Le Corbusier (1887-1965), who developed modernist functionalist ideas and first traveled to Brazil in 1929, gained many collaborators and disciples in the region. Elaborating on this modernist perspective, Spanish American architects added their local traditions, native materials, and unique concepts as the twentieth century progressed.

PERU

In the early twentieth century, modern architecture appeared in Peru with the arrival of the first foreign financial companies and the construction of their headquarters in the historic downtown district of Lima. These buildings include the Bank of Peru and London (J. E. Lattini, 1905), designed with iron structures and colored glass, and the Transatlantic German Bank (Claudio Sahut, 1914), which used reinforced concrete for the first time. The typology of the institutional building became very important in the development of Peruvian architecture in the twentieth century.

Although modernity made its mark in the early twentieth century through the use of new materials and structural systems that were innovative for the period, these institutional buildings retained a relationship with nineteenth-century designs, and so the composite systems of the École des Beaux Arts of Paris were what really defined this architecture. Thus, academicism was the predominant tendency of this period through the 1920s, and the culmination was its adoption in a series of buildings that marked the development of the city of Lima. The Rimac Building (1919), the Pantheon of the Founding Fathers (1924), Archbishop Loayza Hospital (1924), the Palace of Justice (1926–1938), the National Club (1928), and the Reserve Bank (1929) are examples of this architecture of classical and monumental style.

However, indigenist and Hispanist movements also emerged in 1920s, and they spawned the three most important architectural trends of the first half of the twentieth century. Neocolonial, neo-Inca, and neo-Peruvian architecture are all based on the use of an architectural repertoire from the pre-Hispanic or colonial past.

The neo-Inca and neo-Peruvian styles were not widely used in Peru because knowledge of the pre-Hispanic period was still incipient at the time. Their applications were limited to the design of the façades of new projects. The National Museum of Archeology (1924), Peru's Pavilion in the Paris International Exposition (Roberto Haaker and Alberto Jochamowitz, 1937) and the Museum of Anthropology (Hector Velarde, 1940) are examples of this nationalist architectural style. Examples of the neo-Peruvian style can be seen in works such as the Peruvian Pavilion at the Sevilla International Exposition (Manuel Piqueras Cotolí, 1929).

Neocolonialism had an influence in Latin America and became the dominant architectural current based on the reinterpretation of colonial elements adapted to academicist composition. The neocolonial style had more influence in Peru than in other Latin American countries (except Mexico). This was due primarily to the broad tradition of colonial architecture in Peru, which made it possible for both formal and theoretical aspects to be present in the works of neocolonialism's primary representatives: the Peruvian architects Emilio Harth-Terré (1899–1983), Héctor Velarde (1898–1989), José Álvarez Calderón, and Rafael Marquina (1884–1964); the Polish architect Ricardo Malachowski (1887–1972); and the French architect Claudio Sahut. This style used colonial elements such as balconies and portals but organized them around an academicist composition, in buildings such as the Archbishop's Palace (Malachowski, 1916), the Hotel Bolívar (Marquina, 1924), the lateral facade of the Palace of Government (Sahut, 1924–1930), and the Boza and South America Building (Harth-Terré and Álvarez Calderón, 1938). The common characteristic of these buildings was the reinterpretation of colonial elements based on an eminently academic composition.

The art deco and "buque" styles also made their way into the country during this decade. Both styles were linked to the international repertoire and were used either independently or in combination, with the buque style predominant. Buildings that combine the styles include La Casa Ulloa and the Baths of Miraflores (both by Velarde, 1937 and 1938, respectively). The Aurich Building and the Aldabas-Merlchormalo Building (both by Augusto Guzmán, 1933) are examples of the independent use of the art deco style, and the Raffo Building is an example of the buque style (R. Vargas Prada and Guillermo Payet, 1938).

In the mid-1940s, specifically in 1947, the Agrupación Espacio (Space Partnership) was formed with the primary objective of disseminating the principles of modern architecture. The Casa Miró Quesada house (Luis Miró, 1947) is emblematic of the principles of modernity, marking the beginning of the influence of Le Corbusier on Peruvian architecture. Buildings such as the Apartments of Calle Roma (Teodoro Cron), the Central Office of the Lima Yacht Club (Valega), the Casa Truel (Roberto Wakeham), and the Mater Admirabilis Clinic (Paul Linder) also show this influence.

A new period began in the 1950s that incorporated new elements of modernity, such as the use of the curtain wall in Miró Quesada's El Sol Radio Building (1954); the Hotel Savoy (1957) by Bianco; and Cron's Swiss-Peruvian building; as well as some elements of Brazilian architecture in the Atlas buildings (1954) of José Álvarez Calderón and Walter Weberhofer and the El Pacífico building (1957) of Fernando de Osma.

Modern architecture came to Peru in this way during the 1940s. However, its consolidation occurred a few years later, when the military government made it the official architecture. With the military coup of 1968, a process of association began between modern and military architecture, producing an architectural image of unity and homogeneity that the military government wanted to project. The Cartagena Agreement Junta, the Petro-Peru building, the Ministry of Fisheries (today the Museum of the Nation), the Housing Bank, the PIP Operations Center, and several ministry buildings are examples of this style associated with statism and control; it is also associated with nakedness, aggressive materials, and exposed systems.

Modernism remained strong through the rest of the twentieth century, but greater experimentation shaped building and home designs. At the Third International Biennial of Architecture and Urbanism (1978), the Peruvian College of Architecture gave the Peruvian Central Reserve Bank in Lima (Luis Tapia and Manuel Llanos) its top award, the Golden Hexagon. This building was the culmination of a series of institutional projects designed throughout the 1970s in a style known as brutalism.

Previously, the College of Architecture had given the Golden Hexagon to Emilio Soyer's Casa Velarde (First Biennial, 1970) and to the Iquitos Peruvian Armed Forces Villa by Victor Ramírez (Second Biennial, 1972), both designs with strong contextual components. The first project was linked to the search for what is truly Peruvian, without rejecting modern lines, and the second used context by taking into account the climate conditions of the Peruvian jungle where it was located and by using appropriate technology and materials.

In 1978, however, works of a new type began to appear. The Arenales and Higuereta Shopping Centers, for example, were linked fundamentally to the commercial environment and generated some alternatives, albeit timid ones, within the Peruvian architectural spectrum. At the same time, the Ramírez and Smirnoff Continental Bank building was an urban

Plaza de Armas, Santiago, Chile. Modern skyscrapers loom behind the eighteenth-century Metropolitan Cathedral in the center of the city. PHOTOGRAPH BY SUSAN D. ROCK. REPRODUCED BY PERMISSION

landmark whose prophetic location and modern design incorporated a material that was new to the institutional repertoire: the fair-face (*caravista*) brick, which was later adopted for use in various types of buildings, including housing.

The transition from military government to democracy began in Peru in 1978 with the Constituent Assembly, and came to an end with the second election of Fernando Belaúnde Terry as Peru's president in 1980. This turning point in the democratic order began a period of rediscovering architecture, shaped by the possibility of accessing information and new designs developed around the world. In this period, architecture once again became socially significant. The government promoted various competitions, such as the ones for the San Borja Towers and the Limatambo Housing Complex. Designs for use in the National Housing Plan became a big challenge for the new government, but El Niño storms had repercussions on the national economy and, therefore, on architecture.

In these years, something called *Gremco* architecture (Grupo de Empresas Constructoras) appeared in housing projects. Through various designs, this style expressed an alternative to the designs of José García Bryce (b. 1928), such as the Chabuca Granda Housing Complex in the Rimac district (1984–1985). The former had an explicitly commercial interest, whereas the latter was interested in recovering and revaluing historic places such as the traditional neighborhood of Rimac, and in using the architectural repertoire of the place, including the colonial vestibule, patio, and balcony, but with a contemporary language.

Beginning in 1985 Ramírez-Smirnoff made significant modifications to historic downtown Lima, and color was incorporated, especially in public spaces such as the San Martín Plaza and the University campus during the municipal administration of Alfonso Barrantes. At the same time, in the peripheral areas of the city, the government directed the development of places such as the Villa El

Salvador Community, which became an example of urban organization and had a subsequent impact on the restoration of Huaycán.

The 1990s were marked by a variety of heterogeneous alternatives in Peruvian architecture. The beginning of a new government administration coincided with the presentation of the Seventh Biennial's Golden Hexagon Award (1988) to the Molina Credit Bank, designed by Bernardo Fort Brescia's architectural firm American Arquitectonica; this was hugely controversial because it highlighted the contrast between the extreme violence and poverty of Peru's poor with the ostentatious power reflected in the bank's architecture. But this work had significant international influence, and it initiated a more cosmopolitan architecture in Peru. Arquitectonica went on to create a series of key buildings in Lima, including the U.S. Embassy, which combines old motifs of pre-Hispanic looms on its façade with elements of high technology; and the Marriott Hotel and Office Building, a five-star hotel located along the Larco Sea on the edge of Lima. The firm also imposed its postmodern aesthetics on diverse projects such as banks, hotels, and shopping centers.

Municipal governments also provided spaces for active participation in the recovery of the city and public spaces, as in the Plan for Downtown Lima (1996–1997) and the Miraflores Central Park (1992). Outside the capital, cities were restored by projects such as the Las Musas Park in Chiclayo (1994), the Park of Huanca Identity (1994–1996), and projects in the Alameda de Chimbote and in Tumbes and Tacna that show regional presence in Peruvian architecture.

The end of the century brought a variety of designs characterized by their plurality, diversity, and heterogeneity, as can be seen in designs with regional characteristics such as the Sipán Museum in Túcume by Jorge Cosmópolis and the urban renewal of the Malecón de Ilo by Edgardo Ramírez Chirinos, as well as in recovered public spaces such as the Alameda Chabuca Granda in downtown Lima by Javier Artado and the Cultural Park of Lima by Augusto Ortiz de Cevallos. At the same time, the new business centers, five-star hotels, and the big new shopping centers of Lima—such as the Larco Mar Entertainment Center (1996–1998) of Eduardo Figari, Marina Park by Miguel Rodrigo, and the Jockey Plaza Shopping Center (1999) by Arquitectonica—are within the most cosmopolitan and neoliberal current and show a city, and an architecture, in constant change as it enters the era of globalization.

MEXICO

The transformation of Mexican architecture coincided with major social upheaval. In the first ten years of the twentieth century, Mexico was still focused on neoclassical designs. Substantial renovations and large building projects on the Paseo de la Reforma in Mexico City represented national progress and showcased this style. A political crisis in 1910 launched the Mexican Revolution (1910–1917), which significantly disrupted major building construction. As violence and political instability waned in the 1920s, the revolutionary elite began to propose new programs for social policy, economics, and culture. The government's preoccupations affected architectural design because the state began to commission housing for the working classes. Building economical and quality homes coincided with the modernist concern with efficiency and economy.

President Plutarco Elías Calles (1924–1928) initiated these new urban policies and reforms, but the major transition occurred during the presidency of Lázaro Cárdenas (1934–1940). The leader and founder of the Union of Architects in the Fight for Socialism, Juan O'Gorman (1905–1982), was one of Cárdenas's best known hires. For the government O'Gorman designed housing for workers with practical, basic designs, as opposed to the more elaborate buildings of the nineteenth century and the colonial period.

Although Mexican architects followed a basic modernist style, Mexican modernism began to add local tradition, materials, and designs to urban construction. Mural painting with indigenous motifs differentiated Mexican buildings in the postrevolutionary era. Using adobe, stucco, cobblestones, and unfinished wood, Luis Barragán (1902–1988) meshed the local with modern theoretical concerns. Even O'Gorman in later years incorporated an emphasis with national identity. He designed the library at the National Autonomous University of Mexico (1950–1952) with a large mural emphasizing indigenous pride and the plight of the Mexican peasantry.

Mexican postwar architects in the latter half of the twentieth century began to experiment with

The National Congress building in Brasília, late 20th century. Modernism was an important and innovative architectural style, using new materials and technologies, that developed throughout Latin America in the twentieth century. JULIA WATERLOW/EYE UBIQUITOUS/CORBIS

blending the environment and buildings. Barragán designed many of the neighborhoods of Mexico City. Jardines del Pedregal de San Angel became famous for the way in which the houses incorporated the landscape with modernist rationality. Houses followed the natural patterns of the land, rather than trying to impose structure over the environment. Furthermore, Barragán used native vegetation, helping his designs to stand out and appear local.

In 1985 a massive earthquake destroyed many buildings in Mexico City. The rebuilding process was slow because it came during a time of economic malaise and dislocation, but in the late 1990s and the early twenty-first century Mexico City had a construction boom. A trend in Mexican architecture was restoring and reshaping old buildings, creating a blend between the old and the new. This process has occurred in trendy neighborhoods of Mexico City such as La Condesa. Javier Sánchez (b. 1969) gutted an old warehouse there and converted it into loft apartments for professionals. This was a significant change in terms of housing because most mortgages were for larger apartments and only for families. Also, the restoration promoted a new social environment.

Redesigned, the building offered new communal social space with an open interior garden. Ricardo Legorreta (b. 1931) played a major part in restoring the old historic downtown of Mexico City. He designed new apartment complexes that bring together steel and concrete structures with colonial style courtyards and designs.

BRAZIL

New architectural styles emerged in Brazil, as in Mexico, with dramatic social and political changes. In the first few decades of the twentieth century, the architecture reflected lavish classical styles, symbolizing the nation on a road to progress and prosperity. However, in the 1920s, modernists slowly began to appear in Brazil's main cities. For instance, Gregori Warchavchik (1896–1972), a Russian immigrant, designed the Casa Modernista (1927), the first major modernist building in Latin America.

The critical transformation in design and style coincided with the watershed cultural, economic, and social upheaval of the 1930s. After the 1930 military coup, Getúlio Vargas took power and began to implement economic and social reforms. Vargas organized a competition in 1935 to design the Ministry of Health and Education headquarters in Rio de Janeiro. The winners included Brazil's famous twentieth-century architects Lúcio Costa (1902–1998) and Oscar Niemeyer (b. 1907), and their design emphasized Le Corbusier's functionalist ideas. The critic Mauro Guillén described the building as having "a large bloc of reinforced concrete built on 30-feet high pilotis, sun breakers, on the north side and glass on the south side (Rio being in the Southern Hemisphere), and a rooftop garden. The design occupied an entire city block, leaving room for a plaza" (Guillén 2004).

The most notable and largest testament to modernist influence was the construction of Brazil's current capital, Brasília. Costa developed a general master plan that contained numerous references to the automobile, reflecting the overall modernist concern with the mechanical, the industrial, and technical. The city was clearly separated into areas for housing, work, and leisure. Architects and urban planners involved in the project envisioned an urban utopia that would project equality and progress. Despite the effort put into the city, it has not achieved these lofty goals.

After World War II Brazilian architects began to experiment with the brutalist style. Paulo Mendes da Rocha (b. 1928), its best-known practitioner, designed the Brazilian Sculpture Museum in São Paulo (1988). Another important development is the preservation of older styles of architecture. The Brazilian government took on a major preservation project in Salvador, Bahia, which has a large number of colonial buildings in disrepair. In the twenty-first century new wealthy classes have been preserving and moving into old nineteenth-century *fazenda* (plantation) houses designed in the neoclassical and baroque styles.

ARGENTINA

Argentina, like Peru, did not see the early modernist development that Brazil and Argentina did. A possible explanation for this difference might lie in the way radical social and political change occurred in Argentina. At a time when Argentina ranked as one of the wealthiest countries in the world, modernist designs appeared in 1916, but the liberal landowning elite remained in charge until the 1940s and never forcefully demanded modernist designs. When Juan Domingo Perón was elected president in the 1940s he brought major change to politics and public policy,

but he never fully embraced modernism, preferring the older neoclassical styles. Consequently, modernism was received with ambivalence in Argentina.

Indeed, in the 1920s the young modernist architects Martín Noel (1888–1963) and Angel Guido (1896–1960), rather than embracing Le Corbusier as the major Brazilians did, often critiqued his work. These two sought a style and form more strongly associated with Argentina's own traditions. Juan Kronfuss (1872–1944), a Hungarian immigrant, found inspiration in Argentina's colonial designs rather than in the industrial process that influenced modernism. Likewise, Alberto Prébisch (1899–1970) designed buildings such as the Obelisk (1936) and the Gran Rex movie theater (1937), which incorporated the functionality of modernism, but still prominently displayed colonial motifs.

A few architects more fully embraced the ideal premises of the modernist movement. Antonio Ubaldo Vilar (1889–1966) designed many functionalist buildings that lacked notable design and concern for visual reception. His Banco Popular Argentino stood out for its technically advanced structure but its bland presence. Along the same lines, Ubaldo Vilar designed the tallest reinforced concrete building at that time-a technical rather than artistic achievement. In the first half of the twentieth century, at varying degrees and times, Spanish American countries began to use new modernist designs.

Since its arrival in Spanish America, modernity has been present in various ways and forms in architecture, sometimes in an almost solitary and literal relationship to the great principles of Le Corbusier and in other cases fused or integrated with the landscape. Over time, these forms have allowed a closer approximation to what is truly Spanish America architecture.

See also **Art: The Twentieth Century; Cities and Urbanization.**

BIBLIOGRAPHY

Eggener, Keith. "Postwar Modernism in Mexico: Luis Barragán's Jardines del Pedregal and the International Discourse on Architecture and Place." *Journal of the Society of Architectural Historians* 58, no. 2 (June 1999): 122–145.

Fraser, Valerie. *Building the New World: Studies in the Modern Architecture of Latin America, 1930–1960.* New York: Verso, 2000.

Guillén, Mauro. "Modernism without Modernity: The Rise of Modernist Architecture in Mexico, Brazil, and Argentina, 1890–1940." *Latin American Research Review* 39, no. 2 (June 2004): 6–34.

Gutiérrez, Ramón, Eladio Dieste, and Graciela María Viñuales. *Arquitectura latinoamericana en el siglo XX.* Barcelona: Lunwerg, 1998.

Scarpaci, Joseph L. "Architecture, Design, and Planning: Recent Scholarship on Modernity and Public Space in Latin America." *Latin American Research Review* 38, no. 2 (June 2003): 234–252.

ANA PATRICIA QUINTANA MEZA
BYRON CRITES

ARCINIEGA, CLAUDIO DE (1528–1592).

Claudio de Arciniega (*b.* before 1528; *d.* 1592/93), the most important architect of sixteenth-century New Spain. Originally from Burgos, Spain, Arciniega was in the city of Puebla from 1554 to 1558; in 1559, the viceroy, Luis de Velasco, called him to Mexico City and appointed him *maestro mayor de las Obras de Cantería de la Nueva España.* His 1559 monument commemorating the death of Emperor Charles V is known through an illustrated contemporary publication. In a sober Renaissance style sometimes called *purist,* it provides some idea of what his many other works, known only through documents, may have been like. Arciniega was involved in most of the important construction projects of his time in Mexico City, including the cathedral (of which he was the first architect), the viceregal palace, and the churches of the principal religious orders. He also was called upon to give opinions about the cathedrals of Puebla and Pátzcuaro, the fortifications of Veracruz, and the mines of Taxco. In Mexico City elements in the cathedral and the facade of the Church of San Antonio Abad are ascribed to him or to his followers.

See also **Architecture: Architecture to 1900.**

BIBLIOGRAPHY

George Kubler, *Mexican Architecture of the Sixteenth Century* (1948).

Manuel Toussaint, *Claudio de Arciniega, arquitecto de la Nueva España* (1981).

Additional Bibliography

Cuesta Hernández, Luis Javier. "Sobre el estilo arquitectónico en Claudio de Arciniega: su participación en la construcción de los conventos agustinos de Acolman, Actopan y Metztitlán; su papel en la arquitectura novohispana del siglo XVI." *Anales del Instituto de Investigaciones Estéticas* 22: 76 (Spring 2000): 61–88.

CLARA BARGELLINI

ARCINIEGAS, GERMÁN (1900–1999).

Germán Arciniegas (*b.* 6 December 1900, *d.* 29 November 1999), Colombian writer, diplomat, and political figure. Born in Bogotá of Basque descent, Germán Arciniegas became one of Latin America's most colorful and well-known writers. From an early age, he exhibited a talent for combining politics and journalism. In 1921, while attending the law faculty of the National University in Bogotá, he founded the journal *Universidad,* at which time he also attended a discussion group that included future Colombian reform leader Jorge Eliécer Gaitán. In 1924 Arciniegas received an appointment to the faculty of sociology and continued to write for several newspapers and reviews throughout the next decade. He was director of *La revista de las Indias* in 1938 and *El Tiempo* in 1939. Both positions brought Arciniegas into collaboration with Latin America's leading intellectuals.

In 1939 Arciniegas was appointed Colombian chargé d'affaires in Buenos Aires. It was an exciting time to be in that city, and while there Arciniegas met with and was influenced by the community of exiles from Spain, a distinguished group that included José Ortega y Gasset, Ramiro de Maetzu, Ramón Pérez de Ayala, and also with the Argentines Alfredo Palcios and Victoria Ocampo. Arciniegas was also influenced by the cultural elitism of José Enrique Rodó, and he corresponded with such intellectual figures as Stefan Zweig, Alfonso Reyes, and Gabriela Mistral.

Arciniegas was recalled to Colombia to serve as minister of education in 1941–1942, a position he held for a second time from 1945 to 1946. While in office he founded the Popular Library of Colombian Culture and a museum of colonial artifacts, both designed to enhance the public's awareness of Colombian history and culture. When domestic politics made it uncomfortable for Arciniegas to remain in Colombia, he relocated to the United States for a series of professorships at major universities: the University of Chicago (1942, 1944); the University of California at Berkeley (1945); and Columbia University (1943, 1948–1957).

In 1959 Arciniegas resumed his diplomatic career when he was named ambassador to Italy; the next year he was transferred to Israel, where he received an honorary degree from the University of Tel Aviv. He also became ambassador to Venezuela in 1967 and in the 1970s acted as Colombia's emissary to the Vatican. Arciniegas continued his editorial work throughout his life: he was the original force behind *La Revista de América* and subsequently donated his papers and books to the National Library in Bogotá.

Arciniegas has been a controversial figure, eliciting both praise and criticism. His hostility to Spain and the Conquest, coupled with his economic interpretation of history, have led many critics to condemn him as a spokesman for Moscow, but a closer reading reveals that Arciniegas's true vision of America was as a democratic continent free from the fanaticism of Europe. He glorified the nationalist and democratic spirit of America and praised the triple virtues of independence, democracy, and republicanism, an attitude that has appeared in the hundreds of books and articles he wrote during his lifetime. Among his most notable works are: *Amerigo and the New World: The Life and Times of Amerigo Vespucci,* translated by Harriet de Onís (1955); *América es otra cosa: Antología y epílogo de Juan Gustavo* (1992); *Germans in the Conquest of America: A Sixteenth-Century Venture,* translated by Angel Flores (1943); *America in Europe: A History of the New World in Reverse,* translated by Gabriela Arciniegas (1986); *Biografía del Caribe* (1945); *Bolívar y la revolución* (1984); and *El caballero de El Dorado, vida del conquistador Jiménez de Queseda* (Caracas, 1959).

See also **Literature: Spanish America.**

BIBLIOGRAPHY

Federico Córdova, *Vida y obras de Germán Arciniegas* (1950).

Pedro González Blanco, *Against Arciniegas: A Blunt Criticism* (1956).

Antonio Cacua Prada, *Germán Arciniegas: Su vida contada por el mismo* (1990).

Additional Bibliography

Pabón Pérez, Hugo Leonardo, Stella Lamprea, and Martha Sánchez. *Bibliografía de y sobre Germán Arciniegas.* Bogotá: Instituto Caro y Cuervo, 2001.

Tamayo Fernández, Martalucía. *Germán Arciniegas: El hombre que nació con el siglo: Una autobiografía escrita por otro.* Bogotá, Colombia: Fundación Universidad Central, 1998.

KAREN RACINE

ARCOS, SANTIAGO

ARCOS, SANTIAGO (1822–1874). Santiago Arcos (*b.* 25 July 1822; *d.* September 1874), Chilean radical. The son of a Spanish father and a Chilean mother, Arcos was born in Santiago but grew up in Paris, where in 1845 he met his friend Francisco Bilbao (1823–1865). In 1847 he traveled in the United States (part of the time with the Argentine writer and politician Domingo Faustino Sarmiento [1811–1888]) and from there went to Chile (February 1848). With Bilbao and others he formed the radical Sociedad de la Igualdad (Society of Equality) in April 1850. When the society was suppressed in November 1850, he was deported to Peru, from where he set out to visit the California goldfields. Back in Chile in 1852, he wrote (in prison as a subversive) his classic *Carta a Francisco Bilbao* (first printed in Mendoza, Argentina), an acute analysis of the defects of Chilean society. For this, he was swiftly banished to Argentina. In the 1860s he settled in Paris, where he remained for the most part. With the onset of fatal illness, he committed suicide by throwing himself into the Seine.

See also **Chile, Organizations: Society of Equality.**

BIBLIOGRAPHY

Gabriel Sanhueza, *Santiago Arcos, communista, millonario y calavera* (1956).

Cristián Gazmuri, "El pensamiento político y social de Santiago Arcos," in *Historia* 21 (1986): 249–274.

Additional Bibliography

Jobet, Juilio César. "Las ideas sociales y políticas de Santiago Arcos y Francisco Bilbao (Reprinted from *Atenea* no. 208, 1942)." *Atenea* 481–482 (2000): 275–298.

SIMON COLLIER

ARDEN QUIN, CARMELO (1913–).

Carmelo Arden Quin (*b.* 1913), Uruguayan abstract artist. Born in Rivera, Uruguay, Arden Quin was educated in Catholic schools in Brazil. He converted to Marxism in 1930 and began to study art in 1932. In 1935 he met the influential constructivist artist Joaquín Torres García in Montevideo. Moving to Buenos Aires three years later, Arden Quin studied philosophy and literature, and soon joined that city's artistic avant-garde, which included Edgar Bayley, Gyula Kosice, Tomás Maldonado, and Lidy Prati. By the early 1940s, Arden Quin's early cubist style had given way to a geometric abstraction that tentatively rejected the convention of a rectangular frame by employing irregular and cut-out supports for paintings and collages; he pursued this direction in his art throughout the remainder of the decade, as did others in his milieu. He also experimented with sculptures and paintings with movable components, such as his *Coplanal* (1945), a square relief with manipulable geometric figures at each corner.

Along with Kosice and Rhod Rothfuss, Arden Quin was one of the chief contributors to the single issue of the review *Arturo*, published in 1944, and with them he initiated the Grupo Madí in 1946. He and the sculptor Martín Blaszko left the group in 1948, and Arden Quin moved to Paris, where he began to associate with some of the leading figures of European abstract art, including Jean Arp, Auguste Herbin, Michel Seuphor, Constantin Brancusi, Serge Poliakoff, and Nicolas de Staël. One-man exhibitions of Arden Quin's art were held at the Galerie de la Salle, Saint-Paul de Vence, in 1978 and at the Espace Latino-Américain, Paris, in 1983.

See also **Art: The Twentieth Century.**

BIBLIOGRAPHY

Mari Carmen Ramírez, "Re-Positioning the South: The Legacy of El Taller Torres-García in Contemporary Latin American Art," and Florencia Bazzano Nelson, "Carmelo Arden Quin," in Mari Carmen Ramírez, ed., *El Taller Torres-García: The School of the South and Its Legacy* (1992), pp. 260–261, 348–349.

Elizabeth Ferrer, "Carmelo Arden Quin," in Waldo Rasmussen et al., eds., *Latin American Artists of the Twentieth Century* (1993), p. 372.

Additional Bibliography

Goodman, Shelley. Carmelo Arden Quin: *When Art Jumped Out of Its Cage.* Dallas, TX: MADI, 2004.

Maistre, Agnés de, and Carmelo Arden Quin. *Carmelo Arden Quin.* Nice: Demaistre, 1996.

JOSEPH R. WOLIN

ARDÉVOL, JOSÉ (1911–1981). José

Ardévol (*b.* 13 March 1911; *d.* 7 January 1981), Cuban composer. Born in Barcelona, Ardévol began composing as a boy. His father, Fernando Ardévol, conductor of Barcelona's Chamber Orchestra, instructed him in piano, composition, and conducting. At nineteen he studied conducting with Hermann Scherchen in Germany. In 1930 he moved to Cuba, where he taught history and aesthetics at Havana Municipal Conservatory (1936–1941); he also taught composition in the universities of Havana (1945–1950) and Oriente (1949–1951). Ardévol founded the Chamber Orchestra of Havana (1934), conducting it until 1952, and helped found the Grupo de Renovación Musical (1942), of which he was the spokesman and leader. He was very much committed to the Cuban Revolution, directing an underground group called the National Music Committee. In 1959 he was appointed director of the radio orchestras of the Ministry of Education and subsequently national director of music. He also served as editor of the musical magazine *Revolución* and as professor of composition at the Havana Conservatory (1965) and the National School of Music (1968). Ardévol's early music reflects a neoclassical influence mixed with nationalism; by the 1940s he had changed toward serialism and atonality, influenced by Anton von Webern. His works include *Música de cámara, Tres Ricercari, Suites cubanas,* several concerti and other orchestral works, plus a considerable amount of chamber and vocal music. He won the Cuban First National Music Award six times (1938–1953) and the International Ricordi Symphonic Award (1949). His *Música para pequeña orquesta* was a commission that premiered at the First Inter-American Musical Festival in Washington, D.C., in 1958. He died in Havana.

See also **Music: Art Music.**

BIBLIOGRAPHY

Composers of the Americas, vol. 1 (1955).

Alejo Carpentier, *La música en Cuba,* 2d ed. (1961).

Gérard Béhague, *Music in Latin America* (1979); *New Grove Dictionary of Music and Musicians,* vol. 1 (1980).

Additional Bibliography

Ardévol, José. *José Ardévol: Correspondencia cruzada.* Havana: Editorial Letras Cubanas, 2004.

SUSANA SALGADO

ARENA. *See* **Brazil, Political Parties: National Renovating Alliance (ARENA); El Salvador, Political Parties: National Republican Alliance (ARENA).**

ARENALES, JUAN ANTONIO ÁLVAREZ DE (1770–1831).

Juan Antonio Álvarez de Arenales (*b.* 13 June 1770; *d.* 4 December 1831), military and political leader of the Independence era. Born in Spain, Arenales entered on a military career that in 1784 took him to South America. He served in Upper Peru (later Bolivia) where he demonstrated a special interest in the welfare of the Indian population. His involvement in the 25 May 1809 revolution at Chuquisaca led to his arrest and imprisonment, but he escaped to collaborate first with Manuel Belgrano in his campaigns in the Argentine Northwest and Upper Peru and then with José de San Martín in his attempt to liberate Peru. Returning to Salta, where he had married, he became governor in 1823. Arenales sought to emulate the enlightened reformism of Bernardino Rivadavia and the Unitarist faction and also participated in the final mopping up of royalist resistance in Bolivia. However, in the general backlash against the Unitarists' effort to impose a centralist constitution, Arenales was deposed as governor early in 1827. He died in exile in Bolivia.

See also **Peru: From the Conquest Through Independence.**

BIBLIOGRAPHY

Jacinto R. Yaben, *Biografías argentinas y sudamericanas: Perú en 1821,* vol. 1 (1938), pp. 165–173.

Additional Bibliography

Castro Rodríguez, Carlos. *Don Juan Antonio Alvarez de Arenales: soldado de la independencia americana, brigadier general del Ejército Argentino y mariscal de Chile

y del Ejército del Perú.* Sucre: Corte Suprema de Justicia de la Nación, 1997.

DAVID BUSHNELL

ARENAS, REINALDO (1943–1990).

Reinaldo Arenas (*b.* 16 July 1943; *d.* 7 December 1990), Cuban novelist, short story writer, poet, and essayist. Arenas was born in Perronales, a rural area in Oriente Province. His early experiences living in the country in a house full of what he terms "semisingle" women (as depicted in his novels *Singing in the Well* [1982] and *The Palace of the Very White Skunks* [1991]) shaped much of his work and character, as did the friendship and guidance of writers Virgilio Piñera and José Lezama Lima when he was a young man. Although Arenas received little formal schooling as a child, his mother taught him to read and write, and he began writing while very young. In 1959 he joined Fidel Castro's rebel forces, and after the fall of the government of Fulgencio Batista he studied agrarian management in the Oriente town of Holguín and in Havana. His increasing disenchantment and unwillingness to compromise with the new Cuban regime, along with the unabashed homosexuality evident in both his life and his work, caused him to run afoul of the Castro government. Although both his novels *Singing in the Well* (1982) and *Hallucinations* (1971) received some attention in Cuba, he was persecuted, imprisoned, and censored there, even as his work was being published and acclaimed abroad. In 1969 *Hallucinations,* which had been smuggled out of Cuba, was honored in France as one of the best foreign novels. In 1980 he joined the Mariel Boatlift and left for the United States, where he settled in New York City until taking his own life in the final stages of AIDS.

Arenas's work takes the lyrical, ornate, baroque style of Cuban literary tradition and applies it to the themes of rebellion, repression, and the dehumanization that the subjugation of human beings brings upon both victims and perpetrators. Using the specific situations that he lived and knew intimately, he explores the universality of slavery and oppression. Particularly successful examples are his long poem *Leprosorio* (1990) and his novels *Arturo, la estrella más brillante* (1984) and *El asalto* (1991). Shortly before his death he finished his autobiography, *Antes que anochezca* (1992; translated as *Before Night Falls,* 1993). His work has been translated into many languages.

See also **Homosexuality and Bisexuality in Literature.**

BIBLIOGRAPHY

Perla Rozencraig, *Reinaldo Arenas: Narrativa de transgresión* (1986).

Roberto Valero, *El desamparado humor de Reinaldo Arenas* (1991).

Additional Bibliography

Machover, Jacobo. *La memoria frente al poder: Escritores cubanos del exilio: Guillermo Cabrera Infante, Severo Sarduy, Reinaldo Arenas.* Valencia: Universidad de Valencia, 2001.

Soto, Francisco. *Reinaldo Arenas.* London: Prentice Hall, 1998.

ROBERTO VALERO

ARENAS CONSPIRACY. Arenas Conspiracy, a plot to restore Spanish rule in Mexico that was uncovered on 19 January 1827 in Mexico City. The instigator of the plot, a "royal commissioner," was never identified. First arrested was a Spanish friar, Joaquín Arenas, who revealed the conspiracy while attempting to recruit a military commander for the cause. The plan called for the arrest of President Guadalupe Victoria and General Vicente Guerrero on 20 January, the restoration of all Spaniards to their colonial posts, and amnesties and rewards for all who cooperated in the restoration of monarchical government. Only a part of the leadership, including the Spanish generals Gregorio Arana, Pedro Celestino Negrete, and José Antonio Echávarri, was discovered. In the Federal District, Puebla, and Oaxaca, at least sixteen individuals were arrested, five of whom were friars. Fourteen were executed between April 1827 and September 1829, including General Arana and five friars, thus circumventing corporate fueros. The trials became a *cause célèbre,* dividing the two major political parties, the Scottish-rite and York-rite Masons (Yorkinos and Escoceses), with the latter taking the offensive against the Spaniards. The plot spurred the effort of 1827–1834 to expel Spanish-born males from Mexico.

See also **Mexico: 1810-1910.**

BIBLIOGRAPHY

The major sources are Jaime Delgado, *España y México en el siglo XIX,* vol. 1 (1950), pp. 357–375; José María Bocanegra, *Memorias para la historia de México Independiente, 1822–1846,* vol. 1 (1892), pp. 414–440; Juan Suárez y Navarro, *Historia de México y del general Antonio López de Santa Anna,* vol. 1 (1850), pp. 79, 390–395, 417–436, 704–722; and Romeo Flores Caballero, *Counterrevolution: The Role of Spaniards in the Independence of Mexico, 1804–1838,* translated by Jaime E. Rodríguez O. (1974).

Additional Bibliography

Hale, Charles C. *The Transformation of Liberalism in Late Nineteenth-Century Mexico.* Princeton: Princeton University Press, 1989.

Rodríguez, Jaime E.O, ed. *The Divine Charter: Constitutionalism and Liberalism in Nineteenth-Century Mexico.* Lanham, MD: Rowman & Littlefield, 2005.

Thomson, Guy P.C. *Patriotism, Politics, and Popular Liberalism in Nineteenth-Century Mexico: Juan Francisco Lucas and the Puebla Sierra.* Wilmington, DE: Scholarly Resources, 1999.

Wasserman, Mark. *Everyday Life and Politics in Nineteenth-century Mexico: Men, Women, and War.* Albuquerque: University of New Mexico Press, 2000.

HAROLD DANA SIMS

AREQUIPA. Arequipa, a city and department in southern Peru. Founded by Spaniards in 1540, Arequipa became a commercial center during colonial times and the second city of modern Peru.

The city of Arequipa lies on the banks of the Chili River, 7,700 feet above sea level and approximately 60 miles from the Pacific coast. Towering over the city is the volcano Misti (18,990 feet high), a snow-covered, picturesque cone. The region is extremely arid, but irrigation has allowed agriculture to flourish in the Arequipa Valley.

Andean peoples inhabited the valley long before the arrival of the Incas, despite the assertion of Garcilaso de la Vega that Inca Mayta Cápac found the valley unpopulated. The need for pasturage and agricultural products induced Andean ethnic groups to send colonists into the valley. Aymara and even earlier peoples lived along the river. They were still there when the Inca armies arrived. The Incas may have forcibly resettled other peoples to Arequipa as *mitmaqs* (colonizers) for political purposes, but they called all the groups in the valley *mitmaqs* for propaganda, to discredit the existence of early cultures and civilizations.

In 1535, Spaniards first arrived in the region, marauding outward from Cuzco, the Inca capital that had just fallen to the conquistadores. Two years later, Diego de Almagro and his expedition passed through on their return from Chile. By 1539 some Spaniards had received *encomiendas* (grants of Indian labor and tribute) in the valley. The first Spanish attempt to establish a settlement in the region, however, was in 1539 at Camaná on the coast. When that locale proved hot and disease-infested, they received permission from Francisco Pizarro to move inland and founded Arequipa on 15 August 1540.

An oasis in the desert expanses of southern Peru, Arequipa quickly became an agricultural and commercial center. As president of the audiencia (high court) of Lima, Pedro de la Gasca created the *corregimiento* of Arequipa in 1548, the first province in the region. At about the same time a branch (*caja real*) of the royal treasury opened in the city. Residents used light volcanic sillar for construction, and Arequipa soon became known as the "White City." Arequipa distributed merchandise from Lima throughout southern Peru and was a stopping point for traders on their way to the mining camps of Upper Peru. Using the nearby port of Quilca, Arequipa transshipped the royal treasure on its passage from Potosí to Lima.

Around 1600, however, Arequipa's fortunes suffered a prolonged, albeit temporary, setback. The port of Arica became the southern conduit to Upper Peru, to the detriment of Arequipa's commercial life. Volcanic eruptions and earthquakes in 1600 and 1604 devastated the city and its farmlands. (The region is geologically unstable and has suffered severe tremors on many occasions.) The neighboring Vitor Valley, where many residents had vineyards, was particularly hard hit and took several years to recover. At roughly the same time, Arequipa, which had been perhaps the first great Peruvian wine producer, lost the Lima market to vintners around Ica and Pisco. But Arequipan wines retained their dominance in Upper Peru. The rich farmlands generally yielded a surplus of foodstuffs such as wheat, corn, and potatoes, and abundant flocks allowed the development of a significant textile industry. In 1612 it became the episcopal seat of the Arequipa diocese, with jurisdiction over all of southern coastal Peru.

The 1700s brought new prosperity to Arequipa. Local vintners began distilling *aguardiente* (brandy) from their surplus wine and made large profits from its sale in Upper Peru. The Proclamation of Free Trade (1778) increased commercial activity, although higher royal fiscal exactions caused a short-lived rebellion in January 1780. When Charles III established the Peruvian intendancies in 1784, the intendant of Arequipa received jurisdiction over all the provinces of southern coastal Peru. By the 1790s Arequipa was the second largest city in the viceroyalty, with a population of 22,030. It was a royalist stronghold during the wars for independence. Pumacahua and his indigenous soldiers invaded Arequipa in 1814 and killed the intendant, but they were able to hold the city only briefly.

Despite its royalist sentiments, however, Arequipa's economic interests lay less with Lima than with Upper Peru, and following independence Arequipa became a chief opponent of Lima's attempts at political centralization. Foreign commercial interests flocked to Arequipa, attracted by its economy and the access it offered to Bolivia. Arequipa's wine and brandy trade declined, replaced by wool exports. By 1876 railroads linked Arequipa with the coast and with Cuzco via Juliaca, and a Bank of Arequipa opened in 1872. The city has remained a bureaucratic, commercial, and agricultural center, attracting ever greater numbers of migrants from the sierra. Its population in 2005 was 860,000, with 1,140,000 in the department. The late nineteenth-century historical novel *Jorge, el hijo del pueblo* (1892) by María Nieves y Bustamante captures midnineteenth-century Arequipeña society during the time of the 1864 to 1856 civil war.

See also **Charles III of Spain; Gasca, Pedro de la.**

BIBLIOGRAPHY

Germán Leguía y Martínez, *Historia de Arequipa*, 2 vols. (1912–1914).

Victor M. Barriga, *Memorias para la historia de Arequipa*, 4 vols. (1941–1952).

Guillermo Galdos Rodríguez, *La rebelión de los Pasquines* (1967).

Alberto Flores-Galindo, *Arequipa y el sur andino: Ensayo de historia regional (siglos XVIII–XX* (1977).

Alejandro Málaga Medina, *Arequipa: Estudios históricos*, 3 vols. (1981–1986).

Keith A. Davies, *Landowners in Colonial Peru* (1984).

Kendall W. Brown, *Bourbons and Brandy: Imperial Reform in Eighteenth-Century Arequipa* (1986).

Additional Bibliography

Ballón Lozada, Héctor. *Cien años de vida política de Arequipa, 1890–1990.* Arequipa, Peru: Universidad Nacional de San Agustín, 1992.

Chambers, Sarah C. *From Subjects to Citizens: Honor, Gender, and Politics in Arequipa, Peru, 1780–1854.* University Park: Pennsylvania State University Press, 1999.

Nieves y Bustamante, María. *Jorge, el hijo del pueblo: Novela.* Lima: Mejía Baca, 1958.

KENDALL W. BROWN

ARÉVALO BERMEJO, JUAN JOSÉ

(1904–1990). Juan José Arévalo Bermejo (*b.* 10 September 1904; *d.* 7 October 1990), president of Guatemala (1945–1951). Born in Taxisco, Santa Rosa, he graduated from the Escuela Normal in 1922. After working for the Ministry of Education, he spent the duration of the Ubico administration in voluntary exile in Argentina, where he completed his doctorate in philosophy in 1934. The leaders of the October Revolution of 1944 brought him back to campaign for the presidency, which he won overwhelmingly in December 1944.

Arévalo took office on 15 March 1945 with a broad, and ultimately contradictory, populist agenda: to pursue economic development while defending economic nationalism; to create a stable democratic order while greatly increasing political participation; and to expand social welfare while encouraging industrialization. Unable to achieve all of these objectives, the Arévalo administration, nevertheless, changed the legal and institutional structure of the country. Among its major accomplishments were a social security law (1946) guaranteeing workmen's compensation, maternity benefits, and health care; a labor law (1947) legalizing collective bargaining and the right to strike, and mandating a minimum wage (although peasant unions were forbidden); the Social Security Institute (IGSS), which built hospitals and clinics throughout the country; the National Production Institute (INFOP), which provided credit and expertise for small producers; and the creation of a national bank and a national planning office. Foreign investments were to be left intact but subject to government regulation. In 1949 the Congress enacted the Law of Forced Rental, which allowed peasants to rent unused land on large estates. The government also began to distribute lands confiscated from their German owners during World War II.

Arévalo's populist coalition began to unravel early in his administration. Among the causes were the establishment of diplomatic ties with the Soviet Union on 20 April 1945, the emergence of Communist leadership in the Confederación de Trabajadores de Guatemala (Víctor Manuel Gutíerrez Garbín) and the Partido de Acción Revolucionaria (José Manuel Fortuny), the creation of the Communist-oriented Escuela Claridad (1946), and the passing of a Law on the Expression of Thought (1947) that expanded the definition of sedition to include anything urging "disregard of the laws or authorities."

The final blow to the legitimacy of the Arévalo administration was his connivance with his hand-picked successor, Captain Jacobo Arbenz, in the assassination of Arbenz's conservative presidential rival, Major Francisco Javier Arana, on 18 July 1949. The assassination touched off a military rebellion that was put down by students and workers armed by Defense Minister Arbenz. However, stimulated by the "minute of silence" demonstrations commemorating the assassination, many students and professionals joined the conservative opposition. In all, President Arévalo had to contend with over twenty coup attempts against his government.

Although he left Guatemala at the end of his presidency and Arbenz was overthrown in 1954, *arevalismo* remained an important current in Guatemalan politics and was greatly feared by the supporters of the counterrevolution of 1954. His 1962 announcement (from Mexico) that he would once again run for the presidency in 1963 precipitated the demand that a "preventive coup" be launched by the army. On 29 March he secretly crossed the Mexican border, precipitating the overthrow of the Ydígoras Fuentes government. The military government that followed canceled the elections, thereby ending his bid for the presidency. He returned to Guatemala City in the 1980s, where he lived until his death.

See also **Guatemala, Political Parties: Revolutionary Action Party (PAR).**

BIBLIOGRAPHY

Juan José Arévalo, *The Shark and the Sardines* (1961), *Anti-Kommunism in Latin America: An X-Ray of a Process Leading to a New Colonialism* (1963), and *Escritos Políticos y Discursos* (1953).

Archer Bush, *Organized Labor in Guatemala, 1944–1949* (1950).

Piero Gleijes, *Shattered Hope: The Guatemalan Revolution and the United States* (1991).

Stephen Schlesinger and Stephen Kinzer, *Bitter Fruit: The Untold Story of the American Coup in Guatemala* (1982, 1983).

Ronald M. Schneider, *Communism in Guatemala, 1944–1954* (1958).

Leo A. Suslow, *Aspects of Social Reforms in Guatemala, 1944–1949: Problems of Planned Social Change in an Underdeveloped Country* (1950).

Additional Bibliography

Juárez-Paz, Rigoberto. *El pensamiento de Juan José Arévalo, Héctor-Neri Castañeda y otros escritos.* Guatemala: [n.d.], 1996.

LeBaron, Alan. "Impaired Democracy in Guatemala: 1944–1951." Ph.D. diss., University of Florida, 1988.

ROLAND H. EBEL

ARÉVALO MARTÍNEZ, RAFAEL

(1885–1975). Rafael Arévalo Martínez (*b.* 25 d. 1975), one of Guatemala's foremost literary figures. Born in Guatemala City, Arévalo Martínez attended the Colegio de Infantes, a school where children of the rich and the poor studied side by side. Along with other fathers of Guatemalan literature, such as Miguel Ángel Asturias, Enrique Gómez Carrillo, and Máximo Soto-Hall, Arévalo Martínez is credited with introducing modernism to twentieth-century Guatemalan literature. Influen-ced by two of Latin America's foremost modernist poets, Rubén Darío and José Martí y Pérez, Arévalo Martínez exhibits the development of a distinct, yet confident, Latin American consciousness in his novels and poetry.

The ability of Arévalo Martínez to combine aesthetic concerns with a social commitment is undoubtedly his largest contribution to contemporary Latin American prose and poetry. Throughout his long literary career, his unique literary style balanced his personal search for identity with a need to discover his place in society. Among Arévalo Martínez's outstanding works are his 1915 masterpiece, *El hombre que parecía un caballo* (The Man Who Looked Like a Horse), which remains one of the finest pieces of literature in the first quarter of the twentieth century; the psycho-zoological utopian classics, *El mundo de los maharachíasa* (The World of the Maharachías [1939]) and *Viaje a Ipanda* (Journey to Ipanda [1939]); and his critical historical study of the Estrada Cabrera administration, *¡Ecce Pericles! La tiranía de Manuel Estrada Cabrera en Guatemala* (3rd ed., 1983).

See also **Literature: Spanish America.**

BIBLIOGRAPHY

María A. Salgado, *Rafael Arévalo Martínez* (1979).

Additional Bibliography

Nájera, Francisco. *El pacto autobiográfico en la obra de Rafael Arévalo Martínez.* Guatemala: Editorial Cultural, 2003.

WADE A. KIT

ARGENTINA

This entry includes the following articles:
THE COLONIAL PERIOD
THE NINETEENTH CENTURY
THE TWENTIETH CENTURY

THE COLONIAL PERIOD

The territory of what became Argentina in 1853 was incorporated to the Spanish Empire in the middle of the sixteenth century as a marginal area, and it remained so until the end of the eighteenth century. With neither dense indigenous populations nor coveted material resources, these lands received only scant attention from the Spaniards.

EXPLORATION AND SETTLEMENT

The first explorations of the Atlantic coast of the future Argentina came in the aftermath of the discovery of the Pacific in 1513, which prompted efforts to find a passageway from the Atlantic. Trying to find such passage, Juan Díaz de Solís in 1516 reached a vast water mass that he called Mar Dulce, which in time was known as Río de la Plata. In 1520 Ferdinand Magellan finally found the passage to the Pacific Ocean after exploring the whole coast of Patagonia and gathering rich ethnographic observations on the native populations. In 1526 the Spanish crown sent an experienced Italian explorer, Sebastian Cabot, to follow Magellan's route to the Pacific. When Cabot's expedition arrived at the Río de la Plata, it encountered survivors of the failed Solís expedition, who relayed stories about a wealthy king ruling over an inland territory rich in silver. Craving riches, the expedition turned into the Río de la Plata, sailed north along the Paraná River, and established the first settlement in the area, the short-lived fort of Sancti Spiritu (1527). After reaching the Paraguay River and failing to find any silver, Cabot evacuated the fort and sailed back to Spain.

In the 1530s the true conquest and settlement of Argentina began. Spanish expeditions entered the territory following three different routes. In the mid-1530s the Adelantado Don Pedro de Mendoza sailed from Spain to the Río de la Plata area with a very well equipped expedition of 1,500 men that established Buenos Aires in 1536. The city did not prosper, due mainly to indigenous resistance to the Spanish presence. Besieged and starving, Mendoza's lieutenants (the *adelantado* had died of syphilis on his way back to Spain) decided in 1541 to evacuate the city and transfer its residents to the town of Asunción, Paraguay, established in 1537. Thus, Asunción became the center of Spanish colonization in the Río de la Plata area. Its advantages over Buenos Aires were obvious to the settlers: It was located closer to the alleged silver hill and had a dense indigenous population, the agriculturalist Guaraní peoples, who were ready to collaborate with the Spaniards as laborers and soldiers in exchange for a military alliance against their bellicose neighbors. In the 1570s and 1580s people from Asunción—largely mestizos—moved southward to establish the towns of Santa Fe (1573) and Corrientes (1588) and to resettle Buenos Aires in 1580.

BARTERING WITH NATIVES OF PATAGONIA.
*From De Gennes' "Voyage to the Straits of Magellan,"
by the Sieur Froger,* 1698.

Spaniard Bartering with Natives of Patagonia, from de Gennes' *Voyage to the Straits of Magellan*, by the Sieur Froger (1698), from *The Romance of the River Plate*, Vol. I, by W. H. Koebel (1914) (engraving) after German School (17th century). Treaties between Native Americans and Spaniards in Patagonia brought periods of peaceful relations, as depicted here. PRIVATE COLLECTION/ THE STAPLETON COLLECTION/ THE BRIDGEMAN ART LIBRARY

The Spanish exploration and settlement of Argentina's northern area (known as Tucumán in colonial times) came as a result of conflicts over the spoils of the conquest of Peru. From 1550 onward, many unrewarded Spaniards joined the expeditions to Tucumán to find riches. These expeditions established many cities whose survival was helped by the presence of sedentary indigenous populations (most of which had previously been incorporated to the Inca Empire) with rigid social and political hierarchies and accustomed to regular work habits. After three failed attempts at establishing a city in the area, the Spaniards managed finally to found Santiago del Estero in 1553 among Quechua-speaking Indians. Though the Spaniards tried to expand their control to the surrounding territory, they failed to establish another stable city until 1565, when they founded San Miguel de Tucumán.

In the 1570s two major competing but complementary colonizing projects were advanced. Juan de Matienzo, *oidor* (judge) in the Audiencia of Charcas, advocated the continuation of exploration and settlement towards the Atlantic to establish better links with Spain. Viceroy Francisco de Toledo, on the contrary, promoted the consolidation of territories already explored through the founding of new cities among the still-belligerent Indians of Tucumán. Following Toledo's instructions, the cities of Córdoba (1573), Salta (1582), La Rioja (1591), and Jujuy (1593) were established. Based on these cities the Spaniards managed to control the surrounding territories, though indigenous resistance continued in the western parts of Tucumán until the middle of the seventeenth century.

The area to the west of Argentina, known as Cuyo, was settled from Chile from the 1560s onward. The cities of Mendoza (1561), San Juan (1562), and San Luis (1594) were incorporated to the kingdom of Chile, whence their scant population originally came.

By the end of the sixteenth century, all of the colonial towns had already been established. Political and judicial organization ensued. In 1563 the crown created the *gobernación* (province) of Tucumán, placing it under the jurisdiction of the Audiencia of Charcas. This province consisted of the cities of Santiago del Estero, Tucumán, Córdoba, Salta, Jujuy, La Rioja, and Catamarca (the latter established in 1683) and their rural jurisdictions. The oldest city, Santiago del Estero, was made provincial capital (where the governor resided), but the seat of power was transferred to Córdoba in the seventeenth century due to its larger population and economic importance. On the Atlantic side, in 1617 the crown separated the old province of Paraguay from the province of Buenos Aires. The latter included the cities of Buenos Aires (seat of the governor), Santa Fe, and Corrientes and was also placed under the jurisdiction of the Audiencia of Charcas, except for a brief period (1661–1671) when a high court operated in Buenos Aires. The regions of Cuyo became a *corregimiento* (political and military jurisdiction) dependent on Chile. Its territory was thus politically and judicially separated from the other cities that would later become part of Argentina. This political and judicial organization survived until the sweeping reforms of the late eighteenth century altered it considerably.

INDIAN SURVIVAL AND RESISTANCE

In general, the Spaniards managed to control more quickly the sedentary, agriculturalist indigenous populations of Tucumán and Paraguay than the hunter-gatherer, nomadic ones of Chaco, the Pampas, and Patagonia. Whereas several of the sedentary groups maintained fierce resistance to Spanish occupation until the 1660s, the hunter-gatherers survived beyond the Spaniards' control throughout the colonial period. They were called *bárbaros* (savages) by the Spaniards who engaged in frequent confrontations with them.

Tucumán: Encomienda and Indian Labor. From the mid-1550s onwards, the crown distributed the labor of the subdued Indian groups of Tucuman in encomiendas among the Spanish conquistadors. A few of these encomiendas were very large and were located mostly in Jujuy and Salta (such as Casabindo and Cochinoca, given to the marquis of Tojo in 1605 and comprising 2,200 people as late as 1760), but the majority of them were small, encompassing only one or two dozen Indians.

The encomienda system in Tucumán had features that set it apart from other areas in Spanish America. First, the institution took the form of *encomienda de servicio personal* (labor encomienda) as Indians paid their emcomenderos exclusively in labor despite the efforts made by the authorities in the seventeenth century to introduce payment in money, as they had done in the rest of Spanish America. To fulfill their obligations the encomienda Indians worked in the encomenderoś haciendas or wove textiles for them. Some encomenderos even rented their Indians to other Spanish *hacendados* as agricultural labor or as muleteers and porters to transport goods. This last custom was very common in Salta, Jujuy, and Cuyo, where it took the name of *saca de indios* (extraction of Indians) to Chile.

Second, several encomiendas continued to exist in Tucumán until the end of the colonial period, long after they had been abolished in other areas. By 1700 only a handful of Indian communities holding communal lands and ruled by autonomous ethnic authorities existed, mostly located in Jujuy and Santiago del Estero. Called also *pueblos de indios* (indigenous towns), they survived until the first years after independence. The rest of the indigenous population lived on Spanish haciendas, where they worked as day laborers or tenants. Tenancy appeared to have been widespread in

Salta and Jujuy, where Indian peasants paid rent in a combination of kind (sometimes in money) and labor. The day laborers (known locally as *peones*) received a low salary in kind (mostly textiles) or less frequently in money.

Indian Resistance: The Calchaquí Uprisings.

Indian resistance to Spanish settlement was very strong in the Calchaquí Valley, the western mountainous districts of Catamarca, Salta, and La Rioja in Tucumán. The Spaniards had assigned the Indian groups in Calchaquí to encomiendas, but these never materialized due to indigenous resistance. Beginning in the mid-1560s the Indians rose up against Spanish attempts at setting up towns, expelling or killing Spaniards and even priests sent to the area to convert them. Coalitions of several Indian groups participated in two bouts of rebellion against Spanish control, the first in the 1630s and the second in the 1660s. The second Calchaquí uprising was led by a Spanish adventurer named Pedro Bohorques, who managed to convince the Indians that he was a descendant of the Incas. Apparently the Calchaquí groups accepted his leadership, hoping that he would guide them toward elimination of the Spanish presence in the area and possibly restore the old indigenous order. The violence of this uprising and its unified leadership persuaded the Spanish authorities to arm a strong *entrada* (military expedition) to quash Indian insurgence. Governor Alonso Mercado y Villacorta summoned the urban militia, asked the governor of Buenos Aires for military help, entered the Calchaquí area, and crushed the rebels. The defeated Indian groups were divided up and allocated in encomiendas or individually to Spaniards who had participated in the military campaign; some of them were even enslaved. Some groups were uprooted and relocated to distant areas, such as the residents of Quilmes, who were resettled on the outskirts of Buenos Aires.

Frontier Areas.

With the defeat of the Calchaquí rebellion, Indian resistance within Spanish territory came to an end. But the Spaniards could not extend their control on the Chaco, east of Tucumán, and the Pampa and Patagonia areas in the south. On these frontiers Spaniards and Indians engaged in relations that involved violence but also all sorts of commercial and cultural exchanges. In the seventeenth century the cities located near both frontiers were in constant danger of Indian invasions. Local militias were called upon to patrol the border and defend the territory. Hostility was more virulent in Pampa and Patagonia as the Araucanian Indians had mastered horsemanship since the Spanish Conquest. In the eighteenth century, Spanish authorities developed a three-pronged approach to control the Indian frontiers: the establishment of forts and creation of regular military corps (called *partidarios* or *blandengues*) to keep the Indians at bay; the creation of religious missions to convert them to Catholicism and to Spanish work habits, and the organization of military expeditions to expand territorial control. In Pampa and Patagonia, Indians and Spaniards signed treaties that launched a period of stabilized ethnic relations that lasted until independence.

Jesuit Missions.

A unique experiment at controlling Indian populations took place in the northeastern area of the Río de la Plata. Starting in the seventeenth century, the Jesuits established religious missions; there were thirty mission towns by the middle of the eighteenth century. The Jesuit missions attracted a good number of Guaraní Indians, to whom the Jesuits offered protection and shelter against Portuguese *bandeirantes* (slave traders, who enslaved them) and enemy Indian groups. Mission Indians received religious education, knowledge of Spanish literacy skills, and training in music and crafts. They were allowed to hold land in common and to have their own ethnic authorities. Still, the priests supervised most aspects of economic and cultural life in the missions, although they left the solution of daily issues to the Indian authorities. These missions were major players in the colonial economy, especially in the production of *yerba mate* (a very popular infusion then and now), which was commercialized throughout the region. The missions helped also control the border between the Spanish and Portuguese empires. To put an end to a long-standing conflict, in 1750 Spain decided to hand out most of the territory where the missions were located to Portugal in exchange for Colonia do Sacramento. Believing that Portugal was to dissolve the missions, the Indians rebelled against the territorial swap in the Guaraní War, but the rebellion was put down by forces of the two empires combined. After the expulsion of the Jesuits from Spain and its colonies in 1767, the missions entered a period of sharp decline.

ECONOMY AND SOCIETY (1600–1750)

Starting in the late sixteenth century, the cities of Tucumán and Río de la Plata were rapidly integrated into the Andean economic space that revolved around the production and circulation of silver extracted in Potosí (Upper Peru). Throughout most of the colonial period, both areas specialized in the production of primary goods paid for by Potosí's silver and largely consumed by the mining and urban centers of Upper Peru and Peru.

Land, Agrarian Production, and Labor.

Argentina's agrarian history has always been dominated by the image of large cattle ranches inhabited by a roaming rural population, the gauchos. Around the turn of the twenty-first century, historians replaced this image with one of a varied landholding pattern, diversified production, and a more stable population.

In the province of Tucumán, landholding was heavily concentrated in the hands of a small Spanish elite living in the cities. Its members owned large haciendas. In Jujuy and Santago del Estero they were located next to Indian towns that managed to keep control of their communal land, In Tucumán, Salta, and Córdoba they engulfed former Indian communities that had lost their rights to land ownership. Agrarian production was largely organized through encomienda, though Indians and mestizos living within haciendas also were part of the work force. Tenancy was widespread in some areas and tenants (*arrendatarios, agregrados*) were required to pay rent in a combination of labor and kind more than in money. Generally, large rural estates combined agriculture (wheat, corn) with cattle and mule raising and wintering. Some of the estates had lumber works and soap and candle mills.

In the pampas of Buenos Aires and Santa Fe, large ranches were not the prevailing agrarian unit. The rural landscape was dominated by small- and medium-size productive units; therefore, landholding was not fully concentrated in the hands of a landed elite. Tenancy was more general than previously thought and encompassed various arrangements between tenants and landlords that involved payment in money (much more common than in Tucumán) and kind. As encomienda Indians were very few, several labor arrangements existed: Family labor in small and medium units was supplemented with the occasional hire of day laborers (peones); larger *estancias* (cattle ranches) hired tenants and day laborers as temporary labor, and slave workers were common among them. Salaries paid in money were more common than those paid in kind. Some estates specialized in cattle and mule raising, others in agriculture (especially wheat); some establishments combined both.

Trade and Transportation.

The economy of colonial Argentina pivoted around the Andean markets that centered on the production and circulation of silver. Apart from supplying the small urban markets of Río de la Plata and Tucumán, agriculture and pastoral production was exported to the mining centers and cities of Peru and Upper Peru, mainly to Potosí. Mules and cattle; cattle by-products such as grease, tallow, soap, and shoe leather; cheap woolen textiles; low-quality spirits; and wooden items (shafts, beams) were the main products sent to the Andes.

This market was linked by precarious routes trekked by mule caravans and carts. Even distant Buenos Aires—a port city closed to direct legal trade with Spain by its mercantilist economic policies—became dependent on Potosí's silver. In the seventeenth century the city became an important illegal trade outpost. French, Dutch, Portuguese, and English vessels called in its harbor to trade manufactured goods and slaves for the coveted Potosí silver. Around 20 percent of the silver extracted in Potosí was siphoned off to these European countries through Buenos Aires.

Within the domestic market, the circulation of goods fostered the development of the *arriería*, or freight, business. Trains of carts driven by oxen made the three-month trip from Buenos Aires to Jujuy in the summer. As Jujuy was a transference point for goods shipped north (from there on carts could not tread the steep, narrow paths to Upper Peru), muleteers—largely Indians and mestizos from Tucumán—gathered there to transfer the goods from carts to mules. Northward-bound mule trains started the slow and risky crossing of the high plateau towards the Andean markets.

Beginning in the early seventeenth-century, the mule trade developed into a very profitable business that became the central economic activity linking three regions: the pampas of Buenos Aires and Santa

Fe; the wintering and trading posts of Tucumán; and the consuming cities of the Andes. As postmaster Alonso Carrió de la Vandera wrote in 1771, "mules are born and raised in the countryside of Buenos Aires ... finished in the pasture grounds of Tucumán, and work and die in Perú" (Carrió de la Vandera, 1965, p. 64.)

Córdoba, the first hub of this trade, shipped 25,000 mules per year to the Andes by 1650. Salta, and to a lesser extent Jujuy, started to send mules to the Andes in the 1650s and seized the trade from Córdoba from the 1740s onwards. The demand for mules increased throughout the eighteenth century to reach nearly 50,000 per year between 1765 and 1780. Along with mining districts and cities, Indian *corregimientos* were major markets for mules forcefully distributed by *corregidores* (or *repartimientos*) at very high prices. In 1780 the Tupac Amaru rebellion and the ensuing abolition of *repartimientos* brought the prosperous mule trade to a standstill. The crisis lasted between 1780 and 1795; by 1800 the trade was fully recovered, only to come to a halt with the independence war.

In Tucumán the mule trade occupied people of all walks of life. The urban elites owned the land where mules were raised or spent the winter, participated actively in it as merchants, and supplied the muleteers with food and other goods from their stores. Overseers were hired to lead mule trains; they were commonly petty merchants or professional muleteers. Members of the urban plebs, or common people—mestizos, mulattoes, and Indians—were hired as journeymen for wages in cash and kind. Mestizos and Indians from the countryside also participated in the mule business by raising and selling animals in small numbers. The impact of the decline of the mule trade after 1780 was felt by all social sectors and amounted to a serious social and economic crisis.

In Río de la Plata the elite was more concerned with trade than agriculture or livestock raising. They participated actively in the few legal commercial activities allowed and in the many illegal ones. Dealing in contraband was a common practice among the Buenos Aires merchants, with or without the authorities' complicity. Only in the nineteenth century did a landed elite fully develop with the expansion of the agrarian frontier over Indian territory.

REFORM

Located on the margins of the trade system that linked the Andean silver mines with Spain and politically irrelevant, the Río de la Plata area was neglected for more than one and a half centuries. By the middle of the eighteenth century this situation began to change. As a result of Spain's concern about Portugal's advances on the southern border with Brazil, the new Viceroyalty of Río de la Plata was created in 1776. Imperial reforms fostered economic growth and the development of regions hitherto considered unprofitable. Buenos Aires and its surrounding countryside was the area that benefited the most from the Bourbon reforms.

Viceroyalty and Intendencies. In the late 1760s Spain undertook major administrative and military reforms aimed at building up a better defense of its American empire. The Río de la Plata area was far away from the scene of war but still faced a major threat to its security. Across from Buenos Aires, the Portuguese had established Colonia do Sacramento in 1680. The small port city functioned mainly as an outpost for illegal trade by Portugal and Britain. To protect the city a military regiment was stationed in Buenos Aires and militias were organized in all the nearby other cities.

With this enhanced military structure in place, the governor of Buenos Aires, Pedro de Cevallos, occupied the eastern bank of the Río de la Plata, seized Colonia, and expelled the Portuguese in 1776. Immediately afterwards the crown created the Viceroyalty of Río de la Plata, comprising the jurisdictions of the old governorships of Buenos Aires and Tucumán, and added to them Cuyo, which formerly depended on Chile. Buenos Aires was made its capital city and Cevallos its first viceroy. The political role of the city was thus enhanced and a sizable administration was appointed. Also an *audiencia* (royal high court of justice) was established in 1783, and an expanded branch of the Real Hacienda (Royal Exchequer) began to function.

In 1782 Spain introduced a sweeping reform of the colonial political organization through the Real Ordenanza de Intendentes, which was first applied to the Río de la Plata and later to other American viceroyalties. The Ordenanza created eight *intendencies* in the Viceroyalty of La Plata, three of which, Córdoba, Salta, and Buenos Aires, would form Argentina after independence. The Intendency of Córdoba comprised the southern part of the old province of Tucumán (to which Cuyo was added), that of Salta the northern part, and that of Buenos Aires the whole namesake province.

Each *intendency* was headed by an *intendent*. Even though theoretically subordinated to the viceroy, *intendents* concentrated all economic, political, military, and judicial power within their jurisdiction and communicated directly with Spain. The crown's goal of enforcing a more efficient and less corrupt administration clashed with the interests of the local urban elites who wanted to maintain their power. The elites managed to keep some of it by holding the post of *subdelegado* (local magistrate) for one of their own. Yet the autonomy of *cabildos* (town councils) was deeply affected as *intendents* meddled in local affairs.

Economic Reforms. By the mid-eighteenth century the old trade system, which connected Cádiz in Spain to a few ports in Spain's American colonies through convoys of ships, collapsed due to incessant wars. Starting in the 1760s, Spain applied new economic policies to its American colonies. Gradually, the crown opened many ports on both coasts of the Atlantic to trade and, beginning in 1720, authorized individual vessels (*navíos de registro*) to trade with America, thus phasing out the convoys. These policies reflected the shift of economic development from the Pacific to the Atlantic and benefited Río de la Plata, and especially Buenos Aires, immensely.

In 1778 the city was included in the royal decree of *commercio libre*, which opened many Spanish American ports to legal trade with Spain. The same year Viceroy Pedro de Cevallos order the mandatory export of silver from Upper Peru (now part of the Viceroyalty of La Plata) through Buenos Aires. With its improved links to the Atlantic, the city's economy prospered. It became a major exporter of silver and also an important supplier of hides to Europe, especially England. By 1800 the city exported goods worth five million silver pesos per year on average, four million of which were silver and the remainder in hides.

Its newly acquired prosperity and higher political status made Buenos Aires a magnet for both Spanish migrants and inhabitants of interior areas attracted by prospects of economic advancement.

In 1744 the city's population totaled roughly 11,000. By 1810 this figure had increased fourfold to 45,000 people. Buenos Aires was by then the fastest-growing city in the Spanish Empire. This dramatic influx of immigrants had a strong impact on the makeup of the city's elite as the immigrants joined ranks with the recently appointed bureaucrats and military officers stationed there. This new elite had a strong commercial basis and came to dominate the import of European goods and their distribution within the viceroyalty. Testament to its importance, in 1794 the crown authorized the founding of a *consulado* (commercial tribunal) in Buenos Aires. The merchant elite was the foundation of Argentina's nineteenth-century ruling class.

Urban growth and exports fostered the expansion of rural production. Rural establishments of various sizes were brought into the supply of agricultural products and meat to the urban market and hides to the export economy. This economic dynamism led to agrarian expansion on new lands, mainly in Entre Ríos and Uruguay. It also fostered internal migration from Tucumán, Córdoba, and Santiago del Estero to the countryside of Buenos Aires and Santa Fe. Some of these migrants settled in the Buenos Aires countryside while others stayed only temporarily. Slaves were also imported in larger numbers than before. By 1800 roughly one-quarter of the population of Buenos Aires was black and mulatto, both slave and free. Their presence was also sizable in the countryside, where large rural estates employed them as labor.

The impact of economic reforms, namely the expansion of legal trade, was experienced differently by different regions. For Buenos Aires and the Atlantic littoral it inaugurated a period of economic growth that continued after independence. For Tucumán and Cuyo the situation varied, but by and large the impact was negative. Córdoba, for instance, managed to shift its production from textiles to cattle and hides, thus linking with the expanding Buenos Aires and international markets. Other cities suffered the loss of markets for their local products. The cheap wines and liquors manufactured in Cuyo were hit hard by European competition, as were the rough textiles from Tucumán and Santiago del Estero. Salta and Jujuy clung to the mule trade with the Andean markets. All of the cities of Tucumán depended on Buenos Aires for their import of European goods, a situation that would deepen after independence.

THE RISE OF BUENOS AIRES

For about two centuries Buenos Aires had vegetated as a distant outpost located in a forgotten corner of the Spanish Empire, surviving mainly through contraband trade with the Dutch and the Portuguese. From the 1750s on, however, the city's demographic, economic, and political importance was on the rise. This newly acquired importance was taken into account when the city was made viceregal capital and became the link of interior areas of the viceroyalty with the outside world.

In the 1770s the authorities began to improve the urban facilities of the city. Sanitation, safety, and cleanliness were enhanced: A hospital and a poorhouse were established; some streets and sidewalks around the main plaza were paved; and public lighting was installed. In addition the Alameda, a public walkway where the elite promenaded every day, was opened. The first coffeehouse in town, Almacén del Rey, opened in 1764; by 1806 there were already thirteen of them in the city, places where people gathered to drink, play billiards, read, and talk. The first permanent theater opened in 1783 under the viceroy's sponsorship; plays written by local authors were performed there, along with Spanish plays. By the end of the colonial period there were two working theaters in Buenos Aires.

Viceregal authorities also improved educational facilities. In 1772 the old Jesuit school was transformed into a royal school, the Colegio Real de San Carlos. By 1800 three other educational institutions had been created: a school of medicine; an academy of drawing; and an academy of maritime sciences, which was primarily a school of mathematics. Only Córdoba had an older educational institution, the prestigious university established there in 1683.

In 1780 the city incorporated a printing press to its cultural patrimony. The machine had belonged to the Jesuits of Córdoba and was brought to Buenos Aires by viceregal order. Leased to private printers, it was mostly used for publishing official documents and religious and educational books. Argentina's first newspapers appeared in Buenos Aires: the *Telégrafo Mercantil* (1801–1802), *Semanario de Agricultura, Industria y Comercio* (1802–1807), and *Correo de Comercio* (1810–1811). These newspapers were major means for disseminating enlightened ideas throughout the viceroyalty. Copies of them were sold by subscription in all of the provincial towns; as a result a small but active group of men of letters was formed in the viceroyalty. Most of them were children of merchants sent to study at the universities of Charcas, Córdoba, or Salamanca. Many of them became prominent members of the revolutionary generation that took power after 1810.

CRISIS

The last years of Spanish administration in Argentina were tense, especially after 1805. The Napoleonic Wars immensely affected trade between Spain and its colonies. In the late 1790s the colonies were authorized to trade among themselves and with neutral nations (mainly the United States). Therefore, Buenos Aires merchants, by then the richest members of the elites of the Viceroyalty of La Plata, had a taste of real free trade. The Peace of Amiens in 1801 put an end to these liberalized commercial policies. War resumed in 1805; the following year and again in 1807, Buenos Aires was invaded by British troops. The authorities organized the defense by enlisting militias all over the viceroyalty, but especially in the city. The British were expelled but the Spanish authorities saw their power weaken at the hands of the militias under the control of the Buenos Aires merchant elite. In 1810 the militias were the key political actor in the demise of the Spanish regime.

See also **Audiencia; Buenos Aires; Cabot, Sebastian; Captain-General: Spanish America; Consulado; Encomienda; Explorers and Exploration: Spanish America; Intendancy System; Livestock; Magellan, Ferdinand; Mestizo; Oidor; Peons; Pueblos de indios; Repartimiento; Yerba Maté.**

BIBLIOGRAPHY

Assadourian, Carlos Sempat. *El sistema de la economía colonial: El mercado interior, regiones y espacio económico.* México, D. F.: Editorial Nueva Imagen, 1983.

Carrió de la Vandera, Alonso. *El Lazarillo de ciegos caminantes* [1773]. Caracas, Biblioteca Ayacucho, 1985. Translated by Walter D. Kline as *El Lazarillo: A Guide for Inexperienced Travelers between Buenos Aires and Lima.* Bloomington: Indiana University Press, 1965.

Chiaramonte, José Carlos. *La Ilustración en el Río de la Plata: Cultura eclesiástica y cultura laica durante el Virreinato.* Buenos Aires: Puntosur Editores, 1989.

Farberman, Judith, and Raquel Gil Montero, eds. *Los pueblos de indios del Tucumán colonial: Pervivencia y desestructuración.* Buenos Aires: Universidad Nacional de Quilmes, 2002.

Fradkin, Raúl, ed. *La historia agraria del Río de la Plata colonial: Los establecimientos productivos.* 2 vols. Buenos Aires: CEAL, 1993.

Ganson, Barbara. *The Guarani under Spanish Rule in the Rio de la Plata.* Stanford, CA: Stanford University Press, 2003.

Garavaglia, Juan Carlos. *Econmía, sociedad y regiones.* Buenos Aires: Ediciones de la Flor, 1987.

Garavaglia, Juan Carlos, and José Luis Moreno, eds. *Población, sociedad, familia y migraciones en el espacio rioplatense: Siglos XVIII y XIX.* Buenos Aires: Cántaro, 1993.

Garavaglia, Juan Carlos. *Pastores y labradores de Buenos Aires: Una historia agraria de la campaña bonaerense, 1700–1830.* Buenos Aires: Ediciones de la Flor, 1999.

Gelman, Jorge. *De mercachifle a gran comerciante: Los caminos del ascenso en el Río de la Plata colonial.* Huelva, Spain: Universidad Internacional de Andalucía, 1996.

Gelman, Jorge. *Campesinos y estancieros: Una región del Río de la Plata a fines de la época colonial.* Buenos Aires: Los Libros del Riel, 1998.

López de Albornoz, Cristina. *Los dueños de la tierra: Economía sociedad y poder en Tucumán (1770–1820).* Tucumán, Argentina: Universidad Nacional de Tucumán, 2003.

Lorandi, Ana María, ed. *El Tucumán colonial y Charcas,* 2 vols. Buenos Aires: Universidad de Buenos Aires, Facultad de Filosofía y Letras, 1997.

Lynch, John. *Colonial Spanish Administration, 1782–1810: The Intendant System in the Viceroyalty of the Rio de la Plata.* London: Athlone Press, 1958.

Madrazo, Guillermo. *Hacienda y encomienda en los Andes: La Puna argentina bajo el Marquesado de Tojo: Siglos XVII a XIX.* Jujuy, Argentina: Universidad Nacional de Jujuy, 1990.

Mata de López., Sara E. *Tierra y poder en Salta: El noroeste argentino en vísperas de la independencia.* Seville, Spain: Diputación de Sevilla, 2000.

Mayo, Carlos A. *Estancia y sociedad en la pampa, 1740–1820.* Buenos Aires: Biblos, 1995.

Mayo, Carlos A., ed. *Pulperos y pulperías de Buenos Aires, 1740–1830.* Mar del Plata, Argentina: Universidad Nacional de Mar del Plata, Facultad de Humanidades, 1997.

Mörner, Magnus. *The Political and Economic Activities of the Jesuits in the La Plata Region: The Hapsburg Era.* Stockholm: Victor Pettersons Bokindustri Aktiebolag, 1953.

Moutoukias, Zacarías. *Contrabando y control colonial en el siglo XVII: Buenos Aires, el Atlántico y el espacio peruano.* Buenos Aires: Centro Editor de América Latina, 1988.

Punta, Ana Inés. *Córdoba borbónica: Persistencias coloniales en tiempo de reformas (1750–1800).* Córdoba, Argentina: Universidad Nacional de Córdoba, 1997.

Revello, José Torre. *La sociedad colonial (Páginas sobre la sociedad de Buenos Aires entre los siglos XVI y XIX).* Buenos Aires: Ediciones Pannedille, 1970.

Socolow, Susan Migden. *The Merchants of Buenos Aires, 1778–1810: Family and Commerce.* Cambridge, UK: Cambridge University Press, 1978.

Socolow, Susan Migden. *The Bureaucrats of Buenos Aires, 1769–1810: Amor al real servicio.* Durham, NC, and London: Duke University Press, 1987.

Tandeter, Enrique, ed. *La sociedad colonial.* Vol. 2 of *Nueva Historia Argentina.* Buenos Aires: Sudamericana, 2000.

GUSTAVO L. PAZ

THE NINETEENTH CENTURY

As the nineteenth century began, the provinces that later comprised the Argentine Republic all belonged to the Viceroyalty of Río de la Plata, whose capital was Buenos Aires. The province of Buenos Aires, including the capital and its immediate hinterland, was enjoying rapid growth and rising prosperity. This was a result of the easing of overseas trade by late-colonial commercial reforms, the establishment of the viceroyalty in 1776, and the alteration of the trade routes to and from Upper Peru (modern Bolivia) to run through Buenos Aires rather than Pacific ports. The central province of Córdoba, whose capital was second in size only to Buenos Aires—with around 10,000 inhabitants as against nearly 50,000—felt mixed effects from these changes, as did the northwestern provinces of Tucumán and Salta. They benefited from the increase in traffic with Upper Peru, but some of their handicraft industries (such as the ponchos made by Córdoba artisans) suffered from the greater availability of European goods in the Buenos Aires market. Wine producers of the Mendoza and San Juan Provinces in the Cuyo area were likewise at a disadvantage. Much of the interior population, however, was dependent on little more than a subsistence economy, and was little affected by trade routes or trading policies.

Apart from handling silver shipments from Upper Peru and the return flow of imports paid

View of Buenos Aires, an engraving by John Byrne (1785–1847) from Volume 14 of *A General Collection of the Best and Most Interesting Voyages and Travels in All Parts of the World* by John Pinkerton, published 1813 (b/w photo). On the Rio de la Plata, Buenos Aires grew as a major port, economic and political center in the nineteenth century. PRIVATE COLLECTION/ THE BRIDGEMAN ART LIBRARY

for by the silver, Buenos Aires was shipping great quantities of hides from the surrounding pampa to the factories of the industrializing North Atlantic. Its status as an active port also gave it exposure to all manner of new ideas and fashions from Europe, resulting in an intellectual ferment that had its counterparts throughout the Spanish colonies but was more pronounced in Buenos Aires—certainly more so than in the Argentine interior. Then, in 1806, the Río de la Plata felt an external stimulus that aroused decidedly mixed reactions even in Buenos Aires, with its strong orientation to Europe and the North Atlantic.

The attack, although not authorized by the government in London, was a by-product of the Napoleonic Wars in Europe in which, at the moment, Spain was aligned on the side of France against Great Britain. Spain's colonies were thus enemy territory and Buenos Aires a potentially rich prize. It was easily taken by the invaders, who

behaved with moderation and held out the prospect of unrestricted trade with Britain—an offer that was not unwelcome to export producers or to Porteño (Buenos Airean) merchants not tied to metropolitan Spanish trading firms. Yet foreign occupation as such was an affront to the local population, which before the end of 1806 reacted strongly. The Buenos Aires militia, under the French-born officer Santiago Liniers, proceeded to throw out the British forces. It also defeated a second British expedition that arrived early in 1807.

THE COMING OF INDEPENDENCE
The defeat of the British invasions by a largely creole militia gave a major boost to local pride and self-confidence as well as a fund of military experience on which to draw later. Liniers himself became acting viceroy of the Río de la Plata. In 1808, however, the Napoleonic invasion of Spain caused loyal Spaniards and colonials to shift to a British alliance. Liniers was

suspect by virtue of his French origin, even though he professed allegiance to the rump government of Spanish resistance still holding out in southern Spain. A coup attempt against him in Buenos Aires was foiled, but in Montevideo, which also formed part of the viceroyalty, a junta headed by the local Spanish governor breathed defiance. Meanwhile, the arrival in Rio de Janeiro of Carlota Joaquina, sister of King Ferdinand Vii, a captive of the French, became an added complication. The wife of the Portuguese prince regent, she invited Spanish Americans to recognize her as interim head of the empire. The idea proved attractive to a group of Creole professionals at Buenos Aires who felt that such an arrangement might well lead to de facto colonial autonomy.

In the end nothing came of Carlotista intrigues, and Liniers was replaced in late 1809 by a new viceroy sent out directly from Spain; Montevideo then returned to obedience. But the continuing decline of Spanish fortunes in the conflict with Napoleon triggered strong demands for the establishment of a governing junta in Buenos Aires, ostensibly to rule in the name of King Ferdinand until such time as he regained his throne. A junta was created on 25 May 1810 and promptly called on all parts of the viceroyalty to accept its claims. There was resistance in peripheral areas—Uruguay, Paraguay, Upper Peru—and a brief attempt at counterrevolution in Córdoba, led by Liniers, who was the hero of resistance against the British. But all the future Argentine provinces, with varying enthusiasm, recognized the Buenos Aires junta.

With the establishment of a revolutionary junta in Buenos Aires, Argentina had for all practical purposes achieved self-government. The junta itself, however, was soon torn by internal conflict between a radical activist group led by Mariano Moreno and a moderate faction identified initially with the militia officer Cornelio de Saavedra. Moreno, one of the junta's secretaries, took a hard line against any who resisted its authority, while using its newspaper to disseminate the writings of Jean-Jacques Rousseau and to prepare public opinion for outright independence. The moderates, for their part, had more support in the interior; this proved decisive and led to the departure of Moreno to diplomatic exile (he died en route).

Factional strife would be a constant of the revolutionary scene, as junta followed junta over the next few years and other forms of government were tried as well. A constituent assembly that met in 1813 adopted a broad package of liberal reforms, including restrictions on the religious orders, abolition of the Inquisition, and elimination of titles of nobility and Indian forced labor; however, it proved unable to produce a constitution. Meanwhile, Paraguay was permanently lost to the jurisdiction of Buenos Aires, despite a military expedition sent to take control of it in 1811; Uruguay was fought over by Spanish loyalists, Uruguayan autonomists, agents of Buenos Aires, and Portuguese interlopers from Brazil; and a succession of Argentine armies sent to liberate Upper Peru met with temporary success and ultimate failure.

Thanks in part simply to its remoteness, Argentina was the only one of Spain's rebellious colonies that never experienced Spanish reconquest, even in the years 1815–1819, which in other theaters were the low point of the independence movement. During these very years the Argentine provinces experienced an interlude of relative stability under the administration of Supreme Director Juan Martín de Pueyrredón, and in 1816 another constituent congress meeting in Tucumán declared formal independence at last. After moving to Buenos Aires, the congress adopted a first constitution in 1819, which remained largely a dead letter. Meanwhile, with the support of Pueyrredón, an army under the Argentine liberator José de San Martín crossed the Andes into Chile in 1817, to begin the series of campaigns that ultimately took him to Peru.

Even while San Martín was successfully carrying the war across the Andes, the Portuguese were gaining control of Uruguay. Intermittent fighting with the royalists continued in the northwest and Upper Peru. But by 1820 the independence of Argentina proper was assured. At the same time, however, the precarious internal unity achieved under Pueyrredón dissolved, largely as a result of a widespread backlash against the centralism of the abortive 1819 constitution and the intrigues mounted by administration supporters to implant some form of constitutional monarchy.

As of 1820 each province took control of its own affairs, even though few of them had the human or material resources to do so with any chance of success. The principal exception was Buenos Aires, where Governor Martín Rodríguez and his chief minister, Bernardino Rivadavia, consolidated internal order; established a smooth-running provincial administration; and took such progressive steps as founding the University of Buenos Aires, creating a stock exchange, and reforming and simplifying the tax system. By suppressing several small monasteries and seizing church assets, they offended conservative traditionalists. They also sacrificed the interests of the interior by insisting that all foreign trade go through the port of Buenos Aires and by maintaining essentially a tariff primarily for revenue purposes to the detriment of domestic industries seeking protection.

Most key officials and supporters of the Buenos Aires government belonged to the so-called Unitarist faction whose name reflected its commitment to a centralized political system. Despite strong reservations in much of the interior, where opinion was basically federalist, a national congress convoked by Buenos Aires produced another centralist constitution in 1826, and Rivadavia became president of all Argentina under its terms. However, once again the adoption of such a constitution led to violent protest in much of the country. Worse, it happened at a time when war with Brazil over possession of Uruguay—which in 1825 had rebelled against Brazilian rule and rejoined Argentina—made national unity all the more important.

Recognizing his inability to impose the Unitarists' solution on the nation as a whole, Rivadavia resigned in mid-1827 and went into exile. Each province once more assumed full control of its affairs. Buenos Aires this time fell to the local faction of Federalists, led first by Governor Manuel Dorrego—until he was overthrown and murdered in December 1828 in an abortive comeback attempt by the Unitarists—and then Juan Manuel de Rosas. The war with Brazil simply petered out, with Uruguay established under British mediation as an independent nation.

THE ROSAS ERA

Juan Manuel de Rosas, who dominated Argentina from 1829 to 1852, is one of the two most controversial figures of Argentine history, his only rival being Juan D. Perón. Given that Rosas was a wealthy rancher and successful exporter of hides and salt beef,

his political ideal was the stability and tranquility of the colonial era. He felt little sympathy for the Unitarists' reform agenda and dismissed their brand of constitutional centralism as hopelessly impractical. Rosas chose to concentrate instead on protecting the immediate interests of Buenos Aires and his fellow ranchers. At the same time, he skillfully cultivated a wider base of popular support by presenting himself as a defender of traditional values while associating his enemies with unwelcome foreign influences.

Though Rosas assumed the governorship of Buenos Aires Province with dictatorial powers, he still found himself sometimes at odds with the provincial legislature. Therefore, in 1832 he resigned the office to assume leadership of a vast military campaign against the Indian peoples who still occupied much of the choicest land of the Pampa and who, by their raiding parties, were making life precarious for the outermost creole settlements. He was brilliantly successful, pushing the Indian frontier southward to Patagonia and claiming for creole occupation great amounts of land that he divided among his followers or sold on easy terms. Rosas thereby laid the basis for the large-estate system in much of the best land of Argentina.

While Rosas was away, his wife and close adherents in Buenos Aires were stirring up trouble for the governors who succeeded him. The most extreme instance was the rise of a vigilante group known as the Mazorca, which terrorized both Unitarists and lukewarm Federalists (that is, those not strictly beholden to Rosas: see under "Argentina, Movements"). The upshot was that in 1835, the province welcomed Rosas back as governor, this time with the *suma del poder público*, or sum of public power, meaning that he was invested with supreme executive, legislative, and judicial authority. He did not dismiss the legislature or courts, but they now existed simply to do his bidding. Nor did he hesitate to apply terror as needed, whether by means of his official police and military apparatus or by unleashing the Mazorca against his foes. (It should not be forgotten, of course, that Rosas's enemies were not always squeamish about their methods, either.)

Rosas as governor curried favor with the church, but more in words than by action, for he did not return many of the church assets taken by Rivadavia, nor did he reverse the religious toleration that had been another of the Unitarists' achievements. He showed little interest in education but did build up an effective military, with whose help he extended his control beyond the confines of Buenos Aires province, forging alliances with Federalists of the interior and helping them overcome Unitarist or dissident Federalist rivals. He never attempted to create a full-fledged national government, much less issue a constitution. The other provinces of what was dubbed the Argentine Confederation merely delegated to him, as Buenos Aires governor, the right to act for all of them in matters of national security and foreign relations. Rosas was not much interested in how his provincial allies ran their own bailiwicks, only whether they gave unswerving allegiance to him as the leader of all.

Rosas's system had begun to take shape during his first governorship, but it was perfected only after 1835, and it withstood the test of repeated Unitarist conspiracies, including invasions launched from their Uruguayan base in exile. Rosas likewise withstood two efforts to unseat him by European powers in alliance with the Unitarists, the first in 1838 by France and the second in 1845–1848 by France and Great Britain combined. France was seeking redress for real or imaginary injuries suffered by her citizens; the British were angered at Rosas's insistence on keeping the Paraná River closed to foreign navigation and his meddling in Uruguay, where he allied with the Uruguayan Blanco Party in order to counter the Unitarist exiles. Both powers resorted to blockading the Argentine coast, but they were often at cross-purposes with each other and with the Unitarist exiles. Furthermore, they were not prepared to invest resources on the scale that would have been required to humble Rosas. Eventually, they withdrew without achieving their announced objectives. The British did not, however, withdraw from the Falkland Islands, or Islas Malvinas, which they had taken by force in 1833, during Rosas's absence from the governorship.

Rosas was equally effective in defending the economic interests of the Buenos Aires ranchers, whose traditional cattle business was increasingly complemented by sheep raising for the export of wool. He decreed tariff protection for the artisanal industries of the interior provinces, but the policy was halfhearted, as his own agro-exporting class was best served by unhampered foreign trade. To cover military and other expenditures, he resorted to paper-money inflation, which hurt wage earners but not the ranchers whose exports were sold for foreign currency. Also, he kept the Paraná closed. However, the latter policy led to friction with his Federalist allies in the provinces upstream, while his general concentration on Buenos Aires interests tended to weaken his appeal nationally.

Once the threat posed by both Unitarist exiles and European powers had been dispelled, it seemed to many that the time had finally come to get the country properly organized with a federal constitution, yet Rosas still refused to do so. In response, one of his political allies, Justo José de Urquiza—governor of Entre Ríos province up the Paraná River—set out to overthrow Rosas. He enlisted other disaffected Federalists, made peace with the Unitarists in Uruguay, and enlisted the help of Brazil, which had shared much the same grievances against Rosas as Britain and France. The culmination was the battle of Caseros, fought almost at the outskirts of Buenos Aires, in February 1852. Rosas's forces were defeated, and the dictator took ship for England, where he lived the rest of his life as an exile.

NATIONAL ORGANIZATION

Rosas had been the first Argentine leader to forge effective national unity. This achievement, along with his defense of national sovereignty against European intruders, largely accounts for the admiration he continues to receive from many Argentines. Yet he had to go before national unity could be institutionalized on a permanent basis, under the auspices of Urquiza, who called the constituent convention of 1853 that wrote the Argentine constitution which remained in force at the end of the twentieth century. It was federalist in structure but endowed the national authorities with extensive powers, including the right to intervene in a province under certain circumstances, deposing the governor in favor of a presidential interventor—a provision that would lend itself to frequent abuse in coming years. The constitution further incorporated a number of significant liberal reforms, among them the final abolition of slavery in Argentina, and it committed the nation to a course of outward-oriented growth by such features as a clause expressly requiring the government to promote foreign immigration.

Buenos Aires Province refused to ratify the constitution and join the union. After Rosas's fall, it had come under the control mainly of returning Unitarist exiles who soon broke with Urquiza because of personal rivalries and because, in the last analysis, they wanted Buenos Aires to be the dominant partner in any new political arrangement. As a result, the authorities of the reorganized Argentine Confederation established their capital at Paraná, in Urquiza's home province, with Urquiza as president. They effectively opened the Paraná River to foreign trade and were able to bring some colonies of European immigrants to the interior provinces.

But the confederation also became bogged down in a continuing feud with the province of Buenos Aires, which proceeded to organize itself as an independent state. Thanks to its greater resources, this state became a model of progressive change, much as it had been in the 1820s. Domingo Sarmiento, the future "schoolmaster president," presided over expansion of the provincial education system. Construction of the first Argentine railroad was begun in 1854, westward from the city of Buenos Aires into the adjoining pampa. Immigrants came to Buenos Aires, too, and most Argentine trade continued to flow through the port of the separatist province, despite the formal opening of the Paraná River.

The standoff between Buenos Aires and the confederation gave way in 1859–1861 to a series of armed confrontations. At first they favored Urquiza, but in the end the victory went to Bartolomé Mitre, governor of Buenos Aires and shortly to become president of a definitively united Argentina (1862–1868). Some revisions were made in the constitution to ease Buenos Aires's acceptance of it, but these were not substantial. By contrast, some factions in the interior were still unprepared to accept the rule of a liberal Porteño such as Mitre, who had to contend with repeated local uprisings that continued even after Argentina became involved, along with Brazil and Uruguay, in the War of the Triple Alliance against Paraguay (1865–1870). Argentina's primary role in the war was as a route through which Brazilian forces got to Paraguay, as the Brazilians did most of the allied fighting; yet the mere fact of being allied to Brazil, their traditional foe, rankled many Argentines. In the end Argentina settled in her own favor a dispute with Paraguay over territory in the Gran Chaco, but for Argentines their participation in the war has given rise to more historical recrimination than national pride.

Mitre was succeeded as president during the war by Sarmiento (1868–1874), who like Mitre faced scattered uprisings in the interior and like him did not hesitate at times to use brutal tactics against them. However, provincial malcontents were no match for a united national government that was able to purchase the latest military equipment and to move its forces across a steadily growing rail network. Thus, gradually internal peace was established. The government was often high-handed, brandishing the threat of arbitrary military impressment against unruly gauchos, misapplying the constitution's intervention clause against uncooperative governors, and practicing widespread electoral fraud.

Moreover, political power was concentrated in a network of provincial bosses and members of a national mercantile, landowning, and professional elite, with little participation by popular elements. The principal organ of this loose coalition was the Partido Autonomista Nacional (PAN or National Autonomist Party), organized in time to elect Sarmiento's immediate successor, Nicolás Avellaneda (1874–1880). Yet the formal apparatus of constitutional government was maintained, and most civil liberties were respected. Property rights in particular were well protected. The system was thus basically liberal, in the nineteenth-century meaning of the term, even if not democratic, and it was well suited to the mission of fostering economic growth.

From the standpoint of state-building, there were still two important items of unfinished business. One was to incorporate into the effective national territory the southern regions, including most of Patagonia, that were still occupied by largely autonomous Indian groups. This was achieved in 1879–1880 by General Julio A. Roca, Avellaneda's minister of war, in what Argentines called the Conquest of the Desert. Much as happened in the western United States in the same years, the native people were either exterminated or herded into reservations, and the land was opened for white settlement. The other remaining problem was the relationship between the city of Buenos Aires and the national government. Its status as capital of both the nation and its wealthiest, most populous province led to continual tension between the authorities of one and the other; while the mere combination of Buenos Aires city and province created a unit so much stronger than the other provinces that the latter inevitably feared subordination to Buenos Aires's interests. The obvious solution was to detach the city as a separate federal district, which was finally done in 1880 in the aftermath of the government's triumph over the Patagonian Indians. Buenos Aires Province contested the move in a brief civil war, but to no avail. When Roca himself became next president (1880–1886), he ruled from a federal district.

ORDER AND PROGRESS

The consolidation of order was accompanied by a surge of social and economic modernization. One aspect of this was an impressive advance in public education, promoted not just by Sarmiento (who, among other acts, imported female normal school teachers from the United States to show his fellow Argentines what a proper system of free public schools was like) but also by his successors. By the end of the century the literacy rate was approaching 50 percent, as against half that much when Sarmiento assumed the presidency.

To Sarmiento and his collaborators, education ideally should be laic rather than religiously oriented, and this too was achieved for schools under the national government's jurisdiction by a controversial law of 1884, passed during the Roca administration. The law took its place with other measures of the same decade establishing civil registry and civil marriage. The regime's support of secularization—while holding onto traditional state control over the church—led to a temporary rupture of relations with the Vatican but underscored its adherence to cultural and intellectual, if not always political, liberalism.

Most impressive of all was the pace of economic growth. In roughly the half century from the 1870s to World War I, the economy grew at a rate of about 5 percent annually—an achievement matched by no Latin American nation before or since. The growth was based mainly on a steady increase in the production and export of livestock products and grains. An emphasis on ranching was nothing new, though sales of jerked (dried and salted) beef dropped off

sharply by the end of the century, even as fresh meat exports gradually increased. These involved both the sale of cattle on the hoof and refrigerated lamb or mutton. Hides remained another significant item in overseas trade, but wool became—and until the end of the century remained—the country's leading export.

Large-scale grain production was something entirely new. Until the 1870s Argentina was actually an importer of wheat and flour, whereas by 1900 wheat exports were a close second to wool. Previously, there had been no lack of suitable land, but crop farming was labor-intensive and population sparse. Massive European immigration, with over a quarter million persons entering the port of Buenos Aires in the record year 1889, provided the needed agricultural labor, even though not all went to the rural sector and by no means all stayed. Some, indeed, were *golondrinas* (swallows) commuting between Europe and Argentina to work the harvest season in both northern and southern hemispheres.

All this was accompanied by steady growth in transportation and other infrastructure. Most obvious was the consistent advance of railroad construction. Ultimately, it gave Argentina Latin America's largest rail network, stretching nearly 10,000 miles by 1900. Railroads reinforced political unity, and they allowed Tucumán sugar, for example, to be sold in a larger national market; even more importantly they tied all parts of the country to the port of Buenos Aires.

In the building and operation of railroads, foreign capital, technology, and equipment, from Great Britain above all, made an important contribution. Foreign investment likewise played a key role in financial services, with the establishment of branches of foreign banking firms. There was less direct foreign investment in incipient consumer-goods manufacturing, though many of the factories were started by immigrants or sons of immigrants. At least the land itself remained overwhelmingly in native hands, even if unequally distributed. In certain areas of agricultural colonization, landownership was rather widespread, but in the livestock sector and much of crop farming as well, the pattern was one of huge private estates, worked by wage labor or by tenants and sharecroppers.

The national government built some of the railroads in outlying areas unattractive to private investors. Its primary role, however, was to maintain order

Drying leather, Argentina (albumen print on card) by Samuel Boote (fl.1880–1889). Cowhide was Argentina's major export. By 1850, the country supplied Great Britain and the United States with over 20 percent of all their imported leather. PRIVATE COLLECTION/THE STAPLETON COLLECTION/THE BRIDGEMAN ART LIBRARY

and to guarantee, if not the freedom to vote and have one's vote honestly counted, at least freedom of contract. This is what "Peace and Administration," the political slogan of Julio Roca, amounted to in practice. The same Roca, more than anyone else, set the tone for Argentine politics in the late nineteenth century. Both as president himself (including a second term from 1898 to 1904) and then as a power behind the scenes between presidencies, he proved a master manipulator who kept things running smoothly most of the time. To be sure, his immediate successor, Miguel Juárez Celman (1886–1890), was forced to resign amid a financial crisis that he could not solve and had even helped to bring on through speculative mismanagement. But Carlos Pellegrini (1890–1892) then completed the presidential term while skillfully pulling the country out of the crisis.

A greater problem in the end was the exclusivism of the regime and the natural resentment of groups left out. The once free-living gauchos had been tamed by the advent of the sheep raising and a more modern military, and the rural population generally was either ignored or co-opted by the ruling machine. The urban working class, though it was beginning to form unions and its interests were defended by Latin America's first Socialist Party (established in 1896), was for the most part simply ignored. The professional middle class, however, was another matter. As Latin America's largest and best educated, it was fully conscious of its right to a larger voice and increasingly resentful of the regime's restrictive practices. The Unión Cívica Radical (UCR), or Radical Party as it came to be known, was founded in 1890 and had some success in channeling the middle-class discontent. In view of the prevalence of electoral fraud, the Radicals adopted a policy of boycotting elections and kept open the option of revolutionary direct action. Mainly they organized, grew in strength, and waited; they would finally win power in 1916.

The Radicals' message was a bitter condemnation of the existing regime as corrupt and undemocratic, devoted to all the vested interests while oblivious to the needs and desires of the population as a whole. The charges were often vague, but they contained a measure of truth. Revisionist historians of right and left would elaborate on them in succeeding years, giving the rulers of the period a somewhat tarnished image. Then, as one thing after another went wrong in the Argentina of the late twentieth century under populist and military leadership alike, the elitist manipulators of the last quarter of the previous century earned some new respect. They did get things done, and they presided over a process of growth that made Argentina—for a time—Latin America's most developed country.

See also **Avellaneda, Nicolás; Carlota; Conquest of the Desert; Dorrego, Manuel; Falkland Islands (Malvinas); Ferdinand VII of Spain; Juárez Celman, Miguel; Mazorca; Mitre, Bartolomé; Moreno, Mariano; Pampa; Patagonia; Pellegrini, Carlos; Porteño; Pueyrredón, Juan Martín de; Railroads; Rivadavia, Bernardino; Roca, Julio Argentino; Rosas, Juan Manuel de; Saavedra, Cornelio de; San Martín, José Francisco de; Sarmiento, Domingo Faustino; Slave Trade, Abolition of: Spanish America; Urquiza, Justo José de; War of the Triple Alliance.**

BIBLIOGRAPHY

In addition to the treatment in general histories of Argentina, one may consult, for an interpretation of the independence period, Tulio Halperín Donghi, *Politics, Economics, and Society in Argentina in the Revolutionary Period*, translated by Richard Southern (1975); on the early national era, Miron Burgin, *The Economic Aspects of Argentine Federalism, 1820–1852* (1946), John Lynch, *Argentine Dictator: Juan Manuel de Rosas, 1829–1852* (1981), and the classic historical polemic by Domingo F. Sarmiento, *Life in the Argentine Republic in the Days of the Tyrants; or, Civilization and Barbarism* (1868; many later editions); on intellectual history and especially concepts of Argentine nationhood, Nicolas Shumway, *The Invention of Argentina* (1992); on the process of national organization, Tulio Halperín Donghi, *Proyecto y construcción de una nación: Argentina, 1846–1880* (1980), and William H.

Jeffrey, *Mitre and Argentina* (1952); on the late nineteenth century, Douglas W. Richmond, *Carlos Pellegrini and the Crisis of the Argentine Elites, 1880–1916* (1989); on economic and social history, Jonathan C. Brown, *A Socioeconomic History of Argentina, 1776–1860* (1979), James R. Scobie, *Buenos Aires: From Plaza to Suburb, 1870–1910* (1974), and *Revolution on the Pampas: A Social History of Argentine Wheat, 1860–1910* (1964), Richard W. Slatta, *Gauchos and the Vanishing Frontier* (1983), and Mark D. Szuchman, *Order, Family, and Community in Buenos Aires, 1810–1860* (1987); and on British relations, Henry S. Ferns, *Britain and Argentina in the Nineteenth Century* (1960).

Collective works on Argentine History, selected by Hilda Sabato

Nueva Historia Argentina. Buenos Aires, Editorial Sudamericana, 1998–2000. General editor: Juan Suriano. For the nineteenth-century, see Volumes III, IV, and V (directed by Noemí Goldman, Marta Bonaudo, and Mirta Lobato, respectively).

Nueva Historia de la Nación Argentina. Buenos Aires, Planeta, 2000. Edited by the National Academy of History. For the nineteenth-century, see Volumes 4, 5, and 6.

Books on Argentine History, selected by Hilda Sabato

Adelman, Jeremy. *Republic of Capital: Buenos Aires and the Legal Transformation of the Atlantic World.* Stanford, CA: Stanford University Press, 1999.

Alonso, Paula. *Between Revolution and the Ballot Box: The Origins of the Argentine Radical Party in the 1890s.* Cambridge, U.K.: Cambridge University Press, 2000.

Barsky, Osvaldo, and Jorge Gelman. *Historia del agro Argentino. Desde la Conquista hasta fines del siglo XX.* Buenos Aires: Grijalbo/Mondadori, 2001.

Bertoni, Lilia Ana. *Patriotas, cosmopolitas y nacionalistas: La construcción de la nacionalidad Argentina a fines del siglo XIX.* Buenos Aires: Fondo de Cultura Económica, 2001.

Botana, Natalio. *El orden conservador: La política Argentina entre 1880 y 1916.* Buenos Aires: Sudamericana, 1977 (new edition, 1994).

Botana, Natalio y Ezequiel Gallo. *De la república posible a la República verdadera (1880–1910).* Buenos Aires: Ariel, 1997.

Chiaramonte, José Carlos. *Ciudades, provincias, estados: Orígenes de la Nación Argentina (1800–1846).* Buenos Aires: Ariel, 1997.

Cortés Conde, Roberto. *El progreso Argentino, 1880–1914.* Buenos Aires: Editorial.

De la Fuente, Ariel. *Children of Facundo: Caudillo and Gaucho Insurgency During the Argentine State-Formation Process (La Rioja, 1853–1870).* Durham, NC: Duke University Press, 2000.

Devoto, Fernando. *Historia de la inmigración en la Argentina.* Buenos Aires: Sudamericana, 2003.

Gallo, Ezequiel. *La Pampa gringa.* Buenos Aires: Sudamericana, 1993/Edhasa 2004.

Goldman, Noemí, and Ricardo Salvatore, eds. *Caudillismos rioplatenses: Nuevas miradas a un viejo problema.* Buenos Aires, Eudeba, 1998.

Halperin Donghi, Tulio. *Proyecto y construcción de una nación (Argentina, 1846–1880).* Caracas: Biblioteca de Ayacucho, 1980/Buenos Aires, Ariel, 1995.

Halperin Donghi, Tulio. *Politics, Economics, and Society in Argentina in the Revolutionary Period.* Cambridge, U.K.: Cambridge University Press, 1975.

Hora, Roy. *The Landowners of the Argentine Pampas: A Social and Political History, 1860–1945.* Oxford: Oxford University Press, 2001.

Lynch, John. *Argentine Dictator: Juan Manuel de Rosas, 1829–1852.* Oxford: Oxford University Press, 1981.

Myers, Jorge. *Orden y virtud: El discurso republicano en el régimen rosista.* Bernal: Universidad Nacional de Quilmes, 1995.

Rock, David. *Argentina, 1516–1982: From Spanish Colonization to the Falklands War.* Berkeley/Los Angeles: University of California Press, 1985.

Sabato, Hilda. *Agrarian Capitalism and the World Market: Buenos Aires in the Pastoral Age, 1840–1890.* Albuquerque: University of New Mexico Press, 1990.

Sabato, Hilda. *The Many and the Few: Political Participation in Republican Buenos Aires.* Stanford, CA: Stanford University Press, 2001.

Scobie, James. *Revolution on the Pampas. A Social History of Argentine Wheat, 1860–1910.* Austin: University of Texas Press, 1964.

Suriano, Juan. *Anarquistas: Cultura y política libertaria en Buenos Aires, 1890–1910.* Buenos Aires: Manantial, 2001.

Salvatore, Ricardo. *Wandering Paysanos: State Order and Subaltern Experience in Buenos Aires During the Rosas Era.* Durham, NC: Duke University Press, 2003.

Terán, Oscar. *Vida intelectual en el Buenos Aires fin-de-siglo (1880–1910). Derivas de la "cultura científica".* Buenos Aires: Fondo de Cultura Económica, 2000.

Ternavasio, Marcela. *La revolución del voto: Política y elecciones en Buenos Aires, 1810–1852.* Buenos Aires: Siglo XXI, 2002.

DAVID BUSHNELL
BIBLIOGRAPHY UPDATED BY HILDA SABATO

THE TWENTIETH CENTURY

Argentina's position in the global economic order frames its trajectory during the twentieth century. Through lucrative agriculture exports to Europe, in the early 1910s Argentina ranked as one of the richest nations in the world. However, the collapse of international trade and investment following World War I brought economic recession and instability. Political unrest ensued, lasting until the 1980s. Even with this sustained turmoil, by the early twenty-first century Argentina had developed stronger democratic institutions, remained an important cultural center, and was taking advantage of economic globalization.

Due to Argentina's wealth and cultural similarities with Europe, foreigners in the first half of the century lauded the country as a modern, developed nation. On the eve of World War I, Argentina was one of the principal destinations of western European immigration and investment, and one of the chief beneficiaries of a relatively open international trading order. Between 1880 and 1914 the capital city of Buenos Aires had been remodeled to resemble Paris, in the French beaux-arts style. Although located geographically in South America, the country faced east in the sense that the major lines of communication had their terminus in Buenos Aires and other cities of the littoral (particularly Rosario, which was created as a major grain port). Over the nineteenth century, Argentines developed distinctive cultural, culinary traditions and artistic styles, but also found inspiration in Europe, and France in particular.

As London and Paris influenced elite ranchers, lawyers, bankers, and intellectuals, the large wave of Spanish and Italian immigrants diversified the country. A vast immigrant proletariat from Spain and Italy, as well as smaller complements from other countries, tended to regard Argentina as a temporary venue where they could attain the prosperity and well-being denied them by the exhausted countries they had left. They maintained as best they could their connections with their places of origin, particularly the Spanish and Italians, who constituted 80 percent of all foreign residents. Some men commuted back and forth (and probably maintained families in both places).

By some measures, Argentina ranked as one of the five or six wealthiest countries in the world in

1914. Probably the methodologies in use today would raise questions about the ranking, but certainly in terms of the overall value of trade, balance of payments, and prospects for future investment, the assessment was not overdrawn. Argentina on the eve of World War I also possessed something that it has since lost—a sense of unbounded optimism based on the nearly universal assumption that the boom years of 1880 to 1914 could be extrapolated indefinitely into the future. Certainly the notion of Argentina as a country located geographically in Latin America but not really part of it was justified by statistics: In the entire region, no other country except Uruguay (a lost Argentine province that resembles it in many ways) came close to it in prosperity and well-being. And no country was more closely linked economically to the North Atlantic area.

Thirty years later, after two world wars (in which the country remained advantageously neutral), Argentina consolidated much of that promise. The country's infrastructure compared favorably with all but the wealthiest countries of Western Europe. At the same time, the country as a whole had managed to integrate large immigrant communities whose children now spoke Argentine Spanish and thought of themselves as Argentines. Yet, politicians failed to reach a workable consensus. After several unsuccessful attempts at political integration of a new middle class, by 1944 the armed forces, rather than civilian political parties, were the principal arbiters of the country's destiny. Whether in populist or conservative guise, a succession of generals stood at the country's helm for most of the period from 1944 until 1982.

Like other Spanish American countries, Argentina benefited from World War II, which created an unlimited demand for foodstuffs and agricultural raw materials, particularly on the part of Great Britain, the country's principal customer and until recently its chief foreign investor. The intense need for Argentine products, and the inflated prices that the British were willing to pay for them, discouraged any serious thought about technological modernization in the countryside, where local manufacturing and industry slowly grew without concrete government support until the 1940s. Indeed, the Pinedo Plan (1940), laid out a strategy for a more diversified economic growth, but political disagreements halted its implementation.

In the 1950s a sharp economic downtown occurred. Because the war had left Britain virtually bankrupt, international trade waned, and Argentine policy supported industrialization at the expense of agricultural production. By the mid-1950s the country had entered into a gradual but persistent economic decline, which in turn introduced new tensions into the political fabric that exploded into near–civil war in the late 1960s and early 1970s. The consolidation of the European Common Market, combined with the collapse of the Soviet Union, which had become the country's principal purchaser of cereals, weakened the national economy. The economy persevered and recovered. By the mid-1990s the country had diversified its export markets to its Mercosur neighbors, the United States, and Asia, and began to experience more stable economic growth.

This new development was buttressed by changing demographics. As a result of decades of economic stagnation and political conflict, one in ten Argentines now lived abroad, many in the very countries from which their ancestors had emigrated a hundred years before. But one million or more were living in the United States and Canada. Meanwhile, Argentina's relative wealth continued to attract illegal immigration from poorer neighboring countries, particularly Bolivia and Paraguay.

The promise of a closer association with the United States was slow in fulfillment. For one thing, the two countries were competitive in major export lines, particularly cereals. For another, U.S. investors remained distrustful of Argentine political stability and consequently targeted investment in countries such as Chile and Brazil. In the early twenty-first century China and other Asian countries developed large consumer markets for Argentine exports. Rising Asian demand boosted Argentina's commodity prices and helped reduce its reliance on U.S. consumers and financiers.

1900–1943

For the first thirty years of the century Argentina was often held up as a political exemplar for Latin America and indeed for much of southern Europe as well. It had in fact achieved a major transition to democracy through the implementation of universal manhood suffrage (Sáenz Pena Law, 1912), which made possible the election of President Hipólito Irigoyen in 1916, the first such popularly chosen chief executive in all of South America. Irigoyen drew large support from the new middle class and the working class. In part, his cultural politics valorized the popular culture often disdained by the traditional, elite politicians, but, under Irigoyen, Argentina's political system was less competitive and open than it appeared at first glance. The new president regarded his Radical Party as the only legitimate repository of the national will, and himself as little less than indispensable for its actualization. Likewise, the opposition Conservative Party did not consider Irigoyen a legitimate competitor in the political sphere.

Though the Radical Party was originally organized to protest the use of electoral fraud by the country's ruling elites, once in power Irigoyen himself showed scant respect for the outcome of contests in which his party was defeated: He intervened more often than any previous government to overturn the results of provincial elections. Moreover, though Irigoyen stepped down at the end of his first term in 1922, he quarreled with his handpicked successor, Marcelo Torcuato de Alvear, who took a more independent direction. The conflict between the two men split the Radical Party into personalist and antipersonalist wings, and although Irigoyen managed to obtain reelection in 1928 as the candidate of the largest of the two factions, he permanently alienated a large part of his former constituency, which, when the world crisis hit Argentina two years later, made common cause with his enemies and successfully overthrew both him and the existing political order.

Throughout the 1920s Argentina's conservative and provincial parties had struggled mightily to overturn the gathering hegemony of the Radical Party, but to no avail. By the middle of that decade many of Irigoyen's critics became interested in antidemocratic ideologies imported from France and Italy. As with nationalism everywhere, Argentine nationalism reflected a curious amalgam of clerical, militarist, xenophobic, and authoritarian sentiments rather than a coherent ideology. The Argentine Patriotic League epitomized the conservative nationalistic movement, whose followers specialized in breaking up labor demonstrations. Other strongly nationalistic groups included paramilitary leagues, which trained on military bases during off-duty hours; yet another was a new clutch of newspapers and magazines that railed against the excess of cosmopolitan (e.g., immigrant) elements in Argentine life, as well as against British and American influence (imperialism) in high places. In time, Irigoyen and the Radicals became the principal target of all these groups, and the Argen-

Argentina

Population:	40,301,927 (2007 est.)
Area:	1,068,302 sq mi
Official languages:	Spanish
Languages:	Spanish, German, English, French
National currency:	Argentine peso
Principal religions:	More than 90 percent of the population is nominally Roman Catholic, with approximately 20 percent considered to be practicing.
Ethnicity:	Almost all Argentines are white, many are of Spanish or Italian descent. Three percent of the population is made up of minorities, primarily of Native American or Mestizo (mixed white and Native American) heritage.
Capital:	Buenos Aires
Other urban centers:	Córdoba, Rosario, Mendoza, La Plata, San Miguel de Tucumán
Annual rainfall:	Argentina's rainfall varies substantially across its vast area. In Buenos Aires the average rainfall is 37 in. In the northern Chaco region rainfall averages 30 in. Puna de Atacama receives only 2 in of rain in an average year.
Principal geographical features:	*Mountains:* The Andes Mountains run along the entire western border of the country. They include the peaks Aconcagua—which at 22,835 ft is the tallest mountain in the Western Hemisphere—Ojos del Salado (22,572 ft) and Tupungato (22,310 ft). *Rivers:* Río de la Plata and its tributaries the Paraguay, Paraná, and Uruguay; Colorado; Negro *Flatlands:* The fertile plains of the Pampas form the central part of the country. Patagonia is a region of plateaus extending across the southern half of thecountry The Gran Chaco in the north is a low lying region of forests and swamps. *Lakes:* The are many glacier-fed lakes in the western part of the country, including Lago Argentino and Lago Buenos Aires (shared with Chile, where it is called Lago General Carrera). Small lakes can be found in the east, many of them brackish. *Islands:* The large island of Tierra del Fuego in the south is shared with Chile. Argentina claims the British-controlled Falkland Islands (Islas Malvinas) in the Atlantic Ocean.
Economy:	*GDP per capita:* $15,200 (2006 est.)
Principal products and exports:	*Agricultural:* barley, corn, cotton, fruit, linseed oil, livestock, sunflower seeds *Manufacturing:* chemicals, consumer durables, food processing, metallurgy, motor vehicles, printing, steel, textiles *Mining:* aluminum, boron, copper, gold, lead, silver, zinc
Government:	Argentina is a republic. It gained independence from Spain in 1816. The national constitution dates to 1853, but has been suspended or amended many times since then. The president is both head of government and head of state, and is elected along with a vice president to serve a four-year term. The president appoints the cabinet. The National Congress is the legislative branch, with two branches: a 72 seat Senate and a 257 seat Chamber of Deputies.
Armed forces:	The president is commander in chief of the armed forces. *Army:* 41,400 *Navy:* 17,500 *Air force:* 12,500 *Paramilitary:* 31,400
Transportation:	*Rail:* Argentina has 19,282 mi of railway, extending throughout the country but with the network centered on Buenos Aires. *Ports:* Bahia Blanca, Buenos Aires, Concepcion del Uruguay, La Plata, Punta Colorada, Rasario, San Lorenzo-San Martin, San Nicolas *Roads:* 42,756 mi paved, 99,628 mi unpaved *National airline:* Aerolíneas Argentinas *Airports:* 154 paved runway airports, with major facilities at Buenos Aires, Iguazu, and Mendoza.
Media:	Argentina has state-owned media companies, but the market is dominated by private firms. There are over a thousand FM radio stations and several hundred AM stations, as well as 42 television stations. More than 150 daily newspapers are available in Argentina.
Literacy and education:	*Total literacy rate:* 97 percent Education is compulsory for all children ages five to fourteen, and is available at free public schools or through private schools. There are over 46 accredited universities, the largest of which is the University of Buenos Aires.

tine army their chosen instrument. The Radicals and their supporters also invoked nationalism and often attacked the same groups the nationalists targeted. Labor unions, despised by conservatives, griped about foreign control of industries. Irigoyen raised complaints and concerns about international business. Nationalism proved a highly flexible ideology invoked by different actors, depending on the context.

The revolution of 1930 constituted, then, a temporary convergence of two movements. One was democratic but anti-Irigoyen (even Alvear himself, serving as ambassador to France, gave the conspirators his tacit support). The other was not merely anti-Radical but committed to a new vision of the political order. General José Félix Uriburu, the leader of the coup that ousted Irigoyen on 6 September 1930, had firm authoritarian convictions. A combination of political naïveté and a worsening case of cancer forced his retirement in 1932 before he could complete his quasi-fascist project.

General Agustín P. Justo, Alvear's former war minister, struck a deal with the Conservative Party and the anti-Irigoyen Radicals to hold new elections (in which he would be the presidential candidate), but with the important difference that the results would be predetermined by the Interior Ministry. Thus was born the "patriotic fraud," that effectively assured Conservative victories in the presidential contests of both 1932 and 1937, as well as in most races for Congress and the provincial legislatures.

Former president Alvear returned from France in late 1930 expecting to be the victorious presidential candidate in new elections. Instead, he and his associates were temporarily exiled to the extreme Patagonian south. Some antipersonalists continued to support the Justo administration (the so-called Concordancia), but most returned to the parent Radical Party. With Irigoyen's death in 1933, Alvear became the party's undisputed leader, a position he held until his death in 1942. His efforts to negotiate with President Justo to produce a more honest electoral system came to naught. His discussions with President Roberto M. Ortiz (who took office in 1938) seemed to hold more promise, but Ortiz resigned from office in 1940 due to ill health, and his replacement, Ramón S. Castillo, refused to carry the negotiations forward. The political stalemate was finally broken, somewhat unexpectedly, by a military coup in June 1943.

Both Radicals and (later) Peronists have referred to the 1930s as the "infamous decade." In so doing, they are referring not merely to the systematic application of electoral fraud, but also to a series of important changes in economic policy, the centerpiece of which is the Roca-Runciman Treaty concluded with Great Britain in 1933. The treaty was Argentina's response to the threat of imperial preference declared at the Ottawa Conference of 1932. In effect, it saved Argentina's place in British markets in exchange for preferential treatment for British exports in Argentina, accomplished through exchange control,

new tariff walls against non-British goods, and a system of production and trade quotas. Many critics, then and since, have argued that this treaty prevented Argentina from diversifying its economy.

Even though the Argentine economy remained tightly integrated with the British Empire, the trade agreement benefited the Argentine economy during the Great Depression of the 1930s. Argentina weathered the world crisis better than most major countries (including the United States). And it even helped to promote the growth of Argentine industry, though in unintended and unexpected ways. The sudden introduction of commercial discrimination against U.S., German, and other foreign products compelled Britain's major competitors to establish factories in Argentina, and by 1944 the country was producing a wide range of products, from lightbulbs to textiles, that formerly were imported from abroad. This great leap forward was much accelerated by World War II, which deprived Britain of what advantages it had gained in 1933 because its industries were now utterly unable to service the Argentine market.

In many ways the Conservative antipersonalist administrations of the 1930s and early 1940s are among the best the country has ever experienced. Lacking democratic legitimacy and facing social unrest, including labor-union protest, the Conservative governments of the period introduced social investment and public works in an effort to gain greater support. Their accomplishments include a vast program of public works—hospitals, all-weather roads, ports, airports, and waterworks. They created a system of national parks and greatly extended the state railroads to the more remote provinces. They poured significant new investment into Yacimientos Petrolíferos Fiscales (YPF), the state petroleum company. In contrast to the Perón regime and the military regimes that followed, these parastatals were run along orthodox financial lines so that they did not drain on the budget.

Moreover, it was during this period that much of Argentina's modern social legislation was introduced, including the five-and-a-half-day work week, paid vacations, maternity leave, pensions for government employees, and indemnification for discharge from employment. The Justo administration also greatly increased the country's housing stocks by subsidizing low-cost dwellings.

Supporters of Juan Perón, November 1972. With high hopes, a new and younger generation of Peronists welcomes former President Juan Perón to his home in Buenos Aires after seventeen years of exile. Perón won the presidency the following year but his death in 1974 and the sociopolitical turmoil that ensued led to military dictatorship and the Dirty War. © BETTMANN/CORBIS

1943–1966

The Conservatives failed, however, to anchor their accomplishments in the political realm. By 1943 they lacked a presidential candidate. President Ramón Castillo's decision to impose Senator Robustiano Patrón Costas of Salta was unpopular in the Concordancia ranks, and it also led to unrest in the field-grade and flag ranks of the Argentine army. The military had been relatively quiescent since its return to the barracks in 1932, but by the early 1940s the army was rent by intrigues and divisions that took the form of lodges. One such group, the United Officers Group (GOU), was convinced that the Axis powers were about to win the war and concerned that Patrón Costas and the Conservatives (who were thought to be pro-British) might compromise the country's neutrality. This was the proximate cause of the revolution of June 4, 1943.

Between 1943 and 1946 Argentina's military men struggled both to provide programmatic definition for the new regime and to deal with the shifting currents of wartime politics. Three different flag-rank officers held the presidency during these years, each gradually ceding increasing power to Colonel Juan Domingo Perón, who became vice president in 1944 and a presidential candidate in 1946. Although hitherto unknown to the Argentine public, Perón was no stranger to military politics. He was an early member of the Argentine Patriotic League and had been an active conspirator in the revolution of 1930, for which he was rewarded with a position as aide-de-camp to the war minister and subsequently seconded to the Italian army, where he trained with Benito Mussolini's Alpine troops.

A man of considerable charm, charisma, and tactical skills, Perón began building his political base within a few weeks after the coup of June 1943 by taking control of the Secretariat of Labor and Social Welfare. Within eighteen months he had turned it into a political machine dedicated to his own advancement, coopting labor leaders hitherto loyal to the Socialist and even Communist Parties. It was Perón who finally realized Irigoyen's dream of a syndicalist relationship with the labor movement, one that would outlast both his three presidencies and his person. Significantly, he acknowledged the culture and rhetoric of the working class, who often were excluded from the public sphere. Even though Perón embraced long-standing and conservative tenets of Argentine nationalism, his election and his clear support for the proletariat immediately provoked negative reactions from the traditional parties and elites.

Hence, the emergence of Perón in 1946 split the Argentine political community down the middle, dividing virtually all of the country's political forces. The new party attracted disaffected (or opportunistic) Conservatives, Socialists, Communists, and Radicals; most of its actual cadres were recruited from the Radicals. Initially, Perón benefited from the support of the Roman Catholic hierarchy, to whom he had promised that he would not abolish obligatory religious instruction in public schools (established in 1944).

A larger Radical remnant formed the bulk of the Democratic Union, the anti-Peronist coalition created for the 1946 elections, although it too drew support from the leadership of the Conservative, Radical, Socialist, and Communist Parties. Its presidential candidate, José Tamborini (1886-1955), was a colorless career politician who proved no match for the dashing colonel and his fiancée, a small-time actress by the name of María Eva Duarte ("Evita"), who became his wife—and much more—after the elections. Thus the elections of 1946 pitted old politics against new, with the Peronists winning a decisive 54 percent. Even so, the 46 percent that went to the opposition never accepted Perón as a lawful competitor, and they contributed to the long-term polarization in Argentine politics.

The first Perón era (1946–1955) is generally divided into two periods. Up to 1951 the government benefited from the accumulated wartime surpluses of foreign exchange, as well as the high prices for agricultural products generated by the temporary collapse of the Western European economies. This allowed Perón to engage in boom-and-spend populism without producing inflationary pressures or requiring confrontations between different sectors of society. These fortunate conditions came to an end in 1952, reversing economic trends and forcing the president to take refuge in more orthodox policies. This in turn had the effect of neutralizing his primary constituency—the labor movement—while alienating the business community, agriculture, and important elements of Argentina's large urban middle class.

The untimely death of Eva Perón in 1952 weakened the regime, because the president's wife was extraordinarily popular and respected by millions of working-class Argentines, particularly women. Without her antiestablishment discourse, the regime lost much of its popular mystique. A quarrel with the Catholic Church—which Señora Perón would surely have counseled against—eventually provoked unrest in the armed forces. The military eventually removed Perón in September 1955.

During Perón's first period of rule, the most salient feature of the regime seemed to be its authoritarian personalism, which some people mistook for fascism. Perón espoused some aspects of European fascism, but some historians have labeled his policies an "Argentine New Deal," complete with government agencies that preempted much of the economic space formerly reserved to a handful of private businesses and agricultural enterprises. Certainly, Peronism reshaped Argentine politics along more egalitarian lines. The labor movement, the most powerful in Latin America, developed rapidly with Perón's support. Women gained the right to vote. Expanding the social policies and public-works programs of the 1930s, Perón strengthened his political coalition. Like the New Deal, too, the Argentine program often brandished the language of radical economic redress, while actually strengthening the power of the middle class even more than that of the labor movement. That said, organized workers did receive substantial benefits.

However, inefficiency, corruption, and politicization limited the long-term effectiveness of these polices. Loyalty to the president, his wife, and their movement became the overarching criterion of civic virtue—and often, eligibility for government largess. Budget surpluses helped the movement prevail over the opposition in any electoral contest. The economic crisis that began in 1952 brought important changes in public administration. Perón asked his constituency for sacrifice. Furthermore, he abandoned his anti-imperialist banners (by negotiating an agreement with Standard Oil and seeking a rapprochement with the United States). Backing off of his initial social and economic policies, Perón became increasingly vulnerable to attacks from both the Left and the Right.

The overthrow of Perón did not resolve any of the fundamental issues of Argentine politics. The coalition that produced the "Liberating Revolution" (September 1955) was as diverse as the one that had brought Perón to power in the first place, and drew from the same elements (the armed forces and the Catholic Church) that had supported his election in 1946. The military saw the Liberating Revolution as an opportunity to purge Argentine public life of all Peronist influence, a sectarian exercise that took forms (such as total proscription of the party) that even many of its civilian supporters could not fully condone. Even at its lowest points, Peronism still counted for one-third of the electorate, which maintained it as the largest single force in the country, and no one could hope to win a majority at the ballot box without its tacit support. The leader of the Radicals, Arturo Frondizi, surmised as much, and cleverly concluded a pact with Perón (at that point, living in exile) by which the Perón would instruct his followers to vote for Frondizi in the 1958 elections. In exchange, Frondizi would legalize the Peronists four years thence. The agreement assured Frondizi's election, but also his premature overthrow, because when he permitted the Peronists to run under their own names in the elections of 1962, the armed forces quickly deposed him.

In retrospect, the failure of the Frondizi presidency was probably the costliest episode in the country's political history. Frondizi sought to integrate Peronism into the country's democratic life and at the same time to wean away many of Perón's followers to a more moderate and responsible form of populism-cum-nationalism. Unfortunately, the armed forces insisted upon regarding Frondizi himself as some sort of covert leftist, and a dissident faction of his own Radical Party (the so-called Radicals of the People) vehemently objected to any effort to end the proscription of the Peronist Party. These developments eventually canceled out the early achievements of Frondizi's administration—

the attraction of new investment, particularly from the United States, and major initiatives in science and education.

Following Frondizi's overthrow, the military staged new elections in which Arturo Umberto Illia, the candidate of the Radicals of the People, limped into office with a mere 26 percent of the vote. (The Peronists, forbidden once again from presenting their own candidates, registered their protests with blank ballots.) Illia was an austere and honest politician, but clearly a minority president whose very presence in the Casa Rosada depended on the goodwill of the military. Illia ultimately provoked a confrontation with the army that led to his replacement by the commander-in-chief of the Argentine army, General Juan Carlos Onganía, in June 1966.

1966–1973

Between 1966 and 1973 three different generals took turns trying to rule Argentina, none with much success. The purpose of the exercise, which General Onganía insisted on calling the Argentine Revolution, was no longer to eradicate Peronism so much as it was to wait out the death of its leader, at which point elections could be safely convoked. Yet, the military's ineffective economic planning eroded its authority. After two relatively good years, economic deterioration resumed, provoking popular disorder that climaxed in a general uprising in the province of Córdoba in May 1969. Moreover, the generals were beginning to quarrel amongst themselves. Former president General Pedro Aramburu (1955–1958), who had been talking to the civilian politicians, was kidnapped and murdered in 1970 under circumstances that suggest guerrilla collusion with the authorities.

By the early 1970s, what most Argentines remembered about Perón's period of power was that the times had been better (indeed they had). Even his bad period (1952–1955) seemed good by comparison. Nostalgia and the military's poor governance "re-Peronized" important sectors of the middle class. This was politically significant because it suddenly pushed most Argentines into the Peronist camp. (The trade union movement and most unorganized workers—household servants, for example—had never wavered in their loyalty.) Moreover, the new generation of Argentine students had no personal memory of the Perón period, but through family accounts and an

Morgue at Avellaneda Cemetery, late 20th century. Since 1984, human rights organizations and relatives of victims have worked with forensic scientists to locate, exhume, and identify the remains of the thousands of people "disappeared" during Argentina's Dirty War between 1976–1983. JAMES P. BLAIR/NATIONAL GEOGRAPHIC IMAGE COLLECTION

accumulating revisionist literature that equated Peronism with "movements of national liberation" in the third world, Argentine youth developed a romantic vision of Perón. Young radicals expected Peronism to bring radical changes like the Cuban Revolution and the anticolonial revolutions in Africa and Asia.

Perón did not discourage these new ideological assumptions. After brief sojourns in Paraguay, Panama, the Dominican Republic, and Venezuela, in the late 1950s he settled in Franco's Spain, where he perfected a confusing rhetoric that allowed all but the most intransigent anti-Peronists to assume that in the event of his return, their agendas would prevail. At the same time, the Perón residence in Puerta de Hierro became a place of pilgrimage for Argentine politicians of the most varied persuasions, each of whom left the encounter convinced that the former president's return was the sine qua non for Argentina's recovery as a great and prosperous nation.

Perhaps the most important aspect of the Peronist revival of the 1970s was the sudden adherence of young people of middle- and upper-middle-class origins, many of whom began their political careers in formations of the extreme Right or extreme Left. Both groups later contributed to an urban guerrilla movement that specialized in selective assassinations and kidnapping of unsympathetic figures of the military regime. While he refused to take responsibility for these violent actions, Perón also declined to condemn them, cynically declaring that they were the inevitable result of "oligarchical" rule and "surrender to the forces of imperialism." In effect, the Peronist youth and its guerrilla cohorts convinced the generals, already beset with economic problems and growing popular discontent, that only Perón could restore order.

Perón was allowed to return briefly to Argentina in 1972, but he was forbidden from running for president the following year. His stand-in, Héctor José Cámpora, won the race with 49 percent of the vote and assumed office in May 1973. Almost immediately, however, it became apparent that the real power in the new administration lay with the Peronist Youth and the more leftist elements of the party. Perón ordered Cámpora to resign, and his successor to convoke new elections for September. On that occasion Perón returned to power with nearly 62 percent of the vote.

1973–1994

Perón was seventy-eight years old and in poor health. The selection of his third wife, María Estela Martínez (Isabel) de Perón, as his running mate was not particularly reassuring, because she was almost illiterate and possessed of far less native political talent than Eva Duarte. Isabel also held strongly conservative views, putting her at odds with the Left of the party. Although Perón returned to power on a wave of popular euphoria, he quickly became bogged down in the country's intractable economic problems. Furthermore, the regime came into conflict with the Peronist Youth and other leftist elements of his coalition, who regarded Peronism in power as entirely too bland and conservative. By 1974 Perón had expelled these young people from the movement, and they resumed guerrilla actions against the government they had done so much to install. After Perón's death later that year, they accelerated their violent activities, doing much to undercut the fragile credibility of Isabel Perón's succession.

Brief and inglorious, Isabel Perón's tenure lasted as long as it did only because the military had decided to let things deteriorate until there was wide popular clamor for their return. When they finally overthrew her in March 1976, they not only decimated the tiny urban guerrilla movement, but also engaged in a sweep that resulted in the "disappearance" of some 9,000 persons, some of whom had links to terrorism or to the Left, but many more of whom were innocent victims. At incalculable human and moral cost, a semblance of order was restored in Argentina, and for a brief period (1978–1980) the country experienced a modest economic recovery. By 1981, however, huge government deficits and general mismanagement caused a revival of inflation—and of political activity. To neutralize both, in April 1982 President

Argentine troops, many of them young, preparing for the Falklands/Malvinas War, April 1982. Claim to the Malvinas/Falkland has been contested since the nineteenth century. Argentina's reclamation of the British administered islands was widely popular, but the swift military defeat by the British discredited the military dictatorship who resigned, returning the country to civilian rule in 1983. © ALAIN NOGUES/ CORBIS SYGMA

General Leopoldo Fortunato Galtieri decided to invade the Falkland (Malvinas) Islands, long under British occupation but claimed by every Argentine government for more than 150 years.

The recuperation of the Malvinas suddenly reversed the fortunes of the military government, but only briefly. Somewhat unexpectedly, the British (or rather, Prime Minister Margaret Thatcher) decided to dispatch an expeditionary force to retake the islands. By June contingents of the Royal Marines and the British army had defeated the Argentine occupation force, which did not put up much of a fight. The conflict humiliated the Argentine military, and President

Argentina Issues New Currency

U.S. political cartoon about Argentina's economy, 2002. Recession, inflation, unemployment, and debt contributed to economic crisis in the late twentieth and early twenty-first century Argentina. ILLUSTRATION BY JEFF DANZIGER—TRIBUNE MEDIA. REPRODUCED BY PERMISSION

Galtieri was forced to resign. The following year the Radical Raúl Ricardo Alfonsín, one of the chief critics of the military, won the presidency.

Alfonsín's triumph was significant on two counts. It was the first time the Peronists had to go to the polls without Perón—and the first presidential election they had ever lost. The result generated considerable soul-searching and subsequent attempts to modernize and renovate the party. Alfonsín's victory occurred because numerous parties, including the Peronists and the small conservative parties, supported his platform. Radicalism remained the faith of only one out of four voters, and after a brief burst of personal popularity, the new president discovered his limits.

Because Alfonsín ended his term in 1989 several months ahead of time and in a rush of hyperinflation, it is easy to overlook his real accomplishments. He normalized the political scene; he brought the

commanders-in-chief of the armed forces to trial for human-rights offenses; he ordered an investigation of disappearances, which eventually documented their exact number and nature; and he successfully resisted two military uprisings, one sparked by the Left and one by the Right. He also provided Argentina with a new identity as a country at once "Western, nonaligned, and developing." During his rule Argentina was an avid participant in the councils of the nonaligned and a pointed critic of the United States in Central America and elsewhere.

Unfortunately, Alfonsín inherited a large foreign debt and a huge apparatus of money-losing government enterprises. A politician with no training in economics, he was by temperament inclined to seek ideological solutions to concrete problems. He wasted two years trying to divide the Western European countries from the United States on the debt issue, and for practical political reasons chose

Demonstration by relatives and mothers of missing persons, 1982. Since 1977 friends, family, and human rights organizations have staged protests at the Plaza de Mayo in Buenos Aires, seeking information about and demanding justice for their missing loved ones—an estimated 30,000—killed or disappeared during the military dictatorship. © HORACIO VILLALOBOS/CORBIS

not to liquidate or reduce the size of the parastatals. (Had he chosen to do so, however, most likely he would have encountered serious resistance from the Peronists.) Eventually mismanagement—and the larger difficulties Argentina faced in a protectionist world—exacted its price. By 1989 the government had lost control of its own economic situation. There was a massive flight of capital, and the Argentine unit of currency lost value exponentially. In May the Radical candidate for the presidency, Córdoba governor Eduardo Angeloz, was defeated by the Peronist Carlos Saúl Menem. A seven-month transition period had been anticipated between administrations, but within days of Menem's election it was obvious that the Alfonsín government had lost the ability to govern. The inauguration date was accelerated so that Menem could immediately reassure the panic-stricken public.

Menem took office during one of the darkest moments of modern Argentine history. He had served two terms as governor of La Rioja, a small, poverty-stricken province in the northwest where he

had put thousands of his friends and followers on the government payroll, compensating them with scrip redeemable only within provincial boundaries. This was hardly a reassuring preamble to his presidency, but almost from the moment of taking office he reversed course. In effect, Menem took the kind of measures to assure Argentine economic stability that no government, including those dominated by the military, had ever dared to attempt. He also reversed age-old policies that discouraged foreign investment and saving, and most important of all, he proceeded to privatize Argentina's huge public sector. At the same time, he broke the back of the country's powerful labor movement.

Menem also tackled the military question head-on. He pardoned the six commanders-in-chief of the armed forces whom Alfonsín's courts had sentenced to lifetime reclusion for human-rights offenses. This gave him virtually unlimited control of the armed forces, something no Argentine president since 1930 could claim to possess. It also permitted him to slash military budgets, greatly reducing the size of the armed forces, and eventually (in 1994) to eliminate conscription. One attempt to overthrow his government in December 1990 was easily turned aside; the sight of the rebels surrendering army headquarters in downtown Buenos Aires, ordered on their hands and knees by loyalist troops, underscored the low estate into which the praetorian forces in Argentine society had fallen.

By 1993 Argentines had repatriated more than $5 billion of the purportedly $50 billion worth of assets offshore. Foreign investment returned to the country. The Argentine peso was placed on par with the U.S. dollar, a strict fiscal discipline that reduced inflation to single digits. At the same time, dismantling huge parastatals and privatizing essential government services (education, health) opened a new gap in Argentina between rich and poor, and badly frayed the fabric of what had once been Latin America's quintessential middle-class society. Nonetheless, Menem continued to hold the support of more than 40 percent of the Argentine public, whereas his opposition was divided and confused.

At this point the president decided to alter the Argentine Constitution of 1853, which forbade consecutive presidential terms. Somewhat surprisingly, he was able to convince former president Raúl Alfonsín, his archenemy, to endorse the idea of a new charter. The result was to divide the Radical Party yet further, all but assuring Menem's reelection in 1995.

Following the same policies as his first term, Menem's government presided over continued economic growth. However, his decision to peg the peso to the dollar created problems for the next administration, under the Radical president Fernando de la Rúa. When the dollar rose considerably in the 1990s, the expensive Argentine peso made Argentine goods too costly for international trade. The domestic market could not compensate, and in 2000 the economy experienced a severe crisis. Eventually, the government devalued the peso, which eliminated the savings of the middle classes. Then, the government defaulted on its debt. There were large, sometimes violent, demonstrations against the government, and in 2001 de la Rúa resigned. Many commentators feared that Argentina would return to political and economic instability. Instead, the country pulled through the crisis: Even though Argentina went through three different presidents in 2001, democratic institutions prevailed. The military, weakened after the Falkland invasion, never regained its authority with the public and therefore did not have the ability to intervene. A temporary president, Eduardo Duhalde, stabilized the economy and called for new elections in 2003. The Justicialist candidate, Néstor Kirchner, won the presidency. Kirchner has been accused of reviving Latin American populism, using antiforeign rhetoric, and siding with the Left, but politicians in European and North American democracies often engage in similar political positions and styles. Political scientists debate whether democratic institutions have been consolidated in Argentina, but there have been clear improvements from the mid-twentieth century.

Economically, the currency devaluation brought hardship to most Argentines, but in the long term it also spurred an export boom. With a weak currency, Argentina once again sold cattle and agricultural products to its neighbors in the Mercosur trading pact. Another positive development for the Argentine economy has been the rise of China. With China's rapid industrialization, world demand for agriculture products increased substantially in the early twenty-first century, benefiting countries such as Argentina and Brazil. Like its neighbor Chile, Argentina developed new export products. For instance, the Argentine wine industry has gained international respect, specializing in the Malbec grape. Although the debt default may have limited foreign investment in Argentina, recent growth has renewed interest among international investors. Overall, due to the country's population size, the economy will rely greatly on international trade, and will probably feel the effects of future global downturns. Argentina in the early twenty-first century may not have attained the same level of prosperity or optimism that existed a hundred years earlier, but the country survived the difficulties of the twentieth century and emerged as a diverse and stable country with a dynamic cultural and economic potential.

See also **Falklands/Malvinas War.**

BIBLIOGRAPHY

Ciria, Alberto. *Parties and Power in Modern Argentina, 1930–1946*, translated by Carlos A. Astiz with Mary F. McCarthy. Albany: State University of New York Press, 1974.

Crassweller, Robert D. *Perón and the Enigmas of Argentina.* New York: W. W. Norton, 1986.

Estrada, Ezequiel Martínez. *X-Ray of the Pampa*, translated by Alain Swietlicki. Austin: University of Texas Press, 1971.

Falcoff, Mark, and Ronald H. Dolkoff, eds. *Prologue to Perón: Argentina in Depression and War, 1930–1945*. Berkeley: University of California Press, 1975.

Fraga, Rosendo. *Argentina en las urnas, 1931–1991*. Buenos Aires: Editorial Centro de Estudios Union para la Nueva Mayoría, 1992.

Hernández, Pablo José. *Peronismo y pensamiento nacional, 1955–1973*. Buenos Aires: Editorial Biblos, 1997.

Lewis, Paul H. *The Crisis of Argentine Capitalism*. Chapel Hill: University of North Carolina Press, 1990.

Lewis, Paul H. *Guerrillas and Generals: The "Dirty War" in Argentina*. Westport, CT: Praeger, 2002.

Massot, Vicente Gonzalo. *Matar y morir: la violencia política en la Argentina (1806–1980)*. Buenos Aires: Emecé Editores, 2003.

McGee Deutsch, Sandra. *Counterrevolution in Argentina, 1900–1932*. Lincoln: University of Nebraska Press, 1986.

Piglia, Ricardo. *Respiración artificial*. Buenos Aires: Anagrama, 2005.

Reflexiones sobre la nación Argentina. Buenos Aires: Ediciones, Temática, 1982.

Rock, David. *Argentina in the Twentieth Century*. Pittsburgh, PA: University of Pittsburgh Press, 1975.

Rock, David. *Authoritarian Argentina: The Nationalist Movement and Its History, Its Impact*. Berkeley: University of California Press, 1993.

Romero, Luis Alberto. *A History of Argentina in the Twentieth Century*. University Park: Pennsylvania State University Press, 2002.

Torrado, Susana. *Estructura social de la Argentina, 1945–1983*. Buenos Aires: Ediciones de la Flor, 1992.

Waisman, Carlos H. *From Military Rule to Liberal Democracy in Argentina*. Boulder, CO: Westview Press, 1987.

Waisman, Carlos H. *Reversal of Development in Argentina: Postwar Counterrevolutionary Policies and Their Structural Consequences*. Princeton, NJ: Princeton University Press, 1987.

MARK FALCOFF
BYRON CRITES

ARGENTINA, CIVIL CODE.
Argentina's Civil Code, the basis for the country's civil law, is the result of several efforts to codify the law.

The culmination of these efforts came in 1864, when President Bartolomé Mitre commissioned jurist Dalmacio Vélez Sarsfield to write a Civil Code. The bill was passed and became the law of the land through Law No. 340 on September 24, 1869; it went into effect on January 1, 1871. The Civil Code contains 4,051 articles and reflects seventeenth-century principles of liberalism and individualism. After its passage, it was modified several times through various laws in response to developing litigation issues.

Provisions modified in the Code include Law 2393 (1888), establishing the institution of civil matrimony, which may or may not be followed by a religious ceremony; Law 1357 (1926) extended civil rights to women; Laws 11723 (1933) and 22195 (1980) established intellectual property; Law 13512 (1948) established "horizontal property" (or proprietary interest in a cooperative apartment house); and Law 14394 (1954) established a legal code for minors and the family, introducing the concept of the "good of the family" and mandatory joint ownership of the inherited goods of an economic unit.

The most significant changes in the Civil Code were made through Law 17711 (1968), which modified approximately two hundred articles and introduced, among other things, the implicit defeasance clause in contracts, injury as a cause for objection, reparations for moral damages even when contractual responsibility is assumed, the validity of transferring real estate to third-party bona fide purchasers, and the abuse of process principle.

Later, other changes were made via Law 23091 (1984) on urban leases. Law 23264 (1985) changed the regime of *patria potestas* and filiation, making all children equal whether they were adopted or born in or outside of marriage and establishing a shared *patria potestas*. Law 23515 (1987) incorporated divorce *a vinculo matrimonii*; Law 24240 (1993) is the consumer defense law; Law 24481 (1995) made provisions for patents on inventions; Law 24779 (1997) modified the system of adoption, allowing adoption regardless of the civil status of the adopting parties; Law 25236 (2000) protects personal information; Law 25248 (2000) applies to leasing; and Law 25561 (2002) deals with economic emergencies in social, economic, administrative, financial, and exchange matters and reformed the currency exchange regime.

These provisions all contribute to the configuration of the rule of law because they are aimed at avoiding family violence and noncompliance with family obligations, establishing equality among children born to different kinds of unions, extending the institution of adoption, defending consumers, providing minimum guarantees for lessors and lessees, reaching maximum levels of sexual health and responsible parenting for the population, and assuring the comprehensive protection of personal information in archives, records, data banks, or other technical data storage methods.

See also **Argentina: The Twentieth Century; Argentina, Commercial Code; Mitre, Bartolomé; Vélez Sarsfield, Dalmacio.**

BIBLIOGRAPHY

Mirow, Matthew C. *Latin American Law: A History of Private Law and Institutions in Spanish America.* Austin: University of Texas Press, 2004.

Morello, Augusto M., and Néstor L. Portas, eds. *Examen y crítica de la reforma del Código Civil.* La Plata: Editora Platense, 1971.

                                   VIVIANA KLUGER

ARGENTINA, COMMERCIAL CODE.

Argentina's Commercial Code is the collection of provisions that regulate the legal relationships associated with industry and trade in the country. It was written by Dalmacio Vélez Sarsfield and Eduardo Acevedo and adopted first by the Province of Buenos Aires in 1859 and later as code for the Nation of Argentina in 1862. Sources included the Bilbao Ordinances of 1737, and French, Spanish, Portuguese, Dutch, and Brazilian law. After the Civil Code went into effect in 1871, it was necessary to amend the Commercial Code to avoid repetitions. The first modification was made in 1889, affecting the area of corporations and provisions related to the current account, commodity exchange markets, checks, bearer instruments, and mortgage on a vessel. Later, other laws were written that substantially changed the Code or introduced new concepts required by the increase in economic activity. These changes dealt with bankruptcy provisions, trade societies, bonds, insurance, warrants, registered pledges, the transfer of commercial and industrial establishments, financial entities,

patents on inventions and utility models, credit cards, and so on. At the same time, norms detailed in the Commercial Code were eventually incorporated legally, along with specific laws or codes, and autonomous branches of law, such as maritime law and aeronautic law.

The Commercial Code has been vitally important for Argentine economic development because it has provided the legal framework necessary for economic relationships to develop in a context of transparency, predictability, and legal security.

See also **Acevedo Díaz, Eduardo Inés; Argentina: The Twentieth Century; Argentina, Civil Code; Vélez Sarsfield, Dalmacio.**

BIBLIOGRAPHY

Mirow, Matthew C. *Latin American Law: A History of Private Law and Institutions in Spanish America* Austin: University of Texas Press, 2004.

Cámara, Héctor. "Código de Comercio de la República Argentina y reformas o tentativas hasta la actualidad." In *Centenario del Código de Comercio* by the Instituto de Investigaciones Jurídicas. México: Instituto de Investigaciones Jurídicas, 1991.

                                   VIVIANA KLUGER

ARGENTINA, CONSTITUTIONS.

Since its approval, and despite significant revisions, Argentina's Constitution of 1853 has continued to define the workings of the nation's legal system. Up until that time, attempts to legally organize Argentina had failed, mainly because of tensions between the interests of Buenos Aires (which controlled the country's main port) and those of the interior provinces. There had been many attempts at organization, however. Both the Provisional Regulations (1811) and the subsequent Provisional Statutes proved to be short-lived. A Constituent Assembly met in 1813, but failed to approve a constitution, though it managed to establish liberal rules that had significant repercussions for the country. The Provisional Statutes of 1815 also did not establish a sound legal foundation for the nation, but they did prompt the formation of the influential Constituent Congress of 1816, which in 1817 approved a new set of Provisional Regulations to stay in place until the final approval of a constitution.

The only constitutional texts approved before the Constitution of 1853 were the Constitution of 1819 (a product of the Congress of 1816) and the Constitution of 1826. The Constitution of 1819 was particularly important because it assured the organization of a corporate senate (that included members from the military, the church, and academia) and because it made the establishment of a monarchy a possibility. Markedly centralist, it was immediately rejected by a majority of Argentina's provinces. The same fate befell the Constitution of 1826, despite its more federalist nature and its elimination of the more elitist features of the earlier constitutional proposal.

The political crisis that erupted ended with the rise of Juan Manuel de Rosas, who became governor of the province of Buenos Aires in 1829 and later de facto leader of the country, holding power for over two decades. Rosas represented federal interests and, given his resistance to establishing a constitution, he bolstered his power through a series of interprovincial agreements (among them the Federal Pact of 1831).

Rosas's military defeat in 1853 opened the door to the establishment of the Constitution of 1853—a late product of a pact between federalist and centralist forces. Inspired by the work of Juan Bautista Alberdi, this constitution appeared to be "cast in the mold" of the U.S. Constitution of 1787, according to Benjamin Gorostiaga, one of its authors. However, Argentina's constitution differed fundamentally from its U.S. counterpart in significant ways: The U.S. Constitution's system of checks and balances was undermined in the Argentine constitution by the introduction of a stronger presidential system (that included, for instance, the concept of the "state of siege"); the "strongly federal" organization of the U.S. document was weakened in the Argentine (by establishing "federal intervention" over the provinces, for example); and the strict separation of church and state in the U.S. work also was moderated by the Argentine (by Article 2, in which the government "upholds" the Apostolic Roman Catholic faith).

In 1860, as a result of a military conflict originating in Buenos Aires, the constitution was amended for the first time in ten years, to safeguard the autonomy and interests of Buenos Aires. Another reform in 1866 regulated the use of resources from export duties, and another in 1898 specified the number of representatives per inhabitant.

The Constitution of 1853 contributed to a slow democratization of the country, a trend decidedly strengthened with the issue of the Sáenz Peña Act of 1912. This act established universal, secret, and mandatory suffrage, ending a long period of electoral fraud.

In 1930 the first of several military coups in the twentieth century seriously influenced the effective force of the constitutional text. During a period of democratic instability, President Juan Domingo Perón backed the first amending of the constitution, in 1949. The Constitution of 1949 authorized unlimited reelection to the presidency; regulated the state's "social function of ownership" and its intervention in the economy (establishing national ownership of all energy sources); reintroduced military courts; created the concept of the "state of prevention and alarm"; and, most importantly, introduced a long list of social and economic rights, including explicit protection of the traditional family structure and equal rights for men and women in marriage.

In 1955 a military coup reinstalled the former constitution, and a 1957 reform incorporated the present Article 14, which summarized the social commitments of the Constitution of 1959. This reform, for example, established the right to "decent, fair labor conditions," a limited work day, and access to decent housing, and prohibited arbitrary dismissal. In 1972, towards the end of the military interregnum, a constitutional reform (which for the first time did not resort to a Constituent Convention) established the rules to govern the democratic election of 1973, and also contained a number of other amendments that were repealed in 1976 after another military coup.

With the reestablishment of democracy in 1983, new reforming initiatives aimed at ending what was termed the "hyper-presidential" system established by the Constitution of 1853 and thought to have been responsible in good part for a century of democratic instability. The Olivos Pact signed by President Carlos Menem and former president Raúl Alfonsín in 1994 facilitated presidential reelection in exchange for some other reforms aimed at reducing executive powers and modernizing the constitution. The 1994 Constitution included provisions creating the position of cabinet chief, regulating the legislative powers of the president, and introducing a council of magistrates to curb presidential influence on the election of judges. Its reforms were particularly significant with regard to rights: It granted constitutional rank to the principal human-rights conventions signed by the nation; introduced mechanisms of direct democracy; and established equal rights for both sexes, forms of collective action (*amparo colectivo*), and environmental rights.

See also **Alfonsín, Raúl Ricardo.**

BIBLIOGRAPHY

Alberdi, Juan Bautista. *Obras selectas*, edited by Joaquín V. González. Buenos Aires: Librería la Facultad, 1920.

Chiaramonte, José Carlos. *Ciudades, provincias, estados: Orígenes de la nación Argentina, 1800–1846.* Buenos Aires: Ariel, 1997.

Nino, Carlos. *Fundamentos de derecho constitucional.* Buenos Aires: Editorial Astrea, 1992.

Ravignani, Emilio. *Asambleas Constituyentes Argentinas.* 6 vols. Buenos Aires: Casa Jacobo Peuser, 1886.

Sánchez Viamonte, Carlos. *Historia Institucional de Argentina.* México: Fondo de Cultura Económica, 1948.

ROBERTO GARGARELLA

ARGENTINA, FEDERALIST PACTS (1831, 1852).

The Federalist Pacts of 1831 and 1852 were de facto federalist alliances between the Argentine littoral provinces. After the collapse of the Unitarist experiment in the 1820s, local caudillos took control of the provinces. Often seen as the opponents of legal rule, they were nevertheless concerned to forge a framework for reconciling interprovincial relations, because some rules had to be spelled out for relations with foreign governments, customs regulations needed enforcing, and, most important, peace had to be restored between Buenos Aires and other provinces. Moreover, these governors were determined to counter the Liga Unitaria, which united the interior provinces in 1830 under General José María Paz. On 4 January 1831, the governors of Entre Ríos, Santa Fe, and Buenos Aires (later joined by the governor of Corrientes) signed the first federalist pact. In a general sense, this accord served as the skeleton constitution for a decentralized federation of provinces and as the blueprint until the formal 1853 Constitution. The pact embraced the principle of free trade and self-governing provinces but left the issue of control over customs revenues simmering in ambiguity. In effect, Buenos Aires retained its grip over the primary source of the region's fiscal revenues.

This control by Buenos Aires eventually became a factor in bringing down the Buenos Aires caudillo Juan Manuel de Rosas in early 1852. The victorious alliance, led by the Entre Ríos governor, General Justo José de Urquiza, reinvoked the 1831 pact, and on 31 May 1852 a new federal pact was signed, this time involving most of the interior provinces. It gave sweeping powers to Urquiza as interim director but also called for a Constitutional Congress, which a year later approved a new constitution for the Republic. Buenos Aires, however, was loath to join the federation and be stripped of its grip over the customhouse, and eventually seceded from the new confederation. In 1861, after some amendments, Buenos Aires agreed to accept the 1853 Constitution. The federal pacts served as intermediate formulas until full constitutional rule could be consolidated.

See also **Argentina, Constitutions; Buenos Aires; Caudillismo, Caudillo; Entre Ríos; Paz, José María; Rosas, Juan Manuel de; Santa Fe, Argentina; Urquiza, Justo José de.**

BIBLIOGRAPHY

John Lynch, *Argentine Dictator: Juan Manuel de Rosas, 1829–1852* (1981), esp. pp. 138–139.

Haydel Gorostegui De Torres, *Historia argentina: La organización nacional* (1972), esp pp. 19–31.

David Rock, *Argentina, 1516–1982: From Spanish Colonization to the Falklands War* (1985; rev. ed. 1987), esp. pp. 104–120.

JEREMY ADELMAN

ARGENTINA, GEOGRAPHY.

The Argentine Republic is located at the southern end of South America, running southwards from the Tropic of

Capricorn. With an area of 1,072,200 square miles (2,776,900 square kilometers) and a population of 36,260,000, it is bounded by Bolivia, Paraguay, Brazil, Uruguay, and Chile. It is organized as a federation of twenty-three provinces and one autonomous city, Buenos Aires, the federal capital. Its official language is Spanish, although indigenous languages are also spoken in some areas. Seven major natural regions are recognized: The Andes, in the west, has the highest elevations located in the north-central section. (Aconcagua, at 22,834 feet [6,959 meters] above sea level, is the highest peak in the Americas.) These are arid mountains, except in the eastern part of the northern sector, where mountain jungle can be found, and in Patagonia, where there is a cold jungle. In the northern sector is the Puna plateau, which is high, dry, and cold. In the north-central region of the country are the Chaco plains, originally covered by semi-arid forest, with a dry subtropical climate. In the northeastern corner of the country is the dense Missionary Jungle, located on a mountain range, with a humid subtropical climate. The Pampas plains, highly degraded grasslands with a temperate climate, run along the east-central part of the country. The west-central region, which receives the least rainfall, is a long strip of semi-arid wooded vegetation known as the woodlands. In the south is the Patagonian plateau, dry and cold, covered by steppes. Approximately 7 percent of the country is under some type of environmental protection, including the 9.14 million acres that make up the country's thirty-four national parks.

The Río de la Plata (River Plate) Basin covers most of the country. Its principal tributaries are the Paraná, with a broad and active delta, and the Uruguay. The two rivers converge to form the great River Plate estuary.

When the Spaniards arrived, Argentina had an indigenous population of at least 500,000, distributed in relatively dense groups in the northwest and more widely dispersed throughout the rest of the country. The Spanish conquerors settled in the northwest, and to a lesser extent in Cuyo and along the banks of the Paraná, whereas Patagonia and the Chaco remained in indigenous hands until the end of the nineteenth century. At the time of independence (1810), the country had no more than 610,000 inhabitants. The population began to grow gradually from that point onwards, but beginning in the mid-nineteenth century, a strong wave of European immigration accelerated that growth, swelling the

country's numbers to almost 8.2 million by 1914. This wave was subsequently replaced by immigrants from bordering countries. An urbanization trend increased sharply starting in the early twentieth century, driven by the relocation of large masses of people from the northeast and the northwest to the large coastal cities. This resulted in a population that was more than 90 percent urban by 2001, though the tendency toward population concentration has halted. Internal and external migrations transformed the distribution of the population, with the dense settlements of the northwest replaced by those in the Pampas region, followed by settlements in Patagonia, the Chaco, and the Missions territory.

Argentina has a long tradition of public education that goes back to the end of the nineteenth century. The illiteracy rate is relatively low, encompassing less than 4 percent of the adult population. This is reflected in secondary education enrollment, with one-fourth of adults having completed secondary school.

The economy is based on primary production and its related industries. The greatest share of that sector is held by agricultural and livestock production (9% of the GDP), whereas manufacturing occupies the largest share of the secondary sector, with 27 percent of the total. The push to industrialize began dropping off toward the 1970s, and the center of economic activity shifted for a time to the financial and service sectors. Later, the focus returned to primary production, accompanied by the broadening of agriculturally based industries such as food-oil processing and flour mills. The globalization process and the Mercosur common market have promoted industrial diversification, and in many cases Argentina plays a role in international production chains such as those of the automotive and dairy industries. The vast majority of the GDP—80 percent—is generated in the Pampas region. Agricultural activity is centered in this area, where natural conditions allow for the production of all types of cereals (chiefly soy, wheat, and corn), as well as beef and pork. Agriculture has seen great productivity increases through the application of advanced technologies. Each of the remaining regions of the country exhibits a certain degree of agricultural specialization, based on local environmental circumstances. Thus, sugarcane is cultivated in the northwest; cotton in the Chaco; yerba mate, tobacco, and rice in the northeast; wine grapes and olives in Cuyo; and fruit in northern Patagonia. Beef cattle are raised in almost all regions, with varying degrees of technological enhancement, but almost always on natural pastureland (except in the Pampas region). Sheep are raised in Patagonia. Regional production generally targets the domestic market, while the export of cereals and meat as well as their direct derivatives (oil, dairy products) originates chiefly in the Pampas. Fishing activities are increasing significantly in Argentina, particularly in the Patagonian ports.

For many years, timber farming consisted of the irrational use of the native forests of the northern and central parts of the country for the production of tannin, railroad ties, fence posts, firewood, and charcoal. The period since the middle of the twentieth century has seen an increase in reforestation activities linked to the production of cellulose paste. In the early twenty-first century, mining is seeing a surge in activity, concentrated in the western part of the country, where lead, copper, silver, and gold are mined. Oil and gas development is underway in the northeast, Cuyo, and Patagonia. The country is self-sufficient in both, with an exportable surplus. In the realm of energy production, oil and gas are joined by hydroelectric energy, which has great potential, and to a lesser extent, nuclear energy. Most of the country is covered by an interconnected power grid. Industrial activity has tended to concentrate along the Pampas coast. Chief among the industries is food processing (oils, dairy products, meat by-products, sugar, flour). The metalworking and auto industries are located in the vicinity of Buenos Aires, Rosario, and Córdoba. Although the textile and chemical industries are also concentrated around Buenos Aires, they are more widely distributed, as are petrochemicals. The largest industrial centers are in the Buenos Aires Metropolitan Area, on the axis joining San Nicolás, Rosario, and Santa Fe, and the area surrounding the city of Córdoba. At the same time, other areas exhibit greater industrial specialization, for example, winemaking in Mendoza or sugar production in Tucumán.

The railroad network, formerly quite extensive, has virtually disappeared. Only a few branch lines remain in use for cargo shipments. Its disappearance did not coincide with the growth of quality roadways: There are no more than 37,000 miles (59,500 kilometers) of paved roads, and these are generally narrow, in poor condition, and do not cover the entire country. An enormous fleet of buses (the chief means of interurban transportation in Argentina) travels on the nation's highways, interconnecting virtually all of its towns and cities. River and maritime transportation is almost exclusively for cargo. The principal ports are those of Buenos Aires, Rosario, Santa Fe, Bahía Blanca, Quequén, San Antonio Este, and Mar del Plata. An increasing number of private ports specializing in grain shipments have been established along the Paraná River. Argentina has a large network of oil and gas pipelines that extends to neighboring countries. An activity that has grown considerably in Argentina is tourism, both domestic and international. Domestic tourism has stimulated the growth of towns along the Atlantic coast of Buenos Aires and in the Córdoba Mountains, but Argentina is also a growing center of attraction for international tourism. Revenues from international tourism have come to exceed those from livestock industry exports. The greatest attractions for foreign visitors are the city of Buenos Aires, the Iguaçu Falls, the southern lakes, and the Perito Moreno Glacier.

See also **Andes; Buenos Aires; Chaco Region; Córdoba; Cuyo; Iguaçu Falls; Meat Industry; Mercosur; Pampa; Paraná River; Patagonia; Río de la Plata; Wool Industry.**

BIBLIOGRAPHY

Barsky, Osvaldo, and Jorge Gelman. *Historia del agro argentino: Desde la conquista hasta fines del siglo XX.* Buenos Aires: Grijalbo Mondadori, 2001.

Brailovsky, Antonio, and Diana Foguelman. *Memoria Verde: Historia ecológica de la Argentina*, 13th edition. Buenos Aires: Editorial Sudamericana, 2002.

Brown, Alejandro; Ulises Martinez Ortiz, Marcelo Acerbi, and Javier Corchera, comps. *La situación ambiental argentina 2005.* Buenos Aires: Fundación Vida Silvestre, 2006.

Sawers, Larry. *The Other Argentina: The Interior and National Development.* Boulder, CO: Westview Press, 1996.

CARLOS REBORATTI

ARGENTINA, MOVEMENTS

This entry includes the following articles:
FEDERALISTS
UNITARISTS

FEDERALISTS

The Argentine Federalists were a post-Independence faction favoring a national organization allowing provincial autonomy, as against the tightly centralized system sought by the Unitarists. Strong Federalist sentiment in the interior provinces was already evident during the struggle for independence, inspired by resentment of the domineering ways of revolutionary leaders in the former colonial capital, Buenos Aires, and in some instances by differences of economic interest. The national constitutions of 1819 and 1826 proved abortive because much of the interior refused to accept their centralist orientation. Even in Buenos Aires itself there was an influential Federalist faction, led initially by Manuel Dorrego and later by Juan Manuel de Rosas, who first became governor of Buenos Aires Province in 1829. Rosas implanted a personal dictatorship over all Argentina, but without abandoning the Federalist banner and without creating any formal national institutions.

The appeal of Federalists to local sentiment and to Argentine nativism (while depicting the rival Unitarists as beholden to European influence) won them wide popular support in the cities as well as the countryside. However, their most representative figures were large landowners and militia officers like Rosas, who forged close patron-client ties with the rural population of their respective provinces. After the formal adoption in 1853 of a federal-style constitution, Federalism soon ceased to be a distinct political movement.

See also **Dorrego, Manuel; Rosas, Juan Manuel de.**

BIBLIOGRAPHY

Miron Burgin, *The Economic Aspects of Argentine Federalism, 1820–1852* (1946).

Tulio Halperín Donghi, *Politics, Economics, and Society in Argentina in the Revolutionary Period,* translated by Richard Southern (1975).

John Lynch, *Argentine Dictator: Juan Manuel de Rosas, 1829–1852* (1981).

Additional Bibliography

De la Fuente, Ariel. *Children of Facundo: Caudillo and Gaucho Insurgency during the Argentine State-Formation Process (La Rioja, 1853–1870).* Durham, NC: Duke University Press, 2000.

Myers, Jorge. *Orden y virtud el discurso republicano en el régimen rosista.* Buenos Aires: Universidad Nacional de Quilmes, 1995.

DAVID BUSHNELL

UNITARISTS

The Unitarist Party was one of the two major political movements that dominated Argentine politics between 1824 and 1852. Its origins lay in the conflict between centralists and federalists during the decade after 1810. It only emerged as a clearly recognizable political force during the 1824–1827 Congreso General Constituyente, in which it enjoyed a majority. The Unitarist constitution of 1826 summarized the party's basic principles: Buenos Aires should be the capital of the new state; provincial governors should be appointed by the national executive; and provinces should be no more than administrative units. Its leaders were Bernardino Rivadavia, Julián Segundo de Agüero, and Valentín Gómez.

A Federalist reaction in 1827 provoked the party's fall from power. A Unitarist coup d'état conducted by General Juan Lavalle in 1828 led to the military defeat of the Unitarists in Buenos Aires. From 1829 to 1852 the party was proscribed there and its leaders exiled. In the interior of Argentina, Unitarists and Federalists waged a civil war between 1826 and 1832 and again from 1839 to 1848. General José María Paz was able to establish a Unitarist government in Córdoba (1829–1832), while General Lavalle led an unsuccessful invasion of the Argentine Confederation (1839–1841). After the Unitarist government of Corrientes was overthrown in 1848, the party was banned throughout the Confederation. New political forces emerged after 1852 that in effect replaced that party.

See also **Rivadavia, Bernardino.**

BIBLIOGRAPHY

Barba, Enrique M. *Unitarismo, federalismo, rosismo.* Buenos Aires: Centro Editor de América Latina, 1982.

Halperín Donghi, Tulio. *De la revolución de independencia a la Confederación Argentina.* Buenos Aires: Paidós, 1972.

JORGE MYERS

ARGENTINA, ORGANIZATIONS

This entry includes the following articles:
AMERICAN INDUSTRIAL SOCIETY FOR MACHINERY (SIAM)
ARGENTINE CIVIC LEGION (LCA)

ARGENTINE PATRIOTIC LEAGUE (LPA)
ARGENTINE RURAL SOCIETY
ARGENTINE TRADE PROMOTION INSTITUTE (IAPI)
FEDERATION OF ARGENTINE WORKERS (FOA)
GENERAL LABOR CONFEDERATION (CGT)
LIGA FEDERAL, LIGA LITORAL, LIGA UNITARIA
SOCIEDAD DE BENEFICIENCIA
UNITED OFFICERS GROUP (GOU)
YACIMIENTOS PETROLÍFEROS FISCALES (YPF)

AMERICAN INDUSTRIAL SOCIETY FOR MACHINERY (SIAM)

The rise and decline of the industrial manufacturing concern SIAM Di Tella followed that of the Argentine economy. The company was founded in 1910 in Buenos Aires by three Italian immigrants, Torcuato Di Tella and the Allegrucci brothers, to make a dough-kneading machine. Di Tella quickly became the driving force and the Allegruccis withdrew. After Di Tella died in 1948, his management team continued to run the company.

SIAM produced a wide assortment of machinery. After World War I it built gasoline pumps largely for the state-owned oil company, Yacimientos Petrolíferos Fiscales, and ran service stations. SIAM manufactured pumps with a license from a U.S. company, setting a pattern for most of its products. In the 1930s SIAM broke into consumer goods by manufacturing refrigerators. By the early 1960s SIAM was producing a full range of consumer goods, from irons and fans to motor scooters and cars, as well as industrial machinery and steel pipes. It had branches in Uruguay, Brazil, and Chile. It could claim that it was the largest locally owned manufacturing company in Latin America.

Changes in government policies and difficulties in raising capital brought down SIAM. The large number of foreign corporations permitted to build cars hurt SIAM's ability to compete. Lacking adequate capital for new investment, it maintained automobile production too long, thereby weakening the company. Similar problems existed with its other consumer goods products. By 1972, when the government took over SIAM for financial reasons, the firm owed taxes that amounted to 60 percent of its capital. It survived for the next decade largely by selling capital goods to state enterprises, but after the military coup of 1976, the government no longer favored local companies, thus dooming SIAM. When the government attempted to privatize SIAM in 1981–1982, there were no takers. The company had to be broken up.

Although SIAM no longer exists, the Di Tella legacy remains important in the arts and education. After Di Tella's death his foundation created the Instituto Di Tella to support the arts. In 1991 the family foundation and the Instituto Di Tella together founded the nonprofit college Universidad Torcuato Di Tella.

BIBLIOGRAPHY

Thomas C. Cochran and Ruben Reina, *Entrepreneurship in Argentine Culture: Torcuato di Tella and SIAM* (1962).

Jorge Schvarzer, *Expansión económica del estado subsidiario, 1976–1981* (1981).

Paul H. Lewis, *The Crisis of Argentine Capitalism* (1990).

Torcuato S. Di Tella, *Torcuato Di Tella: Industria y política* (1993).

Additional Bibliography

Lucchini, Cristina. *Industrialismo y nacionalidad en Argentina y el Brasil (1890–1950)*. Buenos Aires: Ediciones del Signo [con] Fundación Simón Rodríguez, 2000.

Puiggrós, Adriana, R. Gagliano, and N. Visacovsky. *La fábrica del conocimiento: Los saberes socialmente productivos en América Latina*. Rosario, Argentina: APPEAL: Homo Sapiens, 2004.

JOEL HOROWITZ

ARGENTINE CIVIC LEGION (LCA)

A right-wing paramilitary product of the 1930 revolution that installed General José Félix Uriburu in power, the Argentine Civic Legion arose in early 1931. Its first leader was Dr. Floro Lavalle, a medical doctor, landowner, and founding member of the Argentine Patriotic League; by 1933 Carlos Ribero, a former naval officer, became its head, followed by David Uriburu in the 1940s. The Legion absorbed other paramilitary groups that had been active in the coup and enlisted young aristocrats, Conservative Party members, civil servants (often coercively), military officers, upper-class women, and even schoolchildren. Its opposition to liberal democracy, partisan politics, leftism, and immigration, and its support for hierarchy, family, and religion won the favor of the Uriburu government, which gave it juridical personage and official recognition as its partner in creating order. It also allowed the Legion to use government buildings and services. The group received military instruction at army installations, and weapons and uniforms from the Ministry of War. When thousands of uniformed Legionarios paraded through Buenos Aires in April and May 1931, Uriburu praised the group for protecting the revolution against its enemies.

The Legion became a focus of controversy. Many, including some fellow right-wing nationalists, criticized its ties to the government, military, and Conservative Party. Its spying activities and repression of students suggested that the Legion was an official tool against opponents of the regime, or a means by which Uriburu could perpetuate his rule or bring Conservatives to power. Even potential sympathizers disapproved of recruiting women and children into a militarized organization.

After 1932 the Legion no longer enjoyed official ties to the government. Nevertheless, it continued to occupy government-owned buildings and carry out terrorist acts with impunity. By the mid-1930s it added opposition to Jews and imperialism, and support for state regulation of capital and labor, to its original goals. The Legion's decision to reach out to labor organizations signaled a move away from its elite origins. Furthermore, the Legion adopted a populist rhetoric and critiqued the conservative regime for working too closely with the British. However, it did not hide its sympathy for European fascism and the Axis powers.

See also **Fascism.**

BIBLIOGRAPHY

Carlos Ibarguren, *La historia que he vivido*, 2d ed. (1969).

Alberto Ciria, *Parties and Power in Modern Argentina*, translated by Carlos A. Astiz with Mary F. McCarthy (1974).

Sandra McGee Deutsch, *Counterrevolution in Argentina, 1890–1930: The Rise and Fall of Radicalism* (1986).

Additional Bibliography

Béjar, María Dolores. *El régimen fraudulento: La política en la provincia de Buenos Aires, 1930–1943.* Buenos Aires: Siglo Veintiuno Editores Argentina, 2005.

Deutsch, Sandra McGee. *Las Derechas: The Extreme Right in Argentina, Brazil, and Chile, 1890–1939.* Stanford, CA: Stanford University Press, 1999.

Klein, Marcus. "The 'Legión Cívica Argentina' and the Radicalisation of Argentine 'Nacionalismo' during the 'Década Infame'." *Estudios Interdisciplinarios de América Latina y el Caribe* 13, no. 2 (2002): 5–30.

SANDRA MCGEE DEUTSCH

ARGENTINE PATRIOTIC LEAGUE (LPA)

The Argentine Patriotic League was an antilabor organization that arose in 1919 and was particularly active until the mid-1920s. After World War I, the military and the middle and upper classes feared that the Russian Revolution might spread to Argentina. The general strike that burst into the Semana Trágica (Tragic Week) of January 1919 confirmed their fears. During this week, self-styled civil guards and police attacked worker neighborhoods of Buenos Aires. Other bourgeois citizens formed defense committees against possible labor onslaught. Naval officers coordinated the civil guards and defense committees, giving them arms, vehicles, and military instruction.

After the Tragic Week, a group of naval and army officers invited prominent citizens, other officers, clerics, and society women to create a permanent organization to guard against labor disruptions and leftist views. These people founded the Argentine Patriotic League on 20 January 1919. The defense committees became the first brigades of the League; similar committees that had formed in other parts of the nation were incorporated. The League also organized brigades of property owners and strikebreakers in areas of labor strife. In addition, women in the larger cities formed their own brigades. On 5 April 1919 the brigades elected Manuel Carlés as League president. In the 1920s the League's core included about 820 women and 11,000 men. The majority of its female members and its leaders were upper-class, but the rank-and-file male activists were largely middle-class. A significant number of military officers also belonged to the League.

The League hoped to maintain the status quo through repression and social welfare activities. Male members began to undertake the first task by breaking strikes and attacking unions and radicals in the large cities. When rural strikes broke out from late 1919 to 1921, they shifted their focus to the countryside. For example, in Patagonia they helped the army kill over 1,500 striking ranch workers in 1921. Meanwhile, League men and women established factory schools, employment services, and other social programs. The League publicized the need for such programs and wider measures like social security to divert workers from the class struggle.

When the postwar labor activism ended in the early 1920s—partly thanks to the League—the organization faded from prominence. Yet it participated in the revolution of 1930 against President Hipólito Irigoyen (1916–1922, 1928–1930) and remained in existence at least until the late 1970s.

See also **Semana Trágica.**

BIBLIOGRAPHY

Osvaldo Bayer, *Los vengadores de la Patagonia trágica,* 4 vols. (1972–1978).

David Rock, *Politics in Argentina, 1890–1930: The Rise and Fall of Radicalism* (1975).

Sandra McGee Deutsch, *Counterrevolution in Argentina, 1900–1932: The Argentine Patriotic League* (1986).

Additional Bibliography

Catarina, Luis María. *La Liga Patriótica Argentina: Un grupo de presión frente a las convulsiones sociales de la década del veinte.* Buenos Aires: Corregidor, 1995.

Ospital, María Silvia. *Inmigración y nacionalismo: La Liga Patriótica y la Asociación del Trabajo (1910–1930).* Buenos Aires: Centro Editor de América Latina, 1994.

Rock, David. *Authoritarian Argentina: The Nationalist Movement, Its History, and Its Impact.* Berkeley: University of California Press, 1993.

SANDRA MCGEE DEUTSCH

ARGENTINE RURAL SOCIETY

The Society for Rural Argentina (SRA) is the main voice for the rural interests of the country. It primarily defends the viewpoints of its most powerful sector, the large livestock raisers of the pampas region. Founded in 1866 by a small group of forward-looking ranchers, since its beginnings the SRA has focused on two main objectives: collaborating on technical improvements and setting itself up to represent the interests of the rural sector before the state. In its early years, this modernizing project failed to attract wide support among large landowners. Nevertheless, during the great economic expansion of the 1880s ranchers began to join. By 1910 the SRA had more than 1,000 members and had already become one of the most prestigious institutions of Argentina.

During this foundational period, in which industry and workers held limited power, and in which rural exports boomed, the SRA as a pressure group was not as important as sometimes claimed. After that, however, as the Argentine political economy became more contentious, politics have had an increasing influence on the institution. Since 1912 the SRA has come up against the reform proposals of the Argentina Agricultural Federation (Federación Agraria Argentina, or FAA), an institution originally comprised of small farmers, many of them tenants. With the Great Depression, which strongly affected rural exports, tensions within the rural sector became more intense. New associations of midsized-livestock farmers, also critical of the SRA, formed in those years, such as the Confederaciones Rurales Argentinas (CRA).

The coup d'état of 1943 marked a historical change of direction for the SRA. For the next half century, the state actively promoted industrialization, urban development, and improved living conditions for workers, to some extent at the expense of the rural sector. In addition to increased taxation for the rural sector, successive administrations maintained a freeze on land rents for more than twenty years, which in the long term helped to democratize land ownership. The conflict between the state and the SRA reached its climax during the Perón administration (1946–1955); after that it attenuated but did not disappear altogether. The hostile policies of Perón and his successors towards rural production helped bring the members of the SRA and other representatives of the sector closer together. In the early 1990s Argentina abruptly abandoned industrial protection, and the rural sector once again became the focus of greater attention from the state. Rapid agricultural growth was accompanied by a profound renovation of the entrepreneurial class. Many of the owners of the more modern, technically more complex, agrarian enterprises created since the 1990s do not identify with the SRA. Nevertheless, in the early 2000s the SRA continues to enjoy the advantages provided by its position as the traditional representative of the rural sector, even though the growing complexity of agrarian interests and the importance of other business sectors have reduced its influence considerably.

See also **Agriculture; Argentina: The Twentieth Century; Livestock.**

BIBLIOGRAPHY

Hora, Roy. *The Landowners of the Argentine Pampas: A Social and Political History, 1860–1945.* Oxford, U.K.: Oxford University Press, 2001.

Manzetti, Luigi. "The Evolution of Agricultural Interest Groups in Argentina." *Journal of Latin American Studies* 24, no. 3 (1992): 585–616.

Palomino, Mirta. *Tradición y Poder: la Sociedad Rural Argentina.* Buenos Aires: CISEA–GEL, 1988.

Smith, Peter. *Politics and Beef in Argentina: Patterns of Conflict and Change.* New York: Columbia University Press, 1969.

ROY HORA

ARGENTINE TRADE PROMOTION INSTITUTE (IAPI)

The Argentine Trade Promotion Institute was a government agency created to control the export of important products (chiefly grains and meat) and to purchase key goods abroad. The IAPI was established in March 1946 by the outgoing Edelmiro Farrell government at the suggestion of the advisers of Juan Perón. It was severely modified, stripped of much of its power, in the wake of Perón's fall from power in 1955 and abolished in April 1958.

A crucial economic tool of the Perón regime, IAPI countered efforts by the Allies to purchase food for Europe jointly and also eliminated the unpopular large grain-exporting firms. As a monopoly, IAPI could drive a hard bargain with purchasers of Argentine goods, as well as with producers. IAPI purchased at low prices from producers and sold at high prices. Profits were used to subsidize industrialization. After 1950 the need for more exports led IAPI to encourage greater production.

IAPI remains controversial. Most commentators believe it crippled the agriculture sector by paying low prices, thereby discouraging production and helping to create a balance-of-payments crisis. Charges of corruption were also made. The agency's defenders believe that producers' profits did not suffer as claimed and that IAPI produced higher prices for exports than the falling terms of trade would have permitted under other circumstances.

See also **Perón, Juan Domingo.**

BIBLIOGRAPHY

José Alfredo Martínez de Hoz (h.), *La agricultura y la ganadería argentina en el período 1930–1960* (1967).

Jorge Fodor, "Perón's Policies for Agricultural Exports 1946–1948: Dogmatism or Commonsense?" in *Argentina in the Twentieth Century,* edited by David Rock (1975).

Susana Novick, *IAPI: Auge y decadencia* (1986).

Paul H. Lewis, *The Crisis of Argentine Capitalism* (1990).

Additional Bibliography

Bouzas, Roberto, and Emiliano Pagnotta. *Dilemas de la política comercial externa Argentina.* Buenos Aires: Fundación OSDE: Universidad de San Andrés, 2003.

Novick, Susana. *IAPI: auge y decadencia.* Buenos Aires: Catalogos, 2004.

Viguera, Aníbal. *La trama política de la apertura económica en la Argentina (1987–1996).* La Plata: Ediciones al Margen: Editorial de la U.N.L.P., 2000.

JOEL HOROWITZ

FEDERATION OF ARGENTINE WORKERS (FOA)

Founded in 1901 after a compromise between anarchist and socialist labor leaders, the Federación Obrera Argentina (FOA) changed its name to Federación Obrera Regional Argentina (FORA) in 1904, becoming the representative of the anarchist branch of the Argentine labor movement. The socialists had left the federation in 1903 to form the Unión General de Trabajadores, taking about 1,800 affiliates, while the FOA retained around 7,600 members. By 1904, its membership had grown to 33,000. In 1905 the FORA declared its allegiance to "the economic and philosophical principles of anarcho-communism," rejecting any possible compromise with other ideological tendencies within the labor movement. Government repression of anarchist activism on the one hand, and the absorption of socialist organizations by the growing syndicalist movement on the other, led to a short-lived fusion of anarchist and syndicalist groups in 1914. In 1915 the FORA saw itself divided once again between the so-called FORA IX Congress, standing for the 1915 congress dominated by the syndicalists, and the FORA V

Congress, standing for the 1905 congress, which had proclaimed the principles of anarcho-communism. The two federations remained divided until 1922, when the syndicalist FORA was absorbed by a new syndicalist-dominated organization, the Unión Sindical Argentina. A small hard core of devoted anarcho-communists remained at the FORA V Congress, although the influence of anarchism in the labor movement had become almost negligible. In 1930 the merger of the Unión Sindical Argentina, the socialist Confederación Obrera Argentina, and the remnants of the FORA gave birth to the Confederación General del Trabajo (CGT).

See also **Labor Movements.**

BIBLIOGRAPHY

Diego Abad De Santillán, *La F.O.R.A.: Ideología y trayectoría del movimiento obrero revolucionario en la Argentina,* 2d ed. (1971).

Ruth Thompson, "The Limitations of Ideology in the Early Argentine Labour Movement: Anarchism in the Trade Unions, 1890–1920," in *Journal of Latin American Studies* 16 (1984): 81–99.

Ronaldo Munck, with Ricardo Falcón and Bernardo Galitelli, *Argentina: From Anarchism to Peronism: Workers, Unions and Politics, 1855–1985* (1987).

Additional Bibliography

López, Antonio. *La F.O.R.A. en el movimiento obrero.* 2nd ed. Buenos Aires: Tupac Ediciones, 1998.

Palacios, Héctor A. *Historia del movimiento obrero argentino.* 5 vol. La Plata: H.A. Palacios, 1992–2005.

EDUARDO A. ZIMMERMAN

GENERAL LABOR CONFEDERATION (CGT)

In 1930 union leaders, frustrated by bitter divisions between rival workers' organizations and concerned about labor's tenuous relationship with the state, joined forces and created the Confederación General de Trabajo (CGT). A fusion of the Socialist-controlled Confederación Obrera Argentina, the syndicalist-dominated Unión Sindical Argentina, and several autonomous unions, the CGT would experience major problems in compatibility and commonness of purpose throughout its history. Syndicalist-oriented unions demanded the pursuit of an apolitical course; Socialists wanted a working relationship with sympathetic political groups.

Communist-affiliated unions in the manufacturing and construction trades joined the CGT in 1936, thereby exacerbating the CGT's problems. In 1943 internal bickering resulted in a rupture of the organization into two factions. A new military government, which included among its leadership Juan Domingo Perón, took advantage of the weakened condition of a divided CGT. The Socialist and Communist factions were abolished, and the others, lacking powerful and independent leadership, fell under the control of Perón. CGT delight with Perón's pro-labor policies was offset by the concern of some unions with the growth of Perón's political power and the erosion of CGT independence.

In 1947 Perón, now president of Argentina, completed the consolidation of his power base in the CGT, which now became an appendage of the state with no independence. The CGT had grown powerful, from a membership of 500,000 in 1947 to 2.5 million in 1955.

After Argentina's takeover by the military regime in 1976, the CGT was prohibited and split into factions; nevertheless the organization returned to its adversarial role with the government in 1980. With the fall of the military regime in 1983, the labor movement became increasingly militant throughout the decade as a response to the economic policies and hardships under the new democratically elected president, Raúl Alfonsín. The unions organized not only numerous nationwide protests—including thirteen general strikes—between 1984 and 1987 but also offered their own suggestions to the government for dealing with the economic crisis.

The government's return to Peronism under Carlos Menem in mid-1989 was fully supported by the labor movement. Taking office under dire economic circumstances, Menem prescribed a set of neoliberal reforms that were very distinct from traditional *Peronista* policies. With an emphasis on decreased state intervention in the national economy, the new agenda split the CGT leaders. The CGT was relatively inactive during the early 1990s; the first general strike against Menem's neoliberal policies did not occur until 1996. The destructive splintering of the 1990s continues to inhibit labor's ability to speak with one voice.

See also **Labor Movements.**

BIBLIOGRAPHY

Alexander, Robert J. *A History of Organized Labor in Argentina.* Westport, CT: Praeger, 2003. See pp. 175–212.

Baily, Samuel L. *Labor, Nationalism, and Politics in Argentina.* New Brunswick, NJ: Rutgers University Press, 1967. See pp. 99, 151–192.

Matsushita, Hiroshi. *Movimiento obrero argentino, 1930–1945.* Buenos Aires: Ediciones Siglo Veinte, 1983. See pp. 77–311.

Rock, David. *Argentina, 1516–1982: From Spanish Colonization to the Falklands War.* Berkeley: University of California Press, 1985.

Spalding, Hobart A., Jr. *Organized Labor in Latin America: Historical Case Studies of Workers in Dependent Societies.* New York: Harper & Row, 1977. See pp. 151–206.

PAUL GOODWIN
KARIN FENN

LIGA FEDERAL, LIGA LITORAL, LIGA UNITARIA

The Federal, Littoral, and Unitary leagues were political alliances during the independence and early national periods. The Liga Federal, also known as Liga Litoral and Liga de los Pueblos Libres (League of Free Peoples), was not created through a specific pact but came into being in 1814–1815 as Federalist leaders in the Argentine littoral provinces joined forces with each other and with the Uruguayan leader José Gervasio Artigas in opposition to the *porteño* revolutionists who sought to enforce strict obedience to the central authorities in Buenos Aires. The caudillo José Eusebio Hereñú of Entre Ríos is credited with making the initial move. His province was ultimately joined by Santa Fe, Corrientes, Misiones, and Córdoba, all of which were represented at the Congress of Free Peoples meeting at Concepción del Uruguay, Entre Ríos province, in mid-1815. All proclaimed Artigas as protector. The ultimate objective was an independent Argentina organized as a loose confederation of Platine provinces, which would have included what is now Uruguay. They did not achieve this aim, and Artigas's Uruguay fell to Portuguese occupation. The other provinces continued with varying success, and despite repeated internal dissensions, to resist the control of Buenos Aires. The Federalists' victory at the battle of Cepeda (February 1820) led to the final collapse of the centralist regime, after which the league dissolved.

The Liga Unitaria (also known as Liga Militar), formed in August 1830, was based in the interior province of Córdoba, where the Córdoba-born Unitarist general José María Paz had seized control the year before. By decisively defeating the leading Federalist caudillo of the Argentine interior, Juan Facundo Quiroga, Paz was able to bring nine provinces, extending from Córdoba to the Bolivian border, into his orbit. They formed the Liga Unitaria to create a supreme military power that functioned in practice, under Paz, as a provisional national government. However, it still faced the bitter opposition of Buenos Aires governor Juan Manuel de Rosas and his Federalist allies in the littoral provinces, and it quickly collapsed following the capture of Paz during a skirmish in May 1831.

The Liga Litoral (also known as Liga Federal and Liga de los Pueblos Libres) organized expressly to combat the Liga Unitaria, had its origin in a series of separate understandings among the provinces of the littoral region that were allied with Buenos Aires. Their alliance was formalized in January 1831 by the signing of the Federal Pact, which, in addition to providing for military cooperation against the Unitarists, created an interprovincial representative commission and delegated to Rosas, the governor of Buenos Aires, authority to act in the name of all provinces in foreign relations. As the tide of civil conflict turned against the Unitarists, more provinces became signatories of the Federal Pact; eventually all signed it. While the representative commission never became effective, Rosas took advantage of his special role in foreign relations to secure his personal political control over the country. After the fall of Rosas in 1852, the Liga Federal ceased to exist.

The leaders of these movements held diverse political goals and represented provinces with a range of economic interests. In the late twentieth century, scholars began to examine caudillos' popular supporters, in particular the gauchos, their definitions of Unitarian and Federalist Party identities, and the charismatic appeal of rural leaders. The caudillos' appeal rested on how well they represented culturally specific aspects of their followers—local notions of power, ethnicity, religion, authority, patronage, patriarchy, and even belief in the supernatural.

See also **Argentina, Movements: Federalists; Rosas, Juan Manuel de.**

BIBLIOGRAPHY

Alberto Demicheli, *Formación constitucional rioplatense,* vol. 3, *Los pactos en el proceso de organización* (1955).

John Street, *Artigas and the Emancipation of Uruguay* (1959), pp. 243–328.

Victor Tau Anzoátegui, *Formación del estado federal argentino (1820–1852)* (1965).

José María Paz, *Memorias,* vol. 2 (1968), chap. 16.

John Lynch, *Argentine Dictator: Juan Manuel de Rosas, 1829–1852* (1981).

Additional Bibliography

Chasteen, John Charles. *Heroes on Horseback: A Life and Times of the Last Gaucho Caudillos.* Albuquerque: University of New Mexico Press, 1995.

Chiaramonte, José Carlos. *Ciudades, provincias, estados: Orígenes de la Nación Argentina, 1800–1846.* 2nd Edition. Buenos Aires: Emecé, 2007.

De la Fuente, Ariel. *Children of Facundo: Caudillo and Gaucho Insurgency during the Argentine State-Formation Process (La Rioja, 1853–1870).* Durham, NC: Duke University Press, 2000.

Garavaglia, Juan Carlos. *Poder, conflicto y relaciones sociales: El Río de la Plata, XVIII–XIX.* Rosario, Argentina: Homo Sapiens Ediciones, 1999.

Goldman, Noemí, and Ricardo Donato Salvatore, eds. *Caudillismos rioplatenses: Nuevas miradas a un viejo problema.* Buenos Aires: Eudeba, Facultad de Filosofía y Letras, Universidad de Buenos Aires, 1998.

Halperín Donghi, Tulio. *Historias de caudillos argentinos.* Edited by Jorge Raúl Lafforgue. Buenos Aires: Extra Alfaguara, 1999.

Lynch, John. *Argentine Caudillo: Juan Manuel de Rosas.* Wilmington, DE: SR Books, 2001.

Myers, Jorge. *Orden y virtud: El discurso republicano en el régimen rosista.* Buenos Aires: Universidad Nacional de Quilmes, 1995.

Szuchman, Mark D., and Jonathan C. Brown. *Revolution and Restoration: The Rearrangement of Power in Argentina, 1776–1860.* Lincoln: University of Nebraska Press, 1994.

DAVID BUSHNELL

SOCIEDAD DE BENEFICIENCIA

The Sociedad de Beneficiencia was the major welfare-dispensing agency in Argentina in the nineteenth century. After the Independence Wars, the incipient Argentine government struggled to reassert order. In 1823, Government Minister Bernardino Rivadavia created the Sociedad de Beneficiencia to run the asylums, hospitals, and orphanages of Buenos Aires, in order to keep streets clear of the infirm, diseased, and homeless. Although it was proclaimed illegal during the period 1838–1852, when the dictator Juan Manuel de Rosas considered it an arm of liberal Unitarists, the Sociedad became, by the late nineteenth century, Latin America's most extensive social welfare and public health institution. In particular in the 1860s, mainly as a result of casualties of the War of the Triple Alliance (1865–1870) and disease (such as the cholera epidemic of 1867–1868, and the outbreak of yellow fever in 1871), there was a proliferation of hospitals and clinics. One distinctive feature of the Sociedad was its control and management by women of the Buenos Aires elite. Its importance culminated with the establishment of the Rivadavia Hospital for Women in 1887. The directors came from the city's most prominent families and often bequeathed sizable sums upon their death.

The Sociedad became the most important means for women to participate in the public life of Buenos Aires. They used this position, however, to propagate traditional paternalistic and religious values. In 1880 President Julio A. Roca made the Sociedad de Beneficiencia a national institution. Ultimately, its management of the medical system conflicted with the growing professionalization and male control of medicine, provoking bitter disputes in the 1890s. Furthermore, the city's rapid growth and pressing social problems led to the creation of parallel institutions, especially those controlled by immigrant mutual aid societies. The care of homeless children remained one of the Sociedad's most important tasks; it ran the foundling home, and the girls' and boys' orphanages. As spaces grew scarce, the Sociedad shifted to fostering, the placement of homeless children with families or single persons. In 1946, President Juan Domingo Perón took over its activities and reorganized them under the Dirección Nacional de Asistencia Social, directed by his wife, Eva.

See also **Perón, Juan Domingo; Perón, María Eva Duarte de; Rivadavia, Bernardino; Roca, Julio Argentino; Rosas, Juan Manuel de; War of the Triple Alliance.**

BIBLIOGRAPHY

Carlos Correa Luna, *Historia de la Sociedad de beneficia*, 2 vols. (1923).

Cynthia J. Little, "The Society of Beneficence in Buenos Aires, 1823–1900" (Ph.D. diss., Temple University, 1980).

Additional Bibliography

Moreno, José Luis. *La política social antes de la política social caridad, beneficiencia y política social en Buenos Aires: Siglos XVII a XX*. Buenos Aires: Trama editorial/ Prometeo libros, 2000.

JEREMY ADELMAN

UNITED OFFICERS GROUP (GOU)

There is some dispute on the exact meaning of the acronym GOU, which was one of several secret lodges of Argentine military officers. Robert Potash claims that it was originally formed by twelve members in February or early March 1943 as the Grupo Organizador y Unificador, and that an enlarged organization of nineteen members was formed in July as the Grupo Obra de Unificación. Others have asserted that the initials stood for Gobierno, Orden, Unidad, insinuating a connection with Franco's Spain. It is most commonly referred to as the United Officers Group. Although some members had been German-trained and sympathized with the Nazis, the organization was primarily concerned with military and economic competition with Brazil, industrialization, the acquisition of arms, and domestic political corruption.

On June 6, 1943, three days after a coup ousted Ramón Castillo, the GOU took over and installed General Pedro Ramírez as president. The GOU placed its most prominent officers into high political and military positions. Under Pedro Ramírez, Colonel Juan D. Perón took over the insignificant department of labor. Perón, however, used this position to establish close ties with the labor unions that later helped him get elected president in 1946. Bowing to U.S. pressure, Ramírez broke diplomatic relations with the Axis powers on January 26, 1944. His vice president, General Edelmiro Farrell, condemning the break, replaced him in February. GOU member Colonel Juan D. Perón became Farrell's war minister and vice president. With this transition, the GOU was dissolved on February 23, 1944. The Farrell government lasted until 1946.

See also **Perón, Juan Domingo.**

BIBLIOGRAPHY

Robert A. Potash, *The Army and Politics in Argentina, 1928–1945* (1969).

Marvin Goldwert, *Democracy, Militarism, and Nationalism in Argentina, 1930–1966* (1972).

Alberto Ciría, *Parties and Power in Modern Argentina, 1930–1946* (1974).

Ronald C. Newton, *The "Nazi Menace" in Argentina, 1931– 1947* (1992).

Additional Bibliography

Norden, Deborah L. *Military Rebellion in Argentina: Between Coups and Consolidation*. Lincoln: University of Nebraska Press, 1996.

Romero, Raúl José. *Fuerzas armadas: La alternativa de la derecha para el acceso al poder (1930–1976)*. Buenos Aires: Editorial Centro de Estudios Unión para la Nueva Mayoría, 1998.

ROGER GRAVIL
CHRISTEL K. CONVERSE

YACIMIENTOS PETROLÍFEROS FISCALES (YPF)

Immediately following World War I, powerful international petroleum companies moved into Argentina in an effort to secure the best oil properties. Concerned by their presence, President Hipólito Irigoyen created the YPF in 1922 as a state petroleum monopoly to ensure Argentine control over this vital resource. It was left to his successor, President Marcelo T. de Alvear (1922–1928), to invigorate the agency. To head the YPF, Alvear named Colonel Enrique Mosconi, under whose leadership it became symbolic of Argentina economic independence. In a different context, Mosconi's imprint can be discerned on the state oil companies of Bolivia, Brazil, and Uruguay. In the 1950s and 1960s presidents Juan Domingo Perón and Arturo Frondizi, concerned about maximum productivity and economic development, undermined the idea of a state petroleum monopoly. Gradually, foreign petroleum companies were again invited to participate more fully in the exploitation of the nation's oil fields. To help pay off its public debt, in 1993, the government officially privatized YPF. Initially, a combination of national and international investors took over the company, but a Spanish firm, Repsol, began buying up its shares and took control of the corporation in 1999, making it the tenth largest oil company in the world.

See also **Petroleum Industry.**

BIBLIOGRAPHY

David P. Rock, *Politics in Argentina, 1890–1930: The Rise and Fall of Radicalism* (1975).

Carl E. Solberg, *Oil and Nationalism in Argentina: A History* (1979), pp. 76–111.

Additional Bibliography

San Martín, José N. *El petróleo y la petroquímica en la Argentina (1914–1983): Emergencia, expansión y declinación del nacionalismo petrolero.* Buenos Aires: EC (Ediciones Cooperativas), 2006.

PAUL GOODWIN

ARGENTINA, POLITICAL PARTIES

This entry includes the following articles:
ANTIPERSONALIST RADICAL CIVIL UNION
DEMOCRATIC UNION (UD)
INDEPENDENT SOCIALIST PARTY
INTRANSIGENT RADICALS
JUSTICIALIST PARTY
NATIONAL AUTONOMIST PARTY (PAN)
PERSONALIST RADICAL CIVIC UNION
PROGRESSIVE DEMOCRATIC PARTY
RADICAL PARTY (UCR)
SOCIALIST PARTY
YOUTH ORGANIZATION OF THE RADICAL PARTY (FORJA)

ANTIPERSONALIST RADICAL CIVIC UNION

In 1924 the Antipersonalistas in Argentina emerged as a separate political party when they broke ranks with the Radical Civic Union (Unión Cívica Radical—UCR) and its leader, Hipólito Irigoyen. The appearance of the Antipersonalistas reflected tensions that had typified Argentine radicalism since its birth in 1890.

Vincente C. Gallo, Irigoyen's minister of the interior, led a dissident group within the UCR known as the Azules, or Blues, a faction that later became known as the Antipersonalistas. They represented the old elite wing of the party and actively worked against Irigoyen from 1918 until the end of his term in 1922. Irigoyen's successor in office, Marcelo T. de Alvear, was nominally an Antipersonalista but failed to pursue policies that would assure the survival of the party. A mass base never materialized because the Antipersonalistas were denied access to state patronage, thus lacking the political rewards and positions necessary to gain support. Establishment of a committee structure to organize recruitment in the provinces succeeded only in the province of Santa Fe. Alvear's own ties were with the province of Buenos Aires, and he never established a working relationship with the Antipersonalistas' Santa Fe base.

In order for mass-based politics to succeed, there was need of an administration committed not only to flexible and somewhat inflationary spending of state resources but also, for political purposes, to an expansion of the bureaucracy. Alvear, however, pursued a conservative fiscal policy, and the Antipersonalista influence never effectively spread beyond the borders of Santa Fe.

The Antipersonalistas ran candidates for the presidency in 1928, but Irigoyen won in a landslide. In 1930 the Antipersonalistas supported the revolution that ousted Irigoyen and then joined with conservatives who dominated Argentine politics until the military coup of 1943.

See also **Irigoyen, Hipólito.**

BIBLIOGRAPHY

José Luis Romero, *A History of Argentine Political Thought,* translated by Thomas F. McGann (1963), pp. 224–225.

Robert A. Potash, *The Army and Politics in Argentina, 1928–1945: Yrigoyen to Perón* (1969), pp. 41 n., 47, 59–60.

Paul B. Goodwin, Jr., "The Politics of Rate-Making: The British-Owned Railways and the Unión Cívica Radical, 1921–1928," in *Journal of Latin American Studies* 6 (1974): 257–287.

Additional Bibliography

Gasió, Guillermo. *Yrigoyen: el mandato extraordinario, 1928–1930.* Buenos Aires: Corregidor, 2005.

Giacobone, Carlos Alberto and Edit Gallo. *Radicalismo bonaerense: La ingeniería política de Hipólito Yrigoyen, 1891–1931.* Buenos Aires: Corregidor, 1999.

Persello, Ana Virginia. *El partido radical: Gobierno y oposición, 1916–1943*. Buenos Aires: Siglo veintiuno editores Argentina, 2004.

Tato, María Inés. *Viento de fronda: Liberalismo, conservadurismo y democracia en la Argentina, 1911–1932*. Buenos Aires: Siglo Veintiuno Editores Argentina, 2004.

PAUL GOODWIN

DEMOCRATIC UNION (UD)

Formed in 1945, the Democratic Union of Argentina was a superficially united and diverse front of old-line political parties and interest groups opposed to the presidential candidacy of Juan Domingo Perón. Radicals José P. Tamborini and Enrique N. Mosca headed their ticket in elections scheduled for February 1946. The front's campaign, with its dated slogan, "For Liberty and Against Nazi-Fascism," failed to address the issues that concerned most of the electorate. Moreover, the UD was tainted because of links both to Moscow-oriented Communists and to the U.S. government. Perón won with 52.4 percent of the vote; the UD garnered 42.5 percent.

See also **Fascism.**

BIBLIOGRAPHY

Joseph A. Page, *Perón: A Biography* (1983), chap. 16.

Robert D. Crassweller, *Perón and the Enigmas of Argentina* (1987), pp. 174ff.

Additional Bibliography

Fanel, Luis. *La alternativa ausente: Crisis y ruptura política en Argentina, 1945–1998*. Buenos Aires: Dirple Ediciones, 1999.

Persello, Ana Virginia. *El partido radical: Gobierno y oposición, 1916–1943*. Buenos Aires: Siglo veintiuno editores Argentina, 2004.

Sidicaro, Ricardo. *Los tres peronismos: Estado y poder económico 1946–1955, 1973–1976, 1989–1999*. Buenos Aires: Siglo Veintiuno Editores Argentina, 2002.

PAUL GOODWIN

INDEPENDENT SOCIALIST PARTY

The Independent Socialist Party of Argentina was created in 1927 as the result of a power struggle within the mainline Socialist Party. The new party was led by mostly younger members with a more nationalistic, conservative orientation than the directors of its older predecessor. Entering national congressional elections for the first time in 1928, the Independents came in ahead of the mainline Socialists for second place in the city of Buenos Aires. Two years later they scored an even more impressive victory in a similar contest, besting both the Socialists and the representatives of the incumbent national administration, the Radicals (of the Unión Cívica Radical), to capture a majority of the congressional seats available.

In 1930 the Independents formed an important part of the conservative coalition that contributed to the overthrow of popularly elected President Hipólito Irigoyen (1928–1930). Party leaders Antonio de Tomaso and Federico Pinedo subsequently served as cabinet members under the conservative president Agustín P. Justo (1932–1938). A handful of other party members were elected to the national Congress and to the city council of Buenos Aires in the early 1930s. In Congress and on the council, the Independent Socialists usually allied with the conservative bloc on most major issues, although their opposition to the first mayor (*intendente*) of Buenos Aires appointed by Justo led to his forced resignation a few months after assuming office.

The death of Antonio de Tomaso, the party's main leader, in 1933, coupled with a growing popular reaction against the antidemocratic practices of the conservative regime with which the Independents were associated, caused the party to lose considerable electoral support. By 1936, the Independents were polling less than 3 percent of the total vote in national and local elections and by 1940 had virtually disappeared from the national political scene. While the Independents enjoyed some momentary influence, they are best remembered as one of several examples of recurring divisions within the mainline Socialist Party and of the often ephemeral nature of the many short-lived parties and factions that have characterized much of Argentina's modern political history.

See also **Pinedo, Federico.**

BIBLIOGRAPHY

Horacio Sanguinetti, *Los socialistas independientes* (1981).

Additional Bibliography

Camarero, Hernán, and Carlos-Miguel Herrera. *El Partido Socialista en Argentina: Sociedad, política e ideas a través de un siglo*. Buenos Aires: Prometeo, 2005.

Consigli, Raquel E. *Breve historia del Partido Socialista Argentino, 1893–1943*. Córdoba, Argentina: Prosopis Editora, 2004.

García Sebastiani, Marcela. *Los antiperonistas en la Argentina peronista: Radicales y socialistas en la política Argentina entre 1943 y 1951*. Buenos Aires: Prometeo Libros, 2005.

Walter, Richard J. *The Socialist Party of Argentina, 1890–1930*. Austin: Institute of Latin American Studies, University of Texas at Austin, 1977.

RICHARD J. WALTER

INTRANSIGENT RADICALS

The Intransigent Radicals were a nationalist faction of the Radical Party which emerged during the 1930s in opposition to the undemocratic governments of the period and in repudiation of the more conservative Radical Party faction led by Marcelo T. de Alvear. Vindicating the *yrigoyenista* tradition, they were inspired in the 1930s and early 1940s by the governor of Córdoba, Amadeo Sabattini, who vigorously promoted economic nationalism, an interventionist state, and strict neutrality in World War II, a program encapsulated in the party's founding document, the 1945 Carta de Avellaneda.

Organized as the Movimiento de Intransigencia y Renovación (MIR) after 1945, the Intransigents lost a bitter power struggle with the more conservative faction of their party, the so-called unionists, in the selection of the Unión Democrática ticket chosen to run against Juan Perón in the 1946 election, but dominated the party during the Peronist government (1946–1955). In 1956 they established a separate party, the Intransigent Radical Civic Union (UCRI), which brought Arturo Frondizi to power in the 1958 presidential election. Frondizi's drifting away from many of the party's principles, especially those concerning issues of economic nationalism, weakened the Intransigents' credibility.

Frondizi's ouster in a 1962 coup d'état and his establishment in 1964 of a separate political party, the Movement of Integration and Development (MID), effectively led to the Intransigent Radicals' demise. They ran as a separate party for the last time in the 1963 election won by the Radical Civic Union of the People (UCRP), though they were briefly resuscitated in the 1980s in the form of the Intransigent Party (PI), led by former *intransigente*

governor of Buenos Aires, Oscar Allende. The PI was the most important left-of-center party during the first years of Raúl Alfonsín's Radical administration, though it too eventually disbanded.

See also **Frondizi, Arturo.**

BIBLIOGRAPHY

Marcelo Luis Acuña, *De Frondizi a Alfonsín: La tradición política del radicalismo*, vols. 1 and 2 (1985).

Celia Szusterman, *Frondizi and the Politics of Developmentalism in Argentina, 1955–62* (1993).

Additional Bibliography

Altamirano, Carlos. *Arturo Frondizi, o, El hombre de ideas como político*. Buenos Aires: Fondo de Cultura Económica, 1998.

García Sebastiani, Marcela. *Los antiperonistas en la Argentina peronista: Radicales y socialistas en la política argentina entre 1943 y 1951*. Buenos Aires: Prometeo Libros, 2005.

Persello, Ana Virginia. *El partido radical: Gobierno y oposición, 1916–1943*. Buenos Aires: Siglo veintiuno editores Argentina, 2004.

JAMES P. BRENNAN

JUSTICIALIST PARTY

The Justicialist Party (formerly the Peronist Party) grew out of the electoral coalition that brought Juan D. Perón to power in 1946: the labor-based Laborista Party, the young nationalists of the Union of Radical Civic Renewal (Unión Cívica Radical Renovadora), and the right-wing Independent Centers (Centros Independientes). After the election Perón decreed their merger into the Sole Revolutionary Party (Partido Único de la Revolución), but that sounded too totalitarian, so the name was changed to Peronist Party (Partido Peronista). After Perón was overthrown in 1955, the party was outlawed; it eventually reappeared under the name Unión Popular, since no reference to Perón was permitted.

When neo-Peronists, who sought legalization by repudiating Perón, gained control of the Unión Popular in 1966, Peronist loyalists challenged them under the banner of the Justicialist Party, which is still mainline Peronism's official title. Justicialism, a term coined by Perón himself, refers to his official ideology. In theory it seeks a middle way between democracy and authoritarianism, capitalism and socialism, individualism and collectivism. In practice it aims at what he called "the organized society," which essentially is a corporate state with representation based on government-controlled associations of employers, workers, and professionals.

Under the first Peronist regime (1946–1955) the party acted as an electoral machine, patronage vehicle, and control network. It had a hierarchical structure, with a supreme leader (Perón) at the top, a handpicked Superior Council just beneath him, and a spreading network of provincial (state), departmental (county), and neighborhood, and workplace organizations. Officers were appointed from above, and great emphasis was placed on obedience and discipline. The party also embraced a special trade union wing based on the General Confederation of Labor (Confederación General de Trabajadores; CGT) and the Feminist Peronist Party, which Evita Perón formed in 1949. There was also a leadership school to train future party elites. Though formidable on paper, the party actually had little real vitality, since Perón permitted his subordinates almost no initiative. While Perón was in exile, union leaders like Augusto Vandor led the party. Vandor in particular tried to form an institutionalized party structure, but opposition from Peron and rival labor leaders impeded him.

After Perón's fall the outlawed party was torn between neo- and orthodox Peronists until his return in 1973. Perón's return initially united the party, but Perón this time favored conservatives, causing dissatisfaction among the left and more radical party members. After his death the following year, open warfare broke out between its right and left wings, with the latter eventually forming the Authentic Peronist Party (Partido Peronista Auténtico). When the military took power in 1976, it outlawed all parties.

The restoration of democracy in 1983 found the Justicialist Party weakened, divided, and somewhat discredited by its past, since many people blamed the Peronist government's mismanagement from 1973 to 1976 for bringing on military rule. Consequently, it lost the presidential elections to its main rival, the Radical Civic Union, although it still won control of the Senate and a majority of provincial governorships. During the next six years a reformist faction took control of the Justicialist

Party and gave it a more democratic image. As a result, Justicialists won a majority of the gubernatorial and congressional elections in 1989 and saw their candidate, Carlos Saúl Menem, elected president. In September 1991 the party increased its congressional majority by trouncing the Radicals in midterm elections. Menem departed from many of the standard Justicialist policies. Instead of enacting pro-labor legislation, the Menem government followed neoliberal economics and sold off state-run industries.

Although the economy grew during Menem's presidency, the divisions in the party contributed to its electoral defeat in 1999. The Radicals won the presidency and governed from 1999 until an economic crisis in 2001 caused the collapse of the government. Congress then chose Eduardo Duhalde, a Justicialist politician, to be president until the 2003 elections. The 2003 campaign reflected the intense conflict within the party. Nestor Kirchner, representing the left wing of the party, defeated Menem and won the presidency. This victory did not end the internal fighting. The ideological factions continued to compete in the 2005 races for congress but the Kirchner camp remained dominant.

See also **Duhalde, Eduardo; Kirchner, Néstor; Menem, Carlos Saúl; Perón, Juan Domingo; Perón, María Eva Duarte de; Vandor, Augusto.**

BIBLIOGRAPHY

Partido Peronista, *Directivas básicas del Consejo Superior* (1952).

George Blanksten, *Peron's Argentina* (1953).

Alberto Ciria, *Perón y el justicialismo* (1971).

Additional Bibliography

Altamirano, Carlos. *Peronismo y cultura de izquierda.* Buenos Aires: Temas Grupo Editorial, 2001.

Brennan, James P., ed. *Peronism and Argentina.* Wilmington, DE: SR Books, 1998.

Hernández, Pablo José. *Peronismo y pensamiento nacional, 1955–1973.* Buenos Aires: Editorial Biblos, 1997.

James, Daniel. *Resistance and Integration: Peronism and the Argentine Working Class, 1946–1976.* Cambridge, U.K. and New York: Cambridge University Press, 1988.

Levitsky, Steven. *Transforming Labor-based Parties in Latin America: Argentine Peronism in Comparative*

Perspective. Cambridge, U.K. and New York: Cambridge University Press, 2003.

McGuire, James W. *Peronism without Perón: Unions, Parties, and Democracy in Argentina.* Stanford, CA: Stanford University Press, 1997.

PAUL H. LEWIS

NATIONAL AUTONOMIST PARTY (PAN)

The National Autonomist Party (Partido Autonomista Nacional, PAN) completely dominated politics in Argentina from 1880 to 1916. Even though the opposition was not legally hindered from participating in elections, the PAN won all presidential elections and the great majority of congressional elections during those years. The PAN has been analyzed from various points of view. The Left has seen it as an oligarchic government whose social base was the landowning class (some writers include the business and finance classes as well) that obtained a monopoly on power by appropriating the coercive mechanisms of the national state that had been strengthened during these years. The PAN has also been seen as the inland provinces' political reaction to the traditional power of the province of Buenos Aires. In conquering the dominant province and its resources, however, the inland provinces soon came under the control of the national government once it had consolidated state resources and used them as instruments for controlling and disciplining provincial governments.

Subsequent interpretations, in keeping with political processes occurring within the party, tend to portray the party as a set of competitive and dynamic alliances to share national power. With no degree of internal organization whatsoever or any formal or informal agreements for choosing candidates for elected office (not even for the presidency), the party evolved a political practice of internal competition among those aspiring to national power. In this way, national politics was divided among a series of coalitions, which were continually being reformulated, with a constitution exclusively based on the struggle for power-thus family ties, party traditions, religion, or ideologies did not appear to be relevant at the time that support was needed. Instead, its leaders displayed great pragmatism toward politics and a negative view of political parties and politics itself. The PAN, understood as a set of competitive coalitions among different provincial and national leaders to generate support for presidential candidates, demonstrated great flexibility that would allow the party to adapt and survive for over three decades. But this flexibility was also at the core of its main weakness, because by not organizing or structuring itself internally, it was not able to form stable bonds on the local, provincial, or national levels or a defined strategy or ideology. This weakness allowed the opposition to triumph in the presidential elections for the first time in 1916, subsequent to 1912 when universal male suffrage became obligatory and the vote became secret, and the party did not know how to adapt to the new rules of play.

See also **Argentina: The Nineteenth Century.**

BIBLIOGRAPHY

Alonso, Paula. "La política y sus laberintos: El Partido Autonomista Nacional entre 1880 y 1886." In *La vida política en la Argentina del siglo XIX: Armas, votos y voces*, edited by Hilda Sábato and Alberto Lettieri, 277–292. Mexico and Buenos Aires: Fondo de Cultura Económica, 2003.

Botana, Natalio. *El orden conservador: La política argentina entre 1880 y 1916.* Buenos Aires: Editorial Sudamericana, 1977.

Rock, David. *State Building and Political Movements in Argentina, 1860–1916.* Stanford, CA: Stanford University Press, 2002.

Romero, José Luis. *Las ideas políticas en Argentina.* Buenos Aires: Fondo de Cultura Económica, 1975.

PAULA ALONSO

PERSONALIST RADICAL CIVIC UNION

The Personalist Radicals, also known as Irigoyenistas, were a faction of the Radical Civic Union Party (UCR; Unión Cívica Radical Personalista) active from 1924 to 1933 and loyal to the Radical leader and former president Hipólito Irigoyen. Differences over fiscal policy and party organization led to a split in the Radical Party during the presidency of Marcelo de Alvear (1922–1928). When in power under Alvear, the anti-Personalistas pursued many of the same policies of Irigoyen. However, Irigoyen and the Personalistas employed working-class symbols and rhetoric, whereas the anti-Personalistas seemed a part of an elite oligarchy. As the 1920s came to a close, the dominant pro-Irigoyen wing of the party buttressed its political position by arguing for the nationalization of the country's growing oil industry.

The Personalists' control over Congress and the Radical Party machinery guaranteed the reelection of Irigoyen in 1928.

Although they held a majority in the Argentine Congress, the Personalists accomplished little after 1928. Economic crisis and political confusion contributed to the success of the Revolution of 6 September 1930 that overthrew the elected government. While the Radical Party would recover after World War II, Irigoyen's death in July 1933 led to the Personalist wing's rapid disintegration.

See also **Alvear, Marcelo Torcuato de; Irigoyen, Hipólito.**

BIBLIOGRAPHY

David Rock, *Politics in Argentina, 1890–1930: The Rise and Fall of Radicalism* (1975).

Richard Walter, *The Province of Buenos Aires and Argentine Politics, 1912–1943* (1985).

Additional Bibliography

Gasió, Guillermo. *Yrigoyen: El mandato extraordinario, 1928–1930.* Buenos Aires: Corregidor, 2005.

Giacobone, Carlos Alberto, and Edit Rosalía Gallo. *Radicalismo bonaerense: La ingeniería política de Hipólito Yrigoyen, 1891–1931.* Buenos Aires: Corregidor, 1999.

Persello, Ana Virginia. *El Partido Radical: Gobierno y oposición, 19161943.* Buenos Aires: Siglo veintiuno editores Argentina, 2004.

Tato, María Inés. *Viento de fronda: Liberalismo, conservadurismo y democracia en la Argentina, 1911–1932.* Buenos Aires: Siglo Veintiuno Editores Argentina, 2004.

DANIEL LEWIS

PROGRESSIVE DEMOCRATIC PARTY

The Progressive Democratic Party (PDP) emerged in late 1914 as part of an effort to unite the scattered liberal and conservative political forces of Buenos Aires and the interior into a large national political party. The project, begun in 1912, was the essential complement to the electoral reform of President Roque Sáenz Peña, who sought to integrate radicalism into the political system, but also to defeat it at the polls. The death of Sáenz Peña and the succession of Vice President Victorino de la Plaza in 1914 left the movement without leadership. To make matters worse, the excessive number of potential presidential candidates, such as Lisandro de la Torre (1868–1939), Marcelino Ugarte, Julio A. Roca Jr., and Benito Villanueva (1856–

1933), and the difficult clash between the liberal wing led by de la Torre and the conservative wing led by Ugarte, divided the party and permitted the victory of Hipólito Irigoyen (1852–1933) in 1916. The conservative wing left the province of Buenos Aires, and this led to the PDP being identified with de la Torre, though he had been just one leader among many. The 1916 defeat led to massive desertions from the party, and since then the PDP's strength has been concentrated in the city of Buenos Aires and in the province of Santa Fe, practically the only places where it still exists.

See also **Irigoyen, Hipólito; Roca, Julio Argentino; Sáenz Peña, Roque; Torre, Lisandro de la; Ugarte, Marcelino.**

BIBLIOGRAPHY

Marcor, Darío. *La reforma política en la encrucijada: La experiencia demoprogresista en el Estado provincial santafesino.* Santa Fe, Argentina: UNL (Universidad Nacional del Litoral), 1994.

Malamud, Carlos. "El Partido Demócrata Progresista: Un intento fallido de construir un partido nacional liberal-conservador." *Desarrollo Económico* 138 (1995): 289–308.

CARLOS MALAMUD

RADICAL PARTY (UCR)

The Radical Civic Union (Unión Cívica Radical, or UCR), the first modern party in Argentine history, was founded in 1891. Its modernity was due to four central attributes that differentiated it from other independent factions of nineteenth-century Latin American politics, many of which were mere agreements between *caudillos* or notables. First, the UCR was an organization of national dimensions: The party leadership (that is, the national committee) was composed of four delegates for each province and four for the federal capital. Second, it had a notable level of internal institutionalization, which meant that decision-making processes were channeled through set standards and procedures. The party congresses were conceived as the highest authority within the party. Third, it had a type of territorial construction backed by committees that fulfilled political-electoral functions and other functions of social integration relating to daily needs, from training courses to cheaper food products. These committees also got involved in political affairs, operating as citizenship schools and as mechanisms for political patronage during periods in which the UCR headed the government. Fourth, the UCR was built on an ideology shared by its members—democratic, republican, and federalist—that operated as the foundation for a collective identity with which heterogeneous social sectors could identify.

Both in forming its electoral base and in selecting its leaders, Argentina's Radical Party pulled together a wide range of social actors, including people from the midlevel urban and rural sectors, some rural landowners in the province of Buenos Aires, the merchant bourgeoisie of the city of Rosario, the colonist farmers of east central Santa Fe and southern Córdoba, and the traditional elite of Salta and Córdoba. Their common denominator was their marginal situation with respect to political power (which rested with the conservatives until 1916) and their search for a change in the institutional rules of play. From the perspective of those interests, the establishment of universal, secret, and mandatory suffrage in 1912 was a decisive turning point.

Following the suicide of Leandro Alem in 1896, his nephew Hipólito Irigoyen (1852–1933) became the main party leader. After the death of Leandro Alem—who in 1891 had founded the Unión Cívica Radical in the name of an intransigent rejection to establishing compromise solutions with the conservative regime—his nephew Hipólito Irigoyen became the principle leader of the party. Accused by his rivals of orienting the party around his own personality, he left his mark on radical ideology during the first half of the twentieth century. He took a nationalistic stance with regard to economics and foreign policy—the UCR was in favor of Argentine neutrality during the two world wars—and he was moderately reformist in social matters and laical in the cultural sphere. A professor of philosophy, and strongly influenced by the German Krausism (Karl Christian Friedrich Krause, 1781–1832), transmitted by his Spanish disciples, Irigoyen tended to perceive politics as a branch of Morals. Radicalism had to be a moral force identified with the nation and preach a scrupulous ethical rigor. From his view, the UCR was an expression of nationality and, at the same time, it had the mission of creating it.

The UCR produced six presidencies of Argentina: Irigoyen (1916–1922 and 1928–1930), Mar-

celo T. de Alvear (1922–1928), Arturo Illia (1963–1966), Raúl Alfonsín (1983–1989), and Fernando de la Rúa (1999–2001). Two of these presidencies were overthrown by military coups (Irigoyen in 1930 and Illia in 1966), and strong social convulsions brought early ends to two other Presidential mandate (Alfonsin in 1989 and de la Rúa in 2001). Radicalism played a central role in the process of transition and consolidation of the democracy that was initiated in Argentina at the start of 1983. As in other periods of Argentine history, the stability of the UCR as a governing party was threatened at some points by the weight of corporate powers and at other times by the ravages of Peronism. In the first decade of the twenty-first century, it presents a profile of a party that is lax in its internal discipline and with a strong emphasis on provincial leaders who impose themselves on its national structure and weaken its institutionalization.

See also **Alem, Leandro N.; Alfonsín, Raúl Ricardo; Alvear, Marcelo Torcuato de; Caudillismo, Caudillo; Illia, Arturo Umberto; Irigoyen, Hipólito; Krausismo; Rúa, Fernando de la.**

BIBLIOGRAPHY

Biagini, Hugo, ed. *Orígenes de la democracia argentina: El trasfondo krausista.* Buenos Aires: Fundación Friedrich Ebert, 1989.

Gallo, Ricardo. *Frondizi y la división del radicalismo, 1956–1958.* Buenos Aires: Ed. de Belgrano, 1983.

García Sebastiani, Marcela. "The Other Side of Peronist Argentina: Radicals and Socialists in the Political Opposition to Perón (1946–1955)." *Journal of Latin American Studies* 35, no. 2 (2003): 311–340.

Halperín Donghi, Tulio. *La República imposible (1930–1945).* Buenos Aires: Ed. Ariel, 2004.

Luna, Félix. *Alvear.* Buenos Aires: Hyspamérica, 1986.

Persello, Ana Virginia. *El radicalismo: Gobierno y oposición (1916–1943).* Buenos Aires: Ed. siglo XXI, 2004.

Rock, David. *El radicalismo argentino.* Buenos Aires: Ed. Amorrortu, 1975.

Romero, Luis Alberto, José Luis Fernández, Luis Bertoni, et al. *El radicalismo.* Buenos Aires: Cepe, 1974.

Smulovitz, Catalina. "Opposition and Government in Argentina: The Frondizi and Illia Administrations." Ph.D. diss., Pennsylvania State University, 1991.

Spinelli, María Estela. *Los vencedores vencidos: El antiperonismo y la "revolución Libertadora."* Buenos Aires: Ed. Biblos, 2005.

Tcach, César, and Celso Rodriguez. *Arturo Illia: Un sueño breve.* Buenos Aires: Edhasa, 2006.

Sabattinismo y Peronismo, 2nd edition. Buenos Aires: Ed. Biblos, 2006.

CÉSAR TCACH

SOCIALIST PARTY

Socialist ideas and publications have circulated in Argentina since 1870. *El Obrero* appeared in 1890 to communicate these ideas, and the German socialist club, Vorwärts, initiated the formation of the International Committee, which called on workers in particular to organize themselves and demand protective laws. *La Vanguardia,* a newspaper, founded in April 1894, called for a meeting of socialist groups to form the party. The party was formally established in 1896 when the First Congress approved the Minimum Program. Its Statement of Principles declared that workers were oppressed and exploited by capitalists and that the proletariat was responsible for reforming the situation. To bring about this socioeconomic transformation, the party promoted universal suffrage and worker organization.

The Minimum Program was drawn up, with different variants, on the basis of electoral platforms: an eight-hour work day, improvement of working conditions, elimination of indirect taxes, taxation of large-property ownership and inheritance, extension of the vote to women, separation of Church and state, and divorce. The party encouraged industrial development to increase the power of the worker class, but strongly opposed all protectionism and defended free play of supply and demand. It promoted cooperativism, a mutual support association where people get together by their own free will to solve common economic, social and cultural needs, through the creation of a democratically controlled company.

Juan B. Justo became the indisputable head of the Socialist Party and the defender of gradual and progressive change. The main basis of the party was the ongoing mobilization of its adherents, and it gave priority to the education of workers. It participated in the political system but denounced fraud. Its most resounding triumph was the election of Alfredo Palacios in 1904 as national deputy.

The electoral reform of 1912 set a stage that was more favorable to political organizations. The Socialist Party faced hard competition from the Radical Party, which it considered a part of the old political structure. A significant increase in the electorate in the federal capital, Buenos Aires, resulted in several deputies and senators being elected. Although the electorate of Buenos Aires gave its support to the Socialist Party, the party could not consolidate a solid structure in the country's inland provinces.

The party always had a difficult relationship with workers' organizations and with the diverging opinions of many of its members. Different waves of opinion formed within it, causing several splits. Like Palacios, Manuel Ugarte was considered more nationalist than internationalist. Palacios was expelled from the Socialist Party for challenging its leadership and went on to found the Argentine Socialist Party, which was short-lived and had little success.

In 1912 another faction founded the Karl Marx Studies Center, which defended orthodox Marxism. Tensions increased when party members were forbidden to simultaneously hold membership in the Young Socialists, and due to the group's stance on the 1914 war. Several members were expelled, including José Penelón, Rodolfo Ghioldi, Vittorio Codovilla, and Alberto Palcos, and in 1918 they founded the International Socialist Party, which supported the Russian Revolution and eventually became the Communist Party.

Between 1916 and 1930 Argentine politics underwent an important change that had a significant impact on democratic movements in the country. The military coup of September 6, 1930, broke the continuity of constitutional government, and conflicts within the Socialist Party resurfaced. In the 1930s the party opposition from the Left was expelled and formed the Socialist Workers Party, which in turn underwent several internal crises until its dissolution. An Independent Socialist Party also was formed.

The emergence and consolidation of the Peronist Party drained militants from the Socialist Party, which lost many of its members to the growing Peronist movement. The Socialist Party opposed Peronism, and many of its leaders left for exile. With the fall of

Perón in 1955, the Socialist Party was reactivated, with a renewed hope of attracting members from among the masses, but these new members failed to materialize as workers did not leave the Peronist ranks.

After 1955 Argentina was unstable. Plagued by repeated military coups, the Socialist Party remained on the political scene through its various rifts. In 1958 it split again, forming the Democratic Socialist Party, which continues in the early twenty-first century, as well as the Argentine Socialist Party. The latter was a coalition of socialists, Castroists, and Maoists; their differences prompted the party's division into the Argentine Socialist Party and the Vanguard Argentine Socialist Party, which further split into the Popular Vanguard Party (which self-dissolved in 1972 to join the Justicialist Party) and the Communist Vanguard Party. In 1966 the Argentine Socialist Party split again when Juan Carlos Coral was expelled from the group and joined a Trotskyite group to form the Workers Socialist Party, which ran candidates in the national elections of 1973 and was banned by the military dictatorship in 1976. In 1972 the socialists of the Argentine Socialist Party, along with other scattered minor groups, created the Popular Socialist Party.

See also **Codovilla, Vittorio; Ghioldi, Rodolfo; Justo, Juan B.; Palacios, Alfredo L.; Ugarte, Manuel.**

BIBLIOGRAPHY

Adelman, Jeremy. "El Partido Socialista Argentina." In *Nueva Historia Argentina*, Vol. 5: *El progreso, la modernización y sus límites, 1880–1916*, ed. Mirta Zaida Lobato. Buenos Aires: Sudamericana, 2000.

Aricó, José. *La hipótesis de Justo.* Buenos Aires: Sudamericana, 1999.

Camarero, Hernán, and Carlos Miguel Herrera, eds. *El partido socialista en Argentina: Sociedad, Política, e ideas a través de un siglo.* Buenos Aires: Prometeo, 2005.

Oddone, Jacinto. *Historia del socialismo argentino.* (1934). Buenos Aires: CEAL, 1988.

Walter, Richard. *The Socialist Party of Argentina, 1890–1930.* Austin: University of Texas Press, 1977.

MIRTA ZAIDA LOBATO

YOUTH ORGANIZATION OF THE RADICAL PARTY (FORJA)

Established on 29 June 1935, the Fuerza de Orientación Radical de la Joven Argentina (FORJA; Youth Organization of the Radical Party) tried to revive the Unión Cívica Radical (Radical Party) as a viable political force during the Concordancia (1931–1943).

FORJA appeared as the Radical Party foundered. The overthrow of the second administration of Hipólito Irigoyen in 1930 and the ex-president's death in 1933 weakened the popular or Personalist core of the party. The conservative Anti-Personalist Radical Party faction, led by Marcelo T. de Alvear, lost support when it accepted a minority role in the Concordancia. Rigged elections, the arrest of party activists, and censorship made it difficult to conduct normal operations.

In the face of these challenges, intellectuals, journalists, and activists worked in FORJA with a set of common goals. In books, pamphlets, and articles they challenged the conservative and repressive policies of the national government. They organized meetings to build popular support. They called on the people and the nation to pursue policies that would help Argentina achieve economic and political independence from the power of foreign companies and their allies, the oligarchy within the country. They were particularly critical of the role that Great Britain played in Argentina's development. Most important, they remained loyal to the Radical Party's core faith in popular democracy and open, free, and honest elections.

FORJA's leaders included established Radicals and new figures. They included Luis Dellepiane, Gabriel del Mazo, Arturo Jauretche, and Raúl Scalabrini Ortiz.

As World War II put significant economic and diplomatic pressure on Argentina, FORJA became more militant and extreme. Strongly in favor of Argentina's neutrality, its leadership grew more nationalistic. The military coup of 4 June 1943, restricted its activities. The subsequent rise of Peronism thwarted its efforts to establish a popular political base.

See also **Alvear, Marcelo Torcuato de; Concordancia; Irigoyen, Hipólito.**

BIBLIOGRAPHY

Halperín Donghi, Tulio. *La república imposible.* Buenos Aires: Ariel, 2004.

Juaretche, Arturo. *FORJA y la década infame.* Buenos Aires: Editorial Coyoacán, 1962.

Rock, David. *Authoritarian Argentina: The Nationalist Movement, Its History, and Its Impact.* Berkeley: University of California Press, 1993.

DANIEL K. LEWIS

ARGENTINA, TRUTH COMMISSIONS.

The National Commission on the Disappeared (Comisión Nacional sobre la Desaparición de Personas, or CONADEP) was an Argentine truth commission created by the democratically elected government of President Raúl Alfonsín in 1983. Its main aim was to investigate the violations of human rights committed by the Argentine military dictatorship between 1976 and 1983. The commission published its final report, *Nunca más* (Never again), in 1984 and it was used as key evidence in subsequent trials, including the Trial of the Juntas in 1985.

The dictatorship systemically kidnapped, tortured, and killed between 10,000 and 30,000 Argentine citizens. These killings were not random but carefully planned at the upper levels of the military government. The words *desaparecer* and *desaparecidos* ("to disappear" and "the disappeared") became euphemisms for state-sanctioned assassinations of actual and perceived enemies of the dictatorship. The victims were usually confined in concentrations camps, tortured, eventually executed, and often thrown from military airplanes into the Atlantic Ocean.

The commission gathered files, interviewed the actors, and inspected many of the approximately 340 concentrations camps. It documented 8,960 disappeared citizens but stated that the actual number of victims was certainly higher. It also documented systematic kidnappings and torture of adults and children as well as the fact that many babies were kidnapped with their parents or were born in concentration camps to pregnant prisoners and later "given" to military families. After consulting more than fifty thousand pages of documentary evidence, including thousands of testimonies, the published report concluded that the military engaged in an "organic violation of human rights by the state" (*Nunca más*, p. 8 [author translation]).

See also **Alfonsín, Raúl Ricardo; Dirty War; Truth Commissions.**

BIBLIOGRAPHY

Comisión Nacional sobre la Desaparición de Personas. *Nunca más.* Buenos Aires: EUDEBA, 1984.

Hayner, Priscilla. *Unspeakable Truths: Facing the Challenge of Truth Commissions.* New York: Routledge, 2002.

Vezzetti, Hugo. *Pasado y presente: Guerra, dictadura y sociedad en la Argentina.* Buenos Aires: Siglo XXI, 2002.

Federico Finchelstein

ARGENTINA, UNIVERSITY REFORM.

The university reform movement in Argentina, composed of privileged male students, began in Córdoba in 1918. There, in the country's oldest and most conservative university, student protests successfully effected major changes in the administration of that institution, including direct student participation in the management of university affairs and greater flexibility with regard to entrance requirements, class attendance, and course content. The aim of these reforms was to modernize the traditional, elite-dominated Argentine university, making its curriculum more attuned to contemporary issues and problems and opening its doors to more students of the middle and working classes.

The reform movement spread quickly to Argentina's other universities and eventually to much of the rest of Latin America. While a principal emphasis remained on educational change, reform also stimulated student interest and activism in broader political matters. One consequence of reform was the formation in 1918 of a national student group, the Federación Universitaria Argentina, which served to integrate similar federations at individual universities and articulate student interests nationwide. Soon, students and their organizations in Argentina and elsewhere in Latin America associated with the reform began to make pronouncements and take stands on a number of issues. Generally, they favored democracy over dictatorship, strongly opposed foreign investment and outside intervention in the region—especially on the part of the United States—and advocated improved conditions for the working classes. The students frequently resorted to strikes and demonstrations to support their demands.

Since 1918, the achievements of the university reform movement have provoked controversy in Argentina. There, periods of extreme student activism and influence have alternated with eras of severe repression during which universities have been taken over by national authorities and purged of unwanted professors and students, many of whom have suffered terribly in the process. Moreover, the effects of reform on the overall quality of education have undergone increasing scrutiny. What was once Latin America's finest system of higher education has since experienced serious deterioration. Nevertheless, Argentina still has some of the highest levels of education in Latin America and the world. Since the 1990s, however, critics have accused the government's privatization reforms of undoing many of the accomplishments of the university reform movement by making high-quality education less accessible.

Students continue to be important participants in national life, and the principles of university reform still have considerable force and influence. The Federación Universitaria Argentina has reflected the political diversity and tensions in Argentina since its formation in the early twentieth century. Leftist groups, Peronists and the Radical Party have all competed for and held leadership positions in the organization.

See also **Córdoba, University of; Education.**

BIBLIOGRAPHY

Richard J. Walter, *Student Politics in Argentina: The University Reform and Its Effects, 1918–1964* (1968).

Virginia W. Leonard, *Politicians, Pupils, and Priests: Argentine Education Since 1943* (1989).

Additional Bibliography

Caldelari, María, and Patricia Funes. *Escenas reformistas: A reforma universitaria, 1918–1930.* Buenos Aires: Universidad de Buenos Aires, Programa de Historia Oral y Gráfica, 1998.

Ciria, Alberto, and Horacio J. Sanguinetti. *La reforma universitaria: 1918–2006.* Santa Fe, Argentina: Ediciones UNL, 2005.

Marcó del Pont K., Luis. *Historia del movimiento estudiantil reformista.* Córdoba, Argentina: Universitas, 2005.

Puiggrós, Adriana, ed. *Dictaduras y utopías en la historia reciente de la educación Argentina (1955–1983).* Buenos Aires: Editorial Galerna, 1997.

RICHARD J. WALTER

ARGENTINE CONFEDERATION.

Two different institutions have gone by the name of the Argentine Confederation: the alliance of independent states based on the Federal Pact of 1831, which lasted until the passage of the Constitution in 1853; and the nation organized around that Constitution between 1853 and 1860, without the seceded State of Buenos Aires.

With the failure of the Constituent Congress of 1824 to 1826, the territories that are part of present-day Argentina operated as independent states or provinces. The conflicts between them led those on the coast to sign a treaty of alliance called the Federal Pact. Once their opponents were defeated, all of the other provinces joined the pact, which was the basis for the union, though it lacked confederative institutions. External relations were delegated to the governor of Buenos Aires, Juan Manuel de Rosas, who exercised considerable influence over the rest of the states.

Rosas was defeated by Justo José de Urquiza in 1852 at the Battle of Caseros, and Congress passed the Constitution the following year. Buenos Aires seceded from the confederation, refusing to participate until it was dominated militarily in 1859 and then forced to join in 1860 after its proposals for constitutional reform were accepted. This period of rule by Urquiza also was known as the Argentine Confederation, adopting one of the names mentioned in the Constitution.

See also **Argentina, Constitutions.**

BIBLIOGRAPHY

Martin de Moussy, Victor. *Descripción geográfica y estadística de la Confederación Argentina,* 3 vols. Buenos Aires: Academia Nacional de la Historia, 2005. Originally published in the mid-nineteenth century.

EDUARDO JOSÉ MIGUEZ

ARGUEDAS, ALCIDES (1879–1946).

Alcides Arguedas was a Bolivian writer, politician, and diplomat. Born in La Paz on July 15, 1879, Arguedas is considered one of the initiators of realism in Bolivia, and of *indigenismo* in Latin America. He is well known for his novel *Wata Wara* (1904), which he rewrote and published as *Raza de bronce* (1919). His contact with some of the intellectuals of the Spanish "Generation of 1898," mainly with Miguel de Unamuno and Ramiro de Maeztu, is key to an understanding of Arguedas's view of Bolivian reality, as presented in his highly contested sociological study *Pueblo enfermo* (1909). In this essay Arguedas criticizes his own people for defects of their character, brought on, he suggests, by their oppressive history. This theme was carried over to other books, including his essay *La danza de las sombras* (1934). Arguedas also wrote historical novels, one of the earliest being *Pisagua* (1903), which deals with events of the War of the Pacific. His novels, histories, and essays, though controversial because of his biting criticism of Bolivian reality, at the same time were praised for their candid presentation of the nation's past. Arguedas died on May 6, 1946 in Chulumani.

See also **González Prada, Manuel; Indigenismo; Ingenieros, José; War of the Pacific.**

BIBLIOGRAPHY

Arnade, Charles. "The Historiography of Colonial and Modern Bolivia." *Hispanic American Historical Review* 42 (1962): 333–384.

Sanjinés C., Javier. *Mestizaje Upside-Down: Aesthetic Politics in Modern Bolivia.* Pittsburgh, PA: University of Pittsburgh Press, 2004. See esp. pp. 45–47.

JACK RAY THOMAS
JAVIER SANJINÉS C.

ARGUEDAS, JOSÉ MARÍA (1911–1969).

José María Arguedas was a Peruvian novelist, poet, ethnographer, folklorist, and anthropologist. Renowned for his dedication to indigenous narrative literature and commitment to the survival of indigenous cultures, Arguedas drew on his personal experiences in Quechua communities to portray indigenous culture. Born on 18 January 1911, he was raised by his white father (an itinerant judge) and Quechua Indian caretakers after his mother died. As a result, he spoke Quechua before he learned Spanish. Formally trained in literature and anthropology at the Universidad Nacional Mayor de San Marcos in Peru, he later held posts in various government cultural programs and at museums of folklore and ethnology.

As part of a literary *indigenista* movement in Latin America, Arguedas acknowledged the significance of his Spanish cultural heritage but simultaneously feared its power to destroy the indigenous culture he valued so highly. In his folkloric and ethnological studies, Arguedas aspired to preserve the best of indigenous culture while exposing the cruel treatment and discrimination against indigenous peoples in rural Peruvian communities. His novels and short stories—written in both Spanish and Quechua—reflect his desire to attain a kind of cultural fusion, or *mestizaje*, in which the values of both of Peru's indigenous and Iberian-derived cultures could be joined.

In 1964 Arguedas became head of the Department of Ethnology and professor of Quechua at the Agrarian University. On 28 November 1969, one day after his resignation, he shot himself. It was perhaps his doubt that *mestizaje* would ever be achieved—that in fact indigenous culture would not survive—which led to his suicide. Evidence for this exists in his final unfinished novel, *El zorro de arriba y el zorro de abajo* (The fox from above and the fox from below), published posthumously in 1970. His published works also include *Agua* (Water; 1935), *Yawar fiesta* (The Yawar Party; 1941), *Diamantes y pedernales* (Diamonds and Flint; 1954), *Los ríos profundos* (The Deep Rivers; 1958), *El Sexto* (The Sixth; 1961), and *Todas las sangres* (All of the Bloods; 1964).

See also **Indigenous Languages; Quechua.**

BIBLIOGRAPHY

Aldrich, Earl M., Jr. *The Modern Short Story in Peru.* Madison: University of Wisconsin Press, 1966.

Franco, Sergio R., ed. *José María Arguedas: Hacia una poética migrante.* Pittsburgh, PA: Instituto Internacional de Literatura Iberoamericana, 2006.

Kokotovic, Misha. *The Colonial Divide in Peruvian Narrative: Social Conflict and Transculturation.* Brighton, U.K., and Portland, OR: Sussex Academic Press, 2005.

Oviedo, José Miguel. "Homenaje a José María Arguedas." *Revista Peruana de Cultura* 13 and 14 (1970).

Polar, Antonio Cornejo. *Los universos narrativos de José María Arguedas.* Buenos Aires: Editorial Losada, 1973.

Portugal, José Alberto. *Las novelas de José María Arguedas: Una incursión en lo inarticulado.* Peru: Editorial Fondo PUCP, 2007.

Ortega, Julio. *Revista Iberoamericana* 49, no. 122 (1983). Special issue devoted to Arguedas.

Sandoval, Ciro A., and Sandra M. Boschetto-Sandoval, eds. *José María Arguedas: Reconsiderations for Latin American Cultural Studies.* Athens: Ohio University Center for International Studies, 1998.

CHARLENE VAN DIJK

ARGÜELLES, HUGO (1932–2003).

Hugo Argüelles (*b.* 2 January 1932, *d.* 24 December 2003), Mexican playwright. Born in Veracruz, Argüelles studied at the School of Dramatic Arts of the Instituto Nacional de Bellas Artes (INBA) in Mexico City, where he later taught. He also founded the School of Fine Arts in Puebla. He won, among others, the Premio Nacional de Teatro in 1958 for his play *Los cuervos están de luto* (1958; The Crows Are in Mourning) and the Juan Ruiz de Alarcón award in 1961 for *Los prodigiosos* (1956; The Prodigies). His plays are characterized by black humor and a tone of mockery, capturing the essence of the Mexican spirit. Argüelles enjoys broad recognition for his extensive production of theatrical works, some of which he has successfully directed for television. Other major plays are *La dama de la luna roja* (1970; The Lady of the Red Moon), *El gran inquisidor* (1973; The Grand Inquisitor), *El cocodrilo solitario del panteón rococó* (1985; The Solitary Crocodile of Rococó Pantheon), and *Los gallos salvajes* (1986; The Wild Roosters).

See also **Theater.**

BIBLIOGRAPHY

Heriberto García Rivas, *Historia de la literatura mexicana,* vol. 4 (1974), pp. 478–479.

Emilio García Riera, *Historia documental del cine mexicano,* vols. 8 and 9 (1978), pp. 81–83, 233–235.

Mirta Barrea-Marlys, "Hugo Argüelles," in *Dictionary of Mexican Literature,* edited by Eladio Cortés (1992).

Additional Bibliography

Alcaraz, José Antonio. *Fanfarrias para la dramaturgia de Hugo Argüelles.* México: Universidad Nacional Autónoma de México, Coordinación de Difusión Cultural, Dirección de Literatura, 2002.

Meyer, Juan. *La travesía mágica de Hugo Argüelles: Cuarenta años de dramaturgo.* México, D.F.: Departamento del Distrito Federal, 1997.

JEANNE C. WALLACE

ARGÜELLO, LEONARDO (1875–1947).

Leonardo Argüello (*b.* 1875; *d.* 15 December 1947), Nicaraguan physician, writer, and politician. Born in León, the center of Nicaraguan liberalism, Leonardo Argüello participated in the revolutionary movement of 1911–1912. For his efforts Argüello was made a deputy in and the president of the Nicaraguan Congress. In 1925, Argüello was named minister of public instruction, a position in which he distinguished himself by attempting to broaden education to include the rural population and by allocating more money for schools and libraries. During the 1930s and 1940s, Argüello occupied himself with his writing but was brought from academic life back to politics in February 1947, when Anastasio Somoza García arranged to have Argüello succeed him as president of the nation. Argüello, although already over seventy years old, did not prove to be the puppet that Somoza had anticipated, rather, he began to increase the participation of anti-Somocistas in the government. Three months into his term, Argüello was removed from office by a May 1947 coup led by Somoza's National Guard and forced into exile.

See also **Nicaragua.**

BIBLIOGRAPHY

Sara Barquero, *Gobernantes de Nicaragua* (1937).

Ralph Lee Woodward, Jr., *Central America: A Nation Divided* (1985).

KAREN RACINE

ARGÜELLO, SANTIAGO (1791–1862).

Santiago Argüello (*b.* 1791; *d.* 1862), Spanish military and civilian official in New Spain and Mexican California. Born at Monterey, California, he began his career as an officer in the Spanish army and later served the Mexican government until 1834. Described as tall, stout, and of fair complexion, Argüello was appointed *alcalde* of San Diego in 1836 and prefect of Los Angeles in 1840. He also served as administrator of the former mission at San Juan Capistrano from 1838 to 1840. Argüello's lands included Rancho Tia Juana, Rancho Trabuco, and the San Diego Mission estate, which were granted to him in 1829, 1841, and 1846, respectively. He and his wife, Pilar Ortega, of Santa Barbara, had twenty-two children, many of whom became influential in Mexican California society.

See also **California.**

BIBLIOGRAPHY

Hubert Howe Bancroft, *History of California,* vol. 2 (1885).

Charles Hughes, "Decline of the Californios: The Case of San Diego," in *Journal of San Diego History* 21 (1975): 1–31.

IRIS H. W. ENGSTRAND

ARGÜELLO MORA, MANUEL (1834–1902).

Manuel Argüello Mora is considered to be Costa Rica's first novelist. An orphan, Argüello was raised by his uncle Juan Rafael Mora Porras (1814–1960), who became president of Costa Rica in 1849 and led the nation against William Walker's filibusters in 1856. Forced to leave the country when Mora was overthrown in a coup in 1859, Argüello fictionalized Mora's disastrous attempt to retake power the following year in his most famous short story, "La trinchera" ("The Trench"), and in the short novels *Elisa Delmar* and *Margarita* (all published in 1899).

Argüello's best writing reflects his search for a Costa Rican national identity in the traumatic events of the nineteenth century. By his own count, he produced more than 600 works of historical fiction, journalism, and travel literature. Although modern historians and literary scholars have criticized Argüello's romantic narratives, his writings provide first-hand accounts of important events in the nation's history. By introducing new forms and themes explored by later authors, Argüello Mora assured his place in Costa Rican letters.

See also **Literature: Spanish America; Mora Porrás, Juan Rafael; Walker, William.**

BIBLIOGRAPHY

Argüello Mora, Manuel. *Obras literarias e históricas.* San José, Costa Rica: Editorial Costa Rica, 1963.

RUSSELL LOHSE

ARIAS, ARTURO (1950–).

Arturo Arias (*b.* 22 June 1950), Guatemalan novelist and literary critic. Born in Guatemala City, Arturo Arias is considered one of the leading representatives of the Guatemalan "new" novel. His first novel, *Después de las bombas* (1979; *After the Bombs,* 1990), narrates the mythical and carnivalesque story of a boy's search for his father during the political unrest that followed the Guatemalan counterrevolution of 1954. His second novel, *Itzam Na* (1981), which won the prestigious Cuban Casa de las Américas Award for best novel, is a combination of voices and written documents depicting the social and political alienation of bourgeois Guatemalan youth of the 1970s. His third novel, *Jaguar en llamas* (1989), deals with the indigenous side of Guatemalan history from the Conquest to the present. In 1990 he published his fourth novel, *Los caminos de Paxil,* which also looks at contemporary Guatemalan political history in light of the Mayan past. Arias has also published a collection of short stories, *En la ciudad y en las montañas* (1975), and a collection of essays, *Ideologías, literatura y sociedad durante la revolución guatemalteca: 1944–54* (1979), which won the Casa de las Américas Award for essays; he coauthored the screenplay for *El Norte* (1983). Other works include *Cascabel* (1998); *La identidad de la palabra: Narrativa guatemalteca del siglo veinte* (1998); *The Rigoberto Menchú Controversy* (2001); and *Rattlesnake* (2003). In 1988 he was elected president of the Congress of Central American Writers. Arias has a doctorate in the sociology of literature from the École des Hautes Études en Sciences Sociales in Paris and teaches at San Francisco State University. He served as President of the Latin American Studies Association from 2001 to 2003 and is Director of Latin American Studies at the University of Redlands.

See also **Literature: Spanish America.**

BIBLIOGRAPHY

For a study of Arias's work, see the essays by Dante Liano, Judy Maloof, María Rosa Olivera-Williams, and Ileana Rodríguez in *Cambios estéticos y nuevos proyectos culturales en Centroamérica,* edited by Amelia Mondragón (1994). See also Fernando Alegría, *Nueva historia de la novela hispanoamericana* (1986).

Seymour Menton, *Historia crítica de la novela guatemalteca,* 2d ed. (1985).

Mario Roberto Morales, "La nueva novela guatemalteca y sus funciones de clase," in *Literatura y crisis en Centroamérica: Ponencias*, by Ileana Rodríguez, Ramón Acevedo, and Mario Roberto Morales (1986).

Jorge Campos, "Guatemala: La busca de la salvación en la droga y el viejo mundo indígena," in *Insula: Revista de Letras y Ciencias Humanas* 38 (1983): 11. Arias was interviewed by Lisa Davis and Sonia Rivera for "Guatemala: Hacia la victoria: Conversación con Arturo Arias y María Vázquez," in *Areíto* 10 (1984): 32–35. Criticism by Arias includes his 1993 study, *Postmodernism and New Cultural Tendencies in Latin America*.

Additional Bibliography

Craft, Linda J. *Novels of Testimony and Resistance from Central America*. Gainesville: University Press of Florida, 1997.

ANN GONZÁLEZ

ARIAS, DESIDERIO (1872–1931).

Desiderio Arias (*b.* 1872; *d.* 1931), military figure, politician, and president of the Dominican Republic (17 May 1916–June 1916). Born in Muñoz, Dominican Republic, Arias emerged as a key leader in the Liberal guerrilla movement led by Juan I. Jiménez in the 1910s. Assigned to the post of minister of war and the navy after Jiménez's election, General Arias consolidated his own power and moved against the president in a coup d'état in 1916.

Arias's coup and the civil disorder that followed provoked the United States to intervene, and Arias retired to private life under the watchful eye of the United States. Until the end of his life, Desiderio Arias played a role in his nation's political life as a symbol of the Liberal guerrillas. He died in a rebellion against President Rafael Trujillo Molina.

See also **Dominican Republic.**

BIBLIOGRAPHY

Sumner Welles, *Naboth's Vineyard* (1966).

Additional Bibliography

Herrera Rodríguez, Rafael Darío. *Revueltas y caudillismo: Desiderio Arias frente a Trujillo*. Dominican Republic: Impresos Paulinos, 2002.

Lobetty Gómez de Morel, Olga. *Desiderio Arias: El cacique liniero*. Dominican Republic: Editora Centenario, 1996.

TODD LITTLE-SIEBOLD

ARIAS CALDERÓN, RICARDO (1933–).

Panamanian philosopher and intellectual and former leader of the Christian Democratic Party (PDC) known for his honesty and personal integrity. Ricardo Arias Calderón has a B.A. from Yale University and a doctorate from the University of Paris. He has taught at universities in Panama, Venezuela, and Chile. In the United States he taught at Florida International University from 1972 to 1978. He is considered one of Panama's leading intellectuals, author of many books and articles dealing with philosophical and current political issues. He was forced into exile by the military dictatorship from 1969 to 1978. He joined the PDC in 1964 and was its president from 1980 to 1993. (In 2001 the PDC changed its name to the Partido Popular, or Popular Party [PP]). Arias Calderón was also the president of the Christian Democratic Organization of the Americas from 1981 to 1985 and twice president of the Christian Democratic International (1995–1998; May–October 2000).

In the 1980s, Arias Calderón became one of the leading opponents of the dictator General Manuel Antonio Noriega Moreno (1983–1989). In 1984, he ran for second vice-president on a ticket headed by Arnulfo Arias Madrid in a coalition with the latter's Authentic Panameñista Party (PPA). With the death of Arias Madrid in 1988, the opposition to Noriega was thrown into chaos. In 1989, in preparation for the May elections, the Christian Democrats joined with the majority faction of the Panameñistas, headed by Guillermo Endara Paniza, and other political parties to form a broad anti-Noriega coalition called CivicADO (Democratic Alliance of Civil Opposition). With Endara heading the ticket, Arias Calderón ran for first vice president, with Guillermo Ford (a businessman representing MOLIRENA, a coalition traditional liberal parties associated with the oligarchy), as second vice president.

The Noriega government claimed victory in the elections, but the opposition's count as well as that of independent observers, such as, former U.S. president jimmy Carter, indicated just the opposite. The government later annulled the results. During a demonstration against Noriega's rule, Arias Calderón and Ford were beaten by the dictator's "dignity battalions." CivicADO took over the government after the 1989 U.S. invasion. During his tenure as vice president and minister of justice, Arias Calderón, initiated the process of demilitarization of Panamanian politics and demobilization of the armed forces, which culminated in the 1994 constitutional amendment that abolished the Panamanian Defense Forces (PDF). In its place a new Public Force (FP) was created under the direct control of the Ministry of Justice. Later Arias Calderón purged the new FP of officers who had close associations with the Noriega regime. On 17 December 1992, Arias resigned from his post under pressure from his own party because of disagreements with the Endara administration (the PDC had already pulled out other members from the coalition in April 1991).

Despite battling Parkinson's disease, Arias Calderón remained active in the early twenty-first century, serving as Panama's ambassador to the United Nations. In 2004, the government of Panama awarded him with the Order Basque Nunez de Balboa, in the rank of Grand Cross.

See also **Panama.**

BIBLIOGRAPHY

Panama: A Country Report (1989); Andrew Zimbalist and John Weeks, *Panama at the Crossroads: Economic Development and Political Change in the Twentieth Century* (1991); Eva Loser, ed., *Conflict Resolution and Democratization in Panama: Implications for U.S. Policy* (1992); Mark Falcoff and Richard L. Millet, *Searching for Panama: The U.S.-Panama Relationship and Democratization* (1993); Tom Barry, *et al.*, *Inside Panama* (1995); Orlando J. Pérez, *Post-invasion Panama: The Challenges of Democratization in the New World Order* (2000); Ricardo Arias Calderón, *Democracia sin ejército: La experiencia de Panamá* (2001).

Additional Bibliography

Hernández, Roberto. *Cuatro ensayos de bioética: Aborto, eutanasia, reproducción asistida, colonación humana con tres comentarios críticos del Dr. Ricardo Arias Calderón.* Panamá: Litho Editorial Chen, 2002.

JUAN MANUEL PÉREZ

ARIAS DE ÁVILA, PEDRO. *See* Ávila, Pedro Arias de.

ARIAS DE SAAVEDRA, HERNANDO

(1561–1634). Hernando Arias de Saavedra (Hernandarias; *b.* 1561; *d.* 1634), one of the greatest figures in Argentine history and the first creole to hold public office in Latin America. He was born in Asunción to Captain Martín Juárez de Toledo, a close associate of Alvar Núñez Cabeza De Vaca, and María Sanabria, daughter of the *adelantado* Juan Sanabria y Mencia Calderón. Following a common custom of the period, he was given his paternal grandfather's last name. From a very young age, Hernandarias participated in conquests and explorations and came in contact with important figures of the early history of the Río de la Plata region. He became known for his bravery and was severely wounded more than once.

In 1576, when he was only fifteen years old, he went to work for the governor of Tucumán, Gonzalo de Abrego. In 1577, he entered the service of Hernando de Lerma in Santiago del Estero, and three years later he accompanied Alonso de Vera y Aragón, cousin of the *adelantado* Juan Torres de Vera y Aragón, in a six-month cattle drive from Paraguay to Buenos Aires. In 1582, Hernandarias was with Juan de Garay for the second founding of Buenos Aires. That year he married Garay's daughter, Jerónima Contreras. In 1588, he accompanied Juan Torres de Vera y Aragón in the founding of San Juan de Vera de las Siete Corrientes.

Hernandarias held public office a total of six times, three times between 1590 and 1597 as interim governor of the Río de la Plata, and another three times between 1597 and 1618 as governor. The first time he became governor he was only 29 years old. As governor, Hernandarias proved to be an enlightened administrator. He encouraged commerce among the different provinces; tried to curb the rampant contraband in the Río de la Plata region; protected the Indians and encouraged the creation of Jesuit missions in Paraguay; distributed land among Spaniards, creoles, and mestizos; built schools, churches, and hospitals; and promulgated laws designed to improve the living standards of the population.

Hernandarias's policies created resentment among powerful Spaniards, particularly those engaged in contraband. In 1618, his enemies prevailed against him, and the new governor, Diego de Góngora, had him imprisoned and most of his property confiscated. His wife sought refuge with her brother, General Juan de Garay. Hernandarias's friends took his case to the crown, which sent the *juez pesquisador* (investigating judge) Matías Delgado Flores to investigate. Hernandarias was set free, and he was absolved of any wrongdoing in July 1624 by the *oidor* Alonso Pérez de Sálazar, who had been sent by the Audiencia of Charcas. Hernandarias died in Santa Fe.

See also **Argentina: The Colonial Period.**

BIBLIOGRAPHY

Juan Estevan Guastavino, *Hernandarias* (1928).

Carlos María Aranguren, *Hernandarias* (1963).

Francisco José Figuerola, *Por qué Hernandarias* (1981).

Additional Bibliography

Hernandarias. *Hernandarias*, edited by Walter Rela. Montevideo: Ediciones Galeón, 2001.

JUAN MANUEL PÉREZ

ARIAS MADRID, ARNULFO (1901–1988).

Arnulfo Arias Madrid (*b.* 15 August 1901; *d.* 10 August 1988), Panamanian politician and three-time president (1940–1941, 1949–1951, 1968). A medical doctor by profession and a graduate of Harvard Medical School, Arnulfo Arias was a controversial politician. Elected three times and overthrown on every occasion (the last time after just eleven days in office), Arias dominated Panamanian politics for fifty-seven years. He was highly nationalistic and anti-American. After joining the nationalistic organization *Acción Comunal* in 1930, he was leading it a year later in the revolution that overthrew the corrupt government of Florencio Harmodio Arosemena.

As a populist leader, Arias tried to ingratiate himself with the masses by promoting social revolution and using anti-establishment rhetoric. His platform was embodied in what he called *panameñismo*, translated as "Panama for the Panamanians." His policies against the Chinese and West Indians, whom he stripped of citizenship, and others, such as requiring people in some professions to wear uniforms, made people uneasy. His first presidency constituted a small revolution, challenging the

oligarchy and the United States. He promulgated a nationalistic constitution, created a social security system, gave women the right to vote, attempted a land reform program, and involved the state more actively in the economy. His enemies, the United States in particular, accused him of Nazi tendencies. Arias did not allow the United States to acquire more land for military bases with long-term leases and full jurisdiction as the United States had requested. Arias was trying to avoid the creation of other areas in Panamanian territory over which Panama would not have control. His nationalism and anti-Americanism put him on a collision course with the United States, which in 1941 was involved in his overthrow. In the mid-1980s, Arias became the major figure opposing the dictator General Manuel Antonio Noriega. His followers came to power after the 1989 U.S. invasion and renamed his party the Arnulfista Party of Panama.

See also **Panama.**

BIBLIOGRAPHY

Felipe Juan Escobar, *Arnulfo Arias* (1946).

Jorge Conte Porras, *Arnulfo Arias Madrid* (1980).

Additional Bibliography

Pearcy, Thomas L. "Panama's Generation of '31: Patriots, Praetorians, and a Decade of Discord." *Hispanic American Historical Review* 76 (November 1996): 691–719.

Robinson, William Francis. "Panama for the Panamanians: The Populism of Arnulfo Arias Madrid." In *Populism in Latin America*, edited by Michael L. Conniff. Tuscaloosa: University of Alabama Press, 1999.

JUAN MANUEL PÉREZ

ARIAS MADRID, HARMODIO (1886–1962).

Harmodio Arias Madrid (*b.* 3 July 1886; *d.* 23 December 1962), Panamanian politician and president (1932–1936). Harmodio Arias was a prominent and highly respected politician in the 1920s and one of the leaders of the 1931 revolution that overthrew the government of Florencio Harmodio Arosemena. He and his brother Arnulfo became the leaders of a new and more nationalistic generation of middle-class Panamanians. He was very popular for his opposition to the ratification of the 1926 treaty with the United States. Harmodio became president in 1932 after one of the freest and most honest elections the country had seen.

He came from a modest family. In 1911, he earned a doctorate in law and political science at the University of London. In 1912, President Porras appointed him to a commission charged with drafting a legal code. He was a professor at the law school (1918–1920), deputy to the National Assembly (1920–1924), and Panama's representative to the International Court of Justice at The Hague and the League of Nations. As a member of the National Assembly, he staunchly defended national sovereignty. He also had a very successful law practice.

As president, Harmodio Arias attacked corruption and incompetence, for which he incurred the wrath of those accustomed to using the government for personal gain. He presided over an honest administration. In 1935, Arias founded the University of Panama. In 1936, he negotiated a new treaty with the United States that ended the latter's right to intervene in Panama's internal affairs. As the editor of *El Panamá-América*, he continued to be an influential voice in Panamanian politics after he left the presidency.

See also **Panama.**

BIBLIOGRAPHY

Mélida Ruth Sepúlveda, *Harmodio Arias Madrid: El hombre, el estadista y el periodista* (1983).

Patricia Pizzurno Gelós, *Harmodio Arias Madrid y las relaciones internacionales* (1991).

Additional Bibliography

Araúz, Celestino Andrés. *Antecedentes históricos y balance sobre la obra de gobierno de Harmodio Arias Madrid.* Panama: Editorial Universitaria "Carlos Manuel Gasteazoro," 2003.

JUAN MANUEL PÉREZ

ARIAS SÁNCHEZ, OSCAR (1940–).

Oscar Arias Sánchez (*b.* 13 September 1940), president of Costa Rica (1986–1990, 2006–), awarded the Nobel Peace Prize in 1987 for designing a plan for peace in Central America. Arias Sánchez's father was an early follower of José Figueres Ferrer and an active member of the National Liberation Party (PLN). His mother's family is part of the Costa Rican coffee elite that emerged during the nineteenth-century coffee boom. Arias Sánchez came to international prominence shortly after his inauguration in 1986 when he took bold initiatives to propel Central America into a peace process. His proposals for peace and stability in the region led to an agreement, signed in 1987, between Honduras, Guatemala, Nicaragua, El Salvador, and Costa Rica.

The Arias plan, or Esquipulas II, established the framework for the pacification and democratization of Central America. It provided for the restoration of civil liberties, for amnesty for political prisoners, for free elections, and for genuine dialogue between governments and opposition forces. The plan contributed to the process that brought peace and free elections to Nicaragua and new hope for the eventual demilitarization of the region.

Even though Arias came to the international scene at a relatively young age, he had served a long apprenticeship in the highly competitive arena of Costa Rican party politics and in the rigorous intellectual environment of the University of Costa Rica (UCR). He received his law and economics degrees from the UCR, was awarded a master of arts degree in political science and economics from the London School of Economics (1967), and earned a doctor of philosophy degree from the University of Essex, England (1974). He joined the faculty of UCR in 1969 and served as a member of the ad hoc Commission of the National University (1972–1975). He was a director of the Costa Rican Technological Institute from 1974 to 1977.

Arias began his political career in the PLN and held high elected and appointed positions in the national government and in the party. He served as secretary to the president (1970–1972) during the last José Figueres Ferrer administration. From 1972 to 1977, he held a cabinet-level position as minister of national planning and economic policy. While serving as a member of the National Assembly (1978–1982), he also held other leadership positions. He was secretary of international affairs (1975–1979), and he was elected secretary general in 1979 on a reformist platform that brought a new generation of leaders to the fore. Arias ascended to the presidency chiefly by serving in positions of party leadership and in the administration of President Luis Alberto Monge Álvarez. He won the PLN primary and then defeated Rafael Angel Calderón Fournier in the general election.

Arias has received many awards and honorary degrees from universities in Europe, Central America, and the United States. Since his presidency he has lectured widely on the related questions of world peace and the environment, donating the proceeds from the lectures to the Arias Foundation, which was established to support research on these issues. He has also continued to be active in politics. When the Constitutional Court allowed for reelection, Arias ran for the presidency in 2006. Even though Arias retained considerable credibility from his previous work, leftist rivalry provided considerable competition in the balloting. A manual recount ultimately declared Arias the winner.

See also **Calderón Fournier, Rafael Ángel; Costa Rica, National Liberation Party; Monge Álvarez, Luis Alberto.**

BIBLIOGRAPHY

Oscar Arias Sánchez, *Grupos de presión en Costa Rica* (1971), and *¿Quién gobierna en Costa Rica?* (1976).

John Patrick Bell, "Political Power in Contemporary Costa Rica," in *Journal of Inter-American Studies and World Affairs* 20 (1978): 443–454.

Seth Rolbein, *Nobel Costa Rica* (1989).

Additional Bibliography

Cox, Vicki. *Oscar Arias Sánchez: Bringing Peace to Central America.* New York: Chelsea House, 2007.

Lehoucq, Fabrice Edouard. *Instituciones democráticas y conflictos políticos en Costa Rica.* Heredia, Costa Rica: EUNA, 1998.

JOHN PATRICK BELL

ARICA. Arica is a port city of 180,000 in Tarapacá Province, in the sparsely populated Atacama Desert of northern Chile. The first Europeans to pass through the region were those of the Diego de Almagro expedition. The town was founded by Spaniards in 1570 as San Marcos de Arica. The entrance to the bay is marked by El Morro peak.

During colonial times Arica was a main conduit between Lima and the silver mines of Upper Peru. In the 1680s piracy along the Pacific coast threatened shipping, causing Arica's importance to decline. Proclamation of intra-imperial free trade in 1778 gave Arica renewed vigor as a commercial way station.

Following independence, Arica was initially part of Peru and provided Bolivia a conduit to the sea. During the War of the Pacific (1879–1884), the city surrendered to the attacking Chileans on 7 June 1880, following a bloody siege. The Treaty of Ancón, signed on October 20, 1883, left Arica in Chilean hands; a future plebiscite was to determine Arica's ultimate disposition. Peru and Chile disputed ownership of the province until the United States mediated the Treaty of 1929, which confirmed Chilean possession and gave neighboring Tacna to Peru. The treaty also stipulated that transfer of Arica or other territory in the region to Bolivia required approval of both Peru and Chile, a condition that has led to ongoing and unsuccessful trinational negotiations ever since. Arica's cathedral was designed by Gustave Eiffel. The city is connected by railroad with Tacna in Peru and La Paz; it remains a free port for Bolivia.

See also **Ancón, Treaty of (1883); Chile: The Nineteenth Century; Peru: From the Conquest Through Independence; War of the Pacific.**

BIBLIOGRAPHY

Anaya, Ricardo. *Arica trinacional: Bolivia, Chile, Perú: Una fórmula de paz, integración y desarrollo.* La Paz: Los Amigos del Libro, 1987.

Dagnino, Vicente. *El correjimiento de Arica: 1535–1784.* Arica, Chile: Imprenta La Época, 1909.

St. John, Ronald Bruce. *Boundaries, Trade, and Seaports: Power Politics in the Atacama Desert.* Amherst: University of Massachusetts Press, 1992.

KENDALL W. BROWN

ARIDJIS, HOMERO (1940–). Homero Aridjis (b. 6 April 1940), Mexican writer. Like many of his contemporaries in Mexico, Aridjis has had a varied career, including journalism, diplomatic service, and teaching. Trained as a journalist, he was a member of a writing workshop directed by the noted Mexican short-story writer Juan José Arreola and was awarded fellowships by the Centro Mexicano de Escritores (Mexican Writers Center) and the Guggenheim Foundation.

Aridjis has written poetry and prose, much of it first published in Mexican literary journals and Sunday cultural supplements of newspapers and subsequently appearing in numerous collected works. His many volumes of poetry, among them *Antes del reino* (1963) and *Vivar para ver* (1977), focus on themes of love, life, and death, and are heavily charged with emotion. More recently he has attempted to create the "poema nuclear" (nuclear poem), modifying his use of language and including social and historical themes. As a prose writer of stories and novels, he combines narrative and poetic elements (*Mirándola dormir*, 1964, and *Perséfone*, 1967), autobiography (*El poeta niño*, 1971), and the historical (*1492, vida y tiempos de Juan Cabezón de Castilla*, 1985). Much of Aridjis's writing has been translated into English and other languages. In recent years, he has been actively involved with other intellectuals in the Grupo de los Cien (Group of 100), Mexico's foremost ecological movement.

See also **Literature: Spanish America.**

BIBLIOGRAPHY

Manuel Durán, "Música en sordina: Tres poetas mexicanos. Bonifaz Nuño, García Terrés, Aridjis," in *Plural*, no. 8 (1972): 29–31.

Merlin H. Forster, "Four Contemporary Mexican Poets: Marco Antonio Montes de Oca, Gabriel Zaid, José Emilio Pacheco, Homero Aridjis," in his *Tradition and Renewal: Essays on Twentieth-Century Latin American Literature and Culture* (1975).

Frank Dauster, "Poetas mexicanos nacidos en las décadas de 1920, 1930 y 1940," in *Revista Iberoamericana*, 55, nos. 148–149 (1989): 1161–1175.

Additional Bibliography

Anonymous. "Grupo de los Cien: Alianza Ecológica Latinoamericana." *Integración Latinoamericana* 17:178 (May 1992): 74-76.

Brayman, Matthew. "15 Minutes with Homer Aridjis." *Business Mexico* 13:4 (Apr 2003): 8-11.

GABRIELLA DE BEER

speare's *The Tempest* who in this short book becomes a symbol of the enlightening spirit with which the author aspires to enhance Latin American culture. Written in the aftermath of Spain's imperial collapse in the war of 1898 against the United States and addressed primarily to young Latin Americans, *Ariel* is both an idealistic call to cultural independence and a warning against the tendency toward utilitarian overconfidence that Rodó discerned in North American progressive materialism. The essay is presented as a scholarly final lecture by old Próspero (alluding to the protagonist of *The Tempest*), who exhorts his students as builders of the future to strive individually for standards of excellence. *Ariel* is less a social philosophy than a cultural manifesto, the elitist spirit and erudite style of which have variously been defended or attacked by Latin American readers and writers as Arielismo.

See also **Arielismo; Krausismo; Positivism; Rodó, José Enrique.**

BIBLIOGRAPHY

Alas, Leopold. "Clarín." Prologue to *Ariel* by José Enrique Rodó, 5th edition. Madrid: Espasa-Calpe, 1975.

González Echevarría, Roberto. "The Case of the Speaking Statue: *Ariel* and the Magisterial Rhetoric of the Latin American Essay." In his *The Voice of the Masters: Writing and Authority in Modern Latin American Literature*. Austin: University of Texas Press, 1985.

Fuentes, Carlos. Prologue to *Ariel* by José Enrique Rodó. Translated by Margaret Sayers Peden. Austin: University of Texas, 1988.

Miller, Nicola. "The 1890s–1900s." In her *In the Shadow of the State: Intellectuals and the Quest for National Identity in Twentieth-Century Latin America*, pp. 96–114. London and New York: Verso, 1999.

San Román, Gustavo *This America We Dream Of: Rodó and 'Ariel' One-Hundred Years On*. London: Institute for Latin American Studies, 2001.

Ward, Thomas. "Rodó y las 'jerarquías imperativas,'" In his *Resistencia cultural: La nación en el ensayo de las Américas*, pp. 72–85. Lima: Editorial Universitaria, Universidad Ricardo Palma, 2004.

PETER G. EARLE

ARIEL. *Ariel* is an influential essay by the Uruguayan writer José Enrique Rodó that appeared in 1900. The title alludes to a character in Shake-

ARIELISMO. *Arielismo* refers to an idealistic quality of Hispanic American thought. The term is a neologism derived from José Enrique Rodo's

Ariel (1900), an essay that advocates a harmonious synthesis of the finest attributes of Greco-Roman culture, the Judeo-Christian heritage, and modern (late-nineteenth-century) perspectives. In Latin American intellectual circles it has customarily been associated with elitism, spiritualist aesthetics, and high standards of excellence.

Arielismo has often been used to explain the contrast between refined intellectual activity and high culture on the one hand, and a more direct, pragmatic approach to Latin American problems on the other. Practical-minded critics of the tendency have recognized its value as a cultural ideal and educational stimulus but have considered its advocates to be out of touch with Latin America's most pressing political, social, and economic needs.

Arielismo has had few explicit defenders. However, important twentieth-century writings have shared or revised its spirit, among them: the Peruvian José de la Riva-Agüero's *Carácter de la literatura del Perú independiente* (1905) as well as his compatriot Francisco García Calderón's *Le Pérou contemporain: étude sociale* (1907), the Mexican Alfonso Reyes's *Visión de Anáhuac* (1917), the Venezuelan Mariano Picón-Salas's *Regreso de tres mundos* (1959), and the Dominican Pedro Henríquez Ureña's *Seis ensayos en busca de nuestra expresión* (1928). Its detractors have been more pointed in their reaction: for example, Alberto Zum Felde, *Proceso intelectual del Uruguay y crítica de su literatura* (1941), and Luis Alberto Sánchez, *Balance y liquidación del novecientos* (1941). In 1971 Roberto Fernández Retamar published *Calibán*, a socialist-oriented essay in which the leading roles in Rodó's work are reversed: Now Próspero, the imperialistic magician, symbolizes the United States, and the uncouth Calibán is made over to represent a victimized Latin America.

See also **Ariel; Darío, Rubén; Krausismo; Positivism; Rodó, José Enrique.**

BIBLIOGRAPHY

Aronna, Michael. *"Pueblos enfermos": The Discourse of Illness in the Turn-of-the-Century Spanish and Latin American Essay.* Chapel Hill: University of North Carolina Department of Romance Languages, 1999.

Crow, John A. "Ariel and Calibán." In his *The Epic of Latin America*, 4th edition. Berkeley: University of California Press, 1992.

Nuccetelli, Susana. "Latin Americans, North Americans and the Rest of the World." In her *Latin American Thought: Philosophical Problems and Arguments*, pp. 179–221. Boulder, CO: Westview Press, 2002.

Oviedo, José Miguel. "Bajo las alas de Ariel." In his *Breve historia del ensayo hispanoamericano*, pp. 45–62. Madrid: Alianza, 1990.

Rodríguez Monegal, Emir. "América/utopía: García Calderón el discípulo favorito de Rodó." *Cuadernos Hispanoamericanos* 417 (1985): 166–171.

Stabb, Martin S. "The Revolt against Scientism." In his *In Quest of Identity: Patterns in the Spanish American Essay of Ideas, 1890–1960* Chapel Hill: University of North Carolina Press, 1967.

Ward, Thomas. *La teoría literaria: Romanticismo, krausismo y modernismo ante la globalización industrial.* University of Mississippi: Romance Monographs no. 61, 2004; see pp. 70–91 and 127–138.

Zea, Leopoldo, and Hernán Tabeada, eds. *Arielismo y globalización.* Mexico: Fondo de Cultura Económica, 2000.

PETER G. EARLE

ARISMENDI, JUAN BAUTISTA (1775–1841).

Juan Bautista Arismendi (*b.* 1775; *d.* 23 July 1841), officer in the Venezuelan Emancipating Army. Arismendi was born in La Asunción on Margarita Island. At the commencement of the movement for emancipation from Spain, Arismendi took the pro-independence side and participated in the 1812 expedition to Guyana. He returned to Margarita Island following the expedition only to find it under the control of Coronel Pascual Martínez of the Spanish government. Arismendi's pro-independence leadership led to his arrest and imprisonment first in La Guaira and later on Margarita Island. During his imprisonment, Spanish authority was forcibly ousted and Arismendi was named governor of the island in 1813. That same year he traveled to Caracas to place himself in the service of Simón Bolívar, who put him in charge of the Barlovento campaign.

Arismendi returned to Margarita Island in 1814 and was named its commander in chief. In 1819 he served as vice president of the republic for a short time. Two years later he led his own armed contingent in the battle of Carabobo. He remained on Margarita Island and on more than one occasion during the Southern campaign resisted orders for his recruitment. In 1828 José Antonio Páez appointed him second in command of the army, and in 1830 he was an active participant in the movement that dissolved Gran Colombia. Arismendi was elected senator in the National Congress for the province of Margarita in 1835 and was reelected in 1839.

See also **Margarita.**

BIBLIOGRAPHY

Mariano De Briceño, *Historia de la Isla de Margarita: Biografías del General Juan Bautista Arismendi y de la Señora Luisa Cáceres de Arismendi* (1885).

Horacio Bianchi, *Juicio histórico sobre la vida y obra del General Juan Bautista Arismendi* (1941).

Francisco Javier Yánes, *Historia de Margarita y observaciones del General Francisco Esteban Gómez* (1948).

Additional Bibliography

Bencomo Barrios, Héctor. *El general en jefe Juan Bautista Arismendi: Una vida al servicio de Venezuela* Caracas: Fundación Polar, 2002.

INÉS QUINTERO

ARISMENDI, RODNEY (1913–1989).

Rodney Arismendi (*b.* 22 March 1913; *d.* 27 December 1989), leader of the Communist Party of Uruguay. Arismendi was born in the city of Río Branco in the department of Cerro Largo. He studied law in Montevideo, where he was a prominent student leader. During this period he joined the Communist Party, whose secretary general, Eugenio Gómez, had held the office since the party's inception. Arismendi took over for Gómez as secretary general in 1955 and held the office until 1989. As a journalist and director of the daily *Diario Popular,* he was forced into exile but was elected a representative to Parliament in 1946, and went on to serve a number of terms in the legislature. In 1973 Arismendi was imprisoned by the military regime and later deported; he lived for more than ten years in the Soviet Union. Returning to Uruguay in 1984, he was elected to the senate, an office he held until his death.

Arismendi was one of the principal pro-Soviet Marxist theorists in Latin America, publishing several books on ideological themes and playing an important role in the creation of the leftist Frente Amplio. After his death, he was replaced as secretary general of the Communist Party by Jaime Pérez, a former union leader.

See also **Uruguay, Political Parties: Communist Party.**

BIBLIOGRAPHY

Martin Weinstein, *Uruguay: Democracy at the Crossroads* (1988).

Gerardo Caetano and José Rilla, *Breve historia de la dictadura* (1991).

Additional Bibliography

Barros-Lémez, Alvaro. *Arismendi: Forjar el viento.* Montevideo: Monte Sexto, 1987.

JOSÉ DE TORRES WILSON

ARISTA, MARIANO (1802–1855). Mariano

Arista (*b.* 1802; *d.* 1855), president of Mexico (1851–1853). Arista enlisted as a cadet in the Provincial Regiment of Puebla at the age of fifteen. In June 1821 he joined the Army of the Three Guarantees under the leadership of Agustín de Iturbide to support the Plan of Iguala for autonomy and independence for Mexico. Arista continued to serve in the army, reaching the rank of brigadier general. On 8 June 1833 he rebelled against the radical reforms of President Valentín Gómez Farías, calling on General Antonio López de Santa Anna and the army to preserve the *fueros* (prerogatives) and properties of the regular and secular clergy. Exiled to the United States in November 1833, Arista was able to return to Mexico only after the triumph of the Plan of Cuernavaca, which provided the basis for Santa Anna's formation of a more conservative government. Arista served as a member of various military commissions before being named commanding general of the state of Tamaulipas in 1839. In 1846, Arista was called to lead the Army of the North. On 8 May 1846, at Palo Alto, Tamaulipas, Arista's forces were defeated by a U.S. army contingent under General Zachary Taylor in the first major battle of the war. The next day Arista retreated and turned over command to General Francisco Mejía. Arista served as minister of war from 12 June 1848 to 15 January 1851, on which date he assumed the office of president. He resigned on 6

January 1853 and moved to Europe. He died aboard a British ship en route from Portugal to France, where he hoped to obtain medical treatment. He was buried in Lisbon; his ashes were returned to Mexico in 1880.

See also **Mexico: 1810–1910.**

BIBLIOGRAPHY

Alberto María Carreño Escudero, *Jefes del ejército mexicano en 1847* (1914).

Charles L. Dufour, *The Mexican War: A Compact History, 1846–1848* (1968).

Moisés González Navarro, *Anatomía del poder en México, 1848–1853* (1977); *Diccionario Porrúa de historia, biografía y geografía de México,* 5th ed. (1986).

Additional Bibliography

Costeloe, Michael P. "Mariano Arista and the 1850 Election in Mexico." *Bulletin of Latin American Research* 18 (January 1999): 51–70.

D. F. STEVENS

ARISTIDE, JEAN-BERTRAND (1953–). Jean-Bertrand Aristide (b. July 15, 1953) was president of Haiti in 1991, 1994–1996, and 2001–2004. A onetime Roman Catholic priest, Aristide took office on February 7, 1991, as the country's first democratically elected president since Haitian independence in 1803. Ordained in 1982 and a supporter of liberation theology, he was hailed as a savior by Haiti's poverty-stricken masses but viewed with suspicion by the Haitian elite. Overthrown by a military coup seven months after his inauguration, a Aristide was restored to the presidency in 1994 by a U.S.-led invasion and completed his five-year term in 1996. Constitutionally barred from a second consecutive term, he was succeeded by René Préval, his former prime minister and protégé. Aristide returned to win a second term in a controversial 2000 election, running against six unknown candidates in a vote boycotted by Haiti's organized opposition and by international monitors, except for a small group from Caribbean nations.

Commencing his second term in February 2001, Aristide became increasingly authoritarian, creating his own version—known as *chimères*—of the reviled Tonton Macoute of the twenty-nine-year Duvalier dictatorship ending in 1986. National alienation grew. His base was eventually reduced to pockets of support in the slum neighborhoods of Port-au-Prince, the capital, and the peasant countryside. By late 2003 his position had become untenable against a fractured opposition of university students, the business community, and former members of the Haitian army, dissolved by Aristide in 1991. In the pre-dawn hours of February 29, 2004, Aristide fled the country aboard a U.S. government plane for eventual South African exile. Replaced by a two-year transitional government, new elections were held in February 2006, returning Préval to the presidency and leaving open the prospect for Aristide's eventual return.

See also **Duvalier, Jean-Claude; Haiti; Tonton Macoutes.**

BIBLIOGRAPHY

Works by Aristide

In *The Parish of the Poor: Writings from Haiti,* ed. and trans. Amy Wilentz. Maryknoll, NY: Orbis Books, 1990.

Jean-Bertrand Aristide: An Autobiography, ed. Linda Maloney. Maryknoll, NY: Orbis Books, 1993.

Other Sources

Deibert, Michael. *Notes from the Last Testament: The Struggle for Haiti.* New York: Seven Stories Press, 2005.

Dupuy, Alex. *The Prophet and Power: Jean-Bertrand Aristide, Haiti, the International Community, and Haiti.* Lanham, MD: Rowman and Littlefield, 2007.

Fatton, Robert Jr. *Haiti's Predatory Republic: The Unending Transition to Democracy.* Boulder, CO: Lynn Rienner Publishers, 2002.

Griffiths, Leslie. *The Aristide Factor: A Biography of Haiti's First Democratically Elected President.* Oxford, UK: Lion Publishing, 1997.

DON BOHNING

ARIZONA. Arizona, a colonial territory of Spain (until 1821) and part of the Mexican state of Sonora (until 1853). Jesuit missions, slowly expanding north from Sinaloa after 1630, reached southern Arizona by 1700, led by the noted missionary Father Eusebio Kino. Until the cessation of hostilities with the Apaches in the 1770s, Hispanic population was limited to the missions of San Xavier del Bac and Tumacácori, and to the presidio of Tubac (moved to

Tucson in 1776). Thereafter, the Hispanic population slowly expanded along the Santa Cruz valley and then east to the San Pedro valley, peaking at well over 1,000 in the 1820s. However, the breakdown of the presidial system (including cessation of gift rations to the Apaches) and of the missions (administered by the Franciscans after the Jesuit expulsion of 1767) led to renewed Apache raiding after 1830 that forced a retreat of the Mexican frontier in southern Arizona. When U.S. troops occupied Tucson in late 1846, Mexicans remained only there and at Tubac. In 1848, Apaches forced the complete abandonment of the latter. Through purchase under the Treaty of La Mesilla (December 30, 1853), southern Arizona was joined to the rest of Arizona as a territory of the United States. Arizona remains a site of contention between the United States and Mexico. Mexican immigration into the United States grew rapidly beginning in the 1980s, and the Arizona desert is one of the main crossing points. Many U.S. citizens in Arizona protest this labor movement, but the Mexican government and U.S. immigrants-rights groups argue that the United States should expand legal visa options so that Mexican workers do not continue to cross the dangerous Arizona desert.

See also **United States-Mexico Border.**

BIBLIOGRAPHY

Jay Wagoner, *Early Arizona, Prehistory to Civil War* (1975).

John L. Kessell, *Friars, Soldiers, and Reformers: Hispanic Arizona and the Sonoran Mission Frontier 1767–1856* (1976).

David J. Weber, *The Mexican Frontier, 1821–1846: The American Southwest Under Mexico* (1982).

Additional Bibliography

Weber, David J., and Jorge Ferreiro. *La frontera española en América del Norte.* México: Fondo de Cultura Económica, 2000.

STUART F. VOSS

ARLT, ROBERTO (1900–1942).

Roberto Arlt (*b.* 2 April 1900; *d.* 26 July 1942), Argentine writer. Born in Buenos Aires, Arlt's writing was one of the major critical (re)discoveries of the halcyon, countercultural period between the demise of Juan Perón (1955) and the military coup of 1966. One dimension of the interest in Arlt was a reaction against the emerging international monumentalization of Jorge Luis Borges. Arlt evoked several components of Argentine culture that were judged to be absent in Borges: he was of immigrant extraction; he was unlettered and unencumbered by an immense bookish learning; his literature centered on the urban proletariat, with a heavy emphasis on the socially marginal, misfits, and the aberrant; he was unconcerned by coherent ideologies and, indeed, often seemed to relish the incoherent and the contradictory; and he exemplified the practice of literature, not as an intellectual pastime, but as gainful employment. While today it may seem specious to promote a categoric disjunction between Borges and Arlt, Arlt was championed as an authentic voice of all of the gritty aspects of the Argentine sociopolitical body that the aloof Borges—at least in his world-literature embodiment—seemed to deny. Moreover, in novels like *Los siete locos* (1929; *The Seven Madmen*, 1984), dramas written for the populist theater, such as *Trescientos millones* (1932), and in the hundreds of newspaper columns that constitute a veritable mosaic of the underbelly of the Buenos Aires proletariat and petite bourgeoisie in the watershed years of the Great Depression, Arlt moved the literary registers of Spanish away from the rhetorical and poetic models of modernism and other European standards (including ossified academic norms) toward the beginnings of a true urban colloquiality in Argentine literature, one perhaps less sociolinguistically authentic than it is emblematically authentic. He died in Buenos Aires.

See also **Borges, Jorge Luis; Literature: Spanish America.**

BIBLIOGRAPHY

David William Foster, *Currents in the Contemporary Argentine Novel* (1975), pp. 20–45.

Aden Hayes, *Roberto Arlt, la estrategia de su ficción* (1981).

Enrique Giordano, *La teatralización de la obra dramática, de Florencio Sánchez a Roberto Arlt* (1982); *Review* (Center for Inter-American Relations), no. 31 (1982), special issue devoted to Arlt.

Gerardo Mario Goloboff, *Genio y figura de Roberto Arlt* (1988).

Additional Bibliography

Martínez, Elizabeth Coonrod. *Before the Boom: Latin American Revolutionary Novels of the 1920s.* Lanham, MD: University Press of America, 2001.

Morales Saravia, José, Barbara Schuchard, and Wolfgang Matzat. *Roberto Arlt: Una modernidad argentina.* Madrid: Iberoamericana and Frankfurt am Main: Vervuert, 2001.

Rosenberg, Fernando J. *The Avant-Garde and Geopolitics in Latin America.* Pittsburgh, PA: University of Pittsburgh Press, 2006.

DAVID WILLIAM FOSTER

ARMADA DEL MAR DEL SUR. Armada del Mar del Sur, a small Pacific fleet designed by the Spanish crown to protect Spanish settlements along the Pacific coast of Tierra Firme (South America) and to convoy Spanish shipping in the Pacific. Its construction was originally prompted by the incursions of English, Dutch, and French traders and pirates, which began in the 1570s. Its most important convoy duty was accompanying the merchant fleet that carried Peruvian silver from Callao to Panama in Tierra Firme for the Portobelo fair and returned laden with European goods.

The armada normally consisted of between four and six warships—usually two to four galleons of 600 to 1,000 tons each and a similar number of smaller vessels of 80 to 100 tons. This nucleus was often supplemented in times of distress by various hastily converted merchant vessels.

Despite frequent complaints about poor quality and high costs, viceregal authorities relied on the colonial shipyards at Guayaquil to build the vessels. Given the crown's reluctance to support Pacific defenses, the viceregal treasury in Lima struggled to finance the construction and maintenance of this small defense force. As viceregal finances began to deteriorate by the late seventeenth century, however, the burden of defending the Pacific increasingly fell on private commercial interests.

See also **Fleet System: Colonial Spanish America.**

BIBLIOGRAPHY

The best survey is Pablo E. Pérez-Mallaína and Bibiano Torres Ramírez, *La armada del mar del sur* (1987). Two important articles are Peter T. Bradley, "Maritime Defence of the Viceroyalty of Peru (1600–1700)," in *The Americas* 36, no. 2 (October 1979): 155–175, and Lawrence A. Clayton, "Local Initiative and Finance in Defense of the Viceroyalty of Peru: The Development of Self-Reliance," in *Hispanic American Historical Review*

54, no. 2 (May 1974): 284–304. The best general surveys on Pacific defenses and foreign intrusions are Peter T. Bradley, *The Lure of Peru: Maritime Intrusion into the South Sea, 1598–1701* (1989), and Guillermo Lohmann Villena, *Historia marítima del Perú*, vol. 4, *Siglos XVII y XVIII* (1973).

Additional Bibliography

Goodman, David C. *Spanish Naval Power, 1589-1665: Reconstruction and Defeat.* Cambridge, U.K.: Cambridge University Press, 1997.

KENNETH J. ANDRIEN

ARMED FORCES. The armed forces in Latin America, usually consisting of an army, navy, air force, and often a national police force, have a varied history, but have played an important role in national political life throughout the continent. In the majority of Latin American nations, militaries played a central role in consolidating national identity, although in countries such as Colombia they have played a more limited role. Latin American militaries in many countries enjoy economic, social, and political privileges derived from their postcolonial role in defending newly independent nations as well as establishing domestic order as mandated by many national constitutions. In part as a result of these multiple roles, almost all armed forces in the hemisphere have had historic difficulties balancing their mandate for national defense with respect for civilian oversight and democratic process. As of 2007, armed forces in the Americas ranged from nearly 370,000 members (Brazil) to less than 8,500 members (Honduras), with many having forces of approximately 100,000 (such as Argentina, 74,000; Chile, 72,000; Peru, 113,000; Venezuela, 92,000).

The struggle to establish national military institutions lasted throughout the nineteenth century. Spanish and Portuguese colonial administrations maintained minimal military presence in the Americas. With the exception of major coastal ports and along frontier regions established during the reforms of the eighteenth century and numbering approximately 23,000 American-born members by 1800 (compared with only 6,000 regular Spanish army soldiers), disorganized regional militias played a central role in independence conflicts, sowing the seeds for later military governments and conflicts. Class conflict and elite rivalries over control of new national infrastructures were often channeled through violent clashes between liberal and conservative parties, as in the Chilean civil war of 1891, in which the Conservative Party congress, supported by the navy, fought the Liberal Party president, allied with the army. In many countries, including Peru and Brazil, postindependence leaders were largely military officers; many countries including Mexico and Colombia experienced significant postindependence upheaval, including violent regional rebellions.

Historically, Latin American militaries have been involved in relatively few international conflicts. The century following independence was characterized by three major conflicts: the War of the Triple Alliance (also called the Paraguayan War, 1864–1870), in which Paraguay battled allied Argentina, Brazil, and Uruguay; the War of the Pacific (1879–1884), in which Chile battled allied Bolivia and Peru; and the Chaco War (1932–1935) between Paraguay and Bolivia. Longstanding border tensions between Ecuador and Peru erupted in 1941, 1981, and 1995; tensions over immigration culminated in the so-called Soccer War between Honduras and El Salvador in 1969. The Argentine conflict with Great Britain over the Falkland Islands (Malvinas) played an important role in both countries' domestic politics in 1982.

Latin America played only a limited role in the international conflicts of the twentieth century; most countries remained largely neutral during World War II, siding with the United States only after Pearl Harbor and considerable diplomatic pressure. Only Brazil and Colombia sent troops to fight in Europe, and only Colombia participated in U.S.-led actions in the Korean War. One notable exception was Cuba, which played a major role in the Central African wars of independence; the small Caribbean nation sent more than 100,000 troops between 1975 and 1988.

Foreign military advisors played a critical role in developing Latin American military institutions. Prussian missions trained forces in Argentina, Bolivia, and Chile; Chile in turn was involved in training in Colombia, Ecuador, and El Salvador, and taught Central American, Venezuelan, and Paraguayan officers in the Santiago military school. French officers offered training in Peru and Brazil;

Swiss, Spanish, and Italian military delegations were also involved in training operations. Following World War II, the United States became the major influence on hemispheric military forces. The Inter-American Treaty of Reciprocal Assistance (Rio Treaty) was signed in 1947, followed by the Mutual Security Act of 1951; these documents laid the groundwork for U.S. cooperation with Latin American armies. The United States continues to be the primary influence in the region, providing significant resources and training (at times training more than 80,000 soldiers and police per year). Since the United States vacated Howard Air Force Base in Panama in 1999 the United States no longer maintains any major bases in the region, but has constructed Forward Operating Locations from which air and sea operations are launched in Ecuador, Aruba, Curacao, and El Salvador, primarily targeting narcotics traffic.

Military professionalization and modernization efforts involved increasingly sophisticated weapons, specialized academies for advanced technological training, and standardized measures of accomplishment intended to promote merit rather than family connections. Universal conscription was debated and implemented in most countries, in part to reverse the trend of small standing armies at the turn of the twentieth century (when Peru, for example, had only 7,000 soldiers). Prior to this time, and in some cases (particularly in wartime) well into the late twentieth century, military recruitment was characterized by impressment (forced military service) in which young men were rounded up and forced into the ranks. Obligatory military service became a primary vehicle for many poor and indigenous men to participate in national life and citizenship.

In the early twenty-first century many countries in Latin America have mandatory military conscription; the vast majority (including Mexico, Ecuador, Peru, Chile, Venezuela, Brazil, Bolivia, and Paraguay) actually conscript only a percentage of all eligible men in systems that are highly vulnerable to corruption, contributing to the disproportional representation of young indigenous and poor men. In Colombia, high-school graduates are required to serve less time and are not required to participate in combat operations. Since the end of the Central American wars, Nicaragua and Honduras

Mexican army parade, Mexico City, Mexico, 1988. After successfully helping their respective countries achieve independence from colonial rule, many military forces in Latin America continue to exercise control over national politics. © LIBRA TAYLOR/CORBIS

have voluntary military service and Guatemala and El Salvador do not fully enforce their standing laws on universal conscription. The military remains a primary mode of social mobility for lower-class men. Women play very small roles in official hierarchies and on active duty, but have played important if understudied roles in institutional support services.

The technological advances of World War I weaponry inspired military lobbying for expanded budgets, and in part generated the wave of military intervention in politics throughout the 1930s. Political corruption rewarded politically active officers who, frustrated by limitations on institutional and fiscal power imposed by reformist democratic governments, took power (often later consolidated through electoral fraud and corruption) in personalistic military regimes in Paraguay (Alfredo Stroessner, 1954–1989), Peru (Manuel Odría, 1948–1956), Venezuela (Marcos Pérez Jiménez, 1948–1958), El Salvador (Maximiliano Hernández Martínez, 1931–1944), Nicaragua (Anastasio Somoza Garcia, 1937–1956), and Cuba (Fulgencio Batista, 1952–1959). Among the exceptions to this trend were Colombia's Gustavo Rojas Pinilla (1953–1957) who was put into and removed from power by a coalition of civilian elites in an effort to reduce partisan violence. Mexico instituted successful civilian control of the military in the post-revolutionary period, and in 1948 Costa Rica abolished its military, relying instead on a Police Guard.

The growing strength of military institutions included control of significant economic sectors that developed into entrenched institutional interests. By the 1960s a new wave of military governments swept the continent, often headed by a series of chiefs of staff with military control of many governmental posts and relying on civilian support from within the elite class in the Catholic Church, businesses, and the government; military governments took power in Peru (1962), Brazil (1964), Argentina (1966), Ecuador (1972), Uruguay (1973), and Chile (1973). The majority pushed economic restructuring favoring businesses and international investment with the exception of Peru, where the military government promoted populist reforms. During the 1980s, some Central American and Andean militaries battled insurgencies, leading to increased power for military forces.

With the transition to democracy throughout the hemisphere, civilian rule returned to countries with military governments, first in Ecuador in 1979, followed by Chile in 1989, and insurgent warfare ended with military defeat (Peru) and peace accords (1989 in Nicaragua, 1991 in El Salvador, and 1996 in Guatemala). Central American military forces have declined significantly in their size and influence, although the process of democratization remains incomplete. In Guatemala, for example, intelligence institutions are not yet completely under civilian control; military involvement in law enforcement violates the peace accord's restriction of the military role to external defense; and cooperation by the military with civilian courts investigating and prosecuting human rights violations and common crimes is still weak. Many military forces continue to enjoy significant political and economic independence and many legal privileges. Militaries and civilians alike continue to struggle with the legacy of human rights abuses during the second half of the twentieth century. While many countries established commissions with varying mandates to clarify events and responsibilities during military governments (including El Salvador, Guatemala, Uruguay, Brazil, Chile, Argentina, and Peru), few military officers went to trial. Increasing international acceptance of human rights norms has opened to the doors to ongoing investigations, such as the arrest of General Pinochet in 1998 and the reversal of military immunity laws in Argentina. Armed forces throughout the region continue to exercise considerable autonomy in allocating military budgets, and many are significant economic players in their own right, controlling banking, commercial, and agricultural investments.

With the exception of Colombia, Latin American militaries no longer face the threat of insurgencies that were the hallmark of the cold war period, leading to efforts to redefine the military mission. Issues including counter-narcotics efforts, organized crime, migration, gangs, and terrorism are increasingly being handled by military forces. Latin American militaries have become active participants in international humanitarian and peacekeeping missions, motivated by opportunities for both individual career advancement and institutional prestige. These efforts date back to participation by Brazilian and Colombian battalions in the first United Nations Emergency Force in the Suez Canal sector and the Sinai peninsula from 1956 to 1967. Argentina includes peacekeeping support as one of the military's basic missions, and established the Argentine Centre for Joint Training in Peacekeeping Operations (CAECOPAZ) in 1995; Argentine troops have participated in missions in more than eleven countries. As increased regional integration becomes the norm through trade and other cooperative agreements, regional security operations have increased, such as joint training exercises by forces from Brazil, Uruguay, Chile, and Argentina.

See also **Rio Treaty (1947); Pérez Jiménez, Marcos; Stroessner, Alfredo; Batista y Zaldívar, Fulgencio; Hernández Martínez, Maximiliano; Human Rights; Odría, Manuel Apolinario; Rojas Pinilla, Gustavo; Somoza García, Anastasio.**

BIBLIOGRAPHY

Atlas Comparativo de la Defensa en América Latina. Buenos Aires, Argentina: Red de Seguridad y Defensa de América Latina, 2007. Also available from http://www.resdal.org/libros/Archivo/atlas-libro07.htm.

Beattie, Peter. 2001. *The Tribute of Blood: Army, Honor, Race, and Nation in Brazil, 1864–1945.* Durham, NC: Duke University Press, 2001.

Fitch, J. Samuel. *The Armed Forces and Democracy in Latin America.* Baltimore: Johns Hopkins University Press, 1998.

Pion-Berlin, David, ed. *Civil-Military Relations in Latin America: New Analytical Perspectives.* Chapel Hill: University of North Carolina Press, 2001.

Silva, Patricio, ed. *The Soldier and the State in South America.* New York: Palgrave Macmillan, 2001.

WINIFRED TATE

ARMENDÁRIZ, JOSÉ DE (1670–?).

José de Armendáriz (*b.* 1670; *d.*?) marquis of Castelfuerte and viceroy of Peru, 1724–1736. A native of Rivagorza, Spain, Armendáriz pursued a military career from a young age, serving in Flanders, Catalonia, Naples, Portugal, and Villaviciosa. Captain-general of Guipúzcoa when named viceroy of Peru in 1723, he was probably the most distinguished Spanish military officer to serve in South America.

Armendáriz proved energetic and firm, unlike his predecessor, Fray Diego Morcillo, but was neither an innovator nor a reformer. He stepped up surveillance along the Pacific coast to reduce smuggling by foreign vessels and limited the duration of the Portobelo fairs to deter contraband. Armendáriz also devoted great energy to strengthening colonial defenses throughout the continent. He captured and executed José de Antequera, the former *oidor* (judge) of Charcas, who had installed himself as an independent governor of Paraguay. The execution touched off a serious tumult in Lima, which Armendáriz crushed. Because the guards killed two Franciscan partisans of Antequera in suppressing the uprising, the clergy harshly criticized the viceroy, but the crown fully supported him. He also acted swiftly and severely to defeat the mestizo rebellion of Alejo Calatayud in Cochabamba. Armendáriz attempted to curb the corruption of provincial governors (*corregidores*) and restrict the sale of *aguardiente* (distilled liquor), with little success.

Promoted in 1729 to captain-general, the highest Spanish military rank, Armendáriz received the great honor of membership in the Order of the Golden Fleece upon his return to Spain. He then commanded the regiment of royal guards.

BIBLIOGRAPHY

"Relación del estado de los reynos del Perú que hace el Exmo. Señor Don José Armendaris, marqués de Castel-Fuerte, Á su sucesor el marqués de Villagarcía, en el año de 1736," in Manuel A. Fuentes, ed., *Memorias de los virreyes que han gobernado el Perú*, vol. 3 (1859), pp. 1–369.

J. A. De Lavalle, "La ejecución de Antequera," in *El Ateneo* 2 (1886): 23–35, 66–80.

Rubén Vargas Ugarte, *Historia general del Perú*, vol. 6 (1966), pp. 121–190.

Additional Bibliography

Moreno Cebrián, Alfredo. *El virreinato del marqués de Castelfuerte, 1724-1736: El primer intento borbónico por reformar el Perú*. Madrid, España: Editorial Catriel, 2000.

Moreno Cebrián, Alfredo, and Núria Salai Vila. *El "premio" de ser virrey: Los intereses públicos y privados del gobierno virreinal en el Perú de Felipe V*. Madrid: Consejo Superior de Investigaciones Científicas, Instituto de Historia, 2004.

KENDALL W. BROWN

ARMENDÁRIZ, PEDRO (1912–1963).

Pedro Armendáriz (*b*. 1912; *d*. 18 June 1963), Mexican actor. Born in Mexico City, Armendáriz attended school in San Antonio, Texas, and completed his studies at the California Polytechnic Institute. He worked as a journalist in the United States before returning to Mexico in 1934. Armendáriz debuted in the film *María Elena* (1935) and went on to appear in more than 100 movies. He was a leading actor with the famed team of director Emilio "El Indio" Fernández. Armendáriz's striking screen presence made him one of the most popular leading stars of Mexican cinema. His most memorable films are *Distinto Amanecer* (1943), *María Candelaria* (1943), *Maclovia* (1948), *La perla* (1946), and *Ena-morada* (1947). He was also cast in several Hollywood films, including *Fort Apache* (1948) and *From Russia with Love* (1963). He died in Los Angeles.

See also **Cinema: From the Silent Film to 1990.**

BIBLIOGRAPHY

Luis Reyes De La Maza, *El cine sonoro en México* (1973).

E. Bradford Burns, *Latin American Cinema: Film and History* (1975).

Carl J. Mora, *Mexican Cinema: Reflections of a Society: 1896–1980* (1982).

John King, *Magical Reels: A History of Cinema in Latin America* (1990).

Additional Bibliography

García, Gustavo. *Pedro Armendáriz*, 3 vols. Mexico: Clio, 1997.

DAVID MACIEL

ARMIJO, MANUEL (1801–1853). Manuel

Armijo (*b*. 1801; *d*. 1853), governor of New Mexico (1836–1846). Armijo's administration was notable mainly for its opposition to Anglo-American incursions. He sought to control the illegal activities of American trappers, and in 1841 he led the Mexican forces that defeated a group of Texans, led by General Hugh McLeod, who sought to conquer New Mexico. In 1846 Armijo led the Mexican army that opposed the invasion of the province by General Stephen W. Kearny. In the face of superior U.S. forces, he abandoned the defense of the territory and fled to Mexico, where he remained.

See also **New Mexico.**

BIBLIOGRAPHY

Ralph Emerson Twitchell, *The Leading Facts of New Mexican History,* 5 vols. (1911–1917), and *The Conquest of Santa Fe, 1846,* edited by Bill Tate (1967).

Additional Bibliography

Lecompte, Janet. "Manuel Armijo, George Wilkins Kendall, and the Baca-Caballero Conspiracy." *New Mexico Historical Review* 59 (January 1984): 49–65.

Tyler, Daniel. "New Mexico in the 1820's: The First Administration of Manuel Armijo." Ph.D. diss., University of New Mexico, 1970.

RICHARD GRISWOLD DEL CASTILLO

ARNAZ, DESI (1917–1986). Desi Arnaz (*b.* 2 March 1917; *d.* 2 December 1986), Cuban bandleader, actor, and pioneer television producer. Born Desiderio Alberto Arnaz y Acha in Santiago de Cuba to an influential family, Arnaz and his father went into exile in Miami with the overthrow of President Gerardo Machado in 1933. Discovered there by Xavier Cugat, he joined the Cugat band for a six-month tour. He then returned to Miami and, with his own band, introduced the conga line to the United States, and started a national dance craze. During the 1940s, he appeared on Broadway and made several feature films. While filming *Too Many Girls* in 1940, he met Lucille Ball, marrying her the same year. They were divorced in 1960.

Although popularly known for his role as Ball's husband in the television show *I Love Lucy,* his most important contributions came as the guiding force behind its production company, Desilu. His many innovations created the presentation and format of the situation comedy (sitcom) as it is known today and began the practice of reruns. Desilu bought its own studio and became the most important independent production house in the industry, producing many of the successful 1950s television comedies. Arnaz retired in the early 1960s. He died in Del Mar, California.

See also **Radio and Television.**

BIBLIOGRAPHY

Arnaz chronicled his own life through his divorce from Lucille Ball in his autobiography, *A Book* (1976). His contributions to the music industry are discussed in John S. Roberts, *The Latin Tinge: The Impact of Latin American Music in the United States* (1979). Innovations to the television industry are discussed in William Boddy, *Fifties Television: The Industry and its Critics* (1990).

Additional Bibliography

Sandoval-Sánchez, Alberto. *José Can You See?: Latinos On and Off Broadway.* Madison: University of Wisconsin Press, 1999.

JACQUELYN BRIGGS KENT

ARNS, PAULO EVARISTO (1921–). Paulo Evaristo Arns (*b.* 14 September 1921), archbishop of São Paulo, Brazil (1970–). A Franciscan priest born in Forquilhinha, Santa Catarina, Arns was a relatively unknown figure until he was named auxiliary bishop of São Paulo in 1966. Like most of the hierarchy, Arns supported the 1964 military coup, but after being named archbishop in November 1970, he became a trenchant critic of the military government and one of Brazil's outstanding voices on behalf of human rights. A venerated public figure, Arns denounced the widespread use of torture. In January 1972 he created the Archdiocesan Justice and Peace Commission, which became known for its efforts to defend human rights. In his pastoral work, Arns supported Christian base communities, which became controversial in the 1970s and 1980s because of some activists' support for the labor movement and the Workers' Party. In 1973, he was named a cardinal.

After becoming one of Brazil's most prominent public figures in the 1970s, Arns fell out of favor with the Vatican and was less visible in the 1980s. When John Paul II became pope in 1978, Arns and the archdiocese of São Paulo came under careful scrutiny. In 1980, the pope asked Arns to write a report explaining and defending the church's overt support for a major strike that had taken place that year. Four years later, the Vatican undertook an investigation of seminars in dioceses identified with liberation theology, including the archdiocese of São Paulo, which was admonished to avoid portraying Christ as a revolutionary. In 1989, the pope dismantled and subdivided the archdiocese, which had previously been the largest in the world in terms of its Catholic population. Arns remained archbishop of São Paulo, but it was now a smaller archdiocese, from which most of the poor areas where base communities had flourished were excised. During the 1990s, his archdiocese actively promoted social services and lent help to those suffering from AIDS. In 1998, Arnes retired and became an archbishop emeritus. However, he continued to be a voice against poverty and inequality, critiquing even the leftist government of Lula for not aggressively addressing these matters.

See also **Acquired Immune Deficiency Syndrome (AIDS); Brazil, Political Parties: Workers Party (PT); Catholic Church: The Modern Period; John Paul II, Pope; Liberation Theology.**

BIBLIOGRAPHY

Paulo Evaristo Arns, *Em defensa direitos humanos* (1978).

Helcion Ribeiro, ed., *Paulo Evaristo Arns* (1989).

W. E. Hewitt, *Base Christian Communities and Social Change in Brazil (1991)*, esp. pp. 28–37.

Additional Bibliography

Serbin, Ken P. *Secret Dialogues: Church-State Relations, Torture, and Social Justice in Authoritarian Brazil.* Pittsburgh, PA: University of Pittsburgh Press, 2000.

Sousa, Jessie Jane Vieira de. *Círculos operários: A Igreja Católica e o mundo do trabalho no Brasil.* Rio de Janeiro: Editora UFRJ, 2002.

Vásquez, Manuel A. *The Brazilian Popular Church and the Crisis of Modernity.* Cambridge; New York: Cambridge University Press, 1998.

SCOTT MAINWARING

AROSEMENA, FLORENCIO HARMODIO (1872–1945).

Florencio Harmodio Arosemena (*b.* 17 September 1872; *d.* 30 August 1945), a civil engineer and president of Panama

(1928–1931). Arosemena presided over one of the most corrupt periods in Panamanian history. His only previous political involvement had been a brief period as a councilman in the Panama City government. He became president largely as a result of the manipulations of President Rodolfo Chiari (1924–1928). He and his cronies lined their pockets and used their offices for their own personal businesses. He was overthrown on 2 January 1931 by the nationalistic organization *Acción Comunal.* It was the first time since its separation from Colombia that a constitutionally elected government of Panama had been overthrown.

See also **Panama.**

BIBLIOGRAPHY

Walter La Feber, *The Panama Canal: The Crisis in Historical Perspective* (1978).

Additional Bibliography

Arosemena, Bey Mario and Jorge Conte Porras. *Florencio Harmodio Arosemena, 1872–1945.* Panama, 1982.

JUAN MANUEL PÉREZ

AROSEMENA, JUAN DEMÓSTENES

(1879–1939). Juan Demóstenes Arosemena (*b.* 24 June 1879; *d.* 16 December 1939), jurist, teacher, journalist, member of the Panamanian Academy of History, and president of Panama (1936–1939). Arosemena had a long history of public service. In 1912 he was named chief justice by President Belisario Porras, who appointed him governor of the province of Colón in 1922. He became secretary of foreign relations in the administration of Florencio Harmodio Arosemena (1928–1931).

In 1936 he was the candidate for president of the National Revolutionary Party, which his younger brother, Arnulfo, had helped to organize. He was elected with the backing of President Harmodio Arias Madrid (1932–1936). He died before his term expired and was succeeded by Augusto S. Boyd. Arosemena's regime was basically a caretaker government, paving the way for Arnulfo Arias's ascension to power in 1940.

See also **Panama.**

BIBLIOGRAPHY

Manuel María Alba C., *Cronología de los gobernantes de Panamá, 1510–1967* (1967).

Walter La Feber, *The Panama Canal: The Crisis in Historical Perspective* (1978).

Jorge Conte Porras, *Diccionario biográfico ilustrado de Panamá*, 2d ed. (1986).

JUAN MANUEL PÉREZ

AROSEMENA, JUSTO (1817–1896).

Justo Arosemena (*b.* 1817; *d.* 1896), Panamanian intellectual and statesman. At sixteen he was awarded a bachelor's degree in humanities from the College of San Bartolomé, Colombia. In 1837 he was awarded a doctorate in law by the University of Magdalena. Arosemena spent most of his life in government, serving as minister of foreign relations (1848–1849), speaker of the Chamber of Deputies of the Colombian Congress (1852), senator, president of the Constitutional Convention of Río Negro (1863), and the first president of the Federal State of Panama (1855).

He wrote extensively on law and politics and was a prominent exponent of European liberal ideas. He belonged to the radical faction of the Liberal Party, the Golgotha. Arosemena believed that freedom had to reach everyone in society and that this required sovereignty. He favored autonomy for the isthmus. Arosemena envisioned the potential economic benefits that could be derived from an interoceanic canal, but he warned against foreign domination. Although he admired the U.S. political system, he spoke against U.S. intervention in other countries, particularly after the Mexican War (1846–1848). His most important works are *Examen sobre la franca comunicación entre los dos océanos por el istmo de Panamá* (1846), *Estudios constitucionales* (1852), and *El Estado Federal de Panamá* (1855).

See also **Colombia, Political Parties: Liberal Party.**

BIBLIOGRAPHY

José Dolores Moscote, *La vida ejemplar de Justo Arosemena* (1956).

Octavio Méndez Pereira, *Justo Arosemena*, 2d ed. (1970).

Additional Bibliography

Aparicio, Fernando. *Liberalismo, federalismo y nación: Justo Arosemena en su contexto histórico.* Panama: Editorial Portobelo Instituto del Canal de Panamá y Estudios Internacionales, 1997.

Barraza Arriola, Marco Antonio. *Antología de escritores del istmo centroamericano* 2nd ed. San Tecla, El Salvador: Clásicos Roxsil, 2003.

Dolores Moscote, José, and Enrique J. Arce. *La vida ejemplar de Justo Arosemena.* Panama: Autoridad del Canal de Panamá, 1999.

JUAN MANUEL PÉREZ

AROSEMENA, PABLO (1836–1920).

Pablo Arosemena (*b.* 1836; *d.* 29 August 1920), Panamanian politician and president (1910–1912) and an ardent supporter of classical nineteenth-century liberalism. Arosemena held many important political posts during his long political life. He was attorney general, president of the Sovereign State of Panama in 1875 and 1885 (on both occasions overthrown by the Colombian army), and in 1880 he was elected second vice president to the Colombian presidency. Arosemena continued to be active in politics after Panama's separation from Colombia. In 1904 he became president of the National Constituent Assembly. He served as Panama's president from September 1910 to October 1912, having been appointed by the National Assembly to finish the term of José Domingo de Obaldía following his death. Arosemena succeeded Carlos Antonio Mendoza, who temporarily had assumed the presidency immediately following Obaldía's death.

See also **Panama.**

BIBLIOGRAPHY

Ernesto De Jesús Castillero Reyes, *Historia de Panamá*, 7th ed. (1962).

Gustavo A. Mellander, *The United States in Panamanian Politics: The Intriguing Formative Years* (1971).

Additional Bibliography

Arosemena, Pablo. *Estudios.* Prologue by Jacqueline West de Cochez. Panama: Kiwanis International, 1982.

"Quién era Pablo Arosemena." *Revista Cultural Lotería* 431 (July-August 2000): 103–120.

JUAN MANUEL PÉREZ

AROSEMENA GÓMEZ, OTTO (1925–1984).

Otto Arosemena Gómez (*b.* 19 July 1925; *d.* 20 April 1984), president of Ecuador (1966–1968). A native of Guayaquil who received his law degree from that city's public university, Arosemena entered local politics. Serving as president of the Guayas provincial electoral tribunal (1952) and then as a deputy in the National Congress, he became a prominent businessman as well as a lawyer. He was twice chosen as senator representing coastal commercial organizations. Originally a Liberal, Arosemena broke away to organize his personalistic Coalición Institucionalista Democrática (CID) on 2 February 1965. He was one of three CID members in the 1966 Constituent Assembly, where he made a pact with the Right and was chosen provisional president of the nation (November 1967).

Arosemena remained in office for twenty months, during which a new constitution was adopted and national elections were held. His government was cautious in the area of domestic policy, although Arosemena was outspoken in foreign affairs. Hostility to U.S. policy led him to withhold his signature from the official declaration adopted by the 1967 conference of hemispheric presidents in Punta del Este, Uruguay. He subsequently criticized the Alliance for Progress and after a public exchange with the U.S. ambassador, ordered his expulsion from Ecuador. Once out of office, Arosemena sought to build the CID, but with limited success. His party backed the rightist presidential candidate León Febres-Cordero in the 1984 elections, then swiftly dissolved upon the death of Arosemena.

See also **Ecuador, Political Parties: Overview.**

BIBLIOGRAPHY

John D. Martz, *Ecuador: Conflicting Political Culture and the Quest for Progress* (1972).

Additional Bibliography

Estupiñán Tello, Julio. *El cuarenta de Otto Arosemena Gómez y la Asamblea Nacional Constituyente de 1966-67: los coroneles de la tradición.* Esmeraldas, Ecuador: J. Estupiñán Tello, 2000.

JOHN D. MARTZ

AROSEMENA MONROY, CARLOS JULIO (1919–2004).

Carlos Julio Arosemena Monroy (*b.* 24 August 1919, *d.* 5 March 2004), president of Ecuador (1961–1963). Scion of a wealthy Guayaquil family, Arosemena received his law degree in 1945 from the University of Guayaquil and became active in Liberal politics. By the 1950s he was an ardent nationalist, loyal to José María Velasco Ibarra. He was elected to the Chamber of Deputies in 1952 and 1958, and he became president of the Federación Nacional Velasquista in 1960. In the latter year he was the vice presidential candidate on the slate with Velasco and was swept to office by the Velasquista landslide victory.

Presiding over Congress in his role as vice president of the republic, Arosemena soon broke with Velasco and became an outspoken critic. When Velasco was overthrown in 1961, Arosemena, at age forty-two, succeeded him as president. A supporter of labor and an outspoken nationalist, he espoused moderate reforms while expressing sympathy for the Cuban Revolution. This position aroused traditional domestic interests and angered the United States. His public displays of drunkenness became increasingly frequent, and the opposition hardened. On 11 July 1963 Arosemena was overthrown by the armed forces, which set up their own junta.

Arosemena soon organized his personalistic party, the Partido Nacionalista Revolucionario (PNR), which carried his banner in elections for the 1966 Constituent Assembly and afterward. But the PNR was unable to generate significant popular support. By 1984 its congressional representation consisted of Arosemena himself, and since 1986 the PNR has been moribund.

See also **Ecuador, Political Parties: Overview.**

BIBLIOGRAPHY

Martin C. Needler, *Anatomy of a Coup d'état: Ecuador 1963* (1964).

John D. Martz, *Ecuador: Conflicting Political Culture and the Quest for Progress* (1972).

Additional Bibliography

Arosemena Monroy, Carlos Julio, and Carlos Calderón Chico. *"No me importa el juicio de la historia": (Conversaciones con Carlos Julio Arosemena).* Quito, Ecuador: Planeta, 2003.

JOHN D. MARTZ

AROSEMENA QUINZADA, ALBACÍADES (1883–1958).

Albacíades Arosemena Quinzada (*b.* 20 November 1883; *d.* 8 November 1958), Panamanian president (1951–1952). Arosemena was born in Los Santos. He was a cattleman and a businessman but was also very active in politics, having served as minister of the treasury, treasurer of the Panama City government, and ambassador to Spain and France. Arosemena Quinzada was president after the overthrow of Arnulfo Arias. His period in office was very chaotic, and he was unsuccessful in his attempts to calm the situation.

See also **Panama.**

BIBLIOGRAPHY

Albacíades Arosemena Quinzada. *Edición conmemorativa del centenario de su nacimiento* (1984).

JUAN MANUEL PÉREZ

ARRAES DE ALENCAR, MIGUEL

(1916–2005). The Brazilian populist politician Miguel Arraes was born on 15 December 1916, into a rural middle-class family in Araripe, in the interior of Ceará. He eventually settled in Recife and graduated with a degree in law from the Faculdade de Direito do Recife in 1937. A government job with the Instituto do Açúcar e do Álcool (IAA) and political connections provided by his family led to his appointment as finance secretary of Pernambuco in 1947. In 1950 he was elected state deputy for the Partido Social Democrático (PSD) and in 1954 for the Partido Social Trabalhista (PST). By 1955 he had joined the Frente do Recife, a reformist left-center coalition that reached out to urban popular classes.

Arraes won election as mayor of Recife in 1959 and gained a reputation as a populist by courting poor voters with urban improvement programs. Initially Arraes did not appear to diverge significantly either in content or style from his predecessor, Pelópidas Silveira. However, Arraes expanded his focus beyond that of Silveira and those who had come before. In his mind Recife was "a city in expansion," whose "indomitable population" was confronting not only grave problems in the areas of "housing, transportation . . . and public lighting,"

but more importantly was faced with an inadequate "supply of basic essential food stuffs, high cost of living and schools" (Barros, p. 51).

Although at this point Arraes had not yet evolved into the populist politician that he would later become, his campaign was clearly marked by a new orientation to the popular classes. He appealed to the *povo* (people) not only for their support in the election but for their active help in transforming Recife. Arraes most clearly diverged from past municipal governments when he followed up on his campaign promises to provide more schools by establishing the Movimento de Cultura Popular (MCP). This education program opened up a new sphere of action to Recife's municipal government and was the cornerstone of its social program.

In 1963 Arraes became governor of the state amid rising tensions throughout the country. Arraes, or Arraia, as he was known by the people, implemented a minimum wage for rural workers, expanded farm credit, and promoted unionization in the countryside. Perhaps his most important achievement was the Acordo do Campo. This 1963 agreement between the rural workers unions—the *usineiros*—and the government belatedly brought the Consolidation of Labor Laws (CLT or Consolidação das Leis do Trabalho) to the Zona da Mata. A product of the Estado Novo, or corporatist state of Gétulio Vargas, the CLT brought labor under the control of the state—for example, it established labor courts for resolving disputes between labor and management—but also offered significant gains for workers, including the regulation of wages (establishing a minimum wage and overtime) as well as health and safety. Arraes also pushed to expand rural electrification during his governorship. This further exemplifies both his attempt to appeal to the rural sectors and his drive to modernize Pernambuco.

Like most populists of this period Arraes was a vocal nationalist. As a result he often came into conflict with both SUDENE, Brazil's regional development agency for the Northeast, and the USAID/ Alliance for Progress officials headquartered in Recife. He criticized SUDENE's director, Celso Furtado, for the role that foreign capital played in his Guiding Plans, and he broke relations with USAID in May 1963. In a speech that month he noted, "I will not negotiate with foreign powers. I am not president of the Republic" (Soares, p. 139).

According to Arraes, the states had no right to sign agreements with USAID because this was the responsibility of the federal government. Arraes went on to accuse USAID of being an agent of imperialism and *latifundio*.

Arraes was acting not in isolation but rather within the national context of the presidency of João Goulart (1961–1964) and increasing leftist mobilization throughout the Northeast. The military coup of 1964 led to Arraes's arrest and imprisonment for over a year on Fernando de Noronha and in Rio de Janeiro. He would later go into exile in Algeria, where he spent most of the period 1965–1979. Although not an ally of Goulart, Arraes was accused of radicalizing politics in the Northeast and blamed for successive waves of strikes and lockouts. His support for the Peasant Leagues and agrarian reform made him suspect as well.

Arraes returned to Brazil in September of 1979 under the Lei de Anistia or General Amnesty Law (28 August 1979), and three years later won election to Congress. Using his image as an elder statesman, he ran for governor in 1986 and took office the following year, having been elected by the largest margin in the state's history. During this administration he implemented social welfare programs much in the spirit of his first administration. One such program was Chapéu de Palha (Straw Hat) guaranteed a minimum wage to sugarcane workers of the Zona da Mata region during the five-month period between sugar harvests. He also returned to the project of rural electrification, focusing on bringing electricity to small landowners.

Arraes failed to make a large showing in the primaries for president in 1989 but was elected federal deputy that year for the Partido do Movimento Democrático Brasileiro (PMDB). In 1990 he joined the Partido Socialista Brasileira (PSB). He was elected to his third term as governor of Pernambuco in 1994, with 54 percent of the vote. His final term as governor was marked by economic crisis and political strife. As a result he lost his bid for reelection in 1998 to his former ally Jarbas Vasconcelos. He was elected as a federal deputy again in 2003 and served as national president of the PSB until his death at age eighty-eight on August 13, 2005.

See also **Brazil, Liberal Movements; Brazil, Political Parties: Party of Brazilian Social Democracy (PSDB).**

BIBLIOGRAPHY

Primary Work

Arraes, Miguel. *Palavra de Arraes: Textos de Miguel Arraes.* Rio de Janeiro: Editôra Civilização Brasileira, 1965.

Secondary Works

Barros, Adirson de. *Ascenção e queda de Miguel Arraes.* Rio de Janeiro: Equador, 1965.

Beloch, Israel, and Alzira Alves De Abreu, eds. *Dicionario histórico-biográfico brasileiro, 1930–1983.* Rio de Janeiro: Editora Forense-Universitária, 1984.

Callado, Antônio. *Tempo de Arraes: Padres e comunistas na revolução sem violência.* Rio de Janeiro: José Alvaro, 1964.

Debret, Guita Grin. *Ideologia e populismo: A. de Barros, M. Arraes, C. Lacerda, L. Brizola.* São Paulo: T. A. Queiroz, 1979.

Page, Joseph A. *The Revolution That Never Was: Northeast Brazil, 1955–1964.* New York: Grossman, 1972.

Soares, José Arlindo. *A Frente do Recife e o governo do Arraes: Nacionalismo em crise 1955–1964.* Rio de Janeiro: Paz e Terra, 1982.

Souza, João Francisco de. *Uma Pedagogia da Revolução: A contribuição do governo Arraes (1960–1964) à reinvenção da educação brasileira.* São Paulo: Cortez Editôra, 1987.

TIA MALKIN-FONTECCHIO

ARRAU, CLAUDIO LEÓN (1903–1991).

Claudio León Arrau (*b.* 6 February 1903; *d.* 9 June 1991), Chilean pianist. Early recognized as a prodigy, Arrau became one of the most accomplished Latin American musicians of the twentieth century. As a youth from Chillán, Arrau was sent on a grant from the Chilean government to study at the prestigious Julius Stern Conservatory in Berlin under the tutelage of Martin Krause from 1912 until 1918. During his tenure in Germany he earned numerous honors, including the Liszt and Ibach prizes. Throughout the 1920s and 1930s Arrau toured Europe and the Americas before settling in the United States after the outbreak of World War II.

Arrau was known for his slow tempos and lack of ostentation, a style that emphasized the inherent beauty of the music rather than the skill of the musician. In 1935, Arrau played a series of recitals in Berlin featuring the complete keyboard works of Bach. After this performance, he announced that he would no longer publicly perform any Bach, as he felt the piano could not do the composer justice.

In later years, Arrau brought his talents to Japan, Australia, and Israel, and recorded distinctive versions of major works by Beethoven, Brahms, Chopin, and others. He received many honors, including the UNESCO International Music Prize, and was named a commander in the French Legion of Honor. The cities of Santiago and Chillán both contain streets bearing Arrau's name.

See also **Music: Art Music.**

BIBLIOGRAPHY

Joseph Horowitz, *Conversations with Arrau* (1982).

Ingo Harden, *Claudio Arrau* (1983).

Additional Bibliography

Conversations with Arrau was republished in 1999 with a new title. Horowitz, Joseph. *Arrau on Music and Performance.* Mineola, NY: Dover, 1999.

Montero, Luis Merino. *Claudio Arrau: 100 años.* Santiago de Chile: Universidad de Bio-Bio, 2004.

JOHN DUDLEY

ARREOLA, JUAN JOSÉ (1918–2001).

Juan José Arreola (*b.* 21 September 1918, *d.* 3 December 2001), Mexican writer. Born in Ciudad Guzmán in the state of Jalisco, Arreola received the prestigious Premio Xavier Villaurrutía in 1963 for his only novel, *La feria* (The Fair, 1963). He has also written drama but is best known for his innovation in the short story and other short prose forms. His major collections of stories and prose pieces include *Varia invención* (Various Inventions, 1949), *Confabulario* (Confabulary, 1952), *Palindroma* (Palindrome, 1971), and *Bestiario* (Bestiary, 1972). Together with writers such as José Revueltas and Juan Rulfo, Arreola's works move Mexican literature beyond a parochial consideration of nationalistic themes and address Mexican identity in the context of universal human truths and archetypes. Through the use of humor, satire, irony, fantasy, and linguistic playfulness, he has exp-

lored themes such as religiosity, the absurd, materialism, the commercialism of the United States, and relations between the sexes. He has also played an influential role in Mexican literature as the director of writing workshops and as the editor of two important literary series in the 1950s, *Cuadernos del unicornio* (The Unicorn's Notebooks) and *Los presentes* (Those Present).

See also **Literature: Spanish America.**

BIBLIOGRAPHY

Yulan M. Washburn, *Juan José Arreola* (1983).

Russell M. Cluff and L. Howard Quackenbush, "Juan José Arreola," in *Latin American Writers,* vol. 3, edited by Carlos A. Solé and Maria Isabel Abreu (1989), pp. 1229–1236.

Additional Bibliography

Arreola, Orso. *El último juglar: Memorias de Juan José Arreola.* México: Editorial Diana, 1998.

Paso, Fernando del. *Memoria y olvido: Vida de Juan José Arreola, 1920-1947.* México: Fondo de Cultura Económica, 2003.

DANNY J. ANDERSON

ARRIAGA, PONCIANO (1811–1863).

Ponciano Arriaga (*b.* 1811; *d.* 1 March 1863), Mexican politician and cabinet minister, "Father of the Constitution of 1857." Born in the provincial capital of San Luis Potosí, Arriaga was an ardent federalist and radical liberal. He used his oratorical and writing skills in the movements against President Anastasio Bustamante in 1832 and later against President Antonio López de Santa Anna. Arriaga was deposed as *regidor del ayuntamiento* (president of the city council) of San Luis Potosí and jailed for these activities in 1841, but the following year he was elected to represent his home state in the national congress.

During the war with the United States (1846–1847), Arriaga helped to supply the Mexican army in Coahuila and Nuevo Laredo. He opposed the Treaty of Guadalupe Hidalgo for conceding territory in order to gain peace. He served briefly (13 December 1852–5 January 1853) as minister of justice under President Mariano Arista. When Santa Anna regained the presidency, Arriaga was exiled.

In New Orleans, he met Benito Juárez, Melchor Ocampo, and other liberals. With the triumph of the Revolution of Ayutla (1854), Arriaga returned to Mexico and was elected to the Constituent Congress of 1856–1857. As president of the congress, he was one of the principal authors of the Constitution of 1857. During the War of the Reform (1858–1861), Arriaga supported the Juárez government and later served as republican governor of the state of Aguascalientes (1862–1863) and the Federal District (1863).

See also **Mexico, Constitutions: Constitutions Prior to 1917.**

BIBLIOGRAPHY

Francisco Zarco, *Historia del Congreso extraordinario constituyente de 1856–1857* (1898–1901, repr. 1956).

Jesús Reyes Heroles, *El liberalismo mexicano*, 3 vols. (1957–1961).

Richard N. Sinkin, *The Mexican Reform, 1855–1876: A Study in Liberal Nation-Building* (1979); *Diccionario Porrúa de historia, biografía y geografía de México*, 5th ed. (1986).

Additional Bibliography

Benítez Treviño, V. Humberto. *Ponciano Arriaga: Defensor paradigmático del los pobres.* Toluca: Universidad Autónoma del Estado de México, 1999.

D. F. STEVENS

ARRIERO. *Arriero*, an indigenous, mulatto, mestizo, or humble Spanish man who, from the mid-sixteenth century on, managed four or five mules (and, less often, horses). Typically teamed up with other muleteers or assistants to form *recuas* (strings) of twelve to fifty animals, *arrieros* transported a great variety of goods, often grains, ten to fifteen miles a day, not infrequently along trade routes dating back to pre-Hispanic times. *Arrieros* earned anywhere from twenty-five pesos a year to ten times that amount, with variation corresponding largely to capital investment. Numerous regulations sought to govern arrieros, such as the kind of animals they used, how many animals, where they obtained grain to feed the animals, what goods they transported, and how much they charged. In Mexico, arrieros eclipsed *tlamemes* (pre-Conquest human

carriers), facilitating a much expanded and less onerous interregional trade and transportation system.

See also **Mestizo.**

BIBLIOGRAPHY

Mexican arrieros have received greater scholarly attention than those of other parts of Latin America. Ross Hassig, *Trade, Tribute, and Transportation: The Sixteenth-Century Political Economy of the Valley of Mexico* (1985), is a most useful compilation of data. Biographies of muleteers include John C. Super, "Miguel Hernández: Master of Mule Trains," in *Struggle and Survival in Colonial America*, edited by David G. Sweet and Gary B. Nash (1981); and Richard Boyer, "Juan Vásquez, Muleteer of Seventeenth-Century Mexico," in *The Americas* 37 (April 1981): 421–443.

Additional Bibliography

Suárez Argüello, Clara Elena. *Camino real y carrera larga: La arriería en la Nueva España durante el siglo XVIII.* México, D.F.: Centro de Investigaciones y Estudios Superiores en Antropología Social, 1997.

STEPHANIE WOOD

ARRIETA, JOSÉ AGUSTÍN (1803–1874). José Agustín Arrieta (*b.* 1803; *d.* 1874), Mexican painter. In an effort to explain the Mexicanism, the rustic provincialism, of Arrieta's work, it has been judged according to a single criterion, that of popular painting. It is often forgotten that as a student at the Academy of Fine Arts in Puebla under the direction of Julián Ordóñez and Lorenzo Zendejas, he was competent in genres typical of the academy, such as painting historical themes or representing the human figure, in full or in half, as well as torsos and heads. Although he was not a student at the Academia de San Carlos in Mexico City, he occasionally sent work there from 1850 to 1871.

Arrieta's extensive work stresses two themes: folkloric paintings and dining-room paintings or still lifes. He took pride in an impeccable technical control. His dining-room paintings, which became popular with collectors of rustic art, are full of allusions to European art in their details as well as in some elements of their harmonious composition. His folkloric paintings depict scenes inside homes as well as in public places, such as the street.

His work is replete with subtle implications of popular culture.

See also **Art: The Nineteenth Century.**

BIBLIOGRAPHY

Francisco Cabrera, *Agustín Arrieta, pintor costumbrista* (1963).

Fausto Ramírez, *La plástica del siglo de la independencia* (1985).

Additional Bibliography

García Barragán, Elisa. *José Agustín Arrieta: Lumbres de lo cotidiano.* Coyocán, Mexico: Fondo Editorial de la Plástica Mexicana, 1998.

Palou, Pedro Angel. *Identidad de Puebla: Esencia de mexicanidad: José Agustín Arrieta (1803-1874).* Puebla: Gobierno del Estado de Puebla, 2002.

                                    ESTHER ACEVEDO

ARRIETA, PEDRO DE (1691–1738).
Pedro de Arrieta (*fl.* 1691–*d.* 15 December 1738), Mexican architect. Born in Real de Minas, Pachuca, Arrieta passed the examination to become a master architect in Mexico City in 1691. Four years later he supervised the buildings of the Inquisition, and in 1720 he became *maestro mayor de la catedral y del real palacio,* the highest rank to which an architect in New Spain could aspire. Among the many public and private buildings ascribed to him are the Basilica of Guadalupe (1695–1709); the remodeling of the Jesuit church of the Profesa, contracted in 1714 and completed in 1720; and the Palace of the Inquisition with its peculiar suspended arches (1733–1737). His work is classical in that he insisted on the use of columns and rejected the surface movement of the salomonic baroque with its characteristic spiral columns. Also characteristic of Arrieta's buildings are polygonal arches and narrative reliefs.

See also **Architecture: Architecture to 1900.**

BIBLIOGRAPHY

Manuel Toussaint, *Colonial Art in Mexico* (1967).

Heinrich Berlin, "Three Master Architects in New Spain," in *Hispanic American Historical Review* 27 (1947): 375–384.

María Concepción Amerlinck, "Pedro de Arrieta, su origen y testamento," in *Monumentos históricos* 6 (1981): 27–32.

Additional Bibliography

Fernández García, Martha. *El Palacio de la Escuela de Medicina.* Mexico City: Facultad de Medicina, Universidad Nacional Autónoma de México, 1994.

                                    CLARA BARGELLINI

ARRIVÍ, FRANCISCO (1915–).
Francisco Arriví (*b.* 24 June 1915), Puerto Rican author, dramatist, and theater director. Arriví was born in San Juan and graduated from the University of Puerto Rico in 1938. From 1938 to 1941 he taught at Ponce High School, where his students staged his first plays. After his return to San Juan in 1941, he wrote, directed, and translated dramas and was active in the radio productions of the School of the Air until 1948. He studied drama at Columbia University in New York under a Rockefeller grant in 1949 and was programming director for the Puerto Rican government radio station for ten years. A tireless organizer, Arriví established the Tinglado Puertorriqueño experimental theater company and developed the theater program of the Institute of Puerto Rican Culture, which he directed from 1959 to 1970. He launched the institute's yearly festivals, among them Puerto Rican Theater, International Theater, and the Theater of Ponce. He was instrumental in the creation of the Fine Arts Center in Santurce as a forum for the performing arts in 1981.

In 1959 the Institute of Puerto Rican Literature honored Arriví's *Vejigantes* (Carnival masks, 1958), a powerful drama about racial identity in Puerto Rico, which formed part of a trilogy of plays on the same theme that Arriví entitled *Máscara puertorriqueña* (Puerto Rican masquerade, 1959–1960). Other famous plays by Arriví are *María Soledad* (1947), *Caso del muerto en vida* (The case of a man dead in life, 1951), *Club de solteros* (Bachelors' club, 1953), and *Cóctel de Don Nadie* (The cocktail of Mr. Nobody, 1964). Arriví has also published books of poetry and collections of essays on theater and literature, including *Areyto mayor* (An indigenous festival, 1966) and *Conciencia puertorriqueña del teatro contemporáneo, 1937–1956* (Puerto Rican awareness of contemporary theater, 1967).

See also **Theater.**

BIBLIOGRAPHY

Frank M. Dauster, *Ensayos sobre el teatro hispanoamericano* (1975).

Josefina Rivera De Alvarez, *Literatura puertorriqueña: Su proceso en el tiempo* (1983).

Esthervinda Zacarías De Justiniano, *Francisco Arriví: Bibliografía selectiva* (1986).

Additional Bibliography

Abrams, Dianne Virginia Magee. "Francisco Arrivi: Unmasking Social Injustice." Ph.D. diss., Rutgers University, 2004.

Medina, Georgie. "La mulatez en la dramaturgia puertorriqueña de Tapia y Rivera, Arriví y Rosario Quiles." Ph.D. diss., University of Kentucky, 1998.

ESTELLE IRIZARRY

ARRON, HENCK A. E. (1936–2000).

The leading politician and the first prime minister of the Republic of Suriname at its independence on November 25, 1975, Henck Arron (April 25, 1936–December 4, 2000) was born in Paramaribo, the country's capital, and studied in the Netherlands, then the colonial motherland. He was employed in the Netherlands and afterwards in the banking sector of Suriname. In 1961 he became a member of the directorate of the National Creole Party (NPD), representing the Afro-Surinamese population. In 1963 Arron became a member of parliament. During the elections of 1973 he was the leader of a Creole-Javanese party coalition that won twenty-two of the thirty-nine parliamentary seats.

Assuming the prime ministership he announced, against the wishes of the Hindustani part of the population, the independence of Suriname "before the end of 1975." The Dutch social democratic government, convinced that the Netherlands would be better off without its colony, reacted enthusiastically. Thereupon, a rather bizarre negotiation was initiated between the two governments about the amount of development aid Suriname would receive, a kind of "Golden Handshake" from the Dutch to benefit the new republic. Arron, well aware that he could squeeze more concessions by delaying independence, succeeded in raising the amount of money from an initial offer 700 million to 3.5 billion guilders (€1.6 billion; US$ 2.25 billion) an aid reservoir

that even by 2007 was not completely spent. Arron was ousted from power in 1980 by a sergeants' coup led by Dési Bouterse. After the reestablishment of democracy in 1987, Arron refused the country's presidency, being appointed instead as vice president (1988–1990). After a second coup in 1990, he left politics. His colleague, Ronald Venetiaan, became president in 1991; Venetiaan was re-elected for second and third terms in 2000 and 2005. In 2000 Arron died of cardiac arrest while in the Netherlands.

See also **Bouterse, Desi; Suriname and the Dutch in the Caribbean.**

BIBLIOGRAPHY

Hoogbergen, Wim, and Dirk Kruijt. *De oorlog der sergeanten. Surinaamse militairen in de politiek, 1980–1992* [The Sergeant's War: The Surinamese Military in National Politics]. Amsterdam: Bert Bakker, 2005.

Sedney, Jules. *De toekomst van ons verleden. Democratie, etniciteit en politieke machtsvorming in Suriname* [The Future of Our Past: Democracy, Ethnicity and Political Power Formation in Suriname]. Paramaribo: VACO, 1997.

DIRK KRUIJT

ARROYO ASENCIO.

Arroyo Asencio, a small river in Uruguay near Mercedes, in the department of Soriano. Its importance derives from the fact that from its banks originated the famous Grito de Asencio (28 February 1811), which marked the beginning of the revolution in the Banda Oriental, the old name for what is known today as Uruguay. Outstanding in this event were Pedro Viera and Venancio Benavídes, inhabitants of the area who organized their neighbors into an uprising against the government of Montevideo. Although he was not present, the influence of the caudillo José Artigas, the future head of the revolution in the area, was significant.

See also **Grito de Asencio.**

BIBLIOGRAPHY

Brother Damasceno, *Ensayo de historia patria*, vol. 1 (1950).

John Street, *Artigas and the Emancipation of Uruguay* (1959).

Additional Bibliography

Rodríguez, Jaime E. *The Independence of Spanish America.* New York: Cambridge University Press, 1998.

JOSÉ DE TORRES WILSON

ARROYO DEL RÍO, CARLOS ALBERTO (1893–1969).

Carlos Alberto Arroyo del Río (*b.* 27 November 1893; *d.* 31 October 1969), president of Ecuador (nonelected 1939 and elected 1940–1944). Born in Guayaquil, Arroyo del Río studied law, entered private practice, and taught at the University of Guayaquil, eventually becoming rector in 1932. He became active in the Liberal Radical Party, serving as a member of the *Junta de Beneficencia*, secretary of the Municipal Council (1917–1918), and president of the Municipal Council (1921–1922). In 1922–1923 he represented Guayas Province in congress, serving as president of the Chamber of Deputies in 1923. Elected senator in 1924, he actively opposed the revolution of July 1925 and the Ayora administration, and ten years later (1934–1935) led the congressional opposition to President José María Velasco Ibarra that resulted in the dissolution of congress.

When Aurelio Mosquera Narváez died in office on 15 November 1938, Arroyo del Río assumed executive power as president of the Senate and presided over an extraordinary congress that abrogated the Constitution of 1938 and reinstated the Constitution of 1906. He resigned on 28 May 1944 to run for president. He was elected and took office on 1 September 1940. The supporters of his leading opponent, Velasco Ibarra, charged that the election was fraudulent and attempted a coup. The insurrection failed, and the leaders, including Velasco Ibarra and Carlos Guevara Moreno, were exiled.

Within a few months of Arroyo del Río's inauguration, Peru invaded territory claimed by Ecuador. In 1944, Arroyo del Río was removed from office as a result of the country's defeat in the 1941 border war with Peru, and Velasco Ibarra was recalled from exile to replace the discredited president. Arroyo del Río left the country, going first to Colombia, then to New York City; he returned to Guayaquil in 1948 to resume his legal practice. He remained the target of public attacks until his death.

See also **Ecuador, Constitutions; Ecuador-Peru Boundary Disputes.**

BIBLIOGRAPHY

Oscar Efren Reyes, *Breve historia general del Ecuador,* vol. 2 (1957), esp. pp. 813–827.

David H. Zook, Jr., *Zarumilla-Marañon: The Ecuador–Peru Dispute* (1964).

Enrique Ayala Mora, ed., *Nueva historia del Ecuador: Época republicana IV,* vol. 10 (1983), esp. pp. 105–108.

Additional Bibliography

Gándara Enríquez, Marcos. *El Ecuador del año 1941 y el Protocolo de Río:antecedentes, hechos subsiguientes: Arroyo y su tiempo.* Quito: Centro de Estudios Históricos del Ejército, 2000.

LINDA ALEXANDER RODRÍGUEZ

ARROYO GRANDE, BATTLE OF.

Battle of Arroyo Grande, a major engagement in the Platine civil wars fought on 5 December 1842. In the midst of Uruguay's Guerra Grande, the gaucho army of General Fructuoso Rivera crossed into Argentine territory and campaigned successfully against the military forces of the Buenos Aires strongman Juan Manual de Rosas. At the beginning of December 1842, however, Rosista troops under the command of General Manual Oribe met Rivera's army at Arroyo Grande, on the right bank of the Uruguay River in Entre Ríos, and decisively defeated it, eliminating 3,000 men and capturing a wealth of munitions in the process. This victory made it possible for Oribe to carry the fight immediately onto Uruguayan soil, where his troops were soon besieging Montevideo. A very energetic participant in the Arroyo Grande struggle, under Oribe's command, was Justo José de Urquiza, who at that time was only a minor Entrerriano cavalry officer, but who would soon be the most important political figure in the Littoral provinces.

See also **Rivera, Fructuoso.**

BIBLIOGRAPHY

Telmo Manacorda, *Fructuoso Rivera, el perpetuo defensor de la república Oriental* (1946); *The Cambridge History of Latin America,* vol. 3 (1985), pp 645–647.

Additional Bibliography

Goldman, Noemí, and Ricardo Donato Salvatore. *Caudillismos rioplatenses: Nuevas miradas a un viejo problema.* Buenos Aires: Eudeba, Facultad de Filosofía y Letras, Universdad de Buenos Aires, 1998.

Halperín Donghi, Tulio, and Jorge Raúl Lafforgue. *Historias de caudillos argentinos.* Buenos Aires: Extra Alfaguara, 1999.

Szuchman, Mark D., and Jonathan C. Brown, eds. *Revolution and Restoration: The Rearrangement of Power in Argentina, 1776-1860.* Lincoln: University of Nebraska Press, 1994.

THOMAS L. WHIGHAM

ARRUFAT, ANTÓN (1935–). Antón Arrufat (*b.* 14 August 1935), Cuban playwright and poet. Born in Santiago in Oriente Province, Arrufat studied in his native city as well as at the University of Havana. He has traveled to Czechoslovakia, France, Italy, and England and been very active in promoting literary activity in Cuba. He was editor in chief of the influential *Casa de las Américas* from 1960 to 1965 and has contributed to *Lunes de Revolución, Ciclón, Cuba en UNESCO, La Gaceta de Cuba,* and others. His work has attained such national acclaim as the honorable mentions he received for his play *El vivo al pollo* in the Casa de las Américas competition in 1961 and for his collection of poetry *Repaso final* in the 1963 competition. In 1968 he won the coveted prize given by the Cuban Union of Writers and Artists (UNEAC) for his play *Los siete contra Tebas,* which established him as one of Cuba's leading playwrights and at the same time brought him into temporary disfavor with the Castro regime. After a decade or so of being relegated to the periphery, he was rehabilitated and has become active again. Arrufat remained in Cuba, where he began publishing and participating in cultural activities once again. In 2000 he won the National Literature Prize and the Alejo Carpentier Prize for his novel *La noche del aguafiestas.*

See also **Literature: Spanish America.**

BIBLIOGRAPHY

Barquet, Jesús J. *Teatro y Revolución Cubana: Subversión y utopía en Los siete contra Tebas de Antón Arrufat/ Theater and the Cuban Revolution: Subversion and utopia in Seven against Thebes by Antón Arrufat.* Lewiston, NY: E. Mellen Press, 2002.

Kirk, John M., and Leonardo Padura. *Culture and the Cuban Revolution: Conversations in Havana.* Gainesville, FL: University Press of Florida, 2001.

ROBERTO VALERO

ART

This entry includes the following articles:
PRE-COLUMBIAN ART OF MESOAMERICA
PRE-COLUMBIAN ART OF SOUTH AMERICA
THE COLONIAL ERA
THE NINETEENTH CENTURY
THE TWENTIETH CENTURY
FOLK ART

PRE-COLUMBIAN ART OF MESOAMERICA

Mesoamerican art begins about 1500 BCE, when permanent objects of great craft and skill begin to be imbued systematically with religious and other meanings by their makers. Before that time, craftsmen made finely honed tools and other utilitarian works that have endured, but their religious and ritualistic objects have perished. This era of the union of craft and meaning in enduring, nonperishable works is also the era in which the first civilizations of Mesoamerica arose, most notably the Olmecs of the Gulf Coast. By the end of the second millennium BCE, the Olmecs (a modern name; their name for themselves is lost forever), probably in pursuit of hard stones like jade for making sacred objects, had established trade routes that reached from modern Guatemala and Honduras to the Mexican states of Morelos and Guerrero. Roughly extending from fourteen to twenty-one degrees north latitude, and excluding the Caribbean islands, this region is called Mesoamerica (Middle America), and from about 1500 BCE until the Spanish Conquest in 1521, it was an area of some cultural unity, sharing concepts of religion, the calendar, and cultural practices, such as the ballgame. Dramatically different art styles emerged, however, at different times and places.

OLMEC

The Olmec (ca. 1500 BCE–ca. 400 BCE) built sacred centers along the swampy rivers of the Gulf Coast. At both San Lorenzo and La Venta in southeastern Mexico, millions of cubic feet of earth were formed into earthworks. La Venta exhibits the first known Mesoamerican pyramid, and its shape, a fluted cupcake, suggests derivation from the volcanoes of Central Mexico. Although radiocarbon dating has shown San Lorenzo to have been destroyed before the rise of La Venta, these and other centers of Olmec culture share forms and materials, including

Atlantean supports on the Pyramid of Quetzalcoatl, Tula, Mexico. These fifteen-foot-high statues, created at the start of the tenth century CE, once supported the roof of Quetzalcoatl's pyramid. IMAGE COPYRIGHT GORDON GALBRAITH, 2007. USED UNDER LICENSE FROM SHUTTERSTOCK.COM

colossal portrait heads of their early rulers and altarlike thrones of imported basalt. Without obvious prototypes, the Olmec achieved the most naturalistic and plastic forms found in the New World, including basalt carvings of the human form (for example, the "Wrestler," ca. 800 BCE) and fine kaolin "hollow baby" sculptures.

WEST AND CENTRAL MEXICAN CULTURES
Both provincial and idiosyncratic styles merged in the highlands of West and Central Mexico and treated the human form, particularly in the ceramics of Tlatilco and Xochipala.

West Mexican Cultures. From about 200 BCE until about 500 CE, peoples in West Mexico made monumental architecture and buried their dead in underground shaft tombs, following patterns that seem to be somewhat distinct from the rest of Mesoamerica. The Nayarit, Colima, and Jalisco traditions are best known through their hollow clay tomb sculptures: animated groupings of figures from Nayarit; hollow dogs and parrot vessels from Colima; and warriors with clubs from Jalisco.

Central Mexican Cultures. At the end of the first millennium BCE, new civilizations emerged in Central Mexico, in the Maya region, Oaxaca, and the Gulf Coast; their florescence in the first millennium CE is generally known as the Classic period. In central Mexico, the greatest city of its day arose at Teotihuacán, peaking in the fifth century with a population of about 250,000. The city plan focused on two colossal structures completed by about 200 CE, the pyramids of the Sun and Moon, and followed by a rigid grid that encompassed all constructions, sacred, civil, or domestic. Religious buildings generally have alternating vertical and sloping planes called *talud-tablero*, but buildings of all sorts, including those with elaborate architectural ornament, were painted with brilliant stucco pigments, some with freehand images and others laid out with a template. Featured are devotional images of major deities, especially Tlaloc, god of rain, agriculture, and war, and the great goddess, Spider Woman; these gods are also the subjects of the few surviving stone sculptures.

Teotihuacán artisans fashioned vast quantities of figurines, initially by hand, and then later in molds. They exported these and cylinder tripod vessels to the rest of Mesoamerica. Teotihuacán's decline and eventual demise, 650–800 CE, may have disrupted Mesoamerica, leading to the end of the Classic period.

SOUTHERN MEXICAN CULTURES

Oaxaca. In Oaxaca, the Zapotecs made hilltop Monte Albán their capital and, in front of their buildings, set up two-dimensional reliefs of rulers and their conquests. Three-dimensional figures attached to urns accompanied the noble dead into richly painted tombs set under palaces. Although the Totonacs dominated the Gulf Coast, El Tajín was probably built by the Huaxtecs. To the south, the Totonacs made life-size hollow ceramic sculptures of gods and humans, and the Aztecs later adopted the art.

Wall painting depicting the judgment of captives, Maya (photo) Bonampak, Chiapas State, Mexico. ALAN GILLAM/ MEXICOLORE/ THE BRIDGEMAN ART LIBRARY

Maya Region.   In the Maya region, both in the lowlands, at El Mirador and Cerros, and in the highlands, at Kaminaljuyú, Abaj Takalik, and Izapa (ca. 200 BCE— 250 CE), experiments in art, writing, and architecture led to uniform practices in the Classic (250–900 CE) at dozens of lowland sites. Highland stone stelae pictured rulers and gods and used a writing system to record names and dates. At lowland sites, each setback of pyramids was faced with a giant stucco mask.

At Tikal, carved stelae with flat, linear images of rulers covered with ritual paraphernalia and accompanied by dates counted from a base date that can be correlated to the European calendar, were erected before 300 CE. By 550, the end of the Early Classic, such monuments had been set up at Uaxactun, Copán, Yaxchilán, Caracol, and other sites. The union of ruler portraiture and glyphic historical narrative was unique to the Classic Maya. In a script that represents both the sounds and syntax of languages, these texts illuminate

Maya art from a Maya point of view. Large structures housed royal tombs, shrines for ancestor worship. At both Tikal and Río Azul, monochromatic paintings in red or black covered tomb walls, some with death dates and others with iconography of the underworld. Kings took rich offerings to the grave, including pots, jade masks and jewelry, sacrificial victims, perishable foodstuffs, and cloth. Stone ballcourts were included on most city plans.

During the fourth and fifth centuries, weaponry, fashions, and goods from distant Teotihuacán affected the Maya. Traditional quadrupod and basal-flanged bowls gave way to cylinder tripods on which the Maya began to paint narrative scenes in bright stucco or earth-toned slips.

Widespread sixth-century warfare hindered the development of Maya art, but in the seventh century, city-states flourished. At Palenque, King Pacal the Great initiated interior wall sculpture with multifigural compositions. Before his death, he built the nine-level Temple of Inscriptions for his own memorial, and an interior staircase leads to his tomb. At Copán and Quirigua, seventh- and eighth-century sculptures featured high relief, and portraits of Copán king 18 Rabbit achieve a plastic three-dimensionality. Tikal stone sculpture followed established canons, but the carved wooden lintels of funerary temples bear innovative imagery. Under kings Shield-Jaguar and Bird-Jaguar, Yaxchilán favored lintels recording marriage, bloodletting, and warfare. To the north, King Chaac erected palaces at Uxmal with elegant proportions. At Bonampak, a complete program of paintings treats warfare, bloodletting, and dynastic succession; in subject and style it relates closely to contemporary paintings at Cacaxtla in Central Mexico, which in turn shared an eclectic style with Xochicalco and Seibal. Generally, Mayan art has a changing and individual style. The uniqueness of Mayan art reflects how various Mayan kings looked for new symbols to project power. In the ninth century, most Classic cities were abandoned.

About 900, at both Tula (in Hidalgo) and Chichén Itzá (in Yucatán) new art forms emerged, including chacmool statues, atlantean supports, and serpent columns. Metallurgy arrived in Mesoamerica, and the Chichén Sacred Well (a natural sinkhole) received gold-disk offerings with repoussé designs. Colonnades flank many civil structures; at Chichén Itzá, a stone skull rack adjoins the largest ballcourt in Mesoamerica. Elaborate paintings at Chichén detail massive warfare, perhaps waged by a Toltec and Chichén alliance. Together, these two cities dominated all of Mesoamerica, and along their axis, both Toltec and Mayan iconography and ideology were shared and diffused until these cities were abandoned in the twelfth century. Poorly made architecture characterizes later architecture at Mayapan and Tulúm.

AZTEC

In Central Mexico, the Aztecs founded their island capital, Tenochtitlán, in about 1345. Politically and economically imperialistic, they dominated much of Mesoamerica at the time of the Spanish Conquest, and their wealth supported Tenochtitlán's development as a sacred center where architecture and sculpture replicated the cosmos and the gods. Dedicated to Huitzilopochtli, the Aztec sun god, and to Tlaloc, the main dual pyramid, or *Templo Mayor,* faced a round

temple of Quetzalcoatl, the Feathered Serpent creator and wind god. The Aztec placed three-dimensional basalt sculptures inside religious architecture, including the beheaded Coatlicue with her necklace of hearts and hands. Round two-dimensional stones such as the dismembered Coyolxauhqui, sister of Huitzilopochtli, and the great Calendar stone recording the ages of humanity's destruction were placed flat on the ground or on the surface of a temple. At the same time, simple vegetal and animal forms were formed from hard, semiprecious stones. Aztec nobility dwelt near the sacred precinct in multistoried palaces. Canals replaced streets, and aqueducts brought fresh water from the mainland. Ruler portraits were carved into live rock at nearby Chapultepec, and pools and temples were formed of the live rock of mountains surrounding the Valley of Mexico.

Like most Mesoamericans, the Aztecs had quantities of screenfold genealogies, histories, and religious and divinatory texts. Some skilled scribes may have been foreigners, Mixtecs from Oaxaca, who also practiced metallurgy and featherwork in Tenochtitlán. Little Aztec gold survives, but Mixtec gold from a Monte Albán tomb reveals the skill in lost wax and filigree that the Aztecs admired. Aztec and Mixtec *tlacuilos* also produced pictorials, which have been used to understand their concepts of history and writing.

Within a generation of the Spanish Conquest in 1521, little art in the pre-Columbian tradition was being made. The Spanish sought native tribute lists, histories, and maps of New Spain through the 1580s, some still created in the Nahua or a hybrid style, but by 1600, the elite tradition of native art and architecture had ceased in Mesoamerica.

BIBLIOGRAPHY

Miguel Covarrubias, *Indian Art of Mexico and Central America* (1957).

Michael D. Coe, *America's First Civilization: Discovering the Olmec* (1968).

Richard F. Townsend, *State and Cosmos in the Art of Tenochtitlán* (1979).

Esther Pasztory, *Aztec Art* (1983).

George Kubler, *The Art of Ancient America,* 3d ed. (1984).

Mary Ellen Miller, *The Art of Mesoamerica* (1986).

Linda Schele and Mary Ellen Miller, *The Blood of Kings: Dynasty and Ritual in Maya Art* (1986).

Michael D. Coe, *The Maya,* 4th ed. (1987).

Michael Kan, Clement Meighan, and H. B. Nicholson, *Sculpture of Ancient West Mexico: Nayarit, Jalisco, Colima* (1989).

Linda Schele and David Freidel, *A Forest of Kings: The Untold Story of the Ancient Maya* (1990).

Additional Bibliography

Boone, Elizabeth Hil. *Stories in Red and Black: Pictorial Histories of the Aztecs and Mixtecs.* Austin: University of Texas Press, 2000.

Clark, John E., and Mary E. Pye, eds. *Olmec Art and Archaeology in Mesoamerica.* New Haven: Yale University Press, 2000.

de la Fuente, Beatriz. *Pre-Columbian Painting: Murals of Mesoamerica.* Milan: Jaca Books, 1999.

Guernsey, Julia. *Ritual and Power in Stone: The Performance of Rulership in Mesoamerican Izapan Style Art.* Austin: University of Texas Press, 2007.

Milbrath, Susan. *Star Gods of the Maya: Astronomy in Art, Folklore, and Calendars.* University Park: Pennsylvania State University Press, 2000.

Miller, Mary Ellen. *Maya Art and Architecture.* New York: Thames & Hudson, 1999.

Pasztory, Esther. *Pre-Columbian Art.* Cambridge, U.K.: Cambridge University Press, 1998.

MARY ELLEN MILLER

PRE-COLUMBIAN ART OF SOUTH AMERICA

The Inca Empire or Tahuantinsuyo (1438–1532 CE), crushed by the Spanish invaders, was only the last of many pre-Hispanic cultures in the Central Andes (a geographical and cultural area that includes the Pacific Coast, highlands, and tropical lowlands of modern Peru as well as the Bolivian altiplano), each of which had contributed to a very long and distinguished tradition in the arts. This tradition included architecture, sculpture, and painting as well as textiles, pottery, and metalwork, classes of objects that occupied a paramount position in the symbolic life of the ancient inhabitants of the Central Andes.

CHAVÍN

One theme that runs throughout Andean cultural history is the intimate relationship between architectural monuments and their natural surroundings. This phenomenon is evident at the highlands center of Chavín de Huántar (the seat of Chavín culture, ca. 850–200 BCE), a ceremonial site built in a sacred geographical context. The site is located between two rivers whose waters originate from the melting snows of a sacred mountain; the river water was channeled through tunnels in the main temple to produce a rumbling, thundering sound that emanated from its interior. It is likely that mountain worship was a principal reason for the construction of Chavín de Huántar, and it may have motivated the design of later monuments (such as the Nasca Lines and Tiahuanaku [Tiwanaku] and Inca structures). In fact, the main building may have represented a real or cosmic mountain. Named the Castillo, it is a massive structure faced with cut granite blocks laid in horizontal rows of alternating widths. Inside, a labyrinth of stone-lined galleries, compartments, and ventilating shafts runs through the temple on several irregular levels.

The Castillo was adorned originally with dozens of stone sculptures, such as the Lanzón (14.77 feet tall), which resides in a small, dark chamber deep inside the temple. The Lanzón is carved to represent a costumed anthropomorphic figure with a feline mouth and serpent hair. The conjoining of diverse elements from the natural world in a single figure, combined with a mysterious and awesome setting, evokes an otherworldly experience. The Lanzón was most likely a cult object, perhaps symbolic of natural forces.

PARACAS

Paracas culture (ca. 700 BCE—200 CE) is at present best known through elaborately decorated textiles and well-made ceramic vessels. The largest scientifically documented group of Paracas textiles comes from a burial precinct called the Necrópolis on the Paracas peninsula. Among the hundreds of funerary bundles excavated there, several dozen contained dignitaries, each of whom had been wrapped in stunning woven garments. The brightly colored images of animals and of costumed human impersonators that are embroidered on these garments relay information about the worldview and social roles of the members of Paracas society. Other, more abstract designs likely encode information about ancestral relationships and community supernaturals. The Paracas cultural tradition included two styles of fineware pottery, one a postfire resin-painted ware and the other an

Woollen figure of a jaguar, Paracas Culture, c. 1500 BCE (ceramic) by Peruvian School. PRIVATE COLLECTION/ PHOTO © BOLTIN PICTURE LIBRARY/ THE BRIDGEMAN ART LIBRARY

extraordinarily thin, finely crafted monochrome ware modeled into animal and plant forms.

Few extensive architectural remains are known for Nasca culture (ca. 1–700 CE). Of these, the most prominent is the ceremonial center of Cahuachi, with its forty mounds of varying sizes. The largest construction, the Great Temple, is a 66-foot-high stepped mound formed by encasing a natural rise with elongated, wedge-shaped adobes. Cahuachi's architectural forms were oriented to the spiritual world: the site has a natural spring that was a hallowed landscape feature, and a sunken court on top of one mound opens east toward a sacred mountain associated in local legend with water sources.

The most famous material remains of Nasca culture are gigantic desert markings. The Nasca geoglyphs, which include biomorphic figures, geometric designs, and straight lines, undoubtedly had multiple meanings; one of their functions may have been as ceremonial paths related to some sort of ritual process directed towards a mountain/water/ fertility cult.

Nasca pottery is notable for its rich palette. Images were painted in many different colors of slip clay, which was fired on top of a solid-color ground. They illustrate creatures and plants, as well as human beings wearing facial masks and ritual costumes. Many of these images are similar to some of those embroidered on fabrics from the Paracas Necrópolis, but the use of polychrome slip-based pigments represents a major artistic and technological breakthrough in pottery making on the southern coast.

MOCHE

An important center of Moche culture (ca. 100–750 CE) comprises two adobe structures in the form of truncated stepped platform mounds, the Huaca del Sol and the Huaca de la Luna (in the Moche Valley). Although only a portion of the original remains, the Huaca del Sol is a spectacular landmark, towering 130 feet above the desert plain at its highest point. Across a wide plain, the Huaca de la Luna sits on the steep lower slopes of a hill.

Almost all Moche structures were adorned with polychrome murals, such as one (now destroyed) at Pañamarca in the Nepeña Valley that depicted a religious procession of elaborately costumed figures carrying goblets. The same scene is known from painted depictions on Moche pottery, which carries a pictorial art rich in naturalistic detail. Moche potters also excelled in modeling vessels into realistic, commanding portraits of their rulers.

As shown most beautifully in the tombs of Sipán, Moche metalsmiths—the most sophisticated artists within the Andean metallurgical tradition—crafted masks, beads, and nose, ear, and headdress ornaments as well as bells and rattles for the elite to use as adornments and to display political power and social status and to communicate religious beliefs. They also developed ingenious procedures to impart the colors of gold and silver to objects actually made of alloys. The style of Moche art also represents the political transformations of the time. The Moche gradually dominated the Gallinazo, but did not eliminate its culture. Consequently, ceramic production reflected a mix of the dominant culture and the previous Gallinazo.

TIAHUANACO/TIWANAKU AND HUARI

Confusion exists over the relationship of two principal polities, Tiahuanaco and Huari, that thrived in the Central Andes during the period ca. 550–900 CE. The cities were centers of power that, while culturally distinct in many respects, shared a religious iconography as well as the production of certain art forms (such as interlocked tapestry tunics and knotted hats). Some scholars believe that the earlier Pucara culture was the common heritage of these two, which could help explain the similarities in their art.

The original form of the buildings at Tiahuanaco is uncertain, but set within its palaces, temples, and plazas were impressive large stone sculptures. The so-called Gate of the Sun is a large single block of andesite incised with images of the principal figures in the Tiahuanaco belief system: a central, frontal figure dressed in an elaborate tunic, flanked by rows of staff-bearing human- and condor-headed attendants seen in profile.

The Huari empire extended throughout the highlands and coast of Peru. It boasted both administrative and ceremonial sites with large rectilinear structures, multistory buildings, and edifices with interior galleries and plazas. Tapestry tunics and four-cornered hats are two of its most spectacular artistic expressions; the predominant imagery features the same staff-bearing figures seen on the Gate of the Sun as well as geometric motifs. A limited number of recognizable subjects appear in Huari tunics, but iconography is overshadowed by color patterns. Huari culture is known also through monolithic sculptures and carved miniature figures.

CHIMÚ

Chan Chan in the Moche Valley was the capital city of the Chimú kingdom (ca. 1100–1476 CE). The central core of monumental constructions contains ten huge adobe rectangular enclosures that were major administrative centers of the empire. These palace compounds are enriched with carved clay wall decoration: repeating figures of fish, crustaceans, birds, and anthropomorphs are arranged in bands and panels. Many of the same motifs appear in other media, such as woven garments. For example, pelicans are represented on a stunning set of garments made entirely of undyed white cotton; white birds are brocaded in a checkerboard design on white plain-weave and gauze fabric.

INCA

Chimú metalworking also was highly developed and was so prized by the Incas that they took objects and artisans to the capital when their king, Pachacuti, vanquished the Chimú ruler Minchançaman. Pachacuti undertook the rebuilding of Cuzco, the political and religious capital of Tahuantinsuyo, in what some scholars claim is the physical form of a puma, the animal that symbolized the Inca dynasty. The technically astounding stonework of Inca imperial architecture is evident in Cuzco's main temple, the

Coricancha, with its foundations and freestanding buildings of perfectly cut and fitted basalt (much of this stonework was obscured originally by sheets of beaten gold). Inca rulers had palaces not only in Cuzco but also in the country. The sites of Pisac, Ollantaytambo, and Machu Picchu were royal estates developed by Pachacuti. His architecture focused on the contrast between built and natural form, often incorporating into a building site natural outcrops that were embellished and elaborated with walls, niches, and carving.

The Incas often relocated artisans from other conquered cultures to provincial centers in order to produce crafts for the state. These works displayed Inca cultural symbols, but different ethnic groups continued to produce crafts following their local techniques and traditions.

Like generations of Andeans before them, these last pre-Hispanic peoples embedded symbolic meanings in cloth. In Inca society, dress was a mark of ethnic identity as well as social station (Inca royalty wore the most sumptuous woven garments), material was an important accessory to ritual, weavings were offered as a major sacrificial item, and cloth was exchanged during diplomatic negotiations. Fabric indeed had a social and sacred nature in the Andean world.

See also **Mesoamerica.**

BIBLIOGRAPHY

Alan R. Sawyer, "Tiahuanaco Tapestry Design," in *Textile Museum Journal* 1, no. 2 (1963): 27–38.

John H. Rowe, "Form and Meaning in Chavín Art," in *Peruvian Archaeology: Selected Readings,* edited by John H. Rowe and Dorothy Menzel (1967).

Christopher B. Donnan, *Moche Art of Peru: Pre-Columbian Symbolic Communication* (1978).

John H. Rowe, "Standardization in Inca Tapestry Tunics," in *The Junius B. Bird Pre-Columbian Textile Conference, May 19th and 20th, 1973* (1979).

Michael E. Moseley and Kent C. Day, eds., *Chan Chan: Andean Desert City* (1981).

Ann P. Rowe, *Costumes and Featherwork of the Lords of Chimor: Textiles from Peru's North Coast* (1984).

Johan Reinhard, "Chavín and Tiahuanaco: A New Look at Two Andean Ceremonial Centers," in *National Geographic Research* 1, no. 3 (1985): 395–422.

Walter Alva, "Discovering the New World's Richest Unlooted Tomb," in *National Geographic* 174, no. 4 (1988): 510–549.

Richard L. Burger, "Unity and Heterogeneity Within the Chavín Horizon," in *Peruvian Prehistory,* edited by Richard W. Keating (1988): 99–144.

Susan A. Niles, "Looking for 'Lost' Inca Palaces," in *Expedition* 30, no. 3 (1988): 56–64.

Anthony F. Aveni, ed., *The Lines of Nazca* (1990).

Anne Paul, *Paracas Ritual Attire: Symbols of Authority in Ancient Peru* (1990), and *Paracas Art and Architecture: Object and Context in South Coastal Peru* (1991).

Richard Burger, *Chavín and the Origins of Andean Civilization* (1992).

Anita Cook, "The Stone Ancestors: Idioms of Imperial Attire and Rank Among Huari Figurines," in *Latin American Antiquity* 3, no. 4 (1992): 341–364.

Rebecca Stone-Miller, *To Weave for the Sun: Andean Textiles in the Museums of Fine Arts* (1992).

Richard F. Townsend, ed., *The Ancient Americas: Art from Sacred Landscapes* (1992).

Helaine Silverman, *Cahuanchi in the Ancient Nasca World* (1993).

Walter Alva and Christopher Donnan, *Royal Tombs of Sipán* (1993).

Additional Bibliography

Hayashida, Frances M. "Style, Technology and State Production: Inka Pottery Manufacture in the Leche Vallye, Peru." *Latin American Antiquity* 10(4) (1999): 337-352.

Moore, Jerry D. *Cultural Landscapes in the Ancient Andes: Archaeologies of Place.* Gainesville: University Press of Florida, 2005.

Niles, Susan A. *The Shape of Inca History: Narrative and Architecture in an Andean Empire.* Iowa City: University of Iowa Press, 1999.

Pasztory, Esther. *Pre-Columbian Art.* Cambridge: Cambridge University Press, 1998.

Pillsbury, Joanne. *Moche Art and Archaeology in Ancient Peru.* Washington, DC: Distributed by Yale University Press, 2001.

Stone-Miller, Rebecca. *Art of the Andes: From Chavín to Inca.* London: Thames & Hudson, 2002.

Uceda, Santiago and Elias Mujica. *Moche: Propuestas y perspectivas.* Trujillo: Universidad Nacional de la Libertad, 1994.

ANNE PAUL

THE COLONIAL ERA

The nature of colonization often dictates that art and architecture follow the forms and iconography of the colonizers. Although this was true in Latin

America, varying local conditions made for differences from the colonizing countries as well as among the colonies themselves. The differences were not only in materials and techniques, as could be expected, but also in emphases and interests. Under these circumstances, European stylistic terms can be confusing and so must be extended by terms that reflect Latin American developments more accurately. Although much has been investigated, there still are large gaps in the knowledge of Latin American colonial art, so that serious interpretative studies are difficult, and superficial generalizations are too easily made.

ARCHITECTURE IN SPANISH AMERICA

A type of architecture common to all of Spanish America is the extensive system of coastal fortifications, many of which were designed in the sixteenth century by the Italian engineer Battista Antonelli. However, most of the art and architecture preserved from the early colonial era is concentrated in the monastic establishments. Especially in Mexico, where evangelization was inspired by humanist utopian ideas, monastic complexes often evolved into spectacular, monumental groups of buildings. Erected after the first conversions had been consolidated, the complexes consist of large atriums or enclosed sacred spaces in front of churches. They often were intentionally built on the sites of the indigenous religious structures they replaced. A cross is in the center of the atrium; chapels, called *posas,* are at the corners; and there is some sort of "open chapel" that served for outdoor liturgy, in which great numbers of Indians in the atrium could participate. Open chapels can be complex, separate structures, as was frequent in New Spain; they can be integrated into the church building in the form of balconies, as in Mexico and Peru; or they can simply be sheltered under overhanging roof extensions, as in New Granada.

The church building itself is usually a single nave, although basilican plans also exist. In Mexico sixteenth-century churches generally have one rather squat tower or a belfry wall (*espadaña*) and are vaulted, while in South America there are many examples with wooden roofs. The massive proportions and appearance of sixteenth-century churches in Mexico have given rise to the term "fortress church." Although protection from hostile Indians could be necessary in border areas,

Church of San Francisco, Quito, Ecuador. This church's combination of Italianate and Flemish influences with a symmetrical façade influenced the architecture of many other churches in the Andean region. © CRAIG LOVELL/CORBIS

heavy walls have more to do with the presence of less-than-professional builders coupled with an abundant work force, and crenellations served not defense but a desire to make these buildings into symbols of the fortified City of God. Next to the church is the cloister, where the friars lived and where visitors could be accommodated.

Special mention must be made of San Francisco in Quito. In contrast with New Spain, where less than a generation after the Conquest enormous buildings were being erected, warfare in the Andean area made it impossible to build monumentally until the later sixteenth century. Thus San Francisco was not completed until around 1575. With its Italianate ornament and rustication, filtered through Flemish mannerist sensibilities, and a symmetrical facade between two towers, it is a seminal structure that influenced many later churches of the region.

Architectural styles in the sixteenth century included Gothic, Renaissance (in its plateresque and purist varieties) and Mudéjar. The use of treatises, especially of Sebastiano Serlio's illustrations, can be documented again and again in architectural details everywhere from the steps in front of San Francisco in Quito to the painted coffering of Mexican cloister walks and rooms. The architectural scheme for evangelization created in the sixteenth century continued to be used, with changes in building styles and ornament, throughout the colonial period in frontier areas.

The missions of the Jesuits in Paraguay, eastern Bolivia, northeastern Argentina, and southern Brazil form a separate group. Built between 1609 and the expulsion of the Jesuits from the Americas in 1767, most of the churches are spaces enclosed by curtain walls and supported by wooden columns, such as the eighteenth-century example at Yaguarón, Paraguay. At Trinidad, Paraguay, however, the church is a vaulted stone structure completed about 1740.

Just how much was preserved from the native cultures in artistic matters is still debated. In architecture, beyond certain techniques and materials, there is little. Adobe and *bejareque* (earth-and-stick) constructions and palm or grass roofs were retained, and are still used in many regions. In central Mexico something of the pre-Columbian tradition of stone carving manifested itself in a sixteenth-century style called *tequitqui*, in which European subject matter mingles with respect for the mass of the stone and some native motifs, as can be seen in atrium crosses, facades, and baptismal fonts. Also of native origin are the *quincha* vaults (plaster-coated webs of straw and reeds on wooden frames) of Peru.

Spanish settlements in the New World were generally built on a grid plan, with a cathedral or parish church and a plaza at the center—a scheme that was formalized in Spanish domains by ordinances. Civilized life for the colonist was city life, and much importance was given to regulated public spaces. In the early period most monumental residences were fortresslike, but the sixteenth-century houses of Diego Columbus in Santo Domingo and of Cortés in Cuernavaca have external loggias. Later palaces often have balconies and ground-level porticos. There are also hospitals, schools, and other public buildings. Usually the basic scheme is that of rooms around internal patios.

The cathedrals were being erected at the same time as the last cathedrals of Spain and generally depended heavily on European models and workmen. The first in the New World was the cathedral of Santo Domingo (1512–1541), built by Europeans (like most colonial structures in the Caribbean). Except for examples in that area, such as the wooden-roofed cathedral of Cartagena, most of the cathedrals of the rest of Spanish America are vaulted and follow similar schemes: rectangular plans with a nave and two side aisles and side chapels. Generally the facade is flanked by two towers. In elevation the older cathedrals of Santo Domingo, Mérida, and Guadalajara, as well as the cathedrals of Cuzco and Lima, are of the hall-church type: the roof is the same height over the nave and the aisles. After 1585, at the cathedrals of Mexico City and Puebla, the plans were more tightly centralized and the buildings were given a basilican elevation.

Cathedrals in Latin America, as elsewhere, often took very long to build and thus display a range of styles. Most were finished in the seventeenth century, by which time baroque elements and movement were evident. In ecclesiastical architecture this meant ornate sculpted portals with strong centralizing and ascending tendencies. Everywhere, though later and less frequently in South America, baroque architecture was marked by the use of the twisted salomonic column, initially introduced in retablos (elaborate gilt wooden altarpieces). Some movement also occurs in plans: facades protrude into the spaces before them; niches in the interiors push out the walls.

The most variety in plans occurred in the eighteenth century, when circular and oval buildings were erected. During the seventeenth century, building types varying according to function and regional characteristics became established. Churches other than cathedrals were often built on the Latin cross plan, although the basilican plan also was used. Convent churches, in which the two entrances are at the sides of the nave rather than at the end (which is set aside for the nuns and opens only to the adjacent cloister), developed in New Spain. Sanctuaries often have a centralizing tendency, as at eighteenth-century Esquipulas in Guatemala, with its four corner towers. The dome, elevated on a drum (thereby adding drama to the mass of the building and directing light into the interior), proliferated in New Spain, where its many variations are proof of the presence of local architects and artisans.

In Cuzco and Lima, earthquakes in 1650 and 1656 were followed by extensive building campaigns that resulted in another important group of churches. San Francisco in Lima, the most coherent building of this group, is characterized by retablo portals whose multiple columns protrude and mass toward the center, where broken and curved pediments create a strong vertical movement. Other regional variants are defined to a great extent by technical and material considerations. Examples include the buildings with stucco and glazed tile decoration in the area of Puebla in New Spain and squat churches with broad, screen-type facades, resistant to earthquakes, in southern Mexico and Central America. In the highlands of Peru and Bolivia, centered at the Peruvian towns of Arequipa, Cajamarca, and Puno, is the mestizo architecture of the eighteenth century, characterized by low relief and overall portal carving.

PAINTING AND SCULPTURE IN SPANISH AMERICA

New World painting and sculpture developed from a European base. Although ingredients of colors, feather mosaics, *amate* (fig tree) paper, and sculptures of corn pith, maguey, and local woods were retained from pre-Columbian times, the new Christian subject matter and the forms that clothed suggest a greater European influence. Traveling and resident European artists and works, notably prints, introduced the new iconography and styles. Even when pre-Columbian iconography is depicted, as in some Mexican sixteenth-century wall paintings and manuscripts, the style is European. The Flemish painter Simon Pereyns in Mexico and the Italian Jesuit lay brother Bernardo Bitti, who was also a sculptor and worked in Peru, are examples of European painters who introduced the mannerist style into the New World.

Local painters emerged, especially in New Spain, where the process of the Americanization of art seems to have been quicker, and the workshops they established continued for generations. The style of Francisco de Zurbarán was introduced partly through the importation of some of his works. By the middle of

Madonna and Child, School of Cuzco, Anonymous (c. 18th century). The rich gold detail and triangular shape of the Virgin are typical of the Cuzco School, which flourished from the mid-seventeenth century. ROY MILES FINE PAINTINGS/ THE BRIDGEMAN ART LIBRARY

the seventeenth century Peter Paul Rubens, too, had found his way to the New World via prints and followers such as Diego de la Puente in Peru. Before the end of the century the softer style of Bartolomé Murillo had reached Latin America. In Mexico the paintings of Baltasar de Echave Orio, Luis Juárez, and their descendants (Baltasar de Echave Ibía, Baltasar de Echave Rioja, and Jose Júarez), of Juan Correa, and of Cristóbal de Villalpando covered the seventeenth century. Gregorio Vázquez Ceballos was the most important seventeenth-century painter of New Granada and the only Latin American colonial painter who left a considerable number of drawings. Miguel de Santiago and Nicolás Javier Goríbar worked in Quito. The best painter of Peru was Melchor Pérez Holguín, whose work is concentrated in Potosí.

In Cuzco some painters, among them Diego Quispe Ttito, took a more European direction, while others developed a style, now called the Cuzco school, in which gold patterning was applied especially to the clothing of religious figures, giving them a sumptuous and archaic character. Peculiar to the area, too, are paintings of richly robed Virgins, pyramidal in form. Representations of angels were very popular everywhere, and a special type emerged in the Andean highlands: angels dressed as soldiers and carrying rifles (*arcabuceros*). From the middle of the seventeenth century, in both Mexico and Peru, historical paintings appeared, and a consciousness of the differences that distinguish the New World from the Old emerged. Contemporary occurrences, notably processions, are depicted in a way that reveals the variety of local peoples.

In sculpture, carved wooden gilt and painted retablos were the principal decoration of churches. In the sixteenth century, they were generally executed by European artists in Renaissance style. Andalusian influence was strong in sculpture; European artists came to the New World, and European pieces, often figures of the Virgin, found their way there as well. The Europeans trained native artists, and their successors eventually developed retablo schemes and vocabularies of their own. These are among the most notable creations of the colonial period throughout Latin America.

In the seventeenth century, in accord with baroque tastes, retablo compositions acquired richness, with attention tending to concentrate on the center. The twisted salomonic column proliferated in New Spain after its introduction around mid-century. Important examples are the retablos of Santo Domingo in Puebla, of Meztitlán, and the three in the Capilla de los Ángeles in the cathedral of Mexico City. In South America mannerist scrolls and grotesques seem to have lasted longer into the seventeenth century than they did in New Spain; especially fantastic are the many carved pulpits. After around 1670, however, the salomonic column dominated retablo design. The retablo in the apse of the Compañía in Cuzco (ca. 1670) and that at Cocharcas are considered among the finest. In South America the carved ceiling is also of great importance. San Francisco in Quito is an example of an interior lined with golden retablos and ornament and covered by a gilt carved ceiling.

Variety and imagination in supports and decorative elements continued into the eighteenth century. There also developed a tendency toward polychromy and an emphatic unification in design that drew attention to a single central image or group of images, and subordinated or even eliminated the rest in favor of elaborate, often theatrical, framing devices. The impact of the ephemeral decorations for processions and of stage sets for theater was probably considerable and is only beginning to be assessed. In New Spain the *estípite* was introduced around 1720 and became the identifying hallmark of a style, sometimes called Churrigueresque, which includes rococo elements. As had happened with the salomonic column, it was first used on interior retablos and then moved to the exteriors, notably the facade of the Sagrario in Mexico City in the 1740s. However, unlike the salomonic column, the *estípite* was little used in South America. Rather, richness was enhanced there by further elaborations of earlier, ultimately mannerist forms in retablos and pulpits. The sculpted individual baroque figure acquired movement and often was part of a theatrical ensemble. These trends can be seen in winged Virgins of the Apocalypse of Quito. An urge toward lifelikeness is evident in the many figures made to be dressed in real clothing.

By the mid-eighteenth century it is possible to speak of neoclassical trends. In New Spain this signified a rejection of the *estípite* and a renewed interest in classical elements. In retablos there was a tendency to abstraction and rococo delicacy of ornament along with greater realism in the figures, which no longer were gilt but, rather, painted in naturalistic colors. In painting, a partial return to mannerist coloring mingled with rococo sweetness and simplified compositions, as in the work of Miguel Cabrera in Mexico City and Manuel de Samaniego in Quito. Concern among artists over their position and role coincided with these developments: Cabrera attempted to establish an academy and Samaniego composed a treatise on painting. A generalized secularization of culture is evident in the luxury of furniture and the decorative arts, in the proliferation of portraiture and domestic religious art, and in the increased interest in genre, exemplified in the *casta* paintings—representations of the racial mixes that made up Iberoamerican populations. These casta paintings also reflect a new sense of creole identity. The content of the casta paintings often defended the local culture from Europeans who labeled the Americas as inferior. An important

***De Espagnol y Mestiza: Castiza* by Miguel Cabrera (1695–1768).** The *casta* genre, such as Cabrera's depiction of a Spanish man and mestiza (mixed-race) woman with their child, represented the development of a new creole identity in painting in the eighteenth century. SCALA/ART RESOURCE, NY

factor in the taste for luxury goods was the commerce with the East, which brought to Spanish America great quantities of Oriental wares, on their way to Spain via Mexico. This contact with the East was the origin of the many ivory figures still to be seen, especially in Mexico.

With the establishment of the Academia De San Carlos in New Spain in 1785, academic neoclassicism formally entered the New World. Its introduction was accompanied by a fresh wave of artists from Europe who built severe monuments and buildings from California to the Southern Cone, among them Manuel Tolsá in New Spain, Antonio Bernasconi in Guatemala City, Domingo de Petrés in Colombia, Marias Maestro in Lima, and Joaquín Toesca in Chile. Neoclassicism also affirmed itself in sculpture and painting, notably in portraits, such as those by Rafael Jimeno in New Spain and by José Gil de Castro in Peru.

ART AND ARCHITECTURE IN BRAZIL

Brazil differs from the rest of Latin America in that the artistic relationship with the mother country was stronger, so much so that developments in Brazil were sometimes contemporary and complementary to developments in Portugal rather than derivative. Fortifications were as important as in the Spanish colonies, but urbanization tended to be more medieval in character, so that grid plans are the exception. As in Spanish America, church architecture concentrated talent and effort. Mannerist forms dominate seventeenth-century construction, as at São Benito in Rio de Janeiro (planned in 1617, built in 1670–1680) and in the Jesuit church (now cathedral) of Salvador, rebuilt between 1657 and 1672.

Most of what has been preserved is from the eighteenth century, when the typically Portuguese double-shell, elongated octagonal nave and elaborate *capela-mor* (presbytery) type of church architecture made its appearance. It was to dominate Brazilian colonial art; an early instance is Nossa Senhora da Glória do Outeiro in Rio de Janeiro (1714–1730). Later in the century, rococo curves were introduced into architectural plans and decorations. Although there are important examples of this in various places, such as in buildings by the Italian architect Antonio Giuseppe Landi in Belém, the best known instances are in Minas Gerais, beginning with Nossa Senhora do Rosário dos Prêtos in Ouro Prêto, built around 1785.

Sculpture and painting in colonial Brazil were often closely associated with architecture. As in Portugal, the typical retablo design of the seventeenth century was a series of ornamented concentric arches framing a tiered platform for the cult image. In the eighteenth century the earlier tight designs, like the one at São Francisco at Salvador (1723–1746), were transformed into more open and ascending compositions, exemplified especially in Minas Gerais. Much of the painting that is preserved is ceiling decoration, either within coffered ensembles, as at São Francisco at Salvador, or, after around 1740, in illusionistic compositions. Notable among these is the 1773 ceiling of A Conceição da Praia in Salvador, by José Joaquim da Rocha, and other numerous examples in Minas Gerais. Walls covered with painted tiles, a type of decoration that is ubiquitous in Portugal, also occurs in

Nossa Senhora da Glória do Outeiro (Our Lady of Glory of Outeiro), Rio de Janeiro, Brazil. The elaborate form of church architecture exemplified by Our Lady of Victory dominated Brazilian colonial art during the eighteenth century. © PETER M. WILSON/CORBIS

Brazil; an important example can be seen in the cloister at São Francisco, Salvador.

The flourishing of art in Minas Gerais corresponded to the inland shift in population and wealth of the eighteenth century. Patronage also changed. Art in the coastal cities and settlements had been produced for and often in monastic establishments, but in the interior, lay brotherhoods contracted a great number of works. As in Spanish America, rococo mixed with Oriental elements and there was a progressive secularization of culture, along with the introduction of neoclassical elements toward the end of the eighteenth century. The principal artist of this period in Minas Gerais was the crippled mulatto sculptor and architect Antônio Francisco Lisboa (O Aleijadinho, "Little Cripple"). Among his masterpieces are the Church of São Francisco at Ouro Prêto (1774–1794), a strikingly unified conception whose entrance protrudes between towers, complete with retablo and illusionistic ceiling decoration, and the

sanctuary of Bom Jesus de Matozinhos at Congonhas do Campo (1796–1805), with its sculptures representing the passion of Christ and with twelve prophets carved in soapstone. Although the quality of Aleijadinho's work and his fame have overshadowed his predecessors and contemporaries, artists such as his uncle, the architect Antônio Francisco Pombal, the sculptor Francisco Javier de Brito, and the painters Bernardo Pires da Silva and Manoel da Costa Ataíde, are only a few of the personalities who contributed to this last phase of Brazilian colonial art.

See also **Architecture: Architecture to 1900; Catholic Church: The Colonial Period; Missions: Jesuit Missions (Reducciones); Retablos and Ex-Votos.**

BIBLIOGRAPHY

Diego Angulo Iñiguez, *Historia de arte hispanoamericano,* 3 vols. Barcelona: 1945–1956.

Pál Kelemen, *Baroque and Rococo in Latin America.* New York: Macmillan, 1951.

George Kubler and Martin Soria, *Art and Architecture in Spain and Portugal and Their American Dominions, 1500 to 1800*. Baltimore: Penguin Books, 1959.

Manuel Toussaint, *Colonial Art in Mexico*. Austin: University of Texas Press, 1967.

Ramón Gutiérrez, *Arquitectura y urbanismo en Iberoamérica*. Madrid: Ediciones Cátedra, 1983.

Santiago Sebastián, José De Mesa, and Teresa Gisbert, *Arte iberoamericano desde la colonización a la independencia*. Vol. 29, *Summa Artis*. Madrid: Espasa-Calpe, 1985.

Octavio Paz, "Introduction," in *Mexico: Splendors of Thirty Centuries*. New York: Metropolitan Museum of Art/Boston: Little, Brown, 1990.

Santiago Sebastian, *El barroco iberoamericano* (1990).

Damián Bayón and Murillo Marx, *History of South American Colonial Art and Architecture*. New York: Rizzoli, 1992.

Additional Bibliography

Bailey, Gauvin A. *Art of Colonial Latin America*. New York: Phaidon, 2005.

Carrera, Magali M. *Imagining Identity in New Spain: Race, Lineage, and the Colonial Body in Portraiture and Casta Paintings*. Austin: University of Texas Press, 2003.

Fane, Diana. *Converging Cultures: Art & Identity in Spanish America*. New York: Harry N. Abrams, 1996.

Farago, Claire J, ed. *Reframing the Renaissance: Visual Culture in Europe and Latin America, 1450-1650*. New Haven: Yale University Press, 1995.

Gutiérrez, Ramón, ed. *Pintura, escultura y artes útiles en Iberoamérica, 1500-1825*. Madrid: Cátedra, 1995.

Katzew, Ilona. *Casta Painting: Images of Race in Eighteenth-Century Mexico*. New Haven: Yale University Press, 2004.

Katzew, Ilona, ed. *New World Orders: Casta Painting and Colonial Latin America*. New York: Americas Society, 1996.

Rishel, Joseph J., and Suzanne L. Stratton, eds. *The Arts in Latin America, 1492-1820*. New Haven: Yale University Press, 2006.

CLARA BARGELLINI

THE NINETEENTH CENTURY

The history of nineteenth-century Latin American art has two modes: one emphasizing continuity with European art, including the Eurocentric styles of the colonial viceroyalties, and another emphasizing change, fragmentation, and celebration of local values. The latter has tended to dominate, since the art history of the period has often been organized around political categories, stressing national schools, the break with the colonial past, and the emergence of popular art forms.

The nineteenth century in Latin America did indeed produce great changes, incessant wars and revolts, social upheavals, and both demographic and economic surges. Cities such as Caracas, Buenos Aires, Santiago, and Rio de Janeiro, which were just emerging at the end of colonization, would become important cultural centers by the twentieth century. Patronage also changed, from aristocratic to bourgeois, from centralized to highly dispersed, from religious to secular, with the emergence of a popular market for the arts becoming ever more important as the century progressed. It would, however, be a mistake to ignore the strong relationships of Latin American nineteenth-century art both to the previous viceregal traditions and to contemporary European art. Indeed, the history begins in the late colonial period, with the rise of neoclassicism and romantic art, so that the stylistic transition from the viceregal era to that of independence was initially quite smooth.

NEOCLASSICISM AND THE ACADEMIES

In Mexico, the establishment in 1785 of the Academia De San Carlos on neoclassical principles yielded a strong uniformity in "official" art from 1790, and in many ways it provides an archetype for Latin American art at the end of the colonial era and the early years of independence. Although the academy was in part an imposition of a centralizing Spanish Bourbon regime, it also responded to preexisting local artistic and intellectual currents. By 1811, the younger academic artists, studying under the Valencian painter Rafael Jimeno y Planes (1761–1825), the sculptor-architect Manuel Tolsá (1757–1816), and their Mexican fellow-professors, were using the neoclassical style and historical allusions to promote liberal political ideas (Pedro Patiño Ixtolinque, *King Wamba Threatened by One of His Electors,* relief sculpture, 1817). The interplay of ancient European and Mexican themes would continue to be a hallmark of Mexican academic art, with pre-Hispanic history incorporated by mid-century into the mix of subjects, as in the work of Manuel Vilar (*Tlahuicole,* 1851), José María Obregón (*The Discovery of Pulque,* 1869), and Rodrigo

Gutiérrez (*The Senate of Tlaxcala,* 1875). Furthermore, the importance of the neoclassical architecture of Tolsá (School of Mines, Mexico City) and colleagues such as Francisco Eduardo Tresguerras (Church of El Carmén, Celaya, 1802–1807) in setting the tone for the following century cannot be overstated. One should also note, however, the coexistence of romantic styles on a more personal basis, as in the works of the Mexican artist-patriot José Luis Rodríguez Alconedo (1762–1815).

Neoclassical taste was also established outside Mexico by official commissions and the importation of artists from Europe, most notably in Brazil, Argentina, Chile, and what would become Colombia. Again, architecture provides the best examples, as in the case of the works of Andrés Blanqui, an Italian Jesuit, and the Frenchman Prosper Catelin in Buenos Aires (Cathedral, finished 1823), of Fray Domingo de Petrés in Bogotá (*d.* 1811; Cathedral, Santa Fe de Bogotá), or, especially, of the Italian Joaquín Toesca in Chile (Santiago Mint, 1788–1799).

The Mexico City academy and its younger sibling at Puebla (in operation by 1812; confirmed in 1819) were apparently the only official arts organizations founded in the Spanish viceroyalties during the colonial era (private drawing academies operated sporadically in a number of viceregal cities, including those founded in Lima by Javier Cortés around 1810 and by the Sevillian José del Pozo soon thereafter). By the 1840s, however, there were academies operating in Jalisco (by about 1830), Bogotá, Caracas (chartered 1826, in operation by the mid-1830s), Quito, Cuenca, Buenos Aires (privately from 1818; at the university from 1822), Santiago (by 1849), and perhaps elsewhere (the topic has not been properly studied). Oddly, Lima, which had been such an important viceregal center, continued to rely on private schools, to its great detriment; as we will see, Peruvian artists seeking academic training before 1919 often traveled to Quito or Buenos Aires.

In Brazil, the transfer of the court of Dom João VI to Rio de Janeiro led, in 1816, to the arrival of a group of mostly French artists and architects under the neoclassicist Joachim Lebreton, with a mandate to educate young Brazilians. An academy was begun soon after, and, in 1826, the Académia Imperial de Belas Artes, under the direction of the painter Jean-Baptiste Debret (a cousin of David; 1768–1848), moved to its sumptuous new neoclassical building designed by Auguste-Henri-Victor Grandjean De Montigny (1776–1850), who also designed such important monuments as the Customs House. In Argentina, the teaching of the Swiss painter Johann Guth (in Argentina from 1817) and the Italian Paolo Caccianiga (from the late 1820s) at the university produced several generations of artists aware of both neoclassical and romantic values.

It is impossible to characterize the academies universally, since each organization reflected widely varying local patronage. In Brazil, the academy initially enforced a rigid French classicism, while Mexico City was more eclectic and the Puebla academy, responding to the ethnographic interests of its patrons, developed an important school of genre painting. At Mexico City, genre subjects were admitted in figure competitions early in the century, and landscape painting was an important part of the curriculum. In general, we may say that the academies were centers of continuity, if also of progress. A number of other constants may be cited: the academies were typically Eurocentric, inviting European artists to professorships and tending to suppress interest in the artistic values, if not the subject matter, of pre-Hispanic civilizations and indigenous social groups. The influence of Paris was mediated by that of Rome, particularly in Mexico and Buenos Aires, while Spanish artists often came from the Levant rather than from Madrid, yielding in both cases a more international and eclectic character. Finally, the academies were essential for keeping the Latin American artists abreast of technical developments and for providing a stable base for education and patronage in the midst of often chaotic political and economic situations. Many of the academies, especially in the first two-thirds of the century, maintained the racial openness that had already distinguished the arts in the viceregal era.

HISTORY PAINTING

Nineteenth-century Latin America produced a surprising number of academic history painters of the first rank, almost none of them known outside the field. In Mexico, these include—in addition to the already mentioned Vilar, Obregón, and Rodrigo Gutiérrez— Juan Cordero (1824–1884), Santiago Rebull (1829–1902), Felipe S. Gutiérrez (1824–1904), Félix Parra (1845–1919), and Leandro Izaguirre (1867–1941).

(A particular strength of the Mexican system was its program of sending young artists to Rome.) In Brazil, in addition to Lebreton, Debret, and their colleague Nicolas-Antoine Taunay (1755–1830), there are Vítor Meireles De Lima (1832–1903), Pedro Américo de Figueiredo (1843–1905), Rodolfo Amoêdo (1857–1941), and Manuel de Araújo Pôrto Alegre (1806–1879), an art historian and diplomat as well as a painter. The first half of the long career of Elyseu d'Angelo Visconti (1867–1944; also active in Europe) was dedicated to salon-style history painting; he turned to impressionist and postimpressionist works in the 1920s. In Chile and Peru, the Frenchman Raymond Quinsac Monvoisin (1790–1870; in America, 1845–1861) brought neoclassical principles but found his own style affected by romantic values. In Venezuela, Arturo Michelena (1863–1898) and Martín Tovar y Tovar (1828–1902) were among the many artists contributing to the artistic programs of the regime of Antonio Guzmán Blanco.

SCULPTURE

From the outset, the Mexican and Brazilian academies developed strong programs in sculpture, in part because of sculpture's role in the production of coinage and medals and its value as a communicator of public values, but also because drawing after sculpture was such an important aspect of the academic education. By the time of Alexander von Humboldt's visit in 1803, the Mexico City academy had acquired a sizable collection of plaster casts after ancient and European works, many still in use today. Manuel Tolsá's activities as sculptor-architect and teacher thus began a century-spanning academic dynasty that included his students Patiño Ixtolinque (mentioned earlier) and José María Labastida (active 1830–1849) and their successors, the Catalán Manuel Vilar (1812–1869) and the Mexican Miguel Noreña (1843–1894), with a general trajectory from neoclassicism through romantic appropriation to symbolic realism. In Brazil, Auguste-Marie Taunay (1768–1824), who had accompanied his brother Nicolas in the Lebreton group, served as the first professor of sculpture, establishing the neoclassical style. He was succeeded by João Joaquim Alão.

RELIGIOUS ART

The academies and their circles of patrons (including governments) in nineteenth-century Latin America quickly came to play the dominant role in patronage at the centers of power, replacing the Roman Catholic

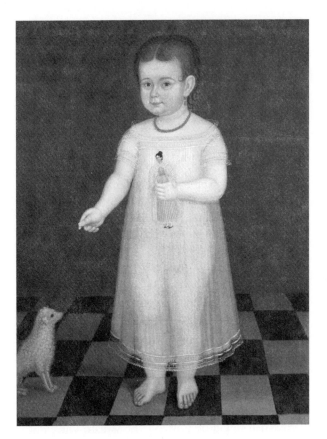

Young Girl with a Doll, 1838 (oil on canvas) by Jose Maria Estrada (c.1800–c.1860). MUSEO BELLAS ARTES, MEXICO/ GIRAUDON/ THE BRIDGEMAN ART LIBRARY

church. Indeed, if there is any one element that signals a break in Latin American culture at the time of Independence it is the collapse of centralized, "official" church patronage. In part due to liberal anticlericalism and the almost universal disestablishment of the church, the collapse was also in part aesthetic, since the new neoclassical principles were often at odds with significant aspects of viceregal religious art, such as the vast gilded retablos (altarpieces). Similarly, with a few notable exceptions, officially commissioned polychromed sculpture became almost purely replicative at the centers of power after about 1830. Although the church hierarchy continued to commission the occasional large-scale painting, religious histories and even devotional pictures were as likely to be the product of academic competitions and the salons as of clerical interest. As a result, much of the best religious art of the nineteenth century was produced for provincial patrons—local parishes, family altars and so forth—by artists with little or no academic training. Polychromed statuary became a significant folk art form, as it remains even in the southwestern United States to this day. Similarly, the *ex voto*, which may be found well back into the viceregal era, moved into the center of art history, with literally thousands of examples, many of extremely high artistic quality, produced in almost every country.

PORTRAITURE

The introduction of neoclassicism at the end of the colonial era meant that the straightforwardly realistic, classically simple bourgeois portrait, often at half-length, had already become dominant by about 1800; among its many virtues was the provision of a format in which provincial painters could express their genius even without benefit of academic training. We therefore see, occasionally in the same work, stylistic continuity and striking change, as the political and social forces unleashed at Independence are commemorated through portraiture by an extraordinarily wide range of artists.

Nonacademic masters have left an indelible image of the years of struggle for independence. The Peruvian José Gil de Castro ("El Mulato Gil"; *d.* ca. 1841), an officer in Bernardo O'Higgins's Chilean independence army, was active as a portraitist in Chile from 1814 to 1822 and thereafter in Argentina and Peru. His portraits of Bolívar and the other leaders of the independence movement are canonical, while his memorial portrait of *The Martyr Olaya* (1823) has come to sum up the entire era. In Mexico, José María Estrada (active ca. 1830–1865), who received provincial academic training in Jalisco, adapted both neoclassical formulas and viceregal traditions, such as the portrayal of deceased nuns, to his deceptively simple images, which can be at once naive and psychologically perceptive (*Don Francisco Torres* [*The Dead Poet*], 1849). That rural activity need not imply technical backwardness is best seen in the works of Hermenegildo Bustos (1832–1907), one of the finest portraitists of his century, who, in spite of describing himself as an "amateur," produced stunning evocations of the provincial bourgeoisie of west-central Mexico (*Don Juan Muñoz and Doña Juliana Gutiérrez*, 1868).

Academic portraiture may be said to have moved from a neoclassical mode, occasionally enhanced by romantic elements, in the first half of the century, to a reliance on the salon values of haute bourgeois European portraiture in the second half—although in both cases, French influence (including that of Franz Winterhalter) was often accompanied by contemporary Italian currents. In Mexico, one can cite Pelegrín Clavé (1810–1880)—the Catalán artist who, with Manuel Vilar, had been called to Mexico in 1846 to restructure and revitalize the Mexico City academy—and Felipe S. Gutiérrez (*Señora Sánchez Solís*, about 1875). (In contrast, Juan Cordero's portraits occasionally extol the *mestizo* origins of his sitters, perhaps as a critique of the Eurocentric values of Clavé and his supporters at the academy.) In Colombia, the autodidact José María Espinosa (1796–1883) produced surprisingly refined neoclassical portraits, while, later in the century, Epifanio Garay (1849–1903) adapted conventions learned in Paris both to portraiture and to history subjects, achieving a vivid bravura realism. Their quieter counterpart in Venezuela was Martín Tovar y Tovar. In Argentina, the Italian Carlos Enrique Pellegrini (1800–1875), originally trained as an engineer, established portraiture on neoclassical realist principles from 1828; he was soon joined by Cayetano Descalzi (born in Italy, active in Argentina after 1830), who, like Pellegrini, initially benefited from the patronage of the dictator Juan Manuel de Rosas and his circle, and by the Argentine Ignacio Baz (1826–1887), who eventually had to flee Rosas's tyranny. The Taunay family, along with Debret and the short-lived José Correia de Lima (1814–1857), developed neoclassical and romantic portraiture in Brazil; their counterparts in Chile were Raimundo Quinsac Monvoisin (1790–1870), Alejandro Cicarelli (1811–1879, to Chile via Brazil, 1848), and Cicarelli's pupil, the polymath Pedro Lira (1845–1912), who adapted oil techniques gained from a study of the seventeenth-century Dutch masters. As with Garay in Colombia and Gutiérrez in Mexico, the salon style of late-nineteenth-century academic portraiture was developed to a high degree of refinement by Rodolfo Amoêdo in Brazil. In Peru, this category suffered from the lack of a local official academy, which in part caused the talented portraitists Daniel Hernández (1856–1932) and Francisco Laso (see Genre, below) to go to Rome and Paris for training and to remain abroad through much of their careers.

LANDSCAPE AND NATURALIST DESCRIPTION

Beginning in the mid-1700s, an important series of naturalist expeditions—Cook (Pacific, 1768–1776), Mutis (northern Andes, 1784–1817), Humboldt (1799–1804), to cite only the best known—visited the Western Hemisphere or Pacific Rim to record previously unclassified flora and fauna. As Bernard

Still life with cat, plucked chicken, fruit, avocado, and olives, José Agustín Arrieta (1802–1874). Arrieta, who painted in Puebla, Mexico, was a chief proponent of still life in the nineteenth century. SCHALKWIJK/ART RESOURCE, NY

Smith has demonstrated, the artistic demands of these expeditions developed an empirical, realist style outside the aesthetic values of the academies, with immense importance for the future. To this we can add, with Stanton Catlin, that the necessarily New World subject matter of both the European and the American artist-recorders, including those who focused on human society as well as natural wonders, turned Latin American art away from dependence on European models and began to focus it on its own social and natural contexts.

Among the other new categories opened in Latin American art during the romantic era was landscape, which had been almost nonexistent in colonial art. Stimulus here came both from abroad, in the form of foreign artists who came in search of the picturesque or who were invited to teach at the academies, and from the national movements themselves, which produced patrons eager to see their independent homelands celebrated in art. Landscape was also affected by what Robert Rosenblum has called "the northern Romantic tradition" of England, Germany, and the United States, and so provided an important counterweight to neoclassical and academic influences. Among many itinerant European painters who came in search of *l'exotisme américain* were Thomas Ender (Austrian, 1793–1875; in Brazil, 1817–1818), Johann Moritz Rugendas (German, 1802–1858; active in Brazil, 1820–1823, Mexico, 1831–1834, Chile, Argentina, Peru, and Uruguay, 1834–1846), and Jean-Baptiste-Louis Gros (French, 1793–1870; in Mexico 1830s). In Mexico, landscape painting was established by Daniel Thomas Egerton (English, *d.* 1842; in Mexico from 1830) and Eugenio Landesio (Italian, 1810–1879; in Mexico from 1855), the latter having been called to teach the subject in the academy. Each was influenced by Claude Lorrain, but while Egerton looked to Lorrain's romantic qualities through Turner's eyes, Landesio stressed the classical aspects derived from the Venetian Renaissance and the Bolognese school, which he couched in a *plein air* realism. The resulting combination of romantic engagement, classical composition, and realist technique found its brilliant fruition in the works of the internationally famous Jóse María Velasco (Mexican, 1840–1912), who is rightfully considered among the greatest landscape masters of any period (*The Valley of México,* 1875). Landscape was established in Argentina by the polymath Prilidiano Pueyrredón (1823–1870), and in Uruguay by Juan Manuel Besnes (1788–1865) and Juan Manuel Blanes (1830–1901). Among its practitioners in Brazil (with a local tradition going back to Post in the seventeenth century) was Agostinho José da Mota (1824–1878). In Ecuador, landscape was introduced by Rafael Salas (1830–1906), perfected by Rafael Troya (1845–1921), and also practiced, in both oils and watercolors, by Joaquín Pinto (1842–1906), especially at the end of his career.

GENRE

Genre painting has strong roots in the colonial period (see the Mexican eighteenth-century *Castas*). In the nineteenth century, genre is dominated by *costumbrista* art, a sometimes contradictory blend of ethnographic realism and romantic celebration of the picturesque, often motivated by civic pride. (The movement affected literature as well as the visual arts.) Genre was thus closely allied with landscape and scientific illustration and often found official or academic as well as private support. As with landscape, visiting European painters made an important contribution and in many cases became residents, training or influencing artists born locally. In addition to Debret (in Brazil 1816–1824) and Rugendas, we may mention Frederick Catherwood (English, 1799–1854; in the Yucatán and Chiapas with the North American archaeologist J. L. Stephens, 1839–1841); Léon Gauthier (French; in Colombia 1850s), Claudio Gay (French, 1800–1873; in Chile 1843–1851), Adolphe d'Hastrel (French, 1805–1870; in Uruguay 1839–1841), Victor Patricio de Landaluze (Spanish, 1828–1889; in Cuba from about 1855), Conrad Martens (English, 1801–1871; in Uruguay 1833–1834; with Darwin to Valparaíso, 1834), Edward Walhouse Mark

(English, 1817–1895; in Colombia 1843–1856), Edouard H. T. Pingret (French, 1788–1875; in Mexico 1852), and Emeric Essex Vidal (English, 1791–1861; in Argentina and Uruguay, 1810s).

At the same time, American-born painters and lithographers, encouraged by local patronage, embraced genre enthusiastically. As has already been noted, Puebla, Mexico, was an important center of *costumbrismo,* with José Agustín Arrieta (1802–1874) the outstanding proponent of both genre and still life. In Mexico City, Felipe S. Gutiérrez blended academic composition with ethnographic realism, as in his *The Farewell,* which also alluded to the biography of the patron, the politician Felipe Sánchez Solís. Works such as *The Wake* (*El velorio,* 1889), by José María Jara (1866–1939), at once cater to and rise above the continued interest of the European salons in ethnic customs.

The best-known Peruvian *costumbrista* is the nonacademic Pancho Fierro (1803–1879), whose lively watercolors and caricatures compare favorably with Goya's drawings. (Fierro also painted murals, which have not survived.) Another Peruvian painter, Francisco Laso (1823–1869), produced what is surely the most stylistically advanced work by a Latin American artist at mid-century, the strikingly modern *Dweller in the Cordillera* (*Indian Potter*), painted in Paris in 1853. Laso's severe yet sensitive image of an indigenous potter—hieratically frontal, silhouetted against an ambiguous light wall, shadowed by a large-brimmed hat, almost symbolist in his isolation—has more in common with the abstracted portraits of Whistler than with the genre pictures of his contemporaries in Latin America. As with certain works by Debret at the beginning, José Correia de Lima in the middle, and Rodolfo Amoêdo or José Ferraz de Almeida Júnior (1850–1899; *The Guitarist,* 1899) at the end of the century in Brazil, Laso's image erases the distinctions between *costumbrismo* and traditional portraiture.

Perhaps because of romantic principles derived from the teaching of Guth and Caccianiga, in the area of the Río de la Plata genre and landscape were early fused. Along with Pueyrredón, the outstanding early exponent of *costumbrismo* in Argentina was the academy-trained painter and lithographer Carlos Morel (1813–1894), whose brilliant career

The Paraguayan in Her Desolate Mother Land (1880), by Juan Manuel Blanes (1830–1901). Images of indigenous people as allegorical figures appear in Latin American art at the end of the nineteenth century. The woman at the center of this painting, which is also known as *Paraguay: Image of Your Desolate Country*, represents Paraguay devastated by war. MUSEO NACIONAL ARTES PLASTICAS, MONTEVIDEO, SPAIN/ INDEX/ THE BRIDGEMAN ART LIBRARY

was curtailed by shock-induced insanity in 1845; there was also the French-trained Juan León Pallière (1823–1887), who worked in Buenos Aires in the 1850s, occasionally in collaboration with Enrique Sheridan (Argentine, trained in Britain, ca. 1835–1860). Perhaps the most extraordinary of the southern artists was Juan Manuel Blanes, the Argentine-born Uruguayan who combined the sweep of the pampas landscape, genre, contemporary history, and allegory in images of an almost symbolist effect (*Paraguay: Image of Your Desolate Country,* ca. 1880; *Review of Rio Negro by General Roca,* 1891). The allegorical use of the human figure, including indigenous types, was widespread at the end of the century, as in the cases of Amoêdo in Brazil or Felipe Gutiérrez and Jesús F. Contreras in Mexico.

GRAPHIC ARTS

The dominant means of expression in the graphic arts for the first half of the century is the archetypically romantic medium lithography, which was used by both visiting artists (such as Humboldt, Debret, and Egerton) and Americans as a means of distributing their images of *costumbrismo* and nationalistic landscape, as well as a vehicle for political cartooning and social satire, often influenced by Daumier. Among the many lithographers active in Latin America was the Englishman Joseph Skinner (active in Peru around 1805); the Italian Claudio Linati (1790–1832; in Mexico from 1825), who first brought lithogra-phy to Mexico; and Linati's contemporary, the German Karl Nebel (1805–1855; in Mexico from 1829), who preceded Catherwood in depicting pre-Hispanic monuments as well as *costumbrista* scenes. From the 1830s, a popular graphic tradition became increasingly dominant, with audiences among both the bourgeoisie and the working classes. The most famous artist active in this sphere was the Mexican José Guadalupe Posada (1851–1913), whose works have become such an important influence on modern artists. Although Posada's audience may not have been as uneducated as is sometimes assumed, his sources in popular art are clear, and his vivid, highly abstracted renderings in a wide variety of graphic media (including direct carving in type metal) had the effect of bridging the worlds of the bourgeois fine arts and the arts of peasants and working people.

ARCHITECTURE

Until mid-century, various local versions of the neoclassical style predominated; as late as 1854–1865 Pueyrredón's designs for Buenos Aires could maintain a basically neoclassical format. Eventually, architecture took up the romantic attitude: one finds Florentine Renaissance villas and even neo-Gothic structures, especially in Brazil, where the colonial use of tiles was often maintained in even the severest Tuscan design. After the 1850s, however, the influence of French urbanism under Baron Haussmann and Beaux-Arts eclecticism gradually predominated, as may be seen in Mexico City's Paseo de la Reforma or in the Alameda and other projects at Santiago de Chile initiated by François Brunet de Baines (called from France in 1849 to organize a school of architecture) and Benjamín Vicuña Mackenna, the superintendent of public works. In 1872, Peru used the plans of French engineer and architect Gustave Eiffel to build the Palacio de la Exposición in Lima, the Fenix Theater in Arequipa and a church in Tacna. (This trend continued in the twentieth century, as the Avenida Rio Branco in Rio de Janeiro [1903–1906] indicates.)

The policies of Porfirio Díaz in Mexico, which encouraged European and North American investment, also opened up Mexican architecture to international influence just at the time that rapid economic expansion made considerable new construction necessary. Ministry buildings (such as that now housing the National Museum of Art) were built in a modified Beaux-Arts style, while the use of boulevards, initiated under Maximilian in the 1860s, continued to be the norm. French influence was often tempered by Italian intervention, most notably in the work of Adam Boari at the turn of the century, including the Florentine Renaissance revival post office and the difficult-to-characterize Palace of Fine Arts, which was completed after 1919 by Antonio Muñoz and Federico Mariscal. A similar phenomenon may be seen in Buenos Aires, where economic expansion at the turn of the century led to the adoption of a neo-baroque Beaux-Arts mode in the works of Alejandro Christophersen (San Martín Palace) and Julio Dormal (final design for the Teatro Colón, 1905–1908). Many of the finest works of nineteenth-century architecture, however, are anonymous or not yet attributed, especially the many suburban villas, rural haciendas, and more modest urban dwellings of the new upper-middle class.

IMPRESSIONISM, SYMBOLISM, AND ART NOUVEAU

For the most part, the development of impressionist and postimpressionist European avant-garde styles is a twentieth-century phenomenon in Latin America. One should cite, however, the paintings of Martín A. Malharro (1865–1911), a precursor of the impressionists active by the 1880s in Argentina, and the symbolist or art nouveau aspects of the work of the Mexican Julio Ruelas (1870–1907) and his follower, Roberto Montenegro (1885–1964), in both painting and the graphic arts. Mexican sculpture, especially in the hands of Jesús F. Contreras (1866–1902; influenced by Rodin) and his younger associates Agustín Ocampo and Fidencio Nava, carried a symbolist decadent mode into the first years of the new century.

See also **Academia de San Carlos; Architecture: Architecture to 1900; Debret, Jean-Baptiste; Posada, José Guadalupe; Tolsá, Manuel.**

BIBLIOGRAPHY

Gabriel Giraldo Jaramillo, *La pintura en Colombia* (1942).

José Maria dos Reis, *Historia da pintura no Brasil* (1944).

Adrián Merlino, *Diccionario de artistas plásticas de la Argentina* (1954).

P. M. Bardi, *The Arts in Brazil* (1956).

José Pedro Argul, *Pintura y escultura del Uruguay* (1958); *Pintura venezolana 1661–1961* (1960).

Antonio R. Romera, *Historia de la pintura chilena* (1960).

Bernard Smith, *European Vision and the South Pacific, 1768–1850* (1960).

Yara Tupynambá, *Tres séculos e meio de pintura no Brasil* (1961).

Jean Charlot, *Mexican Art and the Academy of San Carlos* (1962).

Julio E. Payró, *23 Pintores de la Argentina, 1810–1900* (1962).

José María Vargas, *Historia del arte ecuatoriano* (1964).

Stanton Loomis Catlin and Terence Grieder, *Art of Latin America Since Independence* (1966).

Justino Fernández, *El arte del siglo XIX en México* (1967).

Alfredo Boulton, *Historia de la pintura en Venezuela*, 2 vols. (1968).

Leopoldo Castedo, *A History of Latin American Art and Architecture* (1969).

Josefa Emilia Sabor, *Bibliografía básica de obras de referencia de artes y letras para la Argentina* (1969).

Gaspar Galasz and Milan Ivelic, *La pintura en Chile desde la colonia hasta 1981* (1981).

Caracas, Consejo Municipal del Distrito Federal, *Guzmán Blanco y el Centenario del Libertador, 1883* (1983).

Fausto Ramírez, *La plástica del siglo de la independencia* (1985).

Dawn Ades, *Art in Latin America: The Modern Era, 1820–1980* (1989).

Fausto Ramírez, *Mexico: Splendors of Thirty Centuries* (1990).

Additional Bibliography

Bleys, Rudi. *Images of Ambiente: Homotextuality and Latin American Art, 1810—Today.* New York: Continuum, 2000.

Gutiérrez Viñuales, Rodrigo, and Ramón Gutiérrez. *Pintura, escultura y fotografía en Iberoamérica: Siglos XIX y XX.* Madrid: Cátedra, 1997.

McIntyre, Kellen Kee, and Richard E. Phillips. *Woman and Art in Early Modern Latin America.* Boston: Brill, 2007.

Ortiz Angulo, Ana. *La pintura mexicana independiente de la Academia en el siglo XIX.* México, D.F.: Instituto Nacional de Antropología e Historia, 1995.

Zarur, Elizabeth Netto Calil, and Charles M. Lovell, eds. *Art and Faith in Mexico: The Nineteenth-Century Retablo Tradition.* Albuquerque: University of New Mexico Press, 2001.

MARCUS B. BURKE

THE TWENTIETH CENTURY

Latin American art in the twentieth century reflected the influence of styles and movements that characterized European and North American art of the period. For this reason, it is most important to consider developments in the art of Latin America together with similar developments in places like Paris and New York.

During the first two decades of the century, Latin American art absorbed the combined influences of Spanish realism (exemplified by Joaquín Sorolla and Ignacio Zuloaga), and symbolism. In Mexico, Saturnino Herrán (1887–1918) depicted the Mexican Indians in a nonidealized manner, whereas Joaquín Claussell (1866–1935) painted the native landscape with impressionist techniques. In Brazil, Elyseu d'Angelo Visconti (1867–1944) worked in an impressionist manner, and in Uruguay, Pedro Blanes Viale (1879–1926) produced luminous, sun-drenched landscapes.

Dance in the Courtyard, **by Pedro Figari (1861–1938),** a postimpressionist scene of Buenos Aires social life in the 1920s. ART RESOURCE, NY

Varieties of postimpressionism had a large following, including Armando Reverón (1889–1954) of Venezuela, Pedro Figari (1861–1938) of Uruguay, and Andrés de Santa María (1860–1945) of Colombia. Reverón became the hermit of Macuto beach, where he painted "white" coastal scenes in which he reconverted, or purified, the colors of the spectrum through light back into white. Santa María explored the properties of distortion and artificial light in his interior scenes. Figari, also an essayist, diplomat, and lawyer, painted scenes of salon life in Buenos Aires, as well as the African ritual dances of Montevideo known as the Candomblé, in bright flat colors and patterned compositions reminiscent of Edouard Vuillard in France.

MODERNISM

During this pivotal period throughout Latin America, there was a great deal of exchange in aesthetic practices, philosophies, and ideas between artists and writers. Poets, educators, critics, philosophers, and writers shared space on the pages of various avant-garde journals published throughout the Americas during the 1920s, 1930s, and 1940s. Imagery verbalized in the poetry of the period was often mirrored in aesthetic practice. Modernity here was marked by a strong interest in European movements and, equally, by an interest in investigating indigenous cultural production with the intent to forge the concept of a so-called national art. The most significant part of this development centered on the search for authenticity as a way to validate national culture. This process of authentication involved the recognition, examination, and embracing of historical and diasporic cultures that informed the eclectic character of modern culture and society throughout the Americas. Pre-Hispanic cultures, remnants of colonial European culture, and culture derived from the history of enslaved Africans were all embraced by some artists, writers, and intellectuals as evidence of a genuine national culture. Together with these influences, the language of European avant-garde movements was adapted in order to create a modernist aesthetic that was more specific to this part of the globe. Varying degrees of indigenous, pre-Hispanicizing or Africanizing elements were present, as were equal parts of cubist, surrealist, and abstract tendencies.

Significantly, cubism and futurism exerted a major influence throughout Latin America as a basis for the innovations of the 1920s and after. Diego Rivera (1886–1957) of Mexico was a cubist between 1913 and 1917. In Argentina, Emilio Pettoruti (1892–1971) developed a highly personal version of synthetic cubism with delicately orchestrated colors. Beyond his cubist influence, Pablo Picasso was imitated in all of his stages, especially the work he produced in the 1920s and 1930s.

Throughout the 1920s, artists began to affirm their regional identities by applying a synthesis of cubism, futurism, and expressionism to local themes. An avant-garde emerged in Mexico, Cuba, Argentina, Chile, and Brazil. Each movement made significant advances in terms of developing a visual art with a national ethos. From the start of the 1920s through mid-century, avant-garde groups in capital cities throughout the Americas published periodicals about visual art and culture that included not only visual art, but also fiction, poetry, and essays on the modern condition. Much of the material published in these journals addressed the growing interest in national culture as filtered through a romanticized view of history, particularly the pre-Hispanic past.

One of the significant movements of the early 1920s was the Mexican mural movement. In 1921, after General Álvaro Obregón had consolidated power as president, education minister José Vasconcelos invited a dozen or so artists to paint murals on the walls of public buildings. Among the invited group, three are particularly significant for their contributions: José Clemente Orozco (1883–1949); Diego Rivera; and David Alfaro Siqueiros (1896–1974). In their pre-mural careers, each artist had taken a different route. Orozco had earned his living as a political cartoonist while painting expressionist watercolors of brothel interiors. Rivera had been a bohemian in Paris, experimenting with the style of all the major movements from impressionism to cubism. Siqueiros, who had fought in the Mexican Revolution, was leaving behind the mild impressionism picked up at the Open Air school and was flirting with constructivist as well as futurist approaches to art. These muralists revived the ancient techniques of fresco and encaustic and took revolutionary and indigenous themes as the subjects of their murals. Orozco's view was dark and dystopic, while Rivera and Siqueiros (both committed Communists) were

La Justicia Humana **(Human Justice),** a mural in Mexico's Supreme Court of Justice building by José Clemente Orozco, one of the great muralists of the twentieth century. *Human Justice* is typical of Orozco's dark images of suffering and violence. SCHALKWIJK/ART RESOURCE, NY. © 2007 ARTISTS RIGHTS SOCIETY (ARS), NEW YORK / SOMAAP, MEXICO CITY

painters of revolutionary hope. The mural movement in Mexico became associated with the Syndicate of Technical Workers, Painters, and Sculptors (Syndicato de Trabajadores Técnicos, Pintores y Escultores), whose official organ was the newspaper *El Machete.*

In 1924 the Cuban painter Victor Manuel (1897–1969) introduced modern art in Cuba with the aid of the painters Eduardo Abela (1889–1965), Carlos Enríquez (1900–1957), Fidelio Ponce De León (1895–1949), and Amelia Peláez (1897–1968) and the sculptor Juan José Sicre (1898–1974). These artists were supported by the essayist Jorge Mañach and the editorial staff of the *Revista de Avance.* This publication is significant in that it chronicled the development of cultural nationalism and avant-garde practice in Cuba at the end of the 1920s. Significantly, the journal published a questionnaire that it sent to artists, writers, and critics all over the Americas about art and identity. The results of the questionnaire were published in various issues of the journal, alongside articles about cubism, futurism, modernist poetry, and ruminations on the influence of Africa and indigenous cultures in the Americas.

In Argentina, poets and painters banded together in 1924 to found the review *Martin Fierro.* The group included the painters Juan del Prete (1897–1987), Alejandro Xul Solar (1887–1963), and Emilio Pettoruti, as well as the writers Leopoldo Lugones, Ricardo Guiraldes, and Jorge Luis Borges. Particularly noteworthy in the pages of *Martin Fierro* are the poetry and cubist-inspired images of artists such as Pettoruti. Each issue treated literature and poetry together with discussions of visual art, film, music, and theater.

In Chile, a group called Montparnasse was founded in 1928. It included the painters Camilo Mori (1896–1973) and Pablo E. Burchard ((1875–1964). This group of young painters earned their name because the School of Fine Arts in Chile sent them to study in Paris with their modernist colleagues. Their first exhibition was held in 1923 in Santiago and was a revelation to the public. Challenging the norms of academic painting in Chile at the time, this group of artists favored ordinary subjects and the modernist styles of the French painters. As in other countries, a modernist publication appeared in Chile. Titled *Zig-Zag,* it was first published in 1905 and was linked to the country's most important newspaper, *El Mercurio*.

The most revolutionary movement occurred in Brazil, where the painter Emiliano di Cavalcanti (1897–1976) and several poets organized the Semana de Arte Moderna (Modern Art Week) in São Paulo during 1922. This was a weeklong festival of the arts that included dance, poetry readings, and an art exhibition. Perhaps the greatest innovator within Latin American art of the 1920s was Tarsila do Amaral (1886–1973). A native of São Paulo, Amaral had studied in Paris with Fernand Léger and André Lhote. Her mature style is one of colorful and bold forms. She was a founding member of the Pau Brasil (Brazilian Wood) movement in 1924, as well as of the *movimento antropófago* (anthropophagist movement) in 1928. She collaborated with her husband, the poet Oswaldo de Andrade, in a series of paintings and poems in which native imagery is fused with that of modern industry. Both poet and painter were involved with the magazine *Klaxon*.

SOCIAL REALISM

During the 1920s the Parisian avant-garde was rejected whereas the aesthetics of the Mexican muralists was embraced in the Andean countries. In Peru, José Sabogal (1888–1956) demonstrated a commitment to mural painting as well as to indigenous subject matter. In 1926, in La Paz, Bolivia, the Academia Nacional de Bellas Arte (National Academy of Fine Arts) was founded and later directed by Cecilio Guzman de Rojas (1899–1950), a Bolivian painter trained in Spain who painted Indians in a symbolist style.

The Mexicans' call for a figurative and socially committed art was most influential in countries such as Peru, Bolivia, and Ecuador. Eduardo Kingman (1913–1997) and Oswaldo Guayasamín (1919–1999) were the main representatives of social realism in Ecuadorian painting. In 1933 Siqueiros traveled to Argentina, where the painters Juan Carlos Castagnino (1908–1972), Lino Spilimbergo (1896–1964), and Antonio Berni (1905–1981) collaborated with him on a mural near Buenos Aires. Berni later became known for his large collages, made out of diverse materials salvaged from refuse, as well as for his iconographic characters Juanito Laguna, a poor slum boy, and Ramona Montiel, a prostitute.

Through them, Berni expressed his social and political concerns. In Brazil, a nationalistic mural style was dominated by Cândido Portinari (1903–1962), who painted scenes of local customs and life among the poor with less political emphasis than in the work of the Mexicans.

CONSTRUCTIVISM, SURREALISM, AND ABSTRACTION

Alongside social realism, new avant-garde groups continued to emerge throughout Latin America in the 1930s and 1940s. In 1934 the Uruguayan painter Joaquín Torres-García (1874–1949) returned to Montevideo, where he founded the Asociación de Arte Constructivo as well as his workshop school. Among the artists who studied with the constructivist master were Julio Alpuy (b. 1919), Gonzalo Fonseca (1922–1997), and Washington Barcala (1920–1993), as well as Torres-García's two sons.

A touch of the fantastic had existed in Mexican art throughout the 1920s and 1930s in the paintings of Frida Kahlo (1907–1954) and Juan O'Gorman (1905–1982). Surrealism was introduced in Latin America after the mid-1930s. André Breton visited Mexico in 1938, and in 1942 the surrealist European painters Remedios Vara (1908–1963) and Leonora Carrington (b. 1917) sought refuge there from World War II. The painters Manuel Rodríguez Lozano (1897–1970), Julio Castellanos (1905–1947), and others who were associated with the antimuralist group of poets, Los Contemporaneos, practiced a classicism tinged with surrealist as well as homoerotic overtones. In the mid-1930s the Argentine Juan Battle-Planas (1911–1966) exhibited his paranoiac X-rays in Buenos Aires. In 1939 the Orion group emerged, with the painters Luis Barragán (1902–1988), Vicente Forte (1912–1980), and Leopoldo Presas (b. 1915), who had affinities with the Italian metaphysical school. Raquel Forner (1902–1988), another Argentine painter, went through a surrealist phase before devoting herself to themes of space travel in a vivid, expressionist style.

The Cubans Wilfredo Lam (1902–1982) and Mario Carreño (1913–1999) had affinities with surrealism. The Guatemalan modernist Carlos Mérida (1891–1984) practiced a subtle geometric abstraction with roots in Maya pictographs. The Chileans Roberto Matta (1911–2002) and Nemesio Antúnez (1918–

1993) both studied architecture but later turned to a surrealist or metaphysical abstractionist type of painting. Surrealist variations found many adherents in Chile, including Rodolfo Opazo (b. 1935), Juan Gómez Quiros (b. 1939), Ricardo Yrrárazaval (b. 1931), and Guillermo Núñez (b. 1930). In Mexico, Rufino Tamayo (1899–1991) represented a modernist opposition to the mural movement. His synthesis of pre-Columbian and cubist forms, his use of the colors of contemporary Mexican popular culture, and his call for an apolitical art had a profound effect on the younger generation of artists.

PLURALISM AND THE POSTWAR PERIOD

After the mid-1940s, abstract art took a firm hold, with geometric tendencies becoming more prevalent in the east and informalist ones in the west. In Argentina the Arte Concreto-Invención movement emerged under the leadership of Tomás Maldonado (b. 1922). Informalist abstraction had its exponents in the work of the Argentines Sarah Grilo (b. 1921) and José Antonio Fernández-Muro (b. 1920), the Uruguayan Carlos Paez Villaró (b. 1923), and the Brazilian Manabu Mabe (1924–1997).

In the 1950s a number of new artists emerged in Central America, Cuba, and South America. In Nicaragua Armando Morales (b. 1927) painted flat black-and-white abstractions endowed with mystical meanings before turning to a figurative, more metaphysical style. In Colombia Alejandro Obregón (1920–1992) developed a style derived from Picasso, Antoni Clavé, and informalism, whereas Enrique Grau (1920–2004) painted homoerotic images of chubby male youths. In Ecuador, Manuel Rendón (1894–1982) initiated abstract painting, attracting followers in the younger artists Aníbal Villacis (b. 1927) and Enrique Tábara (b.1930). The Bolivian María Luisa Pacheco (1919–1982) conjured up jagged Andean peaks in glowing textile colors, and the Peruvian Fernando de Szyzlo (b. 1925) painted abstraction in luminous glazes inspired by the poetry and religion of the Incas. In Cuba, René Portocarrero (1912–1986), Mariano Rodríguez (1912–1990), and Cundo Bermúdez (b. 1914) painted neocolonial interiors, roosters, and dancers in a decorative expressionism. The sculptor Roberto Diago was inspired by African forms and used dark, polished wood for his creations that referred to Cuba's complex cultural history.

INFORMALISM, NEOFIGURATION, AND GEOMETRY

The informalist tendency spread to sculpture in the 1940s and 1950s. The Argentine Libero Badii (1916–2001) was very much a part of this current. In the meantime, Francisco Zuñiga (1912–1998), a Costa Rican residing in Mexico, depicted the Indian woman in a monumental style derived from the Mexican muralists. In Cuba, Roberto Estopiñán (b. 1921) brought to his work a neofigurative sensibility that had much in common with the postwar work of Marino Marini in Italy and Henry Moore in Britain.

From the late 1950s and into the 1960s, a violent neofiguration spread throughout the Spanish-speaking Americas. José Luis Cuevas (b. 1934), Marcello Grassman (b. 1925), Julio Zachrisson (b. 1930), Carlos Alonso (b. 1929), and Hermenegildo Sabat (b. 1933) practiced forms of neofiguration exclusively through the media of drawing and printmaking. In Colombia, Fernando Botero (b. 1932) started painting obese figures satirizing Colombian society. Jacobo Borges (b. 1931) of Venezuela worked in an expressionist manner in which vividly colored figures swirled through the pictorial space. In Argentina, Luis Felipe Noé (b. 1933), Ernesto Deira (1928–1986), Rómulo Macció (b. 1931), and Jorge de la Vega (1930–1971) made their appearance under the collective name of Otra Figuración (Other Figuration). These artists specialized in a colorful expressionist drip technique that depicted faces and monstrous creatures, reminiscent of the COBRA painters.

The Mexicans Gunther Gerzso (1915–2000), Vicente Rojo (b. 1932), and Manuel Felguerez (b. 1928) all worked abstractly throughout the 1960s, the latter two favoring hard-edged compositions. Francisco Toledo (b. 1940) followed in Tamayo's footsteps while adding a fantastic, erotic edge to his compositions. The Guatemalan Rodolfo Abularach (b. 1933) turned the human eye into a cosmic icon, first in highly detailed pen-and-ink drawings and etchings and later in oils. Marcelo Bonevardi (1929–1994), an Argentine, embedded polished wooden constructions in flatly painted metaphysical compositions on canvas. In Colombia, variations of constructivism and geometric abstraction were to be found in the work of sculptors Ramírez Villamizar (1923–2004) and Edgar Negret (b. 1920) and

A bronze sculpture by Fernando Botero stands in the Plaza Botero, Medellín, Colombia. Botero's late-twentieth-century images of grossly obese military leaders, clergy, and other elites satirizes the greed of Colombian society.
© FERNANDO BENGOECHEA/BEATEWORKS/CORBIS

painters Om-ar Rayo (b. 1928) and David Manzur (b. 1929). The latter, however, eventually returned to figuration through a reinterpretation of Renaissance themes.

Venezuela and Argentina were the major producers of optical and kinetic art. Jesús Rafael Soto (1923–2005), Alejandro Otero (1921–1990), and Carlos Cruz Diez (b. 1923) were the leading kinetic artists in Caracas. Otero, under the influence first of Paul Cézanne and later of constructivism, produced a series of coffee pots throughout the late 1940s. In the 1950s he began color rhythms, which consisted of superimposed vertical bands painted in bright Duco colors. Soto, expatriated in Paris for many years, created his delicately orchestrated "vibrations" by suspending thin wires from frames or attaching squares to thinly striped canvas or wood panels, creating a rippling effect. Later Soto produced the "penetrables," environments made of densely pac-

ked translucent nylon tubes through which people could walk. Cruz Diez, also living in Paris, executed his "physichromies" by painting along perpendicular vertical strips attached to a flat surface instead of the surface itself. Argentines and Brazilians have explored plastic, metal, light, glass, and other materials in their optical and kinetic work. The leading Argentine artists working in this area have been Rogelio Polesello (b. 1939), Julio Le Parc (b. 1938), Eduardo Mac Entyre (b. 1929), Miguel Angel Vidal (b. 1928), and Ary Brizzi (b. 1930).

In the late 1950s and throughout the 1960s, Puerto Rico produced some major artists in spite of the aggressive avalanche of pop culture from the United States. Julio Rosado del Valle (b. 1922) was a self-taught expressionist who moved between figuration and abstraction. Luis Hernández Cruz (b. 1936) was an abstractionist with constructivist tendencies who produced paintings as well as sculpture. Myrna Baez (b. 1931) was a printmaker and painter who worked with the human figure within a landscape context, whereas Lorenzo Homar (1913–2004) and Rafael Tufiño (b. 1922) were printmakers who were devoted to a social realist aesthetic. Undoubtedly, the island's greatest artist is the portraitist Pancho Rodón (b. 1934), whose artistic production consists of devastating depictions of such Latin American luminaries as Borges, Luis Muñoz Marín, Juan Rulfo, and Rómulo Betancourt.

Critics as diverse as Julio Payro, Luis Cardoza y Aragón, Jorge Romero Brest, José Gómez Sicre, and Marta Traba have documented the development of the visual arts in Latin America in the twentieth century. It is true that Latin America is responsible for no original "ism" in that century, but nevertheless, thanks to its firmly held aim of maintaining connection with its communities by means of visual messages charged with meaning, it has gradually produced an image bank of real importance to the region.

CONTEMPORARY ART

In the early twenty-first century a number of important artists were working throughout the Americas in every medium imaginable. Galleries and private art collections grew, as did institutions dedicated specifically to the exhibition of modern and contemporary art. Nearly every country throughout the Americas boasted a museum of contemporary art and, in some form, a biennial exhibition. This contributed significantly to the growth of the contemporary art market and to the acceptance of various forms of contemporary expression. In addition, many artists of the newer generation lived both in the United States and in their home country, adding another level of significance to their work. Postmodernism allowed artists throughout the Americas to broach a number of current social, political, and aesthetic issues through various expressive modes.

The Dominican Republic developed a strong group of young artists who showed work both at home and abroad. Among this group, Raquel Paiewonski (b. 1969), Quisqueya Hernández, and Jorge Piñeda (b. 1961) stand out. In neighboring Haiti, a group of artists that includes Pierrot Barra (1942–1999), Mireille Délice (b. during 1970–1975), Jeannot Jean-Philippe (1958–1997), and Yves Telemak have been making work that deals with imagery related to particular aspects of Haitian culture, including voodoo. Inspired by pop culture imagery that includes tourism brochures and posters, these artists use nontraditional images to inspire their work in more conventional media such as sculpture and flag decoration.

PUBLIC ART AND INTERVENTIONS

In Puerto Rico, Chemi Rosado Seijo (b. c. 1974), Jennifer Allora (b. 1974), and Guillermo Calzadilla (b. 1971) have made significant contributions to the development of contemporary art. Chemi Rosado Seijo organized a public art project in which the homes of some of the disenfranchised people of the island were treated to a new coat of green paint to strike a balance between the domestic and the environmental. Charles Juhasz-Alvarado (b. 1965) created large-scale public sculpture-based projects. Similarly, since the 1960s, Brazil has had a very strong contemporary art movement, including a number of groups that had undertaken interventions, ephemeral or temporary projects, and other forms of public art practices that address a larger audience than the traditional museum and gallery visitor. Early leaders of this kind of work include Cildo Meireles (b. 1948). He was followed by various groups of younger artists that include Interferencias Urbanas (Urban Interferences, in Rio de Janeiro), Radial, and Azucar Invertido (Inverted Sugar).

Projects such as inSite, which took place on the border between Tijuana, Mexico, and San Diego, brought attention to the relationship between artists working in both countries. The work of Mexican conceptual artist Yoshua Okon (b. 1970) deals with issues around labor, industry, and contemporary politics. Other influential Mexican contemporary artists include Miguel Calderón (b. 1971) and Gabriel Orozco (b. 1962).

CONCEPTUAL ART AND PERFORMANCE

Conceptual art continues to be a significant mode for many artists throughout the Americas. It was a particularly useful mode for challenging authority and for raising questions about thought processes and human existence. This method of working was particularly prevalent from the late 1960s through the 1970s. Perhaps one of the most well-known groups to practice early conceptual and performance art was Tucumán Arde (Tucumán Is Burning), featuring Marta Minujín (b. 1944), working in Buenos Aires. Juan Downey (1940-1992) was a significant early performance artist working in Chile. In Los Angeles, the performance group ASCO (Nausea) had great influence on later generations. Younger conceptual artists have created a more stylized approach, employing sophisticated fabricators in the creation of their projects, in addition to creating their own work. Among noted current practitioners are José Antonio Hernandez Diez (Venezuela, b. 1964), Tunga (Brazil, b. 1952), Doris Salcedo (Colombia, 1958), the collective known as Los Carpinteros (The Carpenters, Cuba), Waltercio Caldas (b. 1946), and Carlos Leppe (b. 1952), among numerous others.

PAINTING AND SCULPTURE

Many artists remained committed to painting and sculpture and to variations on these media, which sometimes included installations. Among the noted are Manuel Mendive (b. 1944, Cuba), Alexis Leyva (Kcho) (b. 1970, Cuba), Graciela Sacco (b. 1956, Argentina), Luis Felipe Noé (b. 1933, Argentina), and Fernanda Brunet (b. 1963, Mexico). Painters favoring a neo-figurative approach included Patricia Villanueva in Peru, Lina Espinoza in Colombia (b. 1964), and Victor Rodriguez (b. 1970, Mexico). Significant painters working in Chile included Claudio Bravo (b. 1936), Fernando de Szyszlo (b. 1925, Peru), and Arturo Duclos (b. 1959). In terms of sculpture, Laura Sánchez and Aldo Shiroma are currently working in Peru and Mateo Lopez in Colombia and Matías Pinto de Aguilar in Chile are also noteworthy. Belkis Ramirez (b. 1960) is a gifted sculptor working in the Dominican Republic.

THE CONTEMPORARY DIASPORA

In terms of contemporary Latin American art, the Latino diaspora cannot be discounted. Some of the most innovative Latin American artists are living and working in the United States or in Europe, where the market for their work is larger, and experimental contemporary art is well supported. They often have careers in both places, as their work is sought after both at home and abroad. Among some of the significant expatriate artists are José Bedia (b. 1959), Maria Magdalena Campos-Pons (b. 1959), Luís Camnitzer (b. 1937), Luís Cruz Azaceta (b. 1942), Eugenio Dittborn (b. 1943), Edouard Duval-Carrié (b. 1954), Leandro Erlich (b. 1973), Nayda Collazo-Llorenz (b. 1968), Alfredo Jaar (b. 1956), Guillermo Kuitca (b. 1961), Marc Latamie (b. 1952), Gordon Matta-Clark (1943–1978), Vik Muñiz (b. 1961), Ernest Neto (b. 1964), Liliana Porter (b. 1941), Ernesto Pujol (b. 1957), Juan Sánchez (b. 1954), Andres Serrano (b. 1950), and Jorge Tacla (b. 1958). There are many more such artists who make their homes and careers in two or more countries. The development of contemporary art and international opportunities for younger artists has encouraged the growth of artistic production and the development of contemporary art venues throughout the Americas.

See also **Alfaro Siqueiros, David; Amaral, Tarsila do; Antúnez, Nemesio; Berni, Antonio; Borges, Jacobo; Botero, Fernando; Bravo, Claudio; Camnitzer, Luis; Carreño, Mario; Carrington, Leonora; Contemporáneos, Los; Cruz Diez, Carlos; Cuevas, José Luis; Da Matta, Roberto; Deira, Ernesto; di Cavalcanti, Emiliano; Dittborn, Eugenio; Felguérez, Manuel; Figari, Pedro; Fonseca, Gonzalo; Forner, Raquel; Gerzso, Gunther; Grau, Enrique; Grilo, Sarah; Guayasamín, Oswaldo; Herrán, Saturnino; Homar, Lorenzo; Jaar, Alfredo; Kahlo, Frida; Lam y Castilla, Wifredo; Macció, Rómulo; Mac Entyre, Eduardo; Mérida, Carlos; Minujin, Marta; Modern Art Week; Modernism, Brazil; Morales, Armando; Noé, Luis Felipe; Obregón, Alejandro; O'Gorman, Juan; Orozco, José Clemente; Otero, Alejandro; Pacheco, María Luisa; Peláez, Amelia; Pettoruti, Emilio; Ponce de León, Fidelio; Porter, Liliana; Portinari, Cándido Torquato; Portocarrero,** René; Reverón, Armando; Rivera, Diego; Rojo, Vicente; Sabogal, José; Santa María, Andrés de; Soto, Jesús Rafael; Szyszlo, Fernando de; Tábara, Enrique; Tamayo, Rufino; Toledo, Francisco; Torres García, Joaquín; Tunga; Vega, Jorge Luis de la; Visconti, Eliseu d'Angelo; Xul Solar; Zachrisson, Julio.**

BIBLIOGRAPHY

Ades, Dawn. *Art in Latin America: The Modern Era, 1820–1980.* New Haven, CT: Yale University Press, 1989.

Arte de América y España: Catálogo general. [Madrid?]: Instituto de Cultura Hispánica de Madrid, 1963.

Catlin, Stanley Loomis. *Art of Latin America since Independence.* New Haven, CT: Yale University Press, 1966.

Damaz, Paul F. *Art in Latin American Architecture.* New York: Reinhold, 1963.

Mexico: Splendors of Thirty Centuries, trans. Edith Grossman et. al. New York: Metropolitan Museum of Art, 1990.

Ramirez, Marí Carmen, and Héctor Olea. *Inverted Utopias: Avant-garde Art in Latin America.* New Haven, CT: Yale University Press, 2004.

Sullivan, Edward, ed. *Latin American Art.* London: Phaidon, 2000.

Zannini, Walter. *História general do arte no Brasil.* São Paulo, Brazil: Instituto Walther Moreira Salles, 1983.

ROCIO ARANDA-ALVARADO

FOLK ART

Folk art is produced by an individual or group working together in response to the religious, ceremonial, cultural, and artisanal traditions of the particular ethnic or tribal group to which he or she or they belong. Called *arte popular, arte folklórico,* or *artesanías* (artisan goods) in Spanish and *artesenato* in Portuguese, the genre includes religious or ceremonial art and sculpture, toys, masks, pottery, basketry, textile arts, musical instruments, decorative items, equestrian gear, jewelry, and other objects that are both artistic and folkloric in nature. The folk artist is generally untrained in academic art, and uses at-hand materials. At its best and most traditional, folk art in Latin America is spontaneous, colorful, whimsical, thought-provoking, and crafted by skilled artisans. At its worst, the work—often derided as "airport art"—is the mass-produced degeneration of traditional folk art forms, produced by impoverished, unskilled workers responding to consumer demand from outside their cultural and economic circle.

In the pre-Columbian era, highly skilled metallurgists, weavers, ceramicists, jewelers, lapidaries, stonemasons, muralists, and other artisans created works of timeless beauty for political and religious elites, primarily in the urban centers of Mesoamerica and the Andes. In the homes and villages of ordinary people, less well-trained artists created objects for their own needs and those of the common folk. Although many fine examples of elite art from this period have survived to the present, little of the pre-Columbian folk art created for the masses exists today, although its influence endures. Much of this work was made of highly perishable materials, such as straw, flowers, and wax.

The arrival of Europeans in the late fifteenth century had a major impact on the folk arts of Latin America. Diseases and mistreatment at the hands of the Iberian conquerors led to the extinction of many native groups and to the irretrievable loss of much knowledge and many artistic skills. Europeans destroyed much of the art, especially that made of precious metals and objects they considered idolatrous.

On the positive side, however, Europeans introduced new materials and technologies into the Americas. Artists were quick to incorporate such novelties as glass, sheep's wool, iron, cowhide, canvas, linen, paper, and silk into their art. Forged iron and steel tools meant improved techniques for working metal, wood, leather, and stone. The pottery wheel and glazing techniques revolutionized ceramic art. Domestic animals, the wheel, oceangoing vessels, written languages, and other imports from Europe led to better communication and transportation, as well as advances in mining, farming, marketing, and supply. The galleon trade between Acapulco and Manila, which began in 1570 and ended with Mexican Independence from Spain in 1821, brought additional new materials and artistic influences to the Americas from the Orient. The galleons, which also called at ports such as Lima and San Salvador de Bahia, introduced Latin America to such Asian influences as glazing techniques and forms in ceramics; silk and metallic threads in textile arts; incrustation of mother-of-pearl and tortoise shell in furniture; ivory carving for religious imagery; and lacquer techniques. Black slaves from Africa brought to many parts of Latin America other artistic techniques and cultural heritages. Their skills at working gold, silver and iron, as well as their textile art traditions, had a lasting impact on popular arts in those regions, where, even during slavery, blacks were allowed to practice their ancient arts. Within a short period after contact with Europe, Latin American folk art, while still an indigenous expression in most regions of the Americas, demonstrated nevertheless the impact of innovations and influences from Europe, Asia, and Africa.

As indentured servants, slaves, or apprentices, native and mestizo craftsmen learned new skills from master European craftsmen. Catholic clergy were also instrumental in instructing natives. They fostered and preserved the arts, although they often destroyed work they believed to be idolatrous. A select few pupils were taught at formal arts-and-crafts schools such as San José de los Naturales, founded in Mexico City by Pedro de Gante about 1526; and the Franciscans' Colegio de San Andrés, founded in Quito in 1552.

During the three centuries of colonial rule, however, native artisans and their output were subjected to strict regulations and controls. Although Europeans appreciated native artistry, they resented the prestige that artisans enjoyed, and feared competition from them. For example, although natives were highly skilled at working metals, in 1550 Philip II of Spain forbade them to possess or work precious metals. Artisans also were not allowed to incorporate native constructs and designs in their work. In the isolated regions of the Americas and in private, however, indigenous people, mestizos, and blacks conserved ancient folk art traditions, passing cultural knowledge and skills from parents to children.

When most parts of Latin America declared their independence from Spain and Portugal in the first quarter of the nineteenth century, the folk arts in the new nations experienced an exuberant revival. Liberated from servitude to the Iberians, the people had more freedom to create objects for their own pleasure and use. Pre-Columbian themes, symbols and flags of the new nations, local flora and fauna, and other conceits previously forbidden by the Iberians appeared in religious and ceremonial art, silver, jewelry, equestrian gear, toys, ceramics, household goods, public art, clothing, textile arts, architecture, and popular painting. The trend continued throughout the political chaos of the nineteenth century, until the twentieth century, when the pervasiveness of a cash economy made increasing demands on people's time and energies. "Folk art occupies the brief interlude between court taste and commercial taste," wrote George Kubler. In those regions of the Americas where barter economies, poverty, and cultural conservatism still prevail, the traditional folk art phenomenon endures, primarily in the Andean highlands, rural Northeastern Brazil, and the Indian regions of Mexico, Guatemala, Panama, and the Amazon basin.

In the mid-twentieth century, when air travel, affluence, and consumerism began to bring tens of thousands of visitors from the Northern Hemisphere to all parts of Latin America, the folk arts underwent a new mutation. Artists who had produced works only for their own use and enjoyment, or for that of their traditional clientele, responded to the new market created by outsiders eager to purchase their work. Increasingly, upper- and middle-class Latin Americans, as well as foreigners, became interested in collecting folk art. The casual output of part-time artists and family workshops was rapidly supplanted by cottage industries producing folk art goods on a near industrial scale and to importers' specifications. By the late 1960s the employment of thousands of workers in the production and exportation of folk art from Latin America had become a burgeoning part of the economies of nearly all countries in the region. Since the 1990s, the Fair Trade movement has reshaped Latin American folk art. Under Fair Trade principles, sellers of local crafts promise to pay artists a socially just wage. Organizations such as Manos Artesanas in Peru have shops and websites where the goods are certified under Fair Trade principles. Stores selling Fair Trade folk art from Latin America have become increasingly popular in the United States and Europe.

The work itself was forever changed. Some of the folk artists, who traditionally work in anonymity, became famous personalities, showing their work in galleries and museums around the world and sharing art critics' columns with artists working in academic modes. The lines between folk art and fine art were blurred. Yet in the villages, alleys, markets, and workshops of Latin America, anonymous folk artists still hover over their workbenches, spontaneously fashioning ordinary materials into objects of delight and beauty, in the exercise of ages-old traditions and the enduring human need for artistic expression.

See also **Manila Galleon; Slavery: Spanish America.**

BIBLIOGRAPHY

George Kubler and Martin Soria, *Art and Architecture in Spain and Portugal and Their American Dominions, 1500 to 1800* (1959).

George McClelland Foster, *Culture and Conquest: America's Spanish Heritage* (1960).

Lilly de Jongh Osborne, *Indian Crafts of Guatemala and El Salvador* (1965).

Elizabeth Boyd, *Popular Arts of Spanish New Mexico* (1974).

Nelson H. H. Graburn, ed., *Ethnic and Tourist Arts: Cultural Expressions from the Fourth World* (1976).

Francisco Statsny, *Los artes populares del Perú* (1979).

August Panyella, *Folk Art of the Americas* (1981); and *Brazil: Arte do Noreste/Art of the Northeast* (1985).

Henry Glassie, *The Spirit of Folk Art: The Girard Collection at the Museum of International Folk Art* (1989).

Chloë Sayer, *Arts and Crafts of Mexico* (1990).

Martha J. Egan, *Milagros: Votive Offerings from the Americas* (1991).

Gloria Fraser Giffords, *Mexican Folk Retablos* (rev. ed. 1992).

Marion Oettinger, *The Folk Art of Latin America: Visiones del Pueblo* (1992).

Liliana Villegas and Benjamin Villegas, *Artefactos: Colombian Crafts from the Andes to the Amazon* (1992).

Additional Bibliography

Bartra, Eli. *Crafting Gender: Women and Folk Art in Latin America and the Caribbean.* Durham: Duke University Press, 2003.

Camayd-Freixas, Erik, and José Eduardo González. *Primitivism and Identity in Latin America: Essays on Art, Literature, and Culture.* Tucson: University of Arizona Press, 2000.

MARTHA J. EGAN

ARTEAGA, ROSALÍA (1956–).

Rosalía Arteaga was Ecuador's first female president, although she held office only for about twenty-four hours. Abdalá Bucaram's running mate in the 1996 presidential elections, Arteaga later distanced herself from Bucaram. During the convoluted events of February 1997 that ended in Bucaram's removal from office, she was appointed president briefly until power went to Fabian Alarcón, president of congress. Arteaga traces these events in her memoirs, *La Presidenta*, and shows how Alarcón came to power through illegal means, thanks in part to the *machista* ideology of the armed forces and to her weakness in congress.

See also **Bucaram, Abdalá; Ecuador: Political Parties.**

BIBLIOGRAPHY

Arteaga, Rosalía. *La Presidenta*. Guayaquil: Edino, 1997.

Cornejo, Diego, ed. *¡Que se vaya! Crónica el bucaramato*. Quito: Edimpres-Hoy, 1997.

Torre, Carlos de la. *Populist Seduction in Latin America: The Ecuadorian Experience*. Athens: Ohio University Center for International Studies, 2000.

CARLOS DE LA TORRE

ARTIGAS.

Artigas, department in northwestern Uruguay, 4,689 square miles in area with 69,200 inhabitants. Founded in 1852 on the bases of the settlement of San Eugenio, the city of Artigas has 35,120 inhabitants (1985). Located on the Quaraí River, it is the provincial capital. The region produces beef, hides, wool, and wheat, and entertains active trade exchanges with neighboring Brazil. The department is named after José Artigas (1764–1850), who fought in the independence movement and against the centralization efforts of Buenos Aires in the postindependence era.

See also **Uruguay, Geography.**

BIBLIOGRAPHY

Additional Bibliography

Galván, Gloria, Antonio De la Peña, and Juan José Píriz. *Artigas*. Montevideo, Uruguay: Editorial Fin de Siglo, 1998.

Grupo Interdisciplinario de Economía de la Energía. *Artigas: Economía del departamento: Análisis y perspectivas al año 2010*. Montevideo, Uruguay: Convenio Unión Trabajadores de la Educación, Universidad de la República, 1996.

CÉSAR N. CAVIEDES

ARTIGAS, JOSÉ GERVASIO (1764–1850). José Artigas was one of the Río de la Plata's first caudillos and became a prominent figure in the Wars of Independence. He was the principal advocate of federalism and autonomy for the provinces that would become Uruguay and Argentina. During the 1810s he joined forces with the revolutionary government in Buenos Aires in the fight for independence in the region and in the Banda Oriental, or the territory that would become Uruguay. Artigas's charisma, knowledge of the countryside, military savvy, and relationships with people from across the social hierarchy helped him acquire a multiethnic group of loyal supporters. Clashes with the Buenos Aires government and the Portuguese occupation of the Banda Oriental eventually led him and his followers into exile in Paraguay. Throughout the 1800s Artigas's reputation fluctuated, but from the late 1800s to the present day there is no doubting his position in the national pantheon as a founding father of Uruguay.

Born June 19, 1764, Artigas studied at the convent of San Francisco in Montevideo and then worked in the countryside. In 1797 he began serving with the Cuerpo de Blandengues, an armed cavalry force charged with policing and maintaining order in rural areas. During the first decade of the 1800s, Artigas moved up in rank in the Cuerpo. His service led him to crisscross the Banda Oriental and allowed him to experience social realities in different parts of the territory. Artigas and his forces established positive relationships with both wealthy landowners (*estancieros*) and rural populations that often worked on the *estancieros'* estates (*estancias*). They also fought briefly against the English during the second invasion of the region in 1807.

In May 1810 a *junta*, or local council, declared self-rule in Buenos Aires, marking one of the key moments in the outbreak of independence, known as the May revolution. When Artigas learned of the events across the river, he abandoned his position as captain in the Cuerpo, and thus his ties to Spanish authorities, and joined revolutionary forces in Buenos Aires. In 1811 the junta charged him with organizing the insurgence against royal forces in the Banda Oriental. Midway through the year he began the campaign against the royalists, and rural inhabitants quickly united with Artigas. In contrast, Montevideo remained a Spanish stronghold. Patriots won a series of battles en route toward Montevideo, and toward the end of May they requested that Viceroy Francisco Javier Elío surrender the city. He refused, and the patriots carried out the first siege of the city. Portuguese forces came to the aid of royalists in Montevideo, which, coupled with the defeat of patriots in Upper Peru, resulted in a deal between the Buenos Aires junta and the viceroy: Insurgents would end the siege, and both patriot and Portuguese forces would quit the Banda Oriental. In what was then called the *redota*, and is now referred to as the "exodus," Artigas led his men north, crossing the Río Uruguay and setting up camp in Ayuí.

In early 1812 the Buenos Aires government decided to back Artigas and his men in hopes of driving out the Portuguese troops, still in the Banda Oriental. Through negotiations the military conflict was avoided, and Portuguese forces left the territory. The fight for independence from Spain was then renewed, resulting in the second siege of Montevideo. In 1813 Artigas sent a delegation to Buenos Aires to propose a set of tenets known as the *instrucciones del año XIII*, calling for independence from the Spanish crown, a federalist system of government with checks and balances for the Argentine provinces, and provincial autonomy from the overbearing influence of Buenos Aires. Representatives in Buenos Aires refused to allow the delegation to participate in the provincial assembly, which led to a rift between the Buenos Aires government and Artigas, declared a traitor to the patriot cause in 1814. Troops from Buenos Aires took control of Montevideo, and skirmishes ensued between them and forces from the Banda Oriental until 1815, when Artigas's idea of provincial autonomy was tentatively accepted and control of the city was given to Orientales (inhabitants of the Banda Oriental). But tensions rose again in 1816. The Buenos Aires government reached out to the Portuguese to control the source of "unruly" federalism, presented as a threat to neighboring Brazil. By the end of the year Portuguese troops had occupied the Banda Oriental and would remain until the mid 1820s.

For the next three years Artigas and his supporters fought unsuccessfully against the Portuguese and for support from Buenos Aires. Toward the end of 1820 he went into exile in Paraguay, where he lived quietly the last thirty years of his life, maintained by José Gaspar Rodríguez de Francia and Carlos Antonio López. Little else is known of the time he spent there, though it is clear that the second part of his life contrasted dramatically with the travels and military missions of the first part.

Artigas's remains were repatriated in 1855, marking the beginning of his rise to the status of national hero. Among certain social circles during the first half of the nineteenth century, a "Black Legend" of Artigas had held sway. Many elite liberals from Argentina and Uruguay considered him a sower of anarchy and a bloodthirsty, self-aggrandizing *caudillo*. This image underwent dramatic changes during the second half of the century, thanks largely to writings by Juan Zorrilla de San Martín and Carlo María Ramírez's book *Artigas*. By 1900 Artigas had been apotheosized. Artists portrayed him in various representations, and gradually the icon of Artigas emerged, first as an old man, and finally as youthful soldier, on stamps and national currency. In his historical paintings Juan Manuel de Blanes depicted a young and hearty Artigas, which became the most widely disseminated image of the leader. The novels of Eduardo Acevedo Díaz also contributed to the construction of a new national hero. In 1923 this status became official, with the inauguration of a statue of Artigas on horseback in Montevideo's Plaza Independencia. In the early twenty-first century his remains rest in a mausoleum beneath the statue, making it the most revered and guarded national monument in Uruguay.

See also **Banda Oriental; Acevedo Díaz, Eduardo Inés; Blanes, Juan Manuel; Caudillismo, Caudillo; Elío, Francisco Javier; Francia, José Gaspar Rodríguez de; López, Carlos Antonio; United Provinces of the Río de la Plata; Uruguay: Before 1900; Wars of Independence: South America.**

BIBLIOGRAPHY

Ramírez, Carlos María. *Artigas. Clásicos Uruguayos*, no. 1. Montevideo: Ministerio de Educación y Cultura, 1985.

Reyes Abadie, Washington. *Artigas y el federalismo en el Río de la Plata, 1810–1820*. Montevideo: Ediciones de la Banda Oriental, 1974.

Ribeiro, Ana. *El Caudillo y el Dictador*, 3rd edition. Montevideo: Planeta, 2005.

Street, John. *Artigas and the Emancipation of Uruguay.* Cambridge, U.K.: Cambridge University Press, 1959.

Zorrilla de San Martín, Juan. *La epopeya de Artigas. Clásicos Uruguayos,* nos. 37–41. Montevideo: Ministerio de Instrucción Pública y Previsión Social, 1963.

WILLIAM G. ACREE JR.

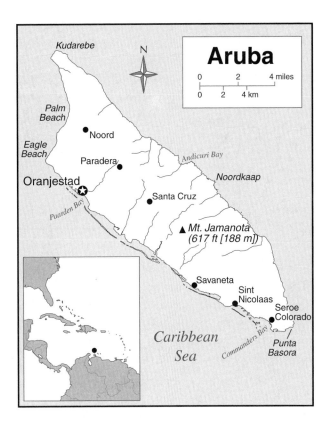

ARUBA. From 1636 to 1986 Aruba was part of the Netherlands Antilles, administered by the government center at Curaçao. Until 1954 the islands were officially referred to as "Curaçao and its dependencies." The dependency on Curaçao has always been a source of resentment for Aruba. In several aspects, Aruba was different from the five other islands of the Netherlands Antilles, even in comparison with Curaçao and Bonaire, although Aruba and these two islands have in common the spoken Papiamento, a Portuguese-based Creole language familiar to the Criolo of Cabo Verde.

In colonial times, slavery in the salt pans of Bonaire was the backbone of the local Netherlands Antillean economy, with Curaçao serving as a shipment point for the slaves. Sugar plantations with slave workers were the principal source of internal revenue. Slavery was rare, however, on Aruba. Aruba's first inhabitants were the Arawak Indians; the European colonists are believed to have mixed with the indigenous population. The Arawak legacy is considered to constitute a component of the Aruban culture. In general, the Aruban population is light-colored, except in the southern cone of the island, where black immigrants from other Caribbean countries came to work in the oil industry. Aruba shares with the other islands of the former Netherlands Antilles a fixation on color and race. Although never explicitly mentioned, the dominance of the "black" governments in Curaçao after 1954, when the Antilles acquired political autonomy, increased antagonism against "colonialist Curaçao."

In 1986 Aruba, at the behest of a political movement insisting on autonomy vis-à-vis Curaçao, seceded from the Netherlands Antilles. Aruba became a separate, autonomous "country" within the kingdom of the Netherlands under the Dutch crown. The *status aparte* granted by The Hague applied to the period between 1986 and 1996, after which Aruba had to become independent—a condition imposed by the Dutch government. Even in 1986 it was clear that Aruba had only agreed with this commitment in order to get its autonomy. Once it had been achieved, independence was not longer a case, and the Netherlands accepted this fait accompli: After 1996, the kingdom of the Netherlands no longer insisted on independence and Aruba continues to be incorporated in the kingdom.

Aruba's economy was dependent on the oil industry for more than fifty years. In 1928 Standard Oil built a refinery on Aruba to process Venezuelan oil. The island economy prospered, and oil processing was the dominant industry until the mid-1980s, when the refinery was closed. After its secession from the other Antilles, Aruba's economy was stagnant, even moribund, for a couple of years. Unemployment rose, a considerable portion of the population migrated, and the number of inhabitants diminished from 65,000 to 50,000. Then the government opted for a huge investment in mass tourism, trying to appeal to U.S. visitors. The effort to finance the hotels and other infrastructure for tourism also attracted illicit funding

Aruba	
Population:	100,018 (2007 est.)
Area:	75 sq. mi
Official language:	Dutch
Languages:	Papiamento (a Spanish-Portuguese-Dutch-English dialect); Spanish; English
National currency:	Aruban guilder/florin
Principal religions:	Roman Catholic 82%; Protestant 8%; other (includes Hindu, Muslim, Confucian, Jewish) 10%
Ethnicity:	Mixed white/Carib Amerindian 80%; other 20%
Capital:	Oranjestad
Annual rainfall:	Averages 24 in
Economy:	*GDP per capita:* US$21,800 (2004)

and drug money. In the 1990s the governments in The Hague and of Aruba (collaborating with U.S. customs and other agencies) were able to curtail considerably the influence of illicit financing and drug-related activities. An elaborated triangular system of cooperation and control was established.

In the meantime, Aruba's tourist industry has been thriving, and the island enjoys one of the highest standards of living in the Caribbean region. Poverty and unemployment rates are very low. About half of the Aruban GNP is tourism related. Yearly, more than a million tourists from the United States, Canada, and the European Union visit the island. As of January 2007, the national population exceeded 100,000 inhabitants; 33 percent were immigrants from the Caribbean island states and Colombia.

See also **Curaçao.**

BIBLIOGRAPHY

Oostindie, Gert. *Paradise Overseas; The Dutch Caribbean: Colonialism and Its Transatlantic Legacies.* Oxford: Macmillan, 2005.

Oostindie, Gert, and Inge Klinkers. *Decolonising the Caribbean: Dutch Politics in a Comparative Perspective.* Amsterdam: Amsterdam University Press, 2003.

DIRK KRUIJT

ARZÁNS ORSÚA Y VELA, BARTO-LOMÉ
(1676–1736). Bartolomé Arzáns Orsúa y Vela (*b.* 1676; *d.* January 1736), Bolivian writer and historian. Born in Potosí of Spanish parents, Arzáns dedicated his life to the writing of his multivolume *Historia de la villa imperial de Potosí,* the most complex and fascinating text of the colonial period in Bolivia. Arzáns did not completely finish the work; his son Diego wrote the final 8 of its 322 chapters. The manuscript was lost for many years, and the first edition was not published until 1965.

In this work, Arzáns attempts to give a complete and detailed history of Potosí, one of the most prosperous cities of the New World during the sixteenth and seventeenth centuries. It was founded in 1545 next to the Mountain of Potosí, a rich silver mining site. In order to capture and convey the splendor and greatness of the city, Arzáns includes historical data, legends, short stories, Indian myths, descriptions of daily events, and details about various aspects of life in the city. The book is an exuberant and baroque depiction of Potosí, with history and fiction intertwined. The *Historia* is crucial to an understanding of Bolivia because of the historical, literary, and ideological information it provides; it can be seen to prefigure post-colonial Bolivian nationalism.

See also **Potosí.**

BIBLIOGRAPHY

Mario Chacón Torres, *Documentos en torno a Bartolomé Arzáns Orsúa y Vela* (1960).

Lewis Hanke and Gunnar Mendoza, Introduction to *Historia de la villa imperial de Potosí,* 3 vols. (1965).

Leonardo García Pabón, *Espacio andino, escritura colonial y pensamiento andino: La historia de Potosí en la narrativa de Bartolomé Arzáns* (Ph.D. diss., University of Minnesota, 1990).

Additional Bibliography

Galarza Sepúlveda, Denise. "City, Myth, and Morality in Bartolomé Arzáns's Historia De La Villa Imperial De

Potosí: A Criollo Project." Ph.D. diss., Emory University, 2002.

Spadaccini, Nicholas, and Luis Martín-Estudillo, eds. *Hispanic Baroques: Reading Cultures in Context.* Nashville: Vanderbilt University Press, 2005.

LEONARDO GARCÍA PABÓN

ARZE, JOSÉ ANTONIO (1904–1955).

José Antonio Arze (*b.* 13 January 1904; *d.* 23 August 1955), Bolivian intellectual and politician. Born in Cochabamba, Arze was the most influential Marxist intellectual and the leading leftist politician in Bolivia during the 1940s. In 1928 he helped found the National Student Federation (FUB), which demanded university reforms on the Argentine model. As the presidential candidate of the FUB in 1940, Arze received almost a fifth of the total vote. Thereafter, he was instrumental in organizing the first effective national leftist party, the Party of the Revolutionary Left (PIR), which rivaled in size and influence the National Revolutionary Movement (MNR) among the opposition parties of the 1940s. Arze again became a presidential candidate in 1951. He was a professor of sociology at the University of San Francisco Xavier in Sucre and founder of the Institute of Bolivian Sociology and its journal, the *Revista del Instituto de Sociología Boliviana*. The author of numerous books and translator of Louis Baudin and Georges Rouma, Arze influenced several generations of leftist politicians in Bolivia.

See also **Bolivia, Political Parties: Party of the Revolutionary Left (PIR).**

BIBLIOGRAPHY

An excellent introduction to Arze and his times is Herbert S. Klein, *Parities and Political Change in Bolivia: 1880–1952* (1969). Short summaries of Arze's life are available in Guillermo Francovich, *El pensamiento boliviano en el siglo XX* (1956), pp. 108–110, and Valentín Abecia Baldivieso, *Historiografía boliviana*, 2d ed. (1973), pp. 451–453.

Additional Bibliography

Taborga, Jesús. *El pensamiento filosófico en Bolivia: Antología: Enfoque crítico-socio-cultural* La Paz: Editorial Gramma, 2001.

ERICK D. LANGER

ASADO. Huge herds of wild cattle roamed much of the pampa until the mid-nineteenth century. Inhabitants of the Río de la Plata, especially the equestrian gaucho, developed a fondness for beef, especially *asado,* which is roasted beef (or lamb or goat). The meat, often a side of ribs, is skewered on a metal frame called an *asador* and is roasted by placing it next to a slow-burning fire. Gauchos favored cooking *asado* with the wood of the quebracho tree because it smokes very little. *Asado,* accompanied by maté tea, formed the basis of the gaucho diet; this technique is still used today. In Brazil, the cooking style is known as *churrasco* and in Peru it can take the form of pot roast.

See also **Churrasco; Gaucho.**

BIBLIOGRAPHY

Félix Coluccio, *Diccionario folklórico argentino,* vol. 1 (1964), pp. 27–28.

Richard W. Slatta, *Gauchos and the Vanishing Frontier* (1983), p. 76.

Additional Bibliography

Assunção, Fernando O. *Historia del gaucho: El gaucho, ser y quehacer.* Buenos Aires: Editorial Claridad, 1999.

Foster, David William, Melissa Fitch Lockhart, and Darrell B. Lockhart. *Culture and Customs of Argentina.* Westport: Greenwood Press, 1998.

Mayo, Carlos A. *Vivir en la frontera: La casa, la dieta, la pulpería, la escuela (1770-1870).* Buenos Aires: Editorial Biblos, 2000.

Nogués, Jacinto P. *El asado argentino.* Buenos Aires: Imaginador, 2003.

RICHARD W. SLATTA

ASCASUBI, HILARIO (1807–1875). Hilario Ascasubi (*b.* 14 January 1807; *d.* 17 November 1875), Argentine poet, journalist, politician, and entrepreneur. His adventurous adolescence took him through Portugal, France, England, and Chile. In 1824 he reorganized an old printing shop in the provincial city of Salta, renaming it Imprenta de la Patria, and began publishing the *Revista de Salta*. Thus began his journalistic career, which he never abandoned. In 1825 Ascasubi began a second career, this time in the army fighting the *caudillaje*

(bossism). As a lieutenant he was in charge of recruiting and tasted defeat in two battles. Under General Juan Lavalle, the hero of the fight against the tyrant Juan Manuel de Rosas, Ascasubi became captain. A prisoner during 1831–1833 in a pontoon in Buenos Aires, he escaped to Montevideo and set up a bakery, becoming rich enough to help Lavalle and the Argentine refugees. At the same time, he managed to continue pursuing his poetic interests, achieving fame with this "gauchescos" *trovos* (popular ballads) published later under the title *Paulino Lucero* (1872).

Ascasubi joined the armies successfully fighting the Rosas dictatorship and, as a lieutenant colonel in the ensuing period (1843–1852), performed various jobs while continuing his writing. From 1853 to 1859 he published *Aniceto el Gallo, Gaceta Joco-Tristona y Gauchi-Patriótica* (Aniceto the Rooster, Humorous-Sad and Gauchi-Patriotic Gazette). Although retired, Ascasubi was sent to France in 1860 to recruit for the Argentine army. In Paris he finished and published his main work, the lengthy *Santos Vega, o Los mellizos de La Flor* (1872), a narrative poem that depicts the pampa, the idiosyncrasies of its inhabitants and their customs, the intimate life within the *estancia,* and the mythological figure of the *payador* (singer). Argentine publisher Stockcero republished *Santos Vega, o los mellizos de la flor* in 2004.

Absorbed by the political events in his country, Ascasubi was not only a chronicler, but an exceedingly active participant. As a writer, he transmitted the everyday happenings, the anecdotes that humanize and draw us near to historical events. As a publisher, he established a number of important newspapers. As a businessman, he brought gas service to Buenos Aires, extended the railroad tracks, and helped erect the Teatro Colón (1857).

See also **Gauchesca Literature.**

BIBLIOGRAPHY

Manuel Mujica Láinez, *Vidas de El Gallo y el Pollo* (1966).

David Lagmanovich, "Tres cautivas: Echeverría, Ascasubi, Hernández," in *Chasqui* 8, no. 3 (1979); 24–33.

Additional Bibliography

Chiappini, Julio O. *Borges y Ascasubi.* Rosario, Argentina: Zeus Editora, 1994.

Fernández, Miguel Angel. "The Capitalist 'Payador': Hilario Ascasubi's *Aniceto el Gallo,*" in *Chasqui* 31 (May 2002): 86–103.

ANGELA B. DELLEPIANE

ASIANS IN LATIN AMERICA. In 1990 Alberto Fujimori, son of Japanese immigrants, became president of Peru. His election underscores the fact that not only Europeans, but Asians as well, have immigrated in significant numbers to Latin America and contributed to the social, cultural, economic, and political development of the region. Every Latin American country received some Asian immigrants in the nineteenth and twentieth centuries.

As early as the seventeenth century, *chinos de manila* were known in Mexico City, Cuba, and other parts of Spanish America, the result of the Manila Galleon trade between Mexico and the Philippines. However, organized, large-scale Asian immigration to Latin America, consisting almost exclusively of Chinese and Japanese, did not take place until the mid-nineteenth century. Most of the Chinese went to Cuba, Peru, Mexico, and parts of Central America, while the Japanese settled largely in Peru and Brazil, and a much smaller number in Bolivia. Whether forced or free, large-scale Asian movement to Latin America was part of the international labor migration of the late nineteenth and early twentieth centuries in the wake of the worldwide development of capitalism and imperialism, and specifically of the decline of slavery in Latin America.

The bulk of the early Chinese and Japanese immigrants worked under harsh agricultural labor conditions, gradually making the transition to independent agricultural or urban commercial activities. The relative prosperity experienced by Asian communities in the early twentieth century resulted in anti-Asian violence and persecution in all these countries, with the worst being the expulsion of the Chinese from northern Mexico during the Great Depression and the deportation and incarceration in the United States of Japanese Peruvians during World War II.

THE CHINESE IN PERU, CUBA, AND MEXICO

From 1847 to 1874 as many as 225,000 Chinese "coolies," under eight-year contracts, almost all male, were sent to Cuba and Peru, with 80 percent or more destined for the sugar plantations. In Cuba, then still a Spanish colony, the Chinese worked alongside African slaves, the chief source of plantation labor, while in Peru, where slavery was abolished in 1854, Chinese coolies supplanted black slaves. Scholars have viewed *la trata amarilla* (the yellow trade) as both a transition from slave to free labor and, even more, a modified form of slavery. Not disputed is the indispensability of Chinese labor to the maintenance of the plantation-based economies of both societies.

In Peru several thousand coolies also helped build the Andean railroad and worked in the off-shore guano mines south of Lima. In the 1870s escaped coolies and free Chinese were among the pioneers who penetrated the Peruvian Amazon, building settlements, introducing trade activities and small-scale manufacturing, and cultivating rice, beans, sugar, and other crops.

In Cuba a small number in the nineteenth century were also employed in domestic service, cigarette factories, and other small manufacturing, as well as by the colonial government in large public-works projects. In the 1860s *chinos mambises* (Chinese freedom fighters) also joined fellow slaves and free blacks in the first armed struggle to overthrow Spanish colonial rule. As men who were neither slave nor free, neither black nor white, the Chinese coolies helped break down the racialist ideology of Cuba's plantation system.

While free Chinese migrants continued to enter Cuba and Peru in the first decades of the twentieth century, the numbers were not large, and both governments sought to limit further Chinese immigration in the face of local protest against perceived Chinese excesses in commercial activities. The gender imbalance from the coolie period was never sufficiently redressed, and subsequent generations were increasingly mestizoized. At the end of the twentieth century, Chinese Peruvians remained a visible minority, their presence captured by the ubiquitous *chifas* (Chinese restaurants). Since the Cuban Revolution of 1959, a large number of Chinese Cubans have left the island as part of the massive exodus of the Cuban middle class.

Free Chinese immigrants began entering Mexico at exactly the same time that the United States enacted Chinese exclusion and Porfirio Díaz took power in Mexico and promoted immigration along with development, particularly of the frontier region between northern Mexico and the United States. Instead of assuming laboring jobs in the mines and railroads, which were filled by Mexicans, the Chinese entered the new economic niche of local commerce and became truck farmers, small manufacturers, and, especially, small shopkeepers, forming in effect a ubiquitous petite bourgeoisie. They prospered even through the turmoil of the Mexican Revolution, in part by provisioning the various revolutionary armies.

Numbering over 24,000, the Chinese had become the largest immigrant community in Mexico by 1927. Besides large colonies in Sonora and Baja California Norte, they had also settled in every state and territory except Baja California Sur and Tlaxcala. Not surprisingly, however, their relative success inevitably generated resentment and sporadic persecution, which culminated in 1929–1930 with the expulsion of the large Chinese colony of Sonora (state bordering Arizona) and subsequent nationalization of their businesses, spelling the decline of the Chinese throughout Mexico.

THE JAPANESE IN PERU AND BRAZIL

Japanese immigration to Peru and Brazil began in 1899 and 1908, respectively, and continued into the 1970s, with the high point (over 60 percent of the total) during the interwar decades of the 1920s and 1930s. Early Japanese immigration to Latin America resembled that of the Chinese in that the vast majority went as contract laborers, but the patterns soon diverged, with three distinguishing features. First, the Japanese contracts were of shorter duration, and the Japanese made a relatively quick transition from plantation labor to independent farming. Second, from the beginning the Japanese government acted to control and regulate migration through licensing immigration companies and protecting the migrants' rights and interests once overseas, including subsidizing immigrant colonization activities. Third, while men still outnumbered women, the Japanese government encouraged the migration of women, ensuring in turn the integrity of migrant families, the formation of new families, and the continuity of Japanese traditions in the adopted homelands.

By 1924 most of the Japanese in Peru had left the plantations for independent farming or for Lima and other cities and towns throughout the country, where they opened up a variety of small businesses in the service and food sectors. Large numbers of free immigrants continued to arrive until after the attack on Pearl Harbor in 1941. During World War II, under pressure from the United States, a willing Peruvian government deported 1,429 Japanese citizens and residents to concentration camps in the United States, while confiscating Japanese-owned property and nationalizing Japanese businesses.

The Japanese community of Peru managed to recover from this act of infamy and to grow in the postwar years. As the largest immigrant community in Peru, they numbered 32,002 in 1966, almost evenly divided between men and women, with more than half living in Lima and the vast majority of them second, third, or fourth generation. Through reproduction and some continual immigration, the population had grown to over 50,000 by the early 1970s and has remained stable.

In 2000, early in Fujimori's third term, a government scandal caused him to go into exile in Japan, where he remained for five years. The Japanese government revealed that he had never given up his Japanese citizenship. Japan denied Peru's extradition requests, but in 2005 Fujimori was arrested in Chile and in September 2007 was extradited to Peru. He awaited trial there on charges of corruption and sanctioning death-squad killings. While his daughter, Keiko Fujimori, was quite popular (she was elected to the Peruvian Congress in 2006), he remained a controversial public figure in Peru.

Japanese immigration to Brazil represents the largest and longest continuous flow of people from Asia to Latin America: A total of 237,466 migrated between 1908 and 1961. By the late 1970s the Japanese Brazilian population had grown to over 700,000 (three-quarters Brazilian-born), making it the largest Japanese community outside Japan and the most prosperous and successful Asian immigrant community in Latin America.

Always heavily concentrated in São Paulo city and state (90 percent in the late twentieth century),

Japanese immigrants have made significant contributions to both the agricultural (rice, cotton, vegetables, and especially coffee) and, later, the industrial-commercial (manufacturing, shopkeeping, international trade) development of the country. They were also instrumental in the early colonization of the vast Amazon region. Although in the immediate postwar years the majority of Japanese Brazilians were a rural middle-class of small and medium landowners—having won the all-important concession to own and lease land—living in hundreds of Japanese settlements, they have become since the 1960s a highly educated, urban middle-class, active in Brazilian economic and political life.

By the late twentieth century the once prominent Chinese immigrant communities of Latin America had declined significantly, the result of absorption into the larger society by miscegenation or assimilation or departure by voluntary exodus or expulsion. In contrast, Japanese immigrants and their descendants in Brazil and Peru continued to grow in size and prominence, retaining their distinctive identity while also increasingly integrating into the national life. Despite this growth, some Japanese Brazilians, called Dekasegi, meaning "working away from home," returned to Japan during the economic turmoil of the 1980s in Brazil. As of the early 2000s over 200,000 Japanese Brazilians live in Japan and are the largest group of Portuguese speakers in Asia.

See also **Mestizo.**

BIBLIOGRAPHY

Anita Bradley, *Trans-Pacific Relations of Latin America* (1942).

Watt Stewart, *Chinese Bondage in Peru* (1951).

C. Harvey Gardiner, *The Japanese and Peru, 1873–1973* (1975).

Denise Helly, *Idéologie et ethnicité: Les chinois Macao à Cuba, 1847–1886* (1979).

Robert J. Smith, "The Ethnic Japanese in Brazil," in *Journal of Japanese Studies* 5, no. 1 (1979): 53–70.

James L. Tigner, "Japanese Immigration into Latin America," in *Journal of Inter-American Studies and World Affairs* 23 (November 1981): 457–482.

Evelyn Hu-Dehart, "Coolies, Shopkeepers, Pioneers: The Chinese of Mexico and Peru (1849–1930)," in *Amerasia Journal* 15, no. 2 (1989): 91–116.

Additional Bibliography

Appelbaum, Nancy P., Anne S. Macpherson, and Karin Alejandra Rosemblatt, eds. *Race and Nation in*

Modern Latin America. Chapel Hill: University of North Carolina Press, 2003.

Herrera Jerez, Miriam, and Mario Castillo Santana. *De la memoria a la vida pública: Identidades, espacios y jerarquías de los chinos en La Habana republicana (1902–1968).* Havana: Centro de Investigación y Desarrollo de la Cultura Cubana Juan Marinello, 2003.

Lesser, Jeffrey. *Searching for Home Abroad: Japanese Brazilians and Transnationalism.* Durham, NC: Duke University Press, 2003.

Masterson, Daniel M., and Sayaka Funada-Classen. *The Japanese in Latin America.* Urbana: University of Illinois Press, 2004.

McKeown, Adam. *Chinese Migrant Networks and Cultural Change: Peru, Chicago, Hawaii, 1900–1936.* Chicago: University of Chicago Press, 2001.

Trazegnies Granda, Fernando de. *En el país de las colinas de arena: Reflexiones sobre la inmigración china en el Perú del s. XIX desde la perspectiva del derecho.* Lima: Pontificia Universidad Católica del Perú, Fondo Editorial, 1994.

EVELYN HU-DeHART

ASIENTO. The *asiento* was a contract granted by the Spanish crown to an individual or company allowing the holder exclusive rights in the slave trade with Spain's American colonies; it constituted the principal legal means of supplying slaves to Spanish America. These monopolistic arrangements specified the number of *piezas de Indias* (standard slave units, each *pieza* being equivalent to a prime male slave) to be delivered annually, ports of entry, and lump sums and head taxes to be paid to the Spanish monarchy. The *asientistas,* holders of the *asiento,* rarely provided their full complement of *piezas de Indias* so that contraband trade in slaves and other goods flourished, often with the complicity of *asientistas* and their agents.

The *asiento* apparently emerged in the 1590s, although similar contracts date from the early 1500s. The Portuguese dominated the *asiento* until Portugal's assertion of independence in 1640 undermined the arrangements. Spain refused to offer commercial rights to "rebels," "heretics," or enemies—categories that seemed, in the mid-1600s, to encompass all possible contractual partners. Not until 1662 did the Spanish, striving to boost royal revenues, revive the *asiento.*

Because Spain lacked adequate commercial and maritime resources and access to the African coast, foreigners continued to dominate the trade. European powers so coveted the contract as an opportunity to penetrate the commerce of the Spanish empire, that the *asiento,* its actual fiscal importance greatly exaggerated, became an instrument of foreign policy and diplomacy. The contract fell to the Dutch in 1675, to the Portuguese in 1694, to the French in 1701, and, finally, to the English in the Peace of Utrecht (1713) as a spoil of war. The Anglo-Spanish agreement survived until 1750, but the monopolistic character of the *asiento* slowly passed into eclipse, and Spain abrogated the system in 1789.

See also **Slave Trade.**

BIBLIOGRAPHY

Colin Palmer, *Human Cargoes: The British Slave Trade to Spanish America, 1700–1739* (1981).

James A. Rawley, *The Transatlantic Slave Trade* (1981).

Additional Bibliography

Cáceres Gómez, Rina. *Rutas de la esclavitud en Africa y América Latina.* San José: Editorial de la Universidad de Costa Rica, 2001.

Landers, Jane, and Barry Robinson. *Slaves, Subjects, and Subversives: Blacks in Colonial Latin America* Albuquerque: University of New Mexico Press, 2006.

Vila Vilar, Enriqueta. *Aspectos sociales en América colonial: De extranjeros, contrabando y esclavos.* Bogotá: Instituto Caro y Cuervo: Universidad de Bogotá "Jorge Tadeo Lozano," 2001.

CARA SHELLY

ASOCIACIÓN CRISTIANA FEMENINA (YWCA). Asociación Cristiana Femenina (YWCA), organization founded (London, 1855; United States, 1858; World YWCA, 1894) for the "temporal, moral, and religious welfare of young women who are dependent on their own exertions for support," with affiliates appearing throughout Latin America in the 1890s. Resident "Yankee teachers" and Englishwomen established a branch in Buenos Aires in 1896; the Mexican YWCA was founded by social reformer María Elena Ramírez. The YWCAs offered temporary housing for women travelers, aid to immigrant women and girls, and recreational and educational programs for young working women. The YWCAs were centers for the discussion of feminist ideas on secular (or progressive Protestant) education, woman suffrage, abolition of prostitution and the white slave trade, and health care and civil rights for women.

See also **Women.**

BIBLIOGRAPHY

Marifran Carlson, *¡Feminismo! The Woman's Movement in Argentina from Its Beginnings to Eva Perón* (1988).

Ward M. Morton, *Woman Suffrage in Mexico* (1962).

Additional Bibliography

Boyd, Nancy. *Emissaries: The Overseas Work of the American YWCA, 1885-1970*. New York: Woman's Press, 1986.

French, William, and Katherine Elaine Bliss. *Gender, Sexuality, and Power in Latin America since Independence*. Lanham: Rowman & Littlefield, 2007.

Lavrin, Asunción. *Women, Feminism, and Social Change in Argentina, Chile, and Uruguay, 1890-1940*. Lincoln: University of Nebraska Press, 1995.

Tarrés, María Luisa, and Luzelena Gutiérrez de Velasco. *Género y cultura en América Latina: Cultura y participación política*. México, D.F.: Colegio de México, 1998-2003.

FRANCESCA MILLER

ASOCIACIÓN DE MAYO. Asociación de Mayo, an Argentine literary group of the early nineteenth century. Following the 1810 separation from Napoleonic Spain and the May 1819 declaration of the Argentine Republic and in the context of the civil strife that led to the tyranny of Juan Manuel de Rosas in 1835, Buenos Aires was fertile ground for an array of social, cultural, and literary activities inspired by French romanticism. The principal reference point for these activities was the Generation of 1837, its principal spokesperson was Esteban Echeverría (1809–1851), and one of its major groups was the Asociación de Mayo. The French influence on figures like Echeverría, Juan María Gutiérrez (1809–1878), and Juan Bautista Alberdi (1810–1884)—all prominent names in Argentine literary history—as well as on a first generation of students at the Universidad de Buenos Aires, which the country's first president, Bernardino de Rivadavia

(elected 1826), had recently established, was evident in the fact that the Asociación's members had originally met between 1835 and 1837 in the salon of the wife of the French consul. In 1837, the group began to meet in the Librería Argentina de Marcos Sastre, where, as the Salón Literario, they pursued their reading and discussion of French cultural texts. It was at Echeverría's suggestion that in 1838 they began to identify themselves under the banner of Joven Argentina or the Asociación de Mayo, both denominations underscoring their commitment to considerations of foundational national identity in conformance with romantic ideological currents that extended beyond a strictly French base. (France was already an organized nation state; thus, the efforts at national sociocultural unity of a country such as Italy offered perhaps more precise reference points for these Argentine literati.) The Generation of 1837, focusing on local realities, developed original ideas and policies regarding national development. While these thinkers have traditionally been described using Conservative and Liberal labels, their complex ideology defies such broad descriptions. After considerable, if frustrated, efforts to influence the course of public and political events— Echeverría's 1846 *Dogma socialista* is the key synthetic document here—the exile imposed in 1839 by the defeat of Juan Lavalle (1797–1841) and the confirmation of Rosas's dictatorial power disbanded the group definitively. After Rosas's fall, however, the constitution of 1853 endorsed many of the political and economic ideas of the Generation of 1837.

See also **Literature: Spanish America.**

BIBLIOGRAPHY

Juan Antonio Solari, *Asociación de Mayo y dogma socialista* (1937).

Antonio Juan Bucich, *Esteban Echeverría y su tiempo* (1938); *Antecedentes de la Asociación de Mayo, 1837–1937* (1939).

Rodolfo A. Borello, "Mayo: Literatura y realidad," in *Universidad* [Santa Fe], no. 64 (1965): 175–206.

Additional Bibliography

Adelman, Jeremy. *Republic of Capital: Buenos Aires and the Legal Transformation of the Atlantic World*. Stanford, CA: Stanford University Press, 1999.

Ghirardi, Olsen Antonio. *La Generación del '37 en el Río de la Plata*. Córdoba, Argentina: Academia Nacional de Derecho y Ciencias Sociales de Córdoba, 2004.

Katra, William H. *The Argentine Generation of 1837: Echeverría, Alberdi, Sarmiento, Mitre*. Madison, NJ: Fairleigh Dickinson University Press, 1996.

Laera, Alejandra, and Martín Kohan. *Las brújulas del extraviado: Para una lectura integral de Esteban Echeverría*. Rosario, Argentina: Beatriz Viterbo, 2006.

DAVID WILLIAM FOSTER

ASPERO. Aspero, one of the largest known Cotton Preceramic Period settlements in Peru. Radiocarbon dates place the peak occupation between 3000 BCE and 2500 BCE. Aspero is located just north of the floodplain of the Supe River on the Pacific coast of Peru. The site is about 5,350,000–7,150,000 cubic feet of ashy midden covering thirty acres. It has at least fourteen corporate labor platform mounds, the largest about 115 feet wide, 165 feet long, and 33 feet high.

The mounds are layers of rooms that were partially demolished and filled in to form an elevated base for new rooms. The rooms were not domestic but rather appear to have been used for ritual activity. Some were decorated with colored paint, clay friezes, and wall niches. In the larger mounds, the rooms were approached from a central stairway and were hierarchically arranged, that is, access to one was through another, with the inner rooms the most highly decorated. The size and complexity of these structures indicate the existence of a complex socio–political organization, most likely a chiefdom, to coordinate the significant labor force needed for their construction.

Artifacts included twined cotton and bast fiber textiles, bags, and nets; reed baskets; gourd bowls; pecked-and-ground stone tools and bowls; carved wood, bone, and shell ornaments; and unbaked clay human figurines. Most of these figurines represented females, some pregnant. All but one were found in a cache sealed between two floors in one of the large mounds, where they appear to have been a symbolic dedicatory burial.

Supporting a sizeable population, the subsistence economy was mixed, with the primary marine food sources—mainly small fish and shellfish—supplemented with fruits, peppers, legumes, and tubers such as achira (*Canna edulis*). While the beans, peppers, tubers, and some fruits were cultivated, most agriculture was directed toward producing raw materials for textiles (cotton) and containers (gourds). Maize too was probably present. Archaeologists have debated the amount of aquatic life and agriculture in the diet of these early coastal inhabitants.

See also **Archaeology.**

BIBLIOGRAPHY

Michael E. Moseley and Gordon R. Willey, "Aspero, Peru: A Reexamination of the Site and Its Implications," in *American Antiquity* 38 (1973): 452–468.

Robert A. Feldman, "Preceramic Corporate Architecture: Evidence for the Development of Non-Egalitarian Social Systems in Peru," in *Early Ceremonial Architecture in the Andes,* edited by C. B. Donnan (1985).

Robert A. Feldman, "Preceramic Unbaked Clay Figurines from Aspero, Peru," in *The New World Figurine Project,* edited by Terry Stocker (1991).

Additional Bibliography

Blake, Michael, ed. *Pacific Latin America in Prehistory: The Evolution of Archaic and Formative Cultures*. Pullman: Washington State University Press, 1999.

Bonavia, Duccio, Claudia Grimaldo, and Jimi Espinoza. *Bibliografía del período precerámico peruano*. Lima: Pontificia Universidad Católica del Perú, Fondo Editorial, Academia Nacional de la Historia, 2001.

Moseley, Michael E. *The Incas and Their Ancestors: The Archaeology of Peru*. New York: Thames and Hudson, 1992.

ROBERT A. FELDMAN

ASPÍLLAGA FAMILY. Aspíllaga Family, Peruvian plantation owners. The matriarch of the family, Catalina Ferrebú de Aspíllaga, immigrated to Lima from Chile in the 1820s. Sons Ramón (d. 1875) and Antonio went into the family's transport business, which operated between Lima and Callao. As partners of financier Julián Zaracondegui, they purchased a large property on the northern coast, Hacienda Cayaltí. Ramón managed the plantation with his sons Antero (1849–1927) and Ramón (1850–1940) and eventually took control of it. Earlier they had purchased a cotton farm in the Pisco Valley, Hacienda Palto. They stocked both enterprises with indentured Asians, whom they overworked with impunity. They then sank the profits into commercial urban real estate and developed close ties with English lenders. Younger brothers Baldomero and Ismael helped out, but the older sons Antero and Ramón ran the family business. The Aspíllagas became linked with other wealthy families of Lima through marriage, and they joined the prestigious Club Nacional.

In politics, the Aspíllagas helped organize the Civilista Party. The younger Ramón sat briefly in the national Chamber of Deputies. After 1906 Antero was elected to the Chamber of Deputies and then moved to the Senate, where he carefully guarded the interests of export planters. He lost as the candidate of the Civilista Party in the presidential elections of 1912 and 1919. On the eve of the ballot count in 1919, Augusto Leguía, a contender for president, conspired with the army to nullify the vote, despite the fact that he probably would have won. Thereafter the family concentrated on its plantation and on mining and banking. Family members sat on the board of directors of the powerful Banco Popular, from which they received large low-cost loans in the 1930s. On the plantations they fiercely opposed all efforts to organize labor and became hated opponents of the American Popular Revolutionary Alliance (APRA), which tried to organize field workers into unions and teach them to read in night classes. The Aspíllagas supported Luís Sánchez Cerro for president in 1931 and General Oscar Benavides thereafter. After World War II they withdrew from direct management of Hacienda Palto but continued in sugar despite shrinking returns. In 1968 the military reform government seized control of the Aspíllaga plantations, compensating the owners with government bonds.

See also **Peru, Political Parties: Civilista Party; Plantations.**

BIBLIOGRAPHY

Dennis Gilbert, *La oligarquía peruana: Historia de tres familias* (1982).

Michael Gonzales, *Plantation Agriculture and Social Control in Northern Peru, 1875–1933* (1985), esp. pp. 29–32, 166–194.

Additional Bibliography

McEvoy, Carmen. *La utopía republicana: Ideales y realidades en la formación de la cultura política peruana, 1871-1919*. Lima, Perú: Pontificia Universidad Católica del Perú, Fondo Editorial, 1997.

Peloso, Vincent C. *Peasants on Plantations: Subaltern Strategies of Labor and Resistance in the Pisco Valley, Peru*. Durham, NC: Duke University Press, 1999.

VINCENT PELOSO

ASSEMBLY OF NOTABLES.

Assembly of Notables, Mexican council that offered the crown to Archduke Maximilian. On 16 June 1863, General Élie-Frédéric Forey ordered the establishment of a thirty-five-member Junta Suprema de Gobierno. This provisional junta appointed a three-man executive power, which consisted of Juan Nepomuceno Almonte, Mariano Salas, and Archbishop Pelagio Antonio de Labastida, and then designated the 215 members of an Assembly of Notables. The assembly met on 8–10 July in the building of the former Chamber of Deputies and included the Conservative Luis G. Cuevas, a former minister, and Pedro Escudero y Echánove, who had sat in the Constituent Congress of 1856–1857. Members tended to be moderates, though some, such as José Fernando Ramírez and Manuel Orozco y Berra, refused to participate. Rejecting both federalism and centralism, the assembly opted for "a moderated, hereditary monarchy as the form of government best suited to Mexico, with a Catholic prince" as emperor of Mexico. The assembly offered a vacant Mexican crown to Archduke Maximilian of Hapsburg. Should Maximilian decline the offer, the opinion of Napoleon III was to be sought.

The assembly was an attempt by the French, then in concert with leading Conservatives and moderates, to provide legitimacy for Maximilian's accession to the throne. The republicans, however, maintained that the Juárez administration, elected in 1861, was the legitimate government and that the assembly was illegal. Ultimately, the conservatives' association with the French occupation tarnished their political movement. Juárez gained greater legitimacy and eventually defeated the French, ushering in an era of liberal rule until the Mexican Revolution in 1910 reoriented Mexican politics.

See also **Labastida y Dávalos, Pelagio Antonio de.**

BIBLIOGRAPHY

Cunningham, Michele. *Mexico and the Foreign Policy of Napoleon III.* Houndmills, U.K., and New York : Palgrave, 2001.

García Cantú, Gastón. *La intervención francesa en México.* México: Clío, 1998.

José, Fuentes Mares. *Juárez, Los Estados Unidos y Europa* (1983), pp. 358–363.

Meyer, Jean A. *Yo, el francés: La intervención en primera persona: Biografías y crónicas.* México: Tusquets Editores, 2002.

Rafael Tafolla Pérez. *La Junta de Notables de 1863* (1977).

BRIAN HAMNETT

ASSIS, JOAQUIM MARIA MACHADO DE.   *See* **Machado de Assis, Joaquim Maria.**

ASSUNÇÃO, LEILAH   (1943–). Leilah Assunção (*b.* 1943), Brazilian playwright, author, and actress. Born Maria de Lourdes Torres de Assunção in Botucatu, São Paulo, Assunção holds a degree in education from the University of São Paulo and has studied acting, fashion design, literary criticism with Antônio Callado, and theater at the Teatro Oficina. Besides writing, she has acted in several plays and worked as a fashion model. In her theater Assunção reveals a humorous sensitivity for the middle class and their problems, and especially for women restricted in their environment and confronting a man's world. Although some of her works were censored in the years of military rule, Assunção's first play, *Fala baixo senão eu grito* (1969), a critical analysis of the heroine's life, won a Molière Prize. Margot Milleret describes *Boca molhada de paixão calada* (1980), perhaps Assunção's most political play, as depicting "a couple in their forties who re-create their past by acting out previous sexual encounters." Assunção is considered one of the most important playwrights in Brazil today, and is one of the few to live exclusively on the earnings from her writing, due in part to the popularity of her television scripts.

See also **Theater.**

BIBLIOGRAPHY

Alcides João De Barros, "A situação social de mulher no teatro de Consuelo de Castro e Leilah Assunção," in *Latin American Theatre Review* 9 (Spring 1976): 13–20.

Margo Milleret, "Entrapment and Flights of Fantasy in Three Plays by Leilah Assunção," in *Luso-Brazilian Review* 21 (Summer 1984): 49–56.

Elzbieta Szoka and Joe W. Bratcher III, eds, *3 Contemporary Brazilian Plays in Bilingual Edition* (1988), esp. pp. 211–216.

Ann Witte, "Feminismo e anti-Feminismo em Leilah Assunção e Millôr Fernandes," in *Dactylus* 9 (1988–1989): 15–20.

Margo Milleret, "(Re)playing the Brazilian Dictatorship," in *Discurso literario: Revista de estudios iberoamericanos* 7, no. 1 (1990): 213–224.

Additional Bibliography

Andrade, Ana Lúcia Vieira de. *Margem e centro: A dramaturgia de Leilah Assunção, Maria Adelaide Amaral e Isis Baião.* São Paulo: Perspectiva, 2006.

Silva, Magda. "Leilah Assunção: History and Feminism of the Sixties and Seventies in Brazil." M.A. Thesis, University of North Carolina at Chapel Hill, 1995.

GARY M. VESSELS

ASTRONOMY.   In contrast with modern cultures, religious beliefs in indigenous societies in the Western Hemisphere played an important role in the development of astronomy. Archaeoastronomy consults written and unwritten sources for information about how these diverse peoples thought about and observed the heavens within the context of their worldview as a whole. For example, the Maya emphasized the special relationship between the Sun and Venus to which they assigned religious significance, whereas current astronomy arranges planets according to distances from the Sun. Mayan inscriptions on stelae (carved monuments) likewise connect important events in the lives of rulers with eclipses and other astronomical events. It is likely that Andean and Mesoamerican peoples shared the belief that time flowed around the horizon, as Mexicans depicted on their calendar wheels. Scholars have discovered that the Maya even constructed buildings in alignment with astronomical events occurring at the horizon, as did peoples in the Central Valley of Mexico, Andean peoples, and those who lived in the present-day U.S. Southwest. The Governor's

Palace at Uxmal, for example, displays over 300 Venus glyphs, and the constructions at Teotihuacán show planning designed in accordance with a solar horizon calendar, as did those at Tenochtitlán. Some suggest that the Caracol, built around 1000 CE at the site of Chichén Itza served as the astronomical observatory behind the written Venus calendar found in the Dresden Codex, which also includes an almanac showing that the Maya could predict solar eclipses. Indeed, five of the sixteen surviving pre-Columbian codices include Venus almanacs used to regulate specific practices of warfare and ritual sacrifice.

Although it is harder to discern astronomical orientations among the indigenous peoples of the present-day U.S. Southwest, Brazil, and the Andean region, suggestive evidence abounds. The Casa Rinconada, from the eleventh-century Anasazi-Pueblo cultures of Chaco Canyon, New Mexico, a huge circular kiva for worship, is perfectly aligned on the pole star and contains a special window, possibly designed to admit the light emanating from the summer solstice sunrise. A sketch of the 1054 supernova was drawn on the walls of the canyon. In Casa Grande, Arizona, buildings contain accurate solar alignments at solstices and equinoxes, and the Chumash people of California carved their astronomical sightings into rocks.

Archaeologists in the twenty-first century unearthed structures in the Brazilian Amazon that have expanded existing knowledge of the region. An ancient stone structure dating from between 3000 to 1600 BCE suggests ancient peoples in present-day Amapá had sophisticated astronomical knowledge; this challenges the previous hypothesis that there were few advanced societies in the Amazon during that period. The structure, which may be a temple or observatory, is composed of more than 127 evenly spaced large stone blocks driven into the ground. Scholars believe the stones' arrangement aided in pinpointing the winter solstice, and that this and other information derived from the stars and Moon helped to determine crop cycles.

Andean peoples, too, watched the skies for information about the future. Manuscripts produced after the Spanish conquest and on-site observations indicate that the Coricancha Temple (Temple of the Sun) in Cuzco possessed an astronomical orientation; opposite inner halls look out toward the June and December solstice sunrise and sunset positions, reflecting the Incas' dualistic, vertical view of the cosmos still held today. It is thought that the Incas built pillars (*huacas*) along the Cuzco horizon to demarcate solar positions and provide information about when to begin planting at what altitudes. Record keepers called *quilcacamayoc* wove astronomical data into textiles. The desert plateaus of coastal Nasca, Peru, contain over 100 geometrical shapes known collectively as the Nasca Lines. Although some scholars have speculated that the lines were the remains of a horizon-based astronomy system, that view has been discredited. Nevertheless, modern Andean peoples believe that a sighting of a bright Pleiades constellation will yield good harvests, and Quechua speakers think the Milky Way (Mayu) continues the river system flowing through the Valley of Cuzco into the heavens. The Guane people of Colombia also developed a calendar based on astronomy.

Since these ancient times, the study of astronomy has continued to develop. Many universities have academic departments of astronomy, and observatories exist throughout the Americas. A leading Mexican astronomer, Guillermo Haro (1913–1988), not only has made many important contributions to the field, but also was a significant promoter of institutional development. Despite a tragic accident in 2003, Brazil continues to press on with its space program. Also the region continues to witness many astronomical events. One of the largest meteors ever recorded, the 37.2-ton Campo del Cielo, landed in Argentina in 1969, generating interest and study.

See also **Aztec Calendar Stone.**

BIBLIOGRAPHY

Alvarez Gutiérrez, Jaime. *Los Guanes: Con el código, las claves, los glifos y la revelación de su increíble calendario.* Bogotá, Colombia: Editorial Cabra Mocha, 2004.

Arias de Greiff, Jorge. *La astronomía en Colombia.* Bogotá, Colombia: Academia Colombiana de Ciencias Exactas, Físicas y Naturales, 1993.

Aveni, A. F., ed., *World Archaeoastronomy* (1989).

Aveni, Anthony F., ed. *Archaeoastronomy in Pre-Columbian America* (1975), and *Native American Astronomy* (1977).

Aveni, Anthony F. *Skywatchers of Ancient Mexico* (1980).

Aveni, Anthony F. *Skywatchers.* Austin: University of Texas Press, 2001.

Baity, Elizabeth Chesley. "Archaeoastromony and Ethnoastronomy So Far," *Current Anthropology* 14 (1973): 389–449.

Bargalló Cervelló, Pedro. *El cielo de Caracas, 1567–1967: 400 años contemplando el paso de las estrellas.* Caracas: Banco Industrial de Venezuela, 1965.

Bauer, Brian, and David S. P. Dearborn. *Astronomy and Empire in the Ancient Andes: The Cultural Origins of Inca Sky Watching.* Austin: University of Texas Press, 1995.

Carlson, John B. "Ancient Skies," *Humanities* 7 (1986): 24–28.

Carlson, John B., and W. James Judge, eds. *Astronomy and Ceremony in the Prehistoric Southwest* (1987).

Carlson, John B. "America's Ancient Skywatchers," *National Geographic Magazine* 177 (1990): 76–107.

Collea, Beth A., and Anthony F. Aveni. *A Selected Bibliography on Native American Astronomy* (1978).

Cuesy, Silvia L. *Cazador de estrellas: La vida del astrónomo Guillermo Haro.* México, D. F: Destino, 2004.

Galindo Trejo, Jesús. *Arqueoastronomía en la América antigua.* Madrid: Editorial Equipo Sirius, 1994.

Jalles, Cíntia, and Maura Imazio. *Olhando o céu da pré-história: Registros arqueoastrônomos no Brasil.* Rio de Janeiro: Museu de Astronomia e Ciências Afins, 2004.

Malmström, Vincent Herschel. *Cycles of the Sun, Mysteries of the Moon: The Calendar in Mesoamerican Civilization.* Austin: University of Texas Press, 1997.

Rice, Prudence M. *Maya Political Science: Time, Astronomy, and the Cosmos.* Austin: University of Texas Press, 2004.

Ruggles, Clive L. N., and Nicholas J. Saunders, eds., *Astronomies and Cultures* (1993).

Sprajc, Ivan. *Venus, lluvia y maíz: Simbolismo y astronomía en la cosmovisión mesoamericana.* México, D.F.: Instituto Nacional de Antropología e Historia, 1996.

Williamson, Ray A., ed. *Archaeoastronomy in the Americas* (1981).

Williamson, Ray A., and Claire R. Farrer, eds. *Earth and Sky: Visions of the Cosmos in Native American Folklore* (1992).

JOHN B. CARLSON

ASTURIAS, MIGUEL ÁNGEL (1899–1974).

Miguel Ángel Asturias (*b.* 19 October 1899; *d.* 9 June 1974), Guatemalan writer and Nobel Prize winner (1967). His country's greatest writer in the twentieth century, Asturias was also one of the forerunners of Latin America's literature boom of the 1960s, along with Jorge Luis Borges of Argentina and Alejo Carpentier of Cuba.

Asturias was born in the old district of La Parroquia in Guatemala City and spent his early years there. His father, a lawyer, fearing persecution by dictator Manuel Estrada Cabrera (1898–1920), moved the family to the small town of Salamá, where they lived from 1903 to 1907. In this town the young mestizo (mixed Mayan and Spanish heritage) came into contact with the Mayan lifestyle, something that would mark him for the rest of his life.

In Guatemala City, Asturias completed his secondary education at the nation's top public institution, Instituto de Varones, and enrolled in the law school of the University of San Carlos in 1918. In April 1920 he became active in the overthrow of dictator Estrada Cabrera, emerging as a student leader after this epic struggle. As a result, he traveled to Mexico City with a student delegation and met Mexico's minister of education, José Vasconcelos, a well-known philosopher on ethnic issues and miscegenation. Young Asturias was greatly influenced by his thinking. Asturias received his law degree in 1923 but never practiced. Already the author of poems, short stories, and essays, he left for Paris in 1924.

In Paris, Asturias studied ethnology under Georges Raynaud, a Mayanist, and came to rediscover his own Mayan roots as a result. He was also a correspondent for *El Imparcial,* one of Guatemala's leading newspapers, and traveled extensively throughout Europe. His first published book was *Leyendas de Guatemala* (Legends of Guatemala, 1930), in which the prehuman forces and creatures of Mayan myth are given new life, and Mayans are placed in that landscape.

In 1933 Asturias returned to Guatemala, then under the control of another dictator, General Jorge Ubico (1931–1944). Unable to make a living as a writer, Asturias was forced to work for the official newspaper, *El Liberal Progresista.* Later he founded the first radio news program in Guatemala, "Diario del Aire" (Radio Newspaper, 1937).

In 1944, when the Ubico dictatorship was overthrown, Asturias fled to Mexico, where he published his best-known novel, *El señor presidente* (The President, 1946). Of this work, critic Gerald

Martin says that it "exemplifies more clearly than any other novel the crucial link between European Surrealism and Latin American Magical Realism" (1989). It remains the single most famous Latin American "dictator novel."

One year later the new democratic government of Juan José Arévalo (1945–1951) named Asturias cultural attaché in Mexico. Three years later he was appointed ambassador to Argentina, where he published his masterpiece, *Hombres de maíz* in 1949 (translated as *Men of Maize* in 1975). Soon after, he began his ideological transition toward leftist politics. *Men of Maize* is considered by some critics to be the first unmistakable magical realist Joycean novel in Latin America, the most ambitious to this day, and perhaps the greatest of the twentieth century. According to Chilean critic Ariel Dorfman (1992), the contemporary Spanish American novel begins with its publication. It anticipates by fifty years many issues popular at the end of the twentieth century, such as ecology, feminism, global consciousness, and a defense of native peoples. Gerald Martin describes it as "a profound meditation on the history of Guatemala, contained within a symbolic history of Latin America since the conquest, contained within the history of humanity's passage from so-called barbarism to so-called civilization since the Greeks, contained within the novelist's own reflections on the human condition."

Asturias was ambassador to El Salvador in 1954 when the country was invaded by a mercenary army and the democratic process was interrupted. He went into exile in Argentina, then moved to Genoa, Italy, where he published his last truly memorable novel, *Mulata de tal* (1963), a work that, fusing the experience of Quetzalcoatl with that of Dante, anticipates Latin America's literature boom.

In 1966 Asturias's old university friend Julio César Méndez Montenegro was elected president of Guatemala and named Asturias ambassador to France. That same year Asturias won the Lenin Peace Prize, and the following year, the Nobel Prize for literature.

When General Carlos Arana Osorio gained control of Guatemala in 1970, Asturias resigned as ambassador and gave the Nobel Prize money to his son, Rodrigo, who apparently used it to found a guerrilla organization. Asturias died in Madrid and is buried in the Père-Lachaise Cemetery in Paris.

Asturias, essentially a novelist, also wrote poetry, plays, and journal articles. His books are *Leyendas de Guatemala* (stories, 1930); *Émulo Lipolidón* (play, 1935); *Alclasán* (play, 1940); *El señor presidente* (novel, 1946); *Sien de alondra* (poetry, 1949); *Hombres de maíz* (novel, 1949); *Viento fuerte* (novel, 1949); *El papa verde* (novel, 1954); *Weekend en Guatemala* (stories, 1955); *Soluna* (play, 1955); *Los ojos de los enterrados* (novel, 1960); *El Alhajadito* (novella, 1961); *Mulata de tal* (novel, 1963); *Clarivigilia primaveral* (poetry, 1965); *Letanías del desterrado* (poetry, 1966); *El espejo de Lida Sal* (stories, 1967); *Maladrón* (novel, 1969); *Tres de cuatro soles* (poetry, 1971); and *Viernes de dolores* (novel, 1972).

See also **Literature: Spanish America.**

BIBLIOGRAPHY

Luis Harss and Barbara Dohmann, "Miguel Ángel Asturias," in their *Into the Mainstream: Conversations with Latin American Writers* (1967).

Richard J. Callahan, *Miguel Ángel Asturias* (1970).

Ariel Dorfman, "Myth as Time and Word," translated by Paula Speck, in *Review 75,* no. 15 (1975): 12–22.

Jean Franco, "Miguel Ángel Asturias," in *Latin American Writers,* vol. 2, edited by Carlos A. Solé (1989), pp. 865–873.

Gerald Martin, *Journeys Through the Labyrinth: Latin American Fiction in the Twentieth Century* (1989).

Ariel Dorfman, *"Hombres de Maíz: El mito como tiempo y palabra* in Gerald Martin, ed., *Asturias's Hombres de Maíz: Critical Edition* (1992).

Additional Bibliography

Asturias Montenegro, G. *Miguel Angel Asturias: Biografía breve* Guatemala: Editorial Cultura, 1999.

Preble-Niemi, Oralia. *Cien años de magia: Ensayos críticos sobre la obra de Miguel Ángel Asturias.* Guatemala: F & G Editores, 2006.

ARTURO ARIAS

ASUAR, JOSÉ VICENTE (1933–).

José Vicente Asuar (*b.* 20 July 1933), Chilean composer and acoustic engineer. Born in Santiago, Asuar began his musical studies with Jorge Urrutia-Blondel (composition) and Juan Orrego-Salas (orchestration) at the Santiago Conservatory. From 1952 to 1958 he studied engineering at the Catholic University of Chile, continuing his education in Germany, at the Technical University of Berlin (1959–1960). While in Germany, he studied with Boris Blacher at the Berlin Hochschule für Musik (1959–1960) and with Jacques Wildberger at the Baden Hochschule für Musik. He studied composition privately under Fritz Winckel and Werner Meyer-Eppler; at Darmstadt University he attended the summer seminars of Boulez, Ligeti, Stockhausen, and Maderna (1960–1962). Back in Santiago, Asuar was director of the electronic music studio (1958–1959) at the Catholic University. In 1960 he returned to Germany to organize an electronic music studio at Karlsruhe. In Caracas from 1965 to 1968, Asuar created and directed the first Venezuelan studio of electronic music. In 1969 he became director of the Department of Sound Technology at the University of Chile. The following year he was awarded a Fulbright grant to study computer music with Lejaren Hiller at the State University of New York at Buffalo.

Asuar has written works for instrumental ensembles, chamber and vocal music, and a considerable number of electronic music pieces. Some of his compositions are *Variaciones espectrales* (1959), *Encadenamientos* (1957), *Preludio a la noche* (1961), *Estudio aleatorio* (1962), *La noche II* (1966), and *Kaleidoscopio* and *Catedral* (1967). He has also written several essays about electronic-music techniques.

See also **Music: Art Music.**

BIBLIOGRAPHY

John Vinton, ed., *Dictionary of Contemporary Music* (1974).

Gérard Béhague, *Music in Latin America* (1979); *New Grove Dictionary of Music and Musicians,* vol. 1 (1980).

Additional Bibliography

Dal Farra, Ricardo. "Something Lost, Something Hidden, Something Found: Electroacoustic Music by Latin American Composers." *Organised Sound* 11 (2006): 131-142.

SUSANA SALGADO

ASUNCIÓN. Asunción, capital city of Paraguay, founded 15 August 1537 (the Feast of the Assumption) by Juan de Salazar y Espinoza on the east bank of the Paraguay River, 956 miles upstream from the port of Buenos Aires, Asunción became the capital of Paraguay on 14 May 1811. Serving as a base for colonial expeditions and Jesuit missionaries, Asunción was an important city in the early history of the Spanish Empire. From Asunción, expeditions founded cities in Argentina, Bolivia, and Brazil. For this reason it is known as the "mother of cities." As the center of the nation's political, economic, religious, and cultural life, Asunción dominates Paraguay's commerce, industry, and communications. It has a humid, subtropical climate with a mean temperature of 84F during the summer (October through March) and an average rainfall of 50 inches, occurring primarily in December and January. By the seventeenth century, Asunción was overshadowed by Buenos Aires, with its more favorable commercial location. Demographic data suggest that Asunción's population surpassed 3,500 by 1565; 7,000 by 1800; 11,000 by 1846; 42,000 by 1900; 203,000 by 1950; and 389,000 by 1972. In 2002 the population reached 508,795 in the city, and more than 1.6 million in the greater metropolitan area *Gran Asunción.*

The town was laid out in a gridiron pattern with a central plaza containing the religious, governmental, and commercial institutions. Within Asunción the competition for commercial dominance between port and plaza was resolved in favor of the plaza. During its first three centuries, Asunción was a nearly economically self-sufficient frontier river town with a Spanish- and Guarani-speaking Mestizo population of limited class divisions. It was subject to indigenous attack as late as the 1740s. The city prided itself on the secondary and religious training available at the Real Colegio y Seminario de San Carlos, which opened in 1783. Construction of public buildings and roads during the Carlos Antonio López administration (1844–1862) reflected increasing affluence. During the War of the Triple Alliance (1864–1870), however, Brazil captured, pillaged, and destroyed much of the city. The export of Asunción's wealth to Buenos Aires destroyed its development and slowed the nation's postwar commercial growth.

Renovated nineteenth-century buildings such as the 1843 cathedral; the government palace, built on the site of the former *cabildo* (city hall) and used by every president since Francisco Solano López (1862–1870); and the railroad station and theater, begun during the Carlos Antonio López administration, are landmarks of contemporary Asunción. The Pantheon of Heroes, a smaller version of the Invalides in Paris, was completed in 1937.

Initially connected to Buenos Aires by river and road and in the twentieth century by rail, and linked by road to Brazil and Bolivia, the city prospered. Beginning in the 1960s, Asunción expanded its telephone, water, sewage, and electrical power services. After World War I, and in particular since the 1960s, better-paying jobs, modern conveniences, and kin in Asunción have attracted increasing numbers of rural migrants and some foreign immigrants. By 2001 the city accounted for more than 25 percent of the nation's total population. Argentina's economic crisis in 2001 hurt Paraguay, and since then street vending and informal activities are a way of survival for many of Asunción's residents. As in the nineteenth century, the region surrounding Asunción produces foods such as corn and rice as well as sugarcane and fruit for the city. Asunción exports tobacco, cotton, hides, meat, and timber to international markets.

Asunción controls the nation. Power resides primarily in the national executive. The judiciary, the two-chamber Congress, and all the public institutions have their headquarters in the city. Municipal government is weak, however, since the president traditionally appoints the mayor. The seat of the archbishop for this primarily Catholic country is Asunción. The city is home to the Universidad Nacional de Asunción (founded 1889) and the Universidad Católica "Nuestra Señora de la Asunción" (founded 1960) as well as the National Theater and a variety of museums.

The seasonal flooding of the Paraguay River from May to July that displaces inhabitants in informal marshland settlements continues to strain the city. Contingent on funding, the municipal and federal governments in cooperation with international agencies are planning an "embankment process" to elevate the marshlands.

Since a military coup overthrew the thirty-five-year reign of General Alfredo Stroessner in 1989, Paraguay has moved toward establishing a democratic system of government. Notwithstanding recent political conflicts and corruption, Paraguay has held relatively clean presidential elections since 1993. In August 2003 President Nicanor Duarte Frutos took office.

See also **Paraguay River.**

BIBLIOGRAPHY

Departmento De Cultura y Arte, Municipal De Asunción, *Historia edificia de la ciudad de Asunción* (1967), provides a series of short sketches by various authors on different aspects of the city, with over half the material after 1870. Mabel Causarano, *Asunción: Análisis histórico-ambiental de su imagen urbana: Álbum gráfico, 450 años* (1987), is a photo-album history of the city. Harris Gaylord Warren, *Paraguay and the Triple Alliance: The Postwar Decade, 1869–1878* (1978), esp. pp. 16–18 and 33–34, also provides descriptive material on the nineteenth century, while Fulgencio R. Moreno, *La Ciudad de la Asunción* (1926, repr. 1968), concentrates primarily on colonial development, including political, demographic, economic, and social information. George F. Masterman, *Seven Eventful Years in Paraguay* (1869), esp. pp. 32–34, provides an excellent description of Asunción in the nineteenth century and the wartime conditions of Paraguay, but his analysis of Francisco Solano López must be approached with caution.

Imas Ruiz, Víctor Julio. *Ante la pobreza, la organización: La emergencia del movimiento barrial en el marco de la transición política en el Paraguay.* Asunción: BASE-ECTA, 1995.

Krüger, Hildegard. *El Cabildo de Asunción: Estructura y función del cabildo colonial.* Asunción: Instituto Cultural Paraguayo-Alemán, 1996.

Lafuente Machain, Ricardo de. *El Fundador: Juan de Salazar de Espinosa.* Asunción: Academia Paraguaya de la Historia: FONDEC, 2004.

Laterza Rivarola, Gustavo. *Historia del municipio de Asunción: Desde sus comienzos hasta nuestros días.* Asunción: GG Servicios Gráficos, 1995.

Prieto, Juan Manuel. *La ciudad en que vivimos.* Asunción: Arandurã Editorial, 2001.

Quevedo, Roberto, Margarita Durán Estragó, and Alberto Duarte. *Actas capitulares y documentos del Cabildo de Asunción del Paraguay, Siglo XVI.* Asunción: Municipalidad de la Ciudad de Asunción, 2001.

Vera Blinn Reber

ASYLUM. Asylum (Sp./Port. *asilo*) is a distinctive diplomatic and political practice employed primarily in Latin America and a major institution for human rights protection in the Western Hemisphere. Asylum may be defined as the right to offer protection to individuals suffering from political persecution. United Nations Resolution 2312 (XIII) of 1967 defines asylum to be a state's right, the concession of which does not constitute a hostile action toward the asylee's original territorial state.

Based on Roman law, the notion of asylum dates to pre-Christian times, although one of its greatest historical expressions has been through canon law. Asylum has evolved principally as a result of custom, rather than legal factors. In the nineteenth and twentieth centuries, the institution of asylum has become largely a Latin American practice. It grew there as a result of local political volatility which manifested itself in the recurrence of uprisings and revolutionary upheavals. Furthermore, for the young Latin American nation-states, concession of immunity in asylum cases implied diplomatic recognition by the major powers.

In modern usage, two types of asylum exist: internal and external. Internal asylum, more commonly referred to as territorial asylum, was the only type of asylum known until relatively recently. It is generally considered a consequence of territorial sovereignty. States grant this type of asylum to foreigners fleeing their own countries. Although a state possesses the right to not admit any person to its territory, no state, after providing a persecuted individual hospitality, may expel him or turn him over to a state which requests him.

External asylum is that granted on an extraterritorial basis and is permitted in legations, embassies, consulates, warships, and military camps. Diplomatic asylum, which applies to the former three locations, is the most common form of external asylum and may be conceded to nationals of the country in which the diplomatic entity is accredited and located. Diplomatic asylum arose when the European states began to maintain permanent representatives abroad and thus since the inception of diplomatic immunity.

EARLY EVOLUTION OF ASYLUM

Diplomatic asylum in Latin America dates to the late nineteenth century and stemmed from the political organization of independent states. Once the ascendency of anticlerical liberals eradicated religious asylum, and as states began to consolidate, the new governments perceived recognition as a significant

priority. Thus, they did not breach the sovereignty of another nation's diplomatic premises. As a result, individuals persecuted for their political beliefs attempted to obtain asylum inside those premises.

Although the practice of asylum became relatively common in the first twenty-five years after Independence, its legal basis remained ambiguous, as reflected in early asylum treaties. In 1865 an agreement was signed in Lima regulating political asylum. In 1867 various European and American legations convened in Lima at a conference which recognized diplomatic asylum as a common practice in the region. The diplomats, however, did not claim that asylum represented a basic rule of international law, nor was it claimed to be a practice native to Latin America. The Lima conference also required that the practice of asylum not interfere with the sovereignty of the American people.

The Convention on the International Penal Law, adopted on 23 January 1889, by the First South American Congress on Private International Law at Montevideo, represented an affirmation of the conclusions of the former conference. The 1889 assembly reasserted the notion that asylum should be regulated through international law. It also recognized the diplomatic asylum of political offenders as a right permitted by the usage, conventions, or laws of the South American countries.

The Sixth International Conference of American States, held in Havana, resulted in the adoption of a Convention Fixing the Rules to Be Observed for the Granting of Asylum on 20 February 1928. The United States was the only American state expressing reservations about the doctrine of asylum. The Convention of Havana established several important principles of diplomatic asylum in Latin America. First, asylum may be conceded only in urgent cases and only for the time strictly necessary for the asylee to secure his safety. Second, asylees may not be disembarked in any part of their national territory nor anywhere near it. Third, as long as asylum lasts, asylees are not permitted to practice acts contrary to public security. Fourth, the right to asylum may be given to political delinquents only in diplomatic legations or military locations. Finally, the government of an asylee's national territory can demand that the asylee be removed from the territory as soon as possible, and the diplomatic agent that has agreed to grant asylum can demand the necessary safe-conducts for the asylee.

In 1933 the Seventh International Conference of American States, held in Montevideo, adopted a Convention on Political Asylum on December 26, 1933. This rather vague agreement permitted the state granting asylum to define the crime of the asylee as political. The significance of this treaty and the 1928 Havana Convention lies in their widespread acceptance. Treaties which declare asylum as a basic human right have not been embraced so inclusively. The Second South American Conference on Private International Law at Montevideo adopted the Treaty on Political Asylum and Refuge on 4 August 1939, revising the 1889 Montevideo treaty.

HAYA DE LA TORRE CASE

On 28 March 1954, the Tenth Inter-American Conference held in Caracas adopted conventions on diplomatic and territorial asylum, partially as a result of the Haya De La Torre case between Colombia and Peru. The Caracas Convention defines territorial asylees as individuals who come from states in which they suffer persecution as a result of political convictions, ideas, or associations or for political crimes. In 1954, Caracas also hosted the Convention on Diplomatic Asylum, which asserted that each state may decide whether to grant or refuse asylum to any individual. The asylum-granting state also was res-ponsible for stipulating the nature of an asylee's crime. It also established the principle of non-refoulement, or the proscription of forced return of an asylum seeker to a country of persecution. Finally, the Convention also expressed the boundaries of rights to freedom of expression, assembly and association. While guaranteeing them, it prohibited asylees from provoking or organizing against a sovereign state.

One of the most important cases in Latin American asylum history has been the Haya de la Torre case. In January 1949, Víctor Raúl Haya de la Torre, leader of the Peruvian APRa party, sought refuge in the Colombian embassy in Lima. Colombia argued that custom represented a sufficient legal foundation for asylum. Peru, by contrast, historically has tended to reject this claim. The two countries carried the case to the International Court of Justice for clarification, because they could not agree on the interpretations of the 1928 Havana Convention regarding the determination of the nature of the asylee's crime and the obligation of a territorial state to concede the necessary safe-conduct.

Following a series of disputes regarding these issues, the International Court of Justice in 1950 produced a jurisprudential doctrine, concluding that Peru was not required to grant Haya de la Torre safe-conduct, that Colombia was not required to turn him over to Peruvian authorities but was required to put an end to the irregularly conceded asylum. After an asylum of five years, Peru issued Haya de la Torre a decree of exile from the country. Colombia agreed to turn him over to the Peruvian minister of justice for one hour for judgment before issuance of the exile decree. Peru reserved extradition rights and demanded that Haya de la Torre never be granted territorial asylum in Colombia. The Haya de la Torre case is important as an example of asylum acting as an impetus for jurisprudence. The involvement of the International Court of Justice as a juridical actor in an asylum case is significant.

FAJARDO, CÁMPORA, AND HONECKER CASES

Two other relevant cases for the legal interpretation of asylum principles and asylum's institutional evolution are the Saúl Fajardo case in Colombia in 1952 and the Hector José Cámpora case in Argentina in 1976. From 17 March to 4 April 1952, the Colombian guerrilla Saúl Fajardo was sheltered in the Chilean embassy in Bogotá. The two governments involved disagreed on the nature of Fajardo's crime, with Colombia declaring the asylum illegal because they considered Fajardo not a political delinquent but rather a common criminal. This case reflects the importance of the distinction between political and common crimes and the weight of political expediency.

Ex-president Hector Cámpora remained in the Mexican embassy for over three years as a result of the Argentine government's refusal to grant him a safe-conduct. The Cámpora case represents the first time an asylum had been so prolonged when the asylee was not charged judicially. With Cámpora were his son Hector Pedro and ex-secretary of the Peronist Movement, Juan Manuel Abal Medina. These individuals requested and were granted asylum in April 1976. In November 1979, ex-president

Cámpora was allowed to go to Mexico, where he was diagnosed with a terminal illness.

The Argentine government, though recognizing the right of asylum and allowing it to function in other cases, refused to grant the safe-conducts necessary for these particular asylees to leave the country. The refusal resulted not from the existence of charges of common crimes, as in the case of Haya de la Torre. Rather, the Argentine government admitted that Cámpora was a political criminal but still refused him the safe-conduct. By late 1979, Mexico threatened to carry the case to the International Court of Justice, using the Haya de la Torre case as a precedent. In effect, the Argentine government denied the obligation of a territorial state to issue the safe-conducts. The Cámpora matter illustrates, first, that the Haya de la Torre case proved to be a precedent in the institution of asylum. Second, it shows that political expediency often shapes, and sometimes undermines, the operation of the institution.

An important contemporary case is that of Erich Honecker, former prime minister of East Germany, who was charged with manslaughter and misappropriation of state funds. Honecker fled his country in March 1991 and lived in the Chilean embassy in Moscow from December 1991 to July 1992. Some members of the post-Pinochet Chilean government, including the Chilean ambassador in Moscow, Clodomiro Almeyda, felt the country owed a debt to Honecker, who had provided asylum to many of Salvador Allende's supporters. Although the Chilean government announced in March 1992 that it would not grant asylum to Honecker, it allowed him to remain in the embassy until Russian authorities determined his future. In July the Chilean government asked Honecker to leave its Moscow embassy. Honecker's trial in Germany began in November 1992, but in January 1993 the German court, recognizing that Honecker suffered from terminal cancer, canceled the trial and allowed Honecker to travel to Chile.

MASSIVE DIPLOMATIC ASYLUM

Although historically asylum has been determined on an individual basis, the establishment of military governments in Brazil, Argentina, Chile, Ecuador, Peru, Bolivia, and Uruguay in the 1960s and 1970s stimulated massive requests for asylum. Most asylees

from these countries sought protection in Mexico, Venezuela, Costa Rica, and to a lesser extent, in Colombia.

The most relevant and visible case of massive diplomatic asylum in modern Latin American history is the case of Chile after the 11 September 1973, military coup in which President Salvador Allende was deposed. In the months following the coup, many embassies, including the missions of countries outside the region, admitted thousands of asylum seekers. Among the asylees were Hortensia B. de Allende, the wife of the assassinated president, who was asyled in the Mexican embassy; most of Allende's cabinet ministers; journalists, intellectuals, professionals, and bureaucrats associated with the deposed regime; and leaders of political parties and labor unions, along with other social activists.

In a different political and international context, another modern case of massive request for diplomatic asylum is that of the Cubans who stormed the Peruvian embassy in 1980 to request asylum. The Cuban government announced that any Cuban who wished to leave the country should go to the Peruvian embassy. More than 10,000 people appeared in three days. Although not all of those who requested asylum did so as a result of political persecution, Peru eventually granted asylum to 740 Cubans. The balance either decided to remain in Cuba or fled to the United States in the Mariel Boatlift which the Peruvian embassy incident precipitated.

Until recently the overwhelming majority of exiles protected by asylum came from relatively prosperous sectors of society and from all sides of the ideological spectrum depending on the country and circumstance. Asylees were typically prominent politicians, skilled workers, social leaders, religious figures, university graduates, intellectuals, artists, businessmen, and women. With variations from case to case and country to country, this was the general profile of asylum seekers from Guatemala after an armed coup deposed the reformist government of President Jacobo Arbenz in 1954; from Cuba after 1959 when Fidel Castro took power and instituted revolutionary trials against thousands of people believed to be associated with the old regime; from Brazil, Argentina, and Uruguay during several years after the military seized power in 1964, 1966, and 1973, respectively; from Chile in 1973 after General Augusto Pinochet deposed the Allende government; and from Nicaragua after Sandinista guerrillas defeated the dictatorship of Anastasio Somoza Debayle in 1979. The social, political, or economic prominence of many asylum seekers accorded this international legal institution particular prestige and relevance in Latin America. Some countries, including Mexico, Venezuela, Costa Rica, and even the United States and Canada, have greatly benefited from often highly qualified, talented, and creative exiles.

REFUGEES

Political conflicts and revolutionary upheavals in South and Central America have increasingly been accompanied by a general decline in economic conditions as an exacerbation of social inequalities in the countries affected. These interrelated political and economic problems have stimulated waves of migrants seeking either safety and protection or employment and better economic opportunities in Latin American nations which are relatively more stable and developed, as well as in the United States, Canada, and Europe.

Although some of these migrants have applied for political asylum in diplomatic missions, the majority of them have left their country without diplomatic aid or protection. Few have applied for territorial asylum. A sizable proportion of migrants escaping political and economic problems in Latin America in the 1980s established residence in other countries or moved from one to another outside the legal protection of the asylum status. Instead, they were refugees using tourist visas and other temporary alien permits or were without documentation. Over time, these circumstances have created considerable confusion and overlapping between the cases of individuals fitting the classical definition of asylees, economic migrants, and the new phenomena of refugees legitimately concerned with their security as a result of membership in communities suffering political repression, such as ethnic groups or residents of areas affected by war and generalized violence.

As a consequence of the economic and political events of the 1980s in the hemisphere, the typical Latin American refugees are no longer persons who enter an embassy in search of protection, assured by their prestige and status of a friendly welcome and good treatment in the recipient country. Nor are they individuals capable of assuring their maintenance and economic well-being with little or no external support. During the 1990s, and directly as a consequence of the political unrest, violence, and economic stagnation in Central America and the Caribbean, large numbers of peasants, unskilled workers, indigenous groups, and marginalized populations have sought protection and welfare assistance outside their country of origin. Since they were migrating under very precarious conditions, their disadvantages are significant and their needs urgent. In contrast with the experience of most traditional exiles protected by the institution of asylum, many refugees of this new type have endured harsh conditions. They have often been perceived and isolated as active supporters of revolutionary movements posing a threat to the security of the host country or as social and economic burdens.

Diplomatic asylum has remained a crucial instrument of human rights protection, particularly at specific times of political crisis or as a mechanism to evade severe travel and migration restrictions imposed upon citizens, as in the case of Cubans storming the Peruvian embassy in Havana in 1980. A more diverse and complex migration process has emerged since 1980, however, extending the narrowly defined notion of asylum to the broader experience of refugees. Given its complexity and magnitude, the Central American and Caribbean refugee phenomena became a source of serious international controversy and a difficult political and economic responsibility for recipient countries and humanitarian organizations. Furthermore, the practical impossibility of clearly defining the borderline between political refugees and economic migrants has resulted in a more restricted application of asylum principles and tighter immigration controls on the part of recipient countries such as Mexico, Costa Rica, and the United States.

Central America and the Caribbean. The most significant waves of refugees in the hemisphere include Nicaraguans, Salvadorans, Guatamalans, Cubans, and Haitians. In 1981 indigenous people from the Atlantic coast of Nicaragua began entering Honduras from the Mocorón region, and in 1986 over 14,000 were in camps run by the United Nations High Commissioner for Refugees (UNHCR). They represented approximately half of the estimated 30,000 indigenous people from Nicaragua who, after the Sandinistas' seizure of power in 1979 and during the U.S.-sponsored anti-Sandinista civil war of the 1980s, escaped into the Miskito region of Honduras, were forcibly relocated, or joined the contra forces fighting the Sandinistas.

Simultaneously, 14,000 Nicaraguans, mostly peasants, crossed the border, either disaffected from the Sandinista regime or forced by the contras to the department of El Paraíso in Honduras, where they settled in camps under the protection of the Red Cross and the UNHCR. The Nicaraguans in El Paraíso represented part of a larger group of Nicaraguan peasants, mainly from the departments of Nueva Segovia, Jinotega, Esteli, and Madriz, in exile in Honduras. As many as 230,000 Nicaraguans also fled to Costa Rica in various waves. Only 30,000 of them were officially recognized as refugees by Costa Rican authorities.

The formal repatriation process of the Indians began in 1986. During 1987, 14,000 Indians repatriated with international assistance. By 1989, only 9,000 indigenous people were registered as refugees by the UNHCR in Honduras. All but a handful returned to Nicaragua after the elections of 1990, when the Sandinistas lost power to a coalition of opposition forces led by Violeta Chamorro. Most of the peasant refugees settled in the El Paraíso region in Honduras were repatriated to Nicaragua after 1989, and the return of refugees from Costa Rica also intensified after that year.

Between 1981 and 1985, 46,000 Guatemalan refugees entering the southern Mexican state of Chiapas, bordering on Guatemala, received refugee status. Initially, local peasant communities helped the refugees settle in camps run by the Catholic Church. Later, the Mexican government and the UNHCR took charge of many of those camps. These officially recognized refugees constituted part of a much larger group of peasants, mostly Indians of several different ethnic and linguistic groups. These refugees were often victims of the counterinsurgency campaign launched by the Guatemalan army in the highlands of the country, an area heavily populated by the Maya-K'iche' Indians. By the end of 1992, only 8,000 Guatemalans exiled in Mexican camps had returned to their country. In 1993 massive repatriations of Guatemalan Indians started under the leadership of the 1992 Nobel Peace Prize winner, Rigoberta Menchú, who was also an Indian refugee.

Between 1980 and 1986, Salvadorans suffering government repression or directly affected by the country's civil war emigrated in massive numbers to neighboring countries. Approximately 21,000 settled in internationally supervised refugee camps in Honduras. In 1987 refugees settled in Honduras began to return to El Salvador in large contingents. By 1990, without the explicit consent of the Salvadoran government, more than 16,000 had forced their return to their country in a series of very large convoys.

Cubans and Haitians have also left their countries in massive numbers, with the primary destination being the United States. Between 1959, when Fidel Castro took power, and 1980, almost 800,000 Cubans migrated to the United States. In 1980 more than 125,000 Cubans left their country in the Mariel boatlift. The Haitian "boat people" began migrating to the United States in large numbers in 1972, and by 1980 more than 1,000 a month were attempting the journey in boats that were often homemade and flimsy.

The examples of Cuban and Haitian immigration into the United States reflect the ambiguities involved in asylum and refugee policy, since one set of refugees, those abandoning Castro's Socialist Cuba, has been welcomed with open arms, while the other, fleeing the repression and poverty of Haiti's elite-dominated society, have been turned back. Cubans have been perceived as immigrating for political reasons, while Haitians have been said to seek improved economic conditions. The administration of U.S. president Jimmy Carter attempted to clarify the immigrant situation by creating the category Cuban-Haitian entrant, which meant that these groups received federal aid and were allowed to remain in the country on a two-year trial basis but did not receive refugee status. This classification was applicable to entrants before 1 January 1981, but it did nothing to halt immigration or resolve the status of later immigrants, particularly Haitians, who continued to enter South Florida at a rate of 10,000 a year.

Devising Solutions. A refugee may be generally defined as "a person outside his or her country of origin, who is unable or unwilling to return there owing to a well-founded fear of being persecuted on grounds of race, religion, nationality, social group, or political opinion." This definition is based on the Convention Relating to the Status of Refugees of July 28, 1951, and the Protocol Relating to the Status of Refugees adopted on 31 January 1967. Although the concept of refuge stems from the tradition of territorial asylum, refugees do not necessarily ask for individual protection; rather, they may seek refuge as a result of persecution due to their membership in some type of group. Refuge is a central aspect of human rights issues.

The Office of the United Nations High Commissioner for Refugees, the foremost international agency responsible for refugees, was created by the United Nations General Assembly on 14 December 1950. It is nonpolitical and its statute brings within the mandate of the United Nations' authority those refugees covered by previous bilateral treaties as well as those resulting from both pre- and post-1951 events or conditions. Since the creation of the UNHCR, the 1951 Convention and the 1967 Protocol have been the principal instruments for international regulation of refugees.

The Cartagena Conference of Experts of 1984 conducted a comparative study of the refugee question in Central America and attempted to formulate a regional solution. Although it is not a legal mechanism, the Cartagena Declaration is significant as a proof of consensus within the region regarding refugees. The Declaration also expanded the definition of a refugee to include persons fleeing not because of specific persecution but rather as a result of more general violence.

The Contadora negotiations of 1984, followed in 1987 by the Esquipulas II peace accords, or the Procedure for the Establishment of a Firm and Lasting Peace in Central America, further attempted to define solutions to the refugee problem in Central America by requiring that the matter be addressed; the parties also agreed to seek international support in their efforts. In response, the International Conference on Central American Refugees, Returnees and Displaced Persons (CIREFCA) was created in 1989. The region's governments have been compelled to collaborate with the UNHCR and other international organizations. Rather than refuge remaining a bilateral question, therefore, it has become

internationalized as third actors have begun to participate actively. The Central American conflict represents a turning point from the Haya de la Torre asylum case, since it implies that the refugee must not only be regulated but also administered by international institutions. Protection of the politically persecuted is now granted internationally rather than based on sovereign national rights.

In the 1990s, the level of violence in Latin America lessened and democratic governments began to take over. Consequently, the number of political refugees has not been as great as it was during the regional wars and military dictatorships of the 1970s and 1980s. Nevertheless, there have been important cases. The civil war in Colombia caused hundreds of thousands of people to leave their homes. Many people in rural areas moved to cities or neighboring countries. Others fled to the United States to escape the violence. Also, while political leaders in Latin America in the past have found asylum in neighboring countries, this tradition has begun to change. In 2007 the former Peruvian president Alberto Fujimori went to Chile. Rather than granting him asylum, the Chilean courts ruled that he had to be returned to Peru to face criminal charges there.

See also **United States-Latin American Relations.**

BIBLIOGRAPHY

S. Prakash Sinha, *Asylum and International Law* (1971).

Atle Grahl-Madsen, *Territorial Asylum* (1980).

Guy S. Goodwin-Gil, *The Refugee in International Law* (1983).

David A. Martin, ed., *The New Asylum Seekers: Refugee Law in the 1890s,* International Studies in Human Rights Series, vol. 10 (1988).

Keith W. Yundt, *Latin American States and Political Refugees* (1988).

F. Markx-Veldjuijzden, *The Right of Asylum: Selective Bibliography* (1989).

Mary Ann Larkin, Frederick C. Cuny, and Barry N. Stein, eds., *Repatriation Under Conflict in Central America* (1991).

Additional Bibliography

Rodríguez de Ita, Guadalupe. *La política mexicana de asilo diplomático a la luz del caso Guatemalteco, 1944–1954.* Mexico: Instituto Mora, 2003.

Sikkink, Kathryn. *Mixed Signals: U.S. Human Rights Policy and Latin America.* Ithaca, New York: Cornell University Press, 2004.

ADOLFO AGUILAR ZINSER

ATACAMA DESERT. Atacama Desert, interior region of southern Bolivia, northern Chile, and northwestern Argentina, 8,250–13,200 feet in elevation. Considered the driest desert of the world, the Atacama expands along a series of elongated, flat-bottomed basins, the remnants of shallow lakes of Quaternary Age. Today, on the floors of the desiccated lakes, borax, natural salt, and nitrate deposits are mined. Along intermittent watercourses fed by the icecaps of Andean volcanoes, pastoral communities of Atacameño Indians were established about 5,000 years ago. They were skilled woodcarvers and expert wool and ceramic artisans who traded with the Incas and the Aymara (Tiahuanaco) Indians to the north and the Diaguitas to the south. Several towns in the Atacama Desert, such as Peine, San Pedro de Atacama, and Lasana, still bear the strong cultural imprints of the old Atacameño culture.

See also **Argentina, Geography.**

BIBLIOGRAPHY

The classic work on this region is Isaiah Bowman, *Desert Trails of Atacama* (1924).

Additional Bibliography

Rivera, Mario A. *Arqueología del desierto de Atacama: La etapa formativa en el área de Ramaditas/Guatacondo.* Santiago: Universidad Bolivariana, 2005.

Vicuña Urrutia, Manuel. *La imagen del desierto de Atacma (XVI–XIX): Del espacio de la disuación al territorio de los desafíos.* Santiago: Editorial de la Universidad de Santiago de Chile, 1995.

CÉSAR N. CAVIEDES

ATACAMES. Atacames, the name assigned to the prehistoric culture occupying the Ecuadorian Esmeraldas coast during the Integration Period (500–1531 CE). Recent archaeological research of the Atacames type site has established three occupational phases: Early Atacames 1 and 2 (700–1100 CE) and Late Atacames (1100–1526 CE). The end point marks the first of Francisco Pizarro's voyages of conquest down the coast of Ecuador.

Early ethnohistorical accounts, which report a densely populated coast, describe the town of Atacames as having over 1,500 houses laid out on a grid plan with streets and open plaza areas. Archaeological investigations conducted in the 1970s by the Spanish archaeologist José Alcina Franch and his colleagues confirmed these early descriptions, having documented a series of large habitation sites with mound groups and extensive cultural refuse all along the coast of Esmeraldas, including Atacames, Tonsupa, Balao, and La Tolita. Most mounds are long, low platforms that supported residential structures, while others are funerary mounds containing numerous urn burials or tall, chimney-type interments of stacked bottomless urns.

At the Atacames site, a progressive expansion in site size and complexity has been documented. The mounds vary considerably in size, from 420 to 5,520 square yards in area and from less than 30 inches to over 80 inches in height. Mounds are predominantly round throughout the sequence, but ellipsoid and irregular shapes occur as well. The overall site configuration experienced temporal shifts throughout the Integration Period, as on-site population levels continued to grow. By Late Atacames times, a regular grid pattern emerged with rows of mounds and open avenues running obliquely from the shoreline.

Atacames pottery is generally less decorated and more poorly crafted than that of the preceding Tiaone culture, although vessel forms remain diverse. These include a range of small olla forms, polypod bowl forms, as well as pedestal cups (*compoteras*) with anthropomorphic faces. Red-on-buff painting is the predominant decorative technique, with geometric designs executed in fine- to medium-width lines. Other pottery artifacts include spindle whorls with a large flat base and small conical top, cylindrical seals or stamps, and modeled zoomorphic whistles.

Also found in abundant quantities are a wide variety of small beads (*chaquira*) used for bodily adornment. These were manufactured from a range of raw materials including lithics, shell, bone, and precious metals such as gold and copper. Although all were widely traded, shell beads seem to predominate, and those made from *Spondylus* were highly prized. Other forms of bodily decoration characteristic of Atacames include dental mutilation and gold-inlaid teeth. The latter may have been the prerogative of high-status individuals.

The large size and internal complexity of towns such as Atacames, together with specialization in craft production and the deferential treatment of the dead, all suggest a fairly complex form of sociopolitical organization, very probably a stratified chiefdom. As was the case with the Jama-coaque II settlements to the south, however, Atacames was probably succumbing to strong Manteño domination prior to the Spanish Conquest.

See also **Archaeology.**

BIBLIOGRAPHY

Francisco De Xerez [1528], "La relación Sámano-Xerez," in *Colección de documentos inéditos para la historia de España*, vol. 5 (1842), pp. 193–201.

Betty J. Meggers, *Ecuador* (1966).

Mercedes Guinea Bueno, *Patrones de asentamiento en la arqueología de Esmeraldas (Ecuador)* (1983).

Robert A. Feldman and Michael E. Moseley, "The Northern Andes," in *Ancient South Americans*, edited by Jesse D. Jennings (1983).

Mercedes Guinea Bueno, "Valoración de las evidencias de intercambio en la desembocadura del Río Esmeraldas: El problema cronológico," in International Congress of Americanists, *Relaciones interculturales en el área ecuatorial del Pacífico durante la época precolombina*, edited by Jean François Bouchard and Mercedes Guinea Bueno, BAR International Series 503 (1989), pp. 127–146.

César M. Heras y Martínez and Jesús Adánez Pavón, "Chimeneas cerámicas: Un rasgo cultural de significación controvertida," in International Congress of Americanists, *Relaciones interculturales en el área ecuatorial del Pacífico durante la época precolombina*, edited by Jean François Bouchard and Mercees Guinea Bueno, BAR International Series 503 (1989), pp. 147–162.

Additional Bibliography

Alcina Franch, José. *La arqueología de Esmeraldas (Ecuador), introducción general.* Madrid: Ministerio de Asuntos Exteriores, Dirección General de Relaciones Culturales, 1979.

Almeida Reyes, Eduardo. *Culturas prehispánicas del Ecuador.* Quito: Viajes Chasquiñan, 2000.

Brezzi, Andrea, and Matthew Leighton. *Tulato, ventana a la prehistoria de América: Cultura Tumaco-La Tolita.* Bogotá, D.C.: Villegas Editores, 2003.

DeBoer, Warren R. *Traces behind the Esmeraldas Shore: Prehistory of the Santiago-Cayapas Region, Ecuador.* Tuscaloosa: University of Alabama Press, 1996.

Ubelaker, Douglas H. *Skeletal Biology of Human Remains from La Tolita, Esmeraldas Province, Ecuador.* Washington, DC: Smithsonian Institution Press, 1997.

JAMES A. ZEIDLER

ATAHUALPA (c. 1498–1533). Atahualpa (or Atahuallpa, Ataw Huallpa in Quechua, called Atabalipa in the Spanish chroniclers) was the Inca ruler at the time of the Spanish Conquest of Peru. Little accurate information exists about his life; even his date and place of birth are uncertain. Some suggest he was born in the imperial center of Cuzco, others that he was from Tomebamba (Cuenca, Ecuador). His father was Huayna Capac, the last undisputed ruler of Tahuantinsuyu, the Inca Empire; his mother was a favorite secondary wife from the north, perhaps from the Schiri nation. Huayna Capac died of smallpox, which swept into the Andes ahead of the Spanish.

The Andean practice of succession was not based on primogeniture. Any male child from the principal or from any of the secondary wives could become *último* Inca (ruler). The division of Cuzco into separate halves (*hanan* and *urinsaya*) with a divided government and the importance of the cults of the lineages (*panacas*) of previous Inca rulers complicated the question of succession. As he lay dying, elder advisers repeatedly asked Huayna Capac about the succession. It seems he favored his youngest child, Ninan Cuyochi, who, however, also contracted smallpox and died. Huayna Capac's second choice was probably Huascar, his son with Ragua Ocllo. Initially the Cuzco religious and political elite supported Huascar. Indeed, the Cuzco leadership proclaimed him heir after Huayna Capac's death. But as Huayna Capac drifted in and out of a coma in his last hours, he also named Atahualpa, a favorite from the north, who had promising military potential. Atahualpa, with the support of great military commanders, moved southward in an attempt to secure control of Tahuantinsuyu. Victorious, Atahualpa's forces captured Huascar outside Cuzco and imprisoned him. General Quizquiz went into Cuzco, attempting to obliterate completely the Huascar faction.

The Execution of the Inca by A. B. Greene, c. 1891. A nineteenth-century interpretation of the execution of Atahualpa, the last Incan emperor. THE LIBRARY OF CONGRESS

Such was the political turmoil in the realm when a band of Spaniards under Francisco Pizarro arrived on their third expedition of 1531. Atahualpa had left commander Rumiñavi in charge of Quito and Chalicuchima in control of the central Andes while he, along with a few thousand troops, traveled to Cajamarca to rest and enjoy the thermal baths nearby. There the Spanish captured him on November 16, 1532, after he dropped or threw the Bible on the ground, saying it did not speak to him. After realizing the European thirst for gold, Atahualpa offered as ransom to fill a room within two months with gold, and twice with silver. Pizarro and the other Europeans were astounded as shipments slowly began to make their way into Cajamarca from throughout the realm. With the completion of the ransom (a total of about 13,420 pounds of 22½-carat gold and 26,000 pounds of good silver), the quandary of what to do with the Inca ruler increased. Atahualpa began to mistrust the promise of release and had probably ordered his commander Rumiñavi to move toward Cajamarca. Around the same time Hernando Pizarro, half brother of Francisco, convinced Chalicuchima to come to Cajamarca with him. Chalicuchima's decision is incomprehensible because it resulted in one of Atahualpa's most formidable generals submitting himself voluntarily to captivity.

Ultimately, a group that included royal officials and the recently arrived Diego de Almagro persuaded Pizarro that it was dangerous to keep the Inca captive and that he should be executed. The principal Atahualpa defenders, Hernando de Soto and Hernando Pizarro, were away at the time the trial took place. Atahualpa was charged with ordering while in jail the execution of his half-brother and preparing a surprise attack against the Spaniards, charges for which he was found guilty and sentenced to die at the stake. Friar Vicente de Valverde succeeded in converting Atahualpa to Christianity, and therefore the Inca was garroted instead of burned, on July 26, 1533. In subsequent years myths evolved (the *Inkarrí* cycle) portraying Atahualpa's return, ushering in a new age during which the yoke of the invaders would be overthrown. This cycle of myths gave rise to actual attempts to overthrow the Spanish colonial regime as late as the 1780s (Tupac Amaru II) and became intertwined with pro-independence ideologies during the nineteenth century.

See also **Huayna Capac; Incas, The; Peru: From the Conquest Through Independence; Pizarro, Francisco.**

BIBLIOGRAPHY

Arguedas, José María. "Mitos quechuas posthispánicos." In *Formación de una cultura nacional indoamericana*, 6th edition. México: Siglo Veintiuno Editores, 1998.

Burga, Manuel. *Nacimiento de una utopía: muerte y resurrección de los incas*, 2nd edition. Lima: Universidad Nacional Mayor de San Marcos/Universidad de Guadalajara, 2005.

Carrión, Benjamín. *Atahuallpa*, 10th edition. Quito: Campaña Nacional Eugenio Espejo por el Libro y la Lectura, 2002.

Cieza de León, Pedro de. *The Discovery and Conquest of Peru: Chronicles of the New World Encounter.* Edited and translated by Alexandra Parma Cook and David Noble Cook. Durham: Duke University Press, 1998.

Hemming, John. *The Conquest of the Incas.* New York: Harcourt, Brace, Jovanovich, 1970. Rev. ed., New York: Penguin, 1983.

Pease G.Y., Franklin. *Los últimos Incas del Cuzco*, 5th ed. Peru: Instituto Nacional de Cultura, 2004.

NOBLE DAVID COOK

ATAHUALPA (JUAN SANTOS) (1710?–c. 1756).

Atahualpa (Juan Santos) (*b.* 1710?; *d.* ca. 1756), leader of an indigenous rebellion in the jungles and mountain slopes of east-central Peru from 1742 to 1752. Not much is known about the early life of Juan Santos, who later took the name Atahualpa. He was born either in Cajamarca or, more likely, Cuzco; he learned Spanish and Latin while studying with the Jesuits. A Jesuit may have taken him to Spain and Africa.

In 1742 Juan Santos appeared in the mountains of Chanchamayo, declaring himself the descendant of Atahualpa, the Inca captured and murdered in 1533 by Francisco Pizarro at the outset of the Spanish conquest of Peru. A charismatic leader, Juan Santos combined Christian and Andean messianism. Raiding from the jungles of the Gran Pajonal, his followers destroyed the region's Franciscan missions. Juan Santos aimed to drive the Spaniards out of Peru but was unable to mobilize the populous central highlands. Nonetheless, several military expeditions against his stronghold failed to defeat him, and the government finally established forts along the frontier to prevent him from invading the highlands. In 1752 Juan Santos's forces seized Andamarca, threatening Jauja, but quickly withdrew. His hostilities then ceased. He probably died in Metraro. His uprising reflected mounting indigenous resistance to the colonial system. Revolts in Tarma (1744) and Lima (1750) supported his call for insurrection, and even after 1752 rumors about the new Atahualpa disturbed Peru.

See also **Movimiento Revolucionario Tupac Amaru (MRTA).**

BIBLIOGRAPHY

Mario Castro Arenas, *La rebelión de Juan Santos* (1973).

Steve J. Stern, "The Age of Andean Insurrection, 1742–1782: A Reappraisal," in *Resistance, Rebellion, and Consciousness in the Andean Peasant World, 18th to 20th Centuries*, edited by Steve J. Stern (1987), esp. pp. 43–63.

Alonso Zarzar, *"Apo Capac Huayna, Jesus Sacramentado": Mito, utopía, y milenarismo en el pensamiento de Juan Santos Atahualpa* (1989).

Additional Bibliography

Dávila Herrera, Carlos. *Juan Santos Atahualpa, paradigma de la rebelión asháninca.* Lima, Perú: Universidad Nacional Mayor de San Marcos, Seminario de Historia Rural Andina, 2002.

Torre y López, Arturo Enrique de la. *Juan Santos Atahualpa.* Lima, Perú: Pontificia Universidad Católica del Perú, Fondo Editorial, 2004.

KENDALL W. BROWN

ATAIDE, TRISTÃO DE. *See* **Lima, Alceu Amoroso.**

ATENEO DE LA JUVENTUD (ATHENAEUM OF YOUTH).

Ateneo de la Juventud (Athenaeum of Youth), a Mexican literary and intellectual society, 1907–1914. Although founded as the Sociedad de Conferencias (Society for Lectures) in 1907 and known as the Ateneo de México (the Athenaeum of Mexico) after 1912, the group was christened the Ateneo de la Juventud in 1909 and it is by this name that it is generally known. Under the leadership of Antonio Caso and Pedro Henríquez Ureña, the society came to include such influential thinkers and writers as Alfonso Reyes, José Vasconcelos, and Martín Luis Guzmán. The Ateneo developed around the short-lived literary journal *Savia Moderna* (Modern Vigor, 1906), whose contributors attempted to depart from *modernista* writing and the influence of French literature. Eventually the society became a forum for questioning the official philosophy of positivism employed by the government of Porfirio Díaz for state administration and social regulation. By organizing annual cycles of lectures, the Ateneo proposed a political, social, and intellectual renovation of Mexican society through the public discussion and broad dissemination of knowledge. In 1912, after the start of the Mexican Revolution (1910), members of the group participated in founding the Popular University and assisted the minister of education, Justo Sierra, in establishing the School of Higher Studies in the National University of Mexico. Although the society disbanded in 1914, its influence was immense during Mexico's post-Revolutionary state-building decades of the 1920s and 1930s.

See also **Literature: Spanish America.**

BIBLIOGRAPHY

Juan Hernández Luna, ed., *Conferencias del Ateneo de la Juventud* (1962).

José Rojas Garcidueñas, *El Ateneo de la Juventud y la Revolución* (1979).

James Willis Robb, "Alfonso Reyes," in *Latin American Writers*, vol. 2, edited by Carlos A. Solé and Maria Isabel Abreu (1989), pp. 693–703.

Gabriella De Beer, "José Vasconcelos," in *Latin American Writers*, vol. 2 (1989), pp. 575–584, and "El Ateneo y los ateneístas: Un examen retrospectivo," in *Revista iberoamericana* 55, no. 148–149 (1989): 737–749.

Additional Bibliography

Curiel, Fernando. *La revuelta: Interpretación del Ateneo de la Juventud, 1906-1929.* México: Universidad Nacional Autónoma de México, Centro de Estudios Literarios, Instituto de Investigaciones Filológicas, 1999.

DANNY J. ANDERSON

ATENEO DEL URUGUAY.

Ateneo del Uruguay, a forum founded in 1877 for intellectuals in Uruguay. It reached its zenith in the 1880s. The Ateneo was a product of the fusion of the Club Universitario with the Sociedad Filo Histórica (1874–1877), the Club Literario Platense (1875–1877), and the Sociedad de Ciencias Naturales (1876–1877). The Ateneo was romantic and spiritualist. It encouraged moderate rationalism, critically debated positivism and philosophical materialism, and rejected artistic realism. Born during the Lorenzo Latorre dictatorship, it brought together a young, professional elite whose members possessed or were heirs to the liberal creed of the "principista" generation of 1870, who were now opposing militarism. From its ranks came politicians and polemicists such as Julio Herrera y Obes, Joaquín de Salterain, and Carlos María Ramírez, who would succeed the militarists. It also provided early schooling for youths who, like José Batlle y Ordóñez, twice president of the republic, would succeed these men. In 1886, the Ateneo merged with Sociedad Universitaria to form the Ateneo de Montevideo. It was eclipsed by new cultural movements toward the end of the nineteenth century, but would again become a political and intellectual rallying point in opposition to the dictatorship of 1933.

See also **Latorre, Lorenzo.**

BIBLIOGRAPHY

Ardao, Arturo. *Espiritualismo y positivismo en el Uruguay* and *La sección filosófica del Ateneo* (1950).

Burgueño, María Cristina. *La modernidad uruguaya: Imágenes e identidades, 1848–1900.* Montevideo, Uruguay: Librería Linardi y Risso, 2000.

Buscio, Jorge. *José Batlle y Ordóñez: Uruguay a la vanguardia del mundo: Pensamiento político y raíces ideológicas.* Montevideo, Uruguay: Editorial Fin de Siglo, 2004.

Felde, Alberto Zum. *Proceso intelectual del Uruguay y crítica de su literatura*, vol. 1 (1930).

FERNANDO FILGUEIRA

ATL, DR.

(1875–1964). Dr. Atl (Gerardo Murillo; *b.* 1875; *d.* 1964), Mexican artist and participant in the Mexican Revolution. A native of

Guadalajara, he became a noted landscape artist and volcanologist. After studying painting at Bellas Artes in Mexico City, he departed in 1896 for Rome, where he later received degrees in philosophy and law. His pseudonym, Dr. Atl (*atl* being the Nahuatl word for "water"), was suggested to him by the writer Leopoldo Lugones in Paris in 1902, and he used this name on his works of art. Returning to Mexico, he hiked up Popocatépetl and Iztaccíhuatl, an experience that led to a lifelong interest, both scientific and artistic, in volcanoes.

After a second stay in Europe, Atl returned to Mexico in 1914 and joined the Constitutionalist movement under Venustiano Carranza. He became a member of the Revolutionary Confederation, a group of military and other Constitutionalist officials formed in 1914 that pressured Carranza to carry out social reforms. He was a close collaborator of General Álvaro Obregón, and helped him attract the support of the Casa de Obrero Mundial and other workers' groups in Mexico City during the Constitutionalist occupation in early 1915. After the Revolution, he returned to painting and authored several books, including works on art and volcanology.

See also **Art: The Twentieth Century.**

BIBLIOGRAPHY

A good biography is Arturo Casado Navarro, *El Dr. Atl* (1984). A beautiful edition of his work is Gerardo Murillo, *Dr. Atl: Pinturas y dibujos* (1974), with a prologue by Carlos Pellicer. Works in English include Mackinley Helm, *Modern Mexican Painters* (1941), pp. 1–20.

Agustín Velásquez Chávez, *Contemporary Mexican Artists* (1937), pp. 45–55.

Additional Bibliography

Saénz, Olga. *El símbolo y la acción: Vida y obra de Gerardo Murillo, Dr. Atl*. Mexico City, El Colegio Nacional, 2005.

LINDA B. HALL

ATLANTIC CHARTER. Atlantic Charter, a declaration of solidarity made by Great Britain and the United States on 14 August 1941. Prior to U.S. entry into World War II, President Franklin Delano Roosevelt met with Winston Chur-

chill, the prime minister of Great Britain. Together the two leaders issued the Atlantic Charter, a broadly conceived statement affirming the two nations' solidarity in the face of impending threats to international security.

The Atlantic Charter cited the rights of all nations to self-determination and "the abandonment of the use of force" in international disputes. The charter was eventually approved by all members of the United Nations, including the countries of Latin America, for whom the charter's repudiation of aggression and insistence on unrestricted free travel on the seas bore particular significance.

See also **World War II.**

BIBLIOGRAPHY

Donald M. Dozer, *Are We Good Neighbors?* (1959).

Additional Bibliography

Coggiola, Osvaldo, and André R. Martin. *Segunda Guerra Mundial: Um balanço histórico*. São Paulo, SP: Xamã, 1995.

Friedman, Max Paul. *Nazis and Good Neighbors: The United States Campaign against the Germans of Latin America in World War II*. Cambridge, U.K.: Cambridge University Press, 2003.

Leonard, Thomas M. and John F. Bratzel. *Latin America During World War II*. Lanham, MD: Rowman & Littlefield, 2007.

JOHN DUDLEY

ATLANTIC ISLANDS, MIGRANTS FROM. Migrants from Atlantic Islands. The Portuguese commonly moved inhabitants of Atlantic possessions (i.e., the Azores and Madeira) to distant portions of their realm. This was expedient for two reasons: it solved the problem of overcrowding in geographic locales already overburdened with growing populations and simultaneously provided stable settlers for the more remote regions of the Portuguese Empire. On occasion, Portuguese settlers in North Africa also were resettled when their communities were threatened by the Moors. Relocation reached its height in the eighteenth century when *açorianos* (Azoreans) were brought in large numbers to Brazil, but it continued into the early years of the nineteenth century.

After Brazil became independent in 1822, the Atlantic islanders fanned out through the English-speaking Caribbean, arriving in substantial numbers in British Guiana in the 1830s and 1840s and later on in Jamaica, Trinidad, Bermuda, and New England. Indeed, the exodus continues to the present; migration is an accepted pattern in the Azores, where limited economic opportunities foster it. Atlantic islanders' migration to Brazil in the eighteenth century, however, bears unique characteristics and deserves scrutiny. The distinguishing feature of this migration is that it was largely agricultural and *voluntary*. One might argue that the incentives were hard to refuse, but relocation to Brazil was a matter of choice for the most part.

The traditional immigrant from the *ilhas* (islands) was a farmer, content to remain on the soil. For eighteenth-century Brazilian administrators such an individual was deemed more desirable than local Brazilians, who were more likely to desert colonization schemes for the recently discovered gold fields. This was especially true in the Far South of Brazil, where efforts to secure the Platine area for the Portuguese had been tenuous since the founding in 1680 of Colônia Do Sacramento across the La Plata estuary from Spanish-held Buenos Aires. Between São Paulo and the fortress of Colônia one small community, Laguna, was the sole deterrent against Spanish aggression. Settlers had been enticed there by offers of free food before the first harvest and sufficient head of cattle to start a livestock business. While the Laguna experiment was successful, the program, initiated and supervised by engineer José da Silva Pais, was considered insufficient to secure the southern boundary. Moreover, it relied exclusively on Brazilian-born recruits. To keep control over the southern regions, therefore, the colonization plan was reformulated in the 1740s to include a massive resettlement of Azorian colonists, a move carefully detailed in a *regimento* (Royal Order) of 1747. The royal orders contained precise instructions on the physical layout of communities built for the Atlantic islanders; each new village was uniformly aligned, and building elements were spaced sufficiently distant from each other to allow for future growth while simultaneously preventing overcrowding. Atlantic volunteers, who were recruited as *casais* (married

couples), were given a house as well as fresh fish each week, two cows, and a ewe.

By 1753 several Azorian communities had been established in Rio Grande do Sul and Santa Catarina. Although the numbers of settlers fell short of the anticipated 4,000 *casais*, at least 950 had settled by 1749, and in the following three years scattered groups continued to arrive. The settlers not only practiced agriculture but also played an important geopolitical role in securing the south for the Portuguese. After 1750, when the notion of *uti possidetis* dominated the boundary demarcations between the Spanish and the Portuguese, the Portuguese minister Alexandre de Gusmão could point to settlement in these new southern communities as a clear example of "effective occupation."

Atlantic island resettlement proved to be attractive elsewhere in Brazil. Indeed, colonial administrators begged for Atlantic colonists, who would not only stabilize a region but also provide models of behavior for the local populace, which was consistently denigrated by officialdom. In the Comarca of Porto Seguro, for example, Indian townships were located next to European settlers' communities, with both groups living in the same type of housing. In the far north, in Amapá, Portuguese administrators created São José de Macapá and Nova Mazagão with immigrant *casais* in order to stabilize the northern borders of the mouth of the Amazon River. Everywhere the Azorian was exalted as the type of settler who would bring prosperity to Brazil. The Portuguese prime minister, the Marquês de Pombal, counted on such infusions of Europeans to make possible his scheme of transforming the wilds of Brazil into a European settlement. Clearly the Portuguese felt a need to "civilize" Brazil, and the sturdy, no-nonsense Atlantic islander was seen as the key to this policy.

BIBLIOGRAPHY

Additional Bibliography

Ribeiro de Medeiros, Octavio H., Artur Boavida Madeira. *Emigração e regresso no concelho da Povoação.* Ponta Delgada [Azores]: Câmara Municipal da Povoação, 2003.

Da Rosa, Victor M.P., Salvato Trigo. *Azorean Emigration: A Preliminary Overview.* Porto, Portugal: Fernando Pessoa University Press, 1994.

ROBERTA M. DELSON

ATUSPARIA REVOLT.

ATUSPARIA REVOLT. Atusparia Revolt of 1885, the largest regional rebellion of primarily peasant composition in nineteenth-century Peru. It was a direct consequence of the Peruvian civil war (1883–1885) between the Reds (a nationalist resistance movement led by Andrés Cáceres) and Blues (a peace-with-Chile faction led by Miguel Iglesias) that followed the disastrous War of the Pacific (1879–1883). In their battles against the Blues, who then controlled the provincial government in the department of Ancash, the rebels were at times led or aided by non-indigenous Red militants. The revolt itself, however—which now bears the name of Pedro Pablo Atusparia, *alcalde ordinario* or district *varayoc* (headman) of the northern half of Huaraz province in 1885—was mobilized by subaltern Indian headmen, who fielded tens of thousands of their compatriots in siege warfare against Blue elements among the mestizo and creole population that dominated the valley towns of the Callejón de Huaylas.

Rebels burned the provincial treasury archive, which held the poll-tax registers. Indians considered the new poll tax to be illegitimate because it did not guarantee access to common lands, as the indigenous head tax had in earlier decades. The *varayoc* signed petitions protesting the postcolonial state's disregard for "Indian rights" and criticized its tendency to collapse into the "criminal projects" of warring caudillos. Rebels controlled the region for two months until Blue counterinsurgency forces from Lima put down the revolt in torrents of blood. After repression and the conclusion of the civil war, however, resistance continued; the poll tax was successfully boycotted until its official abolition in 1895.

See also **War of the Pacific.**

BIBLIOGRAPHY

The most comprehensive treatment of the Atusparia revolt is William W. Stein, *El levantamiento de Atusparia* (1988). It builds on Cesar A. Alba Herrera, *Atusparia y la revolución campesina de 1885 en Ancash* (1985). A more recent study that places the revolt in its historical context is Mark Thurner, "From Two Nations to One Divided" (Ph.D. diss., University of Wisconsin, 1993).

Additional Bibliography

Chambers, Sarah C. *From Subjects to Citizens: Honor, Gender, and Politics in Arequipa, Peru, 1780–1854.* University Park: Pennsylvania State University Press, 1999.

Méndez G. Cecilia. *The Plebeian Republic: The Huanta Rebellion and the Making of the Peruvian State, 1820–1850.* Durham: Duke University Press, 2005.

Soria Casaverde, María Belén. *El Dorado republico: Visión oficial de la Amazonia peruana, 1821–1879.* Lima: Seminario de Historia Rural Andina, 2006.

Thurner, Mark. *From Two Republics to One Divided: Contradictions of Postcolonial Nation Making in Andean Peru.* Durham: Duke University Press, 1997.

MARK THURNER

AUCHMUTY, SAMUEL (1758–1822).

AUCHMUTY, SAMUEL (1758–1822). Samuel Auchmuty (*b.* 22 June 1758; *d.* 11 August 1822), British general who distinguished himself as a commanding officer in the British army during several key battles with the Spanish in Argentina and Uruguay. Born in New York under British rule, Sir Samuel Auchmuty remained loyal to the throne and fought for the British during the American War of Independence. Auchmuty remained in the armed forces and served in India, Egypt, and, beginning in 1806, Latin America, where he took part in the 1806–1807 British invasion at the Río de la Plata and then commanded the occupation of Montevideo, Uruguay. While in Latin America, Auchmuty also published an anti-Spanish newspaper, *La Estrella del Sur,* and fought in a failed attack on Buenos Aires in 1807. He died while serving in occupied Ireland.

See also **British in Argentina.**

BIBLIOGRAPHY

William W. Kaufmann, *British Policy and the Independence of Latin America: 1804–1828* (1951).

JOHN DUDLEY

AUDIENCIA.

AUDIENCIA. Audiencia, a regional high court in Spanish America in the colonial era and the district under its jurisdiction. Audiencias were the highest judicial tribunals in the Spanish colonies, enjoyed executive and legislative authority, and, in the absence of a region's chief executive, served as the executive on an interim basis. The first audiencia was established in 1511, and by 1606 there were eleven colonial tribunals: in Santo Domingo, Mexico City, Panama, Guatemala, Lima, Guadalajara, Santa Fe (New Granada), Charcas, Quito, Chile, and Manila. Panama's tribunal was abolished in 1751, but by the close of the colonial era there were additional tribunals in Buenos Aires, Caracas, and Cuzco. With the exception of Cuzco and Guadalajara, the audiencia districts became, with modest modifications, the territorial bases for nation-states after independence.

Each audiencia had a presiding officer, judges, and at least one crown attorney (*fiscal*). The sizes of the audiencias varied substantially, however. The early audiencias were small, consisting of a president, several judges who handled both civil and criminal cases, and one crown attorney. In 1568, the viceregal tribunals of Lima and Mexico were assigned additional judges to handle criminal cases (*alcaldes del crimen*); the remaining judges (*oidores*) specialized in civil cases. With the expansion of the courts in 1776, each audiencia had a regent who oversaw the overall operation of the tribunal, three or more *oidores*, and two *fiscales*, one for civil and one for criminal cases. The tribunals of Lima and Mexico also had several *alcaldes del crimen*, giving the courts a total of eighteen ministers each. Together, the American audiencias had one hundred ministers.

Audiencia judges and crown attorneys were required to be university-trained lawyers and at least twenty-five years of age when named to a court. Their appointments were for life or the pleasure of the king.

As the most professional branch of the royal bureaucracy and the most important civil institutions under their jurisdiction's chief executive, audiencias held prestige and power in judicial, legislative, and executive matters. Among their judicial responsibilities was first-instance jurisdiction for cases that related to the royal treasury and for certain cases that arose in the capital cities where they resided. As courts of appeal within their districts, audiencias exercised final authority in criminal cases and most civil suits.

The audiencias also had executive and legislative responsibilities. A district's chief executive received the audiencia's advice on all major questions; decisions reached through this consultation had the force of law unless disallowed by the Council of the Indies. In the executive's absence, the court assumed his duties and governed. Audiencias also were required to enforce royal laws, and to that end judges undertook periodic inspection tours within their districts. Judges also often sat with one or more corporate bodies in a colony, such as the merchants' guild.

Audiencias, then, possessed formidable powers. Their role in judicial affairs and in overseeing the implementation of royal legislation made their decisions important for the communities they served. Since appointments of audiencia ministers were for life or royal pleasure, the audiencias provided an element of continuity at the highest level. Incoming executives disregarded their advice only with peril. Armed with far-reaching authority, the audiencias were, always in theory and often in fact, an important check on other institutions of government.

Although the initial audiencia ministers were born in Spain, men born in the New World (creoles) began to receive audiencia appointments in 1585. From that year to 1687, creoles constituted 24 percent of all new appointees. In 1687, the Crown began to sell audiencia appointments during periods of financial crisis and, as a result, Americans secured 44 percent of the appointments until 1750, most through purchase, and many in their district of birth. As a result of securing dispensations from legislation restricting local social and economic ties, many of these purchasers were deeply linked to their region of service, a circumstance that compromised their ability to provide impartial justice. When the Crown stopped sales and began to reassert its authority over the courts in the early 1750s, the percentage of Americans who entered the courts dropped back to 24 percent. This change, which was most pronounced in the appointments immediately following the expansion of the courts' size in 1776, did not go unnoticed by creoles. With regard to the audiencias, their clamor for appointments was not, as was once thought, to gain entry into high positions, but rather to return to an era in which they had enjoyed frequent access to these powerful courts.

See also **Colonialism; Judicial Systems: Spanish America.**

BIBLIOGRAPHY

Recopilación de leyes de los reynos de las Indias, 4 vols. (1681; repr. 1973), *libro* II, *títulos* XV–XVIII.

John H. Parry, *The Audiencia of New Galicia in the Sixteenth Century* (1948).

John L. Phelan, *The Kingdom of Quito in the Seventeenth Century* (1967).

Guillermo Lohmann Villena, *Los Ministros de la audiencia de Lima en el reinado de los Borbones (1700–1821)* (1974).

Mark A. Burkholder and D. S. Chandler, *From Impotence to Authority: The Spanish Crown and the American Audiencias, 1687–1808* (1977), and *Biographical Dictionary of Audiencia Ministers in the Americas, 1687–1821* (1982).

Additional Bibliography

Andrien, Kenneth J. *The Kingdom of Quito, 1690–1830: The State and Regional Development.* Tuscaloosa: University of Alabama Press, 2004.

Barrios, Feliciano. *El gobierno de un mundo: Virreinatos y audiencias en la América hispánica.* Cuenca, Ecuador: Ediciones de la Universidad de Castilla-La Mancha: Fundación Rafael del Pino, 2004.

Hawkins, Timothy. *José De Bustamante and Central American Independence: Colonial Administration in an Age of Imperial Crisis.* Tuscaloosa: University of Alabama Press, 2004.

Sanciñena Asurmendi, Teresa. *La audiencia en México en el reinado de Carlos III.* México: Universidad Nacional Autónoma de México, 1999.

MARK A. BURKHOLDER

At first, jurisdiction of the *audiencia* extended from Panama north to Yucatán and Tabasco, but soon those regions were removed from its district. In the 1560s the Audiencia de los Confines was abolished and a court was reestablished at Panama with administration by the Audiencia of Mexico. However, the *audiencia* in Guatemala was restored by 1570 with jurisdiction from Chiapas to Costa Rica. As the Audiencia of Guatemala, the court maintained this ar-rangement until the end of the colonial period.

See also **Audiencia.**

BIBLIOGRAPHY

For a discussion in Spanish, see Mario Góngora, *El estado en el derecho indiano, época de fundación (1492–1570)* (1951). Various aspects of the *audiencia* are dealt with in Ralph Lee Woodward, Jr., *Central America: A Nation Divided,* 2d ed. (1985); Murdo J. MacLeod, *Spanish Central America: A Socioeconomic History, 1520–1720* (1973); and William L. Sherman, *Forced Native Labor in Sixteenth-Century Central America* (1979).

Additional Bibliography

González Villanueva, Gustavo. *Los primeros cristianos de la Audiencia de los Confines.* San José, Costa Rica: Promesa, 2003.

Jiménez Núñez, Alfredo. *Antropología histórica: La audiencia de Guatemala en el siglo XVI.* Sevilla, Spain: Universidad de Sevilla, 1997.

WILLIAM L. SHERMAN

AUDIENCIA DE LOS CONFINES.

The New Laws of 1542 called for the creation of the Audiencia de los Confines, so named because it was to be situated at Comayagua, a village on the border of Guatemala and Honduras, where the court held its first session in May 1544. In May 1548 the second president, Alonso López De Cerrato, arrived. He recommended the court's removal to Santiago de Guatemala (now Antigua), a much larger and more prosperous settlement that was less isolated. Although Gracias a Dios had only a few poverty-stricken residents, the audiencia had remained there for four years because Governor Alonso Maldonado and his colleagues profited illegally from local business affairs. In 1549 Cerrato moved the court to Santiago, where it occupied the bishop's residence.

AUGUSTINIANS.

Augustinians, a Roman Catholic religious order of priests and brothers named after the fifth-century bishop and saint Augustine of Hippo. The Order of the Hermit Friars of St. Augustine, as it is formally known, adopted Augustine's "rule" at the time of their founding by the Holy See in 1256. Classified as a mendicant order, members are known as friars; they are governed by an elected prior-general, who resides in Rome, and are organized throughout the world into regions called provinces, each governed by an elected prior-provincial. By the fourteenth century, the Aug-ustinians were established in most parts of Europe. Later they expanded into Africa, Asia, and America, within the extensive colonial empires of Portugal and Spain. In addition to preaching and missionary activity, they engaged in many types of ministry, including higher education, writing, and patristic studies. Among their better known friars are Giles of Rome (ca. 1245–1316), Martin Luther (1483–1546), St. Thomas of Villanova (1486–1555), Luis de León (1527–1591), and Gregor Mendel (1822–1884).

On 7 June 1533 seven Spanish Augustinians, led by Francisco de la Cruz, arrived in Mexico City, where they established a large church and friary, San Agustín, which was to be the core of a new Augustinian province and the principal center of their activity in Latin America and, eventually, the Philippine Islands. Augustinian expansion in New Spain (Mexico) was rapid. By the end of the sixteenth century, the number of Augustinians, including both Spaniards and criollos, exceeded 600 friars, located in some seventy-two missions throughout central Mexico, extending from San Luis Potosí in the north to Oaxaca in the south. The growth in the region of Michoacán was especially notable, resulting in the creation of a second Mexican Augustinian province in 1602. The two administrative regions, the provinces of Mexico and Michoacán, continue to exist, and among their churches are several imposing historic monuments, some still occupied by Augustinian friars. Worthy of particular attention for art and architecture are the friaries of Acolman, Cuitzeo, Morelia, and Yuriria. The friary of San Agustín in Mexico City, however, no longer exists; its large church was confiscated in the nineteenth century and converted into the national library in 1884.

The leading Augustinian figure in colonial Mexico was Alonso de la Vera Cruz, a sixteenth-century missionary, educator, writer of philosophical texts, canon lawyer, and administrator. Educated at the University of Salamanca, he was one of the founders and principal lecturers of the University of Mexico, established in 1553. Like his friend and associate Bartolomé de Las Casas, Fray Alonso was keenly interested in defending the rights of the native Indians, a goal he pursued in two of his series of lectures, *Relectio de dominio infidelium et iusto bello* and *Relectio de decimis* (in *The Writings of Alonso de la Vera Cruz*, edited and translated by Ernest Burrus, 1968–1976). His teachings met with opposition, especially from the archbishop of Mexico, Alonso de Montúfar, who denounced him to the Inquisition. Recalled temporarily to Spain in 1562, Fray Alonso defended his views successfully,

was regarded favorably by Philip II, and was therefore able to influence legislation aimed at removing abuses of the Indians. His interest in the native peoples was not merely academic, for he was an active missionary who spoke Tarascan, the language of Michoacán, and advocated full incorporation of the Indians into the sacramental life of the Catholic Church.

Another prominent sixteenth-century Augustinian was Andrés de Urdaneta, the mariner-turned-friar who is credited with discovering the eastbound route across the Pacific Ocean from Manila to Acapulco. Employed by the crown as a navigator, he also led the first group of Augustinian missionaries to the Philippine Islands in 1564–1565. Another early friar was Agustín Farfán, a physician who published the first medical handbook in Mexico, *Tratado de medicina* (1579). Two seventeenth-century authors of note were the historians Juan de Grijalva and Diego Basalenque.

Before the middle of the seventeenth century the Augustinians were to be found in most parts of the Spanish Empire. An extensive development took place in Peru, where the foundations of a new province began at Lima in 1551. The province of Peru was the base from which were organized the provinces of Quito, Ecuador (1573), New Granada (Bogotá, Colombia, 1575), and Chile (Santiago de Chile, 1595), as well as missions in the regions later known as Bolivia and Argentina. The Peruvian missions of the colonial period were grouped principally in the areas of Lima, Trujillo, and Cuzco, and their history has been recorded by two able seventeenth-century chroniclers, Antonio de la Calancha and Bernardo de Torres. A noted Augustinian in the more recent history of Latin America is Diego Francisco Padilla. A patriot and pamphleteer in the independence movement in Colombia, he was a member of the first junta of the revolutionary government in 1810.

The Augustinians, like all the older religious orders, went into severe decline in Latin America in the nineteenth century. Liberation from Spain and the accompanying wars and confiscations, often anticlerical as well as anti-Spanish, greatly reduced the numbers and influence of the friars. In the twentieth century, however, there has been a recovery, accomplished in part with the help of friars from western Europe, especially Spain, and from the United States. In 1990 the Augustinians were active in nearly every country of Latin America, most notably in Mexico and Peru. Mexico had two provinces entirely composed of native-born friars, and Peru had four major mission areas, composed chiefly of foreign-born friars. Besides Mexico, full-fledged Augustinian provinces existed in Colombia, Ecuador, and Chile, and the number of friars in Brazil and Argentina also was considerable. As of 1988 the total number of Augustinians in fourteen countries of Latin America was 714.

See also **Catholic Church: The Colonial Period.**

BIBLIOGRAPHY

For the general history of the Augustinians see *History of the Order of St. Augustine,* 4 vols. (1979–1989); and Roberto Jaramillo, comp., *Los Agustinos en América Latina: Pasado y presente* (1987).

Specialized studies include Gregorio De Santiago Vela, *Ensayo de una biblioteca ibero-americana de la Orden de S. Agustín,* 8 vols. (1913–1931); Avencio Villarejo, *Los Agustinos en el Perú, 1548–1965* (1965); Ernest Burrus, *The Writings of Alonso de la Vera Cruz,* 5 vols. (1967–1975); Manuel Merino, ed., *Crónicas agustinianas del Perú,* 2 vols. (1972); Nicolás P. Navarrete, *Historia de la provincia agustiniana de San Nicolás de Tolentino de Michoacán,* 2 vols. (1978); Alipio Ruiz Zavala, *Historia de la Provincia agustiniana del santísimo Nombre de Jesús de México,* 2 vols. (1984); Arthur Ennis, *Augustinian Religious Professions in Sixteenth Century Mexico* (1986).

Additional Bibliography

Carrasco Notario, Guillermo. *Los Agustinos de Chile y el desarrollo económico y social de Cuyo.* Santiago: Coedición de la Viceprovincia Agustina de Argentina y de la Provincia Agustina de Chile, 1997.

Costales, Piedad Peñaherrera de., and Alfredo Costales Samaniego. *Los agustinos, pedagogos y misioneros del pueblo, 1573–1869.* Quito: IEAG: Abya Yala, 2003.

Lazcano González, Rafael. *Bibliografía missionalia Augustiniana: América Latina, 1533-1993.* Madrid: Editorial Revista Agustiniana, 1993.

Rea, Alonso de la., and Patricia Escandón. *Crónica de la orden de N. Seráfico P.S. Francisco, provincia de S. Pedro y S. Pablo de Mechoacán en la Nueva España.* Zamora: Colegio de Michoacán: Fideicomiso Teixidor, 1996.

ARTHUR J. ENNIS O.S.A.

AURY, LOUIS-MICHEL (c. 1788–1821). Louis-Michel Aury (*b.* ca. 1788; *d.* 30 August 1821), French privateer during the Latin American Wars for Independence (1810–1821). Born in Montrouge, a Paris suburb, Aury grew up during the French Revolution and entered Napoleon's navy at an early age. In 1803 he left his warship at Guadeloupe to join French privateers. Seven years later, with the equivalent of several thousand dollars in prize money, Lieutenant Aury had achieved notoriety as a privateer. He suffered serious setbacks when U.S. officials in New Orleans confiscated his ship in 1810 and a Federalist mob in Savannah burned his ship to the water in 1811, episodes that embittered Aury toward the United States. In 1812 José Pedro Gual, representative of the Cartagena creole government, arranged for Aury to command a refitted privateer. The U.S. declaration of war against Britain had improved conditions for French privateers in America, and Latin American rebel governments had begun to issue patents to those who would carry their struggle against Spain to the high seas. Operating from Cartagena, Commodore Aury's fleet supported Simón Bolívar by devastating Spanish shipping, but a bitter rivalry developed between Aury and the commander of Bolívar's Venezuela squadron, Luis Brión.

After Cartagena fell to the Spanish late in 1815, Aury joined Bolívar in Haiti but refused to serve under Brión's command. Instead, he accepted a patent from Mexican rebels and in 1816 reorganized his fleet in New Orleans, in close association with merchants headed by Edward Livingston. With Aury, they supported General Xavier Mina, a young Spanish rebel who had organized his expedition in Liverpool and brought it to Baltimore with the cooperation of Gual. The New Orleans associates hoped to wrest Florida from Spain and to gain access to Mexico's silver mines. Aury established a government at Galveston only nominally connected with the revolution in Mexico. From Galveston he directed profitable privateering operations in the Gulf of Mexico, channeling the booty back to New Orleans. Mina arrived at the end of 1816, but Aury refused to support his plan for an overland invasion of Mexico, preferring to continue privateering or to make a seaborne assault on Tampico. Mina took most of the forces and invaded Mexico in April

1817, only to be captured by the Spaniards and executed in October 1817.

Aury, meanwhile, sailed to Florida, arriving on 15 September 1817 at Fernandina, Amelia Island, where Gregor MacGregor had established a Republic of Florida, which he turned over to Aury as the representative of the Mexican rebels. Aury began a lucrative commerce with Georgia in slaves and merchandise. These activities embarrassed the Spanish and French governments and were a nuisance to the United States. Thus, on 2 December 1817 President James Monroe ordered U.S. troops to suppress Aury's bases at Fernandina and Galveston. Aury, in collaboration with Gual, abandoned further pretense of operating under the authority of a nonexistent Mexican government and formed an independent Florida Republic on 9 December. Two weeks later U.S. forces took over Amelia Island and remained there until after Spain sold Florida to the United States in 1821.

Aury resumed privateering operations in the Caribbean. Again refusing to serve under Brión, he acquired patents from the governments of Chile and Buenos Aires and established a base at Old Providence Island in the western Caribbean. After a successful raid on Izabal, Guatemala, in May 1819, he plotted with José Cortés Madariaga, envoy of Chile and Buenos Aires to Jamaica, to liberate Central America. His privateering brought prosperity to Old Providence, but his efforts at a rapprochement with Bolívar failed, sabotaged by Brión, even after Aury petitioned Bolívar for incorporation of Old Providence into Gran Colombia. Aury undoubtedly felt his settlement would be more secure attached to Colombia than to distant Buenos Aires. His campaign in April 1820 to take the Spanish forts at Trujillo and Omoa, Honduras, failed, but Aury continued his privateering from Old Providence until a fall from his horse abruptly ended his life.

Aury's attacks on Spanish shipping contributed to the establishment of Latin American independence. Despite his strong commitment to republicanism inherited from the French Revolution, however, he was often suspected of placing his own interests ahead of those of the creole republics whose flags he flew.

See also **Piracy.**

BIBLIOGRAPHY

George Coggeshall, *A History of American Privateers and Letters of Marque During Our War with England …* (1856).

Lewis Bealer, *Los corsarios de Buenos Aires: Sus actividades en las guerras hispanoamericanas de la independencia, 1815–1821* (1937).

L. E. Dabney, "Louis Aury: The First Governor of Texas under the Mexican Republic," in *Southwestern Historical Quarterly* 42, no. 1 (1938): 108–116.

Harris G. Warren, "Documents Relating to the Establishment of Privateers at Galveston, 1816–1817," in *Louisiana Historical Quarterly* 21, no. 4 (1938): 1086–1109.

Stanley Faye, "Privateersmen of the Gulf and Their Prizes," *Louisiana Historical Quarterly* 22, no. 4 (1939): 1012–1094, and "Commodore Aury," in *Louisiana Historical Quarterly* 24, no. 3 (1941): 611–697.

Harris G. Warren, *The Sword Was Their Passport: A History of American Filibustering in the Mexican Revolution* (1943).

Harold A. Bierck, *La vida pública de don Pedro Gual* (1947).

Martin Luis Guzmán, *Javier Mina, héroe de España y México*, 2d ed. (1955).

Clifton B. Kroeber, *The Growth of the Shipping Industry in the Río de la Plata Region, 1794–1860* (1957).

Jaime Duarte French, *Los tres Luises del Caribe: ¿Corsarios o libertadores?* (1988).

Additional Bibliography

Cacua Prada, Antonio. *El corsario Luis Aury: intimidades de la independencia.* Bogota: Academia Colombiana de Historia, 2001.

Reyes Canal, Julio C. *Historia de estas islas: y un cuento marinero.* Bogota: Códice, 1996.

RALPH LEE WOODWARD JR.

AUSTIN, MOSES (1761–1821). Moses Austin (*b.* 4 October 1761; *d.* 10 June 1821), founder of the American lead industry and father of Stephen F. Austin. Reared in Connecticut, Moses Austin moved to Richmond, Virginia, in 1785 to manage a mercantile business. An entrepreneur, he revived the lead business, making considerable money before experiencing business reverses. He then moved to Spanish Upper Louisiana, where he received a land grant for his lead enterprise. He founded Potosi, Missouri, in 1798 and prospered until the

War of 1812. Bankrupt by 1820, Austin saw his economic revival in establishing a colony in Texas, for which he secured permission from the Spanish government. His son, Stephen Fuller, established the colony after his father's death.

See also **Iron and Steel Industry.**

BIBLIOGRAPHY

Eugene C. Baker, *The Austin Papers* (1924–1928) and David B. Gracy II, *Moses Austin: His Life* (1987).

DAVID B. GRACY II

AUSTIN, STEPHEN FULLER (1793–1836).

Stephen Fuller Austin (*b.* 3 November 1793; *d.* 27 December 1836), father of Anglo-American Texas. Born in southwest Virginia, Austin lived and attended school in Spanish Upper Louisiana, Connecticut, and Kentucky before beginning work at age seventeen in his father's mercantile and lead businesses in Missouri. He served in the Missouri territorial legislature, but demonstrated no special business acumen. Loyalty to his father, despite financial reverses, drew him into land speculation in Arkansas (1819) and law studies in Louisiana (1820).

In 1821, Austin determined to carry out his deceased father's plan to settle Anglo-Americans in Spanish Texas. He received or participated in five *empresario* contracts, his first one for 300 families being the only one fulfilled by any *empresario*. Until 1828, Austin was responsible for civil and military affairs of the Anglo-American settlements, an authority he exercised with a patience and tact that minimized friction between the settlers and the Mexican authorities until unrest led to the conventions of 1832 and 1833, which sought changes in unpopular laws and separate statehood within Mexico.

Returning from a trip to Mexico City, where he obtained many of the demands of the conventions of 1832 and 1833, Austin was arrested (1834) on suspicion of inciting insurrection and held in Mexico City for eighteen months. Back in Texas (1835), he supported opposition to the Mexican central government, and during the Texas Revolution (1836) commanded troops, later serving as a commissioner to the United States. Defeated for president of the republic, he became secretary of state but died in office soon after.

See also **Texas.**

BIBLIOGRAPHY

Eugene C. Barber, *The Austin Papers* (1924–1928) and *The Life of Stephen F. Austin* (1925).

Additional Bibliography

Cantrell, Gregg. *Stephen F. Austin, Empresario of Texas.* New Haven: Yale University Press, 1999.

DAVID B. GRACY II

AUTO, AUTO SACRAMENTAL.

Auto Sacramental, a theatrical genre originating from a dramatic form developed especially in the thirteenth and fourteenth centuries, the *miracle* (France) or *auto* (Iberian Peninsula) presented episodes involving a miracle, usually the intervention of the Virgin Mary in favor of a poor sinner, commonly of the lower classes, guilty of some unpardonable crime before the law, human or divine. The theater of the early Renaissance in Spain (Juan del Encina) and Portugal (Gil Vicente) is essentially a stylized form of that of the Middle Ages, combining the religious and the profane with more realistic characterizations and dialogue. Whereas Encina's *autos* were no longer liturgical or ecclesiastical, Vicente continued the medieval tradition and introduced the allegory. In this genre he was a precursor of Calderón de La Barca, whose *autos sacramentales* epitomize the form in content and technique.

All variations were utilized in the New World by the Jesuit missionaries from Spain and Portugal. In their efforts to convert and colonize Indians in their missions, the priests not only followed Iberian models, but also incorporated much that they observed in native settings and culture, including language, in order to present the teachings of the church to their catechumens. These traditions have evolved to the present day, with Ariano Vilar Suassuna as perhaps the chief proponent in Brazil in his *Auto da compadecida* and other works.

See also **Jesuits.**

BIBLIOGRAPHY

Sábato Magaldi, *Panorama do teatro brasileiro* (1962).

Additional Bibliography

Arellano, Ignacio and J. Enrique Duarte. *El auto sacramental.* Madrid: Ediciones del Laberinto, 2003.

Díaz Balsera, Viviana. *Calderón y las quimeras de la culpa: Alegoría, seducción y resistencia en cinco autos sacramentales.* West Lafayette, IN: Purdue University Press, 1997.

Kurtz, Barbara Ellen. *The Play of Allegory in the Autos Sacramentales of Pedro Calderón de la Barca.* Washington, D.C.: Catholic University of America Press, 1991.

Rull Fernández, Enrique. *Arte y sentido en el universo sacramental de Caderón.* Pamplona: Edition Reichenberger, 2004.

RICHARD A. MAZZARA

AUTOMOBILE INDUSTRY. Motor vehicles first arrived in Buenos Aires in 1889, and in 1916 Ford Motor Company established assembly operations in Argentina. While Ford's move marked the beginning of automobile production in Latin America, several North American automakers already maintained distribution networks in major countries there. Throughout the first half of the twentieth century, U.S. firms, eager to supplement slowing domestic growth, dominated the Latin American auto trade. Most began by distributing U.S.-built vehicles; some, such as Chrysler and Kaiser, proceeded to authorize licensing agreements, enabling local manufacturers to assemble their vehicles, while others, including General Motors, established subsidiary operations to assemble vehicles. In either case, early assembly operations were small-scale, designed to build vehicles from complete knockdown kits (CKDs) imported from the United States. The CKDs included virtually all the sheet metal and subassemblies required to produce a vehicle. Following Ford's lead, General Motors built an assembly plant in Brazil in 1925, and before long most of Detroit's major automakers had established assembly operations in the Mexico City area. Auto production stagnated during the Great Depression and World War II, however, and locally built vehicles remained a small portion of vehicles sold in Latin America. Vehicle shortages during the war prompted Latin American governments to end their dependence on imported vehicles, and resultant policies effected a resurgence in the industry. Thereafter, auto manufacturing expanded. In 1992 Brazil and Mexico produced 1.1 million vehicles each, as opposed to 9.7 million units in the United States. The prevalence of automobiles in Latin America still lags behind other industrialized nations, however. In the United States, for example, there was one vehicle for every 1.6 people in 1990; in Mexico, that ratio dropped to one for every 8.9, while in Brazil there was only one vehicle for every 12 people. Brazil and Mexico emerged as dominant producer nations, while Argentina, Chile, Peru, Colombia, and Venezuela played much smaller roles.

After 1945, governments in Brazil, Mexico, Argentina, and Chile supported the development of the automotive industry in order to end dependence on imported vehicles and to increase employment. They encouraged foreign investment, granted tax incentives to heavy industry, and levied high tariffs on imported finished vehicles while maintaining duty-free status for CKDs. Some imposed outright bans on imported vehicles. The incentives, coupled with a car-starved market, resulted in an influx of European manufacturers and renewed growth. During the 1950s, Córdoba, Argentina, became an important automotive center and was home to Fiat and Kaiser assembly plants. Argentina's inducements also attracted General Motors and Rambler. Córdoba became known for its militant labor force, which commanded higher wages; since labor costs in Brazil were lower, Volkswagen constructed its plant in São Paulo, and both General Motors and Ford chose Brazil for future expansion. In Mexico, no fewer than eleven auto firms were represented. By the late 1950s, more than twenty major European, North American, and Japanese manufacturers assembled imported components—far too many entrants to achieve efficiency in such a small market.

Governments realized that the goal of substituting domestic for foreign vehicles needed refinement: manufacturers were unable to achieve the economies of scale necessary to control costs and produce quality products at affordable prices. Since all major producers were foreign-owned and managed, the importation of the components of their vehicles created a drain on foreign exchange. Brazil took the first step by initiating content restrictions, which stipulated that an increasing portion of a vehicle's content must be locally produced. Argentina followed suit in 1958, and in 1960 Mexico not only enacted local-content laws but also rationalized the number of its auto manufacturers. Content laws challenged automakers in two ways: first, they became increasingly responsible for building a complex vehicle, not just a kit; second, they were now subject to the vagaries of local-parts supply, inflation, and infrastructure problems.

Prices of domestically produced vehicles were substantially higher than in Europe or North America owing to production inefficiencies, higher material and financing costs, and taxes. Latin America's markets languished. The large and rapidly growing market sought by the manufacturers remained limited by low incomes. During the 1970s governments and manufacturers began to look beyond domestic markets. They sought to capitalize on the region's low labor costs and believed increased export volume would both lower prices for the domestic market and alleviate trade imbalances. Despite major worldwide economic recessions in the 1970s and the 1980s and spiraling inflation, which eroded cost advantages, the Latin American automobile industry, particularly that of Mexico, reached new production records. While trade barriers and lackluster economies throughout the world have softened demand for new vehicles, the Latin American automobile industry is as vital as ever.

South America's Mercosur Trade Agreement and the North American Free Trade Agreement (NAFTA) have stimulated exports by further eliminating trade barriers between producing nations. Major international carmakers moved to Mexico's side of the border with the United States after the passage of NAFTA. In 2006, Mexico produced two million cars, a record number. Argentina's auto industry has had a difficult time adjusting to international competition and in the early twenty-first century has been restructuring. In Brazil, Renault, Honda, and Toyota set up factories in the 1990s, creating stiff competition there for the traditional industry leaders General Motors, Ford, and Volkswagen. This led to an extremely competitive market and Brazil became a major exporter to Europe and the rest of South America. As of 2007 Brazil still maintains tariffs that protect local auto production. This protection has become a contentious issue during the Doha Round of World Trade Organization (WTO) discussions and future agreements will probably require that Brazil at least lower duties on foreign auto imports.

See also **Mercosur; North American Free Trade Agreement.**

BIBLIOGRAPHY

Deebe Ferris, *Ward's Automotive Yearbook* (1962–1993).

Motor Vehicle Manufacturers Association of the U.S., Inc., *Automobile Facts and Figures* (1967–1992).

Jack N. Behrman, *The Role of International Companies in Latin American Integration* (1972).

Rhys Owen Jenkins, *Dependent Industrialization in Latin America: The Automotive Industry in Argentina, Chile, and Mexico* (1977), and *Transnational Corporations and the Latin American Automobile Industry* (1987).

Ian Roxborough, *Unions and Politics in Mexico: The Case of the Automobile Industry* (1984), pp. 45–46.

Richard S. Newfarmer, ed., *Profits, Progress, and Poverty* (1985), pp. 205–207, 225.

Bernhard Fischer et al., *Capital-Intensive Industries in Newly Industrializing Countries: The Case of the Brazilian Automobile and Steel Industries* (1988).

Additional Bibliography

Arteaga García, Arnulfo. *Integración productiva y relaciones laborales en la industria automotriz en México.* Mexico City: Universidad Autónoma Metropolitana, Unidad Iztapalapa, Plaza y Valdés, 2003.

Brambilla, Irene. *A Customs Union with Multinational Firms: The Automobile Market in Argentina and Brazil.* Cambridge, MA: National Bureau of Economic Research, 2005.

Tuman, John Peter. *Reshaping the North American Automobile Industry: Restructuring, Corporatism, and Union Democracy in Mexico.* London and New York: Continuum, 2003.

JANET M. PLZAK

AUTO RACING. *See* **Sports.**

AVALOS, PACT OF (1820). A last-ditch effort by José Gervasio Artigas to save the ideal of a confederation, the Pact of Avalos was signed on April 24, 1820, in the small town of

Avalos, Corrientes, Provincias Unidas del Río de la Plata (later named Argentina). Only the provinces of Corrientes and Misiones joined Artigas, who represented the Banda Oriental, in the signing of the treaty.

Artigas's Federal League had been moribund since February 23, 1820, the day that Buenos Aires and the caudillos of Santa Fe and Entre Ríos signed the Pact of El Pilar in spite of his adamant opposition. In fact, the Pact of Avalos was an offensive-defensive treaty of Corrientes, Misones, and Banda Oriental, which were not signatories to the Pact of El Pilar. Many of the federalist caudillos had been acting independently of Artigas because he was tied down fighting the Portuguese in the Banda Oriental, leaving them to their devices for their own survival, while facing the ever-present threat of Buenos Aires. The Pact of Avalos bound the signatories to fight for freedom and independence and would allow each province to elect its own governor and manage its internal economy. Artigas was again named the Protector of the Free Peoples, but he was already a beaten man, with no real power to influence events. He then moved to Corrientes and from there to Paraguay, where he died in 1850, never again having enjoyed the political influence he once had.

See also **Artigas, José Gervasio.**

BIBLIOGRAPHY

Lucena Salmoral, Manuel. *José Gervasio Artigas: Gaucho y confederado.* Madrid: Anaya, 1988.

Maggi, Carlos. *La nueva historia de Artigas.* 8 vols. Montevideo: Ediciones de la Plaza, 2005.

Narancio, Edmundo M. *La independencia de Uruguay,* 3rd edition. Montevideo: Editorial Ayer, 2001.

Navarro García, Luis. *José Artigas.* Madrid: Ediciones Quorum, 1987.

Street, John. *Artigas and the Emancipation of Uruguay.* Cambridge, U.K.: Cambridge University Press, 1959.

JUAN MANUEL PÉREZ

AVELLANEDA, NICOLÁS (1837–1885).

Nicolás Remigio Aurelio Avellaneda, who served as president of Argentina from 1874 to 1880, was born in Tucumán. When he was four years old his father, Marco Avellaneda, a prominent member of the opposition party to the dictator Juan Manuel de Rosas, was executed. After studies at the University of Córdoba, Avellaneda returned to his native province and founded the newspaper *Eco del Norte.* In 1857 he moved to Buenos Aires, where he was active as a journalist and also earned a law degree. He taught political economy at the University of Buenos Aires School of Law, and in 1865 published his most important book, *Estudio sobre las leyes de tierras públicas* (Study on the Laws of Public Lands).

Elected as a deputy to the provincial parliament, he resigned to become a minister in the government of Adolfo Alsina (the governor of the province of Buenos Aires). In 1868 President Domingo Faustino Sarmiento named Avellaneda a national minister of justice and public instruction, and he became a key figure in the cabinet. In 1874 he was elected president, but his opponent, former President Bartolomé Mitre, led a revolt against the election. The revolt was finally defeated, and Mitre was sent to jail. In 1877 Avellaneda decreed an amnesty and launched a policy of national reconciliation. As president he continued Sarmiento's policy of expanding primary schooling and improving the national system of higher education. The 1873 economic crisis prompted him to initiate a policy protecting local industry and drastically reducing public expenditures. In 1878–1879 his minister of war, Julio A. Roca, conducted the Conquest of the Desert (the conquest of lands in the hands of the native populations, encompassing the whole Patagonia). Roca was then designated the successor of Avellaneda. Before completing his term, Avellaneda declared the city of Buenos Aires a federal district; as a result of this decree, the province of Buenos Aires would lose control over the customhouse, its main source of revenue. When Carlos Tejedor, the governor of the province, rebelled, Avellaneda left the capital and marched to Belgrano, a suburb, where he organized a counteroffensive. He defeated the rebellion, thus succeeding in separating the city of Buenos Aires from the province. This event is considered the final phase in the consolidation of Argentina's federal state, initiated in 1862 by President Bartolomé Mitre.

After completing his presidency, Avellaneda was elected a national senator from his native province, and shortly thereafter was appointed rector of the Universidad Nacional de Buenos Aires. In 1885 he traveled to Europe with his wife, Cecilia Nóbrego, for medical treatment, but he died en route at the age of forty-eight. The works of Avellaneda, who also had literary inclinations, were published as *Escritos literarios*.

See also **Alsina, Adolfo; Argentina, Political Parties: National Autonomist Party; Argentina: The Nineteenth Century; Conquest of the Desert; Mitre, Bartolomé; Roca, Julio Argentino; Rosas, Juan Manuel de; Sarmiento, Domingo Faustino; Tejedor, Carlos.**

BIBLIOGRAPHY

Avellaneda, Nicolás. *Estudio sobre las leyes de tierras públicas.* Buenos Aires: J. Roldán, 1915.

de Gandía, Enrique. *Nicolás Avellaneda: sus ideas y su tiempo.* Buenos Aires: Comisión Permanente de Homenaje al Dr. Nicolás Avellaneda, 1984.

Páez de la Torre, Carlos. *Nicolás Avellaneda, una biografía.* Buenos Aires: Planeta, 2001.

ELÍAS JOSÉ PALTI

AVERÍA.   Avería, a Spanish tax on the Indies trade that covered the costs of providing armed protection for merchant shipping. First collected in 1521, the *avería* was administered by the Casa De Contratación of Seville, working closely with the *consulado*. There was no fixed rate, the aim being to spread the costs of necessary defense over all commodities, although in 1644 Philip IV guaranteed that the maximum charge would be 12 percent of the value of cargoes. The ad valorem tax was abolished in 1660 in favor of an agreement that the principal merchant houses of Seville would contribute fixed sums toward the costs of defending the transatlantic fleets.

See also **Fleet System: Colonial Spanish America.**

BIBLIOGRAPHY

Guillermo Céspedes Del Castillo, *La avería en el comercio de Indias* (1945).

Clarence H. Haring, *The Spanish Empire in America* (1947), esp. pp. 305–306.

Additional Bibliography

Acosta Rodríguez, Antonio, Adolfo Luis González Rodríguez, and Enriqueta Vila Vilar. *La Casa de la Contratación y la navegación entre España y las Indias.* Sevilla, Spain: Universidad de Sevilla, 2003.

Martínez Shaw, Carlos, and José María Oliva Melgar. *Sistema atlántico español: Siglos XVII–XIX.* Madrid: Marcial Pons Historia, 2005.

Romano, Ruggiero. *Mecanismo y elementos del sistema económico colonial americano, siglos XVI–XVIII.* México: El Colegio de México, Fideicomiso Historia de las Américas, 2004.

JOHN R. FISHER

AVIATION.   Beginning in 1910, Latin American, European, and U.S. aviators in small but growing numbers pioneered airplane flights in Latin America. In aviation's early barnstorming and aerial pathfinding phase, flying in Latin America was characterized by several factors that were natural consequences of the times: the relatively few Latin American aviators came from wealthy families, such as the Brazilian Alberto Santos-Dumont, who in 1906 made the first airplane flight in Europe; and most planes were imported from Europe or the United States—the latter factor would persist indefinitely. As elsewhere, fatal accidents often occurred in the flimsy and underpowered planes of aviation's infancy.

Mexico was the site of several milestones in military aviation. Early in 1911 the regime of Porfirio Díaz, faced with spreading revolution, hired two French barnstormers to fly reconnaissance over rebel forces, the first known combat sorties of an airplane anywhere. As most factions in the revolution came to possess small numbers of planes, almost every facet of aerial warfare, if in microcosm and isolation, was recorded either preceding or concurrent with developments in World War I in Europe—besides reconnaissance, air-to-air combat, tactical air support, and the bombing of population centers occurred. Two noteworthy events occurred in 1914: a Constitutional plane piloted by Gustavo Salinas Carmiña scored a near miss on a Huertista warship off the west coast and U.S. Navy planes flew reconnaissance over Veracruz in the first use of aviation in a U.S. intervention.

In 1915 the Constitutionalists formed what was later the Fuerza Aérea Mexicana; it was soon conducting training, and manufactured a respectable number of airplanes of its own design after World War I restricted foreign supply. Argentina, Brazil, Chile, Cuba, and Uruguay created military air arms before or during World War I.

From 1919 on, most Latin American countries developed air arms with the aid of foreign military missions. They were equipped mainly with hand-me-downs from Europe and the United States, and their operations were for the most part noncombat: training, surveying, security watch. Like their army and naval counterparts, air officers sometimes engaged in volatile politics, a notable example being Marmaduke Grove, who was briefly head of state in Chile in 1931. Periodically Latin American air arms engaged in aerial warfare after 1919; leading examples were operations of the air arms of both Bolivia and Paraguay in the Chaco War (1932–1935); operations of U.S.-equipped fighter squadrons from Mexico in the Philippines and from Brazil in Italy in World War II; and the gallant but doomed fight of the Argentine air force against the British in the South Atlantic War of 1982. Helicopters and strike aircraft hunted guerrillas in the 1970s and 1980s.

Nonexistent until 1919, civil air transport in Latin America stemmed from the failure of surface transportation to blanket an often difficult and diverse geography. It was spurred by an international rivalry with martial implications and was fostered by nationalism.

The international rivalry pitted three non–Latin American groups against one another: Germans, who created airlines in South America, most notably Sociedad Colombo-Alemana de Transportes Aéreos (SCADTA), in Colombia in December 1919, the first lasting airline in the region; U.S. officials, fearing the implied threat to the Panama Canal, and private interests, recognizing a most fertile field for air transport, the latter launching Pan American Airways (1927), which with unprecedented government aid monopolized all U.S. international airline business until World War II; and French private interests, whose heavily subsidized airline Aéropostale developed the world's longest route system, including routes in much of South America, by 1930. The rivalry featured three of the great pioneers in air

transport history—Juan Terry Trippe of Pan American; Peter Paul von Bauer of SCADTA in Colombia; and French-born Marcel Boulloux-Lafont, who resided in South America. In the end, von Bauer secretly sold controlling interest in Depression-weakened SCADTA to Trippe (1931), and Boulloux-Lafont lost Aéropostale when the French government forced it into bankruptcy in 1931 by withdrawing its subsidy.

During World War II, the Germans lost their airlines when Latin American countries, under pressure from the United States, nationalized all German enterprises.

Lines both domestic and international multiplied in the 1930s, some fading as others took to the sky. It was increasingly clear that air transport filled special needs in a region struggling to modernize, but also clear that airlines helped maintain the dependency imbalance. One line, Compañía Mexicana de Aviación (CMA), will serve to illustrate. It was founded in 1924 by U.S. entrepreneurs to fly payrolls to oil fields. With the help of some well-connected Mexicans, CMA added routes and diverse cargo. In 1929 it became a Pan American subsidiary in Mexican guise in order to carry PAA mail and cargo, something foreign lines could not do under Mexican law. CMA became truly Mexican after World War II, in a general trend to divest lines based in Latin America of foreign control, even though these lines still depended on outsiders for equipment such as the jets they began to acquire in the 1960s.

A number of Latin American air forces became involved in air transport. In 1929 Línea Aeropostal Santiago-Arica (later Línea Aérea Nacional, LAN) was founded by Comandante Arturo Merino Benítez as a division of the Chilean air force to carry mail and passengers, in part to counter the presence of PANAGRA, the jointly owned subsidiary of Pan American and the U.S. conglomerate W. R. Grace. It soon became a civil line, and ultimately the major Chilean domestic and international carrier. Other air forces, for example, Argentina's, developed transport divisions to serve sparsely settled areas, such as that from the Pampas to the Chilean border, that would not be profitable for a private-sector airline. Another dimension of Latin American air transport is that it is no longer the preserve of the well-to-do. After World

War II it began to be more available to the less affluent with the rise of low-fare airlines.

Deregulation of the airline industries in the 1990s helped make air travel even more accessible to the general population. When governments lifted restrictions on prices and allowed full competition, ticket prices dropped dramatically. Lower fares helped more people to fly but also caused strains in the air infrastructure of many countries. Brazil suffered two of its worst airline disasters in 2007, and many experts believed that old equipment, an understaffed air traffic control system and crowded airports contributed to these crashes.

Other Latin American nations privatized their national airlines in the early 1990s to pay off large public debts. A mix of national and international investors bought the firms, with mixed results. LAN, Chile's former state-run airline, was bought by the Scandinavian Airlines System (SAS) and successfully expanded into other regions of Latin America. For instance, by 2005 LAN took over Ecuador's former state-run airline Ecuatoriana, which had fallen into bankruptcy after its sale to the Brazilian airline VASP in 1995. In 1990 Iberia, a Spanish airline company, purchased Aerolineas Argentinas, which fell into bankruptcy in 2001. Also, many analysts believe the privatization was corrupt, believing that Argentine officials received kickbacks from Iberia. Despite these problems, Aerolineas Argentinas emerged from bankruptcy, and as of 2007 another Spanish firm, Vieja Marsans, operates it. The Bolivian airline Lloyd Aereo Boliviano collapsed as a private company; VASP bought a controlling interest in 1995, but by the early twenty-first century both VASP and Lloyd Aereo Boliviano encountered financial difficulties. Bolivian investors took over VASP's share but the airline ended service in 2007. Thus, privatization and deregulation have brought, at times, more competition, but also disruption to service.

BIBLIOGRAPHY

Significant works covering one or more aspects of aviation in Latin America are Wesley Phillips Newton, *The Perilous Sky: U.S. Aviation Diplomacy and Latin America, 1919–1931* (1978).

Marylin Bender and Selig Altschul, *The Chosen Instrument: Juan Trippe, Pan Am, the Rise and Fall of an American Entrepreneur* (1982).

R. E. G. Davies, *Airlines of Latin America Since 1919* (1984).

One of the best reference works dealing with the world's air forces (including those of Latin America), their histories, and their relative statuses is Mark Hamish et al., *Air Forces of the World: Illustrated Directory of the World's Military Air Powers* (1979). The British periodical *Air International* has monthly updates on both military and civil aviation around the world.

Many Latin American countries have produced their own historical literature on their aviation. Those on Mexico include José Villela Gómez, *Breve historia de la aviación en México* (1971).

Enrique Sandoval C., *Historia oficial de la fuerza expedicionaria mexicana* (1946), on the Mexican fighter squadron in the Philippines.

Additional Bibliography

Magnusson, Michael. *Latin Glory: Airlines of Latin America.* Osceola, WI: Motorbooks International, 1995.

Potenze, Pablo Luciano. *Historia del transporte aerocomercial.* Buenos Aires: Universidad Argentina de la Empresa, 1997.

WESLEY PHILLIPS NEWTON

ÁVILA, ALONSO DE (c. 1539–1566).

Alonso de Ávila (b. c. 1539; d. 3 August 1566), leader of the so-called Cortés Conspiracy of 1565–1566. Ávila was a leading light of the second, native-born generation of *encomenderos* in Mexico. Less economically secure than their fathers, they grew increasingly resentful of the royal policies that progressively limited their power. They sought a champion in Martín Cortés, the conquistador's son and second marqués del Valle, who arrived in Mexico in 1563. Cortés soon clashed with the viceroy, Luis de Velasco, and his pretensions to political influence increased when Velasco's death left an undersized, three-man *audiencia* as the highest authority in the colony.

In October 1565, Alonso de Ávila, Gil González Dávila (his older brother), and several other members of the colonial elite began actively plotting the overthrow of the government. They planned to assassinate the *audiencia* judges and other high officials and to proclaim Cortés king. But the marqués wavered, refusing explicitly to endorse the conspiracy. His indecision, along with the general indiscretion and ineptitude of the conspirators, allowed the *audiencia* to strike first. On 16 July 1566, the

ENVIRONMENT AND DEVELOPMENT

Vicuñas in Las Vicuñas National Reserve, Chile. The reserve lies within Lauca National Park, declared a World Biosphere Reserve by UNESCO in 1981. Home to many species of birds and mammals, the reserve was the site of controversy in 2007 when the Chilean government approved a mining company's request to explore for minerals there. © Theo Allofs/Corbis

LEFT: **An ecolodge in the Kapawi Ecological Reserve, Ecuador.** Kapawi Lodge, a luxury resort in the Amazon rainforest, is designed to minimize the impact of tourism on the surrounding environment. Buildings stand on stilts to avoid displacing local vegetation and the lodge is powered entirely by solar energy. Ownership of the lodge is being gradually transferred to the indigenous Achuar people. © ALISON WRIGHT/CORBIS

OPPOSITE: **Tourists climbing the Perito Morena Glacier, Patagonia, Argentina.** With the rise of adventure travel and ecotourism, Patagonia, a near neighbor to Antarctica, has become an increasingly popular destination for travelers, bringing both benefits to the local economy and costs to its environment. LIVA CORONA/THE IMAGE BANK/GETTY IMAGES

BELOW: **Golfing in the Atacama Desert, Chile.** Rainfall in Chile's Atacama Desert is almost nonexistent. In order to eliminate the heavy water usage that the grounds of a traditional golf course would require, these grassless greens at the Club de Golf are covered in used motor oil. JOEL SARTORE/NATIONAL GEOGRAPHIC IMAGE COLLECTION

RIGHT: **Shark caught in a gill net off the coast of the Galapagos Islands, Ecuador.** Because gill nets snare everything that swims into them, their use has had devastating effects on coastal marine life. TUI DE ROY/MINDEN PICTURES/GETTY IMAGES

BELOW: **Fishermen at dawn, Bahia de Los Angeles, Baja California, Mexico.** Overfishing by commercial fishing operations has drastically reduced fishing stock in this region, making it difficult for local fishermen to catch enough to earn a living. ANNIE GRIFFITHS BELT/NATIONAL GEOGRAPHIC IMAGE COLLECTION

ABOVE: **Beach pollution at Guanabara Bay, Rio de Janeiro, Brazil, 2007.** Nearly ninety percent of the waste found in Guanabara Bay is recyclable. Large-scale internationally funded efforts have failed to make headway against the contamination. In response, the Rio de Janeiro city government has taken matters into its own hands, recruiting local residents who are paid to pick up the trash they find along and in the city's waterways. © MARCELO SAYAO/EPA/CORBIS

RIGHT: **Oil refinery, Willemstad, Curaçao.** Located off the coast of oil-rich Venezuela, Curaçao is an attractive location for oil companies seeking to build refineries. © ROBERT HARDING WORLD IMAGERY/CORBIS

LEFT: **Preserving caymans from extinction, Aguaro-Guariquito National Park, Venezuela, 2004.** Members of the Venezuelan Ministry of Environment and Natural Resources release caymans from captivity as a part of a government program attempting to save the species from extinction. JUAN BARRETO/AFP/GETTY

LEFT TOP: Deforestation, Santarém, Brazil. What was once lush Amazon rainforest now stands cleared for planting soy. Increased soybean production in Brazil—in response to heavy demands from Europe and China—has dramatically accelerated the rate of deforestation. © COLIN MCPHERSON/CORBIS

LEFT BOTTOM: Clearing the rainforest, Rondônia State, Brazil. Trees smolder as acres of Amazonian rainforest are burned to clear land for pasture for cattle, one of the leading causes of deforestation in the Brazilian Amazon. The Brazilian government's efforts to stem the tide of deforestation have met with setbacks; after an initial decrease, tree felling in the cattle and farming region of Rondônia state rose 602 percent in September 2006. MICHAEL NICHOLS/NATIONAL GEOGRAPHIC IMAGE COLLECTION

RIGHT: Traffic jam on the Marginal Tietê highway, São Paulo, Brazil. As in many of Latin America's growing cities, population growth in São Paulo—a city known for its traffic and smog—overwhelms its infrastructure and places a heavy burden on the local environment. AP IMAGES

BELOW: Manaus harbor, Brazil, 2006. Boats wait on a bank of the Amazon River in the north of Brazil. The Amazon is the chief avenue of transportation for both people and goods in this region. EVARISTO SA/AFP/GETTY IMAGES

RIGHT: **A Colombian police officer uproots poppy plants used to make heroin, 2000.** Years of U.S.-sponsored eradication programs, which involve the widespread spraying of herbicides on illegal drug crops, have caused water and soil quality damage and deforestation in Colombia's rainforests and highlands. AP IMAGES

BELOW: **Public fountain, Rancho Grande, Chaco region of Bolivia, 2007.** A Guarani girl washes her face at a public fountain that was set up with aid from the World Food Programme, UNICEF, and the World Health Organization. Thirty percent of all Bolivian households lack a potable water connection. The UN's Millennium Development Goal for Bolivia is to reduce this number to five percent by 2015. © MARIN ALIPAZ/EPA/CORBIS

audiencia arrested the Ávila brothers and Cortés. After a brief trial, Alonso and Gil were condemned to death—a sentence clearly intended to deter any future conspirators. Both brothers were beheaded in Mexico City's central Plaza.

See also **González Dávila, Gil.**

BIBLIOGRAPHY

Fernando Benítez, *The Century After Cortés,* translated by Joan Mac Lean (1965).

Lesley Bird Simpson, *Many Mexicos* (1966), esp. pp. 119–126.

Jorge Ignacio Rubio Mañé, *El Virreinato,* vol. 2, *Expansión y defensa: Primera parte* (1983), pp. 3–21.

R. DOUGLAS COPE

ÁVILA, JULIO ENRIQUE (1892–1968).

Julio Enrique Ávila (*b.* 4 August 1892; *d.* 1968), Salvadoran poet and intellectual leader. A professor of chemistry and pharmacology, and later dean of the Faculty of Chemistry and Pharmacy at the National University of El Salvador, Ávila became known primarily as a literary figure. His first book, *Fuentes de alma* (1917), established him in the modernist school of Rubén Darío. Subsequent works, especially the poetic novel *El vigía sin luz* (1927) and an anthology, *El mundo de mi jardín* (1927), established him as one of the leading Salvadoran poets of his generation.

See also **Literature: Spanish America.**

BIBLIOGRAPHY

Alfonso María Landarech, *Estudios literarios* (1959), pp. 114–139.

Luis Gallegos Valdés, *Panorama de la literatura salvadoreña del período precolombino a 1980* (1987), esp. pp. 209–216.

David Escobar Galindo, *Índice antológico de la poesía salvadoreña* (1987), pp. 256–257.

RALPH LEE WOODWARD JR.

ÁVILA, PEDRO ARIAS DE (c. 1440–1531).

Pedro Arias de Ávila (Pedrarias Dávila; *b.* ca. 1440; *d.* July 1531), Spanish soldier, governor of Panama (1514–1526) and of Nicaragua (1527–1531), and founder of Panama City (1519). Pedrarias was a member of a prominent noble family of Segovia; his uncle was an archbishop and his older brother was the count of Puñonrostro. He was perhaps of *converso* origins.

In his boyhood Pedrarias was a page in the court of Juan II of Castile and León (1406–1454). In later life he distinguished himself in the war against the Moors in Granada (1482–1492) and as a colonel of infantry fighting in North Africa (1508–1511). Physically imposing and athletic, Pedrarias was nicknamed "the jouster" and "the gallant." After another had declined the honor, he accepted an appointment as captain-general and governor of Castilla del Oro in Darién (also known as Panama), offered in June 1513, despite his being seventy-three years of age.

Information had reached the king about the riches to be found in Panama, and owing to rumors of a great body of water to the south, a large fleet was organized under the command of Pedrarias. Among fifteen hundred or more passengers, the vessels carried a brilliant array of notables, including Pedrarias's wife, Isabel de Bobadilla y Peñalosa, the chronicler Gonzalo Fernández de Oviedo y Valdés, the historian Bernal Díaz Del Castillo, and Hernando de Soto. Altogether, it was perhaps the most distinguished passenger list of any fleet sailing to the New World. Pedrarias embarked for the Indies in April 1514 with orders to assume control of the colony; suspend the acting governor, Vasco Núñez de Balboa; and to bring Balboa to justice on the charge of usurping authority from previous leaders.

The king learned of Balboa's discovery of the Pacific Ocean a few days after the departure of Pedrarias. Accordingly, the crown appointed Balboa adelantado, but he was subject to Pedrarias. It took six months for the commission to reach Panama, and Pedrarias withheld the information from Balboa. Initial contact between the two men was cordial, and Balboa freely shared his knowledge of the land and people of Panama with Pedrarias. Balboa was acquitted in his judicial review, but because of his prestige and popularity, Pedrarias seethed with resentment and jealousy. To help relieve the tension, Bishop Juan de Quevedo arranged the betrothal of Pedrarias's daughter María to Balboa. The aging governor doubtless welcomed a good political match for his eldest daughter, who was in a convent in Seville.

Meantime, lieutenants of Pedrarias led predatory *entradas* in search of gold and slaves, undoing by their brutality much of the goodwill Balboa had established among the natives. Balboa continued his project to build ships to sail down the Pacific coast to explore the rich land of "Biru," of which Indians had spoken. His plans were interrupted when a companion betrayed him, charging that he planned to overthrow the authority of Pedrarias, to whom he was still subject. Balboa was also accused of being more interested in his Indian mistress than in his betrothed. Pedrarias, his parental pride wounded, saw the opportunity to be rid of his rival once and for all. Balboa, apparently innocent of the charge of treason, was found guilty, denied appeals, and beheaded along with three of his friends at Acla in January 1519.

That same year Pedrarias founded the city of Panama, on the south coast of the isthmus. Under his aegis Pascual de Andagoya made an exploratory voyage in 1522 to investigate the great civilization that was said to exist to the south. Later, Pedrarias was a partner in the expedition of Francisco Pizarro that led to his conquest of Inca Peru. In 1522 Pedrarias also dispatched lieutenants northward, and in 1523 Francisco Hernández de Córdoba, who was welcomed by local caciques, founded the cities of León and Granada in Nicaragua. When he plotted with others and renounced the authority of Pedrarias, Hernández de Córdoba was arrested and executed in 1526. Despite mounting criticism, Pedrarias was appointed governor of Nicaragua in 1527.

His daughter María was married to Rodrigo de Contreras, a nobleman of Segovia and later governor of Nicaragua (1534–1544); another daughter, Isabella, became the wife of explorer Hernando de Soto, the future governor of Cuba. His extreme cruelty to Spaniards and Indians alike notwithstanding, Pedrarias enjoyed powerful support, including that of the influential Juan Rodríguez de Fonseca. With such friends back in Spain, as well as extraordinarily good luck, he served as a governor in Central America for seventeen years, a remarkable career for the times. In 1531, at age ninety, the bitter old man died in León. By then he had justly earned the nickname "the wrath of God," bestowed upon him by a contemporary chronicler.

See also **Panama City.**

BIBLIOGRAPHY

The standard biography of Pedrarias is Pablo Álvarez Rubiano, *Pedrarias Dávila: Contribución al estudio de la figura del "gran justador," gobernador de Castilla del Oro y Nicaragua* (1944), although it sees the subject in a more positive light than do most historians. Very convenient and useful are the 152 documents presented in the appendices. Also valuable is Mario Góngora, *Los grupos de conquistadores en Tierra Firme, 1509–1530* (1962). Showing Pedrarias in a very negative role is his contemporary antagonist, the chronicler Gonzalo Fernández De Oviedo y Valdés, *Historia general y natural de las Indias,* 5 vols. (1959); also critical of Pedrarias is the historian Bartolomé De Las Casas, *Historia de las Indias,* edited by Agustín Millares Carlo, 3 vols. (1951). See also Carlos Molina Argüello, *El gobernador de Nicaragua en el siglo XVI* (1949). In English, consult Kathleen Romoli, *Balboa of Darien: Discoverer of the Pacific Ocean* (1953), and Carl Ortwin Sauer, *The Early Spanish Main* (1966).

Additional Bibliography

Castro Vega, Oscar. *Pedrarias Dávila, la ira de Dios.* Costa Rica, 1996.

Mena García, María del Carmen. *Pedrarias Dávila.* Sevilla: Universidad de Sevilla, 1992.

WILLIAM L. SHERMAN

ÁVILA CAMACHO, MANUEL (1897–1955).

Manuel Ávila Camacho (*b.* 24 April 1897; *d.* 13 October 1955), president of Mexico (1940–1946), remembered for his moderate leadership and for his consolidation and refinement of the achievements of his predecessor, Lázaro Cárdenas. His administration was crucial in the final transition from military to civilian political leadership, and in tempering government attitudes toward the Roman Catholic church after he declared himself a believer. He also moderated the nationalism and anti-Americanism of the Cárdenas administration, which had been symbolized by the 1938 nationalization of oil, and allied Mexico with the United States during World War II. As president Ávila Camacho reversed socialist tendencies in public education, repealing constitutional amendments stipulating adherence to that philosophy of education.

Ávila Camacho was born in Teziutlán, Puebla, the hometown of his lifelong friend, the notable labor leader Vicente Lombardo Toledano. (One source claims, however, that his birthplace was Martínez de la Torre, Veracruz.) He was largely raised by his mother, Eufrosina Camacho, and received some preparatory schooling and business training, but instead of continuing his education he joined the Constitutionalists under General Antonio Medina in 1914. He remained in the army as a career officer, serving his mentor, Lázaro Cárdenas, as chief of staff in 1920. Three years later he commanded the 79th Cavalry Regiment in Michoacán, where he opposed the rebellion of Adolfo de La Huerta. Promoted to brigadier general in 1929, he again fought under General Cárdenas against the Escobar rebellion, the last major uprising of disgruntled Revolutionary generals against the government. Between 1929 and 1934 he commanded several important military zones, and when Cárdenas reached the presidency in 1934, Ávila Camacho was appointed *oficial mayor* (executive officer) of the secretariat of national defense, after which he rose to subsecretary and, ultimately, in 1937, to secretary of that agency. He resigned his position 17 January 1939 to run for president on the government party ticket in a heated electoral campaign against Juan Andrew Almazán.

See also **Mexico: Since 1910.**

BIBLIOGRAPHY

Luis Medina, *Historia de la revolución mexicana,* vol. 20, *Del cárdenismo al avilacamachismo* (1978), and vol. 21, *Civilismo y modernización del autoritarismo* (1979).

Additional Bibliography

Buenfil Burgos, Rosa Nidia. *Argumentación y poder: La mística de la revolución mexicana rectificada.* Mexico City: Plaza y Valdés, 2004.

Krauze, Enrique. *El sexenio de Avila Camacho.* Mexico City: Clío, 1999.

Miller, Michael Nelson. *Red, White, and Green: The Maturing of Mexicanidad, 1940-1946.* El Paso: Texas Western Press, University of Texas at El Paso, 1998.

RODERIC AI CAMP

AVILÉS, GABRIEL (1735–1810). Gabriel Avilés (marqués de Avilés: *b.* 1735; *d.* 19 September 1810), viceroy of Peru (1801–1806). Like his predecessor, Ambrosio O'Higgins, Avilés served as captain-general of Chile (1795–1799) before his promotion to Peru, and also briefly as viceroy in Buenos Aires (1799–1801). Avilés played a prominent role in the repression of the Túpac Amaru rebellion (1780–1783), combining firmness as a military commander with denunciation of the social abuses and administrative corruption that had provoked the insurrection. Before his transfer to Chile—as field marshal and second marqués de Avilés—he served as governor of Callao.

During his vice-regency in Peru, Avilés promoted public health, repressed a conspiracy in Cuzco, and oversaw the incorporation into the viceroyalty of Mainas and Guayaquil (in present-day Ecuador). He remained in Peru for four years under his successor Abascal, but refused the offer of appointment as viceroy of the Río de la Plata following the May 1810 revolution. Shortly thereafter he left Lima for Spain, but died in Valparaíso, Chile.

See also **Peru: From the Conquest through Independence.**

BIBLIOGRAPHY

Carlos Alberto Romero, ed., *Memoria del virrey del Perú, marqués de Avilés* (1901).

Additional Bibliography

Mariluz Urquijo, José María. *El Virreinato del Río de la Plata en la época del marqués de Avilés (1799-1801).* Buenos Aires: Academia Nacional de la Historia, 1964.

JOHN R. FISHER

AVIO. Avio, a form of credit and investment used in mining, but also employed in other forms of economic activity. In mining, the *aviador* (financier), who supplied the *avios,* furnished mine owners with cash, mercury, salt, and magistral (crushed copper pyrites) for the general purposes of mining or refining silver. When mine owners were unable to repay these debts because of floods, lack of labor, or exhaustion of veins, *aviadores* frequently acquired ownership of the enterprise. In the south of New Spain, merchants used *avios* to lend money to aspiring Alcalde Mayor candidates who needed substantial resources to purchase the post. In order to repay the loan, the *alcalde* or his lieutenant would force the indigenous people to purchase mules or luxury commodities for which they had to pay by producing cochineal and cotton.

See also **Mining: Colonial Spanish America.**

BIBLIOGRAPHY

Two sources on the *avios* in mining are Peter Bakewell, *Silver Mining and Society in Colonial Mexico-Zacatecas* (1971), and David Brading, *Miners and Merchants in Bourbon Mexico (1763–1810)* (1971). Brian Hamnett's *Politics and Trade in Southern Mexico, 1750–1821* (1971) has a thorough discussion of the system of *avios* and *repartamiento* of merchandise.

Additional Bibliography

Hoberman, Louisa Schell. *Mexico's Merchant Elite, 1590-1660: Silver, State, and Society.* Durham: Duke University Press, 1991.

EDITH COUTURIER

AXAYACATL (c. 1449–1481).

Axayacatl (*b.* ca. 1449; *d.* 1481), Aztec emperor from 1468/69–1481. The sixth Mexica Tlatoani (a "speaker" or ruler), Axayacatl (Watery Visage) was the grandson of two previous rulers: Motecuhzoma I on his mother's side, and Itzcoatl on his father's side. According to one native history, he became ruler at age nineteen. His short reign was devoted to military campaigns. To the expanding Aztec empire he added Toluca, Malinalco, and other Matlatzinca polities west of the Mexica capital of Tenochtitlán; he also subdued the Tuxpan area on the Gulf coast. In 1473 a dispute between Axayacatl and his sister's husband Moquihuix, ruler of Tlatelolco, Tenochtitlán's neighbor to the north, led to Tlatelolco's military defeat. In 1478 Axayacatl led a disastrous campaign against the Tarascans in Michoacán; native histories state that all but 200 of Axayacatl's 20,000 or more soldiers perished in the worst Mexica defeat until the Spanish conquest. Axayacatl was succeeded by his brother, Tizoc. Axayacatl's son, Motecuhzoma II (1466–1520), was ruling when Cortés invaded Mexico.

See also **Aztecs.**

BIBLIOGRAPHY

Diego Durán, *The Aztecs: The History of the Indies of New Spain,* translated by Doris Heyden and Fernando Horcasitas (1964).

Burr Cartwright Brundage, *A Rain of Darts: The Mexica Aztecs* (1972).

Nigel Davies, *The Aztecs: A History* (1980).

Additional Bibliography

Evans, Susan Toby. *Ancient Mexico & Central America: Archaeology and Culture History.* London: Thames & Hudson, 2004.

León Portilla, Miguel. *Fifteen Poets of the Aztec World.* Norman: University of Oklahoma Press, 1992.

LOUISE M. BURKHART

AYACUCHO.

Ayacucho, also known as Huamanga, the principal city (1981 population, 68,535) and capital of the department of the same name (1981 population, 523,821) in south-central highland Peru. Founded by Francisco Pizarro on 9 January 1539 as San Juan de la Frontera, it was moved several miles to its present site on 25 April 1540 by Alonso de Alvarado. It is located about 9,025 feet above sea level on a small plain in an intermountain valley about 224 miles southeast of Lima. During the colonial period Ayacucho became a significant administrative center for the region, a way station on the major route from Lima to Cuzco almost equidistant from both cities, and the residence of miners from neighboring Huancavelica and of local landowners.

On 9 December 1824, the nearby plain of Quinua was the site of the Battle of Ayacucho, which ensured the independence of South America from Spanish control. The city then entered an extended period of decline due to its isolation and limited natural resources, especially water. A railroad intended to link Ayacucho with central Peru and commemorate the centennial of the 1824 battle terminated at Huancavelica. The reopening of the colonial University of San Cristóbal de Huamanga (1677–1886) in 1959 and the completion of an all-weather highway to the coast near Pisco in 1968 revitalized the city. From 1961 to 1972 the population grew from 21,465 to 34,706, but the department remained one of the poorest in the country. In response to the activities of the Shining Path, an insurgent group that originated at Ayacucho in 1980, the city and most of the department were under nearly continuous military control after late 1982. The combination of insurgent activity and military presence contributed to high levels of violence, repression, and forced migration. However, since the late 1990s, with the defeat of most guerrilla forces, there has been much less violence in Ayacucho.

See also **Peru, Revolutionary Movements: Shining Path.**

BIBLIOGRAPHY

Cox, Mark R. *Pachaticray (El mundo al revés): Testimonios y ensayos sobre la violencia política y la cultura peruana desde 1980.* Jesús María, Lima: Editorial San Marcos, 2004.

Degregor, Carlos Iván, *Ayacucho 1969–1979: El surgimiento de Sendero Luminoso* (1900).

Erauso, Catalina de. *Historia de la Monja Alférez, Catalina de Erauso, escrita por ella misma.* Edited by Angel Esteban. Madrid: Cátedra, 2002.

Fowler, Luis R. *Monografía histórico-geográfica del Departamento de Ayacucho* (1924).

Guamán Poma de Ayala, Felipe. *Nueva crónica y buen gobierno.* 3 vols. Edited by John Murra, Rolena Adorno, and Jorge L. Urioste. Madrid: Historia 16, 1987.

Instituto Nacional De Estadística, *Censos nacionales: VIII de población, III de vivienda, 12 de julio de 1981: Departamento de Ayacucho,* vol. 1 (1983).

Sala i Vila, Núria. *Selva y Andes: Ayacucho (1780–1929) historia de una región en la encrucijada.* Madrid: Consejo Superior de Investigaciones Científicas, Instituto de Historia, 2001.

Stern, Steve J. *Peru's Indian Peoples and the Challenge of Spanish Conquest Huamanga to 1640.* Madison: University of Wisconsin Press, 1982.

DAVID SCOTT PALMER

AYACUCHO, BATTLE OF.

Battle of Ayacucho, the final battle of the Wars of Independence, which took place at the hacienda Ayacucho, near the city of Huamanga (later renamed Ayacucho), Peru, on 9 December 1824. Since Simón Bolívar had been notified by the Colombian government that he could no longer command a Peruvian army, he appointed the thirty-two-year-old Bolivian general Antonio José de Sucre to lead the liberation army. Although the royalists outnumbered their opponents by more than two to one, possessed superior artillery, and occupied the strategic heights overlooking the plains, Sucre was able to rally his forces with a desperate calvary charge that routed the enemy and captured the Spanish commander, General José de La Serna. The royalists suffered 1,400 dead and 700 wounded, while total casualties on the patriot side amounted to 900. That evening all royalist forces in the sierra surrendered, followed shortly thereafter by those in Lima. Although a diehard Spanish force managed to hold out in the fortress at Callao until January 1826, Spanish power in South America was ended after more than three centuries of Spanish rule.

See also **Wars of Independence, South America.**

BIBLIOGRAPHY

Timothy E. Anna, *The Fall of Royal Government in Peru* (1979).

Additional Bibliography

Fisher, John Robert. *Bourbon Peru, 1750-1824.* Liverpool: Liverpool University Press, 2003.

Mendizábal, Francisco Javier de. *Guerra de la América del Sur, 1809-1824.* Buenos Aires: Academia Nacional de la Historia, 1997.

PETER F. KLARÉN

AYACUCHO, MARSHALS OF. *See* **Marshals of Ayacucho.**

AYALA, ELIGIO

(1880–1930). Eligio Ayala (*b.* 1880; *d.* 24 October 1930), president of Paraguay (1924–1928) and educator. Born in Mbuyapey of humble parents, Ayala displayed considerable talent at an early age and rose rapidly in the ranks of the Partido Liberal. In the 1890s, he moved to Asunción, where he attended the Colegio Nacional and began teaching in 1904, giving courses in philosophy, civics, psychology, and logic. In 1908 he received a doctorate in law from the university.

At this time, Ayala embarked on a political career. He held office as attorney for the indigent, civil judge, and congressional deputy. After participating in the 1904 and 1911 revolutions as a Liberal stalwart, he left Paraguay and spent the next eight years in Europe.

Upon his return after World War I, Ayala dedicated himself to teaching and journalism. He regained his old congressional seat and in 1920 was appointed finance minister by President Manuel Gondra. Ayala quickly gained a reputation for honesty and level-headedness. Eschewing the jingoism of many Liberals, he took a stand in favor of negotiations with Bolivia over the disputed Chaco Region.

After serving as provisional president of Paraguay in 1923, he was elected to that office one year later. His administration brought the first spate of internal peace in more than twenty years. Bent on reforming the nation's archaic fiscal system, Ayala balanced the national budget, stabilized the currency, and paid off a considerable portion of the government's debt. With Paraguay's renewed access to international credit, Ayala purchased munitions for his fledgling army and two warships for the navy. His emphasis on the professionalization of the armed forces rescued the military from continued partisan strife and prepared it for the upcoming Chaco War, a conflict that Paraguay was unable to avoid after all. Indeed, in the last year of Ayala's administration there was a series of border incidents that overshadowed all the progress he had promoted.

In 1928 Ayala resumed the post of finance minister, this time in the government of his successor, José P. Guggiari. He also retained several key posts in the Partido Liberal. Two years later he was killed in Asunción, the victim of a tragic romantic involvement.

See also **Paraguay, Political Parties: Liberal Party.**

BIBLIOGRAPHY

William B. Parker, *Paraguayans of To-Day* (1921).

Carlos Zubizarreta, *Cien vidas paraguayas,* 2d ed. (1985), pp. 277–280; *The Cambridge History of Latin America,* vol. 5 (1986), pp. 475–496.

Additional Bibliography

Brugada, Arturo, and Leandro Prieto Yegros. *La Revolución de 1904.* Asunción: Editorial Cuadernos Republicanos, 1990.

Llano, Mariano. *Eligio Ayala: el milagro paraguayano.* Paraguay: Editora Ricor Grafic, 1998.

Viola, Alfredo. *Eligio Ayala: presidente constitucional, 1924-1928.* Asunción: Centro de Publicaciones de la Universidad Católica, 2002.

THOMAS L. WHIGHAM

AYALA, EUSEBIO (1874–1942).

Eusebio Ayala (*b.* 15 August 1874; *d.* 4 June 1942), intellectual, statesman, provisional president (1921–1923), and president of Paraguay (1932–1936). Ayala studied law and wrote essays on history, political economy, and international law. In 1900, he obtained his law degree at the National University in Asunción, subsequently teaching in various disciplines. As a diplomat, he displayed a profound knowledge of the major boundary dispute that existed with Bolivia. On 20 August 1920, Ayala was appointed to President Manuel Gondra's cabinet, but because of factional fighting, Gondra was forced to resign. Ayala replaced him in November 1921 as provisional president, only to resign in 1923 in the middle of a civil war. He was elected president in 1932, leading Paraguay through the Chaco War against neighboring Bolivia. After the defeat of the Bolivians, Ayala's government was toppled on 17 February 1936 by a military coup that had civilian support. In spite of his overthrow, Ayala has been regarded as one of the most capable national leaders of his generation.

See also **Chaco War.**

BIBLIOGRAPHY

Paul H. Lewis, *Paraguay Under Stroessner* (1980).

Riordan Roett and Richard Scott Sacks, *Paraguay: The Personalist Legacy* (1991).

Additional Bibliography

Llano, Mariano. *Eusebio Ayala: Ante su patria.* Paraguay: AGR Servicios Gráficos, 2005.

Peña Villamil, Manuel. *Eusebio Ayala y su tiempo.* Paraguay: M. Peña Villamil, 1993.

MIGUEL A. GATTI

AYALA, JOSÉ DE LA CRUZ (1854–1892).

José de la Cruz Ayala (*b.* 1854; *d.* 29 January 1892), Paraguayan politician, journalist, and social critic. Better known by his pen name "Alon," Ayala was a Liberal firebrand who helped crystallize resistance to the Bernardino Caballero and Patricio Escobar governments in the 1880s. Born in the interior town of Mbuyapey, Ayala witnessed the cruelties of Paraguayan politics as a child, when his father and older brother were assassinated in his presence. When he arrived in Asunción in 1877, he was already very much a confirmed rebel. He entered the Colegio Nacional, where he studied the Greek and Roman classics and received a bachelor's degree in 1882.

While at the *colegio,* Ayala cemented his friendship with the young historian Cecilio Báez, who encouraged him to enter the then booming field of journalism. Following Báez's suggestion, he wrote for several newspapers, including *El Heraldo* and *La Democracia.* His editorial pieces, published pseudonymously, attacked the government's policy of selling public lands to foreign entrepreneurs. More generally, he denounced the corruption that had seeped into every level of the Paraguayan body politic. Deeply offended by Ayala's stinging criticisms, President Caballero had him drafted and sent to an isolated army outpost in the Chaco. Ayala managed to escape and, from hiding, smuggled out a series of letters (tellingly entitled *Cartas del infierno*), which appeared in opposition dailies, vexing Caballero and Escobar still further. In 1891 Ayala momentarily came out of hiding to join the Liberals in a civil war, but he was forced to escape to Argentina, where he died one year later.

BIBLIOGRAPHY

Harris G. Warren, *Rebirth of the Paraguayan Republic: The First Colorado Era, 1878–1904* (1985), pp. 64, 73, 81.

Carlos Zubizarreta, *Cien vidas paraguayas,* 2d ed. (1985), pp. 205–207.

Additional Bibliography

Bordón, F. Arturo. *La vida romántica de Alón, José de la Cruz Ayala, mártir de la democracia paraguaya.* Asunción, 1966.

THOMAS L. WHIGHAM

AYCINENA, JUAN FERMÍN DE (1729–1796).

Juan Fermín de Aycinena (*b.* 7 July 1729; *d.* 3 April 1796), first *marqués* of Aycinena. He has been called the most powerful man in the history of Central America. Born in Siga, Navarra, in July 1729, he immigrated to New Spain in 1748 and began his commercial career as a mule runner, principally in Oaxaca, before arriving in Santiago de Guatemala (today Antigua) in 1753 or 1754. Subsequently he became the leading indigo exporter, wholesale merchant, and creditor in the Kingdom of Guatemala, and perhaps its only millionaire. He acquired several estates, especially Salvadoran indigo plantations, many through foreclosure. He was among the leading *trasladistas,* or supporters of the transfer of the capital city after 1773 to Guatemala City, and a generous benefactor of church and state. In 1783 he acquired the only Castilian title in late colonial Central America. In 1794 he became the first prior of the Consulado de Comercio of Guatemala City. Married three times, his numerous offspring became the center of the oligarchy in late colonial and early republican Central America.

See also **Guatemala.**

BIBLIOGRAPHY

Diana Balmori, Stuart F. Voss, and Miles L. Wortman, *Notable Family Networks in Latin America* (1984), pp. 61–69.

Ralph Lee Woodward, *Central America: A Nation Divided,* 2d ed. (1985), pp. 74–75.

Additional Bibliography

Brown, Richmond F. *Juan Fermín de Aycinena: Central American Colonial Entrepreneur, 1729-1796.* Norman: University of Oklahoma Press, 1997.

RICHMOND F. BROWN

AYCINENA, MARIANO DE (1789–1855).

Mariano de Aycinena (*b.* 15 September 1789; *d.* 22 January 1855), chief of state of Guatemala (1827–1829). Aycinena was a leading figure in Central American independence. A younger son of Juan Fermín de Aycinena, first marquis of Aycinena, he was a patriarch of Guatemala's most prominent and powerful family in the late colonial and early republican era. As *síndico* (attorney general) of the *ayuntamiento* of Guatemala City, he helped lead the movement for independence. Afterward he promoted the annexation of Central America to the Mexican empire of Agustín de Iturbide, with whom he had corresponded prior to independence. He became a leader of Central American conservatives in the early republic and an officer of the Consulado de Comercio while managing his family's international trading firm. He was involved in the negotiations that resulted in a British loan to Central America in 1824, the proceeds of which some contemporary politicians and later historians accused him of appropriating.

As chief of state of Guatemala during the presidency of Manuel José Arce, Aycinena was a central figure of the civil war that disrupted the United Provinces of Central America from 1826 to 1829. Aycinena's faction was ultimately defeated by the forces of the Honduran general and unionist hero Francisco Morazán. Exiled after the war, he returned to Guatemala in the late 1830s and lived there for the rest of his life. Although not a prominent participant in Guatemalan government during that time, he enjoyed informal influence through his family, whose members dominated government and society in the Conservative era (1838–1871).

See also **Guatemala.**

BIBLIOGRAPHY

Modern assessments of Aycinena's role in the era of independence are in Mariano Rodríguez, *The Cádiz Experiment in Central America, 1808 to 1826* (1978); and Miles Wortman, *Government and Society in Central America, 1680–1840* (1982). Guatemalan historian Ramón Salazar provides a bitter view in his *Hombres de la independencia* (1899).

RICHMOND F. BROWN

AYCINENA, PEDRO DE (1802–1897).

Pedro de Aycinena (*b.* 19 October 1802; *d.* 14 March 1897), Guatemalan minister of foreign relations (1854–1871) and interim president of Guatemala (1865). Aycinena was a principal minister and adviser to the Conservative regimes of Rafael Carrera (1851–1865) and Vicente Cerna (1865–1871). Son of Vicente Aycinena, second *marqués*

of Aycinena, younger brother of Juan José de Aycinena, and nephew of Mariano de Aycinena, he belonged to one of Guatemala's most prominent families. In 1836 he married his first cousin, Dolores Aycinena y Micheo, daughter of José de Aycinena, Spanish Councilor of State and the Indies under Ferdinand VII. Their son Juan Fermín de Aycinena Aycinena was the eminent Guatemalan poet.

Graduating in civil and canon law from the University of San Carlos in 1821, Aycinena joined the Colegio de Abogados in 1823. He spent much of the 1820s in Europe representing his family's merchant house and returned to Guatemala to manage his family's affairs in the 1830s, following the family elders' expulsion after the civil war of 1826–1829. In the 1840s, with the return to Conservative rule in Guatemala (and most of his brethren to the country), he became involved in government. As foreign minister, he negotiated the controversial Wyke-Aycinena Treaty of 1859, which acknowledged British rights to Belize. He also negotiated Spanish recognition of Guatemalan independence in 1863. He was briefly exiled following the Liberal Revolution of 1871 and returned to pursue law and commerce until his death in 1897, the last of the Guatemalan *serviles* (conservatives).

See also **Guatemala.**

BIBLIOGRAPHY

Diana Balmori, Stuart F. Voss, and Miles L. Wortman, *Notable Family Networks in Latin America* (1984), pp. 61–69. Further details may be found in Roberto Zeceña Flores, "Biografías de Ex-Ministros de Relaciones Exteriores," in *Diplomacia y sociedad* (Guatemala City) 3 and 4 (November–December 1969): 18–19, and Ramiro Ordóñez Jonoma, "La Familia Varón de Berrieza," in *Revista de la Academia Guatemalteca de Estudios Genealógicos, Heráldicos e Históricos* 9 (1987): 644–645.

RICHMOND F. BROWN

AYCINENA PIÑOL, JUAN JOSÉ DE

(1792–1865). Juan José de Aycinena Piñol (*b.* 29 August 1792; *d.* 17 February 1865), third marquis of Aycinena and titular bishop of Trajanópolis (1859). Juan José de Aycinena was the dominant figure of the conservative political faction in nineteenth-century Central America and the Guatemalan Republic, which he helped found. Born in Antigua Guatemala to a family of immense wealth and power, Aycinena trained as an attorney before entering the priesthood in 1817. Although a cleric, he was involved in virtually every area of Guatemalan public life. As a member of the Economic Society, he promoted the development of a Central American silk industry. Most important, he operated in the midst of Central American politics. A promoter of Central American independence from Spain (1821) and annexation to the Mexican Empire (1821–1823), Aycinena was sent into exile in the United States for most of the 1830s with his political faction's (and family's) defeat in the Central American civil war of 1827–1829.

A forceful advocate of constitutional monarchy and of a pronounced secular role for the Catholic church, Aycinena is perhaps best known for a series of political tracts written in exile in the early 1830s. The *Toros amarillos* (yellow-paged polemics) called for the dissolution of the United Provinces of Central America in the name of isthmian peace. Returning to Guatemala in 1837, Aycinena played a central role in the formal breakup of the United Provinces through his newspaper, *El Observador,* and as a delegate to the federal congress.

With the collapse of the federation, Aycinena exercised extraordinary power as Guatemala's minister of government, justice, foreign affairs, and ecclesiastical affairs (1842–1844). Subsequently, as vice president of Guatemala's Chamber of Representatives (1851–1865), as a councillor of state (1856–1865), and especially as rector of the University of San Carlos (1840–1854; 1859–1865), Aycinena helped set the tone of politics and society under Guatemalan strongman José Rafael Carrera (1844–1849; 1851–1865). His biographer, David L. Chandler, asserts, no "single individual [was] more responsible ... for the outlines of society and government that subsequently took shape in Guatemala. ... Father Aycinena became the Conservative prophet of a new era."

See also **Guatemala.**

BIBLIOGRAPHY

David L. Chandler, "Peace Through Disunion: Father Juan José de Aycinena and the Fall of the Central American Federation," in *The Americas* 46 (October 1989): 137–157; and *Juan José de Aycinena: Idealista conservador de la Guatemala del siglo XIX,* translated by Victoria Vázquez, Marina Vázquez, and Lucia Robelo Pereira (1989).

Additional Bibliography

Chandler, David Lee. *Juan José de Aycinena: idealista conservador de la Guatemala del siglo XIX.* Antigua, Guatemala: Centro de Investigaciones Regionales de Mesoamerica, 1988.

RICHMOND F. BROWN

AYLLU. Ayllu, the basic social unit in modern Andean society. An *ayllu* today is a community that consists of a number of unrelated extended families living in a specified area and following common rules of crop rotation under relatively informal leadership. In ancient times there existed a social unit that basically corresponds to the modern *ayllu,* but its exact nature is unclear due to confusion and casualness of Quechua usage in the Spanish chronicles.

Modern anthropologists have often assumed that *ayllus* were clan groups, but there is no unequivocal evidence to prove this assertion. In the Spanish chronicles, the word *ayllu* was used in connection with several different concepts that can refer to lineages of the royal Incas, a moiety, or the community groups referred to above. As John Rowe points out in his classic article on Inca culture, in Quechua the word *ayllu* seems to be a generic term for "kin group," and its specific reference was probably clarified by the context. Moreover, the modern definition of *ayllu,* and what evidence there is for defining the ancient *ayllu,* do not conform to the anthropological definition of clan, particularly in the respect that the *ayllu* seems to lack totemic association with any animal or plant. *Ayllus* were normally named for a person or place.

Under Inca rule, the *ayllu* is defined by Rowe as a kin group with theoretical endogamy, with descent in the male line, and lacking totemism. The *ayllu* owned a specific territory, and each member couple cultivated what they needed for their support. Each year the family plots or fields were redistributed to ensure the proper rotation of crops and that the needs of each family were met. The relationship between the *ayllu* and the *panaca*, a similar social construction, needs to be worked out.

See also **Calpulli; Indigenous Peoples.**

BIBLIOGRAPHY

The best discussion of the meaning of *ayllu* in Inca times is in John H. Rowe, "Inca Culture at the Time of the Spanish Conquest," in *Handbook of South American Indians,* vol. 2 (1946), pp. 183–330. Modern *ayllus* are discussed by Bernard Mishkin, "The Contemporary Quechua," and Harry Tschopik, Jr., "The Aymara," in *Handbook of South American Indians,* vol. 2 (1946), pp. 411–470 and pp. 501–574, respectively.

Adrián Ambía, Abel. *El ayllu en el Perú actual: con un estudio de las normas tradicionales de la comunidad campesina de Amaru, Calca, Cusco.* Lima: Ediciones PUKARA, 1989.

Burga, Manuel. *Nacimiento de una utopía: Muerte y resurrección de los incas.* 2nd Edition. Lima: Universidad Nacional Mayor de San Marcos; Universidad de Guadalajara, 2005.

Rostworowski de Diez Canseco, María. *Historia del Tahuantinsuyu.* 2nd Edition. Lima: IEP, Instituto de Estudios Peruanos, 1999.

GORDON F. MCEWAN

AYLWIN AZÓCAR, PATRICIO (1918–).

Patricio Aylwin Azócar (*b.* 26 November 1918), leader of the Christian Democratic Party (PDC) and president of Chile (1990–1994). One of the original founders of the PDC, he served as the head of the National Falange as well as of the party itself. As the leader of the PDC's more conservative wing, the *oficialistas,* and later, as head of the entire party, he doubted the Allende government's (1970–1973) commitment to respect the nation's constitution. Aylwin increasingly came to believe that President Salvador Allende could not be trusted and, following last-minute negotiations, demanded that the president appoint only military men to his cabinet as proof of his honest intent. When Allende complied only partially, Aylwin apparently sided with the pro-coup forces, believing that the military would restore democracy to the nation.

Following Allende's overthrow in 1973, Aylwin, particularly after the death of Eduardo Frei, slowly emerged as the PDC's most viable spokesman. As the head of Chile's most popular party and one of the leaders of the anti-Pinochet forces, Aylwin became a leader around whom the various diverse parties could unite. In 1989 he managed to forge a coalition of seventeen disparate elements, defeat two opponents, and win the presidency with 55 percent of the vote.

Following his election, Aylwin created a coalition government in an attempt to retain widespread public support. His economic programs consisted of attempting to build on the momentum generated by the Pinochet administration while implementing new laws, and passing new taxes, to protect the working class.

Aylwin's principal problem following his election, as well as before it, was General Augusto Pinochet. The former dictator, although no longer president, still controlled the army. He was intent, moreover, on ensuring that the newly elected government would not punish the armed forces for their activities in overturning Allende or in the succeeding years. Aylwin, however, had to attempt to heal the nation while bringing to justice those who had committed abuses. Aylwin's election marked the return of Chile to its democratic traditions. Since leaving office, Aylwin has focused on fighting poverty. He proposed a UN summit on the subject, which was held in Copenhagen during 1995. Currently, he works as president of the Corporation for Democracy and Justice, a nongovernmental organization that focuses on the elimination of poverty and promoting honest government.

See also **Allende Gossens, Salvador; Chile, Political Parties: Christian Democratic Party (PDC); Frei Montalva, Eduardo; Pinochet Ugarte, Augusto.**

BIBLIOGRAPHY

Paul E. Sigmund, *The Overthrow of Allende and the Politics of Chile, 1964–1976* (1977), 217–218, 220, 223.

Julio Faúndez, *Marxism and Democracy in Chile: From 1932 to the Fall of Allende* (1988), 235.

Additional Bibliography

Aylwin, Patricio, Margarita Serrano, and Ascanio Cavallo. *El poder de la paradoja: 14 lecciones políticas de la vida de Patricio Aylwin.* Santiago de Chile: Grupo Editorial Norma, 2006.

WILLIAM F. SATER

AYMARA. Between approximately 1200 and 1500, at least twelve distinct Aymara-speaking kingdoms dominated the area of the Andean Altiplano (high plateau) between Cuzco in present-day Peru and Potosí in present-day Bolivia. The origins of the Aymara language are not clear, but linguist Alfredo Torero believes that it may have developed in the area of Huari (Wari) culture in the central highlands of Peru. Although the Aymara actually constituted one cultural and linguistic group, there was often fierce competition among them, and consequently the kingdoms were well fortified militarily.

The most basic social and economic unit among the Aymara was the extended family, which in turn belonged to larger groups known as *ayllus*. An *ayllu* is generally understood to be a group of people who hold land in common and who trace their origins to one spiritual or legendary ancestor.

Above the *ayllu* level Aymara society had a dualistic structure that divided human communities into complementary halves. Each kingdom, as well as each village or settlement, was composed of two moieties, or *parcialidades:* a superior one, usually called *hanansaya,* and one of inferior status known as *hurinsaya*. This political division reflected a conception of the universe based on the unity of halves, or opposites. This dualism was symbolized by the male/female relation, and features of the physical world (rocks, mountains, bodies of water) were often conceived of as either male or female.

Each Aymara kingdom had two *kurakas,* or chiefs, one for each *parcialidad;* and on the district and village levels there were usually also leaders for both *hurinsaya* and *hanansaya*. *Kurakas* were responsible for allocating lands to *ayllu* members, ensuring that the proper religious rites were performed, and periodically redistributing some of the community's wealth. In return for performing these functions, *kurakas,* who generally had access to considerably more land than did commoners, had their fields tilled by *ayllu* members and received various other types of labor service as well. This labor for the leaders was viewed as a form of reciprocity by the common people for the generosity the *kurakas* demonstrated in redistributing the society's surplus.

The anthropologist John Murra was among the first scholars to show how agricultural "archipelagos" were used by the Aymara in order to make the best of the Andean region's varied geography. In this "vertical" system, agricultural lands with different altitudes and ecologies were utilized to produce a variety of crops. Most Aymara communities had their primary settlements on the sides of highland valleys or on the *altiplano,* where they were able to graze herds of llamas and alpacas, exploit salt deposits, and grow potatoes and quinoa. Lands in lower valleys provided vegetables, maize, coca leaf, cotton, tropical fruits, and vegetables.

It was through their *ayllus* that families obtained products grown in lowland zones that were more than several hours' walk from their base communities. *Ayllu*-held lands in distant regions were farmed by agricultural colonists (*mitimaes, llacturuna*) who were sent by the highland leaders for this purpose. Most ethnohistorians believe that because of the system of agricultural colonies the Aymara economy was able to function without markets or a medium of exchange. Products from lowland areas most likely were redistributed to community members by the *ayllu* leaders as a form of largesse.

After about 1440, the Inca—a Quechua-speaking ethnic group based in the Cuzco area—began to expand southward and to incorporate the Aymara kingdoms into their state system. The Aymara responded in a variety of ways to the invasions. Kingdoms in the area of Lake Titicaca eventually rose in revolt against increasing Inca demands for land and labor. Further south, Aymara leaders seem to have more readily cooperated with the invaders in return for certain concessions. For instance, the *kurakas* of the Charcas, Caracaras, Chuis, and Chichas were feasted by the Inca leaders, showered with gifts, and made officers in their armies. In general, the main burdens of Inca rule probably fell on the common people, who now, in addition to working the lands of their own *kurakas,* also had to do the same for the Inca leaders and spiritual cults.

The Inca imperial approach of building on preexisting Andean social and political institutions, and the flexibility of the Aymara lords in cooperating with the new state, helped Aymara culture survive to experience the next invasion: that of the Spanish, which began in 1532. During the Conquest and Spanish colonial period Aymara people used a variety of strategies, ranging from revolt to alliances with the colonialists to skillful use of the colonial legal system, in order to survive domination and maintain fundamental aspects of their culture. Since political independence from Spain in 1825 the Aymara have continued as a distinct cultural and linguistic group despite attacks on their communal organizations and system of land tenure, the racism of the dominant mestizo society, and their economic exploitation as peasants and poorly paid workers.

According to the 2001 census, approximately one-third of the population of Bolivia continues to speak Aymara. Although throughout the nineteenth century and well into the twentieth most Aymara people were peasant farmers, now many are urban and have diverse occupations. There are Aymara industrial workers, truck drivers, business people, intellectuals, and professionals. The 2005 election of Evo Morales to the presidency, the Aymara leader of the *Movement Toward Socialism / Movimiento al Socialismo* (MAS), garnered international attention for both Bolivia and indigenous movements. Today Aymara political and cultural organizations have links with other Native American rights groups in Bolivia and other countries.

See also **Art: Pre-Columbian Art of South America; Indigenous Peoples; Tiwanaku.**

BIBLIOGRAPHY

John V. Murra, "An Aymara Kingdom in 1567," in *Ethnohistory* 15, no. 2 (1968): 115–151, and *Formaciones económicas y políticas del mundo andino* (1975).

Nathan Wachtel, *The Vision of the Vanquished* (1977).

Thérèse Bouysse-Cassagne, "L'espace aymara: *Urco* et *uma*," in *Annales*, 33, nos. 5–6 (1978): 1057–1080.

Martha J. Hardman, ed., *The Aymara Language in Its Social and Cultural Context* (1981).

Franklin Pease, "The Formation of Tawantinsuyu: Mechanisms of Colonization and Relationship with Ethnic Groups," in *The Inca and Aztec States, 1400–1800,* edited by George A. Collier, Renato I. Rosaldo, and John D. Wirth (1982), pp. 172–198.

John V. Murra, "The Limits and Limitations of the 'Vertical Archipelago' in the Andes," in *Andean Ecology and Civilization: An Interdisciplinary Perspective on Andean Ecological Complementarity,* edited by Shozo Masuda, Izumi Shimada, and Craig Morris (1985).

Xavier Albo, ed., *Raíces de América: El mundo Aymara* (1988).

Additional Bibliography

Ricardo Díaz, *Evo: Rebeldía de la coca* (2004).

ANN ZULAWSKI

AYMARA (LANGUAGE).

The Aymara people are a transnational ethnic group in South America, currently comprising farming and herding communities located around Lake Titicaca, on the altiplano of Peru, Bolivia, and Chile. They are distinguished by speaking the language of the same name, Aymara, and they call themselves the Aymara Nation.

The Spanish gave the name *Aymara* to the language spoken by this group, which was earlier called the "language of the *qollas*" (the language of the altiplano people). Aymara was the name of one of the pre-Inca cultures living on the altiplano, and after 1559 the word was attributed to one of the more widespread languages in the area but spoken by ethnic groups other than the Aymara. During their empire, the Incas called these ethnic groups the *qollas*, which is why the province they lived in was called the Qollasuyu. The first grammar and dictionary of the Aymara language, *Vocabulario de la Lengua Aymara,* was published in 1612 by Jesuit priest Ludovico Bertonio, who wrote it using Spanish orthography based on his research in Chuchito, Juli, in Puno, Peru. This work is fundamental for any student of the Aymara language.

The Aymara people are of pre-Hispanic origin; the oldest Aymara culture is Tiwanaku (in Aymara, *Taypi qala,* or "central stone," according to chronicler Bernabé Cobo) dating from 2000 BCE. Various Aymara-speaking nations existed in the same age as the Incas and were gradually integrated into the Inca Empire or Tawantinsuyu, forming the province of Qollasuyu. The last Aymara nation to be incorporated into the Tawantinsuyu was the Lupaca.

The pre-Hispanic civilizations of the Andes raised llama and alpaca, which provided them with meat and wool and served as beasts of burden. They were civilizations that domesticated the potato, oca, mashua, olluco, and quinua, and always maintained contact with the inter-Andean valleys to obtain corn, yucca, sweet potato, and coca.

Tiwanaku was abandoned for years. Thousands of its stones were used to build churches and buildings in neighboring towns. In the early twentieth century, Arthur Posnanski came to Bolivia and drew world attention to these archeological remains, especially to the gate renowned for its depiction of a mythical being holding two scepters. This culture, based on farming and raising livestock in the high Andean altitude, began to collapse as a result of great ecological changes, possibly freezes, droughts, or famines.

In July 1538, Pizarro decided to conquer the fourth *suyu* or Inca province. He sent an expedition of two hundred Spanish soldiers and five thousand indigenous people to the altiplano. The Lupaca were able to resist, but other opposing groups gradually yielded. Pizarro governed the new territories through the cities and the "residents," to whom he granted lands and Indians. Thus, the city of Chuquisaca (Charcas) was founded in December 1538. The rich mines of Potosí were not discovered until 1545 and by 1561 there were three Spanish cities in the area, Chuquisaca, Porco, and Potosí. La Paz was founded in 1548 (with forty-two residents, all Spanish *encomenderos*).

Under Spanish rule, thousands of Aymara died, especially in the Potosí mines. The Aymara participated in the struggle for independence, particularly in the uprising of Tupaj Katari. In 1824, when independence was won at the battle of Ayacucho, the Aymara people were located within Peruvian territory, in an area called Alto Peru. In 1825, however, Alto Peru became the independent republic of Bolivia and the Aymara people were thus divided, some remaining in Peru and a larger portion in Bolivia.

In 1870, when Chile won the war of the Pacific, it seized territory that had mainly been inhabited by the Aymara from both Bolivia and Peru. Thus in the early twenty-first century these people live in three different countries. There are currently 1,600,000 Aymara speakers, and they share a strong ethnic identity. The 1993 Peru census and the 1992 Bolivia and Chile censuses counted 1,237,658 Bolivian Aymara, 296,465 Peruvian Aymara, and 48,477 Chilean Aymara.

See also **Precontact History: Latin America in the Precontact Period; Quechua; Tiwanaku.**

BIBLIOGRAPHY

Bertonio, Ludovico. *Vocabulario de la Lengua Aymara.* Cochabamba, Bolivia: Centro de Estudios de la Realidad Económica y Social, 1984.

CARMEN ESCALANTE

AYOLAS, JUAN DE (1539?–?). Juan de Ayolas (*b.* 1539; *d.* ?), Spanish explorer active in Argentina and Paraguay. Ayolas was born a Hidalgo in the Briviesca region of Spain. Thanks to his long-time friendship with Pedro de Mendoza, he received a commission as *mayordomo* when the latter organized an expedition to explore the basin of the Río de la Plata in the early 1530s.

The voyage from Spain was not without its problems. Ayolas discovered a plot against Mendoza by dissident Spaniards while the small fleet was off the Brazilian coast. His quick action saved the adelantado and placed Ayolas in a good position to play a major role in the exploration of the Plata.

After the founding of Buenos Aires in 1536, Mendoza chose his friend to lead a new expedition inland to find a viable route to the silver districts of Upper Peru (what he optimistically termed the *Sierra de la Plata*). Ayolas ascended the Río Paraná with three vessels and two hundred men. He received succor along the way from various groups of Guaraní Indians, especially in the vicinity of what would one day become the city of Asunción. Proceeding upriver from that point, he finally halted in February 1537 at a spot some 120 miles to the north. There he divided his men, leaving behind forty under the command of Domingo Martínez de Irala and setting out on foot with the remaining 160 to cross the inhospitable Chaco region to Peru.

What occurred next is not entirely clear and is based exclusively on the testimony of a converted Chané Indian boy named Gonzalo. According to this eyewitness, after many tribulations, Ayolas and his party actually reached the Andes. He left a number of Europeans at an improvised camp in the hill country and, ferrying a quantity of silver taken from the resident Incas, recrossed the Chaco to the Río Paraguay, where the exhausted Ayolas expected to find Martínez de Irala and the three vessels awaiting his return. Irala, however, had gone south after a year in order to find provisions and to repair his ships. While Ayolas pondered his next move, a large band of Payaguás invited the weary Spaniards to take refuge with them, and then, at a prearranged signal, fell upon them and killed them to a man. Only the boy Gonzalo escaped to report what he had seen to Irala. The latter campaigned hard against these same Payaguáes over the next few years, but he never recovered the bodies of his comrades.

See also **Explorers and Exploration: Spanish America.**

BIBLIOGRAPHY

Harris Gaylord Warren, *Paraguay: An Informal History* (1949), pp. 34–50.

Carlos Zubizarreta, *Cien vidas paraguayas*, 2d ed. (1985), pp. 21–23.

Additional Bibliography

Miranda Silva, Fidel. *Asunción fue fundada el 15 de agosto de 1536 por Juan de Ayolas: Trabajo de investigación bibliográfica*. Ciudad del Este, Paraguay: F. Miranda Silva, 2005.

                                    THOMAS L. WHIGHAM

AYORA CUEVA, ISIDRO (1879–1978).

Isidro Ayora Cueva (*b*. 31 August 1879; *d*. 22 March 1978), president of Ecuador (nonelected 1926–1929 and elected 1929–1931). Born in Loja, Ayora studied medicine in Quito, did postgraduate work in Berlin, and completed an internship in Dresden. After returning to Ecuador in 1909, he developed a private practice and taught obstetrics at Central University, where he accepted the post of director of maternity (1917). Elected deputy of Loja in 1916 and president of the cantonal council for 1924–1925, Ayora was appointed rector of Central University and director of the Civil Hospital of Quito in 1925. On 10 January 1926 he became a member of the provisional governing junta and minister of social welfare, labor, and agriculture. On 1 April 1926 he accepted the position of provisional president.

Ayora concluded an agreement with Princeton economist Edwin W. Kemmerer to head an advisory mission whose purpose was to propose solutions to the nation's financial problems. In October 1926 the mission drafted laws to modernize and strengthen Ecuadorian financial institutions and procedures to eliminate budget deficits. Ayora, with the backing of the military, was able to enact most of the sweeping reforms proposed by the Kemmerer Mission.

Ayora was elected to the presidency in 1929 but suffered increasing public criticism for his policies, many of them based on the recommendations of the Kemmerer Mission. Public dissatisfaction mounted as internal conditions deteriorated in response to disruptions in the world economy. Critics blamed the Ayora government for exacerbating the nation's problems. When popular discontent erupted in mass demonstrations in Quito, Ayora resigned on 24 August 1931. He returned to his medical practice and remained active in professional organizations and administrative positions.

See also **Ecuador: Since 1830.**

BIBLIOGRAPHY

Linda Alexander Rodríguez, *The Search for Public Policy: Regional Politics and Government Finances in Ecuador, 1830–1940* (1985), esp. pp. 131–133, 137–164.

Additional Bibliography

Coral Patiño, Héctor. *Isidro Ayora*. Quito: Abrapalabra Editores, 1995.

Febres Cordero, Francisco. *De Flores a flores y miel*. Quito: Ojo de Pez, 1996.

                            LINDA ALEXANDER RODRÍGUEZ

AZAR, HÉCTOR (1930–2000).

Héctor Azar (*b*. 17 October 1930, *d*. 11 May 2000), Mexican playwright who founded the Centro de Arte Dramático (CADAC, 1975), a respected theater school. Azar, born in Atlixco, Puebla, studied in the United States under the direction of Max Reinhardt at Actors' Studio. His first plays (both 1958), *La Apassionata* and *El alfarero*, depicted social problems from a stylized point of view. *Olímpica* (1962), his best-known work, and *Inmaculada* (1963) are poetic dramas that deal mainly with feminine frustration. His collection of short pieces, *Juegos de azar* (1973), includes a religious mystery play, *La seda mágica*, and a Renaissance farce, *Doña Belarda de Francia*. A more traditional drama, *Los muros vacíos* (1974), contrasts with his later experimental works, such as the farcical trilogy *Diálogos de la clase medium* (1979–1986) and a poetic drama that pays homage to the Mexican painter Rufino Tamayo, *Las alas sin sombra* (1980). His critical essays are collected in *Funciones teatrales* (1982).

See also **Theater.**

BIBLIOGRAPHY

María Del Carmen Millán, "Prólogo," in *Los juegos de Azar* (1973).

Jacquelin Eyring Bixler, "Zoon Theatrykon: Azar y la búsqueda teatral," *Texto crítico*, no. 10 (1978): 42–54.

Additional Bibliography

Alvarado, Luis F. "El discurso postmoderno en el texto dramático de Hector Azar." Ph.D. diss., University of Cincinnati, 1995.

GUILLERMO SCHMIDHUBER

AZARA, FÉLIX DE (1746–1821).

Félix de Azara (*b.* 18 May 1746; *d.* 20 October 1821), scientist and writer. Spanish military man and enlightened scientist, Azara spent twenty years (1781–1801) traveling throughout the viceroyalty of the Río de la Plata, gathering information about the area and conducting experiments. He was born in Aragon, and after studying philosophy at the University of Huesca, entered the Military Academy at Barcelona. Commissioned as *alférez* (ensign) in the Company of Engineers, he participated as an officer in the Algiers campaign of 1775. By 1781, with the rank of lieutenant colonel, Azara was in America to participate in the boundary commission charged with fixing the limits between the Spanish and Portuguese dominions in South America. Upon returning to Spain in 1802, Azara wrote scientific treatises as well as general descriptions of the area. Best known are *Descripción é historia del Paraguay y del Río de la Plata* (1847) and *Viajes por la América meridional* (1809).

See also **Science.**

BIBLIOGRAPHY

Enrique Udaondo, *Diccionario biográfico colonial argentino* (1945), pp. 122–123.

Additional Bibliography

Alterach, Miguel Angel. *La expulsión de los jesuitas: Misión Bucareli y Ursúa y "Memoria histórica-" de Doblas para Felix de Azara*. Buenos Aires, 2000.

Mones, Alvaro, and Miguel A. Klappenbach. *Un ilustrado aragonés en el virreinato del Río de la Plata: Félix de Azara, 1742-1821: estudios sobre su vida, su obra y su pensamiento*. Montevideo: Museo Nacional de Historia Natura, 1997.

SUSAN M. SOCOLOW

AZCAPOTZALCO.

Azcapotzalco (Place of the Ant Hill), the capital city of the Tepanecs and the dominant military and political power in the Basin of Mexico from the mid-fourteenth century through the first quarter of the fifteenth century. Located on the western edge of Lake Tetzcoco, Azcapotzalco's preeminence coincides with the reign of its greatest ruler, Tezozomoc. Under this ambitious and long-lived ruler, the Tepanecs successively conquered cities to the west, south, east, and finally north of the lake. Following Tezozomoc's death in 1426, the legitimate heir was deposed. In the revolt that followed, Azcapotzalco was conquered in 1428 by a coalition of forces led by Mexico Tenochtitlán and Tetzcoco, former tributaries of Azcapotzalco, and Tlacopán, its former ally. The political strategies and administrative policies of Tezozomoc's Tepanec Empire served as a model for the so called Triple Alliance that was subsequently formed by the victorious new powers. Present-day Azcapotzalco is a part of Mexico City.

See also **Precontact History: Mesoamerica.**

BIBLIOGRAPHY

Nigel Davies, *The Toltec Heritage: From the Fall of Tula to the Rise of Tenochtitlán* (1987).

Additional Bibliography

Carlos Santamarina Novillo and José Luis de Rojas y Gutiérrez de Gandarilla, *El sistema de dominación azteca: El imperio tepaneca* (2006).

ELOISE QUIÑONES KEBER

AZCÁRATE Y LEZAMA, JUAN FRANCISCO DE (1767–1831).

Juan Francisco de Azcárate y Lezama (*b.* 11 July 1767; *d.* 31 January 1831), Mexican lawyer, writer, and leader of the struggle for Mexican independence. Azcárate studied jurisprudence and in 1790 became a lawyer of the

Royal Audiencia. He taught courses at the University of Mexico and became a member of the Academy of Jurisprudence and the College of Lawyers. A distinguished lawyer, Azcárate was also interested in politics, becoming a member of the city council of Mexico City in 1803.

Azcárate played an important role during the imperial crisis provoked by Napoleon's invasion of Spain and the abdication of the Spanish monarchs, when the capital's city council, dominated by creoles, decided to promote autonomist interests. He was the author of the council's *representación* of 19 July 1808 to the viceroy against the recognition of any monarch but the legitimate one. An active participant in the meetings convened to discuss the creation of a governing junta, Azcárate was imprisoned during the coup d'état of 15 September. Freed in 1811, he rejoined the city council in 1814. He was a member of the governing junta in 1821 and one of the signers of the Declaration of Independence. Azcárate served in various diplomatic posts during the Augustín de Iturbide regime. In 1827 he was a member of the Committee of Public Education and the following year of the Tribunal of War and Marine.

See also **Mexico, Wars and Revolutions: War of Independence.**

BIBLIOGRAPHY

Enrique Lafuente Ferrari, *El Virrey Iturrigaray y los orígenes de la independencia de México* (1941).

José María Miquel I Vergés, *Diccionario de insurgentes* (1969), pp. 59–61.

Lucas Alamán, *Historia de Méjico*, vol. 1 (1985); *Diccionario Porrúa de historia, biografía y geografía de México*, 5th ed., vol. 1 (1986), pp. 244–245.

VIRGINIA GUEDEA

AZCÁRRAGA MILMO, EMILIO (1930–1997).

Azcárraga Milmo was an entrepreneur, television pioneer, and chief executive officer of Televisa, Latin America's largest media network. Born on September 6, 1930, he was the son of the radio and television mogul Emilio Azcárraga Vidaurreta and Laura Milmo, a member of a prominent Mexican entrepreneurial family. His father founded the firm Telesistema Mexicano (which would later become Televisa) with the former Mexican president Miguel Alemán and the entrepreneur Rómulo O'Farrill. The Azcárraga family held a controlling interest in the Televisa media empire, which came to dominate Mexican programming and Spanish-language periodicals.

Azcárraga Milmo graduated in 1947 from Instituto Patria, an influential Jesuit preparatory school, and studied at the Culver Military Academy in Indiana but did not earn a degree. He began his career modestly, selling the *Encyclopaedia Britannica*. He worked in sales at Station XEW and then became director of the business accounts for Channel 2, Televisa's leading station. Eventually he served as vice president of production for Televisa. After his father's death he became president of Televisa in 1973, and, according to *Forbes* magazine, his family reached a net worth in 1994 of $5.4 billion. *Fortune* magazine ranked his family's wealth as thirty-ninth in the world the previous year. After his own death on April 16, 1997, his son Emilio Azcárraga Jean took over the leadership of Televisa and, as of 2000, owned 51 percent of Televicentro, the Televisa holding company.

Azcárraga Milmo was known for his aggressive and occasionally flamboyant style, earning him the nickname of "El Tigre," the tiger. He also continued his family's policy of generous support for the arts. He was president of the Friends of the Arts in Mexico and a major sponsor of *Mexico: Splendors of Thirty Centuries*, an exhibit that appeared in New York, San Antonio, and Los Angeles in 1990 and 1991. Despite his wealth and influence, he never became a member of Mexico's most influential entrepreneurial organization, the Mexican Council of Businessmen. Under Azcárraga Milmo's leadership, Televisa's news programs became identified with the Institutional Revolutionary Party and the Mexican government, a posture that he publicly and vociferously supported. Under his son's leadership, after an internal struggle within the company, efforts were made to alter Televisa's image and provide politically neutral news coverage.

See also **Radio and Television.**

BIBLIOGRAPHY

Fernández, Claudia, and Andrew Paxman. *El tigre Emilio Azcárraga y su imperio Televisa*. Mexico: Grijalbo, 2000.

Orme, William A., Jr. *A Culture of Collusion: An Inside Look at the Mexican Press.* Coral Gables, FL: North-South Center Press, University of Miami, 1997.

RODERIC AI CAMP

AZCONA HOYO, JOSÉ SIMÓN

(1927–2005). José Simón Azcona Hoyo (*b.* 26 January 1927, *d.* 24 October 2005), president of Honduras (1986–1990). José Azcona received his degree in civil engineering from Tegucigalpa's National Autonomous University in 1963. He studied and worked in Mexico, Costa Rica, and the United States intermittently during the 1960s and 1970s but maintained his ties to the Liberal Party in Honduras. He served in a variety of political positions, including congressional deputy (1982–1985) and minister of communication (1982–1983). Azcona broke with incumbent president Roberto Suazo Córdova in 1985 and led a faction of the Liberal Party known as the Rodista Dissent Movement, after his mentor Modesto Rodas. Under a new electoral system, in which the two main parties alternate terms in power, Azcona won the 1985 presidential race even though he did not receive a plurality. Despite this successful transition of power between civilian presidents, the strength of the Honduran military grew during Azcona's administration. Although he was widely viewed as responsible and trustworthy, Azcona was a weak president faced with increasingly complicated domestic and foreign issues: the presence in his country of Nicaraguan contras, rapidly expanding U.S. involvement in the area, Salvadoran refugees, and the appearance of a guerrilla threat.

See also **Honduras, National Party (PNH).**

BIBLIOGRAPHY

James A. Morris, *Honduras: Caudillo Politics and Military Rulers* (1984).

James Dunkerley, *Power in the Isthmus* (1988).

Roy Gutman, *Banana Diplomacy* (1988).

Additional Bibliography

Azcona Bocock, José S. *Construyendo una Honduras mejor.* Tegucigalpa: Graficentro Editores, 2005.

KAREN RACINE

AZCUÉNAGA, MIGUEL DE (1754–1833). Miguel de Azcuénaga (*b.* 4 June 1754; *d.* 19 December 1833), Argentine military man. Born in Buenos Aires, the son and grandson of prominent Basque merchants (Vicente de Azcuénaga and Domingo Basavilbaso), Azcuénaga was related by blood or marriage to many of the more conservative Spanish monopoly traders in Buenos Aires. After studying in Spain, he returned in 1773 to the city of his birth as a commissioned military officer. Between 1776 and 1800 he served as a member of the *cabildo,* a colonel in the militia, and the chief of militia in Buenos Aires. He was especially active as the commander of a volunteer infantry battalion during the English invasions of 1806–1807.

A participant in the *cabildo abierto* (open town council meeting) of 23 May 1810, Azcuénaga was a fervent supporter of the end of viceregal rule. He served in the first independence government and was especially active in organizing the military forces of the new government. Dismissed from the government as the result of political intrigue, Azcuénaga later held a variety of posts, including *gobernador intendente* of Buenos Aires (1813), president of the War Commission, and Buenos Aires deputy to Congress (1818). He died in Buenos Aires.

See also **Argentina: The Colonial Period.**

BIBLIOGRAPHY

Enrique Udaondo, *Diccionario biográfico colonial argentino* (1945), p. 125.

Bernardo González Arrili, *Hombres de Mayo* (Buenos Aires, 1960), pp. 47–50.

Additional Bibliography

Lesser, Ricardo. *La infancia de los próceres: Belgrano, Rivadavia, Moreno, Castelli, Azcuénaga.* Buenos Aires: Editorial Biblos, 2004.

SUSAN M. SOCOLOW

AZEVEDO, ALUÍSIO (1857–1913).
Aluísio Azevedo (*b.* 14 April 1857; *d.* 21 January 1913), Brazilian novelist. Aluísio Azevedo was the major figure of Brazilian naturalism, a movement

influenced by the novels of Émile Zola and other European naturalists, but also firmly grounded in the social and historical context of Brazil at the end of the empire period. Azevedo appears to have seen literature as a way to get ahead in life, and his first naturalist novel, *O mulato* (1881) was a scandalous success. He published three more naturalist novels, including his masterpiece, *O cortiço* (1890), but simultaneously turned out a number of romantic potboilers. Azevedo abandoned fiction after he was appointed to the Brazilian diplomatic corps in 1895, at the age of thirty-eight. While his works exhibit his gift for describing places, from the provincial city that is the setting for *O mulato* to the Rio de Janeiro slums in *O cortiço,* all Azevedo's novels are weakened by their improbable plots and stereotypical characters. His Brazilian contemporaries were shocked and titillated by the heavy-handed treatment of sexuality in Azevedo's novels—the English translation of *O cortiço,* published in 1926 as *A Brazilian Tenement,* had to be drastically censored for North American audiences—but today's critics view his works primarily as historical documents. While he and his contemporaries saw these works as innovative attempts to modernize and renew the Brazilian novel, the underlying themes of his naturalism are pessimism about Brazil's future and fear of all the changes that the future might bring: the family skeletons that abolition of slavery might uncover, the white population's prospect of increased competition from mulattos and immigrants, and the education and emancipation of women.

See also **Literature: Brazil.**

BIBLIOGRAPHY

Dorothy S. Loos, *The Naturalistic Novel of Brazil* (1963).

Sônia Brayner, *A metáfora do corpo no romance naturalista* (1973).

Lúcia Miguel-Pereira, *Prosa de ficção de 1870 a 1920,* 3d ed. (1973), pp. 142–159.

Jean-Yves Mérian, *Aluísio Azevedo, vida e obra* (1988).

Additional Bibliography

Klock, Sheldon C. Jr. *Themes in the Novels of Aluísio Azevedo.* Toronto, ON, Canada: York Press, 1999.

Sedycias, João. *The naturalistic novel of the New World: A comparative study of Stephen Crane, Aluísio Azevedo, and Federico Gamboa.* Lanham, MD: University Press of America, 1993.

DAVID T. HABERLY

AZEVEDO, FERNANDO DE (1894–1974). Fernando de Azevedo (*b.* 2 April 1894; *d.* 19 September 1974), Brazilian educator, editor, sociologist, and cultural historian. As city director of public education from 1926 to 1930, Azevedo led in the implementation of school reforms in Rio de Janeiro. Later he was secretary of education and culture in São Paulo. In 1934 he founded and then later directed the humanities faculty of the University of São Paulo. As editor of the Biblioteca Pedagógica Brasileira and Brasiliana series, he introduced new ideas and revived Brazilian classics.

Azevedo wrote on sports and physical education, classical Latin literature, educational sociology, and the sociology of sugar mills and railroads. His major work was *A cultura brasileira* (1943), published as a supplement to the 1940 census. This ambitious survey combines a social and psychological history of the development of the Brazilian people with an institutional history of the Catholic church, the professions, literary and artistic achievements, and the sciences. It interprets Brazilian culture through the history of education from colonial times through the 1930s, calling for a unified system of public education to build national unity.

See also **Education.**

BIBLIOGRAPHY

Fernando De Azevedo, *História da minha vida* (1971), and *A cultura brasileira* (1943), translated by William Rex Crawford, under the title *Brazilian Culture* (1950).

Maria Luiza Penna, *Fernando de Azevedo: Educação e transformação* (1987).

Additional Bibliography

Teixeira, Anísio, and Diana Gonçalves Vidal. *Na batalha da educação: correspondência entre Anísio Teixeira e Fernando de Azevedo (1929-1971).* Bragança Paulista: EDUSF, 2000.

DAIN BORGES

AZEVEDO, THALES DE (1904–1995).

Thales de Azevedo (*b.* 26 August 1904, *d.* 5 August 1995), Brazilian social scientist and first director of the Instituto de Ciências Sociais at the Universidade Federal da Bahia. Thales Olimpio Góis de Azevedo was born in the city of Salvador, Bahia. He studied medicine and later anthropology and ethnography. Dedicated to the creation of a center for social sciences at Universidade Federal da Bahia, he was one of the authors of the proposal calling for the establishment of such a center. In 1961 the president of the university founded the Instituto de Ciências Sociais and appointed Azevedo the first director.

Azevedo's publications include *Gaúchos, notas de antropologia social* (1943); *Uma pesquisa sobre a vida social no estado da Bahia* (with Charles Wagley and Luís de Aguiar Costa Pinto, 1950); *Civilização e mestiçagem* (1951); *Les élites de couleur dans une ville brésilienne* (1953); *O catolicismo no Brasil* (1955); *Atualidade de Durkheim* (with Nelson Sampaio and A. L. Machado Neto, 1959); *Ensaios de antropologia social* (1959); *Social Change in Brazil* (1963); *Cultura e situação racial no Brasil* (1966); *A evasão de talentos* (1968); *Integração intercultural* (1974); *Democracia racial, ideologia e realidade* (1975); *A religião civil brasileira: Um instrumento político* (1981).

See also **Sociology.**

BIBLIOGRAPHY

Florestan Fernandes, *A etnologia e a sociologia no Brasil* (1958).

Karl N. Degler, *Neither Black nor White: Slavery and Race Relations in Brazil and the United States* (1971).

Márcio Moreira Alves, *A igreja e a política no Brasil* (1979).

Additional Bibliography

Maio, Marcos Chor. "UNESCO and the Study of Race Relations in Brazil: Regional or National Issue?" *Latin American Research Review* 36:2 (2001): 118-136.

ELIANA MARIA REA GOLDSCHMIDT

AZORES.

Azores, an archipelago consisting of nine islands (Flores, Corvo, Terceira, São Jorge, Pico, Fayal, Graciosa, São Miguel, and Santa María) and several islets in the North Atlantic, 800 miles off the coast of Portugal. First mentioned by the Arab geographer, Edisi in the twelfth century, the Azores were discovered by the Portuguese in 1427 during their voyages of discovery. These expeditions were financed by the military order of Christ, which was headed by Prince Henry the Navigator. Initially the explorers visited the central islands and, to the east, Santa María and São Miguel. Twenty-five years later the western Azores were discovered by Diogo de Teive, a Madeiran sugar merchant and navigator.

The Azores played an important role in the exploration of and, later, the trade with the New World. Columbus's ship, the Niña, visited Santa María in 1493 on its return from his first voyage to America. His crew was briefly detained by the islanders until Columbus could negotiate their release. Later, the Azores served as a post between Europe and the Americas where Portuguese ships would stop in order to pick up fresh food and water before continuing their journey across the Atlantic.

Woad, a dyestuff planted by the Flemish, who had established settlements there in the fifteenth century, was an important export until it was replaced by indigo from Brazil.

See also **Explorers and Exploration: Spanish America.**

BIBLIOGRAPHY

T. Bentley Duncan, *Atlantic Islands* (1972).

Additional Bibliography

Brown, A. Samler. *Guía de Madeira, las Canarias y las Azores.* Gran Canaria: Departamento de Ediciones, 1999.

Moniz, Miguel. *Azores: World Bibliographical Series.* Santa Barbara, CA., 1999.

Symington, Martin. *Portugal with Madeira and the Azores.* New York: D.K. Pub., 1997.

SHEILA L. HOOKER

AZTEC CALENDAR STONE.

The Aztec Calendar Stone is the most widely recognized emblem of pre-Columbian Mesoamerican civilization. Although it was sculp-ted by anonymous Aztec artisans during the reign of King Axayácalt (1469–1481), only forty years prior to the Spanish Conquest, it embodies a rich cultural tradition that extends back another two thousand years through the Toltec, Maya,

Aztec Calendar Stone. More correctly known as the Sun Stone, the Aztec Calendar Stone was once used in rituals honoring the sun god Tonatiuh. IMAGE COPYRIGHT TOMASZ OTAP, 2007. USED UNDER LICENSE FROM SHUTTERSTOCK.COM

and Olmec civilizations. It is less a representation of a practical calendar than of the Aztec cosmic worldview and a monument to their principal deity, the sun god Tonatiuh. Consequently, it is more correctly called Piedra del Sol, the Sun Stone. The earliest description of the Sun Stone was by Antonio B. León y Gama, writing in 1792.

The stone is a massive, 24.5-ton, round basaltic monolith, three feet thick and nearly twelve feet in diameter, intricately carved on one face and originally replete with bright colors. It was apparently meant to be mounted horizontally to serve as a sacred repository for the ritualistic feeding of the hearts and blood of captured warriors to the sun god. The stone was buried during the Spanish defeat of Tenochtitlán (present-day Mexico City) in 1521, but it was recovered in 1790 during the repaving of the Plaza Mayor. The stone is exhibited at the Museo Nacional de Antropología de Mexico in Mexico City.

Despite extensive studies of the iconography of the stone and its connections to Aztec religion and cosmology, a definitive interpretation is impossible,

largely because verbal traditions were only imperfectly conveyed to and recorded by post-Conquest Spanish scholars. The Aztecs viewed existence as a series of cycles of creation and destruction, not only for humans but for the gods as well. Close familiarity with astronomical sky cycles, most notably by the famously accomplished Maya astronomers, undoubtedly intensified their cyclic mythology. The theme of the stone can be said to be cosmic time cycles, and its circular shape is a metaphor for repeating time.

The outer half of the stone's face consists of concentric circular bands, each with a distinct series of carvings. On the outermost border are two Xiuhcoatl fire serpents, and thrust out of their opened mouths and confronting one another are the heads of two gods, probably Tonatiuh and Xiuhtecutli (the fire god). In the stone's original orientation, with the top oriented toward the East, the serpents are following the diurnal motion of the sun toward the West. The innermost two circular bands represent the so-called Calendar Round, a fifty-two-year cycle of four concurrently running series of day counts: two numerical and two symbolic, with names linked to a sequence of rituals. The end of a Round marked a dangerous time that demanded a solemn cleansing and renewal ceremony (the "Binding of the Years") and the symbolic rekindling of the Sun to ensure its continued motion through the heavens.

The heart of the stone contains the glaring face of the sun god Tonatiuh embedded in the six-lobed day-sign for *ollin*, or movement. Movement here is associated with the motion of the sun through the sky and possibly movement through cosmic time; it is also the symbol for earthquakes. The four square panels of the *ollin* sign arranged in a large X-shape depict the four cosmic eras (or "suns") thought to have preceded the current era (the Fifth Sun). Although the gods struggled to make Earth fruitful and secure, humankind was destroyed in four successive catastrophes—devoured by jaguars, swept away by raging hurricanes, incinerated by a rain of fire, and drowned in a great flood. The fifth era began with the self-immolation of the god Nanhuatzin on behalf of humanity. To prevent a cataclysm of violent earthquakes predicted by a date on the *ollin* symbol, the Aztecs assiduously offered the sun god the regular nourishment of blood sacrifices to help him maintain the diurnal cycle of day and night and thereby ensure their survival. This grim obligation is symbolized by a tongue-shaped sacrificial flint knife that protrudes from the god's mouth and, at either side of his face, a claw gripping a human heart. Many similar features can be found in other Aztec sacrificial carvings, but the Sun Stone is the most magnificent example and stunningly captures the vibrant and exotic cosmos of the Aztecs.

See also **Aztecs; Calendars, Pre-Columbian; Precontact History: Mesoamerica.**

BIBLIOGRAPHY

Aveni, Anthony F. *Skywatchers*. Austin: University of Texas Press, 2001.

Bernal, Ignacio. *100 Great Masterpieces of the Mexican National Museum of Anthropology*. New York: Harry N. Abrams, l969.

Boone, Elizabeth Hill. *The Aztec World*. Montreal: St. Remy Press, and Washington, DC: Smithsonian Books, 1994.

Matos Moctezuma, Eduardo, and Felipe Solís. *El Calendario azteca y otros monumentos solares*. Mexico:

Consejo Nacional para la Cultura y las Artes, Instituto Nacional de Antropología e Historia, Grupo Azabache, 2004.

Montes, Augusto Molina. "The Building of Tenochtitlán." With paintings by Felipe Dávalos. *National Geographic* 158 (1980): 753–775.

Nicholson, H. B. "The Problem of the Identification of the Central Image of the 'Aztec Calendar Stone.'" In *Current Topics in Aztec Studies: Essays in Honor of Dr. H. B. Nicholson*, ed. Alana Cordy-Collins and Douglas Sharon. *San Diego Museum Papers* 30 (1993): 3–15.

ROBERT W. O'CONNELL
VIRGINIA L. TEGTMEYER

AZTECS.   *Aztec* (native of Aztlan) is a popular term widely used in Europe and the United States, but it is very imprecise. Although generally used in referring to the inhabitants of Mexico Tenochtitlan, it is usually broadened to include the inhabitants of the twin city, Mexico Tlatelolco. At other times it is used in referring to the Nahuatl-speaking groups of central Mexico and even to all the peoples in that region whether they spoke Nahuatl or not.

Strictly speaking, *Aztec* is a name for the inhabitants of a place called Aztlan, where the inhabitants of Tenochtitlan and Tlatelolco are said to have originated. But, as indicated by their own chronicles, when they left that location they changed their name to *Mexica* as commanded by their patron god, Huitzilopochtli. Furthermore, the other Nahua groups never used the term *Aztec* to refer to themselves, whereas those who inhabited Tenochtitlan called themselves *Mexicas* or *Tenochas*. So it is more correct to speak in general terms of *Nahua* groups when referring to all Nahuatl speakers of central Mexico and to use *Mexica*, *Tenochca*, or *Tlatelolca*, as applicable. This article will give preference to use of the term *Mexica*.

HISTORY

Since the late twentieth century, investigation into the historical development of the Mexica people has focused on understanding the significance that recounting their own past had for them rather than trying to establish the factual reality of the events involved. Accordingly it can be said that, for the Mexica, the story of their migration from Aztlan to their founding of Tenochtitlan and their subsequent military expansion to the height of their splendor was seen as the fulfillment of the promise that the god Huitzilopochtli had made to his people at the beginning of their history. The story says that the god Huitzilopochtli promised them that if they left Aztlan, they would ultimately gain fame, glory, untold wealth, and dominion over other peoples. In exchange, the Mexica were to devote a sumptuous religious cult to the deity and, particularly, to offer him human sacrifices. Wealth and power, plus the victims offered as human sacrifices, would be obtained through war. This was exactly the situation at the height of their splendor: a city receiving material resources as tribute from an extensive area of central Mexico.

This new understanding of the image that the Mexica themselves created for their reality as a hegemonic people in the Late Post-Classic period in Mesoamerica certainly sheds light on the issues involved in their response to the Spanish Conquest and the construction of the new colonial order of New Spain.

ECONOMY, SOCIETY, AND POLITICS

Studies of their economic, social, and political organization have been less prevalent in the early twenty-first century. Nevertheless, there have been important contributions, mainly with regard to the colonial period and fewer to the pre-Hispanic era. Focus has been given to the significant continuities between the Mesoamerican world and that of the early colonial period.

Certainly one of the greatest problems encountered in gaining knowledge of Mesoamerican societies in general and of Nahua society in particular has to do with the terminology that scholars have used. The problem begins with the Spanish writers of the sixteenth and seventeenth centuries, who employed their own terms to describe the new situation they saw before them. They used a medieval language, compared very different institutions to each other, and made comparisons of social elements that were in principle quite distinct. This approach has a strong legacy for modern scholars, who continue to speak of kings and empires, of tributaries and slaves, of nobles and plebeians, solely because a sixteenth-century friar or conquistador thought that is what they were. However, neither can scholars simply resort to the expedient of using Nahuatl terms if they are not clearly explained and if their content and meaning are not well understood. The solution to this problem lies in a deep analysis of the Nahua categories of their own society and in the qualified and thoughtful use of a modern language.

These problems become evident with the extensive use in recent years of the Nahuatl term *altépetl* (*alt* meaning "water" and *petl* meaning "mountain"), when it is conceived of as a city-state governed by a monarch, an understanding that does not coincide with the majority of historiographic sources that use *altépetl* in referring to populations of highly diverse aspects, with different forms of government, from simple peasant farmer villages to enormous hegemonic metropolises. Furthermore, the chronicles give much more weight to the governing lineages of each locality than to the *altépetl* as political entities. Greater importance is also given to smaller units called *calpulli* (large houses) that were linked by kinship, engagement in a common economic activity, or worship of a particular god. It must be recognized that a full understanding of the basic structures of the social and political organization is still problematic, including that of the *calpulli* itself and such political structures as *tlahtocáyotl* (government of a tlatoani), *tecuhcáyotl* (government of a *tecuhtli*) and the largest political form we know of, the Triple Alliance or Excan Tlatoloyan (the triple seat of power).

WORLDVIEW AND RELIGION

Without a doubt, the most numerous and most published studies by far are those of the Mexica worldview and religion. Three conditions favor such studies, one of which is that there is more source information on these topics; another is that there has been a long series of studies on the subject since the nineteenth century. Some of the most eminent scholars who have studied the Mexica have devoted themselves specifically to the field of religious thought. The greatest contributions are in the general worldview and in the study of the mythology, particularly the works of Alfredo López Austin on the common source of Mesoamerica's religious structures and traditions.

The third condition favoring research on these topics lies in the studies of the archaeological reports on the Great Temple and the learned works based on traditional sources. Overall, there has been more study of the beliefs and myths of the Mexicas but very little of their religious institutions, so that the institutional foundations of the operation of the religious apparatus are still unclear. The natural foundations of Nahua religious beliefs have been studied by Gabriel Espinosa and Johanna Broda.

ART AND LITERATURE

The study of Nahuatl literature has posed various problems from the beginning. The first is conceptual, since the etymological meaning of literature tends to the literal, to the written script, hardly applicable in principle to a cultural universe in which the recording forms were oral or pictographic. Consequently scholars have resorted to the concept of oral literature proposed from literary studies. According to this concept, any oral production with meaning is a text and can be considered literature. The second problem is the question of the literary genres applicable to that literature. The pioneer in these studies, Ángel María Garibay, was aware of the insufficiency of European literary genres in understanding and defining Nahuatl cultural phenomena but, for educational reasons, made constant use of them in his works.

Miguel León-Portilla, however, has reviewed the matter and taken a different position, critical of Garibay. This scholar proposes that there are two great genres: *cuícatl* (songs) and *tlahtolli* (discourses). *Cuícatl* is generally characterized as being a form of oral public expression accompanied by music, that is, these works were sung. The *cuícatl* were sung by individuals specially prepared for the task, such as priests and young cantors from the power group, who also composed them. *Tlahtolli* are described as a form of public oral expression without music, very similar to declamation or recitation. The *tlahtolli* were declaimed by individuals specially prepared for the task, generally elderly men, priests, and governors, who also composed them.

SOURCES

Study of the sources that provide the history and culture of the ancient Nahua in general and those of the Mexica in particular have been slowly receiving the stimulus and depth they deserve. The potential for gaining greater knowledge depends to a great extent on the quality of the basic work material and the skill of the researchers in understanding the sources in their context. There are two prominent, different but complementary, paths of research. One is the critical publication of the sources themselves, and the other is the analysis of the sources from the historiographic perspective.

In the field of publication of sources, there are three important trends. One is the facsimile edition, with appropriate introductory studies, of the pictographic documents known as codices. Another is the work of translating the Nahuatl texts, which requires sufficient knowledge of Nahuatl and a good critical apparatus. The third trend is the need for critical publications of the texts written in Spanish. Prominent in this field are recent technical innovations in the reproduction of facsimiles that provide today's specialist with materials highly faithful to the originals, in such aspects as use of color, calligraphic details, and composition of the paper. Some of the translations worthy of mention are those done by the Chalca chronicler Chimalpahin Cuauhtlehuanitzin, and among the publications of Spanish-language texts is *Historia de Tlaxcala* by Diego Muñoz Camargo.

In regard to analysis of the sources themselves from the historiographic perspective, significant contributions have been made in both the study of works and of specific writers–such as the work of José Rubén Romero Galván on the Mexica chronicler Hernando Alvarado Tezozómoc–and the broad perspective of the studies coordinated by Romero himself and those prepared by Miguel Pastrana Flores. These studies have revealed the need to understand the chronicles of indigenous tradition within a social process of strong cultural change, combining the ancient worldview of the Mesoamerican peoples with European historiographic forms.

BIBLIOGRAPHY

Studies

Carrasco, Pedro. *Estructura político territorial del Imperio tenochca: La Triple Alianza de Tenochtitlan, Tetzcoco y Tlacopan.* Mexico: Fondo de Cultura Económica El Colegio de México, 1996.

Clendinnan, Inga. *Aztecs: An Interpretation.* Cambridge, U.K., and New York: Cambridge University Press, 1991.

Espinosa Pineda, Gabriel. *El embrujo del lago: El sistema lacustre de la cuenca de México en la cosmovisión mexica.* Mexico: Universidad Nacional Autónoma de México, Instituto de Investigaciones Históricas, 1996.

León-Portilla, Miguel. *El destino de la palabra: De la oralidad y los códices mesoamericanos a la escritura alfabética.* 2nd ed. Mexico: Fondo de Cultura Económica / El Colegio Nacional, 1997.

León-Portilla, Miguel, ed. *Bernardino de Sahagún. Quinientos años de presencia.* Mexico: Universidad Nacional Autónoma de México, Instituto de Investigaciones Históricas, 2002.

López Austin, Alfredo. *Los mitos del tlacuache: Caminos de la mitología mesoamericana.* Mexico: Alianza, 1990.

López Austin, Alfredo. *Tamoanchan y Tlalocan.* Mexico: Fondo de Cultura Económica, 1994.

López Luján, Leonardo. *Las ofrendas del Templo Mayor de Tenochtitlan.* Mexico: Instituto Nacional de Antropología e Historia, 1993.

Pastrana Flores, Miguel. *Historias de la Conquista: Aspectos de la historiografía de tradición náhuatl.* Mexico: Universidad Nacional Autónoma de México, Instituto de Investigaciones Históricas, 2004.

Pastrana Flores, Miguel. *Entre los hombres y los dioses: Acercamiento al sacerdocio de calpulli entre los antiguos nahuas.* Mexico: Universidad Nacional Autónoma de México, Instituto de Investigaciones Históricas, 2007.

Romero Galván, José Rubén, ed. *Historiografía novohispana de tradición indígena.* Mexico: Universidad Nacional Autónoma de México, Instituto de Investigaciones Históricas, 2003.

Sources

Alvarado Tezozómoc, Fernando. *Crónica mexicana.* Edited by Gonzalo Díaz Migoyo. Madrid: Información e Historia, 1997.

Bautista, Juan. *Anales.* Edited by Luis Reyes García. Mexico: CIESAS / Biblioteca Lorenzo Boturini, 2001.

Buenaventura Zapata y Mendoza, Juan. *Historia cronológica de la noble ciudad de Tlaxcala.* Edited by Luis Reyes García and Andrea Martínez Baracs. Mexico: Universidad Autónoma de Tlaxcala / CIESAS, 1995.

Chimalpahin Cuauhtlehuanitzin, Domingo Francisco de San Antón Muñón. *Memorial breve acerca de la fundación de la ciudad de Culhuacan.* Edited by Víctor M. Castillo F. Mexico: Universidad Nacional Autónoma de México, Instituto de Investigaciones Históricas, 1991.

Chimalpahin Cuauhtlehuanitzin, Domingo Francisco de San Antón Muñón. *Primer amoxtli libro: 3a relación de las Différentes histoires originales.* Edited by Víctor M. Castillo F. Mexico: Universidad Nacional Autónoma de México, Instituto de Investigaciones Históricas, 1997.

Chimalpahin Cuauhtlehuanitzin, Domingo Francisco de San Antón Muñón. *Primera, segunda, cuarta, quinta y sexta relaciones de las Différentes histoires originales.* Edited by Josefina García Quintana, Silvia Limón, Miguel Pastrana, and Víctor Castillo. Mexico: Universidad Nacional Autónoma de México, Instituto de Investigaciones Históricas, 2003.

Chimalpahin Cuauhtlehuanitzin, Domingo Francisco de San Antón Muñón. *Séptima relación de las Différentes histoires originales.* Edited by Josefina García Quintana. Mexico: Universidad Nacional Autónoma de México, Instituto de Investigaciones Históricas, 2003.

Códice de Tepetlaoztoc (Códice Kinsgsborough) Estado de México. Facsimile ed. Perla Valle Study. Mexico: El Colegio Mexiquense, 1994.

Códice Fejérváry-Mayer: El Tonalámatl de los pochtecas. Edited by Miguel León-Portilla. Mexico: Raíces, 2005.

Códice Techialoyan García Granados. Facsimile ed. Introductory note by Xavier Noguez. Toluca: El Colegio Mexiquense / Gobierno del Estado de México, 1992.

Códice Tudela. Facsimile ed. Madrid: Testimonio / Ministerio de Educación, Cultura y Deportes / Agencia Española de Cooperación Internacional, 2002.

Códice Veitia. Facsimile ed. Madrid: Testimonio Compañía Editorial / Patrimonio Nacional, 1986.

Matrícula de Tributos. Facsimile ed. Edited by Ma. Teresa Sepúlveda et al. Mexico: Raíces, 2003.

Muñoz Camargo, Diego. *Historia de Tlaxcala: MS 210 de la Biblioteca Nacional de París.* Edited by Luis Reyes García. Mexico: CIESAS / Gobierno del Estado de Tlaxcala / UAT, 1998.

Olmos, Andrés de. *Arte de la lengua mexicana.* Facsimile ed. Edited by Ascensión Hernández and Miguel León-Portilla. Mexico: Universidad Nacional Autónoma de México, Instituto de Investigaciones Históricas, 2002.

MIGUEL PASTRANA FLORES

AZTLÁN. Aztlán, legendary homeland of the Mexicas (Aztecs). It was from Aztlán that the Mexicas were said to have begun their odyssey to the promised land, Tenochtitlán. Scholars are in disagreement as to the geographical location of Aztlán, placing it anywhere from present New Mexico to California. Some see it as a spiritual rather than a real place. In contemporary times, the term *Aztlán* became an integral part of the political ideology of the Chicano movement, referring to the U.S. Southwest or other areas of large Chicano population. The usage of *Aztlán* by Mexican-American political activists and writers was particularly significant in the early phase of the Chicano movement (1965–1976).

See also **Aztecs.**

BIBLIOGRAPHY

Ángel Julián García Zambrano, *Pasaje mítico y paisaje fundacional en las migraciones mesoamericanas* (2006).

David Carrasco, Eduardo Matos Moctezuma, Scott Sessions, *Moctezuma's Mexico: Visions of the Aztec World* (2003).

Refugio I Rochin and Dennis Nodín Valdés, *Voices of a New Chicana/o History* (2000).

DAVID MACIEL

AZUELA, MARIANO (1873–1952). Mariano Azuela (*b.* 1 January 1873; *d.* 1 March 1952), Mexican writer. Azuela wrote more than twenty novels, numerous short stories, three plays, biographies, and books of essays. He was born in Lagos de Moreno, Jalisco, and studied medicine in Guadalajara. From early on he alternated between practicing that profession and writing. He published his first book, the short novel *María Luiza,* in 1907, but did not receive international or even national recognition until the mid-1920s, when *Los de abajo* (*The Underdogs*) was "discovered" and praised as a great novel reflecting the cultural heritage of the Mexican Revolution. This book had originally appeared in serial form and then was published in one volume at the end of 1915 in El Paso, Texas, but the definitive edition was published by the author himself in 1920, when he moved to Mexico City. Azuela's narrative work is a vast mural on which appear the changes and critical characters of Mexican society in the first half of the twentieth century, beginning with the years immediately preceding the Revolution.

Honoré de Balzac and Émile Zola were decisive influences on his work. Latin American *modernista* literature (not to be confused with European and North American modernism) was clearly imprinted in Azuela's style.

Two qualities distinguish Azuela as a twentieth-century artist: the acuity with which he captures his characters as social actors, and the lucid way in which he insists, throughout all of his work, that Mexico's social and political problems are rooted in the moral decay of society. No one was better than he at portraying the opportunism, social climbing, resentment, and greed that arose during the Mexican Revolution and later spread throughout all of Mexican society.

Azuela's vision, however, was static and prototypical. His characters are not psychologically complex or capable of dramatic change, and his moralistic clarity becomes at times an obsession. This gives his work the air not of a great human comedy, but of a gallery of scenes with vivid, precise, and incisive images that lack perspective and movement. This mixture of strengths and defects explains why critical judgment and history have almost unanimously declared *Los de abajo* Azuela's masterpiece. It is not by chance that the subtitle of the book is *Cuadros y escenas de la Revolución Mexicana* (Sketches and Scenes of the Mexican Revolution) by which the author himself clearly shows that his vision is more episodic than dramatic. With all its defects, *Los de abajo* continues to be the most intense description of the revolutionary masses and all their contradictions.

Azuela's intense and austere realism influenced other major works, such as Martín Luis Guzmán's *El águila y la serpiente* (1928), Nellie Campobello's *Cartucho* (1931), Rafael F. Muñoz's *Vámonos con Pancho Villa* (1931), and Juan Rulfo's *Pedro Páramo* (1955). His works are available in *Obras completas,* edited by Francisco Monterde, 3 volumes (1958–1960).

See also **Literature: Spanish America.**

BIBLIOGRAPHY

Luis Leal, *Mariano Azuela* (1971), and "Mariano Azuela," in *Latin American Writers,* edited by Carlos A. Solé and Maria Isabel Abreu, vol. 2 (1989), pp. 457–464.

Stanley L. Robe, *Azuela and the Mexican Underdogs* (1979).

Additional Bibliography

Azuela, Arturo. *Prisma de Mariano Azuela.* Mexico City: Plaza y Valdés, 2002.

Leal, Luis. *Mariano Azuela, cuentista.* Santa Barbara: University of California, 2003.

JORGE AGUILAR MORA

B

BABYLONIAN CAPTIVITY. Babylonian Captivity (1580–1640), the period when Spain ruled Portugal. Since Portugal first declared her independence in the twelfth century, Spaniards had yearned to regain control of the western kingdom. The successive deaths of Sebastian (1578) and Cardinal Henry (1580) without issue made it possible for Philip II of Spain to claim Portugal and her empire. Thereafter three successive sovereigns, Philip II, III, and IV, ruled Portugal from a distance via councils of regency and with the aid of an itinerant advisory body, the Council of Portugal, but proved unable to honor pledges to preserve the integrity of the empire. As the eastern empire began to crumble in response to indigenous pressures and challenges posed by Holland and England, the Portuguese also witnessed the loss of much of their navy and, for a time, of the sugar-producing captaincies of northeastern Brazil as well as the growth of commodities prices and taxes used to defend Spanish but not Portuguese interests. A series of protest revolts in 1637 were indications of widespread discontent within the kingdom. On 1 December 1640 a group of young nobles entered the royal palace in Lisbon, compelled the resignation of Margaret of Mantua, the last Spanish regent, and acclaimed João, duke of Bragança, as the first king of the restored monarchy.

See also **Bragança, House of; João IV of Portugal.**

BIBLIOGRAPHY

Joel Serrão, ed., *Dicionário de história de Portugal*, 4 vols. (1971).

Joaquim Veríssimo Serrão, *História de Portugal*, vol. 4 (1979).

Additional Bibliography

Stella, Roseli Santaella. *Brasil durante el gobierno español, 1580-1640*. Madrid: Fundación Histórica Tavera, 2000.

DAURIL ALDEN

BACA FLOR, CARLOS (c. 1865–1941). Carlos Baca Flor (*b.* ca. 1865; *d.* 20 February 1941), Peruvian artist. Born in Islay, formerly Peruvian now Chilean territory, Baca Flor moved with his family to Santiago, Chile, in 1871. At age fifteen he entered the School of Fine Arts in Santiago, where he studied with Cosme San Martín and the Italian Giovanni Mochi. Awarded the Prix de Rome in 1887, he declined the prize rather than renounce his Peruvian citizenship. He moved to Lima shortly thereafter, where the government granted him a fellowship to study at the Royal Academy of Fine Arts in Rome. Three years later he went to Paris to study with Benjamin Constant and Jean-Paul Laurens at the Julian Academy. He never returned to Peru.

For many years Baca Flor lived in extreme poverty, but his luck changed when he obtained first prize at the Salon des Artistes in 1907. Soon afterward, banker John Pierpont Morgan commissioned him to do his portrait. Subsequently, he obtained portrait commissions from major personalities in the financial world. He painted one hundred and fifty portraits, among them that of Cardinal Eugenio

Pacelli, later Pope Pius XII. In 1926 he was elected a member of the Academy of Fine Arts in Paris.

Baca Flor died in Neuilly-sur-Seine, considering himself a Peruvian although he had spent only eight years in his native country. His impeccable technique, at times brilliant composition, and the amazing realism of his portraits are recognized even by those who perceive his academic style as anachronistic.

See also **Art: The Twentieth Century.**

BIBLIOGRAPHY

Juan E. Ríos, *La pintura contemporánea en el Perú* (1946), pp. 25–27.

Additional Bibliography

Jochamowitz, Alberto. *Baca-Flor, hombre singular; su vida, su carácter, su arte.* Lima, Peru: Imprenta Torres Aguirre, 1941.

MARTA GARSD

BACHARÉIS.

Bacharéis, term employed in nineteenth-century Brazil to designate all those who had graduated from an educational institution. More specificially, it referred to graduates in law from Coimbra University or from one of the Brazilian law schools, São Paulo or Olinda. This educational experience provided them with a common cultural and political outlook that was inherited from the Portuguese Enlightenment. During the reign of Pedro II (1840–1889), the *bacharéis* occupied all the important positions in the state bureaucracy and distinguished themselves as ministers, senators, representatives, and attorneys. They became the most evident symbol of the political world of the elite.

See also **Education: Overview.**

BIBLIOGRAPHY

Alberto Venancio Filho, *Das arcadas ao bacharelismo* (1982).

Richard Graham, "Locating Power," in his *Patronage and Politics in Nineteenth-Century Brazil* (1990).

Additional Bibliography

Abreu, Sérgio França Adorno de. *Os aprendizes do poder: O bacharelismo liberal na política brasileira.* Rio de Janeiro: Paz e Terra, 1998.

Kirkendall, Andrew J. *Class Mates: Male Student Culture and the Making of a Political Class in Nineteenth-Century Brazil.* Lincoln: University of Nebraska Press, 2002.

LÚCIA M. BASTOS P. NEVES

BACHATA.

Bachata is a ballad-style music and accompanying dance with roots in the Dominican Republic that has grown in international popularity since the 1990s. Once a very marginal genre in the Dominican Republic, *bachata* was socially stigmatized throughout the twentieth century because it was played in bars, cabarets, and brothels in low-income neighborhoods on the outskirts of the capital, Santo Domingo. Its association with sexual references in a *doble sentido* (double-meaning) style contributed to its negative reputation among elite classes, whereas it had widespread popularity among working-class Dominicans. Instruments traditionally used in *bachata* music, such as the metal-tubed *güira* and percussive *tambores*, made with cheap materials such as aluminum cans and goat hides, reflect the historical poverty of its artists. *Bachata*'s stigma is disappearing, however, as it increasingly gains international fame and new audiences. These changes are connected to the extensive migration of Dominicans to the northeast United States since the 1960s. *Bachata* artists such as Juan Luis Guerra and the New York–based band Aventura have elevated international recognition of the genre, which is widespread throughout Latin America, the United States, and Europe in the early twenty-first century.

See also **Music: Popular Music and Dance.**

BIBLIOGRAPHY

Hernandez, Deborah Pacini. *Bachata, a Social History of a Dominican Popular Music.* Philadelphia: Temple University Press, 1995.

HANNAH GILL

BACHELET, MICHELLE (1951–).

Michelle Bachelet, who became the first female president of Chile on 15 January 2006, was born in the Chilean capital of Santiago on 29 September 1951. Her father, Alberto Bachelet (1922–1974), had been an important figure in the government of

Salvador Allende, and he was arrested after the 1973 coup that brought Augusto Pinochet to power, and he died in prison in 1974. In January 1975 both Michelle and her mother, Ángela Jeria, were arrested and tortured for their allegiances to the Socialist Party. After they were released they went into exile in Australia and Germany, but maintained allegiance to the Socialist Party.

In 1979 Bachelet returned home to Chile, and in 1982 she completed her medical training at the University of Chile. Although the political allegiances of her family made it difficult for her to secure employment, she eventually found work at a medical clinic that specialized in treating those who had been tortured under Pinochet. She later worked for a nongovernmental organization assisting children whose parents were victims of the military regime.

Bachelet moved into politics in 1995, when she was named to the Socialist Party Central Committee. In 2000 the Chileans elected another Socialist president, Ricardo Lagos Escobar. Escobar appointed Bachelet as Chile's minister of health. In 2002 she became the first female Latin American defense minister.

In 2005 the Socialist Party of Chile selected her as its presidential candidate. Her presidential campaign platform was based on continuing Chile's free-market economic policies and maintaining the country's close ties with the United States, while increasing social benefits, especially for women, the retired, and the poor. Despite the popularity of her platform, her personal life (as a divorced mother of three and an admitted agnostic) was difficult for her to overcome in a country as Catholic as Chile. In the first round of voting she won the most support but did not receive a majority of the vote. Her victory was finally secured with a January 2006 runoff vote, where she gathered 53.3 percent of popular support.

During her presidency she worked to implement the goals of her platform. She made free public healthcare more readily available for the elderly poor, and she increased retirement pensions for Chile's most disadvantaged groups by 10 percent. When Augusto Pinochet died on 10 December 2006, she did not organize a government funeral for the ex-dictator. This decision was in keeping with general public sentiment; on the day that he died, thousands of demonstrators celebrated in the streets of Santiago.

See also **Chile, Political Parties: Socialist Party.**

BIBLIOGRAPHY

Guzmán Bravo, Rosario, and Gonzalo Rojas Donoso. *La hija del tigre.* Santiago de Chile: RiL Editores, 2005.

Subercaseaux, Elizabeth, and Malú Sierra. *Michelle: Desde la cárcel a la presidencia de Chile.* Barcelona: RBA Libros, 2006.

Worth, Richard. *Michelle Bachelet.* New York: Chelsea House, 2007.

EMILY BERQUIST

BACHILLER Y MORALES, ANTONIO

(1812–1889). Antonio Bachiller y Morales (*b.* 7 June 1812; *d.* 10 January 1889), Cuban writer, historian, and archaeologist. Born in Havana, Bachiller y Morales became a lawyer and a university professor. He was persecuted and exiled by the Spanish authorities when the Ten Years' War (1868–1878) began because he favored Cuba's autonomy from Spain. He is best known for his extensive and tireless research, the basis of studies in which he brought together information that had not previously attracted attention. Perhaps the most important of these studies is his three-volume history of Cuban letters and education (*Apuntes para la historia de las letras y instrucción publica de la isla de Cuba,* 1859–1860), but he also made significant contributions on the period of the British domination of Havana (*Cuba: Monografía histórica . . . desde la perdida de la Habana hasta la restauración española,* 1883) and on the pre-Columbian inhabitants of Cuba (*Cuba primitiva,* 1880). Although Bachiller y Morales made quite a few mistakes in his haste to gather information, the efforts of modern historians would have been far less fruitful without his dedication and spadework. He died in Havana.

See also **Cuba: The Colonial Era (1492–1898).**

BIBLIOGRAPHY

In the absence of English materials see Max Henríquez Ureña, *Panorama histórico de la literatura cubana* (1963), vol. 1, pp. 361–364. See also José Martí's piece on Bachiller y Morales, *Obras completas* (1963), vol. 5, pp. 141–153.

JOSÉ M. HERNÁNDEZ

BACKUS AND JOHNSTON.

Backus and Johnston, a company started in 1889 by American engineers Jacob Backus and J. Howard Johnston, with the first customized smelter in the copper center of Casapalca, Peru. A few years later the company reduced the cost of transporting copper for export, making use of the arrival in the high Andes in 1893 of the Central Railway. As the company gained control of mineral transport, it lowered the amounts paid for copper to rival producers. This practice soon drove many Peruvian producers out of copper mining and led to a virtual foreign copper monopoly. By the end of World War I the New York–based Cerro De Pasco Corporation had taken over Backus and Johnston, and by 1930 few other locally owned mining smelters remained. A large measure of the profitability of Andean copper can be attributed to the low cost of labor. The cheap labor force of villagers had left the nearby villages, attracted by the cash offered for work in the mines. Bad working conditions, low pay, and company inattention soon led to strikes. After years of struggle miners won the right to an eight-hour day and other concessions. Labor conditions remained poor, and mine workers continued to be organized and militant.

See also **Copper Industry.**

BIBLIOGRAPHY

Rosemary Thorp and Geoffrey Bertram, *Peru, 1890–1977: Growth and Policy in an Open Economy* (1978), esp. pp. 73–83.

Florencia Mallon, *The Defense of Community in Peru's Central Highlands: Peasant Struggle and Capitalist Transition, 1860–1940* (1983), esp. pp. 126, 135–136.

Additional Bibliography

Jochamowitz, Luis. *Hombres, minas y pozos: 1896-1996: Un siglo de minería y petróleo en el Perú.* Lima: Sociedad Nacional de Minería y Petróle, 1996.

VINCENT PELOSO

BÁEZ, BUENAVENTURA (1812–1884).

Buenaventura Báez (*b.* 1812; *d.* 1884), five-time president of the Dominican Republic. Báez was born in Azua to a wealthy landowner and his African slave. During the Haitian occupation of Santo Domingo, Báez represented Azua in the Haitian Congress and Constituent Assembly. He distrusted the Dominican independence movement and refused to recognize its authority after the proclamation of independence on 27 February 1844. Throughout his political career, Báez sought to place his country under the protection of a major foreign power, believing that the Dominican Republic did not have the strength to maintain genuine independence. With the aid of his future archrival, General Pedro Santana, he assumed the presidency for the first time in 1849.

First Presidential Term (24 September 1849–15 February 1853) Báez negotiated with both France and England for their possible acquisition of the Dominican Republic. He became the champion of the interests of the upper and middle classes by promoting the development of industry and furthering the educational system through the opening of national colleges at Santo Domingo and Santiago de los Caballeros. Báez concluded a concordat with the Vatican by which the Roman Catholic church was permitted to provide religious instruction in Dominican public schools. During his first term, the country suffered frequent attacks by Haiti, all of which were repelled. In 1853 Báez was forced into exile by Santana.

Second Presidential Term (8 October 1856–12 June 1858) Báez began his second term by unleashing a fierce persecution of Santana and his followers. He issued paper currency, which led to a devaluation of the peso and the ruin of many landowners, particularly the tobacco cultivators of the Cibao. A revolt in that fertile agricultural region toppled Báez, who fled to Spain. While still in exile there, he advocated Spain's annexation of the Dominican Republic.

Third Presidential Term (8 December 1865–29 May 1866) During his third term, Báez established a truly despotic regime marked by his effort to crush all opposition. He antagonized Dominican patriots by negotiating a deal with U.S. Secretary of State William H. Seward, by which the Dominican Republic would allow the United States to acquire the Samaná Peninsula in return for economic aid. Once again, a revolt in the Cibao forced Báez to flee the country.

Fourth Presidential Term (2 May 1868–January 1874) Báez's fourth term was the bloodiest and the most anarchic of his five terms. It is known in Dominican history as the "Regime of the Six Years." After failing to sell Samaná to the United States for $2 million, Báez offered the entire country to Washington. This plan met with a positive response from U.S. President Ulysses S. Grant, but the determined resistance of Senator Charles Sumner of Massachusetts prevented the annexation. By 1874, revolutionary forces compelled Báez to flee to Curaçao.

Fifth Presidential Term (27 December 1876–2 March 1878) Báez began his final term by promising democratic, liberal reforms, but he was soon indulging in familiar repressive measures. He also renewed his efforts to incorporate his country into the United States. His final exile from Santo Domingo began in March 1878. He died in Puerto Rico.

See also **Dominican Republic.**

BIBLIOGRAPHY

Emilio Rodríguez Demorizi, *Papeles de Buenaventura Báez* (1969).

Ian Bell, *The Dominican Republic* (1981).

Additional Bibliography

Cruz Sánchez, Filiberto. *La guerra de los seis años: La guerra contra los planes anexionistas de Buenaventura Báez, 1868-1874.* Santo Domingo: Nuevo Diario, 2005

Sang, Mu-Kien A. *Buenaventura Báez, el caudillo del Sur: 1844-1878.* Santo Domingo: Instituto Tecnológico de Santo Domingo, 1991

KAI P. SCHOENHALS

BÁEZ, CECILIO (1862–1941).

Cecilio Báez (*b.* 1 February 1862; *d.* 18 June 1941), politician, intellectual, diplomat, public servant, and provisional president of Paraguay (1905–1906). Cecilio Báez was one of the founders of the Liberal Party in 1887 and later its president. He was a deputy in Congress for several terms, beginning in 1895. He might be remembered most as the party's leading theoretician. Báez was also known for denouncing Francisco Solano López, the controversial leader who led Paraguay into disastrous War of the Triple Alliance in 1864. He was appointed provisional president on 9 December

1905 for eleven months. Because of his influence, he was often able to keep the Liberals somewhat united in spite of their tendency to splinter into factions. By profession a doctor of law and a historiographer, Báez was instrumental in shaping a national education program. His prolific writings dealt with Paraguayan history as well as literary, legal, and political issues. He was a great advocate of democracy as well as a strong critic of the Catholic Church. Báez was the National University's rector throughout the 1920s and 1930s. After the Chaco War with Bolivia, Báez, as foreign minister, signed the peace treaty on 28 July 1938.

See also **Paraguay, Political Parties: Liberal Party.**

BIBLIOGRAPHY

Paul H. Lewis, *Paraguay Under Stroessner* (1980).

Harris Gaylord Warren, *Rebirth of the Paraguayan Republic* (1985).

Riordan Roett and Richard Scott Sacks, *Paraguay: The Personalist Legacy* (1991).

Additional Bibliography

Aguero Wagner, Luis. *Historia ocultada: La policía de la cultura y otros capítulos negados de la historia paraguaya.* Asunción: 2006.

Dávalos, Juan Santiago. *Cecilio Báez como ideólogo.* Asunción: Escuela Técnica Salesiana, 1967.

Farcau, Bruce W. *The Chaco War: Bolivia and Paraguay, 1932-1935.* Westport, CT: Praeger, 1996.

MIGUEL A. GATTI

BAHAMAS, COMMONWEALTH OF THE.

Commonwealth of the Bahamas, an archipelago of over 700 islands, stretching from less than fifty miles off the coast of Florida south toward Haiti. The total land area is over 5,000 square miles, but only sixteen of the islands are populated to any large extent (2007 population: 305,655). The capital, Nassau, is located on the central island of New Providence. Historically, the Bahamas' claim to fame lies in the fact that its easternmost island, San Salvador, formerly called Guanahani and then Watlings Island, was the first land discovered by Christopher Columbus on October 12, 1492. "Bahamas" comes from the Spanish *bajamar*, meaning "shallow water," and refers to the shallow waters that surround the

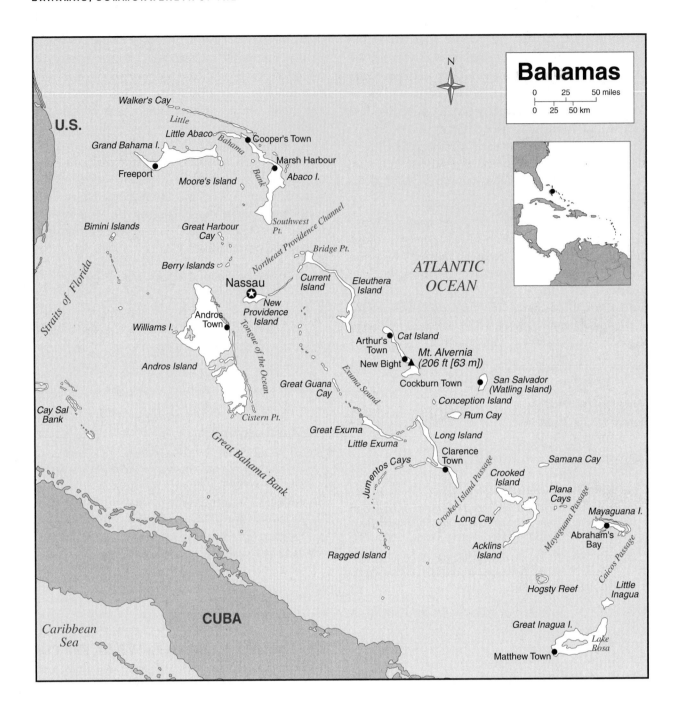

islands, making them ideal harbors. The Spanish made no attempt to colonize the islands, however, because they were settled by an indigenous population, the Arawaks, who had no apparent treasures or developed civilization. Almost all of the Indians died from contact with the Spanish or were dragged off to work in the mines of Hispaniola.

In 1629, the islands were granted to Sir Robert Heath, attorney general of England. In 1647 the Crown made another grant to the Company of Eleutherian Adventurers, who colonized the island of Eleuthera. The Eleutherian Adventurers, the first English settlers of the Bahamas, came from Bermuda under the direction of Sir William Sayle, seeking liberty and freedom of religion. In 1670, a third grant was issued by Charles II to six lord proprietors from Carolina.

The eighteenth century brought a flurry of activity to the islands. The first royal governor, Sir Woodes Rodgers, was sent by the Crown to Nassau

Commonwealth of the Bahamas

Population:	305,655 (2007 est.)
Area:	5,382 sq mi
Official language:	English
Languages:	English, Creole
National currency:	Bahamian dollar (BSD)
Principal religions:	Baptists, 35%; Anglicans, 15%; other Protestant Christians, 24%; Roman Catholics, 13.5% (2000)
Ethnicity:	Roughly 85% of the population is descended from African slaves; most of the remainder is white, primarily of British heritage.
Capital:	Nassau
Other urban centers:	Freeport
Annual rainfall:	50 in
Principal geographical features:	The Bahamas are an archipelago of over 700 islands in the Atlantic Ocean. Some of the largest include Andros, Abaco, Grand Bahama, and Great Inagua. The capital is on New Providence island, near the center of the archipelago. The terrain is mostly low and flat, with the highest point being Mt. Alvernia (206 ft) on Cat Island.
Economy:	*GDP per capita:* $21,600 (2006 est.)
Principal products and exports:	The economy of the Bahamas is centered on tourism and finance.
Government:	Gained independence from the United Kingdom in 1973. The Bahamas are a constitutional parliamentary democracy. The chief of state is the king or queen of the United Kingdom, who is represented by a governor general. The parliament is bicameral. The 41 members of the House of Assembly are directly elected, and the leader of the majority in the House is the prime minister and head of government. Leading House members advise the governor general on the appointment of a 16 member Senate.
Armed forces:	In 2005 the Royal Bahamian Defense Force consisted of 860 active personnel and operated 8 ships and 4 aircraft.
Transportation:	*Ports:* Freeport, Nassau, South Riding Point *Roads:* 961 mi paved / 713 unpaved (1999) *National airline:* Bahamas Air *Airports:* 24 paved field airports and 1 heliport, with the largest in Nassau and Freeport.
Media:	3 daily newspapers: *Freeport News, Nassau Daily Tribune, Nassau Guardian;* 5 private and 1 state-owned radio stations; 1 private and 1 state-owned television stations
Literacy and education:	*Total literacy rate:* 96% Education is compulsory for children ages 5 to 16. The College of the Bahamas offers the nation's only associate and bachelor's degree programs.

in 1718. By the middle of the century, Nassau had become the hub of activity for pirates because of the island's strategic location. During the American Revolution, loyalists fled to the islands along with many freed slaves. In 1782, the Spanish attacked New Providence, which was finally ceded to Great Britian in exchange for East Florida under terms of the Treaty of Paris (1783). The influx of loyalists spurred economic development, but not without competition from the landed elite. Both fared well, however, owing to the profitability of the cotton harvests before the devastation caused by the chenille bug in 1788.

The islands experienced relative peace throughout the nineteenth century. The abolition of slavery in 1838 brought social and economic reconstruction, although a high percentage of the slaves were freed before that date. During the U.S. Civil War, the colony prospered owing to its ideal situation as a depot for vessels running the blockade of the Confederacy.

The House of Assembly, formed in 1729, remains the most important political institution. It was controlled almost exclusively by white merchants and settlers throughout the nineteenth century. In the twentieth century the oligarchy was run by a group of merchants known as the Bay Street Boys, named after Nassau's main commercial downtown street. Politics changed in 1962 when the House voted for universal suffrage. With the formation of the popularly supported Progressive Liberal Party (PLP), white minority rule ended in 1967.

The PLP began a program of national development and controlled migration, and instituted a highly successful Bahamianization program in 1973. The islands gained their independence on July 10 of that year but retain ties with Great Britain through the Commonwealth. The leader of the PLP, Sir Linden Oscar Pindling, was prime minister from 1967 to 1992. Hubert A. Ingraham of the Free National Movement was elected prime minister in 1992. The PLP returned to power in 2002 with the election of Perry Christie, but Ingraham again became prime minister in 2007.

The main source of foreign currency for the Bahamas is tourism, followed by the well-developed offshore banking system for international investors. Because of the lack of taxes, and the relatively stable political situation, the Bahamas is an attractive tax haven. It is home to hundreds of European, American, and Canadian investors. In the early twenty-first century, the islands continue to rely on tourism but have suffered several significant setbacks. After the 11 September 2001 attacks on the United States, tourism declined for a couple of years. Then in 2004 and 2005, large hurricanes damaged the islands.

The Bahamas had a series of conflicts with the United States in the 1980s over its financial secrecy laws, which have allowed some U.S. investors to avoid taxation in the United States, and also about drug trafficking. Consequently, the Bahamas was excluded from the U.S. Caribbean Basin Initiative. After 1985, however, relations improved. In 1989 the U.S. Senate voted against a bill proposing to make the Bahamas ineligible for U.S. aid. In the 1990s the United States and the Bahamas had increased collaboration to curb the drug trade, which had grown significantly throughout the Caribbean.

See also **Pindling, Lynden Oscar; San Salvador.**

BIBLIOGRAPHY

Alan Burns, *History of the British West Indies* (1965).

Michael Craton, *A History of the Bahamas,* 2nd ed. (1968).

Gordon K. Lewis, *The Growth of the Modern West Indies* (1968).

Paul Albury, *Story of the Bahamas* (1975).

For more statistical information see *The Caribbean Yearbook 1979/80* (1980) and *The Bahamas Handbook* (annual). See also Tony Thorndike, "Bahamas," in *South America, Central America, and the Caribbean 1991* (1990).

Additional Bibliography

Johnson, Whittington Bernard. *Post-Emancipation Race Relations in the Bahamas.* Gainesville: University Press of Florida, 2006.

Saunders, Gail. *Bahamian Society after Emancipation.* Rev. ed. Kingston, Jamaica: Ian Randle, 2003.

DARIÉN DAVIS

BAHIA.   A state in Northeastern Brazil, Bahia has an area of 216,612 square miles. The population of 13,950,146 million (2006) is 67 percent mulatto, 27 percent white, and 11 percent black. The capital city is Salvador.

The Baía de Todos os Santos (All Saints Bay), discovered by Amerigo Vespucci in 1501, gave its name to the state. The Portuguese launched a plan to colonize Bahia in 1530. The main product was sugarcane, cultivated in the fertile soil of the Recôncavo, the region surrounding the bay. Cotton and tobacco were also grown, the latter a valuable item in the slave trade. The expansion of cattle raising led to the occupation of the interior of the state. The educational and cultural life of the colony was organized primarily by the Jesuits, who also worked on the conversion of the Indians to Christianity.

In spite of the Dutch invasion (1623–1624), the seventeenth century was the apogee of colonial life in Bahia, thanks to the expanding production of both sugar and tobacco, which responded to the higher demands in the European and African markets, respectively. The social structure was hierarchical, oligarchic, and repressive. Administrative positions were filled by whites, with the slaves brought from Africa constituting the labor force. Indian labor was used mostly in cattle raising in the interior. Salvador was the most important city of the colony until the second decade of the nineteenth century, when the coffee industry vaulted Rio de Janeiro and São Paulo to paramount importance.

Due to strong resistance by the Portuguese, Bahia did not gain its independence (1823) until one year after the rest of the country did. Even though many *baianos* occupied prominent positions in the national administration, Bahia became a second-class province during the empire (1822–1889), primarily because of the declining importance of its exports. Economic stagnation lasted until 1907, when cacao, cultivated in the southern part of the state, became the major export.

The coming to power of Governor José Joaquim Seabra (1912), with his politics of national salvation aimed at ending the powerful oligarchies in the country, typified the ascension of sectors of the urban middle class to positions of command. The sugar barons, dominant in the earlier period, had lost both the economic power and the political influence that they had previously enjoyed. The administrative decentralization of the empire was replaced by centralized governments in the republic, which aimed to integrate a fragmented country.

Oligarchic and conservative, the government of Bahia opposed the Revolution of 1930. The political movement, however, stirred up popular demonstrations. The depression of the 1930s was extremely severe in the state, due to its heavy dependence on cacao exports, which fell drastically. Social instability and strike attempts were curbed by strong state repression. Bahia was then governed by Juraci Magalhães who, influenced by Franklin D. Roosevelt's New Deal, launched a small-scale program of public works and succeeded in enhancing the economic situation of the state.

The Estado Novo (1937–1945) of Getúlio Vargas installed a dictatorial government under which the states were ruled by intervenors appointed by Vargas. Otávio Mangabeira, who served as governor from 1947 to 1951, is considered the most outstanding political figure in the state after Rui Barbosa.

Agriculture and commerce remain the main activities of the state. After the creation of the Industrial Park of Aratu during the 1970s, however, Bahia became the industrial leader in the Northeast, although its capital-intensive industries have not created much local employment. Given Bahia's attractive beaches, more attention is being paid to the development of tourism.

Culturally, Bahia is known for its lasting influence from slave times. The Yoruba religious system of Candomblé as well as the martial art of Capoeira are distinguishing components of this region. In addition, it is the birthplace of some of Brazil's most famous artists and thinkers, including João Gilberto, Gilberto Gil, Caetano Veloso, and Luiz R. B. Mott.

See also **Guangala.**

BIBLIOGRAPHY

Azevedo, Thales de. *Povoamento da cidade do Salvador*, 3rd edition. Salvador: Editora Itapuã, 1969.

Costa, Ana Alice Alcantara. *As donas no poder: Mulher e política na Bahia*. Salvador, Brazil: Núcleo de Estudos Interdisciplinares sobre a Mulher, FFCH/UFBA, 1998.

Kraay, Hendrik. *Afro-Brazilian Culture and Politics: Bahia, 1790s to 1990s*. Armonk, NY: M. E. Sharpe, 1998.

Mattoso, Katia M. De Queirós. *Bahia, século XIX: Uma provinia no Império*, 2nd edition. Rio de Janeiro: Editora Nova Fronteira,1992.

McGowan, Chris. *The Brazilian Sound: Samba, Bossa Nova, and the Popular Music of Brazil*. Philadelphia: Temple University Press, 1998.

Novais Sampaio, Consuelo. "Crisis in the Brazilian Oligarchical System: A Case Study on Bahia, 1889–1937." Ph.D. diss., Johns Hopkins University, 1979.

Reis, João José. *Slave Rebellion in Brazil: The Muslim Uprising of 1835 in Bahia*, trans. Arthur Brakel. Baltimore, MD: Johns Hopkins University Press, 1993.

Russell-Wood, A. J. R. *Fidalgos and Philanthropists: The Santa Casa da Misericórdia of Bahia, 1550–1755*. Berkeley: University of California Press, 1968.

CONSUELO NOVAIS SAMPAIO

BAHÍA. Bahía, the name given to one of several prehistoric cultures in coastal Ecuador during the Regional-Developmental Period (500 BCE–500 CE). Bahía is named after the large bay at the mouth of the Chone River, Bahía de Caráquez, but its territory extends 90 miles down the coast to southern Manabí Province. It was formally defined by Ecuadorian Emilio Estrada in the late 1950s, on the basis of his deep excavations in the modern city of Bahía de Caráquez and nearby sites. Other Bahía occupations have been documented at Los Esteros and Tarquí (near modern Manta), Salango, and La Plata Island.

Where not destroyed by modern settlement, some sites appear to have been true urban centers with ceremonial precincts and rectangular platform mounds having a formal grid plan. La Plata Island served as an important religious sanctuary where regular pilgrimages were made for ritual events and where votive offerings of figurines and other objects were repeatedly deposited. Ceremonial activity has also been documented at Salango, in southern coastal Manabí, where archaeologists have uncovered the remains of a 120-square-yard, adobe-walled temple structure bordered by deep wall trenches, stone alignments, and linear posthole patterns. Given the large number of Bahía burials uncovered and the richness of their associated grave offerings, the structure has been interpreted as a ceremonial/mortuary one for elite sectors of Bahía society.

Apart from these scientific excavations, much knowledge of this culture comes from the elaborate ceramic artifacts that have been unearthed both by professional archaeologists and by commercially motivated looters. Although some traits show continuity with the earlier Chorrera culture (such as iridescent painting), new vessel forms, decorative techniques, and thematic imagery also appear in Bahía pottery. New types of ceramic artifacts include miniature house models, head rests, and "golf-tee" ear plugs said to represent Asiatic influences, presumably through trans-Pacific contact. Anthropomorphic figurines appear in a wide variety of forms and sizes, including the small, solid, mold-made Esteros type and the larger, hollow La Plata type. The latter are decorated with multicolored postfire pigments similar to those of Jama-coaque figurines. Crudely shaped anthropomorphic figures also appear on tusk-shaped stone pendants. One artifact type unique to the Bahía culture is the carved stone plaque made from volcanic tuff, which is apparently restricted to La Plata Island. Typically these are decorated on one side with carved geometric designs in a quadripartite layout, usually small incised circles inside an X-shaped figure. No contextual information is available, but suggested functions range from gaming pieces to navigational devices.

The urban character, elaborate ceremonialism, and mortuary ritual of the largest Bahía sites indicate considerable sociopolitical complexity, very likely a stratified chiefdom, or *señorío*, with a well-defined regional settlement hierarchy. In spite of the littoral nature of the site thus far studied, the Bahía culture probably had a strong agricultural base supported by a tributary population of inland farmers and craft specialists. External contacts were most intensive with adjacent Regional-Developmental chiefdoms to the north, south, and east, although long-distance voyaging for exotic resources, such as precious stones, may have occurred.

See also **Guangala; Precontact History: Latin America in the Precontact Period.**

BIBLIOGRAPHY

Emilio Estrada, *Arqueología de Manabí central* (1962).

Matthew Stirling and Marian Stirling, "Tarquí: An Early Site in Manabí Province, Ecuador," in *Smithsonian Institution, Bureau of American Ethnology, Bulletin* 186 (1963): 1–28.

Jorge G. Marcos and Presley Norton, "Interpretación sobre la arqueología de la Isla de la Plata," in *Miscellánea antropológica ecuatoriana* 1, no. 1 (1981): 136–154.

Robert A. Feldman and Michael E. Moseley, "The Northern Andes," in *Ancient South Americans,* edited by Jesse D. Jennings (1983).

Presley Norton et al., "Excavaciones en Salango, provincia de Manabí, Ecuador," in *Miscelánea antropológica ecuatoriana* 3 (1983): 9–80.

Additional Bibliography

Cummins, Thomas B.F., Julio Burgos Cabrera, and Carlos Mora Hoyos. *Huellas del pasado: Los sellos de jama-coaque.* Quito: Museos del Banco Central del Ecuador, 1996.

Currie, Elizabeth J. *Prehistory of the Southern Manabí Coast, Ecuador: López Viejo.* Oxford: Tempvs Reparatvm, 1995.

Marcos, Jorge G. *Arqueología de la costa ecuatoriana: Nuevos enfoques.* Quito: Corporación Editora Nacional; Guayaquil, Ecuador: Escuela Politécnica del Litoral, Centro de Estudios Arqueológicos y Antropologicos, 1986.

Pearsall, Deborah M. *Plants and People in Ancient Ecuador: The Ethnobotany of the Jama River Valley.* Belmont: Wadsworth/Thompson Learning, 2004.

Raymond, J. Scott, Richard L. Burger, and Jeffrey Quilter, eds. *Archaeology of Formative Ecuador: A Symposium at Dumbarton Oaks, 7 and 8 October 1995.* Washington, DC: Dumbarton Oaks Research Library and Collection, 2003.

Reitz, Elizabeth Jean, and Maria A. Masucci. *Guangala Fishers and Farmers: A Case Study of Animal Use at El Azúcar, Southwestern Ecuador.* Pittsburgh, PA: University of Pittsburgh, Department of Anthropology; Quito: Libri Mundi, 2004.

Zeidler, James A., and Deborah M. Pearsall. *Regional Archaeology in Northern Manabí, Ecuador.* Pittsburgh, PA: University of Pittsburgh, Dept. of Anthropology, 1994.

JAMES A. ZEIDLER

BAHÍA, ISLAS DE. Islas De Bahía. The Bay Islands of Honduras, just off the north coast of that country, constitute the smallest and most distinctive of the eighteen departments of the Republic of Honduras. The elongated cluster of eight islands and sixty-five cays has a total land area of just under ninety-two square miles. The major islands (from west to east, Utila, Roatán, Barbaret, and Guanaja) are continental in geological structure and surrounded by reefs in unusually clear water. Perhaps no other part of the Caribbean has experienced more cultural diversity than these islands; they have been occupied by nine distinct groups since aboriginal times. Occupants have included Pech (Paya) Indians, colonial Spaniards, multinational pirates, Englishmen, Garífuna (Black Caribs), Anglo-Antilleans, Afro-Antilleans, North Americans, and Spanish Hondurans.

While the earlier archeological record indicates that aboriginal islanders were influenced by the high cultures of Mesoamerica (primarily Maya), later pre-Columbian artifacts are similar to those of the adjacent mainland, the home of Indians identified as Pech. Columbus visited these islands in 1502 during his fourth voyage, the first to Central America.

The native islanders, during the first century of uncontested Spanish colonization, were enslaved, Christianized, and used as a labor supply. Bartolomé de Las Casas exaggerated the contact population, saying it was "more than 150,000 souls"; it was more likely only several thousand strong when first encountered by the Spaniards. By 1544, documents show that only about 1,000 remained. The census of 1639 counted 400 souls. Shortly afterward, the Spaniards depopulated the islands because the natives were aiding pirate intruders.

Non-Spanish raiders found the islands particularly strategic and attractive because the gold-carrying Honduras Fleet called at nearby Trujillo, and other shipping routes passed nearby. Deep embayments on Roatán's south coast were the best refuges in the region. The largest attack was perhaps that of William Jackson, who with 1,500 men and sixteen vessels took Trujillo in 1642. The buccaneers wintered on Roatán.

The English military continued to disrupt the Spanish influence over the islands, particularly during 1742–1749 and 1779–1782. The ruined English fortifications around Port Royal, dating from these two major occupations, can still be seen. Anthony's Cay, also on Roatán, was another English site of this period.

In 1797, the British-organized importation of some 2,000 Black Caribs (now called Garífuna) from the island of Saint Vincent in the Windward Islands introduced another culture to the islands. This marked the beginning of a permanent settlement pattern that has persisted until today. Most of the Garífuna settled the beachlands around the Bay of Honduras, but their first village was Punta Gorda, on the north coast of Roatán.

English speakers, still dominant in the islands, became firmly established after Cayman Islanders arrived in 1835, a year after the abolition of slavery. For a decade during the mid-nineteenth century, when the English claimed the islands as a crown colony, the traditions and social inclinations of Anglo- and Afro-Antilleans became well embedded.

North Americans visited the islands in the 1860s, as traders in the banana and coconut commerce with New Orleans; since then they have come as tourists who enjoy diving and fishing in the clear waters.

A relict English-speaking enclave on the rimland of the western Caribbean, the Bay Islands are experiencing a modern Hispanicization from the mainland populations. Although the Republic of Honduras has had formal political power in the islands since 1859, only since the 1970s have there been effective attempts to incorporate the islands into the mainland system. Attracted primarily by economic opportunities represented by a developing tourism industry, Spanish-speaking Ladinos from the mainland are increasing their proportion of the population and asserting their culture. According to the national census of May 1988, the islands are home to 22,062 people, roughly three-fourths of whom live on Roatán, the most developed island. The largest settlements are the capital, Coxen Hole, on Roatán (3,901); Bonacca, the quaint stilt house settlement off Guanaja (2,027); Oak Ridge, on Roatán (1,304); and East Harbour, on Utila (1,261).

See also **Honduras.**

BIBLIOGRAPHY

William V. Davidson, *Historical Geography of the Bay Islands, Honduras: Anglo-Hispanic Conflict in the Western Caribbean* (1974).

Elissa Warantz, "The Bay Islands English of Honduras," in *Central American English,* edited by John Holm (1983).

Additional Bibliography

Jacobson, Susan K., Thorn, Sherry L., and Alevizon, William S. *The Bay Islands: Nature and People.* Honduras: Bay Islands Conservation Association, 1992.

Lytton Regalado, Alexandra; Trujillo, Federico; Vallerani, Andrea, and Rodas, César. *Las Islas de la Bahía.* El Salvador: Laffite Bloch, 2002.

WILLIAM V. DAVIDSON

BAHÍA BLANCA. Bahía Blanca, city at the southern edge of the Argentine province of Buenos Aires (2001 census population of 276,546) located on a natural bay. Founded in 1828 as a military outpost against roaming Pampa Indians, it was used by Juan Manuel de Rosas as a stronghold against the Indians in 1833. Following the Campaign of the Desert (1879–1883), a concerted effort by the Buenos Aires government to clear the Indians from the Pampa to make room for agrarian colonists, and the completion of a railway link with Buenos Aires in 1885, it became an important center of colonization and the end station of the General Roca railway. The hinterland was settled predominantly by families of Italian ancestry who managed successful farmsteads and cattle ranches and founded urban enterprises in the city. Nearby Puerto Galván is the site of an oil refinery that processes crude oil brought from Plaza Huincul, at the foot of the Andes. Packing plants, tanneries, transportation workshops, grain-processing mills, and a large chemical plant that uses petroleum derivatives dominate the economic activities of the city, which has also developed into a cultural center of the southern pampa. The Universidad Nacional del Sur, founded in 1956, has more than 15,000 students. Bahía Blanca is connected by major highways with Mar del Plata and Buenos Aires. Puerto Belgrano is an important strategic base for the navy and the air force.

See also **Argentina, Geography.**

BIBLIOGRAPHY

Pedro González P., *Bahía Blanca como capital de una nueva provincia* (Bahía Blanca, 1962).

María E. Rey, *Historia de la industria en Bahía Blanca* (Bahía Blanca, 1980).

Additional Bibliography

Cernadas de Bulnes, Mabel Nelida. *Historia, política y sociedad en el sudoeste bonaerense.* Bahía Blanca: Universidad Nacional del Sur, 2001.

Gallardo, Juan Luis. *Vida y circunstancia de Enrique Julio: Fundador de La Nueva Provincia.* Bahía Blanca: Edición de La Nueva Provincia, 1998.

Llull, Laura. *Prensa y politica en Bahía Blanca: La nueva provincia en las presidencias radicales, 1916–1930.* Bahía Blanca: Universidad Nacional del Sur, 2005.

Viego, Valentina. *El desarrollo industrial local en territorios periféricos: El caso de Bahía Blanca.* Bahía Blanca: Departamento de Economía, Universidad Nacional del Sur, 2004.

Zingoni, José María. *Arquitectura industrial: Ferrocarriles y puertos: Bahía Blanca, 1880–1930.* Bahía Blanca: Editorial de la Universidad Nacional del Sur, 1996.

CÉSAR N. CAVIEDES

BAIÃO. Baião, a popular form of music, dance, and song in northeastern Brazil, typically played by trios of accordion, triangle, and *zabumba* (bass drum). The *baião*, and related genres such as the *baiano* and *abaianada*, most likely originated in the nineteenth century as a social dance music and musical pattern in rural northeastern Brazil among the mestizo population. The name probably comes from an early association with the state of Bahia. The music and dance elements of *baião* were influenced by, if not derived from, Afro-Brazilian styles. An urban form of the *baião* was created and popularized nationally in the 1940s by Luiz Gonzaga, who mixed a rhythm played on the *viola* (a ten-string folk guitar) by northeastern bards with drum patterns from Bandas De Pífanos (fife-and-drum bands). In the 1950s and 1960s it became a national symbol of the Northeast when millions of northeasterners migrated to the South (especially to São Paulo) in search of work. Baião is not as popular as samba or bossa nova, but it has influenced important contemporary musicians, such as Gilbert Gil. Musically, the *baião* is characterized by a syncopated duple rhythm played on the *zabumba* and a melodic scale featuring a flatted seventh. The songs' texts dwell on love and on the natural beauty and chronic problems of the Northeast. They are usually told from a male perspective, often in slang and a heavy northeastern accent.

See also **Banda de Pífanos; Bossa Nova; Cantoria; Gil, Gilberto; Samba.**

BIBLIOGRAPHY

José Ramos Tinhorão, *Pequena história da música popular: Da modinha ao tropicalismo,* 5th ed. (1986), esp. pp. 219–229.

Mundicarmo Maria Rocha Ferretti, *Baião dos dois: A música de Zédantas e Luiz Gonzaga...* (1988).

Chris Mc Gowan and Ricardo Pessanha, *The Brazilian Sound: Samba, Bossa Nova, and the Popular Music of Brazil* (1991), esp. pp. 135–136.

Additional Bibliography

Crook, Larry. *Brazilian Music: Northeastern Traditions and the Heartbeat of a Modern Nation.* Santa Barbara, CA: ABC-CLIO, 2005.

Murphy, John P. *Music in Brazil: Experiencing Music, Expressing Culture.* New York: Oxford University Press, 2006.

Santos, José Farias dos. *Luiz Gonzaga: A música como expressão do Nordeste.* São Paulo: IBRASA, 2004.

LARRY N. CROOK

BAJA CALIFORNIA. Baja California, a peninsula about 850 miles long in the extreme northwestern part of the Republic of Mexico, extending southward from the boundary with California and separated from the mainland of Mexico by the Gulf of California. Physiographically, it is formed by a fault-block mountain with a steep escarpment facing east and a gentle slope toward the Pacific. The southern tip of the peninsula and the extreme north have a climate similar to that of the Mexican mainland and receive summer rains totaling 10–25 inches per year, but the rest of the peninsula is extremely arid, with virtually no surface water. Today, it is divided into two states: Baja California, which became a state in 1952, with a population of about 1.6 million in 1990, and Baja California Sur, which became a state in 1974, with a population of approximately 375,000 in 1990.

Occupied since pre-Columbian times by simple hunting and gathering societies, the peninsula was discovered by the Spaniards in the early 1530s and explored by Fortún Jiménez de Bertadoña in 1534, Hernán Cortés in 1535, and Francisco de Ulloa in 1539. The Jesuits established the mission of Loreto in 1697, and by the time they were expelled in 1767, they operated 19 missions and associated settlements for some 6,000 Indians. Through the nineteenth century, Baja California was characterized by scattered settlements that focused on stock raising and by a limited agriculture based on well irrigation. In 1888, it was divided into two territories.

In the early twentieth century, railway connections to California and irrigation from the Colorado River began to transform northern Baja California, and in 1948 it was connected to the rest of Mexico by railroad. The northern irrigated valleys became centers for producing wine grapes, olives, vegetables (especially tomatoes), wheat, and barley. The region became Mexico's major wine producer after an expansion of vineyard plantings in the 1970s. Tijuana has gained great importance as a tourist center, drawing many North Americans since the Prohibition era and World War II, and still offers a race course, gambling, and a flavor of the exotic to the more than 30 million tourists who cross the border each year.

Baja California Sur has followed a different economic course. After centuries of isolation, it was linked to the mainland by ferry service in 1924, and in 1973 a paved highway from south of Ensenada to La Paz was completed. Resorts have been developed at San José del Cabo, Cabo San Lucas, and outside La Paz.

BIBLIOGRAPHY

Pablo Martínez, *A History of Lower California* (1960).

Robert Cooper West, ed., *Handbook of Middle American Indians,* vol. 1 (1964), pp. 55–56, 369–370.

Adrián Valadés, *Historia de la Baja California: 1850–1880* (1974).

Jorge L. Tamayo, *Geografía moderna de Mexico,* 9th ed. (1980), pp. 49–50, 58–59, 378–379.

Robert Cooper West and John P. Augelli, *Middle America: Its Lands and Peoples,* 3d ed. (1989), pp. 245, 359–360.

Additional Bibliography

Enciso Lizárra, Sayra Selene. *Mapas, planos y diseños de Baja California, siglos XVIII y XIX.* La Paz, Baja California Sur: Instituto Sudcaliforniano de Cultura, 2006.

Kopinak, K. "Maquiladora Industrialization of the Baja California Peninsula: The Coexistence of Thick and Thin Globalization with Economic Regionalism." *International Journal of Urban and Regional Research,* 27, no. 2 (2003): 319–336.

Laylander, Don, and Moore, Jerry D., eds. *The Prehistory of Baja California: Advances in the Archaeology of the Forgotten Peninsula.* Gainesville: University Press of Florida, 2006.

Pesenti C. and Dean, K. S. "Development Challenges on the Baja California Peninsula: The Escalera Náutica." *Journal of Environment and Development,* 12, no.4 (2003): 445–454.

JOHN J. WINBERRY

BAJÍO. Bajío, an area recognized since colonial times as the "Granary of Mexico" because of its fertile soils and production of corn, beans, and wheat. Formed by the basins of Guanajuato and Jalisco, it covers parts of the states of Jalisco, Guanajuato, Querétaro, and Michoacán. The Bajío lies at an altitude of about 6,500 feet, and its surface is covered by thick lacustrine sediments enriched with volcanic ash. It receives about 25 inches of rainfall a year, almost all of which falls during the summer months.

During the pre-Columbian era, the Bajío was on the northern frontier of Mesoamerica and was occupied largely by nomadic Chichimecs. Opened to Spanish colonization after the Mixtón War of 1541, the area drew Otomí and Tarascan farmers from the south and east, followed by Spanish missionaries, who began producing wheat, and by ranchers, who introduced herds of livestock. The discovery of silver at Zacatecas in 1546, at Guanajuato in 1563, and later at sites to the north and east, created markets for agricultural products, and garrison towns such as Celaya (1571) were established to protect the silver route from Zacatecas to Mexico City from hostile Indians.

By the mid-seventeenth century, the Bajío was Mexico's major wheat-producing area. With this success came the expansion of cultivated land, the decline of livestock, the development of large estates, and the rapid growth of population, especially during the eighteenth century. Irrigation also became important; Spanish *hacendados* used springs but also irrigated with water from the Lerma River and its tributaries. The earliest of these works, dating from 1648, was the dam on the Laguna de Yuriria. For the most part, wheat was grown on irrigated land, and maize was raised on nonirrigated plots. During the colonial period a textile industry based on wool, and later cotton, grew up in the cities of the Bajío, especially Querétaro, Celaya, and Salamanca.

The Bajío remained Mexico's most productive agricultural region until the 1950s, when new lands were opened in the irrigated valleys of the northwest. Even though much of the Bajío was broken up into *ejidos* during the 1930s, the region remains important for farming, growing wheat, truck crops (especially strawberries), alfalfa, corn, and beans. New irrigation complexes such as the Solís dam on the Lerma River (1949) have replaced the old systems, whose relict features are still visible in the landscape today.

See also **Agriculture.**

BIBLIOGRAPHY

D. A. Brading, *Haciendas and Ranchos in the Mexican Bajío: León, 1700–1860* (1978).

Michael E. Murphy, *Irrigation in the Bajío Region of Colonial Mexico* (1986).

Robert Cooper West and John P. Augelli, *Middle America: Its Lands and Peoples,* 3d ed. (1989), pp. 258–260, 304–305.

Additional Bibliography

Cárdenas García, Efraín. *El Bajío en el clásico: Análisis regional y organización política.* Zamora, Michoacán: El Colegio de Michoacán, 1999.

JOHN J. WINBERRY

BAKER, LORENZO DOW (1840–1908). Lorenzo Dow Baker (*b.* 15 March 1840; *d.* 21 June 1908), native of Wellfleet, Massachusetts, leading Cape Cod shipowner, and a principal founder of the modern banana-exporting industry in the Caribbean. Captain Baker first brought a small cargo of bananas from Jamaica to New Jersey in 1870. In subsequent years he greatly expanded this trade, developing it between Jamaica and Boston. In 1884 he led the formation of the Boston Fruit Company, which in 1899 merged with Minor C. Keith's Tropical Trading & Transport Company and other banana interests to become the United Fruit Company. Baker continued to serve the company as its representative in Jamaica until just before his death in Boston. His development of the banana industry contributed to considerable economic growth in Jamaica.

See also **Banana Industry.**

BIBLIOGRAPHY

Frederick U. Adams, *Conquest of the Tropics: The Story of the Creative Enterprises Conducted by the United Fruit Company* (1914); *National Cyclopædia of American Biography*, vol. 14 (1917), pp. 350–351.

Philip K. Reynolds, *The Banana: Its History, Cultivation and Place Among Staple Foods* (1927).

Charles M. Wilson, *Empire in Green and Gold* (1947).

Additional Bibliography

Bartlett, Wilson Randolph. "Lorenzo Dow Baker and the Development of the Banana Trade Between Jamaica and the United States, 1881-1890." Ph.D. diss., American University, 1977.

SUE DAWN MCGRADY

BALAGUER, JOAQUÍN (1907–2002).

Joaquín Balaguer, born in Villa Bisonó on 1 September 1907, was a Dominican author, lawyer, politician, and three-time president of the Dominican Republic (1960–1962, 1966–1978, 1986–1996). He studied law at both Santo Domingo and Paris, receiving a doctorate of law from each. In 1930 he became involved in the conspiracy of Rafael Estrella Ureña against president Horacio Vásquez, which brought Rafael-Leónidas Trujillo Molina to power. Balaguer served the Trujillo regime in important ambassadorial posts abroad and as minister of education, vice president (1957–1960), and president (1960–1961) at home. Whereas most members of Trujillo's government used their positions for personal enrichment, Balaguer continued to lead his modest bachelor existence.

In the wake of Trujillo's assassination in 1961, Balaguer served as an important transitional figure between the end of the era of Trujillo and the presidential elections in 1962. He initiated a number of reforms that were designed to persuade the Organization of American States to lift its sanctions against the Dominican Republic. Balaguer opposed the attempt of Trujillo's brothers José Arismendi and Héctor Bienvenido to resurrect Trujilloism without Trujillo. He presided over the Council of State that ruled the country until the inauguration of the new president in February 1963. As the nation's political situation became volatile in late 1962, Balaguer decided upon exile in New York City. Thus he was absent from the Dominican Republic during Juan Bosch's ephemeral presidency (1963); the military coup and subsequent triumvirate headed by Donald Reid Cabral, and the 1965 revolution, civil war, and foreign intervention.

During the presidential elections of 1966, Balaguer was the candidate of the Reformist Party (PR), which he founded during his years in exile. He won 57 percent of the vote. Thus began the twelve-year era of Balaguer, which witnessed his reelection as president in 1970 and 1974. The era was marked by massive aid from the United States, an economic boom triggered by the rise in world sugar prices, and a large building program that included the restoration of the colonial part of Santo Domingo.

After an interlude of presidents belonging to the Dominican Revolutionary Party (PRD) from 1978 to 1986, Balaguer was elected president in 1986 and reelected in 1990 and 1994. During these years, he engaged in an extensive public works campaign that included building schools, housing projects, roads, libraries, sports complexes, and museums. However, the Dominican economy was too weak to support such projects, and his final legacy was one of heavy debts and economic stress. By 1996, international pressure against him caused him to voluntarily leave office two years before his term was up.

In the 2000 election, he ran again for president but was defeated. That same year, he refused to testify in a trial resulting from a 1975 incident involving a left-wing journalist, Orlando Martínez, who criticized his presidency and was later executed by a death squad that included Dominican Republic military officers. In 2000, the death squad members were sentenced to the maximum possible jail time for their crimes.

Balaguer, blind and frail, died on 14 June 2002, at the age of ninety-five. His political career had spanned seven decades, with twenty–two years as president. Despite the many controversies that surrounded him, Balaguer is remembered as the Dominican Republic's outstanding statesman of the twentieth century. His contributions to Dominican literature are significant, especially his critical history, *Historia de la literatura dominicana* (1956), other works of literary criticism, historical works on the Trujillo era, including *Memorias de un cortesano* (1989), and his work on

Dominican relations with Haiti, *La isla revés: Haiti y el destino dominicano* (1983). Balaguer's intense rivalry with Bosch extended to literary as well as political pursuits.

See also **Dominican Republic; Trujillo Molina, Rafael Leónidas.**

BIBLIOGRAPHY

Balaguer's writings also include *La política internacional de Trujillo* (1941), *Semblanzas literarias* (1948), *Entre la sangre del 30 de mayo y la del 24 de abril* (1983), *La voz del capitolio* (1984), and *Memorias de un cortesano de la "era de Trujillo"* (1988). See also James Nelson Goodsell, "Balaguer's Dominican Republic," in *Current History* 53, no. 315 (1967): 298–302.

Additional Bibliography

Bosch, Brian J. *Balaguer and the Dominican Military: Presidential Control of the Factional Officer Troops in the 1960s and 1970s.* Jefferson, NC: McFarland, 2007.

Estrella Veloz, Santiago. *Tres maestros de la política.* Santo Domingo, Dominican Republic: Editora Callado, 2005.

Gómez Bergés, Victor. *Balaguer y yo: La historia.* Santo Domingo, Dominican Republic: Cuesta–Veliz Ediciones, 2006.

Infante, Fernando A. *12 años de Balaguer: Cronología histórica, 1966–1978.* Santo Domingo, Dominican Republic: Editorial Letra Gráfica, 2006.

Rodríguez de León, Francisco. *Trujillo y Balaguer: Entre la espada y la palabra, 1930–1962.* Santo Domingo, Dominican Republic: Nostrum, Letra Gráfica, 2004.

KAI P. SCHOENHALS

BALAIADA. Balaiada, a rural uprising of 1838–1841 in the Brazilian provinces of Maranhão and Piauí. A relatively numerous peasantry had developed in connection with the cotton plantations in northern Maranhão. They, along with slaves, and cowboys from the cattle areas of southern Maranhão and Piauí, were the principal supporters of the movement. Arbitrary military recruitment, personal grievances, and resentment against the Portuguese elite, which had managed to remain influential after independence, were the main reasons for the revolt. In the cattle areas of southern Maranhão and in Piauí, the movement was initially supported by fazendeiros (ranchers) as well. In Piauí the particular target was the arbitrary rule of the governor, the viscount of Parnaíba.

The rebels adopted the demands of the former Patriot Party, now the Liberal Party—expulsion of the Portuguese and suspension of the police chiefs responsible for recruitment—and claimed recognition for their officials. The liberal elite refused to join a popular movement led by cowboys like Raimundo Gomes Vieira, peasants like Balaio (Manuel Francisco dos Anjos Ferreira), and maroons like Cosme Bentos das Chagas.

During the uprising, which began in December 1838, the rebels managed to control large parts of the interior and twice occupied the city of Caixas. Government troops proved inefficient because of numerous desertions and lack of experience with guerrilla warfare. The new commander in chief, Luís Alves de Lima E Silva, the future duke of Caixas, arrived with reinforcements from Rio de Janeiro in February 1840. He divided the rebels by granting amnesty to those who captured runaway slaves.

Defections led to a radicalization of the remaining *balaios* around Gomes and an alliance with the rebellious slaves led by Cosme, but they could not long resist the numerous and now well-organized government troops. By January 1841, Maranhão and Piauí were considered pacified. Many prisoners were executed.

See also **Brazil: 1808–1889.**

BIBLIOGRAPHY

José Ribeiro Do Amaral, *Apontamentos para a história da revolução da Balaiada na província do Maranhão*, 3 vols. (1898–1906).

Maria Januária Vilela Santos, *A Balaiada e a insurreição de escravos no Maranhão* (1983).

Maria Amélia Freitas Mendes De Oliveira, *A Balaiada no Piauí* (1985).

Matthias Röhrig Assunção, *A guerra dos Bem-te-vis: A Balaiada na memória oral* (1988).

Additional Bibliography

Leandro, Eulálio de Oliveira. *A Marinha e as camadas populares no Maranhão, 1872.* Imperatriz: Edtirca, 2002.

Octavio, Rodrigo. *A Balaiada, 1839: Depoimento de um dos heróis do cerco de Caixas sobre a Revoluçao dos "Balaios."* São Paulo: Editoria Sicilano, 2006.

Ribeiro, Francisco de Paula. *Francisco de Paula Ribeiro: Desbravador dos sertões de Pastos Bons: A base geográfica e humana do Sul do Maranhão.* Imperatriz: Etica, 2005.

Ribeiro, Francisco de Paula. *Memorías dos sertões maranhenses.* São Paulo: Editorial Siciliano, 2002.

MATTHIAS RÖHRIG ASSUNÇÃ O

BALBÁS, JERÓNIMO DE (?–1748).

Jerónimo de Balbás (*d.* 22 November 1748), retablo master. Balbás was born in Zamora, Spain, and lived in Cádiz in the early eighteenth century; later he worked in Seville and in Marchena. In 1718 he was in New Spain. Reminiscent in design of his principal retablo for the Sagrario of the cathedral of Seville (1706–1709, destroyed 1824), his Retablo de los Reyes for the cathedral of Mexico City (1718–1737), with four large *estípites,* determined the direction that much of the art of New Spain was to take for the rest of the century. The final breakdown of the Renaissance grid scheme in retablo design and the introduction of the *estípite* along with a new vocabulary of motifs are due to Balbás's work in the cathedral of Mexico City. He stayed on in New Spain and executed numerous other retablos, including the altar of Pardon and the central free-standing retablo, or *ciprés,* of the cathedral; only the first survives, reconstructed after a fire in 1967.

See also **Retablos and Ex-Votos.**

BIBLIOGRAPHY

Manuel Toussaint, *Colonial Art in Mexico* (1967).

Concepción Amerlinck, "Jerónimo de Balbás, artista de vanguardia, y el retablo de la Concepción de la Ciudad de México," *Monumentos históricos* 2 (1979): 25–34.

Guillermo Tovar De Teresa, *México barroco* (1981), pp. 86–87.

Additional Bibliography

Tovar de Teresa, Guillermo. *Géronimo de Balbás en la Catedrál de México.* Mexico City: Asociación Amigos de la Catedral Metropolitana, 1990.

CLARA BARGELLINI

BALBÍN, RICARDO (1904–1981).

Ricardo Balbín (*b.* 29 July 1904; *d.* 9 September 1981), Argentine political leader and one of the principal Radical Party figures in the postwar period. Originally from Buenos Aires, Balbín was elected in 1930 as a Radical congressman from La Plata but was unable to serve because of the military coup of that same year. He was one of the leading *intransigentes* (Intransigent Radicals) who, with Arturo Frondizi, was cofounder of the Movimiento de Intransigencia y Renovación (MIR) in 1945. With Frondizi, Balbín (as party whip) led the Radicals in the Argentine congress under Juan Perón until 1949, when the government began a campaign against him, which led to his forced resignation as congressman and imprisonment. In the 1951 election, he was the unsuccessful Radical presidential candidate against Perón.

Balbín broke with Frondizi and the *intransigentes* after Perón's ouster and in 1956 established the Radical Civic Union of the People (UCRP), a more conservative and decidedly anti-Peronist party, which nominated him in the election won by Frondizi in 1958. With the demise of the *intransigentes,* Balbín emerged as the principal leader of the Radical Party and was one of the country's most important political figures until his death. In 1970 he led his party in a broad civilian front, La Hora del Pueblo (The People's Turn), working on behalf of the restoration of civilian rule, and was again defeated in his bid for the presidency in the 1973 elections.

In the wake of the electoral defeat, a left-wing faction within the party, the Movimiento de Renovación y Cambio, led by Raúl Alfonsín, emerged to challenge his leadership, critical of both his backroom-style politics and conservative program. Following the 1976 coup, he was an outspoken critic of the military government and twice imprisoned.

See also **Argentina, Political Parties: Radical Party (UCR).**

BIBLIOGRAPHY

Gabriel Del Mazzo, *El radicalismo: Notas sobre su historia y su doctrina,* vol. 3 (1959).

Marcelo Luis Acuña, *De Frondizi a Alfonsín: La tradición política del radicalismo,* vol. 2 (1984).

Additional Bibliography

Arrondo, César A. *Balbín entre rejas: La prisión de Ricardo Balbín en 1950.* Buenos Aires, Editorial de la Universidad de La Plata, 2002.

Pignatelli, Adrián. *Ricardo Balbín, el presidente postergado.* Buenos Aires: Centro Editor de América Latina, 1992.

JAMES P. BRENNAN

BALBOA, VASCO NÚÑEZ DE (c. 1475–

1519). Vasco Núñez de Balboa (*b.* ca. 1475; *d.* January 1519), a Spanish conquistador from Jerez de los Caballeros in Estremadura, and the first known European to see the Pacific Ocean. A poor, illiterate hidalgo, he sailed for the New World in 1501 with the expedition of Rodrigo de Bastidas, exploring the northern coast of modern Colombia. After settling on Hispaniola, he failed as a farmer, and in 1510 he escaped his creditors by stowing away on a vessel bound for the coast of Urabá (Colombia). The expedition, led by Martín Fernández de Enciso, sailed to relieve the settlement founded near Cartagena by Alonso de Ojeda, and now led by Francisco Pizarro, which was in desperate straits. Balboa, accepted as a common soldier, advised moving the colony west across the Gulf of Urabá, a region he had visited with Bastidas. The wretched settlers took the advice and found a plentiful supply of food, much gold, and Indians without poisoned arrows.

Seen as the savior of the colony, Balboa quickly gained popularity and respect among the men. The settlement of Santa María de la Antigua del Darién was founded in 1510 in Panama (then called Darién and, later, Castilla del Oro) under the jurisdiction of Diego de Nicuesa. Therefore, Balboa noted, Enciso had no authority. When Nicuesa appeared, the colonists of Antigua forced him aboard an unseaworthy ship, and he disappeared at sea. The pompous Enciso was then charged with usurping the authority of Nicuesa and was expelled from the colony. He returned to Spain, where he leveled charges of usurpation against Balboa, who realized that he needed to counter them with a spectacular achievement. In late 1511 the king had named Balboa interim governor of Darién, and in 1513 he was appointed supreme commander of the colony. He also received word of an impending order directing him to return to Spain to face charges. Instead, Balboa moved with some urgency to find the great body of water south of the isthmus, of which a friendly cacique had spoken.

On 1 September 1513, Balboa set out with 190 Spaniards, 1,000 Indian porters, and some bloodhounds. After extreme hardships—cutting through dense jungle and swamps, crossing rough mountains, and fending off hostile natives—the expedition finally reached its objective. Advancing alone to a peak on 25 (or 27) September, Balboa gazed upon the vast "South

Balboa's First Sight of the Pacific Ocean, September 25, 1513, from *The American Continent and Its Inhabitants before Its Discovery by Columbus* by H. E. Philippoteaux, 1890. WASHINGTON D.C., USA/ THE BRIDGEMAN ART LIBRARY

Sea," subsequently called the Pacific. Four days later he waded into the surf, claiming for Spain the ocean and the shores washed by it. The enterprise succeeded brilliantly for Balboa because he had subjugated many tribes without the loss of a single Spaniard, and he returned triumphantly to Antigua in January 1514 with a fortune in gold, pearls, and slaves.

Balboa is often portrayed as having treated the Indians humanely, but this is true only in a relative sense. More than most conquistadores, he befriended Indians, enjoying good relations with some thirty caciques. He also kept various mistresses. Yet he did not hesitate to fight those whom he considered obstinate. He was a man of his time and circumstances, sometimes enslaving Indians and punishing them severely. Among other atrocities, he ordered Indian homosexuals burned at the stake, and dogs were set upon recalcitrant caciques.

Meanwhile, the king—ignorant of Balboa's great achievement, and persuaded by Enciso and others of his culpability—appointed a new governor of Darién. He was Pedro Arias de Ávila (Pedrarias Dávila), the aging scion of a prominent family. Sailing for Panama with a large fleet in April 1514, Pedrarias carried orders to suspend Balboa's authority and bring him to justice. Initial inquiry acquitted Balboa, and Pedrarias came to resent his popularity, especially after Balboa's deeds became known in Spain. Though still subject to Pedrarias, Balboa was appointed adelantado of the Southern Sea and captain-general of the provinces of Coiba and Panama in 1515. Relations between the two rivals appeared to improve when Pedrarias's daughter María was betrothed to Balboa in 1516. In fact, the rancorous old man nursed a grudge. While the "son-in-law" made plans to explore the Pacific coast of Panama on his own, he was betrayed by a friend, who accused him of ignoring Pedrarias's authority. Balboa was arrested on trumped-up charges of treason. Found guilty, and denied an appeal to Spain, he was decapitated at Acla.

See also **Ávila, Pedro Arias de; Colombia, Pacific Coast.**

BIBLIOGRAPHY

The best biography of Balboa in English is Kathleen Romoli, *Balboa of Darien: Discoverer of the Pacific Ocean* (1953). In Spanish, the standard work is Angel De Altolaguirre y Duvale, *Vasco Núñez de Balboa* (1914). Very useful are Carl Ortwin Sauer, *The Early Spanish Main* (1966), and Hubert Howe Bancroft, *History of Central America*, vol. 1 (1882), both of which have good maps. See also the work of the official chronicler and contemporary of Balboa, Gonzalo Fernández De Oviedo y Valdés, *Historia general y natural de las Indias*, 5 vols. (1959).

Additional Bibliography

Lucena Salmoral, Manuel. *Vasco Nuñez de Balboa: Descubridor de la Mar del Sur.* Madrid: Ediciones Anaya, 1988.

Martínez Rivas, J. R. *Vasco Núñez de Balboa.* Madrid: Historia 16, 1987.

WILLIAM L. SHERMAN

BALBUENA, BERNARDO DE (c. 1562–1627). Bernardo de Balbuena (*b.* ca. 1562; *d.* 11 October 1627), a major poet of colonial Spanish America. Balbuena was born in Valdepeñas, La Mancha, but immigrated to Mexico, possibly with his father, about 1564. He studied first in Guadalajara and then in Mexico City. In 1585 while at the University of Mexico, he won the first of several prizes for poetry. Beginning in 1586, he occupied a series of ecclesiastical posts in the Guadalajara region, where he composed most of the poetry that would bring him fame. Balbuena returned to the capital to oversee publication of his *Grandeza mexicana* (1604), an idealized description and eulogy of Mexico City that presaged and contributed to the development of creole patriotism. Thereafter, however, his career in the church took precedence. He went back to Spain to resume his studies, earning a doctorate in theology from the University of Sigüenza in 1608. Appointment as *abad mayor* (abbott) of Jamaica soon followed, and in 1619 he was named bishop of Puerto Rico, an office he held until his death.

Balbuena also published *Siglo de oro en las selvas de Erífile* (1608), a pastoral romance, and *El Bernardo, o Victoria de Roncesvalles* (1624), an epic poem largely composed before 1600 glorifying Spain's past and present. His poetry displays a baroque mixture of erudition; fertile invention; vigorous, evocative language; and rich (perhaps excessive) ornamentation.

See also **Literature: Spanish America.**

BIBLIOGRAPHY

For biographical information see J. Rojas Garcidueñas, *Bernardo de Balbuena: La vida y la obra* (1958). A convenient collection of some of Balbuena's best work is in Bernardo De Balbuena, *Grandeza mexicana, y fragmentos del Siglo de oro y El Bernardo*, 3d ed. (1979). Scholarly criticism has focused on the epic *El Bernardo*. The most complete study is John Van Horne, *El Bernardo of Bernardo de Balbuena* (1927). For a more recent view see Gilberto Triviños, "Bernardo del Carpio desencantado por Bernardo de Balbuena," in *Cuadernos Americanos* 236 (May–June 1981): 79–102.

Additional Bibliography

González, Serafín. "Bernardo de Balbuena y la admirable belleza del mundo." In *Memoria y literatura: Homenaje a José Amezcua* edited by María José Rodilla, Alma Mejía, and José Amezcua. Mexico City: Universidad Autónoma Metropolitana, 2005.

Rodilla, María José. *Lo maravilloso medieval en El Bernardo de Balbuena.* México: Universidad Nacional Autónoma de México, 1999.

Serna, Mercedes. *Poesía colonial hispanoamericana, siglos XVI y XVII* . Madrid: Cátedra, 2004.

R. DOUGLAS COPE

BALCARCE, MARIANO (1807–1885).

Mariano Balcarce (*b.* 8 November 1807; *d.* 20 February 1885), Argentine diplomat. The son of Antonio González Balcarce, a military hero of the struggle for independence, Mariano Balcarce was born in Buenos Aires. He spent most of his life in diplomatic service in Europe. His first assignment, at age twenty-four, was as an assistant to the Argentine minister to Great Britain. He later moved to Paris, where he was living at the time of his death. Balcarce negotiated the treaty by which Spain recognized Argentine independence, and he assiduously publicized the attractions of Argentina for prospective immigrants. He befriended numerous Argentine and other Latin American visitors to France and established a particularly close relationship with José de San Martín during the latter's years of exile in France; he married Mercedes de San Martín, the Liberator's daughter, in 1832.

See also **Argentina: The Nineteenth Century.**

BIBLIOGRAPHY

Diccionario histórico argentino, vol. 1 (1953), p. 415.

César H. Guerrero, *San Martín y su familia* (1978), pp. 81–89.

DAVID BUSHNELL

BALDOMIR, ALFREDO (1894–1948).

Alfredo Baldomir (*b.* 1894; *d.* 1948), president of Uruguay (1938–1943). Baldomir was the brother-in-law of President Gabriel Terra, who chose him as his potential successor. Baldomir had been chief of police in Montevideo at the time of Terra's 1933 coup.

The 1938 election was a family affair for the Colorado-backed president. Terra had the party offer two candidates: his brother-in-law, Baldomir, who received 121,000 votes, and his father-in-law, Eduardo Blanco Acevedo, who received 98,000. The Colorado Party, with a total of 219,000 votes, thus defeated the Herrerist Blancos (National Party), which offered only one candidate, who had 114,000 votes.

With an economic upturn and a resurgence of the Batllist tradition, Baldomir felt that Terra's alliance with the Blancos, led by Luis Alberto de Herrera, as defined in the 1934 Constitution, had outlived its usefulness. The Blancos were opposed to much of Baldomir's domestic program and were critical of his cooperation with the United States at the start of World War II. Their guaranteed control of half of the seats in the Senate left them with a strong veto power. Consequently, on 21 February 1942 Baldomir postponed the upcoming March elections, dissolved Congress, and called for a constitutional plebiscite to restore the normal functioning of the electoral system. He created a Council of State, to which he submitted his constitutional proposal on 29 May. The new constitution did away with the division of the Senate between the 1933 coup leaders (Terra and Herrera) and restored full constitutional democracy. Baldomir is quoted as having said, "We have the costliest electoral system on the continent, but it is cheaper than revolution."

See also **Uruguay, Political Parties: Colorado Party.**

BIBLIOGRAPHY

Philip B. Taylor, Jr., *Government and Politics of Uruguay* (1960).

Additional Bibliography

Frega, Ana, Mónica Maronna, and Ivette Trochon. *Baldomir y la restauración democrática, 1938-1946*. Montevideo: Ediciones de la Banda Oriental, 1987.

MARTIN WEINSTEIN

BALDORIOTY DE CASTRO, RAMÓN

(1822–1889). Ramón Baldorioty de Castro (*b.* 28 February 1822; *d.* 30 September 1889), a leading member of Puerto Rico's autonomy movement. Of humble roots, Baldorioty received his early education from Padre Rufo Fernández, who recognized the youth's superior intellect. In 1846, Fernández arranged for Baldorioty to study at the University of Madrid. After returning to Puerto Rico, Baldorioty taught at the School of Commerce, Agriculture, and Navigation (1854–1870).

A member of Puerto Rico's Liberal Reformist Party, Baldorioty served in the Constitutional Cortes of 1869 and as a deputy in the Cortes of 1870–1871. After the Spanish monarchy was restored in 1875, Baldorioty went into exile to Santo Domingo for four years.

As a Liberal Reformist, Baldorioty advocated basic civil rights, abolition of slavery, and administrative decentralization. However, the party split into two factions, one favoring assimilation into Spain's political system and the other seeking autonomy. Upon his return from exile in 1878, Baldorioty steered liberals toward the Republican Autonomist wing of the Liberal Reformist Party. He led efforts to reorganize the party along autonomist lines, and at the Assembly of Ponce, in 1887, he presided over the newly created Puerto Rican Autonomist Party. The Autonomists eventually secured Puerto Rican autonomy from Spain in late 1897, eight years after Baldorioty's death.

See also **Puerto Rico, Political Parties: Overview.**

BIBLIOGRAPHY

Edward J. Berbusse, *The United States in Puerto Rico, 1898–1900* (1966).

Lidio Cruz Monclova, *Baldorioty de Castro (Su Vida—Sus Ideas)* (1966).

Pilar Barbosa De Rosario, *De Baldorioty a Barbosa: Historia del autonomismo puertorriqueño, 1887–1896* (1974).

Luis González Vales, "The Challenge to Colonialism (1866–1897)," in *Puerto Rico: A Political and Cultural History*, edited by Arturo Morales Carrión (1983).

Additional Bibliography

Vega Ramos, Luis, ed. *Baldorioty ahora*. San Juan, PR: PROELA, 2002.

JOHN J. CROCITTI

BALLAGAS Y CUBEÑAS, EMILIO

(1908–1954). Emilio Ballagas y Cubeñas (*b.* 7 November 1908; *d.* 11 September 1954), Cuban poet and essayist. Born in Camagüey, Cuba, Ballagas's writing career began with a 1926 essay about Cuban patriot José Martí, which won him a scholarship sponsored by the *Revista Martiniana* to study at the University of Havana. Better known as a poet, he published his first compositions in *Antenas* in 1928 and in the avant-garde *Revisita de Avance* the following year. While a student at the university, Ballagas published his much-acclaimed "Elegía de Mariá Belén Chacón" in *Revista de Avance* (1930). One year later he published *Júbilo y fuga,* which confirmed Ballagas's importance as a national and international poet and signaled the first of three stages in his poetry.

Ballagas completed his Ph.D. in pedagogy in 1933 and taught at the Normal School for teachers in Santa Clara, becoming its director the following year. His *Cuaderno de poesía negra* (1934) and *Antología de la poesía negra hispanoamericana* (1935) exemplify the tradition of Afro-Cuban poetry. Although many of Ballagas's poems highlight the folkloric aspects of Afro-Cuban traditions, some speak to the economic and social conditions of blacks on the island.

During a trip to Paris in 1937 to research Amerindian languages at the Bibliothèque Nationale, Ballagas met many of the best-known poets of the period. In 1939 he published *Sabor eterno,* a collection of poems about love, written with the intense emotions that characterized the second stage of his poetry. Ballagas completed a second Ph.D. in 1946 and published his dissertation, "Situación de la poesía afroamericana," in the *Revista Cubana* and the anthology *Maps de la poesía negra americana* (1946). He traveled to New York and became associated with the Institute for the Education of the Blind.

Ballagas's religious feelings, which are expressed in the third stage of his poetry, are evident in *Nuestra Señora del Mar* (1943), dedicated to the patron saint of Cuba, the Virgen de la Caridad del Cobre. He continued his religious poems in *Cielo en rehenes,* which won the National Prize for Poetry in 1951, although it was not published until 1955, and *Décimas por el júbilo martiano en el centenario del apóstol José Martí,* a patriotic as well as spiritual book, which won the Centenario Prize in 1953, commemorating Martí's birth. Ballagas died in Havana.

See also **Literature: Spanish America.**

BIBLIOGRAPHY

Cintio Vitier, *Lo cubano en la poesía* (1958).

Samuel Feijóo et al., *Lunes de Revolución* 26 (1959).

Argyll Pryor Rice, *Emilio Ballagas, poeta o poesía* (1966).

Rosa Pallas, *La poesía de Emilio Ballagas* (1973).

Rogelio De La Torre, *La obra poética de Emilio Ballagas* (1977).

Argyll Pryer Rice, "Emilio Ballagas," in *Latin American Writers,* edited by Carlos A. Solé and Maria Isabel Abreu (1989), pp. 1081–1087.

Julio A. Martínnez, ed., *Dictionary of Twentieth-Century Cuban Literature* (1990), pp. 43–50.

Additional Bibliography

Barquet, Jesús J., and Norberto Codina, eds. *Poesía cubana del siglo XX: Antología.* Mexico: Fondo de Cultura Económica, 2002.

WILLIAM LUIS

performance catalog published yearly by the Instituto Nacional de Bellas Artes.

Additional Bibliography

Dallal, Alberto. *La danza en México.* México: Universidad Nacional Autónoma de México, Instituto de Investigaciones Estéticas, 2000.

Ramos Smith, Maya, and Patricia Cardona. *La danza en México: Visiones de cinco siglos.* México: Consejo Nacional para la Cultura y las Artes, Instituto Nacional de Bellas Artes, 2002.

GUY BENSUSAN

BALLET FOLKLÓRICO DE MÉXICO.

Ballet Folklórico de México, form of popular entertainment that emerged in Mexico in the mid-1940s to promote popular cultural nationalism, usually with government support. The best-known company is Amalia Hernández's Ballet Folklórico de México, which performs in the Bellas Artes Palace in Mexico City and sponsors an international touring group. An early concern with folk culture was gradually supplanted by emphasis on spectacular choreography and dramatic costumes. Similar folk-dance groups arose in Cuba and Venezuela, where they focused on the African and other traditional heritages of the people.

The concern for the preservation of authentic folk dance and for regionalism has stimulated the creation of many groups, especially at universities and among ethnomusicologists, in Mexico, Santo Domingo, Puerto Rico, Panama, Colombia, Peru, Argentina, and Brazil. Folkloric material is increasingly available through recordings, brochures, televised festivals, and videotapes. In the southwestern United States, Hispanics have established dance groups in their schools in efforts to maintain their culture and support political and union activities. A major dance competition is held annually in Tucson, Arizona.

See also **Music: Popular Music and Dance.**

BIBLIOGRAPHY

"Ballet Folklórico Nacional de México," video released by RTC (1987); and *Ballet Folklórico de México,*

BALL GAME, PRE-COLUMBIAN.

Pre-Columbian Ball Game, also known as *ulama* or *tlachtli,* a very complex game played with a rubber ball by the ancient civilizations of Mesoamerica (Mexico, Guatemala, and adjacent territories). Rubber, native to the New World, was unknown in Europe until Columbus brought back a solid rubber ball. In 1528 Hernán Cortés brought a team of Aztec players to demonstrate the game before the Spanish court.

The pre-Columbian game was played a bit like soccer, except that the feet were not employed to advance the ball. Players could strike it with hips, legs, or elbows. The fifteen-pound rubber ball was deflected from a U-shaped yoke worn over the hips. Protective padding was worn around the waist and on the arms and knees, and gloves protected the hands. There were probably training games. Official games were performed within stone-masonry ball courts with side enclosures and end zones. The ball was deflected back and forth into the narrow court from sloping benches and vertical walls that sometimes held stone rings for scoring. A point was lost if the ball touched the paved court.

This ball game was played in all regions of Mesoamerica, with variations, for 3,000 years (1500 BCE–1500 CE). It still survives in Sinaloa, Mexico. In the Classic Period, prior to Aztec times, the game was more of a religious ritual than a team sport. It also had political and military overtones. However, its fundamental symbolism reflected Mesoamerican philosophy pertaining to the maintenance of agricultural fertility and the cosmos itself. The rubber ball, ideally kept constantly in motion, represented the sun, the moon, or Venus.

At the conclusion of a ritual game the loser (or perhaps the winner) was decapitated. This sacrifice was believed to aid the sun on its journey from day to night and its reappearance at dawn, after having defeated the lords of the underworld. Like the sun, the chosen ball player was metaphorically transformed and reborn. The symbolism of the ball game was characteristically dualistic: dry season–rainy season, sky–underworld, day–night, sun–moon, and death–rebirth.

Spanish chroniclers recorded eyewitness accounts of the Aztec game, and archaeology provides us with narrative carved stone sculpture and ceramics depicting the pre-Columbian cult and its meanings. Among the finest surviving portable stone objects from Mesoamerica are the decorated hip yokes and associated paraphernalia. These were probably ceremonial replicas of the wood or leather equipment used in the game.

See also **Indigenous Peoples; Popol Vuh; Precontact History: Mesoamerica.**

BIBLIOGRAPHY

Gerard Van Bussel, Paul Von Dongon, and Ted J. J. Leyenaar, eds., *The Mesoamerican Ball Game* (1991).

Vernon Scarborough and David Wilcox, eds., *The Mesoamerican Ball Game* (1991).

Additional Bibliography

María Teresa Uriarte, *El juego de pelota en Mesoamérica: Raíces y supervivencia* (1992).

LEE ALLEN PARSONS

BALLIVIÁN, JOSÉ (1805–1852).

José Ballivián (*b.* 30 November 1805; *d.* 16 October 1852), president of Bolivia (1841–1847). Born in La Paz, he is perhaps best known as the victorious general in the 1841 battle of Ingaví, in which the Bolivian army beat the Peruvian invaders under the leadership of General Agustín Gamarra, forever ending Peruvian plans to annex Bolivia. Ballivián was also a capable administrator and one of the best nineteenth-century Bolivian presidents. Although he joined the military early in life, having fought as a teenager in the Spanish and patriot armies, Ballivián was a self-taught man who fostered science and culture. He was fortunate that during his government the country enjoyed relative prosperity

due to revenues from taxes on guano from the Pacific coast, quinine from the eastern foothills, and a silver boomlet. Most important was his attempt to consolidate Bolivia's eastern frontier regions. He founded the department of Beni in the Amazon basin of northeastern Bolivia, promoted the exploration of the Otuquis River region in Santa Cruz, and attempted but largely failed the exploration, military conquest, and settlement of the Chaco.

See also **Bolivia: Since 1825.**

BIBLIOGRAPHY

The recent publication in Spanish of Janet Groff Greever's 1957 dissertation *José Ballivián y el oriente boliviano*, translated by José Luis Roca (1987), is one of the few widely available works on the Ballivián administration. Humberto Vázquez-Machicado, "Sobre la vida del General José Ballivián (1804–1852)," in *Obras completas de Humberto Vázquez-Machicado y José Vázquez-Machicado*, vol. 4 (1987), provides important information on Ballivián's life. Though the interpretation is dated, the most inclusive political narration of the Ballivián administration is Alcides Arguedas, *Historia de Bolivia: Los caudillos letrados, 1828–1848* (1923).

ERICK D. LANGER

BALMACEDA FERNÁNDEZ, JOSÉ MANUEL (1840–1891).

José Manuel Balmaceda Fernández (*b.* 19 July 1840; *d.* 19 September 1891), diplomat, politician, and president of Chile (1886–1891). The son of politically prominent and wealthy parents, Balmaceda briefly studied at a seminary, an experience that may have contributed to his anticlericalism. Although a large landowner, he also became involved in a variety of tasks: editor of various newspapers, private secretary to a president, and a diplomat. Not surprisingly, he won, at age twenty-four, the first of his many congressional elections. While serving as a deputy he also undertook certain diplomatic missions, arranging a border settlement with Argentina. During the administration of Domingo Santa María (1881–1886), he held the posts of minister of foreign relations, minister of war, and the more important position of minister of the interior. Since he was handpicked by Santa María, his election to the presidency was virtually assured, thanks to his mentor's massive intervention in the political process.

Balmaceda took over Chile at a transitional time. Increasingly, the nation's economy, and its revenue base, rested on the mining and exporting of nitrates. The new president had clear ideas of what he wanted to do with these funds: build railroads and public buildings, expand educational facilities, modernize the military, colonize the newly opened southern territories, and reward his political henchmen and their families with lucrative government positions and contracts.

Certain forces, however, stood in the way of Balmaceda's programs. The politicians wanted their place at the public trough. They particularly disliked the fact that the newly created ministry of public works seemed so powerful and that Balmaceda often used his executive powers to create jobs without consulting the legislature. The deputies and senators resented that the president alone seemed to have the power to dispense largess.

The second problem was the nature of the nitrate trade. Nitrates, while an essential component of fertilizers and explosives, were still a commodity whose value fluctuated with the state of the world economy. When prices fell, the nitrate producers, or *salitreros,* generally responded by limiting production, in hopes of driving up the mineral's value. While such production cutbacks proved beneficial to the mining interests, they hurt the government, which depended upon the export levy on nitrates to sustain the régime and its various public-works projects. Hence, Balmaceda viewed as an enemy anyone who could reduce production. His particular bête noire was John Thomas North, an English financier who owned much of what was worth owning in the nitrate-rich province of Tarapacá: a bank, a supply company, the local source of water, and the railroad that carried the *salitre* from the pampas to the port of Iquique.

The conflict between these two men became quite hostile. North, by keeping prices high for transport, increased the cost of the nitrate and hence limited its sale. Balmaceda, who resented the loss of potential income, tried to break North's monopoly on the nitrate-transportation network by offering railroad concessions to other foreign financiers. North deeply resented Balmaceda's efforts and tried to marshal his friends in the Chilean Congress to prevent the president from implementing his policies.

Balmaceda's principal problem was not North or his associates but his own methods of ruling.

Although Balmaceda had initially enjoyed the support of a majority of the congress, he began to lose popularity. In part, various politicians, including some in his own party, disliked the way Balmaceda had been elected president. Others resented his seemingly unlimited control over patronage, particularly his willingness to appoint men to positions on the basis of talent, not political connections.

Legislative animus toward the president increased when he ruthlessly intervened in the 1888 congressional elections. Worse, Balmaceda lost his majority in Congress when the legislators concluded that he would select Enrique Salvador Sanfuentes to succeed him. It became obvious that if he wished to rule, Balmaceda would have to consult the legislature.

Balmaceda went on the offensive, demanding a strengthening, not a diminution, of presidential powers. Doubtless, these proposals shocked the Congress, which might have expected compromise. Clearly, the nation had reached an impasse: throughout 1890 the Congress demanded that the president create a cabinet to its liking before the legislature would approve the budget. Balmaceda refused. Since the president and the Congress seemed more intent on insulting each other than on addressing the country's pressing problems, the nation stagnated.

Thanks to the intervention of Archbishop Mariano Casanova, Balmaceda succeeded in forming a new cabinet acceptable to the legislature. When it collapsed, Balmaceda formed one composed of his friends, further antagonizing the Congress, which still refused to pass a budget.

Increasingly, Balmaceda ruled by decree, which created more uncertainty than it solved problems. Believing that the president might act illegally, his legislative foes created a junta to coordinate their efforts should it be necessary to resist his government. They soon had a reason: in January 1891, Balmaceda, citing the legislature's earlier refusal to approve his request for funding, unilaterally declared that he would use the budget authorized for 1890 for 1891 instead. Considering this act a violation of the 1833 Constitution, the junta rebelled, thereby initiating the Revolution of 1891.

Balmaceda's military efforts seemed as ill-fated as his political programs. Since the rebels controlled the nitrate-rich north, they had more money than the legitimate government. Worse, the rebels, who enjoyed naval supremacy, successfully prevented Balmaceda from taking possession of two cruisers under construction in Europe. All the president could do was mobilize his army, whose morale seemed to have deteriorated as much, if not more than many of their weapons, and await the ultimate invasion.

The attacks came in August. By the end of the month, the rebels controlled Santiago. As the congressionalist mobs looted the homes of his supporters and killed his officers, Balmaceda took refuge in the Argentine embassy. He remained there until 19 September 1891, the day after his term of office expired. Then he shot himself.

It is easier to say what Balmaceda was not than what he was: his willingness to deal with foreign investors other than North indicated that he was not an economic nationalist; his cynical manipulation of elections demonstrated that he was not a democrat; his brutal suppression of strikes showed that he was not a friend of the worker. While he was perhaps a visionary, his political methods seemed more typical of a bygone era than of a nation groping its way toward democracy.

See also **Chile, Constitutions; Chile, Revolutions: Revolution of 1891; Nitrate Industry.**

BIBLIOGRAPHY

Harold Blakemore, "The Chilean Revolution of 1891 and Its Historiography," in *Hispanic American Historical Review* 45, no. 3 (1965): 393–421, and his *British Nitrates and Chilean Politics, 1886–1896: North and Balmaceda* (1974): Hernán Ramírez Necochea, *Balmaceda y la contrarevolución de 1891,* 2d ed. (1969).

Ricardo Salas Edwards, *Balmaceda y el parlamentarismo en Chile,* 2 vols. (1925).

Julio Bañados Espinosa, *Balmaceda: Su gobierno y la revolución de 1891* 2 vols. (1894).

Maurice H. Hervey, *Dark Days in Chile: An Account of the Revolution of 1891* (1892).

José Miguel Yrarrázaval Larrain, *El presidente Balmaceda,* 2 vols. (1940).

Crisóstomo Pizarro, *La revolución de 1891* (1971).

WILLIAM F. SATER

BALSAS RIVER. Balsas River originates in the southeastern Mesa Central and empties into the Pacific Ocean near the city of Lázaro Cárdenas,

Michoacán. Forming one of the largest basins in Middle America (44,828 sq. mi.), it flows from east to west in a low depression bounded on the north by the Cordillera Neovolcánica, on the south by the Sierra Madre del Sur, and on the east by the Sierra de Oaxaca. Cut off by these ranges from moisture-bearing winds off both the Pacific and the Gulf of Mexico, the Balsas basin is hot and dry. Near its origin, the river is called the Mezcala; about halfway through its course to the Pacific, it becomes the Balsas. Approximately 60 miles inland from its mouth, it is joined by the Tepalcatepec, which flows south through the northwestern extension of the Balsas depression; thereafter the Balsas flows through a narrow canyon to the Pacific.

During pre-Columbian times, the Balsas basin was an important source of the gold given as tribute to the Aztecs. Colonial settlement of the region was typified by scattered Indian and mestizo subsistence farmers, and cattle raising was the most important economic activity. In 1907, however, the Italian émigré Dante Cussi established Nueva Italia and Lombardia haciendas under a contract with the federal government to develop the area. He introduced irrigation and limited commercial agriculture, but most of these lands were collectivized in 1938.

In 1947 the Comisión del Tepalcatepec was created for the integrated development of that 7,000-square-mile segment of the Balsas basin. The commission, headed by ex-President Lázaro Cárdenas, was given broad powers to construct dams for irrigation and hydroelectricity, to develop lines of communication and transportation, to create and expand settlement centers, and to deal with agricultural and credit matters. In 1960 it was absorbed by the Comisión del Río Balsas, with Cárdenas again as director.

The largest project on the Balsas is El Infiernillo dam, built in 1964 about 35 miles inland from the Pacific. Forming a lake 65 miles long, it provides the lower Balsas with irrigation water and central Mexico with nearly 1 million kilowatts of electricity. In 1971 a smaller dam, La Villita, was built downstream to provide electricity to the iron and steel complex at Lázaro Cárdenas.

See also **Michoacán.**

BIBLIOGRAPHY

Robert Cooper West, ed., *Handbook of Middle American Indians,* vol. 1 (1964), pp. 106, 381.

David Barkin and Timothy King, *Regional Economic Development: The River Basin Approach in Mexico* (1970).

Jorge L. Tamayo, *Georgrafía moderna de México,* 9th ed. (1980), pp. 55, 139–140.

Robert Cooper West and John P. Augelli, *Middle America: Its Lands and Its Peoples,* 3d ed. (1989), pp. 28–29, 350.

Additional Bibliography

Fabián Ruiz, José. *Lerma y Balsas, crónica de dos ríos.* Morelia, México: Foro Cultural Morelos, 1998.

MacNeish, Richard S. and Eubanks, Mary W. "Comparative Analysis of the Rio Balsas and Tehuacan Models for the Origin of Maize." *Latin American Antiquity* 11(2000): 3–20.

Shepard F.P., and Reimnitz E. "Sedimentation Bordering the Rio Balsas Delta and Canyons, Western Mexico." *Geological Society of America Bulletin,* 92, no. 6 (1981): 395–403.

Soto Nuñez, José Carmen and Sousa Sánchez. *Plantas medicinales de la cuenca del Río Balsas.* México, D.F.: Universidad Nacional Autónoma de México, 1995.

JOHN J. WINBERRY

BALSEIRO, JOSÉ AGUSTÍN (1900–1992).

José Agustín Balseiro (*b.* 23 August 1900; *d.* 1992), Puerto Rican writer and professor. Balseiro earned a law degree from the University of Puerto Rico (1921), and an honorary doctorate from the Catholic University of Chile. His writings are varied. His three novels move from the biographical mode of *La ruta eterna* (1923) to the indictment of social ills in *La gratitud humana* (1969). His poetry began emphasizing love and wine (*La copa de Anacreonte,* 1924) and ended with love and transcendence (*El ala y el beso,* 1983). His best-known critical works are *Novelistas españoles modernos* (1933), *Expresión de Hispanoamérica* 2 vols. (1960–1963), and *The Americas Look at Each Other* (1969).

Balseiro's critical essays, his creative works, his teaching (at the University of Illinois–Urbana, Duke University, and elsewhere), and his many lectures throughout Latin America won him wide recognition, including membership in the Spanish Royal Academy, Madrid's Center of Historical Studies, Mexico's Academy of Letters, and Argentina's Sarmiento Institute. He received the Orders of Isabel la Católica (Spain) and Vasco Núñez de Balboa (Panama). Balseiro also served as Puerto Rico's senator-at-large.

See also **Literature: Spanish America.**

BIBLIOGRAPHY

Juan Enrique Colberg, *Cuatro autores clásicos contemporáneos de Puerto Rico* (1966); *Diccionario de literatura puertorriqueña,* vol. 2, pt. 1 (1974).

Nicolás Kanellos, ed., *Biographical Dictionary of Hispanic Literature in the United States* (1989).

Additional Bibliography

Balseiro, José Agustín. *Obra selecta de José Agustín Balseiro.* Rio Pedras, PR: Editorial de la Universidad de Puerto Rico, 1990.

MARÍA A. SALGADO

BALTA, JOSÉ (1814–1872).

José Balta (*b.* 1814; *d.* 26 July 1872), president of Peru (1868–1872). A soldier of common background and strong convictions, he led troops from Chiclayo on the northern coast against the government when President Mariano Ignacio Prado issued decrees to curb the political power of Catholic bishops. With army support, Balta remained in power for a full presidential term. Convinced that Peru must escape its financial dependence on local guano consignees, he placed the Ministry of Finance in the hands of Nicolás de Piérola and approved his policy of domestic spending of income earned by contracting for a guano monopoly with the Dreyfus Company of France. Thereafter military salaries and pensions rose, and public facilities improved. Contractors laid hundreds of miles of new rail lines throughout the country, including the famous Central Railway linking Lima with the mining center of La Oroya in the Andean highlands. But expenditures quickly outran income from all sources, and public sentiment soon associated the military with public waste. Balta and Piérola clashed repeatedly until Piérola resigned in 1871. Balta then incurred new debts to the Dreyfus Company. At the end of Balta's term, Peru faced a foreign debt of £49 million, a tenfold increase over what it had been when he took office. By the election of 1872 military leadership was in disrepute. Balta's secretary, Ricardo Palma, and North American entrepreneur Henry Meiggs, among others, persuaded him not to prevent the inauguration of his successor. In the military uprising that followed this decision, Balta was imprisoned and shot dead in his cell by guards.

See also **Guano Industry.**

BIBLIOGRAPHY

Fredrick B. Pike, *The Modern History of Peru* (1967), esp. pp. 125–126, 131–132.

Henry F. Dobyns and Paul L. Doughty, *Peru: A Cultural History* (1976), esp. pp. 191–194.

Additional Bibliography

Valdizán Ayala, José. *José Balta Montero.* Lima, Peru: Editorial Brasa, 1995.

VINCENT PELOSO

BALTIMORE INCIDENT.

Baltimore Incident, an 1891 diplomatic dispute between the United States and Chile. Following the September collapse of the Balmaceda government, Captain Winfield Schley permitted some of the sailors serving on the cruiser U.S.S. *Baltimore* to have shore leave on 16 October in Valparaíso. Schley failed to realize that the presence of uniformed American sailors might fan latent Chilean hostility into a firestorm of confrontation.

Various brawls between American servicemen and Chileans erupted in Valparaíso's sleazy waterfront saloons and brothels. By the evening's end, the police had jailed seventeen Americans, and two U.S. sailors had died from knife wounds.

The Americans charged that the police not only failed to protect them but had joined the crowds in beating the sailors. The Chilean courts disagreed with the American charges, however, concluding that the U.S. sailors had started the brawl. Benjamin Harrison, the American president, regarded the incident as an insult to the United States and demanded an apology and compensation from the Chilean government. Refusing to apologize, Chile's foreign minister, Manuel Antonio Matta, publicly described Harrison as either stupid or a liar. The irate American president sent an ultimatum to the Chilean government: either apologize for injuring the American servicemen and offer compensation, or the United States would declare war.

Chile, having only recently ended a costly revolution, was ill prepared for a confrontation with the United States. Worse, Santiago feared that Argentina, Bolivia, and Peru would take advantage of a war with the United States to attack Chile. Finally, Chile's allies in Europe—Germany and Great Britain—indicated that they would not attempt to restrain Washington. Friendless and surrounded by potential enemies, Chile acceded to Washington's demands, paying compensation and apologizing for the episode. The *Baltimore* incident remained a sore point in relations with the United States because many Chileans regarded the diplomatic confrontation as yet another example of American imperialism.

See also **United States-Latin American Relations.**

BIBLIOGRAPHY

Joyce S. Goldberg, *The "Baltimore" Affair* (1986).

William F. Sater, *Chile and the United States: Empires in Conflict* (1990), 61, 66–68.

Additional Bibliography

Collier, Simon, and William F. Sater. *A History of Chile, 1808-2002.* Cambridge: Cambridge University Press, 2004.

Morales Pérez, Salvador E. *La diplomacia mexicana y conflictos chilenos en 1891.* México, D.F.: Centro de Investigación Científica "Ing. Jorge L. Tamayo," 1996.

Núñez P., Jorge. *1891, crónica de la guerra civil.* Santiago [Chile]: LOM Ediciones, 2003.

WILLIAM F. SATER

BANANA INDUSTRY.

The rise of ocean-going steamships during the latter third of the nineteenth century stimulated banana exports from the Caribbean region to the United States and Europe, and later from South America and Africa. Bananas, in many varieties, are a tropical grass of the Musaceae family. Of Far Eastern origin, they spread to Africa and in the sixteenth century were brought by Canary Islanders to Latin America, where they became a common local food. Banana exports began in the era of rapid sailing ships after 1850, but did not become important until steamships made the export of perishable fruit more practical after 1860.

Bananas on the deck of a cargo ship, Darien, Panama, 1996. The banana trade in Central America continues to be chiefly controlled by U.S. corporations but they have been joined by an increasing number of national companies. © DANNY LEHMAN/CORBIS

A Boston ship captain, Lorenzo Baker, was among the early banana shippers, developing trade between Jamaica and Boston. Baker and Andrew Preston led the formation of the Boston Fruit Company in 1885, which greatly expanded this enterprise. Meanwhile, other shippers developed banana exports along the Caribbean coast of Central America, where banana production and export became closely associated with railroad construction. Minor C. Keith was especially important with his Tropical Trading and Transport Company in developing Costa Rican banana exports, which amounted to more than a half million stems annually by 1885. Other shippers based on the American Gulf Coast developed banana exports from Colombia, Nicaragua, and Honduras before the turn of the century. Boston Fruit and Tropical Trading and Transport merged in 1899, creating the United Fruit Company, which came to dominate the industry. Samuel Zemurray's Cuyamel Fruit Company and the Vacarro brothers' Standard Fruit And Steamship Company were important competitors.

In the early twentieth century these companies were fiercely competitive as they gained land, railroad concessions, and shipping and distribution rights for the production and export of bananas. In 1929 United Fruit purchased Cuyamel; Zemurray soon emerged as the chief executive at United Fruit and led it to an even more dominant position in the industry by 1950. The tendency was for banana production to shift from the Caribbean islands to the Caribbean and Pacific lowlands of Central America and to Panama, Colombia, and Ecuador, although since 1960 there has been renewed development of banana production in the eastern Caribbean.

Large-scale export of bananas required substantial capital investment in production, pest and disease control, and transportation. Bananas were thus an important agroexport for the liberal development schemes of the late nineteenth and early twentieth centuries and provided considerable revenue for modernization in Jamaica, Central America, and

Leading Latin American banana producers, 1948–2005 (metric tons)

Country	1948–1952	1970	1975	1980	1985	1987	1989	2005
Brazil	2,084	6,408	5,311	6,736	4,815	5,188	5,502	6,703
Dominican Republic	208	775	799	901	914	1,045	1,193	547
Colombia	354	780	1,050	1,030	1,200	1,340	3,550	1,764
Costa Rica	434	1,146	1,121	1,092	1,008	925	1,335	2,352
Ecuador	360	2,700	2,544	2,269	1,970	1,962	3,336	6,118
Guatemala	185	487	520	650	690	709	420	1,070
Honduras	802	1,200	852	1,330	1,091	1,020	1,220	887
Mexico	412	1,136	1,194	1,515	1,151	1,489	1,185	509
Panama	249	947	989	1,050	1,067	907	1,030	439
Venezuela	756	968	860	983	989	1,000	1,636	536

SOURCE: Data from James W. Wilkie, ed. *Statistical Abstract of Latin America*, vols. 20–28 (1980–1990); Economic Commission for Latin America and the Caribbean, *Statistical Yearbook for Latin America and the Caribbean* (1990); Food and Agricultural Organization of the United Nations.

Table 1

Ecuador as close ties developed between the fruit companies and the governments. Costa Rica was the leading exporter in the early twentieth century, but by the 1940s Honduras had taken over that position, to be replaced by Ecuador in 1951. The major Latin American producers and exporters of bananas in recent years are indicated in the accompanying table.

Because of heavy damages from storms or disease, especially Sigatoka or Panama disease, the companies required large expanses of land for their plantations and were often criticized for making much of the land unfit for future cultivation because of excessive cultivation and use of pesticides. Yet the banana companies also greatly improved the transportation and communication systems, paid better wages than native-owned firms dealing in agroexports such as coffee, and contributed to educational and health improvements in the countries where they operated.

Growing opposition to the powerful foreign banana interests eventually supported nationalist efforts to curtail their power, so that in the second half of the twentieth century, some of their lands were expropriated, they were taxed more heavily, and incentives for native-owned production resulted in more native ownership and in more competition among the foreign companies. United Fruit was taken over by Eli Black, and then went bankrupt,

being succeeded by United Brands in the early 1970s (United Brands became Chiquita Brands International in 1990); Castle and Cooke had taken over Standard Fruit by 1968. These companies were joined in production by a rising number of national companies.

Banana production has raised debates and conflicts in the twenty-first century over issues of trade and globalization. European countries give trade preferences to their former colonies in the Caribbean, but the United States has pressured the European Union to change these policies. Many specialists believe that this change would benefit producers in Central American countries, where the trade is largely controlled by U.S. companies.

See also **Fruit Industry; United Fruit Company; Zemurray, Samuel.**

BIBLIOGRAPHY

Frederick Upham Adams, *Conquest of the Tropics* (1914, repr. 1976).

Philip Keep Reynolds, *The Banana: Its History, Cultivation and Place Among Staple Foods* (1927).

Charles David Kepner, Jr., and Jay H. Soothill, *The Banana Empire: A Case Study of Economic Imperialism* (1935, repr. 1967).

Charles M. Wilson, *Empire in Green and Gold: The Story of the American Banana Trade* (1947).

Leading Latin American banana exporters, 1950–2005 (metric tons)

Country	1950	1960	1970	1975	1980	1985	1987	2005
Brazil	152	242	204	147	67	105	81	226
Colombia	144	191	262	486	692	783	962	1,389
Costa Rica	223	273	867	1,077	1,027	857	943	1,601
Ecuador	165	1,076	1,246	1,450	1,437	1,075	1,402	4,159
Guatemala	160	198	220	260	336	366	380	1,126
Honduras	351	363	812	420	987	872	904	509
Panama	189	263	601	558	505	686	676	328

SOURCE: Data from James W. Wilkie, ed. *Statistical Abstract of Latin America*, vols. 20–28 (1980–1990); Economic Commission for Latin America and the Caribbean, *Statistical Yearbook for Latin America and the Caribbean* (1990); Food and Agricultural Organization of the United Nations.

Table 2

Stacy May and Galo Plaza, *The United Fruit Company in Latin America* (1958).

Henry B. Arthur, James P. Houck, and George L. Beckford, *Tropical Agribusiness Structures and Adjustments—Bananas* (1968).

Wilhelm Bitter, *Die wirtschaftliche Eroberung Mittelamerikas durch den Bananen-Trust* (1971).

Organization of American States, Executive Secretariat for Economic and Social Affairs, *Sectoral Study of Transnational Enterprises in Latin America: The Banana Industry* (1975).

Thomas Mc Cann, *An American Company: The Tragedy of United Fruit,* edited by Henry Scammell (1976).

Wilson Randolph Bartlett, Jr., "Lorenzo Dow Baker and the Development of the Banana Trade between Jamaica and the United States, 1881–1890," (Ph.D. diss., American University, 1977).

Thomas L. Karnes, *Tropical Enterprise: The Standard Fruit and Steamship Company in Latin America* (1978).

Maurice Brungardt, *The United Fruit Company in Colombia* (1987).

Robert Thomson, *Green Gold: Bananas and Dependency in the Eastern Caribbean* (1987).

Additional Bibliography

Barahona, Marvin, and Julio C. Rivera. *El silencio quedó atrás: Testimonios de la huelga bananera de 1954.* Tegucigalpa: Editorial Guaymuras, 1994.

Bucheli, Marcelo. *Bananas and Business: The United Fruit Company in Colombia, 1899–2000.* New York: New York University Press, 2005.

Clegg, Peter. *The Caribbean Banana Trade: From Colonialism to Globalization.* Basingstoke, Hants, U.K. and New York: Palgrave Macmillan, 2002.

Frank, Dana. *Bananeras: Women Transforming the Banana Unions of Latin America.* Cambridge, MA: South End Press, 2005.

Striffler, Steve, and Mark Moberg. *Banana Wars: Power, Production, and History in the Americas.* Durham, NC: Duke University Press, 2003.

RALPH LEE WOODWARD JR.

BANANEROS. *See* **Colombia, Great Banana Strike.**

BANCO COMERCIAL Y AGRÍCOLA (ECUADOR).

Banco Comercial y Agrícola (Ecuador), a leading financial institution from 1895 to 1926, located in the prosperous port of Guayaquil, the nation's commercial center. The bank handled much of the proceeds from coastal Ecuador's successful cacao export trade. The governing Liberal Party's (1895–1944) heavy borrowing, however, dangerously depleted bank reserves, leaving currency issues improperly backed. Highland critics of the Liberal Party objected to the emerging close relationship between government and the bank. Criticism grew more urgent after the economic collapse of 1922. Following a 1925 coup by young military officers, the government closed the Banco Comercial y Agrícola and created a new central bank. Some historical interpretations depict 1895–1925 as an era of "bank rule" over Ecuador.

See also **Urvina Jado, Francisco.**

BIBLIOGRAPHY

The best treatment of fiscal and monetary issues is Linda Alexander Rodríguez, *The Search for Public Policy: Regional Politics and Government Finances in Ecuador, 1830–1940* (1985). For the broader political economic context see Osvaldo Hurtado, *Political Power in Ecuador,* translated by Nick D. Mills, Jr. (1985). Detailed discussion of banking can be found in Julio Estrada Ycaza, *Los bancos del siglo XIX* (1976). The socioeconomic context is analyzed in the path-breaking study by Lois Crawford De Roberts, *El Ecuador en la época cacaotera* (1980).

Additional Bibliography

Pineo, Ronn F. *Social and Economic Reform in Ecuador: Life and Work in Guayaquil.* Gainesville: University Press of Florida, 1996.

RONN F. PINEO

BANCO DE AVÍO.

The Banco de Avío para Fomento de la Industria Nacional, the first industrial development bank founded in Latin America, was set up by the Mexican government on 16 October 1830 to provide long-term loans at low rates of interest to the nation's fledgling cotton textile industry. Capitalized by a levy of 20 percent on the duties from cotton textile imports, the bank was to have capital of 1 million pesos. During its twelve years of operation it made loans to twenty-nine industrial enterprises. Most of the bank's loans went to cotton and wool textile firms, but it also extended credit to paper mills, iron foundries, and other enterprises. The capital it provided supplemented the equity capital raised by the industrialists; roughly 6 percent of the capital invested in the textile industry came from the bank. The bank was dissolved on 23 September 1842 by order of General Antonio López de Santa Anna, who had already alienated much of its assets in an attempt to obtain cash for a bankrupt fisc.

See also **Banking: Since 1990.**

BIBLIOGRAPHY

Linda Ivette Colón Reyes. *Los orígenes de la burguesía y el Banco de Avío* (1982).

Robert A. Potash, *The Mexican Government and Industrial Development in the Early Republic: The Banco de Avío* (1983).

Additional Bibliography

Flores Clair, Eduardo. *El Banco de avío minero novohispano: Crédito, finanzas y deudores.* México, D.F.: Instituto Nacional de Antropología e Historia, 2001.

Gómez Galvarriato, Aurora. ed. *La industria textil en México.* México, D.F.: Instituto Mora: Colegio de Michoacán: Colegio de México: Instituto de Investigaciones Históricas-UNAM, 1999.

STEPHEN H. HABER

BANCO DE LA REPÚBLICA (COLOMBIA).

Banco de la República (Colombia), Colombia's central bank. The second central bank in Latin America (the first was Peru's), it was established in 1923 to serve as a lender to Colombia's commercial banks, to administer its international reserves, to issue its currency, and to serve as the government's banking agent. Since 1951 the bank has played an active role in managing Colombia's money supply and in promoting national economic development through credit facilitation. The institution has gone through three stages in its management of the money supply: the first (1923–1931), under the gold standard; the second (1932–1950), when it gradually gained influence over Colombia's money management; and the third (1950 to the present), when it controlled the money supply.

The historical reasons for the creation of the bank in 1923 were several. Major among them was the fact that Colombia (within Latin America) was one of the nations with the least foreign investment. This situation drove the Colombian government to seek better relations with the financial markets in New York and London. By 1922 it had become clear that Colombia's finances needed expert guidance. This was provided by the Edward Kemmerer Mission (1923), which recommended the creation of the Banco de la República. This, in turn, led to substantial increases in foreign investment from the United States and Great Britain.

During the financial crisis of 1929–1931, the bank took over the management of Colombia's salt and emerald mines, as collateral for its stabilization of the currency and finances. Its nonfinancial roles include the promotion and protection of Colombia's cultural heritage, the establishment of modern research facilities, and the sponsorship of many cultural activities. These include the Museo del Oro (Bogotá), organized in 1939, and the Biblioteca Luis Ángel Arango (named for a former director of the bank), formally founded in 1958, with branches in every major Colombian city.

See also **Banking: Since 1990.**

BIBLIOGRAPHY

Julie Jones and Warwick Bray, *Preconquest Goldsmiths' Work of Colombia in the Museo del Oro, Bogotá* (1957).

Adolfo Meisel Roca Et Al., *El Banco de la República: Antecedentes, evolución y estructura* (1990).

Additional Bibliography

Kemmerer, Edwin Walter, Adolfo Meisel Roca, Alejandro López Mejía, et al. *Kemmerer y el Banco de la República: Diarios y documentos.* Bogotá: Banco de la República, 1994.

Sánchez, Fabio, ed. *Ensayos de historia monetaria y bancaria de Colombia.* Bogotá: Tercer Mundo Editores, 1994.

J. León Helguera

BANCO DE LONDRES Y MÉXICO.

Banco de Londres y México, originally (1863) the London Bank of Mexico and South America. It first had two branches, one in Mexico City and one in Lima, but in the late nineteenth century both became domestic banking institutions—the Banco de Londres y México in 1889 and the Banco del Perú y Londres in 1897—with a combination of local and European shareholders. The Banco de Londres y México, as it was known from the 1860s, introduced modern banking practices in various Mexican cities, although it was surpassed in importance by the Banco Nacional de México (1884), against which it struggled for preeminence until the outbreak of the Mexican Revolution in 1910. In the 1930s and 1940s the Banco de Londres regained some of the business it had lost due to the revolution and subsequent civil war. It was absorbed by the SERFIN financial group of Monterrey in 1977 and today continues its activities under that name.

See also **Banking: Since 1990.**

BIBLIOGRAPHY

David M. Joslin, *A Century of Banking in Latin America* (1963); *100 años de banca en México: Primer centenario del Banco de Londres y México, S.A. (1864–1964)* (1964).

Additional Bibliography

Maurer, Noel. *The Power and the Money: The Mexican Financial System, 1876-1932.* Stanford: Stanford University Press, 2002.

Carlos Marichal

BANCO DE MÉXICO.

Founded on September 1, 1925, Banco de México (Banxico) is Mexico's central bank. Obeying a mandate of the 1917 Mexican constitution, Alberto J. Pani, minister of finance under Plutarco Elías Calles, took the political and organizational initiative to order the establishment of a Banco Único de Emisión (Unique Bank of Emission), as the bank was originally known, as an institutional mechanism to control the monetary disorder inherited from the revolution years.

Banco de México immediately held legal control over monetary emissions, but it would take more than six years and a worldwide economic depression for the Mexican central bank to achieve the confidence of the Mexican population. Only after 1931 were the central bank's bills widely accepted by the Mexican public. During the following decades, the Banco de México played an important role in the Mexican model of development, not only regulating monetary supply and the availability of credit, but also funding Mexican government deficits.

During the 1970s and early 1980s, expansive monetary policies and high inflation rates damaged the bank's public credibility. As a result, the government initiated a series of reforms, the most important of which took effect in April 1994: Banco de México was given constitutional autonomy from the executive branch of Mexican government. This reform allowed it to stop funding government deficits and focus its policy instruments on inflation control.

See also **Banking: Since 1990; Calles, Plutarco Elías.**

BIBLIOGRAPHY

Banco de México. Available from http://www.banxico.org.mx.

Cárdenas, Enrique. *La hacienda pública y la política económica, 1929–1958.* México: Fondo de Cultura Económica, 1994.

Menéndez Romero, Fernando. *El Banco de México y la reserva federal de Estados Unidos de América.* México: Porrúa, 1994.

SERGIO SILVA-CASTAÑEDA

BANCO DE SAN CARLOS (POTOSÍ).

Banco de San Carlos (Potosí), a mining bank in Potosí (1779–1825) that was the amplification of earlier credit institutions. The first of these was a private company created by leading *azogueros* (refiners) in 1746–1747 to provide loans and supplies. This establishment was taken under partial royal direction in 1752 as a *banco de rescates,* a bank that bought raw silver from the refiners, for cash, at a discount. It had mixed success. In 1779 Jorge Escobedo y Alarcón, governor of Potosí, resolved to take the bank fully into royal control as the Banco de San Carlos. It continued to buy silver at a discount and now also was charged with collecting the 10 percent crown royalty on silver produced. Fed by the discount, the loan fund grew large. Loans, however, were rarely invested productively, since the *azogueros*—the social elite among Potosí refiners, not known for their entrepreneurship—contrived to take most of the funds themselves.

See also **Banking: Overview.**

BIBLIOGRAPHY

Rose Marie Buechler, *The Mining Society of Potosí, 1776–1810* (1981).

Guillermo Miro Delli-Zotti, *El Real Banco de San Carlos de Potosí y la minería altoperuana colonial, 1779–1825* (Banco de España, 1991).

Additional Bibliography

Sánchez Gómez, Julio, Guillermo Claudio Mira Delli-Zotti, and Rafael Dobado. *La savia del imperio: Tres estudios de economía colonial.* Salamanca: Ediciones Universidad de Salamanca, 1997.

PETER BAKEWELL

BANCO DE SAN CARLOS (SPAIN).

Banco de San Carlos (Spain), the first national bank of Spain, established in 1782 in Madrid during the reign of Charles III. Its original purpose was to stabilize the credit of the government, servicing the state bonds called *vales reales* that had been issued to cover the expenses incurred by the monarchy in its European and American wars at the end of the eighteenth century. Although essentially a government bank, the Banco de San Carlos was privately owned. Among its stockholders were Spanish capitalists, French rentiers, and, surprisingly, a large group of Indian community treasuries of Mexico. The bank continued to provide financial services to the Spanish government during the Napoleonic Wars and most of the reign of Ferdinand VII (1814–1833), but in 1828 it was restructured and became the Banco de San Fernando. Today it is known as the Banco de España.

See also **Banking: Overview.**

BIBLIOGRAPHY

Earl Hamilton, "Plans for a National Bank in Spain, 1701–1783," in *Journal of Political Economy* 58, no. 3 (1949): 315–336.

Pedro Tedde, *El Banco de San Carlos (1782–1829)* (1988).

Additional Bibliography

Calderón Quijano, José Antonio. *El Banco de San Carlos y las comunidades de indios de Nueva España.* Sevilla: Banco de España, Escuela de Estudios Hispano-Americanos, 1963.

Tedde, Pedro, and Carlos Marichal. *La Formación de los bancos centrales en España y América Latina (siglos XIX y XX).* 2 vols. Madrid: Banco de España, Servicio de Estudios, 1994.

CARLOS MARICHAL

BANCO DO BRASIL.

Banco do Brasil, Brazil's first formal bank and Latin America's first modern-style bank, founded in 1808 after the Portuguese prince-regent Dom João VI established his court in Rio de Janeiro. As a mixed institution under state control, the Banco do Brasil served as a commercial bank, the government's fiscal agent, and Brazil's first bank of issue. The bank realized great profits but played an inadequate commercial role because it concentrated on financing government deficits. It greatly expanded its issues of currency, particularly to finance Brazil's war in the Banda Oriental (today Uruguay) between 1825 and 1828. When Dom João left Brazil for Portugal in 1821, he took all of the precious metals that backed the bank's issues. This first Banco do Brasil tottered and finally closed its doors in 1829.

The second Banco do Brasil was founded in Rio in 1851 by the entrepreneur Baron of Mauá as a private commercial bank with a capital of 10,000 contos (about £1.2 million or $5 million). Two years later Parliament merged this bank with another private bank and eventually with three provincial banks to form the third Banco do Brasil. A bank of issue, it also served as the country's largest financial institution and the government's banker. Although its stocks were held privately, it often benefited from government contracts and loans and was an important vehicle for enacting public policy.

The Banco do Brasil lost its dominant position during the explosion of new banks created during the Encilhamento between 1889 and 1891. In 1894 Congress merged the Banco do Brasil with the country's largest bank, the Banco da República dos Estados Unidos do Brasil, to create the Banco da República, capitalized at 200,000 contos (about $40 million). This was again a semipublic bank with a government-appointed president who had veto power. It was the sole government agency for affecting the exchange rate, collecting and depositing tax revenues, servicing the foreign debt, and lending to the federal treasury, while also being the largest commercial bank in the country. Severely weakened by many poor loans granted during the Encilhamento, the Banco da República had to be bailed out by the state in 1900.

In 1905 the institution reformed its charters, reduced its capital to 70,000 contos, and again assumed the name Banco do Brasil. The new bank, now with one-third public ownership, continued its previous public functions but refrained from investment banking. The bank's branches spread throughout the country; by 1930 it had over eighty. Although an attempt in the early 1920s to give the bank many of the powers of a central bank proved short-lived, after 1937 it played an important role in long-term industrial and agricultural loans.

The Banco do Brasil continues as one of the most important semipublic banks in the country, acting as a commercial lender and a government agent. By 1964 it was the twenty-eighth largest bank in the world and the largest in Latin America and the entire third world. But as the state's institutionalized financial presence increased after the 1950s with the creation of a central bank, the Banco Nacional do Desenvolvimento Econômico e Social (BNDES), the Banco Nacional da Habitação (BNH), and public banks in all of the states, the Banco do Brasil's importance as an agent of state policy declined. The growth of private Brazilian and foreign banks has reduced its relative commercial position as well. Even so, it continues to be, as it has been for most of its history, the largest bank in Brazil.

See also **Banking: Overview; Banking: Since 1990.**

BIBLIOGRAPHY

Victor Viana, *O Banco do Brasil: Sua formção, seu engrandecimento, sua missão nacional* (1926).

Claudio Pacheco, *História do Banco do Brasil,* 4 vols. (1973).

Steven Topik, "State Enterprise in a Liberal Regime: The Banco do Brasil, 1905–1930," in *Journal of Inter-American Studies and World Affairs* 22, no. 4 (1980): 401–422.

Additional Bibliography

Medeiros, Cezar. *O banco universal contemporâneo: Uma estratégia para financiar os investimentos: O papel do Banco do Brasil, dos demais bancos oficiais e dos fundos de pensão.* Rio de Janeiro: INsight Editorial, 1996.

Rodrigues, Lea Carvalho. *Metáforas do Brasil: Demissões voluntárias, crise e rupturas no Banco do Brasil.* São Paulo: Annablume, 2004.

Triner, Gail D. *Banking and Economic Development: Brazil, 1889-1930.* New York: Palgrave, 2000.

STEVEN TOPIK

BANDA DE PÍFANOS.

Banda de Pífanos, a fife-and-drum ensemble—also called *zabumba, banda cabaçal,* and *esquenta mulher*—common among the mestizo populations of northeastern Brazil. Most likely brought to Brazil by Portuguese settlers as early as the sixteenth century, these ensembles are used for the rituals of folk Catholicism (prayer sessions, pilgrimages, processions) and for such secular functions as dramatic and social dances and revelry. The musicians, who are almost always male, learn to play strictly by ear and are typically rural agricultural workers or urban laborers. The bands comprise four to six instruments, including two *pífanos* (cane flutes), a *zabumba* (bass drum), a *tarol* (snare drum), a *surdo* (tenor drum), and *pratos* (hand cymbals). The repertoire consists of devotional music for the veneration of saints as well as music for social dancing and secular festivities. For religious occasions such as a novena (prayer session devoted to a saint), *bandas de pífanos* accompany the singing of hymns and praise songs, and play devotional music in honor of the saint in march and waltz rhythms. Secular dance music, such as Baião, *forró,* and *xote,* is played for community parties, in commercial dance halls, and on radio shows. *Bandas de pífanos* perform frequently during the June festivals honoring Saint Anthony, Saint John, and Saint Peter.

See also **Music: Popular Music and Dance.**

BIBLIOGRAPHY

César Guerra-Peixe, "Zabumba: Orquestra nordestina," in *Revista brasileira de folclore* 10, no. 26 (1970): 15–38.

Additional Bibliography

Crook, Larry. *Brazilian Music: Northeastern Traditions and the Heartbeat of a Modern Nation.* Santa Barbara: ABC-CLIO, 2005.

Murphy, John P. *Music in Brazil: Experiencing Music, Expressing Culture.* New York: Oxford University Press, 2006.

LARRY N. CROOK

BANDA ORIENTAL.

BANDA ORIENTAL. Banda Oriental, historical designation of the northeastern region of the Río De La Plata estuary used to distinguish it from the southern shores, the traditional core of the Argentine Republic. The name was applied by custom to the relatively well-populated stretch of land between the lower course of the Uruguay River, south of Fray Bentos, and the city of Rocha, near the Atlantic coast. It became official when the province joined the United Provinces of the Río De La Plata (1812), represented by José G. Artigas (1764–1850).

The regional strife that colored most of the early years of independence in the Río de la Plata region contributed to alienating the inhabitants of the northeastern shores, a feeling that intensified when the Congress of Tucumán (1816) ratified the independence of the United Provinces without mentioning the Banda Oriental, politically controlled at that time by Artigas. In 1817, taking advantage of the isolation and relative weakness of the province, Brazilian troops invaded the territory and exiled Artigas to Paraguay. The Brazilian occupation continued until 1825, when Colonel Juan A. Lavalleja and his famous Thirty-Three Companions stormed Montevideo to liberate the Banda Oriental. With the help of Argentine troops, liberation was achieved in Ituzaingó in February of 1827, and in the following year Argentina and Brazil relinquished their claims to the Banda Oriental. Under the name of Uruguay it became an independent country.

See also **Argentina, Geography; United Provinces of the Río de la Plata.**

BIBLIOGRAPHY

Lucía Sala De Touron, *Evolución económica de la Banda Oriental* (Montevideo, 1967).

José C. Williman, *La Banda Oriental en la lucha de los imperios: 1503–1818* (Montevideo, 1975).

Additional Bibliography

Barrios Pintos, Aníbal. *Historia de los pueblos orientales: Sus orígenes, procesos fundacionales, sus primeros años.* 2nd. ed. Montevideo: Academia Nacional de Letras, 2000.

Hudson, W. H. *The Purple Land: Being the Narrative of One Richard Lamb's Adventures in the Banda Orientál, in South America, as Told by Himself.* New York: Dutton, 1916.

Kleinpenning, Jan M. G. *Peopling the Purple Land: A Historical Geography of Rural Uruguay, 1500–1915.* Amsterdam: CEDLA, 1995.

Verdesio, Gustavo. *La invención del Uruguay: La entrada del territorio y sus habitantes a la cultura occidental.* Montevideo: Editorial Graffiti: Editorial Trazas, 1996.

CÉSAR N. CAVIEDES

BANDEIRA, MANUEL CARNEIRO DE SOUZA

BANDEIRA, MANUEL CARNEIRO DE SOUZA (1886–1968). Manuel Carneiro de Souza Bandeira (*b.* 19 April 1886; *d.* 13 October 1968), Brazilian poet. Born in Recife,

Pernambuco, Bandeira moved to Rio at the age of ten. He planned to be an architect, but his studies were interrupted by tuberculosis. While ill, he wrote verses that filled his idleness and alleviated his suffering, but eventually he began to write great poetry. His health improved, and in 1917 he published his first volume of poetry, *A cinza das horas* (The Ashes of the Hours).

He lived for thirteen years in a working-class suburb of Rio and later taught literature at the Pedro II School and what is now the Federal University of Rio de Janeiro.

Bandeira's work has been divided into two not very distinct phases. The first comprises his three earliest collections of poems. *A cinza das horas* follows symbolist and Parnassian ideals. *Carnaval* (1919) reveals independent traits that depart from the literary conventions of the time and includes "Os Sapos," later a national anthem of the modernists. *O ritmo dissoluto* (Dissolute Rhythm, 1924) contains unconventional themes and forms.

Libertinagem (Libertinage, 1930) is the first volume of Bandeira's second phase. It reveals a transition to the modernistic aesthetic in several ways: the adoption of Portuguese as spoken in Brazil; prosaic themes; popular aspects of Brazilian culture; and humor, varying from fine irony to straight jokes. Additional works by Bandeira include *Estrela da manhã* (Morning Star, 1936), *Lira dos cinqüent'anos* (Lyrics of Fiftieth Birthday, 1940), *Belo, Belo* in his *Poesias Completas* (3d ed., 1948), *Mafuá do malungo* (2d ed., 1954), *De poetas e poesia* (1954), *A Brief History of Brazilian Literature* (1958), *Estrela da tarde* (Evening Star, 1963), *Estrela da vida inteira* (Whole Life Star, 1966), *Andorinha, andorinha* (1966), and *Poesia completa e prosa* (4th ed., 1983). *This Earth, That Sky: Poems by Manuel Bandeira,* translated by Candice Slater, appeared in 1988.

Bandeira continued to be open to new approaches, even having written concretist poems. He always remained, however, an essentially lyric poet. His poetry, often tinged with irony, melancholy, and tragic humor, betrays reminiscences of his own life. He is also recognized as a literary critic, anthologist, essayist, and translator.

See also **Literature: Brazil.**

BIBLIOGRAPHY

Gilda E Antônio Cândido, "Introdução," in *Estrela da vida inteira* (1966).

Claude L. Hulet, "Manuel Bandeira," in *Brazilian Literature,* edited by Claude L. Hulet, vol. 3 (1975), pp. 9–24.

Joaquim Francisco Coelho, *Biopoética de Manuel Bandeira* (1981), and *Manuel Bandeira, pré-modernista* (1982).

Emmanuel De Morais, "Uma vida cada vez mais cheia de tudo," in Bandeira's *Vou-me embora pra Pasárgata* (1986).

Gilberto Mendonça Teles, "Manuel Bandeira," in *Latin American Writers,* edited by Carlos A. Solé and Maria Isabel Abreu, vol. 2 (1989), pp. 629–641.

MARIA ISABEL ABREU

BANDEIRAS. Bandeiras, large companies of armed colonists and Indian warriors that left the captaincy of São Vicente and penetrated the vast wilderness to the north, west, and south in search of gold and Indian slaves in the sixteenth, seventeenth, and eighteenth centuries. The *bandeirantes* (participants in the *bandeiras*) are responsible for the exploration of the great Brazilian west, numerous discoveries of gold, and the enslavement of thousands of Indians.

The first *bandeiras* were organized in the late sixteenth century as prospecting expeditions in search of gold and precious minerals, but the failure to find significant lodes shifted the focus to Indian slaving. Outfitted in the town of São Paulo, *bandeiras* included whites, Mamelucos, and Indians. They carried arms, gunpowder, lead, collars, chains, bows, and arrows. Gone for months, even years, at a time, the expeditions subsisted off of manioc flour and food hunted from the forest. These expeditions were financed privately from São Vicente by investors who expected to be rewarded with gold or Indian slaves.

The Guarani Indians living in Jesuit missions became the targets of the slaving *bandeiras*. Manoel Preto led attacks against the missions in the 1610s. In 1628, Antônio Rapôso Tavares led a *bandeira* of some three thousand men to Guairá, where he attacked and burned several missions, enslaved the Indians, and marched them back to São Vicente. Later *bandeiras* led by André Fernandes and Paulo de Amaral destroyed other missions. Soon thereafter the Jesuits moved their remaining missions to what is today Rio Grande do Sul, Uruguay, Paraguay, Argentina, and Mato Grosso. The *bandeiras* followed them and continued to take slaves.

In response to intense lobbying by the Jesuits, Pope Urban VIII issued a bull (1639) which reiterated the freedom of Indians and excommunicated those who held Indians in servitude. In São Paulo an angry town council responded by expelling the Jesuits from São Vicente. The Jesuits also received permission to arm their Indians in self-defense. The fortified missions then repulsed the *bandeiras*. A *bandeira* led by Pascoal Leite Paes was turned back in 1639, as was another at the Mbororé River in 1641. Thereafter, the *bandeiras* left the missions alone. Slaving continued, however, against tribal Indians.

A new phase of *bandeirante* activity began in the 1690s, when the first substantial discoveries of gold were made in Minas Gerais. Large *bandeiras*, led by former Indian slavers, were mounted to search for precious metals. Veteran *bandeirante* Bartolomeo Bueno da Silva, the younger, trekked through Goiás, where he discovered gold in the 1720s. Fernão Dias Pais sought emeralds in a quixotic quest that yielded only tourmalines.

The Crown used *bandeiras* for political ends. Some expeditions were outfitted to wage war against Indian enemies or runaway slaves. A *bandeira* led by Domingos Jorge Velho destroyed the quilombo of Palmares in the 1690s. Antônio Rapôso Tavares led a *bandeira* across South America in 1647 to reconnoiter a possible route to Peru. His expedition logged 7,000 miles through the Chaco, the eastern Andes, and down the Madeira and Amazon rivers to the Atlantic Ocean. *Bandeirantes* explored the far west and claimed it for Portugal. They were soon followed by a wave of prospectors, slaves, farmers, and traders who effectively won the far west for Brazil.

See also **Entrada; Gems and Gemstones; Gold Rushes, Brazil; Mining: Colonial Brazil; Slavery: Brazil.**

BIBLIOGRAPHY

Richard M. Morse, *The Bandeirantes: The Historical Role of the Brazilian Pathfinders* (1965).

Alcantra Machado, *Vida e morte do bandeirante* (1978).

John Hemming, *Red Gold: The Conquest of the Brazilian Indians* (1978).

Additional Bibliography

Guimarães, Acyr Vaz. *A saga bandeirante: De São Vicente ao Chuí, dos campos de Piratininga às minas do Cuiabá*. Campo Grande-MS: UCDB, 2004.

Santos, Márcio. *Estradas reais: Introdução ao estudo dos caminhos do ouro e do diamante no Brasil*. Belo Horizonte: Editora Estrada Real, 2001.

ALIDA C. METCALF

BANDITRY. Banditry can be defined simply as the act of taking property from another by using force or the threat of force. But Latin American bandits have appeared in varied and complex guises. Some common criminals simply brutalized and abused their fellow men. However, banditry also arose because throughout Latin American history, elite rule restricted access to economic opportunity and political expression. Runaway slaves or maroons sometimes became highwaymen, stealing from travelers to survive. Domination by the wealthy forced the rural masses to defend their interests through various means. Eric J. Hobsbawm coined the term "social bandits" to describe Robin Hood–style outlaws who championed the oppressed peasants.

When elites denied them access to land or to a living wage, the rural masses struck back using legal and extralegal tactics, including banditry. In early twentieth-century southern Bolivia, the peasants used banditry, mass mobilization, or litigation, depending on the strength of their corporate identity and cohesiveness. During the Mexican Revolution, peasants formed regional bandit gangs to combat the encroachment of large haciendas or other forces of change that disrupted traditional Indian village life.

Some outlaws gained reputations as social bandits and were celebrated in folklore and music. The Latin American masses sometimes viewed bandits as heroes striking a blow against their rich oppressors. Argentina's rural poor identified with the persecution suffered by legendary gauchos like Juan Moreira and Martín Fierro. Lampião (Virgolino Ferreira da Silva) and Antônio Silvino in Brazil, Pío Romero in Bolivia, and Manuel García in Cuba became symbols of popular resistance to oppression.

But bandit myth, like most myth, expresses only half-truths. Peasant stories about bandits exhibit what Erick D. Langer has termed "a selective memory." Such tales romanticize bandits and ignore their ignoble deeds, such as robbing, terrorizing, and killing peasants. Few romanticized bandits actually lived the heroic, idealized lives attributed to them in popular culture or in Hobsbawm's social bandit model.

Myth and folklore color some famous bandits so completely that accurate historical depiction is difficult. To compound matters, official government sources often purposely blur the distinction between bandit and revolutionary. Elitist officials typically labeled as bandits any groups that threatened their political monopoly. The U.S. press and government officials of the 1920s termed Augusto Sandino's Nicaraguan forces "bandits" to discredit them. Sixty years later Ronald Reagan publicly referred to members of the Sandinista government as "thugs." The unduly positive images of historical bandits generated in folklore were offset by the negative images from politically motivated government sources.

MOTIVES AND SUPPORT

Why did bandits steal? A desire for profit motivated many gangs. Unlike mythical bandits, however, actual gangs acted more often on the basis of self-interest and opportunism than in the defense of peasant-class interests. As Paul J. Vanderwood has shown, the marginalized rural poor fomented disorder, including bandit attacks, and profited from the resulting conflict. Guerrilla bandits (discussed below) are one example of those who profited from disorder.

Eleodoro Benel (1873–1927), a bandit leader in northern Cajamarca, Peru, was one of many such grasping, rural petty tyrants whose main goal was self-aggrandizement. Such profiteers formed whatever alliances they deemed useful. Bandit leaders cooperated more often with the powerful, not the humble, elements of society.

Economic self-interest also motivated many nineteenth-century bandits, as in Cuba's La Habana Province, where they consciously pursued their own personal gain in an opportunistic fashion. Manuel García's career as a profit-minded bandit

antedated his service to the Cuban independence movement.

In addition to a desire for economic gain, personal and familial conflict drove some men to banditry. Family feuds, endemic to the Brazilian backlands, moved Lampião to take up the outlaw life. The Brazilian "good thief," Antônio Silvino, followed the leads of his father and godfather into bandit life. And the gauchos of the Argentine plains often turned into outlaws after killing someone in a knife fight. There were so many *cimarrón* (wild, feral) bandits on the rural roads between central Peru and Salta in Argentina that they became a favorite topic in fiction, such as the short novels of Juana Manuela Gorriti, *Gubi Abaya* and *El ángel caído*.

Local elites, not the peasant masses, generally provided the support, material assistance (food, arms, clothing), hiding places, and intelligence needed by bandit gangs. In Brazil, Silvino and Lampião cooperated with elites, not the peasant masses. Bandits in Peru, Mexico, and Argentina operated in a similar fashion. These elite-bandit alliances helped keep local oligarchies in power and gave a degree of legitimacy to the outlaws. A politically powerful family could insulate bandits from police and legal authorities.

GUERRILLA BANDITS

If officials labeled revolutionaries as bandits, bandits sometimes professed to have political aims, to cover their crimes with a veneer of legitimacy. Christon Archer coined the term "guerrilla bandits" to describe opportunists who used war as an excuse to pillage. Marginal rural people became guerrilla bandits, drawn to war by coercion or by promises of booty. They exhibited little loyalty and switched sides according to their assessment of the best potential profit. Guerrilla banditry became common in Venezuela, Mexico, Cuba, and elsewhere during the wars for independence and civil wars of the nineteenth century.

POLITICAL BANDITS

Unlike pre-political social bandits or self-serving guerrilla bandits, political bandits had a consciousness of and loyalty to a larger political movement. They did not switch sides for financial gain but instead labored for a political, partisan, or regional agenda. They exhibited clear partisan rather than class leanings. Political banditry was evident in independence-era Cuba, early-twentieth-century

Cajamarca, Peru, and the Colombian *Violencia* of 1945–1965, which left between 100,000 and 300,000 people dead. The Cuban independence period illustrates both political banditry and the interpretive debates going on in the study of banditry. Louis A. Pérez, Jr., sees banditry in western rural Cuba as motivated by peasant resentment of their marginalization by expanding sugar plantations. In contrast, Rosalie Schwartz argues that western Cuba's banditry reflects neither class conflict nor social banditry. First, many bandit gangs emerged before the process of sugar plantation expansion began. Second, the land concentration that Pérez considers a cause of banditry in fact came after many bandit gangs had emerged.

The peasant villages that purportedly supported and sustained social bandits did not exist in the bandit-infested areas of western Cuba. Manuel García put banditry and extortion at the service of the independence movement. His letters and broadsides show a clear political agenda, not typical of Hobsbawm's social bandit.

The Colombian *Violencia* offers another example of banditry, which even Hobsbawm acknowledges to be "in essence more political than social." The *serrano* (mountain region) uprisings during the Mexican Revolution offer another good example of political banditry cutting across class barriers. In both cases, conflict and banditry broke down along partisan or regional, not class, lines. In both cases, there was a political consciousness and agenda at work, a situation not typical of the prepolitical social bandit. Even Gilbert Joseph, who defends to a degree Hobsbawm's views, agrees that the political strategies of the peasants were not archaic "in the sense of being outmoded or prepolitical."

Banditry, then, can be an expression of mass discontent, a means of achieving a political agenda, or a yearning for economic betterment. Banditry could be a tactic of rural elites as well as the rural poor; outlaw networks often cut across class lines. Many bandit gangs developed and profited from close ties to regional and local power brokers: the Caudillos (political bosses) or *coroneis* (planter elite).

What about female bandits? We know that a woman called María Bonita died with Lampião in a hail of gunfire in 1938. And "La Carambada," a female bandit who dressed in male clothing, robbed

travelers in Querétaro, Mexico, during the mid-nineteenth century. Women most likely lived with male bandit gangs at their hideouts.

A more recent phenomenon has come to light regarding Salvadoran gang members. Many of these hoodlums learned their trade in exile in Los Angeles and other U.S. locations and were later deported back to Central America, where they have been applying what they learned.

Richard Slatta, Gilbert Joseph, and others have begun placing Latin American banditry in a broader, more comparative perspective. Wider comparisons highlight the similarities and differences among bandits as well as the roles of culture, regionalism, and other variables. Yet more research is needed. Instead of blithely accepting bandit images from folk legends and literature as fact, scholars must use them as lenses for viewing peasant cultures. Even if folk views of heroic bandits do not reflect historical reality, they do reflect much about the yearnings and values of Latin America's rural masses.

In sum, Latin American elites and masses both participated in banditry. The rural poor sometimes used banditry to express political sentiments. At other times banditry represented an economic alternative in a world of opportunity narrowly restricted by the elite. On occasion, economic self-interest and political rebellion came together, as in the case of guerrilla banditry.

Latin American elites long have recognized the dangerous political potential of banditry and have made vigorous efforts to contain it. But although they have been victimized by the elite, the rural poor have not remained passive victims. If denied legitimate means of survival and participation, people will strike back violently at their oppressors.

See also **Gangs; Maroons (Cimarrones); Quiroga, Juan Facundo.**

BIBLIOGRAPHY

Billy Jaynes Chandler, *The Bandit King: Lampião of Brazil* (1978).

Eric J. Hobsbawm, *Bandits*, rev. ed. (1981).

Paul J. Vanderwood, *Disorder and Progress: Bandits, Police, and Mexican Development* (1981).

Christon I. Archer, "Banditry and Revolution in New Spain, 1790–1821," in *Biblioteca Americana* 1, no. 2 (1982): 58–89.

Gonzálo G. Sánchez and Donny Meertens, *Bandoleros, gamonales y campesinos: El caso de la Violencia en Colombia* (1983).

Richard W. Slatta, ed., *Bandidos: The Varieties of Latin American Banditry* (1987).

Erick D. Langer, *Economic Change and Rural Resistance in Southern Bolivia, 1880–1930* (1989).

Louis A. Pérez, Jr., *Lords of the Mountain: Social Banditry and Peasant Protest in Cuba, 1878–1918* (1989).

Rosalie Schwartz, *Lawless Liberators: Political Banditry and Cuban Independence* (1989).

Richard W. Slatta, "Banditry as Political Participation in Latin America," in *Criminal Justice History: An International Annual* 11 (1990): 171–187.

Gilbert M. Joseph, "On the Trail of Latin American Bandits: A Reexamination of Peasant Resistance," in *Latin American Research Review* 25, no. 3 (1990): 7–53.

Additional Bibliography

Balboa Navarro, Imilcy. *La protesta rural en Cuba: Resistencia cotidiana, bandolerismo y revolución 1878–1902*. Madrid: Consejo Superior de Investigaciones Científicas, 2003.

Gorriti, Juana Manuela. *Dreams and Realities: Selected Fiction of Juana Manuela Gorriti*. Translated by Sergio Waisman. New York: Oxford University Press, 2003.

Solares Robles, Laura. *Bandidos somos y en el camino andamos: Bandidaje, caminos y administración de justicia en el siglo XIX, 1821–1855: El caso de Michoacán*. Morelia, Mexico: Instituto Michoacano de Cultura; Instituto de Investigaciones Dr. José María Luís Mora, 1999.

Zilberg, Elana. "Fools Banished from the Kingdom: Remapping Geographies of Gang Violence between the Americas (Los Angeles and San Salvador)." *American Quarterly* 56, no. 3 (September 2004): 759–779.

RICHARD W. SLATTA

BANKING

This entry includes the following articles:
OVERVIEW
SINCE 1990

OVERVIEW

Although several special types of credit institutions emerged in Latin America in the late colonial period, it was not until the third quarter of the nineteenth century that modern banks and banking practices became permanently established in the hemisphere's republics. At that time the expansion of trade and the financial requirements of national governments impelled the creation of new types of credit institutions and the reform of monetary systems throughout the area. By the end of the century there existed a broad variety of banks, both domestic- and foreign-owned, mostly concentrated in commercial and mortgage banking as opposed to industrial finance.

In the 1920s the trend toward greater specialization in banking accelerated, a process reflected in the creation of central banks in most nations. The establishment of state development (industrial, agricultural, and foreign trade) banks was perhaps the characteristic feature of Latin American banking during the 1930s and 1940s. In subsequent decades private banking was diversified on a local and regional basis, foreign banks multiplied in various financial centers, and new types of banking instruments and institutions linked to burgeoning capital markets were developed.

THE EARLIEST BANKS

Historians have not yet satisfactorily explained the impact of banking on the overall processes of economic development in Latin America, concentrating instead mainly on institutional histories. It is should be emphasized, however, that, during the nineteenth century, the birth of banking was the result of a slow process of expanding and maturing credit markets that served the needs of agriculture, ranching, mining, manufacturing, and, of course, trade. In addition, the larger banks served the financial needs of governments, always a critical function.

The first banks, which were not destined to survive, were closely tied to government finance. Neither the first Banco Do Brasil, established in 1808, nor the Banco de Buenos Aires, founded in 1822, nor the Banco De Avío of Mexico, created in 1830, was able to weather the financial crises generated by deficit-ridden governments. Only in Brazil did commercial banking begin to flourish with the establishment of banks in Rio de Janeiro (1838), Maranhão (1844), and Bahia (1844). After the 1850s, however, banking institutions began to multiply in other nations, some of which were to prove more durable. Among the more important national banks were the Banco de la Provincia de

Buenos Aires (1854), the Banco Nacional de Chile (1865), the Banco del Perú (1863), the Banco Español de la Isla de Cuba (1856), and the Crédito Inmobiliario y Fomento Cubano (1857).

BANKING CRISES

The first regionwide banking crisis occurred as a result of the world recession that began in 1873. Numerous banks in Chile, Peru, Argentina, and Brazil failed, thinning the ranks of the financial institutions in many cities. However, in the 1880s a new banking boom took place, a reflection of the general process of economic modernization in most Latin American nations. This development included the building of railway systems, the introduction of tramways, establishment of telephone and electrical enterprises in the larger cities, and the expansion of the leading export sectors: agriculture, ranching, and mining. To finance these activities it became necessary to create many new banks, not only in the capitals but also regionwide. The leaders in this process were the larger state banks—the Banco Nacional (Argentina), the Banco Nacional de México, and the Banco do Brasil—which began to engage heavily in branch banking and to dominate the commercial credit markets through their branches in both the capital and many secondary cities. In the late 1880s provincial governments began to stimulate the establishment of regional banks, modeled to a large degree on the U.S. free banking system. This new practice, carried out with great speed, combined with the rapid expansion of burgeoning stock markets in Rio de Janeiro, Buenos Aires, and Santiago de Chile to spur a wave of feverish financial speculation.

A second great financial crisis shook many Latin American capitals in the early 1890s. In Argentina virtually all the state-owned banks were forced to close in the midst of a general financial panic that brought the government to its knees. In Brazil the financial craze (Encilhamento) that marked the transition from empire to republic in 1889 soon led to financial crisis and banking retrenchment. In Chile the banking boom of the late 1880s was cut short by the civil war that toppled the administration of President José Balmaceda in 1891.

THE GROWTH OF SPECIALIZED BANKING

From 1900 to 1914 there was a new stage in the history of banking in Latin America as specialization became more important. The largest domestic banks concentrated on lending to the government but also participated in commercial banking, providing loans to merchants and landowners. At the same time, there emerged a large number of specialized mortgage banks that helped finance the rapid development of cities such as Buenos Aires, Rio de Janeiro, São Paulo, Mexico City, and Havana. The mortgage banks also provided funds to rural property owners, who prospered with the expansion of exports. There simultaneously developed additional and different specialized banking institutions: cooperative banks; a few mining and industrial banks; many private financial companies (mostly involved in real estate speculation); and a large number of foreign banks.

Foreign banks had actually begun playing an important role in the 1860s with the establishment of British-owned commercial banks in Buenos Aires, Rio de Janeiro, Lima, Santiago, and Mexico City. Some of these expanded rapidly—for example, the Bank of London and the Río de la Plata, which quickly established branch offices not only in various cities in Argentina but also in Uruguay and Paraguay. British banks dominated foreign banking in Latin America until the 1890s, when a number of German-owned banks were established in the principal cities of the region. In contrast to the British banks, which tended to be independent companies, the German banking firms were direct subsidiaries of the biggest German commercial banks, the Deutsche, Disconto, and Dresdner banks. In any case, the foreign-owned banks in Latin America tended to specialize principally in the financing of foreign trade, in foreign exchange transactions, and in providing loans to such foreign-owned enterprises as railways, mines, and public utilities.

In 1914 the outbreak of World War I provoked a brief financial crisis in many Latin American countries, but subsequently most banks prospered with the export boom generated by war demand. A new development at the time was the penetration of U.S. banking houses in the region, particularly in the Caribbean but also in several South American capitals. Here the National City Bank took the lead, controlling most of the new branches.

CENTRAL BANKING

During the 1920s central banks began to be established in various Latin American nations. The first such banks were created largely as a result of financial advisory missions led by Edwin W. Kemmerer, a Princeton University professor, to Chile, Peru, Bolivia, Ecuador, and Colombia, all of which established central banks in the 1920s through his direct inspiration. In Mexico the central bank, the Banco de México, was set up in 1925 under the guidance of local financial and legal experts, such as the lawyer Manuel Gómez Morín, who later played an important role in conservative political circles. In Argentina central banking came more slowly: it was not until 1935, after the onset of the Great Depression and the mission to Buenos Aires of Bank of England director Sir Otto Niemeyer in 1932, that the government decided to establish the Banco Central de la Repúblic Argentina, the first president of which was the illustrious economist Raúl Prebisch. In Brazil the Getúlio Vargas administration (1930–1945) adopted a different banking strategy, deciding to continue using the services of the Banco Central da Republica do Brasil to manage most government finance. Not until 1965 was the Brazilian central bank established.

The state took an even more direct role in the banking sector in the 1930s and 1940s in most Latin American nations, creating a great array of specialized agricultural, industrial, and mining credit institutions. In Mexico this was the period of the founding of the Nacional Financiera (1934), the Banco de Crédito Ejidal (1935), the Banco Nacional de Comercio Exterior (1938), and several other financial agencies. In Peru the Banco Agrícola was set up in 1931, the Banco Industrial in 1937, and the Banco Minero in 1941. In Argentina the Banco de Crédito Industrial, set up in 1941, was transformed into the Banco Nacional de Desarrollo in 1971. In Chile the Corporación de Fomento de la Producción (CORFO) was set up in 1939, and in Brazil the Banco Nacional do Desenvolvimento Econômico e Social was established in 1952; there also were several state-promoted regional development banks, such as the Banco de Crédito da Amazônia, set up in 1942, and the Banco do Nordeste, in 1952. In Venezuela the role of the Corporación Venezolana de Fomento (CVF) must be underscored because it has been the main agency for promoting public investment in basic infrastructure, as well as in the industrial and agricultural sectors, since the 1950s.

REGIONAL BANKING

A major innovation in the 1960s was the establishment of regional, multilateral development banks, the most important being the Inter-American Development Bank (IDB), headquartered in Washington, D.C. This bank pooled the resources of many Latin American countries and also tapped the international capital markets for additional funds. Under its first president, Felipe Herrera, the IDB established a new financial strategy consisting of providing long-term loans to governments and state agencies to help modernize infrastructure, agriculture, education, and selected industries. As a multilateral institution it has proved as durable and successful as its elder colleague, the World Bank, and has provided the region with a high volume of development financing on reasonable terms. Other regional development banks have been established by governments in Central America and the Caribbean, although they remain relatively small.

Whereas the commercial banks dominated Latin American credit markets until World War II, in the second half of the twentieth century many different specialized companies developed to provide financing for private enterprise and investment. The growth of private financial institutions other than commercial banks began in the 1950s and 1960s. In the mid-1960s the assets of the private financial companies (*financieras*) equaled those of the commercial banks and later surpassed them. Nonetheless, it should also be kept in mind that many *financieras* and insurance firms are owned or controlled by a banking group, a fact that confirms both the trend toward financial specialization and the traditional high level of concentration of banking capital in most of Latin America.

A PERIOD OF CHANGE

The 1980s were a period of dramatic change in the Latin American banking world. Following an enormous wave of financial speculation fueled by a foreign debt boom in the late 1970s came a series of economic crises that deeply affected the solvency of many Latin American banks, including a major drop in petroleum prices in the early 1980s, a foreign debt crisis that began in 1982, and domestic economic recessions that plagued most Latin American economies during the decade. As a result, several governments took measures to restructure their banking systems.

In August 1982 President José López Portillo of Mexico announced the nationalization of virtually the entire commercial banking system and the expropriation of dollar deposits from tens of thousands of depositors. The losses suffered by private citizens were on the order of several billion dollars, but the government absorbed the external debts of the banks, which surpassed $10 billion. The former stockholders of the commercial banks were subsequently compensated with approximately one-third of the stock of the state-owned banks and with facilities for the establishment of many new private financial companies, mostly involved in stock market operations.

In Peru in 1987 President Alan García announced the nationalization of commercial banks, but the uproar and opposition were so great that his action helped spur the political campaign of the writer Mario Vargas Llosa against the García administration. Eventually the Peruvian authorities were forced to water down their measures and begin a gradual process of reprivatization. In 1989 Brazilian President Fernando Collor de Mello announced the nationalization of all commercial bank deposits, which were then valued at more than $100 billion. Despite great opposition, the government maintained this control for eighteen months, after which there began a renewed process of liberalization of the banking system. Meanwhile, in Mexico the government of Carlos Salinas de Gortari began a process of reprivatization of the Mexican commercial banks in 1990, which for some time proved a financial success and a source of considerable income for the government.

See also **Banco Comercial y Agrícola (Ecuador); Banco de Avío; Banco de la República (Colombia); Banco de Londres y México; Banco de México; Banco de San Carlos (Potosí); Banco de San Carlos (Spain); Banco do Brasil; Economic Development; Inter-American Development Bank (IDB); World Bank.**

BIBLIOGRAPHY

Inter-American Development Bank, *Annual Report* (1961–1991).

David Joslin, *A Century of Banking in Latin America* (1963).

Centro De Estudios Monetarios De Latinoaméricos (CEMLA), *Annual Report* (1980–1990) and specialized country studies.

José Manuel Quijano, *La banca: Pasado y presente (problemas financieros mexicanos)* (1983).

Javier Marquez, *La banca mexicana: Septiembre de 1982–junio de 1985* (1987).

Barbara Stallings, *Banker to the Third World: U.S. Portfolio Investment in Latin America, 1900–1986* (1987).

Paul W. Drake, *The Money Doctor in the Andes: The Kemmerer Mission, 1923–1933* (1989).

CARLOS MARICHAL

SINCE 1990

Since the late twentieth century, banking systems in Latin America have undergone profound changes. Despite wide differences in these systems, stemming from the particular history of each country, certain elements are common to the region as a whole. For many years state intervention, described by scholars as financial repression, was the norm. Such financial policy frameworks as directed credit policies, restrictive schemes of reserve requirements, and interest rate ceilings date back to the post–World War II period but were intensified during the 1970s, when the public sector experienced a greater expansion. By the end of that decade, the use of external debt led to high public indebtedness. As a result of financial repression, Latin American economies and banking systems experienced a wave of crises between 1980 and 2001. Argentina's bank crisis, between 1980 and 1982, preceded a generalized Latin American debt crisis, which exploded in 1982. Chile's 1982 crisis was a severe shock to that country's banking system.

The banking systems of other nations faced serious problems but not full-fledged crises. In Mexico, because banks were expropriated in 1982, the crisis had a minor impact on the stability of the banking system. In 1984 and 1985 Colombian and Peruvian banking systems faced problems; in Peru the situation was so severe that the government attempted to nationalize the banks in 1987. During the 1980s the economic recession in the region had affected the quality of banks' assets, as well as their capacity to expand. At the same time, macroeconomic instability, mainly inflation and devaluation of local currency, impinged on the value of assets and increased risks faced by banks. In addition, because of strong state intervention, substantial financing was being used to alleviate the public sector deficit. For example, in the case of Mexico, after the 1982 expropriation of private commercial banks the government used the banking system to fund its deficit. In Brazil there was also a flow of banks' resources to the public sector. With the debt crisis weakening banking systems, the stage was set for further crises later on.

From the mid-1980s to the beginning of the 1990s, the liberalization process in the financial sector was initiated in most countries in the region, prompting significant changes in banking and financial systems. Financial liberalization consisted of the opening of banking markets (privatization and elimination of barriers to market entry), the opening to external flows of capital, the liberalization of interest rates, and reduced participation by the state. Preceding the liberalization trend, the first such financial reforms in the region had taken place in 1974 in Chile under the military dictatorship. However, Chile's liberalization was not accompanied by an adequate prudential regulation, leading to the worst banking crisis in the country's history in 1982. The crisis restored the presence of the state to the banking sector.

Mexico initiated the general financial liberalization in 1988. The reforms began with the opening of the capital account to foreign investment and ended with bank reprivatization. Nevertheless, banks were weakened after having been under the control of the state and years of macroeconomic instability. In addition, corruption and other irregularities beset the process of reprivatization. As in other countries, there was inadequate prudential regulation, a policy that would have monitored risks faced by banks. In late 1994 a severe banking crisis exploded, with the cost of this crisis estimated at 6.5 percent of Mexico's GDP.

In Brazil the presence of the state remained strong until the 1990s, as a result of which the state internalized many of the problems faced by banks. Brazil's most severe banking crisis occurred in 1994, with Panama, Venezuela, and Ecuador also facing crises. Argentina had undergone another banking crisis in 1989 and 1990, with banks whose assets represented 40 percent of the entire financial system's assets going into bankruptcy. In 2001 Argentina fell again into a severe banking crisis, in which a significant amount of deposits were frozen, thus damaging mainly individual savers; this phenomenon was known as *el corralito* (little pen). Since the successive crises of this era, banks in the region have adopted stricter prudential regulation measures.

In the early twenty-first century, bank regulation is in line with the Basel Agreement, an accord developed at a central bankers' meeting in Basel, Switzerland, in 1975 that established guidelines for supervision of banks.

The most important transformation in the region's banking systems has been their internationalization. Since 1994 large international bank corporations have entered the Latin American banking markets, to the extent that in many countries they have managed to control an important part of the banking industry. Thus banks are no longer the property of local control groups, mainly industrial and financial conglomerates, but rather are subsidiaries of international banks. International banks have become an important factor in the banking systems of Mexico, Chile, Peru, Paraguay, and Brazil; to a lesser extent, they have also entered Bolivia, Colombia, Costa Rica, El Salvador, and Venezuela. In Cuba, Ecuador, Guatemala, and Nicaragua, entry by foreign banks has been minimal or nonexistent. Entry strategies have been related mainly to the purchase of local banks. Among the international banks that have been more aggressive in their entry strategies are the Spanish and English banks, followed by those from other European countries and the United States and Canada.

The entry into the financial sector of new actors that compete and complement bank operations has changed Latin American financial systems. The systems most affected have been private pension funds, which saw the need to open up the market, and specialized financial intermediaries, "non-bank banks" that look for increasing the availability of credit in specific market segments. Chile was a pioneer in developing a model pension funds system.

Another emerging trend affecting the region in the twenty-first century is microfinance, financial services aimed at the poor that engage in transactions of small amounts for individuals, micro enterprises, and small family businesses. Historically, in all Latin American nations the financial system penetration has been weak, and most of their populations have little or no access to financial services. In microfinance, financial intermediaries try to reach those who historically have lacked access to the formal financial system, the "unbanked." Many clients are women or small groups of people from one town or village. Modalities and operation styles vary among microfinance institutions. Microfinance development has made notable strides in Bolivia, Ecuador, and El Salvador; greater expansion of this sector has occurred in Brazil, Mexico, Peru, and Chile. Large commercial banks have also started to enter into this sector throughout the region. Many economists believe that microfinance will allow greater financial penetration and increased access to formal financial systems across the region.

See also **Economic Development; Economic Integration; Inter-American Development Bank (IDB).**

BIBLIOGRAPHY

Bank for International Settlements. "Evolving Banking Systems in Latin America and the Caribbean: Challenges and Implications for Monetary Policy and Financial Stability." BIS Paper No. 33 (February 2007). Available from http://www.bis.org.

Del Angel, Gustavo, ed. *La Banca en América Latina: Lecciones del pasado, retos al futuro.* Mexico: CIDE, 2003.

Del Angel, Gustavo, Carlos Bazdresch, and Francisco Suárez, eds. *Cuando el Estado Se Hizo Banquero: Consecuencias de la Nacionalización Bancaria en México.* Mexico: Fondo de Cultura Económica, Colección Lecturas del Trimestre 96, 2005.

Foro Regional Sobre Asuntos Relacionados a la Estabilidad Financiera. "Análisis de los efectos del incremento de la actividad de la banca extranjera en América Latina y el Caribe." *Monetaria* 25 3 (2002): 205–246.

Gruben, William C., Jahyeong Koo, and Robert R. Moore. "When Does Financial Liberalization Make Banks Risky? An Empirical Examination of Argentina, Canada and Mexico." Federal Reserve Bank of Dallas, Working Paper 0399. 1999. Available from *Ideas*, University of Connecticut, Department of Economics. http://ideas.repec.org/p/fip/feddwp/0399.html#provider.

Haggard, Stephen, Chung H. Lee, and Sylvia Maxfield, eds. *The Politics of Finance in Developing Countries.* Ithaca, NY: Cornell University Press, 1993.

Hausmann, Ricardo, and Liliana Rojas-Suárez, eds. *Banking Crises in Latin America.* Washington, DC: Inter-American Development Bank, 1996.

Minushkin, Susan. "*Banqueros* and *Bolseros*: Structural Change and Financial Market Liberalisation in Mexico." *Journal of Latin American Studies* 34, no. 4 (2002): 915–944.

GUSTAVO DEL ANGEL

BANK NATIONALIZATION. The most significant case in modern history of private banks nationalization or expropriation by a Latin American government took place on September 1, 1982, in Mexico, when Mexican president José López Portillo issued a decree whereby Mexican private commercial banks were nationalized. The nationalization or expropriation of Mexican private commercial banks has been one of the banking appropriations of greater magnitude in modern history and was an unprecedented event with major consequences on the Mexican economy.

The bank nationalization in Mexico was preceded by the outbreak of the debt crisis in Latin America in August 1982. In this context, the arguments to seize banks were to implement an exchange rate control, and to bring to an end the outflow of funds from the country to foreign nations. However, the underlying causes differ from those officially advocated. Previously a political rupture between the government and bankers had taken place. Moreover, there was an ideological element, since there were groups in the government in favor of an expropriation of commercial banks, who deemed such appropriation as a necessary measure to support the country economy.

Consequences are summarized in three key points: a) banks were used by the government to finance public deficit; b) the structure of ownership and corporative control in the banking sector changed, thus influencing the behavior and performance of this industry; c) the relations between the State and the Mexican private sector changed dramatically, thus generating direct effects in the political scene.

In 1990, Mexican president Carlos Salinas reprivatized banks. However, this process was implemented through a weak institutional framework which implied strong irregularities in the process; these reached the public domain during the 1995 banking crises. In the process, some of the bank charters were granted to entrepreneurs that mismanaged the banks and conducted their institutions to bankruptcy. The newly privatized banks also had weak structures for assessing credit risks, an inheritance from their previous status as government financial entities. A deficient conduction of many Mexican banks, and the lack of an adequate prudential regulation aggravated the financial situation of the banking system at the moment when the 1994 Peso crisis exploded. After the crisis, the Mexican banking sector had to open its doors for capital injections from global financial intermediaries. As a consequence, today's Mexican banks are property of international financial conglomerates.

Conceptually speaking, the bank nationalization was an expression of the State's capacity to alter private property rights. Mexican banks were always exposed to an expropriation risk throughout the twentieth century (Haber, 2005). However, there were several factors, inherent to the relationship between the banking sector and the government that inhibited an expropriation or reduced expropriation risk before 1982 (Del Angel, Bazdresch and Suárez, 2005).

Other Latin American experiences which preceded the Mexican case include Costa Rica, where in June 1948 the four most important banks of this country were nationalized. In July 1979, the government of Nicaragua nationalized all the banking system. In May 1980, the government of El Salvador nationalized the entire banking system.

Subsequent to the Mexican case, in Peru, president Alan García announced the nationalization of private commercial banks in 1987. The reasons for such expropriation in Peru are similar to those in Mexico. However, García did not count on an effective authoritarian governmental steering mechanism as in Mexico. The action could not take place due to strong civil opposition, including the media. One of the leaders in the campaign against the nationalization was Mario Vargas Llosa, who after this event started to fully participate in Peruvian politics.

See also **Banking: Overview; Banking: Since 1990; García Pérez, Alan; López Portillo, José; Salinas de Gortari, Carlos; Vargas Llosa, Mario.**

BIBLIOGRAPHY

Del Angel, Gustavo, Carlos Bazdresch, and Francisco Suárez, eds. *Cuando el Estado Se Hizo Banquero. Consecuencias de la Nacionalización Bancaria.* Fondo de Cultura Económica, Colección Lecturas del Trimestre #96. México, 2005.

Haber, Stephen. "Mexico's Experiments with Bank Privatization and Liberalization, 1991-2003." *Journal of Banking and Finance* 29: 8-9. August-September 2005. pp. 2325-2353.

GUSTAVO A. DEL ANGEL

BANZER SUÁREZ, HUGO (1926–2002).

Bolivia's military dictator from 1971 to 1978, Hugo Banzer became an important actor in the country's democratic transition and its elected president in 1997. Born May 10, 1926, in Concepción, he studied at military schools in Bolivia, Argentina, Brazil, and the United States, including its School of the Americas in Panama. His military career brought him to politics after General René Barrientos Ortuño's coup in 1964, when he became minister of education. Following subsequent government posts he emerged as the leader of a conservative faction of the military that twice attempted to overthrow General Juan José Torres González. The second attempt, on August 21, 1971, succeeded, and Banzer became president. Initially governing with a civilian coalition, he banned all political parties in 1974 and increasingly relied on repressive tactics. Although he survived numerous coup attempts, he was forced from office in 1978. In March 1979 he founded the Acción Democrática Nacionalista (ADN) and competed in the annulled presidential contests of 1979 and 1980. Banzer received the most popular votes in the 1985 presidential election but lost to the Movimiento Nacionalista Revolucionario (MNR) in the second round when congress made the final selection among the candidates. Nevertheless, Banzer formed a governing pact with the MNR that helped stabilize Bolivia's democracy after the tumultuous period that began in 1979. Banzer ran again in 1989, 1993, and 1997, when he took the presidency once again. He pursued an aggressive coca eradication policy until cancer forced him to resign on August 6, 2001, and transfer power to Vice President Jorge Quiroga Ramírez. Banzer died on May 5, 2002.

See also **Bolivia, Political Parties: Nationalist Democratic Action (ADN); Military Dictatorships: Since 1945.**

BIBLIOGRAPHY

Malloy, James M., and Eduardo Gamarra. *Revolution and Reaction: Bolivia 1964–1985.* New Brunswick, NJ: Transaction, 1987.

ROBERT R. BARR

BAPTISTA, MARIANO (1832–1907).

Mariano Baptista (*b.* 16 July 1832; *d.* 19 March 1907), president of Bolivia (1892–1896). One of the greatest political orators of Bolivia, Baptista is also considered the ideologist of the Conservative (or Constitutionalist) Party, which prevailed from 1884 to 1899. Dedicated to politics all his adult life, Baptista was a supporter of the dictatorship of José María Linares (1857–1861). As a diplomat, Baptista represented Bolivia well in border negotiations with virtually all neighboring countries. Elected vice president during the Gregorio Pacheco administration (1884–1888), Baptista became one of the most important Conservative politicians. He wrote profusely in various newspapers in favor of the Catholic church, mining interests, and railroad development, and against the anticlerical Liberal Party. When Baptista was elected president in 1892 he had the misfortune of presiding over the collapse of international silver prices and the economic crisis it triggered in Bolivia. During his administration he fostered railroad construction and the exploitation of rubber resources in the Acre region of northeast Bolivia.

See also **Bolivia, Political Parties: Conservative Party.**

BIBLIOGRAPHY

There is no biography of Baptista. The best source on his life is his monumental *Obras completas* (1932). References to Baptista are in Herbert S. Klein, *Bolivia: The Evolution of a Multi-Ethnic Society* (1982), pp. 159–161.

ERICK D. LANGER

BAQUEDANO, MANUEL (1826–1897).
Manuel Baquedano (*b.* 1826; *d.* 1897), Chilean military leader. Born in Santiago, Baquedano ran away at the age of twelve and sailed as a stowaway in the expedition sent to destroy the Peru-Bolivia Confederation. In 1839 he fought in the battles of Portada de Guias and Yungay. During the civil war of 1851 he fought in the battle of Loncomilla against his father. In 1854 he was separated from military service by the government of Manuel Montt but was reinstated in 1859. Baquedano fought against the Araucanian Indians in 1868 and was a brigadier general when the War of the Pacific (1879–1883) broke out. In February 1880 he commanded 14,800 men during the campaign against Tacna and Arica. Following this series of victories,

he commanded 26,500 troops in the attack on Lima. On 13 and 15 January 1881 he won the bloody battles of Chorillos and Miraflores, which led to the capitulation of Lima and drove Peru to accept defeat.

Following the war Baquedano was promoted to generalissimo. In 1881 the Conservative Party proclaimed him their presidential candidate, but he refused to accept. Between 1882 and 1894 he served in the Chilean Senate. In early 1891 the Chilean Congress asked Baquedano to support its position against President José Manuel Balmaceda, but he declared neutrality and took no part in the revolution of 1891. Following Balmaceda's 1891 suicide, Baquedano took command of the nation until those opposed to Balmaceda could take charge.

See also **Chile, Political Parties: Conservative Party; Military Dictatorships: 1821–1945.**

BIBLIOGRAPHY

Jorge Carmona Yañez, *Baquedano*, 2d ed. (1978); *Historia militar de Chile*, 2d ed., 3 vols. (1984).

Additional Bibliography

Ekdahl, Guillermo, and Carlos Valenzuela Solis de Ovando. *Baquedano general victorioso: Los Angeles, Tacna, Arica, Chorrillos, Miraflores.* Santiago de Chile: Edit. Andújar, 2003.

ROBERT SCHEINA

BAQUERIZO MORENO, ALFREDO
(1859–1951). Alfredo Baquerizo Moreno was president of Ecuador from 1916 to 1920. Born September 28, 1859, in Guayaquil, Baquerizo Moreno earned distinction as a writer of prose and poetry before embarking on a career in politics. He held various government posts, including mayor of Guayaquil, secretary to the minister of the Superior Court in Guayaquil, minister of foreign relations, senator for Guayas Province, president of the Senate, vice president, and acting president (in August 1912). Serious fraud allegations marred his 1916 election as the hand-picked successor to Leónidas Plaza Gutiérrez. In office Baquerizo Moreno continued Ecuador's "liberal era" (1895–1925) reforms, signing legislation in 1918 that legally ended debtors' prisons and *concertaje* (forced labor), even if the laws were not always

enforced. His administration helped the Rockefeller Foundation carry out a successful anti-yellow fever campaign in Guayaquil in 1919. A former professor at the University of Guayaquil, he sought to advance public education in Ecuador. His administration's efforts were undermined by a weakened economy, as sales of Ecuador's leading export, cacao, declined sharply. In foreign policy Baquerizo Moreno resolved Ecuador's lingering boundary dispute with Colombia with the Muñoz Vernaza-Suarez Treaty of 1916. At age seventy-two, Baquerizo Moreno briefly served as interim president, from September 1931 to August 1932. He died in New York City on March 20, 1951.

See also **Cacao Industry; Ecuador: Since 1830; Plaza Gutiérrez, Leonidas.**

BIBLIOGRAPHY

Pike, Fredrick B. *The United States and the Andean Republics: Peru, Bolivia, and Ecuador.* Cambridge, MA: Harvard University Press, 1977.

Rodriguez, Linda Alexander. *The Search for Public Policy: Regional Politics and Government Finances in Ecuador, 1830–1940.* Berkeley: University of California Press, 1985.

RONN PINEO

BAQUIANO.

Gauchos of the Río de la Plata developed a wide range of equestrian skills. The *baquiano* (or *baqueano;* guide or scout) provided a particularly important service on the seemingly trackless pampa. Skilled gaucho *baquianos* led military expeditions, wagon trains, herds of cattle, and foreign travelers across vast stretches of open plains. They navigated by the stars, landmarks, and even the taste of the grass. Because of the demand for their knowledge of terrain, trails, water holes, and such, scouts earned higher wages than the average ranch hand. Domingo F. Sarmiento singled out the *baquiano* as one of four special gaucho types that he described in 1845.

See also **Gaucho.**

BIBLIOGRAPHY

Domingo F. Sarmiento, *Life in the Argentine Republic in the Days of the Tyrants,* translated by Mary Mann (1971).

Richard W. Slatta, *Gauchos and the Vanishing Frontier* (1983).

Additional Bibliography

Assunção, Fernando O. *Historia del gaucho: El gaucho, ser y quehacer.* Buenos Aires: Editorial Claridad, 1999.

Lynch, Ventura R., and Pedro Luis Barcia. *Folklore bonaerense.* Buenos Aires: Secretaría de cultura de la nación en coproducción con RML Ediciones, 1994.

RICHARD W. SLATTA

BAQUÍJANO Y CARRILLO DE CÓRDOBA, JOSÉ DE (1751–1817).

José de Baquíjano y Carrillo de Córdoba (*b.* 13 March 1751; *d.* 24 January 1817), Peruvian intellectual, educator, and high court judge. The precocious and ambitious son of a wealthy, titled family in Lima, Baquíjano obtained a doctorate in canon law from Lima's University of San Marcos at the age of fourteen. After an unsuccessful trip to Spain seeking a high court (*audiencia*) appointment (1773–1776), he returned to Lima and in 1778 joined the faculty at San Marcos.

In 1781 Baquíjano delivered the university's welcoming eulogy for Viceroy Augustín de Jáuregui. Royal censure of the published text, replete with references to prohibited literature, was followed by unsuccessful efforts to win either the rectorship of San Marcos or the senior chair of civil law.

Baquíjano's fortunes improved in the 1790s. He wrote articles for the *Mercurio peruano,* secured the senior chair in canon law at San Marcos, and again set off for Spain to pursue an appointment to Lima's *audiencia.*

Persistence paid off. After being named a criminal judge on the Lima court in 1797, an unusual accomplishment for a native son at the time, Baquíjano advanced to the civil chamber in 1806. Although he was named to the Council of State by the Cortes of Cádiz in February 1812, Baquíjano was never seated. By the time he reached Spain, Ferdinand VII had returned and nullified the Cortes' actions. Baquíjano died in Seville, still loyal to the Spanish monarchy.

See also **Audiencia.**

BIBLIOGRAPHY

Mark A. Burkholder, *Politics of a Colonial Career: José Baquíjano and the Audiencia of Lima* (1980).

Additional Bibliography

Arcilas Farias, Eduardo. *El pensamiento económico hispanoamericáno en Baquiujano y Carrillo.* Caracas, Venezuela: Consejo Nacional de la Cultura, Centro de Estudios Latinoamericanos Romulo Gallegos, 1976.

Puente Brunke, José de la. *José Baquijano y Carrillo.* Lima: Editorial Brasa, 1995.

MARK A. BURKHOLDER

BARAGUA, PROTEST OF. *See* Zanjón, Pact of.

BARALT, RAFAEL MARÍA (1810–1860).

Rafael María Baralt (*b.* 3 July 1810; *d.* 4 January 1860), Venezuelan writer and historian. After spending his childhood in Santo Domingo, Baralt returned to Venezuela in 1821. His first task as a historian was to accompany Santiago Mariño on the western campaign and organize and publish the documents pertaining to it. During the administration of José Antonio Páez, he traveled to Caracas and mingled with the intellectuals of the city. He joined the Economic Society of the Friends of the Country and participated with Agustín Codazzi in editing the *Resumen de la geografía de Venezuela* (1841) and the *Atlas físico y político de Venezuela* (1840). He also prepared one of his best-known works, the *Resumen de la historia de Venezuela,* published in Paris in 1841. The government placed Baralt in charge of studying the border disputes with British Guiana.

In September 1841 Baralt left for Europe, working in the Spanish archives and making connections in the Spanish literary world. He settled permanently in Spain, where he was intensely active intellectually and published numerous works. In 1853 Baralt was elected a regular member of the Royal Academy of the Spanish Language, and he held important public posts in Spain. He was director of the official periodical, *Gaceta de Madrid,* and administrator of the National Printing House.

See also **Venezuela, Organizations: Economic Society of the Friends of the Country.**

BIBLIOGRAPHY

Augustín Millares Carlo, *Rafael María Baralt (1810–1860): Estudio biográfico, crítico y bibliográfico* (1969).

Pedro Grases, *Biografía de Rafael María Baralt, 1810–1860* (1973).

Additional Bibliography

Morón Montero, Guillermo. "Elogio a Rafael María Baralt." *Boletín de la Academia Nacional de Historia* (Venezuela) (Oct.–Dec. 2004): 35–46.

INÉS QUINTERO

BARBADOS.

Barbados, the most easterly of the Caribbean islands with an estimated population of 280,946 (2007). It has one of the highest population densities in the world (1,542 per square mile). Under the direction of William Courteen, the British settled and colonized Barbados in 1627. There was a lack of agricultural production and a scarce supply of indigenous labor.

Consequently, the British imported Arawak Indians from what is today known as Guyana to begin indigo and tobacco production. With the introduction of sugar to the island, the smallholdings economy was transformed into a plantation economy, and thousands of African slaves were imported to work in the fields. The harshness of slavery led to several revolts, the most famous occurring in 1702 and 1816. Slavery, although abolished in 1838, left intact a highly stratified class-based society, organized in part on color. The landed elite, who had established a parliamentary system to represent their interests in 1639, remained in power as politics excluded the majority of the population until the 1930s.

In 1938 the Barbados Progressive League was formed under the direction of Grantley Adams; it was renamed the Barbados Labour Party (BLP) in 1946. In 1944, this popular-based party gained a minority in the House of Assembly. Three years later, after a successful campaign that extended the franchise, the BLP was able to secure a majority in the elections. After the introduction of universal adult suffrage in 1951, the BLP won sixteen of the twenty-four seats. Adams became premier of Barbados, and in January 1958 prime minister of the newly formed West Indies Federation, which sought regional cooperation among the English-speaking Caribbean islands. Meanwhile, the Democratic Labour Party, headed by Errol Barrow, began to call for independence, which was granted by Great Britain in 1961. Barrow became the country's first prime minister in that year and remained in office until his death in 1987.

Today the primary sources of foreign currency for Bajans, as Barbadians are called, are tourism and the sugar industry, to which 80 percent of the agricultural land is dedicated.

See also **Adams, Grantley Herbert.**

BIBLIOGRAPHY

Ronald Tree, *A History of Barbados,* 2d ed. (1977).

M. S. Dann, *Everyday Life in Barbados: A Sociological Perspective* (1979).

Ingrid Kowler, comp., *What You Should Know About the Caribbean* (1980).

Hilary Beckles, *A History of Barbados: From Amerindian Settlement to Nation-State* (1990).

Additional Bibliography

Beckles, Hilary. *Great House Rules: Landless Emancipation and Workers' Protest in Barbados, 1838-1938.* Kingston; Miami: I. Randle; Oxford: J. Currey, 2004.

Gmelch, George, and Sharon Gmelch. *The Parish Behind God's Back: The Changing Culture of Rural Barbados.* Ann Arbor: University of Michigan Press, 1997.

Gragg, Larry. *Englishmen Transplanted: The English Colonization of Barbados, 1627-1660.* New York: Oxford University Press, 2003.

Howard, Michael McGregor. *The Economic Development of Barbados.* Kingston, Jamaica: University of the West Indies Press, 2006.

Howe, Glenford D., and Don D. Marshall. *The Empowering Impulse: The Nationalist Tradition of Barbados.* Barbados: Canoe Press, 2001.

Menard, Russell R. *Sweet Negotiations: Sugar, Slavery, and Plantation Agriculture in Early Barbados.* Charlottesville: University of Virginia Press, 2006.

Schomburgk, Robert H., Sir. *The History of Barbados: Comprising a Geographical and Statistical Description of the Island, a Sketch of the Historical Events since the Settlement, and an Account of Its Geology and Natural Productions.* London: F. Cass, 1971.

DARIÉN DAVIS

BARBERO, ANDRÉS (1877–1949). Andrés Barbero (*b.* 28 July 1877; *d.* 14 February 1949), Paraguayan physician, scientist, and philanthropist. Born into a very wealthy Asunción family, Barbero decided at an early age to pursue a career in the sciences, despite the backwardness of his country's scientific establishment. Accordingly, he studied medicine, graduating in 1904. His practice lasted only a short time, however, and he soon abandoned it to dedicate himself to teaching and scientific research.

In 1921 Barbero founded the Sociedad Científica del Paraguay together with naturalists Guillermo Tell Bertoni and Emilio Hassler. He also established a journal, the *Revista Científica del Paraguay,* which he edited for many years and which he filled with his own erudite pieces on Paraguayan flora and fauna.

Barbero's greatest contribution came in the field of philanthropy. He almost single-handedly created and maintained the Paraguayan Red Cross, the School for Rural Obstetrics, the National Cancer Institute, and a dozen other institutions emphasizing public health. After his death in 1949, his family donated still more funds for a new foundation, La Piedad, which supported efforts in many fields, from investigations into the indigenous languages of the Chaco to the care of retirees in the capital city, to the maintenance of various museums.

See also **Paraguay: The Twentieth Century.**

BIBLIOGRAPHY

William Belmont Parker, ed., *Paraguayans of To-Day* (repr. 1967), pp. 115–118.

Carlos Zubizarreta, *Cien vidas paraguayas,* 2d ed. (1985), pp. 239–241.

Additional Bibliography

Soler, Carlos Alberto. *Andrés Barbero: Su vida y su obra.* Asunción: Fundación La Piedad, 1977.

THOMAS L. WHIGHAM

BARBOSA, DOMINGOS CALDAS (1738–1800). Domingos Caldas Barbosa (*b.* 1738; *d.* 9 Nov. 1800), Brazilian poet, singer, and songwriter. The son of a slave woman and a Portuguese merchant, Barbosa studied at Jesuit schools in Rio. His early satires got him into trouble with the authorities and led to a military assignment in a distant province until 1762. He went to Portugal with the hope of entering the university, but his father's death prevented him from doing so. Introduced by family friends to the Lisbon court, he gained favor as a poet and performer of original songs. As a composer, he was a central figure in the emergence and dissemination of the *modinha* and Afro-Brazilian *lundu* song forms. With the aid of his protectors, Barbosa also took holy orders. His case is an example of the symbiosis of religious and secular spheres in his day.

Barbosa was a founding member and first president of the stylish Nova Arcádia literary club. His poems, collected in the two volumes of *Viola de Lereno* (1798, 1826), exemplify both neoclassicism and innovative applications of Afro-Brazilian language. Father Barbosa's work is both transitional, ranging from a strict continental style to a more flexible New World expression, and synthetic, drawing on erudite as well as popular sources.

See also **Music: Popular Music and Dance.**

BIBLIOGRAPHY

Jane M. Malinoff, "Domingos Caldas Barbosa: Afro-Brazilian Poet at the Court of Dona Maria I," in *From Linguistics to Literature: Romance Studies Offered to Francis M. Rogers,* edited by Bernard H. Bichakjian (1981).

David Brookshaw, *Race and Color in Brazilian Literature* (1986).

Additional Bibliography

Tinhorão, José Ramos. *Domingos Caldas Barbosa: O poeta da viola, da modinha, e do lundo (1740-1800).* São Paulo: Editora 34, 2004.

                                              CHARLES A. PERRONE

BARBOSA, FRANCISCO VILLELA

(1769–1846). Francisco Villela Barbosa (*b.* 20 November 1769; *d.* 11 September 1846), marqués of Paranaguá and minister of the Empire of Brazil. Born in Rio de Janeiro, where his father dealt in commerce, Barbosa graduated in 1796 with a degree in mathematics from the University of Coimbra, later becoming a professor of geometry at the Royal Navy Academy in Lisbon.

His political role was particularly important during the reign of Pedro I (1822–1831). After serving as Rio de Janeiro's representative to the Lisbon Cortes, he returned to Brazil in 1823 and was appointed minister of the empire and of foreign affairs. He also held, on various occasions, the post of navy minister (1823, 1825, 1826, 1829, 1831, and 1841). He supported the dissolution of the Constituent Assembly and participated in the framing of the Constitution of 1824. He was a state councilor, and in 1825 he took part in the negotiations to recognize Brazil's independence. In 1826, Barbosa was appointed a senator, but his fidelity to Pedro I forced him to withdraw, temporarily, from public life after Pedro's abdication in 1831. Later, he championed the project that advanced the coming of age of Pedro II. He wrote several works, chiefly treatises on geometry.

See also **Brazil, The Empire (Second).**

BIBLIOGRAPHY

Januário Da Cunha Barbosa, "Biografia dos brasileiros distintos por letras, armas, virtudes, etc.: Francisco Villela Barbosa," in *Revista do Instituto Histórico e Geográfico Brasileiro* 9 (1847): 398–408.

Moacir Werneck De Castro and Francisco De Assis Barbosa, "Marquês de Paranaguá," in *Enciclopédia Mirador Internacional,* vol. 16 (1983), p. 8, 598.

                                   LÚCIA M. BASTOS P. NEVES

BARBOSA DE OLIVEIRA, RUI

(1840–1923). Rui Barbosa de Oliveira (*b.* 5 November 1840; *d.* 1 March 1923), Brazilian statesman, jurist, writer, and diplomat. Barbosa was a leader in many of the great causes that transformed Brazil in the late nineteenth century, leading to the abolition of slavery, the fall of the empire, the creation of the republic, the development of a federal system, and the separation of church and state all within a period of two years. Born in Salvador, Bahia, Barbosa attended law school in Recife and São Paulo, returning to Salvador to practice law. He quickly turned to journalism, becoming a defender of civil rights and a proponent of abolition. Barbosa first served as a representative from Bahia in the imperial parliament, and later as a senator from 1891 to 1923.

While he joined the republican cause only shortly before the fall of Dom Pedro II in 1889, he became one of its greatest leaders, helping to consolidate the new government. Barbosa acted as the first minister of finance for the provisional government of the republic (1889–1891), in which capacity he instituted sweeping banking and monetary reforms, established high tariffs, and abandoned the gold standard. Credited by some historians with being the first minister of finance (and the only one up until the 1930s) to break with liberal economics in order to spur industrial development, Barbosa is characterized by others as doing so simply to curry favor with the elite banking community in order to appease criticism of the new regime. Industrial development and the beginnings of import-substitution were fortuitous byproducts.

Barbosa was the principal author of the Constitution of 1891, which he based to an important extent on the United States Constitution, especially in the design of federalism. This naturally gave to U.S.–Brazilian relations "an intimate approximation," in Barbosa's words, though he was not as ready as the great foreign minister, the baron of Rio Branco, to follow the lead of the United States in international matters as part of an "unwritten alliance." This reluctance became especially evident at the Second International Peace Conference at The Hague in 1907, which Barbosa attended at the foreign minister's request. Barbosa (and Brazil) gained international renown at the conference for his eloquent arguments in defense of the equality of all nations and, specifically, in favor of the right of small or weak nations to equal representation on an International Court of Justice. This position was at odds with that of the United States and other powers, which sought a smaller court dominated by them. The conference ended without a decision on the court but with Brazilian prestige and Barbosa's popular reputation significantly enhanced.

Barbosa ran for the presidency in 1910 and 1919, touring the provinces and taking issues directly to the voting public for the first time in Brazilian politics. Both bids for higher office were unsuccessful, however, undermined in part by the opposition of influential members of the military, whose involvement in government Barbosa had attacked repeatedly throughout his career. Barbosa was elected to the Brazilian Academy of Letters in 1908 and served as its president until 1919. His published works on finance, civil liberties, education, and the law number more than 150 volumes.

See also **Brazil: Constitutions.**

BIBLIOGRAPHY

Raymundo Magalhães, Jr., *Rui: O Homem e o mito* (1964).

E. Bradford Burns, *The Unwritten Alliance: Rio-Branco and Brazilian-American Relations* (1966).

Pinto De Aguiar, *Rui e a economia brasileira* (1973).

José De Arruda Penteado, *A consciência didática no pensamento pedagógico de Rui Barbosa* (1984).

Steven Topik, *The Political Economy of the Brazilian State, 1889–1930* (1987).

Additional Bibliography

Pinto, José Augusto Rodrigues, and José Teixeira Cavalcante Filho. *Ruy Barbosa, 150 anos.* Salvador, Bahia: Faculdade de Direito da Universidade Federal da Bahia, 2000.

ELIZABETH A. COBBS

BARBOSA-LIMA, CARLOS (1944–).

The Brazilian guitarist Carlos Barbosa-Lima began his studies at an early age, and by his early teens was an accomplished performer, appearing on television and radio as well as in concerts. He later studied with Isaias Sávio and the legendary Andrés Segovia. Since his American debut in 1967, he has enjoyed an active concert and recording career. Many important composers have written for Barbosa-Lima, including Alberto Ginastera, whose *Sonata*, Opus 47 the guitarist premiered. He has performed with many of the world's major orchestras, is a busy chamber musician, and is a constant participant in prestigious music festivals. Musically his tastes run from Bach through Joplin to contemporary composers, and he has performed and recorded music by such diverse Brazilian composers as Heitor Villa-Lobos, Luiz Bonfá, and Antonio Carlos Jobim, among many others. Among his published transcriptions are works by Scarlatti, Bach, and Handel, and he has arranged works by Bernstein, Sondheim, Cole Porter, and many Brazilian classical and popular music composers. His discography comprises more than thirty-five recordings, including baroque, Beatles, and Brazilian music. For many years he was a professor at the Manhattan School of Music in New York and then a resident of Puerto Rico.

See also **Ginastera, Alberto Evaristo; Jobim, Antônio Carlos "Tom"; Music: Popular Music and Dance; Villa-Lobos, Heitor.**

BIBLIOGRAPHY

Del Casale, Lawrence. "Carlos Barbosa-Lima (The Chameleon, Part I, 1944–1982)." *Soundboard* 25:2 (Fall 1999), 7–11.

Del Casale, Lawrence. "Carlos Barbosa-Lima (The Chameleon, Part II, 1982–1997)." *Soundboard* 25:3 (Winter 1999), 23–26.

Henken, John. "Barbosa-Lima's Music Is the Sum of Its Ethnic Parts." *Guitar Review* 90 (Summer 1992), 30–31.

Saba, Therese Wassily. "Carlos Barbosa-Lima." *Classical Guitar* 17 (October 1998), 11–12.

THOMAS GEORGE CARACAS GARCIA

BARBOSA Y ALCALÁ, JOSÉ CELSO

(1857–1921). José Celso Barbosa y Alcalá (*b.* 27 July 1857; *d.* 21 September 1921), Puerto Rican politician and physician. Born in the town of Bayamón to a humble family of African descent, Barbosa rose to a position of prominence in the political life of Puerto Rico. He earned a medical degree at the University of Michigan (1880) and then returned to his homeland to become a fervent advocate of annexation to the United States, which he saw as the only way to free Puerto Rico from the bonds of Spanish colonialism. Barbosa joined the Liberal Reform Party in 1883, and he spent the rest of his life leading the movement for Puerto Rico's incorporation as an autonomous unit within the United States. In 1898 he formed what a year later became known as the Republican Party of Puerto Rico, which he led until his death. From 1900 to 1917, Barbosa served on an executive council arranged by the Foraker Act. This post allowed him further participation in Puerto Rico's early attempt to settle its status after independence from Spain.

See also **Puerto Rico.**

BIBLIOGRAPHY

José Celso Barbosa, *José Celso Barbosa, pionero en el cooperativismo puertorriqueño, siglo XIX* (1982).

Raymond Carr, *Puerto Rico, a Colonial Experiment* (1984).

Robert J. Alexander, ed., *Biographical Dictionary of Latin American and Caribbean Political Leaders* (1988).

TODD LITTLE SIEBOLD

BARBUDA.

Barbuda, a 62-square-mile Leeward Island in the Caribbean, located about 30 miles north of Antigua. A dependency of Antigua, Barbuda was settled by the British in the mid-1630s shortly after the colonization of Antigua. In 1674, Sir Christopher Codrington established the first major sugar plantation in Antigua and subsequently leased the island of Barbuda to cultivate food for the estate. Blacks brought from Africa to work in Barbuda became unwilling subjects of a breeding experiment to produce physically larger and stronger slaves. Evidence of this experiment can be seen today in their descendants; the people of the island are recognized for their large stature. The current population of some fifteen hundred are predominantly African in descent and live in the island's only village, named after Codrington.

Politically, Barbuda remains linked to Antigua. In 1967, Antigua received full self-government as an associated state of the United Kingdom, and in November 1981, Antigua and Barbuda acquired independence as a single territory. Attempts by Barbuda to obtain independence from Antigua have failed.

See also **Caribbean Sea, Commonwealth States.**

BIBLIOGRAPHY

Carleen O'Loughlin, *Economic and Political Change in the Leeward and Windward Islands* (1968), pp. 30–32.

Ben Box and Sarah Cameron, eds., *1992 Caribbean Island Handbook* (1991), pp. 318–321, 327.

Additional Bibliography

Lazarus-Black, Mindie. *Legitimate Acts and Illegal Encounters: Law and Society in Antigua and Barbuda.* Washington DC: Smithsonian Institution Press, 1994.

D. M. SPEARS

BARCO VARGAS, VIRGILIO (1921–
1997). Virgilio Barco Vargas (*b.* 17 September
1921; *d.* 20 May 1997), president of Colombia
(1986–1990). From a prominent Cúcuta family,
Barco combined study in the United States (including doctoral work in economics at MIT) with politics in his home city. In the 1960s he held several
cabinet posts and was highly regarded as mayor of
Bogotá (1966–1969); he later served as ambassador
in Washington, D.C. After an aborted candidacy for
president in 1982 he won a landslide victory in
1986. The economy performed creditably under
his administration, but the Barco years were better
known for the upward spiral of violence propagated
by guerrillas, right-wing death squads (which acted
with suspicious impunity), and drug traffickers.
Colombia's drug cartels stepped up their attacks
on judges, journalists, and officials, culminating in
the murder of Barco's presumptive successor, Luis
Carlos Galán, in August 1989. Over the next several
months hundreds were killed in cartel-ordered
bombings, while the government's hard line produced few results. The definitive incorporation of
the M-19 guerrilla movement into legal politics,
near the end of Barco's term, brightened the scene
somewhat. In 1992, Barco retired from politics. He
died in 1997.

See also **Drugs and Drug Trade.**

BIBLIOGRAPHY

Ignacio Arizmendi Posada, *Presidentes de Colombia, 1810–
1990* (1990), pp. 301–305.

Additional Bibliography

Chacón Medina, Pablo. "Virgilio Barco Vargas, estadista y
político." Boletín de Historia y Antigüedades 86 (July-
Sept 1999): 843-847.

Deas, Malcolm and Carlos Ossa, eds. *El gobierno Barco:
Política, economía y desarrollo social en Colombia,
1986-1990.* Bogotá: Editorial Nomos, 1994.

RICHARD J. STOLLER

BAREIRO, CÁNDIDO (1838–1880).
Cándido Bareiro (*b.* 1838?; *d.* 4 September 1880),
Paraguayan diplomat and president (1878–1880).
Bareiro was one of a score of young Paraguayans
sent to Europe for advanced study by the Carlos
Antonio López government in the late 1850s.
Bareiro's field was diplomacy, and within a few years
he received an appointment as minister to Paris and
London. His stay in the European capitals coincided
with the War of the Triple Alliance (1864–1870), in
which Paraguay faced the combined military might
of Brazil, Argentina, and Uruguay. Bareiro's loyalty
to the López regime and his unceasing efforts to
counter Allied propaganda in Europe brought him
some acclaim among those few Paraguayans then
living abroad.

He finally returned to a wrecked and occupied
Asunción in 1869. At once he became the focus of
a Lopizta group that included Bernardino Caballero and Patricio Escobar, both war heroes. Other
conservatives, many with Brazilian connections,
came to join this same group, which, after Bareiro's
death evolved into the Colorado Party. Bareiro
himself manipulated various Paraguayan factions,
as well as the Brazilian occupiers, during the
1870s. In this, he worked hard to oppose the
liberals who had tried to undercut the influence
of the traditional rural elites.

Bareiro was elected president in 1878. Though
his administration was short lived and his attempts
to resuscitate the economy woefully inadequate, he
did make an honest attempt to curb the corruption
that had seeped into Paraguayan politics since the
war. He also had the satisfaction of seeing Paraguayan claims over the Chaco Boreal upheld in an
arbitration award.

Bareiro died suddenly of a stroke while working at his desk in the presidential palace.

See also **Paraguay, Political Parties: Colorado Party.**

BIBLIOGRAPHY

Harris Gaylord Warren, *Paraguay and the Triple Alliance: The
Postwar Decade, 1869–1878* (1978), pp. 52–57, 73–74,
180–181, 274–275, and *Rebirth of the Paraguayan Republic: The First Colorado Era, 1878–1904* (1985), pp. 41–50.

THOMAS L. WHIGHAM

BARILOCHE. Bariloche is a city of 75,468 in-
habitants (2001) located on the eastern shore of
Nahuel Huapi Lake, at the southern fringe of

Argentina's Río Negro Province. Jesuit Nicolás Mascardi founded San Carlos de Bariloche in 1670 as a mission for the Mapuche Indians who wandered between southern Chile and southern Argentina. In the Conquest of the Desert (1858–1861), the young Argentine republic went to war against the Indians and then opened the region for colonization by war veterans as well as German and Italian homesteaders. Settlements were established on the picturesque Nahuel Huapi Lake and into the upper reaches of Limay River, an Andean tributary of the Río Negro. The development of the entire region received a boost when Bariloche became a favorite summer and winter resort for the European-rooted bourgeoisie of Buenos Aires in the 1920s. In the early twenty-first century the city also attracts Andean tourists via the scenic route of Laguna Fría, Puerto Blest, and Paso Puyehue. During winter, modern hotels accommodate guests from Argentina, Uruguay, and Brazil, as well as North Americans and Europeans taking advantage of the winter sports opportunities during their native summers.

Bariloche is an administrative and educational center for the Andean region of Rio Negro Province and site of the Museo de la Patagonia. Daily flights connect Bariloche with Buenos Aires, and railroads depart for San Antonio Oeste, on the Atlantic coast, and Bahia Blanca, in the south of Buenos Aires Province.

See also **Argentina, Geography; Conquest of the Desert.**

BIBLIOGRAPHY

Neuman, Andrés. *Bariloche*. Barcelona: Editorial Anagrama, 1999.

CÉSAR N. CAVIEDES

BARING BROTHERS.

Baring Brothers, a London merchant bank founded in 1763 by the Baring family to finance trade with the United States and India. During the Napoleonic Wars it was engaged in substantial operations for the British treasury. The firm soon became one of the major powers in international finance. Between 1820 and 1870 it provided numerous government loans for France, Spain, Portugal, Russia, and Canada, among others. In Latin America it placed a Buenos Aires foreign loan in 1824, a Chilean railway loan in 1858, and a Venezuelan loan in 1862. During the 1880s it became the principal banker to the governments of Argentina and Uruguay, leading international banking syndicates in issuing six Argentine national loans and three Uruguayan loans. However, its excesses led to bankruptcy in November 1890, causing a major financial crisis in London, known as the Baring panic. Upon its reorganization in 1892, the firm reassumed its role as leading banker to Argentina, issuing eight loans for that nation between 1907 and 1914. In later years its importance in Latin American finance declined, although it continued to maintain close ties with the Argentine government until 1946, when Argentine president Juan Domingo Perón liquidated the foreign debt of the government. In other fields of international finance, Baring Brothers remained active on the London money market, particularly as investment counselor to British firms operating abroad. In the 1970s Baring Brothers once again began placing international loans for Latin American governments, frequently as a member of the banking syndicates that issued external bonds. Rash speculation in the Far East brought the firm to the brink of collapse in 1995 and it was later sold.

See also **Banking: Overview.**

BIBLIOGRAPHY

Ralph Hidy, *The House of Baring in American Trade and Finance: English Merchant Bankers at Work, 1763–1861* (1949).

Armando O. Chiapella, *El destino del empréstito Baring Brothers* (1975).

Philip Ziegler, *The Sixth Great Power: A History of One of the Greatest of All Banking Families, the House of Baring, 1762–1929* (1988).

Additional Bibliography

Leeson, Nicholas W., and Edward Whitley. *Rogue Trader: How I Brought Down Barings Bank and Shook the Financial World*. Boston: Little, Brown, 1996.

Ortega Peña, Rodolfo, and Eduardo Luis Duhalde. *Baring Brothers y la historia política argentina; La banca británica y el proceso histórico nacional de 1824 a 1890*. Buenos Aires Editorial Sudestada, 1973.

CARLOS MARICHAL

BARNET, MIGUEL

BARNET, MIGUEL (1940–). Miguel Barnet (*b.* 28 January 1940), Cuban novelist, poet, essayist, and ethnologist. Born in Havana, educated in a local American primary school, and later a student of the distinguished ethnographer Fernando Ortíz, Miguel Barnet came of age during the final years of the Fulgencio Batista dictatorship. With the triumph of the Cuban Revolution, he became an active contributor to the process of literary experimentation and cultural reclamation it set in motion. Barnet first came to national attention as the poet of *La piedra fina y el pavorreal* (1963) and the much-praised *La sagrada familia* (1967), a lyrical autopsy of petit bourgeois domestic life. Publication of *Biografía de un cimarrón* (1966; *The Autobiography of a Runaway Slave*, 1968), the first in an ethnic tetralogy of documentary narratives, brought almost immediate international acclaim and established him as an innovating pioneer of the testimonial genre in contemporary Latin America. *La canción de Rachel* (1969; *Rachel's Song*, 1991), *Gallego* (1981), and *La vida real* (1986) confirmed his reputation as Cuba's premier exponent of the documentary novel.

Barnet explores the common ground between anthropology and literature, blending the methods and procedures of the novelist's and biographer's art—oral history—and the ethnographer's record of popular life and culture. Each work is a vivid textual re-creation of the spoken voice of ordinary, often-disdained or socially slighted Cuban citizens: a runaway black slave; a small-time mestizo female cabaret entertainer of the 1940s; a Spanish immigrant to the island; and a peasant migrant to the United States. The individuals usually absent from conventional history thus become emblematic personifications of Cuba's evolving historical experience and ethnocultural development; those lost to national recollection are reclaimed for the collectivity: "Memory, as a part of the imagination," Barnet notes in the prologue to *La vida real*, "...[is] the essential key of all my work of testimony."

Barnet has been a professor of folklore at Havana's School for Art Instructors (1961–1966), a researcher for the Institute of Ethnology and Folklore of the Cuban Academy of Science, and most recently a member of the editorial board of *Unión*, the journal of the Union of Cuban Artists and Writers (UNEAC). His other collections of poetry include *Isla de Guijes* (1964), *Orikis y otros poemas* (1980), and *Carta de noche* (1982).

See also **Literature: Spanish America.**

BIBLIOGRAPHY

Seymour Menton, *Prose Fiction of the Cuban Revolution* (1975), esp. pp. 83–85.

Roberto González Echevarría, "*Biografía de un cimarrón* and the Novel of the Cuban Revolution," in *Novel* 13, no. 3 (1980): 249–263.

Julio A. Martínez, ed., *Dictionary of Twentieth Century Cuban Literature* (1990), pp. 59–64.

Emilio Bejel, *Escribir en Cuba: Entrevistas con escritores cubanos, 1979–1989* (1991), pp. 15–29.

Additional Bibliography

Azougarh, Abdeslam. *Miguel Barnet: Rescate e invención de la memoria.* Genéve: Slatkine, 1996.

Howe, Linda S. *Transgression and Conformity: Cuban Writers and Artists after the Revolution.* Madison: University of Wisconsin Press, 2004.

Luis, William and Ann González, eds. *Modern Latin-American Fiction Writers.* Second Series. Detroit: Gale Research, 1994.

Sklodowska, Elzbieta. "Miguel Barnet: Hacia la poética de la novela testimonial." *Revista de Crítica Literaria Latinoamericana* 14 (1988): 139–149.

ROBERTO MÁRQUEZ

BARNOLA, PEDRO PABLO

BARNOLA, PEDRO PABLO (1908–1986). Pedro Pablo Barnola (*b.* 28 August 1908; *d.* 12 January 1986), Venezuelan writer and educator. As a student at the Academy San Ignacio de Loyola in Caracas, Barnola was the first Venezuelan to join the Jesuits after their reestablishment in the country. He completed his studies first in Europe (1925–1932) and later in the United States (1935–1940). Ordained a priest in 1938, he dedicated himself to teaching at the Academy San Ignacio. He was director of the magazine *SIC,* rector of the Andrés Bello Catholic University, editorial director of the *Obras completas de Andrés Bello* (1951), and member of the editorial commission for the *Obras completas de Rafael María Baralt.* He was a regular member of the Royal Academy of the Spanish Language and an outstanding defender of the purity of Castilian Spanish. He collaborated with

Professor Ángel Rosenblat on the first volume of the *Diccionario de Venezolanismos* (1983). He is the author of numerous works of literary criticism. The principal ones include: *Altorrelieve de la literatura venezolana* (1970); *Estudios crítico-literarios* (1945, 1953, 1971); and *Raíz y sustancia de la civilización latinoamericana* (1953).

See also **Spanish Language.**

BIBLIOGRAPHY

Horacio Jorge Becco, *Pedro Pablo Barnola, S.J., Bibliografía (1935–1985)* (1986).

INÉS QUINTERO

BARRACAS. Barracas, old borough of the city of Buenos Aires, Argentina, located close to the mouth of the Río de las Matanzas, also known as Riachuelo, flowing into the estuary of Río De La Plata. It was named thus for the numerous warehouses for hides and agricultural products located in this area in colonial and early republican times. With the arrival of Italian immigrants in the 1880s and their establishment in this sector of the city there emerged the borough of La Boca, which increased in importance when port facilities for domestic navigation were built on the Riachuelo, communicating with the estuary by means of the Southern Canal. Toward the end of the twentieth century Barracas lost significance as a warehouse and port district and has become mostly a residential area for lower-middle-class families.

See also **Buenos Aires.**

BIBLIOGRAPHY

Additional Bibliography

Alvarez de Celis, Fernando. *El sur en la Ciudad de Buenos Aires: Caracterización económica territorial de los barrios de La Boca, Barracas, Nueva Pompeya, Villa Riachuelo Villa Soldati, Villa Lugano y Mataderos.* Ciudad Autónoma de Buenos Aires: Centro de Estudios para el Desarrollo Económico Metropolitano, 2003.

Puccia, Enrique Horacio. *Barracas, su historia y sus tradiciones, 1536–1936.* Buenos Aires: Tall. Gráf. de la Compañía General Fabril Financiera, 1968.

CÉSAR N. CAVIEDES

BARRADAS, FRANCISCA VÍVEROS.
See **Paquita la del Barrio.**

BARRADAS, RAFAEL (c. 1890–1929). Rafael Barradas (*b.* c. 4 January 1890; *d.* 12 February 1929), Uruguayan painter. Born in Montevideo, Barradas had a brief career as an illustrator and journalist for newspapers and magazines such as *El Tiempo, Bohemia,* and *La Semana;* in 1913 he founded the periodical *El Monigote* (The Bumpkin). Barradas traveled to Europe that year and settled in Spain, where he worked as an illustrator for the magazines *La Esquella de Torratxa,* in Barcelona, and *Paraninfo,* in Zaragoza. He exhibited at the Galerías Dalmau in Barcelona in 1916 and the following year in the Salón de los Humoristas in Madrid. In his first solo exhibition at the Galerías Layetanas (1918), he introduced an aesthetic conception which he called *vibracionismo,* his interpretation of futurism and cubism.

During the early 1920s Barradas worked in Madrid as scenographer and toy and poster designer. He also illustrated editions of books by Charles Dickens, Alexandre Dumas, and Félix Lope de Vega and was costume designer for Federico García Lorca's *El maleficio de la Mariposa.* He frequented the *Ultraístas,* a group of poets that included Jorge Luis Borges, and collaborated with the latter on the magazine *Tableros.* He worked on *Los Magníficos,* portraits of popular Spanish types, rendered in monumental geometric forms. He devised *clownism,* an expressionistic style in which he painted picturesque details of busy urban areas. In 1924 he was awarded the Grand Prix at the International Exhibition of Decorative and Industrial Arts in Paris. Back in Barcelona, he painted a series of watercolors called *Estampones de Montevideo* (Prints of Montevideo), humorous views of that city.

In 1928 Barradas returned to Montevideo, where he died a few months later. His last work was a series of madonna and child images rendered in a postcubist style. Barradas, who produced his most significant work in Spain, is considered an innovative personality in the history of Uruguayan art.

See also **Art: The Twentieth Century.**

BIBLIOGRAPHY

Angel Kalenberg, *Seis maestros de la pintura uruguaya: Juan Manuel Blanes, Carlos Federico Sáez, Pedro Figari, Joaquín Torres-García, Rafael Barradas, José Cuneo* (1987).

Dawn Ades, *Art in Latin America: The Modern Era, 1820–1980* (1989).

Raquel Pereda, *Barradas* (1989) and *Rafael Barradas* (1992).

Additional Bibliography

Casal, Julio J. *Rafael Barradas.* Buenos Aires: Editiorial Losada, 1949.

Jardí, Enric. *Rafael Barradas a Catalunya i altres artistes que passaren la mar.* Barcelona: Generalitat de Catalunya, Comissió América i Catalunya, 1992.

MARTA GARSD

BARRAGÁN MORFIN, LUIS (1902–1988).

Luis Barragán Morfin (*b.* 9 March 1902; *d.* 22 November 1988), Mexican architect and landscape architect. Barragán trained as a civil engineer at the Escuela Libre de Ingeniera, in his native Guadalajara, Jalisco, and received his diploma 13 December 1923, after which he presented his admission thesis for the architecture program. Upon admission, he left for a year's study and travel in Europe (1924–1925). He returned to a Mexico radically changed by revolution and land reform and found his architecture program disbanded. As the youngest son of a landowning family, he joined his brother's construction firm in the development of urban Guadalajara. Without formal design training Barragán found the need to overlap architecture with civil engineering and, working with his brother Juan José Barragán, produced a number of projects, including the house for Enfraín González Luna (1929–1931).

At the invitation of architect-engineer José Luis Creixell and the primitive painter Jesús (Chucho) Reyes Ferreira, Barragán began work in Mexico City on several International Style buildings. Barragán's twenty-year design and intellectual collaboration with Reyes and the émigré sculptor Mathias Goeritz was a major turning point in modern architectural design and theory. They worked separately or in consultation with one another, each taking the lead in their individual discipline. Barragán, the architect, treated a building site like a transparent solid defined by its light, natural configuration, and context. He moved through the site to find indications of forms and connections as a sculptor would explore the volume of a block of stone to find its contained figure. Program requirements and circulation then cut the volume, disciplined the light, and defined enclosures from a plan diagram sketched on the ground for workmen or on a scrap of paper for a client's information. Barragán, Reyes, and Goeritz took the indigenous architectural style of Mexico through the filter of the International Style into the intellectual abstraction and pragmatism of projects like the Towers of Satellite City and Casa Gilardi in Mexico City, then returned to the memory of Barragán's childhood home, Hacienda de Corrales, near Mazamitla, Jalisco, to design projects like the contemporary equestrian hacienda San Cristobal, near Mexico City (1967–1968). In the more than fifty international projects attributed to Barragán, the hacienda form always alludes to Mexico.

One of Mexico's most important architects and architectural design theorists, Barragán was a founding member of the Mexican Society of Landscape Architects and its honorary president for life (1973), a recipient of the Premio Nacional de Artes (first prize for architecture; 1976), and honorary fellow of the American Institute of Architects (1976), the second winner of the Pritzker Prize for Architecture (1980), and an honorary member of the American Academy and Institute of Arts and Letters (1984). His architecture was the subject of exhibitions at the Museum of Modern Art in New York (1976) and the Museo Rufino Tamayo in Mexico City (1985) and a traveling exhibition organized by *Montage Journal* of Boston (1989–1994). Luis Barragán's death in Mexico City was honored by a memorial exhibition at the Palacio de Bellas Artes.

See also **Architecture: Modern Architecture.**

BIBLIOGRAPHY

Emilio Ambasz, *The Architecture of Luis Barragán* (1976).

Luis Barragán, *Luis Barragán: The Pritzker Architectural Prize* (acceptance speech, 1980).

Luis Barragán et al., *Ensayos y apuntes para un bosquejo crítico: Luis Barragán* (1985); "Luis Barragán, arquitecto," in *Arquitectura*, 70 (March 1989): 51–85.

José Checa Alvarez and Manuel Ramos Guerra, *Obra construida: Luis Barragán Morfin, 1902–1988* (1989).

Max Underwood, "Architect of the Intangible," in *Americas* 43, no. 4 (1991): 6–15.

Armando Salas Portugal, *Photographs of the Architecture of Luis Barragán* (1992).

Estelle Jackson et al., *Luis Barragán: The Architecture of Light, Color, and Form* (catalog for *Montage Journal* traveling exhibition, 1995).

Additional Bibliography

Barragán: The Complete Works. With preface by Alvaro Siza. New York, NY: Princeton Architectural Press, 2003.

ESTELLE JACKSON

René De La Pedraja Toman, *Energy Politics in Colombia* (1989).

Additional Bibliography

Aprile Gniset, Jacques. *Génesis de Barrancabermeja: Ensayo.* Colombia: Instituto Universitario de la Paz, 1997.

Coghlan, Nicholas. *The Saddest Country: On Assignment in Colombia.* Montreal: McGill-Queen's University Press, 2004.

Toro Puerta, Mario Rafael. *Pendientes de un hilo: El proceso de desafiliación en un sector de Barrancabermeja.* Bogotá: Editorial Bonaventuriana, Universidad de San Buenaventura, 2004.

DAVID SOWELL

BARRANCABERMEJA.

Barrancabermeja, a Colombian port and refinery town. This Magdalena River town of 191,403 people (2005 est.) in the department of Santander developed in tandem with the Colombian petroleum industry. Commonly referred to as "Barranca" after the red clay banks of the river, the town remained quite small until the discovery of petroleum in the early twentieth century. The 1921 de Mares concession of oil fields to Jersey Standard (later Exxon) authorized refinery construction shortly thereafter. Under the restrictive Petroleum Law of 1919, the concession reverted to national control forty years later. In 1951, Exxon and Ecopetrol jointly expanded the capacity of the refinery. Its 150,000 barrels per day capacity as of 2007 represents two-thirds of the country's potential. Jersey Standard's concession came in the midst of intense nationalist feeling over the 1903 separation of Panama, which was quite visible in the 1920s. Labor strife has been common in the Barrancabermeja refinery, with major conflicts in 1925, 1936, 1948, 1963, and in the 1980s. Throughout the 1990s the city witnessed major violence, conflict, and displaced refugees in the civil war between paramilitary and armed opposition groups. In response, international human rights organizations denounced the violence. Some of these groups maintain a physical presence in Barrancabermeja and the surrounding rural regions.

See also **Petroleum Industry.**

BIBLIOGRAPHY

A. Eugene Havens and Michel Romieux, *Barrancabermeja: Conflictos sociales en torno a un centro petrolero* (1966).

BARRANCA YACO.

Barranca Yaco, site in the Argentine province of Córdoba where the Federalist chieftain Juan Facundo Quiroga was assassinated on 16 February 1835. Quiroga was returning to Buenos Aires from a mission to the Argentine northwest when an armed band murdered him. An investigation and trial ordered by the Buenos Aires strongman Juan Manuel de Rosas put the blame on the Reinafé brothers, who controlled the province of Córdoba; they were later executed. Rosas's enemies alleged that he himself was behind the crime, hoping to eliminate a potential rival, but there is no evidence to support the charge. However, Rosas used the crime as proof that internal security was in peril and as justification for his own return to the governorship of Buenos Aires with "the Sum of Public Power."

See also **Quiroga, Juan Facundo.**

BIBLIOGRAPHY

Domingo F. Sarmiento, *Life in the Argentine Republic in the Days of the Tyrants; or, Civilization and Barbarism* (1974), chap. 13.

John Lynch, *Argentine Dictator: Juan Manuel de Rosas 1829–1853* (1981).

Additional Bibliography

Cárdenas de Monner Sans, María Inés. *Juan Facundo Quiroga: Otra civilización.* Buenos Aires: Libreria Histórica, 2004.

Carrasco Quintana, Martín. *Cómo se mata a un caudillo: Papeles de Barranca Yaco.* Buenos Aires: El Calafate, 2004.

DAVID BUSHNELL

BARRANQUILLA. Barranquilla, a city 12 miles (19 kilometers) from the mouth of the Magdalena River, near the Caribbean coast of Colombia, is the capital of that country's department of Atlántico. In the 2005 census, the city had a population of 1,113,016, making it the fourth largest in Colombia.

Founded in 1629, the city developed slowly as a river port. Its growth was hindered by a shifting sandbar at the mouth of the Magdalena that obstructed passage of large, oceangoing vessels. In 1870–1871 a railroad bypassing the sandbar was built, linking Barranquilla with nearby satellite ports on the Caribbean. Barranquilla then became Colombia's principal port, but the railroad solution was still far from ideal, and the twentieth century saw efforts to dredge and maintain a navigable channel linking the city directly to the sea. Nevertheless, by midcentury Barranquilla had lost its leadership to Buenaventura on the Pacific; later it was overtaken by Cartagena as well. In the meantime, however, it had become an important manufacturing center, producing processed foods and beverages, textiles, and petrochemicals. It proved more attractive than Colombia generally to immigrants, including an important Middle Eastern contingent. Yet as elsewhere in coastal Colombia, popular culture retained a strong Afro-Colombian imprint—clearly evident in Barranquilla's yearly carnival, the best-known in Latin America outside Brazil.

See also **Magdalena River.**

BIBLIOGRAPHY

Nichols, Theodore E. "The Rise of Barranquilla." *Hispanic American Historical Review* 34 (1954): 158–174.

Posada Carbó, Eduardo. *Una invitación a la historia de Barranquilla*. Bogota: Fondo Editorial CEREC, 1987.

DAVID BUSHNELL

BARREDA, GABINO (1818–1881). Gabino Barreda (*b.* 1818; *d.* 1881), Mexican philosopher and educator. Born in Puebla, Barreda is credited with introducing Comtian positivism to Mexico. After studies in Mexico at the Colegio de San Ildefonso, he entered law school but later abandoned it to pursue his passion for the natural sciences in the Mining School and School of Medicine. After enlisting as a volunteer in the war against the United States, he left in 1847 for Paris, where he took courses with Auguste Comte. Returning to Mexico in 1851, he completed his degree as a medical doctor and taught in the School of Medicine.

In 1867 President Benito Juárez appointed him to preside over a commission to reorganize Mexican education. The resulting *Leyes orgánicas de la educación pública* in 1867 and 1869 made public schooling lay, free, and obligatory for the Federal District and territories. Professional school programs were reformed to eliminate speculative thinking and emphasize the positive sciences. Attention was focused on the founding of the Escuela Nacional Preparatoria for men in the old Colegio de San Ildefonso, with Barreda its director.

With a uniform curriculum based on Comte's interpretation of the physical and social sciences, the school addressed what Barreda believed were the causes of Mexican backwardness: a disdain for productive labor and entrepreneurialism; a proclivity for clericalism, which had inhibited the development of a scientific attitude; and a liberal preoccupation with abstract principle. Like Comte, Barreda believed in a hierarchical social order in which a team of social engineers would aid captains of industry to ensure orderly economic progress.

Opposition to Barreda's positivist ideas on the part of Liberals and Catholics led to his appointment in 1878 as ambassador to Germany. However, his intellectual contribution was great. He is credited with the formation of a generation of Mexican positivists, many of whom successfully combined statesmanship and business, among them Francisco Bulnes, Francisco G. Cosmes, Joaquín Casasús, José Yves Limantour, Pablo Macedo, Justo Sierra, Roberto Núñez, Rafael and Emilio Pardo, Porfirio Parra, Rafael Reyes Spíndola, Rafael Hernández Madero, and Miguel Macedo.

See also **Education: Overview.**

BIBLIOGRAPHY

William Dirk Raat, "Leopoldo Zea and Mexican Positivism: A Reappraisal," in *Hispanic American Historical Review* 48 (1968): 1–18.

Leopoldo Zea, *El positivismo en México* (1968); Mary Kay Vaughan, *The State, Education, and Social Class in Mexico, 1880–1928* (1982).

Francisco Javier Guerra, *México, del antiguo regimen a la revolución*, vol. 1 (1988).

Charles A. Hale, *The Transformation of Mexican Liberalism* (1989).

Additional Bibliography

Robledo Mesa, José Antonio. *Gabino Barreda y la mitologema liberal*. Puebla, Mexico: Gobierno del Estado de Puebla: Benemerita Universidad Autonoma de Puebla, 2003.

Ruis, Rosaura Gutierrez. "Gabino Barreda and the Introduction of Darwin in Mexico." In *Mexican Studies in the History and Philosophy of Science,* edited by Santiago Ramirez and R.S. Cohen. Boston, MA: Kluwer Academic Publishers, 1995.

MARY KAY VAUGHAN

BARREDA Y LAOS, FELIPE (1888–1973).

Felipe Barreda y Laos (*b.* 1888; *d.* 1973), Peruvian historian, lawyer, diplomat, educator. He was educated in a Jesuit school and at the University of San Marcos in Lima, where he became a professor. He was the author of several books, including treatises on intellectual currents in colonial Peru, Hispanic culture, and other diplomatic, educational, and historical subjects. Initially influenced by positivism, his view of the colonial past was critical of the influence of the scholastic tradition in Peru. In later works, however, he emphasized the unity of the peninsular and American Hispanic tradition and the beneficial effects of Hispanic culture in America. He also assumed a continental view in his diplomatic works.

See also **Positivism.**

BIBLIOGRAPHY

See his *Dos Américas: Dos mundos* (1952) and *Vida intelectual del virreinato del Perú*, 3d ed. (1964).

ALFONSO W. QUIROZ

BARREIRO, ANTONIO (c. 1780–1835).

Antonio Barreiro (*b.* ca. 1780; *d.* after 1835), *assessor* (legal adviser) of New Mexico during the 1830s.

Barreiro was sent by the Mexican government in 1831 to establish a judicial system. After a year in the territory, Barreiro published his report, *Ojeada sobre Nuevo-México.* The work synthesized data collected earlier in the century by Alexander von Humboldt, reports of soldiers of the presidio of Sante Fe, and the reports of the representatives to the first National Congress in Mexico.

Barreiro's *Ojeada* represents a plea for Mexico City to provide a modicum of investment in the rich territory he described. Government support to aid in the building of stone bridges, for example, would ease the difficult conditions for transport and export. Strengthening the powers of the governor and New Mexican courts of first instance could aid in the punishment of petty crime and greater deliberation on matters of import to the citizens. National warehouses, an adequate building in which to house the public treasury, and stronger defenses along the New Mexican frontier would increase and secure tariff revenues, encourage and streamline trade, and dissuade both the raids of "wild Indians" and the grasping Americans interested in extending "the boundary of Louisiana to the left bank of the Bravo or North River" (Rio Grande). Barreiro concluded, "Only the attention of the government toward this country, which is worthy of a better fate, will remove all the obstacles to its welfare. Only an extraordinary effort on the part of the government will develop the valuable elements which lie submerged there and which will some day raise it to the height of prosperity."

Partly due to the publication of his report, Barreiro won election in 1834 and 1835 as New Mexico's deputy to the Mexican Congress. With a printing press imported from Missouri in 1834, Barreiro published the first New Mexican newspaper, *El Crepúsculo de la Libertad.*

See also **New Mexico.**

BIBLIOGRAPHY

Pedro Bautista Pino, Antonio Barreiro, and José Agustín De Escudero, *Three New Mexico Chronicles,* translated and edited by H. Bailey Carroll and J. Villasana Haggard (1942).

Frances Leon Swadesh, *Los Primeros Pobladores: Hispanic Americans of the Ute Frontier* (1974).

Pearce S. Grove, Becky J. Barnett, and Sandra J. Hansen, *New Mexico Newspapers: A Comprehensive Guide to Bibliographical Entries and Locations* (1975).

David J. Weber, *The Mexican Frontier, 1821–1846: The American Southwest under Mexico* (1982).

ROSS H. FRANK

BARRERA, ISAAC J. (1884–1970).

A journalist, literary critic, historian, and biographer, Isaac J. Barrera was a prodigious intellectual who dedicated himself to the study of the culture and history of Ecuador. As a journalist, he promoted the modernist movement in Ecuador through regular columns in *El Comercio* and by founding and directing the literary magazine *Letras*. As a biographer, he wrote several studies of prominent figures of Ecuador, including Vicente Rocafuerte, an important leader of Ecuador's independence movement. As a historian he wrote a study of colonial Quito, traced the history of journalism in Ecuador, offered a general account of the formation of the republic, and provided a synopsis of Ecuadoran historiography. Barrera is most widely recognized, however, for his *Historia de la literatura ecuatoriana* (1944). At the time the work was published, it represented a revision of Ecuadoran literary history. It grouped authors by genre and offered comparative analyses of their works, and also examined the literary theories behind them. According to Barrera's own understanding of literature, the *Historia* is not merely a literary history. As he indicates at the beginning of the work, it is a study of the intellectual history of a nation and gets at the true nature of the Ecuadoran people.

See also **Ecuador: Since 1830.**

BIBLIOGRAPHY

Arias, Augusto. *Panorama de la literatura ecuatoriana.* Quito: Editorial LaSalle, 1961.

Sánchez Astudillo, Miguel. *Barrera, Isaac J. Espécimen de letrado y de hombre.* Quito: Casa de la Cultura Ecuatoriana, 1964.

Thomas, Jack Ray. *Biographical Dictionary of Latin American Historians and Historiography.* Westport, CT: Greenwood Press, 1984.

KENNETH ATWOOD

BARRERA BARERRA, EULALIA BEATRIZ (1918–).

Eulalia Barrera B., a Quito-born Ecuadorian writer and newspaperwoman, had a period of fertile literary activity writing *tradiciones* and short stories as well as editing collections of them with her sister Inés. The writing of *leyendas* (legends), integral to Romanticism, was imported to Latin America, where the genre helped inspire a new trend, the *tradición*, "invented" by the Peruvian Ricardo Palma and the Venezuelan Juan Vicente Camacho. The *tradición*, unlike the mere *leyenda* with no equivalent in Anglo-American literature, added to the story line a deeper meaning that could be linguistic analysis, satire, or even a political explanation. Barrera, instead of nationalizing the form as Palma did, revised it from the perspective of gender analysis. Her most interesting *tradiciones*, "Flor de amor" and "Capilla del Consuelo," turn to Spanish medieval and Renaissance themes to examine the social structures that subordinate women. By looking at previous times and places, Barrera could criticize the place of women in contemporary Ecuadorian society. Many of her pieces published in the Ecuadorian press lie uncollected and forgotten, waiting to be rediscovered.

See also **Palma, Ricardo; Tinajero Martínez de Allen, Eugenia.**

BIBLIOGRAPHY

Barrera B., Inés, and Eulalia Barrera B. *Tradiciones y leyendas del Ecuador.* Quito: Empresa Editora "El Comercio," 1947.

Barrera B., Inés, and Eulalia Barrera B. *Los mejores cuentos ecuatorianos.* Quito: Empresa Editora "El Comercio," 1948.

Ward, Thomas. "Perú y Ecuador." *La narrativa histórica de escritoras latinoamericanas*, edited by Gloria da Cunha, pp. 271–305. Buenos Aires: Ediciones Corregidor, 2004.

THOMAS WARD

BARRETO, PAULO. *See* Rio, João do.

BARRETO DE MENEZES, TOBIAS JR. (1839–1889).

Tobias Barreto de Menezes Jr. (*b.* 7 June 1839; *d.* 26 June 1889), Brazilian philosopher and jurist, founder of the Recife School. Born in Campos, in the province of Sergipe, to a family of very modest circumstances, Barreto learned Latin from a priest and, from the age of fifteen, made his living teaching humanities. He studied law in Recife and became known for his poetical disputes with Antônio de Castro Alves. As a member of the Generation of 1870 he fought for intellectual renewal in the Brazilian Empire.

Unlike most of his generation, who turned to French positivism, Barreto found inspiration in German authors. In the areas of religious criticism (Georg von Ewald, Ludwig Feuerbach), political ideas (von Gneist, Frobel), and law (von Ihring), they seemed to him to offer views more suitable to combat the spiritualist and neo-Thomist eclecticism then dominant in Brazil. His "Germanism" produced a model for solving Brazilian problems and enabled him to criticize the French-inspired Brazilian liberals, the francophile elite of the Southeast, and the dominant juridical conceptions.

Although he was married to the daughter of a Liberal *fazendeiro* (rancher), Barreto suffered social and racial discrimination as a result of his mixed heritage. After a brief and not very successful involvement in local and regional politics (he was a Liberal member of the provincial assembly in 1878–1879), he gained influence by becoming a professor at the law faculty of Recife in 1882. In his lectures he defended the view that law is neither divine nor natural, but a product of history. A supporter of philosophical monism, he was responsible for the wide dissemination of Ernst Haeckel's theories in Brazil and became famous for his polemics against ultramontanist and idealist positions.

Although Barreto was widely attacked, his views were supported by his friend, the literary critic Sílvio Romero, and by a group of students who played major roles during the Old Republic: Clóvis Beviláqua, Higinho Cunha, Benedito Leite, and Artur Orlando.

See also **Philosophy: Overview.**

BIBLIOGRAPHY

Tobias Barreto, Jr., *Obras completas,* 10 vols. (1925–1926).

Hermes Lima, *Tobias Barreto: A época e o homem* (1939).

Paulo Mercadante and Antonio Paim, *Tobias Barreto na cultura brasileira: Uma reavaliação* (1972).

Centro De Documentação Do Pensamento Brasileiro, *Tobias Barreto: Bibliografia e studos críticos* (1990).

Additional Bibliography

Kirkendall, Andrew J. *Class Mates: Male Student Culture and the Making of a Political Class in Nineteenth-Century Brazil.* Lincoln: University of Nebraska Press, 2002.

MATTHIAS RÖHRIG ASSUNÇÃO

BARRETT, RAFAEL (1876–1910).

Rafael Barrett (*b.* 1876; *d.* 17 December 1910), Anglo-Spanish anarchist writer who influenced an entire generation of Paraguayan radical intellectuals. Born in Santander, Spain, in 1876, Barrett moved to Asunción in 1904. Working days in the general statistics office, he devoted his nights to journalistic efforts, churning out article after article of social criticism, focusing especially on the plight of poor workers in the yerba plantations of eastern Paraguay. His principal writings, compiled in a volume entitled *El dolor paraguayo* (1910), have been favorably compared with the works of Peru's Clorinda Matto De Turner, Ecuador's Jorge Icaza Coronel, and Bolivia's Alcides Argüedas. Afflicted with tuberculosis, Barrett left his Paraguayan wife and children behind at San Bernardino and returned to Europe, where he died at Arcachón, France.

See also **Paraguay: The Nineteenth Century.**

BIBLIOGRAPHY

Rafael Barrett, *El dolor paraguayo* (1978).

Carlos Zubizarretta, *Cien vidas paraguayas,* 2d ed. (1985), pp. 248–251.

Additional Bibliography

Muñoz, Vladimiro. *Barrett.* Asunción: Germinal, 1994.

THOMAS L. WHIGHAM

BARRIENTOS ORTUÑO, RENÉ (1919–1969).

René Barrientos Ortuño (*b.* 1919; *d.* 27 April 1969), army officer and president of Bolivia (1966–1969). Barrientos, a native of Cochabamba, graduated in 1943 from the military academy from which he had earlier been expelled for supporting the government of President Germán Busch (1937–1939). He played an active though very junior role in the 1944 peasant congress sponsored by the regime of President Gualberto Villarroel

(1943–1946) and the Movimiento Nacionalista Revolucionario (MNR). Although he stayed in the army after the overthrow of Villarroel, he was retired for participating in an MNR insurrection against the conservative government.

He participated in the 1952 MNR revolution that launched the Bolivian National Revolution. While the MNR was in power, he became head of the air force and of the "military cell" of the MNR. In the 1964 election, as a result of military pressure, the civilian selected to run as the MNR candidate for vice president with President Víctor Paz Estenssoro was forced to step down. René Barrientos was put in his place. Even before becoming vice president in August, Barrientos was leading a conspiracy to overthrow Paz Estenssoro, which came to fruition on 4 November 1964. For some time after Paz Estenssoro's overthrow, Barrientos and General Alfredo Ovando were "copresidents." During that period, there were violent clashes between the regime and organized labor, particularly the miners. The mining camps were occupied by troops and many miners and members of their families were either killed or wounded.

In 1966 General Barrientos was elected president. Although his regime continued to rule in a highhanded fashion and was particularly hostile to organized labor, it did enjoy wide support among the peasantry. Barrientos spoke Quechua, and spent much time traveling in rural areas. He also continued to support the land redistribution that had taken place under the MNR government as well as extensive programs of extending technical help to the Indian peasants. Peasant support was of key importance in helping the Barrientos government to defeat the guerrilla effort launched in 1967 by Ernesto "Che" Guevara. Guevara was executed by the Bolivian army unit that captured him. Barrientos died in the mysterious crash of a helicopter he was piloting.

See also **Bolivia, Political Parties: Nationalist Revolutionary Movement (MNR).**

BIBLIOGRAPHY

Christopher Mitchell, *The Legacy of Populism in Bolivia: From the MNR to Military Rule* (1977).

Additional Bibliography

Soto S., Cesar. *Historia del Pacto Militar Campesino.* Cochabamba, Bolivia: Ediciones CERES, 1994.

ROBERT J. ALEXANDER

BARRILLAS, MANUEL LISANDRO

(1844–1907). Manuel Lisandro Barrillas (*b.* 1844; *d.* 1907), president of Guatemala (1885–1892). Barrillas was appointed provisional president in 1885 after the death of Justo Rufino Barrios and was constitutionally elected the following year. Like Barrios, he was a coffee grower who participated in the Liberal Revolution that swept the Conservatives from power in 1871. His liberal credentials and vast coffee holdings in San Marcos and Retaluleu ensured a smooth rise to power. The Barillas administration rested largely on its ability to induce the nation's Indian majority to labor on large coffee *fincas*. When the Indians resisted, his government, with the aid of the military, resorted to a number of forced-labor schemes that included the *mandamiento*, debt bondage, and a vagrancy law.

The Barrillas government coincides with a tremendous expansionary period for Guatemala's coffee industry. In the late 1880s and early 1890s world prices for Guatemalan coffee reached record high levels. Coffee cultivation was introduced to large new tracts of land to take advantage of the favorable world market. It is in this period that Guatemala gained its reputation as a producer of one of the world's finest mild coffees.

See also **Coffee Industry.**

BIBLIOGRAPHY

Sanford A. Mosk, "The Coffee Economy of Guatemala, 1850–1918: Development and Signs of Instability," in *Inter-American Economic Affairs* 9 (1955): 6–20.

WADE A. KIT

BARRIOS, AGUSTÍN (1885–1944).

Agustín Barrios (*b.* 23 May 1885; *d.* 7 August 1944), Paraguayan musician and composer. Born in San Juan Bautista in the Paraguayan Misiones, Barrios came from an impoverished background. He nonetheless attained fame early on as a local prodigy with the guitar. At the end of the century, he was discovered by Gustavo Sosa Escalada, the country's most famous guitarist, who helped Barrios to develop his skill with the instrument. After studying at the Colegio Nacional in Asunción, Barrios began a concert tour of South America in 1910. The tour lasted fourteen years, and included extended stays in Chile, Argentina, Uruguay, and Brazil.

In his presentations, Barrios often appeared in Indian costume, replete with feathers, and went under the stage name of *Cacique Mangoré*. Throughout this time Barrios also composed pieces for the guitar, a good many of which he attributed to obscure European composers in the belief that they would then be taken more seriously.

After a brief return to Paraguay in the mid-1920s, Barrios again left the country, this time in the company of a diplomat, Tomás Salomini, who served as his patron and who arranged recitals for him in Cuba, Mexico, and, in 1934, in several European capitals. Barrios was the first major Latin American musician to play before European audiences. He has frequently been compared to Andrés Segovia as an interpreter, and to Niccolò Paganini as a virtuoso. He evidently wrote over a hundred works, though many of these are now lost. His extant corpus includes *Danza paraguaya, El catedrál,* and *Rapsodia andaluza.* Starting in 1939, Barrios taught at the National Music Conservatory in San Salvador, El Salvador, where he died.

See also **Music: Popular Music and Dance.**

BIBLIOGRAPHY

Peter Sensier, "Augustín Barrios," *Guitar* 2: 12 (1974), p. 22.

Bacón Duarte Prado, *Agustín Barrios: Un genio insular* (1985).

Additional Bibliography

Stover, Richard D. *Six Silver Moonbeams: The Life and Times of Agustín Barrios Mangore.* Clovis, CA: Querico, 1992. [Translated into Spanish by Rafael Menjivar Ochoa. *Seis rayos de plata: Vida y tiempo de Agustín Barrios Mangore.* San Salvador, El Salvador: CONCULTURA, Dirección de Publicaciones e Impresos, 2002.]

MARTA FERNÁNDEZ WHIGHAM

BARRIOS, EDUARDO (1884–1963).

Eduardo Barrios (*b.* 25 October 1884; *d.* 13 September 1963), Chilean novelist, short-story writer, and playwright. Known primarily for his psychological novels, Barrios subordinated action to character portrayal in his works. Many of his protagonists are will-less, alienated men destined to fail. His first collection of stories, *Del natural* (1907), reflects the tenets of nineteenth-century realism and Émile Zola's naturalism. The unifying theme is love, which Barrios examines within the context of middle-class mores. The title story of his second collection, *El niño que enloqueció de amor* (1915), is a psychological study of a nine-year-old boy who becomes enamored of an older woman and goes mad when he discovers her with her boyfriend. The story re-creates the imaginary world of a child who is increasingly alienated from adults. Critics have seen precursors of modernism in the extreme delicacy of the boy's portrait. Barrios's novel *Un perdido* (1918) combines a subtle character analysis with a detailed description of the Chilean middle class. *El hermano asno* (1922), which deals with the repressed erotic yearnings of a friar named Lázaro, has been called anticlerical because Lázaro witnesses an apparent crime and Church authorities try to silence him. *Tamarugal* (1944) and *Gran señor y rajadiablos* (1948) are set in rural areas; the former deals with life in the nitrate mines in the north of Chile, while the latter portrays life on a typical Chilean farm around the turn of the century. *Los hombres del hombre* (1950) is a psychological portrait of a man who suspects his wife of infidelity. Barrios also wrote a number of plays, including *Lo que niega la vida* (1913), *Vivir* (1916), and *¡Ante todo la oficina!* (1925).

See also **Literature: Spanish America.**

BIBLIOGRAPHY

Jaime Peralta, "La novelística de Eduardo Barrios," in *Cuadernos Hispanoamericanos* 173 (1964): 357–367.

Manuel E. Ramírez, "Some Notes on the Prose Style of Eduardo Barrios," in *Romance Notes* 9 (1967): 40–48.

Jerry L. Benbow, "Grotesque Elements in Eduardo Barrios," in *Hispania* 51 (1968): 86–91.

Ned J. Davidson, *Eduardo Barrios* (1970).

Silvia Martínez Dacosta, *Dos ensayos literarios sobre Eduardo Barrios y José Donoso* (1976).

John Walker, *Metaphysics and Aesthetics in the Works of Eduardo Barrios* (1983).

Luis A. Mansilla, "Eduardo Barrios," in *Araucaria de Chile* 28 (1984): 141–144.

Silvia Martínez Dacosta, *Los personajes en la obra de Eduardo Barrios* (1988).

BARBARA MUJICA

BARRIOS, GERARDO (1813–1865).

Gerardo Barrios (*b*. 3 October 1813; *d*. 29 August 1865), general and president of El Salvador (1859–1863). Born to a wealthy, well-connected family in the department of San Miguel, Barrios remains a popular figure in the history of modern El Salvador. He was the first president in Central America to introduce reforms based on liberalism-positivism, and set the course for the modernization of Salvadoran society.

Barrios's family had extensive landholdings, on which they grew indigo. Young Gerardo felt a vocation for the military and joined the militia at a young age. By 1840 he had already participated in the overthrow of one president, José María Cornejo, and fought in battles at Mixco, San Miguelito, Espíritu Santo, Perulapía, and in Guatemala. He joined other Central American leaders in the struggle against the American filibuster William Walker in Nicaragua in the 1850s. In this campaign Barrios earned a reputation as a skillful leader and formed a close relationship with the Guatemalan president Rafael Carrera. In July 1858, Carrera decorated Barrios with the Cross of Honor. This friendly association was not destined to last long, however, for Barrios was more of an ideologue than Carrera, and friction developed after Barrios succeeded to the presidency of El Salvador when President Miguel de Santín de Castillo's health failed in 1858.

Barrios then embarked on a remarkable new course that revealed his deep admiration for the United States and Europe. In fact, Barrios often spoke of the perfection of the British and French political institutions. He undertook the modernization of the Salvadoran government: an expansion and centralization of the bureaucracy, the restoration of San Salvador as the national capital, and the transfer of the Supreme Court back to San Salvador. Barrios next overhauled the legal system by drafting new civil and penal codes and altering the process of justice. The right to collect taxes was removed from local jurisdiction and decreed a national responsibility. He repatriated the remains of the great Liberal leader of independence Francisco Morazán, who was actually Honduran, and buried them in San Salvador with much ceremony. Barrios extended the term of the presidency from two to six years, increased the role of the executive branch at the expense of the legislative, and upheld the democratic transfer of office. He returned office to Santín upon the latter's recovery late in 1859, but arranged to have himself elected the following year.

In 1860, Barrios began to promote the production of coffee on a large scale, by lowering production taxes on the new crop, exempting the coffee labor force from military service, and distributing land to those promising to grow coffee on two-thirds or more of the area. Barrios's government took an unprecedented, active role in the economy of the nation when it purchased a boat and attempted to export coffee to California itself. Furthermore, Barrios followed the French model and transformed the old-style Salvadoran militias into a modern national army; he also created a military academy with a Colombian as its head.

By 1862, Barrios's liberalism had begun to encroach on the privileged position of the Roman Catholic church. Although he was not an enemy of the church, as president Barrios stressed the ultimate authority of secular over religious authorities. He required all priests to declare obedience to the state, thereby provoking conflict with the Vatican and stirring up fears among other Central American leaders. In 1862, Barrios reached a concordat with the Holy See in which priests agreed to swear loyalty to the Constitution but not to the actual government. Barrios's main efforts were concentrated in education and the expansion of transportation and communication. By 1863, he had many enemies both within El Salvador and across Central America. He repelled a Guatemalan invasion in early 1863, but before the end of the year Carrera returned and conquered El Salvador. Barrios was caught in Nicaragua while trying to escape. He languished in jail and was executed in 1865. Thus ended the first liberal-positivist experiment in Central America.

See also **El Salvador.**

BIBLIOGRAPHY

Government of El Salvador, *Gerardo Barrios: Héroe nacional de El Salvador* (n.d.).

Emiliano Cortés, *Biografía del capitán general Gerardo Barrios* (1965).

José Dolores Gámez, *Gerardo Barrios ante la posteridad* (1965).

Ítalo López Vallecillos, *Gerardo Barrios y su tiempo*, 2 vols. (1967).

KAREN RACINE

BARRIOS, GONZALO (1902–1993).

Gonzalo Barrios (b. 1902; d. 30 May 1993), Venezuelan politician. The son of a well-to-do family from Portuguesa State, Barrios studied law at the Central University of Venezuela, where he was a prominent member of the Generation of 1928. After returning from a European exile in 1936, he became a founder of the Venezuelan Organization (Organización Venezolana—ORVE), the National Democratic Party (Partido Democrático Nacional—PDN), and Democratic Action (Acción Democrática—AD). During the AD *trienio* (1945–1948) he served as a member of the revolutionary junta, secretary of the presidency, and governor of the Federal District. After 1958 he held a series of important positions in AD (including secretary-general) and in government (minister of the interior, senator). After running as AD's unsuccessful presidential candidate in 1968, he continued to play an active role in party and national affairs. He died in 1993 in Caracas.

See also **Venezuela, Political Parties: Democratic Action (AD).**

BIBLIOGRAPHY

John D. Martz, *Acción Democrática: Evolution of a Modern Political Party in Venezuela* (1966).

Robert J. Alexander, ed., *Biographical Dictionary of Latin American and Caribbean Political Leaders* (1988).

Additional Bibliography

Sant Ros, José. *Los verdaderos golpistas.* Venezuela: Kariña Editores, 1998.

WINFIELD J. BURGGRAAFF

BARRIOS, JUSTO RUFINO (1835–1885).

Justo Rufino Barrios (b. 19 July 1835; d. 2 April 1885), president of Guatemala (1873–1885). Born in San Lorenzo, department of San Marcos, Guatemala, Justo Barrios was the son of Ignacio Barrios, a prominent dealer in horses and cattle and landowner, and Josefa Auyón de Barrios. He led the Liberal Reforma of 1871 and represented the shift in power from the Conservative elite of Guatemala City to the Liberal coffee interests of the western highlands.

Barrios received his elementary and secondary education from tutors and schools in San Marcos, Quetzaltenango, and Guatemala City, where he studied law and earned his certificate as a notary in 1862. In Guatemala City he came under the influence of leading Liberals, Miguel García Granados and Manuel Dardón, but he returned to his family lands in 1862 and especially developed his estate, "El Malacate," along the Mexican border.

In 1867 Barrios joined the Liberal insurgency against President Vicente Cerna. When an attack on the barracks at San Marcos failed, Barrios fled into Chiapas, in southern Mexico, where in 1869 he organized a rebel force in collaboration with Field Marshal Serapio Cruz. After Cruz's death in 1870, García Granados joined the movement and formed a provisional government early in 1871, with Barrios as military commander. They quickly gained control of the western highlands, and in a manifesto issued at Patzicía on 3 June 1871 they stated the goals of their revolution. The crucial battle came at San Lucas Sacatepéquez, on the heights above Guatemala City, where on 29 June, Barrios routed Cerna's army. On the following day he marched into the capital victorious. García Granados served as the first president under the Reforma. Barrios wanted more sweeping reforms, however, and in 1873 he won election as president of Guatemala.

Barrios quickly forged a strong dictatorship, eliminating the Conservative opposition and greatly strengthening the power of the state. He represented the coming to power in Guatemala of the liberal-positivist philosophy that would remain dominant until at least 1944. Barrios promoted strongly anticlerical legislation, suppressed the tithe, abolished the regular orders, expropriated church property, and greatly reduced the number of priests in the country; he also established religious liberty, civil marriage and divorce, and state collection of vital statistics. He launched a public education system at all levels and took the University of San Carlos out of the control of the church, making it the state university and establishing other secondary and normal schools. His educational reforms, however, benefited primarily the upper and middle classes of Guatemala City and Quetzaltenango. Most rural Guatemalans continued to have little access to education and often now lost their village priests, who formerly had provided some education to parishioners. Barrios's restructuring of the university emphasized professional and technical education at the expense of the humanities and liberal arts, another reflection of positivist thinking.

Barrios put great emphasis on material progress. Coffee exports increased enormously as he encouraged the encroachment of ladino planters on Indian communal lands and made their labor more accessible to planters, began a railroad system, and developed ports and roads. He facilitated formation of banks and other financial institutions to provide credit for economic development and modernization. New ministries of agriculture, development, and education reflected this emphasis on economic growth as well as the increased role of the state. Barrios also attracted immigration and investment from overseas; German and U.S. influence increased notably. His administration codified the laws and promulgated a new constitution in 1879, under which he was reelected in 1880. His policies spurred substantial modernization of both Guatemala City and Quetzaltenango.

In foreign affairs Barrios played an important role in the neighboring states of El Salvador and Honduras, and in 1882 he settled differences with Mexico at the cost of giving up Guatemalan claims to Soconusco and other parts of Chiapas. He renewed the Guatemalan claim to Belize, however, repudiating the Wyke-Aycinena Treaty of 1859 with Great Britain. He also tried to revive the unionist spirit of Francisco Morazán and sought to reestablish the Central American federation by means of Guatemalan military power. That effort, however, ended abruptly in 1885 when Salvadoran forces defeated the Guatemalan army at Chalchuapa, where Barrios died in battle.

Barrios established a new "coffee elite" centered in the western highlands around Quetzaltenango, reducing the power of the Guatemala City merchant elite that had dominated the country since the late colonial period. At the same time, he greatly accelerated exploitation of the indigenous population and moved Guatemala more rapidly into an export-led economy dependent on foreign markets and investment. Although celebrated in Guatemalan history as the "Reformer" who ended the long Conservative dictatorships of Rafael Carrera and Vicente Cerna (1839–1871),

his own dictatorial rule and strengthening of the military established a pattern of repressive government for subsequent Liberal governments even to the present. Barrios's personal wealth increased enormously during his rule, especially in comparison with earlier Guatemalan presidents. In this, too, he set a pattern that many of his successors would emulate.

See also **Central America; Education.**

BIBLIOGRAPHY

Although there is an extensive literature on Barrios in Spanish, there is relatively little in English. The standard biography is Paul Burgess, *Justo Rufino Barrios: A Biography* (1926, 2d ed. 1946). Jim Handy, *Gift of the Devil: A History of Guatemala* (1984), has a useful chapter on the Barrios period. Excellent for understanding his economic policy is David J. McCreery, *Development and the State in Reforma Guatemala, 1871–1885* (1983). Two helpful doctoral dissertations are available in English, but have been published only in Spanish: Hubert J. Miller, *La iglesia y el estado en tiempo de Justo Rufino Barrios* (1976); and Thomas R. Herrick, *Desarrollo económico y político de Guatemala durante el período de Justo Rufino Barrios (1871–1885)* (1974). Among the many works by Central American authors, the most useful are Pedro Joaquín Chamorro Zelaya, *El patrón: Estudio histórico sobre la personalidad del General Justo Rufino Barrios* (1966); Carlos Wyld Ospina, *El autócrata: Ensayo político-social* (1929); Víctor Miguel Díaz, *Barrios ante la posteridad* (1935); and Casimiro D. Rubio, *Biografía del general Justo Rufino Barrios, reformador de Guatemala: Recopilación histórica y documentada* (1935).

RALPH LEE WOODWARD JR.

BARRIOS DE CHAMORRO, VIOLETA (1929–).

Violeta Barrios de Chamorro (*b.* 18 October 1929), president of Nicaragua (1990–). Elected president as the representative of the fourteen-party National Opposition Union (Unión Nacional Opositora—UNO) coalition, Barrios de Chamorro seemed an unlikely candidate. She was born in the southern Nicaraguan province of Rivas to wealthy, landowning parents and attended Catholic schools. In 1950 she married Pedro Joaquín Chamorro Cardenal, a leader of the middle-class opposition to the dictatorship of the Somoza family. Nonetheless, her political participation during the decades of the 1950s, 1960s, and 1970s was confined to that of supportive wife and mother.

In January 1978 Chamorro Cardenal was assassinated, probably by a member of the Somoza family. The assassination set off a wave of strikes and mass insurrection that helped carry the Sandinista Liberation Front (Frente Sandinista de la Liberación Nacional—FSLN) into power. Doña Violeta, as she is called, was named a member of the five-person ruling junta. She resigned from that body less than a year later.

For the remainder of the 1980s, her political participation was confined to criticizing the FSLN and supporting the Contra war from her position as owner of the daily newspaper *La Prensa*, which she inherited from her late husband. Other members of her family took more prominent roles in politics.

Barrios de Chamorro reentered formal politics when she ran for president in 1990. Running on the promises to end the Contra war and repair the economy, she portrayed herself as the traditional mother who would reconcile the Nicaraguan family just as she had reconciled her own politically torn family. She won the election with 55 percent of the vote.

Since Barrios de Chamorro's election, the civil war has ended, for the most part. Massive devaluations and cuts in real wages (now among the lowest in the hemisphere) have eliminated hyperinflation. Her relative independence from the United States, whose support was essential in putting her into power, came as something of a surprise to both her supporters and detractors. Her administration often chose to govern in coalition with moderates in the FSLN rather than with the far-right members of the UNO. This choice hastened the disintegration of the inherently unstable fourteen-party UNO coalition. While many within Nicaragua critiqued her neoliberal economic reforms, these changes did help stabilize the economy and promote economic growth, even though poverty remains a considerable problem. In 2006 Barrios de Chamorro's old opponent and the leader of the Sandinistas, Daniel Ortega, won the presidency. While the United States felt that a leftist government would harm democratic institutions, Barrios de Chamorro, who did not support Ortega, stated that democracy would survive his presidency.

See also **Chamorro Cardenal, Pedro Joaquín; Nicaragua; Nicaragua, Sandinista National Liberation Front (FSLN); Ortega Saavedra, Daniel.**

BIBLIOGRAPHY

Salman Rushdie, "Doña Violeta's Version," in *The Jaguar Smile: A Nicaraguan Journey* (1987), pp. 145–153.

Denis Lynn Daly Heyck, "Violeta Chamorro," in *Life Stories of the Nicaraguan Revolution* (1990), pp. 37–52.

Karen Kampwirth, "The Mother of the Nicaraguans: Doña Violeta and the UNO's Gender Agenda" in *Latin American Perspectives* (1995).

Additional Bibliography

Lacayo Oyanguren, Antonio. *La difícil transición nicaragüense en el gobierno con Doña Violeta*. Nicaragua: Colección Cultural de Centro América, 2005.

KAREN KAMPWIRTH

BARROS, ADHEMAR DE (1901–1969).

Adhemar de Barros (*b*. 22 April 1901; *d*. 12 March 1969), three-time governor of São Paulo (1957–1961), and frequent populist candidate for president (1955, 1960, 1965).

The Barros family lived on its extensive coffee lands and owned businesses in the interior of São Paulo. Adhemar attended high school in the capital, completed his medical training in Rio, and interned in Europe. His political career began with Getúlio Vargas's surprise appointment as state interventor in 1938. Adhemar seized the opportunity to build hospitals, roads, clinics, and schools, making a name for himself as a vigorous administrator.

In 1945 Adhemar formed the populist-style Social Progressive Party (PSP) and ran for governor in 1947. Finding his upper-class background a hindrance, he adopted the image of a rough-and-tumble provincial. Spending both his own and illicitly raised money, he hired publicity experts, conducted polls, purchased media exposure, and flew his own airplane to expand his following. In office he stressed building programs—schools, hospitals, highways, and dams—that glorified his image as "the manager." Tempted by the presidency in 1950, he withdrew in favor of Vargas with the understanding that the latter would support him in 1955.

Adhemar's flamboyant career was blocked by the meteoric rise of Jânio Quadros, who defeated him in the 1954 gubernatorial election. An indictment for corruption stalled his campaign for president the following year. Absolved of the charges and vindicated by his mayoral victory in 1957 and his gubernatorial defeat of Quadros in 1963, Adhemar hoped to win the presidency in 1965. The military revoked his political rights because of graft, however, and he died three years later in self-imposed exile.

See also **Brazil: Since 1889.**

BIBLIOGRAPHY

Thomas E. Skidmore, *Politics in Brazil, 1930–1964* (1967).

Guita Grin Debert, *Idelogia e populismo* (1979).

Regina Sampaio, *Adhemar de Barros e o PSP* (1982).

Israel Beloch and Alzira Alves De Abreu, comps., *Dicionário histórico-biográfico brasileiro, 1930–1983* (1984).

Additional Bibliography

Cannabrava Filho, Paulo. *Adhemar de Barros: Trajetória e realizaçoes.* São Paulo: Editora Terceiro Nome, 2004.

Kwak, Gabriel. *O trevo e a vassoura: Os destinos de Janio Quadros e Adhemar de Barros.* São Paulo: A Girafa, 2006.

Pomar, Pedro Estevam da Rocha. *A democracia intolerante: Dutra, Adhemar, e a repressão ao Partido Comunista, 1946-1950.* São Paulo: Arquivo do Estado: Imprensa Oficial do Estado, 2002.

MICHAEL L. CONNIFF

BARROS, JOÃO DE (c. 1496–1570). João de Barros (*b.* ca. 1496; *d.* 21 October 1570), bureaucrat, humanist, lord-proprietor (*donatario*) in Brazil, historian. The son of a member of the lower nobility, João de Barros served as a page to Prince João, future king of Portugal. From 1525 to 1528 he was treasurer of the Casa da India, Mina, e Ceuta. In 1532 Barros became factor (*feitor*) of the Casa da India e Guiné (also called the Casa da India e Mina), a post he held until 1567. He was the author of *Clarimundo* (1522), a romance of chivalry, and *Ropica Pnefma* (1532), an allegory greatly influenced by Erasmus.

In 1535 Barros became the seventh of the twelve lords-proprietor to be awarded hereditary captaincies in Brazil between 1534 and 1536. He received several grants of land on the northern coast of Brazil along with two other lords-proprietor, Aires da Cunha and Fernão Álvares de Andrade. In 1535 the three lords-proprietor financed an expedition to explore and settle their lands, but most of the fleet was shipwrecked and little came of the effort. In 1555 or 1556, Barros sent another expedition that included his sons, Jerónimo and João, but this effort, too, was unsuccessful, leaving Barros in very serious financial straits. Many historians, unaware of the second expedition, have combined the two into one and have asserted, without evidence, that Barros's sons were on the 1535 voyage. After suffering a stroke in 1567, Barros retired to his country estate, São Lourenço do Ribeiro de Alitem, near Pombal, where he died.

Published between 1552 and 1615, Barros's most important literary work was the four-volume *Décadas de Asia,* modeled on Livy's *History.* Covering Portugal's overseas activity to 1538, the work is of great value to historians because of Barros's access to materials as factor of the Casa da India e Guiné, his incorporation of Portuguese translations of Asian chronicles and other documents that have since disappeared, and his use of eyewitness accounts of those Portuguese returning from overseas.

See also **Explorers and Exploration: Brazil.**

BIBLIOGRAPHY

A very good biography in English is Charles R. Boxer, *João de Barros: Portuguese Humanist and Historian of Asia* (1981). A number of documents regarding the career of Barros were published by António Baião, "Documents inéditos sôbre João de Barros," in *Boletim da segunda classe,* vol 11, edited by Academia das Sciências de Lisboa (1916–1917), pp. 202–355. The major documents for the grant of his captaincy in Brazil, and not included in the preceding work, are transcribed by António Baião in his introduction to the fourth edition of *Asia de Joam de Barros* (1932), the first of the *Décadas.* Also useful in assessing Barros's role as a humanist strongly influenced by Erasmus is José V. De Pina Martins, *Humanismo e Erasmismo na cultura portuguesa do século XVI: Estudo e textos* (1973).

FRANCIS A. DUTRA

BARROS ARANA, DIEGO (1830–1906). Diego Barros Arana (*b.* 16 August 1830; *d.* 14 November 1906), Chilean historian and diplomat. One of Chile's premier scholars, Barros Arana graduated from the Instituto Nacional, Chile's finest secular high school. As a liberal historian he tended to equate conservative ideology with backwardness; consequently, his works tended to flay both the Roman Catholic church and the authoritarian regime of Manuel Montt. He was a professor at the University of Chile and later was the director of the Instituto Nacional. He enjoyed an active political life, serving as a deputy for the Liberal Party. Barros Arana's articles in various newspapers so incensed Montt that Barros Arana fled his homeland.

Upon his return, he took up once again a life of scholarship and public service. An extremely prolific historian, Barros Arana published a variety of biographies as well as a multivolume history of Chile. He also acted as Chile's minister to Argentina, where he negotiated a treaty resolving the question of the ownership of Patagonia. Rather than follow his instructions, Barros Arana gave up Chile's claim to the disputed territory, permitting the Argentines to occupy Tierra del Fuego. This act not only compromised Chile's claims to vast territory but also threatened Santiago's vital trade routes to Europe. Recalled in disgrace to Chile, he became an object of public scorn, although he continued in public life, serving as a deputy. Barros Arana's scholarship had a lasting impact on Chilean intellectual life, influencing subsequent generations.

See also **Chile, Political Parties: Liberal Party; Patagonia.**

BIBLIOGRAPHY

Gertrude Yeager, *Barros Arana's Historia jeneral de Chile: Politics, History, and National Identity* (1981).

Allen Woll, *A Functional Past: The Uses of History in Nineteenth-Century Chile* (1982).

WILLIAM F. SATER

BARROSO, ARY (1903–1964). Ary Barroso (*b.* 7 November 1903; *d.* 9 February 1964), Brazilian songwriter. Barroso was one of his country's most influential composers of samba music; his songs were renowned for their beautiful melodies and picturesque language, and often celebrated Brazil, its people, and culture. Barroso's "Aquarela do Brasil" (known elsewhere simply as "Brazil")

ranks among the world's best-known popular tunes of the twentieth century.

Born in Ubá, Minas Gerais, Barroso moved in 1920 to Rio, where he played for dance-hall orchestras and later became a successful writer of hit songs for Carnaval. He helped develop the genre called *samba-canção*, a softer, more sophisticated samba that emphasized melody more than rhythm and featured more complex harmonies. With "Aquarela do Brasil" (Watercolor of Brazil), Barroso created another style, *samba-exaltação*, so-called for its characteristic grand, epic songs with soaring melodies that "exalted" a particular subject. Among his other standards are "Na batucada da vida" (A Strong Indictment of Poverty), "No tabuleiro da baiana" (On the Baiana's Tray), "Na baixa do sapateiro" (also called "Bahia"), "Rio de Janeiro," and "Inquietação" (Disquiet).

For the last fifty years, Barroso has been one of the most recorded Brazilian composers both inside and outside his country, and his songs have reached the world through the animated films of Walt Disney (such as *The Three Caballeros*), movies such as Terry Gilliam's *Brazil* (1985), and countless interpretations by world pop and jazz artists. "Aquarela do Brasil" rivals "The Girl From Ipanema" as the most internationally famous Brazilian tune of all time.

See also **Music: Popular Music and Dance.**

BIBLIOGRAPHY

Vasco Mariz, *A canção brasileira*, 5th ed. (1985).

Chris McGowan and Ricardo Pessanha, *The Brazilian Sound: Samba, Bossa Nova, and the Popular Music of Brazil* (1991).

Additional Bibliography

McCann, Bryan. *Hello, Hello Brazil: Popular Music in the Making of Modern Brazil*. Durham, NC: Duke University Press, 2004.

Moraes, Mário de. *Recordações de Ary Barroso: Ultimo depoimento*, 2nd ed. Rio de Janeiro: Edição FUNARTE, 2003.

CHRIS MCGOWAN

BARROSO, GUSTAVO DODT (1888–1959). Gustavo Dodt Barroso (*b.* 29 December 1888; *d.* 3 December 1959), Brazilian writer, journalist, and politician. Barroso was a pioneer of the

Brazilian folklore movement known as Northeastern Regionalism. Under the pen name João do Norte he wrote *Terra de sol* (1912), in which he praised the backlands peasantry for hard work, devotion to family, religious zeal, and closeness to nature. In *Heróes e bandidos: Os cangaceiros de Nordeste* (1917), he adopted the view that backlands bandits such as Antonio Silvino were predisposed to crime because of their race, lack of education, and the "savagery" of their environment. In the 1930s he became a supporter and one of the most influential propagandists of *integralismo*, the Brazilian variant of fascism.

Born in Fortaleza, Ceará, Barroso studied in Ceará, attended the Law School of Fortaleza from 1907 to 1909, and graduated in 1911 from the Law School of Rio de Janeiro. In 1914 he was appointed secretary of justice and interior for the state of Ceará and later directed *Diário Oficial*. A prolific writer, he published 128 books, including folklore, short stories, history, biography, criticism, plays, poetry, essays, a dictionary, memoirs, translations, and children's readers. He founded and directed the National Historic Museum, edited the Rio magazines *Fon-Fon* and *Selecta,* and served on the 1919 Brazilian delegation to the Versailles Peace Congress. In March 1923 he was elected a member of the Brazilian Academy of Letters. Other writings include *O integralismo em marcha* (1933) and *O que o integralista deve saber* (1935).

See also **Literature: Brazil.**

BIBLIOGRAPHY

Raimundo De Menezes, *Dicionário literário brasileiro, ilustrado* (1969).

Ralph Della Cava, *Miracle at Joaseiro* (1970).

Additional Bibliography

Gonçalves, Cláudio do Carmo. *Ficções do patrimônio: Raízes de memória em Gustavo Barroso e Mário de Andrdade.* Rio de Janeiro: Editora Agora da Ilha, 2002.

Maio, Marcos Chor. *Nem Rotschild nem Trotsky: O pensamento anti-semita de Gustavo Barroso.* Rio de Janeiro: Imago Editora, 1992.

TERESA MEADE

BARROW, ERROL WALTON (1920–1987).

Errol Walton Barrow (21 January 1920–1 June 1987), who ultimately became prime minister of Barbados, was born to middle-class black parents in the parish of St. Lucy in Barbados. An honor student, Barrow joined the Royal Air Force in 1940, and despite his experiences with racism, he rose through the ranks to become personal navigation officer to the commander-in-chief of the British Army in occupied Germany.

Upon his return from service he entered politics as a member of the Barbados Labour Party (BLP). After gaining a seat in parliament in 1951 and serving the BLP for four years, Barrow left the party to form the Democratic Labour Party (DLP). This was the beginning of the extraordinarily stable two-party system on the island. It was also a period of major social change fought for against two powerful opponents: colonialism and the power of the white local plantocracy. Barrow won both battles without engendering hatreds or bitterness.

Barrow served as premier of Barbados from 1961 until independence in 1966, when he became the island's first prime minister. In 1986, after serving in the opposition for ten years, Barrow led his party to a decisive electoral victory and was reelected prime minister. He died a year after his election, on 1 June 1987. His legacy of broad and deep democratic and developmental achievement is widely recognized throughout the region, and he has been declared a national hero in Barbados.

See also **Barbados.**

BIBLIOGRAPHY

Morgan, Peter. *The Life and Times of Errol Barrow.* Bridgetown, Barbados: Caribbean Communications, 1994.

ANTHONY P. MAINGOT

BARRUNDIA, JOSÉ FRANCISCO (1787–1854).

José Francisco Barrundia (*b.* 12 May 1787; *d.* 4 August 1854), proponent of Central American independence, ideological leader of the radical liberals during the early national period. The son of prominent Guatemalan creoles Martín Barrundia and Teresa Cepeda y Coronado, Barrundia was a brilliant lawyer, orator, and writer. Educated in Guatemala, he was among the intellectual elite of the late colonial period. In 1811 he translated John Milton's *Paradise Lost* and several classical Italian works into Spanish.

As a *regidor* (alderman) on the Guatemala City Council, Barrundia revealed his liberal political views. He participated in the ill-fated Belén Conspiracy of 1813 but escaped capture and a death sentence by hiding from the police of Captain General José Bustamante y Guerra for the next five years. As a member of the Tertulia Patriótica, along with José María Castilla, Pedro Molina, Manuel Montúfar, Marcial Zebadúa, and José Beteta, he plotted Guatemalan independence. He also joined with Molina in editing the pro-independence newspapers *El Editor Constitucional* and *El Genio de la Libertad*. When Barrundia opposed annexation to Mexico, Captain General Vicente Filísola branded him a terrorist and "dangerous subject." Upon the separation of Central America from Mexico in 1823, Barrundia served on the Council of Government (1823–1825) and was a coauthor of the Constitution of 1824. In 1825 he was elected as the first vice president of the United Provinces of Central America but refused the office.

Barrundia's erudite writings in periodicals, several of which he edited, made him one of the most influential liberals of his era. His strident, uncompromising liberalism made him appear arrogant to some, but he was foremost among the so-called *exaltados,* or *fiebres,* of the early national period. He served briefly as president of the United Provinces (26 June 1829–16 September 1830), but it was in the legislatures of both Central America and Guatemala that his leadership was most prominent. In the election of 1830, Francisco Morazán defeated him for the presidency of Central America, but the speech Barrundia delivered in turning over the office of president to Morazán was eloquent and gracious. He was elected governor of Guatemala in the same year, but he refused that office, preferring to remain in the legislature. His essays and other political writings formed a major part of the liberal polemic in Guatemala for the first thirty years of independence.

Under Governor Mariano Gálvez (1831–1838) Barrundia served as minister of education, and he was also the major advocate for Guatemala's 1836 adoption of Louisiana's Livingston Codes of penal law, which he translated from English. Division among the liberals led him to oppose Gálvez in 1837 and collaborate briefly with Rafael Carrera, the peasant guerrilla leader, to bring down Gálvez's government in 1838. He was unable to control the rebel caudillo, however, and spent much of the remainder of his life in exile, actively conspiring to overthrow the Conservative Carrera. He played a prominent part in the brief Liberal Revolution of 1848 in Guatemala but was once more forced into exile.

Barrundia spent his last years in Washington, where he served from 1852 until his death (in New York) as the Honduran minister to the United States. He was the leading ideologue and champion of the liberal cause in Central America and a strong supporter of Francisco Morazán and Central American union.

See also **Guatemala.**

BIBLIOGRAPHY

David Vela, *Barrundia ante el espejo de su tiempo,* 2 vols. (1956–1957), is the standard work on Barrundia. In English, Mario Rodríguez, *The Cádiz Experiment in Central America, 1808 to 1826* (1978), and *A Palmerstonian Diplomat in Central America* (1964), both contain insight on Barrundia's career, as does Ralph Lee Woodward, Jr., *Rafael Carrera and the Emergence of the Republic of Guatemala, 1821–1871* (1993).

RALPH LEE WOODWARD JR.

BARRUNDIA, JUAN (1788–c. 1843).

Juan Barrundia (*b.* 8 October 1788; *d.* c. 1843), first governor of the state of Guatemala (12 October 1824–6 September 1826) following its organization within the United Provinces of Central America in 1824. Like his better-known brother, José Francisco Barrundia, he was among the radical liberals (*fiebres*) who supported the independence movement. In 1826 federal president Manuel José Arce deposed and imprisoned him. After his release, Barrundia hid out in Suchitepéquez until Francisco Morazán's military triumph of 1829. Morazán restored Barrundia as governor of Guatemala, and Barrundia served from 30 April 1829 until 30 August 1829, when the legislature elected Pedro Molina to succeed him. Doctor Mariano Gálvez defeated Barrundia for the governorship in the election of 1831. In 1836 Barrundia presided over the federal congress in San Salvador. With a conservative change in government, he went into exile at San Cristóbal de las Casas, Chiapas, Mexico, where he died.

See also **Guatemala.**

BIBLIOGRAPHY

David Vela, *Barrundia ante el espejo de su tiempo,* 2 vols. (1956–1957).

Additional Bibliography

Flemion, Phillip F. "States' Rights and Partisan Politics: Manuel José Arce and the Central American Union." *Hispanic American Historical Review* 53 (November 1974): 600-618.

RALPH LEE WOODWARD JR.

BASADRE, JORGE (1903–1980). Jorge Basadre was Peru's most prolific and renowned twentieth-century historian. Born in Tacna on February 12, 1903, he was educated in the schools of Lima and at the National University of San Marcos, where he earned the LittD and LLD degrees. In 1928 he joined the Faculty of Letters at San Marcos as professor of history and then, in 1931, the Faculty of Law. In addition to teaching, he administered the university library for two terms in the 1930s and 1940s. During World War II he directed the National Library, which he successfully rebuilt after a devastating fire. More than a decade later he served as minister of education (1956–1958).

Basadre received many honors and visiting appointments that took him abroad, from institutions including the Carnegie Foundation, the Universities of Sevilla and Virginia, and the Pan American Union in Washington, D.C. During a long career that spanned sixty years, he wrote a prodigious number of historical studies, which began to appear in the 1920s. Perhaps, his most profound were *La iniciacion de la republica* (2 vols., 1929–1930), *La multitud, la ciudad y el campo en la historia del Perú* (1929), and *Perú: problema y posibilidad* (1931); a historiographical trilogy today universally acclaimed as classics.

The first edition of his monumental, three-volume *Historia de la republica del Perú, 1822–1933* appeared in 1939 and was later revised and expanded in five subsequent editions to seventeen volumes (1969). This colossal work is notable for its diversity of topics, ranging from politics, economics, and sociology to science and technology, education, and art and literature. In all of his works Basadre sought to discover what constituted the essence of Peru—the nation, its racially and ethnically diverse people, and what came to be called *lo peruano* (to be Peruvian). Always attuned to the contemporary Peruvian scene, he also wrote numerous articles for newspapers and journals both in Peru and abroad, which were collected in a single volume, *La vida y la historia* (1975). Basadre died on June 29, 1980.

See also **Peru: Peru Since Independence.**

BIBLIOGRAPHY

Basadre, Jorge. *Memoria y destino del Perú: Textos esenciales.* Edited by Ernesto Yepes del Castillo. Lima: Fondo Editorial del Congreso del Perú, 2003.

O'Phelan Godoy, Scarlett, and Mónica Ricketts Sanchez-Moreno, eds. *Homenaje a Jorge Basadre: El hombre, su obra, y su tiempo.* Lima: Instituto Riva-Agüero, Pontificia Universidad Católica del Perú, 2004.

PETER KLARÉN

BASALDÚA, HECTOR (1895–1976). Hector Basaldúa (*b.* 29 September 1895; *d.* 21 February 1976), Argentine painter, printmaker, stage designer, and illustrator. Basaldúa was born in Pergamino, Buenos Aires Province. In 1914 he studied in the capital city at the private academy of the Italian artist Bolognini, and later at the National Academy of Fine Arts under Pío Collivadino. Between 1923 and 1930 he studied in Paris under Charles Guérin, André Lothe, and Othon Friesz. Basaldúa received a gold medal for stage design at the Paris International Exhibition, in 1937, and first prize for painting at the Argentine National Salon of Plastic Arts. He visited the United States to study theater techniques in 1946, and was the designer of opera and ballet sets at the Teatro Colón, Buenos Aires. In 1980 the National Museum of Fine Arts, in Buenos Aires, held a retrospective of his works. A quick perception of reality and an unerring feeling for decorative effect are basic to Basaldúa's work. His activity as a stage designer and book illustrator gave to his work an artificial tone related to rapidly captured images.

See also **Art: The Twentieth Century; Theater.**

BIBLIOGRAPHY

Museum of Modern Art in Latin America (1985).

Vicente Gesualdo, Aldo Viglione, and Rodolfo Santos, *Diccionario de artistas plásticos en la Argentina* (1988).

AMALIA CORTINA ARAVENA

BASEBALL. *See* Sports.

BASEL, TREATY OF (1795).

Treaty of Basel (1795), an agreement between France and Spain that restored to Spain peninsular territory lost during the Franco-Spanish War (1793–1795) and gave France Santo Domingo. Spain was ill prepared for war, and when defeat appeared inevitable, Manuel de Godoy led the way out, an effort which earned him the title "Prince of Peace." His justifications for making peace were economic difficulties, a shortage of troops, and lack of money—hardly novel conditions in eighteenth-century Spain. The treaty angered the British, who subsequently renewed a vigorous and damaging attack on Spanish shipping; in October 1796, Spain declared war on Great Britain. In 1797 the British navy imposed a total blockade on Cádiz and reduced the number of ships that arrived from 171 in 1796 to nine in 1797.

See also **French-Latin American Relations; Godoy, Manuel; Santo Domingo.**

BIBLIOGRAPHY

Andrés Muriel, *Historia de Carlos IV* (1959): John Fisher, *Commercial Relations Between Spain and Spanish America in the Era of Free Trade, 1778–1796* (1985).

SUZANNE HILES BURKHOLDER

BASES ORGÁNICAS.

Bases Orgánicas, Mexican constitutional charter. In October 1841, General Antonio López de Santa Anna took control of Mexico following a successful revolt against the incumbent president, Anastasio Bustamante. To the surprise of many observers, Santa Anna permitted the election of a congress that was charged with drawing up a new constitution for the country. The congress met in 1842, but dominated by liberals and federalists, it proposed a constitution that Santa Anna did not like. Hence, as he had done in 1834, he used the army to force the closure of the congress. To replace it, he nominated an assembly of prominent citizens who were likewise charged with producing a new charter. They duly obliged with what was known as the Bases Orgánicas, promulgated on 14 June 1843. These comprised 202 articles that were to form the constitution of the nation. They stipulated a highly centralized government with political power firmly vested in the center and in the dominant social and financial elite. The Bases Orgánicas were replaced in 1846 when Mexico reverted to a federal form of government with the mercurial Santa Anna once again at its head.

See also **Mexico, Constitutions: Constitution of 1917; Santa Anna, Antonio López de.**

BIBLIOGRAPHY

For the text of the Bases Orgánicas, see Felipe Tena Ramírez, *Leyes fundamentales de Mexico, 1808–1971* (1971), pp. 405–436.

Additional Bibliography

Fowler, Will. *Mexico in the Age of Proposals, 1821–1853.* Westport, CT: Greenwood Press, 1998.

MICHAEL P. COSTELOE

BASQUES IN LATIN AMERICA.

People from the Basque provinces of Spain (Alva, Guizpúcoa, and Vizcaya) immigrated to the Spanish colonies from the first discoveries through the colonial and national periods. Basques established themselves in every colony and country, and to a lesser extent also in Brazil. During the colonial period Mexico received the largest number, but wherever trading possibilities prevailed these industrious and energetic Spaniards established their import-export, wholesale, retail, and artisanal operations. Some went into mining, others into agriculture. Basques became prominent in all areas of the economy, and they also held high positions in the royal bureaucracy and the clergy.

Basque migrants to Spanish America were almost always either bachelors or husbands who left their wives and families in Spain. Once they set up their businesses they routinely brought other Basques to colony and country to work for them. Intimate relatives or simply men from their hometowns or regions, these men often rose in the business and not infrequently established their own. When married Basques thrived, they usually brought their wives and families to the New World.

Most Basques resided in port towns and the larger interior urban centers. It was there that trading and business opportunities held the most promise for them. A smaller number migrated to rural areas and established agricultural enterprises, and some of these developed into large and influential holdings. Sometimes Basque merchants of prominence purchased landed estates for the social prestige conveyed by land ownership but also to add real property to their portfolios to use as collateral for loans and as tangible wealth to bequeath to their families. In 1767 the Spanish crown sold off the estates of the Jesuits. Some Basque merchants, especially in Chile, purchased their large and highly productive landed properties. Some also purchased titles of Castile, thus becoming nobles.

Basques were also enormously influential through the trading companies they formed to conduct trade between Spain and the colonies under the protection of royal monopolies. The most famous was the Royal Guipuzcoan Company of Caracas, established in 1728 to conduct trade with Venezuela. Because of its success, other trading companies were formed. Wherever they traded in the colonies they established offices and agents and thus further increased the Basque presence in the colonies.

Wherever Basques resided in considerable numbers they formed confraternities that served their religious and social needs. They have continued to form Basque associations through the modern period. In many of the Spanish colonies, Basque merchants and employees introduced their game of *pelota*, the forerunner of jai alai. After work Basques often took vigorous exercise playing this fast and difficult game.

Compared to Spaniards from other parts of Spain, the Basques were small in number but distinguished in accomplishment. Their greatest relative influence came during the colonial period. The enterprise of empire, with its restrictions on trade and foreign immigration, benefited the Basques. After independence their influence continued, but they were never again so distinctively prominent. One reason for this is that the Basques attempted to secure their place in society by forming large family networks, preferably with other Basque families but sometimes with non-Basques.

See also **Spain.**

BIBLIOGRAPHY

Azcona Pastor, José Manuel. *Possible Paradises: Basque Emigration to Latin America*, translated by Roland Vásquez. Reno: University of Nevada Press, 2004.

JAY KINSBRUNER

BASSOLS, NARCISO (1897–1959).

Narciso Bassols (*b*. 22 October 1897; *d*. 24 July 1959), Mexican intellectual and public official, a member of the intellectual generation of 1915, whose leaders, the "Seven Wise Men," included Alfonso Caso y Andrade, Manuel Gómez Morín, and Vicente Lombardo Toledano.

Born in Tenango del Valle, Bassols was the great-nephew of President Sebastián Lerdo de Tejada and the son of a humble judge, Narciso Bassols. He attended the National Preparatory School in Mexico City (1911–1915), and graduated from the National School of Law on 29 May 1920, after which he taught at both institutions. At the law school he made his mark as a brilliant professor, and scores of his students went on to become leading public officials. As dean of the law school from 1928 to 1929, he attempted to introduce academic reforms, including a trimester system, which provoked a student rebellion. Meanwhile, in addition to his academic duties, he wrote the agrarian law of 1927. He continued teaching law, becoming professor of constitutional law and of writs and guarantees, but left teaching in 1931 to pursue a career in public life.

Bassols employed his multiple talents in reconstructing Mexico's modern banking system in 1930 and 1931. He also became a key cabinet member in the six-year interregnum between the presidencies of Plutarco Elías Calles and Lázaro Cárdenas, serving as secretary of public education (1931–1934) and secretary of government (1934). He served as secretary of the treasury in the first cabinet of Cárdenas, but believing loyalty and integrity to be more important than political expediency, he resigned in 1935, when Cárdenas broke with Calles. Bassols later served as ambassador to London, Paris, and Moscow. Disenchanted with the direction of public policy, in 1941 he founded the League of Political Action with Vicente Lombardo Toledano, and in 1947 he was one of the founders of the Popular Party, the forerunner of the Popular Socialist Party, which for many years was the only leftist opposition party in Mexico.

See also **Mexico: Since 1910.**

BIBLIOGRAPHY

Narciso Bassols: En memoria (1960).

John W. F. Dulles, *Yesterday in Mexico: A Chronicle of the Revolution, 1919–1936* (1961).

Narciso Bassols, *Obras* (1964).

Roderic Ai Camp, *Mexican Political Biographies, 1884–1935* (1991).

Additional Bibliography

Bassols, Narciso. *Narciso Bassols, pensamiento y acción: Antología.* Introduction by Alonso Aguilar Monteverde Mexico: Fondo de Cultura Económica, 1995.

RODERIC AI CAMP

BASSO MAGLIO, VICENTE (1889–1961).

Vicente Basso Maglio (*b.* 22 December 1889; *d.* 15 September 1961), Uruguayan poet, writer, journalist, and editor. His career in journalism began when he was an editor for *La Reforma, El Día,* and *La Razón,* all in Montevideo. Subsequently he was director of *El espectador* and its subsidiary broadcasting system, Difusoras del Uruguay. Basso Maglio's most acclaimed poetry collection, *Canción de los pequeños círculos y de los grandes horizontes* (1927), features the poet's transcendental, mystical comprehension of the relationship between man and God. His dense, hermetic expression sometimes reveals an excessive confidence in abstract symbols to communicate the complex web of relationships linking inner and outer reality. Other works by Basso Maglio include the acclaimed *La expresión heróica* (1928) and *Tragedia de la imagen* (1930), a work on modern art.

See also **Uruguay: The Twentieth Century.**

BIBLIOGRAPHY

Sarah Bollo, *Literatura uruguaya, 1807–1965,* vol. 2 (1965).

Francisco Aguilera and Georgette Magassy Dorn, *The Archive of Hispanic Literature on Tape: A Descriptive Guide* (1974).

WILLIAM H. KATRA

BASTIDAS, RODRIGO DE (c. 1460–1526).

Rodrigo de Bastidas (*b.* ca. 1460; *d.* 1526), early Spanish explorer. With a royal commission to explore and trade, Bastidas sailed from Cádiz in 1500 or 1501 with three ships carrying more than fifty people, including some women. He was neither a pilot, an adventurer, nor a man of arms; rather, he was a successful and respected notary in Triana (Seville). He was also unusual among leaders of early expeditions because of his relatively humane treatment of the Indians. Exploring regions not previously seen by Europeans, he discovered the Magdalena River, the Gulf of Urabá, and eastern Panama. By contrast with most later expeditions in the area, his was remarkable for its comparatively good relations with the local inhabitants, whose wealth of gold and pearls was willingly traded for Spanish trinkets. Though his ships were wrecked, Bastidas salvaged seventy-five pounds of gold and pearls, returning to Spain a rich man. He moved his family to Hispaniola, where he prospered as a cattleman. Made governor of Santa Marta in 1520, Bastidas was assassinated in Cuba by an ambitious lieutenant.

See also **Explorers and Exploration: Spanish America.**

BIBLIOGRAPHY

Bastidas is discussed at some length in Hubert Howe Bancroft, *History of Central America,* vol. 1 (1882). See also Kathleen Romoli, *Balboa of Darien, Discoverer of the Pacific* (1953), and Carl Ortwin Sauer, *The Early Spanish Main* (1966).

Additional Bibliography

Bermúdez Bermúdez. *Arturo E. Don Rodrigo de Bastidas, adelantado de Santa Marta.* Colombia: Fondo Mixto de Promoción de la Cultura y las Artes de Magdalena, 2000.

WILLIAM L. SHERMAN

BASURTO, LUIS (1920–1990).

Luis Basurto (*b.* 11 March 1920; *d.* 9 July 1990), Mexican playwright, actor, director, producer, and critic. A native of Mexico City, Basurto studied law, philosophy, and literature at the National Autonomous University of Mexico and began his career as a journalist. For many years he wrote film and theater reviews and a regular Thursday column in the *Crónica de México*. He was a tireless performer known throughout the Hispanic world. When he was awarded the Juan Ruiz de Alarcón Prize for literature shortly before his death, it was fitting tribute to a man who brought enormous talent and energy to the Mexican theater for more than fifty years.

Several of Basurto's twenty-six plays, some of which date from the 1940s, have become classics of the Mexican repertory. In more than 7,000 performances *Cada quien su vida* (1955) has shown with compassion and understanding the realities of Mexico's marginal classes during a New Year's Eve celebration. Other major works include *Los reyes del mundo* (1959), *Con la frente en el polvo* (1967), and *El candidato de Dios* (1986). At the time of his death Basurto was directing *Corona de sangre* (1990), the history of Padre Pro, who was executed for treason without trial in 1927 but had recently been beatified by the Vatican. Many of his plays have strongly Catholic themes. Basurto was adept at mixing sensational and often degenerate aspects of society with a strong social message.

See also **Journalism in Mexico; Theater.**

BIBLIOGRAPHY

Frank Dauster, *Historia del teatro hispanoamericano (siglos XIX y XX)*, 2d ed. (1973).

Additional Bibliography

Pacheco, Cristina, and Mauricio Sanders, eds. *Al pie de la letra: Entrevistas con escritores*. México: Fondo de Cultura Económica, 2005.

GEORGE WOODYARD

BATÁN GRANDE.

Batán Grande, region in the mid–La Leche Valley at the northern end of the north coast of Peru. Much of the area comprises the *yunga* life zone, which is characterized by year-round humidity and intense sun. From the early twentieth century until 1969, Batán Grande was owned by the Juan Aurich hacienda, which produced cacao, citrus and other fruits, and rice. Since the 1969 agrarian reform, intensive commercial cultivation of sugarcane has predominated. In 1991, 13,400 hectares of the Batán Grande became a protected reserve. This national park attracts both scholars and tourists from around the world interested in the archeological ruins, flora, and fauna found in the region.

The extensive forest of algarrobo (*Prosopis pallida*) situated in the western portion of Batán Grande is the largest (at least 25 square miles) of its kind remaining on the Peruvian coast today. Protected as the Poma National Archaeological and Ecological Reserve, it provides a refuge area for diverse fauna that has largely disappeared elsewhere on the coast, such as iguana, squirrels, anteaters, parrots and numerous other bird species, and even boa constrictors. The reserve also protects at least thirty major archaeological sites (spanning ca. 2000 BCE to 1532 CE), including the site of Sicán, the capital of the Middle Sicán religious state that controlled or influenced much of the Peruvian coast from circa 900 to 1100 CE. Cemeteries around these mounds contain numerous shaft tombs endowed with impressive quantities of precious and base metal objects. Organized grave looting, beginning in the 1930s—some of the worst ever seen in the New World—has brought infamy to the region.

Batán Grande was a major pre–Hispanic metallurgical center from circa 900 CE up to the time of the Spanish Conquest. In fact, the name Batán Grande derives from the numerous metal–working tools in its vicinity. The *batán* is a large anvil stone with a shallow central concavity used in conjunction with a rocking stone, called a *chungo*, to crush ore for and slag from arsenical copper (a type of bronze) smelting.

At the time of the Conquest, local inhabitants spoke the now extinct Muchik language and belonged to the ethnic polities of Jayanca and Túcume, according to Sebastián de la Gama's *Visita de Jayanca* (1540).

See also **Sicán.**

BIBLIOGRAPHY

Paul Kosok, *Life, Land, and Water in Ancient Peru* (1965), pp. 115–180.

Susan Ramírez, "Social Frontiers and the Territorial Base of Curacazgos," in *Andean Civilization and Ecology*, edited by Shozo Masuda, Izumi Shimada, and Craig Morris (1985), pp. 423–442.

Izumi Shimada, "Temples of Time: The Ancient Burial and Religious Center of Batán Grande, Peru," in *Archaeology* 34, no. 5 (1981): 37–45.

Izumi Shimada, "Cultural Continuities and Discontinuities on the Northern North Coast, Middle–Late Horizons," in *The Northern Dynasties: Kingship and Statecraft in Chimor,* edited by Michael E. Moseley and Alana Cordy–Collins (1990), pp. 297–392.

Izumi Shimada and Jorge Montenegro, *Cultura Sicán: Dios, riqueza y poder en la Costa Norte del Perú.* Lima: Fundación del Banco Continental para el Fomento de la Educación y la Cultura, Edubanco, 1995.

IZUMI SHIMADA

BATISTA, CÍCERO ROMÃO (1844–1934).

Cícero Romão Batista (Padre Cícero) (*b.* 24 March 1844; *d.* 20 July 1934), Brazilian priest and political leader of Ceará. Born at Crato in Juàzeiro, in 1865 Cícero entered the seminary at Fortaleza and was one of its first graduates. Ordained in 1870, he began his clerical career as a teacher in Crato. Two years later he was appointed to the chaplaincy in Juàzeiro. In 1889, a communion wafer Cícero administered reportedly turned to blood in the mouth of one of his parishioners. This "miracle" gave him religious power, which he later converted into political strength; he became one of the most influential political bosses in the Northeast, and the village of Juàzeiro became a site for religious pilgrimages. Although the church disavowed the "miracle" and restricted his religious activities, it made no attempt to remove him, for the peasants of the interior regarded him as a saint. Although he clashed with both ecclesiastical and governmental authority, his movement did not seek to destroy political or religious order, but rather attempted to improve the social and economic conditions of his followers. Juàzeiro do Norte became the economic and industrial center of the backlands under his leadership. His followers marched on Fortaleza, bringing about the downfall of its state government. Padre Cícero continues to be regarded as an unofficial saint in the Northeast,

and each year large numbers of pilgrims gather at his grave in Juàzeiro.

See also **Catholic Church: The Modern Period.**

BIBLIOGRAPHY

Ralph Della Cava, *Miracle at Joaseiro* (1970).

Ronald M. Schneider, *"Order and Progress": A Political History of Brazil* (1991).

Additional Bibliography

Aquino, Pedro Ferreira de. *O santo do meu nordeste: Padre Cícero Romão Batista.* São Paulo: Letras & Letras, 1997.

MICHAEL L. JAMES

BATISTA Y ZALDÍVAR, FULGENCIO

(1901–1973). Fulgencio Batista y Zaldívar (*b.* 16 January 1901; *d.* 6 August 1973), the Cuban army's strongman in the 1930s, elected president in the 1940s, and dictator in the 1950s. The son of a farm and railroad laborer, Batista was born in Banes, Oriente Province. He spent his early years in poverty and attended a Quaker missionary school. At twenty he joined the Cuban army because it offered an opportunity for upward mobility. He attended evening classes at the National School of Journalism, from which he graduated. In 1928 he was promoted to sergeant and assigned as stenographer at Camp Columbia in Havana.

The deepening economic depression and the overthrow of Gerardo Machado's dictatorship in 1933 had released a wave of uncontrolled anger and anxiety. Unhappy with a proposed reduction in pay and an order restricting their promotions, the lower echelons of the army began to conspire. On 4 September 1933, Batista, together with anti-Machado student leaders, assumed the leadership of the movement, arrested army officers, and overthrew the provisional government of Carlos Manuel de Céspedes. They appointed a five-man junta (the Pentarchy) to rule Cuba and, on 10 September, named Ramón Grau San Martín as provisional president. Grau's nationalistic and revolutionary regime was opposed by the United States, which refused to recognize it. Batista soon became a colonel and chief of staff of the army.

On 14 January 1934, the alliance between students and the military collapsed. Batista forced Grau to resign, thus frustrating the revolutionary process that had begun with Machado's overthrow. Batista ruled through puppet presidents until 1940, when he was elected president. Desiring to win popular support, he sponsored an impressive body of welfare legislation. Public administration, health, education, and public works improved. He legalized the Cuban Communist Party and in 1943 established diplomatic relations with the Soviet Union. Immediately following the Pearl Harbor attack, Batista brought Cuba into World War II on the Allied side. Air and naval bases were made available to the United States, which purchased all of Cuba's sugar production and provided generous loans and grants. In 1944 Batista allowed the election of his former rival, Grau San Martín.

Batista settled in Daytona Beach, Florida, where he wrote *Sombras de América* (published in Mexico in 1946). In 1948, while still in Florida, he was elected to the Cuban Senate from Santa Clara province. He returned to Cuba that same year, organized his own party, and announced his presidential candidacy for the June 1952 elections. On 10 March 1952, however, Batista, joined by a group of army officers, overthrew the constitutionally elected regime of President Carlos Prío Socarrás. Batista suspended Congress and the 1940 constitution, canceled the elections, and dissolved all political parties. University students soon began to show their opposition by rioting and demonstrating. On 26 July 1953, young revolutionaries led by Fidel Castro unsuccessfully attacked the Moncada military barracks in Oriente Province. Some of the attackers were killed and others, including Castro, were jailed.

In a rigged election in November 1954, Batista was reelected for a four-year term. Corruption in his administration reached unprecedented proportions, leading students to increase their protests. After his release from prison in 1956, the revolutionary leader Fidel Castro went to Mexico to prepare an expedition that landed in Cuba in December of that year and began guerrilla operations. On 13 March 1957, an attack on the Presidential Palace by students and followers of deposed President Prío nearly succeeded in killing Batista. The Batista government met terrorism with counterterrorism.

By 1958 national revulsion against Batista had developed. Finally, defections from the army precipitated the fall of the regime on 1 January 1959. Batista escaped to the Dominican Republic and later to Madeira. He died at Guadalmina, near Marbella, Spain.

See also **Cuba, Revolutions: Revolution of 1933; Cuba, Twenty-Sixth of July Movement; Military Dictatorships: Since 1945.**

BIBLIOGRAPHY

Hugh Thomas, *Cuba: The Pursuit of Freedom* (1971).

Jaime Suchlicki, *Historical Dictionary of Cuba* (1988) and *Cuba: From Columbus to Castro,* 3d ed. (1990).

Additional Bibliography

Argote-Freyre, Frank. *Fulgencio Batista.* New Brunswick, NJ: Rutgers University Press, 2006.

Fuente, Alejandro de la. *A Nation for All: Race, Inequality, and Politics in Twentieth-Century Cuba.* Chapel Hill: University of North Carolina Press, 2001.

Whitney, Robert. *State and Revolution in Cuba: Mass Mobilization and Political Change, 1920-1940.* Chapel Hill: University of North Carolina Press, 2001.

JAIME SUCHLICKI

BATLLE, LORENZO (1810–1887).

Lorenzo Batlle (*b.* 10 August 1810; *d.* 8 May 1887), general and president of Uruguay (1868–1872). When the Great War (Guerra Grande) began in 1839, Batlle became a captain on the side of the Colorado Party (Unitario) and played an active role in the circle associated with the *Defensa* of Montevideo. From 1847 to 1851, he was minister of war and the navy in the cabinet of Joaquín Suárez and became a central figure in the postwar period, which was characterized by political experimentation, efforts toward a stable peace, and the ongoing debate concerning political parties. First he joined the ranks of the so-called Conservative Party, a Colorado group with an oligarchic slant and strong support from the military and financial sectors. He subsequently became a member of the Liberal Union and then returned to the Colorados. He became minister of finance in the government of Gabriel Antonio Pereira (1856–1857) and minister of war and the navy again during the dictatorship of Venancio Flores (1865–1868).

Batlle was elected president in 1868, introducing a "politics of partisanship" with a decided elitist bent. During his administration, he faced a grave economic crisis, permanent conflict with his party's regional caudillos, and the outbreak of the so-called Revolution of the Lances led by the Blanco caudillo Timoteo Aparicio. After his presidency, he went into a long period of retirement from public life, interrupted only in 1886 when he became a leader of the Quebracho Revolution against the dictatorship of General Máximo Santos. Batlle died in poverty a year later.

See also **Uruguay, Political Parties: Colorado Party.**

BIBLIOGRAPHY

Juan E. Pivel Devoto, *Historia de los partidos políticos en el Uruguay,* 2 vols. (1942).

José P. Barrán and Benjamín Nahum, *Historia rural del Uruguay moderno,* vol. 1 (1967).

Lucía Sala De Tourón and Rosa Alonso Eloy, *El Uruguay comercial, pastoril y caudillesco,* vol. 2 (1990).

GERARDO CAETANO

BATLLE BERRES, LUIS CONRADO

(1897–1964). Luis Conrado Batlle Berres (*b.* 1897; *d.* July 1964), president of Uruguay (1947–1951). Luis Batlle Berres was the nephew of the great leader of the Colorado Party and founder of modern Uruguay, José Batlle y Ordóñez. He began his political career in the 1920s as a deputy in Congress for Montevideo. Elected vice president in 1946, he succeeded to the presidency upon the death of Tomás Berreta. Smart and ambitious, "Lusito," as he was known, found himself constrained by the Batllist faithful, the adoring but increasingly conservative followers of José Batlle led by his sons Lorenzo and César. In 1948 Batlle Berres had signaled his independence by starting his own newspaper, *Acción,* as a voice separate from *El Día,* the Colorado newspaper founded by José Batlle and run by his sons. He thus distanced his own political movement, List 15, from his cousins' List 14. His faction proved to be dominant within the party in the 1950 elections.

Batlle Berres favored the continuation of a presidential system, even in the face of an almost religious demand by the Batllist faithful to create a *Colegiado* (collegial executive system). Batlle Berres's urban populist coalition had swept his faction to such a convincing victory in 1950 that the Blanco (National Party) leader, Luis Alberto de Herrera, was willing to join with Lorenzo and César in support of a collegial executive in order to prevent a new political dynasty. Unable to withstand the List 14 and Herrerist calls for constitutional reform, Batlle Berres supported the 1951 plebiscite that gave Uruguay a collegial executive system under the new 1952 Constitution. Nevertheless, Batlle Berres's List 15 continued to dominate Colorado voting, giving him the most powerful voice in Uruguayan politics through the mid-1950s. Following his death, the leadership of List 15 passed to his son Jorge Batlle, and this sector of the party became known as Radical Batllism.

See also **Batllismo; Uruguay, Political Parties: Colorado Party.**

BIBLIOGRAPHY

Philip R. Taylor, Jr., *Government and Politics of Uruguay* (1960).

Santiago Rompani, ed., *Luis Batlle: Pensamiento y acción,* 2 vols. (1965).

Martin Weinstein, *Uruguay: The Politics of Failure* (1975).

MARTIN WEINSTEIN

BATLLE Y ORDÓÑEZ, JOSÉ (1856–1929). José Batlle y Ordóñez (*b.* 21 May 1856; *d.* 20 October 1929), journalist and president of Uruguay (1903–1907, 1911–1915). One of the most important and influential personalities in Uruguayan history, José Batlle y Ordóñez's first avocation was philosophy rather than politics. With an initial Catholic education, he was influenced as a youth by the ideas of Karl Christian Friedrich Kraus. His transition to a rationalist, spiritualist philosophy would mark his later public career. Also early in his life, he began a lifelong journalism career, writing for such periodicals as *La Razón, La Lucha,* and *El Espíritu Nuevo.*

FROM ANTIMILITARISM TO SOCIAL REFORM

Batlle y Ordóñez began his political life between 1876 and 1886, confronting the military dictatorships of Lorenzo Latorre and Máximo Santos. He participated in the 1886 Quebracho Revolution against Santos, which, despite military defeat, marked the beginning of a political transition toward civilian rule. In this same year he founded the newspaper *El Día*, which served as a mouthpiece for the Colorado Party. From its pages, he led the opposition to the Santos regime. After its early financial problems and government repression, *El Día*'s low price and street distribution caused it to become the foremost newspaper in Uruguayan history.

With Santos out of power, Batlle y Ordóñez—part of the group of allies of then Minister Julio Herrera y Obes—was appointed as political chief of the department of Minas by President Máximo Tajes. This was his first position as a public servant, and it lasted only six months. Already deeply involved in the political militancy of the Colorado Party, he was elected to the Chamber of Deputies in 1893 and the Senate in 1896. He opposed the oligarchic practices of President Herrera y Obes (1890–1894) and worked intensely on the organization of a popular faction within the Colorado Party. He adamantly opposed the presidency of Juan Idiarte Borda, who, assassinated in 1897, never finished his term.

Batlle y Ordóñez supported the rise to power of Juan L. Cuestas, which began a dramatic political ascent that would win him the presidency of the Senate. He supported the 10 February 1898 coup led by Cuestas and formed part of the interim state council. He was considered a favorite to succeed to the presidency in 1903, but in 1901 he seemed to lose all chances when he strongly rejected the Blancos (Nationalists) and was displaced from the presidency of the Senate. Cuestas withdrew his support for Batlle y Ordóñez due to the latter's proven independence of character. Conservative Uruguayans also began to oppose Batlle. They saw him as a "war candidate," due to his growing ill-will toward the Nationalists and his doctrinaire defense of the "politics of partisanship," which threatened the system of *coparticipación*. They also mistrusted some of the reformist ideas he outlined in his critiques of the gold-supporting oligarchy in 1891 and in his editorials supporting workers' movements in 1895.

GOVERNMENT AND CIVIL WAR

With arduous effort, Batlle y Ordóñez won over the internal factions of the Colorados along with a group of dissident Blancos. This assured him a majority among the legislators. He was elected president by the General Assembly on 1 March 1903. His first presidency was marked by the Blanco uprisings of 1903 and 1904 led by the caudillo Aparicio Saravia. Batlle y Ordóñez was also confronted by two antagonistic visions of the political future of the country: the continuance and deepening of *coparticipación* versus the "politics of partisanship." Saravia's death in 1904 marked the end of the revolution and the consolidation of "partisanship."

Reformist measures adopted during the first administration of Batlle y Ordóñez included the abolition of the death penalty, legalization of divorce by mutual consent, a law of labor regulation, expansion of public education, creation of the Colleges of Commerce and of Agronomy and Veterinary Science, and a plan for public works and roads. At the end of his presidential term in 1907, Batlle y Ordóñez left almost immediately on a trip to Europe and the Near East that lasted almost four years. In 1907 he participated in the Second International Peace Conference in The Hague. While visiting many European countries, he studied their social conflicts and joined in ideological debates, thereby polishing many of the ideas and proposals that constituted the reformist plan he would implement during his second presidential term. He returned to Uruguay in February 1911 and on 1 March was again elected president by an overwhelming majority of legislators in the General Assembly. (The Blanco Party had abstained from the legislative elections in 1910 after another attempt at revolution failed.)

THE RISE AND FALL OF REFORM

The second presidency of Batlle y Ordóñez constituted the decisive period during which his reformist plan was implemented. The debate over a broad range of initiatives dominated the public stage. These reforms generated strong resistance from the Blanco Party (which abandoned its abstentionist posture in 1913), from management guilds, from foreign capital (especially British), and from the army.

The Batllist plan was organized around six major reforms. First, economic reform was based on the nationalization of strategic sectors and industrialization through protectionist legislation. Second, social reform centered on "critical support" for unions, "protective" social legislation for workers and other philanthropic measures. Third, rural reform was aimed at the gradual elimination of large ranches, the promotion of a more balanced and automated livestock industry, and the transformation of rural poverty. Fourth, fiscal reform sought tax increases for the wealthy, a decrease in taxes on consumption, the use of economic pressure as an instrument of social justice, and the stimulation of economic development. Fifth, moral reform promoted the concept of a cosmopolitan nation, secular politics, and various feminist principles. Finally, political reform promoted public debate and supported proposals that the executive branch be organized in a collegiate system.

Not all of these reforms came to fruition, due in some cases to strong opposition and in others to ambiguity among the Batllists themselves. Also, proposals for political reform did not include essential democratic changes that the opposition demanded, such as the secret ballot, proportional representation, and guarantees against electoral fraud. The essence of the reform plan was implemented before the democratization of the political system, which occurred with the second constitution in 1919. Batllism suffered a defeat in the decisive elections of 30 July 1916 for members of the National Constituent Assembly. Batlle's successor to the presidency, Feliciano Viera, adopted the so-called "halt politics," which drastically decreased proposals for reform. From 1916 to the end of the 1920s, the predominant atmosphere in public policy favored putting the brakes on reform. Batllism gradually lost its political initiative and strength.

THE LAST YEARS
Although with less power than earlier, Batlle y Ordóñez continued to be politically active throughout the last years of his life. He was one of the fundamental backers of the political accord from which sprang the new constitution. In 1921 and 1927 he served briefly as president of the National Council of Administration, the central component of the new collegiate executive branch. He was a major force behind the effort to attain electoral unity among distinct Colorado Party factions. He made exhausting tours of the country, seeking grassroots support for his reforms, and until his death he led the often acerbic debates in the inner recesses of the Colorado Party. Even in the midst of political uproar, he constantly promoted political debate from the pages of El Día.

Batlle y Ordóñez died just a few days before the great stock market crash on Wall Street. The Great Depression had its effects on Uruguay, among them putting a halt to a good part of the reformist projects of Batllism. Most of the first three decades of the twentieth century in Uruguay are referred to by historians as the Batllist Era. Whether in a spirit of polemic or agreement, the ideas and symbols associated with Batlle y Ordóñez remain present in the Uruguayan public debate.

See also **Uruguay, Political Parties: Colorado Party.**

BIBLIOGRAPHY

Milton Vanger, *José Batlle y Ordóñez of Uruguay, the Creator of His Times, 1902–1907* (1963) and *El país modelo* (1983).

Carlos Real De Azúa, *El impulso y su freno* (1964).

Göran Lindahl, *Batlle, fundador de la democracia en el Uruguay* (1971).

José P. Barrán and Benjamín Nahum, *Historia rural del Uruguay moderno*, vols. 5–7 (1977–1978), and *Batlle, los estancieros y el Imperio Británico*, 8 vols. (1979–1987).

Carlos Zubillaga, *El reto financiero: Deuda externa y desarrollo en el Uruguay, 1903–1933* (1982); *El primer batllismo: Cinco enfoques polémicos* (1985); Raúl Jacob, *Modelo batllista: ¿Variacíon sobre un viejo tema?* (1988).

Gerardo Caetano, *La República Conservadora, 1916–1929*, 2 vols. (1992–1993).

Additional Bibliography

Buscio, Jorge. *José Batlle y Ordóñez: Uruguay a la vanguardia del mundo*. Montevideo: Editorial Fin de Siglo, 2004.

Peluas, Daniel. *José Batlle y Ordóñez: el hombre*. Montevideo: Editorial Fin de Siglo, 2001.

GERARDO CAETANO

BATLLISMO. Batllismo, the political philosophy and social program of José Batlle y Ordóñez (1856–1929), president of Uruguay (1903–1907,

1911–1915). It was a philosophy that emphasized nationalism and social, political, and economic development. While recognizing economic inequalities, Batlle did not subscribe to Marxist interpretations of class struggle. For him, the best way to solve the differences in society was by creating an interventionist state to regulate the imbalances of society and work for a more equitable distribution of wealth. *Batllismo* held that a modern state could operate only with a politically active population aware of its rights and obligations. Therefore, elections and mechanisms for political participation were considered to be very important. While in office, Batlle enacted an extensive social program and nationalized industries.

See also **Batlle y Ordóñez, José.**

BIBLIOGRAPHY

Roberto B. Giudici, *Batlle y el batllismo* (1928), and *Los fundamentos del batllismo*, 2d ed. (1947).

Martin Weinstein, *Uruguay: The Politics of Failure* (1975).

Additional Bibliography

Claps, Manuel Arturo, and Mario Daniel Lamas. *El batllismo como ideología.* Montevideo: Cal y Canto, 1999.

Panizza, Francisco E. *Uruguay: Batllismo y después. Pacheco, militares, y tupamaros en las crisis del Uruguay batllista.* Montevideo: Ediciones de la Banda Oriental, 1990.

Pelúas, Daniel. *José Batlle y Ordóñez: El hombre.* Montevideo: Editorial Fin de Siglo, 2001.

JUAN MANUEL PÉREZ

BATON ROUGE, BATTLE OF.

Battle of Baton Rouge, a conflict between British and Spanish troops on 21 September 1779. Baton Rouge, Louisiana, which had formerly been French, became part of British West Florida in the 1763 Treaty of Paris. Spain decided to take the frontier post when it declared war on Britain during the American Revolution. After taking Fort Bute, General Bernardo de Gálvez led a force of over 1,000 men from New Orleans in an attack on the British fort commanded by Lieutenant Alexander Dickson. Gálvez laid siege to the main redoubt with ten heavy cannons during the night of 20 September and began a devastating bombardment the following morning. With the fort damaged beyond repair, the British surrendered that afternoon with

little loss of life on either side. Dickson also surrendered British claims to Natchez, thereby giving Spain the entire Mississippi River Valley.

See also **Spanish Empire.**

BIBLIOGRAPHY

John W. Caughey, *Bernardo de Gálvez in Louisiana, 1776–1783* (1934).

Jack D. L. Holmes, *The 1779 "Marcha de Gálvez": Louisiana's Giant Step Forward in the American Revolution* (1974).

J. Barton Starr, *The American Revolution in West Florida* (1976).

Additional Bibliography

Beerman, Eric. *España y la independencia de Estados Unidos.* Madrid: Editorial MAPFRE, 1992.

Chavez, Thomas E. *Spain and the Independence of the United States: An Intrinsic Gift.* Albuquerque: University of New Mexico Press, 2002.

LaFarelle, Lorenzo G. *Bernardo de Gálvez: Hero of the American Revolution.* Austin: Eakin Press, 1992.

LIGHT TOWNSEND CUMMINS

BATRES JUARROS, LUIS (1802–1862).

Luis Batres Juarros (*b.* 7 May 1802; *d.* 17 June 1862), Guatemalan politician and businessman. Born in Guatemala City, Batres Juarros received a law degree from San Carlos University in 1823. He fought against Francisco Morazán in the civil war and then immigrated to the United States for a time. After 1839 he became a very important figure among supporters of the Guatemalan conservative regime. He served several terms as a representative in Congress and was a minister of war, of finance, and of the interior. He also held the positions of mayor of Guatemala City (1845), state advisor, and attaché to the consulate of commerce. He played a key role in the drafting of the Constitution of the Republic in 1851, reorganized the mint, and defended the reestablishment of the Jesuits in 1851.

See also **Guatemala.**

BIBLIOGRAPHY

Noticia biográfica del Señor Don Luis Batres (1862).

Lorenzo Montúfar y Rivera Maestre, *Reseña histórica de Centro América*, 7 vols. (1878–1888).

Miguel García Granados, *Memorias del General García Granados* (1952).

Mario Rodríguez, *A Palmerstonian Diplomat in Central America: Frederick Chatfield, Esq.* (1964).

Luis Beltranena Sinibaldi, *Fundación de la República de Guatemala* (1971).

Pedro Tobar Cruz, *Los montañeses* (1971).

Agustín Estrada Monroy, ed., *Hombres, fechas y documentos de la patria* (1977).

                    ARTURO TARACENA ARRIOLA

BATRES MONTÚFAR, JOSÉ (1809–1844).

José Batres Montúfar (*b.* 18 March 1809; *d.* 9 July 1844), Guatemalan writer, soldier, and politician. Born in San Salvador, in 1824 he entered the Cadet School, and with the rank of second lieutenant of artillery, he participated in the Federal War at the side of President Arce. He was taken prisoner in the battle of Mexicanos in 1828. While in prison he learned English and began to read Byron, who inspired his later literary work. In 1829 he returned to Guatemala and began his career as a writer. Of primary note are his lyrical compositions in the romantic style, especially *Tradiciones de Guatemala*, which consists of three satirical pieces—the last unfinished—in which he describes the lifestyle and mentality of the dominant class in Guatemala at the beginning of the nineteenth century. These are written along the lines of the *Novelle galanti* of Giovanni Casti.

In 1836, Batres Montúfar graduated from the Academía de Estudios, and as a surveyor he participated in the 1837 engineering commission that, under the direction of John Baily, explored the San Juan River of Nicaragua for the possible development of an interoceanic canal. His younger brother Juan died during this endeavor. He was named political head of Amatitlán in 1839, and in 1840 fought as captain of artillery, defending Guatemala City against Francisco Morazán. In 1842 he was elected as a representative to Congress from the department of San Marcos.

See also **Guatemala.**

BIBLIOGRAPHY

José Batres Montúfar, *Poesías de José Batres y Montúfar* (1845).

Fernando Cruz, "El poeta D. José Batres," in *Biografías de literatos nacionales,* vol. 1 (1889), pp. 153–260.

Antonio Batres Jáuregui, *José Batres Montúfar* (1910).

José Arzú, *Pepe Batres íntimo. Su familia, su correspondencia, sus papeles* (1940).

Adrián Recinos, "Introducción," in *Poesías de José Batres Montúfar* (1940).

Thomas Irving, "Pepe Batres, poeta de Guatemala," in *Revista Iberoamericana* 23, no. 45 (1958): 93–111.

Additional Bibliography

José Batres Montúfar. *Obras completas.* Guatemala: Editorial Piedra Santa, 2003.

                    ARTURO TARACENA ARRIOLA

BAUXITE INDUSTRY.

Bauxite, the commercial source of aluminum and its compounds, has been mined in and exported from Latin America since World War I. Surinam, Guyana, Jamaica, Venezuela, Brazil, and on a much lesser scale Argentina, Haiti, Mexico, and the Dominican Republic have been or are involved in the bauxite-aluminum industry.

Early known South American deposits of bauxite were located in northern South America. British Guiana (now Guyana) and Netherlands Guiana (now Surinam) were producing two-thirds of the world's bauxite by the end of World War II. During that war, the bauxite reserves in Jamaica were seriously assessed, and Alcan aluminum, a Canadian company, began large-scale mining development, including the construction of Port Esquivel, during the 1950s. Two U.S.-based companies, Kaiser Bauxite and Alcoa (Aluminum Company of America), began Jamaican bauxite operations in the early 1960s. Haiti and the Dominican Republic were also mining bauxite on a much smaller scale.

By the 1960s, Latin American leaders were becoming alarmed because the mining of bauxite, a nonrenewable resource, was not proving beneficial to the countries of origin. Bauxite is strip-mined, and the work is not labor intensive. The ore was being shipped overseas for processing, and aluminum prices and production were controlled by multinational corporations. Regional authorities began to negotiate for a larger share of the profit, local construction of alumina refineries and smelters, and more local control over the decision-making process. Guyana's bauxite gave rise to political maneuvers that became volatile. In 1964 the victorious political faction guaranteed Alcoa the right to the peaceful removal of bauxite at constant 1938 prices, but the People's National Congress Party won a majority in 1973 and assumed control of all foreign trade in 1974, in part to meet the government policy of gaining a larger share of bauxite profits. Jamaica, with a growing sense of nationalism, demanded—and got—a 600 percent increase in its share of the profits and the right to purchase 51 percent of the Kaiser and Reynolds operations.

Venezuela's bauxite industry was developed during the 1960s and 1970s, using power from the government-built Guri Dam on the Caroni River to process Caribbean bauxite. Venalum, a subsidiary of Corporación Venezolana de Guyana (CVG), runs the largest alumina smelter in the world, and Interalumina, another CVG unit, operates a billion-dollar alumina-processing plant built in 1983 to handle bauxite discovered at Los Pijiguaos. Thus, CVG created the first fully integrated aluminum industry in the developing world, with all three stages (bauxite mining, alumina smelting, and aluminum production) under its control. At least half of the final product is contracted to a Japanese syndicate.

Bauxite was mined in Minas Gerais, in southeastern Brazil, before 1967, but until that year, when aerial side-looking radar surveys became possible, little was known about the huge bauxite deposits in Brazil's Amazon region. Brazil's mining and aluminum-processing facilities have expanded greatly since the original Trobetas project was completed in 1979, some 540 miles west of Belém, by the Mineração Rio do Norte (MRN). Throughout the 1980s, using a variety of financial and ownership arrangements with Alcan, Billiton Metais (a Shell subsidiary), Norsk Hydro (Norway), Reynolds Alumino (a Reynolds Aluminum subsidiary), and Nippon Amazon Aluminum (Japan), several Brazilian companies began bauxite, alumina, and aluminum production in the states of Pará, São Paulo, and Rio de Janeiro for domestic use and export primarily to Japan, Norway, and the United States.

Competition in the world's bauxite-aluminum industry is intense. Guinea and Australia have developed their huge bauxite deposits, and multinational companies remain dominant. Aluminum prices are strongly affected by recessionary times. (For example, in October 1990 the price of aluminum was 88 cents per pound; by September 1991 it had fallen to 56 cents per pound.) A continuing emphasis on using recycled aluminum has also reduced world demand. Venezuela and Brazil have managed to maintain competitive prices, but Jamaican production dropped 40 percent after 1980, and Surinam, which has been plagued by recurring civil disorder since gaining independence in 1975, has been unable to guarantee delivery of the only known abrasive-grade bauxite in the Western Hemisphere. By 2005 Brazil had become the second leading producer behind Australia. Prices in the late twentieth century recovered partly due to the rapid industrialization of China, which created much higher demand. Industries that utilize this substance for precise grinding and metal finishing have thus turned to sources outside Latin America.

See also **Mining: Modern.**

BIBLIOGRAPHY

Eduardo Galeano, *Open Veins of Latin America: Five Centuries of the Pillage of a Continent* (1973).

Rosemary D. F. Bromley and Ray Bromley, *South American Development: A Geographical Introduction* (1982).

United Nations, *Latin American Development in the 1980s* (1982).

Robert N. Gwynne, *Industrialization and Urbanization in Latin America* (1986).

U.S. Department of the Interior, Bureau of Mines, *Minerals and Materials* (1987, 1988, 1989).

Henry R. Ensiminger, *The Mineral Industry of Brazil* (1988).

Clive Y. Thomas, *The Poor and the Powerless: Economic Policy and Change in the Caribbean* (1988).

Errol D. Sehnk and Patricia A. Plunker, *Bauxite, Alumina, and Aluminum* (1989).

U.S. Department of the Interior, Bureau of Mines, *Minerals Yearbook Area Reports* (1990).

Additional Bibliography

Barboza, Frederico Lopes Meira, and Alfredo C. Gurmendi. *Economia mineral do Brasil*. Brasília: Departamento Nacional de Produção Mineral, 1995.

Munroe, Trevor. "Partnership Building: Reflections on the Michael Manley Accord in the Bauxite/Alumina Industry." *Caribbean Quarterly* 48, no. 1 (March 2002): 94–97.

LESLEY R. LUSTER

BAUZÁ, MARIO (1911–1993). Mario Bauzá, multi-instrumentalist, arranger, and composer, was one of the foremost figures in the creation of a new style of music that mixed together jazz and Afro-Cuban music. He was born April 28, 1911, in Havana. The son of a black cigar maker, he was raised by his white godfather, a military man of wealth and family. He studied classical music and by age sixteen was playing bass clarinet with the Havana Symphony Orchestra. He first visited New York in 1927 as a member of a Cuban dance band. He took up saxophone and trumpet and moved to New York for good in 1930. By 1933 he was playing with the great swing band of drummer Chick Webb at the Savoy; Webb made him musical director in the following year. In 1939 he joined the band of Cab Calloway, whom he encouraged to hire his friend, Dizzy Gillespie.

Bauzá's dream of marrying jazz and Cuban music came true with the founding of a band led by his brother-in-law, Machito and his Afro-Cubans, in 1940. He was lead trumpeter and musical director of that band for decades thereafter. This group played for Latin audiences at the Palladium in New York as well as for African American audiences at the Savoy and Renaissance ballrooms. Surprisingly, the band did not play in Bauzá's native country. Nevertheless, it was one of the most influential bands of the day. Bauzá left Machito's band in 1975 and created his own orchestra, which he led until his death on July 12, 1993.

See also **Music: Popular Music and Dance.**

BIBLIOGRAPHY

Austerlitz, Paul. *Jazz Consciousness: Music, Race, and Humanity.* Middletown, CT: Wesleyan University Press, 2005.

Loza, Steven. *Tito Puente and the Making of Latin Music.* Urbana: University of Illinois Press, 1999.

Orovia, Helio. *Cuban Music from A to Z.* Durham, NC: Duke University Press, 2004.

ANDREW J. KIRKENDALL

BAYLY LETTS, JAIME (1965–). Jaime Bayly Letts, a Peruvian journalist, writer, and television show host, was born in Lima on February 19, 1965. He started working on the conservative newspaper *La Prensa* in the early 1980s. A right-winger, he promoted Mario Vargas Llosa's presidential candidacy in 1990. The late-night show *1990 en América* was his first success in Peruvian TV; he interviewed celebrities and politicians with provocative and almost disrespectful questions, copying the style of the American talk-show host David Letterman. In Miami, he hosted late-night shows for the CBS and Telemundo networks.

Bayly presents himself as a bisexual; his first novel *No se lo digas a nadie* (1996, Don't Tell Anybody), became a gay fiction bestseller and later a movie in 1998. He has written ten novels. *La noche es virgen* (1997, Night Is a Virgin) won the Spanish *Herralde* prize in 1997. His most recent novel is *Y de repente, un ángel* (1995, And Suddenly, an Angel). He was distinguished in May 2007 with a media award from the gay and lesbian alliance against defamation (GLAAD) in South Florida.

See also **Homosexuality and Bisexuality in Literature; Radio and Television.**

BIBLIOGRAPHY

Ruiz Bravo, Patricia. *Subversiones masculinas: Imágenes de los varones en la narrativa joven* [Masculine Subversions: Male Images in the Young's Narrative.] Lima: Flora Tristán, 2001. A critical work about *No se lo digas a nadie* (Don't Tell Anybody).

Spanish News Agency EFE. "Jaime Bayly, una figura destacada de la nueva literatura en español." *El Mundo,* Barcelona, October 22th, 2005. Available from http://www.elmundo.es/elmundo/2005/10/16/cultura/1129463511.html.

JACQUELINE FOWKS

BAY OF PIGS INVASION. Known in Cuba as Batalla de Girón, the Bay of Pigs Invasion was a U.S.-sponsored military venture of Cuban exiles against revolutionary Cuba in mid-April 1961. Launched with a force of about 1,500 Cuban exiles, the invasion was the result of growing antagonism between exiled Cubans and Fidel Castro's increasingly radical regime as well as U.S. desire to topple Castro against the backdrop of the cold war. The failed invasion stands as a pivotal moment both for the Cuban revolution and Cuba-U.S. relations.

Training of Cuban exiles began in March 1960. Led by José Pérez San Román, the exile force eventually came to be known as Brigade 2506. Manuel Artime served as the brigade's political chief. The invasion's primary goal was to secure a beachhead for the establishment of a temporary government by the Cuban Revolutionary Council under the leadership of centrist former prime minister José Miró Cardona. While not enthusiastic about the plans, newly elected president John F. Kennedy agreed to go forward but was adamant about limiting and concealing U.S. involvement.

The attack began on 15 April, when U.S. planes bearing Cuban marks bombarded several military installations. Air raids scheduled for 16 April, however, were canceled by direct orders from Kennedy. On 17 April approximately 1,300 brigade troops landed on the southern coast locations of Girón Beach and the Bay of Pigs; the landing sites proved to be inauspicious owing to swampy conditions, isolation, and reefs that surrounded the area. After two-and-a-half days of intense fighting, Cuban militia and army troops under Castro's command defeated Brigade 2506. Instrumental in the Cuban army's victory were elite cadet troops led by Captain José Ramón Fernández as well as successful air strikes by Cuban fighter planes. The final death toll on the brigade's side was somewhere around 125; another 1,197 were taken prisoner, ten of whom died while being transported to Havana in an overcrowded and airtight truck container. According to Cuban official statistics, 157 Cuban army and militia troops were killed in action. Most other sources, however, place the estimate much higher, between 1,800 and 2,200. After months of intense negotiation, brigade captives were released in exchange for $53 million in medicine and food.

The causes of the Bay of Pigs defeat have been the subject of much reflection and study. Among the most salient ones stand the failure of the Kennedy administration to provide adequate air and naval support and the CIA's overestimation of discontent of the Cuban people toward the revolution. CIA agents and operatives also alienated the exile force.

The Bay of Pigs invasion turned out to be a fiasco for the U.S. government. Kennedy later reminisced that it had been "the worst experience of [his] life." For the exiles, the defeat represented a major setback in the struggle against Castro, but many continue to commemorate the battle as a heroic attack against a much larger and better-equipped force. Castro, for his part, took credit for having stopped the imperial aggression of the world's mightiest military power. The Bay of Pigs not only demonstrated revolutionary Cuba's military effectiveness but also demonstrated the extent of popular support for the revolution. The failed invasion allowed Castro to consolidate his power over the island and to declare openly the socialist nature of the revolution. In terms of U.S.-Cuba relations, the invasion marked the end of any possible rapprochement and pushed Cuba deeper into the Soviet orbit.

See also **Castro Ruz, Fidel; Cuban Missile Crisis; United States-Latin American Relations.**

BIBLIOGRAPHY

Johnson, Haynes. *The Bay of Pigs: The Leaders' Story of Brigade 2506.* New York: Norton, 1964.

Kornbluh, Peter, ed. *Bay of Pigs Declassified: The Secret CIA Report on the Invasion of Cuba.* New York: New Press, 1998.

Wyden, Peter. *Bay of Pigs: The Untold Story.* New York: Simon & Schuster, 1980.

LUIS MARTÍNEZ-FERNÁNDEZ

BAZAINE, FRANÇOIS ACHILLE

(1811–1888). François Achille Bazaine (*b.* 13 February 1811; *d.* 23 September 1888), French military commander in Mexico (1863–1867). Born near Metz, Bazaine joined the French Foreign Legion in 1832, serving in Algeria and Spain. He served with General Élie-Frédéric Forey in the Crimea (1854–1856) and in the Italian campaign (1859). Bazaine took North African troops with him to Mexico in 1863, and Napoleon III appointed him on 16 July 1863 as supreme commander of French Intervention forces, replacing Forey.

In Mexico, Bazaine's aim was to reconcile the various factions and win over moderate opinion to the empire. He disliked the Mexican Conservatives and followed Napoleon's policy of blocking any reversal of the Reform Laws. He became critical of Emperor Maximilian's indecision. The peak of

Bazaine's career was the Oaxaca campaign of 1865. With 8,000 men he took the city on 9 February and captured Porfirio Díaz, the Liberal military commander. He put into effect Napoleon's evacuation policy during 1866 and left Mexico on the last convoy on 12 March 1867, returning to France without military honors, since Mexico had already become an embarrassment to Napoleon.

At the outbreak of the Franco-Prussian War in 1870, Bazaine commanded the 103,000 men of the Third Army Corps, with headquarters at Metz. Although he held down a Prussian army in Lorraine, he was unjustly accused of treason for surrendering Metz in October 1870 after a seventy-day siege. After returning from captivity in Germany and seventeen months of house arrest, he was court-martialed on 6 October 1873 and sentenced to twenty years on the prison island of Sainte Marguerite, from which he escaped on 10 August 1874. He spent the last years of his life in Spain.

See also **French Intervention (Mexico); Miramón, Miguel.**

BIBLIOGRAPHY

Jack Autrey Dabbs, *The French Army in Mexico, 1861–1867* (1963).

Alfred. J. Hanna and Kathryn A. Hanna, *Napoleon III and Mexico: American Triumph over Monarchy* (1971).

BRIAN HAMNETT

BAZÁN, JUAN GREGORIO (?—1570).

Juan Gregorio Bazán (*d.* 1570), conquistador of Tucumán province and lieutenant governor. Begun in 1549, the permanent occupation of Tucumán was characterized by jurisdictional conflicts between Spaniards. Bazán, born in Talavera de la Reina, Spain, was present at the founding of Santiago del Estero (1553) and of San Miguel de Tucumán (1565), and became governor of the town of Esteco in 1567. He unsuccessfully combed the countryside for Indians to serve as laborers for newly founded towns. The Lules Indians attacked him and his party on their return from Peru, where he had gone to meet his newly arrived family. Bazán was killed, as was his son-in-law, Diego Gómez de

Pedraza, who uttered a phrase during the battle that has remained part of Argentine folklore: "Caballero soy y no voy huyendo" ("I am a gentleman, and I do not flee").

See also **Conquistadores.**

BIBLIOGRAPHY

Roberto Levillier, *Descubrimiento y población del norte argentino* (1943).

Ricardo Levene, *A History of Argentina* (1963).

Additional Bibliography

Serrano Redonnet, Jorge. A. *La sangre del conquistador Juan Gregorio Bazán.* Buenos Aires: Ediciones Dunken, 1997.

NICHOLAS P. CUSHNER

BEAGLE CHANNEL DISPUTE. Beagle Channel Dispute, the territorial conflict between Argentina and Chile that brought the two countries to the brink of war in 1978. The Beagle Channel (named after Charles Darwin's ship) lies at the tip of South America, just south of Tierra Del Fuego. An 1881 treaty between Argentina and Chile established the Beagle Channel as their international border for part of the Tierra del Fuego area, but the treaty did not specify the exact location of the channel. Of particular interest was whether the Beagle Channel—and thus the border—ran north of the three key islands of Picton, Lennox, and Nueva (which would make them Chilean), or south of the islands (which would make them Argentine). The issue was not the islands themselves, which are cold and barren, but rather that ownership of them might allow Chile to claim sovereignty or establish an exclusive economic zone 200 miles into the South Atlantic, inhibiting Argentina's ability to project its influence into that region, its key islands (including the Falkland Islands), and Antarctica.

In July 1971 Argentina and Chile agreed to accept Great Britain as arbitrator in an arrangement under which the crown would either accept or reject the recommendation of an expert panel of international jurists. The panel decided in favor of Chilean sovereignty of the three islands, and in May 1977 the British government accepted their recommendation. Argentina rejected the award on narrow technical grounds, and both countries began to prepare for possible conflict. At what seemed to be the last minute before hostilities broke out, the two nations agreed to Vatican mediation in December 1978. This mediation led to the 1984 Treaty of Peace and Friendship, which awarded the islands to Chile, but prohibited Chile from claiming sovereignty or establishing an economic zone in the South Atlantic.

See also **Boundary Disputes: Overview.**

BIBLIOGRAPHY

Jack Child, *Geopolitics and Conflict in South America: Quarrels Among the Neighbors* (1985), esp. pp. 77–85.

Michael A. Morris, "Southern Cone Maritime Security After the 1984 Argentine-Chilean Treaty of Peace and Friendship," in *Ocean Development and International Law* 18, no. 2 (1987): 235–254.

Philip Kelly and Jack Child, eds., *Geopolitics of the Southern Cone and Antarctica* (1988), esp. pp. 36–39 and 75–77.

Additional Bibliography

Benadava, Santiago. *Recuerdos de la mediación pontificia entre Chile y Argentina, 1978-1985.* Santiago de Chile: Editorial Universitaria, 1999.

Passarelli, Bruno. *El delirio armado: Argentina-Chile, la guerra que evitó el Papa.* Buenos Aires: Editorial Sudamericana, 1998.

JACK CHILD

BEALS, CARLETON (1893–1979). Carleton Beals (*b.* 13 November 1893; *d.* 26 June 1979), leftist journalist from the United States who specialized in Latin America. Born in Kansas and educated at the University of California, Berkeley, Beals covered political unrest and social change from Mexico in the latter years of Venustiano Carranza (1914–1920) to the Cuba of Fidel Castro. An outspoken opponent of U.S. threats against the Mexican government's ostensibly radical policies in the mid-1920s, he was also one of the few observers to criticize President Plutarco Elías Calles's abandonment of these plans and movement toward authoritarianism.

Beals's most dramatic feat was his interview with Nicaraguan rebel Augusto Sandino in the war-torn jungles of Nicaragua in February 1928.

While not entirely uncritical, his series of articles in *The Nation* conveyed the strengths of the Sandino movement at a crucial point in the debate concerning the U.S. military intervention.

A member of the cosmopolitan intellectual community of Mexico City in the 1920s, Beals met and wrote about many of Latin America's political and cultural leaders of the era, including the Mexican muralist Diego Rivera and the Peruvian politician-intellectual Víctor Raúl Haya de la Torre. He was one of the few reporters to deplore the 1954 overthrow of Guatemala's leftist government by the United States. The final chapter in his Latin American career was his coverage of Fidel Castro's revolution in Cuba in the 1950s. Later Beals wrote popular fiction and local U.S. history.

See also **Journalism.**

BIBLIOGRAPHY

Two of Beals's many books are *Mexican Maze* (1931) and *Banana Gold* (1932). See also John A. Britton, *Carleton Beals: A Radical Journalist in Latin America* (1987).

Additional Bibliography

Pineda Franco, Adela Eugenia, and Leticia M. Brauchli, eds. *Hacia el paisaje del mezcal: Viajeros norteamericanos en México, siglo XIX y XX.* México, D.F.: Editorial Aldus, 2001.

JOHN A. BRITTON

BEANS. Beans, widely cultivated legumes that have nourished the people of Latin America for millennia. Throughout the region, few meals lack beans. In Mexico, people typically eat mashed beans with corn tortillas, whereas in Brazil, since colonial times, a ladle of soupy beans poured over rice is the core component of many daily diets. In this way, the majority of Latin Americans survive on the near complete protein provided by a mixture of beans and rice or maize.

While hundreds of species exist, many of them indigenous to the American tropics, the multiple varieties of the common bean (*phaseolus vulgaris*), including dried black, pinto, and red beans, are the most widespread in Latin America. Another species, commonly known as lima or butter beans (*phaseolus lunatus*), is also widely grown in the region. Both were among the earliest domesticated plants of the Western Hemisphere, with evidence of their cultivation dating from 7000–5000 BCE.

Archaeologists differ over the locations in which bean agriculture first developed in America, but it is now believed that it occurred independently in Mexico's Tamaulipas desert and Peru's highland Callejon de Hayulas valley. The culture gradually spread throughout North and South America well before 1492. After Columbus, Europeans eventually recognized the utility of dried beans on long ocean voyages, and their journeys helped introduce American beans throughout the world.

The production of beans has generally been taken for granted in Latin America. Their low cost and high nutritional value assured that they were always being cultivated by someone. Indians grew them with maize, weaving the vines between stalks of corn. On sugarcane plantations, captive Africans commonly received small plots of land in order to grow beans to feed themselves. Peasants invariably mixed beans with other subsistence crops. Coffee growers frequently left extra space between the rows of trees in order to intercrop beans and other vegetables.

Competing export crops and livestock land uses have caused problems for bean farming in Latin America. The expansion of soybean agriculture in the last decades of the twentieth century reduced the land devoted to growing common beans, and in Brazil the once ubiquitous black bean nearly disappeared from the market. At the same time, the population explosion caused increased demand, and bean prices skyrocketed. To keep underpaid workers fed, some governments subsidized bean farmers, while many others artificially manipulated prices. All the same, as late as 1980, small family farmers produced more than three-quarters of the beans grown in Latin America, revealing the continued decentralization of bean cultivation.

Bean supply shortages and price hikes worsened as Latin American governments tried to liberalize their economies. Strapped by heavy foreign debt burdens, officials simultaneously encouraged foreign exchange–earning export crops while cutting back on subsidies for staple crops like beans.

In the inflation-plagued 1980s and 1990s, fluctuations in the availability of beans and other basic foodstuffs contributed to social and political unrest in Peru, Argentina, and Venezuela. In Brazil, the looting of supermarkets in cities such as Rio de Janeiro became commonplace in 1992.

In the twenty-first century, soybean production has continued to expand, due to the large demand from China. However, this expansion has sparked debate because Brazil in 2005 lifted its ban on genetically modified (GM) crops. GM soybeans are productive but both environmental and consumer groups have raised concerns about their unknown effects. The increase in soybean production has also been a major driver of Amazon deforestation.

See also **Coffee Industry; Nutrition; Soybeans.**

BIBLIOGRAPHY

Alvin Silverstein and Virginia Silverstein, *Beans: All About Them* (1975).

Luis López Cordovez, "Trends and Recent Changes in the Latin American Food and Agriculture Situation," in *CEPAL Review* (April 1982): 7–41.

Charles B. Heiser, Jr., *Seed to Civilization: The Story of Food*, new ed. (1990).

Additional Bibliography

Carillo, Ana María. *La cocina del tomate, frijol y calabaza.* Mexico City: Clío, 1998.

Long, Janet, and Luis Alberto Vargas. *Food Culture in Mexico.* Westport, CT: Greenwood Press, 2005.

CLIFF WELCH

BEAR FLAG REVOLT. Bear Flag Revolt, an 1846 uprising by Anglo-American settlers against Mexico. On 14 June 1846 a group of thirty-three Anglo-American California settlers led by a trapper named Ezekiel Merritt took control of the plaza in the town of Sonoma north of San Francisco and proclaimed a California Republic. When the Mexican garrison in Sonoma capitulated without a fight, the Bear Flaggers took Colonel Mariano G. Vallejo, commander of the garrison, and his brother Salvador to Captain John C. Frémont's camp near the confluence of the Sacramento and San Joaquin rivers. Frémont, on a topographical mission for the U.S. government, covertly encouraged the proclamation of the California republic but remained officially aloof.

The Bear Flaggers controlled Sonoma until July 1846, when U.S. forces began the occupation of Alta California. Although rumors of war between Mexico and the United States had been circulating through the U.S. naval force off the California coast, the Bear Flag proclamation was the immediate catalyst for the U.S. conquest of the province. Commodore John D. Sloat, commander of the U.S. Pacific squadron, assuming that Frémont had already received news of the Mexican-American War, calculated that blame could be shifted to Frémont if the occupation of California proved premature. Thus, on 7 July 1846, Sloat landed a force of marines at Monterey, initiating the conquest of California.

See also **California.**

BIBLIOGRAPHY

Robert S. Smilie, *The Sonoma Mission* (1975).

David J. Weber, *The Mexican Frontier, 1821–1846: The American Southwest Under Mexico* (1982).

Additional Bibliography

Papp, Richard Paul. *Bear Flag Country: Legacy of the Revolt: A History of the Towns and Post Offices of Sonoma County, California.* Forestville, CA: Analecta, 1996.

Phelps, William Dane. *Frémont's Private Navy: The 1846 Journal of Captain William Dane Phelps.* Glendale, CA: A.H. Clark Co., 1987.

Walker, Dale L. *Bear Flag Rising: The Conquest of California, 1846.* New York: Forge, 2000.

Warner, Barbara R. *The Men of the California Bear Flag Revolt and Their Heritage.* Spokane: Sonoma Valley Historical Society, 1996.

ROBERT H. JACKSON

BECAN. Becan, an ancient city-state located in the Mexican state of Campeche, near the geographical center of the Yucatán Peninsula. Occupation dates from about 600 BCE to 900 CE. The fortress of Becan, built probably by a classic Maya group about 350 CE, consists of a dry moat nearly 1.5 miles in circumference. The moat originally measured about 52 feet across and 16 feet deep with an earthen parapet on the interior lip of the moat, giving a total height from the bottom of about 45

feet. The seven narrow causeways that led into the fortress were all cut in the fourth century CE, indicating that the city was threatened at that time. This was a general period of warfare among the aristocratic rulers of various city and regional states as they attempted to expand their boundaries and power.

Becan appears to have fallen into a period of disuse after circa 500, another time of general disruption in the Maya lowlands. Between about 650 and 840 the city was revitalized, the moat cleaned out, and many large structures built. These buildings are in the Río Bec and Chenes architectural styles, with large "earth monster" mouth doorways and much serpent symbolism. Corner towers and the famed "false temple towers" of the Río Bec style are typical at Becan as well as at the site of Río Bec itself. Storage rooms, multi-apartment palaces, and reservoirs made the fortified zone highly functional.

The nearby sites of Río Bec, Xpuhil, and Chicanna were contemporary, and in the eighth century the surrounding countryside was packed with people and gridded with stone walls. Over 4,000 square miles of terraced hillsides and nearby wetland gardens in swamps attest to intensive food-production systems. The aristocrats of the Late Classic period in this region appear to have lived mainly on their country estates in small and large palaces.

A generalized feudal system characterized Late Classic social structure here. Warfare must have been a threat, however, considering that Becan was reactivated in the Late Classic period. Raids from Maya states farther to the north occurred at other sites and may have been feared here. In any event, the great collapse of southern Maya civilization was only slightly delayed in the Río Bec region, perhaps for a hundred years. By 1000 even the rural zone was deserted.

See also **Archaeology.**

BIBLIOGRAPHY

R. E. W. Adams, "Río Bec Archaeology and the Rise of Maya Civilization," in *The Origins of Maya Civilization*, edited by R. E. W. Adams (1977), and "Settlement Patterns of the Central Yucatan and Southern Campeche Regions," in *Lowland Maya Settlement Patterns*, edited by Wendy Ashmore (1981).

Sylvanus Griswold Morley and George W. Brainerd, *The Ancient Maya*, 4th ed., revised by Robert J. Sharer (1983), pp. 302–304.

Additional Bibliography

Luz Evelia Campana, *Nuevas imágenes de Becan, Campeche*. In *Arqueología mexicana* Vol. 10, no. 56 (2002), p. 64-9.

R. E. W. ADAMS

BECERRA-SCHMIDT, GUSTAVO

(1925–). Gustavo Becerra-Schmidt (*b*. 26 August 1925), Chilean composer. Becerra was born in Temuco and studied at the National Conservatory and at the Faculty of Musical Arts, University of Chile, under the guidance of Pedro Humberto Allende and Domingo Santa Cruz. He taught composition and musical theory from 1953 to 1956. From 1958 to 1961 he was the director of the renowned Institute of Musical Extension and its research publication, *La revista musical chilena*. In 1969 he was elected to the Fine Arts Academy of Chile and two years later received the Premio Nacional de Arte. For a number of years he resided in Europe, serving as the cultural attaché at the Chilean embassy in Bonn. In 1974 he became a professor of composition at the University of Oldenburg (Germany).

At the beginning of his career Becerra cultivated a neoclassical style, but soon started using more contemporary techniques, including dodecaphonism. The pointillism he practiced during the late 1950s and the 1960s gave way to a more romantic *Klangfarbenmelodie* (tone-color melody) and the use of what Becerra called a "complementary polychordal system." His String Quartets nos. 4, 5, and 6 (1958, 1959, 1960) and his Symphony no. 2 (1955–1958) are good examples of those techniques. Becerra also tried to combine more accessible musical elements into his works, like Chilean folk music and Javanese music, which he used with very modern devices.

During the 1960s Becerra experimented with aleatoric techniques, as in his Symphony no. 3 (1960), the Guitar Concertos nos. 1 and 2 (1964, 1968), and his oratorio *Macchu Picchu* (1966), with words by Chilean poet Pablo Neruda. Becerra composed works of pure experimental theater, such as *Juegos* (Games) for piano, Ping-Pong balls, and live recording (1966). Other important works by Becerra include String Quartet no. 7 (1961); Quintet for

piano and string quartet (1962); a leftist political composition *Chile 1973*, for voice and small orchestra (1973–1974); Trio for flute, violin, and piano (1958); *Saxophone Quartet* (1959); *Llanto por el hermano solo* for choir (1966); *Responso para José Miguel Carrera* for voice, wind quintet, piano, and percussion (1967); *Morula, gastrulay blastula* (1969), for piano and tape (1969); *Provocation* (1972), a minidrama; *Parsifae* (1973), an opera; and *Diez trozos para ocho solistas* (1977).

See also **Music: Art Music.**

BIBLIOGRAPHY

Primer festival de música de América y España (1964), pp. 59, 63.

Luis Merino Montero, "Los cuartetos de Gustavo Becerra," in *Revista musical chilena* 19 (1965): 44–78.

John Vinton, ed., *Dictionary of Contemporary Music* (1974), p. 61.

Gérard Béhague, *Music in Latin America: An Introduction* (1979), pp. 320–321; *New Grove Dictionary of Music and Musicians* (1980).

ALCIDES LANZA

BECKMAN REVOLT.

Beckman Revolt (1684), a rebellion that resulted in the expulsion of the Jesuits from the captaincy of Maranhão and the removal of its governor. Both were responses to the actions of the Portuguese crown in 1680 prohibiting enslavement of the Brazilian Indians in the state of Maranhão, assigning their welfare to the Jesuits, and establishing a Lisbon-based company of merchants who pledged to furnish the state with 600 African slaves annually in return for a monopoly on its exports. Manoel Beckman, the wealthy planter who led the uprising, and many other rebels were hanged; five others received lesser sentences.

See also **Slavery: Brazil.**

BIBLIOGRAPHY

Murray Graeme Mac Nicoll, "Seventeenth-Century Maranhão: Beckman's Revolt," in *Estudios Ibero-Americanos*, 4 (1978): 129–140.

John Hemming, *Red Gold: The Conquest of the Brazilian Indians* (1978).

Additional Bibliography

Assunçao, Paulo de. *Negócios Jesuíticos: O cotidiano da administraçao dos bens divinos.* São Paulo: Edusp, 2004.

Castelnau-L'Estoile, Charlotte de. *Operários de uma vinha estéril: Os jesuítas e a conversão dos indios no Brasil, 1580–1620.* Bauru: Edusc, 2006.

Cohen, Thomas M. *The Fire of Tongues: António Vieira and the Missionary Church in Brazil and Portugal.* Stanford: Stanford University Press, 1998.

Vilar, Soccoro de Fátima Pacífico. *A invençao de uma escrita: Ancheita, os Jesuitas, e suas histórias.* Porto Alegre: EDIPUCRS, 2006.

DAURIL ALDEN

BEDOYA, ALFONSO (1904–1957).

Alfonso Bedoya worked as a character actor in Mexican and U.S. cinema from the late thirties to the late fifties. Born on April 16, 1904, in Vicam Sonora, he left his small town as a child and briefly attended a private school in Texas. After dropping out and working odd jobs in the United States, he moved to Mexico City. Bedoya appeared in more than 175 Mexican films. Among his films were *La Golondrina* (The Swallow, 1938); *El Gavilán* (The Hawk, 1940); *Los de abajo* (The Underdogs, 1940); *Los tres mosqueteros* (The Three Musketeers, 1942); *Flor Silvestre* (1943); *Gran Casino* (1946); *Doña Bárbara* (1943); *Las Abandonadas* (The Abandoned, 1944) and *La Perla* (The Pearl, 1945). Bedoya's first role in U.S. cinema was in John Huston's classic *Treasure of the Sierra Madre* (1948), which also starred Humphrey Bogart and Tim Holt. In this film, he played a vicious Mexican bandit leader named Gold Hat and uttered the lines that he is most remembered for: "Badges? We ain't got no badges! We don't need no badges. I don't have to show you any stinking badges!" Although Bedoya starred in other U.S. movies, none brought him as much success. He died of reasons related to heavy drinking in Mexico City on December 15, 1957.

See also **Cinema: From the Silent Film to 1990.**

BIBLIOGRAPHY

"Bedoya, Alfonso." Obituary. *New York Times,* December 17, 1957.

SOPHIA KOUTSOYANNIS

BEDOYA DE MOLINA, DOLORES (1783–1853).

Dolores Bedoya de Molina (Bedoya González, María Dolores; *b.* 20 September 1783; *d.* 9 July 1853), Guatemalan politician. Like most of her brothers, Bedoya was from early on an advocate of Central American independence. She married the statesman Pedro Molina in 1804 and moved to Granada, Nicaragua, where he served as doctor for the fixed battalion until 1811. On returning to Guatemala in 1814, she lent her support to her brother Mariano, imprisoned as a result of the Belén conspiracy against Captain General José de Bustamente in 1813. She supported Molina's campaign for independence in the pages of *El Editor Constitucional,* and during the proclamation of independence from Spain on 15 September 1821, she led a crowd of advocates for independence outside the Palace of Government. Emancipation brought with it the conflict between republicans and those who favored annexation with the Mexican Empire of Iturbide. This conflict resulted in the assassination of Mariano Bedoya by the government's annexationist forces on 29 November 1821 and the exile of the Molina-Bedoya family to Verapaz. Bedoya always supported the political career of her husband, whether it was as leader of the Liberal Party, chief of state, or political exile.

See also **Guatemala.**

BIBLIOGRAPHY

Carlos Gándara Durán, *Pedro Molina* (1936).

Rubén Leyton Rodríguez, *Doctor Pedro Molina* (1958).

José Antonio Mobil, *100 personajes históricos de Guatemala* (1979).

Additional Bibliography

Morales, Fabiola. *Mujer y libertad: Dolores Bedoya de Molina.* Guatemala: Editorial Cultura, 1996.

ARTURO TARACENA ARRIOLA

BEDOYA REYES, LUIS (1919–).

Luis Bedoya Reyes (*b.* 1919), Peruvian politician and lawyer, charismatic mayor of Lima for two terms (1964–1969), and a contender for the presidency of Peru in the elections of 1980 and 1985. His political activities started with his support of the civilian president José Luis Bustamante y Rivero (1945–1948). In 1956 he contributed to the formation of the centrist Christian Democratic Party (PDC) and became its first general secretary. His close links with Popular Action, headed by his friend Fernando Belaúnde Terry, led to his nomination as minister of justice when Belaúnde was elected president in 1963. He renounced this ministerial post to run for mayor of Lima in 1964.

Clearly at odds with the PDC's leader, Héctor Cornejo Chávez, Bedoya formed the Christian Popular Party in 1966. Extremely popular in Lima, Bedoya headed the Right's feeble opposition to the military dictatorship between 1974 and 1980. In 1978, Bedoya received the second most votes as representative to the Constituent Assembly. He has since been associated with the political right, which suffered sound defeats in the presidential elections of 1985 and 1990.

After retiring from politics, Bedoya opened a law firm in Lima, where he specializes in civil, commercial, and public law. He also serves on the Consultation Board of the University of Lima Law School.

See also **Peru, Political Parties: Popular Action (AP).**

BIBLIOGRAPHY

Pedro Pablo Kuczynski, *Peruvian Democracy Under Economic Stress: An Account of the Belaúnde Administration, 1963–1968* (1977).

John Crabtree, *Peru Under García: An Opportunity Lost* (1992).

Additional Bibliography

Amiel Meza, Ricardo and Luis Bedoya Reyes. *La fe social cristiana de Luis Bedoya Reyes: Derrotero de un compromiso doctrinario*. Lima: s.n., 2000.

Bedoya Reyes, Luis, Ricardo Amiel Meza, and César Madrid Isla. *Bedoya en la Constituyente*. Peru: Studios Madrid, 1990.

ALFONSO W. QUIROZ

BEDREGAL DE CONITZER, YOLANDA

DA (1918–). Yolanda Bedregal de Conitzer (*b.* 21 September 1918), Bolivian poet, novelist, and artist. Probably the best-known Bolivian female poet, Bedregal is called simply "Yolanda of Bolivia." She has received the most prestigious literary awards of Bolivia, among them, the Erich Guttentag National Prize for her novel *Bajo el oscuro sol* (1971). Her poetry covers a variety of themes and styles, but its most prominent characteristic is a special sensibility for childhood—she has written several books of poetry for children. Another very important subject in her writing is the land and native people of Bolivia. Although at times Bedregal casts the Indian in a romantic light, she grasps the spirit of Indian culture (especially Aymara culture). In her latest poetry, such as the collection *Nadir* (1950), strongly religious (even mystical) motifs are evident.

See also **Literature: Spanish America.**

BIBLIOGRAPHY

Despite her importance to Bolivian literature, very few critical works have been published about Bedregal. For a general survey see Majorie Agosin, "Para un retrato de Yolanda Bedregal," *Revista iberoamericana* 52, no. 134 (1986): 267–270.

Additional Bibliography

Bedregal, Yolanda. *Poesía de Bolivia, de la época precolombina al modernismo.* Buenos Aires: Editorial Universitaria de Buenos Aires, 1964.

Salgado, María Antonia. *Modern Spanish American Poets. First Series.* Detroit: Gale Group, 2003.

LEONARDO GARCÍA PABÓN

BÉJAR, HÉCTOR (1935–). Héctor Béjar, Peruvian author, journalist, and Castroist guerrilla leader in the 1960s. Béjar was born in 1935 and became involved in radical politics during his time in art and law school. It was then that he formed and led the Army of National Liberation (ELN), which launched a guerrilla campaign in 1965. In prison after 1966, he contributed to the understanding of the character, limitations, and rigidities of the Peruvian guerrilla movement by writing a treatise prized and first published in Cuba. The guerrilla movement, he explained, developed out of the climate of rebellion and oppression after the end of General Manuel Odría's dictatorship. Freed by the military government after the amnesty of 1970, Béjar accepted a government post to conduct official propaganda among peasants. This organization, which is still active, is called SINAMOS—literally, "sin amos," or "without masters" in Spanish.

See also **Peru, Revolutionary Movements: Army of National Liberation (ELN).**

BIBLIOGRAPHY

Héctor Béjar, *Peru 1965: Notes on a Guerrilla Experience* (1970).

ALFONSO W. QUIROZ

BELALCÁZAR, SEBASTIÁN DE (1490–1551).

Sebastián de Belalcázar (also Benalcázar: *b.* 1490?; *d.* 30 April 1551), Spanish conquistador. Born probably as Sebastián Moyano, like many illiterate and humble folk, Belalcázar changed his name to that of his home town: Belalcázar, province of Córdoba. His later fame and success demonstrated the possibilities for social mobility in the New World. Belalcázar came to Santo Domingo in 1507, joined Vasco Núñez de Balboa in Darién in 1513, received an *encomienda* in Panama in 1519, and became first *alcalde* of León, Nicaragua, in 1523. Participating as captain in the capture of the Inca Emperor Atahualpa at Cajamarca, Peru, in 1532, he received 2.25 of the 217 shares of the booty amassed from Atahualpa's treasure and became rich.

Investing in new expeditions and freeing himself from the authority of Francisco Pizarro, Belalcázar moved north and conquered southern Colombia. He helped found the cities of Quito in 1534, Guayaquil in 1535, and Cali and Popayán in 1536. In 1538 he pushed even farther north toward the gold and dense population of the Chibcha (Muisca) Indians, but Gonzalo Jiménez De Quesada and Nicolás Féderman and their expeditions from Santa Marta and Coro, respectively, had already arrived. They each claimed the Chibcha territory but agreed in 1539 to journey to Spain together to resolve the dispute there.

Although unsuccessful in his Chibcha claim, Belalcázar received many honors in Spain. He was made governor of Popayán for life, had his three mestizo children legitimized, and married his son to a Spanish noblewoman. Back in Cali in 1542, he found himself reluctantly drawn into the Peruvian civil wars; he survived even when on the losing side,

as in Viceroy Blasco Núñez Vela's defeat at Iñaquito in 1546. While others lost their heads, as Núñez Vela did, or were shunted aside, as Jiménez and Féderman were, Belalcázar successfully defended his governorship in southern Colombia against all comers from 1536 until his 1550 *residencia* (impeachment) and death sentence. That sentence, based on his 1546 execution of Jorge Robledo for encroaching on the Popayán territory, was being carried by Belalcázar to Spain for appeal when he died in Cartagena.

See also **Conquistadores.**

BIBLIOGRAPHY

A comprehensive biography is Diego Garcés Giraldo, *Sebastián de Belalcázar: Fundador de ciudades, 1490–1551* (1986). An older and never finished work detailing Belalcázar's day-by-day activities is Jacinto Jijón y Caamaño, *Sebastián de Belalcázar*, 3 vols. (1936–1949). For documents on Belalcázar, see Jorge A. Garcés G., ed., *Colección de documentos ineditos relativos al adelantado capitán don Sebastián de Belalcázar, 1535–1565* (1936). In English a succinct account can be found in James Marvin Lockhart, *The Men of Cajamarca* (1972), pp. 122–129. A lively read is John Hemming, *The Search for El Dorado* (1978).

Additional Bibliography

Avellaneda Navas, José Ignacio. *La expedición de Sebastián de Belalcázar al Mar del Norte y su llegada al Neuvo Reino de Granada.* Santa Fé de Bogotá, D.C.: Banco de la Republica, 1992.

MAURICE P. BRUNGARDT

BÉLANCE, RENÉ (1915–2004).

René Bélance (*b.* 28 September 1915, *d.* 11 January 2004.), Haitian poet. After graduating from the École Normale (Port-au-Prince), Bélance entered government service (departments of justice and commerce). He wrote for *Le nouvelliste, Conjonction,* and *Optique,* among other journals. In an interview in *Callaloo,* he says he was mistakenly labeled a surrealist because his *Luminaires* (1943) was published at the same time as the "hermetic" work of Magloire Saint-Aude. After spending several years in Puerto Rico, Bélance settled in the United States and taught at Brown University. Although he wrote some metrical verse, he favors free verse and poetic prose, with deep roots in African rhythms and dance. He writes with a deceptive simplicity—"Je sais des musiques sereines / au charme délicieux." L.-S. Senghor saw him as "the most gifted of the young Haitian poets" (*Anthologie de la nouvelle poésie nègre et malgache*, 2d ed., 1969). Other poetical works by René Bélance include *Rythme de mon coeur* (1940), *Pour célébrer l'absence* (1943), *Survivances* (1944), *Épaule d'ombre* (1945), and *Nul ailleurs* (1983). Bélance died in January 2004 at the age of 89.

See also **Literature: Spanish America.**

BIBLIOGRAPHY

Naomi M. Garret, *The Renaissance of Haitian Poetry* (1963), pp. 175–184.

F. Raphaël Berrou and Pradel Pompilus, *Histoire de la littérature haïtienne illustrée par les textes,* vol. 3 (1977), pp. 389–393.

René Bélance, "Poems and Interview," in *Callaloo* 15, no. 3 (1992): 601–610.

Additional Bibliography

Saussy, Haun. "A Note on René Belancé." *Callaloo* 22 (Spring, 1999): 351-354.

CARROL F. COATES

BELAÚNDE, VÍCTOR ANDRÉS (1883–1966).

Víctor Andrés Belaúnde (*b.* 15 December 1883; *d.* 14 December 1966), Peruvian intellectual, educator, publisher, and diplomat. Born in Arequipa and educated as a lawyer at the universities of Arequipa and San Marcos in Lima, Belaúnde taught history at San Marcos and the Catholic University. In addition to his academic activities, he headed the Boundaries Section of the Ministry of Foreign Affairs during the crucial period of international disputes with Ecuador, Colombia, and Chile between 1907 and 1911. His main intellectual contributions address the issues of Peruvian nationality and its role in solving national problems. Belaúnde was initially influenced by positivism before embracing French idealist and Catholic philosophies. He believed in the need to integrate Peruvians of disparate historical backgrounds within a Peruvian national ideal. He named this ideal *peruanidad* ("Peruvianness"). Peruvian social problems should not lead to revolutionary changes, as proposed by José Carlos Mariátegui and Víctor Raúl Haya de la Torre, but to social and cultural conciliation. Only through a strong feeling of national unity and a deep understanding of the genuine contributions of Peruvian history would Peru be able to form part of the community of modern nations.

Belaúnde publicized Peruvian cultural contributions as the editor of a new and third version of the landmark *Mercurio Peruano,* first published in 1791–1795. The new *Mercurio Peruano,* which appeared with brief interruptions between 1918 and 1978, published articles on a wide variety of national and international subjects. It became the longest-lasting cultural journal in Peru.

Exiled for his political opposition to President Augusto Leguía (1919–1930), Belaúnde taught in several U.S. universities, including Columbia, Virginia, Miami, and Chicago. On his return to Peru in the early 1930s, he helped successfully mediate the border dispute between Colombia and Peru. As president of the Catholic University and minister of foreign affairs in 1957, he achieved national stature as an intellectual eminence. In his later years Belaúnde held a high diplomatic post at the United Nations in New York City, where he died.

See also **Mercurio Peruano.**

BIBLIOGRAPHY

See his *La realidad nacional* (1931), *Peruanidad* (1957), and *Meditaciones peruanas* (1963).

Frederick Pike, *The Modern History of Peru* (1967).

Additional Bibliography

Gonzales, Osmar. *Sanchos fracasados: Los arielistas y el pensamiento politico peruano.* Lima: Ediciones PREAL, 1996.

Santiváñez Vivanco, Martín. *El concepto de peruanidad en Victór Andrés Belaunde ante el nuevo milenio.* Lima: Universidad de Lima, Fondo de Desarrollo Editorial, 2003.

ALFONSO W. QUIROZ

BELAÚNDE TERRY, FERNANDO (1912–2002).

Fernando Belaúnde Terry (*b.* 7 October 1912; *d.* 4 June 2002), Peruvian politician, twice president of Peru (1963–1968, 1980–1985). Representing civilian centrist political forces opposed to militarism and the Peruvian Aprista Party's established influence, Belaúnde received enthusiastic initial support of his populist modernizing ideology. He was born in Lima to a family of intellectuals and politicians from Arequipa. His father, Rafael, brother of the distinguished nationalist intellectual Víctor Andrés Belaúnde, went into exile in France during Augusto B. Leguía's regime in the early 1920s. Thus, Fernando was able to study mechanical and electrical engineering in Paris between 1924 and 1930 and later architecture at the universities of Miami and Texas, from which he graduated in 1935.

Upon his return to Lima, Belaúnde established in 1937 the professional journal *El Arquitecto Peruano,* which became an influential means of spreading modern ideas on urbanization. Belaúnde also became professor of urban studies and founder of the Institute of Urban Studies. In 1944, Belaúnde supported the successful bid for the presidency by José Luis Bustamante y Rivero's National Democratic Front. He consequently was elected congressional deputy for Lima. After Bustamante's ouster by a military coup in 1948, Belaúnde resumed his professional and teaching activities. With the return of democracy in 1956, Belaúnde's presidential candidacy was supported by the Front of Democratic Youth. Although he was not elected, Belaúnde was soon able to establish a new political party, Popular Action, which, together with the support of the Christian Democratic Party, would be the base for his second and successful candidacy for the presidency in 1962.

During his first presidency Belaúnde had to face the powerful opposition coalition of the Aprista Party and the Odriista National Union. He tried to carry out a program of extensive public works financed by foreign and domestic credit. However, between 1965 and 1968 inflation increased and political scandals (corruption, contraband, and unpopular agreements with a foreign oil company) were uncovered. Military pressure mounted as a consequence of the substantial authority ceded to the army to fight the guerrilla movement of 1965. The military ousted Belaúnde in 1968 and continued to govern until 1980. Reelected as president in 1980, Belaúnde again confronted daunting economic problems and the growth of a new rural and urban armed struggle led by Shining Path (Sendero Luminoso). His popularity, and that of his party, fell as a consequence of an overall inefficient government between 1980 and 1985. He and his party lost that election to Alan García of the Alianza Popular Revolucionaria Americana (American Popular Revolutionary Alliance [APRA]) party. When Belaúnde handed over power to Garcia, the event marked the first peaceful transition of power among democratically elected presidents in his lifetime.

Because Belaúnde served as president under the 1979 Constitution, after his term he was appointed to a life-long seat in the Peruvian senate. (This privilege for former presidents was abolished by Peru's 1993 Constitution.) In 2002, he died in Lima after suffering from a brain hemmorhage and cancer. He was 89 years old.

See also **Peru, Political Parties: Popular Action (AP).**

BIBLIOGRAPHY

Fernando Belaúnde Terry, *Peru's Own Conquest* (1965).

Pedro Pablo Kuczynski, *Peruvian Democracy Under Economic Stress: An Account of the Belaúnde Administration, 1963–1968* (1977).

Additional Bibliography

Belaúnde Terry, Fernando, and Enrique Chirinos Soto. *Conversaciones con Belaúnde: Testimonio y confidencias.* Lima: Editorial Minerva, 1987.

García Belaúnde, Victór Andrés. *Los ministros de Belaúnde: 1963-68, 1980-85.* Lima: s.n., 1988.

Melgar, Jorge. *A Belaúnde lo que es de Belaúnde.* Lima, 1973.

Moscoso Perea, Carlos. *El populismo en América Latina.* Madrid: Centro de Estudios Constitucionales, 1990.

ALFONSO W. QUIROZ

BELÉM. Belém, city in Brazil near the mouth of the Amazon River. Belém is located on the south bank of the Pará River, about 60 miles from the Atlantic Ocean. Long the capital of the state of Pará, it had more than 1.38 million inhabitants in 2007. The region was densely settled by native peoples when the Europeans first reconnoitered it in 1500.

Within a hundred years, several British and Dutch agricultural colonies sprang up in the vicinity. In 1616 Francisco Caldeira Castelo Branco (Capitão Mor of Rio Grande do Norte) founded the modern city, called Santa María de â Belém. He and a lieutenant, Pedro Teixeira, used Belém as a base from which to drive out the foreigners. In addition to its location, Belém offered maritime passage and anchorages protected from the awesome tidal bore that swept up the Amazon River.

Belém served the Portuguese as a strategic gateway to the entire Amazon basin. In the 1660s it became the economic emporium of the Amazon Region, and governors often resided there instead of in the capital at São Luís. By the eighteenth century, Belém merchants had organized shipyards, trade, and Indian slaving expeditions throughout the region.

At the height of the rubber boom in the early 1900s, U.S. entrepreneur Percival Farquhar built modern docks to accommodate oceangoing ships. The collapse of the boom only temporarily deflated Belém's economy, and today the city provides governmental, political, economic, financial, educational, and defense services for the local population and the country as a whole.

See also **Brazil, Geography.**

BIBLIOGRAPHY

John Ure, *Trespassers on the Amazon* (1986).

Additional Bibliography

Chesnut, R. Andrew. *Born Again in Brazil: The Pentecostal Boom and the Pathogens of Poverty.* New Brunswick: Rutgers University Press, 1997.

Cruz, Ernesto Horácio da. *História de Belém.* Belém: Universidade Federal do Pará, 1973.

Pereira, Magnus Roberto de Mello, Maria Angélica Soller, and Maria Izilda Santos de Matos. *A cidade em debate: Belém, Recife, Rio de Janeiro, São Paulo, Santos, Uberlândia, Curitiba, Porto Alegre.* São Paulo: Editora Olho d'Agua, Sociedade e Cultura, 1999.

Sarges, Maria de Nazaré. *Belém: Riquezas produzindo a belle-époque (1870-1912).* Bélem: Paka-Tatu, 2002.

Slater, Candace. *Entangled Edens: Visions of the Amazon.* Berkeley: University of California Press, 2002.

Zetter, Roger, and Georgia Butina Watson. *Designing Sustainable Cities in the Developing World.* Burlington: Ashgate, 2006.

MICHAEL L. CONNIFF

BELÉN, CATAMARCA.

Belén, a town of 12,252 inhabitants (2001), is the capital of the department of the same name in the province of Catamarca in Argentina. It was founded in 1607 under orders of Alonso de Ribera—Governor of Tucuman—by Gaspar Doncel, lieutenant governor of La Rioja, as a major Spanish center at the foot of the Sierra de Famatima, in Calchaquí Indian territory. In 1683, after repeated Indian uprisings and natural catastrophes, the regional administrative seat was moved to a safer location on the colonial road between Tucumán and Mendoza and named San Fernando del Valle de Catamarca.

Having lost its administrative significance, Belén was left to providing services to pastoral groups, small mining outposts, and subsistence farmers. In the early twenty-first century the region produces early grapes, corn, tobacco, soybeans, and alfalfa. Whereas the irrigated valleys allow intensive cattle ranching, traditional goat herding has survived in the semiarid foothills of the Sierra. The development of Catamarca into a flourishing agricultural valley has arrested the further growth of Belén, and the whole *departmento* has been losing population to Santiago del Estero, Tucumán, Mendoza, Córdoba, and Buenos Aires.

See also **Argentina, Geography; Catamarca.**

BIBLIOGRAPHY

Morandini, Norma. *Catamarca.* Buenos Aires: Planeta, 1991.

CÉSAR N. CAVIEDES

BELÉN CONSPIRACY.

Belén Conspiracy, an attempt made in December 1813 to secure Guatemala's independence from Spain. Alienated by the political repression imposed by Captain General José de Bustamante, a group of Guatemalan creoles seeking independence met in the cells of the Convent of Belén in Guatemala City near the end of 1813. There they planned to seize Bustamante, Guatemala's Archbishop Ramon Casaus y Torres, and principal military officers. Bustamante had originally seemed sympathetic to the creoles' concerns but soon acted against their interests. A number of rebellions occurred throughout the region in 1813, illustrating disgruntlement with and rejection of Bustamante's control, and by extension that of the Cortes of Cádiz as well. In

March, creoles revolted in El Salvador, and in December of that year, creoles in León and Granada rebelled. The revolts were put down and the participants imprisoned by Bustamante.

The Belén conspirators sought to free the soldiers of the patriot army of Granada held prisoner by Bustamante and, more important, ultimately to declare independence. Their plans fell apart when they were discovered and arrested by local soldiers. Among those captured were Joaquín Yudice, Tomás Ruiz, and Fray Víctor Castrillo. The ringleaders and ten lesser participants were sentenced to hang but were later pardoned on 2 May 1818. Others were sent to Africa for ten years hard labor. José Francisco Barrundia escaped capture but was sentenced in absentia. He spent six years in hiding in Guatemala.

See also **Guatemala.**

BIBLIOGRAPHY

Mario Rodríguez, *La conspiración de Belén en nueva perspectiva* (1965).

Richard E. Moore, *A Historical Dictionary of Guatemala* (rev. ed. 1973).

Ralph Lee Woodward, Jr., *Central America: A Nation Divided* (1976).

Mario Rodríguez, *The Cádiz Experiment in Central America, 1808 to 1826* (1978).

J. Daniel Contreras R., *Breve historia de Guatemala* (1983).

Additional Bibliography

Dym, Jordana. *From Sovereign Villages to National States: City, State, and Federation in Central America, 1759–1839.* Albuquerque: University of New Mexico Press, 2006.

Dym, Jordana, and Christophe Belaubre. *Politics, Economy, and Society in Bourbon Central America, 1759–1821.* Boulder: University Press of Colorado, 2007.

Kramer, Wendy. *Encomienda Politics in Early Colonial Guatemala, 1524–1544: Dividing the Spoils.* Boulder: Westview Press, 1994.

Quesada S., Flavio J., Mario Alfonso Bravo Soto, and Sandra Herrera. *Estructuración y desarrollo de la administración política territorial de Guatemala: En la colonia y la época independiente.* Guatemala: Universidad de San Carlos de Guatemala, 2005.

HEATHER K. THIESSEN

BELGIAN COLONIZATION COMPANY.

Encouraged by King Léopold I of Belgium, a small group of investors in 1841 organized the Belgian Colonization Company to take advantage of economic opportunities in Guatemala. In 1842 the limited-liability company purchased 8,000 *caballerías* (264,000 acres) of undeveloped lands and assumed concessions and obligations for immigration, construction of a deep-water port, and other economic development in the department of Santo Tomás on Guatemala's north coast. In return the company received monopolies and exemptions favoring its commerce over all competitors. It could collect tolls for ten years on the planned road between the port and the Motagua River, and it would hold a ten-year monopoly on steam navigation on the river. Foreign immigrants to the Santo Tomás colony automatically became Guatemalan citizens and enjoyed a twenty-year exemption from most taxes. They were exempt from all commodity monopolies (*estancos*) but were prohibited from introducing goods under *estanco* from the colony into the interior. Although obligated to serve in the municipal militia, the colonists were exempt from service to Guatemala.

Conceptually the enterprise promised public and private rewards, but in fact it experienced problems on both sides of the Atlantic. In Belgium the organizers and directors—speculators and close friends of Léopold I—tried, against the wishes of his anticolonialist legislature, to acquire overseas territories using the private sector. The company enjoyed royal and ministerial subsidies and favors, and it reported regularly, though confidentially, to Léopold and his cabinet. In Guatemala the political scene was reversed. The Liberal government of the 1830s, which favored foreign investment, had been succeeded by Rafael Carrera's xenophobic Conservative ministers, although members of the Constituent Assembly with business and commercial interests championed the Belgian proposals. The company bribed prominent advocates for the enterprise, paying through a Guatemalan firm (Pullieiro, Balcárzel, and Associates) in Izabal and Santo Tomás whose public-works concessions and constructions the company promised to buy. Two Conservative members of the Assembly argued that Guatemala would suffer as badly from a future Belgian commercial monopoly at Santo Tomás as from the present British monopoly exercised from Belize. They predicted that a Belgian enclave would threaten Guatemalan sovereignty over its Caribbean coastline and the adjacent littoral province. The Assembly nevertheless approved the contract on 4 May 1842.

In May 1843 a communitarian settlement began at Santo Tomás. In the first year the company sent fewer than 200 temporary settlers and workers, with inadequate provisions. The landless residents fell prey to disease, dissension, and intrigue. The colonial administration changed personnel four times. In March 1844, Major Augustin Scévola Guillaumot arrived as the new colonial director, with extraordinary powers to institute a "military regime" for order and work. He also held covert instructions to lay the foundation for a future action to separate the District of Santo Tomás from Guatemalan jurisdiction. He raised the immigrant population to 800 civilians and 48 Belgian soldiers, like himself, who were officially on leave but posted to service with the company.

Guillaumot began surveying and clearing lands. Sealing off Santo Tomás as an ethnic enclave, he fired the Indian workers, drove the native-born residents from the colony, and rejected proposals from Guatemalan and Belize merchants to establish branch outlets at Santo Tomás. He violated the company's customs exemptions by importing luxury goods duty free for sale in the interior. The commandant of Izabal, Gerónimo Paiz, entered Santo Tomás in May 1844 with a detachment of soldiers and reestablished a national presence. He installed a port authority and customs director subordinate to his authority. In November, Carrera created a Permanent Commission on Santo Tomás Affairs and appointed General Manuel José Arce as *corregidor*. Guillaumot resigned. The settlement faltered. Many of the colonists moved inland to the capital or relocated in Belize or Honduras. The colonial population plunged to 280.

Both the company in Brussels and its settlement at Santo Tomás struggled unsuccessfully through the next decade. Léopold tried to save the enterprise in 1846. Through his minister of foreign affairs he ordered the Belgian minister to Mexico, Édouard Blondeel van Cuelebrouck, to negotiate the transfer of Santo Tomás in full sovereignty to Belgium. The Guatemalan government rejected any proposal that ceded sovereignty or conveyed rights of extraterritoriality, insisting that a Guatemalan commission be assigned to Santo Tomás with full authority to intervene in all operations of the colony. Meanwhile a change of government in Brussels in March 1846 brought to power a cabinet unsympathetic to Léopold's overseas adventurism. The new cabinet withdrew support. The company attempted to reorganize in order to prevent bankruptcy. Guatemala permitted the Belgian Colonization Company to struggle on until no hope remained that it could meet its contractual obligations. Carrera finally implemented the Decree of Forfeiture in 1854.

See also **Guatemala.**

BIBLIOGRAPHY

For the early years of the colony, see Joseph Fabri, *Les belges au Guatemala (1840–1845)* (1955). The origins of the Belgian interest in Guatemala may be found in William J. Griffith, *Empires in the Wilderness: Foreign Colonization and Development in Guatemala, 1834–1844* (1965), esp. pp. 217–250. Company documents and correspondence are printed in Nicolas Leysbeth, *Historique de la colonisation belge à Santo-Tomas, Guatemala* (1938). A comprehensive history is Ora-Westley Schwemmer, "The Belgian Colonization Company, 1840–1858" (Ph.D diss., Tulane University, 1966).

Additional Bibliography

Pompejano, Daniele. *La crisis del antiguo régimen en Guatemala (1839-1871)*. Guatemala: Editorial Universitaria, Universidad de San Carlos de Guatemala, 1997.

Woodward, Ralph Lee. *Rafael Carrera and the Emergence of the Republic of Guatemala, 1821-1871*. Athens: University of Georgia Press, 1993.

WES SCHWEMMER CADY

BELGRANO, MANUEL (1770–1820).

Manuel Belgrano (*b.* 3 June 1770; *d.* 20 June 1820), Argentine independence leader. Born into a wealthy merchant family, Belgrano was educated in his native Buenos Aires and at the University of Salamanca in Spain. He was admitted to the practice of law and in the last years of the colonial regime also belonged to a circle of creole professional men, all influenced by enlightenment thought, who were eager to promote economic development and practical improvements in infrastructure. Becoming secretary of the Buenos Aires Consulado, or merchant guild, he worked to encourage new productive activities and to improve the system of education. He also served in the local militia forces opposing the British invasions of 1806–1807.

Belgrano's initial response to the Spanish imperial crisis of 1808 was to support a project for constitutional monarchy in the American colonies under Princess Carlota Joaquina, sister of King Ferdinand VII, a captive of Napoleon. She was currently in Rio de Janeiro as wife of the Portuguese prince regent. This scheme came to nothing, and following the May Revolution of 1810 Belgrano threw in his lot frankly with the patriot cause. He served on the Buenos Aires junta itself, but in early 1811 set off for Paraguay as commander of an expedition sent to bring that province under control of the new authorities. He was defeated militarily, but soon afterward Paraguayans carried out their own revolution against Spain, for which Belgrano's proselytizing efforts in Paraguay had helped prepare the ground.

In 1811 Belgrano assumed command of patriot forces in the Argentine northwest, facing the royalists in Upper Peru (later Bolivia). He won some victories, but his own invasion of the Bolivian Andes in 1814 ended in defeat. Having yielded his command to José de San Martín, Belgrano traveled to Europe in 1815 as part of a diplomatic mission that hoped to negotiate an agreement with Spain for an independent Argentine monarchy under a prince of the Spanish royal family. The idea was flatly rejected by Spain. On his return to Argentina, Belgrano worked both to obtain a formal declaration of independence (as finally effected on 9 July 1816) and to create a constitutional monarchy under a descendant of the Incas. In his final years, he again served militarily on the northern front while trying to mediate in political quarrels among various bands of patriots.

Among the leaders of Argentine independence, Belgrano is second only to San Martín in the esteem of later generations, although no great military or political triumphs are associated with his name. None of the forms of constitutional monarchy that he backed ever took hold. However, he served his country steadily and disinterestedly, enjoying the respect, if not always winning the agreement, of his fellow revolutionaries.

See also **Argentina: The Nineteenth Century.**

BIBLIOGRAPHY

The classic study is Bartolomé Mitre, *Historia de Belgrano y de la Independencia Argentina* (1857; many later editions). A good modern study, by one of his descendants, is Mario Belgrano, *Historia de Belgrano,* 2d ed. (1944). In English the highlights of his career are covered in both John Lynch, *The Spanish American Revolutions, 1808–1826,* 2d ed. (1986), chaps. 2 and 3, and Tulio Halperín-Donghi, *Politics, Economics, and Society in Argentina in the Revolutionary Period,* translated by Richard Southern (1975).

Additional Bibliography

Cacua Prada, Antonio. *El general Manuel Belgrano: Maestro de la libertad argentina.* Santa Fé de Bogotá, D.C.: Plaza y Janés, 2000.

García Enciso, Isaías José. *Manuela Belgrano: La hija del general.* Buenos Aires: Editorial Sudamericana, 2003.

DAVID BUSHNELL

BELIZE. A 1997 newswire article posed the question: Is Belize Caribbean or Central American? The comment was made in May, when Belize sent its deputy prime minister, Dean Barrow, to a historic Caribbean-U.S. summit in Bridgetown, Barbados, attended by U.S. president Bill Clinton, while Prime Minister Manuel Esquivel chose to attend a Central American summit in Costa Rica. As the only Central American country in the fourteen-member Cari-bbean Community (CARICOM), Belize has sometimes been described as being a "remote" state of the Caribbean. Barrow commented that while trying to draw closer to Central America, CARICOM re-mained more important for this former British colony, because it was Belize's first line of support in its longstanding diplomatic struggle with Guatemala. On September 25, 2006, Belize joined the Central American Bank for Economic Integration (CABEI), established by the governments of Guatemala, El Salvador, Honduras, Costa Rica, and Nicaragua with the aim of contributing to the social and economic development of the region. Prime Minister Said Musa noted that Belize's integration in the Central American region had been much slower, "but we are well poised to take advantage of our geographic position in the Central American isthmus" (http://channel5belize.com/archive).

CONTEMPORARY BELIZE

In the early twenty-first century, Belize has moved ethnically, religiously, and economically from a

Caribbean perspective to a more Central American one. In the 2005 mid-year updates to the decennial 2000 census, Belize's population stood at 291,800, up 3.3 percent from the previous year and almost equally divided between urban (50.2 percent) and rural (49.8 percent). In 2000 the Cayo District in the west was the fastest-growing district, with population up 29.3 percent over the census of 1991. Belize and Stann Creek, two districts that had experienced high rates of emigration, grew substantially over the decade as well, yet it was unclear whether this represented a slowing of emigration or high levels of immigration. Belizeans began immigrating to the United States in the 1970s, first to New York and afterward to Los Angeles. Approximately 45,000 to 55,000 Belizeans and their U.S.-raised children currently reside in greater Los Angeles, representing about 45 percent of the total number in the United States.

Demography. Mestizos (the term originally applied to individuals of mixed Spanish and Yucatecan Mayan descent but now applied to immigrants from Guatelamala and El Salvador as well) are now the largest ethnic group in Belize, making up 48.7 percent of the population, followed by Creoles (individuals of mixed African and European ancestry), accounting for 24.9 percent. This continued a pattern noted in the 1991 census. For the first time, both urban and rural areas were predominantly Mestizo. Of Belize's six districts, Mestizos were the largest ethnic group in Corozal (76 percent), Orange Walk (77 percent), and Cayo (63.7 percent), while Creoles predominated in Belize (59 percent), Garifuna (Black Caribs) in Stann Creek (31 percent), and Mayas in Toledo (65.4 percent). Almost half of the population (49.6 percent) was Roman Catholic. Surprisingly, only 53.6 percent claimed to speak English well, whereas 52 percent claimed to speak Spanish well. The literacy rate was 76.5 percent in 2000, up 5.2 percent from 1991. Some 85 percent of the population was native born, with the remainder being immigrants from the Central American countries of Guatemala (42.5 percent), El Salvador (17.6 percent), and Honduras (14 percent).

Economy. With an economy based primarily on tourism and the export of primary products, a small domestic population base, weak infrastructure, and heavy consumer demand influenced by

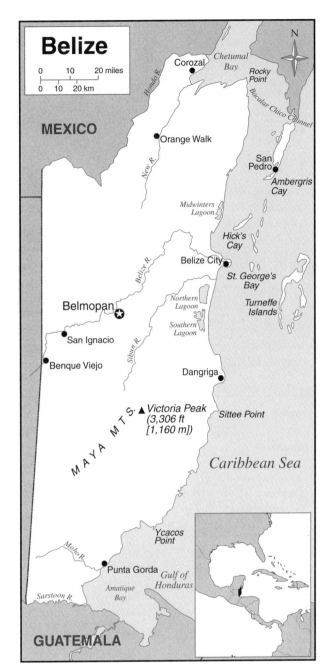

the saturation of cable television from the United States since the 1980s, Belize has struggled in its efforts to grow its economy. After World War II the economy became more diversified, and sugar replaced mahogany as the leading export. In the first decade of the twenty-first century, the leading exports were citrus (orange and grapefruit concentrate), marine products (white farm shrimp and lobster), sugar, bananas, garments, and papayas. These totaled US$206.64 million in 2005. These were dwarfed by imports totaling US$592.92

million. The United States was Belize's leading trading partner, taking 52.27 percent of its exports and providing 39.11 percent of its imports. While the inflation rate at 3.7 percent was up more than a percentage point in 2005, unemployment at 11 percent remained a serious problem. Gross domestic product (GDP) grew by 3.7 percent.

Belize was once a colonial backwater, but tourism has become a major source of revenue over the past several decades. While most of the tourists have been attracted to the offshore islands for skin and scuba diving, recent governments have encouraged ecotourism and archaeological exploration. By 2004 approximately 42 percent of Belize's land area was under some form of protective status. This included 988,000 acres of forest reserves, 408,000 acres of national parks, 388,000 acres of wildlife sanctuaries, 306,000 acres of private reserves, 111,000 acres of nature reserves, and 28,000 acres of archaeological reserves. In the late 1990s Belize began cooperating with Mexico, Guatemala, and Honduras to promote Mundo Maya, offering tourist ventures in the former Maya areas. In 2000 Carnival Cruise Lines joined Norwegian and several smaller lines in making Belize City a stop on their Caribbean cruises. By January 2007 the Belize Tourism Board reported tourist arrivals at the Philip Goldson International Airport up 2.9 percent from 2005 to about 250,000. Cruise passenger arrivals, which reached a peak of 850,000 in 2004, declined to 650,000 in 2006. The opening of a new Southside cruise port planned for 2008 might help, but the future of the cruise industry remained uncertain. There is also fear that the big-spending adventure travelers will go elsewhere if Belize becomes a mass tourist spot. The average cruise passenger spends only $45 in Belize. The $18 million Las Vegas Casino opened in Corozal in September 2006. Located between the northern border checkpoint and the commercial free zone in Corozal, it is designed to cater to

Belize

Population:	294,385 (2007 est.)
Area:	8,867 sq mi
Official language:	English
Languages:	English, Spanish, Creole, Mayan languages, Garifuna, German
National currency:	Belizean dollar (BZD)
Principal religions:	Roman Catholics, 49.6%; Pentecostals, 7.4%; Anglicans, 5.3%; Seventh-day Adventists, 5.2%; Mennonites, 4.1%; Methodists, 3.5%.
Ethnicity:	Mestizo, 48.7%; Creole, 24.9%; Maya, 10.6%; Garifuna, 6.1%; Other, 9.7%.
Capital:	Belmopan
Other urban centers:	Belize City
Annual rainfall:	The north of the country has 50 in of rain on average, the south, over 150 in.
Principal geographical features:	*Mountains:* Cockscomb, Maya *Rivers:* Belize, Hondo, New *Islands:* Ambergris Cay, Hicks Cay, Turneffe Islands, numerous reefs.
Economy:	*GDP per capita:* $8,400 (2006)
Principal products and exports:	*Agricultural:* sugar, bananas, citrus, fish. *Industrial:* clothing, forest products
Government:	Belize became independent of the United Kingdom in 1981 and governed as a parliamentary democracy. The legislature is a bicameral National Assembly made up of a 12-seat Senate and a 29-seat House of Representatives. The head of government is the prime minister. The head of state is a governor general appointed by the monarch of the United Kingdom. Representatives are directly elected. Senators are appointed by the prime minister, governor general, and leading institutions.
Armed forces:	The Belize Defense Force maintains an Army, Maritime Wing, Air Wing, and Support group. There were approximately 1,050 active duty and 700 reserve personnel in 2005.
Transportation:	*Ports:* Belize City, Big Creek, Corozol, Punta Gorda. *Roads:* 303 mi paved / 1,481 mi unpaved *Airports:* 4 paved runway airports, 40 unpaved. International airports at Belize City and Punta Gorda.
Media:	Major weekly newspapers include *Amandala, Belize Today,* and *The Reporter.* 10 private and 1 government radio stations, 2 private television stations.
Literacy and education:	*Total literacy rate:* 76.5% (2000) Education is free and compulsory for children ages 5 to 14. The University of Belize provides higher education.

thousands of Mexicans visiting the free zone. Tourism revenues were estimated at BZ$312.4 million (US$158.36 million) in 2003.

Crime and Health.

Serious social problems of recent vintage also threaten the country and its tourist industry. Once a small domestic producer of marijuana, Belize has become an important transshipment spot in the Colombian cocaine trade. Los Angeles–style gangs began to appear in Belize City in the 1990s, accompanied by crack cocaine. The murder rate soared. While the police department has been reluctant to make crime statistics public, both murders and burglaries were on paths toward record highs in 2007. Channel 5 Belize reported 87 murders in 2006. This was up from 2005 when there were 81 murders and 1,660 burglaries. By July of 2007 there had been 49 homicides, many gang related. One reporter dubbed Belize the "big league of flying bullets" and spoke of an epidemic of violence plaguing the country. In less than twenty years AIDS has become a very serious problem. The national prevalence rate now exceeds 2 percent of the population. Men and women were equally affected in the 434 new infections reported in 2005. AIDS was the number one killer of those aged thirty to forty-nine. One optimistic sign was that more Belizeans were being tested.

Oil.

One of the most positive economic developments in recent years was the discovery of oil near Spanish Lookout in western Belize in 2006. Dating back to the colonial period, the oil and gas industry experienced more than fifty dry wells before striking pay dirt. Belize Natural Energy Ltd. (BNE), made up of more than seventy small investors from Ireland, drilled five successive wells before hitting a dry hole. Production has stabilized at 2,700 barrels of oil per day. With no infrastructure in place, getting the oil to refineries will require new investment. Belize joins Guatemala and Cuba as the only oil and gas producers in the western Caribbean.

HISTORY

Once referred to as a "colonial dead end" or "the place that is no place," by the twenty-first century Belize was a struggling democracy dedicated to ecotourism and a center of intensive archaeological investigation. It was

the setting for countless mystery novels, whose killers drifted off to Belize never to be seen again.

The Maya.

Projectile points discovered near Ladyville tend to confirm the presence of early humans in Belize around 9000 BCE. Settled farming communities began to appear between 2500 and 2250 BCE. There is evidence of maize cultivation, pottery production, and trade in jade and obsidian at several pre-Classic sites (1250 BCE–250 CE). There are indications of terracing and canal building at Pulltrouser Swamp and Cerros, in northern Belize, and at Nohmul, near Orange Walk Town. A manufacturing industry produced oval axes, hoes, and adzes at Colha, near Cerros. Pyramids typical of the Classic period of Maya architecture were constructed at Nohmul.

Excavation of Maya sites in Belize is ongoing and accelerated during the 1990s and the first decade of the 2000s. The major sites include Actun Balam, Altun Ha, Cahal Pech, Caracol, Cerros, Cuello, Lamanai, Lubaantun, Nim Li Punit, Nohmul, Pusilha, Uxbena, and Xunantunich.

At Altun Ha, a site near the north coast of Belize that flourished from c. 800 BCE to 925 CE, with a later reoccupation in the fifteenth century, archaeologist David Pendergast, from the Royal Ontario Museum, discovered large quantities of carved jade, including a 5.9-inch-high, 9.74-pound, full-round head of Kinich Ahau, the sun god. In 2007 Arlen and Diane Chase of the University of Central Florida began their twenty-third excavation season at Caracol, the largest known Classic Maya city in the southern Maya lowlands. In 650 CE the urban area of Caracol had a radius of approximately six miles and may have boasted a population of 140,000 people. These were supported by an immense agricultural field system and elaborate planning. Lamanai in the Orange Walk District was also excavated by the Royal Ontario Museum from 1974 to 1986. It is the first known southern Maya lowlands site with continuous occupation from c. 1500 BCE to 1650–1700 CE. In 1997 Belize's largest speleo-archaeological project was launched as part of the Belize Valley Archaeological Reconnaissance Project directed by archaeologist Jaime Awe. He has also conducted excavations at Cahal Pech, Baking Pot, and many other sites. Some of the most exciting research by Heather McKillop from Louisiana State University describes salt production along the eastern Maya littoral. While searching underwater for evidence of these salt factories in the Punta Ycacos Lagoon in the Toledo District in 2004, her crew discovered the first completely intact, full-sized Maya canoe wooden paddle.

Most Maya centers in the lowlands of Belize experienced political and economic decline in the tenth century for reasons still not understood. Some populations dispersed along lakeshores and rivers. However, the arrival of the Spanish in the sixteenth century found many communities still flourishing and engaging in an extensive trading network.

The Spanish. Hernán Cortés (1485–1547) may have passed through Belize en route to Honduras in 1524–1525. However, it was not until 1544 that the province of Chetumal, which included portions of Belize, was successfully conquered. Belize was incorporated into the two newly created provinces of Chetumal (north) and Dzuluinicob (south). A contributing factor in the ease of conquest may have been pre-Conquest population decline. Population in the region went down between 1517 and 1542 from about 800,000 to about 250,000.

For almost a century, from 1544 to 1638, the Spanish dominated communities at Tipu in the west and Lamanai in the northwest. Indians in these areas were granted in *encomienda* to Spaniards and were forced to supply labor and cacao beans. Anti-Spanish rebellions occurred during 1567 and 1568. In 1638 Lamanai and Tipu joined in a widespread rebellion that expelled the Spaniards from most of Belize until after 1695.

The Bay Settlement. The date of the first British settlement in the Bay of Honduras has not been documented. Legends tell of a settlement along the Cockscomb Coast in the 1630s, whereas others argue that a Scottish-born privateer, Peter Wallace, founded a settlement in 1638. Sustained settlement by British settlers owed its origin to the logwood tree. According to *The Dyer's Assistant* by James Haigh et al. (1870), logwood—when cut into small shavings or chips—was useful for making a great number of colors and shades, from sedan blacks to shades of gray to fine violets, but most commonly for purples. These were used in the European woolen, linen, cotton, and hat manufacturing industries.

While the Treaty of Madrid (1670) between England and Spain marked the first acknowledgement that England had some rights in the West Indies, these were never clearly defined. If logwood cutters viewed this treaty as supporting their territorial claims along the Central American coast, neither the British or Spanish governments ever supported their claims.

This illegal settlement in the heart of the Spanish Empire was under frequent attack from Spanish authorities in Yucatán, and it was abandoned and resettled several times. Article 17 of the Anglo-Spanish Treaty of 1763 gave the settlement some legitimacy by legalizing the cutting, loading, and carrying away of logwood. By the time logwood cutting was legalized, the baymen had turned to the more profitable cutting of mahogany. Mahogany, used in shipbuilding and in the English furniture industry, remained the principal export of the settlement until the mid-twentieth century. Because the baymen were said to prefer hard liquor to hard labor, they began importing African slaves after 1724 to cut timber. Several slave revolts between 1765 and 1773, plus the large number of runaways who sought asylum in Yucatán, suggest that while slavery in Belize may have differed from slavery on the sugar plantations in the Caribbean, it was probably no less onerous. In 1769 Lieutenant James Cook made a trip from the Belize River to the Rio Hondo and thence cross-country to Merida. He wrote that "in traveling through the swamps it is very troublesome, the mules being knee deep, in the dry season, in a stiff blueish mud, often times nearly sticking fast, and the boughs of the logwood trees so low, as to oblige you to lay flat on the mules shoulders whilst the animal is all that time plunging in endeavoring to extricate himself from the mire" (Cook 1769, n.p.).

The earliest form of government in the settlement was the public or town meeting. In these gatherings, magistrates were elected to administer a code based on common law and ancient usage called Burnaby's Code, written by Admiral Sir William Burnaby, commander in chief at Jamaica.

By 1779 the bay settlement consisted of plantations along the banks of several rivers, with settlers numbering about five hundred and slaves totaling about three thousand. Saint George's Cay, a small island just off the coast, was the nominal capital. The Spaniards successfully attacked the cay in 1779, forcing the settlers and their slaves to march overland to Mérida. Four years later, in compliance with the Treaty of Versailles (1783), the Spanish granted the British logwood concessions between the Hondo and Belize rivers. Three years after that the treaty was extended by the Convention of London (1786) to permit the extraction of both logwood and mahogany as far south as the Sibún River. The treaty also forced the British to abandon settlements at Roatán and along the Mosquito Coast. Some 2,214 settlers and their slaves from these settlements moved to Belize.

A writer for the *Britannic Magazine* (1794) stated that trade with "Honduras" was far greater than imagined. He estimated that it involved fifteen hundred seamen shipping twelve thousand tons, giving employment to thirty thousand cabinetmakers and dyers in an enterprise worth one and a half million pounds annually. Annual exports were between five and six million feet of mahogany, two thousand tons of logwood, fustic, ironwood, lignum vitae, zebrawood, brazilwood, cedar and several other woods, turtle shell, sarsaparilla, deerskins, gums, and live turtle. The number of inhabitants in 1790 amounted to about four thousand, of whom four-fifths were slaves. The principal food was salt beef, pork, turtle, and fish.

In 1798 the Spanish, under the command of the captain-general of Yucatán, Arturo O'Neil, launched an unsuccessful attack on the bay settlement, known since as the Battle of Saint George's Cay. The settlers' success in this battle is commemorated on September 10th. Well-prepared and armed with advance intelligence from spies in Havana, the British repelled a much larger Spanish force, although one weakened by yellow fever. This represented the last serious attempt by the Spanish to dislodge the Baymen from their settlement.

The Central American Republics.

With the onset of the independence of Central America in 1821, the British threat had been reduced to the single settlement of Belize (they had largely abandoned settlements in Nicaragua, Honduras, and the Bay Islands). The thirty years after independence saw the reestablishment of the settlement of the Bay Islands, the reassumption of the British protectorate over the Mosquito Coast, the expansion of the boundaries of Belize, and a tremendous expansion of commercial relations between Great Britain and Central America, with most of the trade passing through Belize. The

absence of any deepwater port along the Caribbean coast dictated that British goods be shipped to Belize and then transshipped in coastal vessels to Central American ports. The British entrance into the Central American retail trade coincided with the appearance of commission houses and branches of British commercial companies in Belize. By 1831, considering the British Caribbean as a whole, Belize ranked second only to Jamaica as an importer of British manufactures. However, unable to induce the British to relinquish their position in Belize and unable to develop a satisfactory alternate commercial route, Central Americans became increasingly hostile over the status of Belize.

In 1828 Great Britain claimed the territory of Belize on the basis of conquest, long use, and custom and in 1835 asked Spain to cede the territory. When no response was forthcoming, the British began to exercise more formal jurisdiction over the territory. By the time the Clayton-Bulwer Treaty (1850) between Great Britain and the United States was negotiated, Britain's position was that it had acquired rights of possession.

To legitimize its jurisdiction, Britain signed a treaty with Guatemala on April 30, 1859. The first six articles defined the boundaries of Belize. Article 7 provided for the construction of a road from Guatemala City to the Caribbean coast. Guatemala viewed this as compensation for its loss of territory. When Guatemala failed to ratify a supplementary convention to this treaty in 1863, the end of the stipulated period, the Britain felt that it was now released from the obligation under Article 7. This was disputed by Guatemala. The dispute has festered for more than a century and a half. Guatemala continues to question whether Britain legitimately occupied the territory of Belize.

The bay settlement formally became the Crown Colony of British Honduras in 1862. It was administered by a lieutenant governor who was under the nominal supervision of the governor of Jamaica. When this tie with Jamaica was severed in 1884, the position of lieutenant governor was elevated to governor.

A Depressed Economy.

After 1850 Belize's lucrative reexport trade to Central America declined severely and the economy became dependent on the country's own natural resources. The mahogany trade dominated the economy until well into the twentieth century. The peak year in the nineteenth century was 1846, when exports totaled 13.7 million feet. Thereafter, the wholesale cutting of young trees and the exhaustion of almost all accessible trees seriously depleted the country's timber resources. The increased costs of extracting less accessible reserves combined with declining prices in Europe led to declining profits. By 1870 exports totaled only 2.75 million feet. Levels of exports equal to those of 1846 were not reached again until 1906, when 11 million feet were exported.

Land ownership was increasingly monopolized by a small number of families that developed partnerships with metropolitan companies. Four companies—Young, Toledo and Company; Sheldon Byass and Company; John Carmichael; and the British Honduras Company—owned most of the land by 1870. In 1875 the British Honduras Company became the Belize Estate and Produce Company. That same year, after it acquired property from Young, Toledo, and Company, it became the largest landholder in the colony, owning about half of all privately held land.

The emancipation of the slaves in the 1830s brought little economic improvement in their lives. Through use of a "company store" approach, the freedpersons were kept permanently in debt to the lumber companies. Advances on wages were paid to mahogany workers just prior to the Christmas season. This money being quickly expended, supplies for the cutting season had to be purchased on credit from the employer at exorbitant markups.

A limited trade in chicle, the coagulated latex of the sapodilla tree, began in the late nineteenth century. This tree extract, used in the manufacture of chewing gum, was shipped to the United States. Wrigley's was the predominant purchaser. Exports reached a peak in 1930 with more than four million pounds. Thereafter, the industry went into a decline brought on by overtapping of the trees, the world depression, and a switch to synthetics.

Bananas were first exported in 1890. Between 1896 and 1912 annual exports averaged 500,000 bunches. Prospects appeared bright until 1913, when Panama disease struck the area and exports began a rapid decline. In the same area of the Stann Creek Valley where bananas had previously been grown, a grapefruit industry was established in the 1920s. By 1933 more than 13,000 cases

were being exported. Although several attempts were made to develop the sugar industry prior to World War II, none proved very successful.

By 1890 Belize had a population of about thirty thousand. Twelve thousand people (largely Creoles of African and Caucasian descent) lived in Belize City. Another ten thousand Spanish-speaking Mestizos, refugees from the Caste War in Yucatán, were living in the Corazal District. Four thousand Kekchi and Maya were living in the southern and western regions. Three thousand Garifuna, who had arrived in the colony in the early 1800s from Honduras, lived in Stann Creek and Punta Gorda and surrounding villages. Small numbers of East Indians, imported to work on sugar estates, lived in the south.

However, for most of the period the capital, Belize City, was the colony. The Creoles dominated the political and social life of the colony, and together with a small group of Europeans, they also controlled the economy.

From Colony to Independence, 1862–1981.

In 1871 the crown colony system of government was introduced. The Legislative Assembly was replaced by a Legislative Council composed of five official and five unofficial members, all appointed by the lieutenant governor. This council remained in existence until 1936, when elections resumed. By 1945 six members of the council were elected and four were appointed by the governor. New constitutions in 1954 and 1960 increased the role of elected officials vis-à-vis the governor. Membership in the Legislative Assembly, which included six cabinet ministers, was expanded to eighteen, eleven of whom were elected. The governor's powers were curbed, and he was required to act with the advice of the ministers.

The 1964 constitution granted internal independence. However, the continuing dispute with Guatemala delayed the event until 1981. In preparation, a new capital, Belmopan, was constructed some fifty miles west of Belize City. Disastrous hurricanes in 1931, 1955, and 1961 had made this a necessity. On September 21, 1981, Belize achieved full independence with a parliamentary democracy based on the Westminster system.

A prime minister and cabinet make up the executive branch, while a twenty-nine member elected

A view of downtown Ambergris Cay, 1994. As in much of Belize, tourism is now the main industry in this former quiet fishing village. © DAVID SAMUEL ROBBINS/CORBIS

House of Representatives and an eight-member appointed Senate form a bicameral legislature. The British monarch is the titular head of state and is represented in Belize by a governor-general, who must be a Belizean.

Political Developments since 1945. Considerable labor agitation was provoked in the 1930s by the rapid decline in the mahogany industry during the preceding decade, the Great Depression, and a hurricane of September 10, 1931, which killed one thousand people. Antonio Soberanis Gómez (1897–1975) lobbied for improved wages and work for the unemployed. A barber by trade, he created and led the laborers and unemployed association in the 1930s. The country's first trade union was founded in 1943. It later merged interests with a growing nationalist movement to form Belize's first political party, the People's United Party (PUP), in 1950. Shortly thereafter, George Price, one of its founders, was elected party leader.

Price won an unbroken series of local and national elections until 1984. Over a thirty-year period the PUP obtained continuous mandates from the electorate, first to launch a final attack against colonialism and then to lead the new nation into economic prosperity.

The principal opposition party, the United Democratic Party (UDP), was founded on September 27, 1973, from three smaller parties. Manuel Esquivel served as party chairman from 1976 to 1982 and party leader from 1982 to 1998. In 1984 he led the UDP to a stunning victory (twenty-one of twenty-eight seats) and became Belize's second prime minister. During a five-year term, sound fiscal management and encouragement of foreign investment in tourism and manufacturing helped invigorate the country's economy. However, intraparty wrangling, charges of corruption, and a series of contested party caucuses led to a surprising electoral defeat in 1989. By winning fifteen of the twenty-eight seats that year, the PUP was restored to power and George Price once again became prime minister.

Following the PUP's return to power, the government led by Price steered a course similar to his predecessor's by encouraging agricultural exports and expanding textile manufacturing. Belize took a leadership role in the new ecotourist movement, which seeks to promote preservation of flora and fauna while providing expanded opportunities for the ecologically minded traveler. Several major new hotels were completed in Belize City and a new deepwater port completed at Big River. Improvements were also made in the country's infrastructure, although construction of a much-needed hospital in Belize City suffered repeated delays. By 1992 Belize's economy was suffering from a worldwide recession.

Buoyed by the municipal elections of March 1993, Price decided to call a general election before the end of his term. Soon after this fateful decision, though, a series of events developed in rapid succession that contributed to his government's defeat on June 30. These included Britain's announcement that it would withdraw all of its defense forces from Belize by January 1994 and a 25 May coup in Guatemala. Before the June election, the opposition UDP attacked the Price government for failing to address satisfactorily the security implications for Belize of these two events.

The UDP won sixteen of twenty-nine seats in the new parliament and on July3, Manuel Esquivel was sworn in again as prime minister. He quickly made good on several of his campaign promises by introducing free education at all levels and announced structural reforms to depoliticize the public service. Seeking long-term solutions to Belize's economic problems and under pressure from the International Monetary Fund (IMF), the Esquivel government in October 1995 announced plans to cut government spending by eliminating civil service jobs and freezing teacher wages. This prompted protest marches on Belmopan in October and November. Unmoved, in December the government fired seven hundred public servants, just before Christmas. At the Equivel government's behest, a Value Added Tax (VAT) was passed on April 1, 1996. While these moves appeased Belize's foreign creditors, they were unpopular at home and sealed the fate of the UDP for more than a decade.

Despite predictions of a tight election, on August 27, 1998, the PUP, with its new leader, Said Musa, crushed the Esquivel government, winning twenty-six of twenty-nine seats in the House. The former prime minister lost his own seat and resigned as party leader in favor of Dean Barrow. The new prime minister, a native of San Ignacio, had served as a cabinet minister in the previous Price administrations and was a lawyer trained in the United Kingdom. He had played a key role in drafting Belize's Constitution of 1981. Having campaigned hard on the theme of the need to get the economy moving again, that became a top priority.

During its first term (1998–2003) the Musa government approved the establishment of the University of Belize, made up of five tertiary institutions. At the September celebration of independence in 2000, it recognized the former prime minister, George Price, now senior minister, as a National Hero of Belize. Complaining of the economic mess it had inherited, the government was cautious in introducing measures to spur investment. With the opposition still in disarray, Musa, running on a platform of "No Turning Back," led his party to a resounding victory in the national and municipal elections of March 5, 2003. Winning twenty-two of twenty-nine legislative seats, his became the first government to win two consecutive elections. Because of frequent rumors of corruption at high levels, Musa asked all cabinet members to sign a code of conduct.

Thereafter, the government made a series of economic blunders that further weakened the economy. In 2004 it allowed the Social Security Board (SSB) fund to invest in more than eighteen hundred private mortgages valued at more than $53 million and loaned a further $43 million through a newly created Development Finance Corporation (DFC) to promote economic development. When some borrowers defaulted, Belizeans began to worry about future pensions. Economic woes worsened when the government decided to raise money by selling its majority share in BTL (Belize Telecommunications Ltd) to an American company, Innovative Communication, chaired by Jeffrey Prosser, on April 1, 2004. In November of that year, *Forbes* magazine reported that Prosser had a mountain of debt and was in Washington, D.C., trying to stave off creditors and regulators. Several months later, on February 10, 2005, the government announced that it had taken back BTL and ousted Prosser, who had defaulted on payments. Continuing economic problems, investigations of misconduct at the SSB and DFC, and lowered credit ratings prompted civil unrest and widespread protests and strikes by teachers, students, and public employees in April 2005, with protestors no doubt egged on by the opposition UDP.

On March 2, 2006, this growing economic crisis led to a UDP landslide in the municipal elections. The UDP captured a majority of seats in two cities and seven towns, winning sixty-four of sixty-seven council seats and capturing 60 percent of the popular vote. It now seemed poised to reclaim the national government in the elections of 2008. While Belize signed a partial scope agreement with Guatemala on June 28, 2006, aimed at increasing trade, no progress was made on the long-standing boundary dispute. A report from the International Narcotics Control Strategy complained that Belize continued to be a transshipment point in the cocaine trade in partnership with Mexican and Colombian drug dealers.

As Belize celebrated its twenty-fifth anniversary of political independence on September 21, 2006, Prime Minister Musa noted that his government was implementing a comprehensive package of fiscal, monetary, and financial-sector reforms. These included a 10 percent general sales tax introduced on July 1. For Belize's creditors, however, it was a case of too little, too late. With external debt reaching US$1.1 billion, Belize was forced to default and seek cooperation from the country's private creditors. The government blamed the costs associated with rebuilding from four hurricanes and two major storms between 1998 and 2002. Financial critics blamed fiscal recklessness on the part of the government. In February 2007 Belize became the first country in seventy years to use a collective action clause to restructure a sovereign bond governed by New York law, thus quickly restructuring half of its debt.

See also **Altun Ha; British-Latin American Relations; Caracol; Caribbean Common Market (CARIFTA and CARICOM); Cerros; Clayton-Bulwer Treaty (1850); Creole; Drugs and Drug Trade; International Monetary Fund (IMF); Madrid, Treaty of (1670); Mestizo; Musa, Said; Price, George.**

BIBLIOGRAPHY

General and Pre-1900 Diplomatic Histories

Cook, Lieutenant James. *Remarks on a Passage from the River Balise in the Bay of Honduras, to Merida.* London: Printed for C. Parker, 1769.

Dobson, Narda. *A History of Belize.* Port of Spain, Trinidad and Tobago: Longman Caribbean, 1973.

Grant, C. H. *The Making of Modern Belize: Politics, Society, and British Colonialism in Central America.* Cambridge: Cambridge University Press, 1976.

Humphreys, R. A. *The Diplomatic History of British Honduras, 1638–1901.* New York, Oxford University Press, 1961.

Recent Sources on the Maya

About Caracol. Available from http://www.caracol.org.

Chase, Diane Z., and Arlen F. Chase. *Studies in the Archaeology of Caracol.* 1994. San Francisco: Pre-Columbian Art Research Institute (Monograph 7), 1994.

Garber, James F., ed. *The Ancient Maya of the Belize Valley: Half a Century of Archaeological Research.* Gainesville: University Press of Florida, 2004.

McKillop, Heather. *Salt: White Gold of the Ancient Maya.* Gainesville: University Press of Florida, 2002.

McKillop, Heather. *In Search of Maya Sea Traders.* College Station: Texas A&M University Press, 2005.

Spain, Britain, and the Maya

Jacobi, Keith P. *Last Rites for the Tipu Maya: Genetic Structuring in a Colonial Cemetery.* Tuscaloosa: University of Alabama Press, 2000.

Jones, Grant D. *Maya Resistance to Spanish Rule: Time and History on a Colonial Frontier.* Albuquerque: University of New Mexico, 1984.

Jones, Grant D. *The Conquest of the Last Maya Kingdom.* Stanford, CA: Stanford University Press, 1998.

Naylor, Robert A. *Penny Ante Imperialism: The Mosquito Shore and the Bay of Honduras, 1600–1914: A Case Study in British Informal Empire.* Rutherford, NJ: Fairleigh Dickinson University Press, 1989.

Eighteenth and Nineteenth Centuries

Bolland, O. Nigel. *Colonialism and Resistance in Belize: Essays in Historical Sociology,* 2nd edition. Benque Viejo del Carmen, Belize: Cubola Productions, 2003.

Clegern, Wayne M. *British Honduras: Colonial Dead End, 1859–1900.* Baton Rouge: Louisiana State University Press, 1967.

Finamore, Daniel. "Pirates of the Barcadares: Early Mariners in Belize Left Archaeologists Tantalizing

Traces of Their Lives but No Buried Treasure." *Natural History,* November 2002.

Johnson, Melissa A. "The Making of Race and Place in Nineteenth-Century British Honduras." *Environmental History* 8, no. 4 (2003): 598–617. Also available from http://historycooperative.press.uiuc.edu/journals/eh/8.4/johnson.html.

Simmons, Donald C., Jr. *Confederate Settlements in British Honduras.* Jefferson, NC: McFarland, 2001.

Twentieth and Twenty-First Centuries

Arvigo, Rosita. *Sastun: My Apprenticeship with a Maya Healer.* San Francisco, CA: HarperSanFrancisco, 1994.

McClaurin, Irma. *Women of Belize: Gender and Change in Central America.* New Brunswick, NJ: Rutgers University Press, 1996.

Macpherson, Anne S. *From Colony to Nation: Women Activists and the Gendering of Politics in Belize, 1912–1982.* Lincoln: University of Nebraska Press, 2007.

Palacio, Myrtle. *Who and What in Belizean Elections: 1954–1993.* Belize: Glessima Research, 1993.

Roessingh, Carel et al. *Entrepreneurs in Tourism in the Caribbean Basin: Case Studies from Belize, the Dominican Republic, Jamaica and Surinam.* Amsterdam: Dutch University Press, 2005.

Shoman, Assad. *Party Politics in Belize.* Belize: Cubola Productions, 1987.

Shoman, Assad. *13 Chapters of a History of Belize.* Belize City, Belize: Angelus Press, 1994.

Sutherland, Anne. *The Making of Belize: Globalization in the Margins.* Westport, CT: Bergin and Garvey, 1998.

Wiegan, Krista E. "Nationalist Discourse and Domestic Incentives to Prevent Settlement of the Territorial Dispute between Guatemala and Belize." *Nationalism and Ethnic Politics* 11 (2005): 349–383.

Ethnic Studies

Koop, Gerhard S. *Pioneer Years in Belize.* Belize City, Belize: G. S. Koop, 1991.

Loewen, Royden. *Diaspora in the Countryside: Two Mennonite Communities and Mid-Twentieth-Century Rural Disjuncture.* Toronto: University of Toronto Press, 2006.

Palacio, Joseph O. *The Garifuna: A Nation Across Borders—Essays in Social Anthropology.* Benque Viejo del Carmen, Belize: Cubola Productions, 2005.

Roessingh, Carel. *The Belizean Garifuna: Organization of Identity in an Ethnic Community in Central America.* West Lafayette, IN: Purdue University Press, 2001.

Wilk, Richard W. *Household Ecology: Economic Change and Domestic Life among the Kekchi Maya in Belize.* Tucson: University of Arizona Press, 1991.

Wright, Peggy, and Brian E. Coutts, comps. *Belize.* 2nd ed. Santa Barbara, CA: CLIO Press, 1993. Also a Net Library e-book (2002).

Online Sources

Attorney General's Ministry. Available from http://www.belizelaw.org.

Belize Free Press. Available from http://belizefreepress.com.

Central Statistical Office (CSO). Available from http://www.cso.gov.bz.

Elections and Boundaries Department of Belize. Available from http://www.belize-elections.org/index.html.

Government of Belize. Available from http://www.belize.gov.bz/index.php.

BRIAN E. COUTTS

BELLEGARDE, LUIS DANTÈS (1877–1966). Luis Dantès Bellegarde (*b.* 18 May 1877; *d.* 14 June 1966), Haitian educator, politician, diplomat, and author. A native of Port-au-Prince, Bellegarde taught at the secondary and university levels before entering politics. He joined the Ministry of Foreign Affairs around 1905 and was minister of public instruction and agriculture in 1918–1921. In 1950 he was president of the Constituent Assembly. Bellegarde's diplomatic activity included service as ambassador to France and the Vatican (appointed 1921) and as ambassador to the United States (appointed 1931) and to the United Nations.

Bellegarde was coauthor of almost twenty books on Haitian history, politics, and sociology. Among them are *La nation haïtienne* (1938), written with Sténio Vincent, and *Haïti et son peuple* (1953), written with Mercer Cook.

Bellegarde remains controversial for his pro-French, Christian, and Western views. Nevertheless, his contributions to Haitian social thought; foreign, financial, and economic policy; and education are clear. He died in Port-au-Prince.

See also **Haiti.**

BIBLIOGRAPHY

Paul Blanchet, "Sur la tombe de Dantès Bellegarde," in *La Nouvelliste,* 17 June 1966.

Patrick Bellegarde-Smith, *In the Shadow of Powers: Dantès Bellegarde in Haitian Social Thought* (1985).

ANNE GREENE

BELLI, GIOCONDA (1948–). Gioconda

Belli (*b.* 9 December 1948), Nicaraguan poet and novelist. Best known for her autobiographical, erotic, and feminist celebration of sexuality and the female body, Belli has published four books of poetry: *Sobre la grama* (1974); *Línea de fuego* (1978), winner of the Cuban Casa de las Américas Prize; *Truenos y arcoiris* (1982); and *De la costilla de Eva* (1987; *From Eve's Rib*, 1993). In testimony to her rising reputation in Central America, all four books were republished together as *Poesía reunida* (1989). An ardent supporter of the Sandinista revolution, Belli wrote eloquently of the loss of friends and comrades in the fighting. Her first novel, *La mujer habitada* (1988; *The Inhabited Woman*, 1994), recounts the struggle of a Latin American woman to transcend the politics of individualistic bourgeois feminism and join the broader historical struggle of all oppressed peoples. Her second novel, *Sofía de los presagios* (1990), depicts the feminist struggles of a woman in contemporary Nicaragua. In addition to English, much of Belli's work has been translated into German.

See also **Literature: Spanish America; Nicaragua.**

BIBLIOGRAPHY

For studies of Belli's narrative, see María Salgado, "Gioconda Belli, novelista revolucionaria," and Vicente Cabrera, "La intertextualidad subversiva en *La mujer habitada*," in *Monographic Review/Revista Monográfica* 8 (1992): 229–242 and 243–251; Luis T. González Del Valle, ed., *Critical Essays on the Literatures of Spain and Spanish America* (1991); Lady Rojas Trempe, "La alteridad indígena y mágica en la narrativa de Elena Garro, Manuel Scorza y Gioconda Belli," in *Alba de América: Revista Literaria* 9 (1991): 141–152. For studies of her poetry, see Kathleen March, "Gioconda Belli: The Erotic Politics of the Great Mother," in *Monographic Review/Revista Monográfica* 6 (1990): 245–257; and Electra Arenal, "Two Poets of the Sandinista Struggle," in *Feminist Studies* 7, no. 1 (1981): 19–27.

Additional Bibliography.

Barbas-Rhoden, Laura. *Novels of Testimony and Resistance from Central America.* Gainesville: University Press of Florida, 1997.

Belli, Gioconda. *The Country under My Skin: A Memoir of Love and War.* New York: Knopf, 2002.

Belli, Gioconda. *The Inhabited Woman.* Willimantic, CT: Curbstone Press, 1994.

Belli, Gioconda. *The Scroll of Seduction: A Novel.* New York: Harper Collins, 2006.

Rodríguez, Ileana. *House/Garden/Nation: Space, Gender, and Ethnicity in Post-Colonial Latin American Literatures by Women.* Durham, NC: Duke University Press, 1994.

ANN GONZÁLEZ

BELLINATI, PAULO (1950–). Guitarist,

composer, and arranger Paulo Bellinati is a native of São Paulo, Brazil. He studied with Isaias Sávio, graduated from São Paulo's Conservatory of Drama and Music, and lived in Switzerland for several years, studying at the Conservatory of Geneva and teaching at the Conservatory of Lausanne. He has toured extensively, and has recorded and performed with many of Brazil's most important artists. Bellinati has won numerous awards as a performer, arranger, and producer, including the Prêmio Sharp, Brazil's equivalent of a Grammy, in 1994. His many compositions and arrangements for guitar solo and chamber music have been performed and recorded by important Brazilian and international musicians, including Caetano Veloso, Chico Buarque, Carlos Barbosa-Lima, John Williams, the Assad Brothers, and the Los Angeles Guitar Quartet. He has also transcribed and recorded works by Garoto, one of Brazil's most important popular music guitarists.

See also **Music: Popular Music and Dance.**

BIBLIOGRAPHY

Ferguson, Jim. "Brazilian Complications." *Classical Guitar* 10: 5 (January 1992), 11–12.

Ferguson, Jim. "Paulo Bellinati—Brazilian Soul, Classical Mind." *Guitar Player* 30 (September 1996), 22.

Hodel, Brian. "Paulo Bellinati." *Guitar Review* 88 (Winter 1992), 4–6.

Martinez, Emma. "Paulo Bellinati." *Classical Guitar* 16: 12 (August 1998), 32–33.

THOMAS GEORGE CARACAS GARCIA

BELLO, ANDRÉS (1781–1865). Andrés

Bello (*b.* 29 November 1781; *d.* 15 October 1865), Venezuelan polymath and public servant, the most distinguished Latin American intellectual of his (and perhaps any other) century. Born and educated in Caracas, Bello accompanied Simón Bolívar (1783–1830), whom he had briefly taught, as a member of the first Venezuelan diplomatic mission to Britain (1810). The collapse of the Venezuelan Republic stranded him in London, where he lived, often penuriously, for more than eighteen years. In the 1820s he coedited the influential Spanish-American journals *La Biblioteca Americana* (1823) and *El Repertorio Americano* (1826–1827), and worked as an official of the Chilean and Colombian legations. At the invitation of the Chilean government, he moved to Santiago in 1829. He was employed thereafter as senior official in the foreign ministry, as editor of the government gazette *El Araucano,* and as first rector of the newly founded University of Chile (1843–1865)—still colloquially known in Chile as *la casa de Bello* (Bello's house). He was a senator from 1837 to his death.

The extraordinary range of Bello's genius was reflected in prolific writings on international and Roman law, philosophy, literature, drama, grammar, and science. His poems, especially the two great London poems, "Alocución a la poesía" (Allocution to Poetry, 1823), and "A la agricultura de la zona tórrida" (Agriculture in the Torrid Zone, 1826), have often been seen as the true starting point of all postcolonial Latin American literature. Bello's work as a jurist was crowned by his single-handed authorship of the classic Civil Code of the Republic of Chile (1855). His numerous writings on language culminated in the *Gramática de la lengua castellana destinada al uso de los americanos* (Grammar of the Spanish Language for the Use of Americans, 1847), which won him honorary membership in the Real Academia in Spain. He made radical proposals to modify the orthography of Spanish; several features of his scheme remained in use in Chile until around 1910. His guidance also shaped a school of Chilean historians.

Bello's influence on the intellectual life of nineteenth-century Chile is incalculable. At the heart of all Bello's work lay the belief that Latin America, now politically free, needed to create its own cultural and intellectual traditions, traditions that would be authentically Latin American, without repudiating the achievements of European civilization. At his funeral in 1865 the scientist Ignacio Domeyko (1801–1889) doubted "that one man, in one lifetime, could know so much, could do so much, could love so much." Bello's bicentennial in 1981 was extensively commemorated throughout Spanish America.

See also **Chile: The Nineteenth Century; Literature: Spanish America.**

BIBLIOGRAPHY

Rafael Caldera, *Andrés Bello,* translated by John Street (1977).

John Lynch, ed., *Andrés Bello: The London Years* (1982).

Additional Bibliography

Jaksic, Ivan. *Andrés Bello: Scholarship and Nation-Building in Nineteenth-Century Latin America.* New York: Cambridge University Press, 2001.

SIMON COLLIER

BELLY, FÉLIX (1816–1886). Félix Belly (*b.* October 1816; *d.* 3 November 1886), French journalist and promoter of a Nicaraguan transisthmian canal. Belly visited Nicaragua and received a canal concession in 1858 from the government of General Tomás Martínez. Belly's settlement of a boundary dispute between Nicaragua and Costa Rica cleared the way for work to begin. Yet Belly faced other problems. The U.S. government disapproved of Belly's work, fearing that he was an agent of French imperialism. More serious still was a shortage of investment capital. Belly surveyed a canal route, but financial problems and renewed border disputes terminated the project.

See also **French-Latin American Relations.**

BIBLIOGRAPHY

Cyril Allen, *France in Central America: Félix Belly and the Nicaraguan Canal* (1986).

David I. Folkman, Jr., *The Nicaragua Route* (1972).

STEVEN S. GILLICK

BELMOPAN. Belmopan, capital of Belize. Discussion of the need for a new capital for the British colony of British Honduras took place for years before it was actually built. Four reasons were advanced: first, the old capital, Belize City, lying a scant eighteen inches above sea level, had been devastated by major hurricanes in 1931 and 1955.

Second, planners hoped to reduce the overwhelming centralization of educational, economic, political, and cultural functions in Belize City. Third, some people believed that Belize City, with its squalid slums, inadequate sanitation, and severe overcrowding, had reached the limits of urbanization. Finally, the government hoped to focus attention on the neglected interior of the country.

Planning began in earnest following Hurricane Hattie, which struck Belize City on 31 October 1961 and killed 262 people and destroyed or damaged 75 percent of the city's structures. A site near Roaring Creek Village, some 50 miles southwest of Belize City, was selected. Safe from the onslaught of hurricanes, it had an abundant supply of potable water from the Belize River and was located at the intersection of two of the country's major highways.

Designed to be built in five stages over a twenty-year period, only $12 million was initially available in the form of loans and grants from the British government. Of 8,100 acres purchased for the site, 450 acres were cleared. Construction began in 1966, and the new capital opened officially in 1970. By then buildings to house the national government, civil servants, and essential public services had been completed. The central area for public buildings includes three plazas, government, civic administration, and commercial, which are connected by pedestrian walkways. The government complex, in the shape of a Mayan temple, includes a series of gray concrete-block buildings that house the principal ministries and is crowned by the National Assembly.

Twenty years after the first offices were occupied, the buildings, with their cell-like offices, were severely overcrowded, and in 1991 construction began on two massive new office structures. Other buildings completed since 1970 include the government printery, the public works department, a police training complex, the national archives, and Belize House, the residence of the governor general. Municipal buildings housing police, fire officials, a post office, and a civic center have also been completed. The commercial sector has grown more slowly. More than eight hundred residences have been constructed and occupied since 1970. In 2000, the town of Belmopan was incorporated.

While some early planners envisioned a busy city of thirty thousand people with tree-lined avenues by the 1980s, population growth has been modest. In 2005 the population was estimated at 13,500. Nevertheless, since the 1980s Belmopan has attracted refugees from neighboring Central American countries, many of whom have settled on the city's outskirts. The new capital has spurred agricultural and commercial development in the center of the country and now is an important transportation hub. Since the 1990s Belmopan has experienced growth: a number of foreign governments relocated their embassies from Belize City, and it is home to the main campus of the University of Belize. On the negative side, few industries have relocated to Belmopan. Many civil servants continue to commute from Belize City.

See also **Belize.**

BIBLIOGRAPHY

Belmopan, Belize C. A., Miscellaneous Collection #97 (ca. 1970), National Archives (26–28 Unity Blvd., Belmopan, Belize).

Peter Furley, "A Capital Waits for Its Country," in *Geographical Magazine* 43, no. 10 (1971): 713–716.

Kevin C. Kearns, "Belmopan: Perspective on a New Capital," in *Geographical Review* 63, no. 2 (1973): 147–169.

M. Day, G. Gruszczynski, and K. Schuparra, "Belmopan, the Hummingbird Highway, and Other Regional Influences," in *Environment and Resources in the Hummingbird Karst of Central Belize,* University of Wisconsin–Milwaukee, Department of Geography, Occasional Papers Series, no. 2 (1987): 42–49, and figs. 9 and 10, pp. 15–16.

Additional Bibliography

Probst, Heinz J., and Helmut Nuhn, eds. *Polarization and Capital Relocation in Belize: Case Studies in Urban Development and Planning.* Hamburg, Germany: Wayasbah, 1990.

Woods, Louis A., Joseph M. Perry, and Jeffrey W. Steagall. "The Composition and Distribution of Ethnic Groups in Belize: Immigration and Emigration Patterns, 1980–1991." *Latin American Research Review* 32, no. 3 (1997): 63–88.

BRIAN E. COUTTS

BELO HORIZONTE.

Belo Horizonte is a major industrial center and the capital of Minas Gerais, the second most populous state in Brazil. Located on a plateau in the mountains of southeastern Brazil at an elevation of approximately 2,500 feet, greater Belo Horizonte has a population of more than 4 million. It is the third largest city and industrial center in Brazil.

State politicians and planners created the city in the 1890s to replace the small, isolated state capital at Ouro Prêto. They hoped to create a new and dynamic political and economic center for the state. After a contentious debate, the state government decided to build the new capital on the site of Curral del Rei, a small hamlet with some eight thousand inhabitants, located in the center of the state. Inspired by the examples of Washington, D.C., and Paris, planners designed the central area of the city using a geometric grid plan.

From its inauguration in 1897 until World War II, Belo Horizonte served mainly as a bureaucratic and administrative center, with a growing population but little heavy industry. By the early 1940s the city had a population approaching a quarter million.

Over the next four decades Belo Horizonte rapidly industrialized, becoming a major center for the production of iron and steel, automobiles, and cement. Located in the heart of a region rich in iron ore, bauxite, manganese, and gold, the city has also developed into a major center for mining and construction companies.

Belo Horizonte has become a more dominant economic and political capital for Minas Gerais than its planners ever envisioned. State planners and politicians now search for ways to decrease the concentration of nearly one-third of the state's industrial production in a single city.

See also **Automobile Industry; Iron and Steel Industry; Mining: Modern.**

BIBLIOGRAPHY

Eakin, Marshall C. "Creating a Growth Pole: The Industrialization of Belo Horizonte, Brazil, 1897–1987," *Americas* 47 (1991): 383–410.

Eakin, Marshall C. *Tropical Capitalism: The Industrialization of Belo Horizonte, Brazil.* New York: Palgrave, 2001.

Wirth, John D. *Minas Gerais in the Brazilian Federation, 1889–1937.* Stanford, CA: Stanford University Press, 1977.

MARSHALL C. EAKIN

BELTRÁN, LOLA (1932–1996). Lola Beltrán (María Lucila Beltrán Ruíz) was a Mexican ranchera singer who achieved superstar status. Known as "Lola la Grande" (Lola the Great), Beltrán was the most successful female ranchera singer after Lucha Reyes (1906-1944). She was born on 7 March 1932, in El Rosario, Sinaloa, like Reyes into a lower-class family. She was working as a secretary at a radio station (XEW) in Mexico City in the 1950s when she was discovered by the singer Matilde Sánchez. With the help of Sánchez and Miguel Aceves Mejía, she made her debut as a singer. During her career she recorded more than a hundred records, with hits such as "Cucurrucucú paloma," "Huapango torero," and "Paloma negra." She also worked extensively in film, mainly musicals, including *El tesoro de la muerte* (1954), *Cucurrucucú paloma* (1965), and *Una gallina muy ponedora* (1982). In the 1970s she was in the television soap opera *Mi rival.* Besides her noteworthiness as a female singer in an otherwise male-dominated field, she is significant for bringing ranchera music, a traditional Mexican style related to mariachi, to the international stage, and is informally known as the "Ambassador of the Ranchera." She was the first ranchera artist to perform at the Palacio de Bellas Artes in Mexico City. Beltrán influenced many singers working in the genre, including Rocío Dúrcal and Linda Ronstadt. She died suddenly on 24 March 1996, in Mexico City.

See also **Music: Popular Music and Dance.**

BIBLIOGRAPHY

Garcia-Orozco, Antonia. "Cucurrucucú Palomas: The Estilo Bravío of Lucha Reyes and the Creation of Feminist Consciousness via the Canción Ranchera." Ph.D. diss., Claremont Graduate University, 2005.

Nájera-Ramírez, Olga. "Unruly Passions: Poetics, Performance, and Gender in the Ranchera Song." In *Chicana Feminisms: A Critical Reader*, edited by Gabriela F. Arredondo et al., pp. 184-210. Durham, NC: Duke University Press, 2003.

CARYN C. CONNELLY

BELTRÁN, LUIS (1784–1827). Luis Beltrán (*b.* 7 September 1784; *d.* 8 December 1827), Franciscan friar and chaplain of several Platine armies during the struggle against Spain. Born near Mendoza, Argentina, Fray Beltrán entered the Franciscan order when barely sixteen years old and soon moved to the convent in Santiago, Chile. His military career started after he joined José Miguel Carrera's army as chaplain and took part in the battle of Hierbas Buenas in 1812. Although this battle was disastrous for the rebels, it allowed Beltrán to demonstrate his skills at military engineering. He later held, for example, the post of director of ordnance (1820–1824) for the Chileans and worked in that same capacity under Simón Bolívar in Peru in 1824. An argument with Bolívar, however, led to a suicide attempt by Beltrán and dimmed his work and health thereafter. Lieutenant Colonel Beltrán left the army in 1827 and retired to Buenos Aires, where he renewed his interest in the religious life he had never formally abandoned. He was named "heroic defender of the nation" by Buenos Aires. He died in Buenos Aires.

See also **Franciscans.**

BIBLIOGRAPHY

Alfredo Gargaro, *Pedro Regalado de la Plaza, director de la maestranza del ejército de los Andes* (1950).

Ricardo Piccirilli Et Al., *Diccionario histórico argentino*, vol. 1 (1953), pp. 520–521.

FIDEL IGLESIAS

BELTRÁN, LUIS (SAINT) (1526–1581).

Luis (Saint) Beltrán (*b.* 1 January 1526; *d.* 10 October 1581), Spanish Dominican missionary and patron saint of Colombia. Born in Valencia and ordained in 1547, Beltrán arrived in Cartagena in 1562. After proselytizing among the Indians of the northern coast, he served for three years as *doctrinero* of Turbará, near present-day Barranquilla. A letter from Bartolomé de Las Casas warning him to be careful of how he confessed and absolved *encomenderos* of their sins may have led him to a more determined defense of the Indians. Appearing before one banquet table of *encomenderos*, Beltrán dramatically squeezed the corn *arepas* (pancakes), the fruit of Indian labor, so hard that blood supposedly trickled onto the white tablecloth. His conflicts with *encomenderos* and his fame as a holy man grew. Brought back to Cartagena as a preacher and fundraiser,

Beltrán addressed audiences all along the Caribbean coast from Nombre de Dios to Santa Marta. On his way to serve as prior of the Dominican friary in Bogotá, he was ordered back to Spain, where he arrived in 1569. Chosen to head several Spanish religious houses, he died in Valencia. He was beatified by Paul V in 1608 and canonized by Clement X in 1671.

See also **Dominicans.**

BIBLIOGRAPHY

See Juan Manuel Pacheco, S.J., *Historia extensa de Colombia*, vol. 13, *Historia eclesiástica*, tomo 1, *La evangelización del Nuevo Reino, siglo xvi* (1971), esp. pp. 485–488.

MAURICE P. BRUNGARDT

BELTRÁN, MANUELA (1724–?). Man-

uela Beltrán (*b.* 1724; *d.* ?), Comunero insurgent. A heroine of the Comunero Revolt that swept through the uplands of New Granada in 1781, Manuela Beltrán remains an obscure figure. Born of Spanish ancestry in Socorro, province of Tunja, she appears to have been a woman of modest means. Her home, a prosperous agricultural, commercial, and textile manufacturing town, was hit hard by the ambitious, intemperately applied revenue measures of Regent Visitor Gutiérrez de Piñeres. Riots erupted in Socorro on 16 March 1781 following the promulgation of the decree separating the collection of the Alcabala and the Armada de Barlovento taxes, which people mistakenly believed to be a new tax. Emerging from the angry crowd, Manuela Beltrán, in the midst of riotous applause, dramatically tore down the Armada de Barlovento ordinance, an act that at least symbolically marked the beginning of the Comunero revolt. Thereafter, Beltrán disappeared from history, but she is representative of the prominent role that women so often played in the popular protests of the eighteenth century.

See also **Comunero Revolt (New Granada).**

BIBLIOGRAPHY

Pablo E. Cárdenas Acosta, *El movimiento comunal de 1781 en el Nuevo Reino de Granada (reivindicaciones históricas)*, vol. 1 (1960), esp. p. 101.

John Leddy Phelan, *The People and the King: The Comunero Revolution in Columbia, 1781* (1978), esp. pp. 46–60.

ALLAN J. KUETHE

BELTRÁN, PEDRO (1897–1979).

Pedro Beltrán (*b.* 17 February 1897; *d.* 16 February 1979), Peruvian landowner, economist, publisher, and politician. Born in Cañete, he became a distinguished representative of liberal interests among the economic elite of coastal Peru. He studied at San Marcos University and in London at Kings College and the London School of Economics, from which he received a master's degree in economics in 1918. On his return to Peru, he promoted agricultural modernization and organized cotton and sugar producers. By 1929, Beltrán had become the president of the influential National Agrarian Society and a member of the board of directors of the Peruvian Reserve Bank.

After the fall of President Augusto B. Leguía in 1930, Beltrán continued to exercise his influence as a leading exporter of agricultural goods through the daily newspaper *La Prensa*, which he bought in 1934. Between 1944 and 1946, Beltrán was the Peruvian ambassador to the United States and presided over the Peruvian delegation at the Bretton Woods conference. He vigorously opposed state controls over imports and foreign currency exchange under president José Luis Bustamante y Rivero (1945–1948). In 1956, Beltrán was imprisoned by Manuel Odría for his opposition as head of the National Coalition, a civilian political group. In 1959–1960, during the second Prado administration, he served as minister of finance. In 1974 the military government expropriated his newspaper. He lived thereafter in exile in New York City, where he died.

See also **Peru, Organizations: National Agrarian Society.**

BIBLIOGRAPHY

Rosemary Thorp and Geoffrey Bertram, *Peru, 1890–1977: Growth and Policy in an Open Economy* (1978).

Gonzalo Portocarrero Maisch, *De Bustamante a Odría* (1983).

ALFONSO W. QUIROZ

BELTRÁN, WASHINGTON (1885–1920).

Washington Beltrán (*b.* 7 February 1885; *d.* 2 April 1920), Uruguayan lawyer, journalist, and politician. While earning very high grades in Montevideo's National University, School of Law and Social Sciences, Beltrán published several articles of note in scientific and literary journals. Later, he extended his expertise into philosophical and legal terrains, with the publication of articles such as "Los filósofos del siglo XVIII," "*El contrato social*," and "Fallos de la Alta Corte de Justicia en materia civil, penal, comercial, administrativa y de lo contencioso administrativo" in Buenos Aires's *Revista de Derecho* between 1908 and 1909. With Carlos Roxlo he directed the newspaper *El Civismo* and later wrote on political issues for *La Democracia* and other newspapers. He also served in the Justice Department. As codirector and principal writer of *El País*, he consistently opposed the socialist and populist program of Colorado Party leader José Batlle y Ordóñez, during Batlle's second term as president from 1911 to 1915. In 1914 Beltrán was elected deputy to the National Congress. Between 1916 and 1917 he served as a member of the National Constituent Assembly, which approved a two-party governing council, the Colegiado, to replace the presidency. Beltrán was killed in 1920 during a pistol duel with Batlle.

See also **Uruguay: Constitutions.**

WILLIAM H. KATRA

BELZU, MANUEL ISIDORO (1808–1865).

Manuel Isidoro Belzu (*b.* 4 April 1808; *d.* 27 March 1865), president of Bolivia (1848–1855). Born into a poor artisan family in La Paz, Belzu was educated at the Franciscan monastery. At thirteen he ran away from the monks and joined an army fighting Spanish forces. He fought for various generals, including Agustín Gamarra of Peru and Andrés Santa Cruz, José Ballivián, and José Miguel de Velasco of Bolivia. He became minister of war in the Velasco government in February 1848.

Belzu seized control of the government in December 1848. Employing populist rhetoric, he was the first general to base his regime on the urban artisans and Cholos (people of mixed Indian and European heritage). Although he remained in power until 1855, when he "constitutionally" handed the presidency to his son-in-law, General Jorge Córdova, Belzu failed to consolidate control. He survived one assassination attempt in 1850 and forty-two revolutions against his authority. From 1855 to 1857, he represented Bolivia in Europe, where he remained until 1865. That same year he returned to Bolivia in order to prevent the assumption of power by Mariano Melgarejo, who had him assassinated.

See also **Bolivia: Since 1825.**

BIBLIOGRAPHY

Julia Díaz Arguedas, *Los generales de Bolivia (rasgos biográficos) 1825–1925* (1929), pp. 431–439.

Herbert S. Klein, *Bolivia: The Evolution of a Multi-Ethnic Society* (1982), pp. 128–131, 133–135.

Oficina Nacional De Estadística De Bolivia, *De siglo a siglo, hombres celebres de Bolivia* (1920), pp. 85–89.

Fausto Reinaga, *Belzu: Precursor de la revolución nacional* (1953).

Additional Bibliography

Molina Céspedes, Tomás. *Belzú, quien lo mató?* Cochabamba: T. Molina Céspedes, Editora J.V., 2001.

ERWIN P. GRIESHABER

BEMBERG, MARÍA LUISA (1922–1995).

Argentine filmmaker María Luisa Bemberg is an exception to many norms: She was a member of the Argentine oligarchy, by definition a minority group; she was one of the few successful women directors in Latin America; she made her first feature when she was a grandmother in her late fifties; and finally, of the handful of films she made, most enjoyed some degree of success either nationally or internationally. The extensive bibliography on Bemberg and her work is testament to her significance in Latin American cinema, and particularly cinema by women.

Up to a point Bemberg followed the rules for a woman of her social group. Born 14 April 1922, she married early within her class, and went on to have four children. Contrary to the rules, however, she divorced some ten years later. During the time her children were growing up, she dabbled in feminist activities, but did not get into film until the 1970s, when two of her screenplays were adapted by well-known male directors. It was the combination of her dissatisfaction with how her stories were adapted and her privileged economic status that led her to directing her own films. Her directorial debut came in 1981 with *Momentos*, made when she was 59 years old.

Bemberg's films clearly reveal her feminist orientation in that they focus on female characters, most often of the upper class, and always trapped by social conventions. Some of them are more contemporary in setting, whereas others are historical pieces. One of her most successful films, *Camila*, for example, is based on the true story of the ill-fated romance of a young upper-class woman, Camila O'Gorman, and a local priest in nineteenth century Argentina. While thematically her films are feminist in their approach, formally they follow a classic narrative structure and in some instances may be classified as melodramas—categorizations that seem to undermine the challenges of her feminist politics. At the same time, many critics have noted how in her work she repeatedly subverts the "male gaze" of classic narrative cinema by granting the power of looking to the female characters.

Films directed by Bemberg include *Momentos* (1981); *Señora de nadie* (1982); *Camila* (1984; Academy Award nomination, Best Foreign Language Film); *Miss Mary* (1986; Best Film, Best Actress, Best Set Design, Havana Film Festival, 1986); *Yo, la peor de todas* (1990; Organisation Catholique Internationale du Cinéma et de l'Audiovisuel [OCIC] Award, and Honorable Mention, Venice Film Festival, 1990); and *De eso no se habla* (1993; Best Screenplay [with Jorge Goldenberg] and Special Jury Prize, Havana Film Festival, 1993). Bemberg died in Buenos Aires on 7 May 1995.

See also **Cinema: From the Silent Film to 1990.**

BIBLIOGRAPHY

Carbonetti, Maria de los Angeles, Rita de Grandis, Monica Escudero, and Omar Rodriguez. "Representation of Women in the Films of Maria Luisa Bemberg" in *Women Filmmakers: Refocusing*, ed. Jacqueline Levitin, Judith Plessis, and Valerie Raoul. Vancouver: University of British Colombia Press, 2003.

De Grandis, Rita, ed. *María Luisa Bemberg: Entre lo político y lo personal.* Special Issue, *Revista Canadiense de Estudios Hispánicos* 27, no. 1 (Otoño 2002).

King, John, Sheila Whitaker, and Rosa Bosch, eds. *An Argentine Passion: María Luisa Bemberg and Her Films.* London and New York: Verso, 2000.

Salas, Hugo. "Some Girls Are Bigger than Others: María Luisa Bemberg." *Senses of Cinema* 22 (September–October 2002). Available from http://www.sensesofcinema.com/contents/02/22/bemberg.html.

Stone, Cynthia L. "Beyond the Female Gaze: María Luisa Bemberg's Sor Juana Inés de la Cruz." *CiberLetras* 13 (July 2005). Available from http://www.lehman.cuny.edu/ciberletras/.

Vásquez, Lourdes. *De identidades: María Luisa Bemberg, filmografía y bibliografía.* SALALM Latin American Information series, No. 6. Available from http://www.libs.uga.edu/lais/laisno6.html.

CARYN C. CONNELLY

BEMBERG, OTTO (1827–1895).
Otto Bemberg (*b.* 1827; *d.* 1895), German-born businessman in Argentina. Bemberg arrived in Buenos Aires in the 1850s and established a prosperous import-export business. He married the daughter of the influential Senator Mariano Ocampo and served as Argentine consul in Paris during the War of the Triple Alliance (1865–1870). He became involved in the arms trade with Argentina, and following his return to Buenos Aires, he became an agent for many important French industrial companies, especially the Schneider firm, which exported railway and other heavy equipment to the Río de la Plata.

With offices in Buenos Aires and Paris, Bemberg began to specialize in financial dealings, and he was the agent for a large number of Argentine provincial loans issued on the Paris Stock Exchange in the 1880s. He was an agent to various French banks and helped arrange financing for a French-owned railway in Argentina and for the construction of the port works in Rosario.

In 1888 Bemberg established the Quilmes Beer Company, long the largest brewery in Argentina, which remains owned by the Bemberg family. The brewery expanded production spectacularly between 1900 and 1925 and also bought competing breweries to establish its dominance. The company was nationalized by the government of Juan D. Perón in 1947 and was returned to the Bemberg family in 1955.

See also **Germans in Latin America.**

BIBLIOGRAPHY

José Luis Torres, *Algunas maneras de vender patria* (Buenos Aires, 1973).

CARLOS MARICHAL

BENALCÁZAR, SEBASTIÁN DE. *See* Belalcázar, Sebastián de.

BENAVENTE, TORIBIO DE. *See* Motolinía, Toribio de.

BENAVIDES, ALONSO DE (1579–c. 1636).
Alonso de Benavides (*b.* before 1579; *d.* ca. 1636), Franciscan missionary and propagandist in New Mexico. The personification of Christian spiritual conquest, Benavides acted in New Mexico in the seventeenth century with a zeal reminiscent of his sixteenth-century brethren. He was born at San Miguel, in the Azores, and entered the Franciscan order in Mexico City, serving subsequently in various capacities. Appointed superior of the New Mexico missions and agent of the Inquisition, Benavides presented his credentials to Governor Felipe de Sotelo Osorio at Santa Fe early in 1626. During his three-year term, Benavides labored actively not only among Pueblo Indians, but also among Apaches. When the ardent friar returned to Mexico City in early 1630, Franciscan authorities sent him to Spain to lobby at court. His sanguine report of missionary progress and potential in New Mexico, published the same year, and a revised version prepared for the pope in 1634 remain valuable ethnohistorical sources.

See also **Missions: Spanish America.**

BIBLIOGRAPHY

Frederick Webb Hodge Et Al., eds., *Fray Alonso de Benavides' Revised Memorial of 1634* (1945).

Peter P. Forrestal, trans., and Cyprian J. Lynch, ed., *Benavides' Memorial of 1630* (1954).

Additional Bibliography

Benavides, Alonso de, and Baker H. Morrow, trans. *A Harvest of Reluctant Souls: The Memorial of Fray Alonso de Benavides, 1630.* Niwot, CO: University Press of Colorado, 1996.

Hodge, Frederick Webb. *Bibliography of Fray Alonso de Benavides.* New York: Museum of the American Indian, Heye Foundation, 1919.

JOHN L. KESSELL

BIBLIOGRAPHY

David Werlich, *Peru: A Short History* (1978), pp. 201–337.

Alfonso W. Quiroz, "Financial Development in Peru Under Agrarian Export Influence, 1884–1950," in *The Americas* 47 (1991): 447–476.

ALFONSO W. QUIROZ

BENAVIDES, OSCAR RAIMUNDO

(1876–1945). Oscar Raimundo Benavides (*b.* 1876; *d.* 1945), Peruvian general and twice de facto president of Peru (1914–1915, 1933–1939). Born in Lima, he was one of the first professional officers to graduate from the Peruvian Military School in the 1890s. He completed studies in science at the San Marcos University in 1905 and his military training in France in 1907. In 1911 he became nationally known for his swift mobilization of an army he led to Iquitos during the military actions arising from a dispute between Peru and Colombia over a jungle area.

As chief of staff of the Peruvian army in 1913, he did not endorse President Guillermo Billinghurst's bid to enhance his executive power. Consequently, Benavides was temporarily ousted from the army. Soon, however, he led the first institutional military coup in Peruvian history against Billinghurst in 1914. In 1915 constitutional order was restored. Benavides continued his military service into the 1920s, when his opposition to President Augusto B. Leguía resulted in his exile to Guayaquil, where he continued to conspire. When Colonel Luis M. Sánchez Cerro overthrew Leguía in 1930, he appointed Benavides ambassador to Spain and Great Britain and then called him back to Peru during the brief war with Colombia in 1932.

After Sánchez Cerro was assassinated in 1933, the Peruvian Congress designated Benavides president of the republic. During his administration he proscribed the APRA movement and in 1936 held elections which were nullified because of the electoral victory of the candidate supported by the APRA. He established the social security system and carried out a program of public works in the midst of a slow economic recovery after 1933. In 1939, Benavides handed over power to his relative, civilian Manuel Prado.

See also **Peru, Political Parties: Peruvian Aprista Party (PAP/APRA).**

BENEDETTI, MARIO (1920–). Mario

Benedetti, born on September 14, 1920, in Paso de los Toros (Tacuarembó), is a Uruguayan author of novels, poems, stories, essays, plays, songs, and literary criticism. More than seventy of his books have been translated into twenty languages and adapted to film, theater, radio, and television. As a result of his political exile, mostly in Spain, from 1973 to 1983, his works reached readers in many regions and of varying backgrounds. He is considered one of the most renowned intellectuals from the Uruguayan Generation of 1945 and is one of the most highly acclaimed writers in Latin America.

The uniqueness of his work lies in his exploration of the seemingly dull existence of the anonymous urban middle class. Over the course of half a century, Benedetti has revisited certain themes— loneliness, boredom, envy, nostalgia, conformism, mediocrity, social justice, democracy—in what can be seen as three periods. In the first period, comprising his initial works up to 1973, he introduced the apathetic middle class, listlessly accepting political corruption. The second period spans the devastating years of the Uruguayan military dictatorship, with its persecutions, imprisonments, torture, death, and exile. In the third period, from 1983 on, his books portray the human adaptation to new social, political, and literary realities, and, since the turn of the twenty-first century, emphasize the dehumanizing effects of technology and globalization.

Although he has worked in diverse genres, his books achieve unity and cohesion by illuminating and enhancing each other. Beneditti, well known for his *vocación comunicante*, strives to maintain a dialogue with his readers. To achieve this goal, he employs a conversational prose style, generating the immediate identification and trust of readers and listeners, his *lector-mi-prójimo*, those near him to whom he writes. Benedetti has received honorary doctorates and major literary prizes, such as the Golden Flame from Amnesty International (1987), the Queen Sofía Ibero-American Poetry Prize (1999), and the Menéndez Pelayo International Prize (2005).

See also **Literature: Spanish America.**

BIBLIOGRAPHY

Novels by Benedetti

La tregua (1960, 125 editions). Madrid: Alianza, 1997.

Gracias por el fueg. (1965, 57 editions). Madrid: Alianza, 1999.

El cumpleaños de Juan Ángel (1971, 37 editions). Madrid: Alfaguara, 1996.

Short Story Collections by Benedetti

Montevideanos (1959, 35 editions). Barcelona: Suma de Letras, 2000.

La muerte y otras sorpresas (1968, 34 editions). Madrid: Santillana, 1994.

Geografías (1984, 17 editions). Madrid: Alfaguara, 1994.

El porvenir de mi pasado. Madrid: Alfaguara, 2003.

Poetry

Poemas de la oficina (1956, 18 editions). Madrid: Visor, 1989.

Cotidianas (1979, 14 editions). Madrid: Visor, 2001.

El olvido está lleno de memoria (1995, 9 editions). Buenos Aires: Planeta Argentina, 1999.

Inventario uno (1963, 55 editions). Madrid: Visor, 1986.

Inventario dos (1994, 7 editions). Mexico City: Patria, 1995.

Inventario Tres. Madrid: Visro, 2003.

Plays by Benedetti

Ida y vuelta. Buenos Aires: Talía, 1963.

Pedro y el capitán (1979, 32 editions). Madrid: Alianza, 1999.

Essays by Benedetti

El país de la cola de paja (1960, 9 editions). Montevideo: Arca, 1973.

El escritor latinoamericano y la revolución posible (1974, 12 editions). Mexico: Nueva Imagen, 1981.

Subdesarrolloy letras de osadía. (1987). Madrid: Alianza, 2002.

La realidad y la palabra. Madrid: Ediciones Destinos, 1991.

Literary Criticism by Benedetti

Letras del continente mestizo, 3rd edition. Montevideo: Arca, 1974.

El recurso del supremo patriarca, 9th edition. Mexico: Nueva Imagen, 1979.

El ejercicio del criterio, 6th edition. Madrid: Alfaguara, 1995.

Works on Benedetti

Alemany, Carmen, Remedios Mataix, and José Carlos Rovira, eds. *Inventario cómplice.* Alicante: Universidad de Alicante, 1998.

da Cunha, Gloria. *El exilio, realidad y ficción.* Montevideo: Arca, 1992.

da Cunha, Gloria. *Mario Benedetti y la nación posible.* Alicante: Universidad de Alicante, 2001.

Lago, Sylvia. *Mario Benedetti: Cincuenta años de creación.* Montevideo: Universidad de la República, 1996.

Manssur, Mónica. *Tuya, mía, de otros: La poesía coloquial de Mario Benedetti.* Mexico City: Universidad Nacional Autónoma de México, 1979.

Mathieu, Corina. *Los cuentos de Mario Benedetti.* New York: P. Lang, 1983.

GLORIA DA CUNHA

BENEDICTINES. Benedictines are a religious order of the Roman Catholic Church consisting of both monks and nuns. Members of the Benedictine Order, known for their formative influence in the Christianization of Europe, were relegated to a secondary status in the European settlement of Latin America. Unlike the other major religious orders of Europe (the Jesuits, Franciscans, and Dominicans), the Benedictines played a minor role in the colonizing and evangelization of Latin America. This was due in part to the control exercised by Spanish and Portuguese monarchs under the Royal Patronage of the Indies promulgated by Pope Julius II in 1508. Philip II of Spain, while encouraging missionary ventures of the mendicant orders from Spain and Portugal, was reluctant to give approval to petitions of the monastic orders to establish foundations in the New World. Many of the monastic communities were themselves reluctant to undertake large-scale missionary activity in the sixteenth and seventeenth centuries. The principal reason for this reluctance was due to Benedictine efforts to reestablish a contemplative way of life, a process that was at odds with the call to evangelize Latin America.

BRAZIL

Nonetheless, there was a Benedictine presence in Latin America from the sixteenth century—primarily in Brazil. From 1582–1598, monks of the Portuguese Benedictine Congregation established monasteries at Bahia (1581), Rio de Janeiro (1586), Olinda (1586) and São Paulo (1598). These communities exerted a considerable influence on the pastoral and liturgical life of the Brazilian Catholic church. After Brazil obtained its independence from Portugal in 1822, all Benedictines in Brazil were united into the Benedictine Brazilian Congregation (1827). Repressive laws of the Brazilian government reduced the numbers and influence of the congregation to the point where, in 1894, there were only ten monks remaining. At this juncture, the German Beuron Congregation of Benedictines committed themselves to revivify monastic life in Brazil. Within fifteen years, they restored six abbeys, several priories and smaller houses, and sent monks to do missionary work among the Indians of the Amazon River Basin. The twentieth century was marked by a renewed growth in the numbers and influence of the Benedictine Brazilian Congregation, which by 1985 had grown to seven abbeys and 170 monks. In 2005, Brazil had 13 monasteries and 110 monks.

OTHER PARTS OF LATIN AMERICA

Outside Brazil, the period from 1500 to 1900 was practically devoid of organized Benedictine activity. Individual missionary monks, a number of Benedictine bishops, and a few communities of Benedictine women appeared throughout these centuries, but it was only at the end of the nineteenth century that an aggregate presence began with the foundation of a number of new houses.

In 1899 monks of Belloc Abbey in France founded the Abbey of Niño Dios in Argentina. Like the first Brazilian abbey three centuries earlier, this monastery grew rapidly and exerted much influence. In 1903 monks of Silos Abbey in Spain started the first of what were intended to be several foundations in Mexico. Successive persecutions by the Mexican government forced the monks to flee that country in 1915, and to settle in Buenos Aires, where they started the Abbey of San Benito. At the same time, Silos established the first Benedictine foundation in Chile (Nuestra Señora de las Nieves del Puente). Two more foundations in Chile followed in 1920 and 1977. Another Chilean house was the monastery of Las Condes (1938), eventually taken over by the Beuronese Congregation. German-speaking monks from Einsiedeln, Switzerland, were also responsible for the establishment of the Abbey of Los Toldes in Argentina (1948). Noteworthy in the wave of new houses after World War II were seven monasteries of Benedictine sisters.

NEW FOUNDATIONS AND REFORMS

In March 1960 Pope John XXIII urged the superiors of North American religious communities to intensify their missionary efforts in Latin America. A wave of new foundations followed in both Central and South America as a result of this appeal, including several of the Cistercian Order of Strict Observance (Trappist) in Argentina and Chile. This thrust toward a more contemplative religious life was affirmed by the Latin American bishops in their historic meeting in Medellín, Colombia, in 1968.

One of the fruits of the reform of religious life in the Roman Catholic Church brought about by Vatican Council II (1962–1965) was the organization of all Benedictine monasteries in Latin America into the Congregation of Cono-Sur in 1970. This congregation then divided itself into three geographic areas: CUMBRA (Brazil), ABECA (Caribbean, Central America), and Cono-Sur (the remaining South American nations). The congregation's members have held triennial reunions since 1972 and have become a vital component of the Latin American church, staffing schools, serving as centers for prayer and scholarship, and providing pastoral care. By 2005, the congregation numbered over 8,000 monks and 16,000 Benedictine women worldwide.

See also **Catholic Church: The Colonial Period; Catholic Church: The Modern Period.**

BIBLIOGRAPHY

Antonio Linage Conde, *El monacato en España e Hispano-américa* (1977), esp. pp. 619–660.

Oliver Kapsner, "The Benedictines in Brazil," in *American Benedictine Review* 28 (1977):113–132.

Jean Leclercq, "Espasione monastica fuori dell'Europa: America Latina," in *Dizionario degli Istituti di Perfezione* 5 (1978):1734–1735.

Mauro Matthei, "Implantación del Monacato Benedictino Cisterciense en el Cono Sur," in *Cuadernos Monásticos* 52 (1980):21–128.

Leander Hogg, "Philip II of Spain and the Benedictines in the New World," in *American Benedictine Review* 35 (1984):364–377.

Additional Bibliography

Andrade Cernadas, José Miguel. *El monacato benedictino y la sociedad de la Galicia Medieval: Siglos X al XIII.* Sada, A Coruña, Spain: Edicios do Castro, 1997.

Barry, Patrick, OSB. *A Cloister in the World: The Story of the Manquehue Apostolic Movement, a Benedictine Movement of the Laity and Its Work in Chile.* St. Louis, MO: Abbey of Saint Mary and Saint Louis, Outskirts Press, 2005.

Luna, Joaquim G. de. *Os monges beneditinos no Brasil: Esbôço histórico.* Rio de Janeiro: Edições "Lumen Christi," 1947.

JOEL RIPPINGER O.S.B.

BENÍTEZ, GREGORIO (1834–1910).

Gregorio Benítez (*b.* 1834; *d.* 1910), Paraguayan diplomat and author. Born in the interior town of Villarrica, Benítez received his education there and at Asunción. In the early 1850s, he was noticed by officials of the Carlos Antonio López government, who decided to groom him for a career in the state bureaucracy. In 1856, he received an assignment to act as secretary to the president's son, General Francisco Solano López, who was at that time war minister. Benítez later accompanied the younger López to Buenos Aires on a mission to mediate a dispute between that province and the Argentine Confederation.

His position as a diplomat established, Benítez was designated secretary of legation at London in 1860. After the beginning of the War of the Triple Alliance in 1864, he went to the continent to solicit European support for the Paraguayan cause. He became his country's chief diplomatic representative in Prussia, France, and Britain before journeying to the United States in 1868. In Washington and other cities, Benítez tried to gain North American help in arranging peace negotiations with

Argentina and Brazil, but these efforts were rebuffed by the two nations, who went on to defeat the Paraguayans in 1870.

Benítez reemerged on the diplomatic scene more than twenty years later when he negotiated an 1894 boundary agreement with the Bolivians that set limits on expansion in the Gran Chaco territory. Though this treaty, jointly issued with Bolivian diplomat Telmo Ichazo, was tragically short-lived, it nonetheless permitted some respite from the escalation of tensions between the two countries.

Benítez wrote several informative memoirs, including *La triple alianza de 1865: Escapada de un desastre en la guerra de invasión al Paraguay* (1904) and *Anales diplomático y militar de la guerra del Paraguay* (1906).

See also **Paraguay: The Nineteenth Century.**

BIBLIOGRAPHY

Luis G. Benítez, *Historia de la cultura en el Paraguay* (1976).

Harris Gaylord Warren, *Rebirth of the Paraguayan Republic: The First Colorado Era, 1878–1904* (1985).

MARTA FERNÁNDEZ WHIGHAM

BENÍTEZ, JAIME (1908–2001). Jaime

Benítez (*b.* 29 October 1908; *d.* 30 May 2001), Puerto Rican intellectual, politician, and member of the United States Congress (1973–1977), and one of the architects of modern Puerto Rico, especially its system of higher education. He was born in Vieques and educated in public schools in Puerto Rico; he received a master's degree in law from Georgetown University in 1931 and a master of arts from the University of Chicago in 1938. From 1931 to 1942, Benítez taught political science at the University of Puerto Rico and served as chancellor and then president of the university—and the entire university system—from 1942 until 1971. As president, he directed a complete reorganization of the university, publishing his plan in *La reforma universitaria* (1943). He established a university museum and a research library in the university's main campus at Río Piedras. Benítez attracted major intellectuals to teach at the university, among them the Spanish poets Pedro Salinas and Juan Ramón Jiménez, and founded and contributed to the literary review *La Torre*.

Benítez wrote influential books on education, including *Education for Democracy on a Cultural Frontier* (1955), *Etica y estilo de la universidad* (1964), *Junto a la Torre: Jornadas de un programa universitario* (1963), and *La universidad del futuro* (1964). He wrote for *Sur* and *Cuadernos Americanos*, the most prestigious cultural journals of Latin America, was a member of the United States National Commission for UNESCO (1948–1954), and lectured at many universities around the world. Benítez worked closely with Puerto Rican statesman Luis Muñoz Marín to establish the Commonwealth of Puerto Rico. He was a member of the Constitutional Convention of Puerto Rico and served as chairman of the Committee on Bill of Rights (1951–1952). He was a delegate to the Democratic National Convention in 1976 and was elected as a Popular Democrat to the U.S. House of Representatives in 1972 for a four-year term. From 1980 to 1986 he was a professor of government at the Inter-American University in Puerto Rico, and in 1984 he became a professor of government at the American College in Bayamón, Puerto Rico. While there he focused on finding faculty positions for scholars who were refugees from dictatorial regimes in Spain and other countries. He died on May 30, 2001, in San Juan, Puerto Rico.

See also **Puerto Rico.**

BIBLIOGRAPHY

Cesáreo Rosa-Nieves, *Biografías puertorriqueñas: Pérfil histórico de un pueblo* (1970); *Hispanic Members of Congress, 1822–1994* (1996).

GEORGETTE MAGASSY DORN

BENÍTEZ ZENTENO, RAÚL (1931–2006).

Raúl Benítez Zenteno began publishing detailed and prescient scholarly work on Mexico's population in the 1960s and quickly emerged as one of Mexico's most prominent demographers. With a scholarship from Mexico's Institute of Social Investigations at the National Autonomous University of Mexico (IISUNAM), Benítez Zenteno became the first Mexican to study at the United Nations Center of Latin American Demography. His 1961 publication, *Análisis demográfico de México*, examined birth trends, death rates, and migration movements to construct models and scenarios of the nation's future size. The analysis produced two principal projections, one of which estimated the future population of Mexico. Further Benítez Zenteno studies, commissioned by the Bank of Mexico, helped the government to develop planning policies, which took into account tremendous expansion of the population and the economy. Examining the relationship between historical demography and economic development in other works, Benítez Zenteno inspired younger scholars to analyze the effects of population trends over the long term. He worked as a professor at UNAM and later became director of IISUNAM. Benítez Zenteno directed the demographic journal *Demos*, which became well-known for its analyses of national and international human growth patterns.

See also **Economic Development.**

BIBLIOGRAPHY

Benítez Zenteno, Raúl. *Análisis demográfico de México*. Mexico City: Instituto de Investigaciones Sociales, Universidad Nacional, 1961.

Pick, James B., and Edgar W. Butler. *The Mexico Handbook: Economic and Demographic Maps and Statistics*. Boulder, CO: Westview Press, 1994.

BYRON CRITES

BENNETT, MARSHALL (1775–1839).

Marshall Bennett (*b.* before 1775; *d.* 1839) Belize entrepreneur. Bennett was involved with every major enterprise in the Bay of Honduras. His foresight, enterprise, and success were unique for the time. A commanding figure in the oligarchy that ruled Belize, he was first elected magistrate in 1789 and served consecutively from 1813 to 1829. Besides being chief magistrate and the wealthiest merchant, Bennett was the senior judge of the Supreme Court, colonel commander in the militia, agent for Lloyds of London, a major shipowner, and the only Belize merchant to open a branch in Guatemala, where he spent most of his time after 1828.

The mahogany trade was Bennett's prime concern, and he had separate arrangements with Guatemalan chief of state Mariano Gálvez and Central American Federation President Francisco Morazán to control mahogany lumbering on the Caribbean coast. Although apparently trusted and respected by his many associates, he was accused of breaking up Gregor MacGregor's settlement at Black River, reneging on a colonization contract with Gálvez, and manipulating the Eastern Coast of Central America Company for his own purposes.

See also **Belize.**

BIBLIOGRAPHY

Mario Rodríguez, *A Palmerstonian Diplomat in Central America: Frederick Chatfield, Esq.* (1964).

William Jay Griffith, *Empires in the Wilderness: Foreign Colonization and Development in Guatemala, 1834–1844* (1965).

O. Nigel Bolland, *The Formation of a Colonial Society: Belize from Conquest to Crown Colony* (1977).

Robert A. Naylor, *Penny Ante Imperialism: The Mosquito Shore and the Bay of Honduras, 1600–1914* (1989).

Additional Bibliography

Revels, Craig Stephen. "Concessions, Conflict, and the Rebirth of the Mahogany Trade." *Journal of Latin American Geography* 2: 1 (2003): 1–17.

ROBERT A. NAYLOR

BENSON, NETTIE LEE (1905–1993). Nettie Lee Benson, historian, librarian, and teacher, was born in Austin, Texas. Educated at the University of Texas, she began her lifelong association with that university's Latin American collection in 1942, while working on her doctorate. As head librarian over the next thirty-three years, she developed a world-class research library using innovative acquisitions strategies such as personal visits to publishers, bookstores, authors, and government agencies in various Latin American countries. Benson was a founding member of the Seminar on the Acquisition of Latin American Library Materials (SALALM) in 1956, and from 1960 to 1962 she traveled to Latin America as an agent for the Latin American Cooperative Acquisitions Program (LACAP), a consortium of U.S. research libraries.

Benson taught Mexican and Latin American history at Texas from 1962 until 1985, and Latin American bibliography and the book trade from 1964 to 1975. She served with distinction as chairperson of the Bolton Prize Committee, Conference on Latin American History (1970); as president of the Fourth International Conference of U.S. and Mexican Historians (1973); and on the editorial board of the *Hispanic American Historical Review* (1974–1979).

Benson's work was widely recognized. After her retirement in 1975 the university Board of Regents renamed the Latin American collection in her honor, and in 1979 the president of Mexico bestowed on her the Order of the Aztec Eagle for her contributions to Mexican history.

See also **Hispanic American Historical Review.**

BIBLIOGRAPHY

Benson, Nettie Lee. *Diputación provincial y el federalismo mexicano.* Mexico City: El Colegio de México, 1952, 1980. Revised English edition: *The Provincial Deputation in Mexico: Precursor of the Mexican Federal State.* Austin: University of Texas Press, 1992.

Benson, Nettie Lee. "Texas as Viewed from Mexico, 1820–1834." *Southwestern Historical Quarterly* 90:3 (January 1987), 219–291.

Benson, Nettie Lee, ed. *Mexico and the Spanish Cortés, 1820–1834: Eight Essays* [by students in Benson's history seminar]. Austin: University of Texas Press, 1966. Spanish edition, *México y el Cortés Español.* Mexico City: Camara de Diputados del Congreso, 1985.

LAURA GUTIERREZ-WITT

BENT'S FORT. Bent's Fort, largest of the trading posts located outside of Mexican territory to capitalize on the potential offered by the Santa Fe trade. Originally known as Fort William, it was built in 1833 near the confluence of the Arkansas and Purgatoire rivers in what is now Colorado. Owners Charles Bent and Ceran St. Vrain profited not only from the fur trade and the sale of merchandise to surrounding Athabascan–speaking peoples, Mexicans, and Anglos, but also from the traffic in arms and ammunition to Navajos, Apaches, and other native groups who used these weapons to raid northern Mexican settlements. The booty taken in livestock was often sold to Bent's Fort or similar trading emporiums. In this way, U.S. traders influenced shifts in the traditional balance of power and trading relationships among indigenous peoples and Mexicans, which further weakened Mexico's tenuous hold on its far northern territory. With the decline of the fur trade, Bent's Fort lost its strategic importance and was abandoned in 1849.

BIBLIOGRAPHY

David Lavender, *Bent's Fort* (1954).

David J. Weber, *The Mexican Frontier, 1821–1846: The American Southwest Under Mexico* (1982).

Additional Bibliography

Comer, Douglas C. *Ritual Ground: Bent's Old Fort, World Formation, and the Annexation of the Southwest.* Berkeley: University of California Press, 1996.

Hyslop, Stephen G. *Bound for Santa Fe: The Road to New Mexico and the American Conquest, 1806-1848.* Norman: University of Oklahoma Press, 2002.

SUSAN M. DEEDS

BERBEO, JUAN FRANCISCO (1729–1795).

Juan Francisco Berbeo (*b.* 17 June 1729; *d.* 28 June 1795), a leader (*capitán*) of the Comunero Revolt in New Granada (1781). Berbeo was a member of the second-tier elite of his native Socorro, politically well connected but economically in modest circumstances. In April 1781, after a month of popular protests against new taxes, he led the Socorro *cabildo* into an alliance with the protesters, thus confirming Socorro's leading role in the rebellion. With Archbishop Antonio Caballero y Góngora Berbeo negotiated the June 1781 agreement that led to the demobilization of the *comuneros'* army of several thousand—an agreement that Caballero soon nullified—and in 1782 Berbeo and almost all of the other participants were pardoned. Berbeo claimed that he joined the rebellion in order to moderate its course and to preserve Socorro's ultimate obedience to the crown, but the Socorro elite doubtless sympathized with many of the plebeians' complaints against the fiscal and administrative effects of recent Bourbon Reforms.

See also **Comunero Revolt (New Granada).**

BIBLIOGRAPHY

John Leddy Phelan, *The People and the King: The Comunero Revolution in Colombia, 1781* (1978).

RICHARD STOLLER

BERENGUER, AMANDA (1921–).

Amanda Berenguer (*b.* 1921), Uruguayan poet. Born in Montevideo, she began her literary career in earnest with the publication of her third book of poems, *Elegía por la muerte de Paul Valéry* (1945). Her first two publications, *A través de los tiempos que llevan a la gran calma* (Through the Times That Lead to the Great Calm, 1940) and *Canto hermético* (1941), had very limited circulation. With *El río* (1952) and *La invitación* (1957), Berenguer begins to develop a personal and original poetic voice; *Contracanto* (1961) is a collection of brief poems. With *Quehaceres e invenciones* (Chores and Inventions, 1963), Berenguer reaches linguistic and lyrical precision in poems of oneiric and enigmatic landscapes.

She is considered a representative of a new and daring voice in Uruguayan poetry. In *Declaración conjunta* (Joint Statement, 1964), *Materia prima* (Raw Material, 1966), and *Composición de lugar* (To Lay One's Plans, 1976), the lyric voice searches for a vision of the world that rejects tradition through the creation of new poetic structures. Her *Poesía 1949–1979* (1980) includes her complete works up to that time, except for the first three books of poems. *Identidad de ciertas frutas* (The Identity of Certain Fruits, 1983) continues to construct peculiar and innovative imagery. In 1986 Berenguer received the Reencuentro de Poesía Award granted by the University of the Republic in Montevideo. She is considered one of the main poets of contemporary Uruguay by Angel Rama, Mario Benedetti, and others. In 2006, she was named an honorary member of the Uruguayan National Academy of Letters.

See also **Literature: Spanish America.**

BIBLIOGRAPHY

Emir Rodríguez Monegal, *Literatura uruguaya de medio siglo* (1966).

Alejandro Paternain, *Treinta y seis años de poesía uruguaya* (1967).

Additional Bibliography

Scott, Renée Sum. *Escritoras uruguayas: Una antología crítica*. Montevideo, Uruguay: Ediciones Trilce, 2002.

Sosnowski, Saúl and Louise B. Popkin, eds., trans. Louise B. Popkin. *Repression, Exile, and Democracy: Uruguayan Culture*. Durham, NC: Duke University, 1993.

MAGDALENA GARCÍA PINTO

BERESFORD, WILLIAM CARR (1768–1854).

William Carr Beresford (*b.* 2 October 1768; *d.* 8 January 1854), British general who led the troops that accompanied Sir Home Popham in his invasion of Buenos Aires in 1806. Having begun his service in the British army at the age of seventeen, Beresford enjoyed great success as an officer in Egypt and South Africa between 1799 and 1805. It was after victory at Capetown, South Africa, in 1806 that Beresford and his troops were assigned to join Popham in his expedition to the Río de la Plata. In June 1806, Beresford's troops captured Buenos Aires and placed the area under British rule. In believing the Spanish-Americans to be on the verge of rebellion, Popham and Beresford misjudged the citizens' loyalty to Spain and encountered some opposition among the people of Buenos Aires before Santiago de Liniers's reconquest of the city less than two months later.

After escaping from imprisonment by the conquering Spaniards, Beresford returned to England, where he served as one of Wellington's lieutenants in numerous battles with the French.

See also **British in Argentina.**

BIBLIOGRAPHY

Alexander I. Shand. *Wellington's Lieutenants* (1902).

Enrique Williams Alzaga, *Fuga del General Beresford, 1807* (1965).

Additional Bibliography

Lozier Almazán, Bernardo P. *Beresford, gobernador de Buenos Aires*. Buenos Aires: Editorial Galerne, 1994.

JOHN DUDLEY

BERGAÑO Y VILLEGAS, SIMÓN (1784–1828).

Simón Bergaño y Villegas (*b.* 1784; *d.* 1828), Guatemalan journalist. Bergaño y Villegas was born in Escuintla, Guatemala. Biographers think that, due to his limited economic resources, he was self-educated. Owing to an accident in his youth, he had to use crutches throughout his life and had to spend much time in a wheelchair.

Bergaño y Villegas was both an excellent journalist and a poet. From 1804 to 1807 he edited the *Gazeta de Guatemala*, which, at the time, was a sixteen-page weekly containing the writings of various intellectuals. Bergaño y Villegas's encyclopedic knowledge made his writings a threat to the conservative ideas of the time. Some of his writings in the *Gazeta de Guatemala* appeared under the pseudonym Bergoñer de Segiliú. Nevertheless he was tried for his writings by the Inquisition in 1808 and sentenced to exile in Spain. He was taken to Havana, where he fell ill and spent several months in a hospital, thus evading transport to Spain. In Cuba he founded the periodical *Correo de las Damas* (1811), which was shut down by the bishop of Havana. In 1812 he founded the *Diario Cívico*. He died in Havana.

See also **Journalism.**

BIBLIOGRAPHY

Salomón Carrillo Ramírez, *El poeta Villegas, precursor de la independencia de Centro América*, 2d ed. (1960).

Carlos C. Haeussler Yela, *Diccionario general de Guatemala* (1983), vol. 1, pp. 235–236.

José A. Mobil, *100 personajes históricos de Guatemala* (1991), pp. 142–144.

OSCAR G. PELÁEZ ALMENGOR

BERGES, JOSÉ (late 1820s–1868).

José Berges (*b.* late 1820s; *d.* 21 December 1868), Paraguayan diplomat and jurist. Berges was a charming, quick-witted man whose social skills and intelligence were early recognized by President Carlos Antonio López, who appointed him to the office of district judge in the mid-1840s. His success in this position was such that López soon transferred him to the diplomatic service, where he distinguished himself on several key occasions. In 1851 he negotiated an agreement in Montevideo whereby Paraguay agreed to support a military alliance against the Argentine dictator Juan Manuel de Rosas. Five years later he went to Rio de Janeiro to work with Brazilian diplomats on a mutual trade and boundary treaty.

Berges's finest moment as a diplomat, however, came in 1860, when he journeyed to Washington, D.C., to argue Paraguay's case before an arbitration commission called to decide culpability in the Water Witch dispute with the United States. The decision of the chief arbitrator favored the Paraguayans, and when Berges returned to Asunción, his fame had grown so much that some even spoke of his succeeding the aging López.

When López died in 1862, he was instead succeeded by his eldest son, General Francisco Solano López. The new president, though in many ways an egomaniac, saw no reason to hold Berges's popularity against him and soon appointed him foreign minister. In this capacity, he sent notes of protest to Brazil when that country intervened in Uruguay in 1864. These protests were only a prelude to the six-year War of the Triple Alliance, which commenced shortly thereafter. During the course of the fighting, the Paraguayan army invaded northeastern Argentina, and Berges was named to organize a short-lived puppet regime at Corrientes.

After López abandoned his Argentine campaign in late 1865, Berges returned to Asunción, where he headed up virtually all public administration in the Paraguayan capital. Three years later he was accused of conspiring against the Solano López regime. After being subjected to merciless torture, he confessed and was then summarily shot along with other supposed plotters.

See also **Water Witch Incident.**

BIBLIOGRAPHY

Arturo Bray, *Hombres y épocas del Paraguay* (1957), vol. 2, pp. 69–98.

Charles J. Kolinski, *Historical Dictionary of Paraguay* (1973), p. 25.

Carlos Zubizarreta, *Cien vidas paraguayas*, 2d ed. (1985), pp. 142–145.

THOMAS L. WHIGHAM

BERMAN, SABINA (1955–).

Sabina Berman, born August 21, 1955, is a Mexican playwright, screenwriter, novelist, and poet. Her work has earned both commercial success and critical acclaim. The plays *Yankee, Herejía, Rompecabezas,* and the children's play *La Maravillosa Historia del Niño Pingüica,* each were awarded the Mexican National Theatre Prize. Much of Berman's work combines spectacular stage effects and witty repartee with an exploration of identity in Mexico, including the gender experiments of *El suplicio del placer,* inquiries into the colonial inquisition of a Jewish family in *Herejía,* and campy interpretations of national myth in *Entre Villa y una mujer desnuda.* Berman has expanded her focus to international subjects, with hit plays on Sigmund Freud and Molière. She has also adapted English-language texts, such as the play *eXtras,* for the Mexican stage. Berman's political concerns emerge in her screenplay *Backyard,* about the unsolved murders of hundreds of women near the U.S.-Mexican border, and the nonfiction work *Democracia cultural* on the state of government-funded arts in Mexico.

See also **Literature: Spanish America; Theater.**

BIBLIOGRAPHY

Adler, Heidrun, and Jaime Chabaud, eds. *Un viaje sin fin: Teatro mexicano hoy.* Frankfurt: Vervuert; Madrid: Iberoamericana, 2004.

Berman, Sabina. *The Theatre of Sabina Berman: The Agony of Ecstasy and Other Plays.* Translated by Adam Versényi. Carbondale: Southern Illinois University Press, 2003.

Bixler, Jacqueline E., ed. *Sediciosas seducciones: Sexo, poder y palabras en el teatro de Sabina Berman.* Mexico: Escenología, 2004.

Niebylski, Dianna C. "Caught in the Middle: Ambiguous Gender and Social Politics in Sabina Berman's Play *Entre Villa y una mujer desnuda.*" *Revista de Estudios Hispánicos* 39, no. 1 (2005): 153–177.

EMILY HIND

BERMEJO, ILDEFONSO (1820–1892).

Ildefonso Bermejo (*b.* 1820; *d.* 1892), Spanish publicist and writer active in Paraguay. A budding journalist with experience in Madrid, Bermejo first came to Asunción in 1855 at the behest of the

Carlos Antonio López government, which had hired him to help launch several projects of a cultural nature. Over the next few years, Bermejo was the main force behind such state-sponsored newspapers as *El Semanario de Avisos y Conocimientos Útiles, El Eco del Paraguay,* and *La Época.* More important, he trained a team of young Paraguayans in the field of journalism, and his flair and erudition appeared in much of their subsequent work. In 1860, for instance, they produced *La Aurora,* an ambitious literary and scientific review, the first publication of its kind in the still very isolated Paraguay.

Aside from his journalistic work, Bermejo founded several secondary-level educational institutions, including the Aula de Filosofía. He also wrote plays for the newly constructed Teatro Nacional.

Bermejo had an irascible character that all too often conflicted with the rather conservative members of the Asunción elite. After disagreements with officials of the Francisco Solano López regime in 1863, he returned to Europe, where he published a scathing account of his Paraguayan experiences, *Repúblicas americanas: Episodios de la vida privada, política, y social de la República del Paraguay* (1873), in which he lampooned the López family and the country he had left behind.

See also **Journalism.**

BIBLIOGRAPHY

Rafael Eladio Velázquez, *Breve historia de la cultura en el Paraguay* (1980), pp. 156–157, 169–171.

Efraím Cardozo, *Apuntes de historia cultural del Paraguay* (1985), pp. 248–274 passim.

Additional Bibliography

Bermejo, Ildefonso Antonio. *Episódio da vida privada, política e social na república do Paragui.* Porto Alegre: EDIPUCRS, 2002.

THOMAS L. WHIGHAM

BERMEJO RIVER. Bermejo River, waterway that arises in southern Bolivia, crosses the Chaco, and flows 650 miles through shifting channels to join the Paraguay River south of the Paraguayan port of Pilar, in Argentine territory. Along with the Pilcomayo, it is one of the two main tributaries of the Paraguay River. First explored in 1778, the river is navigable by small craft for 158 miles at all times and for 399 miles during high waters. The river, which carries large amounts of sediment, is difficult to navigate and serves few colonists. As a result of the Machaín–Irigoyen arbitration treaty signed by Paraguay and Argentina on 3 February 1876, the Pilcomayo River, rather than the Bermejo, became the western boundary separating Argentina and Paraguay.

See also **Paraguay River.**

BIBLIOGRAPHY

Although Thomas J. Page, *La Plata, the Argentine Confederation, and Paraguay* (1859), is a major primary source on Carlos Antonio López, it also provides an excellent description of Paraguayan rivers. Emilio Castro Boedo, *Estudios sobre navegación del Bermejo y colonización del Choco* (1873), focuses on the historical significance of the Bermejo. United States Army Corps of Engineers, *The Paraguayan River System* (1954), esp. pp. 18–19, evaluates the degree of navigability of Paraguayan rivers in the 1950s, with suggestions for development. Harris Gaylord Warren, *Paraguay and the Triple Alliance: The Postwar Decade, 1869–1878* (1978), esp. pp. 258–261 and 280–283, includes some economic, geographic, and social information.

Additional Bibliography

Binational Commission for the Development of the Upper Bermejo and Grande de Tarija River Basin, and Organization of American States. *Transboundary Diagnostic Analysis of the Binational Basin of the Bermejo River.* Buenos Aires, Argentina: Organization of American States, 2000.

Starck, Daniel, and Gallardo, Eduardo. *Guía excursion Corte de las Sierras subandinas en el Río Bermejo (límite entre Bolivia y Argentina).* Salta, Argentina: Universidad de Salta, 1999.

VERA BLINN REBER

BERMÚDEZ, JOSÉ FRANCISCO (1782–1831). José Francisco Bermúdez (*b.* 23 January 1782; *d.* 15 December 1831), officer in the Venezuelan Emancipating Army. Bermúdez was involved with the cause of independence from 1810. In 1812 he participated in the Barcelona campaign, and with the fall of the First Republic that year, he left for Trinidad. With Santiago Mariño, he invaded Venezuelan territory in 1813 and participated in the liberation of eastern Venezuela. When the Second Republic fell in 1815, he went to Cartagena and the Antilles and joined the troops of Mariño to participate in the Guiana campaign (1816–1817). Simón Bolívar appointed him commander in chief of the province of Cumaná in 1817 and later commander in chief of the Army of the East. He participated in the Battle of Carabobo in 1821 and in the battles which finally consolidated the liberation of Venezuelan territory. With the creation of Gran Colombia, he was appointed intendant and commander of the department of Orinoco. Between 1828 and 1830, he put down various insurrections in eastern Venezuela. The following year he retired from public life.

See also **Venezuela: The Colonial Era.**

BIBLIOGRAPHY

Santos Erminy Arismendi, *De la vida del General José Francisco Bermúdez* (1931).

Ministerio De La Defensa, *Próceres del ejército (biografías): Generales José Francisco Bermúdez, Francisco Mejía* (1980).

José Francisco Bermúdez, *General en jefe José Francisco Bermúdez: Bicentenario de su nacimiento* (1982).

INÉS QUINTERO

BERMÚDEZ VARELA, ENRIQUE

(1932–1991). Enrique Bermúdez Varela (*b.* 11 December 1932; *d.* 16 February 1991), former colonel in the Nicaraguan National Guard and military commander of the Nicaraguan Democratic Forces (Fuerzas Democráticas Nicaragüenses—FDN), an anti-Sandinista counterrevolutionary organization. Educated primarily at the Military Academy of Nicaragua, Bermúdez entered the National Guard in 1952. As a military engineer, he occupied various positions within the Department of Transit and the Department of Roads. In 1965, Bermúdez served with the Inter-American Peace Force in the Dominican Republic and later obtained appointment as military attaché to the Nicaraguan embassy in Washington, D.C. In 1981, Bermúdez helped establish the FDN, a radical group devoted to the overthrow of the Sandinista government.

See also **Contras; Inter-American Organizations.**

BIBLIOGRAPHY

Christopher Dickey, *With the Contras: A Reporter in the Wilds of Nicaragua* (1985).

Roy Gutman, *Banana Diplomacy: The Making of American Policy in Nicaragua, 1981–1987* (1988).

D. M. SPEARS

BERNAL JIMÉNEZ, MIGUEL (1910–

1956). Miguel Bernal Jiménez (*b.* 16 February 1910; *d.* 12 July 1956), Mexican composer and musicologist. Born in Morelia, Michoacán, Bernal Jiménez started his musical career as a choirboy at the Morelia cathedral and began musical studies at the Colegio de Infantes with Mier y Arriaga and Aguilera Ruiz. Later he entered the Escuela Superior de Música Sagrada in Morelia. After his graduation in 1928 he went to Rome to study organ, composition, Gregorian chant, and musicology at the Pontificio Istituto di Musica Sacra, graduating in 1933. He returned to Morelia, where he began teaching at the Escuela Superior de Música Sagrada, where in 1936 he became director. While there, he started the magazine *Schola Cantorum*. During this period he toured Mexico and the United States, performing organ concerts, conducting choirs, and giving lectures. From 1954 to 1956 he was dean of music at Loyola University in New Orleans, where he taught until his death in León, Guanajuato, Mexico.

Bernal wrote several works for the stage, among them *Tata Vasco* (1941), an opera commemorating the fourth centenary of the arrival of Vasco de Quiroga, first bishop of Michoacán, and two ballets: *Tingambato* (1943), based on a Tarascan legend, and *Los tres galanes de Juana* (1952). He also wrote the *Suite michoacana* (1940), and *Noche en Morelia* (1941), as well as a considerable number of major compositions and sacred vocal music. He has also written a number of important musicological essays based on his researches.

See also **Music: Art Music.**

BIBLIOGRAPHY

B. I. Harrison, "Old Mexican Organs," in *Diapason* 56 (June 1955): 35.

M. Querol Gavaldá, "Bernal Jiménez, Miguel: La técnica de los compositores," in *Anuario Musical* 10 (1955): 224ff.; *New Grove Dictionary of Music and Musicians*, vol. 2 (1980).

Additional Bibliography

Díaz Núñez, Lorena. *Como un eco lejano: La vida de Miguel Bernal Jiménez.* México, D.F.: Consejo Nacional para la Cultura y Artes, 2003.

SUSANA SALGADO

Additional Bibliography

Bernal y García Pimentel, Ignacio. *Apuntes para la historia de la infraestructura en México.* México: Banco Nacional de Obras y Servicios Públicos, 1998.

MICHAEL D. LIND

BERNAL Y GARCÍA PIMENTEL, IGNACIO (1910–1992).

Ignacio Bernal y García Pimentel (*b.* 13 February 1910; *d.* 24 January 1992), Mexican archaeologist. Born in Paris, Bernal came from a family of illustrious Mexican historians: he was the grandson of Luis García Pimentel and the great-grandson of Joaquín García Icazbalceta. In 1943 he joined Alfonso Caso in the Monte Albán excavations and began his lifelong interest in the archaeology of Oaxaca. Bernal received a doctorate from the Universidad Nacional Autónoma de México in 1949. His books *Urnas de Oaxaca* (1952, with Caso) and *La cerámica de Monte Albán* (1967, with Caso and Jorge Acosta) established the foundations of Oaxaca archaeology. From 1949 to the 1960s he directed excavations at seven sites in Oaxaca, including Yagul and Dainzú. In 1962 he was chosen the first director of the Museo Nacional de Antropología e Historia; he retired in 1976. Despite a heavy schedule of teaching and administration, Bernal produced 270 publications.

See also **Archaeology.**

BIBLIOGRAPHY

Among Bernal's most important publications are *Bibliografía de arqueología y etnografía: Mesoamérica y el norte de México 1514–1960* (1962); *Mexico Before Cortez,* translated by Willis Barnstone (1963); "Archaeological Synthesis of Oaxaca," in *Handbook of Middle American Indians,* vol. 3, edited by G. R. Willey (1965), pp. 788–813; "The Mixtecs in the Archaeology of the Valley of Oaxaca," in *Ancient Oaxaca,* edited by John Paddock (1966), pp. 345–366; *The Olmec World,* translated by Doris Heyden and Fernando Horcasitas (1969); *The Ballplayers of Dainzú,* with Andy Seuffert, translated by Carolyn B. Czitrom (1979). See also Wigberto Jiménez Moreno, "Ignacio Bernal," in *Notas mesoamericanas,* no. 10 (1987); Kent V. Flannery, "Ignacio Bernal," in *American Antiquity* 59, no. 1 (1994): 72–76.

BERNARDES, ARTUR DA SILVA (1875–1955).

Artur da Silva Bernardes (*b.* 8 August 1875; *d.* 23 March 1955), president of Brazil (1922–1926). Bernardes was born in Viçosa, Minas Gerais, the son of a Portuguese solicitor. He attended the Lazarist school in Caracas and studied law in Ouro Prêto, where he was a leader in the *Bucha,* a secret student society inspired by the German *Burchenschaft.* After completing his studies, he returned to Viçosa to work as a lawyer, and in 1903 he married Clélia Vaz de Melo.

Bernardes began his political career in the early 1900s, holding various posts in Minas Gerais, including president of the municipal chamber, chief executive of Viçosa, and state deputy. Between 1909 and 1915, he served as a federal deputy. As his political career advanced, Bernardes became the secretary of finances for the state of Minas Gerais in 1910, serving until 1914. Four years later, he was elected governor of Minas Gerais.

Elected president of Brazil in 1922, Bernardes, however, ruled the country under a state of siege during most of his presidency, with challenges coming from both the Right and the Left. The most celebrated opposition faction was led by the Communist revolutionary leader Luís Carlos Prestes.

President Bernardes implemented constitutional reforms that strengthened executive powers and sought reductions in public expenditures. He withdrew Brazil from the League of Nations in 1926 because it refused to admit Germany as a member nation.

After his presidential term ended, Bernardes (a senator from 1929 to 1932) helped organize the unsuccessful Constitutionalist Revolution against Getúlio Vargas in 1930. He was exiled to Portugal in 1932 for five years. Elected federal deputy upon his return to Brazil, Bernardes continued his nationalistic campaign in which he advocated exploitation of the country's natural resources solely by Brazilians. He lost reelection in 1937 but returned to politics in

1945, when he organized the political party União Democrática Nacional (UDN). Soon after, however, he broke with this party and founded the Partido Republicano (PR), of which he was president until his death in 1955.

See also **Brazil, Political Parties: National Democratic Union of Brazil (UDN); Republican Party (PR).**

BIBLIOGRAPHY

Neves Fontoura, *A Aliança Liberal e a Revolução de 1930* (1963); *Almanaque Abril* (1994).

IÉDA SIQUEIRA WIARDA

BERNI, ANTONIO (1905–1981).

Antonio Berni (*b.* 14 March 1905; *d.* 13 October 1981), Argentine painter. Berni was born in Rosario, where in 1916 he studied at the Centre Catalá under Eugenio Fornels and Enrique Munné. In 1925 he went to Madrid, and then to Paris, where he studied at the Académie de la Grande Chaumière under André Lothe and Othon Friesz. The influence of the surrealists Salvador Dali and Giorgio de Chirico is evident in his early works. Berni met the Mexican David Alfaro Siqueiros in Buenos Aires in 1933, after which he favored representation in his work. In the following decades Berni developed his style in neorealistic, narrative compositions. His creation of two folk figures, "Juanito Laguna" and "Ramona Montiel," constitutes the visual and conceptual synthesis of his attempts to incorporate decorative elements in his art. Berni's creative imagination and enthusiasm were manifest until his last days, when he created three-dimensional animals in assemblages with mannequins, a curious return to the surrealistic output of his early years. Berni received the first prize for painting at the National Salon of Buenos Aires (1937) and the Grand Acquisition Prize, also at the National Salon (1940).

See also **Art: The Twentieth Century.**

BIBLIOGRAPHY

José Viñals, interviewer, *Berni, palabra e imagen* (1976).

Vicente Gesualdo, Aldo Viglione, and Rodolfo Santos, *Diccionario de artistas plásticos en la Argentina* (1988).

Additional Bibliography

Glusberg, Jorge. *Antonio Berni.* Buenos Aires: Museo Nacional de Bellas Artes, 1997.

AMALIA CORTINA ARAVENA

BERRETA, TOMÁS (1875–1947).

Tomás Berreta (*b.* 22 November 1875; *d.* 1 August 1947), president of Uruguay (1947). Berreta was from the department of Canelones, where he was a farmhand, cattle driver, policeman, chief of police (1911–1916), and quartermaster general (1917). He was elected to Parliament in 1923 and served as minister of public works (1943–1946) during the presidency of Juan José de Amézaga before being elected president. He died five months into his term.

A man of humble background and a descendant of Italian immigrants, Berreta exemplified through his career the changing nature of Uruguayan society in his day. At age seventeen he met José Batlle y Ordóñez while delivering a report to the newspaper *El Día*. Their friendship helped launch Berreta's political career from a department that was still rural and in which the ideas of Batllismo were just beginning to blossom.

See also **Batlle y Ordóñez, José; Batllismo.**

BIBLIOGRAPHY

Daniel Vidart, *Tomás Berreta: Apología de la acción* (1946).

Juan Carlos Pedemonte, *Los presidentes del Uruguay* (1984).

Martin Weinstein, *Uruguay: Democracy at the Crossroads* (1988).

Additional Bibliography

Cigliuti, Carlos Walter. *Vida de Don Tomás Berreta: Las opciones de la democracia.* Montevideo, Uruguay: Imprenta Rosgal, 1975.

JOSÉ DE TORRES WILSON

BERRÍO, PEDRO JUSTO (1827–1875).

Pedro Justo Berrío (*b.* 28 May 1827; *d.* 14 February 1875), Antioquian (Colombian) statesman. A leader in the department of Antioquia's struggle for self-determination, Berrío, a native of Santa Rosa de Osos, received his doctorate in law at Bogotá in

1851. He subsequently served in the Antioquian Assembly (1852–1853), as a magistrate (1854), and in the national Congress (1856–1857). A Conservative, he led the partisan forces that in December 1863 overthrew the Liberal regime of Antioquia. Berrío's nearly universal support in the department won his government formal recognition from the national Liberal president, Manuel Murillo Toro, on 18 April 1864. As governor (10 January 1864–7 August 1873), he actively promoted internal improvements such as the Antioquia Railroad. Berrío's importance derives from his success in keeping Antioquia out of the Colombian economic and social turmoil of the 1860s and early 1870s. Antioquia's economy and prosperity expanded considerably during his tenure. Berrío died in Medellín.

See also **Antigua; Colombia, Political Parties: Conservative Party.**

BIBLIOGRAPHY

Joaquín Emilio Jaramillo, *Vida de Pedro Justo Berrío* (1927).

Estanislao Gómez Barrientos, *Del Dr. Pedro Justo Berrío y del escenario en que hubo de actuar* (1928).

Javier Gutiérrez Villegas, *Pedro Justo Berrío* (1975).

Additional Bibliography

Villegas Botero, Luis Javier. *Las vías de legitimación de un poder: La administración presidida por Pedro Justo Berrio en el estado soberano de Antioquia: 1864-1873.* Bogotá: Colcultura, 1996.

J. LEÓN HELGUERA

BERRO, CARLOS (1853–1930). Carlos Berro (*b.* 17 January 1853; *d.* 15 October 1930), Uruguayan politician. Berro was born in Montevideo, but his family, exiled for belonging to the Blanco (National) Party, resettled in Santiago, Chile, where he received with honors his doctorate in jurisprudence. He returned to his homeland in 1873 and was named counseling judge of the department of Colonia. In 1885 he was elected national representative for the department of Lavalleja. In 1890 he was appointed minister of justice, culture, and public education by President Julio Herrera y Obes. Between 1891 and 1896 he represented the department of Treinta y Tres in the Senate.

In the uprisings of 1894 and 1897, Berro joined with the revolutionary forces of Aparicio Saravia, the military leader of the Partido Nacionalista. In 1898 he was elected national representative for the department of Montevideo, and in 1907 he was elected first vice president of the Directorate. An active militant in the Blanco Party, he participated in the constituent assembly, which in 1917 enacted the first constitutional reform in the history of Uruguay.

Berro's career illustrates the evolution of the Blanco Party at the turn of the century. A student in exile, graduate of a foreign school, and noted lawyer, judge, legislator, revolutionary, and party boss, he later returned to civil activities and participated in the transformation of the Blanco Party into a force that disputed power at the ballot box rather than through revolution. In the elections for the constituent assembly of 30 June 1916 (the first elections in Uruguay to use the secret ballot and proportional representation), Berro was elected, and he helped to write the Constitution of 1917.

See also **Uruguay, Constitutions; Uruguay, Political Parties: Blanco Party.**

BIBLIOGRAPHY

José M. Fernández Saldaña, *Diccionario Uruguayo de biografías, 1810–1940* (Montevideo, 1945).

Brother Damasceno, *Ensayo de historia patria*, vol. 2 (1950).

JOSÉ DE TORRES WILSON

BERTONI, MOISÉS (1858–1929). Moisés Bertoni (*b.* 1858; *d.* 19 September 1929), Swiss-born naturalist active in Paraguay. A native of the Alpine cantor of Tessin, Bertoni left an indelible mark on scientific investigation in Paraguay. He attended the universities at Geneva and Zurich where he studied science before arriving in South America in 1884. Advised by the French geographer Elisée Reclus that the Misiones region of northeastern Argentina boasted flora and fauna found nowhere else, Bertoni relocated across the Paraná River to Paraguay in 1887. On the edge of the river, he built a fine home and laboratory at an isolated camp from which he conducted all manner of biological research. He published scores of articles and papers on such topics as yerba mate, ethnobotany, and the habits of aquatic mammals.

President Juan Gualberto González brought Bertoni to Asunción in the early 1890s to head the Jardín Zoológico and the newly established agricultural school. In 1893, while serving in that latter post, he recruited a number of Swiss colonists to settle at Colonia Guillermo Tell (later called Puerto Bertoni) in southeastern Paraguay. He acted as patron to these immigrants, a good many of whom stayed on in the country despite the fact that the colony did not prosper. For his part, Bertoni continued to edit scientific journals and write works on natural history, many of which were printed on a primitive press at Guillermo Tell. His magnum opus, *Descripción física y económica del Paraguay,* filled seventeen volumes, but Bertoni was only able to print four before his death.

See also **Science.**

BIBLIOGRAPHY

Carlos Zubizarreta, *Cien vidas paraguayas,* 2d ed. (1985), pp. 257–261.

Harris Gaylord Warren, *Rebirth of the Paraguayan Republic: The First Colorado Era, 1878–1904* (1985), pp. 292–293.

Additional Bibliography

Baratti, Danilo, and Patrizia Candolfi. *Vida y obra del sabio Bertoni: Moisés Santiago Bertoni, 1857-1929: Un naturalista suizo en Paraguay.* Asunción: Helvetas, 1999.

THOMAS L. WHIGHAM

BERTRAND, FRANCISCO (1866–1926).

Francisco Bertrand (*b.* 1866; *d.* 1926), president of Honduras. Francisco Bertrand served as president of Honduras three times between 1911 and 1919. Through a policy of reconciliation and control, he imposed order on Honduras's traditionally unstable political system. His first term, 28 March 1911 to 31 January 1912, arose out of an agreement between the government of General Miguel Dávila and rebels led by General Manuel Bonilla. Under the Tacoma Pact of 1911, these parties agreed to end hostilities. Bertrand was appointed provisional president and oversaw elections that Bonilla won without opposition. In the succeeding administration, Bertrand

became secretary of government and justice, and later vice president. Following Bonilla's death in 1913, Bertrand served as interim president from 20 March 1913 to 28 July 1915. Six months before the end of his presidency, he resigned to campaign for a third term. His third term, from 1 February 1916 to 9 September 1919, was one of relative stability. Bertrand's attempt to impose his own successor, however, led to a rebellion and a return to political chaos. On 9 September 1919, Bertrand resigned from office and left the country.

See also **Honduras.**

BIBLIOGRAPHY

Lucas Paredes, *Drama político de Honduras* (1958), esp. pp. 241–268.

Raúl Arturo Pagoaga, *Honduras y sus gobernantes* (1979), esp. pp. 46–49.

PETER A. SZOK

BERUTI, ANTONIO LUIS (1772–1841).

Antonio Luis Beruti (*b.* 2 September 1772; *d.* 3 October 1841), military officer in the struggle for Argentine independence. Born in Buenos Aires, Beruti studied in Spain but even before the 1810 revolution was involved with other creole patriots in conspiracy against the colonial regime. He became a strong supporter of the May Revolution of 1810 and of Mariano Moreno against rival revolutionary factions. Beruti held military positions in both Buenos Aires and the interior and accompanied José de San Martín in his crossing of the Andes in 1817. After independence he was an active Unitarist and opponent of the dictatorship of Juan Manuel de Rosas. As such he took part in the civil wars against Rosas, and following the Unitarists' defeat at Rodeo del Medio, Mendoza, in September 1841, he suffered an attack of delirium from which he soon died.

See also **Argentina, Movements: Unitarists.**

BIBLIOGRAPHY

Jacinto R. Yaben, *Biografías argentinas y sudamericanas,* vol. 1 (1938), pp. 578–579.

DAVID BUSHNELL

BERUTTI, ARTURO (1862–1938).

Arturo Berutti (*b.* 27 March 1862; *d.* 3 January 1938), Argentine composer. Born in San Juan, Argentina, Berutti studied composition with his father, a composer and pianist, and with Ignacio Álvarez. Later, in Buenos Aires, he was a student of Nicolás Bassi's. At twenty he published his fantasia *Ecos patrióticos* and began writing a series of articles in the *Revista Mefistófeles* to promote musical nationalism. After winning an official scholarship, Berutti traveled to Germany and enrolled at the Leipzig Conservatory (1884), where he studied with Carl Reinecke and Salomon Jadassohn. In 1887 the Stuttgart Orchestra premiered his *Obertura Andes.* He composed two symphonies on Latin American subjects; *Rivadavia* and *Colombiana* (both in 1888). After traveling to Paris, he settled in Milan, where he wrote the *Sinfonía Argentina* (1890) and *Vendetta,* his first opera, which premiered at the Teatro Lirico in Vercelli. In 1893 his *Evangelina* was performed at Milan's Teatro Alhambra.

Berutti, like the Brazilian Antônio Carlos Gomes, was one of the few South American composers whose operas met with success in Italy. He composed *Pampa* (1897), the first Argentine opera based on the native drama of Juan Moreira. It was followed by *Taras Bulba* (1895), which premiered at the Teatro Regio in Turin, *Yupanki* (1899), *Khrysé* (1903), and *Los héroes* (1909), based on an incident of the de Rosas period. He also composed *Facundo Quiroga* and *El espectro,* both unpublished, and *Horrida Nox,* the first Argentine opera with a Spanish libretto. Although based on Latin American subjects, all of Berutti's operas—as was true of other Latin American operas of the time—were European and classical in style and musical structure. While he was a passionate promoter of nationalism, as a composer Berutti is aesthetically linked to the romantic tradition. With short trips to Argentina, he resided in Europe until 1903, when he returned to Buenos Aires, where he continued to compose until his death. In addition to operas and symphonies, he composed orchestral works and vocal and piano pieces.

See also **Music: Art Music.**

BIBLIOGRAPHY

Rodolfo Arizaga, *Enciclopedia de la música argentina* (1971).

Gérard Béhague, *Music in Latin America* (1979); *New Grove Dictionary of Music and Musicians,* vol. 2 (1980).

Additional Bibliography

Aguilar, Gonzalo Moisés. "The National Opera: A Migrant Genre of Imperial Expansion." Translated by Kathryn Auffinger. *Journal of Latin American Cultural Studies* 12:1 (March 2003): 83–91.

SUSANA SALGADO

BETANCES Y ALACÁN, RAMÓN EMETERIO (1827–1898).

Ramón Emeterio Betances y Alacán was born in Cabo Rojo, Puerto Rico on April 8, 1827, to Felipe Betances Ponce and Maria del Carmen Alacán. His parents were a well-off Dominican–Puerto Rican mulatto family. When Betances reached primary-school age, he was sent to get a college degree in southern France, where he received the support and nurturing of a French-Puerto Rican family. In 1846 Betances earned a B.A. in philosophy, and after a brief stay in Puerto Rico he returned to France to pursue a degree in medicine, which he earned in 1855. That same year Betances returned to Puerto Rico and established his residence and medical practice in the town of Mayagüez. There he earned an excellent reputation as a doctor, risking his life when he controlled successfully an outbreak of cholera in Puerto Rico. Because he offered his services for free to the poor, he was given the name *Doctor de los pobres* ("Doctor of the poor people").

In addition to treating the poor, Betances was an abolitionist who bought the freedom of many children born into slavery. In his famous proclamation "Ten Commandments of Free Men" (1867), Betances called for the abolition of slavery, freedom of speech, freedom of worship, and the right to elect one's officials. The proclamation appears to be inspired by the Haitian Revolution, and scholars affirm that Betances sought in the revolution a model to emulate against colonialism and slavery. In addition to his abolitionist activities, Betances organized the first rebellion against Spanish colonial rule in Puerto Rico, known as El Grito de Lares ("The Cry of Lares"), in 1868. The rebellion was a failure, and Betances fled to New York City in April 1869. In the 1860s Betances traveled throughout the United States and the Caribbean, where he succeeded in establishing contacts with important Cuban and Dominican revolutionary leaders such as Ramón Estrada Palma and Gregorio Luperón, who became the president of the Dominican Republic in 1879. In recognition of Betances's aid in the Dominican struggle against Spain, President Luperón appointed Betances an ambassador to Paris and London. Betances never returned to Puerto Rico. He dedicated the last twenty-five years of his life to the cause of an Antillean Confederation, with Haiti as the lead country. After the Spanish-American War the United States established a new system of colonial rule in the Caribbean, and until the last moment of his life, Betances vehemently rejected the outcome of the war. Betances passed away on September 16, 1898 in Neuilly, France. In 1920 his remains were brought to his hometown of Cabo Rojo. Puerto Ricans celebrate his birthday as a national holiday.

See also **Slavery: Spanish America.**

BIBLIOGRAPHY

Bonafaux, Luis. *Betances.* San Juan, Puerto Rico: Instituto de Cultura Puertorriqueña, 1970.

Estrade, Paul, and Félix Ojeda Reyes. *Pasión por la libertad: Actas, Coloquio Internacional "El Independentismo Puertorriqueño, de Betances a Nuestros Días."* San Juan, Puerto Rico: Instituto de Estudios del Caribe, Editorial de la Universidad de Puerto Rico, 2000.

Jiménez de Wageheim, Olga. *Puerto Rico's Revolt for Independence: El Grito de Lares.* Princeton, NJ: M. Wiener Publishers, 1993.

Maldonado Denis, Manuel. *Betances, revolucionario antillano y otros ensayos.* Río Piedras, Puerto Rico: Editorial Antillana, 1970.

Ojeda Reyes, Félix. *La manigua en París: correspondencia diplomática de Betances.* City: San Juan, PR: Centro de Estudios Avanzados y del Caribe Publisher, 1984.

Ramos Mattei, Andrés A. *Betances en el ciclo revolucionario antillano: 1867–1875.* San Juan, Puerto Rico: Instituto de Cultura Puertorriqueña, 1987.

Suárez Díaz, Ada. *El doctor Ramón Emeterio Betances y la abolición de la esclavitud.* San Juan, Puerto Rico: Instituto de Cultura Puertorriqueña, 1980.

MILAGROS DENIS

BETANCOURT, RÓMULO (1908–1981).

Rómulo Betancourt (*b.* 22 February 1908; *d.* 28 September 1981), president of Venezuela (1945–1948, 1959–1964). The founder of contemporary Venezuelan democracy, Betancourt was also a hemispheric leader and symbol of democratic values and practices. A strong critic and opponent of both Marxist and right-wing authoritarianism, he personified enlightened democratic reformism in the Americas. He was also the founder and organizational genius of Venezuela's political party Democratic Action (Acción Democratica—AD), which he regarded as among his most important achievements. Betancourt's AD has remained a dominant force in Venezuelan politics for a full half-century and survived his death.

Born to a modest family in Guatire, a town east of Caracas, Betancourt became absorbed by politics during his student days. Emerging as a leader of the Generation of '28, he was a major participant in the uprising which protested the government of long-time dictator Juan Vicente Gómez. The February 1928 uprising led to the exile of Betancourt and other young Venezuelans until Gómez's death in 1935. It also nourished their intellectual and political hunger for democracy in Venezuela, and led to a search for new political and doctrinal solutions to national problems, especially those related to the overwhelming influence of petroleum on society and national life.

Betancourt assumed a major role in building a reformist political organization following his 1936 return to Caracas. (He returned again in 1941.) He built the nucleus for what later became AD, formally established in September 1941. Having purged Marxist elements from the organization, Betancourt stressed the need for open debate and discussion of petroleum policy and other major issues. When the AD and lesser opposition parties were effectively barred from meaningful participation in elections set for 1945, Betancourt and his colleagues joined with junior military officers to overthrow the existing regime. This so-called October Revolution (1945) introduced a three-year period, the *trienio,* which was marked by dramatic and far-reaching reforms.

For more than two years a seven-person junta headed by Betancourt led Venezuela toward an institutionalized open political system. The Constituent Assembly wrote a new constitution (signed into law 5 July 1947) and national elections held 14 December 1947 brought to office a government headed by the AD's Rómulo Gallegos early in 1948. Betancourt and other members of the junta had pledged not to seek office in the next administration. When the government of Gallegos, an eminent writer but inexperienced politician, was overthrown less than a year after being inaugurated, Venezuela entered a decade of military authoritarianism dominated by Marcos Pérez Jiménez.

Betancourt spent a decade of exile in Cuba, Costa Rica, and Puerto Rico. Other prominent party leaders had similar experiences, and those in the underground were persecuted and killed. When a massive civic protest finally led to the collapse of the Pérez Jiménez government in January 1958, Betancourt and other democratic leaders returned home. They created a new arrangement of power sharing, and Betancourt won election to the presidency in December 1958. Although he took office with the support of other democratic parties, he experienced an extraordinarily difficult incumbency.

Remnants of rightist militarism instigated two substantial uprisings. An assassination attempt planned by the Dominican strongman Rafael Leónidas Trujillo killed a member of Betancourt's party; Betancourt's hands were burned and his equilibrium was affected. Meanwhile, young admirers of Fidel Castro and the Cuban revolution mounted an armed insurgency that brought violence and terrorism in the cities of Venezuela at a time when Betancourt was grappling with a depressed economy left by the corrupt military dictatorship.

Betancourt courted the private sectors, encouraged properly controlled foreign investment, and moved toward a meaningful program of agrarian reform. Labor was supported, education received special attention, and other measures sought to correct social injustices. Betancourt also established warm relations with the Kennedy administration in Washington. The personal friendship of the two presidents grew strong as Venezuela emerged as the model of democratic reformism in Latin America.

As required by the 1961 Constitution, Betancourt left office after his five-year term (1959–1964). Once power had been transferred to Raúl Leoni, another member of the AD's founding generation, Betancourt went into exile for nearly five years, during which time he recuperated from the serious injuries suffered during the attempted

assassination. After returning, he declined to run for the presidency in 1973, instead backing Carlos Andrés Pérez.

In his final years Betancourt was still a powerful force in AD. A tenacious defender of democratic values, he brooked no opposition to his vision of representative government throughout the hemisphere. He died after suffering a stroke during a visit to New York City and was buried in Caracas.

See also **Venezuela, Political Parties: Democratic Action (AD); Venezuela: Venezuela since 1830.**

BIBLIOGRAPHY

Robert J. Alexander, *The Venezuelan Democratic Revolution* (1964) and *Rómulo Betancourt and the Transformation of Venezuela* (1982).

Charles J. Ameringer, *The Democratic Left in Exile: The Anti-Dictatorial Struggle in the Caribbean, 1945–1959* (1974).

Rómulo Betancourt, *Venezuela: Politics and Oil,* trans. Everett Baumann (1979).

Juan Liscano and Carlos Gottberg, *Multimagen de Rómulo: Vida y acción de Rómulo Betancourt en gráficas,* 5th ed. (1978).

John D. Martz, *Acción Democrática: Evolution of a Modern Political Party in Venezuela* (1964).

John D. Martz and David J. Myers, eds., *Venezuela: The Democratic Experience,* rev. ed. (1986).

Franklin Tugwell, *The Politics of Oil in Venezuela* (1975).

Ramón J. Velásquez, J. F. Sucre Figarella, and Blas Bruni Celli, *Betancourt en la historia de Venezuela del siglo XX* (1980).

Additional Bibliography

Schwartzberg, Steven. *Democracy and U.S. Policy in Latin America.* Gainesville: University Press of Florida, 2003.

JOHN D. MARTZ

BETANCOURT CISNEROS, GASPAR

(1803–1866). Gaspar Betancourt Cisneros (*b.* 28 April 1803; *d.* 20 December 1866), Cuban advocate of annexation to the United States. Born in Camagüey, Betancourt Cisneros, also known by his pen name El Lugareño, was a progressive businessman who sponsored the establishment of schools, built bridges, and promoted the construction of the first railroad in his native province of Camagüey. A firm believer in constitutionalism and deeply influenced by physiocratic ideas, he distributed a large portion of his estate to peasants at a minimal cost. He also rejected slavery as the worst evil. Always concerned with Cuba's future, in 1823 Betancourt Cisneros went in search of Simón Bolívar in order to request his support for overthrowing the Spanish yoke. Later he advocated Cuba's annexation to the United States, although, in his view, "Annexation is not a sentiment but a calculation ... it is the sacred right of self-preservation." Toward the end of his life, however, he returned to his advocacy of independence as he came to distrust U.S. intentions. Betancourt Cisneros died in Havana.

See also **Cuba: The Colonial Era (1492–1898).**

BIBLIOGRAPHY

For a discussion of some of Betancourt Cisneros's ideas, see Geraldo E. Poyo, *"With All, and for the Good of All"* (1989); also, Ramiro Guerra, *Manual de historia de Cuba* (1975).

Additional Bibliography

Monal, Isabel, and Olivia Miranda Francisco, eds. *Pensamiento cubano, siglo XIX.* La Habana: Editorial de Ciencias Sociales, 2002.

José M. Hernández

BETANCUR CUARTAS, BELISARIO

(1923–). Belisario Betancur Cuartas (*b.* 4 February 1923), president of Colombia (1982–1986). The second of twenty-two children of a poor family from Amagá, Antioquia, Betancur received a law degree in Medellín in 1947 and worked in Conservative journalism there. In the 1960s he served in the congress and as minister of labor. In 1979 he was appointed ambassador to Spain. After two unsuccessful runs for the presidency, Betancur finally won in 1982. He inherited a banking crisis and a developing recession, which he handled with relative success. His major domestic initiative was an opening to Colombia's guerrilla groups, culminating in truce agreements with three of the four largest in May–August 1984. But by late 1985 these truces collapsed, as dramatically illustrated by M-19's seizure of the Palace of Justice in Bogotá in 1985.

Increased pressure against cocaine traffickers, after years of official nonfeasance, led to the assassination of Betancur's minister of justice in April 1984. On the international front, Betancur's advocacy for developing countries at the United Nations in October 1983 won wide applause, as did his role in the Contadora peace process for Central America. After the end of his political career, he became involved in many international organizations and associations, including the Commission for Truth in the El Salvadorian Peace Process.

See also **Colombia: Since Independence; Colombia, Revolutionary Movements: M-19.**

BIBLIOGRAPHY

Ignacio Arizmendi Posada, *Presidentes de Colombia, 1810–1990* (1990), pp. 295–300.

Olga Behar, *Las guerras de la paz* (1985).

Ana Carrigan, *The Palace of Justice* (1993).

Additional Bibliography

Betancur Cuartas, Belisario. "Perspectivas económicas y políticas de America Latina." In *Democracía y desarrollo en América Latina*, edited by Fernando Cepeda Ulloa. Buenos Aires: Grupo Editor Latinoamericano, 1985.

Ramírez, Socorro and Luis Alberto Restrepo. *Actores en conflicto por la paz: El proceso de paz durante el gobierno de Belisario Betancur (1982–1986.)* Mexico: Siglo Ventiuno, 1988.

Restrepo, Laura. *Historia de una traición.* Bogotá: Plaza & Janés, 1986.

Vázquez Carrizosa, Alfredo. *Betancur y la crisis nacional.* Bogotá: Ediciones Aurora, 1986.

Richard J. Stoller

BETHANCOURT, PEDRO DE SAN JOSÉ DE

(1626–1667). Pedro de San José de Bethancourt (also Betancur; *b.* 21 March 1626; *d.* 25 April 1667), founder of charitable institutions in Guatemala. Born in Villaflor, Canary Islands, Hermano Pedro (as he is known today) traveled to Guatemala in 1650–1651 by way of Cuba. He studied for the priesthood in Santiago de Guatemala but gave up after three years. While he was in nearby Petapa, a vision of the Virgin came to him. Newly encouraged, he returned to Santiago, where, upon relating his experience to his confessor, he was admitted to the Third Order of the Franciscans. Inspired to help the poor and sick, he established a primary school and hospital in a straw hut, becoming known as the "Servant of God." Through charity he raised funds to build a hospital and formed a group of followers whom he called Bethlehemites, in recognition of the importance he placed on the Nativity as a period of Christian devotion each year. When he died, leadership for his work passed to Rodrigo de Arias Maldonado, known as Rodrigo de la Cruz. Hermano Pedro was buried in the Chapel of the Third Order in the San Francisco church in Santiago (now Antigua), where his tomb continues to be a much-visited shrine. Many miraculous healings have been attributed to him. The request for his beatification was considered from 1712 to 1771, when Pope Clement XIV granted him the status of "Servant of God." Beatification waited until 22 June 1980.

See also **Bethlehemites.**

BIBLIOGRAPHY

David Vela, *El Hermano Pedro* (1935).

Maximo Soto Hall, *Pedro de San José Bethencourt: El San Francisco de Asís americano* (1949).

DAVID L. JICKLING

BETHLEHEMITES. Bethlehemites, a religious order founded in Guatemala to extend health care and education to the poor. Pedro de San José de Bethancourt received great popular support for his work with the poor as a Franciscan lay worker in the last half of the seventeenth century in Santiago de Guatemala. In 1658 he founded a convalescent hospital in Santiago, which received royal approval in 1660. His followers and fellow workers became known as Bethlehemites, in recognition of the importance he attached to the Nativity as a period of Christian devotion each year. When Hermano Pedro died in 1667, leadership of the movement passed to his assistant, Rodrigo de Arias Maldonado, known as Rodrigo de la Cruz. The local bishop, Payo Enríquez de Ribera, was another enthusiastic

supporter of the hospital and educational work of the Bethlehemites. When he was transferred to Mexico in 1668, he called for the Bethlehemites to establish a hospital in Mexico City and later in Veracruz.

The formal creation of the order, with branches for both men and women, was approved by Pope Clement X in 1674. Two provinces were established: one in Peru with twenty-two centers and the second in Mexico, Guatemala, and Cuba with eleven centers. Many men and women from Spain joined the order through the Convent of Belem in Havana.

The early history of the order and of its founders was written in 1723 by a Spanish theologian, Joseph García de la Concepción. During the smallpox epidemic of 1736 the order was acclaimed for its outstanding services to the stricken in the countries where its members worked. Today the Bethlehemites continue their activities in Guatemala and Spain.

See also **Catholic Church: The Colonial Period.**

BIBLIOGRAPHY

Joseph García De La Concepción, *Historia Belemitica*, 2d ed. (1956).

Additional Bibliography

Mayo, Carlos A. *Los betlemitas en Buenos Aires: Convento, economía y sociedad (1748-1822)*. Sevilla: Excma. Diputación Provincial de Sevilla, 1991.

DAVID L. JICKLING

BIANCO, JOSÉ (1908–1986). José Bianco (*b.* 21 November 1908; *d.* 24 April 1986), Argentine writer, editor, and literary critic. Born in Buenos Aires, Bianco served from 1938 to 1961 as editorial director of Victoria Ocampo's influential literary and intellectual review *Sur*. After he broke with Ocampo over a visit he made to Cuba (the Cuban Revolution occasioned many partings in Argentine cultural life in the 1960s), Bianco played a major role in the development of the University of Buenos Aires Press, one of the significant axes of cultural development in Argentina until the university was taken over by the military regime in 1966. Throughout his life, Bianco published his critical essays in an impressively diverse array of forums, from the oligarchic daily *La Nación* to the Cuban revolutionary journal *Casa de las Américas. Ficción y reflexión* (1988) is an anthology of Bianco's literary criticism.

Bianco's creative literature is most identified with early texts: *Sombras suele vestir* (1941), a novel that anticipates the formal experimentation of works twenty years later in its utilization of a fragmented point of view and the counterpoint between narrative shifts and the cruel human drama it chronicles; and *Las ratas* (1943), where a plot turning on murder-suicide displaces the traditional omniscience of the mystery story with the relativization of narrative knowledge. *Las ratas* was enthusiastically acclaimed by Jorge Luis Borges at a time when the latter was particularly interested in detective fiction, a genre with a long record of influence in Argentine literature.

See also **Literature: Spanish America.**

BIBLIOGRAPHY

Antonio Prieto Taboada, "El poder y la ambigüedad en *Sombras suele vestir,* de José Bianco," in *Revista Iberoamericana* 49, no. 125 (1983): 717–730; "Ficción y realidad de José Bianco, 1908–1986," in *Revista Iberoamericana* 52, no. 137 (1986): 957–962; "Entrevista: José Bianco," in *Hispamérica* 17, no. 50 (1988): 73–86.

Hugo Beccacece, "Estudio preliminar," in *José Bianco, Páginas de José Bianco* (1984), pp. 11–31.

DAVID WILLIAM FOSTER

BICALHO OSWALD, HENRIQUE CARLOS

(1918–1965). Henrique Carlos Bicalho Oswald (*b.* 1918; *d.* 1965), Brazilian engraver and painter. The son of the painter Carlos Oswald, Bicalho Oswald enrolled in the mid-1940s in the National School of Fine Arts in Rio de Janeiro. While in Paris in 1958, he became acquainted with the printmaker Johnny Friedlaender. Upon his return from Europe in 1959, Henrique settled in Salvador and accepted a position as head of the printmaking department at the University of Bahia. Alongside Hansen-Bahia (Karl Heinz Hansen) and Mario Cravo, Bicalho Oswald helped popularize engraving in Bahia. Although he executed religious canvases and decorative and abstract works, Henrique is best known for figurative works documenting the landscape and daily life of Bahia, including *Inflation, Alone,* and *Northeastern Migrants.*

See also **Art: The Twentieth Century.**

BIBLIOGRAPHY

Dawn Ades, *Art in Latin America* (1989), p. 339.

CAREN A MEGHREBLIAN

BIDLACK TREATY (TREATY OF NEW GRANADA, 1846).

Bidlack Treaty (Treaty of New Granada, 1846) was an agreement between the United States and New Granada recognizing New Granada's sovereignty over the Isthmus of Panama. U.S. minister Benjamin Alden Bidlack negotiated the pact without specific instructions, except to supply information on isthmian transit and to prevent other powers from obtaining transit rights. New Granada viewed the Moskito Indian king, who had claim to land from Panama up to Nicaragua, and the General Juan José Flores expedition being organized in London as elements in a concerted British plan to dominate all the isthmian routes. The United States was also concerned with a French transit company that had commissioned an excellent study and map of a canal route. Under the agreement the United States assured the "perfect neutrality" of, and New Granada's sovereignty over, the isthmus. In return New Granada, in clause XXXV of the treaty, gave the United States exclusive rights of transit "upon any mode of communication that now exists, or that may be, hereafter, constructed." Simultaneously with the transit treaty, Bidlack and New Granada's commissioner Manuel María Mallarino negotiated a commercial treaty, which was signed on 12 December 1846 and proclaimed 12 June 1848.

The Bidlack Treaty was the only pact in the nineteenth century in which the U.S. government agreed to defend a Latin American state's sovereignty at the request of that state. Clause XXXV served as the basis for protecting the Panama Railroad, completed in 1855. It also was used in the 1880s to justify maintaining U.S. vessels at Panama during the Ferdinand de Lesseps canal venture. International law specialist John Basset Moore used clause XXXV in 1903 to argue that the United States had the "right of way" necessary to build a canal without Colombia's consent.

See also **Panama Canal; United States-Latin American Relations.**

BIBLIOGRAPHY

David Hunter Miller, ed., *Treaties and Other International Acts of the United States of America,* vol. 5 (1937), pp. 115–160.

E. Taylor Parks, *Colombia and the United States, 1765–1934* (1935).

Charles I. Bevans, ed., *Treaties and Other International Agreements of the United States of America,* vol. 6 (1971), pp. 865–881.

David Mc Cullough, *The Path Between the Seas: The Creation of the Panama Canal, 1870–1914* (1977).

John E. Findling, *Dictionary of American Diplomatic History,* 2d ed. (1989).

THOMAS SCHOONOVER

aesthetic experimentation, the bienals have become institutionalized and have restricted creativity.

See also **Art: The Twentieth Century.**

BIBLIOGRAPHY

Mario Pedrosa, "A bienal de ca' para lá," in *Arte Brasileira Hoje,* edited by Ferreira Gullar (1973); *Arte no Brasil,* vol. 2 (1979), pp. 897–899.

Additional Bibliography

Alambert, Francisco, and Polyana Canhête. *As Bienais de São Paulo: Da era do Museu à era dos curadores (1951-2001).* São Paulo: Boitempo, 2004.

Matarazzo Sobrinho, Francisco, and Agnaldo Farias. *Bienal de São Paulo, 50 anos, 1951-2001= 50 years of the São Paulo Biennial: Homenagem a Francisco Matarazzo Sobrinho.* São Paulo: Fundação Bienal de São Paulo, 2001.

CAREN A. MEGHREBLIAN

BIENAL DE SÃO PAULO.

Bienal de São Paulo, an international art exhibition held in São Paulo every two years. Inaugurated in 1951, the first Bienal de São Paulo was organized by Laurival Gomes Machado, the director of the São Paulo Museum of Modern Art, and Sérgio Milliet, art critic. The model they envisioned for São Paulo resembled that established for the Venice Biennale: to stimulate artistic production and creativity, provide international exposure for young artists, and enable artists to compete internationally and be judged by an international committee. Locally, it contributed to ending Brazil's artistic and cultural isolation while exposing Brazilians, and specifically Brazilian artists, to the major international artistic movements of the twentieth century.

In the first São Paulo Bienal, artists from nineteen countries exhibited 1,800 works of art. Little-known Brazilian artists such as Lasar Segall, Cândido Portinari, Di Cavalcanti, and Vítor Brecheret had the opportunity to exhibit alongside such internationally established artists as Picasso and Léger. By the second Bienal in 1953, artists from forty countries participated. Di Cavalcanti received a best-painter prize, while Eliseu Visconti was allocated a special room to exhibit his works. Over the years, critics claim, however, that rather than opening the door to new

BIGAUD, WILSON (1931–).

Wilson Bigaud (b. 29 January 1931), Haitian painter who has been an integral part of the renaissance of Haitian art. He is hailed as an innovator of the *vraiment naïf* genre with his paintings of pop-eyed rural folk and people with disproportionate bodies. The renowned artist Hector Hyppolite took Bigaud as an apprentice when the latter was only fifteen years old. Bigaud joined the Centre d'Art in Port-au-Prince in 1946 and shortly thereafter painted his masterpiece, *Miracle at Cana* (1950–1951), for the Holy Trinity Cathedral. In this work, all Bigaud's trademark elements are present: a jungle murder, a cemetery, drums, and voodoo images, all bathed in a rich yellow light. His *Adam and Eve* is considered the best of all Haitian primitive paintings. In the late 1950s Bigaud suffered a series of nervous breakdowns that interrupted and changed his style, after which he became a recluse.

See also **Art: The Twentieth Century.**

BIBLIOGRAPHY

Selden Rodman, *The Miracle of Haitian Art* (1974).

Eleanor Ingalls Christensen, *The Art of Haiti* (1975).

Madame Shishi, *"Les Naïfs Haitiens": An Introduction to Haitian Art and History* (1982).

Additional Bibliography

Benson, LeGrace. "Kiskeya-Lan Guinee-Eden: The Utopian Vision in Haitian Painting." *Callaloo.* 15 (Summer 1992) 726–734.

KAREN RACINE

BIGNONE, REYNALDO (1928–).

Argentine military man Reynaldo Bignone was de facto president between July 1982 and December 1983. Born January 21, 1928, he began his military career in 1947 at the Advanced School of Warfare. In 1975 he was named secretary of the Army High Command. After participating in the 1976 military coup, he directed large-scale illegal operations that were carried out by military "task forces." In 1980 he was named head of the High Command of Military Institutes. He was a political ally of de facto President Jorge Rafael Videla (1976–1981), and after Videla's resignation asked for voluntary retirement.

In 1982, after Argentina's defeat in the Malvinas War (or Falklands War), with the economy in deep crisis and the de facto regime disarticulated, the army named Bignone president of the republic and expected him to lead the process of democratic transition. During his short administration, he legalized the activity of political parties and called for elections but followed an irresponsible monetary and economic policy. Bignone passed the National Pacification Law, giving self-amnesty to members of the military for crimes committed during the dictatorship (a law revoked at the beginning of the democratic government of Raúl Ricardo Alfonsín).

In 1985 he was sent to prison for his role in ordering the torture and disappearance of political opponents. He was freed in 1986 but then sentenced to jail again in 1998 for ordering the kidnapping of the babies of political opponents who gave birth in jail during the military government. He regained his freedom in 2005.

See also **Alfonsín, Raúl Ricardo; Argentina: The Twentieth Century; Dirty War; Falkland Islands (Malvinas); Videla, Jorge Rafael.**

BIBLIOGRAPHY

Acuña, Carlos, ed. *La nueva matriz política argentina.* Buenos Aires: AR Nueva Visión, 1995.

Novaro, Marcos, and Vicente Palermo. *La dictadura militar, 1976–1983.* Buenos Aires: Paidós, 2003.

VICENTE PALERMO

BIG STICK POLICY.

"Big Stick Policy" was a phrase attributed to President Theodore Roosevelt (1901–1909), who described his guiding philosophy in dealing with Latin America as "Speak softly and carry a big stick." More than any U.S. leader, Roosevelt argued that forceful diplomatic policies and occasional landings of U.S. troops were necessary to preserve U.S. strategic interests in Latin America, especially in the Caribbean and Central America, and to safeguard foreign lives and property when national governments were unable or unwilling to carry out their obligations. Roosevelt integrated the policy into the Roosevelt Corollary to the Monroe Doctrine. Latin American critics charged that the professed reasons for employing the Big Stick—a form of gunboat diplomacy—were guises to conceal U.S. efforts to create an "informal empire" in Latin America and especially in the Caribbean and Central America, to advance the interests of U.S. business. Although he insisted his purpose lay in upholding law and order in places where local governments would not or could not do so, Roosevelt used the Big Stick in Cuba (1902–1903, 1906–1909), Panama (1903), the Dominican Republic (1904–1905), Central America (1906–1907), and in the Venezuelan debt crisis of 1902–1903. In Central America Roosevelt's purpose was both laudable and political: to create a mechanism for peaceful settlement of disputes and to chastise the anti-U.S. government in Nicaragua for its alleged meddling in the internal affairs of its neighbors. In some cases the policy served to rouse greater antipathy toward the United States throughout the region and led to even deeper U.S. involvement in the internal affairs of several Caribbean and Central American republics.

See also **Clark Memorandum; Monroe Doctrine; Roosevelt, Theodore; Roosevelt Corollary; United States-Latin American Relations.**

BIBLIOGRAPHY

Collin, Richard H. *Theodore Roosevelt's Caribbean: The Panama Canal, the Monroe Doctrine, and the Latin*

American Context. Baton Rouge: Louisiana State University Press, 1990.

Healy, David. *Drive to Hegemony: The United States in the Caribbean, 1898–1917.* Madison: University of Wisconsin Press, 1988.

Langley, Lester D. *The Banana Wars: United States Intervention in the Caribbean, 1900–1934.* Lexington: University Press of Kentucky, 1983.

LESTER D. LANGLEY

BILAC, OLAVO (1865–1918). Olavo Bilac (*b.* 16 December 1865; *d.* 18 December 1918), Brazilian poet. Declared in 1907 "the prince of Brazilian poets," Bilac was one of the greatest figures in Parnassianism. This movement in poetry, like naturalism in the novel, displayed the same antiromantic revolt that dominated the literary scene at the end of the nineteenth century. Bilac was born in Rio de Janeiro. His first book of poems, *Poesias* (1888), was warmly received, and the author was lauded by the leaders of Parnassianism. In the first poem of the collection, "Profissão de fé" (Profession of Faith), the author insists on the Parnassian ideal of language perfection. He viewed the poet's task as similar to that of a goldsmith fashioning delicate jewels: "When I write, I envy the goldsmith / I imitate the love / With which he, in golden relief / Creates his flowers." He expressed his love for the Portuguese language in "Língua Portuguesa": "I love your agrestic lushness and your aroma / Of virgin forests and large oceans! / I love your rude and dolorous idiom." He conserved this spirit throughout his life.

Bilac worked with a great variety of themes—personal and historical—the latter ranging from classical Rome to Brazilian history. His lyrical production diverges from exaggerated sentimentalism to sensualism. In "Ouvir estrelas" he converses with the stars, explaining, "Love and you will understand them. / Only one in love is / Able to listen to and understand the stars." His love poems, the best of his work, are still very much alive. Part of the contemporaneous force of Bilac's lyrics lies in the plasticity of the universe created by his verse: forms, colors, textures, sounds, and movements breathe life into his imagined world.

Bilac had illustrious careers in government and literature. He was a founding member of the Brazilian Academy of Letters, and he was above all a revered poet whose verse resounds in the voice and heart of his people. Additional works by Bilac include *Poesias* (2d ed., 1902), *Conferências literárias* (1906), *Ironia e piedade* (1916), and *Últimas conferências e discursos* (1924).

See also **Literature: Brazil.**

BIBLIOGRAPHY

Eloi Pontes, *A vida exuberante de Olavo Bilac* (1944).

Manuel Bandeira, in *Apresentação da poesia brasileira* (1946), pp. 108–118.

Eugênio Gomes, in *Visões e Revisões* (1958), pp. 126–133, 134–141, 215–295.

Fernando Jorge, *Vida e poesia de Olavo Bilac* (1963).

Claude L. Hulet, "Olavo Bilac," in *Brazilian Literature,* vol. 2 (1974), pp. 78–94.

Marisa Lajolo, *Os melhores poemas de Olavo Bilac* (1985).

Additional Bibliography

Botelho, André. *Aprendizado do Brasil: A nação em busca dos seus portadores sociais.* Campinas: Editora da Unicamp, FAPESP, 2002.

MARIA ISABEL ABREU

BILBAO BARQUÍN, FRANCISCO (1823–1865). Francisco Bilbao Barquín (*b.* 9 January 1823; *d.* 19 February 1865), Chilean radical. Born in Santiago and educated at the Instituto Nacional, Bilbao quickly revealed radical tendencies. His controversial article "La sociabilidad chilena" (The Nature of Chilean Society), published in the journal *El Crepúsculo* (June 1844), was immediately condemned by the authorities as blasphemous and immoral, though not subversive. In October 1844 Bilbao left for Europe, staying in Paris and making the acquaintance of the French thinkers Hugh-Félicité-Robert Lamennais (1782–1854), Jules Michelet (1798–1874), and Edgar Quinet (1803–1875). From autumn 1847 to summer 1848 he traveled in Germany, Austria, and Italy: he was in Paris in time to witness revolutionary activity there.

In February 1850 Bilbao returned to Chile where, with Santiago Arcos and others, he formed the Sociedad de la Igualdad (Society of Equality) in

April 1850. The society's leaders took nicknames from figures of the French Revolution: Bilbao's was Vergniaud, a testimony to his considerable talent for oratory. He went into hiding when the society was suppressed in November 1850. He fought in the Santiago insurrection of 20 April 1851 and later went into hiding and then into exile in Peru; he never returned to Chile. In 1855 he moved to Europe and in 1857 he made his final move to Argentina.

Bilbao's writings, liberal and democratic in content, are high-flown and often very lyrical. His works *La América en peligro* (America in Danger, 1862) and *El evangelio americano* (The American Gospel, 1864) highlight the contrast between the free and prosperous United States and the "disunited states" of Spanish America.

See also **Chile, Organizations: Society of Equality.**

BIBLIOGRAPHY

Alberto J. Varona, *Francisco Bilbao, revolucionario de América* (1973).

Solomon Lipp, *Three Chilean Thinkers* (1975), chap. 1.

SIMON COLLIER

BILLINGHURST, GUILLERMO ENRIQUE (1851–1915).

Guillermo Enrique Billing-hurst (*b.* 1851; *d.* 1915), Peruvian populist president (1912–1914), heir to the dictatorial tradition of civilian caudillo Nicolás de Piérola. Born in Arica to a family whose wealth originated in the nitrate business, Billinghurst supported, financially and politically, Piérola's forceful actions to become president.

In 1894–1895 Billinghurst financed Piérola's forces fighting a civil war against General Andrés Cáceres. Following Piérola's success in 1895, Billinghurst became first vice president and president of the Chamber of Senators. In 1898 he was in charge of negotiating a settlement over the Chilean-occupied territories of Tacna and Arica, which was turned down by the Chilean legislature. Failing to obtain official support due to Piérola's pact with the Civilista Party, Billinghurst lost the presidential elections of 1899. However, after reorganizing Piérola's former Democratic Party in

1908, Billinghurst became mayor of Lima (1908) and in 1912 was finally elected president of the republic. Attempting to establish stronger executive and protectionist changes, he faced a strong opposition by the Civilistas. When he tried to close the legislature in 1914, Billinghurst was ousted by a military coup led by General Oscar Benavides. Billinghurst died in Iquique.

See also **Peru: Peru Since Independence.**

BIBLIOGRAPHY

Jorge Basadre, *Historia de la República del Perú*, vol. 8 (1964).

Steve Stein, *Populism in Peru* (1980).

Additional Bibliography

Gonzales, Osmar. *Los orígenes del populismo en el Perú: El gobierno de Guillermo E. Billinghurst, 1912–1914.* Lima: [s.n.], 2005.

ALFONSO W. QUIROZ

BIMINI.

Bimini (Biminis), a large cay and two small islands running southward approximately fifty miles from the east coast of Florida. It is a popular tourist site, especially for sailing and fishing. Local legends suggest that the mythological Atlantis lies submerged beyond North Bimini, while others state that it is the site of Ponce de León's Fountain of Youth. With a total land area of only nine square miles, Bimini is home to about 1,700 inhabitants. It is part of the Bahama archipelago and has two main settlements: Alice Town and Bailey Town. Alice Town is the site of the Lerner Marine Laboratory, operated by the American Museum of Natural History and is the place where Ernest Hemingway wrote his novel *Islands in the Stream*.

See also **Bahamas, Commonwealth of the.**

BIBLIOGRAPHY

One of the best general surveys is *Bahamas Handbook* (annual). See also James E. Moore, *Pelican Guide to the Bahamas* (1980).

Additional Bibliography

Saunders, Ashley B. *History of the Bahamas: Bimini: A Case Study.* Bimini, Bahamas: New World Press, 1990.

Saunders, Ashley B. *History of Bimini*. Alice Town, Bimini, Bahamas: New World Press, 2000.

Warner, David T. *Bimini: Tales of an Island Getaway*. Montgomery, AL: River City Pub., 2003.

DARIÉN DAVIS

BINGHAM, HIRAM (1875–1956).

Hiram Bingham (*b.* 19 November 1875; *d.* 6 June 1956), U.S. explorer, scholar, author, and politician who sought the fabled Incan "lost city" of Vilcabamba and instead encountered (1911) and later popularized the ceremonial site of Machu Picchu in the Urubamba canyon of Cuzco, Peru. Born to a distinguished family of Protestant missionaries in Honolulu, Bingham studied at Yale to become a pastor and later at Berkeley and Harvard, where he specialized in Latin American history. Married to an heir of a wealthy Connecticut family, Bingham was able to finish his graduate studies and embark on several expeditions to South America. These included field trips to Colombia, Venezuela, and Peru between 1909 and 1915, when he was an assistant professor at Yale. Finding academic life too stifling, Bingham joined the U.S. military as an aviator during World War I. Later he entered politics in Connecticut, where he was elected lieutenant governor in 1922, governor in 1924, and U.S. senator in 1924, serving until 1933. He died in Washington, D.C. He wrote several books, including *Inca Land* (1922), *Elihu Yale* (1939), and *The Lost City of the Incas* (1948).

See also **Archaeology.**

BIBLIOGRAPHY

Alfred M. Bingham, *Portrait of an Explorer* (1989).

ALFONSO W. QUIROZ

BÍO-BÍO RIVER.

The Bío-Bío River is the largest stream of continental Chile (380 km) with sources in the Andean lakes Galletué and Icalma. Major affluents are the Laja, Renaico, Malleco, and Vergara rivers. Its upper course, in the Lonquimay Valley, is famous for its Mapuche native inhabitants. On its lower course lie several important cities and industrial centers (2002 census): Concepción (216,061), Talcahuano (250,348), Los Angeles (166,566), and Chiguayante (81,302).

Since the late 1970s the Region of Bío-Bío, the Eight Region, has surpassed in population (1,861, 400) and economic significance the Region of Valparaíso-Aconcagua (the Fifth Region), once the country's second hub. A steel mill, paper mills, textile factories, building materials manufacturing, and the main navy base at Talcahuano contribute to the economic strength of the region. Concepción, the regional capital, is famed for its first-class university.

During colonial times the Bío-Bío River was the southernmost boundary of Spanish colonization. To the south stretched the territory of the indomitable Araucanian Mapuche who submitted to Chilean rule only in 1881. In the early republican years (1818–1830) the unruly aristocracy of Concepción challenged the supremacy of the noblemen in the capital of Santiago, but eventually they submitted. During the 1960s and early 1970s the Bío-Bío region was a stronghold of the militant Left and suffered harsh treatment under the rule of General Augusto Pinochet (1973–1988).

See also **Chile, Geography; Concepción, Chile; Mapuche; Pinochet Ugarte, Augusto.**

BIBLIOGRAPHY

Instituto Geográfico Militar. "Región del Bíobío." *Geografía de Chile*, Vol. 9. Santiago de Chile: Author, 1986.

CÉSAR N. CAVIEDES

BIOY CASARES, ADOLFO (1914–1999).

Adolfo Bioy Casares (*b.* 15 September 1914; *d.* 8 March 1999), Argentine novelist, essayist, and short-story writer. Born in Buenos Aires, he studied law and philosophy and letters, but chose instead to run his family's estancia. In 1932 he became a close friend of Jorge Luis Borges, with whom, under the pseudonyms of H. Bustos Domecq, B. Suárez Lynch, and B. Lynch Davis, he wrote several detective stories. He is chiefly identified as a writer of fantastic literature due to his novel *La invención de Morel* (1940; *The Invention of Morel and other Stories,* 1964), which was awarded the Municipal Prize for Literature in 1941. This book marks the beginning of the modern science-fiction narrative in Argentine literature. In the same year, he wrote and published, together with his wife, the writer Silvina Ocampo, and Borges, the now classic *Antología de la literatura fantástica*.

Bioy demonstrated a wide range of narrative interests, from thrillers to love stories, with existentialist, Gothic, and pseudoscientific themes, and displayed his ability for light humor as well as dark irony and hallucinatory fantasies. He wrote about thirty books, many of which have been made into movies and television productions in Argentina and Italy, and he received the Cervantes Prize (Spain, 1991), the Mondello Award (Italy, 1984), and the National Literary Award (Argentina, 1962 and 1967). In 1973 he was awarded the major literary prize of his country, the Grand Prize of the Argentina Society of Writers. In 1990 he was the recipient of the Cervantes Prize, the highest prize of Hispanic letters. He died on March 8, 1999, in Buenos Aires.

See also **Science Fiction in Latin America.**

BIBLIOGRAPHY

David P. Gallagher, "The Novels and Short Stories of Adolfo Bioy Casares," in *Bulletin of Hispanic Studies* 52 (1975); 247–266.

Suzanne J. Levine, *Guía de Adolfo Bioy Casares* (1982).

Thomas C. Meehan, "Temporal Simultaneity and the Theme of Time Travel in a Fantastic Story by Adolfo Bioy Casares," in *Kentucky Romance Quarterly* 30, no. 2 (1983): 167–185.

Additional Bibliography

Bioy Casares, Adolfo. *Memorias. Infancia, adolescencia y cómo se hace un escritor*. Barcelona: Tusquets Editores, 1994.

Camurati, Mireya. *Bioy Casares y el alegre trabajo de la inteligencia*. Buenos Aires: Ediciones Corregidor, 1990.

Navascúes, Javier de. *El esperpento controlado: La narrativa de Adolfo Bioy Casares*. Pamplona: Ediciones Universidad de Navarra, 1995.

Orrego Arismendi, Juan Carlos. "Adolfo Bioy Casares y Jorge Luis Borges: La historia de una falsa paternidad." *Revista Universidad de Antioquia* 257 (July-Sep 1999): 59-65.

Villordo, Oscar Hermes. *Genio y figura de Adolfo Bioy Casares*. Buenos Aires: EUDEBA, 1983.

ANGELA B. DELLEPIANE

BIRD, VERE CORNWALL (1909–1999).

Vere Cornwall Bird Sr. (December 7/9?, 1909–June 29?, 1999) was born to a working-class single mother in St. John's in what was then the British colony of Antigua. Although he had only a primary school education, Bird gained organizational experience through his work with the Salvation Army in Trinidad and Grenada. Following region-wide labor unrest in the late 1930s, Bird joined the fledgling trade union movement and in 1939 was elected to the executive board of the Antigua Trades and Labour Union (ATLU). In 1944 he was elected to the colonial legislature. When Britain granted partial internal self-government to the island in 1960, Bird led his Antigua Labour Party (ALP) to power and became Antigua's first chief minister. In 1967 Antigua was granted full self-rule, and Bird became its first premier, becoming Antigua's first prime minister when independence was granted in 1981. Bird (with his two sons, Vere Jr. and Lester) governed Antigua (corruptly, it is alleged) until 1994, when, at age 83, he retired. Bird brought a measure of development to Antigua as he oversaw the difficult economic shift from sugar to tourism. He was an avid promoter of regionalism and was one of the founders of the Caribbean Free Trade Association (CARIFTA). He was the first person to be declared a national hero of Antigua and Barbuda.

See also **Antigua; Barbuda.**

ANTHONY P. MAINGOT

BISHOP, MAURICE (1944–1983). Maurice Bishop was raised in a family of meager means in Grenada. He eventually rose to become the country's prime minister, then was murdered in a series of events that precipitated U.S. intervention. Bishop studied law in London, where he became interested in leftist politics and fascinated with the Black Power movement. Upon his return to Grenada in 1973, the charismatic Bishop founded the New Jewel Movement (NJM), a Marxist political party. He was elected to parliament, and for several years served as the opposition leader in Grenada's House of Representatives, where he was a vocal critic of strongman Prime

Minister Eric Gairy and his government. In 1979 Bishop used Gairy's trip to the United Nations as an opportunity to stage a coup, and quickly moved to declare himself prime minister and suspend the constitution and parliament. All parties other than the NJM were outlawed while Bishop ruled by decree.

Once in power, Bishop set out to invigorate Grenada's economy. His efforts were aided by Cuba, the Soviet Union, and later the Nicaraguan Sandinistas. A crucial goal of Bishop's government was the construction of an airstrip, justified under the pretext of increasing tourism to the tiny English-speaking island. This raised tensions with the United States, which viewed the 9,000-foot runway as a conduit for infiltration of the Caribbean by Cuba and the Soviet Union. Bishop found himself in an increasingly difficult position, with the election of the tough anticommunist president Ronald Regan in the United States, on the one hand, and the uncompromising Marxist-Leninists in his own cabinet on the other. On 19 October 1983, Bishop and several of his supporters were rounded up by the military supporters of Deputy Prime Minister Bernard Coard (b. 1944), lined up against a wall, and shot. Six days later, after almost continuous curfew, the United States intervened with 6,000 Marines to reinstate order in Grenada. Maurice Bishop's four-year reign marked the end of socialist movements in the Caribbean.

See also **Grenada; New Jewel Movement.**

BIBLIOGRAPHY

Bhola, Ron. "Grenada Struggles with Its Past." BBC news. October 30, 2003. Available from http://news.bbc.co.uk/1/hi/world/americas/3228111.stm.

Williams, Gary. "Prelude to an Intervention: Grenada 1983." *Journal of Latin American Studies* 29, no. 1 (February 1997): 131–169.

Woodward, Bob. *Veil: The Secret Wars of the CIA, 1981–1987.* New York: Simon and Schuster, 1987.

SEAN H. GOFORTH

BLACK CARIBS. *See* **Caribs.**

BLACK LEGEND, THE. The Black Legend, a body of traditional literature hostile to Spain, its people, and its culture. The national stereotype derived from this literature portrays the Spanish as uniquely cruel, bigoted, lazy, and ignorant.

The term was apparently coined by Julián Juderías in his book *La Leyenda negra y la verdad histórica* (1914). The author of revisionist works on a variety of topics, Juderías was convinced that Spain and its culture had been systematically vilified by foreign authors who were inspired by Protestantism or the Enlightenment. His book, which was extremely popular in Spain, is basically a defense of Spanish accomplishments. In 1944 the Argentine scholar Rómulo Carbia applied the concept to the historical treatment of the Spanish conquest of America and linked the Black Legend specifically to the work of Bartolomé de Las Casas, whose *Brevísima Relación de la destrucción de las Indias* had been widely circulated in translation since the sixteenth century. In Carbia's view, Las Casas had exaggerated the brutality of the Conquest in an effort to secure improved treatment for the Indians, and in so doing he had provided Spain's political and religious enemies with a rich source of propaganda. Like Juderías, Carbia was primarily interested in defending the Spanish record.

The publication of Lewis Hanke's *The Spanish Struggle for Justice in the Conquest of America* (1949) opened a North American debate over the Black Legend and placed Las Casas squarely at its center. Hanke contended that the efforts of Las Casas and the legislation that resulted from them were unique in the history of colonizing powers. Only Spain had attempted to place its conquests on a moral footing. Though the works of Las Casas were misused by Spain's enemies, his career in itself was a partial refutation of the Black Legend. This position was hailed by Ramón Menéndez Pidal in his *El Padre Las Casas, su doble personalidad* (1963), a curious work that went on, somewhat inconsistently, to accuse Las Casas of paranoia. Opposition to Hanke's views came primarily from Benjamin Keen (1969), who noted that neither the bishop nor his reforms had done the Indians much good, and that the Spanish Conquest was as brutal and unprincipled as Las Casas had claimed. The Black Legend, in other words, was not legend but

Engraving of an execution and attempted conversion in the Caribbean, sixteenth century. According to some scholars, much of the Western world once based their view of Spain on a body of literature that described Iberians as devious, slothful, and uneducated. Events such as the Spanish Inquisition from the late fifteenth to early nineteenth centuries offered evidence, for some, to perpetuate the stereotype. BILDARCHIV PREUSSISCHER KULTURBESITZ/ART RESOURCE, NY

fact. Francisco López de Gómara, Girolamo Benzoni, and other chroniclers of the Conquest provided independent support for the accusations of Las Casas, and their works, too, had been widely circulated throughout Europe. Keen warned against the promulgation of a White Legend by those sympathetic to Spanish culture.

The Keen–Hanke debates narrowed the Black Legend to the single issue of the Conquest, but the broader accusations of Juderías had not been forgotten. The work of Sverker Arnoldsson (1960), William Maltby (1971), and others showed that anti-Spanish attitudes predated the publication of Las Casas and had multiple roots. Italy, Germany, England, and the Netherlands developed "Black Legends" of their own, in most cases as a reaction to the development of Spain as a world power in the sixteenth century. In a collection of documents published in 1971, Charles Gibson recognized this fact

and provided examples of anti-Spanish writing from the sixteenth century to the twentieth that reflect a wide spectrum of political and intellectual hostility. Though generally balanced in his approach, Gibson was more sympathetic to Hanke than to Keen.

These disputes were clouded from the beginning by problems of definition. With few exceptions, contributors to the debate failed to distinguish the Black Legend as a body of anti-Spanish literature from the Black Legend as a component of popular mentality. The process by which propaganda, much of it ephemeral, was absorbed and converted into broadly held stereotypes therefore remained unclear, and the usefulness of the Black Legend as a case history in the development of national consciousness went largely unexplored. Additional confusion arose from Keen's refusal to compare Spanish behavior with that of other nations. As Gibson pointed out, if the term "Black

Legend" is to have meaning, it must refer to the assumption that Spanish actions were *uniquely* evil. This crucial point has not always been acknowledged. No one has claimed that the Spanish were without guilt, but were they in fact worse than their imperial rivals? If they were not, then the Black Legend was by definition false.

Whatever its intellectual limitations, the controversy over the Black Legend eventually resulted in a rough consensus. Most scholars came to agree that there is in fact a body of literature which portrays Spain, its history, and its people in a consistently unfavorable light. This literature achieved a measure of acceptance in the non-Hispanic world and resulted in a widespread perception that the Spanish people were uniquely cruel, lazy, bigoted, and ignorant, and that their culture had contributed little of value to Western civilization.

The origins of this literature and of the perceptions embedded within it were recognized as multiple. Propaganda aimed at resisting Spanish imperial policies in the sixteenth and seventeenth centuries was common to virtually every western European nation. The revolt of the Netherlands alone produced hundreds of pamphlets that were reprinted and translated into other languages until the end of the Thirty Years' War. The work of Las Casas was often appropriated by these propagandists, but given the bishop's polemic intent, his writings would in any case have created a negative impression. Other accounts of the Conquest, though not necessarily intended as polemics, tended to corroborate Las Casas, for Spanish behavior in the Conquest was appalling. It was not, however, unparalleled; and there is merit in Hanke's claim that no other imperial power made equivalent efforts, even in theory, to protect indigenous populations.

The Black Legend was further reinforced by Spain's historic role as a champion of Catholicism. The implacable hostility of Protestant authors, most of them Dutch or English, was echoed during the Enlightenment when Voltaire and others found in Spanish culture a symbol of the superstition and ignorance they sought to combat. The Inquisition, itself the subject of a vast and often sensational literature, was seen as an expression of the Spanish character. The result of these efforts was cumulative because writers tended to repeat the stories of their predecessors, creating episodes in Spanish history that were in the truest sense legendary.

More recently, anti-Spanish propaganda was disseminated in the United States to justify the Spanish-American War, and negative interpretations of Spanish colonial rule were revived in parts of Latin America by the movement known as Indigenismo. The *indigenistas* sought to promote Indian cultural values as a fundamental component of nationalism, but their effort was in one respect self-defeating. Those outside the Hispanic world have rarely made distinctions among the Spanish-speaking peoples. In North America, where anti-Spanish characterizations were at one time common in popular literature, films, and school textbooks, the traditional image of the cruel and lazy Spaniard was easily transferred to Latin Americans and Hispanic Americans. By the end of the twentieth century increased sensitivity to racial and ethnic stereotypes had modified the textbooks, but unsympathetic portrayals of Hispanic characters remained common in the movies and on television. Fictional Mexicans, Cubans, and Colombians had come to display the negative traits formerly attributed to Spaniards.

Meanwhile, in scholarship the Black Legend had lost some of its virulence. Since the publication of *España defendida* (1604) by Francisco Gómez de Quevedo y Villegas, Spanish writers and publicists had attacked the Black Legend with varying degrees of skill. Their efforts were often little known outside the Iberian Peninsula, but Keen was right to point out that some Yankees, too, were "more sympathetic than is generally supposed." At least three generations of scholarship have produced a more balanced appreciation of Spanish conduct in both the Old World and the New, while the dismal records of other imperial powers have received a more objective appraisal. If few scholars would now argue that Spain's reputation was beyond reproach, fewer still would claim that it was uniquely reprehensible. Remaining echoes of the Black Legend were heard primarily in the acrimonious debate over the Columbus Quincentenary and in works that deplored the integration of non-European peoples into the world economy. The targets were pervasive Eurocentrism and the mythology of development capitalism rather than Spanish culture, but the parallel with earlier uses of anti-Spanish material was troubling. In the Anglo-Saxon world, where true appreciation of either

Spanish or Latin American culture is rare, the death of the Black Legend cannot be taken for granted.

See also **Las Casas, Bartolomé de.**

BIBLIOGRAPHY

Julián Juderías y Loyot, *La Leyenda negra y la verdad histórica* (1914).

Rómulo D. Carbia, *Historia de la leyenda negra hispano-americana* (1944).

Lewis Hanke, *The Spanish Struggle for Justice in the Conquest of America* (1949) and *Bartolomé de Las Casas: Bookman, Scholar and Propagandist* (1952).

Sverker Arnoldsson, *La Conquista española de América según el juicio de la posteridad: Vestigios de la leyenda negra* (1960) and *La Leyenda negra: Estudios sobre sus orígenes,* translated by Mateo Pastor-López and others, in *Acta Universitatis Gothoburgensis* 66, no. 3 (1960).

Benjamin Keen, "The Black Legend Revisited: Assumptions and Realities," *Hispanic American Historical Review* 49, no. 4 (1969): 703–719.

Charles Gibson, *The Black Legend: Anti-Spanish Attitudes in the Old World and the New* (1971).

William S. Maltby, *The Black Legend in England: The Development of Anti-Spanish Sentiment, 1558–1660* (1971).

Additional Bibliography

Garcia Càrcel, Ricard. *La leyenda negra: Historia y opinión.* Madrid: Alianza Editorial, 1992.

Hillgarth, J.N. *The Mirror of Spain, 1500–1700: The Formation of a Myth.* Ann Arbor: University of Michigan Press, 2000.

WILLIAM S. MALTBY

BLACK PEOPLES. *See* **African Brazilians, Color Terminology; Africans in Hispanic America.**

BLAINE, JAMES GILLESPIE (1830–1893). James Gillespie Blaine (31 January 1830–27 January 1893) was a U.S. representative and senator who served twice as secretary of state. Blaine's second stint as secretary of state (1889–1892), under President Benjamin Harrison, stood in marked contrast to his earlier service under James Garfield (1881). (He resigned when Garfield was assassinated.) Harrison, a more dynamic leader than Garfield, forged many of his own foreign policy

initiatives, thereby restraining Blaine's inclinations. In addition, Blaine himself had changed since the early 1880s: A combination of wisdom and ill health, both perhaps the products of advanced age, moderated Blaine's earlier impetuosity while teaching him tact, a skill needed by all diplomats. Although committed to advancing U.S. economic interests in Latin America, he also supported the incipient Pan American movement. And while hoping to obtain coaling stations for the U.S. Navy and the building of a Panama Canal, he also encouraged reciprocal trade treaties with Latin America. Blaine would also preside over the first meeting of the Pan American nations in 1890. Blaine did not bear responsibility for supposed U.S. involvement in Chile's 1891 revolution, which alienated the victorious government of Vice-Admiral Manuel Montt. Similarly, Blaine was not involved in the *Baltimore* incident of 1891, a crisis that owed its origin to the failure of Chilean authorities to prevent and punish the maltreatment and murder of some U.S. sailors on liberty in Valparaíso. In fact, the highly nationalistic President Harrison was the author of the tough U.S. stance vis-à-vis Chile—a diplomatic confrontation that almost led to war—because Blaine's ill health sidelined the secretary during the resolution of the crisis. Personal tragedy, the death of two of his children plus the worsening of the Bright's Disease from which he suffered, prevented Blaine from exercising his responsibilities. He died within six months of resigning his office in June 1892.

See also **Baltimore Incident; Panama Canal; Pan-Americanism; United States-Latin American Relations; Valparaíso.**

BIBLIOGRAPHY

Healy, David. *James G. Blaine and Latin America.* Columbia: University of Missouri, 2001.

Sater, William F. *Chile and the United States: Empires in Conflict.* Athens: University of Georgia, 1990.

WILLIAM F. SATER

BLANCO, ANDRÉS ELOY (1897–1955). Andrés Eloy Blanco (*b.* 6 August 1897; *d.* 21 May 1955), Venezuelan poet, journalist, and statesman. A prolific author of poetry, theater, stories and anecdotes, innumerable articles in periodicals, and political speeches, Blanco is chiefly remembered today for his very popular poems in a folkloric vein and for his humorous writings. He was also, however, a lifelong (and frequently imprisoned or exiled) opponent of successive dictatorships and an important figure in the evolution of what came to be the Acción Democrática Party. He is credited with important contributions in the drafting of the 1947 Constitution, and he served as minister of foreign affairs during the brief presidency of Rómulo Gallegos (February–November 1948). In his poetry he was among the earliest in this century to reabsorb traditional Hispanic popular forms and themes into contemporary poetic practice; many of his works in this mode are charming, some are memorable. Juan Liscano and Efraín Subero note an underlying Christian attitude in his hopeful celebrations of common people and his vision of the nation. Subsequent generations of poets have turned away from Blanco's regionalist or nativist manner. Some of his verses have entered oral tradition, and he remains widely read by the general public, for whom he stands alone among modern Venezuelan poets as a national icon.

See also **Literature: Spanish America; Venezuela, Constitutions; Venezuela, Political Parties: Democratic Action (AD).**

BIBLIOGRAPHY

Andrés Eloy Blanco, *Obras completas* (1973), is the best available presentation of the texts and contains excellent essays by various specialists. Efraín Subero has edited *Apreciaciones críticas sobre la vida y la obra de Andrés Eloy Blanco*, 2d ed. (1974), a valuable compendium of studies and essays, many of them by Blanco's contemporaries. For detailed discussion of his place in Venezuelan literary history, see José Ramón Medina, *Ochenta años de literatura venezolana* (1981), and Juan Liscano, *Panorama de la literatura venezolana actual* (1984).

Additional Bibliography

Ramírez, Alfonso. *Biografía de Andrés Eloy Blanco.* Caracas: Comisión Presidencial del Centenario del Natalicio de Andrés Eloy Blanco, 1997.

MICHAEL J. DOUDOROFF

BLANCO, JOSÉ FÉLIX (1782–1872).

José Félix Blanco (*b.* 24 September 1782; *d.* 18 March 1872), officer in the Venezuelan Emancipating Army, politician, and historian. Blanco studied in the seminary of Caracas and was ordained a priest in 1809. At the beginning of the movement for independence in 1810, he joined the patriotic forces as an army chaplain. He participated in numerous campaigns from 1812 to 1817, when Simón Bolívar assigned him to the administration of the missions of Caroní. Blanco attended the Congress of Cúcuta in 1821. Political and military activities distanced him from his priestly duties and, in 1833, he requested (of Rome) and was granted secularization. Over the next two decades, Blanco was commandant of Maracaibo, secretary of war and the navy, a candidate for vice president and president of the Republic, and secretary of finance and foreign affairs.

After leaving public life in 1854, Blanco repeatedly sought reordination, which was finally granted in 1863. From 1855 until his death, he dedicated himself to the compilation and organization, with Ramón Azpurua, of the documents and testimonies relative to the history of the emancipation. The voluminous collection was published after his death under the title *Documentos para la historia de la vida pública del Libertador* (1875–1877). Its fourteen volumes constitute, even today, one of the most important collections of documents on Latin American emancipation.

See also **Venezuela: The Colonial Period.**

BIBLIOGRAPHY

Lino Iribarren Celis, *El padre Blanco, ilustre prócer de la independencia* (1961).

Carole Leal Curiel, *Convicciones y conversiones de un republicano: El expediente de José Félix Blanco* (1985).

INÉS QUINTERO

BLANCO, JUAN (1919–).

Juan Blanco (*b.* 29 June 1919), Cuban composer. Born in Havana, Blanco began his traditional composition studies at the Municipal Conservatory in Havana and then studied at the University of Havana under the guidance of Harold Gramatges and José Ardévol. During the mid-1950s he taught himself the techniques of *musique concrète*, electronic music, recording, as well as the use of sound for films. In 1969 he became the main musical adviser for the House of the Americas in Havana. Blanco is a prolific writer and critic who has published many articles and written criticism for several Cuban magazines and newspapers. Almost all his compositions since 1965 involve the use of electronic techniques and mixed media. Blanco has done extensive research with "spatial techniques," in some cases utilizing multiple loudspeaker networks. *Poema espacial,* no. 3 ("Viet-Nam," 1968), combines sound and light and requires the use of four tape tracks distributed among thirty-seven loudspeakers.

Other important compositions are *Canto a la paz* for soloists, mixed choir, and orchestra (1952); Elegy for orchestra (1956), a memorial to the fighters who died during the Cuban Revolution; *Divertimento* for string orchestra (1954); Quintet for winds, timpani, and piano (1972); *Música para danza* (1961); Études, nos. 1 and 2 for tape (1962–1963); *Texturas* for orchestra and tape (1963–1964); *Pirofonías* (1976); Episodes for orchestra (1964); *Contrapunto espacial,* no. 1 (1965–1966); *Erotofonías* for orchestra and tape (1968); and *Erotofonías,* no. 2 (1974) for tape. Blanco composed tape music for the Cuban Pavilion at Expo '67 and Expo '70 and for the São Paulo Biennial in 1988. For several years he has produced and directed the International Festival of Electroacoustic Music in Varadero, Cuba.

See also **Music: Art Music.**

BIBLIOGRAPHY

John Vinton, ed. *Dictionary of Contemporary Music* (1974), pp. 84–85; *Primer festival latinoamericano de música contemporánea* (1977), p. 34.

Gérard Béhague, *Music in Latin America: An Introduction* (1979), p. 301.

Additional Bibliography

Leonard, Neil III. "Juan Blanco: Cuba's Pioneer of Electoracoustic Music." *Computer Music Journal* 21 (Summer 1997): 10-20.

White, Charles W. "Report on Music in Cuba Today." *Latin American Music Review* 13 (Autumn 1992) 234-242.

ALCIDES LANZA

BLANCO ACEVEDO, EDUARDO

(1894–1971). The Uruguayan surgeon and politician Eduardo Blanco Acevedo was born in Montevideo on March 19, 1894, and received his medical degree in 1908 from the *Facultad de Medicina* in Montevideo. After joining the diplomatic corps, he served as attaché to the Uruguayan embassy in France in 1909 and undersecretary at the Uruguayan embassy in Belgium in 1912. From 1914 to 1919 he worked as a surgeon in French hospitals, attending wounded troops, and was appointed chief surgeon of the Rothschild Hospital in 1915. The French government conferred on him the title of *chevalier* of the Legion of Honor, and he was appointed to the Parisian Society of Surgeons, as well as other French medical societies. After returning to Uruguay in 1919, he began teaching and practicing medicine and held several administrative positions in Uruguayan hospitals, as well as the post of minister of public health (1934–1936). His family was historically associated with the Colorado Party and was related to president and later dictator Gabriel Terra, whose regime, in which Blanco Acevedo participated, began March 31, 1933. When Terra's mandate ended, Blanco Acevedo was one of the candidates who hoped to succeed him in the 1938 elections. Rival candidate General Alfredo Baldomir, also from the Colorado Party, won the election, thanks, it is said, to the women's vote, exercised for the first time that year in Uruguay. Nevertheless, Blanco Acevedo's politics—*Blanco Acevedismo*—remained a conservative force within the Colorado Party, and Blanco Acevedo was an adviser to the *Consejo Nacional de Gobierno* (National Council of Government) from 1952 to 1955. His brother was the prominent historian Pablo Blanco Acevedo.

See also **Baldomir, Alfredo; Terra, Gabriel; Uruguay, Political Parties: Colorado Party.**

BIBLIOGRAPHY

Peña, José M. *Eduardo Blanco Acevedo: historia de una vida integral.* Montevideo: n.p., 1950.

Scarone, Arturo. *Uruguayos Contemporáneos: Nuevo Diccionario de Datos Biográficos.* Montevideo: A. Barreiro y Ramos, 1937.

JOSÉ DE TORRES WILSON

BLANCO ENCALADA, MANUEL

(1790–1876). Manuel Blanco Encalada (*b.* 21 April 1790; *d.* 5 September 1876), first president of Chile, first commander of the Chilean navy, and longest-surviving hero of Chile's Wars of Independence. Born in Buenos Aires, he served in the Spanish navy before returning to South America to play his part in the struggle for independence, during which he fought in numerous actions in Chile. In June 1818 he was named commander of the newly formed Chilean navy, handing it over to Lord Thomas Alexander Cochrane at the end of that year; but when Cochrane left Chile in January 1823, Blanco Encalada resumed command.

As president of Chile from July to September 1826, he was the first Chilean head of state to be called President rather than Supreme Director. In 1837 he was given command of the first Chilean offensive against the Peru–Bolivia Confederation. His assent to the Treaty of Paucarpata (17 November 1837), entailing Chilean withdrawal from Peru, was repudiated by the government and led to his court-martial, but he was acquitted. He was later intendant of Valparaíso (1847–1852) and minister to France (1852–1858).

See also **Chile: Foundations Through Independence.**

BIBLIOGRAPHY

Benjamin V. MacKenna, *El teniente general don Manuel Blanco Encalada* (1917).

SIMON COLLIER

BLANCO FOMBONA, RUFINO (1874–1944).

Rufino Blanco Fombona (*b.* 17 June 1874; *d.* 17 October 1944), Venezuelan writer. One of the most widely read Latin American authors of his generation, Blanco Fombona began his career as a politician at the age of eighteen when he participated in a movement against President Raimundo Andueza Palacio. At twenty, he went to Philadelphia as Venezuelan consul. Two years later he moved to The Hague in the same capacity. Between 1900 and 1905 he served the government of Cipriano Castro as secretary general of the state of Zulia (1900), consul to the Netherlands (1901–1904), and governor of the Amazon Territory (1905). His political career ended in 1910, when Juan Vicente Gómez forced him into exile in France and Spain until 1936. In exile, Blanco Fombona carried on an ardent campaign against Gómez, and fought despotism in

his writings and through participation in a number of abortive anti-Gómez revolts.

Both before and during his exile, Blanco Fombona wrote a number of important essays and novels. His works reflected his life, often in an autobiographical manner, and his commitment to expressions of Spanish Americanism. Like Leopoldo Lugones in Argentina and José Vasconcelos in Mexico, he relied on creole themes that dealt with political corruption, anti-imperialism, and celebration of the best aspects of Spanish-American society. Several times nominated for the Nobel Prize in literature, he produced works that included a wide range of subjects and genres, from poetry to history, from literary criticism to political commentary.

See also **Literature: Spanish America.**

BIBLIOGRAPHY

Angel Rama, *Rufino Blanco Fombona y el egotismo latinoamericano* (1975).

Guillermo Servando Pérez, "Rufino Blanco Fombona," in *Latin American Writers,* edited by Carlos A. Solé, vol. 2 (1989), pp. 503–511. Works by Rufino Blanco Fombona: Poetry—*Trovadores y trovas* (1899); *Pequeña ópera lírica* (1904); *Cantos de la prisión y del destierro* (1911). Novels—*El hombre de hierro* (1907); *El hombre de oro* (1916); *La mitra en la mano* (1927); *La Bella y la Fiera* (1931); *El secreto de la felicidad* (1933). Literary criticism—*Grandes escritores de América* (1917); *El modernismo y los poetas modernistas* (1929). History—*La evolución política y social de Hispanoamérica* (1911); *El conquistador español del siglo XVI* (1921); *Bolívar y la guerra a muerte: Época de Boves, 1813–1814* (1942); *Mocedades de Bolívar: El héroe antes del heroismo* (1942); *El espíritu de Bolívar* (1943).

Additional Bibliography

Blanco Fombona, Rufino. *La obra poética de Rufino Blanco Fombona.* Caracas: L. Carrera, 2002.

WINTHROP R. WRIGHT

BLANCO GALDÓS, HUGO (1934–).

Hugo Blanco Galdós (*b.* 1934), Quechua-speaking agronomist, Trotskyist, and former student leader. Born in Cuzco in 1958, Blanco organized the small tenant farmers of the coffee-growing valleys of La Convención in the high jungle north of Cuzco into a peasant federation that challenged the traditional landlord class. After a series of strikes, land invasions, and armed clashes with the police as well as the spread of such tactics into the southern and central sierra, the government of Manuel Prado was compelled to establish a commission to study the possibility of agrarian reform. Imprisoned in 1963, Blanco was later released, served as an adviser to the government of Juan Velasco on agrarian reform, and continued to be active in leftist politics.

See also **Agrarian Reform; Prado y Ugarteche; Velasco, Juan de.**

BIBLIOGRAPHY

Hugo Blanco, *Land or Death: The Peasant Struggle in Peru* (1972).

Additional Bibliography

Blanco, Hugo. *Workers and peasants to power! A revolutionary program for Peru.* New York: Pathfinder Press, 1978.

Blanco, Hugo. *4 caminos al poder.* Lima: Educación Popular Chaupimayo, 1987.

"Entrevista con Hugo Blanco." *Servicio Europeo de Universitarios Latinoamericanos, S.E.U.L.* 7 (Feb–Mar 1978): 21–27.

Villanueva, Victor. *Hugo Blanco y la Rebelión Campesina.* Lima: Mejía Baca, 1967.

PETER F. KLARÉN

BLANCO GALINDO, CARLOS (1882–1953). Carlos Blanco Galindo (*b.* 12 March 1882; *d.* 3 October 1953), president of Bolivia (June 1930–March 1931). Born in Cochabamba to a patrician family with roots going back to the time of Bolívar, Blanco Galindo was an urbane scholar and army officer with a long history of public and international service. Upon the dissolution of the Hernando Siles Reyes government in May 1930, a military junta chaired by Blanco Galindo assumed power. As the new acting president, he was determined not to stay in power, however, and prepared the way for an elected civilian government, that of Daniel Salamanca, who was inaugurated on 5 March 1931. Blanco Galindo's short term was one of the most productive in Bolivia's history. Among its achievements was an educational reform that included

university autonomy. After 1931 Blanco Galindo continued to serve the nation and Cochabamba but stayed aloof from the squabbles of the military during the tragic Chaco War. He died in Cochabamba.

See also **Bolivia: Since 1825.**

BIBLIOGRAPHY

Quien es quien en Bolivia (1942), pp. 45–46.

Porfirio Díaz Machicao, *Historia de Bolivia*, vol. 2, *Guzmán, Siles, Blanco Galindo* (1955), pp. 139–165.

CHARLES W. ARNADE

BLANDENGUES. Blandengues, a special militia created in 1797 by Spanish authorities in the Río De La Plata region to protect frontier settlements from Indian attack and to combat banditry. In some areas the troops also fought smuggling and the illegal slaughter of wild cattle by traders of dried hides. An early decree authorizing the creation of the force called for eight companies of 100 men each, but these numbers were never reached. Manuel Belgrano, Ernesto Quesada, José Rondeau, José Gervasio Artigas, and other future leaders of the independence movement acquired valuable military experience in their ranks. The Blandengues were particularly important in the pre-independence period of the Banda Oriental (present-day Uruguay). Artigas, joining in 1797, fought with this group against the British invasions of 1806 and 1807, rising to the position of *capitán*. After declaring his commitment to the independence movement in 1811, he commanded his former Blandengue soldiers in important early victories against Spanish royalist forces.

See also **Wars of Independence, South America.**

BIBLIOGRAPHY

Additional Bibliography

Azcuy Ameghino, Eduardo. *La otra historia: Economía, estado y sociedad en el Río de la Plata colonial.* Colección Bitácora argentina. Capital Federal: Imago Mundi, 2002.

Rodriguez Otheguy, Victor A., and Nelson Dellepiane. *Cabalgando en la frontera: Historia de los blandengues orientales.* Montevideo: [s.n.], 1997.

WILLIAM H. KATRA

BLANES, JUAN MANUEL (c. 1830–1901).

Juan Manuel Blanes (*b.* c. 1 June 1830; *d.* 15 April 1901), Uruguayan artist, regarded as the founder of Uruguayan art. Born in Montevideo, Blanes abandoned school at age eleven to work and help his humble family. Around 1843 he moved with his mother and brothers to El Cerrito, returning to Montevideo in 1853, where he made his living as a typographer. In 1855 Blanes moved to the town of Salto, where he taught painting at the School of Humanities and painted commissioned portraits. In 1856 he painted eight pictures of Justo José de Urquiza's military victories for the general's San José Palace. He returned to Montevideo at the outbreak of a yellow fever epidemic, which he documented in a now lost painting (1857). At Urquiza's request he painted the general's family as well as religious themes for the chapel at San José Palace. In 1860, on a grant from the Uruguayan government, he moved to Paris, then to Florence, where he studied at the Florentine Academy with Antonio Ciseri. From then on academic neoclassicism marked his artistic production.

In 1865 Blanes returned to Uruguay and for the next fifteen years received commissions to paint the portraits of famous Latin American personalities, including Paraguayan President Francisco Solano López. His historical paintings earned him prestige in Argentina and Chile. Blanes revealed a naturalistic approach to painting when dealing with subjects of contemporary significance (*Yellow Fever in Buenos Aires,* 1871) and in his series of gauchos (*Dawn*). From 1879 to 1883 he was living once again in Florence, where he painted *Paraguay: Image of Your Desolate Country* (c. 1880), an allegorical image of Paraguay after the devastating War of the Triple Alliance. After returning to Montevideo in 1883, he worked on a portrait of Uruguayan general José Artigas. The Argentine government commissioned his renowned *Review of Río Negro by General Roca and His Army.* Blanes moved to Pisa in 1898, where he died. He was buried at the Pantéon Nacional in Montevideo.

See also **Art: The Nineteenth Century; Urquiza, Justo José de; War of the Triple Alliance.**

BIBLIOGRAPHY

Angel Kalenberg et al., *Seis maestros de la pintura uruguaya* (1987).

Dawn Ades, *Art in Latin America: The Modern Era, 1820–1980* (1989), pp. 28–30, 68.

Additional Bibliography

Cerisola, Roberto Amigo, and Gabriel Peluffo Linari, eds. *Juan Manuel Blanes: La nación naciente, 1830–1901.* Montevideo, Uruguay: Museo Municipal de Bellas Artes Juan Manuel Blanes, 2001.

García Esteban, Fernando. *Juan Manuel Blanes, pintor: Revisión histórico crítica y algunas orientaciones estimativas.* Montevideo, Uruguay: Academia Nacional de Letras, 1977.

Goldaracena, Ricardo. *Juan Manuel Blanes.* Montevideo, Uruguay: Arca, 1978.

MARTA GARSD

BLEST GANA, ALBERTO (1831–1920).

Alberto Blest Gana was a Chilean writer and diplomat. Some of his more outstanding novels are *La Aritmética en el amor* (1860), *Martín Rivas* (1862), *El Ideal de un calavera* (1863), *Durante la Reconquista* (1897), *Los Trasplantados* (1904), and *El Loco Estero* (1909). He pursued military engineering studies in France from 1847 to 1851. On his return to Chile he was made a section chief in the Ministry of War and the Navy. In 1870 Blest Gana was elected as deputy to the National Congress. From 1871 until his retirement from diplomatic service in 1887 he served successively as minister plenipotentiary to Washington, London, and Paris.

Blest Gana belongs to a generation of nineteenth-century Latin American novelists who felt responsible for reflecting on and producing a genuine nationalization of literature as both a reading and writing practice. In Chile, this process was the result of decisive cultural changes. One of them was the emergence of a proto-mass audience of readers of printed material. Blest Gana posited the new national novel (i.e., a novel capable of representing the national for a national reading public) as a cultural mediation between two mid-nineteenth century poles affecting the status of the novel as a genre and of reading as a cultural practice. On the one hand, magazine and journalistic reading for pleasure was socially perceived as feminine and unproductive while on the other, the reading of classic (Greek and Latin) and serious literature was seen as masculine and productive. One was viewed as an easy waste of time and energies while the other was seen as involving hard work and a sure cultural return on the investment. In this context, Blest Gana's key contribution was his proposal of the national novel and its reading as legitimate forms of mediating between those oppositions. Located between the open space of the reading and publishing marketplace where he always sought his success, and the cultural discourse of nation-building which he produced from his university and state positions, Blest Gana allows us to see the participation of new reading publics in the formation of national cultures whose control was by then disputed between the state and the Catholic church—the two other actors of nation-building in the Latin American nineteenth century.

See also **Literature: Spanish America.**

BIBLIOGRAPHY

Kaempfer, Alvaro. "*De Nueva York al Niágara* (1867) de Alberto Blest Gana: A todo vapor fuera de Occidente." *Ciberletras* 4 (January 2001).

Kaempfer, Alvaro. "Alberto Blest Gana's *Durante la Reconquista* (1897): Subalternity and the Legibility of the Popular." *Journal of Latin American Cultural Studies* 13, no. 1 (March 2004): 2–34.

Poblete, Juan. "La construccion social de la Lectura y la novella nacional: El caso chileno." *Latin American Research Review* 34 (1999).

JUAN POBLETE

BLOQUEO DE 1902, EL.

El Bloqueo de 1902, blockade of the Venezuelan coast by the German and British navies to demand payment of the public foreign debt. From the start of the twentieth century, Venezuela, under President Cipriano Castro, had suspended payments on the debt because of the grave fiscal and political crises throughout the country. On 9 December 1902, German and British warships took the principal ports of Venezuela, landing troops and capturing ships as a means of pressing for payment on debts that Venezuela owed those countries. The blockade was also supported by Italian forces and received the backing of France, Belgium, Holland, and other European powers. The debt was 165 million bolívars, which reached 186 million bolívars when war claims and other

damages suffered by nationals of those countries were added. The situation was critical, since Venezuelan revenues were less than 30 million bolívars annually, and the Venezuelan government did not acknowledge the elevated amount of the claims.

Through the mediation of the United States, the conflict was resolved on 13 February 1903 with the signing of the Washington Protocols, through which Venezuela agreed to reinitiate payment on the debt, once the sum of the claims was dropped from 186 million to 39 million bolívars. Venezuela agreed to use 30 percent of its customs receipts to pay off its debts.

BIBLIOGRAPHY

Holger H. Herwig and J. León Helguera, *Alemania y el bloqueo internacional de Venezuela, 1902–1903* (1977).

Manuel Rodríguez Campos, *Venezuela, 1902: La crisis fiscal y el bloqueo, perfil de una soberanía vulnerada*, 2d ed. (1983).

Additional Bibliography

Herwig, Holger H. *Germany's Vision of Empire in Venezuela, 1871-1914.* Princeton, NJ: Princeton University Press, 1986.

McBeth, B. S. *Gunboats, Corruption, and Claims: Foreign Intervention in Venezuela, 1899-1908.* Westport, CT: Greenwood Press, 2001.

INÉS QUINTERO

BLUE BOOK.

Blue Book, U.S. State Department publication with the full title *Consultation Among the American Republics with Respect to the Argentine Situation* (1946). Compiled at the direction of Spruille Braden, who had been ambassador in Buenos Aires before returning to Washington late in 1945 as under secretary of state for American Republic affairs, the *Blue Book* documented Argentina's wartime relations with the Axis powers. Braden's intention was to discredit Juan Perón, the leading candidate in the Argentine presidential election of February 1946. Using captured German archives and decoded Axis telecommunications, State Department investigators produced the *Blue Book* in time for the election. Its data are generally accurate but pertain chiefly to the period prior to Perón's political rise in 1944; its interpretations are heavily biased against Argentina. The *Blue Book* boomeranged: Argentine voters saw it as U.S. interference in their internal affairs. Urged on by the slogan that the United States had handed the Peronists, "¿Braden o Perón?," they elected Perón president.

See also **World War II.**

BIBLIOGRAPHY

Spruille Braden, *Diplomats and Demagogues: The Memoirs of Spruille Braden* (1971).

Additional Bibliography

Guillermo Frontera, Carlos. *Las relaciones argentino-norteamericanas, 1943-1946.* Buenos Aires: Editorial Dunken, 2006.

Newton, Ronald C. *The "Nazi Menace" in Argentina, 1931-1947.* Stanford: Stanford University Press, 1992.

Peltzer, Enrique. *Diez años de conflicto entre la Casa Rosada y la Casa Blanca, 1936-1946.* Buenos Aires: Ethos, 2002.

RONALD C. NEWTON

BLUEFIELDS. Bluefields, a Nicaraguan town at the mouth of the Escondido River on the Bay of Bluefields on the Caribbean Sea and home to an estimated 50,000 people. Protected by a series of islands, it has the best harbor in eastern Central America, through which bananas, mahogany, and cedar passed in the nineteenth and early twentieth centuries. Later, the chief exports included palm and coconut oil and alligator skins. The town was founded by the British and was claimed by them as part of their protectorate over the Miskito people during the nineteenth century. Jamaican and other Caribbean blacks and their descendants, known as Creoles, dominate the town's population, followed by Miskitos, Hispanic Nicaraguans, and North Americans. Other peoples of African descent residing in Bluefields include the Garifuna. English-speaking Creoles were once the coast's most powerful merchants and civic leaders, distinguishing themselves from Spanish-speaking Catholics in the practice of the Protestant faith brought by Moravian missionaries in 1847. In 1855 the Moravians expanded their work to include indigenous peoples, particularly Miskitos. After 1865, the town took on the ambience of an antebellum southern city of the United States as many southerners fled there to escape Reconstruction. Their presence increased tension with the British and Nicaraguans, which climaxed in 1894 when José Santos Zelaya claimed sovereignty over the community. The U.S. government sided with Zelaya to drive the British from Bluefields, but the conflict between the North American residents and the Nicaraguan president remained. Bluefields became a center of revolutionary activity when the Americans there allied themselves with the Nicaraguan factions that succeeded in ousting Zelaya in 1909. From then until the U.S. withdrawal from Nicaragua in 1933, Bluefields served as a port of entry for U.S. Marines sent to the country to maintain order. Until the Sandinista revolution in 1979, the fiercely independent Miskito Indians governed the region with little allegiance to the central government in Managua. The Miskitos resisted the Sandinistas—at times violently—and some of them joined the contra war to overthrow the FSLN regime. The Miskito resistance, the contra war, and concomitant economic hardships forced the Sandinistas to abandon their efforts to control Bluefields. Nevertheless, the Miskito struggle led the Sandinistas to include provisions in the 1984 constitution guaranteeing indigenous people their land. Moreover, in 1987 the government created two autonomous regions: the Región Autónoma del Atlántico Sur (RAAS), of which Bluefields is the municipal and regional center; and the Región Autónoma del Atlántico Norte (RAAN), with Puerto Cabezas as its center. These are denoted as self-governing, autonomous regions and theoretically guarantee land rights and cultural autonomy.

The Universidad de las Regiones Autónomas de la Costa Caribe Nicaragüense (URACCAN) was founded in 1992. Since the 1990s government privatization and economic liberalization has brought changes to the city. Nevertheless, most Bluefields residents, *Costeños*, continue to earn their livelihood from wood exploitation and fishing.

See also **Nicaragua; Zelaya, José Santos.**

BIBLIOGRAPHY

Lester B. Langley, *The Banana Wars: An Inner History of American Empire, 1900–1934* (1983).

Craig L. Dozier, *Nicaragua's Mosquito Shore: The Years of British and American Presence* (1985).

Roy Gutman, *Banana Diplomacy: The Making of American Policy in Nicaragua, 1981–1987* (1988).

Additional Bibliography

Dennis, Philip A. *The Miskitu People of Awastara*. Austin: University of Texas Press, Teresa Lozano Long Institute of Latin American Studies, 2004.

Gordon, Edmund T. *Disparate Diasporas: Identity and Politics in an African Nicaraguan Community*. Austin: University of Texas Press, Institute of Latin American Studies, 1998.

Hale, Charles R. *Resistance and Contradiction: Miskitu Indians and the Nicaraguan State, 1894–1987*. Stanford, CA: Stanford University Press, 1994.

Martínez Cuenca, Alejandro, et al. *Regiones y municipios: La agenda pendiente*. Managua: Foro Democrático, 1998.

Romero Vargas, Germán. *Las sociedades del Atlántico de Nicaragua en los siglos XVII y XVIII*. Managua: Fondo de Promoción Cultural-Banic, 1995.

THOMAS M. LEONARD

BOAL, AUGUSTO (1931–).

This theatrical director, writer, and politician has been a major public intellectual in Brazil since the 1960s. Boal led the development of the politically and socially engaged *Teatro de Arena* (Arena Theater) with others such as the late Gianfrancesco Guarnieri and Oduvaldo Viana Filho in São Paulo. Here he presented several plays, such as *Revolucão na América do Sul* (Revolution in South America) based in his notions of the *teatro do oprimido* (theater of the oppressed), influenced by Paulo Freire's "pedagogy of the oppressed." Arrested by the dictatorship in 1971, Boal suffered torture and sought exile first in Argentina and then in Paris, where for twelve years he created Centers for the Theater of Oppressed. With his innovative ideas of active audience participation, Boal developed the Forum Theater device, which allowed spectators to change the script, to liberate the play from oppressive conditions or relations. He created the Invisible Theater, where plays are presented in settings other than a theater (such as a restaurant); the Image Theater, which employs the body to create images; and other innovations that are internationally recognized. Among other prizes, Boal won the UNESCO Pablo Picasso Medal in 1994. The author has participated prominently in Brazilian politics for the last twenty years, on behalf of the Partido dos Trabalhadores (Labor Party).

See also **Theater.**

BIBLIOGRAPHY

Boal, Augusto. *Theatre of the Oppressed*. New York: Theatre Communications Group, 1985.

Boal, Augusto. *Teatro de Augusto Boal*. Rio de Janeiro: Hucitec, 1992.

PAULA HALPERIN

BOBADILLA, FRANCISCO DE (?–c. 1502).

Francisco de Bobadilla (*d.* ca. 1502), governor and judge of the island of Hispaniola. Bobadilla was probably from an Aragonese family, although the date and place of his birth are uncertain. Appointed on 21 May 1499, he was given authority superseding that of Christopher Columbus. The purpose of the royal appointment was to end instability and strife in the colony. Arriving in Santo Domingo on 23 August 1500, Bobadilla might have seen the executed enemies of Columbus while disembarking. He had Columbus jailed upon his return from an expedition into the interior in September 1500. It was Bobadilla's intention to send him to the Spanish court for trial, where a powerful group rejecting the pretensions of the Italian explorer was active.

As planned, both Columbus and his brother Bartholomew were returned under arrest to Spain. The crown, however, convinced that Bobadilla had exceeded the authority of his instructions, freed the Columbus brothers soon after their arrival in Spain. Bobadilla, disgraced for acting too strongly against Columbus, embarked for Spain in 1502. Unfortunately, that June his fleet was caught in a powerful hurricane in which almost all the ships were lost and much of the documentation involving the early administration of the island destroyed. The historian Oviedo characterized Bobadilla as "honest and religious."

See also **Columbus, Bartholomew; Columbus, Christopher.**

BIBLIOGRAPHY

J. Marino Inchaustequi, *Francisco de Bobadilla: Tres homónimos y un enigma colombino decifrado* (1964).

Additional Bibliography

Casco Guido, Alicia. *Culturas indígenas de Nicaragua*. Managua, Nicaragua: Editorial Hispamer, 1998.

Varela, Consuelo and Isabel Aguirre. *La caída Cristóbal Colón: El juicio de Bobadilla*. Madrid: Marcial Pons, 2006.

NOBLE DAVID COOK

BOBO, ROSALVO (?–1929).

Rosalvo Bobo (*d.* 1929), Haitian populist leader of the Cacos rebellion of 1915. On 28 July 1915, U.S. Marines landed at Port-au-Prince in response to the orders of Admiral William B. Caperton to restore civil order following the death of President Jean Vilbrun Guillaume Sam. They were also to prevent Rosalvo Bobo, Sam's political opponent and critic of U.S. imperialism in Haiti, from assuming the presidency.

Bobo opposed the McDonald contract, an attempt by a U.S. company to build a railroad through northern Haiti that would have involved the seizure of Haitians' property through eminent domain. He was also against U.S. receivership of Haitian customs. Thus the United States blocked his election to the Haitian presidency in 1915, instead ensuring that of Philippe-Sudré Dartiguenave, a puppet ruler. Bobo fled to Cuba, then to Jamaica, and finally to France, where he died.

See also **Haiti, Caco Revolts.**

BIBLIOGRAPHY

James Leyburn, *The Haitian People* (1941).

Hans Schmidt, *The United States Occupation of Haiti* (1971).

David Nicholls, *From Dessalines to Duvalier: Race, Colour and National Independence in Haiti* (1979).

THOMAS O. OTT

BOCAIÚVA, QUINTINO (1836–1912).

Quintino Bocaiúva (*b.* 4 December 1836; *d.* 11 July 1912), journalist and a founding father of the Brazilian Republic. Born Quintino Ferreira de Souza, Bocaiúva was the main author of the Republican Manifesto of 1870, in which he defended the idea of a Liberal and federalist republic to be engendered through pacific means, by "evolution" rather than "revolution." He also criticized the isolation of Brazil as a monarchy among the neighboring republics. "We belong to America and want to be Americans" is one of the most quoted phrases of the manifesto. Elected president of the Republican Party in May 1889, Bocaiúva was prominent among those who instigated the military question and, through it, promoted the alliance of the Republicans with the army, the "yellow button" as they termed it. For this reason he was called a militarist and even an opportunist by his fellow Republicans.

When the Republic was proclaimed, on 15 November 1889, Bocaiúva was the only civilian leader to head the military parade alongside Marshal Deodoro da Fonseca and Lieutenant Colonel Benjamin Constant Botelho De Magalhães. A prominent figure of the new regime, he was Minister of Foreign Affairs until the collective resignation of the first Republican ministry on 20 January 1891 and senator for Rio de Janeiro, elected in 1890 and reelected several times until his death. From 1901 until 1903, he served as governor of the state of Rio de Janeiro.

See also **Brazil, Political Parties: Republican Party (PR).**

BIBLIOGRAPHY

George C. A. Boehrer, *Da Monarquia à República: História do Partido Republicano no Brasil, 1870–1889,* translated by Berenice Xavier (1954), is still the main source for the study of the Republican Party during the monarchy. For the life and political ideas of Bocaiúva, see Eduardo Silva, ed., *Idéias políticas de Quintino Bocaiúva*, 2 vols. (1986).

EDUARDO SILVA

BODEGA Y QUADRA, JUAN FRANCISCO DE LA (1737–1794).

Juan Francisco de la Bodega y Quadra (*b.* 22 August 1737; *d.* 26 March 1794), Spanish naval officer, explorer of the Pacific Northwest. Born in Lima, Peru, Bodega became a Spanish naval officer and was posted to the department of San Blas in 1774. The following year he had command of the *Sonora* on its voyage to southern Alaska. Bodega was promoted to ship's lieutenant in 1776 and commanded *La Favorita*, which sailed to Alaska, in 1779. He remained in

San Blas in 1780–1781, then went to Peru to obtain artillery in 1782. After serving in Spain from 1783 to 1789, Bodega returned to San Blas as its commandant in 1790. He was at Nootka in 1792 as the Spanish commissioner under the 1790 convention with Great Britain. With his British counterpart, George Vancouver, Bodega circumnavigated the island later named for both men. After returning to San Blas in 1793, he retired because of poor health. Bodega died in Mexico City.

See also **Explorers and Exploration: Spanish America.**

BIBLIOGRAPHY

Michael E. Thurman, *The Naval Department of San Blas, 1767–1798* (1967).

Warren L. Cook, *Flood Tide of Empire: Spain in the Pacific Northwest, 1543–1819* (1973).

W. MICHAEL MATHES

BOERO, FELIPE (1884–1958). Felipe Boero (*b*. 1 May 1884; *d*. 9 August 1958), Argentine composer and teacher. Born in Buenos Aires, Boero studied with the composer Pablo Berutti until 1912, when, as a winner of the *Premio Europa* (Europe Prize) established by the Argentine Ministry of Culture, he traveled to France to study at the National Conservatory in Paris under Paul Vidal and Gabriel Fauré (1912–1914). Upon his return to Argentina he founded the National Music Society—later known as the Argentine Association of Composers—which was dedicated to the promotion of Argentine works. A high point in his pedagogic career came in 1934, when the National Council of Education commissioned Boero to create and direct a choral group of two thousand voices. In 1935 he became a member of the National Fine Arts Committee and was appointed music professor and choir director at both the Mariano Acosta Normal School for Teachers and the Manuel Belgrano Institute.

Boero's first opera, *Tucumán,* which premiered in 1918 at the Teatro Colón in Buenos Aires, was the first opera on a Spanish libretto to be composed in the nationalist style; it won the Municipal Prize. Boero wrote seven more works for the stage: the opera-ballet *Ariana y Dionysos* (1916) and the operas *Raquela* (1918), *Siripo* (1924), *El Matrero*

(1925), *Zincalí* (1933), plus two incidental works: *Las bacantes* (1925) and *El inglés de los "güesos"* (1938). *El Matrero,* premiered at the Colón in 1929 under the baton of Ettore Panizza, became the most performed, most popular Argentine opera of the first half of the twentieth century, and was recorded by RCA Victor. Boero composed several orchestral works, among them *Suite de danzas argentinas* (1920–1930), *Madrugada en la pampa* (1930), *Suite argentina* (1940), a Mass (1918) on Latin text, as well as works for vocal soloist and orchestra, for orchestra with choir, choral works, songs, many works for piano, and a collection of children's songs.

See also **Music: Art Music.**

BIBLIOGRAPHY

Rodolfo Arizaga, *Enciclopedia de la música argentina* (1971).

Gérard Béhague, *Music in Latin America* (1979); *Composers of the Americas,* vol. 15 (1969), pp. 29ff.; *New Grove Dictionary of Music and Musicians,* vol. 2 (1980).

Additional Bibliography

Schwartz-Kates, Deborah. "Argentine Art Music and the Search for National Identity Mediated through a Symbolic Native Heritage: The 'Tradición Gauchesca' and Felip Boero's *El matrero.*" *Latin American Music Review* 20:1 (Spring–Summer 1999): 1–29.

SUSANA SALGADO

BOFF, LEONARDO (1938–). Leonardo Boff (*b*. 14 December 1938), Brazilian theologian. A Franciscan priest born in Concordia, Brazil, Boff is arguably Brazil's best-known theologian and is one of the world's foremost liberation theologians. He studied theology in Brazil and Germany, where he did his doctoral work, and was ordained in 1964. His book *Jesus Christ, Liberator,* which portrayed Christ as a liberator of the poor, brought him international visibility and acclaim after its publication in 1972 (English trans. 1978). Since then, Boff has published scores of books that deal with a wide range of themes. In 1972 he was named editor of Brazil's foremost theological journal, the *Revista eclesiástica brasileira.*

In the late 1970s, as Brazil's military regime began to show signs of unraveling and as the opposition conquered new spaces for contestation, Boff became more involved in writing about explicitly political themes. He expressed his support for the leftist Workers' Party and, in the mid-1980s, declared his admiration for the Soviet Union.

In the mid-1970s, the Vatican began investigating Boff's work on the grounds that it strayed too far from Catholic orthodoxy. Boff's life after the publication of *Church: Charisma and Power* (1981; English trans. 1985) was marked by increasing controversy as his work came under attack by conservative theologians and clerics. Calling for a church born from the faith of the poor, Boff's book criticized the Catholic church for being authoritarian and excessively concerned with power. Conservatives counterargued that Boff was unduly critical of the institution, and that the pope and bishops must assume responsibility for leadership in the church. In this view, popular religion therefore holds no special claim to truth in the church.

In September 1984, Boff went to Rome to defend his writings. After several months of deliberation, the Vatican formally criticized Boff's work in May 1985, imposing a silence that was lifted the following year. Because Boff was so prominent, this sanction was broadly perceived as an attack upon the liberation theology movement. In May 1991, Boff was again sanctioned by the Vatican, which required him to resign as editor of the *Revista Eclesiástica Brasileira* and ordered him not to publish any works for a year. In 1992, Rome tried to silence him again, by preventing him from participating in the Earth Summit in Rio de Janeiro that year. In response, he abandoned the priesthood and the Franciscan order.

See also **Catholic Church: The Modern Period.**

BIBLIOGRAPHY

Luis Marcos Sander, *Jesus, o Libertador: A Cristologia da libertação de Leonardo Boff* (1986).

Harvey Cox, *The Silencing of Leonardo Boff: The Vatican and the Future of World Christianity* (1988).

Additional Bibliography

Boff, Leonardo. *The Lord Is My Shepherd: Divine Consolation in Times of Abandonment.* Maryknoll, NY: Orbis Books, 2006.

Boff, Leonardo. *Experimentar a Dios: La transperencia de todas las cosas.* Santander: Sal Terre, 2003.

Cadorette, Curt. *Liberation Theology: An Introductory Reader.* Eugene, Oregon: Wipf & Stock, 2004.

Chauí, Marilena de Souza, and Juárez Guimarães. *Leituras da crise: Diálogos sobre o PT, a democracía brasileira e o socialismo.* São Paulo: Editora Fundacão Perseu Abramo, 2006.

SCOTT MAINWARING

BOGGIANI, GUIDO (1861–1901). Guido Boggiani was an explorer, photographer, and ethnographer of Paraguay's Chaco. Born in Italy, Boggiani studied painting and piano before traveling to Argentina and Paraguay in 1887. An adventurer at heart, he explored the remote Gran Chaco, keeping copious notes and recording detailed drawings of scenes of indigenous life. After returning to Europe and publishing his travelogue, *I Cadvuei (Mbaya or Guaycuru), Viaggi d'un artista nell' America Meriodionale*, in Rome in 1895, Boggiani returned to the Chaco in 1897 to continue his research; he published extensively and took more than three hundred photographs. His work comprises the classic ethnography of the Caduveo and Chamacoco peoples. In a death whose circumstances recall that of the famed conquistador Alejo García in 1526, Boggiani was killed during internecine fighting among the Chaco groups in 1901.

See also **Chaco Region; Chaco War; Paraguay: The Nineteenth Century.**

BIBLIOGRAPHY

Boggiani, Guido. *Boggiani y el Chaco: Una aventura del siglo XIX: Fotografías de la collecíon FRIC.* Buenos Aires: Museo de Arte Hispanoamericano Isaac Fernández Blanco, 2002.

Krebs, Edgardo. "High Noon in the Rain Forest." *American Anthropologist* 104, no. 2 (2002): 649–651.

RICHARD K. REED

BOGOTÁ, SANTA FE DE. The capital and largest city of Colombia, Santa Fe de Bogotá is also the capital of the department of Cundinamarca. In 2005 the city had a population of 7.8 million. It is located in the Eastern Cordillera of the Andes on the eastern edge of a basin known as the *sabana* of Bogotá at an elevation of about 8,600 feet. Rising sharply above the city to the east are two peaks, Monserrate and Guadalupe. Because of its altitude, Bogotá has a cool climate with an average temperature of 57° F.

Although Bogotá has been an important administrative, cultural, and economic center since the sixteenth century, its growth was long impeded by its inland location and high altitude. Before the advent of modern modes of transportation, access to the Magdalena River and the Caribbean Sea required a long and arduous journey. Communication with the Pacific Ocean and other regions of Colombia was equally difficult.

In the 1530s the area around modern Bogotá was part of the domain of the powerful Chibcha chieftain, or *zipa*, called Tisquesusa. Spaniards under Gonzalo Jiménez De Quesada (*d.* 1579) reached the *sabana* in 1537 and proceeded to subjugate the region despite Chibcha resistance. There is some confusion about the circumstances of the founding of Bogotá. The traditional date for the city's foundation is 6 August 1538. According to historian Juan Friede, Jiménez laid claim to the *zipa*'s territories in the latter's capital, called Bogotá (Bacatá), on 6 August 1537. However, the formal establishment of the Spanish city of Santa Fe took place on 27 April 1539, at a nearby site called Teusaquillo.

Santa Fe (Santafé) quickly became the principal city of the Kingdom of New Granada, which embraced most of modern Colombia. An audiencia, or high court, was installed in Santa Fe in 1550; a bishopric was established in 1553 and elevated to the rank of archbishopric in 1564. In the eighteenth century, the Spanish government selected Santa Fe as the capital of the new Viceroyalty of New Granada.

Despite its status as a colonial capital, Santa Fe de Bogotá grew slowly; its population was only about 28,000 in 1761. In the late eighteenth and early nineteenth centuries, the city's intellectual life was stimulated by the scientific teachings and projects of José Celestino Mutis (1732–1808), a Spanish botanist who lived in Santa Fe from 1761 to 1808. This period also saw the establishment of the city's first newspapers and journals, notably the *Papel Periódico* (1791–1797) and the *Semanario... del Nuevo Reino de Granada* (1808–1810).

The city played a major role in Colombia's independence movement from Spain. A dispute in Santa Fe between a Creole and a Spaniard on 20 July 1810 helped to trigger the deposition of the viceroy, an event commemorated as Colombia's national holiday. After independence, Santa Fe, now renamed Bogotá, became the capital of Gran Colombia and later (1831) of New Granada or Colombia.

Colombia's political instability and sluggish economy during the first decades after independence inhibited change in Bogotá, which had a population of only about 30,000 in 1851. The heart of the city was still the square on which the eighteenth-century cathedral was located. The square was given its present name of Plaza de Bolívar after a statue of Simon Bolívar was erected there in 1846. In 1848 President Tomás Cipriano de Mosquera laid the cornerstone of the national capitol on the southern side of the square, but work on the project soon halted (1851).

After 1870, the expansion of commercial agriculture, especially the development of coffee exports, brought modest economic growth to Colombia, which was reflected in Bogotá. The population grew from about 41,000 in 1870 to 121,000 in 1912. Colombia's first successful bank, the Banco de Bogotá, opened its doors in 1871, followed by the Banco de Colombia in 1875 and others. Although Bogotá lagged behind Medellín in textile manufacturing, numerous industries were established during this period, among them the brewery Bavaria (1891) and Cementos Samper (1909). Work was resumed on the capitol (though it remained incomplete until the mid 1920s), and on other public buildings, such as the Teatro Colón, which was modeled on the Paris Opéra. Efforts were also made to improve the quality of urban life through improved paving and the construction of sewers, aqueducts, parks, and bridges. Gas lighting was introduced in 1876 and illumination by electricity in the early 1890s.

During these years affluent Bogotanos began moving north to the nearby hamlet of Chapinero, which was annexed to the city in 1885. By this time a trolley line extended from the Plaza de Bolívar along the Carrera Séptima, the city's main thoroughfare, to Chapinero. Between the 1880s and 1909, Bogotá was gradually connected by rail to the Magdalena as well.

Throughout the nineteenth century, Bogotá's elites enjoyed a reputation for sardonic wit and literary distinction and boasted of the city's claim to be the "Athens of South America." They were also noted for their conservative political views and, like the city's population as a whole, for their devotion to Catholicism. William L. Scruggs (1836–1912), who served as U.S. minister in the 1870s and 1880s, observed that "there is probably no city on the continent where the external forms of religion are more rigidly observed."

Scruggs was also impressed by the insubordination of the lower classes, who were mainly Mestizos. The economic quickening of the late nineteenth century brought dislocation to many workers, and government monetary policy contributed to an inflationary trend in the 1890s. In 1893 the publication of a series of articles in a leading newspaper accusing the lower classes of drunkenness and immorality produced a riot that left from forty to forty-five persons dead. During the disorders the rioters attacked police stations as well as the homes of public officials.

Bogotá's growth accelerated after 1930 for several reasons. With the expansion of commercial agriculture and import-substitution industrialization, Colombia's economy was growing at a more rapid rate than before. Bogotá became more important as a manufacturing center, accounting for 29 percent of the nation's industrial employment by 1975. The enlarged socioeconomic role of the state increased the size of the bureaucracy and gave birth to numerous public agencies headquartered in the capital. Agricultural modernization and endemic rural violence displaced many peasants who migrated to Bogotá. As a result, by 1973 Bogotá contained 13.6 percent of Colombia's population as compared to 4.1 percent in 1938. In 1964 more than 50 percent of the city's population had been born in other parts of the country.

The aspirations and tensions fueled by these changes contributed to the rise of the charismatic Liberal leader Jorge Eliécer Gaitán (b. 1898), who served as mayor of Bogotá in 1936–1937. During the violence that followed his assassination in 1948 (referred to as the Bogotazo), hundreds of buildings and shops in the central business district were damaged or destroyed, including the departmental headquarters of Cundinamarca, the ministries of justice and interior, and two buildings of the archdiocese. (In 1985 a government assault against guerrillas who had taken possession of the Palace of Justice severely damaged the building and cost nearly one hundred lives.)

Since 1930 the northward drift of the upper and upper-middle classes has continued, accompanied by a similar movement of offices and commercial establishments. Lower-income residential areas have become concentrated in the central, southern, and western sectors, with much self-built irregular housing in the latter two. In 1983 municipal authorities created the Corporación Candelaria to restore and preserve fifty-four blocks in the city's central district, mainly in the historical quarter called the Candelaria.

In 1954 the national government incorporated Bogotá into a Special District (Distrito Especial) that also included six nearby municipalities: Bosa, Engativá, Fontibón, Suba, Usaquén, and Usme. The chief executive officer, or Alcalde Mayor, of the Special District was appointed by the president until 1986, when the position was made elective. In the constitution of 1991 the Special District was renamed the Capital District (Distrito Capital). It was to be governed by an elective mayor and district council, along with neighborhood officials. The constitution also restored to the city its colonial name of Santa Fe de Bogotá.

Between 2002 and 2006 violence in Colombia decreased: Murders fell by 37 percent, kidnappings by 78 percent. There is a much larger police presence on the streets of the capital city, and new restaurants and bike paths have opened. Yet, for an estimated one-fifth of the more than three million who fled or were displaced from civil war–torn areas, affordable housing and basic services are still needed.

See also **Colombia: From the Conquest through Independence.**

BIBLIOGRAPHY

Pedro M. Ibáñez, *Crónicas de Bogotá*, 4 vols., 2d ed. (1913–1923).

Juan Friede, *Invasión del país de los Chibchas: Conquista del Nuevo Reino de Granada y fundación de Santafé de Bogotá* (1966).

Alan Gilbert, "Bogotá: Politics, Planning, and the Crisis of Lost Opportunities," in *Latin American Urban Research*, vol. 6: *Metropolitan Latin America: The Challenge and the Response*, edited by Wayne A. Cornelius and Robert V. Kemper (1978), pp. 87–126.

Enrique Durand, "Bogotá: Echoes of the Past," in *Américas* 39 (November–December 1987):24–30.

David Sowell, "The 1893 *Bogotazo*: Artisans and Public Violence in Late Nineteenth-Century Bogotá," in *Journal of Latin American Studies* 21 (1989): 267–282.

Additional Bibliography

Castillo Daza, Juan Carlos del. *Bogotá: El tránsito a la ciudad moderna 1920–1950*. Bogotá: Universidad Nacional de Colombia, 2003.

Corradine Angulo, Alberto. *Apuntes sobre Bogotá: Historia y arquitectura*. Bogotá: Academia Colombiana de Historia, 2002.

Díaz, Rafael Antonio. *Esclavitud, región y ciudad: El sistema esclavista urbano–regional en Santafé de Bogotá, 1700–1750*. Bogotá: Centro Editorial Javeriano, 2001.

Mejía P., Germán. *Los años del cambio: Historia urbana de Bogotá, 1820–1910*. Bogotá: Centro Editorial Javeriano, 1998.

Pérgolis, Juan Carlos. *Bogotá fragmentada: Cultura y espacio urbano a fines del siglo XX*. Bogotá: TM Editores (Universidad Piloto de Colombia), 1998.

Preciado Beltrán, Jair, Robert Orlando Leal Pulido, and Cecilia Almanza Castañeda. *Historia ambiental de Bogotá, siglo XX: Elementos históricos para la formulación del medio ambiente urbano*. Bogotá: Fondo de Publicaciones Universidad Distrital Francisco José de Caldas, 2005.

Rentería Salazar, Patricia, and Oscar Alfredo Alfonso Roa. *La ciudad–transformaciones, retos y posibilidades*. Bogotá: Centro Editorial Javeriano, 2002.

HELEN DELPAR

BOGOTÁ, SANTA FE DE: THE AUDIENCIA.

The audiencia of Santa Fe de Bogotá was first installed in 1550, with jurisdiction over the area that today constitutes most of the modern republics of Colombia and Venezuela. Spanish settlements on the Caribbean coasts were previously under the jurisdiction of the audiencias of Panama and Santo Domingo, but after Spaniards had penetrated into the Andean interior (where they established the Kingdom of New Granada in 1539), Charles I decided to create the new Audiencia of Santa Fe in order to impose royal control over New Granada's unruly conquerors and encomenderos, and to enforce the New Laws of 1542. By 1563 the audiencia's territorial jurisdiction had taken the shape that it was to retain for most of the colonial period. This extended over much of modern Colombia, apart from the great southern territory of the province of Popayán, which became part of the Audiencia of Quito (established in 1563), and most of modern Venezuela, except Caracas which remained within the jurisdiction of the Audiencia of Santo Domingo.

The first audiencia tribunal consisted of four Oidores (judges), all lawyers, one of whom was appointed as president. The first president died en route to Bogotá, however, and the presidency was not subsequently exercised until 1563, by Andrés Venero de Leiva (1563–1574). Government then returned to the audiencia as a collegiate body until the presidency was revived under Antonio González (1590–1597) and Francisco de Sande (1597–1602). The first half-century of the audiencia's life was one of considerable turbulence, characterized by conflicts with *encomenderos,* clergy, and among the *oidores* themselves.

In 1605, the Crown sought to strengthen the audiencia's authority and efficiency by altering its presidency. Juan de Borja became governor and captain-general of New Granada and *presidente de capa y espada,* with military duties and powers. From 1630, the Crown tried further to consolidate the audiencia's authority by appointing Spanish nobles as presidents, in a largely ineffective effort to counter the power of local elites.

During the eighteenth century, the audiencia underwent fresh alterations to its jurisdiction, power, and composition. Reform began in 1717, following a crisis within the audiencia in 1715 when the *oidores* deposed and imprisoned President Francisco de Meneses. The Audiencia of Santa Fe was enlarged to include Panama in its jurisdiction, and in 1719 the first viceroy of New Granada replaced the audiencia's president as the Crown's leading official. Suppressed in 1723, the Viceroyalty of New Granada was reestablished in 1739, and Santa Fe again became an audiencia, with the viceroy as governor and captain-general of New Granada and ex-officio president of the audiencia.

The second Bourbon reform of the audiencia stemmed from Charles III's program of colonial reform and was implemented in New Granada during the *visita general* of 1778–1783. The audiencia was expanded in 1776 to include a regent and a *fiscal del crimen* (crown criminal prosecutor). Also, another *oidor* was added. Furthermore, it was

"Europeanized" by the appointment of peninsular lawyers who were free of local ties. To further reduce their susceptibility to local interests, they now served for shorter periods and were discouraged by the Madrid government from marrying into local Creole society. Subordinated to the viceroys in Santa Fe, the eighteenth-century audiencia reflected the general shift from the consensual government of the Hapsburg monarchy to the centralized, absolutist model favored by the Bourbons.

The audiencia judges were forced to leave Bogotá when viceregal government was overthrown in 1810, and the audiencia moved to Panama until New Granada was reconquered by Spain in 1815. When Spanish rule ended in 1819, the Viceroyalty and Audiencia of Santa Fe were supplanted by republican government.

See also **Audiencia; Colombia: From the Conquest Through Independence.**

BIBLIOGRAPHY

R. B. Cunningham Graham, *The Conquest of New Granada, Being the Life of Gonzalo Jiménez de Quesada* (1922).

Manuel Lucena Salmoral, *Nuevo Reino de Granada, Real Audiencia y Presidentes: Presidentes de Capa y Espada (1605–1628)* (1965) and *Nuevo Reino de Granada, Real Audiencia y Presidentes: Presidentes de Capa y Espada (1628–1654)* (1967).

Sergio Elías Ortíz, *Nuevo Reino de Granada, Real Audiencia y Presidentes: Presidentes de Capa y Espada (1654–1719)* (1966).

Anthony McFarlane, *Colombia Before Independence: Economy, Society, and Politics Under Bourbon Rule* (1993).

Additional Bibliography

Mayorga García, Fernando. *La Audiencia de Santa Fé en los siglos XVI y XVII*. Bogotá: Instituto Colombiano de Cultura Hispánica, 1991.

Ortiz de la Tabla Ducasse, Javier, Agueda Rivera Garrido, and Montserrat Fernández Martínez. *Cartas de cabildos hispanoamericanos. Audiencia de Santa Fe.* Sevilla, Spain: Escuela de Estudios Hispano-Americanos, Consejo Superior de Investigaciones Científicas, 1996.

ANTHONY MCFARLANE

BOGOTÁ CONFERENCE (1948). *See* **Pan-American Conferences: Bogotá Conference (1948).**

BOGOTAZO. Bogotazo, also known as the Nueve de Abril, was a riot in Bogotá, Colombia, after the fatal shooting of Jorge E. Gaitán on 9 April 1948. Gaitán, head of the Liberal Party, was a popular hero whose death enraged his lower- and middle-class followers. A mob soon murdered the assassin, Juan Roa Sierra. The rioters then turned their fury on institutions associated with the ruling Conservative Party and the existing social order, such as government buildings, churches, the Jockey Club, and *El Siglo*, a Conservative newspaper. Many shops were looted, and hundreds were killed or wounded before order was restored on 11 April. Disturbances also took place in other cities. The Bogotazo interrupted the Ninth International Conference of American States attended by the foreign ministers of twenty-one nations, including U.S. secretary of state George C. Marshall. Also present was Fidel Castro, who was in Bogotá to attend a student conference sponsored by the Peronist government of Argentina and took part in the rioting, which represented his first exposure to a revolutionary situation.

In the event, the army remained loyal to the Conservative president, Mariano Ospina Pérez, who rejected calls to resign. He blamed the riot on a communist plot and added Liberals to his cabinet, but the Bogotazo exacerbated partisan tensions and contributed to the deepening *violencia*. Secretary Marshall declared that the Soviet Union was responsible for the Bogotazo. The inter-American meeting resumed on April 14, approved a resolution denouncing communism, and completed work on the charter of the Organization of American States by the end of the month.

See also **Gaitan, Jorge Eliécer; Organization of American States (OAS); Ospina Pérez, Mariano.**

BIBLIOGRAPHY

Alape, Arturo. *El Bogotazo: Memorias del olvido*, 2nd edition. Havana: Casa de las Américas, 1983.

Braun, Herbert. *The Assassination of Gaitán: Public Life and Urban Violence in Colombia*. Madison: University of Wisconsin, 1985.

Henderson, James D. *Modernization in Colombia: The Laureano Gómez Years, 1889–1965*. Gainesville: University Press of Florida, 2001.

HELEN DELPAR

BÓIA-FRIA. *Bóia-fria*, a Brazilian rural manual laborer who is hired temporarily and has no relationship to the place of employment. The name *bóia-fria* literally means the cold food included as part of a worker's wages. Alternate names for these migrant workers include: *avulso* (separate), *contínuo* (messenger), *clandestino* (clandestine [in the northwest]), *volante* (from *voar*—to fly), *safrista* (from *safra*—sugar harvest), *eventual* (for the event), *diarista* (daily), and *temporário* (temporary). The practice originated in industries that required a large number of seasonal manual laborers, such as those engaged in the harvest of coffee beans, and was adopted by others that required a reduced labor force on a full-time basis but employed temporary workers to improve commercial yield. The practice provoked a rural exodus. *Bóia-frias* typically live in the urban periphery and at harvest time move to the fields, where they live in extreme poverty. Their level of education is low, and illiteracy predominates. Their basic diet consists of plain rice or rice and beans.

See also **Agriculture.**

BIBLIOGRAPHY

Maria Da Conceição De Mello Lucas, *O bóia-fria: Acumulação e miséria*, 2d ed. (1975).

Aurélio Buarque Holanda Ferreira, *Novo dicionário da língua portuguesa*, 2d ed. (1986).

Additional Bibliography

Dias, Wilka Coronado Antunes. *Vidas construidas na terra: O ir e vir dos trabalhadores rurais.* Ph.D. diss., 1999.

Jannuzzi, Paulo de Martino. *Migração e mobilidade social: Migrantes no mercado de trabalho paulista.* Campinas-SP: Editora Autores Associados, 2000.

Welch, Cliff. *The Seed Was Planted: The São Paulo Roots of Brazil's Rural Labor Movement, 1924-1964.* University Park: Pennsylvania State University Press, 1999.

DALISIA MARTINS DOLES

BOISO–LANZA PACT (1973). Boiso–Lanza Pact (1973), an agreement guaranteeing the Uruguayan military an advisory role and participation in political decision making. The military and, at that time constitutional, president Juan María Bordaberry were the principal parties to the February 1973 agreement, which was openly recognized by the military through such institutions as the National Security Counsel (Cosena) and the Joint Chiefs of Staff (Esmaco). On 9 February of that year, the military had published communiqués outlining a confusing program that contained some hints of populism. A few days later, in a meeting at the Boiso-Lanza military base in the department of Montevideo, the military presented its demands to President Bordaberry, who was seeking a corporate-style reorganization of the state without precedent in the political tradition of the country. On 27 June 1973, Bordaberry dissolved the Parliament and severely limited civil liberties, beginning the military regime that would last until 1 March 1985.

See also **Bordaberry, Juan María; Uruguay: The Twentieth Century.**

BIBLIOGRAPHY

Angel Cocchi, *Nuestros partidos*, vol. 2 (1984).

Gerardo Caetano and José Rilla, *Breve historia de la dictadura* (1991).

JOSÉ DE TORRES WILSON

BOLAÑO, ROBERTO (1953–2003). The writer Roberto Bolaño, born in Santiago de Chile, led a rather nomadic existence. At fifteen he was living in Mexico, where he began to work as a journalist and became a Trotskyite. In 1973 he returned to Chile in time to witness the military coup. He signed up with the resistance and ended up a prisoner. Some childhood friends who had become policemen recognized him and managed to get him out of jail after a week. He then went to El Salvador, and in 1977 he moved to Spain, where he worked at a variety of jobs—dishwasher, waiter, night watchman, garbage collector, stevedore, and grape harvester. In the 1980s, having won several literary competitions, he was finally able to support himself as a writer. He published *La pista de hielo* (The ice rink) in 1993 and *La literatura nazi en América* (Nazi literature in the Americas) in 1996; his novel *Los detectives salvajes* (*The Savage Detectives*), published in 1999, won the Herralde and Rómulo Gallegos awards.

His fame increased with works such as *Monsieur Pain* (1999), *Nocturno de Chile* (2000; *By Night in Chile*), *Putas asesinas* (2001; Murdering whores), *Amberes* (2002; Ambers), *El gaucho insufrible* (2003; The insufferable gaucho), and above all, *2666*, a novel of more than a thousand pages that he was still finishing at the time of his death (in Spain, of a liver disorder) and that is considered his masterpiece. Through his powerful prose style, his knowledge of world literature, his masterful ability to keep the reader in suspense, the originality of his themes, and his potent sense of humor, Bolaño earned the admiration of readers and critics, many of whom regard him as the most important writer of his generation.

See also **Chile: The Twentieth Century; Literature: Spanish America.**

BIBLIOGRAPHY

Works by the Author Available in English

Amulet. Translated by Chris Andrews. New York: New Directions, 2006.

By Night in Chile. Translated by Chris Andrews. New York: New Directions, 2003.

Distant Star. Translated by Chris Andrews. New York: New Directions, 2004.

Last Evenings on Earth. Translated by Chris Andrews. New York: New Directions, 2006.

The Savage Detectives. Translated by Natasha Wimmer. New York: Farrar, Straus and Giroux, 2007.

Works on the Author

Corral, Will H. "Portrait of the Writer as Nobel Savage." *World Literature Today* 80, no. 6 (2006): 47–50.

Siddhartha, Deb. "The Wandering Years: Roberto Bolano's Nomadic Fiction." *Harper's Magazine* 314 (April 2007): 99–105.

Zalewski, Daniel. "Vagabonds." *New Yorker* (March 26, 2007): 84–89.

ANGEL ESTEBAN

BOLAÑOS, CÉSAR (1931–). The Peruvian avant-garde composer César Bolaños, born June 4, 1931, in Lima, was among the first in his country to write electronic, computer, and music theater works making use of multimedia and indeterminacy in which chance procedures affect both composition and performance. Since 1970 he has concentrated on his research as a musicologist, specializing in ancient and traditional Andean musical instruments and practices, including dance, as well as modern Peruvian music and electronic media. In his native Lima, Bolaños was a pupil of European émigré composer and musicologist Andrés Sas, and in 1958 he went to New York City, studying electronic music at the RCA Institute of Electronic Technology (1960–1963).

His most fruitful period as a composer took place at the Latin American Center for Advanced Musical Studies at the Torcuato di Tella Institute in Buenos Aires (1963–1970), both as student (of composers Luigi Dallapiccola, Alberto Ginastera, Olivier Messiaen, and Luigi Nono) and as professor (of electroacoustic composition and audiovisual theory and practice). He was also instrumental in the foundation of the center's electronic music laboratory, and created there his first electronic tape composition, *Intensidad y altura* (1964), based on a poem by César Vallejo. His computer music was influenced by his collaboration with mathematician Mauricio Milchberg, and Bolaños explicitly used the acronym ESEPCO—for *estructuras sonora-expresivas por computación* (digital sonic-expressive structures)—in the titles of two of his works from 1970. Upon his return to Lima in 1973 he became director of the National Cultural Institute (INC), and also taught at the National Conservatory of Music and Lima University.

Other important compositions by Bolaños include Divertimento no. 3 for chamber ensemble (1967); *Alfa-Omega* for two narrators, theatrical mixed choir, electric guitar, double bass, two percussionists, two dancers, tape, slide projections, and lights (1967), which utilizes biblical texts; *I-10-AIFG/Rbt-1* for three narrators, horn, trombone, electric guitar, two percussionists, two operators for keyboard controlled lights and six radios, nine slide projectors with automatic synchronization, tape, and instrumental amplification, with black lights for the reading of scores and "programmed conducting" using synchronized light signals (1968); and *Ñacahuasu* for chamber orchestra and narrator (1970), based on texts from Che Guevara's Bolivian diary. After an almost fifteen-year hiatus, he composed *Pucayaku* for piano and percussion (1984).

See also **Guevara, Ernesto "Che"; Music: Art Music; Vallejo, César.**

BIBLIOGRAPHY

Béhague, Gerard. "Countercurrents: Since 1950." In *Music in Latin America: An Introduction*. Englewood Cliffs, NJ: Prentice-Hall, 1979.

Estensoro, Juan Carlos. "Bolaños, César." In *The New Grove Dictionary of Music and Musicians*, 2nd edition, edited by Stanley Sadie. New York: Grove, 2001.

Iturriaga, Enrique. "Bolaños Vildoso, César." In *Dicionario de música española e hispanoamericana*, edited by Emilio Casares Rodicio. Madrid: Sociedad General de Autores y Editores, 1999.

Pan American Union, Music Section. "César Bolaños." In *Compositores de América: Dados biográficos y catálogo de sus obras*, Vol. 17. Washington, D.C.: Secretaria General, Organización de los Estados Americanos, 1971.

Pinilla, Enrique. "La música en el siglo XX: Tercera generación." In *Historia del Perú*, Vol. 9, *Procesos e instituciones*. Lima: J. Mejía Baca, 1980.

Pinilla, Enrique. "César Bolaños." In *La música en el Perú*. Lima: Patronato Popular y Porvenir pro Música Clásica, 1988.

ALCIDES LANZA
LUIZ FERNANDO LOPES

BOLAÑOS, LUIS DE (1549–1629).

Luis de Bolaños (*b.* 1549; *d.* 11 October 1629), Franciscan missionary. Called the Apostle of Paraguay, Bolaños was born in Marchena, Spain, in Andalusia. He joined the Franciscan order as a youth and was ordained a deacon. In 1572 he volunteered to serve as a missionary in the Río de la Plata and left Spain with his mentor and friend Fray Alonso de Buenaventura. After arriving in Paraguay in 1575, the two friars preached to Guaranis near Asunción and then in the northern area of the Jejui Guazú River, where the followers of Cacique Overá were resisting Spanish pressure. There in 1580, the missionaries founded Altos, the first enduring reduction of Paraguay. Later, Bolaños and Buenaventura founded Ypané, Atyrá, Tobatí, Itá, Yaguarón, Yuty, and Caazapá, which all survive. Bolaños attempted to work in the part of Guairá that is now the state of Paraná in Brazil, but the Spanish colonists there expelled him for blocking their exploitation of Native American labor. After mastering the Guarani language, Bolaños wrote a Guarani grammar and vocabulary and became the primary translator into Guarani of the catechism of the Council of Lima of 1583, the basis for instruction in the Franciscan reductions and the later Jesuit missions of Paraguay.

In 1585 Bolaños was ordained a priest, and after 1600 he cooperated with Governor Hernando Arias De Saavedra, Bishop Martín Ignacio de Loyola, and colonizer Juan de Garay to extend Spanish secular and religious authority. The more famous Jesuit reductions of Paraguay founded after 1610 were partly the fruition of the methods of Franciscans like Bolaños, who advised Father Manuel de Lorenzana and other members of the Society of Jesus. Though famous as a missionary, Bolaños was also an able administrator. At the end of his life, he retired to the Franciscan house in Buenos Aires, where he died. In 1979 his body was returned to Asunción, Paraguay, where he is a national hero.

See also **Franciscans.**

BIBLIOGRAPHY

Buenaventura Oro, *Fray Luis Bolaños, apóstol del Paraguay y Río de la Plata* (1934).

Andrés Millé, *Crónica de la Orden Franciscana en la conquista del Perú, Paraguay y el Tucumán y su convento del antiguo Buenos Aires, 1612–1800* (1961).

Margarita Durán Estrago, *Presencia franciscana en el Paraguay*, vol. 1 (1987).

Additional Bibliography

Durán Estragó, Margarita. *El hechicero de Dios: Fray Luis Bolaños*. Asunción, Paraguay: Editorial Don Bosco, 1995.

Salas, José Luis. *La evangelización franciscana de los guaranies: su apóstol fray Luis Bolaños*. Asunción, Paraguay: J. L. Salas, 2000.

JAMES SCHOFIELD SAEGER

BOLEADORAS.

Boleadoras, also known as *bolas*, a leather and stone weapon of the Pampas. Indigenous civilizations strongly influenced the material culture and language of the Río de la Plata. They developed the *boleadoras* which was then adopted by the gaucho. The dangerous weapon consists of two or three rawhide thongs, each tipped with leather-covered rocks or metal balls that are bound together at one end. After whirling the *boleadoras* around his head, the Indian or gaucho would fling it at the feet of a fleeing rhea, horse, or bull. Entangled in the thongs, the animal crashed to the ground. In addition to its utility in hunting, the weapon proved effective in cavalry warfare. The indigenous peoples of the pampas reputedly trained their horses to run and escape even when entangled in *boleadoras*.

See also **Gaucho.**

BIBLIOGRAPHY

Richard W. Slatta, *Gauchos and the Vanishing Frontier* (1983), esp. pp. 8, 87.

Additional Bibliography

Assunção, Fernando O. *Historia del gaucho: El gaucho, ser y quehacer.* Buenos Aires: Editorial Claridad, 1999.

De la Fuente, Ariel. *Children of Facundo: Caudillo and Gaucho Insurgency during the Argentine State-Formation Process (La Rioja, 1853-1870).* Durham, NC: Duke University Press, 2000.

Mandrini, Raúl. *Los pueblos originarios de la Argentina: La visión del otro.* Buenos Aires: Editorial Universitaria de Buenos Aires. EUDEBA, 2004.

RICHARD W. SLATTA

BOLERO. Bolero, a form of Latin American music that originated in southern Spain. It was rhythmically modified in late colonial Cuba and made more lyrical in the Yucatán. During the 1930s the powerful radio station XEW helped to popularize the form in Mexico City, where by 1940 it had acquired a sophisticated smoothness that suited it to the dance floor. With the ascendance of ranchera music and rock and roll in the 1950s, the bolero lost its dominance. Still, the dance remains popular and Mexican pop stars often play bolero tunes.

Many regional Mexican songs were recast in the slightly syncopated 2/4 bolero rhythm (eight beats, with the third left out). Well-known guitar trios such as the widely traveled Los Panchos, Las Calaveras, and Los Diamantes helped make the romantic bolero international and gave it a similar sound in Mexico, Spain, Puerto Rico, Peru, and Argentina. Some of the most famous boleros are "Solamente una vez" by Agustín Lara, "Muñequita linda" (also called "Te quiero dijiste") by María

Grever, "Perfidia" by Alberto Domínguez, and the best-selling recording of all, "Bésame mucho" by Consuelo Velásquez.

See also **Music: Popular Music and Dance.**

BIBLIOGRAPHY

See *New Grove Dictionary of Music* (1980).

Claes Af Geijerstam, *Popular Music in Mexico* (1976).

Iris Zavala, *El bolero* (1991).

Additional Bibliography

García Medina, Antonio. *Brevísima historia de la canción y el bolero en México.* Guadalajara: A. García Medina, 2000.

Pedelty, Mark. *Musical Ritual in Mexico City: From the Aztec to NAFTA.* Austin: University of Texas Press, 2004.

Peza, Carmen de la. *El bolero y la educación sentimental en México.* México, D.F.: Universidad Autónoma Metropolitana, Unidad Xochimilco: Muguel Ángel Porrúa, 2001.

GUY BENSUSAN

BOLÍVAR, SIMÓN (1783–1830). Simón Bolívar (*b.* 24 July 1783; *d.* 17 December 1830), foremost leader of Spanish American independence. Born in Caracas to a wealthy landed family with slave-worked cacao plantations, Simón Bolívar received little formal education, although his private tutor, Simón Rodríguez, helped instill in him an admiration for the thinkers of the European Enlightenment. Bolívar traveled to Europe in 1799, and in Madrid in 1802 he married María Teresa Rodríguez de Toro, the daughter of a Caracas-born aristocrat. Upon her death soon after they returned to Venezuela, he made a second trip to Europe, during which he vowed to work for the liberation of Spanish America.

EARLY CAREER

When the Napoleonic invasion of Spain triggered the crisis of the Spanish monarchy in 1808–1810, Bolívar played a minor role in the various attempts to set up a governing junta in Caracas. However, once a junta was created, in April 1810, he became an active participant in the revolutionary movement. After heading a diplomatic mission sent to

Liberation of the Slaves by Simon Bolívar, undated painting by Fernandez Luis Cancino (19th century). Bolívar is portrayed here as a liberator of slaves as well as of nations, although slavery was only gradually eliminated in Gran Colombia under Bolívar's rule. GIRAUDON/ART RESOURCE, NY

London, he pressed for an outright declaration of independence, which was issued on 5 July 1811.

Having served as a colonial militia officer, though without formal military training, Bolívar was eventually given military command of the key coastal fortress of Puerto Cabello, whose loss in July 1812 served to hasten (though it hardly caused) the collapse of Venezuela's First Republic. When the Venezuelan dictator Francisco de Miranda accepted the inevitable and signed a capitulation to the royalists, Bolívar was one of those who angrily arrested him and by preventing his escape in effect turned Miranda over to the Spanish. Bolívar himself soon escaped to Curaçao and from there to Cartagena in New Granada, where he issued the Cartagena Manifesto (the first of his major political documents) and sought assistance for a new attempt to liberate Venezuela. With help from the United Provinces of New Granada, he invaded his homeland in 1813, and in less than three months swept into Caracas. This *campaña admirable* (admirable campaign), as it has been called, first earned Bolívar the title of "Liberator" and made him the acknowledged political as well as military leader of Venezuela.

Bolívar chose not to restore the federal constitution adopted in 1811 by the First Republic, believing that federalism was a dangerously weak form of government. The Second Republic that he then created, a frank military dictatorship, was no more successful than its predecessor, for it was soon being worn down by the assault of royalist guerrilla bands. Appealing to the Venezuelan masses to reject an independence movement whose principal figures (like Bolívar) were drawn from the creole elite, the royalists found a favorable response especially among the rough cowboy population (*llaaneros*) of the Orinoco plains. Before the end of 1814, Bolívar was again a fugitive in New Granada.

Despite his distaste for federalism, Bolívar repaid the New Granadan federalists grouped in the United Provinces for the aid they had given him by helping them subdue Bogotá, whose leaders favored a strong central authority. But he had little desire to take part in this or other internecine conflicts of the New Granadan patriots, especially when the defeat of Napoleon in Europe and restoration of Ferdinand VII to his throne now permitted Spain to redouble its efforts to suppress colonial rebellion. In mid-1815 Bolívar left New Granada, shortly before the arrival of the Spanish expeditionary force that would reconquer most of it for the king. Bolívar went first to Jamaica, where in his "Jamaica Letter" he offered a keen analysis of the present and future state of Spanish America. He next moved to Haiti, where he obtained help from the Haitian government for a new attempt to liberate Venezuela—and for a second attempt when the first ended in failure. By the end of 1816, he had regained a foothold and made contact with revolutionary bands still active in northeastern Venezuela.

In July 1817, Bolívar's forces seized Angostura (today Ciudad Bolívar), on the lower Orinoco River. The port of Angostura gave Bolívar a link to the outside world, while the Orinoco River system facilitated contact with pockets of patriot resistance in other parts of the Orinoco Basin, including the Apure region, where José Antonio Páez had won increasing numbers of llaneros over to the patriot cause. When Páez accepted Bolívar's leadership, the Liberator gained a critically important ally. As a llanero himself, Páez helped to give the independence struggle a more popular image. So did Bolívar's declaration (issued soon after his return to Venezuela in 1816) making abolition of slavery one of the patriot war aims. The mostly llanero cavalry of Bolívar and Páez could not dislodge the veteran Spanish troops occupying Andean Venezuela; but neither could the royalists make much headway on the Orinoco plains.

VICTORIOUS MOMENTUM
Bolívar sought to institutionalize the revolutionary movement by calling elections for a congress, which assembled at Angostura in February 1819 and ratified his leadership. Yet Bolívar's long-term objectives were not limited to Venezuela. In May 1819 he embarked on the campaign that took him westward across the llanos and over the Andes to central New Granada, where on 7 August he won the decisive battle of Boyacá. The victory opened the way to Bogotá, occupied three days later, and gave Bolívar control of an area with important reserves of recruits and supplies. It also gave him a victorious momentum that he never entirely lost.

Bolívar placed the New Granadan officer Francisco de Paula Santander in charge of the recently liberated provinces and then returned to Angostura, where, at his urging, in December 1819, the congress proclaimed the union of Venezuela, New Granada, and Quito (Ecuador) a single Republic of Colombia (usually referred to as Gran Colombia). The following year Bolívar turned his attention to the part of Venezuela still under royalist control. Military operations were suspended temporarily by an armistice of November 1820, but the victory at Carabobo, in June 1821, brought the war in Venezuela to a close except for royalist coastal enclaves that held out for another two years.

Meanwhile Gran Colombia was given a constitution by the Congress of Cúcuta, meeting in 1821 on the border between Venezuela and New Granada. The document was not entirely to Bolívar's liking, but he agreed to serve under it when the Congress named him first constitutional president, with Santander as vice president. Since Bolívar intended to continue leading the military struggle against Spain, Santander became acting chief executive in the Colombian capital of Bogotá, charged with organizing the home front and mobilizing resources.

After a local uprising in Guayaquil threw off royalist control of that port city, Bolívar sent his trusted lieutenant Antonio José de Sucre to Ecuador with a Colombian auxiliary force. While Bolívar fought his way through southern New Granada, Sucre penetrated the Ecuadoran highlands. After Sucre defeated the royalists at the battle of Pichincha (May 1822), on the outskirts of Quito, Bolívar entered Quito as well. Continuing to Guayaquil, he obtained its semivoluntary incorporation into Gran Colombia just before he met there with the Argentine liberator José de San Martín. The exact substance of their discussions was never revealed, but it would seem that one thing they disagreed on was how to complete the liberation of Peru, where San Martín controlled the coastal cities but not the highlands. Soon afterward, San Martín abandoned Peru, and Bolívar accepted a call to take his place.

LAST GREAT CAMPAIGN

Once he reached Peru, in September 1823, Bolívar found Peruvian collaboration to be somewhat fickle, but by mid-1824 he was ready for his last great campaign. On 6 August he scored an important victory at Junín, in the central Peruvian Andes, and on 9 December, in the battle of Ayacucho, his army (commanded by Sucre) obtained the surrender of the main royalist army. In the following weeks Sucre mopped up remnants of royalist resistance in Upper Peru (modern Bolivia).

A few days before Ayacucho, Bolívar, from Lima, issued a call to the Spanish American nations to meet at Panama and create a permanent alliance. He did not have a Pan-American gathering in mind, for he failed to invite the United States, Brazil, and Haiti—even while hoping that Great Britain would send an observer. The United States and Brazil were invited by the administration of Vice President Santander in Bogotá, though in the end they did not take part; and neither did the Panama Congress of 1826 produce the hoped-for league of Spanish American states. Bolívar's design for the congress, however, revealed his ambivalence toward the United States, whose institutions he admired in principle but considered unsuited to Latin American conditions and whose growing power he foresaw as a long-term threat. His interest in having British representation clearly reflected both his belief that British friendship was essential for the security and economic development of the new republics as well as his deep admiration for Great Britain and its system of constitutional monarchy.

Bolívar soon followed Sucre to Upper Peru, where he assumed provisional direction of the newly independent nation that was to name itself Bolivia in his honor. Bolívar did not stay there long, but when the Bolivians invited him to draft their first constitution, he gladly accepted. The proposal that he later submitted (in May 1826) had some progressive features, yet its centerpiece—a president serving for life with power to name his successor—aroused wide criticism as a disguised form of monarchy. Bolívar was gratified that both Bolivia and Peru adopted, at least briefly, the main lines of his scheme. However, his hope that Gran Colombia, too, would adopt some form of it was never realized.

Bolívar's interest in reforming Colombian institutions was heightened by the rebellion of Páez in April 1826 against the government of Santander. The Liberator returned home before the end of the year, settled Páez's rebellion with a sweeping pardon, and added his support to demands for an immediate reform of the constitution. These actions led to a conflict with Santander, who became a leader of the opposition to Bolívar at the constitutional reform convention that met at Ocaña from April to June 1828. When the sessions ended in deadlock, Bolívar's supporters called on him to assume dictatorial powers to "save the republic," and he agreed to do so.

As dictator, Bolívar rolled back many of the liberal reforms previously enacted in Gran Colombia, including a reduction in the number of monasteries and abolition of Indian tribute. He did not necessarily oppose the reforms in question; he merely decided they were premature. And he did not touch the free-birth law that Gran Colombia had adopted for gradual elimination of slavery.

Bolívar's dictatorship was bitterly opposed by the adherents of Santander, some of whom joined in the abortive September 1828 attempt to assassinate Bolívar. After that, political repression became harsher, and Santander was sent into exile, but scattered uprisings still broke out. Also, serious disaffection arose in Venezuela, which was ideologically the most liberal part of the country as well as generally resentful of being ruled from Bogotá. The last straw was an intrigue by Bolívar's cabinet to recruit a European prince to succeed him as constitutional monarch when the Liberator died or retired. Páez again rose in rebellion in late 1829, and this time Venezuela became a separate nation.

Another convention that met in Bogotá in January 1830 did produce a new constitution, but it could not stem dissolution of the union. Ailing and disheartened, Bolívar stepped down from the presidency in March 1830 and set off for self-imposed exile. He died at Santa Marta before he

Mural of Simón Bolívar, Venezuela, 2002. Bolívar remains to this day a symbol of independence throughout South America. © MACDUFF EVERTON/CORBIS

could board ship, though not before Ecuador seceded from the union and newly autonomous Venezuela prohibited its most famous son from setting foot on its soil.

Though at the end it seemed to Bolívar that his work had been in vain, he is revered today as the one person who made the greatest contribution to Spanish American independence. His contribution was not just military but also political, in the articulation of patriot objectives and the establishment of new states. Moreover, he has been claimed as a precursor by every ideological current, from the revolutionary Left (which admires him for his opposition to slavery and distrust of the United States) to the extreme Right (which approves his authoritarian tendencies): there is something about Bolívar to appeal to every taste and every age.

See also **Wars of Independence: South America.**

BIBLIOGRAPHY

The best English-Language biographies are Gerhard Masur, *Simón Bolívar* (1948; rev. ed 1969); the highly critical Salvador De Madariaga, *Bolívar* (1952; repr. 1979).

Augusto Mijares, *The Liberator,* translated by John Fisher (1983). Bolívar can be studied in his own words in *Selected Writings of Bolívar,* compiled by Vicente Lecuna, edited by Harold A. Bierck, Jr., translated by Lewis Bertrand, 2 vols. (1951), and in those of his Irish aide in Daniel F. O'Leary, *Bolívar and the War of Independence,* translated and edited by Robert F. McNerney, Jr. (1970). His campaigns are exhaustively covered in Vicente Lecuna, *Crónica razonada de las guerras de Bolívar,* 3 vols. (1950); and on his political ideas, Víctor Andrés Belaúnde, *Bolívar and the Political Thought of the Spanish American Revolution* (1938) is still useful. His relations with Europe and European perceptions of Bolívar are the subject of Alberto Filippi, ed., *Bolívar y Europa en las crónicas, el pensamiento político y la historiografía,* 2d ed. (1988). A special issue of the *Hispanic American Historical Review* 63, no. 1 (1983), contains essays by a group of specialists on particular aspects of his career. The subsequent image of

Bolívar is brilliantly analyzed in Germán Carrera Damas, *El culto a Bolívar* (1969).

Additional Bibliography

Bushnell, David. *Simón Bolívar: Hombre de Caracas, proyecto de América: Una biografía.* Buenos Aires: Editorial Biblos, 2002.

Elliott, J. H. *Empires of the Atlantic World: Britain and Spain in America, 1492-1830.* New Haven: Yale Univeristy Press, 2006.

Hernández Sánchez-Barba, Mario. *Simón Bolívar: Una passion política.* Barcelona: Ariel, 2004.

Rodríguez O., Jaime E. *The Independence of Spanish America.* Cambridge, U.K.: Cambridge University Press, 1998.

DAVID BUSHNELL

BOLIVIA

This entry includes the following articles:
THE COLONIAL PERIOD
SINCE 1825

THE COLONIAL PERIOD

CONQUEST AND SETTLEMENT

The first substantial Spanish incursion into the lands now called Bolivia took place in 1535, the year Diego de Almagro led his great expedition south from Peru toward Chile. On its way, the expedition passed over the high Bolivian plateau now known as the altiplano.

A little south of Cuzco, Almagro moved from Quechua-dominated territory into Aymara lands. Over the previous several centuries, the Aymara speakers had organized themselves into more than a dozen substantial polities. Prominent among these were the Colla, around the northern and western shores of Lake Titicaca, and the Lupaqa, great raisers of llamas on the southwest fringes of the lake. Two hundred and fifty miles southeast of Titicaca were the less rich and powerful Charca, whose name became attached to the Spanish highland region that developed around and south of the lake and embraced most of the Aymara peoples. The province of Charcas was the direct ancestor of modern Bolivia. (The highland region was also known up to about 1700 as the Provincias de Arriba, or "Upper Provinces," and after that as Alto Perú, or "Upper Peru.")

The Aymara polities had been incorporated into the Inca Empire about 1460, becoming the province named Collasuyo. But loss of independence brought surprisingly little change in politics, economy, and society. Extraction of tribute and the implantation of Quechua-speaking colonies (*mitmaq*)—for example, in the valleys of Cochabamba—were the main exceptions.

Permanent Spanish occupation of Aymara lands did not begin until 1538, and was facilitated by native conflicts. In that year, the Lupaqa, probably prompted by the anti-Spanish rebel leader Manco Inca, attacked the Colla. The Colla had been stubbornly pro-Spanish since the Inca war of succession, in which they had supported Huascar in his struggle against his brother Atahualpa. (Huascar had been assassinated by Atahualpa; the newly arrived Spaniards then propitiously executed the latter.) At the Lupaqa attack, the Colla called for Spanish help. The ranking Spanish leader in Cuzco, Hernando Pizarro, decided to oblige. A quick Spanish victory at the Desaguadero River, at the southern tip of Titacaca, opened the way into the remaining Aymara lands. Many Aymara yielded peacefully, but not all. In the eastern Andean ranges (now known as the Cordillera Real), the Chicha polity, encouraged by Manco's agents, led other Aymara in opposition. Late in 1538, a fierce battle ensued in the Cochabamba Valley, in which the Spanish, now under Gonzalo Pizarro, and a number of Incas loyal to them prevailed, though barely. By 19 March 1539, Gonzalo Pizarro was back in Cuzco, bringing with him Aymara leaders who had surrendered.

At about the same time, the Spaniards accomplished two other objectives in Aymara territory that had enduring effects. The first, the work of Pedro Anzures de Campo Redondo, a subordinate of the Pizarros, was the foundation, possibly in mid-1538, of Villa de Plata in a temperate valley 140 miles south of Cochabamba. This town, which soon became the city of La Plata (renamed Sucre in 1839), was the political and administrative capital of the colonial province of Charcas from 1559 until independence and then, to 1898, of the sovereign state of Bolivia. Its name, "Silver," reputedly commemorates a 1538 event of still greater moment for Bolivian history: the Spanish location, 70 miles

Colonial church, Laja, Bolivia. DAVID JOHNSON/CORBIS

southwest of the town's site, of the silver deposits of Porco, worked by the Incas and doubtless by the Aymara and others before them. The Pizarros immediately seized a major interest in Porco. Henceforth, "Charcas" became synonymous with silver.

That association was vastly strengthened in 1545 with the discovery of the Cerro Rico (Rich Hill) at Potosí, between Porco and La Plata. The mines of Rich Hill and of the area around Potosí yielded about half the silver produced by Spanish America from 1550 to 1650 and continued yielding abundantly until the 1890s. Potosí itself soon attracted tens of thousands of inhabitants, becoming before 1600, despite its altitude of over 13,000 feet, one of the three largest cities of Spanish America—matched only by Lima and Mexico City in size and wealth. Its growth conjured into existence, or at least stimulated the rise of, many smaller towns in the Bolivian highlands. One such town was La Paz, founded in 1548 some 40 miles southeast of the lower end of Titicaca. The aim here was to safeguard from native attack the increasingly important road linking Spanish Peru with Potosí, Porco, and La Plata. In due course La Paz became a large trading and agricultural center in its own right, the main Spanish city in northern Charcas, and, from the 1890s on, the de facto capital of Bolivia.

Among the areas that sold goods to Potosí were the eastern interior lowlands. Here, in conquest and settlement, there was a great contrast with the highlands, since the impetus had come from the southeast in a series of expeditions across the Gran Chaco from Paraguay between 1537 and 1547. The result, in 1561, was the foundation of the city of Santa Cruz de la Sierra, 160 miles northeast of La Plata, by ñuflo de Chávez. The city lay at the foot of the Andes' easternmost salient into the interior and was from the start the key Spanish center in lowland Charcas. It has grown in recent decades to rival La Paz in wealth and political influence.

While the native people of the plains posed little threat to Spanish settlement, those of the *montaña* region, the wide foothill zone east and southeast of La Plata, were a different matter. The Spaniards called them, generically, Chiriquanos. This expansive and bellicose culture, reportedly of Guaraní origin, proved as resistant to Spanish incursions as it had been to the Incas'. The threat it posed to the main Spanish centers in Charcas was contained by the founding of defensive frontier towns such as Tarija (1574) and Tomina (1575). But from mountain retreats the Chiriguanos continued to threaten until the end of the colonial period.

EARLY COLONIAL GOVERNMENT AND ECONOMY

The Chiriguanos were, however, only a small worm in the opulent apple of Charcas. Once the richness of Potosí became apparent, Spaniards flooded in, closely pursued by the Spanish state in the form of the Audiencia of Charcas. This blend of high court and governing council was formally created in 1558–1559, with its seat in La Plata. There it remained, the main administrative body of Charcas, until independence. Its jurisdiction embraced what is now Bolivia and large parts of present-day Chile, Peru, Paraguay, and Argentina. Within this vast territory arose several regional governorships, each to some degree independent of the audiencia. The only substantial one falling inside what is now Bolivia was that of Santa Cruz de la Sierra, created in the 1590s.

State influence in Charcas grew by another quantum leap in the 1570s with the arrival of Don Francisco de Toledo, fifth viceroy of Peru. Toledo is renowned for the five-year *Visita General* (general inspection) he made of the central part of his viceroyalty; half of the time (late 1572–mid-1575) was spent in Charcas. There, as in Peru itself, he directed the relocation (*reducción*) of native people to new communities, fewer and larger than their traditional ones. The aim here was multiple: to separate the people from their familiar surroundings, so that they could be more easily Hispanicized (in, for example, religion and civil government); to simplify organization of their labor; and to facilitate tribute collection. Many of the displaced people abandoned the new towns, but Toledo certainly achieved permanent disruption of old patterns. He reassessed tributes and generally redefined them as cash rather than kind for convenience of collection. This change forced Andeans to participate in the money economy of the Spanish world by selling either their goods or their labor for cash. Toledo also extended the reach of the state by introducing *corregidores* (district officers) to administer indigenous affairs in rural areas. He organized the founding of Cochabamba in 1570 or 1571, partly as a barrier against the Chiriguanos. The city then grew rapidly as the focus of a large and fertile farming region closely tied to the Potosí market.

It was in Potosí that Toledo wrought his best-remembered reforms. First he organized the notorious Mita, the system of forced labor that brought to Potosí each year, at least initially, more than 13,000 native men to work in mines and refineries. Forced labor had been sent to Potosí before Toledo's time; but he systematized and enlarged the practice (see also slavery). Many *mita* workers, with their families, stayed in Potosí after their year of service was over, adding to its population. Others left but did not return home. For various reasons they preferred to join the swelling number of displaced people that was one notable outcome of Spanish colonial practices throughout the central Andes in the sixteenth century.

Toledo's other major effort at Potosí was to promote the refining of ores by amalgamation with mercury. The technique, developed in Mexico about 1555, had been slow to reach the Andes, though it was poised for advance there when Toledo decided to push it forward. He first stimulated mercury production at Huancavelica, southeast of Lima. Then he encouraged experts to demonstrate the method in Potosí. The outcome of this innovation, allied with cheap and plentiful *mita* labor, was a phenomenal boom that reached its peak in 1592. But the gain was at great cost to the native people. Not only were they uprooted and forced into dangerous work at low pay but they were driven from the central role they had played in silver production. Expensive refining mills were needed to make amalgamation profitable, and such investment was beyond the Indians' capacity.

By 1600, the best ores at Potosí had been mined, though vast quantities of lesser material remained. This depletion led to a search for new silver deposits all over highland Charcas. The richest discovery was at a site on the altiplano 120 miles southeast of La Paz. The ores proved so good and plentiful that in 1607 a new town, Oruro, was created nearby. Production there never equaled Potosí at its peak, but it remained important. Other

Miners panning for gold in a Bolivian river, undated engraving. Mining, which relied on the forced labor of native workers, played a significant part of the economy of colonial Bolivia. © BETTMANN/CORBIS

and lesser deposits were briefly exploited around Potosí throughout the seventeenth century. Their effect was only briefly to interrupt the downward trend of the district's output. By the early 1700s, production had returned to the levels of the 1560s (pre-*mita* and pre-amalgamation). It stayed there until the 1740s, when a 1736 reduction from a fifth to a tenth in the royalty taken by the Crown on silver production and a later increase in the labor impositions on the *mita* workers spurned a modest recovery, which lasted the rest of the century.

Whatever the fluctuations in silver output, the mining towns (above all Potosí) needed food and multitudinous other goods. This led, from about 1550 on, to the articulation of a vast economic zone to supply their requirements. The valleys around Cochabamba, and Mizque to the southeast of it, were early and lasting examples of these backward linkages from mining. Their livelihood depended on sales of maize, wheat, sugar, and livestock in Potosí. The Yungas (steep valleys) east of La Paz on the inland Andean slopes became a prime source of coca for the mines; though coca also came to Potosí from far more distant areas near Cuzco. On the lands around Lake Titicaca the ancient tradition of llama breeding continued, now directed particularly to the freighting of ores and the raw materials of silver production. What is now northwest Argentina grew in settlement before 1600 in response to the demand for its products—cotton cloth, mules, sugar, wine—in the mining zone. Possibly half or more of the silver drawn from the mines went to buying supplies through a far-flung network of interregional trade.

EARLY COLONIAL SOCIETY

Most of the supplies that went to mining towns were produced on land owned by colonists, not communal holdings. By the 1560s, *chacras* (small farms) had appeared, for example, in the deep valleys around Potosí. And over the next century haciendas (larger estates) developed in the more fertile regions of Charcas, especially in the eastern middle-altitude valleys. Some of the lands taken for *chacras* and haciendas had fallen free because of native population losses, caused by newly introduced diseases and the general disruption of the Conquest and its aftermath of settlement. The population decline in some parts of highland Charcas between the 1570s and the 1680s reached almost 60 percent and had probably been severe before 1570 as well.

Some of the record loss, it is true, was the result of movement of people rather than of deaths or lack of births. Migrants (*mitayos*) were hard, sometimes even impossible, to count. Many left their original villages to escape tribute and *mita,* going to cities and towns (such as Potosí), to estates and farms owned by colonists, or to other native communities (where they would be classed as Forasteros, or outsiders, and as such, under Spanish law, exempted from forced labor and tribute). Migrants provided much of the labor needed by Spanish landowners and by miners outside Potosí, since hardly any *mitayos* were sent to the district mines.

Native community life survived despite all the pressures applied to it, as a visitor to highland Bolivia can see today. Nine-tenths of Charcas's people remained rural, and nearly all of them were peasants who spoke only their indigenous language. Viceroy Toledo had ordered that the *reducciones* into which he tried to congregate these people in the 1570s should have a Spanish style of town government, with aldermen, magistrates, constables, and the like. But these positions generally went to the same sort of men who had held authority before the Conquest: the responsible and conservative elders of the communities. Similarly, the *curacas* (regional nobles) of pre-Spanish times continued to exist and to exercise authority. They generally had power over several villages, with rights to use community labor and lands. From the start they were crucial to Spanish control of native society, acting as links between colonial officials and local village leaders. Their position was often hard. They might be obliged, for example, to produce a constant yield of tribute or draft laborers from a shrinking population; they would have to make up any

shortfall themselves. Under such pressures, *curacas* might maltreat their own people or partially Hispanicize themselves by engaging in profit-oriented trade or market agriculture to gain the cash they needed to meet Spanish demands. Thus, in the long term, old social and political relationships tended to change and weaken. But native institutions were resilient; and, suitably adapted to new demands, a distinct Andean culture was still in place when the colonial era ended.

Long before then, however, Charcas had taken on a clear identity of its own in several respects besides the native. The wealth and urban growth associated with mining gave it high status in Spanish America. In 1609, for instance, the see of La Plata was raised to an archbishopric, becoming junior in South America only to Lima. (No other archdiocese was created anywhere else in the Indies before 1700). Four years before, bishoprics had been created in La Paz and Santa Cruz de la Sierra, which now became suffragan, along with Tucumán and Asunción, to La Plata. In 1624 the city of La Plata added to its cathedral and audiencia the University of San Francisco Xavier, where Jesuits trained priests and, after 1681, lawyers, for much of southern South America.

Despite the decline of mining, there was much building and decoration of churches in Charcas in the seventeenth century. A growing number of Amerindian and mestizo craftsmen participated in this work, and distinctive styles took shape. For instance, in 1592 a sculptor named Tito Yupanqui made the famous image of the Virgin that has remained the object of such devotion at Copacabana, at the southern end of Titicaca. By 1700, clear schools of native and mestizo painting were emerging in La Plata, Potosí, and the La Paz–Titicana region (the Colla school). The painters' subjects were mainly devotional.

THE EIGHTEENTH CENTURY
Broadly speaking, the eighteenth century in Upper Peru saw the reversal of trends established after 1600. Silver production at Potosí stopped falling about 1725 and began to rise again at mid-century. (Oruro's low point had in fact come in 1660–1680; after that its output gently rose for a century.) Native population stabilized, probably after a devastating epidemic of influenza or pneumonic

plague that spread from Buenos Aires up into the central Andes in 1719–1720. Generally, thereafter, rural peasant populations grew, though the population of the Spanish-dominated towns languished for much of the century, reflecting the weakness of mining and hence of the demand for supplies in the mining centers. The exception was La Paz, which, thanks to its governmental and marketing role amid a relatively dense native population, continued to grow, though slowly. By 1750 it was, with 40,000 people, the largest town in Upper Peru.

Among the most notable reversals in the eighteenth century was the reimposition of state power. Charcas, like most of Spanish America, had since about 1600, been under ever less effective Spanish control. Like most of the empire, it felt a revived presence of the state once the Bourbons came to power in 1700. The first serious sign came in the late 1720s with the *revisita* (recount) of the population ordered by the viceroy, the marqués de Castelfuerte (1724–1736). Castelfuerte's aim was, first, to find out how much of the central Andean population had died in the epidemic of 1719–1720, and, second, with this new count, to improve the collection of Indian tribute, which, he rightly thought, had become slack and corrupt.

The full weight of reform did not fall on Upper Peru until much later in the century. The greatest change of all came in 1776, when the province was shifted from the Viceroyalty of Peru into the newly formed Viceroyalty of Río de la Plata. Now its exports and imports passed largely through Buenos Aires, and internal trade patterns also changed, reorienting southward. In 1784 the centralizing system of local government by intendants was installed, replacing the rule by *corregidores* put in place by Toledo. Now Upper Peru was divided into four intendancies: La Paz, Cochabamba, Potosí, and Chuquisaca (La Plata). The Spanish government also tried to stimulate mining by, for example, taking over the mining bank, the Banco De San Carlos, in Potosí, improving the supply of mercury, and sending in foreign experts to demonstrate (unsuccessfully, in the event) new refining methods.

A rash of revolts throughout the central Andes was one outcome of this growing state presence after 1700. In Upper Peru the first outbreak occurred at Cochabamba in November 1730, when mestizos, who were exempt from tribute, took

General Rodil surrendering to Simón Bolívar, undated illustration. Independence in the region was achieved gradually as the Spanish were defeated in battle after battle and royalist support evaporated. © BETTMANN/CORBIS

exception to Castelfuerte's attempt to increase tribute income by reclassifying them as Indians. The mestizos were encouraged by creoles (American-born white settlers), who had their own grievances against Spaniards. The anti-Spanish alliance of different classes and ethnic groups was even more striking in the Oruro plot of 1739, a creole and mestizo reaction to increasing taxation. The leader, Juan Vélez de Córdoba, claimed descent from the Incas. The plotters' manifesto promised a restoration of the Inca monarchy, with equality for creoles, mestizos, and Indians, and abolition of tributes, *mita* (draft) labor, and *reparto* (the forced sale) of goods to Indians by *corregidores*. The Oruro plot, like the earlier disturbance at Cochabamba, was easily put down. But the Oruro manifesto, a true rebel program, may have been an inspiration for the far more widespread rebellion led by Túpac Amaru in Peru in 1780–1781.

That great and menacing movement—a reaction in the short term to a recent increase in sales tax, the creation of internal customshouses that imposed taxes and restrictions on interregional trade, and the abuses of *reparto,* which had been legalized in 1756—was centered just south of Cuzco. This rebellion was followed by a derivative revolt in Upper Peru, led by a native trader named Julián Apasa, who took the pseudonym Túpac Catari. Apasa laid siege to La Paz in 1781 before he was captured by Spanish forces late in that year. In the same year a creole movement, with strong links to Túpac Amaru and allied with local Indians and mestizos, took Oruro out of Spanish control. This insurrection, too, was put down by the end of 1781.

INDEPENDENCE

The risings of 1781 in Upper Peru, like that of Túpac Amaru farther north, were not bids for independence. However, they did demonstrate the strong aversion to the state's increasing exactions that became the fundamental motive for the pursuit of independence three and four decades later. Bolivia's advance to independence was set in motion, like the other Spanish American movements, by Napoleon's invasion of Spain in 1808. The Bourbon monarchy was unseated; political disarray descended on Spain and the empire. In the confusion, a group of radical creoles in La Paz, led by Pedro Domingo Murillo, decided to make a bid for autonomy. In July 1809, the group declared itself to be a governing junta ruling in the name of Ferdinand VII. The movement never had time to prove the authenticity of this allegiance; it was suppressed by the end of January 1810 by troops sent in from Peru. Still, this had been the first declaration of independence in Spanish America, and Bolivians remember Murillo proudly.

After this defeat, events proceeded much more slowly. Bolivia was the last Spanish mainland territory to become independent. The problem was twofold. First, the proximity of Peru, which was the Spanish stronghold in South America, made for easy suppression of dissidence in Upper Peru, as the Murillo episode had shown. Second, the government of the Río de la Plata (the incipient Argentina), where home rule was permanently achieved in 1810, had long sought to bring Upper Peru under its control. Buenos Aires therefore sent no fewer than four expeditionary forces into Upper Peru between 1810 and 1817. Although these found many local allies against Spanish forces from Peru, the Upper Peruvians had little enthusiasm for rule from Buenos Aires, so no lasting anti-Spanish alliance developed. The result was much fighting in and over Upper Peru for several years, and much loss of life and property, without conclusive change. Matters were not advanced by the activities of several dozen *caudillos* (pro-independence local leaders) who between 1810 and 1816 fought guerrilla style outside the towns.

After 1816, destruction and exhaustion greatly hindered further internal bids for freedom; and Buenos Aires finally realized that Chile would be a better assault route on Peru. Resistance to Spain therefore dwindled in the province until 1823, when a mestizo from near La Paz, Andrés de Santa Cruz, once a royalist officer and now an independence leader under Antonio José de Sucre, Bolívar's chief lieutenant, inflicted defeats on the Spanish at Zepita and elsewhere in the north. The Spanish were able to dislodge Santa Cruz, but by this time Bolívar's Venezuelan and Colombian forces were assembling in Peru, and the writing was on the wall. In 1824 Bolívar and Sucre defeated the Spanish twice in Peru, at Junín and at Ayacucho. After these victories there remained only a shadow of royalist resistance in Upper Peru. Royalist troops in fact deserted to Sucre as he entered the region in January 1825. Thus freedom came quietly and anticlimactically to the country that in August 1825 would call itself Bolivia after the man responsible for its final liberation.

See also **Almagro, Diego de.**

BIBLIOGRAPHY

Arthur F. Zimmerman, *Francisco de Toledo, Fifth Victory of Peru, 1569–1581* (1938, repr. 1968).

Charles Arnade, *The Emergence of the Republic of Bolivia* (1957).

Eduardo Arze Quiroga, *Historia de Bolivia. Fases del proceso hispanoamericano: Orígenes de la sociedad boliviana en el siglo XVI* (1969).

John Hemming, *The Conquest of the Incas* (1970).

Josep M. Barnadas, *Charcas: Orígenes históricos de una sociedad colonial, 1535–1565* (1973).

Bartolomé Arzáns De Orsúa y Vela, *Tales of Potosí,* edited by R. C. Padden (1975).

Orlando Capriles Villazón, *Historia de la minería boliviana* (1977).

Nicolás Sánchez-Albornoz, *Indios y tributos en el Alto Perú* (1978).

Herbert S. Klein, *Bolivia: The Evolution of a Multi-Ethnic Society* (1982).

Scarlett O'Phelan Godoy, *Rebellions and Revolts in Eighteenth-Century Peru and Upper Peru* (1985).

Thérèse Bouysse Cassagne, *La identidad aymara: Aproximación histórica (siglo XV, XVI)* (1987).

Olivia Harris, Brooke Larson, and Enrique Tandeter, comp., *La Participación indígena en los mercados surandinos: Estrategias y reproducción social, siglos XVI a XX* (1987).

Brooke Larson, *Colonialism and Agrarian Transformation in Bolivia: Cochabamba, 1150–1900* (1988).

Roger N. Rasnake, *Domination and Cultural Resistance: Authority and Power Among an Andean People* (1988).

Additional Bibliography

Escobari de Querejazu, Laura. *Caciques, yanaconas y extravagantes: la sociedad colonial en Charcas s. XVI-XVIII.* La Paz: Embajada de España en Bolivia: Plural Editores, 2001.

Gutiérrez Brockington, Lolita. *Blacks, Indians, and Spaniards in the Eastern Andes: Reclaiming the Forgotten in Colonial Mizque, 1550–1782.* Lincoln: University of Nebraska Press, 2006.

Mangan, Jane E. *Trading Roles: Gender, Ethnicity, and the Urban Economy in Colonial Potosí.* Durham, NC: Duke University Press, 2005.

Serulnikov, Sergio. *Subverting Colonial Authority: Challenges to Spanish Rule in Eighteenth-Century Southern Andes.* Durham, NC: Duke University Press, 2003.

Zulawski, Ann. *They Eat from their Labor: Work and Social Change in Colonial Bolivia.* Pittsburgh, PA: University of Pittsburgh Press, 1995.

PETER BAKEWELL

SINCE 1825

Bolivian history after independence can be characterized as primarily a struggle to integrate the extremely diverse country into a cohesive whole. Three basic issues defined this struggle: first, the way in which indigenous peoples participated in the political and economic life of the country; second, export-oriented trade versus internal economic development; and third, the extension of the Creole-led state into the sparsely inhabited frontier areas.

Bolivia was in many ways an artificial creation, as were virtually all other states in Spanish America. Antonio José de Sucre, the Venezuelan-born patriot general who favored an independent upper Peruvian state, effectively appealed to Simón Bolívar's vanity by naming the new polity after the Liberator. Bolivian leaders could only point to the rather flexible jurisdiction of the colonial high court, the Audiencia of Charcas, as the basis for the new state. Indeed, the events that spawned the Bolivians' sense of separateness took place only a few decades before independence. First, the Spanish crown's decision in 1776 to split Upper Peru from the Viceroyalty of Lima and to integrate the territory into the new Viceroyalty of Buenos Aires severed ties with the rest of Peru. Then, despite the early efforts of Bolivian patriot forces during the Wars of Independence, the Audiencia of Charcas remained a bastion of royalism and so became separated from independence-minded Argentina.

BOLIVARIAN DREAMS

When patriot forces under Sucre's command finally liberated Upper Peru, the region had been wracked by almost sixteen years of civil war. Despite the flooded silver mines, the periodic looting of the royal mint by patriot and royalist forces, and the devastated countryside, Bolivia was one of the most powerful and prosperous countries in South America. It had large numbers of tribute-paying Andean peasants, access to silver (albeit on a reduced scale in comparison with that of the colonial period), and a relatively stable centralized government during the first few decades after independence. Sucre's presidency (1825–1828), though brief, brought about administrative reforms and anticlerical legislation, wresting away much of the power of the Catholic Church.

Andrés de Santa Cruz, another warrior from the independence wars, ruled Bolivia for ten years (1829–1839). He felt powerful enough to recreate the Bolivarian dream of a union of Spanish American republics by annexing Jujuy, the northernmost province of Argentina, and by creating the Peru-Bolivian Confederation (1836–1839). Under the confederation, Peru was divided into a northern and a southern section, with Bolivia remaining whole. Internal opposition forces, both Peruvian and Bolivian, and the invasion by Chile destroyed these plans and led to Santa Cruz's downfall.

Unlike the decades-long attempts to reconstitute larger political units, the social and economic reality of Bolivia quickly set limits to the liberal idealism of the patriot generals who took over the

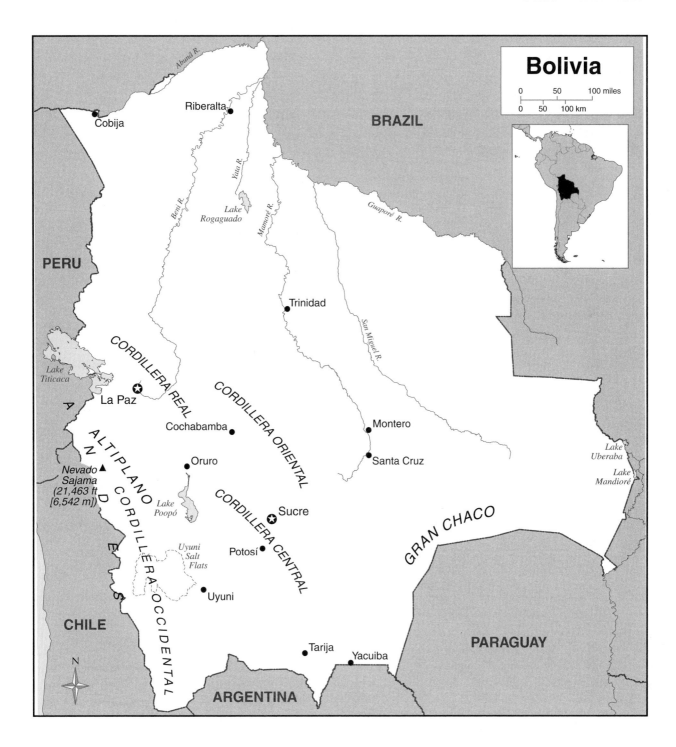

new country's government. Despite a number of economic missions by British agents, the London stock market crash of 1825 eliminated the promised large investments slated to revitalize the mining industry. Local elites and southern import-export merchants financed most mining activity but were unable to come up with the huge sums required to reactivate on any large scale the colonial silver mines. Indeed, without the effective state

subsidies of the colonial Mita (forced Indian mine labor), abolished at independence, mining activity only sporadically paid off.

The most vibrant part of the economy rested on the shoulders of the Andean peasants, who in many ways controlled the economic pulse of the nation. As urban centers lost population, the rural economy took on greater importance, and trade, often

Bolivia

Population:	9,119,152 (2007 est.)
Area:	424,164 sq mi
Official languages:	Spanish, Quechua, Aymara.
National currency:	Boliviano
Principal religions:	Roman Catholic, 95%; Protestant, 5%.
Ethnicity:	Quechua, 30%; mestizo, 30%; Aymara, 25%; white, 15%.
Capital:	La Paz (administrative capital); Sucre (constitutional capital)
Other urban centers:	Cochabamba, Oruro, Potosí, Santa Cruz
Annual rainfall:	Rainfall is plentiful in the northeast but decreases to the west and south.
Principal geographical features:	*Mountains:* Cordillera Occidental and Cordillera Oriental ranges of the Andes. *Rivers:* Beni, Guaporé, Madre de Dios, Manoré, Pilcomayo *Lakes:* Titicaca, Poopó *Other:* The high Altiplano plateau between the Cordillera Occidental and Cordillera Oriental makes up roughly 28% of the country and ishome to more than half the population.
Economy:	*GDP per capita:* $3,100 (2006 est.)
Principal products and exports:	*Agricultural:* coffee, cotton, soybeans, sugar *Mining:* natural gas, petroleum, tin, zinc
Government:	Bolivia gained independence from Spain in 1825. The government is a republic, lead by a president who is both head of state andhead of government. The bicameral legislature is elected through a mix of direct and proportional party list elections, and consists of a 27-seat Chamber of Senators and a 130-seat Chamber of Deputies.
Armed forces:	Males as young as age 14 can be conscripted when there are insufficient volunteers to meet recruitment goals. *Army:* 25,000 *Navy:* 3,500 *Air force:* 3,000 *Paramilitary:* 31,100 national police and 6,000 narcotics police
Transportation:	*Rail:* 2,177 mi *Ports:* Puerto Aguirre *Roads:* 2,329 mi paved; 36,493 mi unpaved *National airline:* Lloyd Aéreo Boliviano *Airports:* 16 paved, over 1,100 unpaved; international airports in La Paz and Santa Cruz
Media:	13 newspapers, including *El Diario, La Razon, El Deber, Los Tiempos,* and *El Mundo.* 171 AM and 73 FM radio stations. 48 television stations including one government station.
Literacy and education:	*Total literacy rate:* 86.7% (2001) Eight years of education for children are compulsory and free of charge. There are 33 universities, including the University of San Andrés and the University of San Francisco Xavier.

crossing national boundaries, depended largely on the participation of the indigenous population. Even export activities, such as silver mining and wool, depended heavily on Indians for transport and the provision of foodstuffs and other goods, including most of the wool itself.

The Bolivian state treasury also depended largely on the Indians. Although Bolívar had abolished tribute payments in 1824 and again in 1825 and had decreed that Indian community lands should be distributed among the peasants and the surplus land sold, these laws were never implemented. The communities continued to control between one-third and three-quarters of all lands in the highlands, the most densely populated regions of the country. Already under the Sucre administration a uniform tax on all citizens had to be abandoned and Indian tribute reinstituted under a different name, the *contribucíon indígenal.* Santa Cruz formalized this arrangement, for tribute was one of the few constant sources of income that, unlike taxes on mining and trade, did not fluctuate substantially. Tribute payments thus provided the resources for Santa Cruz to project Bolivian power beyond its own borders and help create temporarily his version of the Bolivarian pan–Spanish American union.

During this period, governments were also concerned with securing the far-flung Bolivian frontiers. On the eastern frontiers, toward the densely forested slopes and plains of the Amazon and Chaco basins, Santa Cruz fostered the growth of small-scale cattle ranching through liberal land grants. To the west, in the bone-dry Atacama Desert, the Sucre and Santa Cruz administrations invested heavily in developing ports, particularly Cobija, that would provide access to world markets and goods from European countries. The lack of water and later, under the Peru-Bolivian Confederation, the natural advantages of the Peruvian port of Arica condemned these efforts to eventual failure.

Thus, on balance, the first two decades of Bolivian independence were positive. Bolivia remained a militarily powerful force and had a relatively stable and efficient government. However, an economy based largely on internal trade, the relatively low productivity of silver mines, and the predominance of Indian communities made for relatively slow growth.

POLITICAL STRIFE, 1841–1880

The battle of Ingaví (1841), in which Bolivian forces led by José Ballivián vanquished the invading Peruvian army under Agustín Gamarra, was a turning point in Bolivian history, showing the futility of the Bolivarian goal of establishing supranational political units. Ballivían, who proceeded to rule Bolivia from 1841 to 1847, was more concerned with domestic matters. He attended to expanding control of the eastern lowland regions, creating the Beni Department out of the northeastern section of the country. Ballivián also financed expeditions into the Chaco region and construction of a series of fortresses against the Chiriguano and Chaco tribes, the most serious military threat of the southeastern frontier. Later regimes continued many of these policies and extended the eastern frontier significantly through the use of Franciscan missions, fortresses, and land grants to military veterans.

Ballivián's fall in 1847 brought about increasing political strife. Even those presidents who were able to hold on to power were constantly threatened by new uprisings. The most important political figures of the period, Manuel Isidoro Belzú (1848–1855), José María Linares (1857–1861), and Mariano Melgarejo (1864–1870), repeatedly had to suppress uprisings to remain in power. Belzú's regime fostered internal production, and his power resided in the urban artisans and, to a lesser extent, the Indian community. Despite Belzú's political support among protectionist artisans and Indians, this period is marked by the rise of the export-oriented silver-mining economy and, closely related, the triumph of liberal and free-trade policies.

During the 1850s new entrepreneurs took over the ailing silver mines of central and southern Bolivia. Most were merchants connected to Chilean interests, which provided some capital. These new owners modernized the machinery and mining methods, improved production, and brought about steady export growth. In the 1870s silver and nitrate production grew rapidly on the Pacific coast, but this activity from the start was dominated by Chileans, both as mine owners and workers. The growth of export activities strengthened the hand of liberals, who saw free trade as a way to compete effectively on world markets. This was especially true of the new freedom to export silver ore, which previously had to be sold to the state mint.

The growing strength of liberal ideologues can be seen even during the notorious regime of Mariano Melgarejo, when the government used liberal ideology to justify many abusive policies. Both Brazil and Chile were beneficiaries of new treaties that gave away Bolivian territory for little or no compensation. More important, legislation in 1866 and 1868 authorized the first systematic attacks on Indian community lands. Community members were to purchase their own fields within a ninety-day period, otherwise the land would be sold to the highest bidder. Melgarejo's army brutally crushed Indian resistance and, in the south at least, creoles permanently wrested away many community lands. In the more heavily Indian north, Melgarejo's cronies and relatives usurped even more land, but during the massive Indian rebellion of 1869–1870 that helped topple the caudillo's regime, the communities repossessed most of their fields by force.

As a result of the political turmoil in the country, the Pacific coast region had been virtually ignored. The substantial economic growth of the region remained poorly controlled by the Bolivian governments. Instead, Chilean interests dominated the region. Finally in the 1870s Bolivia attempted to counteract Chilean power by allying itself closely with Peru. A dispute over taxing the riches of the Atacama Desert precipitated a Chilean invasion in 1879. Even with the aid of Peruvian forces the allies lost quickly and decisively. After only a few months of combat Bolivia had lost its coastal region and thereafter remained essentially sidelined from the war while the Chileans concentrated on destroying the Peruvian military and occupying that country. Thus the period of internal strife and caudillo rule after the battle of Ingaví had disastrous consequences. Bolivia lost much of its territory and, with the application of liberal policies to promote corrupt practices, also much of its economic and military power.

REIGN OF THE SILVER OLIGARCHY, 1880–1899

The War of the Pacific completely discredited the military and its caudillos, permitting the silver-mining interests to take power directly. This period also marks the beginning of a two-party system, in which ideologies became more important than the personal charisma of party leaders. The Liberal Party followed liberal precepts such as restricting the power of the Catholic Church; it also was in favor of continuing the war with Chile. However, from 1880 to the end of the century the Conservative (or Constitutionalist) Party, representing the Sucre-based silver-mining oligarchy, ruled the country. The Conservatives elected the most important silver miners as their presidential candidates, and they imposed an essentially liberal model of economic development on the country. Their program consisted of four planks: the encouragement of free trade; the creation of a railroad network facilitating the export of minerals; the creation of a rural land market through the abolition of Indian communities; and, in an effort to prevent a reoccurrence of the War of the Pacific fiasco, the development of frontier regions by promoting missions and the sale of land grants.

The Conservatives' program was generally successful, though it did not benefit all sectors of the population equally. For example, the war with Chile and the advent of free trade turned the elites of the southernmost department, Tarija, from contrabandists into important merchants who supplied imports to the silver mines of southern Potosí as well as to the rapidly expanding Chaco frontier. The mine owners also gained as a result of a vigorous railroad building program, financed largely by Chile, which connected the silver mines with the Pacific coast and so drove down transportation costs. At the same time, however, the combination of cheap transport to the coast with no improvements in internal communications hurt Bolivian agrarian interests, because the fertile valleys were not connected to the highland mining areas. The railroads harmed regions such as the fertile Cochabamba Valley, which could not compete with the import of cheap foodstuffs over the railroads.

Efforts to populate the frontiers also met with only limited success. The state put frontier territory up for sale in large units but at low prices per hectare. Despite the obligation of grantees to live on the land or bring in families to live on the grants, few actually followed the letter of the law. Instead, huge tracts came under the control of largely absentee landowners. As a result, frontier development took place in a limited manner; only extensive agriculture such as cattle ranching took up vast extents of fertile land.

This period also marks the subjection of tribal peoples who had remained largely outside the state's jurisdiction. The most important group, the Chiriguanos, more than 100,000 strong, finally submitted to the frontier colonists after numerous engagements in the southeastern Andean foothills. The wars of 1874–1877 and the messianic uprising of 1892 led to the defeat of the Chiriguano forces, the killing of many warriors, the enslavement of women and children, and the distribution of Chiriguano land among the victors. Only the Franciscan missions of the region provided some refuge, but even they over the long run changed indigenous culture substantially.

The situation of indigenous peoples in the highlands also degenerated. The abolition of Indian communities, legislated in 1874 but not implemented until 1880, adversely affected the indigenous population in the highlands. After the plots of each individual community member were measured, the land became available for sale. Most commonly, purchasers used methods such as getting the Indians into debt (by advancing money to pay for their land titles), outright fraud, or coercion to acquire parcels of community land. In the south, Indians sold only small portions of their total holdings at any one time; but this also significantly weakened the communities over the long term. In northern Potosí, Oruro, and elsewhere, communities remained virtually intact. As earlier, the attack on Indian lands was strongest in the north, around La Paz and Lake Titicaca. There, whole communities lost their lands, and the purchasers, mainly elites from La Paz and the surrounding towns, turned the Indians into peons of the newly formed haciendas.

The animosity of the highland Indians toward government land-sale policies helped tip the balance against the Conservatives in the Federalist War (1898–1899). When the deputies from Sucre rammed through legislation in 1898 that would keep the capital permanently in that city, the deputies from La Paz walked out and conspired with the opposition Liberal Party to overthrow the Conservative regime. The Conservatives, tied so closely to the silver-mine owners, were already weakened, for the declining price of silver had precipitated a severe financial crisis for the government.

That same year the city of La Paz rose in revolt under the aegis of the Federalist and Liberal parties. The Liberals also urged the Indian communities of the Altiplano, under the leadership of Zárate Willka, to rebel. In turn, the Liberals promised relief from the land usurpations. With the Altiplano under the control of the Indians, the Conservative army was unable to advance much past Oruro. In the final battle, the Indians and the *paceño* (La Paz residents) forces under Liberal General José Manuel Pando beat the Conservatives. Willka, however, massacred a detachment of Liberal troops and declared war on all whites. The creoles united and beat Willka's forces. In turn, Pando and the Liberals did not honor their agreement with the Federalists other than to make La Paz the de facto capital. Thus, the Federalist War marked the end of Conservative Party dominance, the transfer of the capital from Sucre to La Paz, and a shift away from silver as the principal export.

THE TIN BOOM, 1900–1932

Fortuitously for Bolivia a new product, tin, rapidly took the place of silver as the principal export. Using the railroad system built for silver export as well as Chilean, British, and North American capital, tin production expanded quickly during the first decades of the twentieth century. Like the silver-mining oligarchy, the three most important tin miners were Bolivian nationals. Indeed, the Aramayo family was able to make the transition from silver to tin. The other major tin miners were Mauricio Hochschild and Simón Patiño. Patiño clearly dominated, controlling about 50 percent of the total exports from the early twentieth century to the nationalization of mines in 1952. The mining of tin required much larger infusions of capital than silver, however, and the most important tin miners closely allied themselves with U.S.,

British, or French companies. Patiño's main backer was National Lead, headquartered in the United States. In conjunction with this company, Patiño by the 1920s had extended his holdings to British smelting works and Malaysian tin mines. His Bolivian holdings became only a small portion of his business empire.

The tin boom brought unheard-of prosperity to the northern part of Bolivia. La Paz replaced Sucre as Bolivia's financial center, and many of the city's elite participated in the tin boom. The continued sale of Indian community land helped foster this boom atmosphere, for many elite *paceños* purchased large extents of community lands to use as collateral for shares in mining ventures. Thus, notwithstanding Liberal promises to stop the usurpation of community lands and the Altiplano Indians' decisive participation in the Liberal victory during the Federalist War, the sale of community lands increased during the two decades of Liberal Party dominance.

As during the Conservative epoch, the north was more affected than the southern regions of the Bolivian highlands. Only the Indian rebellions of Jesús de Machaca (1921) and Chayanta (1927), although brutally repressed by the army, convinced the government to make the acquisition of Indian lands much more difficult. By the 1920s, however, the haciendas had expanded to encompass two-thirds of the highlands; only one-third remained in the hands of the Indians. This almost exactly reversed the land-holding patterns of forty years earlier. The expansion of the haciendas at the expense of the Indian communities marginalized the highland Indian from mainstream society and the national economy, a process that was reversed only in the middle of the twentieth century. Also, the integration of large numbers of previously free Bolivian peasants into haciendas caused much resentment. The relatively recent usurpation of their land helped create a climate of resistance that would combine with other factors to bring about widespread rebellion in the 1940s and 1950s.

The indigenous peoples of the eastern Bolivian frontiers did not fare much better than those in the highlands. The Amazonian rubber boom (1871–1912) greatly affected those living in the northeastern quarter of the country. There, virtual slaving expeditions provided the rubber barons with laborers to work in the jungle. In 1905 a Brazilian-aided rebellion in the northeastern jungles of the Acre region brought about the loss of that rubber-rich territory to Brazil despite General José M. Pando's personal efforts to suppress the uprising. As a result, the Liberal administration eased requirements for the purchase of frontier lands, thereby alienating vast amounts of tribal lands. The anticlerical government also restricted frontier missions and began to secularize many; because colonists almost immediately displaced the mission Indians from their land, many indigenous peoples were prevented from doing anything but becoming hacienda peons on the frontier. In addition, the Liberals reorganized frontier territories, which they began to militarize. Relations between the army and the indigenous peoples on the frontier were never good; the poorly disciplined soldiers in the tiny frontier forts usually enforced the rule of the large frontier landholders and in so doing did not endear themselves to the Indians. Frontier economic development projects by foreign companies, such as the vast land grant to a German merchant firm around the secularized Franciscan missions of Villa Montes, only brought about the alienation of lands with little actual development.

Serious opposition to the Liberal regime developed only after 1914, when a dissident group of Liberals formed the Republican Union. This was also a reaction to Ismael Montes, undisputed leader of the Liberals and twice president of Bolivia (1904–1909, 1913–1917), whose autocratic style antagonized fellow politicians during the brief but severe downturn in the Bolivian economy at the beginning of World War I.

Convinced that the Liberals would not give up power through peaceful means, the Republicans revolted successfully in 1920, remaining in power until 1934. Republican leaders generally carried out policies similar to those of the Liberals but were also more responsive to lower-class demands. This resulted in some contradictory behavior. Republicans were as beholden to the tin interests as the Liberals. Although President Saavedra Mallea (1921–1925) created the first rudimentary labor and social legislation, he also permitted the 1923 massacre of mine workers and their families in Uncía. Likewise, although the sale of Indian community lands virtually ended when the Republicans took over, the army under the Hernando

Siles Reyes government (1926–1930) killed hundreds of Indians during the Chayanta uprising of 1927.

The militarization of the Chaco frontier also became problematic when, after 1927, armed clashes between the small frontier garrisons of Bolivian and Paraguayan soldiers became increasingly frequent. Indeed, Republican president Daniel Salamanca's decision to launch an offensive against Paraguayan positions in 1932 started the Chaco War (1932–1935), which led to a costly defeat and initiated a process that would result in the 1952 revolution, the second twentieth-century social revolution (after Mexico) in Latin America.

THE CHACO WAR AND ITS AFTERMATH, 1932–1952

In the beginning of the Chaco War, it appeared that the German-trained Bolivian army would easily beat the poorly outfitted Paraguayan forces. This was almost certainly Salamanca's calculation. He was an intense nationalist who was coming under increasing domestic pressure when the Great Depression wiped out large parts of the Bolivian economy. But the Bolivians faced severe supply problems, poor military leadership, a heavy reliance on mobilized highland Indians who were unaccustomed to the lowland heat and dense underbrush, and the hostility of the poorly treated indigenous peoples in the Chaco. Consequently, they suffered defeat after defeat at the hands of the much better adapted Paraguayan forces. Only in 1935 was the Bolivian military able to reverse the tide of war and win back at least the oil-bearing Andean foothills around Villa Montes.

By the end of the war the Bolivian army had lost a quarter (65,000) of its soldiers, a huge number out of a total population of about 2 million inhabitants. The military began to meddle in national politics, helping to overthrow Salamanca in 1934. The home front had also fallen apart, with widespread resistance to military recruitment in the countryside. Banditry flourished behind the front, often fueled by armed deserters. The Indians who had been sent to the front, from the communities and the haciendas, learned about military organization and how to use weapons, and they came into greater contact with the highly politicized urban working classes. The ignominious defeat of Bolivian forces led to the radicalization of workers, the small but important middle sectors, and even significant elements of the Bolivian army. As after the War of the Pacific, revulsion towards the political and social systems that had brought about defeat led to significant change. However, by now a much larger segment of the population participated in one way or another in politics, and more radical options were discussed.

The military ruled Bolivia from 1936 to 1939, and under the presidencies of General David Toro (1936–1938) and Germán Busch (1938–1939) the "military socialist" governments tried to institute populist and reformist measures. Toro created a ministry of labor and in 1937 nationalized the Bolivian holdings of Standard Oil of Bolivia, which controlled virtually all oil production in the country. In the new constitution of 1938 the state took on a much more active role in the country's economy, reversing the laissez-faire Liberal constitution of 1880. In 1939, however, Busch suspended the constitution and became dictator. After his suicide the same year and the brief rule of General Carlos Quintanilla (1939–1940), elections placed General Enrique Peñaranda, another Chaco War veteran but with a more traditional political vision, in the presidency (1940–1943).

During the political ferment in the aftermath of the Chaco War, political parties became more class-based, and a number of important radical and moderate leftist parties arose. On the basis of José Antonio Arze's extremely strong showing in the 1939 elections, in which he garnered 10,000 votes out of a total of 58,000 despite having no organized party, the leftists formed the Party of the Revolutionary Left (Partido de la Izquierda Revolucionaria; PIR). Another important revolutionary leftist party was the Revolutionary Workers Party (Partido Obrero Revolucionario; POR), which was Trotskyist in orientation. In turn, the more moderate and middle-class left in 1940 formed the National Revolutionary Movement (Movimiento Nacionalista Revolucionario; MNR), heavily influenced by the success of fascist ideology in Europe because of its nationalistic emphasis. All of these parties called for the nationalization of the tin mines, and a struggle ensued to attract the tin-mine workers to their cause. Only the POR and the PIR addressed rural problems in any coherent way, advocating the abolition of personal servitude on the haciendas and expropriation of the Latifundia, or the very largest estates.

In 1943 Major Gualberto Villarroel, with the help of the MNR, overthrew the Peñaranda government. An alliance of the MNR and the POR permitted the formation of the first national miners' union under the leadership of POR leader Juan Lechín Oquendo. In turn, Villarroel, styling himself a new Inca, in 1945 called for an Indigenous Congress, which attracted more than a thousand Indian caciques from throughout highland Bolivia. Villarroel decreed the abolition of the hated unpaid labor services on the haciendas and promised to provide the Indian communities with schools. These laws were never put into effect, for in 1946 a civilian mob overthrew the increasingly repressive Villarroel regime and hanged the president from a lamppost in the main plaza of La Paz.

Nevertheless, contacts between radicalized mine workers and hacienda peons, especially in the Cochabamba area and near the mines, became increasingly common and led to the subversion of the hacienda regime from within. The most important rebellion, which occurred in 1947 in Ayopaya, Cochabamba, involved hundreds of hacienda workers. Elsewhere, as in the Cinti district of southern Bolivia, revolts also flared on the haciendas. The rule of haciendas, previously based on paternalistic ties between landowners and peons, was increasingly undermined by this activity and owners resorted to brutal repression.

The Conservative governments that followed Villarroel, in alliance with the PIR, had increasing difficulty ruling the country. The miners, backed by the POR, and the middle-class MNR adopted more radical positions as the PIR ministers were forced to deal with the unrest. Thus in 1947 the PIR minister of labor sent troops into the Catavi mines and massacred striking workers. These actions destroyed the PIR's popular base and made the POR and MNR more revolutionary than ever. In 1949 the MNR attempted to take over the country in a civilian coup, but their efforts failed after two months of intense fighting in all major Bolivian cities. The MNR became more popular and won the 1951 presidential elections with Víctor Paz Estenssoro as their candidate, but he was prevented from taking power by military intervention. Denied political power through legitimate means, the MNR rose in revolt again in 1952. After three days of warfare, in which the miners came down from the mountains and the conquered armories were opened to the public, the army was finally beaten.

THE BOLIVIAN SOCIAL REVOLUTION, 1952–1986

The 1952 revolution marks a watershed in Bolivian history. The traditional parties had been discredited and the army destroyed. The miners had helped with the brief civil war and were the only ones who had weapons. The new regime, with Víctor Paz Estenssoro at the head, decreed the nationalization of the tin mines, creating Comibol, the state-run mining company. MNR leaders dropped literacy requirements for voting, suddenly enfranchising the Indian masses.

These events created momentum for change in the countryside as well. With the help of mine workers, the peons of the highlands mounted attacks on the hacienda system. Landowners fled the countryside and the largely Indian masses took over the haciendas, burning some to the ground. Under pressure from these developments, the Paz government decreed a land reform package in 1953 that led to the expropriation of most medium-sized and large estates in the highlands. These reforms legalized the de facto takeover of the haciendas, but they also created a long, drawn-out process that soon sapped the rural movement of its strength and tied the peasants to the MNR regime. The government created *sindicatos* (unions) of peasants, which were beholden to the MNR. The Indian communities, in turn, received very little and even lost lands where they had rented them out to outsiders.

These reforms meant that the peasants, once they had their land, became a conservative political force, because they had no reason to wish for other radical change in the country. During its twelve-year reign (1952–1964), the MNR used the peasants to counterbalance the much more radical mine workers. Their conservatism persisted even after the overthrow of the MNR by the revitalized army in 1964, when charismatic General René Barrientos Ortuño fashioned the so-called military-peasant pact. This arrangement, recalled numerous times when the military gained power, essentially meant that peasant leaders promised to remain quiescent if the military did not attack their interests. The arrangement apparently worked even in 1966 when the Argentine revolutionary Ernesto ("Che") Guevara established a guerrilla campaign in the southeastern Andean foothills. The guerrillas received no significant peasant support, and after a year they were captured; some, including Guevara, were executed after a massive army campaign.

The effects in the eastern lowlands were quite different from those in the highlands. Rather than bringing about much social change, most large landowners maintained control over their estates. Moreover, in an effort to stimulate the lowland economy as a way of attracting peasants from the overcrowded highlands, the MNR regime and the United States sent vast amounts of capital into the region. Most of the capital went to the large landlords, who established sugar and, briefly in the 1970s, cotton plantations. As a result, the economy of Santa Cruz boomed, bringing about rapid population growth in the city of Santa Cruz and increasing political and economic clout for Santa Cruz landlords.

After Barrientos's death in an accident in 1969, the army continued to rule but was unable to remain united. In 1970 General Juan José Torres González took over the government, leading the country sharply to the left. Before he could effect major changes, however, he was overthrown in 1971 in a bloody coup led by General Hugo Banzer Suárez, who established a right-wing military dictatorship. During the Banzer years, true economic growth took place. Utilizing many of the infrastructural developments begun under the MNR government, such as those in the Santa Cruz area, the Banzer regime diversified exports and expanded the production of foodstuffs. Road building, new airports, and other infrastructural improvements continued as well.

Economic growth began to slow in the late 1970s, however, and Banzer also came under pressure from the administration of President Jimmy Carter in the United States to hold free elections. After hunger strikes by the opposition, elections were finally held in 1979. A period of political confusion resulted. For two years military and civilian regimes alternated, with the MNR splitting into two major factions, one center-right led by former president Víctor Paz Estenssoro and the other led by left-leaning former president Hernán Siles Zuazo (1956–1960). In addition, a more radical leftist party, the Movement of the Revolutionary Left (Movimiento Izquierda Revolucionaria; MIR), and a new right-wing party, the Nationalist Democratic Action (Acción Democrática Nacionalista; ADN), with former General Hugo Banzer at the helm, also became significant political forces. In 1980 General Luis García Meza took over in what became known as the cocaine coup because many members of the military government had close ties to cocaine trafficking, which had been growing in Bolivia since the 1970s. However, internal resistance and the regime's inability to receive international recognition forced García Meza to resign in 1982. After a brief transition, Hernán Siles Zuazo and his leftist alliance, the Democratic and Popular Union (Union Democratica y Popular; UDP), assumed the presidency they had won in elections just prior to the 1981 coup. However, Siles proved unable to unite his diverse supporters. With tin prices falling and an overblown bureaucracy, the state experienced a severe fiscal crisis, making it impossible to fulfill the long-repressed demands of labor and other groups. As a result, government and the economy spun out of control, with inflation reaching 40,000 percent in 1985. Exhausted, Siles called elections early. The 1952 revolutionary model, with heavy participation by the state, had clearly failed in this multiparty environment.

NEW PATTERNS AFTER 1986

In the 1985 elections three parties, the MNR, the MIR, and the ADN, won almost equal shares of the votes. After intense negotiation, the MNR's Víctor Paz Estenssoro became president with the support of the leftist MIR. However, Paz forged an alliance with the ADN and proceeded to dismantle virtually all of the old revolutionary institutions he himself had built thirty years earlier. He dismantled the state mining company (Comibol), opened up the country to almost unrestricted free trade, and emasculated the mine workers and their unions by "relocating" many of the miners and their families in the subtropical jungle. Significantly, he attempted to impose a new unitary rural land tax that encompassed both peasant lands and commercial estates, but peasant resistance brought about its repeal.

Many "relocated" miners migrated to urban centers, others went into the subtropical jungles of the Chaparé to grow coca. Indeed, to a large extent the money brought in by the cocaine trade helped support the Bolivian economy. Moreover, Bolivian drug dealers increasingly began producing more refined products in an effort to cut out the largely Colombian middlemen.

The 1989 elections again resulted in a deadlock, with no party receiving a plurality. This time, in a surprise move, the leftist MIR allied itself with the right-wing ADN, and MIR leader Jaime Paz Zamora became president. In fact, the neoliberal course that the Paz government had embarked on could not be changed given the demise of state-centered models of economic growth. As a result, the MIR moved to the center and also used its power to break even further the strength of the once-powerful unions. Among the members of the revolutionary alliance, only the peasantry, representing the largest voting block, remained a powerful force within Bolivian politics.

THE AGE OF NEOLIBERALISM, 1986–2000

Neoliberalism, a philosophy that makes market capitalism the underlying rationale for government, would seem an unlikely candidate for implementation in Bolivia, with its thirty-five year history of state-directed economic policy. Yet because of the country's economic crisis and the conditions that the international community placed on offering financial assistance, Bolivia instituted a series of neoliberal economic reforms, beginning in 1986. Initially introduced to avert economic collapse, the institution of balanced budgets, free markets, and free trade became the basis for changing the levers of political power and the relationship between the Bolivian state and its citizens.

For two decades after the 1985 election, closely matched political parties, none of which attracted a majority of the electorate, resulted in multiparty coalition governments. A Democracy Pact enabled the septuagenarian MNR chieftain, Victor Paz Estenssoro, to gain the presidency in alliance with the leftist MIR. Despite his age, Paz proved himself a nimble and ruthless politician, forging a working relationship with Hugo Banzer, who represented the rational right of the Bolivian political spectrum. This alliance sponsored a New Economic Plan, designed to alleviate the nation's economic crisis. The most pressing challenge was hyperinflation, the extremity of which resembled that of Germany's Weimar period. Paz chose to combat the problem by applying "orthodox shock"—constricting the money supply, cashiering public employees, and reducing deficit spending, all conditions demanded by the IMF for its assistance. Once the architect of a program of state ownership and direction of important segments of the national economy, Paz now issued decrees that closed some state enterprises, opened Bolivian markets to imports and foreign ownership, and incapacitated the miner-dominated labor federation.

The late 1980s mark several important transitions in Bolivian political history. A resilient group of politicians, all of whom rose to prominence with the 1952 revolution, passed from the scene, ceding leadership to a generation born after 1930. At the same time, Bolivia's indigenous majority began to exert influence commensurate with its numbers. A *cholo* elite, urban-dwelling and university-trained indigenous people, assumed political prominence, especially in the capital. Much of this emerging sector lived in El Alto, the heights above La Paz, which on receiving its municipal charter in 1987 immediately became Bolivia's third-largest city. And as a further show of strength, the peasant labor confederation, Unique Confederation of Rural Laborers of Bolivia (Confederación Sindical Única de Trabajadores Campesinos de Bolivia; CSUTCB), displaced miners as the most important component of the labor movement.

In 1989 the electorate again divided almost equally for three contending candidates. Although he finished third in the voting, Jaime Paz Zamora of the MIR emerged as president in an alliance with Banzer and the ADN. This election witnessed the emergence of Conscience of the Fatherland (Consciencia de Patria; CONDEPA), a populist party appealing to the indigenous population in La Paz, under the leadership of a popular radio personality. Despite his leftist background, Paz Zamora continued down the neoliberal economic path opened in 1986. He never attempted to roll back the policies of his MNR predecessor and even expanded privatization in the mining sector. Paz Zamora promoted progressive social policies, championed by a group of young political advisers. He greatly expanded the national system of environmentally protected areas, recognized the importance of indigenous rights by greeting Amazonian Indians during their March for Dignity and Territory, and began the process of judicial and electoral reform.

A national census, conducted in 1992, documented a series of significant demographic changes. The national population, though still small at 6.5 million, had grown by more than a quarter since it was last measured in 1976. The census showed that the population had shifted from its traditional north-south axis (La Paz-Oruro-Potosí) to a west-east orientation (La Paz-Cochabamba-Santa Cruz). Perhaps most significantly, Bolivians were now 57 percent urban and 80 percent literate, reflecting the movement and education of the nation's Indian majority. The Bolivian economy had undergone change, as well. Tin, for a century the major source of foreign exchange, underwent a precipitous decline in the 1980s with the collapse of world demand for the mineral. Agricultural exports, especially soy, and hydrocarbons replaced tin as primary exports, and displaced tin miners migrated to the cities and to tropical regions of the country.

Gonzalo Sánchez de Lozada (b. 1930), Goni to friend and foe alike, became the most influential politician of his generation. Running as a candidate of the MNR, he was elected deputy and then senator before serving as Paz Estenssoro's Minister of Planning and Coordination. As minister he began a campaign to institute neoliberal reforms that would last nearly twenty years. Unsuccessful in his attempt to succeed Paz Estenssoro in 1989, Goni gained the presidency four years later through an alliance with the indigenous leader, Víctor Hugo Cárdenas, and his Movimiento Revolucionario Tupaj Katari de Liberación (MRTKL) party. Cárdenas, an Aymara politician and intellectual, became the first native American to hold the Bolivian vice-presidency and was instrumental in steering the administration toward legitimizing the rights and customs of Bolivia's indigenous majority.

Goni's first presidency proved the high water mark of Bolivian neoliberal reform. He intended nothing less than transforming Bolivia from a centrally governed political system with a state-directed economy to a decentralized, liberal democracy that regulated free market capitalism. His administration's policies, collectively called Plan de Todos (Plan for All), had three major components. One part of the plan was to privatize Bolivia's major state monopolies: the national airline, railroad network, telecommunications, and most of the petroleum industry. A large part of the sales revenues were to be invested in a privately managed pension fund, the Bonosol, intended to bail out what was a bankrupt system of state-funded social security. The other major programs of the plan were education reform, which began significant investments in the long-neglected rural school system, and political decentralization through the Law of Public Participation (LPP). Education reform significantly increased national literacy rates, especially in the countryside. LPP transformed local government in Bolivia by creating more than three hundred new municipalities and distributing 20 percent of the nation's tax revenues to them. It forced national political parties to pay attention to local issues and created a base for the rise of new groups of political actors.

The MNR-MRTKL administration also sponsored new land reform legislation, embodied in the Instituto Nacional de Reforma Agraria (INRA), which recognized the legitimacy of communal land ownership (a stance that contradicted neoliberal orthodoxy), accelerated the registration of land titles, and reformed the system of taxation on rural property. Moreover, the administration significantly amended Bolivia's 1967 constitution to extend suffrage; introduce more, though not universal, direct election of legislators; and recognize Bolivia as a multiethnic, multicultural nation. Although subsequent events would undermine the legacy of his Plan for All, Goni left office in 1997 convinced that Bolivia had entered a new period in its history, one that would replace a backward, inefficient, corrupt system with a rational, transparent, and democratic successor.

Goni's presidency produced no political coattails for the MNR. In 1997 the party's share of the presidential vote fell below 20 percent, trailing both the ADN and the MIR, which together garnered more than 40 percent of the electorate. Hugo Banzer formed a second coalition with the MIR and emerged from parliamentary voting as president. Despite their traditional antipathy for the MNR, Banzer and his conservative supporters hastened to join Goni's economic legacy. They were to encounter another legacy, a mounting opposition to neoliberalism that first burst forth in the city of Cochabamba.

Encouraged by the World Bank, Banzer authorized the sale of Cochabamba's municipal water system to a subsidiary of the Bechtel Corporation in 1999. As consumers recognized that the new owners intended to levy substantial rate increases, they organized a protest that eventually became the water war of March and April 2000. Banzer first opposed

the protesters' demands, then imposed martial law in the city; but the demonstrators' solidarity and determination forced him to rescind the contract. The Banzer presidency also acquiesced to external pressure to intensify coca eradication. Supported by funds, equipment, and military advisers from the United States, the Bolivian army launched a series of campaigns in the Chapare to destroy harvested coca leaves and extirpate the plants themselves. Growers' opposition to the loss of their livelihood established the Chapare as a zone of low-intensity combat that alienated public opinion and organized the resistance that would eventually underlie a political movement. Banzer's failing health forced him to resign the presidency in 2001, two years before the expiration of his six-year term. He was succeeded by Vice President Jorge Quiroga.

FORCES OF POPULAR RESISTANCE SINCE 2000

In some quarters the Cochabamba water war was hailed as the first successful challenge to neoliberalism. However, Bolivian activists see it as part of a constellation of opposition movements—*cocaleros*, indigenists, anti-imperialists—that had been building for a decade. In the first decade of the twenty-first century, this coalition of opposition, never seamless and often fractious, continuously challenged the neoliberal hegemony, overthrowing its principal Bolivian proponent and eventually electing a vigorous opponent to the presidency.

Sánchez de Lozada gained a second presidential term in 2002. His campaign, advised by U.S. operatives, including James Carville, former aide to President Bill Clinton, stressed that Goni offered the best chance of averting impending chaos. The electorate showed marked indifference to these blandishments, giving the MNR-led coalition 22.5 percent of the vote and forcing Goni to craft a coalition of very strange bedfellows to gain a working majority in the legislature. The water war served as a prelude to the organized opposition that forced Sánchez de Lozada to resign the presidency in October 2003.

Goni and his vice president and successor, Carlos Mesa, were trapped by the unfulfilled promises of neoliberalism. Scandal plagued the sale of some government monopolies and the Bonosol, and most of the substantial investments made by the new owners went for capital goods rather than jobs. Revenues that state monopolies once provided to the treasury were now replaced largely from value-added taxes on consumption. Despite an increase in gross national product following the economic reforms of 1994–1995, poverty indicators remained unchanged, and the lives of ordinary Bolivians showed little improvement. Goni also seemed politically tone deaf as he proposed the construction of a gas pipeline to the Chilean port of Arica. This not only exposed him to criticism of the bargain-basement contracts signed with multinational petroleum companies, but also revived traditional animosity toward Chile. Although gas succeeded water as the focus of opposition, unrest continued. Roadblocks, organized in part by the charismatic *cocalero* Evo Morales and the indigenous leader Felipe Quispe, disrupted critical transportation networks in the highlands connecting La Paz with Cochabamba and Santa Cruz. Protests became an almost daily occurrence in the capital. On October 17, 2003, Goni departed for the United States, and after a very brief honeymoon, Mesa found himself unable to govern. He resigned the presidency and was succeeded by the chief justice of the Bolivian supreme court, Eduardo Rodriguez Veltze, in 2005.

Over a decade, Evo Morales became the leader of what seemed in the early 2000s to be a dramatic readjustment of Bolivian politics. Displaced from the highlands by collapse of the tin mines and intense droughts in the mid-1980s, he found his way to the Chapare. There he became a coca grower, a leader in the resistance to its eradication, and a national legislator. Under the banner of the Movement Toward Socialism (Movimentio al Socialismo; MAS) party, Morales ran for the presidency in 2002, finishing a very close second but shunned by the MNR-led coalition. Then, in 2005, Morales and his fellow MAS candidates won a majority (53%) of votes cast for president and 72 of 130 seats in the chamber of deputies. Morales's indigenous heritage, Yankee-baiting invective, and friendships with Cuban leader Fidel Castro and Venezuelan president Hugo Chávez brought him to international attention. But within Bolivia, Morales's support stems from his life experience. He passed much of his youth in extreme hardship, came to prominence in opposition to what many Bolivians see as imperialist machinations, and developed an effective, direct style of political communication.

As of 2007, Morales's major accomplishment seems to have been the assembly of an able set of close advisers and administrators. He has also managed to keep the MAS party unified during often fractious parliamentary debates over Bolivian federalism and the role of the state in the economy. But whatever the future holds for the Morales administration, Bolivia's indigenous majority seems poised for an ongoing role in national leadership.

See also **Arze, José Antonio; Aymara; Ballivián, José; Banzer Suárez, Hugo; Barrientos Ortuño, René; Bolívar, Simón; Bolivia, Political Parties: Overview; Bolivia, Political Parties: Movement of the Revolutionary Left (MIR); Busch Becerra, Germán; Cacique, Caciquismo; Cárdenas, Víctor Hugo; Chaco War; Chayanta, Revolt of (1927); Chiriguanos; Cholo; Federalist War (1898-1899); García Meza, Luis; Guevara, Ernesto "Che"; Hochschild, Mauricio; Indigenismo; La Paz; Lechín Oquendo, Juan; Melgarejo, Mariano; Montes, Ismael; Morales, Evo; Neoliberalism; Pando, José Manuel; Patiño, Simón Iturri; Paz Estenssoro, Víctor; Paz Zamora, Jaime; Peñaranda del Castillo, Enrique; Quiroga, Jorge; Quispe, Felipe; Saavedra Mallea, Bautista; Salamanca, Daniel; Sánchez de Lozada Bustamante, Gonzalo; Santa Cruz, Andrés de; Siles Zuazo, Hernán; Sucre; Sucre Alcalá, Antonio José de; Toro, David; Villarroel López, Gualberto; War of the Pacific; Wars of Independence, South America; Zárate Willka, Pablo.**

BIBLIOGRAPHY

Baptista Gumucio, Mariano. *Historia contemporanea de Bolivia, 1930–1978*, 2nd ed. La Paz: Gisbert, 1978.

Fellmann Velarde, Jorge. *Historia de Bolivia*, 2nd ed. 3 vols. La Paz: Editorial Los Amigos del Libro, 1978–1981.

Finot, Enrique. *Nueva historia de Bolivia: Ensayo de interpretación sociológica de Tiwanaku a 1930*, 5th ed. La Paz: Gisbert, 1976.

Guzmán, Augusto. *Breve historia de Bolivia*. La Paz: Editorial Los Amigos del Libro, 1969.

Klein, Herbert S. *Parties and Political Change in Bolivia: 1880–1952*. London: Cambridge University Press, 1969.

Klein, Herbert S. *Bolivia: The Evolution of a Multi-Ethnic Society*, 2nd ed. New York: Oxford University Press, 1992.

Klein, Herbert S. *A Concise History of Bolivia*. Cambridge, U.K., and New York: Cambridge University Press, 2003.

Kohl, Benjamin H., and Linda C. Farthing. *Impasse in Bolivia: Neoliberal Hegemony and Popular Resistance.* London and New York: Zed Books, 2006.

Mesa, José de, Teresa Gisbert, and Carlos D. Mesa Gisbert. *Historia de Bolivia,* 4th ed. La Paz: Editorial Gisbert y Cia, 2001.

ERICK D. LANGER
DAVID BLOCK

BOLIVIA, AGRARIAN REFORM.

Agrarian reform in Bolivia consisted of legal measures enacted in 1953 as a result of the 1952 social revolution. Land tenure has been a divisive issue in Bolivian history. The census of 1950 was the last one before the 1953 land reform and it was used as the basis for the land reform law. The data has been interpreted by authors in different ways. It is agreed that 90 percent of the land was under semifeudal cultivation and was owned by just 6 percent of the proprietors, who held from 1,000 to 10,000 hectares (1 hectare equals 2.47 acres). Also all but 9.3 percent of the land was owned by absentee landowners. Of the land not owned by absentees, just 2.8 percent still belonged to Indian communities, who at the time of the creation of an independent Bolivia in 1825 had held most of the land. Furthermore, the rural workers on the estates, nearly all of whom were classified as Indians, had to provide legally sanctioned personal services.

The agrarian reform's key purpose was to disperse land ownership, promote the breakup of large holdings, and abolish servitude. Besides mandating the redistribution of land and the end of unpaid services, the law encouraged the restoration of Indian communities with modern means of cultivation. This did not happen, but strong peasant unions emerged as a unit of rural organization and production. The strength and number of these *sindicatos* varied from region to region. The law strongly encouraged an increase in agricultural production, protection of natural resources, and internal migration to the less populated eastern regions.

The 1953 law defined six types of land tenure systems, each with different reform requirements. Twenty years later, more than 250,000 new titles, some for expropriated land totaling about 16.25 million acres, had been issued. With the breakup of many large estates, a decline in production occurred. The new freeholders were mostly subsistence far-

mers. But in the 1990s the positive effects of the reform are generally cited, those effects being a relatively peaceful countryside with a rural population that enjoys full political and economic rights. After land again became concentrated in the 1980s, the government in 1996 passed a law creating the National Institute of Agrarian Reform (INRA). The goal was to redistribute land and establish community land titles. However, the slow pace of reform caused Evo Morales, who was elected president in 2005, to pass a new agrarian reform bill in 2006. While not fundamentally different than the 1996 law, the new measure sought to improve implementation.

See also **Agrarian Reform.**

BIBLIOGRAPHY

Benton, Jane. *Agrarian Reform in Theory and Practice: A Study of the Lake Titicaca Region of Bolivia.* Aldershot, U.K.; Brookfield, VT: Ashgate, 1999.

Hernáiz, Irene, and Diego Pacheco. *La Ley INRA en el espejo de la historia: Dos siglos de reformas agrarias en Bolivia.* La Paz: Fundación Tierra, 2000.

Klein, Herbert S. *Parties and Political Change in Bolivia, 1880–1952.* New York: Cambridge University Press, 1969.

Morales, Waltrund Queiser. *Bolivia: Land of Struggle.* Boulder, CO: Westview Press, 1992.

CHARLES W. ARNADE

BOLIVIA, CONSTITUTIONS

This entry includes the following articles:
OVERVIEW
CONSTITUCIÓN VITALICIA

OVERVIEW

Since its declaration of independence on 6 August 1825, Bolivia has had sixteen constitutions, all providing for a representative government, a strong and centralized executive power, the protection of human rights, independent legislative and judicial branches, and a semirigid constitutional amendment process. The constitutions can be broadly classified into three groups, according to their ideological orientation: liberal-republican, socialist, and nationalist.

The liberal-republican phase began in 1826 with the constitution drafted specifically for Bolivia by

Simón Bolívar. It established a popular representative form of government divided into four branches (electoral, legislative, executive, and judicial) and expressly guaranteed civil liberties, property rights, and equality of all before the law. It also set the precedent for a strong executive. One of its most controversial clauses provided that the president serve for life. In addition, the president had the power to name local government officials (such as mayors and prefects) and was exempted from any responsibility for his administration's actions.

In the Bolivarian constitution, the legislative, judicial, and electoral branches were independent of the executive. The tricameral legislative branch was divided into two houses with fixed terms—the tribunes (4 years) and senators (8 years)—and one with a life term—the censors. The judicial branch was made up of a Supreme Court and lower district courts in each department, as well as justices of the peace for each town or village. The electoral branch was composed of representatives popularly elected in each province (one representative per 100 citizens). Although this Constitution claimed to establish popular-representative government, voting rights were restricted by age, literacy, and job/occupation requirements.

The 1826 constitution remained in effect for only two years and was modified by the 1831 constitution, which eliminated the censors and substituted a four-year presidential term for the lifetime term. In addition, the 1831 constitution stated that if no candidate managed to win an absolute majority of the vote (50 percent plus one), the Congress would have to choose among the top three candidates. This provision, which remained in force, became crucial to the political process due to the inability of any party to obtain an absolute majority. Despite its short lifespan, the Bolivarian constitution, together with the 1831 amendments, laid the foundation for all future constitutions, and in subsequent versions very few substantive changes have been made.

The nine constitutions ratified between 1834 and 1880 reflect the intense political instability that plagued Bolivia. During this period constitutions were used to reflect the personal political whims of the current president rather than to introduce real changes in the political system. Among the most

significant changes were the introduction of the responsibility of the president (1834); the elimination of the president's power to sign federation or alliance treaties, following the disastrous Peru–Bolivian Confederation (1836–1839); the establishment of a one-term waiting period before the president could seek reelection (1839); and the direct election of the president by secret ballot (1839). In addition, although the 1843, 1851, 1861, 1868, and 1871 constitutions sought to increase the power of the executive, the 1878 constitution gave the legislative branch more extensive powers. The 1878 constitution, which was ratified in the 1880 constitution and modified in 1931, remained in effect until 1938.

The 1938 constitution, of which the 1945 and 1947 constitutions were expansions, was the first one based upon socialist doctrine. It incorporated the principle of social justice and gave the state more responsibility for guaranteeing human rights such as health and education. Workers were given the right to organize, conduct collective bargaining, and strike.

The National Revolution of 1952 ushered in the nationalist phase of Bolivia's constitutional history. The 1961 constitution, drafted by the Nationalist Revolutionary Movement (MNR) regime, incorporated the reforms instituted by the 1952 National Revolution: universal suffrage, agrarian reform, nationalization of the mines, popular militias, and a larger role of the state in the economy. It also instituted the requirement of party affiliation for deputies to seek election, and it gave more power to the legislature by removing the president's veto power over its resolutions.

The constitution of 1967, which remained in effect until August 1994, was very similar to that of 1961. The main difference is that it established a one-term waiting period between reelections and provided basic guidelines for the electoral bodies and political parties. The constitution can be amended by a two-thirds vote of the legislature, and the reforms cannot be vetoed by the executive. Despite the seemingly large number of constitutions, scholars such as Ciro Trigo, Tomás Elío, and Floren Sanabria G. have argued that there has in fact been only one constitution since 1826 that, although modified repeatedly, has remained in effect until the present day. With the reestablishment of democracy in 1982, however, there has been growing consensus in favor of further constitutional reform, designed to reflect more accurately the altered political circumstances of the country. This consensus finally materialized in reforms adopted in August 1994 when Congress approved a sweeping law that amended thirty-five articles of the constitution through the Constitutional Amendments Law. The 1994 reforms include direct election of half of the members of the lower house of Congress from single-member districts; an increase of the terms for presidents, members of parliament, mayors, and municipal council members to five years, with general and municipal elections alternating every two and a half years; clear procedures favoring the direct election of the president and all mayors; voting age lowered to eighteen; increased powers for departmental prefects; and departmental assemblies composed of national representatives doing double duty as the assembly members in the departments from which they had been elected; the establishment of an independent human rights ombudsman; and the establishment of a constitutional tribunal. Citing the need to give better representation to indigenous groups, President Evo Morales in 2006 convened a Constituent Assembly to rewrite the constitution. In 2007 the Constituent Assembly continued to debate major changes. Controversial proposals included removing term limits for the president.

See also **Bolivia, Political Parties: Nationalist Revolutionary Movement (MNR); Morales, Evo; Peru-Bolivia Confederation.**

BIBLIOGRAPHY

Ciro Félix Trigo, *Las constituciones de Bolivia* (1958).

Tomás Manuel Elío, "Discurso del Dr. Tomás Manuel Elío, presidente honorario del Colegio de Abogados de La Paz, sobre la unidad de la constitución política," in Ramón Salinas Mariaca, *Las constituciones de Bolivia* (1989).

Floren Sanabria G., *La constitución política de Bolivia: 1967* (1990).

Additional Bibliography

Cristóbal Urioste, Juan. *Constitución política del Estado: Historia y reformas.* Bolivia: Fundación Milenio, 2003.

Van Cott, Donna Lee. *The Friendly Liquidation of the Past: The Politics of Diversity in Latin America.* Pittsburgh, PA: University of Pittsburgh Press, 2000.

ANNABELLE CONROY

CONSTITUCIÓN VITALICIA

Simón Bolívar, who in 1825 guided the creation of Bolivia, presented the new nation with its first constitution. Composed by Bolívar, it was approved by the Bolivian assembly in November 1826 but never used.

This 132-article constitution, which represented Bolívar's personal political philosophy, combined various constitutional models, beginning with Athenian democracy. Powers were divided among the electors and the legislative, executive, and judicial branches. The legislature was tricameral: tribune, senate, and censors. Suffrage was broader than was usual for the early nineteenth century. Every ten citizens selected one elector who served for four years. Electors presented candidates for the legislature and local offices and chose censors, who held office for life and were the ultimate guardians of the constitution and individual liberties. The judiciary was independent and selected by the senate from a list prepared by the electors. The executive department was headed by a life-term president who selected his successor. The president, who could appoint only treasury officials, was commander of the army and could not be impeached or held responsible by the other branches. The constitution was officially abrogated with the Treaty of Piquiza with Peru on 6 July 1828.

See also **Bolívar, Simón.**

BIBLIOGRAPHY

Manuel Ordoñez, ed., *Constitución política de la república de Bolivia, leyes y disposiciones más usuales,* vol. 2 (1917).

Victor Andrés Belaunde, *Bolívar and the Political Thought of the Spanish American Revolution* (1938).

Plácido Molina Mostajo, *El libertador en Bolivia* (1975).

Additional Bibliography

Lynch, John. *Simón Bolívar: A Life.* New Haven, CT: Yale University Press, 2006.

Parra Dávila, Alvaro. *El pensamiento político del libertador Bolívar y la Constitución de Bolivia.* Caracas, Venezuela: Ediciones El Centauro, 2000.

CHARLES W. ARNADE

BOLIVIA, ORGANIZATIONS

This entry includes the following articles:
BOLIVIAN STATE PETROLEUM CORPORATION (YPFB)
BOLIVIAN WORKERS CENTRAL (COB)
FEDERATION OF BOLIVIAN UNIVERSITY STUDENTS
SYNDICAL FEDERATION OF BOLIVIAN MINEWORKERS
  (FSTMB)

BOLIVIAN STATE PETROLEUM
CORPORATION (YPFB)

The government-owned Yacimientos Petrolíferos Fiscales Bolivianos (YPFB) was established in 1937 when the government of Colonel David Toro (1898–1977) expropriated the Bolivian holdings of the Standard Oil Company of New Jersey, which had been given the monopoly to explore and exploit the petroleum resources of Bolivia.

Until the Bolivian National Revolution in 1952, the YPFB was unable to keep up with the country's demand for petroleum and its derivatives. A marked increase in output between 1952 and 1956, however, fulfilled the national demand and provided a small amount for export. The revolutionary government, hoping that petroleum could take the place of the declining tin-mining industry as the country's major source of foreign exchange, ended the monopoly of the YPFB. A new petroleum code allowed foreign oil companies to enter the petroleum business, and the Gulf Oil Corporation began to exploit deposits, and built a pipeline to the Chilean port of Arica. The Gulf concession was expropriated by the government of General Alfredo Ovando Candía (1918–1982) in 1969.

Under President Hugo Banzer Suárez (1926–2002) in the 1970s, foreign oil firms were again authorized, but those that obtained concessions were more interested in natural gas than in petroleum. YPFB continued to be the country's largest oil company and to refine all the oil processed in the country. It also exported natural gas to Argentina and Brazil. Popular pressure against attempts by the governments of Presidents Jaime Paz Zamora (b. 1939) and Gonzalo Sánchez de Lozada (b. 1930) in the early 1990s to privatize government firms, including the YPFB, delayed such efforts.

By 1997 most of the assets of YPFB had been sold to foreign companies. Brazil's national oil corporation Petrobras became the largest investor in Bolivia's oil development. However, in 2006 the leftist president Evo Morales (b. 1959) renationalized the oil and natural gas industries, but YPFB did not have the resources or the expertise to take over oil exploration and production. Consequently, foreign firms, as of 2007, remain an important part of Bolivia's oil sector.

See also **Banzer Suárez, Hugo; Morales, Evo; Ovando Candía, Alfredo; Paz Zamora, Jaime; Toro, David.**

BIBLIOGRAPHY

Aillón Gómez, Tania. *Monopolios petroleros en Bolivia la formación de sus ganancias extraordinarias.* Cochabamba, Bolivia: Agencia Sueca para le Desarrollo Internacional, 2004.

Alexander, Robert J. *The Bolivian National Revolution.* New Brunswick, NJ: Rutgers University Press, 1957.

Lora, Guillermo. *A History of the Bolivian Labour Movement.* Cambridge, U.K.: Cambridge University Press, 1977.

Mitchell, Christopher. *The Legacy of Populism in Bolivia: From the MNR to Military Rule.* New York: Praeger Publishers, 1977.

Robert J. Alexander

BOLIVIAN WORKERS CENTRAL (COB)

Established immediately following the Bolivian National Revolution in April 1952, the Bolivian Workers Central quickly came to include most of the country's trade unions. It was headed from the beginning by Juan Lechín, who was also executive secretary of the Mine Workers Federation (FSTMB).

In its first few months, the COB was controlled by the Trotskyist Partido Obrero Revolucionario (POR), because Lechín and other union leaders belonging to the National Revolutionary Movement (MNR), which had come to power with the Revolution, were principally occupied as members of the new government. However, in October 1952, when the Trotskyists put the COB on record against major parts of the proposed government decree nationalizing the big mining companies, the MNR unionists moved immediately to remove the Trotskyists and to assure their own party's control of the COB.

During the first administration of President Victor Paz Estenssoro (1952–1956), the COB officially co-governed with the MNR, its leaders naming and holding the ministries of mines, labor and peasant affairs. However, that situation ended in 1957, when the COB leaders came into conflict with the price stabilization policies of President Hernán Siles.

The COB leadership finally broke with the revolutionary government of the MNR in 1964, when Juan Lechín was denied the party's presidential nomination. They supported the overthrow of President Paz Estenssoro in November 1964, but soon were in conflict with the new military regime. During much of the period 1965–1969, the COB was outlawed.

When General Alfredo Ovando seized power in mid-1969, he formed an alliance with the COB. When he was overthrown by a military coup the following year, the COB was successful in imposing General Juan José Torres as his successor. Under Torres the COB took the lead in establishing the Popular Assembly, which the Trotskyists and others looked upon as an embryonic "soviet," à la Russia in 1917. However, with the overthrow of General Torres by General Hugo Banzer in 1971, there began an eleven-year period of military rule in which the COB was clandestine much of the time.

With the inauguration late in 1982 of President Hernán Siles, with COB backing, the COB rebounded, reaching the height of its political influence. During the three years of Siles's second government, the COB successfully fought by demonstrations and general strikes any effort to impose an economic stabilization policy.

Siles finally called elections in 1985, one year early, and Paz Estenssoro returned to power. This time, however, he was determined not only to enforce a stabilization policy but to close down much of the unprofitable tin-mining sector and to privatize some other government-owned parts of the economy. When the COB sought to carry out a general strike against these policies, the Paz Estenssoro government broke the strike.

This showdown with Paz Estenssoro, and particularly the closing of a large part of the mining industry, greatly reduced the power of the Central Obrera Boliviana, the mine workers having been for forty years the backbone of the COB. It was no longer, along with the armed forces, one of the major power centers of the country's politics. One casualty of this change was Juan Lechín, who for the first time since 1952 ceased to be the president of the COB. In the early twenty-first century, the

COB recovered some of its power and aligned with the many social movements protesting privatization. The confederation has pressed for state control of the country's natural gas reserves.

See also **Labor Movements.**

BIBLIOGRAPHY

Robert J. Alexander, *Organized Labor in Latin America* (1965).

Guillermo Lora, *A History of the Bolivian Labour Movement* (1977).

Additional Bibliography

Alexander, Robert J. *A History of Organized Labor in Bolivia*. Westport, CT: Praeger, 2005.

Baldivia Urdininea, José and Bruno Rojas. *Obreros y gremiales en el proceso democrático*. La Paz: Fundación Milenio, 1995.

Pimentel, José. *Principios históricos del movimiento sindical*. La Paz: Friedrich Ebert Stiftung, ILDIS, 1994.

Vargas Arze, Amadeo. *Historia política de la C.O.B.* Cochabamba, Bolivia: A. Vargas Arze, 1996.

ROBERT J. ALEXANDER

FEDERATION OF BOLIVIAN UNIVERSITY STUDENTS

The Federation was a student organization founded in 1928 by radical intellectuals at Cochabamba with the support of the government of Hernán Siles. Its manifesto was influenced by the university reform movement in Argentina and by Marxism, Indigenismo, and nationalism. The Federation's primary concerns were the socialization of natural resources, agrarian reform, the integration of Indians, strong support for the nascent labor movement, and the complete reintegration of the Pacific littoral.

The Federation lost momentum during the 1930s but was rejuvenated in 1939, when it declared itself the intellectual workers' vanguard and called for social revolution. In 1940 the Federation signed a pact of unity with various regional leftist groups and supported the candidacy of Marxist José Antonio Arze in the presidential elections. It continued to support Arze, who had been the key leader of its 1928 convention, and the radical Revolutionary Party of the Left (PIR), which he founded in mid-1940.

The Federation opposed the fascist leanings of the Gualberto Villarroel government. It ceased to play a role in politics after 1946 because of its support for the discredited PIR, and was dissolved in 1952.

See also **Bolivia, Political Parties: Party of the Revolutionary Left (PIR).**

BIBLIOGRAPHY

Herbert Klein, *Parties and Political Change in Bolivia, 1880–1952* (1971), esp. pp. 99–101, 298–302, 329–331.

Additional Bibliography

Lorini, Irma. *El nacionalismo en Bolivia de la pre y posguerra del Chaco, 1910–1945.* La Paz, Bolivia: Plural Editores, 2006.

MARIA LUISE WAGNER

SYNDICAL FEDERATION OF BOLIVIAN MINEWORKERS (FSTMB)

The FSTMB, a national union of mineworkers, was established in 1944 under the government of Colonel Gualberto Villarroel, a coalition of young military men and the National Revolutionary Movement (MNR) that came to power in December 1943. The first permanent secretary was Juan Lechín, a white-collar employee of Patiño Mines, who was also a local soccer hero and former subprefect in the Catavi area. In 1945 Lechín was elected to the new post of executive secretary, which he was to hold for almost half a century.

During the Villarroel regime, the FSTMB became the largest and most powerful labor organization in Bolivia. However, in the six years following the overthrow and murder of Villarroel in 1946, there was continuing conflict between the federation and succeeding governments. During this period the MNR and the Trotskyist Revolutionary Workers Party (POR) were the principal groups within the union. With the Bolivian National Revolution in April 1952, which brought the MNR to power, Lechín became minister of mines, and the FSTMB became the most important part of the new Bolivian Workers Central (COB). The miners federation was given workers' control in the newly nationalized mining industry, with union officials having virtual veto power over the mine managers. This power virtually ended in the administration of Hernán Siles (1956–1960), and with the overthrow of the MNR regime in November 1964, the FSTMB opposed the government's efforts to raise efficiency and productivity in the mines.

During the administrations of General Alfredo Ovando (1969–1970) and General Juan José Torres (1970–1971), the FSTMB enjoyed a rapprochement with the government, but it was forced underground during most of the 1971–1982 period, when military regimes ruled Bolivia. By contrast, during the second administration of President Siles (1982–1985), the FSTMB was a major factor in preventing the enactment of an economic stabilization program. When Siles was succeeded by President Victor Paz Estenssoro (1985–1989), the power of the miners federation was largely destroyed. In 1986 Juan Lechín was defeated for reelection as executive secretary of the FSTMB. He also resigned as head of the COB. Subsequently, joining with other social movements, the FSTMB regained some political clout, successfully pressuring for the state-owned mining group, Comibol, to regain control of tin mining operations in Huanuni from foreign investors. Still, conflict between union affiliated miners and the thousands laid off in the 1980s, who then survived in mining cooperatives, remains. The struggle over Bolivia's important gas reserves was anticipated to further shape the FSTMB's future.

See also **Bolivia, Organizations: Bolivian Workers Central (COB); Villarroel López, Gualberto.**

BIBLIOGRAPHY

Robert J. Alexander, *The Bolivian National Revolution* (1958).

Guillermo Lora, *A History of the Bolivian Labour Movement* (1977).

Additional Bibliography

Brown, Jonathan C., ed. *Workers' Control in Latin America, 1930–1979.* Chapel Hill: University of North Carolina Press, 1997.

García Linera, Alvaro. *La condición obrera: Estructuras materiales y simbólicas del proletariado de la minería mediana, 1950–1999.* La Paz: Muela del Diablo Editores, 2001.

Grez Toso, Sergio, Francisco Zapata, and Moira Mackinnon. *Formas tempranas de organización obrera.* Buenos Aires: La Crujía: Instituto Torcuato Di Tella/Programa de Naciones Unidas para el Desarrollo, 2003.

Lechín Oquendo, Juan. *Memorias.* La Paz: Litexsa Boliviana, 2000.

Rodríguez Ostria, Gustavo. *El socavón y el sindicato: Ensayos históricos sobre los trabajadores mineros, siglos XIX–XX.* La Paz: ILDIS, 1991.

ROBERT J. ALEXANDER

BOLIVIA, POLITICAL PARTIES

This entry includes the following articles:

OVERVIEW

Political parties in Bolivia have rarely been strong organizations with coherent ideological programs and stable followings. Instead, typically they have served as instruments of access to state patronage, their rise and fall being a function of the fate of their leader. The personal nature of political parties, together with their purely instrumental function, accounts both for the lack of a stable party system and for the strange alliances that are sometimes formed between parties with seemingly opposing ideologies.

Political parties emerged in Bolivia only toward the second half of the nineteenth century. Until then the most common means of accessing power was through military force, and the followers of a particular caudillo (military leader) were referred to by his name. Thus the followers of Andrés de Santa Cruz were referred to as *crucistas*, those of José Ballivián as *ballivianistas*, and so on. The end of the War of the Pacific (1879–1883), involving Bolivia, Chile, and Peru, ushered in the Liberal-Conservative period (1884–1935), in which party lines were drawn according to the economic interests of large traditional landowners and the silver-mining entrepreneurs of the south. The Liberal Party, by contrast, became associated with *la Rosca*, a derogatory term referring to the tin-mining oligarchy and the personnel it used to influence policy making.

The 1930s and 1940s saw the rise of three types of political parties, each with a different proposal for resolving the nation's problems. The nationalist revolutionary type, represented by the Nationalist Revolutionary Movement (Movimiento Nacionalista Revolucionario, MNR), believed that economic and social development could come about only through the creation of a strong centralized state directed by middle-class technocrats and supported by a multiclass alliance. Marxist-style parties originated among the working class, particularly the mine workers, and in the universities. They were broadly divided into Trotskyists, represented by the Revolutionary Workers Party (Partido Obrero Revolucionario, POR) and Stalinists, represented by the Leftist Revolutionary Party (Partido de la Izquierda Revolucionaria, PIR). Finally, nationalist-authoritarian parties, represented by the Bolivian Socialist Falange (Falange Socialista Bolivana, FSB), advocated a corporatist national economic order and a federal political system.

The MNR, which came to power with the 1952 Bolivian Revolution, had a significant impact on the development of party politics and provided a model for the development of many of the subsequent political parties. By forming a multiclass support base, the MNR enjoyed single-party dominance between 1952 and 1964. However, the increasingly conflicting agendas housed under the MNR umbrella soon led a number of factions to break away from the party.

The post-transition period, which began in Bolivia in 1978, was initially characterized by an explosion in the number of political parties, although most of these were small and short-lived. The exceptions were the MNR, the Nationalist Democratic Action (Acción Democrática Nacionalista, ADN) and the Movement of the Revolutionary Left (Movimiento de Izquierda Revolucionaria, MIR), parties that came to dominate the electoral process from 1985 until the end of the 1990s. Despite their dominance of the electoral arena, however, the inability of any one party to obtain an absolute majority in national elections produced a significant trend toward the formation of political pacts and coalitions. Coalition governments did make possible the short-term stability of the democratic process in Bolivia. However, their inability to successfully address the protracted economic crisis—as well as incidents of corruption, abuse of power, and the continued political exclusion of important sectors of the population—eventually led to the delegitimation of traditional political parties.

The disenchantment with the dominant political class, represented by the MNR, ADN, and MIR parties, resulted in two significant changes to the party system. The first was the introduction of reforms to the electoral system. Among the most important of these were the introduction in 1996 of single-member districts to elect 68 of the 130 members of the chamber of deputies and the 2004 Ley de Agrupaciones Ciudadanas y Pueblos Indígenas (Law of Citizen Groups and Indigenous People). These reforms have weakened the traditional political parties and have led to the emergence of a more independent local and indigenous leadership.

The second change, increasingly aided by the reforms already noted, is the rise of antisystemic political parties. These parties challenge existing political and economic arrangements and are headed by populist leaders who draw their support mainly from the marginalized urban and rural poor. Such was the case with the Movement toward Socialism (Movimiento al Socialismo, MAS), the party led by Evo Morales Aima. In December 2005 the MAS made history by not only winning the presidential contest, but doing so with an absolute majority—the first time a party had managed to do this since the transition to democracy in 1978.

See also **Caudillismo, Caudillo.**

BIBLIOGRAPHY

Bueno Saavedra, Ramiro. *Sistema electoral, sistema de partidos y democracia en Bolivia: Efectos políticos del sistema electoral sobre el sistema de partidos (1980–2002)*. La Paz: Universidad Mayor de San Andrés, Carrera de Ciencias Políticas, Instituto de Investigaciones en Ciencia Política, 2004.

Klein, Herbert S. *Bolivia: The Evolution of a Multi-Ethnic Society*, 2nd edition. New York: Oxford University Press, 1992.

Malloy, James M., and Eduardo Gamarra. *Revolution and Reaction: Bolivia, 1964–1985*. New Brunswick, NJ: Transaction, 1988.

Morales, Waltraud Q. *A Brief History of Bolivia*. New York: Facts on File, 2003.

Rolón Anaya, Mario. *Política y partidos en Bolivia*, 2nd edition. La Paz: Librería Editorial Juventud, 1987.

Van Cott, Donna Lee. *From Movements to Parties in Latin America: The Evolution of Ethnic Politics*. Cambridge, U.K., and New York: Cambridge University Press, 2005.

ANNABELLE CONROY

BOLIVIAN COMMUNIST PARTY (PCB)

The first Communist Party in Bolivia was established in the late 1920s under the guidance and patronage of the Communist International. Although it was underground, it gained considerable influence in the nascent organized labor movement, and was represented in 1929 at the Congress of Latin American Communist Parties in Buenos Aires. The party was obliterated during the Chaco War between Bolivia and Paraguay (1932–1935). In 1940 a new Communist-controlled party was established. The Party of the Revolutionary Left (PIR) was headed by José Antonio Arze, who ran for president in the election of that year and did surprisingly well in the country's principal cities, although he was badly defeated by the government nominee, General Enrique Peñaranda.

In the following years, the PIR emerged as a major element in the labor movement, coming to control the Confederación Sindical de Trabajadores de Bolivia. During the government of President Gualberto Villarroel, which encouraged the organization of the mineworkers union (FSTMB) under the leadership of the Movimiento Nacionalista Revolucionario (MNR), the PIR was in strong opposition, and Arze spent most of the period in the United States, where he taught at the Communist Party's training school in New York City.

In the six years following the overthrow of the Villarroel regime in July 1946, the PIR cooperated closely with the reactionary government of the period. As a consequence, the youth of the party withdrew to form the Partido Comunista (PCB) in 1950, and the PIR was dissolved.

The PCB strongly opposed the MNR regime (1952–1964) and began to gain some influence in organized labor, particularly among the mineworkers. It supported the 1964 overthrow of the MNR government by Generals René Barrientos and Alfredo Ovando. In 1964 a pro-Maoist faction split from the PCB to form the Partido Comunista de Bolivia (Marxista-Leninista). Both parties refused to join the guerrilla operation of Ernesto "Che"

Guevara in eastern Bolivia in 1966–1967, and both participated in the so-called Popular Assembly during the government of President Juan José Torres (1970–1971).

The pro-Maoist faction declined in the 1970s and 1980s, while the pro-Soviet party continued to be a major force in organized labor. In 1985 and again in 1987, the PCB's former secretary-general, Simón Reyes, was elected executive secretary of the FSTMB, which had been headed since its establishment almost half a century before by Juan Lechín Oquendo. Neither Communist faction, however, became a major factor in national politics.

See also **Bolivia, Political Parties: Party of the Revolutionary Left (PIR).**

BIBLIOGRAPHY

Hoover Institution, *Yearbook of International Communist Affairs* (1970s, 1980s).

Additional Bibliography

Lavaud, Jean-Pierre. *El embrollo boliviano: turbulencias sociales y desplazamientos políticos, 1952–1982.* Lima, Peru: IEFA, 1998.

Vargas Arze, Amadeo. *El trotzkysmo en Bolivia.* Cochabamba, Bolivia: Editora ILAM, 1995.

ROBERT J. ALEXANDER

BOLIVIAN SOCIALIST FALANGE (FSB)

Founded in Santiago, Chile, in 1937 by Oscar Unzaga de la Vega, Hugo Arias, and Germán Aguilar Zenteño, the Bolivian Socialist Falange was once considered the second largest party in Bolivia. Inspired by the nationalist rhetoric of the Spanish Falange and right-wing Catholic movements in Spain, the FSB was once at the forefront of calls for the nationalization of the Bolivian tin mines. Following the 1952 revolution, however, the FSB led all opposition efforts against the ruling Nationalist Revolutionary Movement (MNR). As a result, prominent members of the FSB were imprisoned and systematically persecuted.

In 1964, the FSB was one of the principal civilian forces that helped the military bring down the MNR. In an ironic twist, seven years later, the MNR and FSB leadership joined forces with then Colonel Hugo Banzer Suárez to overthrow a populist faction of the armed forces. The FSB did not survive the military period mainly because the space it once occupied was filled by the Nationalist Democratic Action (ADN), a party founded by General Banzer Suárez in 1979. By the mid-1980s the FSB had become just another of Bolivia's numerous minuscule political parties. Under David Añez Pedraza, who became the FSB's leader in 1982, the party attempted to move toward the left, precipitating an internal battle that led to the formation of the Socialist Movement (MAS).

See also **Banzer, Suárez, Hugo.**

BIBLIOGRAPHY

Alberto Cornejo, *Programas políticos de Bolivia* (1949).

James Dunkerley, *Rebellion in the Veins: Political Struggle in Bolivia, 1952–1982* (1984).

Additional Bibliography

Irurozqui, Marta. *"A bala, piedra y palo": La construcción de la ciudadanía política en Bolivia, 1826–1952.* Sevilla, Spain: Diputación de Sevilla, 2000.

Lavaud, Jean-Pierre. *El embrollo boliviano: Turbulencias sociales y desplazamientos políticos, 1952–1982.* Lima: IEFA, 1998.

Lorini, Irma. *El nacionalismo en Bolivia de la pre y posguerra del Chaco (1910–1945).* La Paz, Bolivia: Plural Editores, 2006.

EDUARDO A. GAMARRA

CONSERVATIVE PARTY

Formally known as the Constitutional Party, the Conservative Party was formed in the aftermath of the Chilean defeat of Bolivian forces during the War of the Pacific (1879–1884). The Conservatives and Liberals were the first formal political parties in Bolivia based on ideology rather than personalistic leadership. The Conservatives ruled Bolivia from 1884 to 1899 and were the principal political force during the last two decades of the nineteenth century, which is frequently called the period of the Conservative oligarchy. Led primarily by wealthy silver miners from the southern part of the country with close ties to Chilean capitalists, the Conservatives favored a peace treaty and closer ties with Chile. Their vision of the country's economic development rested upon the building of railroads to foster silver exports, the creation of a dynamic land market (at the expense of Indian communities), and the settlement of Bolivia's eastern frontiers. Under the influence of party leader and chief ideologue Mariano Baptista (president of Bolivia, 1892–1896), the Conservative Party also favored the Catholic Church. Although they differed over religious issues, the Conservatives favored the same economic liberalism as their principal political opponents, the Liberal Party.

See also **War of the Pacific.**

BIBLIOGRAPHY

The best analysis in English of the formation of the Conservative Party is Herbert S. Klein, *Parties and Political Change in Bolivia: 1880–1952* (1969), chap. 1. See also Mariano Baptista, *Obras completas* (1932–1934). On the Conservatives' Indian land policies, see Tristan Platt, *Estado boliviano y ayllu andino* (1982).

Additional Bibliography

Irurozqui, Marta. *La armonía de las desigualdades: Elites y conflictos de poder en Bolivia, 1880–1920.* Madrid, Spain: Consejo Superior de Investigaciones Científicas; Cuzco, Peru: Centro de Estudios Regionales Andinos Bartolomé de las Casas, 1994.

Irurozqui Victoriano, Marta. "Political Leadership and Popular Consent: Party Strategies in Bolivia, 1880–1899." *Americas* 53, no.3 (January 1997): 395–423.

ERICK D. LANGER

CONSTITUTIONALIST PARTY

The Constitutionalist Party, whose program was based on the writings of its founder, Mariano Baptista, and on the Bolivian constitution of 1878, represented the interests of the landowning and mining elite. After Bolivia's defeat in the War of the Pacific (1880), the party favored a quick peace settlement with Chile that would include indemnification for lost territory and enable Bolivia to construct a railroad for mining exports.

In the presidential elections of 1884 the Constitutionalists supported Gregorio Pacheco of the Democratic Party, which had proclaimed itself the party of national reconciliation. During Pacheco's presidency, the Constitutionalist Party became known as the Conservative Party and played an important role under the leadership of Baptista.

Its primary concerns were the creation of a powerful parliamentary regime, the promotion of economic growth based on massive railroad construction, and the defense of the interests of the Roman Catholic Church.

Following its defeat by the Liberals in 1899, the Constitutionalist Party began to decline.

See also **Baptista, Mariano.**

BIBLIOGRAPHY

Herbert Klein, *Parties and Political Change in Bolivia, 1880–1952* (1971).

Guillermo Lora, *Historia de las partidos políticos de Bolivia* (1987).

Mario Rolon Anaya, *Política y partidos en Bolivia,* 2d ed. (1987).

Additional Bibliography

Irurozqui, Marta. *La armonía de las desigualdades: Elites y conflictos de poder en Bolivia, 1880–1920.* Madrid, Spain: Consejo Superior de Investigaciones Científicas; Cuzco, Peru: Centro de Estudios Regionales Andinos Bartolomé de las Casas, 1994.

Irurozqui, Marta. "Political Leadership and Popular Consent: Party Strategies in Bolivia, 1880–1899." *Americas,* 53, no.3 (January 1997): 395–423.

MARIA LUISE WAGNER

DEMOCRATIC POPULAR UNITY

The Democratic Popular Unity was founded on 13 April 1978 as a "popular, nationalist, anti-imperialist and revolutionary" opposition political front. It grouped the Nationalist Revolutionary Movement of the Left (Movimiento Nacionalista Revolucionario de la Izquierda—MNRI), the Movement of the Revolutionary Left (Movimiento de la Izquierda Revolucionaria—MIR), the Bolivian Communist Party (Partido Comunista Boliviano—PCB), and other, minor parties under a single banner.

The UDP participated in the 1978, 1979, and 1980 elections but was unable to achieve a majority until 1982, when the Congress voted the UDP into office. Under the leadership of Hernán Siles Zuazo, the party governed the country between 1982 and 1985. Faced with the most severe economic crisis in Bolivian history and plagued by debilitating internal divisions stemming from the conflicting agendas of the coalition's parties, the UDP was forced to call early elections in 1985. By 1986, the MIR, the

PCB, and the Christian Democrats had abandoned the UDP, which then ceased to exist as a party.

See also **Bolivia, Political Parties: Overview; Siles Zuazo, Hernán.**

BIBLIOGRAPHY

Additional Bibliography

Ibáñez Rojo, Enrique. "The UDP Government and the Crisis of the Bolivian Left, 1982–1985." *Journal of Latin American Studies.* 32, no. 1 (February 2000): 175–205.

Lavaud, Jean-Pierre. *El embrollo boliviano: Turbulencias sociales y desplazamientos políticos, 1952–1982.* Lima: IEFA, 1998.

ANNABELLE CONROY

LIBERAL PARTY

The Liberal Party came to power in 1899 after defeating the Conservative Party in the Federalist War (1898–1899) and remained in power until 1920. The Liberals continued many of the programs of the Conservatives, such as encouraging the sale of Indian community lands and developing the infrastructure for the export economy, especially the railroad network that carried minerals to the Pacific coast. This era coincided with the tin-mining boom, which utilized the rail network first developed by the Conservatives for silver exports. After unsuccessful attempts to put down Brazilian filibustering expeditions, the Liberal administration was forced to sell the Acre region in the northeastern part of the country to Brazil in 1903. The party then began to promote a liberal land-grant policy in 1905 to settle frontier lands. Only when it became clear that wealthy absentee landowners had purchased vast extents without populating the frontiers was this policy stopped in 1915. Although the party had been founded by Eliodoro Camacho in 1883 as a force advocating the continuation of the War of the Pacific (1879–1884), it was the most important Liberal president, Ismael Montes, who signed the definitive peace treaty with Chile. The Liberal Party era was one of political peace and prosperity, during which Bolivia modernized rapidly.

See also **War of the Pacific.**

BIBLIOGRAPHY

The best description of the Liberal Party era is Herbert S. Klein, *Parties and Political Change in Bolivia: 1880–1952* (1969),
pp. 31–63. See also Juan Albarracín Millán, *El poder minero en la administracíon liberal* (1972).

Additional Bibliography

Irurozqui, Marta. *La armonía de las desigualdades: Elites y conflictos de poder en Bolivia, 1880–1920.* Madrid, Spain: Consejo Superior de Investigaciones Científicas; Cuzco, Peru: Centro de Estudios Regionales Andinos Bartolomé de las Casas, 1994.

Irurozqui, Marta. "Political Leadership and Popular Consent: Party Strategies in Bolivia, 1880–1899." *Americas* 53, no. 3 (January 1997): 395–423.

ERICK D. LANGER

MOVEMENT OF THE REVOLUTIONARY LEFT (MIR)

Founded in 1971 by Jaime Paz Zamora and others, the Movimiento de la Izquierda Revolucionaria (MIR; Movement of the Revolutionary Left) evolved from a student organization to one of Bolivia's three main parties. Originally associated with the Socialist International and a target for repression, the MIR joined the governing coalition in 1982 after Bolivia's transition to democracy. It took the presidency in the 1989 election as Paz Zamora adopted a social democratic orientation and formed an unlikely coalition with former dictator Hugo Banzer. Abiding by its agreement with Banzer, the MIR supported his unsuccessful bid for the presidency in 1993, hurting the party. The MIR ran Paz Zamora twice more with declining results and eventually lost all national-level presence.

See also **Banzer Suárez, Hugo; Paz Zamora, Jaime.**

BIBLIOGRAPHY

Gamarra, Eduardo A., and James M. Malloy. "The Patrimonial Dynamics of Party Politics in Bolivia." In *Building Democratic Institutions: Party Systems in Latin America*, edited by Scott Mainwaring and Timothy R. Scully. Stanford, CA: Stanford University Press, 1995.

ROBERT R. BARR

MOVIMENTIO AL SOCIALISMO (MAS)

Movimentio al Socialismo (MAS; Movement toward socialism) is a Bolivian political party whose candidates gained the presidency and legislative majority in 2005 national elections. The Instrumento para la Soberanía de los Pueblos (IPSP; Instrument for the peoples' sovereignty) an alliance forged for the 1998 general elections, adopted the MAS acronym; MAS-IPSP is closely linked to its leader, Evo Morales, who rose to prominence by defying Bolivia's traditional political system. Unlike nativist political parties of the past, MAS succeeded in appealing to Bolivia's Indian majority without alienating other segments of the electorate.

MAS's success in the early twenty-first century can be attributed as much to Bolivian economic and political conditions as to its own policies. Despite its name, the party has never been so much Marxist as it is anti-imperialist and opposed to neoliberal economic policies. Its platform stresses a renationalization of strategic economic areas, especially natural resources, respect and preservation of native traditions, and the defense of national sovereignty. In 2005 MAS's political discourse resonated with a population weary of economic stagnation and angered by the past government's proposals to sell natural gas at discounted prices to the developed world via a pipeline passing through Chile.

See also **Morales, Evo.**

BIBLIOGRAPHY

MAS Movimiento al Socialismo. Available from http://www.masbolivia.org/index.html.

Van Cott, Donna Lee. "From Exclusion to Inclusion: Bolivia's 2002 Elections." *Journal of Latin American Studies* 35, no. 4 (2003): 751–775.

DAVID BLOCK

NATIONALIST DEMOCRATIC ACTION (ADN)

Founded in 1979, the conservative Nationalist Democratic Action (Acción Democrática Nacionalista, ADN) party played a key role in Bolivia's transition. Hugo Banzer Suárez, the party's nominee in the 1979, 1980, 1985, 1989, 1993, and 1997 elections, created it to help defend him against charges stemming from his authoritarian tenure. The ADN formed governing pacts in 1985 and 1989, and finally took the presidency in 1997. When Banzer resigned because of poor health in 2001, the reins passed to Vice President Jorge Quiroga. The party then virtually collapsed: It received less than 4 percent of votes in 2002, did not compete in 2005, and received less than 2 percent of votes in the 2006 constituent assembly elections.

See also **Banzer Suárez, Hugo; Bolivia, Political Parties: Overview.**

BIBLIOGRAPHY

Crabtree, John, and Laurence Whitehead, eds. *Towards Democratic Viability: The Bolivian Experience.* Houndmills, Basingstoke, U.K., and New York: Palgrave, 2001.

ROBERT R. BARR

NATIONALIST REVOLUTIONARY MOVEMENT (MNR)

Founded in 1941 by Víctor Paz Estenssoro, Hernán Siles Zuazo, Walter Guevara Arze, and Augusto Céspedes, among others, the Nationalist Revolutionary Movement (Movimiento Nacionalista Revolucionario, MNR) was until the early twenty-first century Bolivia's most important political party. Originally populist, it launched the 1952 revolution, pushed through universal suffrage and land reform, and nationalized Bolivia's mining industry. It was the governing party until 1964, when General René Barrientos Ortuño led a successful coup d'état. By this time Guevara, Paz, and Siles had formally split; the party continued to splinter through the 1970s, when there were at least thirty factions. It saw a substantial realignment in the 1980s as a number of factions joined Paz's Historic MNR (MNR-H). By the mid-1980s the MNR-H had dropped the H and reclaimed the MNR. Hernán Siles Zuazo led the most significant alternative faction, the MNR de Izquierda ("of the Left"; MNRI), from 1971 until the 1980s, when it gradually disappeared.

The MNR returned to power with the elections of 1985, when Paz took the presidency once again. It formed a governing coalition (the "pact for democracy") with the Nationalist Democratic Action (Acción Democrática Nacionalista, ADN) party, a move that many credit for helping consolidate Bolivia's nascent democracy. The MNR also launched the New Economic Policy, which began to dismantle the statist economic system that the MNR itself had initiated in the 1950s. In 1989 the party nominated Gonzalo Sánchez de Lozada, the principal architect of the economic reforms, but lost the contest in the congressional runoff vote, despite winning the most votes in the first round. It was successful in 1993, however, again running Sánchez de Lozada. Significant reforms during his tenure, including an unusual form of privatization and an extensive decentralization program, did not stem the gradually declining support for the MNR. By the late 1990s many voters had grown weary of the dominant political class, including the MNR, and sought alternatives. Nevertheless, the MNR narrowly took the presidency again in 2002, with only 22.5 percent of the popular vote. Again its president, Sánchez de Lozada faced a series of social crises that led to his resignation in 2003. The MNR, along with other traditional parties, has continued to lose support since then, earning only 6.5 percent of the vote in the 2005 general elections and 3.4 percent in the 2006 constituent assembly contest.

See also **Guevara Arze, Walter; Paz Estenssoro, Víctor; Sánchez de Lozada Bustamante, Gonzalo; Siles Zuazo, Hernán.**

BIBLIOGRAPHY

Dunkerley, James. *Rebellion in the Veins: Political Struggle in Bolivia, 1952–1982.* London: Verso, 1984.

Grindle, Merilee S., and Pilar Domingo, eds. *Proclaiming Revolution: Bolivia in Comparative Perspective.* Cambridge, MA: David Rockefeller Center for Latin American Studies, Harvard University, 2003.

Mayorga, René Antonio. "La crisis del sistema de partidos políticos en Bolivia: Causas y consecuencias." *Canadian Journal of Latin American and Caribbean Studies* 30, no. 59 (2005): 55–92.

ROBERT R. BARR
EDUARDO A. GAMARRA

PARTY OF THE REVOLUTIONARY LEFT (PIR)

As is true of other mid-twentieth-century Bolivian parties, the roots of the PIR lie in the disappointment of the young members of the middle class over Bolivia's backwardness and defeat in the Chaco War. The PIR was organized in Oruro in July 1940 and the next year issued a detailed program marking it as a socialist party. Its leaders were the charismatic José Antonio Arze and Ricardo Anaya, both law professors from Cochabamba. For about three decades the PIR was an important party but never achieved a national electoral victory. It disbanded in 1952 following the victory of the Nationalist Revolutionary Movement (Movimiento Nacionalista Revolucionario—MNR) but regrouped in 1956. Eventually it faded into oblivion. The PIR's program, genuinely Marxist but unaffiliated with world communism, was closer to the prevalent Latin American socialist-indigenist thinking. It was strongly anti-imperialist, which its members interpreted as opposition to the pervasive

influence of the United States. During the 1960s, the PIR began to break up. Some members formed the Communist Party of Bolivia. Internal conflicts continued to weaken and eventually ended the PIR.

See also **Arze, José Antonio; Bolivia, Political Parties: Bolivian Communist Party (PCB).**

BIBLIOGRAPHY

Alberto S. Corneyo, *Programas políticos de Bolivia* (1949), pp. 180–294.

Herbert S. Klein, *Parties and Political Change in Bolivia, 1880–1952* (1969).

Additional Bibliography

Klein, Herbert S. *A Concise History of Bolivia.* Cambridge, U.K., and New York: Cambridge University Press, 2003.

Lavaud, Jean-Pierre. *El embrollo boliviano: Turbulencias sociales y desplazamientos políticos, 1952–1982.* Translated by Luis H. Antezana. Lima: IEFA; La Paz: Hisbol, 1998.

Lorini, Irma. *El nacionalismo en Bolivia de la pre y posguerra del Chaco, 1910–1945.* La Paz: Plural Editores, 2006.

CHARLES W. ARNADE

PATRIOTIC AGREEMENT (AP)

In August 1989 General Hugo Banzer Suárez's Nationalist Democratic Action (ADN) and Jaime Paz Zamora's Movement of the Revolutionary Left (MIR) established the Acuerdo Patriótico (AP). Essentially a gentleman's agreement between both men, the pact served both to end an impasse in the Congress between the three top vote getters in the May 1989 elections and to elect Paz Zamora as president of Bolivia. Paz Zamora and Banzer signed no documents, arguing that they would prove that their word could be trusted. Despite the rather unholy nature of the alliance between two erstwhile enemies—Paz Zamora was imprisoned during Banzer's seven-year dictatorship in the 1970s—the AP held office for four years. A bipartisan council (Consejo Político del Acuerdo Patriótico) headed by General Banzer was established to sort out relations between the ADN and the MIR. As part of the original agreement, Luis Ossio Sanjinés, the ADN's vice-presidential candidate in May 1989, was named vice president of the country. In December 1989 and December 1991, the AP, now a political party, ran a single slate of candidates for municipal elections; General Banzer ran as the party's candidate for the 1993 general elections. Following Banzer's defeat at the polls, the AP ended rather unceremoniously in August 1993.

See also **Bolivia, Political Parties: Movement of the Revolutionary Left (MIR); Bolivia, Political Parties: Nationalist Democratic Action (ADN).**

BIBLIOGRAPHY

Eduardo A. Gamarra, "Crafting Political Support for Stabilization: Political Pacts and the New Economic Policy in Brazil," in *Democracy, Markets, and Structural Reform in Latin America,* edited by William C. Smith, Carlos H. Acuña, and Eduardo A. Gamarra (1994), and "Market-Oriented Reforms and Democratization in Bolivia," in *A Precarious Balance,* edited by Joan M. Nelson, vol. 2 (1994).

Additional Bibliography

Mayorga, Fernando. *Neopopulismo y democracia: Compadres y padrinos en la política boliviana (1988–1999).* Cochabamba, Bolivia: Centro de Estudios Superiores Universitarios: Centro de Planificación y Gestión; La Paz, Bolivia: Plural Editores, 2002.

Soria Saravia, Margot. *Democracia e izquierda en Bolivia: La compleja alianza entre la izquierda y la derecha.* La Paz, Bolivia: s.n., 2002.

EDUARDO A. GAMARRA

REPUBLICAN PARTY

The Republican Party, formally called the Republican Union, was formed in 1914 by an offshoot of the Liberal Party and other opposition groups and ruled Bolivia from 1921 to 1934. Marred by continual infighting, the Republicans espoused a traditional liberal ideology like their predecessors, the Liberals. Juan Bautista Savedra, the first Republican president (1921–1925), passed some social legislation but also permitted the massacre of miners at Uncía in 1923. Hernán Siles Zuazo, president from 1926 to 1930, supported university reform, but had to deal with the beginnings of the Great Depression. Siles tried to remain in office past his term, but a military junta overthrew his government and in 1931 gave the reins of power to Daniel Salamanca, one of the founders of the party. As the economic and social situation worsened, Salamanca dragged Bolivia into the disastrous Chaco War, bringing about his own downfall in 1934 and the demise of the Republican Party as a political force.

See also **Bolivia, Political Parties: Nationalist Revolutionary Movement (MNR).**

BIBLIOGRAPHY

The best analysis of the Republican period is in Herbert S. Klein, *Parties and Political Change in Bolivia: 1880–1952* (1969), pp. 64–159. See also David Alvéstegui, *Salamanca, su gravitación sobre el destino de Bolivia,* 4 vols. (1957–1970); Porfirio Díaz Machicado, *Historia de Bolivia,* vols. 1–3 (1954–1955).

Additional Bibliography

Irurozqui, Marta. *"A bala, piedra y palo": La construcción de la ciudadanía política en Bolivia, 1826–1952.* Sevilla, Spain: Diputación de Sevilla, 2000.

Lorini, Irma. *El nacionalismo en Bolivia de la pre y posguerra del Chaco (1910–1945).* La Paz, Bolivia: Plural Editores, 2006.

ERICK D. LANGER

BOLOGNESI, FRANCISCO (1816–1880).

Francisco Bolognesi (*b.* 1816; *d.* 1880), Peruvian national hero and military commander in charge of the defense of the Peruvian garrison in Arica during the War of the Pacific (1879–1883). Together with Alfonso Ugarte, Bolognesi is considered the premier military hero. Both died in the battle of Arica (1880) and are credited with heroic self-sacrifice in defense of Peru. However, the battle and the war resulted in sound defeats for the Peruvian army. This legacy is a cornerstone of official Peruvian nationalism.

Bolognesi was typical of those military officers who were trained during the struggles among military chieftains during the mid-nineteenth century in Peru, as opposed to the professional military cadre that appeared in the 1890s. Bolognesi supported General Ramón Castilla against Generals José Rufino Echenique and Manuel Ignacio Vivanco in 1853–1858. He studied artillery in Europe and became commander general of artillery in 1862. During the War of the Pacific he led the Third Division in the battles of San Franciso, Tarapacá, and Arica. Outnumbered by Chilean forces in Arica he refused to surrender and rallied his soldiers to "fight until firing the last bullet."

See also **War of the Pacific.**

BIBLIOGRAPHY

Jorge Basadre, *Historia de la República del Perú*, vol. 5 (1963).

Additional Bibliography

Cayo Córdoba, Percy. *Francisco Bolognesi Cervantes*. Lima: Editorial Brasa, 1996.

ALFONSO W. QUIROZ

BOLTON, HERBERT EUGENE (1870–1953).

While teaching at the University of Texas from 1901 to 1909, Herbert E. Bolton was awakened to the role of the Spanish in Texas history. He became an important early twentieth-century voice in the promotion of the non-Anglo history of the United States and the importance of inter-American relations, which he felt would lead to a comprehensive understanding of the history of the Americas. Although historians agreed that his ideas were new and creative, he never developed an Americas school of historians. The history of the Spanish Borderlands remains primarily regional history. Many historians have agued that the Americas do not have a common history.

Over the years Bolton taught thousands of students and his Americas approach had a positive impact on them. Some of them included John Francis Bannon, S.J., A. P. Nasatir, Lawrence Kinniard, George P. Hammond, John Caughey, Mary Ross, and J. Manuel Espinosa. These students and others went on to promote the study of the Borderlands and Latin American history through publications, teaching, archival work, and positions in the U.S. State Department, where they had a positive impact.

Through the influence of Bolton, the study of the Spanish Borderlands continues to flourish. The study of the history of the Americas has evolved into the study of the history of the Atlantic world.

See also **Borderlands, The; Hispanics in the United States; United States-Mexico Border.**

BIBLIOGRAPHY

Bannon, John F., ed. *Bolton and the Spanish Borderlands*. Norman: University of Oklahoma Press, 1964.

Bannon, John F., ed. *Herbert Eugene Bolton: The Historian and the Man*. Tucson: University of Arizona Press, 1978.

Hanke, Lewis. *Do the Americas Have a Common History?: A Critique of the Bolton Theory*. New York: Alfred A. Knopf, 1964.

Magnaghi, Russell M. *Herbert E. Bolton and the Historiography of the Americas*. Westport, CT: Greenwood Press, 1998.

RUSSELL M. MAGNAGHI

BOMBAL, MARÍA LUISA (1910–1980).

María Luisa Bombal (*b.* 8 June 1910; *d.* 6 May 1980), Chilean novelist, born in Viña del Mar. Two highly original novels, *La última niebla* (1935) and *La amortajada* (1938), translated into English by the author herself as *The House of Mist* (1947) and *The Shrouded Woman* (1948), attest to María Luisa Bombal's outstanding position among Latin American writers. Educated in France, she lived most of her life away from her country.

An innovative novelist, Bombal was very influential in the development of contemporary narrative in Latin America, and she has had a profound effect on the development of a feminine perspective among Latin American women writers because of her treatment of the feminine characters in her work. Her novels are perfect narratives of fantasy and feminine sensitivity. She is a good representative of the feminist will to surpass the limitations imposed on women by society, and her works are an example of the stylistic experimentation of the period.

After having accomplished both an expression of women's views and the development of a new style, Bombal ceased to publish new works. In her old age she returned to her native country and enjoyed a brief recognition of her influence on younger writers, particularly women. Today, a literary prize for novels is given in her name.

See also **Literature: Spanish America.**

BIBLIOGRAPHY

Hernán Vidal, *María Luisa Bombal: La feminidad enajenada* (1976).

Mercedes Valdivieso, "Social Denunciation in the Language of 'The Tree' by María Luisa Bombal," in *Latin American Literary Review* 9 (1976): 70–76.

Lucía Guerra-Cunningham, *La narrativa de María Luisa Bombal: Una visión de la existencia femenina* (1980), and "María Luisa Bombal," in *Spanish American Women Writers* (1990): 41–52.

Additional Bibliography

Gac-Artigas, Priscilla, ed. *Reflexiones: Ensayos sobre escritoras hispanoamericanas contemporáneas.* New Jersey: Ediciones Nuevo Espacio, 2002.

Hintze, Gloria, ed. *Escritura feminina: Diversidad y género en América Latina.* Mendoza, Argentina: Universidad Nacional de Cuyo, Facultad de Filosofía y Letras, 2004.

S. DAYDÍ-TOLSON

BONAMPAK.

BONAMPAK. Bonampak, a small pre-Hispanic Maya site in the southern Maya lowlands of Chiapas, Mexico. Bonampak is known for its stunning full-color fresco murals. The murals occupy the interior wall and ceiling surfaces of a small masonry building with three corbel-vaulted rooms. The long wall of the building, facing into a large plaza, has a separate entrance for each room.

The murals, preserved by a thin coating of limestone caused by roof seepage, are famed for the richness of information they provide about elite Maya society in the Late Classic Period (790 CE). The (probably historical) narrative scene depicts preparations for a raiding party, its successful return with captives, their torture, and finally the celebration of the event.

The mural of the first room includes preparations notable for the presence of a Maya band with trumpets, rattles, tortoise shells struck with deer antlers, and large drums and for conferences between the ruling chief and his nobles. The second room shows the raiding party and the torture of the captives (their fingernails drip blood). In the third room, the celebration includes dancing on the steps (those in front of the building) and ritual bloodletting rites by the ruler and his family.

The detail in the murals shows several changes of fine clothing, especially woven cloth and featherwork, loincloths of captives, footwear, weaponry, musical instruments, ceremonial rituals, paraphernalia, and sacrifices. They include hieroglyphic inscriptions with names of the participants, dates of the events, and descriptions of the ceremonies.

The site is 19 miles south of Yaxchilán, on the Usumacinta River, and has Yaxchilán emblem glyphs, but none of its own. The earliest and latest Maya long counts are 9.8.9.0.0. (602 CE) and 9.18.0.0.0. (790 CE).

See also **Maya, The.**

BIBLIOGRAPHY

See Carnegie Institution of Washington, *Ancient Maya Paintings of Bonampak, Mexico,* suppl. publication 46 (1955), for full color reproductions of the Tejeda paintings and two Healy photographs. See also Sylvanus G. Morley and George W. Brainerd, *The Ancient Maya,* 4th ed. (1983), esp. pp. 315, 416–421.

Additional Bibliography

Miller, Mary Ellen. *Maya Art and Architecture.* New York: Thames & Hudson, 1999.

Miller, Mary Ellen. *The Murals of Bonampak.* Princeton, NJ: Princeton University Press, 1986.

Reyes-Valerio, Constantino. *De Bonampak al Templo Mayor: El azul maya en Mesoamérica.* México, D.F.: Siglo Veintiuno Editores: Agro Asemex, 1993.

WALTER R. T. WITSCHEY

BONAPARTE, JOSEPH

BONAPARTE, JOSEPH (1768–1844). Joseph Bonaparte (*b.* 7 January 1768; *d.* 19 July 1844), king of Spain. The oldest brother of Napoleon Bonaparte, Joseph was born into a family of the minor nobility in Corte, Corsica. He became a lawyer in 1788 and held a series of posts in Corsica and, after 1793, in France, where he and his family found refuge after the British seized the island. As Napoleon rapidly rose through the French military ranks (he was proclaimed emperor in 1804), Joseph's career gradually became entwined with the military successes of his ambitious brother. Napoleon's dream of a French empire extending across all Europe led him to invade Portugal in 1807 and Spain in 1808, forcing the abdication of the ruling Spanish Bourbon family (first Charles IV and then Ferdinand VII). With the monarchs now absent, Napoleon proclaimed the reluctant Joseph king of Spain in June 1808. These unpopular actions sparked the Peninsular War, a fierce Spanish guerrilla resistance to French incursions that was aided militarily and financially by Great Britain. As king, Joseph's actions were dictated by Napoleon's interests. His tremendous unpopularity led Spaniards to nickname him Pepe Botella (Pepe the Tippler), a vice he was not known to possess.

The rupture of legitimate monarchial power created a crisis of political legitimacy and a power vacuum in Spain's American colonies. French usurpation of the Spanish crown set in motion the Spanish American movements for independence, the causes of which had been developing for several decades. Influential criollo leaders, long discontented with the contradictions and restrictions of Spanish colonial administration, aware that their interests and those of Spain were different, and disillusioned by the rapid decline of the once powerful Spanish metropolis, saw in this turn of events an opportune moment to assert their independence. Joseph died in Florence, Italy.

See also **French-Latin American Relations; Napoleon I.**

BIBLIOGRAPHY

William Spence Robertson, *France and Latin American Independence* (1939; repr. 1967).

Gabriel H. Lovett, *Napoleon and the Birth of Modern Spain,* 2 vols. (1965).

Owen Connelly, *The Gentle Bonaparte: A Biography of Joseph, Napoleon's Elder Brother* (1968).

Michael Ross, *The Reluctant King* (1976).

Additional Bibliography

Cambronero, Carlos. *José I Bonaparte, el rey intruso: Apuntes históricos referentes a su gobierno en España.* Madrid: Alderabán, 1997.

Esdaile, Charles J. *The Peninsular War: A New History.* New York: Palgrave Macmillan, 2003.

Moreno Alonso, Manuel. *Sevilla napoleónica.* Sevilla: Ediciones Alfar, 1995.

Stroud, Patricia Tyson. *The Man Who Had Been King: The American Exile of Napoleon's Brother Joseph.* Philadelphia: University of Pennsylvania Press, 2005.

J. DAVID DRESSING

BONFIM, NOSSO SENHOR DO.

Nosso Senhor do Bonfim (Our Lord of the Good Ending), a term that refers to the patron saint of Bahia, also identified as Jesus Christ, and to the church of the same name in Salvador, Bahia. Some Brazilians identify Jesus with the West African Yoruba deity Oxalá from the Afro-Brazilian religion Candomblé. The Festa da Lavagem do Nosso Senhor do Bonfim, one of Brazil's most traditional celebrations, is held in January on the second Sunday after Epiphany (Day of Kings). Its origins and practices are both Portuguese and African. In the traditional style of Portuguese pilgrimages, visitors and devotees engage in a carnival-like atmosphere of feasting, drinking, singing, and dancing in the church's neighborhood. Located on a hill and outlined in electric lights at night during the celebration, the church can be seen from over 7.5 miles away. On Thursday preceding the Sunday celebration, the faithful march from the Nossa Senhora da Conceição da Praia church in Salvador's commercial center to Bonfim accompanied by musical groups as a preview of Carnival. The governor of Bahia and the mayor of Salvador often appear at the church. Priestesses and women practitioners in the Candomblé religion participate in the procession and the ritual washing of the gleaming white steps of the church though Catholic Church officials intermittently prohibited their involvement through the 1950s. Some claim that the church steps are the sacred stones of Oxalá. The water used is drawn from the well of Oxalá. Sweeping and washing churches for "promises"—pledges to God to do something special if God grants a request—is a Portuguese tradition. A Miracle Room in the church contains innumerable ex-votos, including wood, plaster, and wax reproductions of human body parts and photographs, letters, and paintings. These objects are hung on the walls and from the ceiling in gratitude for cures and other special favors performed by Nosso Senhor do Bonfim.

See also **African-Latin American Religions: Brazil.**

BIBLIOGRAPHY

Ruth Landes, *The City of Women* (1947), esp. pp. 232–244.

Luís Da Câmara Cascudo, *Dicionário do folclore brasileiro,* 2d ed. (1962), pp. 128–129.

Additional Bibliography

Amado, Jorge. *Bahia de Todos os Santos: Guia das ruas e dos mistérios da cidade do Salvador.* São Paulo: Martins, 1967.

Carvalho, José Eduardo Freire de. *A Devoção do Senhor J. do Bonfim e sua historia.* 2nd ed. Salvador: Imprensa Oficial, 1944.

Groetelaars, Martien Maria. *Quem é o Senhor do Bonfim?: O significado do Senhor do Bonfim na vida do povo da Bahia.* Petrópolis: Vozes, 1983.

Ickes, Scott A. "'Adorned with the Mix of Faith and Profanity that Intoxicates the People': The Festival of the Senhor do Bonfim in Salvador, Bahia, Brazil, 1930-1954." *Bulletin of Latin American Research* 24 (2) (April 2005): 181–200.

ESTHER J. PRESSEL

Additional Bibliography

Suárez Pasquel, Lucía. *Fondo Neptalí Bonifaz* Quito: Banco Central del Ecuador, 1984.

Troncoso, Julio C., and Neptalí Bonifax Ascásubi. *Odio y Sangre: Hombres y hechos de la época.* Quito: Fray Jodoco Ricke, 1958.

RONN F. PINEO

BONIFAZ ASCASUBI, NEPTALÍ (1870–1960?).

Neptalí Bonifaz Ascasubi (also Ascazubi; b. 29 December 1870; d. 1960?), was elected president of Ecuador in 1931 but did not serve. A wealthy sierra landowner, in 1925 he became president of Ecuador's newly created Central Bank. His successful election bid brought together an unlikely coalition of small businessmen, artisans, campesinos, and workers—conservatives, liberals, and socialists—all adversely affected by the Great Depression. His platform, the Compactación Obrera Nacional (National Workers' Compact, 1932), called for mildly progressive reform. Bonifaz defeated his Liberal opponent, Modesto Larrea Jijón, in Ecuador's first free election in nearly forty years. However, Liberals still controlled Congress, and they distrusted Bonifaz, believing that he would favor banking and landowning interests. Congress voted to disqualify president-elect Bonifaz in 1932 on the grounds that he was not born in Ecuador. The charge was true: the son of a diplomat, Bonifaz had been born at the Peruvian embassy in Quito—technically not Ecuadorian soil. More seriously, Bonifaz had listed his citizenship as Peruvian until he was forty-six years old. Following Congress's action, Bonifaz lost an ensuing military struggle over the presidency, the War of Four Days. Hundreds died in bitter house-to-house combat in Quito.

See also **Velasco Ibarra, José María.**

BIBLIOGRAPHY

Brief treatment of Bonifaz and the War of Four Days can be found in David W. Schodt, *Ecuador: An Andean Enigma* (1987), and in Osvaldo Hurtado, *Political Power in Ecuador*, translated by Nick D. Mills, Jr. (1985). Fredrick B. Pike, *The United States and the Andean Republics* (1977), provides the standard account of twentieth-century Ecuadorian politics. Rafael Quintero López, *El mito del populismo en el Ecuador* (1980), offers an extended reinterpretive discussion.

BONIFAZ NUÑO, RUBÉN (1923–).

Rubén Bonifaz Nuño (b. 12 November 1923), Mexican writer. Born in Córdoba, Veracruz, Bonifaz Nuño received a law degree from the National University but has devoted himself primarily to literature, mostly poetry, since the publication of *La muerte del ángel* (The Death of the Angel) in 1945. He won a scholarship from the Centro Mexicano de Escritores for the 1951–1952 academic year. In 1953 he published *Imágenes* (Images), a collection of poems that combined classical Greek and Latin influences with Nahuatl. He turned even more fully to the indigenous world in *Siete de espadas* (Seven of Spades), published in 1966, followed by *El ala del tigre* (The Wing of the Tiger) in 1969. In 1974 he was awarded the National Literature Prize. He is also known for his translations of the *Georgics* by Virgil (1963) and the *Eclogues* by Dante (1965), as well as for his essays.

Critics have placed Bonifaz Nuño in the "generation of the 1950s" with Jaime Sabines, Rosario Castellanos, and Jaime García Terres. Whether he is addressing the themes of solitude, disillusionment, misery, immortality, or hopelessness, Bonifaz's poetry is defined by a preference for urban spaces, experimental innovations with traditional poetic forms, a unique mixture of high and popular cultures, and a profound belief in the power of language and poetry to unmask enigmas and reinvent the world. A member of El Colegio Nacional and the Mexican Language Academy, he also directed the Instituto de Investigaciones Filológicas at the National University.

See also **Literature: Spanish America.**

BIBLIOGRAPHY

Marco Antonio Campos, "La poesía de Rubén Bonifaz Nuño," in Klahn and Jesse Fernández, eds., *Lugar de encuentro: Ensayos críticos sobre poesía mexicana actual* (1987), pp. 59–65.

Frank Dauster, "Rubén Bonifaz Nuño: The Shadow of the Goddess," in his *The Double Strand: Five Contemporary Mexican Poets* (1987), pp. 103–133.

Additional Bibliography

Eudave, Cecilia. "La tradición clásica y la poesía de lo cotidiano en Rubén Bonifaz Nuno." *Texto Crítico* 1 (July–Dec 1995): 109–119.

Fick, Marlon L. *The River Is Wide: Twenty Mexican Poets: A Bilingual Anthology = El río es ancho.* Albuquerque: University of New Mexico Press, 2005.

Paz, Octavio. *Poesía en movimiento: México 1915-1966.* México: Siglo Ventiuno, 2000.

Reyes Coria, Bulmaro. *Del poeta humanisto Rubén Bonfiaz Nuno.* México, D.F.: El Colegio Nacional, 2005.

NORMA KLAHN

BONILLA, POLICARPO (1858–1926).

Policarpo Bonilla (*b.* 17 March 1858; *d.* 11 September 1926), president of Honduras, 1894–1899. Bonilla emerged as the Liberal Party's heir apparent during Céleo Arias's failed bid for the presidency in 1887. Upon Arias's death in 1890, the Liberals chose Bonilla to be their candidate against the Progressive Party's nominee, Ponciano Leiva, in the 1891 elections. The Progressives stole the election, then harried the opposition Liberals into exile. From his Nicaraguan asylum, don Policarpo invaded Honduras, unleashing that country's bloodiest civil war. Bonilla's forces, amply supported by Nicaraguan strongman José Santos Zelaya, managed to overthrow the government after more than two years' struggle.

As diligent in office as he had been intransigent in the field, Bonilla rewrote the nation's constitution in 1894 to reflect his brand of doctrinaire liberalism, established in it the preeminence of the executive branch, and revamped public administration at every level. He firmly believed that disciplined political parties competing in honest electoral contests would cure much of what ailed Honduras, but he made little headway in persuading his fellow Hondurans to accept this Anglo panacea. Although mildly xenophobic (his legal practice exposed him to the seamy side of international capitalism), Bonilla continued his predecessors' efforts to foster development through mining and banana export, and he tried unsuccessfully to refund his country's enormous foreign debt.

A lifelong Unionist, Bonilla took the lead in a misguided attempt to revive the Republic of Central America shortly before leaving office in 1899. Hoping to return to law or retail trade after his term in office, he instead spent much of his remaining years in jail, in exile, or abroad on diplomatic missions. He represented Honduras at Versailles after World War I, courageously speaking against trying German leaders as war criminals and challenging Woodrow Wilson to redefine the Monroe Doctrine to fit League of Nations principles. He ran for president in 1923 but lost. Three years later he died in New Orleans.

See also **Central America; Honduras.**

BIBLIOGRAPHY

Aro Sanso (pseud., Ismael Mejía Deras), *Policarpo Bonilla: Algunos apuntes biográficos* (1936).

William S. Stokes, *Honduras: An Area Study in Government* (1950).

Lucas Paredes, *Drama político de Honduras* (1958), chaps. 13–20.

Charles Abbey Brand, *The Background of Capitalistic Underdevelopment: Honduras to 1913* (Ph.D. diss., University of Pittsburgh, 1972).

Richard L. Millett, "Historical Setting," in *Honduras: A Country Study,* edited by James D. Rudolph (2d ed., 1984).

Kenneth V. Finney, *In Quest of El Dorado: Precious Metal Mining and the Modernization of Honduras, 1880–1900* (1987), pp. 70–75.

Additional Bibliography

Zelaya, Gustavo. *El legado de la Reforma Liberal.* Tegucigalpa: Editorial Guaymuras, 1996.

KENNETH V. FINNEY

BONILLA CHIRINOS, MANUEL

(1849–1913). Manuel Bonilla Chirinos (*b.* 1849; *d.* 21 March 1913), president of Honduras (1903–1907 and 1912–1913). The offspring of poor country folk, Manuel Bonilla began his career as a soldier and Liberal partisan. He rose to brigadier general during Marco Aurelio Soto's regime (1876–1883) and served his party as commander during the 1892–

1894 Liberal insurgency. After serving part of a term as vice president and minister of war, General Bonilla broke with the Liberal Party and went into exile.

In 1902 he formed the National Party to run for president in 1903. Although he received more votes than the other candidates, he did not receive a majority, and Congress gave the presidency to Juan Ángel Arias. General Bonilla responded by ousting Arias and installing himself as president. When dissident Liberal legislators, led by Dr. Policarpo Bonilla, challenged the régime, General Manuel Bonilla sent his chief of police, Lee Christmas, to arrest the congressmen and close the Congress. During his first administration, he rewrote the constitution, gave a decided push to education and the North Coast banana companies, submitted the Nicaraguan border dispute to international arbitration, and tried to form peaceful alliances with his Central American neighbors.

In late 1906, dissident Hondurans invaded Honduras from Nicaragua to topple President Bonilla. The rebels occupied Tegucigalpa in March, 1907, sending Bonilla into exile. Four years later, General Bonilla, backed by Samuel Zemurray, unleashed a counterrevolution on the North Coast. After U.S. diplomatic negotiation with the belligerents, an election was held, which Bonilla won (1912). He died the next year.

See also **Honduras.**

BIBLIOGRAPHY

Aro Sanso (pseud., Ismael Mejía Deras), *Policarpo Bonilla: Algunos apuntes biográficos* (1936).

William S. Stokes, *Honduras: An Area Study in Government* (1950).

Lucas Paredes, *Drama político de Honduras* (1958), chaps. 21–30, 32.

Charles Abbey Brand, "The Background of Capitalistic Underdevelopment: Honduras to 1913" (Ph.D. diss., University of Pittsburgh, 1972).

Richard L. Millett, "Historical Setting," in *Honduras: A Country Study,* edited by James D. Rudolph (2d ed., 1984).

Additional Bibliography

O'Brien, Thomas F. *The Revolutionary Mission: American Enterprise in Latin America, 1900–1945.* Cambridge: Cambridge University Press, 1996.

KENNETH V. FINNEY

BONNET, STEDE (?—1718). Stede Bonnet (*d.* 1718), British pirate. A retired officer and successful Barbados planter, Major Bonnet was an unlikely, latecoming pirate. His decision to turn to piracy has been attributed both to the desire to flee a nagging wife and to Bonnet's own mental instability. Captaining the *Revenge* (later the *Royal James*), he plundered several ships along the Atlantic seaboard before briefly joining the infamous Blackbeard (Edward Teach) in August 1717. At Blackbeard's suggestion, he surrendered to the King's Pardon (offered by Britain's King George I) in September, only to find that Blackbeard had used the occasion of his capitulation to steal his loot. Abandoning plans to privateer in the war against Spain, he unsuccessfully pursued Blackbeard, then recommenced pirating off the Carolina coast. Captured twice (he escaped the first time) by Colonel William Rhet, he was brought to trial, sentenced, and hanged in Charleston.

See also **Piracy.**

BIBLIOGRAPHY

Captain Charles Johnson [Daniel Defoe?], *A General History of the Robberies and Murders of the Most Notorious Pirates,* edited by Arthur L. Layward (1926), pp. 67–84.

Robert E. Lee, *Blackbeard the Pirate: A Reappraisal of His Life and Times,* 2d ed. (1976), pp. 30–33, 37–39, 52–53.

Additional Bibliography

Johnson, Charles. *Pirates.* London: Creation, 1999.

Zepke, Terrance. *Pirates of the Carolinas.* Sarasota, FL: Pineapple Press, 2005.

PHILIPPE L. SEILER

BONNY, ANNE Anne Bonny, an early-eighteenth-century pirate. Born near Cork, Ireland, Anne Bonny was the illegitimate daughter of an adulterous lawyer and his maid. At first, her father attempted to disguise her as a young male relative. When this ruse failed, he openly took up residence with Anne and her mother. His law practice suffered as a result of this affair, and he decided to immigrate to South Carolina along with Anne and her mother. He became a successful merchant in Charleston and later purchased a sizable plantation.

Anne's potential inheritance attracted many suitors, yet she eloped with James Bonny, a sailor of questionable integrity. The couple moved to New Providence in the Bahamas, a well-known pirate's haven. As part of his campaign to impose royal authority on the island, Captain Woodes Rogers offered to pardon James Bonny for whatever past crimes he had committed. Bonny not only accepted the pardon, but also spied on his former shipmates.

In the meantime, Anne had fallen in love with Captain "Calico Jack" Rackam and sought a divorce by sale from her husband. When he refused, Rackam and Anne, who posed as a seaman, hijacked a ship and fled the island. Together they raided coastal areas from Jamaica to Cuba. Her continuing masquerade did not prohibit intimate contact with Rackam and at one point she remained ashore in Cuba to bear their child. She had rejoined Rackam when they accepted the royal decree of amnesty for pirates in 1717. They later enlisted on the *Griffin,* a privateering ship, on which they mutinied and returned to piracy. Still disguised as a man, Anne became infatuated with another sailor. The object of her affections turned out to be Mary Read, another woman impersonating a seaman. The triangle formed by the two women and Rackam naturally led to a complex set of accusations, relationships, and clandestine rendezvous.

Anne fought courageously as a pirate and vehemently resisted capture by authorities. At her trial on 28 November 1720, Anne suprised the court with the revelation that she was an expectant mother. Anne's condition saved her from the gallows and she even mocked Rackam on the day of his execution. Anne spent time in prison for her crimes, although she occasionally was granted leaves. Her life after prison passed without notoriety.

See also **Piracy; Read, Mary.**

BIBLIOGRAPHY

Charles Johnson, *A General History of the Robberies and Murders of the Most Notorious Pirates from Their First Rise and Settlement in the Island of Providence to the Present Year,* edited by Arthur L. Hayward (1926).

George Woodbury, *The Great Days of Piracy in the West Indies* (1951).

Rafael Abella, *Los piratas del Nuevo Mundo* (1989).

Additional Bibliography

Black, Clinton V. *Pirates of the West Indies.* Cambridge, U.K.: Cambridge University Press, 1995.

Canfield, Rob. "Something's Mizzen: Anne Bonny, Mary Read, 'Polly,' and Female Counter-Roles on the Imperialist Stage." *South Atlantic Review* 66 (Spring 2001): 45–63.

Lorimer, Sarah, and Susan Synarski. *Booty: Girl Pirates on the High Seas.* San Francisco: Barnes and Noble Books, 2005.

Rediker, Marcus Buford. *Villains of all Nations: Atlantic Pirates in the Golden Age.* Boston: Beacon Press, 2004.

Zepke, Terrance. *Pirates of the Carolinas.* Sarasota, FL: Pineapple Press, 2005.

JOHN J. CROCITTI

BONPLAND, AIMÉ JACQUES (1773–1858).

Aimé Jacques Bonpland (*b.* 29 August 1773; *d.* 11 May 1858), naturalist. Bonpland was born in La Rochelle, France, and studied medicine at the University of Paris. However, his real interest was in natural science. From 1799 to 1804 he accompanied Alexander von Humboldt on his travels to South America, where he collected 60,000 plants. Bernardino Rivadavia invited Bonpland to visit Buenos Aires. In 1817, with his wife and two assistants, he did so, and stayed. In 1818 he was named naturalist of the Río de la Plata and became deeply interested in the possibility of cultivating *yerba maté* in the former Jesuit reducciónes. Bonpland practiced medicine in Buenos Aires, and in 1821 was named to the chair of medicine of the Instituto Médico Militar. While traveling to the old Jesuit missions, he ran afoul of the dictator of Paraguay, José Gaspar Rodríguez de Francia, who kept him in Paraguay from 1822 to 1831.

Bonpland spoke out against the Rosas dictatorship and became involved in anti-Rosas activity. He remained in the provinces of Misiones and Corrientes, and in 1854 was named director of the Museo de la Provincia in Corrientes. Bonpland conducted numerous scientific expeditions, sending back to France and Germany flora and fauna of the Río de la Plata. He died in São Borja, Brazil.

See also **Science.**

BIBLIOGRAPHY

Adolphe Brunel, *Biographie d'Aimé Bonpland: Compagnon de voyage et collaborateur d'Al* (1871).

Guillermo Furlong Cardiff, "En el centenario de Aimé Bonpland, 1858–1859," in *Anales de la Academia argentina de geografía,* no. 2 (1958).

Additional Bibliography

Helferich, Gerard. *Humboldt's Cosmos: Alexander von Humboldt and the Latin American Journey that Changed the Way We See the World.* New York: Gotham Books, 2004.

Humboldt, Alexander von, et al. *Personal Narrative of Travels to the Equinoctial Regions of America during the Years 1799-1804.* Boston, MA: Indypublish.com, 2005.

Zea, Leopoldo, and Alberto García Saladino. *Humboldt y América Latina.* México: Programa Universitario de Difusión de Estudios Latinoamericanos: Instituto Panamericano de Geografía e Historia: Fondo de Cultura Económica, 2000.

NICHOLAS P. CUSHNER

BORAH, WOODROW (1912–1999). Wood-

row W. Borah (December 23, 1912– December 10, 1999) was recognized as one of the most influential scholars in the field of Latin American history. He received his doctorate at the University of California, Berkeley, with a dissertation on the colonial Mexican silk industry that was pioneering for its use of provincial archives and interdisciplinary range. He taught briefly at Princeton University and during World War II served in the Latin American Division of the Office of Strategic Services. He returned to Berkeley in 1948 as member of the speech faculty but moved to the History Department in 1962, retiring in 1980. Together with Sherburne F. Cook, Borah established the so-called Berkeley School of Latin American history, with a unique focus on historical demography. But Borah's research and publications extended to other aspects of colonial Spanish America, with emphasis on Mexico. In 1967 he headed the Conference on Latin American History and in 1986 received a Distinguished Service Award from the American Historical Association.

See also **Silk Industry and Trade.**

BIBLIOGRAPHY

Nettel, Patricia. "Borah, Chevalier y Gibson: Los autores clásicos y la historiografía económica y social del México colonial." *Historias* 41 (1998): 15–36.

Wilkie, James W., and Rebecca Horn. "An Interview with Woodrow Borah." *Hispanic American Historical Review* 65 (August 1985): 401–441.

DAVID BUSHNELL

BORBA GATO, MANUEL DE (c. 1628–

1718). Manuel de Borba Gato (*b.* ca. 1628; *d.* 1718), explorer and administrator in Brazil's mining region. One of the most famous *bandeirantes* (São Paulo explorers who sought wealth and slaves in frontier regions), Borba Gato participated in expeditions, in search of gold and jewels, that crossed the frontier region between his native São Paulo and Bahia. From 1674 to 1681 he accompanied his father-in-law, Fernão Dias Pais, on one of the largest and best organized of these missions. Although it failed in its quest for emeralds, the expedition opened up new areas for other mining and for eventual settlement. Then, implicated in the 1682 murder of the general administrator of mines, Dom Rodrigo de Castelo Branco, near Sumidouro, Borba Gato fled to the Rio Doce region. Never ceasing to look for mineral wealth, he remained in voluntary exile for nearly twenty years.

Borba Gato's exoneration of the murder charge came through the intervention of political allies in 1700. In that same year Borba Gato revealed that he had found gold in the Rio das Velhas area, a discovery that would make him one of the mining zone's richest men. With wealth came power, and he moved quickly into administrative posts. Beginning as the chief customs officer of Rio das Velhas, he rose in 1702 to general administrator of mines for the region.

When civil war flared up in 1708 between those who had come to the mines from São Paulo and the *emboabas* (outsiders), people from other areas, Borba Gato at first showed sympathy for his Paulista compatriots. Siding with two of his kinsmen in a dispute with the *emboabas'* leader, Borba Gato called the latter a thief and ordered his banishment from the area. He never carried out this order, however, and in fact tried to effect a reconciliation. Throughout the war he maintained a position of neutrality. After hostilities ended in 1709, Borba Gato received royal grants of land and the position of superintendent of mines as a reward for his loyal service.

See also **Banderias; Mining: Colonial Brazil.**

BIBLIOGRAPHY

Manoel S. Cardozo, "The *Guerra dos Emboabas:* Civil War in Minas Gerais, 1708–1709," in *Hispanic American Historical Review* 22, no. 3 (1942): 470–492.

Charles R. Boxer, "The Gold Rush in Minas Gerais" and "Paulistas and Emboabas," chaps. 2 and 3 in his *The Golden Age of Brazil, 1695–1750* (1962).

Additional Bibliography

Donato, Hernâno, and Mozart Couto. *O cotidiano brasileiro no século XVIII.* São Paulo: Melhoramentos, 1998.

Fausto, Boris. *A Concise History of Brazil.* Cambridge: Cambridge University Press, 1999.

ROGER A. KITTLESON

BORDABERRY, JUAN MARÍA (1928–).

Juan María Bordaberry (*b.* 1928), president of Uruguay (1972–1976). The constitutional period of his presidency ended in June 1973 with his dissolution of Congress. From then until his deposition in 1976 for refusing to negotiate a return to constitutional government, he headed a military regime (1973–1985).

Bordaberry started his political career as a member of Benito Nardone's populist *ruralista* movement, which played a major role in the National (Blanco) party's election victory of 1958. He later joined the Colorado Party of Jorge Pacheco Areco, was elected a senator (1969–1971), and was nominated for president by Pacheco Areco. In the 1971 elections Bordaberry's slate of candidates received only 22 percent of the total vote. The narrow Colorado victory over the Blanco candidate, Wilson Ferreira Aldunate, is widely believed to have been the result of fraud.

Bordaberry's government was characterized by vigorous repression of all popular protest movements and the persecution of the Tupamaro urban guerrilla movement, which, according to military sources, was defeated in 1972. Following passage of the State Security Bill of 1972, arbitrary

detentions, torture, and attacks by paramilitary groups became endemic. In 1973–1974 all opposition media were shut down, and all political and trade union activity was proscribed. In an essay titled "Las opciones" (1980) and during a speech at the National University in Santiago de Chile (1987), Bordaberry maintained that due to divine right, rulers are not obliged to seek legitimation by democratic vote. He has not held public office since 1976.

On November 17, 2006, Bordaberry and his former foreign minister, Juan Carlos Blanco, were arrested in connection with four political killings during the military rule of the 1970s. They were accused of involvement in the abduction and murder of two legislators and two political rebels who opposed their dictatorship.

See also **Ferreira Aldunate, Wilson; Pacheco Areco, Jorge; Uruguay, Political Parties: Colorado Party.**

BIBLIOGRAPHY

Juan María Bordaberry, *Hacia una doctrina política nacional* (1974).

Oscar H. Bruschera, *Las décadas infames: Análisis político, 1967–1985* (1986).

Martin Weinstein, *Uruguay: Democracy at the Crossroads* (1988).

Additional Bibliography

Campodónico, Miguel Angel. *Antes del silencio: Bordaberry: Memorias de un presidente uruguayo.* Montevideo: Linardi y Risso, 2003.

Fischer, Diego. *Sobremesa presidencial.* Montevideo: Fundación Banco de Boston, 1994.

Lessa, Alfonso. *Estado de guerra: De la gestación del golpe del 73 a la caída de Bordaberry.* Montevideo: Editorial Fin de Siglo, 1996.

Pernas, Walter. *La caída: El dictador Bordaberry y su canciller presos.* Montevideo: Ediciones Cauce, 2006.

DIETER SCHONEBOHM

BORDERLANDS, THE.

The Borderlands is a term popularized by historian Herbert Eugene Bolton (1870–1953) for those parts of the United States once occupied by Spain. It refers to an area mostly south of an imaginary sagging line from the Chesapeake Bay west to San Francisco Bay and sometimes includes the northern states of Mexico. Thanks to explorations undertaken by Hernando de Soto, Francisco Vázquez de Coronado, and Juan Rodríguez Cabrillo between 1539 and 1543, Spaniards had a remarkably accurate early idea of the vastness and variety of the region. Spanish occupation flowed from the Caribbean and central New Spain, driven piecemeal by the search for exploitable resources, Christian missionary zeal, concern for the defense of the more central provinces, and advantage in the imperial contest for North America. Through almost three centuries, the Caribbean rim and the northern frontier of New Spain remained a thinly peopled fringe of civil outposts, missions, and presidios. From the humid Gulf Coast of greater Florida, Louisiana, and Texas, through the arid, basin-and-range high desert of New Mexico, and on up California's foggy shore; from hunting-fishing-gathering Karankawas, Seris, and Chumashes, through Plains Apaches, Comanches, Navajos, and Pimas, to the Pueblo dwellers of New Mexico and Arizona; from St. Augustine (1565) and Santa Fe (1610), through El Paso (1683), Pensacola (1698), and San Antonio (1718), to Tucson (1776) and San Francisco (1776), the only thing that binds the Borderlands together is the history and heritage of the colonial encounter between Spaniards and Native Americans.

Although many scholars have abandoned the term Borderlands and indeed the concept of the region, no one has devised an acceptable alternative. Studies of the western Borderlands (from Texas and the Mexican state of Tamaulipas to both Californias) have proceeded with little attention to the eastern Borderlands (the coastal Carolinas, Georgia, Florida, Alabama, Mississippi, and Louisiana) and vice versa. Recently, however, a reunification seems to be taking place. Indicative of the trend are David J. Weber's *The Spanish Frontier in North America, 1513–1821* (1992); the three-volume *Columbian Consequences*, edited by David Hurst Thomas and subtitled, respectively, *Archaeological and Historical Perspectives on the Spanish Borderlands West* (1989), *Archaeological and Historical Perspectives on the Spanish Borderlands East* (1990), and *The Spanish Borderlands in Pan-American Perspective* (1991); and the *SMRC-Newsletter*, published since 1967 by the Southwestern Mission Research Center in Tucson and which includes studies about the Borderlands from the Atlantic to the Pacific.

Since the late 1980s, two notable Hispanic-Latino thinkers writing inside the United States have given new vigor and direction to this ideological construct by politicizing it. Gloria Anzaldúa, writing from a Chicana vantage point in her *Borderlands/La Frontera: The New Mestiza* (1987), juxtaposes the Nahuatl term *nepantla*, to be divided, with the Spanish term *mestizo* for racial fusion. In his *Local Histories/Global Designs: Coloniality, Subaltern Knowledges, and Border Thinking* (2000), Walter Mignolo, a professor at Duke University, takes Anzaldúa's *nepantlismo* as a starting point and develops a hypothesis of global colonialities from it. Renewed interest in globalization dating from the 1992 quincentenary of Columbus's arrival in the new world implies further interest in a politicized Borderlands theory.

See also **Bolton, Herbert Eugene; United States-Latin American Relations; United States-Mexico Border.**

BIBLIOGRAPHY

Anzaldúa, Gloria. *Borderlands/La Frontera: The New Mestiza*. San Francisco: Spinsters/Aunt Lute, 1987; 2nd edition, 1999.

Badger, R. Reid, and Lawrence A. Clayton. *Alabama and the Borderlands: From Prehistory to Statehood*. University, AL: University of Alabama Press, 1985.

Bannon, John F. *The Spanish Borderlands Frontier, 1513–1821*. Albuquerque: University of New Mexico Press, 1974.

Bannon, John F., ed. *Bolton and the Spanish Borderlands*. Norman: University of Oklahoma, 1964.

Bolton, Herbert E. *The Spanish Borderlands: A Chronicle of Old Florida and the Southwest*. New Haven, CT: Yale University Press, 1921.

Hadley, Drummond. *The Voice of the Borderlands*. Tucson, AZ: Rio Nuevo Publishers, 2005.

Keating, Ana Louise. *Entre Mundos/Among Worlds: New Perspectives on Gloria E. Anzaldúa*. New York: Palgrave, 2005.

Mignolo, Walter. *Local Histories/Global Designs: Coloniality, Subaltern Knowledges, and Border Thinking*. Princeton: Princeton University Press, 2000.

Stoddard, Ellwyn R., Richard L. Nostrand, and Jonathan P. West, eds. *Borderlands Sourcebook: A Guide to the Literature on Northern Mexico and the American Southwest*. Norman: University of Oklahoma Press, 1983.

Thomas, David Hurst, ed. *Spanish Borderlands Sourcebooks*, 27 vols. New York: Garland, 1991–1992. Consists mostly of reprinted documents and articles.

JOHN L. KESSELL
THOMAS WARD

BORGE, TOMÁS (1930–).

Tomás Borge (*b.* 13 August 1930), Nicaraguan leader and cofounder of the Sandinista National Liberation Front. Tomás Borge was born into the family of a drugstore owner in Matagalpa. His political experience began in 1946 with the Independent Liberal Party's student arm, the Democratic Youth Front. He mobilized high school and university students in traditional Liberal areas against the Somoza family. He met Carlos Fonseca and Silvio Mayorga in 1954, upon entering law school at the National Autonomous University in León. Two years later he was arrested in connection with the assassination of Anastasio Somoza García and convicted on the basis of false testimony. After being severely tortured, he escaped to Costa Rica in 1959. In 1960 he sought support from Fidel Castro for the nascent revolutionary movement in Nicaragua. He helped found the Sandinista National Liberation Front in July 1961.

In 1963 Borge led combatants in the attack on the National Guard post in Río Coco. Two years later he became an organizer of the short-lived Republican Mobilization movement. This venture failed in 1966, so he returned to guerrilla warfare, participating in the ill-conceived battle at Pancasán in 1967. Borge fled to Costa Rica, then spent time in Peru and Cuba before returning to Nicaragua in 1971. The National Guard captured him in 1976 and again subjected him to torture. The Sandinista takeover of the National Palace in August 1978 led to Borge's release from prison. He subsequently assumed the leadership of the Prolonged Popular War faction with Henry Ruíz and Bayardo Arce.

After the July 1979 Sandinista victory and Somoza's exile, Borge became minister of the interior, in charge of the police and security forces. He also managed the government's relations with the indigenous peoples on the Atlantic coast. In the 1980s he wrote on many subjects, including human rights, national sovereignty, and revolutionary ideology. While in power, Borge was considered the principal representative of the intransigent, Marxist-Leninist wing of the Sandinista regime. He was replaced as minister of the interior by the Chamorro government in April 1990. As of 1993 he was writing articles for Latin American, North American, and European journals.

See also **Nicaragua, Sandinista National Liberation Front (FSLN).**

BIBLIOGRAPHY

Tomás Borge, "Tomás Borge Speaks on Human Rights in Nicaragua," in *International Press,* 16 March 1981, pp. 245–250.

David Nolan, *The Ideology of the Sandinistas and the Nicaraguan Revolution* (1984).

John Booth, *The End and the Beginning: The Nicaraguan Revolution,* 2d ed. (1985).

Additional Bibliography

Borge, Tomás. *Los primeros pasos: La revolución popular Sandinista.* México: Siglo Ventiuno Editores, 1981.

Borge, Tomás. *The Patient Impatience: From Boyhood to Guerrilla: A Personal Narrative of Nicaragua's Struggle for Liberation.* Willimantic, CT: Curbstone Press, 1992.

Borge, Tomás. *Women and the Nicaraguan Revolution.* Managuá: Departamento de Relaciónes Públicas, Ministerio del Interior, 1982.

Díaz Polanco, Hector. *Nicaragua: Autonomía y revolución.* Panamá: Centro de Capacitación Social, 1986.

Paternostro, Silvia. "The Last Sandinista?" *The Nation* 263 (November 4, 1996): 22-25.

MARK EVERINGHAM

BORGES, JACOBO (1931–).

Jacobo Borges (*b.* 28 November 1931), Venezuelan artist. Born in a rural area near Caracas, Borges attended only primary school. In 1949–1951 he studied painting at the Cristóbal Rojas School of Fine and Applied Arts in Caracas while simultaneously working for an advertising agency and drawing comic strips. In 1952 he won a scholarship from Metro-Goldwyn-Mayer as part of a promotion of its film *An American in Paris* to study in Paris, where he joined the Young Painters' group and developed an expressionist style with social and political implications. Upon his return to Caracas in 1956, he became a very active artist and soon held his first solo exhibition. Selected as one of the Venezuelan entries to the São Paulo Bienal in 1957, he won an honorable mention. From 1957 until 1965 he was a member of the Round Table Group and Whale Group cooperative. From 1965 until 1971, Borges stopped painting and devoted himself to theater and film design. He returned to painting in 1971, and five years later an exhibition of forty-eight of his canvasses, "Magic of a Realist Critic," was presented in Caracas and Mexico City. He wrote and illustrated *The Mountain and Its Era* (1979). In 1988 he represented Venezuela at the Venice Biennale and was included in the Latin American Spirit show at the Bronx Museum, New York, and the Guggenheim Museum exhibit, "Fifty Years: Anniversary Collection." Major retrospectives of his work have been held in the Staatliche Kunsthalle (Berlin, 1987) and the Museo de Arte Contemporáneo (Caracas, 1988). In Caracas in 1994, the Museo Jacobo Borges opened to honor his life's work.

See also **Art: The Twentieth Century.**

BIBLIOGRAPHY

Roldán Esteva Grillet, *Siete artistas venezolanos siglo XX: Rafael Monasterios, Armando Reverón, Héctor Poleo, Alejandro Otero, Carlos Cruz Diez, Jesús Soto y Jacobo Borges* (1984).

Jacobo Borges (CDS Gallery, New York, 1990), with introductory essays by Carlos Fuentes and Dore Ashton.

Additional Bibliography

Acha, Juan. "Jacobo Borges: Del grito al espacio alegórico." *Revista Nacional de la Cultura (Venezuela)* 51 (Jan–Mar 1990): 241–254.

Borges, Jacobo, and Carter Ratliff. *60 obras de Jacobo Borges: Museo de Arte Contemporáneo Internacionál Rufiño Tamayo, Ciudad de México, México Agosto-Octubre 1987: de la Pesca- al Espejo de aguas: [exposición itinerante].* Monterrey: Museo de Monterrey, 1987.

Borges, Jacobo. *Jacobo Borges.* Buenos Aires: Der Brücke Ediciones, 1990.

Esteva Grillet, Roldán. *Siete artistas venezolanos del siglo XX: Rafael Monasterios, Armando Reverón, Héctor Poleo, Alejandro Otero, Carlos Cruz-Diez, Jesús Soto y Jacobo Borges.* Mérida, Venezuela: Museo de Arte Moderno de Mérida, 1984.

BÉLGICA RODRÍGUEZ

BORGES, JORGE LUIS (1899–1986).

Jorge Luis Borges (*b.* 24 August 1899; *d.* 14 June 1986), Argentine writer. Born in Buenos Aires, Borges attended the Collège de Calvin in Geneva during World War I. In the period immediately after the war, he became involved with ultraism, an avant-garde movement in Madrid, and on his return to Argentina helped start an Argentine ultraist group. His earliest surviving poems are iconoclastic, showing concern with the trench warfare of the Great War and sympathy for the Bolshevik Revolution. In the 1920s Borges published three books of poetry (*Fervor de Buenos Aires, Luna de enfrente,* and *Cuaderno San Martín*) and three books of essays (*Inquisiciones, El tamaño de mi esperanza,* and *El idioma de los argentinos*); his writings of the period are imbued with cultural nationalism, in keeping with his support for the populist leader Hipólito Irigoyen.

In the early 1930s Borges worked for a time on the literary supplement of Natalio Botana's innovative daily *Crítica;* it was there that he first published the sketches of the lives of various gangsters, pirates, imposters, and murderers that became his first book of fiction, *Historia universal de la infamia* (1935). In 1937 he became an employee at the Miguel Cané Municipal Library in Buenos Aires, a job that afforded him abundant time for reading and writing. From 1939 to 1953 he produced his most famous stories, collected as *Ficciones* (1944) and *El Aleph* (1949). These years also saw the publication of the essays in *Otras inquisiciones* (1952), most of which were first delivered as lectures in Argentina and Uruguay after Borges was fired from his job in the municipal library for signing a petition against the alliance of the Argentine military with the Nazis. His lectures and essays were no doubt celebrated in part because he was viewed as a symbol of opposition to Juan Domingo Perón. When Perón fell in 1955, Borges was named director of the National Library, a job he held until the return of Peronism.

The final years of Borges's life were marked, or perhaps marred, by celebrity. Beginning in 1961 when he was awarded the Formentor Prize (an international publishers' prize, which he shared with Samuel Beckett), Borges's work was translated into many languages and became the subject of an ever more vast critical bibliography. Borges was also pursued by students of literature and by journalists; even one of Woody Allen's characters in *Manhattan* boasts of her intentions to interview him. As a result, we know Borges's opinions on soccer, politics, Richard M. Nixon, Argentina, blacks, the English language, Federico García Lorca, and so forth, and for a time these (often misinformed or bigoted) opinions seemed to eclipse Borges's own work. Even years after his death, the details of his life seem to have the power to fascinate or titillate the public, particularly the Argentine public; revelations on his love life, brushes with psychoanalysis, proxy marriage, and death in Geneva have all, rather improbably, been major news in Argentina and elsewhere. The first English language compilation of all his short stories was published as *Collected Fictions* in 1998.

Of greater interest in the long run, perhaps, are Borges's complex relations to Argentine culture, history, and politics. His initial populist nationalism (and enthusiasm for Irigoyen) included a measure of intolerance for "low-brow" Argentine culture: he condemned the poet Alfonsina Storni for what he termed her shrill sentimentality, and he made similar attacks on Carlos Gardel's tangos in the 1920s and 1930s. The national tradition to which he was to prove most faithful was liberal and cosmopolitan, as defined in his lecture "The Argentine Writer and Tradition" in 1951 (later included in the second edition of *Discusión* in 1957); his version of the Argentine national tradition necessarily competed with a number of others, and one of them, that of Perón, was to prove rather more decisive.

Two stories written in the late 1940s illustrate Borges's complex relations to the time in which he lived. "La fiesta del monstruo," written (in collaboration with Adolfo Bioy Casares) in 1947 but not published until after the fall of Perón, is a ferocious satire on the Peronist mass meetings in the Plaza de Mayo in the first years of the new regime; the "Monster" of the story is Perón himself, who inspires his followers from afar in their torture and killing of a Jewish passerby. The story is narrated by a brash young Peronist and is an obvious recasting of two crucial liberal texts of the nineteenth century by opponents of the government of Juan Manuel de Rosas: Esteban Echevarría's short story "El matadero" and Hilario Ascasubi's gauchesque poem "La refalosa."

In 1948 Borges's sister and mother were arrested for taking part in a demonstration against the new Peronist constitution (which among other things, of course, gave women the right to vote). A few months later, Borges wrote a curious story,

"Historia del guerrero y de la cautiva," which (when compared to "La fiesta del monstruo") is a rather more nuanced reflection on the need for political action. The character Droctulft, the Germanic invader of Italy who changes sides to join the inhabitants of Ravenna in the defense of their city, is an unequivocal convert to "civilization" but is offset in the story by an English captive woman who chooses to remain with her Indian husband. The captive's story is retold later by Borges's English grandmother, Fanny Haslam de Borges, in a way that barely alludes to the two events that consolidate her feelings of solidarity with the captive woman she saw so many years before on the pampas: her husband, Colonel Francisco Borges, was killed in the civil war in 1874 when he chose to follow Bartolomé Mitre against Adolfo Alsina; the English captive's husband was no doubt to be captured or killed in the "Conquest of the Desert" in 1879. Who is to know, Borges seems to be saying, whether one ultimately is taking the part of civilization or of savagery?

See also **Literature: Spanish America.**

BIBLIOGRAPHY

For details of Borges's life, see Emir Rodríguez Monegal, *Jorge Luis Borges: A Literary Biography* (1978), though the text is sometimes rather untrustworthy; of great interest also is Estela Canto, *Borges a contraluz* (1989). Sylvia Molloy, *Las letras de Borges* (1979), translated as *Signs of Borges* (1994), is the best critical book on the author; see also Beatriz Sarlo, *Jorge Luis Borges* (1993) and Daniel Balderston, *Out of Context* (1993). A good article on Borges's cultural nationalism is Graciela Montaldo, "Borges: Una vanguardia criolla," in *Yrigoyen, entre Borges y Arlt (1916–1930)*, edited by David Viñas (1989), pp. 213–232. Reference works include Daniel Balderston, *The Literary Universe of Jorge Luis Borges* (1986), which indexes most of Borges's works; Evelyn Fishburn and Psiche Hughes, *A Dictionary of Borges* (1990), which focuses on the stories; and Ion Agheana, *Reasoned Thematic Dictionary of the Prose of Jorge Luis Borges* (1990).

Additional Bibliography

Alvarez, Nicolás Emilio. *Discurso e historia en la obra narrativa de Jorge Luis Borges: Examen de Ficciones y El Aleph.* Boulder, CO: Society of Spanish and Spanish American Studies, 1998.

Gómez López-Quiñones, Antonio. *Borges y el nazismo: Sur (1937–1946).* Granada: Universidad de Granada, 2004.

Salas, Horacio. *Borges: Una biografía*. Buenos Aires: Planeta, 1994.

Woodall, James. *The Man in the Mirror of the Book: A Life of Jorge Luis Borges*. London: Hodder & Stoughton, 1996.

DANIEL BALDERSTON

BORGES DE MEDEIROS, ANTÔNIO AUGUSTO

(1863–1961). Antônio Augusto Borges de Medeiros (*b.* 19 November 1863; *d.* 25 April 1961), Brazilian statesman and political boss of Rio Grande do Sul (1903–1930). Born the son of an imperial judge in Capavaca, Rio Grande do Sul, Borges graduated from the Recife Law School in 1885 and agitated for the republic in his native province. A member of the federal Constituent Assembly, he supported Júlio de Castilhos's coup in 1892 and fought the rebels in the Federalist Revolt of 1893–1895. Picked by Castilhos as governor in 1898, Borges served the Riograndense Republican Party boss until Castilhos's death in 1903. Borges then became party leader and ruled the state until 1930, serving as governor a total of twenty-five years.

Like Castilhos, a Comtian positivist, Borges used the former's autocratic constitution to promote public education and rural property taxes; he also balanced the budget and practiced labor paternalism. With Senator Pinheiro Machado, Borges made the Riograndense Republicans contenders in national politics against counterparts in Minas and São Paulo. The gauchos opposed the Paulistas successfully in 1910, played arbiter in 1919, lost in 1922 and 1930, but then incited a revolt, overthrowing the regime. Riograndense economic interests, which were tied to the domestic foodstuffs market, often collided with those of the export-oriented Paulistas.

In 1928 Borges made Getúlio Vargas governor, and he backed Vargas's revolution in 1930. He soon broke with Vargas, supporting São Paulo's Constitutionalist Revolt (1932). Following the defeat of that movement and his imprisonment in Pernambuco, Borges de Medeiros received the second largest number of votes for the presidency in the Constituent Assembly of 1933–1934, losing to his protégé Vargas. Elected to Congress in October 1934 on the opposition ticket, Borges advocated a parliamentary regime to preclude a presidential

dictatorship. His fears were realized three years later, when Vargas declared the authoritarian Estado Nôvo regime and closed Congress, effectively terminating Borges's political career.

See also **Brazil, Populist Republic, 1945–1964.**

BIBLIOGRAPHY

João Neves Da Fontoura, *Memorias*. Vol. 1, *Borges de Medeiros e Seu Tempo* (1958).

Joseph L. Love, *Rio Grande do Sul and Brazilian Regionalism, 1882–1930* (1971).

Carlos E. Cortés, *Gaúcho Politics in Brazil* (1974), pp. 1–88.

Israel Beloch and Alzira Alves De Abreu, eds., *Dicionário histórico-biográfico brasileiro, 1930–1983* (1984), pp. 2142–2151.

Luiz Carlos Barbosa Lessa, *Borges de Medeiros* (1985).

Additional Bibliography

Félix, Loiva Otero. *Coronelismo, borgismo, e cooptação política*. Porto Alegre: Editora da Universidade, Universidade Federal do Rio Grande do Sul, 1996.

Franco, Sérgio da Costa. *A pacificação de 1923: As negociações de Bagé*. Porto Alegre: Editora da Universidade, Universidade Federal do Rio Grande do Sul, 1996.

Pesavento, Sandra Jatahy. *Borges de Medeiros*. Porto Alegre: IEL, 1996.

JOSEPH L. LOVE

BORJA CEVALLOS, RODRIGO (1935–).

Rodrigo Borja Cevallos (*b.* 19 June 1935), president of Ecuador (1988–1992). Born in Quito of a family descended from early Spanish settlers, Borja graduated with distinction from the law school of the Universidad Central in 1960. Already a member of the Liberal Party, he soon entered politics and was first elected to Congress in 1962. Borja was later a central figure among the young Liberals who broke with the traditional leadership to found a new political party, the Izquierda Democrática (Democratic Left—ID) in 1977. Borja was elected congressman from the province of Pichincha in 1970. When constitutional rule was suspended by military *golpe* (1972), he turned to building and developing the ID as Ecuador's first national, mass-based political party.

When military rule came to an end, Borja ran for the presidency in 1978, finishing fourth but establishing himself and his party as a major political contender. Subsequently seated in Congress in honorary office, Borja became a leading spokesman of Ecuador's center Left, and in 1984 he was narrowly defeated in the presidential race. Continuing as the leading opposition congressman, Borja was again the ID candidate in 1988 and won by a comfortable margin. Inaugurated in August 1988, he faced high inflation, economic recession, a huge foreign debt, and declining oil prices. Despite his prestige as a leader of Latin American social democracy, he was forced to adopt basically neoliberal policies, such as cutting subsidies and using free-market practices. Continuing austerity and economic hardship cost his party popular support, and the ID lost its majority in the 1990 congressional elections. Constitutionally prohibited from a second consecutive term as president, Borja continued to grapple with economic pressures as his administration drew to a close. He twice more ran for president, both times unsucessfully. In 1998, he earned 12 percent of the vote and was the third place candidate, while in 2002 the 14 percent that he earned only brought him to fourth place.

See also **Ecuador, Political Parties: Democratic Left (ID).**

BIBLIOGRAPHY

Osvaldo Hurtado, *Political Power in Ecuador,* translated by Nick D. Mills, Jr. (1980).

John D. Martz, *Politics and Petroleum in Ecuador* (1987).

Additional Bibliography

Bacigualpo, Dalton. *Discursos desde el poder.* 2nd ed. Quito: Artes Gráficas Señal Impreseñal, 2005.

Gerlach, Allen. *Indians, Oil, and Politics: A Recent History of Ecuador.* Wilmington, DE: SR Books, 2003.

Striffler, Steve. *In the Shadows of State and Capital: The United Fruit Company, Popular Struggle, and Agrarian Restructuring in Ecuador, 1900–1995.* Durham, NC: Duke University Press, 2002.

JOHN D. MARTZ

BORJA Y ARAGÓN, FRANCISCO DE

(1583–1658). Francisco de Borja y Aragón (Príncipe de Esquilache; *b.* 1583; *d.* 26 September 1658), twelfth viceroy of Peru. The prince of Esquilache, scion of a distinguished Spanish family related to Pope Alexander VI and Saint Francis Borja, was one of the most cultured of royal bureaucrats, an accomplished poet, patron of the arts, and

administrator. Esquilache was appointed viceroy in 1614, when he was only thirty-two years old. His rule was marked by its concern with the practice of idolatry among the Indians and with the security of the empire in the face of continuing Dutch threats. His correspondence with the crown was copious and became a model for other viceroys. Nevertheless, there is debate over Esquilache's personal involvement in governing Peru, since it is possible that he left many details to his well-trained staff. Anxious to hurry back to the court to greet the new monarch, Philip IV, he left the viceroyalty in 1621, before his successor arrived. He spent the last thirty years of his life writing poetry.

See also **Peru: From the Conquest through Independence.**

BIBLIOGRAPHY

Juan Wyskota Z., *El virrey poeta: Seis años de administración de don Francisco de Borja y Aragón en el Perú (1615–1621)* (1970).

Additional Bibliography

Jiménez-Belmonte, Javier. "Un príncipe en la república de las letras: Las obras en verso del Príncipe de Esquilache y la formación del campo literario español de la primera mitad del XVII." Ph.D. thesis. Columbia University, 2002.

JOHN F. SCHWALLER

BORNO, JOSEPH LOUIS E. ANTOINE FRANÇOIS

(1865–1942). Joseph Louis E. Antoine François Borno (*b.* 1865; *d.* 19 July 1942), president of Haiti (1922–1930). Before becoming president, Borno served as minister of foreign affairs and ambassador to the Dominican Republic. He was an advocate of the U.S. intervention in Haiti, inducing the Haitian government to sign the 1915 treaty by which it pledged total cooperation with the United States.

On 12 April 1922, Borno was elected to his first term as president of Haiti. He was reelected in 1926. His first term was relatively stable, but the second ended in crisis with the United States. The combination of the poor economic conditions and the tensions arising from the U.S. occupation led to an uprising against the U.S. Marines in 1929. In 1930, he accepted President Herbert Hoover's investigating committee's recommendations that

U.S. Marines be gradually withdrawn and that popular elections be held. He agreed to step down and supported the U.S. selection of Eugene Roy as provisional president until elections could be held. Roy was replaced by Stenio Vincent.

See also **Haiti.**

BIBLIOGRAPHY

Three works that relate to the U.S. occupation of and involvement in Haiti, 1915–1934, are Hans Schmidt, *The United States Occupation of Haiti, 1915–1934* (1971); Arthur C. Millspaugh, *Haiti Under American Control, 1915–1930* (1970); and Robert D. Heinl, Jr., and Nancy G. Heinl, *Written in Blood: The Story of the Haitian People* (1978).

Additional Bibliography

Blancpain, François. *Haïti et les Etats-Unis: 1915–1934: Histoire d'une occupation.* Paris: L'Harmattan, 1999.

Renda, Mary A. *Taking Haiti: Military Occupation and the Culture of U.S. Imperialism, 1915–1940.* Chapel Hill: University of North Carolina Press, 2001.

Shannon, Magdaline W. *Jean Price-Mars, the Haitian Elite and the American Occupation, 1915–1935.* New York: St. Martin's Press, 1996.

DARIÉN DAVIS

BORRERO Y CORTÁZAR, ANTONIO

(1827–1911). Antonio Borrero y Cortázar (*b.* 28 October 1827; *d.* 9 October 1911), president of Ecuador (1875–1876). A moderate politician, Borrero was selected by Conservative president Gabriel García Moreno (1861–1865, 1869–1875) to run for the vice presidency in 1863. Borrero won in a landslide despite the fact that he did not want the job. He immediately resigned, disgusted by García Moreno's rigging of the election. When García Moreno was assassinated in 1875, Borrero won the subsequent election for president. He hoped to be a healer, peacemaker, and reconciler for a nation so often bloodied by regional and ideological battles. However, in seeking to find a middle road between Liberals and Conservatives, he managed only to antagonize both.

General Ignacio de Veintimilla overthrew Borrero in 1876. After seven years in exile in Peru, Borrero returned to serve as governor of Azuay province (1888–1892). A man of laws, a well-read—if not

well-traveled—intellectual, Borrero was known by contemporaries as the "Cato of Cuenca," or the "Washington of Azuay." Borrero is sometimes viewed by historians as the first Progresita, the grouping of pragmatic political moderates that governed Ecuador from 1883 to 1895. He died in Cuenca, his birthplace.

See also **Alfaro Delgado, José Eloy.**

BIBLIOGRAPHY

On Ecuadorian politics, see Osvaldo Hurtado's interpretive history, *Political Power in Ecuador,* translated by Nick D. Mills, Jr. (1895); and Frank MacDonald Spindler's descriptive *Nineteenth Century Ecuador: An Historical Introduction* (1987). For summary treatment of nineteenth-century Ecuadorian political economy, consult David W. Schodt, *Ecuador: An Andean Enigma* (1987).

Additional Bibliography

Borrero Vintimilla, Antonio. *Filosofía, política y pensamiento del presidente Antonio Borrero y Cortázar, 1875-1876: Aspectos de la política del Ecuador del siglo XIX.* Cuenca, Ecuador: Universidad del Azuay, 1999.

RONN F. PINEO

BOSCH GAVIÑO, JUAN (1909–2001).

Juan Bosch Gaviño (*b.* 30 June 1909; *d.* 1 November 2001), Dominican novelist, sociologist, historian, politician, and president of the Dominican Republic (1963). Bosch, a native of La Vega, published his first collection of short stories, *Camino Real,* in 1933. One year later, Rafael Leónidas Trujillo Molina arrested Bosch for conspiracy against his regime. Released in 1935, Bosch became literary editor of the Dominican Republic's most prestigious newspaper, *Listín Diario.* In 1936 he published one of his most popular novels, *La Mañosa.* Unable to live under the Trujillo dictatorship, he fled his country in 1938. During the next twenty-three years of exile, Bosch resided in Cuba, Costa Rica, Bolivia, Chile, and Venezuela. He was one of the organizers of the Dominican Revolutionary Party (PRD), which was founded in 1939 at Havana. Later, he served as secretary to Cuban President Carlos Prío Socarrás (1948–1952) and helped to organize the abortive attempt to overthrow Trujillo, known as Cayo Confite.

After Trujillo's assassination in 1961, Bosch returned to his native land in order to organize the PRD on Dominican soil. In December 1962, he won the first presidential elections held in the Dominican Republic since 1930. Inaugurated in February 1963, he was deposed after only seven months by a military coup backed by elements of the military (under General Elías Wessín y Wessín), the landowning and business elites, the hierarchy of the Roman Catholic Church, and the military attachés of the United States. Bosch was once again forced into exile, from which he did not return until 1966.

The regime installed by the military coup in September 1963 proved to be most unpopular and was removed by a revolution that occurred on 24 April 1965. The chief aim of the revolutionaries, who called themselves Constitutionalists, was to return Bosch to the presidency of the nation. In order to prevent this possibility, U.S. President Lyndon Johnson dispatched U.S. Marines to Santo Domingo on 28 April. Some historians have claimed that Bosch was a coward for not returning to his country to lead the Constitutionalists in their battle against the Loyalists of Wessín y Wessín and the interventionist forces of the United States. Bosch has responded to this criticism by stating that agents of the Federal Bureau of Investigation surrounded his residence in Puerto Rico in order to prevent his return to Santo Domingo.

Both Bosch and his rival, Joaquín Balaguer, returned from exile for the presidential elections of 1966, in which they were the candidates for the Dominican Revolutionary Party, and the Reformist Party, respectively. Balaguer possessed decisive advantages during the electoral campaign and won the election. In 1973 Bosch broke with the Dominican Revolutionary Party, which he had helped to found, and formed his own political movement, the Party of Dominican Liberation (PLD). When the PLD ran for the first time in 1978, it obtained only an insignificant number of votes, but by the elections of 1982, it was represented in the Dominican Congress by six deputies. In 1986 the PLD obtained 18.3 percent of the vote as well as sixteen deputies and two senators in the Congress. With the disintegration of the Dominican Revolutionary Party into various factions, the PLD emerged as the main challenger of Balaguer's Reformist Party.

During the presidential elections of 1990, Bosch and Balaguer faced each other once again, the latter winning by a narrow margin. Bosch accused his opponent of electoral fraud and threatened to take the dispute to the streets, a move from which he was dissuaded by former U.S. President Jimmy Carter, who mediated between the octogenarian rivals. In 1994 he ran again and again lost. He died on November 1, 2001, in Santo Domingo. Although deeply involved in Dominican politics for over five decades, Bosch will probably be remembered more for his literary achievements than for his accomplishments in the political realm.

See also **Dominican Republic.**

BIBLIOGRAPHY

Bosch's writings include *Cuentos escritos en el exilio* (1962), *The Unfinished Experiment* (1966), *Composición social dominicana* (1970), *El oro y la paz* (1976), and *33 artículos de temas políticos* (1988). See also John Bartlow Martin, *Overtaken by Events: The Dominican Crisis from the Fall of Trujillo to the Civil War* (1966); and Comité Pro Homenaje A Juan Bosch, *Juan Bosch: Un hombre de siempre* (1989).

Additional Bibliography

García Cuevas, Eugenio de J. *Juan Bosch: Novela, historia, y sociedad.* San Juan, PR: Isla Negra, 1995.

González, Raymundo. *Política, identidad y pensamiento social en la República Dominicana, siglos XIX y XX.* Madrid: Doce Calles, 1999.

San Miguel, Pedro Luis. *The Imagined Island: History, Identity, & Utopia in Hispaniola.* Chapel Hill: University of North Carolina Press, 2005.

KAI P. SCHOENHALS

BOSSA NOVA.

Bossa Nova, Brazilian music genre that emerged in Rio de Janeiro in the late 1950s. It became highly popular around the world in the 1960s due to its casual sophistication, light breeziness, and infectious swing. Bossa has been characterized by rhythmic elements of samba, a highly syncopated style of playing guitar, a generally subdued vocal style when sung, and harmonic influences from both American cool jazz and classical music. Guitarist-vocalist João Gilberto developed the characteristic bossa rhythmic style on guitar. Antônio Carlos ("Tom") Jobim was the genre's most influential composer, and pianists João Donato and Luis Eça, guitarists Luiz Bonfá and Baden Powell, vocalist

Nara Leão, singer-songwriters Carlos Lyra, Roberto Menescal, and Ronaldo Bôscoli, and poet-lyricist Vinícius de Moraes were other key figures.

"Chega de saudade" (1958), performed by Gilberto and written by Jobim and de Moraes, is considered the first bossa single; Gilberto's 1959 LP of the same name was the style's first album. The 1959 French-Brazilian movie *Orfeu Negro* (*Black Orpheus*), which included songs by Bonfá, Jobim, and de Moraes, popularized the bossa tunes "Manhã de Carnaval" and "A felicidade" around the world. Charlie Byrd and Stan Getz's 1962 album "Jazz Samba," with songs by Jobim, de Moraes, Bonfá, and Powell, was a smash hit and launched bossa in North America. A boom ensued, and dozens of jazz musicians recorded bossa compositions. In 1964, the style had reached the peak of its popularity with the release of "Getz-Gilberto," an album that teamed saxophonist Getz with Gilberto and Jobim. The LP earned four Grammys, spent ninety-six weeks on the pop charts, and included the now-famous tune "The Girl From Ipanema" (sung by Gilberto and his wife Astrud). Bossa nova had an enormous musical influence on American jazz and international pop in general in the 1960s, and since then has continued to be one of Brazil's most popular styles.

See also **Gilberto, João; Music: Popular Music and Dance.**

BIBLIOGRAPHY

Ruy Castro, *Chega de saudade* (1991).

Chris McGowan and Ricardo Pessanha, *The Brazilian Sound: Samba, Bossa Nova, and the Popular Music of Brazil* (1991).

Additional Bibliography

Castro, Ruy. *Bossa Nova: The Story of the Brazilian Music that Seduced the World*. Chicago: A Cappella, 2000.

Murphy, John P. *Music in Brazil: Experiencing Music, Expressing Culture*. New York: Oxford University Press, 2006.

Naves, Santuza Cambraia. *Da bossa nova à tropicália*. Rio de Janeiro: Jorge Zahar Editor, 2001.

Sola, José Antonio. *Bossa nova: O movimiento que ampliou os limites da MPB*. São Paulo: J.A Sola, 2000.

Távola, Artur da. *40 años de bossa nova*. Rio de Janeiro: Sextante, 1998.

CHRIS MCGOWAN

BOSTON FRUIT COMPANY.

Boston Fruit Company, a banana import firm in the United States. In 1885, when twelve New Englanders under the leadership of Captain Lorenzo D. Baker and Andrew W. Preston invested $15,000 to establish the Boston Fruit Company, the enterprise joined at least sixty other banana companies founded late in the nineteenth century to transport bananas from Central America and the West Indies to the United States. By 1890, when the company was incorporated in Massachusetts, Boston Fruit had become the most successful banana company in the United States. The initial investment had grown to $531,000. There were several reasons for the company's success in transporting and marketing one of the world's most perishable fruits. Replacing sailing vessels with steamships, the company soon purchased two of the fastest cargo ships operating in the Caribbean. Because Boston Fruit established extensive banana plantations in Jamaica, the company was assured a steady supply of the golden fruit—upward of 250,000 stems a year by 1892. In order to expand the distribution and sales of its bananas, Boston Fruit formed the Fruit Dispatch Company, which allowed it to reach U.S. inland markets. In 1899 Boston Fruit merged with Minor C. Keith's three banana companies, with extensive holdings in Costa Rica, Panama, and Colombia, to form the United Fruit Company.

See also **Banana Industry; Fruit Industry.**

BIBLIOGRAPHY

Charles M. Wilson, *Empire in Green and Gold: The Story of the American Banana Trade* (1947), pp. 69–97.

Stacy May and Galo Plaza, *The United Fruit Company in Latin America* (1958), pp. 5–7.

Wilson Randolph Bartlett, Jr., "Lorenzo Dow Baker and the Development of the Banana Trade Between Jamaica and the United States, 1881–1890" (Ph.D. diss., American University, 1977).

Additional Bibliography

Bucheli, Marcelo. *Bananas and Business: The United Fruit Company in Colombia, 1899-2000*. New York: New York University Press, 2005.

Clegg, Peter. *The Caribbean Banana Trade: From Colonialism to Globalization*. New York: Palgrave Macmillan, 2002.

Striffler, Steve, and Mark Moberg. *Banana Wars: Power, Production, and History in the Americas.* Durham: Duke University Press, 2003.

DIANE STANLEY

BOTA DE POTRO. Gauchos made much of their clothing and equipment from leather, plentiful on the livestock-rich pampa. To fashion supple, open-toed riding boots, gauchos killed a colt and stripped the hide from its back legs. The soft skin covered the gaucho's foot, calf, and thigh. As with other elements of gaucho dress, these boots were likely first developed by indigenous peoples who lived on the pampa. The fragile boots wore out after a few months, so another colt would have to be killed. Ranchers called for outlawing the boots because they believed that gauchos stole colts just to fashion them. As wild horses became less plentiful on the plains during the late nineteenth century, imported machine-made boots replaced the homemade variety.

See also **Gaucho.**

BIBLIOGRAPHY

Madaline Wallis Nichols, *The Gaucho* (1968), p. 13.

Richard W. Slatta, *Gauchos and the Vanishing Frontier* (1983), pp. 74–75.

Additional Bibliography

Assunção, Fernando O. *Historia del gaucho: El gaucho, ser y quehacer.* Buenos Aires: Editorial Claridad, 1999.

RICHARD W. SLATTA

BOTERO, FERNANDO (1932–). Fernando Botero is a Colombian artist. Born in Medellín on April 19, 1932, Botero began his career as a writer and illustrator for the Sunday literary supplement of *El Colombiano,* a Medellín newspaper, where his articles on Picasso and Dalí resulted in his expulsion from Jesuit secondary school. He moved to Bogotá in 1951, when he had had his first one-man show. The following year he went to Madrid, where he enrolled in the Real Academia de San Fernando and studied the works of Goya and Velazquez in the Prado. He then went to study art history and fresco painting at the Academia San Marco in Florence. In 1955 he returned to Bogotá, and exhibited at the Biblioteca Nacional. His work was not well received, however, and he moved to Mexico City the following year. From 1958 to 1960 he taught at the Escuela de Bellas Artes at the National University in Bogotá. Botero received the award for the Colombian section of the Guggenheim international exhibition in 1960. That same year he moved to New York, where he lived until 1973. In 1961 the Museum of Modern Art of New York acquired his painting *Mona Lisa at Age 12.* This period reflects his fascination with the Renaissance masters.

In 1973 Botero moved to Paris. Although his subject matter continued to center on small-town Colombia, as evidenced by satirical images of clerics, military men, politicians, and marginals, Botero soon turned to sculpting the images and figures that appeared in his paintings. He had retrospective exhibitions in Germany (1970), Colombia (1973), the Netherlands (1975), the United States (1979–1980), and Germany (1979–1980). After his retrospective at the Museum of Contemporary Art in Caracas in 1976, the Venezuelan government awarded him the Order Andrés Bello, reserved for outstanding figures in Latin American culture. The department of Antioquia honored him with the Cruz de Boyaca for services to his nation. Botero's work has appeared at exhibitions at the Bronx Museum (New York, 1988) and at the Indianapolis Museum, the Hayward Gallery (London), and Centro de Arte Reina Sofia (Madrid), all in 1989.

Botero's popularity continued to grow. In 1992 a painting of a brothel scene was sold at auction for $1.5 million. In the fall of 1993, Botero's work was at the center of a controversy in New York City, when some Park Avenue residents opposed an outdoor public exhibition of his sculptures, fearing it would draw disruptive crowds to their neighborhood. In 1994 Christie's auction house staged a special sale of eleven Botero paintings, only to find that the work featured on the cover of the catalog was in fact a forgery. A collection featuring works he owned as well as 123 of his own works is on permanent display at the Museo Botero, a Spanish colonial-style house in downtown Bogotá.

See also **Art: The Twentieth Century.**

BIBLIOGRAPHY

Eduardo Serrano, *Cien años de arte colombiano* (1985).

Edward J. Sullivan, *Ferdinand Botero* (1993).

Additional Bibliography

Botero, Fernando. *Botero.* Edited by José Maria Faerna. Translated by Alberto Curotto. New York: Cameo/Abrams, 1997.

Botero, Fernando. *Fernando Botero: Paintings and Drawings.* Edited by Werner Spies. Munich and New York: Prestel, 1997.

Botero, Fernando, and Carlos Fuentes. *Botero: Women.* New York: Rizzoli International, 2003.

Lodoño Vélez, Santiago. *Botero: La invención de una estética.* Bogotá: Villegas Editores, 2003.

Sillevis, John. *The Baroque World of Fernando Botero.* Alexandria, VA: Art Services International, 2006.

BÉLGICA RODRÍGUEZ

BOUCHARD, HIPÓLITO (1783–1837).

Hipólito Bouchard (*b.* 13 August 1783; *d.* 5 January 1837), naval hero of Argentine independence. Born in France, Bouchard had been active in his country's merchant marine and in privateering by the time he reached Buenos Aires in 1809. There he stayed, and after the May Revolution of 1810 he was one of the cadre of foreign sailors who gave the Argentine patriots a respectable naval force, especially for corsair operations. Bouchard was naturalized as an Argentine citizen in 1813. He sailed with Admiral Guillermo Brown to the Pacific in 1815 and starting in 1817 commanded the frigate *Argentina* on a privateering voyage that took it around the world. He was a member of the expedition in 1820 that carried José de San Martín to Peru. Thereafter he continued serving Peru, where he acquired a sugar estate and spent the last part of his life as *hacendado*.

See also **Argentina: The Colonial Period.**

BIBLIOGRAPHY

Lewis Winkler Beeler, *Los corsarios de Buenos Aires, sus actividades en las guerras hispano-americanas de la independencia, 1815–1821* (1937).

Héctor Raúl Ratto, *Capitán de navío Hipólito Bouchard,* 2d ed. (1961).

Additional Bibliography

Marco, Miguel Angel de. *Corsarios argentinos: Héroes del mar en la Independencia y en la Guerra con el Brasil.* Buenos Aires: Emecé, 2005.

Uhrowczik, Peter. *The Burning of Monterey: The 1818 Attack on California by the Privateer Bouchard.* Los Gatos, CA: Cyril Books, 2001.

DAVID BUSHNELL

BOULLOSA, CARMEN (1954–).

Carmen Boullosa, novelist, poet, and playwright, was born in Mexico City in 1954. In addition to being a prolific and widely published author Boullosa is also a distinguished teacher and humanitarian, having cofounded with Salman Rushdie the Mexico City House for Persecuted Writers and as of 2007 working on a second under the auspices of the City University of New York.

Many of her novels encompass historical themes—the time of Moctezuma, the colonial era in Mexico, the life and times of seventeenth-century pirates in the Caribbean, the life of Cleopatra. Intrinsic to Boullosa's historical interpretation of these eras are her concepts of memory and the authority of the author. Memory for Boullosa is fluid and ever-changing; it relies on individuals' perception of reality and how they interpret it, depending on their personal desires and fears. Similarily narrative meaning for Boullosa is not constructed based solely on the author's intention; instead she requires active reader participation, often characterized by an open dialogue with her readers that pulls them into the narrative by addressing them directly and inciting them to construct, for themselves, the meaning of what they are reading.

There are also postmodern tendencies in Boullosa's writing, such as the questioning and challenging of predetermined notions of female identity and the inherent struggle women undertake for the power of authentic uncensored self-expression within the patriarchal socio-cultural context. Boullosa does not profess to be a feminist writer, but rather, a writer who also happens to be a woman. Her writing embodies a belief in the philosophical liberation of consciousness from predetermined and restrictive roles, and recognizes that the sociopolitical issues that affect women's perception of self-identity also affect men. Many of Boullosa's fictional protagonists recognize not only the value of language but also the control it exercises over their lives, and in so doing enable themselves to appropriate it, with all its figurative limitations, for their own self-expressive uses.

See also **Castellanos, Rosario; Literature: Spanish America.**

BIBLIOGRAPHY

Selected Works by Boullosa; Essays and Narrations

Papeles irresponsables [Irresponsible Papers]. Publicac, Mexico: Universidad Autónoma Metropolitana, 1989.

Selected Works by Boullosa; Novels

Mejor desaparece [Better Disappear]. México, D. F.: Oceano, 1987.

Antes [Before]. Mexico, D. F.: Vuelta, 1989.

Son vacas, somos puercos: Filibusteros del mar Caribe. Mexico, Ediciones Era, 1991. Translated by Leland H. Chambers as *They're Cows, We're Pigs.* New York: Grove Press, 1997.

Llanto: Novelas imposibles [Cry: Impossible Novels]. Mexico, D. F.: Ediciones Era, 1992.

El médico de los piratas: Bucaneros y filibusteros en el Caribe [The Pirates' Doctor: Buccaneers and Freebooters in the Caribbean]. Madrid, Spain: Ediciones Siruela, 1992.

La milagrosa. México, D. F.: Ediciones Era, 1993. Translated by Amanda Hopkinson as *The Miracle Worker.* London: Cape, 1994.

Duerme [Sleep]. Madrid: Alfaguara; New York: Vintage Books, 1994.

Quizá [Perhaps]. Caracas: Monte Avila Editores, 1995.

Cielos de la Tierra [Earth Skies]. México, D. F.: Aguilar, Altea, Taurus, Alfaguara, 1997.

Treinta años. Col. del Valle, México, D. F.: Alfaguara. 1999. Translated by Geoff Hargreaves as *Leaving Tabasco.* New York: Grove Press, 2001.

Prosa rota: Cuatro novelistas en una sola autora [Broken Prose: Four Novelists in only One Author]. México, D. F.: Plaza and Janés, 2000.

De un salto descabalga la reina. Madrid, Spain: Debate, 2002. Translated by Geoff Hargreaves as *Cleopatra Dismounts.* New York: Grove Press, 2003.

La otra mano de Lepanto. México, D. F.: Fondo de Cultura Económica, 2005. Translated as *Lepanto's Other Hand.* México, D. F.: Fondo de Cultura Económica 2005.

La novela perfecta: Un cuento largo [The Perfect Novel: A Long Short Story]. México, D. F.: Alfaguara, 2006.

Selected Works by Boullosa; Plays

Teatro herético [Heretical Theater]. Puebla: Universidad Autónoma de Puebla, 1987.

Pesca de piratas [Fishing for Pirates]. México, D. F.: Radio Educación, 1993.

Mi versión de los hechos [My Version of the Facts]. México, D.F.: Arte y Cultura Ediciones, 1997.

Los Totoles [The Totoles]. México, D. F.: Alfaguara, 2000.

Selected Works by Boullosa; Poetry

El hilo olvida [The Thread Forgets]. México, D. F.: La Máquina de Escribir, 1979.

Ingobernable [Ungovernable]. México, D. F.: Universidad Nacional Autónoma de México 1979.

Lealtad [Loyalty]. México, D. F.: Taller Martín Pescador, 1981.

Abierta [Open]. México, D. F.: Delegación Venustiano Carranza, 1983.

La salvaja [The Savage Woman]. Michoacán: Taller Martín Pescador, 1989.

Soledumbre [Solitude]. México, D. F.: Universidad Autónoma Metropolitana, 1992.

Envenenada: Antología personal [Poisoned: A Personal Anthology]. Caracas, Venezuela: Pequeña Venecia, 1993.

Niebla [Fog]. Michoacán: Taller Martín Pescador, 1997.

La Delirios. México, D. F.: Fondo de Cultura Económica, 1998.

Jardín Elíseo [Eliseo Garden]. Monterrey: Artegráfico, 1999.

Agua [Water]. Michoacán: Taller Martín Pescador, 2000

La bebida [The Drink]. México, D. F.: Fondo de Cultura, 2002.

Salto de mantarraya [Leap of the Manta Ray]. México, D. F.: Fondo de Cultura Económica, 2002.

Secondary Sources

Castro, Holanda. *Caos y productividad cultural.* Fair Haven, NJ: Ediciones Nuevo Espacio, 2001.

Croquer Pedrón, Eleonora. *El Gesto de Antígona: Herida y Representación en las Escrituras de Clarice Lispector, Diamela Eltit y Carmen Boullosa.* Santiago, Chile: Editorial Cuarto Propio, 2003.

D'Lugo, Carol Clark. *The Fragmented Novel in Mexico: The Politics of Form.* Austin: University of Texas Press, 1997.

Dröscher, Barbara and Carlos Rincón, eds. *Acercamientos a Carmen Boullosa: Actas del Simposio "Conjugarse en infinitivo—la escritora Carmen Boullosa."* Berlin: Verlag Walter Frey, 1999.

Gunderman, Eva. *Desafiando lo abyecto: Una lectura feminista de Mejor desaparece de Carmen Boullosa.* Frankfurt: Peter Lang, 2002.

Santos, Cristina. *Bending the Rules in the Quest for an Authentic Female Identity: Clarice Lispector and Carmen Boullosa.* New York: Peter Lang, 2004.

Vilches Norat, Vanessa. *De(s)madres o el rastro materno en las escrituras del Yo. A propósito de Jacques Derrida, Jamaica Kincaid, Esmeralda Santiago y Carmen Boullosa.* Santiago, Chile: Editorial Cuarto Propio, 2003.

CRISTINA SANTOS

BOUNDARY DISPUTES

This entry includes the following articles:
OVERVIEW
BRAZIL

OVERVIEW

Latin American countries have a long tradition of settling boundary disputes peacefully. Approximately seventeen border conflicts have been effectively resolved, more than in any other region of the world, since the Independence era. These were concluded through arbitration and mediation by European nations, the United States, Latin American countries, and tribunals of jurists. Generally these conflicts have been adjudicated as a response to immediate crises. In addition, the Inter-American System since the turn of the century and the Organization of American States (OAS), founded in 1948, created mechanisms for the peaceful conclusion of border controversies. Several pending boundary disputes in the late twentieth century are still based on the diverse claims of a colonial legacy. However, they have taken on new dimensions because the territories with rival claims contain energy and economic resources of great value. Strategic areas, too, are sources of future conflict, as are tensions arising between states from the migration and dislocation of people.

THE COLONIAL LEGACY

Boundaries in Latin America have been shaped by the colonial heritage of the Spanish and Portuguese empires in the New World. Independent states inherited demarcation lines that were once administered by Portuguese and Spanish ecclesiastical, civil, and legal bodies, each of which influenced the establishment of independent countries. Boundaries were confirmed by the principle of *uti possidetis juris,* which holds that new nations adopt the same boundaries as the colonial entity they replace. Since Independence in the early nineteenth century, there have emerged numerous boundary conflicts which reflect confusion over the jurisdiction of colonial viceroyalties and their subdivisions, such as captaincies-general, presidencies, and *audiencia*s. The boundaries of these smaller administrative units were frequently as vague as the larger entities of which they were once a part. As of 2007, at least twelve countries from Mexico to the Antarctic have unsettled boundary issues and territorial claims against one or more of their neighbors. Each of them can be traced back through three hundred or more years of history, beginning with the competing imperial interests of Spain, Portugal, and their European rivals for domination of the American continent.

SOUTH AMERICA: THE NORTHERN TIER

At the northern tier of South America, boundary issues occupy a major portion of the diplomatic activity of the region's nations. For most of the nineteenth century and on into the twentieth, Colombia and Venezuela struggled to establish an acceptable boundary. An agreement in 1881 gave Colombia the entire Guajira Peninsula, which juts out into the Caribbean Sea. In 1894 Bogotá agreed to cede the eastern portion of this territory, but Venezuela rejected the compromise and demanded that the matter be submitted to arbitration. Since the 1920s partial boundary markings have been agreed on, but a definitive demarcation line including the Guajira Peninsula has yet to be established. In the late twentieth century, sea rights in the Gulf of Venezuela, the entryway from the Caribbean to Venezuela's petroleum fields in Lake Maracaibo, with possible oil resources of its own, have been a major issue in a boundary dispute between these nations. A 1980 accord gave 75 percent of the Gulf and an archipelago at its mouth to Venezuela and

The *Zona en Reclamación*. Venezuelan president Hugo Chávez uses a map to illustrate boundary disputes that exist between Venezuela and Guyana. Venezuela has claimed all of Guyana west of the Río Essequibo since the 1840s, calling it "the Zone to Be Reclaimed." JOSE VARELLA/ AFP/GETTY IMAGES

set up provisions for sharing equally any oil that might be found there.

Since the mid-nineteenth century, Venezuela has had a border dispute with Guyana (formerly British Guiana) in which it claims a 53,000-square-mile area west of the Essequibo River—well over half of Guyana's territory. The area contains bauxite, aluminum, timber, potentially vast hydroelectric power, and possible oil deposits off the northern coast. Since 1966 several attempts have been made to establish a boundary. Both countries have agreed to use diplomatic means to resolve the conflict, namely the good offices of a mediator. Venezuela has suggested the secretary general of the United Nations, and Guyana had proposed that the International Court of Justice rule in the matter. Like Venezuela, Guyana has an unsettled boundary with its eastern neighbor, Suriname. The dispute originates from a late-eighteenth-century conflict between British and Dutch settlers. The issue centers on the validity of a boundary formed by the Courantyne-Kutari rivers and the New River.

SOUTH AMERICA: THE ANDEAN STATES

Most of South America's Andean countries have as yet been unable to establish definitively accepted boundary lines. Disagreement has arisen over vast unsettled lands of earlier colonial powers and new-found mineral and sea resources in the region.

The War of the Pacific (1879–1882), one of the great conflicts in South American history, arose from vague boundaries. Chile, Bolivia, and Peru vied for the vast nitrate and guano resources in the Atacama Desert. The conflict also had roots in a disputed boundary between Bolivia and Chile that stemmed from their imperial colonial legacy. Territory belonging to the Bolivian department of Atacama on the Pacific Ocean had been designated as part of the Viceroyalty of the Río de la Plata (with its capital Buenos Aires) in 1776. When Bolivia became independent, the area in question joined the new nation.

In the 1840s Peru issued licenses to companies exploiting resources in its territory of Tacna, Arica, and Tarapacá. Chile meanwhile claimed territory up to twenty-three degrees south latitude, a claim Bolivia rejected outright, saying it was an encroachment into its domain. In 1874 Chile and Bolivia established their boundary of 24 south latitude while agreeing to share resources between the twenty-third and twenty-fifth parallels through a condominium arrangement. When Peru nationalized all private mines in its nitrate-producing area of Tarapacá in 1875 to create a national monopoly, Chilean mine owners in the territory resisted the action. Bolivia in turn proposed a new tax on nitrates exported from its Atacama region in 1878. The Anglo Chilean Nitrate and Railroad Company, which had been granted a concession by Bolivia, refused to pay an export tax on its nitrate exports.

The intense rivalry among the Andean states for the vast resources in the Atacama along with a Bolivian-Peruvian treaty alliance resulted in war. When Chile ended Peru's control of the sea and defeated its army, Bolivia could no longer remain in the conflict and lost its Atacama territory. The Treaty of Ancón (1883), which ended the conflict, stipulated that Chile could hold Tacna and Arica for ten years. A plebiscite would decide the future disposition of the two areas. In 1929 Arica was ceded to Chile and Tacna to Peru. Bolivia lost its outlet to the sea.

Bolivia continues to look for access to the Pacific Ocean through territory it lost to Chile. It wants a free port on the Pacific Ocean and unimpeded access to it without paying compensation to Chile. Bolivia has presented its case for resolution before the OAS as a "hemisphere problem." This conflict is further complicated by the fact that the only corridor that Chile feels would be feasible is located along its northern border with Peru and consists of territory taken from the latter in the War of the Pacific. Peru has a treaty right, dating from 1929, to approve any arrangement involving its former territory should Chile decide to cede it to a third party. In 2007, Bolivia offered an economic incentive by promising to export its natural gas to Chile in return for access to the coastline; Chile refused the offer.

Peru and Colombia had conflicting claims to Leticia, a 4,000-square-mile area near the Putumayo River in the northeastern Peru–southeastern Colombia region. The dispute emerged from the confusion of boundaries between the colonial viceroyalties of Peru and New Granada and the existence of rubber in the region. The borders agreed upon in 1924 gave Colombia much of the disputed area between the Putumayo and Amazon rivers, including the town of Leticia. Although both sides ratified the treaty, Peru—resenting the loss of land—invaded Leticia in 1932. The League of Nations created a Commission of States (Spain, Cuba, the United States, and Brazil) to regulate the disputed region. In 1934 both nations accepted the boundaries set by the 1924 agreement, and the disputed area was then ceded to Colombia.

Vague colonial jurisdiction in a 100,000-square-mile jungle, bounded by the eastern slopes of the Andes, the Ecuadorian-Colombian border, and the Marañon River, brought Peru and Ecuador to war in 1941. Oil and rubber resources made land claims in this area valuable. The Rio Protocol of 1942, drawn up by mediators (the United States, Argentina, Brazil, and Chile as guarantor powers) and signed by both countries, gave most of the disputed territory to Peru. In 1960 Ecuador, smarting under the 1942 accord, formally declared the Rio Protocol null and void. That same year, fighting broke out in a still-unmarked area between the two states that was believed to have oil resources. Again in 1981, armed conflict erupted in the same region, known as the Cordillera del Condor. Ecuador called for the OAS to convene a meeting of its foreign ministers to deal with the issue. The four guarantor states of 1942 again arranged a cease fire in 1981. In the mid-1990s, Ecuador still demanded that the 1942 Rio Protocol be renegotiated. Peru asked that only the remaining unmarked border of 125 miles be established. After another conflict in 1995, the same guarantor states brokered another agreement, which Peru and Ecuador signed in 1998.

Paraguay and Bolivia lost substantial territory in two nineteenth-century conflicts: Paraguay in the Paraguayan War (1864–1870), or War of the Triple Alliance, and Bolivia in the War of the Pacific. They had conflicting territorial claims in the Chaco, an area of 150,000 square miles believed to have oil deposits. Boundaries were not established in the area either during the colonial era or after independence. Although both nations lay claim to the Chaco under the principle of *uti possidetis juris,* Paraguay began colonization projects in the 1930s to assert effective occupation, or *uti possidetis actual*. The three-year Chaco War (1932–1935) ended with that nation occupying a substantial part of the Chaco. In 1938 a peace treaty establishing boundary lines did not give Bolivia the access to the Atlantic by way of the Río de la Plata waterway system that it wanted. However, the mediating powers did give some of the territory under Paraguayan military occupation to Bolivia. A buffer zone of approximately 60 miles was established to separate Paraguay from Bolivia's oil deposits in the Camiri region in the Chaco.

Boundaries between Argentina and Chile were settled rather easily in the late nineteenth and early twentieth centuries. The Great Andean Range, stretching 2,900 miles and separating the two states, was considered an easily recognizable divide. Between 1881 and 1905 the boundary along the northern portion of the Andes was set at a point "that divided the waters." Later erosion by rivers flowing eastward toward Argentina pushed the watershed west of the Andes to Chile. Consequently, Argentina pressed for the water divide, while Chile favored the crest. By 1905 arbitration had set a boundary line agreeable to both countries.

Further south, a more contentious boundary dispute erupted between Argentina and Chile over the ownership of three islands, Lennox, Picton, and Nueva, in the Atlantic mouth of the Beagle Channel, north of Cape Horn. The key issues were whether the channel entered the Atlantic north or south of the islands and where the channel ended and the Atlantic Ocean began. The dispute also included jurisdiction over surrounding waters, which involved potential offshore rights to rich fishing areas and undersea oil as well as strategic access to the Antarctic.

Both states agreed to submit the issue for arbitration by the British crown. A special tribunal selected by Argentina and Chile from the World Court assisted England in six years of study that resulted in awarding the three islands to Chile in 1977. Argentina rejected the decision. Three years later, under the good offices of the Vatican, Chile would receive all the disputed islands but only limited offshore rights in the Atlantic meridian passing through Cape Horn. Both countries would share scientific and economic ventures in the archipelago as well. Chile, which owned 12 miles of

territorial waters east of the islands, would have to share resource development in the outer 6 miles of that strip. Argentina, sovereign in a 200-mile area into the Atlantic, would have to allow Chile to take part in resource development there, too. In 1984, with still no resolution to the issues, Pope John Paul II drafted a friendship pact, signed by both countries, which provided for continued mediation of this boundary and territorial issue. Later in the year, both countries accepted a treaty that was essentially the same as the 1980 proposal.

Brazil concluded boundary settlements with all of its neighbors (mostly Spanish American states) in the first decade of the twentieth century. Since the colonial era, Brazil had been expanding in all directions either through treaty agreements with Spain or later through occupation in the vast unchartered lands of the southern continent. In the so-called Age of Territorial Diplomacy (1880–1900), Brazil fixed its borders with countries contiguous to it mostly through the latter method.

In 1903 boundary settlements with Bolivia concerning the rubber-producing Acre region gave the territory to Brazil. In return Brazil paid about $10 million to Bolivia for the construction of a railroad to the sea by way of the Amazon River. Other boundaries were fixed in a treaty agreement with French Guiana (1900), in a convention with Argentina (1910) ratifying a treaty concluded in 1898, and in treaties with Peru (1904), Colombia (1928), Venezuela (1929), and Dutch Guiana (1931).

CENTRAL AMERICA, MEXICO, AND THE UNITED STATES

Boundary disputes in Central America have been similar in origin to those in the Southern Hemisphere. Conflicting territorial claims and the existence of valuable economic resources have been prominent among the sources of these disputes. When the Central American Federation broke up in 1838, disputes over boundaries occurred throughout the region. Yet in the twentieth century, demarcation lines have generally been established peacefully. There have been exceptions to this trend, most notably the El Salvador–Honduras War (Soccer War) in 1969. Honduras claimed territory corresponding to the colonial bishopric of Honduras. El Salvador asserted its sovereignty based on administrative areas established during Spanish rule. When Honduras expelled

Salvadoran migrants from the disputed area, war broke out. The OAS was called upon to step in and mediate the issue. It took ten years for it to do so, but the result was a peace treaty signed in 1980. The agreement established a boundary for 135 miles. A commission of representatives from both nations was formed to determine the remaining areas for demarcation, mainly in the Chalatenango, La Unión, and the Goascoran River delta.

A Guatemala-Belize (formerly British Honduras) dispute as well as a Nicaragua-Colombia conflict over several Atlantic islands reflect more than border issues. They involve territorial claims of each state. As has been common in all of Latin America, conflicting colonial jurisdictions have been the main cause of the dispute between Nicaragua and Colombia over nine islands off the former's eastern coast. Nicaragua claims sovereignty over five of them. The dispute began when Spain gave the viceroyalty in New Granada (Colombia) responsibility for defending San Andrés and Providencia islands in 1803. This order was rescinded in 1806, and similar authority was given to the captaincy-general of Guatemala, of which Nicaragua was a part. During the U.S. military intervention in Nicaragua, Managua was persuaded in 1928 to recognize Colombian sovereignty over San Andrés, Providencia, and Santa Catalina islands. Nicaragua abrogated the treaty in 1980. The dispute continues unresolved. As of 2007, the dispute was before the International Court of Justice for a final settlement.

The Guatemala-Belize controversy originated with Great Britain's effective occupation of Spain's eastern Central American territory in the seventeenth century. Guatemala claims the area on the principle of *uti possidetis juris,* asserting sovereignty based on colonial jurisdiction. When British Honduras (later Belize) declared its independence in September 1981, it became a member of the British Commonwealth and the United Nations over Guatemala's protest. In a Heads of Agreement (Britain, Belize, and Guatemala) document drawn up the same year, Guatemala yielded on the territorial claim and Belize granted it permanent and unimpeded access to its isolated port of Puerto Barrios on the Gulf of Honduras. However, negotiations have not yet resolved this dispute definitively, and Guatemala still maintains its claim to about half of Belize's territory.

The Treaty of Guadalupe–Hidalgo (1848), ending the Mexican–American War (1846–1848), established the middle portion of the Rio Grande as the boundary between Mexico and the United States. Floods and torrential rains in 1864 forced the river southward around an area in the El Paso–Ciudad Juárez vicinity called the Chamizal. This left Mexican territory on the north bank. The United States assumed the boundary had changed by erosion. Mexico in turn claimed the course of the Rio Grande had altered suddenly, leaving its land on the north bank of the river. A subsequent boundary dispute in 1884 over the Morteritos Island at the Texas-Tamaulipas border concluded that the demarcation line would move if the river shifted gradually. An International Border Commission was created in 1889 to implement the new guideline and deal with future disputes of this kind.

The commission was unable to resolve the disputed Chamizal area, as both states recognized that its proximity to the expanding urban centers of El Paso and Ciudad Juárez made the area valuable. Yet Mexico and the United States agreed to arbitrate the issue in 1910. The appointed commission concluded that the Rio Grande had changed course in a sudden and violent shift in 1864. Therefore, the boundary was to be reestablished as it existed in 1864. Although Washington rejected the decision, various governments attempted to resolve the controversy.

Finally, in 1963 the Kennedy administration concluded that Washington's rejection of the commission's decision had been a mistake. The dispute was resolved so that Mexico received 630 acres of the Chamizal area, including Córdova Island, an area that juts into United States territory. The latter, in turn, received 193 acres. A final agreement was signed by presidents Lyndon B. Johnson and Gustavo Díaz Ordaz in October 1967. The resolution of this protracted controversy was cited as a model for the peaceful settlement of border disputes by American states. Washington, therefore, created the Chamizal National Memorial and Mexico built a park in Ciudad Juárez commemorating the settlement. While the official border has been settled, the increased immigration into the United States from Mexico has caused U.S. politicians to focus on border security. Some U.S. politicians have called for a wall to be built on the border to keep out Mexican labor, but others hope to establish a guest worker program for Mexican migrants.

CONTEMPORARY BOUNDARY AND TERRITORIAL DISPUTES

Causes of the Argentine-British Falklands-Malvinas War (1982) over a group of disputed islands go back to the sixteenth century, when both Spain and England made claims of discovery. England, France, and Spain established settlements there in the seventeenth and eighteenth centuries. After independence Buenos Aires claimed the islands, located some 300 miles east of the Patagonian city of Río Gallegos. However, Britain took effective control of them in 1833. Argentina seized the islands in April 1982, but Britain recaptured them two and a half months later after a brief war. Although diplomatic relations were restored between the two countries in 1990, as of 1994 there was no final settlement.

Several Latin American countries, namely Argentina, Brazil, Chile, Ecuador, and Peru, have laid claim to territory in Antarctica. They have done so because of the area's geological and political continuity with the South American mainland. These states have asserted interest in a quadrant between longitude 0 and 90 west in which they have overlapping claims. But issues such as sovereignty, resources, and the presence of non–Western Hemisphere countries pose a threat to their claims there.

Chile, Argentina, and Brazil have also viewed their interests in the Antarctic as part of a wider strategic role in the South Atlantic. The Antarctic Treaty of 1959, ratified by mid-1961 by the twelve states named in the preamble (thirty-nine states by 1994) might prevent a Latin American power struggle there, but a confrontation was considered a possibility.

See also **War of the Pacific; War of the Triple Alliance.**

BIBLIOGRAPHY

Gordon Ireland, *Boundaries, Possessions, and Conflicts in South America* (1938).

William J. Dennis, *Tacna and Arica: An Account of the Chile-Peru Boundary Dispute and of the Arbitrations by the United States* (1967).

Peter Calvert, *Boundary Disputes in Latin America* (1983).

Jack Child, ed., *Maintenance of Peace and Security in the Caribbean and Central America* (1984).

Jack Child, *Geopolitics and Politics in South America: Quarrels Among Neighbors* (1985).

William I. Krieg, *Ecuadorian-Peruvian Rivalry in the Upper Amazon*, 2d ed. (1986).

J. R. V. Prescott, *Political Frontiers and Boundaries* (1987).

Jorge Gumucio Granier, *The United States and the Bolivian Seacoast* (1988).

Alan C. Lamborn and Stephen P. Mumme, *Statecraft, Domestic Politics, and Foreign Policy Making: The El Chamizal Dispute* (1988).

Stephen P. Mumme, *The United States-Mexico Boundary* (1991).

Marshall Bertram, *The Birth of Anglo-American Friendship: The Prime Facet of the Venezuelan Boundary Dispute* (1992).

Paul Ganster and Eugenio O. Valenciano, eds., *Mexican-U.S. Border Region and the Free Trade Agreement* (1992); and Ronald B. St. John, *Boundaries, Trade, and Seaports: Power Politics in the Atacama Desert* (1992).

Additional Bibliography

Domínguez, Jorge I., and David R Mares. *Boundary Disputes in Latin America.* Washington, DC: United States Institute of Peace, 2003.

Farcau, Bruce W. *The Ten Cents War: Chile, Peru, and Bolivia in the War of the Pacific, 1879–1884.* Westport, CT: Praeger, 2000.

Moraes, Antonio Carlos Robert. *Bases da formação territorial do Brasil: O território colonial brasileiro no "longo" século XVI.* São Paulo: Editora Hucitec, 2000.

Parodi, Carlos A. *The Politics of South American Boundaries.* Westport, CT: Praeger, 2002.

Passarelli, Bruno. *El delirio armado: Argentina–Chile, la guerra que evitó el Papa.* Buenos Aires: Editorial Sudamericana, 1998.

Simmons, Beth A. *Territorial Disputes and Their Resolution: The Case of Ecuador and Peru.* Washington, DC: United States Institute of Peace, 1999.

Stoddard, Ellwyn R. *U.S.–Mexico Borderlands Issues: The Binational Boundary, Immigration, and Economic Policies.* El Paso, TX: The Promontory, 2001.

Van Dijck, Pitou et al. *Cruzando fronteras: Reflexiones sobre la relevancia de fronteras históricas, simbólicas y casi desaparecidas en América Latina.* Quito: Ediciones Abya-Yala, 2004.

Winders, Richard Bruce. *Crisis in the Southwest: The United States, Mexico, and the Struggle over Texas.* Wilmington, DE: SR Books, 2002.

THOMAS DODD

BRAZIL

At independence, Brazil, the largest Latin American country and fifth largest country in the world, shared ill-defined boundaries with every South American country and territory except Chile. Between 1895 and 1909, under the leadership of diplomat Barão do Rio Branco and utilizing the principle of *uti possidetis* (ownership by occupation rather than claim), the Brazilian government succeeded in delineating approximately 9,000 miles of frontier, adding nearly 342,000 square miles to its national territory in the process. Aided by his diplomatic training abroad, and employing skilled Brazilian geographers and cartographers to illustrate Brazil's claims, Rio Branco sought international arbitration to resolve Brazil's boundaries. In 1895 U.S. president Grover Cleveland arbitrated the settlement of the boundary of Misiones, between Argentina and Brazil, in Brazil's favor. In 1900, in an agreement arbitrated by the president of the Swiss Confederation, France relinquished the entire territory of Amapá to Brazil, resolving the Brazil-French Guiana border. In 1904 the king of Italy arbitrated settlement of the boundary shared by Brazil and British Guiana; Brazil and Peru reached an amicable agreement along the lines proposed by Brazil in 1909.

The desire to secure the potentially rubber-rich Amazon Basin during the rubber boom (c. 1875–1912) was a driving force behind Brazil's diplomatic offensive and was central in the volatile controversy over the Bolivian territory of Acre, which lay along Brazil's central-eastern boundary. By 1900 nearly 60,000 rubber gatherers had migrated from northeast Brazil into the nominally Bolivian territory. In 1899 and again in 1902 the Brazilian migrants rebelled against Bolivian attempts to assert authority in the region and attempted to force the Bolivian government to relinquish the territory to Brazil. The dispute was settled by the Treaty of Petrópolis (17 November 1903), in which Bolivia ceded the territory of Acre (73,000 square miles) to Brazil in exchange for lands bordering the Madeira River, a Brazilian commitment to construct the Madeira-Mamoré railroad to provide an Atlantic outlet for Bolivian goods, and an indemnity of $10 million.

In 1906 Brazil reached agreement with the Netherlands on the Brazil–Dutch Guiana boundary, and in 1907 negotiated successfully with Colombia to confirm Brazilian title to lands involving approximately one-third of the state of Amazonas. An agreement with Venezuela in 1905 settled the northern frontier.

See also **Brazil, Geography.**

BIBLIOGRAPHY

Gordon Ireland, *Boundaries, Possessions, and Conflicts in South America* (1938).

E. Bradford Burns, *Nationalism in Brazil* (1968).

Rollie E. Poppino, *Brazil: The Land and People* (1968).

Harold Eugene Davis et al., *Latin American Diplomatic History* (1977).

Additional Bibliography

Moraes, Antonio Carlos Robert. *Bases da formação territorial do Brasil: O território colonial brasileiro no "longo" século XVI.* São Paulo: Editora Hucitec, 2000.

Parodi, Carlos A. *The Politics of South American Boundaries.* Westport, CT: Praeger, 2002.

Villacrés M., Jorge W. *La lucha de los estados por su dominación de la región amazónica.* Guayaquil, Ecuador: Universidad de Guayaquil, Vicerrectorado Académico, 1992.

FRANCESCA MILLER

BOURBON REFORMS. Bourbon Reforms, commonly defined as the reorganization of the military, commercial, and administrative structures that the Bourbon dynasty inherited in 1700 from its Hapsburg predecessors. Accomplished by ambitious innovations in the collection and generation of royal revenues, this reorganization aimed to modernize the mercantile system, strengthen the royal government administratively and financially, and improve the military position of the Spanish Empire in the face of fierce international competition. The reforms began in the reigns of Philip V (1700–1724, 1724–1746) and Ferdinand VI (1746–1759), but the colonial reorganization reached its fullest expression through the ambitious measures advanced under Charles III (1759–1788) and sustained by Charles IV (1788–1808). Although introduced piecemeal and unevenly in the several colonies, these reforms altered profoundly the character of colonial governance and, by the final decade of the eighteenth century, approximated a unified program.

Innovations in each category of reform occurred under the early Bourbons. For the administration, Philip in 1721 definitively transferred the primary responsibility for governing the empire from the Council of the Indies to the newly created Ministry of the Navy and the Indies, which in 1754 was divided into separate units. In America, he reestablished the Viceroyalty of New Granada in 1739. At mid-century, Ferdinand halted the sale of audiencia offices. And overall, in a multitude of minor steps, the reforms increasingly extended royal authority through centralization.

In the sphere of commercial policy, a series of actions dating from the late 1730s and extending into the early 1750s—highlighted by the work of ministers José del Campillo y Cossío and the Marqués de la Ensenada— curbed the vast privileges of the powerful Consulado (Merchant Guild) of Cádiz, which held a legal monopoly over the American trade. To break the lingering power of Seville, from which the *consulado* had been transferred in 1717, the crown reformed the method of electing officers and liberalized the regulations governing membership. It also developed plans to deregulate radically the colonial trade, opening America to all the ports of Spain. Although this step was thwarted during the reaction following the fall of Ensenada in 1754, the fleet system to South America was nevertheless abolished in favor of register ships. Other measures designed to broaden commercial access to the American marketplace entailed the establishment of privileged trading companies, including those of Caracas (1728), Havana (1740), and Barcelona (1755).

Additional innovations also pointed toward the future. In the regular army, fixed battalions with modernized command structures replaced garrisons comprised of separate companies, beginning with Havana (1719), continuing with Cartagena (1736), Santo Domingo (1738), New Spain (1740), and Panama (1741), and eventually including the other strongpoints of America.

The Crown also experimented with new royal monopolies to enhance its income. In 1717 it established a tobacco monopoly in Cuba, primarily to supply the royal factory in Seville. Tobacco monopolies were also organized in Peru (1745), Chile (1753), and Upper Peru (1755). In New Granada the Crown installed an *aguardiente* (brandy) monopoly in 1736

and a decade later extended it to the presidency of Quito.

Soon after Charles III became king, the 1762 British capture of Havana exposed the vulnerability of imperial defense, imposing urgency on the reformist agenda and elevating military concerns to unparalleled primacy. In 1763, when he regained Havana at the price of Florida in the Treaty of Paris, Charles dispatched to Cuba a reform commission led by the Conde de Ricla as governor and Alejandro O'Reilly as sub-inspector general of the army, and at court he established an interministerial commission, the Junta de Ministros, to coordinate the colonial reorganization. O'Reilly expanded Havana's regular army, but more importantly he involved Cubans directly in the task of defense through the establishment of a disciplined militia. This system provided for the systematic arming and training of the colonial population and granted militiamen the *fuero militar* (military privilege).

Minister of War and Finance Marqués de Esquilache, who dominated the Junta de Ministros at court, worked closely with Ricla to find the means to help support the expanded military. The *alcabala* was increased from 2 to 6 percent, and excise taxes were placed on the sale of colonial liquors. A military intendant was installed with supreme authority over the treasury. Finally, the royal decree of 1765 conceded to Cuba and the other Caribbean islands free trade with the major ports of Spain, thus encouraging legal commerce, stimulating economic growth, and enhancing royal revenues. Meanwhile, a modernization of the royal mail service improved communications with the colonies.

In 1764 the Crown extended the military reform to New Spain through the mission of Lieutenant General Juan de Villalba, which both reorganized the regular army and established a disciplined militia, and in 1765, O'Reilly also reformed the Puerto Rican military. Royal orders to raise disciplined militias were sent to the governors of Caracas and Buenos Aires and the viceroy of Peru. To improve royal finance, Esquilache established a program to make the tobacco monopoly virtually universal in the colonies. In 1765 he commissioned José de Gálvez as visitor-general to New Spain, which was financially responsible for both its own military costs and enormous subsidies to the Caribbean islands. Gálvez improved the collection and administration of royal revenues and placed the new tobacco monopoly on a workable footing. In naming officials, Gálvez angered colonists through his blatant favoritism of Spaniards over what he believed were less reliable Americans. Although the pace of reform slowed following the fall of Esquilache in 1766, Alejandro O'Reilly, now inspector-general of the American army, brought Santo Domingo, Cartagena, and Panama into the new defense system immediately following the Falkland Islands crisis of 1770–1771.

The colonial reorganization resumed its vigor when Gálvez became minister of the Indies in January 1776, on the eve of the American Revolution. Gálvez commissioned José Antonio de Areche and Juan Francisco Gutiérrez De Piñeres to lead reform missions—similar to his own in New Spain—to Peru and New Granada as well as subvisits to Chile and Quito by Tomas Álvarez de Acevedo and José García-Pizarro. Massive resistance led by Túpac Amaru of Peru and the Comuneros of New Granada swept the upland interiors, blunting the successes of these undertakings and leaving enduring scars. Meanwhile, military reform continued to progress. Miners' guilds with broad powers to promote production were installed in New Spain (1777) and Peru (1787), and to improve mining practices, the crown sent technical missions to both of these viceroyalties and to New Granada during the 1780s.

The Intendancy System of provincial governance provided the administrative underpinning for fiscal reform. In 1776 an intendancy was established in Caracas on the same basis as that in Cuba. Six years later, when Gálvez introduced this institution into Río de la Plata, the office was broadened to include government and justice, thereby effecting a rationalization and centralization of the instruments of provincial administration. On this basis, the intendant system was extended to Peru in 1784 and New Spain, Guatemala, and Chile in 1786, but not to volatile New Granada. Other innovations included the establishment in 1776 of the Viceroyalty of the Río de la Plata and the Commandancy General of the Interior Province of New Spain, and, in 1777, the captaincy General of Caracas.

Commercial deregulation constituted the capstone of the colonial reorganization. Following the concession of imperial free trade to the Caribbean islands in 1765, the crown cautiously pursued liberalization, a process highlighted by the incorporation of Yucatán into the Caribbean system in 1770 and, four years later, the legalization of intercolonial trade on the Pacific coast. As minister, Gálvez quickened the tempo of deregulation through a series of measures culminating in the Regulation of Free Trade of October 1778, which definitively broke the Cádiz monopoly, although certain restrictions lingered on the commerce of New Spain and Caracas.

Charles IV sustained this reformist agenda, although his government set a moderate tone in the enforcement of revenue regulations and attempted to limit conflicts with the colonial elites. Caracas and New Spain were incorporated fully into the system of free trade during 1788–1789; the slave trade of Cuba, Santo Domingo, Puerto Rico, and Caracas was opened to all Spanish subjects; and, beginning with Havana in 1794, a host of new colonial merchant guilds were organized, breaking the grip of Lima and Mexico City on the colonial marketplaces. Following the death of Gálvez in 1787, the Ministry of the Indies was split into two portfolios, and in 1790 their functions were assigned to the corresponding Spanish ministries, a step toward standardizing metropolitan and colonial governance.

The Bourbon Reforms produced mixed results. Spain reconquered Florida during the American Revolution and the empire stood well defended as the century advanced, but by arming Americans effectively and granting them military privileges, the crown risked losing political control, a danger destined to become reality during the independence movement of the early nineteenth century. Commercial deregulation undoubtedly stimulated legal commerce. The tariffs collected on this trade, when combined with record royal income from other sources—especially from mining taxes, the *alcabala,* and the tobacco monopoly—brought unparalleled wealth to the royal treasury, but much of this revenue was squandered on the military, while, on another level, tensions between Spain and its colonies lingered. Although the intendancies made provincial governance more efficient, their powers produced stress within the administrative hierarchy, and their subdelegates, operating at the local level, came to resemble the Corregidores they had replaced.

The wars of the French Revolution and Napoleon I interrupted the reformist process, placing burdens on the imperial system that could not have been anticipated. The program of Charles III never had a long-term opportunity to be fully tested.

See also **Charles III of Spain.**

BIBLIOGRAPHY

John Lynch, *Spanish Colonial Administration, 1782–1810: The Intendant System in the Viceroyalty of the Río de la Plata* (1958).

John R. Fisher, *Government and Society in Colonial Peru: The Intendant System, 1784–1814* (1970).

D. A. Brading, *Miners and Merchants in Bourbon Mexico, 1763–1810* (1971).

Christon I. Archer, *The Army in Bourbon Mexico, 1760–1810* (1977).

Jacques A. Barbier, "The Culmination of the Bourbon Reforms," in *Hispanic American Historical Review* 57 (1977): 51–68.

Mark A. Burkholder and D. S. Chandler, *From Impotence to Authority: The Spanish Crown and the American Audiencias, 1687–1808* (1977).

John R. Fisher, *Commercial Relations Between Spain and Spanish America in the Era of Free Trade, 1778–1796* (1985).

Allan J. Kuethe, "Towards a Periodization of the Reforms of Charles III," in *Iberian Colonies, New World Societies: Essays in Memory of Charles Gibson*, edited by Richard L. Garner and William B. Taylor (1985), and *Cuba, 1753–1815: Crown, Military, and Society* (1986).

Allan J. Kuethe and Lowell Blaisdell, "French Influence and the Origins of the Bourbon Colonial Reorganization," in *Hispanic American Historical Review* 71 (1991): 579–607.

Additional Bibliography

Dym, Irene, and Christophe Belaubre, eds. *Politics, Economy, and Society in Bourbon Central America, 1759–1821*. Boulder: University Press of Colorado, 2007.

Katzew, Ilona. *Casta Painting: Images of Race in Eighteenth-century Mexico*. New Haven, CT: Yale University Press, 2004.

Río, Ignacio del. *La aplicación regional de las reformas borbónicas en Nueva España: Sonora y Sinaloa, 1768–1787*. México: Universidad Nacional Autónoma de México, Instituto de Investigaciones Históricas, 1994.

Taylor, William B. *Magistrates of the Sacred: Priests and Parishioners in Eighteenth-century Mexico*. Stanford, CA: Stanford University Press, 1996.

Walker, Charles. *Smoldering Ashes: Cuzco and the Creation of Republican Peru, 1780–1840*. Durham, NC: Duke University Press, 1999.

                                                    ALLAN J. KUETHE

BOUTERSE, DESI (1945–). The military dictator of Suriname between 1980 and 1987 and the most important offstage politician afterward, Desi Bouterse was born on October 13, 1945, in a small village in that nation. Educated by Catholic friars, he became a sergeant-major in the Dutch army. He returned in 1975 to Suriname to become a leading noncommissioned officer in the small national army. Involved in a labor conflict about the rights of the union of NCOs with the post-colonial government, he staged a coup in 1980 Bouterse became the army leader, a full colonel, and the de facto ruler of Suriname with a series of façade civilian cabinets. In 1981 he proclaimed himself the leader of a socialist revolution. He gradually was implicated in illicit business activities.

In December 1982 the military murdered fifteen civilian opposition leaders, a watershed in Suriname politics. A growing civilian opposition produced a period of transition governments, followed by free elections in 1987. However, a guerrilla movement of the Maroon population (descendants of former run-away slaves) in Eastern Suriname created a rationale for the involvement of the army and the continuance of Bouterse as army commander. Around Christmas 1990, Bouterse staged a second coup. In 1993 a new civilian government found the courage to dismiss him as army commander and discharged his supporters as well. Bouterse, now a born-again Christian, is the leader of a multiethnic party that won 25 percent of the votes in May 2005. He lives the comfortable life of a millionaire entrepreneur and senior politician. In early 2007 the Surinamese government announced a process against Bouterse and his former allies who were allegedly involved in the 1982 murders.

See also **Suriname and the Dutch in the Caribbean.**

BIBLIOGRAPHY

Bouterse, Desi, and Ludwich van Mulier. *Dekolonisatie en nationaal leiderschap* [Decolonization and National Leadership]. Nijmegen: MASUSA.

Hoogbergen, Wim, and Dirk Kruijt. *De oorlog der sergeanten. Surinaamse militairen in de politiek, 1980–1992* [The Sergeant's War: The Surinamese Military in National Politics]. Amsterdam: Bert Bakker, 2005.

DIRK KRUIJT

BOVES, JOSÉ TOMÁS (1782–1814).

José Tomás Boves (*b.* 18 September 1782; *d.* 5 December 1814), officer in the Spanish army. A native of Spain, Boves received his nautical education in Asturias, obtained his pilot's license in 1803, and joined a mercantile business with interests in Venezuela. He was accused of smuggling, imprisoned in Puerto Cabello, and later confined in the town of Calabozo. When the War of Independence broke out, Boves declared himself to be on the side of emancipation. But he then became suspect when he supported the royalist leader, Domingo Monteverde, and was imprisoned in 1812 at Calabozo. That same year he joined the royalist ranks under the command of Eusebio Antoñanzas, who released him from prison, and was appointed commander in chief of Calabozo.

Boves rapidly attained great popularity among the inhabitants of the plains for his favorable attitude toward sacking and looting. His detailed knowledge of the plains territory brought him numerous victories over republican troops. In testimonies of the time and in the collected writings on Venezuelan independence, Boves stands out for his fierceness and cruelty to those he defeated. He rebelled against his immediate superior and ignored the authority of the royal *audiencia*. After his death at the battle of Urica, the royalist cause lost popularity among the people of the plains.

See also **Venezuela: The Colonial Era.**

BIBLIOGRAPHY

Juan Uslar Pietri, *Historia de la Rebelión de 1814* (1954).

Acisclo Valdivieso Montaño, *José Tomás Boves, caudillo hispano* (1955).

Germán Carrera Damas, *Boves: Aspectos socioeconómicos de la independencia*, 3d ed. (1972).

Additional Bibliography

Mondolfi, Edgardo. *José Tomás Boves: (1782-1814)*. Caracas: Editora El Nacional, 2005.

Pérez Tenreiro, Tomás. *Para acercarnos a don Francisco Tomás Morales, mariscal de campo, último capitán general en Tierra Firme, y a José Tomás Boves, coronel, primera lanza del rey*. Caracas: Academia Nacional de la Historia, 1994.

Semprún, José. *La división infernal: Boves, vencedor de Bolívar*. Madrid: Ediciones Falcata Ibérica 2002.

INÉS QUINTERO

BOX, PELHAM HORTON (1898–

1937). Pelham Horton Box (*b.* 29 March 1898; *d.* 23 May 1937), British historian who applied modern research methods to the study of Paraguay in the 1930s. The University of Illinois awarded him the Ph.D. in 1927 and in 1930 published his dissertation, *Origins of the Paraguayan War*, which was translated into Spanish in 1936. This revisionist work viewed José Gaspar Rodríguez de Francia (1766–1840) as a revolutionary dictator who ruled with the consent of the peasantry and blamed the War of the Triple Allliance on Francisco Solano López. Now dated, the book remains a starting point for researchers. Box taught for several years at Birkbeck College and two years at King's College, London.

See also **War of the Triple Alliance.**

BIBLIOGRAPHY

Pelham Horton Box, *The Origins of the Paraguayan War* (1930, repr. 1967); *Times* (London), 28 May 1937, p. 18b.

Additional Bibliography

Box, Pelham Horton. *Los orígenes de la Guerra del Paraguay contra la triple alianza*. Asunción: El Lector, 1996.

VERA BLINN REBER

BOXER, CHARLES RALPH (1904–

2000). C. R. Boxer enjoyed several distinct careers in his long and productive life, and upon his death at ninety-six, colleagues and former students counted more three hundred scholarly and popular publications, reflecting his hugely diverse interests. His primary research interests focused upon the first great epoch of modern European expansion into Asia, Africa and the Americas, especially the efforts of the Portuguese and Dutch as they constructed their vast trading empires after 1400. Boxer's dedication to research and uncanny ability to construct a definitive narrative made him one of the best known and widely read historians of the twentieth century.

Born on the Isle of Wight to a distinguished military family, Boxer entered the British army after completing his education at Sandhurst. As a young lieutenant he developed an interest in all things Japanese, including early Dutch and Portuguese economic and military activities there. His growing facility in both Japanese and Dutch led him to study the lives of sailors, merchants, missionaries, imperial officials, slavery, race relations, ship design, maritime history, European enclaves and colonies, and the reaction of local peoples to the sudden appearance of Europeans in their harbors and ports.

Boxer was the ranking British intelligence officer in Hong Kong in the late 1930s as the Pacific war loomed. Although severely wounded during the invasion and later imprisoned, he helped lead covert resistance against the Japanese occupation. Remarkably, throughout the remainder of his life, he betrayed little bitterness over events of that war and resumed his scholarly study of European interaction with Asia and Japan.

He resigned his army commission in 1947, beginning five decades of teaching and research at universities in Britain and the United States. Boxer's early publications and interest in Portuguese maritime expansion led to his appointment to the Camoens chair in Portuguese studies at the University of London. He also visited and lectured at dozens of universities in Asia, Brazil, Africa, and the United States, and was the sometimes-reluctant recipient of many honors and awards, including the Pedro II Gold Medal in 1986. His major works include *The Dutch Seaborne Empire 1600–1800* (1965), *The Portuguese Seaborne Empire 1415–1825* (1969), and *Race Relations in the Portuguese Empire, 1415–1825* (1963).

The publication of *Race Relations*, coming at a time of increasing world scrutiny and criticism of both the Salazarist regime in Portugal and its truculent determination to hold onto the remains of its empire in Africa temporarily cost Boxer the friendship of some acquaintances and many officials in Portugal.

His wife, Emily Hahn, who died in 1997, was a distinguished author and shared many of Boxer's adventures and travels.

See also **Portuguese Empire.**

BIBLIOGRAPHY

Alden, Dauril, assisted by James S. Cummins and Michael Cooper. *Charles R. Boxer: An Uncommon Life.* Lisbon: Fundação Oriente, 2001.

Boxer, C. R. *The Dutch Seaborne Empire, 1600–1800.* New York: Knopf, 1965.

Boxer, C. R. *Race Relations in the Portuguese Empire, 1415–1825.* Oxford: Clarendon Press, 1963; Westport, CT: 1985.

Boxer, C. R. *The Portuguese Seaborne Empire, 1415–1825.* London: Hutchinson; New York: Knopf, 1969.

CRAIG HENDRICKS

BOYACÁ, BATTLE OF.

Battle of Boyacá, the most decisive engagement of Colombian independence. The culmination of a campaign begun by Simón Bolívar in late May on the Venezuelan llanos, the clash took place on 7 August 1819 at Boyacá, about 9 miles southwest of Tunja on the road to Bogotá. With an army of Venezuelans, New Granadans, and British legionnaires, Bolívar crossed the eastern plains, scaled the Andes, and emerged in the series of upland valleys leading to the capital of the Viceroyalty of New Granada. After several inconclusive engagements, Bolívar consolidated his foothold and on 5 August occupied Tunja, placing himself between the main royalist army under Colonel José María Barreiro and Bogotá. When Barreiro tried to outflank Bolívar and secure the road to the capital, fighting broke out at a small bridge over the Boyacá River. Numerically, forces were evenly matched—about 2,850 patriots against 2,700 royalists—but the patriots were in better fighting condition. Combat lasted two hours, and neither side suffered major casualties. However, the patriots claimed the field and took most of the enemy prisoner, including Barreiro. Three days later Bolívar entered Bogotá, and with the momentum gained in this victory, the patriots fanned out through most of the rest of central New Granada.

See also **Wars of Independence, South America.**

BIBLIOGRAPHY

Juan Friede, ed., *La batalla de Boyacá, 7 de agosto de 1819, a través de los archivos españoles* (1969).

Camilo Riaño, *La campaña libertadora de 1819* (1969).

Daniel Florencio O'Leary, *Bolívar and the War of Independence,* translated and edited by Robert F. McNerney, Jr. (1970), pp. 162–165.

Additional Bibliography

Earle, Rebecca. *Spain and the Independence of Colombia 1810-1825.* Exeter: University of Exeter Press, 2000.

Ibáñez, José Roberto. *La campaña de Boyacá.* Santafé de Bogotá, Colombia: Panamericana, 1998.

Thibaud, Clément. *Repúblicas en armas: Los ejércitos bolivarianos en la guerra de Independencia en Colombia y Venezuela.* Lima: Instituto Francés de Estudios Andinos, 2003.

DAVID BUSHNELL

BOYER, JEAN-PIERRE (1776–1850).

Jean-Pierre Boyer (b. 1776; d. 9 July 1850), ruler of Haiti (1818–1843). The regime of Jean-Pierre Boyer marked a vital watershed in the development of Haitian government and society in the nineteenth century. Born in Port-au-Prince, Boyer began his career when he joined the revolutionary forces led by Pierre Dominique Toussaint L'ouverture that abolished slavery and freed Haiti from French colonial domination. In the power struggles dividing Haitians after independence, Boyer, himself a mulatto, sided with mulatto leader Alexandre Sabès Pétion and, in March 1818, succeeded Pétion as head of the Republic of the South. In 1821, after the death of his major rival in the North, Henri Christophe, Boyer unified the country. Under his auspices, Haiti began to consolidate its status as an independent nation. In 1822, out of fear of French plans for reprisal, Boyer sent his troops to the vulnerable eastern half of Hispaniola, which, with Boyer's encouragement, had recently declared its independence from Spain. He remained in control of the region for the remainder of his twenty-five-year reign. In 1825, Boyer obtained France's diplomatic recognition (by paying an indemnity of 150 million francs), an achievement that had eluded earlier leaders of the young nation and that marked the end of Haiti's status as an international pariah. Recognition from the British

came in 1826, after which other countries followed suit.

Despite these successes on the international front, Boyer faced serious challenges at home. The most significant problem was trying to reconcile the needs and interests of two major sectors of the population: the mulatto elite and the black peasantry. During his early years in power, Boyer tried to win the loyalty of the peasantry through land distribution. This popular policy was started by Pétion and contributed to the predominance of small-scale, subsistence agriculture, especially in the South. Yet, Boyer also responded to the demands of mulatto landowners for a restoration of plantation agriculture. In May 1826, he implemented the Code Rural in an attempt to force peasants to work for the large estates. The code stipulated that all peasants were to contract themselves to an estate owner or be considered "vagabonds" liable to arrest and forced labor on public-works projects. It also provided for a rural police force to inspect plantations and keep order in the countryside. Yet, because of government laxness as well as lack of cooperation from some estate owners, it was impossible to enforce the code. Thus, Boyer witnessed the decline of Haiti's once-productive plantation system and the rise of subsistence farming as a way of life for most Haitians.

Boyer's regime also saw a hardening of social and class divisions based on skin color as well as property ownership. In general, government fell into the hands of the more educated, Westernized mulattoes while blacks dominated the military. This split helped undermine the success of Boyer's effort to entice free blacks from the United States to settle in Haiti. During the Boyer period, about 13,000 blacks arrived on the island with the hope of becoming property owners and living in a more egalitarian society; yet, due to problems created by language and cultural differences as well as mulatto social prejudice against blacks, little more than half that number stayed. The revolt of 27 January 1843 led to his exile on 13 March, first in Jamaica and later in Paris. In sum, Boyer not only brought about Haitian unity and consolidated his nation's claim to sovereignty but also oversaw the emergence of a society with color and class divisions that have continued to shape Haitian society and politics to this day.

See also **Haiti.**

BIBLIOGRAPHY

James Graham Leyburn, *The Haitian People* (1968).

David Nicholls, *From Dessalines to Duvalier: Race, Colour and National Independence in Haiti* (1979).

Frank Moya Pons, "Haiti and Santo Domingo, 1790–ca. 1870," in *The Cambridge History of Latin America,* vol. 3, edited by Leslie Bethell (1985), pp. 237–275.

Michel-Rolph Trouillot, *Haiti: State Against Nation* (1990).

Additional Bibliography

Dubois, Laurent. *Avengers of the New World: The Story of the Haitian Revolution.* Cambridge, MA: Belknap Press of Harvard University Press, 2004.

Dubois, Laurent. *A Colony of Citizens: Revolution and Slave Emancipation in the French Caribbean, 1787–1804.* Chapel Hill: University of North Carolina Press, 2004.

Geggus, David Patrick, ed. *The Impact of the Haitian Revolution in the Atlantic World.* Columbia: University of South Carolina, 2001.

PAMELA MURRAY

BOZZO, LAURA (1951–). Born August 19, 1951, in Lima, Perú, Bozzo is a lawyer, former city councillor of Lima, and popular television talk show host. In 1996 she hosted the talk show *Intimidades.* But it was after Bozzo began hosting *Laura en América* in 1998 that she became famous. The program presented bizarre and sensationalistic dramas about poor people.

Bozzo was prosecuted in 2002 for illicit association and receiving money to support Alberto Fujimori's presidential reelection bid of 2000. After three years of house arrest, the judiciary was required to set her free in 2005 because it had not presented charges against her on time. The judiciary changed from house arrest to "appearance." The court sentenced her in July 2006 to four years of conditional prison in July 2006, but because she had been under house arrest for three years she did not have to go to jail.

See also **Radio and Television.**

BIBLIOGRAPHY

Works by Bozzo

Rompiendo Cadenas: Las voces de la violencia. Lima, Peru: Editora Nacional, 2000.

Secondary Sources

Vargas, José Luis. *Adiós a la vergüenza: Los talk shows en el Perú.* Arequipa-Perú: Editorial Universidad Nacional San Agustin (UNSA, 2000). An academic analysis of Bozzo's program *Laura en América.*

JACQUELINE FOWKS

BRACERO. Bracero, the program developed through a series of agreements by the governments of Mexico and the United States (1942–1964) to import temporary Mexican farm workers into the United States. The term *bracero* comes from the Spanish word *brazo* (arm). A bracero, thus, was also the worker who participated in the bracero program.

The United States experienced a shortage of labor during World War II that led to the formal agreement with Mexico in 1942 for temporary admittance into the United States of mainly agricultural workers. By the terms of the initial accord, the U.S. Department of Agriculture administered the program, recruiting workers, placing them with private employers, and guaranteeing acceptable wages and working conditions. The Mexican government established regional recruiting centers where individuals applied for contracts to work in the United States. Once chosen, workers were transported to a U.S. reception center to sign government-standardized work contracts with employers. The contracts provided wage rates equivalent to those of U.S. workers for comparable work, adequate housing at no cost, low-priced meals, a guarantee of work for 75 percent of the contract term, insurance, and return transportation to Mexico at the end of the contract. Some 300,000 braceros participated in the program during World War II, and by the end of the program in 1964 more than 4 million Mexican nationals had worked in the United States under the program.

This labor agreement was at times a source of conflict. When renegotiating the agreement in 1953, Mexico took a firm position for control of bracero wage rates. The United States responded to the impasse in negotiations with an "open border policy," that is, not impeding the flow of illegal immigrants to the United States. When thousands of workers flocked to the northern border, Mexican officials, and even the army, attempted to prevent them from crossing into the United States. This border incident of 1954 came to a head when the braceros marched in protest and the Mexican government ended its attempt to prevent immigration. A new accord was reached in March 1954, and in June U.S. authorities initiated Operation Wetback to deport Mexican workers who were illegally in the United States in order to discourage further illegal entry and to force U.S. employers to hire contract labor under the bracero program.

Despite the problems, the program had benefited both countries. The United States obtained low-cost labor for work where it was difficult to attract Americans. Mexico was able temporarily to export surplus labor, and the remittances of the braceros were a significant source of foreign exchange and income to the impoverished sending communities. Since termination of the bracero program, the labor flows have continued through migration of undocumented workers. Uncontrolled labor migration from Mexico to the United States remains a major issue between the two countries. Labor migration increased rapidly beginning in the 1980s. During his presidency George W. Bush proposed a new guest worker program for undocumented workers, but this proposal was highly contentious and legislation implementing it as of 2007 had not been passed by Congress.

See also **United States-Mexico Border.**

BIBLIOGRAPHY

Ernesto Galarza, *Merchants of Labor: The Mexican Bracero Story* (1964).

Richard B. Craig, *The Bracero Program* (1971).

Peter Kirstein, *Anglo over Bracero: A History of the Mexican Worker in the United States from Roosevelt to Nixon* (1977).

Manuel García y Griega, *The Importation of Mexican Contract Laborers to the United States, 1942–1964: Antecedents, Operation, and Legacy* (1981).

Kitty Calavita, *Inside the State: The Bracero Program, Immigration, and the I.N.S.* (1992).

Additional Bibliography

Alanís Enciso, Fernando Saúl. *El primer programa bracero y el gobierno de México, 1917–1918.* San Luís Potosí: Colegio de San Luís, 1999.

Alanís Enciso, Fernando Saúl, ed. *La emigración de San Luís Potosí a Estados Unidos, pasado y presente.* Monterrey: Senado de la República, Colegio de San Luís, 2001.

Driscoll, Barbara A. *The Tracks North: The Railroad Bracero Program of World War II.* Austin: CMAS Books, Center for American Studies, University of Texas at Austin, 1999.

Gamboa, Erasmo. *Mexican Labor and World War II: Braceros in the Pacific Northwest, 1942–1947.* Seattle: University of Washington Press, 1999.

Gonzalez, Gilbert G. *Labor and Community: Mexican Citrus Worker Villages in a Southern California County, 1900–1950.* Urbana: University of Illinois Press, 1994.

PAUL GANSTER

BRADEN, SPRUILLE (1894–1978). Spruille Braden (*b.* 13 March 1894; *d.* 10 January 1978), U.S. mining entrepreneur and diplomat. Born in Elkhorn, Montana, and educated at Yale, Braden managed numerous copper-mining and business ventures in South America, particularly in Chile. By the early 1930s, he was owner or director of power and light companies in South America and of diverse North American firms. He served intermittently as a diplomat in the 1920s and turned to full-time public service in 1935, when President Franklin D. Roosevelt named him ambassador-delegate to the Chaco Peace Conference. Braden was among the first to sound the alarm over Axis incursions into the Western Hemisphere. As ambassador to Colombia (1938–1941), he struggled against German-controlled airlines in that country (and against the Germans' partner, Pan-American World Airways). He gained further fame for his anti-Axis operations as ambassador to Cuba (1941–1944).

The apogee and collapse of Braden's career came in 1945–1947. In 1945 he was named ambassador to Argentina, with which the State Department had been feuding since Argentina's refusal to join the hemispheric anti-Axis front in 1942. He clashed with Colonel Juan Perón, Argentina's emerging strongman, as well as with the Rockefeller (that is, Latin Americanist or liberal) faction of the State Department and with the British, both of whom urged conciliation with Argentina. Braden rallied the Argentine opposition to Perón and later attempted to use Argentina's flirtation with the Axis (documented in the Blue Book) to influence the election of 1946. These acts were considered violations of diplomatic norms and were also failures: Argentina was admitted to the United Nations at the San Francisco Conference (1945) and Perón was elected president (1946). Confirmed as under secretary of state for American Republic affairs late in 1945, Braden imposed his anti-Peronism on U.S. foreign policy; however, this policy became irrelevant in the cold war. The ensuing stalemate between Braden and Ambassador George Messersmith in Buenos Aires was resolved in June 1947 when Secretary of State Dean Acheson dismissed the ambassador and allowed Braden to resign. In retirement, Braden became a vocal cold warrior.

See also **Perón, Juan Domingo.**

BIBLIOGRAPHY

Spruille Braden, *Diplomats and Demagogues: The Memoirs of Spruille Braden* (1971).

Roger R. Trask, "Spruille Braden Versus George Messersmith: World War II, the Cold War, and Argentine Policy, 1945–1947," in *Journal of Interamerican Studies* 26, no. 1 (February 1984): 69–95.

RONALD C. NEWTON

BRADEN COPPER COMPANY. *See* **Gran Minería.**

BRAGANÇA, HOUSE OF. House of Bragança, noble house of Portugal whose members founded the Bragança dynasty that ruled Portugal from 1640 to 1910 and Brazil from 1822 to 1889. Descended from Dom Afonso (natural son of Dom João I of Portugal) and Dona Beatriz Pereira Alvim (daughter of Condestável Nuno Alves Pereira), who married in 1401; the family takes its name from the city of Bragança, in the northeastern extremity of Portugal. Land donations by Dom João and Condestável Pereira formed the nucleus of the dukedom, which later included extensive holdings in a large number of villages, manors, and fortresses. The dukes appointed ecclesiastical, administrative, judicial, and fiscal authorities throughout their lands and they enjoyed the prerogatives of royal princes outside the line of succession: they granted titles of nobility, and attended meetings of

the Council of State, presiding in the king's absence. Despite such privileges, the House of Bragança entered into conflict with Dom João II, of Aviz, who at the beginning of his reign (1481–1495) sought to strengthen his royal power by demanding from the nobility a pledge of allegiance according to a new formula that linked and subordinated the nobles to royal power far more than the previous pledge. The duke of Bragança, Dom Fernando II, protested the wording of the new formula as too rigorous and demeaning to his dignity. Although the duke eventually swore allegiance, when Dom João II ordered a new survey of all the land in the kingdom, without exception, Dom Fernando and other other nobles conspired against the king. Dom Fernando was brought to trial, decapitated, his family exiled, and all the holdings of the House of Bragança confiscated and distributed among the favorites of Dom João II. In 1497 all rights were restored to the house.

In 1580 the Aviz dynasty ended with the death of Dom Henrique I. Philip II of Spain assumed the Portuguese crown, and Portugal remained united to Spain until 1640. In 1637 the idea of restoration began to take root, and the natural choice for a sovereign was Dom João II, eighth duke of Bragança. The duke and his followers used the outbreak of the Catalunian rebellion in Spain to proclaim the separation of Portugal from Spain, and in 1640 the duke became João IV, king of Portugal. The Braganças governed Portugal during some of its most challenging periods: the recovery from the economic and fiscal devastation left by its former union with Spain, the threat of Spanish military intervention, the animosity of the pope who supported Spain, and the Dutch conquest of Brazil. During the eighteenth century the dynasty experienced a golden age under João V, impelled by his administrative and political acumen and the wealth from the Brazilian gold mines. The nineteenth century brought the Napoleonic invasion, the escape of the Bragança in 1809 to Brazil (where they remained until 1821), and finally the loss of Brazil.

In 1822 Dom Pedro, prince regent of Brazil and heir to the Portuguese throne, proclaimed Brazilian independence and became Pedro I of Brazil. The Brazilian branch of the Bragança dynasty came to govern Brazil and Portugal under constitutional monarchies. Pedro I became Pedro IV of Portugal upon his father's death in 1826, but in the same year he abdicated the throne of Portugal in favor of his daughter, Maria II, and 1831 he abdicated the throne of Brazil in favor of his son, Pedro II. The last Bragança monarchs tried, without success, to forestall the republic but the Republic of Brazil was proclaimed in 1889, and Pedro II exiled. Portugal was proclaimed a republic in 1910, causing Dom Manuel II to leave the country.

See also **Pedro II of Brazil.**

BIBLIOGRAPHY

João Ameal, *História de Portugal* (1968).

Neill Macaulay, *Dom Pedro* (1986).

Additional Bibliography

Dias, Paulo. *Real panteão dos Bragança: Arte e memoria.* Porto: Antília Editora, 2006.

Howe, Malcolm S. *The Braganza Story: A Visit to the Royal Pantheon of Portugal.* London: British Historical Society of Portugal, 1999.

Machado, José Carlos L. Soares. *Os Braganças: História genealógica de uma linhagem medieval (séculos XI a XIII).* Lisbon: J.C.L.S. Machado, 2004.

LYDIA M. GARNER

BRAMUGLIA, JUAN ATILIO (1903–1962).

Juan Atilio Bramuglia (*b.* 19 January 1903; *d.* 4 September 1962), Argentine labor lawyer, foreign minister, and supporter of Juan Domingo Perón. As legal counsel for the railroad workers' union, Bramuglia showed strong initial support of Perón which earned him appointments in the government. In 1944 he was named general director of social welfare, and from 1944 to 1945 he served as federal intervenor in the province of Buenos Aires. When Perón was elected president in 1946, Bramuglia became foreign minister. Bramuglia sought recognition of Argentine claims in Antarctica and the Falkland Islands (Malvinas) and achieved some success in presenting Perón's third position in international affairs. In 1948 he was provisional president of the Third Assembly of the United Nations in Paris, and in 1949 he was elected chairman of the United Nations Security Council. After incurring the displeasure of Evita Perón, Bramuglia resigned from government and pursued scholarly activities. His published works include *Jubilaciones ferroviarias* (1941) and *La previsión social Argentina* (1942).

See also **Antarctica; Falkland Islands (Malvinas); Perón, Juan Domingo.**

BIBLIOGRAPHY

Samuel L. Baily describes Bramuglia's importance in Perón's first administration in *Labor, Nationalism, and Politics in Argentina* (1967). Joseph A. Page, *Perón, a Biography* (1983), discusses his role in Perón's nationalization of the labor movement. Evita's dislike of Bramuglia is covered in Eduardo Crawley, *A Nation Divided: Argentina, 1880–1980* (1984), esp. pp. 116–117.

Additional Bibliography

Rein, Raanan. *In the Shadow of Perón: Juan Atilio Bramuglia and the Second Line of Argentina's Populist Movement.* Trans. Martha Grenzeback. Stanford, CA: Stanford University Press, 2007.

JAMES A. BAER

BRAÑAS GUERRA, CÉSAR (1899–1976).

César Brañas Guerra (*b.* 13 December 1899; *d.* 22 February 1976), Guatemalan poet, journalist, and writer, and one of the founders of the influential Guatemalan daily *El Imparcial* (1922–1985). Born in Antigua, Brañas was the best-known of a family of important literary figures. His father was an immigrant from Galicia and his mother a schoolteacher in Antigua. His prolific output of poetry, novels, historical works, and critical essays was highly influential in mid-twentieth-century Guatemala. Like Miguel Ángel Asturias, he contributed to a social consciousness among the Guatemalan intelligentsia. His large library, a part of the University of San Carlos, is especially useful for study of the nineteenth and early twentieth centuries.

See also **Journalism.**

BIBLIOGRAPHY

Francisco Albizúrez Palma and Catalina Barrios y Barrios, *Historia de la literatura guatemalteca*, 3 vols. (1981–1987), vol. 2, pp. 167–203.

Carlos C. Haeussler Yela, *Diccionario general de Guatemala* (1983), vol. 1, p. 260.

Additional Bibliography

Asturias, Miguel Angel, César Brañas, et al. *Fragmentos de una correspondencia: Brañas-Asturias, 1929–1973.* Guatemala: Editorial Universitaria, Universidad de San Carlos de Guatemala, 2001.

Grandin, Greg. *The Blood of Guatemala: A History of Race and Nation.* Durham, NC: Duke University Press, 2000.

RALPH LEE WOODWARD JR.

BRANDÃO, IGNÁCIO DE LOYOLA

(1936–). Ignácio de Loyola Brandão (*b.* 31 July 1936), Brazilian author. Brandão's writing career began at the age of sixteen, when he was a movie reviewer for a newspaper in Araraquara, his hometown, in the hinterland of the state of São Paulo. Soon after his twenty-first birthday, he moved to the state capital, where he became a journalist. The peculiarities and problems of urban life made a profound impression on him, and for the next eight years he witnessed the people's increasing mistrust in the government, and the resulting turmoil that led to a military coup in 1964. Being a reporter, Brandão had firsthand knowledge of the turbulence of the metropolis, intensified by a period of extreme violence between police and militants following the coup. This environment pervades his fiction. His first book, *Depois do sol* (1965, After the Sun), a collection of short stories, was followed by *Bebel que a cidade comeu* (1968, Bebel, Swallowed Up by the City). Both books portray the social and psychological crises of 1960s Brazil, resulting from political oppression and economic unrest. Brandão eventually abandoned his career as a journalist and devoted himself to his fiction, though his novels and short stories retain a journalistic feel, revealing the author's analytical mind and stylistic irreverence, which often extends to graphic layouts emulating newspapers. His criticism of the government led to censorship of his novel *Zero*, which was banned from publication in Brazil for six years (1969–1975). He became, then, the first Brazilian writer to resort to publication abroad; *Zero* was printed in Italy (1974) before its publication in Portuguese. The

first English-language translation was published in the United States in 1984. Brandão also wrote travelogues, including *Cuba de Fidel: viagem à ilha proibida* (1978, Fidel's Cuba: Voyage to a Forbidden Island) and *O verde violentou o muro: visões e alucinações alemãs* (1984, The Greenery that Shook the Wall: German Visions and Hallucinations). Brandão is a prolific writer whose work has evolved with the times; he remains faithful to his primary vision of a world unredeemable in its unfairness and cruelty.

See also **Brazil, Revolutions: Revolution of 1964; Literature: Brazil.**

BIBLIOGRAPHY

Erilde Melillo Reale, *Il Doppio Segno di Zero* (1976) and *Raccontes in un Romanzo* (1979).

Emilio Rodrígues Monegal, "Writing Fiction Under the Censor's Eyes," in *World Literature Today* (1979).

Ute Hermanns, *Mithos and Realität im Roman Zero* (1984).

Larry Rother, "Life Under the Mili-Tech," review of *Não Verás País Nenhum*, New York Times, 29 September 1985.

Candace Slater, "Brazilian Literature: Zero," *Review* 32 (January–May 1994).

Additional Bibliography

Besa, Pedro Pirres. *Loyola Brandão: A televisão na literatura.* Juiz de Fora, Brazil: Editora da Universidade Federal de Juiz de Fora, 1988.

Bollinger, Rosemarie. "Tres escritores brasileños." *Cuadernos hispanoamericanos* 439 (Jan 1987): 85–98.

Krabbenhoft, Kenneth. "Ignació de Loyola Brandão and the Fiction of Cognitive Estrangement." *Luso-Brazilian Review* 24 (Summer 1987): 35-45.

Martins, Juca. *São Paulo capital.* São Paulo: Instituto Moreira Salles, 1988.

REGINA IGEL

BRANNON DE SAMAYOA CHINCHILLA, CARMEN (1899–1974). Carmen

Brannon de Samayoa Chinchilla (pseud. Claudia Lars; *b.* 1899; *d.* 1974), Salvadoran modernist writer. The daughter of an Irish-American father and Salvadoran mother, Lars grew up on a *finca* (farm) in Sonsonate. She was educated by nuns in Santa Ana and exhibited a literary inclination from a very early age. In her youth she fell in love with the Nicaraguan poet Salomón de la Selva, who introduced her to the world of European romantic literature and served as her mentor. However, her father disapproved of the match and sent her to live with relatives in New York. Upon her return to El Salvador, Lars fell in with a group of modernist and humanist writers known as the Generation of the 1930s, which had assembled around Alberto Masferrer's newspaper *La Patria* and included Serafin Quiteño and Salarrué. Lars immigrated to San Francisco in 1944, where she experienced the drudgery of working in a biscuit factory. In 1974 she returned to El Salvador. The theme of the mysteries of life and the cosmos dominates her major novels and poems. Lars is considered one of the first great modern female literary figures of Hispanic America.

See also **Literature: Spanish America.**

BIBLIOGRAPHY

Claudia Lars, *Estrellas en el pozo* (1934); *Canción redonda* (1937); *Donde llegan los pasos* (1953); *Tierra de infancia* (1958); and *Obras Escogidas* (1973).

Juan Felipe Toruño, *Desarrollo literario de El Salvador* (1958), pp. 325–328.

Matilde Elena López, "Prólogo" to *Obras Escogidas* (1973).

Luis Gallegos Valdés, *Panorama de la literatura salvadoreña* (1981), pp. 225–238.

Additional Bibliography

Bosteels, Bruno, and Tina Escaja, eds. *Delmira Agustini y el modernismo: Nuevo propuestas de género*. Rosario, Argentina: B. Viterbo Editora, 2000.

Lars, Claudia. *Poesía completa*. Ed. Conmemorativa del centenario de su natalacio. San Salvador: CONCULTURA, 1999.

KAREN RACINE

BRASÍLIA. Brasília, the capital of Brazil since 1960 (2007 estimated population 2.3 million). Like many seats of national government, Brasília was a deliberate creation rather than a city that arose spontaneously and organically. The idea of relocating the capital of Brazil from Rio de Janeiro to the backward, sparsely inhabited interior to encourage settlement and development was talked about as early as 1761. In 1891, 5,500 square miles of the Planalto Central were set aside for the site of the future Federal District, but the project did not begin in earnest until 1955, when five possible sites were evaluated in detail by Belcher Associates of Ithaca, New York. The final choice, made in 1956, was located 35 miles southeast of the small town of Planaltina.

The city would probably never have been built had it not been for the efforts of the remarkably dynamic Juscelino Kubitschek, who had risen from humble origins in the state of Minas Gerais to become the president of Brazil in 1956. Kubitschek promised in his campaign to bring Brasília to reality. Presidents were allowed to serve only one term, and Kubitschek, realizing he had to present his successor with a fait accompli, knew he only had five years to get the city built. To design the city he commissioned the architect Oscar Niemeyer, who had designed the barrio of Pampulha in Belo Horizonte, the capital of Minas Gerais, when Kubitschek was governor. Niemeyer was a disciple of Le Corbusier, the father of the modern glass tower, which was beginning to dominate the skylines of many Latin American cities, symbolizing their yearning for progress. Niemeyer devoted himself to Brasília's public buildings. He drew a central square as monumental and majestic as Mexico's prehistoric Teotihuacán, with two rows of green-glass ministries leading down to the Congress, whose two chambers, offset by white towers, resemble two bowls, one face up, the other down; to the president's delicately arched white-marble Planalto Palace; and to the serenely lyrical Itamariti Palace, headquarters of the Ministry of Foreign Affairs, a low-slung structure sitting in water and accessible only by ramps, with an outer sheath of tall, slender arches that were, like the Planalto Palace's, a stylization of colonial architecture. The Costa e Silva Bridge, another of the city's architectural wonders, whose 500-foot free span was the greatest of any suspension bridge in Latin America, took six years to finish.

An open competition for the city plan was won by Niemeyer's Rio de Janeiro colleague, Lúcio Costa. Niemeyer and Costa shared a vision of an egalitarian utopia where all classes would live together and the slums that marred Brazil's other cities would be avoided. Costa's Pilot Plan was shaped like an airplane whose fuselage was devoted to Niemeyer's design for the public buildings, and whose wings were the residential areas, each with sixty "superquadras," which were minicommunities patterned after a medieval town and serviced by their own schools, churches, and shopping areas. Each six-story block of apartments was separated by green space and was raised on pilings so children could play under it.

Many criticized the city for its sterile modernity. At the time of its inauguration on 21 April 1960, Brasília seemed to some visitors too rational, too programmed. If one wanted to have a night on the town, for instance, one did this in the Sector of Diversions. To minimize the number of intersections, street corners, and stoplights and thus ensure the unimpeded circulation of traffic, Costa had created a "speedway city" with a convoluted system of ramps, cloverleafs, and pedestrian overpasses. The problem with this was that it increased the distance to everything and discouraged pedestrian travel. Brasília became the hub of a vast highway system, with interstates shooting off to distant cities like Belém, Cuiabá, Belo Horizonte, and Salvador. The dream of national integration was achieved, but at a cost of several billion dollars, which sent inflation spiraling, created social unrest, and led to the 1964 military coup.

Brasília made aesthetic waves, but the hoped-for social revolution did not take place. After 1960 the apartments in the blocks were placed on the open real-estate market, and the construction workers who had built the city and been affectionately dubbed *candangos* by Kubitschek (most were dark-skinned poor from the Northeast) were bought out and forced to live in unplanned satellite cities 20 miles away. Today the federal district's population is about 3 million. Less than a million live in the Pilot Plan itself; the rest live in the satellite cities. The rich live in mansions along two artificial V-shaped lakes below the Pilot Plan created by Paranoá dam, an area that Niemeyer and Costa planned as a park for everybody but, Niemeyer complained, was "usurped by the bourgeoisie." The surrounding *cerrado*, or savanna, studded with small, warped trees, is spectacularly open. With the concrete slabs of many buildings cracked and coated with black mildew, the city's modernity is no longer so shocking. André Malraux, on a 1959 visit, called Brasília the Capital of Hope, but five years later it became the headquarters of twenty-five years of brutal military dictatorship. With the return to civilian rule in 1985, Brasília has become a symbol of appalling political corruption.

See also **Architecture: Modern Architecture.**

BIBLIOGRAPHY

Norma Evenson, *Two Brazilian Capitals* (1973).

Juscelino Kubitschek, *Por que construi Brasília* (1975).

Alex Shoumatoff, *The Capital of Hope* (1980).

Additional Bibliography

Bursztyn, Marcel, and Carlos Henrique Araújo. *Da utopia à exclusão: Vivendo nas ruas em Brasília.* Rio de Janeiro: Garamond; Brasília: Codeplan, 1997.

Couto, Ronaldo Costa. *Brasília Kubitschek de Oliveira.* Rio de Janeiro: Editora Record, 2001.

Dahdah, Farès. *Lucio Costa: Brasilia's superquadra.* London: Prestel, 2005.

El-Khoury, Rodolphe, and Edward Robbins. *Shaping the City: Studies in History, Theory and Urban Design.* New York: Routledge, 2004.

Goncalves, Maria da Conceição Vasconcelos. *"Favelas teimosas": Lutas por moradia.* Brasília: Thesaurus, 1998.

Gorelik, Adrián. *Das vanguardas a Brasília: Cultura urbana e arquitetura na América Latina.* Belo Horizonte: Editora UFMG, 2005.

Gouvêa, Luiz Alberto de Campos. *Brasília: A capital da segregação e do controle social: Uma avaliação da ação governamental na área da habitação.* São Paulo: Annablume, 1995.

Lopes, Luís Carlos. *Brasília: O enigma da esfinge, a construção e os bastidores do poder.* Porto Alegre: Editora da Universidade, Universidade Federal do Rio Grande do Sul; São Leopoldo: Editora Unisinos, 1996.

Paviani, Aldo, and Ignez Costa Barbosa Ferreira. *Brasília: Dimensões da violência urbana.* Brasília: Editora UNB, 2005.

Sinoti, Marta Litwinczik. *Quem me quer, não me quer: Brasília, metrópole-patrimônio.* São Paulo: Annablume, 2005.

ALEX SHOUMATOFF

BRÁS PEREIRA GOMES, WENCESLAU (1868–1966).

Wenceslau Brás Pereira Gomes (*b.* 26 February 1868; *d.* 15 May 1966), president of Brazil (1914–1918). After serving as governor of the state of Minas Gerais (1908–1910) and vice president under Hermes da Fonseca (1910–1914), Brás was elected president of Brazil in 1914. The Brás presidency marked the end of the extreme federalism of Brazil's early republican years, as the federal government took an increasingly active role in directing state politics and the national economy. Under Brás, force and intimidation were used in several federal interventions into the internal affairs of politically weak states, as well as for the suppression of the Contestado Rebellion along the Santa Catarina-Paraná border. Brás's presidential policies favored the most powerful states. São Paulo and Minas Gerais, which were allied in a power-sharing arrangement known as the politics of *café-com-leite* (an allusion to the prominent coffee-growing and ranching economies of São Paulo and Minas Gerais, respectively).

Aside from declaring war on the Central Powers in 1917, thus making Brazil the only South American republic to join the Allies, Brás is best known for signing the Civil Code of 1917. The Brás presidency is also notable for a rise in domestic industrial production stimulated by the disruptions of international trade and credit brought on by World War I. In November 1918 Brás left office amid a Spanish flu epidemic that ravaged Rio de Janeiro. He subsequently returned to Minas Gerais to lead a private life out of the public spotlight.

See also **Brazil, Civil Code.**

BIBLIOGRAPHY

Raúl Alves Da Souza, *História política dos governos da república* (1927), pp. 195–216.

John D. Wirth, *Minas Gerais in the Brazilian Federation, 1889–1937* (1977).

E. Bradford Burns, *A History of Brazil* (1980).

Additional Bibliography

Viscardi, Cláudia Maria Ribeiro. *O teatro das oligarquias: Uma revisão da "política do café com leite".* Belo Horizonte: Editora C/Arte, 2001.

                                        DARYLE WILLIAMS

BRASSEUR DE BOURBOURG, CHARLES ÉTIENNE (1814–1874).

Charles Étienne Brasseur de Bourbourg (*b.* 8 September 1814; *d.* January 1874), French prelate, antiquarian, and pioneer ethnohistorian. Ordained in 1845, Brasseur enjoyed a variety of postings in the Americas, where he was able to make most of his lasting contributions. Among the countries he visited were Canada (1845–1846), the United States (on at least two occasions, in 1848 and 1854), Mexico (1848–1851, 1863–1866, and 1871), Nicaragua and El Salvador (1854), Guatemala (1855–1857 and 1863), and Honduras (1863).

Brasseur is significant today primarily for his discovery, translation, and publication of several important colonial sources concerning Mesoamerican Indians, principally the Maya. These include Diego de Landa's *Relación de las cosas de Yucatán,* the Popol Vuh, the *Título de los señores de Totonicapán,* the Troano Codex, and the *Memorial de Tecpán Atitlán,* or *Annals of Cakchiquels.* He also compiled and published linguistic materials for both highland Maya (primarily Quiché, including the *Rabinal Achí* drama) and lowland Maya (Yucatecan) peoples that continue to be useful to scholars. Unfortunately, Brasseur's historical interpretations of the documents he worked so tirelessly to discover were judged even by his contemporaries to be seriously flawed. Of little use to present-day scholars on the region, his pronouncements retain only a documentary interest.

To his credit Brasseur did much to promote American studies in his native France, through cofounding the Société Américaine de France (1857) and participating in the subsequent Société d'Ethnographie and the Société de Géographie of Paris. He also raised popular consciousness concerning the indigenous peoples and civilizations of Mesoamerica through his publication of many episodes and discoveries made during his travels.

See also **Indigenous Peoples; Mesoamerica.**

BIBLIOGRAPHY

Adrián Recinos, "Cien años de la llegada del Abate Brasseur de Bourbourg a Guatemala," in *Anales de la Sociedad de Geografía e Historia,* 29 (January–December 1956): 12–17.

Carroll Edward Mace, "Charles Étienne Brasseur de Bourbourg, 1814–1874, in *Handbook of Middle American Indians,* vol. 13, *Guide to Ethnohistorical Sources,* part 2, edited by Robert Wauchope, Howard F. Cline, and John B. Glass (1973), pp. 298–325.

Additional Bibliography

Dufétel, Dominique. "Charles-Etienne Brasseur de Bourbourg, 1814–1874. (Accompanied by the original

French and an English translation by Gregory Dechant)." *Artes de México* 43 (1998): 34–35.

ROBERT M. HILL II

BRATHWAITE, EDWARD KAMAU

(1930–). Edward Kamau Brathwaite (*b.* 11 May 1930), Caribbean historian, poet, and critic. Born in Bridgetown, Barbados, Brathwaite attended high school at Harrison College in Barbados, and college at Cambridge University. He was a professor of history at the University of the West Indies and later became a professor of comparative literature at New York University. As a historian, Brathwaite's scholarly publications include the important works *The Folk Culture of the Slaves in Jamaica* (1969; rev. ed. 1981) and *The Development of Creole Society in Jamaica, 1770–1820* (1971). He is the author of ten collections of poetry and several plays. *The Arrivants: A New World Trilogy* (1973) secured his reputation as a major poet of the Caribbean. In *Roots* (1993), a collection of literary scholarship and criticism, and in other critical writings, Brathwaite shows himself to be foremost among the theorists of Caribbean literature and culture. In 2006 he was declared the international winner of the prestigious Griffin Poetry Prize for his collection, *Born to Slow Horses.*

Major themes of Brathwaite's poetry are Caribbean history and identity; slavery and colonization are integrally connected to the themes of fragmentation and alienation. Brathwaite's poetry attempts to provide a "whole, living tradition" out of which can be derived a new consciousness.

See also **Literature: Spanish America.**

BIBLIOGRAPHY

Gordon Rohlehr, "The Historian as Poet," in *The Literary Half-Yearly* 11 (July 1970): 171–178, and "Islands," in *Caribbean Studies* 10 (January 1971): 173–202.

Kenneth Ramchand, "Edward Brathwaite," in *An Introduction to the Study of West Indian Literature* (1976), pp. 127–142.

Maureen Warner-Lewis, *Notes to Masks* (1977).

Mervyn Morris, "This Broken Ground: Edward Brathwaite's Trilogy of Poems," in *New World Quarterly* 23 (June–September 1977): 91–103.

Lloyd Brown, "The Cyclical Vision of Edward Brathwaite," in *West Indian Poetry* (1978), pp. 139–158.

N. Mackey, "Edward Brathwaite's New World Trilogy," in *Caliban* 3 (Spring–Summer 1979): 58–88.

Velma Pollard, "The Dust—A Tribute to the Folk," in *Caribbean Quarterly* 26 (March–June 1980): 41–48.

Additional Bibliography

Brown, Stewart. *The Art of Kamau Brathwaite.* Bridgend, Mid Glamorgan, Wales: Seren, 1995.

Irele, Abiola. *The African Imagination: Literature in Africa and the Black Diaspora.* New York: Oxford University Press, 2001.

Rowell, Charles H. *Making Callaloo: 25 Years of Black Literature, 1976-2000.* New York: St. Martin's Press, 2002.

Williams, Emily Allen. *Poetic Negotiation of Identity in the Works of Brathwaite, Harris, Senior, and Dabydeen: Tropical Paradise Lost and Regained.* Lewiston, NY: Edwin Mellen Press, 1999.

EVELYN J. HAWTHORNE

BRAVO, CLAUDIO

(1936–). Claudio Bravo (*b.* 8 November 1936), Chilean artist. A virtuoso of realism in painting, drawing, and lithography, Bravo was born in Valparaíso into a wealthy family. He attended Miguel Venegas Cienfuentes's art school from 1947 to 1948. In 1961, he moved to Spain, where he earned his living painting realistic portraits of the Spanish aristocracy. In the mid-1960s, he turned to trompe l'oeil paintings of isolated objects, such as motorcycle paraphernalia, clothing, folded and crumpled pieces of papers, wrapped canvases (*Homage to St. Teresa,* 1969; oil on canvas), and packages (*Blue Package,* 1971). His emphasis on texture, angled lighting, and narrow foreground planes derived from his studies of Francisco de Zurbarán's *bodegones.* Bravo replaced the Spanish master's empty backgrounds with skyscapes and white walls. The realism of Bravo's painting contrasts with his avoidance of all contextual references. His rendering of commonplace objects, biblical themes, and kneeling figures in undefined places or empty space has been interpreted as a surrealist trait. In 1972 Bravo moved to Tangier, Morocco. In 1981, he had his first show with the Marlborough Gallery in New York, which still represented him as of 2007. In 1994, he had his first show at the Museo Nacional de

Bellas Artes in Santiago, Chile. As of 2007, he split his time between Chile and Tangier.

See also **Art: The Twentieth Century.**

BIBLIOGRAPHY

William Dyckes, "The New Spanish Realists," in *Art International: The Lugano Review* 17 (September 1973): 29–33, 45.

Edward J. Sullivan, *Claudio Bravo* (1985).

Additional Bibliography

Bowles, Paul, Francisco Calvo Serraller, and Edward J. Sullivan. *Claudio Bravo: Paintings and Drawings (1964–2004).* New York: Rizzoli; Madrid, Lerner & Lerner, 2005.

Bravo, Claudio and Edward J. Sullivan. *Claudio Bravo: Painter and Draftsman.* Madison: Elvehjem Museum of Art, University of Wisconsin–Madison, 1987.

Colle, Marie-Pierre. *Latin American Artists in Their Studios.* New York: Vendome Press, 1994.

MARTA GARSD

BRAVO, LEONARDO (1764–1812).

Leonardo Bravo (*b.* 1764; *d.* 14 September 1812), Mexican insurgent leader. The Chilpancingo-born patriarch of a large family, Bravo joined the insurgent movement in May 1811, along with his son Nicolás and his brothers Miguel, Víctor, and Máximo, when Hermenegildo Galeana came to his hacienda of Chichihualco. Bravo became one of José María Morelos's most distinguished officers. He played a major role, first in the fortification, and later in the defense, of Cuautla, where the insurgents, besieged by the royalists, held out for seventy-two days despite a lack of supplies. When the siege was lifted at the beginning of May 1812, Bravo traveled to the hacienda of San Gabriel, where he was captured by partisans of the colonial regime. He was taken to Mexico City, where he was tried and executed despite the efforts of his relatives, and even of Morelos, to obtain a pardon in return for the exchange of a sizable group of royalist prisoners.

See also **Mexico: 1810–1910.**

BIBLIOGRAPHY

José María Miquel I Vergés, *Diccionario de insurgentes* (1969), 85–86.

Virginia Guedea, *José María Morelos y Pavón: Cronología* (1981).

Ernesto Lemoine, *Morelos y la revolución de 1810* (1984).

VIRGINIA GUEDEA

BRAVO, MARIO (1882–1944). Mario

Bravo was an Argentine Socialist congressman and senator. Bravo, who was elected a national deputy from the city of Buenos Aires four times (1913–1914, 1914–1918, 1918–1922, and 1942–1946) and a senator twice (1923–1931 and 1932–1938), was one of the leading Argentine Socialist Party politicians of the early twentieth century. Born in the city of Tucumán on July 27, 1882, he received his law degree from the University of Buenos Aires and joined the Socialist Party soon thereafter. He rose rapidly through the party's ranks, becoming its general secretary in 1910. The Socialist Party, which grew quickly from its foundation in 1896, remained a minority party throughout the period. Electoral fraud until 1912 and the popular strength of the urban middle-class party Unión Cívica Radical (Radical Civic Union, or Radical Party) between 1916 and 1930 kept the Socialists from any real chance of forming a government.

As a legislator, Bravo was best known for initiating measures to democratize the selection process of the *consejo deliberante* (city council) of the federal capital, a change that took effect in 1918, as well as for bringing attention to the conditions of sugar plantation workers in his home province of Tucumán. Notwithstanding the electoral fraud after the military coup of 1930, which he denounced in the pages of *La Vanguardia*, the main Socialist newspaper, Bravo returned to Congress in 1932. For this period he is remembered for his criticism of the repression of the Communist Party. A well-regarded poet, his literary efforts focused primarily on social issues. Collections of his poems include *Poemas del campo y de la montaña* (1909) and *Canciones y poemas* (1918).

See also **Argentina, Political Parties: Radical Party (UCR); Argentina, Political Parties: Socialist Party.**

BIBLIOGRAPHY

Cantón, Darío. *Elecciones y partidos políticos en la Argentina, Historia, interpretación y balance: 1910–1966.* Buenos Aires: Siglo XXI, 1973.

Suriano, Juan, ed. *La cuestión social en Argentina, 1870–1943*. Buenos Aires: La Colmena, 2000.

RICHARD J. WALTER

BRAVO, NICOLÁS (c. 1784–1854).

Nicolás Bravo (*b.* ca. 1784–1792; *d.* 22 April 1854) Mexican independence leader and politician. Born in Chilpancingo, Bravo and his family joined the insurgency, in which he distinguished himself in a series of campaigns against the royalists. Captured in 1817, he was imprisoned until October 1820. He supported the Plan of Iguala in 1821, emerging as one of the major political figures of the new order.

Although Bravo served in the regency in 1822, he later opposed Emperor Agustín de Iturbide, eventually becoming part of the government that replaced the emperor. Elected vice president in 1824, he became the Grand Master of the "aristocratic" Escoceses (Scottish rite Masons), and in January 1828 joined a conservative revolt against the growing power of the radical Yorkinos (York rite Masons), which failed and led to his exile to South America.

Upon his return, Bravo served as commander of the Army of the North, deputy to Congress, and interim president in 1839, 1842–1843, and 1846–1847. During the U.S. invasion in 1847, Bravo commanded troops in battles in Puebla, the defense of the capital, and the last stand in Chapultepec Castle, where he was captured. Although invited to join the revolution of Ayutla, he declined because of illness.

See also **Plan of Iguala.**

BIBLIOGRAPHY

Leonard Parrish, "The Life of Nicolás Bravo, Mexican Patriot" (Ph.D. diss., University of Texas, 1951).

Jaime E. Rodríguez O., "The Struggle for the Nation: The First Federalist-Centralist Conflict in Mexico," in *The Americas* 49 (July 1992): 1–22.

Additional Bibliography

Trueba, Alfonso. *Nicolás Bravo: El mexicano que perdonó.* Mexico: Editoral Jus, 1976.

JAIME E. RODRÍGUEZ O.

BRAY, ARTURO (1898–1974).

Arturo Bray (*b.* 1 April 1898; *d.* 2 July 1974), Paraguayan military figure and writer. Born in Asunción to an English father and a Paraguayan mother, Arturo Bray was educated in Asunción and departed for England in 1914 to study medicine. The next year he enlisted in Lord Kitchener's New Armies as a private. He served for two years on the Western Front during World War I, rising to the rank of lieutenant in the infantry. After the war, he returned to Paraguay and quickly received a commission.

During the 1922 military rebellion, Bray remained loyal to the government and held a number of posts in the 1920s. In 1930 he was named director of the Escuela Militar; the following year he was appointed interim chief of police of Asunción. At the outbreak of the Chaco War, Bray was promoted to lieutenant colonel, becoming a divisional commander in 1933. He commanded a unit of infantry at the battle of Boquerón that year. A failed military operation in late 1933 led to his detention until 1935 and left him permanently embittered against many Liberal colleagues within and without the army. Eventually he was cleared of charges and in 1936 participated as chief of the Paraguayan military delegation to the Chaco Peace Conference.

The *Febrista* coup of 1936 resulted in his dismissal from the army and his arrest. With the Liberal restoration in the late 1930s Bray again became chief of police of Asunción; he was promoted to colonel and in 1938 served as minister of the interior. Differences (dating back to the Chaco War) with José Félix Estigarribia and other Liberals led to Bray's diplomatic "exile" as minister to Spain and Portugal (1939–1940) and minister to Chile (1940–1941). The 1941 seizure of power by Higinio Morínigo after the death of President Estigarribia spelled the end of Bray's public career.

During his military career, Bray had published professional articles in Paraguayan and foreign newspapers and periodicals. As a private citizen after 1941, he devoted himself to writing. *Hombres y épocas del Paraguay* (1943) and *Solano López, soldado de la gloria y infortunio* (1946) are his best-known works. Later he added another volume to *Hombres y épocas.* He also translated several historical works from English to Spanish. He died in Asunción in 1974.

See also **Chaco War; Paraguay, Political Parties: Febrerista Party.**

BIBLIOGRAPHY

Carlos R. Centurión, *Historia de la cultura paraguaya*, vol. 2 (1961), pp. 435–438.

Arturo Bray, *Armas y letras*, 3 vols. (1981).

Additional Bibliography

Farcau, Bruce W. *The Chaco War: Bolivia and Paraguay, 1932-1935.* Westport, CT: Praeger, 1996.

Rahi, Arturo. *El Chaco paraguayo: Una historia de despejos, renuncias, mutilaciones, y entregas.* Asunción: F17, 2006.

JERRY W. COONEY

BRAZ, WENCESLAU. *See* Brás Pereira Gomes, Wenceslau.

BRAZIL

This entry includes the following articles:
THE COLONIAL ERA, 1500-1808
1808-1889
SINCE 1889

THE COLONIAL ERA, 1500–1808

FIRST CONTACTS

The first European presence in what was initially called the Land of the True Cross (Terra da Vera Cruz) and later Brazil (in recognition of red dye-wood [*pau brasil;*cb) was the arrival in April 1500 of the fleet commanded by the Portuguese Pedro Alvares Cabral. After notifying the king, the fleet continued around Africa to India. As follow-up fleet to that of Vasco da Gama, which had inaugurated the sea route from Lisbon to India (1498), Cabral's ships had been destined for India. By sweeping out into the Atlantic to avoid the doldrums, Cabral sailed so far off course to the west as to encounter, by chance, the South American continent. In accordance with the Treaty of Tordesillas (1494), he claimed the new land for Portugal. Although the Spaniard Vicente Yáñez Pinzón had

preempted Cabral by a few months, this claim was not challenged. Other early travelers included the Florentine pilot Amerigo Vespucci, who sailed the coastline of Brazil to the Río de la Plata naming topographical features (1501–1502). The following quarter of a century was to witness landfalls on the coast, or residence, by other Europeans.

In a 1 May 1500 letter to King Manuel I, professional scribe Pero Vaz de Caminha reported on the coastal Tupinambá. He described well-built men, physically attractive and modest women, as well as their good health, nakedness, and bodily decoration. The Portuguese pursued a policy of pacification, and relations were cordial. The Tupinambá offered bows, arrows, cloths and hats made of feathers, parrots, and special beads, and received from the Portuguese red caps, linen bonnets, bracelets, and rosaries. Masses were said on shore. Vaz de Caminha extolled the beauties of the land, its agricultural promise, the innocence of the people, and their rich potential for conversion to Christianity.

PEOPLING BRAZIL

Native American populations were the first victims of the European arrival. Friendly encounters gave way to hostilities, barter to slavery. Campaigns against the local people were initiated by Mem de Sá in Bahia in the 1570s. Indian-European relations were to be characterized by tension. To survive, Amerindians accommodated to European pressures, retreated beyond European spheres of influence, or resisted. By the end of the sixteenth century, they had been ousted from most coastal regions. But they could not escape European diseases (smallpox, measles, and common cold) to which they had no immunity, European mores (alcohol consumption and use of clothing), forced relocations, long migrations, and destruction of their beliefs. They were victims of *paulista* slaving Bandeiras, official and unofficial slaving expeditions in the Amazon, forced labor, unjustified attacks, and systematic genocide. In the sixteenth century, Amerindian peoples were enmeshed in Gallo-Portuguese hostilities, and the struggle against the Dutch in the seventeenth century found indigenous peoples divided in their loyalties, even within the same family. Gold rushes to Goiás and Mato Grosso took Europeans farther into Indian territories. European intrusions into Amazonia also had fatal results. The Amazonian population

Drawing of African slaves working in a Brazilian mill, crushing cane to make sugar, 17th century. Brazil's colonial sugar prosperity from the sixteenth to the eighteenth century was made from the labor of enslaved Africans. THE GRANGER COLLECTION. REPRODUCED BY PERMISSION.

guesstimated at 2.4 million in 1500 had probably declined by half by 1808.

This drastic decline was in sharp contrast to the population increases of persons of Portuguese and African birth or descent. The number of Portuguese grew through immigration in the sixteenth and seventeenth centuries and, more slowly, through natural reproduction as more white women became available. Push and pull factors stimulated migration from Portugal and the Atlantic islands. Crown-sponsored migration occurred in the eighteenth century. The typical migrant was male, in his twenties or early thirties, from north of the Tagus, and of limited financial means. The absence of adequate regulatory procedures meant the virtual absence of immigration data. A greater crown presence, suppression of hostile groups, and economic upturns spurred migration in the seventeenth and eighteenth centuries. This was accelerated by news of gold strikes in Brazil, which drained Portugal of three thousand to four thousand emigrants annually.

The third major component of Brazil's population was of African origin. Brazil was the major importer of slaves to the Americas. Estimates put this forced migration at between 4 and 5 million by 1810. The trade was dictated by supply and demand, internal conditions in Africa, and changing fads in Brazil. Its composition was characterized by a number of males double that of females, some young adults, and few children. Slaves in Brazil had low rates of natural reproduction and high mortality. In regions of greatest economic intensity, sugar and mining, there was a slave majority. By 1808, slaves made up about 38 percent and whites, free blacks, and mulattoes each about 28 percent of Brazil's population.

Excluding its indigenous, Brazil's population was about 30,000 in 1600, 300,000 by 1700, 2 million by 1776, and about 3 million by 1808. At the end of the colonial period, Amerindians in settled areas numbered only 6 percent of the population.

SETTLEMENT

The two centuries following Cabral's landfall was characterized by reticence in going beyond coastal regions to the interior of the territory claimed by Portugal. Even along the coast, settlement was irregular. Only in the late sixteenth century were there tentative, and individual, moves away from the coast. In the seventeenth century, there was movement inland from coastal enclaves of Salvador and Recife to the *agreste* and *sertão* and northward to Belém and into the lower Amazon. People traveled from Rio de Janeiro and São Paulo to the west and south. Increasing immigration from Portugal, Madeira, and the Azores, and internal migration fueled such moves. There was a variety of actors: slaves accompanied by owners; missionaries were pioneers to the far north, Amazonia, and far south; cattle ranchers went to Ceará, Piauí, Maranhão, and Minas Gerais; clerics and friars, authorized and unauthorized, roamed the colony; there were few white women or families. *Bandeirantes,* or pioneers, commonly associated with São Paulo but also from Bahia and Pernambuco, came closest to the stereotype of frontiersmen. They splayed out across Brazil as far as the Andes, the Platine region, and the far west.

In the mid-seventeenth century the *bandeira* of Antônio Rapôso Tavares traversed Brazil from São Paulo to Belém using interlocking river systems, and Fernão Dias Pais died searching for silver and emeralds in São Paulo and Minas Gerais (1681). Such treks, which lasted years, pioneered fluvial and terrestrial routes, and were undertaken strictly for profit in the form of Indian slaves, gold, and precious stones. Their predations on the periphery of Portuguese territories bordering on Upper Peru and New Granada, and to the south, with attacks into Spanish Guairá and Tape, disturbed Luso-Spanish relations.

Sparked by gold-rush fever, the first sustained moves to the west came in the eighteenth century. The São Francisco River and the river systems of Amazon-Madeira-Mamoré-Guaporé and Tieté-Paraná-Paraguay made the interior accessible. Portugal faced boundary disputes with Spain, notably in the Río de la Plata region. Through the treaties of Madrid (1750), Pardo (1761), and San Ildefonso (1777), and surveys of questionable accuracy, Portugal sought resolution of such disputes. By 1808, much of Brazil—not only on the peripheries but in the vast expanses between settlement nuclei—still was unsurveyed, and unknown and unsettled by Europeans. Settlements were isolated, huddled together around a major town. The frontier was a mathematical conundrum and geopolitical concept rather than a known quantity.

A yardstick for measuring such settlement is the establishment of townships. With the exception of São Paulo, before the eighteenth century urban development was predominantly on the coast. Urbanization was synonymous with port towns and cities—Belém, São Luís, Recife, Salvador, Rio de Janeiro, Santos— which played multiple roles as commercial emporia, administrative centers, and defensive barriers. In the eighteenth century, the crown attempted to stabilize and regulate this moving population by elevating mining encampments to town status in Minas Gerais, Goiás, and Mato Grosso. By 1808, the greatest concentration of urban population was in the northeast. Salvador counted about 51,000; Recife, 25,000; and Rio de Janeiro, 50,000. São Paulo numbered about 24,000 in 1803 and Vila Rica 7,000 inhabitants in 1804. The population of Brazil was predominantly rural.

CROWN AND LOCAL GOVERNMENT

The Portuguese crown was slow to establish a royal presence in Brazil. It declared the dyewood trade a royal monopoly, and farmed it out to contractors. Spurred by French interlopers and threats of foreign occupation, João III (1521–1557) granted hereditary captaincies to twelve donataries. Each comprised 50 leagues of coast and had no western limit. Each donatary had jurisdiction in civil and criminal cases, made appointments, granted land allocations, and was responsible for defense, colonization, and conversion of the indigenous. In return, he received revenues and certain privileges and prerogatives.

Only ten captaincies were settled. Lack of capital, initiative, and leadership doomed some; disaffected colonists and local resistance undermined others. The only successes were Pernambuco under Duarte Coelho Pereira and São Vicente under Martim Afonso de Sousa. Flemish capital underwrote the latter, but the shared prosperity was founded on cultivation of sugarcane.

Disenchantment led the Crown to induce some donataries to forfeit their rights, a precondition to appointment of a captain-general. In 1549 Tomé de Sousa took up his post and established a capital at Salvador on the Bay of All Saints. Crown government was consolidated under Governor-General Mem de Sá (1558–1572), who ousted the French from the Bay of Guanabara, founded Rio de Janeiro, defeated coastal peoples, encouraged Jesuit missionaries, and brought order to administration.

Until 1808, the senior crown representative in the colony was a governor-general or, after 1720, a viceroy, who reported to the Casa da India, founded in Lisbon in 1503 in recognition of the importance of Asia to Portugal. The shift in power in Asia from Portugal to the United Provinces in the seventeenth century led to the establishment in 1642 of an Overseas Council in Lisbon with umbrella responsibility for the administration of the Portuguese empire. The council, along with viceroys and governors-general, acted in consultation with the sovereign, whose decisions were final. No Casa do Brasil was created to administer Portuguese America nor was a special bureaucracy assembled. Colonial policy was formulated in Lisbon, senior civil servants were mostly Portuguese-born and Portuguese-trained, and institutions were modeled on—or extensions of—metropolitan counterparts.

The Estado do Brasil underwent administrative restructurings, usually of short-lived duration. From 1621 to 1652 and from 1654 to 1772 the captaincies of Maranhão, Pará, and some smaller captaincies formed the Estado do Maranhão e Grão-Pará. The southern captaincies were detached from the authority of the governor-general in Bahia, united as the Repartição do Sul, and placed under Governor-General Salvador Correia de Sá E Benevides in 1658. This was in recognition of his service to king and country. After his death, they reverted to the jurisdiction of the governor-general in Salvador. New captaincies were created to meet new needs for administrative control stemming from demographic growth, changing commercial emphases, and strategic concerns. Gold strikes and immigration to the west led to the creation of the captaincies-general of São Paulo (1720), Minas Gerais (1720), Goiás, and Mato Grosso (1748). By 1800, there were ten captaincies-general and seven subordinate captaincies.

The centralized government of the state of Brazil was in the hands of a governor-general or viceroy, resident in Salvador from 1549 to 1763 and, with the transfer of the capital, thereafter in Rio de Janeiro. He exercised far-reaching jurisdiction over administrative, military, commercial, and fiscal matters; presided over the High Court; assumed responsibility for pacification and protection of Indians; distributed land grants; and made appointments subject to royal approval. He received instructions from the Overseas Council or from the king and reported to Lisbon. Beginning in the latter seventeenth and continuing into the eighteenth century, however, the governors of the captaincies gradually usurped his authority. Although they were subordinate to governors-general or viceroys according to the chain of command, governors often acted without consultation or bypassed the king's senior representative in the colony and dealt directly with the council or king in Lisbon. Gomes Freire de Andrade, governor of Rio de Janeiro (1733–1763), saw his jurisdiction expanded so that by 1748 captaincies subordinate to him were more strategically sensitive, commercially important, and extensive than those under the jurisdiction of the viceroy.

During the eighteenth century there were some superb administrators: Pedro de Noronha and Vasco Fernandes Cezar de Menezes were viceroys in Portuguese India and later in Brazil; André de Mello de Castro was governor of Minas Gerais and later viceroy. Among governors, Lourenço de Almeida saw service in India and as governor of Pernambuco and Minas Gerais.

Fiscal matters fell under the jurisdiction of the treasurer-general in the capital, who acted in consultation with a treasury council that included four High Court judges. Each captaincy had a crown-appointed treasurer and staff of whom only the most senior was dispatched from Portugal. The treasury was responsible for overseeing royal financial interests and leasing crown monopolies on such a variety of commodities and services as brazilwood, salt, whale fishery, tobacco sales, or river crossings. Some were leased in Lisbon, as was the case of the lucrative diamond contract. The treasury did not itself collect taxes. This was farmed out in a competitive bidding system and included collection of tithes—an ecclesiastical tax (*dízimos*) inappropriately used as general funds—of 10 percent on all agricultural production, customs dues, and import and export dues on all commodities, including slaves. Such contracts and proprietary offices spurred self-interest, extortionary practices, corruption, and mismanagement, and defaults were frequent.

The Desembargo do Paço in Lisbon appointed magistrates and undertook judicial reviews. Only in 1609 was a high court (*relação*) established in Salvador. This was suppressed in 1626 and reestablished in 1652. A second high court was created in Rio de Janeiro in 1751. These were the supreme courts, from which there was appeal to the Casa Da Suplicação in Lisbon. The chancellor was the chief officer of the High Court, which was manned by ten judges who were well paid, enjoyed privileges and exemptions, and, like all crown appointees, were trained at the University of Coimbra.

Captaincies in Brazil counted one or more judicial Comarcas, whose chief officer was an *ouvidor geral*. The crown also appointed *juízes de fora*. Career magistrates, including those who were Brazilian born, were rotated. Constraints against engaging in commerce or contracting marriages locally were intended to preserve judicial impartiality but were of limited success. Judges administered Portuguese laws. No codification was made specifically for Brazil, nor was there a counterpart to the Spanish *Código Negro*.

The administration of law was cumbersome; the appeals process was protracted; self-interest and venality in the bureaucracy and among the judiciary made it nigh impossible for all but the very rich and very poor to obtain a fair hearing. Judicial tours of inspection by district judges were too irregular to be effective. The magistracy exercised jurisdiction over areas not strictly judicial and reported to the king on the political, economic, and social state of their regions. As such, they formed part of the checks and balances of colonial administration and contributed indirectly to royal decision making for Brazil.

Forts were built and irregular marine patrols were mounted to defend the 4,603 miles of coast against foreign attacks. Professional officers commanded troops of the line, but defense of the colony depended on militia regiments under honorary masters-of-the-field or colonels. The quality of military personnel was low. They were ill equipped, underpaid, often without formal training, and wore ragged uniforms. The exceptions were two troops of dragoons posted to the Diamond District in the 1720s to impose stability and curb contraband in diamonds. Regular and militia troops escorted bullion shipments, attacked Amerindians, suppressed groups of runaway slaves, and crushed revolts. Free blacks and mulattoes had their own regiments and distinguished themselves fighting against the Dutch. They won a hard-fought and protracted battle to have officers of their own color, the same privileges and exemptions granted to their white counterparts, and eligibility for promotion.

Crown government in Brazil was undermined by difficulties of communication to and from Lisbon and within the colony. Rugged terrain and vast distances made law enforcement difficult, military campaigns logistic nightmares, and tax collection partial. Effectiveness of crown government declined in proportion to increased distance from administrative centers. Viceroys, governors-general, and governors were forced to react to local crises, often without adequate consultation. They were exposed to charges of *lèse-majesté*, to detractors maligning them at court, and to formal administrative reviews during (*devassas*) and concluding (*residências*) their terms. Renewals of triennial terms made crown officials vulnerable to local pressures. Many invested financially, politically, socially, and emotionally in Brazil. Although the most senior crown officials were often well trained, effective, impartial, and honest administrators, the standard deteriorated rapidly in subordinate positions. Disputes over jurisdiction and ill-defined mandates led to turf wars between different branches of government as well as individuals. Ecclesiastics did not hold high public offices. Nor, with rare exceptions, did persons of African or Jewish descent.

MUNICIPAL GOVERNMENT

The Senado Da Câmara was the local town council. Elections occurred annually. Eligibility requirements included age, property ownership, financial and social standing, and civil status. Clerics were excluded, as were, for the most part, persons of African descent. Two ordinary judges presided over a council of three, and there was a procurator. Paid appointees included a scribe, attorney, doctor, and in some cases a surgeon and public health and law enforcement officers. Responsibilities included price regulation, setting professional standards, overseeing guild exams, licensing, public health, marketing regulations, taxation, all public services, public works, maintaining public order, and celebrating religious and civil holidays. The judges, who usually lacked legal training, had limited jurisdiction in civil cases of the first instance.

Municipal councils had a high degree of autonomy and enough political and economic clout to influence legislation and policies by bringing pressure to bear on a viceroy or governor and at court. The Crown attempted to bring councils to heel by appointment of a *juiz de fóra* in an oversight capacity, but with limited effect. Councillors enjoyed privileges and exemptions and pressed for privileges granted to councillors in Lisbon and Oporto. Passions and tensions ran high at election time and rigging was not unknown. Councils were not self-perpetuating oligarchies, but membership represented powerful family and other corporate groups. Policies reflected self-interest as well as the public good.

CHURCH AND RELIGION

By virtue of Padroado Real conceded by papal bulls predating establishment of royal government in Brazil, the Crown could create archbishoprics and bishoprics, make appointments, and set ecclesiastical and missionary policy. By 1808, Brazil counted one archbishopric in Salvador (established in 1676) and six bishoprics: Pernambuco, Rio de Janeiro, Maranhão, Mariana, São Paulo, and Pará. There were ecclesiastical courts. Although ecclesiastical dignitaries were of high caliber, priests were often poorly educated, poorly paid, and vulnerable to venality, self-interest, and profit. Many depended on their congregations for financial support, levied outrageous fees for services, and engaged in contraband and commerce. The church never formally opposed the institution of slavery and had a mixed record in evangelization and religious education of slaves but, although there were examples aplenty of backsliding and syncretism, Roman Catholicism was generally the accepted norm. The church owned landed estates, urban properties, and slaves, and often clashed with the religious orders, the Society of Jesus in particular.

The Holy Office, or Inquisition, had no separate tribunal in Brazil. Clerics resident in the colony were designated to represent it in enquiries. Agents of the Inquisition from Portugal made special visits to Bahia (1591–1593 and 1618), Pernambuco (1593–1595) and Belém (1763–1769), but the most intensive period of enquiries throughout Brazil was the first half of the eighteenth century. Expulsion of Jews from Portugal led many to come to Brazil in the sixteenth century. Emigration was particularly heavy between 1587 and 1601, when Jews were permitted to sell their goods before leaving Portugal. Jewish emigrés established congregations in Pernambuco in the seventeenth century. The rumor that many Catholic priests were Judaizers (secret Jews) called into question the sincerity of forced conversions. Crypto-Jews could not escape the charge of being "of tainted blood" (*de sangue infecta*). Denunciations against them were made in secret. There were few charges of heresy; most crypto-Jews were accused of sexual deviance, bigamy, adultery, blasphemy, and practice of Jewish rites. Seventeen Judaizers were extradited from Brazil to Portugal in the first half of the seventeenth century and eight in the second. Most were from Bahia. In the eighteenth century most were from Rio de Janeiro. There was intensive persecution of Judaizers who were extradited. Between 1644 and 1748, eighteen Brazilian Jews were executed by the Inquisition in Lisbon. Other punishments included flogging, the galleys, jail, and property confiscation.

Religious orders in the colony included Jesuits, Franciscans, Dominicans, Benedictines, Augustinians, and Carmelites. The fact that half of the bishops in Brazil came from their ranks indicates their strength. The orders played roles of varying importance in evangelization and missionary activities. They provided social services such as hospitals, apothecaries, prison assistance, and alms. The religious orders became wealthy as owners of estates and urban properties and engaged in commerce as well. In the absence of a banking system, they played a major role in the colonial economy as the only sources for credit and loans. All maintained monasteries. Because of their wealth and large numbers, they were charged as drains on colonial resources; although many were Brazilian-born, few became provincials, posts most often held by Portuguese.

The first of many convents for women was established in Salvador in 1677. Such institutions owed their genesis less to religious than secular factors: first, to obviate the practice of predominantly elite families sending daughters to convents in Portugal rather than having them marry in Brazil; second, to curb the currency drain from the colony in the form of dowries. Convents in Brazil were places of seclusion or retreat for young women, for the divorced or separated, or for wives whose husbands were absent. After a probationary period, supplicants took vows and were admitted as nuns in one of two categories, namely of the black or the white veil, a distinction which reflected the social background of the supplicants, with nuns of the black veil enjoying higher status. The majority of women were in temporary vows. Convents owned properties, engaged in commercial activities, and made interest-generating loans. Visitors to Brazil lauded the musical and culinary skills of such conventuals and speculated on sexual activities, but could not undermine the religious devotion of such nuns.

The Society of Jesus, unchallenged as the most influential, wealthiest, and most commercially active religious entity in the colony, also numbered the best-trained and educated religious and most dedicated missionaries. Manuel da Nóbrega, José de Anchieta, and Antônio Vieira, whose missionary zeal carried him to the Amazon, spearheaded evangelization, especially among the original Brazilians. The Jesuits operated the only post-secondary schools, which did not exclude persons of African descent; their colleges made a unique contribution to education in the colony.

The Jesuits protected the indigenous from labor-hungry colonists by collecting them in Aldeias. The *aldeias,* with regular work days, organization, and prohibitions of nudity and polygamy, however, eroded Amerindian authority and cultural traditions and isolated rather than prepared the indigenous for integration into mainstream colonial society. The control of the *aldeias* as well as the Jesuit activity on the peripheries, in Maranhão and Pará, and in the disputed borderlands to the south, created suspicion that resulted in temporary and regional expulsions of the Jesuits, culminating in the expulsion of the society from Brazil in 1759.

THE ECONOMY

The Portuguese crown regarded Brazil as a "milch cow" to be exploited for the benefit of the metropolis as a source of raw materials where production was heavily regulated and imports and exports (including slaves) were taxed repeatedly. The economy, in which the crown held monopolies, was export-oriented. Colonists were also expected to contribute to the costs of royal marriages, the rebuilding of Lisbon after the 1755 earthquake, the upkeep of garrisons, and the extraordinary expenditures of the Crown. Tithes (*dízimos*) on agricultural products, a 20 percent tax on extractive industries, and prohibition of manufacture that might compete with Portuguese industry heavily discouraged colonial economic and commercial initiatives.

The mainstay of the Brazilian economy was agriculture, and sugar was preeminent. Colonists built on experience gained in Madeira and São Tomé. Sugarcane was introduced into Brazil during the captaincy period. Bahia and Pernambuco retained their preeminence, but there was also production in Rio de Janeiro and elsewhere. By 1570, Brazilian production rivaled that of Madeira and São Tomé. The industry thrived until 1610, when production flagged, but it recovered during the seventeenth century despite Dutch destruction of mills. The industry was vulnerable to inflation, rising costs, prices on European markets, global demand, competition from the Caribbean, and changing labor-supply conditions in Africa. In Brazil, transportation inadequacies, crop disease, ants, and weather affected productivity and distribution. But sugar was the most consistent generator of revenue throughout the colonial period.

Production demanded heavy capital investment in labor, land, and machinery. Smaller plantations with thirty to forty slaves predominated, although some had two hundred or more. Cane was crushed in oxen- or water-driven mills, and the juice boiled, scummed, and purged before the syrup was collected in earthernware jars where it crystallized. The only technological innovation was in the early seventeenth century when the three-roller vertical mill replaced the two-roller vertical mill. There were two basic grades: white and *muscavado*. An important derivative was rum.

Tobacco from Bahia, dipped in molasses after curing, was exported to West Africa in exchange for slaves. For smoking, or when taken as snuff, it found markets in Europe and even Asia. Other regional export economies included cacao and, later, rice, cotton, and coffee. Brazil produced a wide range of tropical crops. In the subsistence sector manioc, maize, beans, and wheat were important. Urban demands led to manipulation of supply to force up prices. Livestock-raising was important in the interior of the northeast, the north, Minas Gerais, and Rio Grande do Sul. There was a domestic market for meat, tallow, and salted meat. Hides were used in-country as well as exported.

The extractive industries came to importance in the eighteenth century. Gold production in Minas Gerais peaked in the 1730s but strikes in Goiás (1725), Mato Grosso (1734), and elsewhere led to overall production increases into the early 1750s. Alluvial panning was predominant. There was some gallery mining, but the industry was characterized by labor intensity. Inefficient modes of production and absence of technological innovation contributed to its decline as much as overregulation. A variety of expedients to tax production, including capitation taxes, quotas, and smelting houses, did not stem endemic contraband. Gold production provided an important incentive to subsistence agriculture and stimulated commerce and merchant communities in port cities, notably Rio de Janeiro.

Diamonds were officially discovered in the 1720s near Vila do Príncipe. After flooding the European market, the Crown controlled production through demarcating a closely supervised Diamond District and accepting bids for the diamond contract. In 1771, however, the contract was abolished and operation reverted to the crown.

Brazil was part of a global trade network that included Europe, Africa, India, and East Asia. There was a thriving but illegal trade from Spanish America through Río de la Plata and the Portuguese Colônia do Sacramento (founded 1680). Brazil was superbly endowed with deep-water ports which became commercial emporia. Imports from Portugal and Europe included farm animals, flour, salt, olive oil, cod, cheese, wine, textiles, manufactured goods, and machinery, which were exchanged for agricultural products, gold, and diamonds. Slaves from Africa were paid for in tobacco and even bullion, and homeward-bound East Indiamen unloaded silks, china, and oriental exotica. From Africa came bananas, plantains, certain gourds, okra, squashes, and oils, in return for sweet potatoes, peanuts, manioc, maize corn, squashes, pumpkins, and capsicums. In the sixteenth and seventeenth centuries much of the carrying was in Dutch bottoms. There was a thriving domestic trade along the coast and inland by land and navigable rivers; there were also local and regional networks for distribution.

FOREIGN INTERLOPERS

Brazil's prosperity, coupled with changing alliances in Europe, made it vulnerable. At the forefront of the brazilwood trade through the 1540s, the French seized the Portuguese factory at Itamacá in 1531. In 1555 Nicolas Durand de Villegagnon established a settlement in the Bay of Guanabara until dreams of "La France Antarctique" were ended by Mem de Sá in 1565. The French also established São Luis but were expelled from Maranhão in 1615. They briefly occupied Rio de Janeiro in 1711. The ascension of Spain's Philip II to the Portuguese throne led to the union of Portugal with Spain (1580–1640).

Brazil bore the brunt of the predations of the Dutch West India Company: the seizure of Brazilian vessels, the invasion and occupation of Bahia (1624–1625), and the occupation of Pernambuco (1630–1654). The Dutch period in Pernambuco was at its height during the governorship (1637–1644) of Count Johan Maurits of Nassau-Siegen. Artists, botanists, and zoologists recorded in words and pictures the flora and fauna of Brazil. Religious toleration made Dutch Brazil a haven for Jews and Judaizers. But wars of attrition devastated the northeast and revenues from sugar failed to reach Dutch expectations. Beginning with a 1645 revolt led by João Fernandes Vieira, the Dutch were ousted in 1654.

The British did not invade or occupy Brazil but were influential in commerce from the seventeenth century when Charles II took a Portuguese bride (1662). England enjoyed commercial concessions and provided a market for Brazilian sugar in exchange for British manufactured goods, notably textiles and, in the eighteenth century, grain. British exports to Portugal were reexported to Brazilian markets. Portuguese wines and then Brazilian gold paid for such purchases. The British provided credit for Luso-Brazilian merchants in the eighteenth century and were a constant presence in colonial commerce. After 1776 U.S. vessels regularly put into Brazilian ports.

LABOR

Amerindian laborers were co-opted for collection of brazilwood. They worked on sugar plantations of the northeast, often alongside African slaves, until their phasing out in favor of Africans by the

1630s. Despite prohibitions on enslavement except in special circumstances, indigenous labor continued legally and illegally, especially in São Paulo, Rio de Janeiro, and the north. Demands for more labor led the Portuguese to extend to Brazil a trade structure already institutionalized between West Africa and the Atlantic Islands and Portugal in the mid-fifteenth century.

African slaves were the field hands of plantations and cattle ranches and worked in diamond and gold placer mining as well as in domestic service. Some had skills as artisans, porters, or boatmen. In the fields and mines, especially, they had terrible conditions, long hours, physically demanding labor, and suffered harsh punishments. They lived in crowded quarters, were exposed to diseases, suffered dietary deficiencies, and had a low average life expectancy. Domestic slaves may have had less arduous working conditions but were also subject to physical and mental abuse. Some negotiated agreements with owners whereby they could practice a trade or other occupation without direct supervision on condition that a portion of their income be given to the owner. While encouraging illegal activities such as prostitution and contraband, and spurring some to run away, this system enabled slaves to acquire money enough to buy their freedom.

There was a free wage-labor sector which included the indigenous and persons of African descent. The former were employed in regional industries such as making rope out of fibers, gathering fruits, logging, and sailmaking, and in expeditions as scouts. The latter worked as overseers, drovers, ferrymen, and tradespeople. But the majority of skilled jobs were held by whites who dominated the guilds, owned taverns and shops, and held supervisory positions.

SOCIETY

Colonial Brazil was paradoxical in that it bore the European legacy of a society of estates, yet permitted increasing (especially in the eighteenth century) social and financial mobility and blurring of lines of social or racial demarcation. Place of birth, pedigree, religious orthodoxy, occupation, wealth, civil status, and legal status as free or slave were less subject to interpretation than were skin hues and attributes based on perception. Among persons of European descent, there were tensions between Portuguese born and Brazilian born; among persons of African descent, between those of different African "nations," between mulattoes and blacks, between free and slave, and even between those who had been born free or had bought their own freedom, or had been given their freedom by an owner. In a society characterized by miscegenation and subjective racial classifications for persons of mixed blood (*caboclo, mameluco, mestiço* for Indian-Caucasian; *mulato, pardo* for African-Caucasian; *cafuzo* for Indian-African), division by racial phenotypes is inappropriate. Although eligibility for public office was denied to persons of African descent and New Christians, there were exceptions. Prominent persons with African blood included Henrique Dias, the black veteran guerrilla leader who distinguished himself in the War of Divine Liberty against the Dutch; João Fernandes Vieira, commander of a force of blacks and mulattoes who was described in an official document as the "prime cause" of the Portuguese capture of Pernambuco from the Dutch; and António Vieira, the Jesuit who championed the cause of black slaves and Amerindians. Fluidity and not rigidity increasingly characterized social and racial relations in colonial Brazil.

The ruling class was usually white, of Portuguese descent, and landowning. Families such as the Albuquerque Coelho in Pernambuco, Correia de Sá in Rio de Janeiro, or Dias d'Avila in Bahia were all-powerful. Sugar planters and mill owners (*senhores de engenhos*) and cattle ranchers, often characterized as "poderosos do sertão" (powerful men of the backlands), exerted strong control over the social, commercial, and political life of the colony. In the eighteenth century they were joined by an emerging merchant and business community, especially in Salvador and Rio de Janeiro. Mining entrepreneurs dominated Minas Gerais, Mato Grosso, and Goiás. Dignitaries of church and state also belonged to the ruling class.

An urban middle class was composed of lawyers, doctors, surgeons, businessmen and merchants, priests and friars, and low-ranking civil servants at the upper end and, at the lower, artisans, store and tavern owners, and free-wage laborers. In the eighteenth century, increasing manumissions created an African community of freepersons engaged in commerce. The underclass included "tame" Indians, slaves, and a large number of poor and destitute who were stricken by disease and malnutrition, and reduced to begging.

The basic social unit was the family, either nuclear or extended, with linkages through marriage or godparenthood. Usually marriages were between persons of equal social or economic standing and civil status. For the white elite and upper classes, marriage was an instrument to consolidate and extend a family's reputation and fortune. The female partner was often younger than the male, sometimes disproportionately so. Dowries were important and took the form of currency or land, property, or cattle.

There was a double standard governing female and male behavior: white females were expected to be chaste, faithful, and secluded; for the male, no shame or sanctions were attached to sexual promiscuity, extramarital relations, and the taking of a concubine. There was a double standard (among whites) also regarding white and nonwhite women: the latter were expected to be sexually available and have lower moral standards. Recent studies, however, undermine the stereotype of the patriarchal family as the norm for the colony. While accurate for the upper classes, many middle- and lower-class families were headed by women. Desertion and widowhood, not infrequent, threw responsibilities onto women. Among whites, widows administered ranches, estates, and mines; women of African descent—both slave and free—played a crucial role in marketing. Exorbitant fees led to a low incidence of legal marriages. Marriages between free persons of African descent and slaves were less common. The civil status of offspring followed that of the mother. Some slaves would find a free or freed woman of color or Indian woman to bear their children. Indian-black or Indian-white unions were less frequent than white-black unions.

URBAN CULTURE

Only Salvador, Rio de Janeiro, and, fleetingly, Vila Rica do Ouro Preto developed an urban culture. Urban planning was not absent, but topography dictated city configurations after the initial phase. The central area had (where appropriate) governor's and bishop's palaces; city chambers; main church; Jesuit college; monasteries; and the Santa Casa da Misericórdia, a charitable organization. Portugal maintained a cultural hegemony over colonial Brazil. Despite requests, no university was authorized, nor was there a legal printing press, and the book trade was closely supervised. Brazilian students attended the University of Coimbra or other European universities. Institutions of higher education were limited to Jesuit colleges.

In the eighteenth century, literary academies came into being but were usually of short duration and little lasting impact. Theater was a form of recreation. Religious music showed mainly European antecedents, while secular music bore both Portuguese and African imprints. Religious art and architecture also derived from Europe, but Brazilian baroque, which found its greatest expression in Minas Gerais, was unique. There were few examples of secular art of any quality and the fine arts were not prominent. A number of persons of African descent were sculptors, painters, instrumentalists, and composers. The lay brotherhoods were major promoters of architecture and decorative arts in the building of churches and chapels, but there was no tradition of artistic patronage among the elites or merchant classes. The colonial literary scene included clerically penned treatises, histories, and poetry, ranging from the satirical Gregório de Matos to the epic *O Uruguai*, written by José Basílio da Gama.

LATE COLONIAL PERIOD

The reign of João V (1706–1750) was a watershed in terms of absolutist rule. José I (1750–1777) appointed Sebastião José de Carvalho e Mello, later marqués of Pombal, secretary of state for foreign affairs and war. José continued the centralization of power: the authority of the Overseas Council was eroded by ministerial appointments; new administrative captaincies were created; and the capital was moved from Salvador to Rio de Janeiro in 1763. A new Royal Treasury was created in Lisbon and treasury boards were established in each captaincy. Boards of inspection were established in major port cities.

In an attempt to nationalize the Luso-Brazilian economy, monopoly trading companies, such as Company of Grão-Pará e Maranhão (1755) and Company of Pernambuco e Paraíba (1759), were created to offer more regular shipping, promote exports, and provide labor. The fleet system was abolished and prohibitions lifted on coastal trade. The economic center of Brazil moved from the northeast to the center-southern region.

Pombal's measures could not rectify the mid-century economic downturn prompted by the decline in gold production, but his measures did stimulate Brazilian agriculture. Toward the end of the century sugar exports increased, tobacco was flourishing, exports of hides were up, and newer crops of cotton, cacao, and coffee found European markets. New regions—Pará (cacao) and Maranhão (cotton and rice)—became major producers. There was diversification in the agricultural economy. Cotton moved into second place behind sugar as the major export crop. Pombal's attempts to shore up merchants and make them less dependent on foreign capital and thence more competitive led to a decrease in British imports and a downturn in Britain as a market for Brazilian exports while stimulating commerce between captaincies. Some of Pombal's reforms and initiatives were rejected by his successors, but he had set in motion an inexorable momentum for change.

During this period the Jesuits were expelled from Brazil (1759) and the remaining religious orders weakened. Amerindian *aldeias* were placed under secular control. Pombal abolished the distinction between Old and New Christians (1773). But he did not remove the double standard applied to persons of African descent and Indians or products of Indian-white liaisons; laws to benefit the indigenous in terms of personal freedoms, ownership, and right to trade were not matched by legislation favoring Africans.

Earlier Luso-Spanish rivalries in the Río de la Plata region escalated into warfare, which cost both parties a great deal of money and manpower. Spanish attacks on Colônia do Sacramento culminated in its conquest in 1762 and subsequent Spanish invasion of Rio Grande do Sul. Colônia was returned, but a Spanish expeditionary force under Pedro Antônio de Cevallos took Colônia and Santa Catarina in 1777. The Treaty of San Ildefonso (1777) returned Santa Catarina and Rio Grande do Sul to Portugal, but the Portuguese ceded Colônia. In 1801 Portugal made incursions into Siete Missiones and held the conquered lands.

Brazil had not been devoid of collective uprisings, born of social tensions within the colony or reflecting resentment toward decisions taken in Lisbon which favored metropolitan interests over those of the colonists of Portuguese America. Such were short-lived and of local impact: the Beckman Revolt in Maranhão (1684); Guerra dos Emboabas

(1708–1709) in Minas Gerais; Guerra dos Mascates in Pernambuco (1710–1711); and the uprising over proposed foundry houses in Vila Rica (1720). The Enlightenment spurred colonial self-assessment vis-à-vis the metropolis and fanned aspirations if not of separation from Portugal at least of more control over colonial affairs. Two such movements were aborted. The 1789 Inconfidência Mineira in Minas Gerais was made up of a good measure of elite self-interest, reaction against proposed supplementary taxation, and a corrupt governor. Its hero and front man, and the only one to be hanged, was Joaquim José da Silva Xavier, better known as Tiradentes. The Conspiracy of the Tailors in Bahia (1798) involved a group of mulattoes espousing ideals of liberty, equality, and fraternity, as well as a Bahian church.

At the end of the colonial era Brazil was prosperous: exports and domestic commerce were growing; population had increased; cities were growing. When Napoleon invaded Portugal in 1807, the prince regent Dom João, with British assistance, evacuated his court from Lisbon in November 1807. After touching at Salvador, he disembarked in Rio on 7 March 1808. Dom João opened the ports of Brazil to trade with all friendly nations and rescinded prohibitions on colonial manufacturing, unknowingly paving the way toward Brazilian independence. While still a colony of Portugal, Brazil was the residence of a European monarch and his court and the seat of metropolitan government—a distinction unique in Latin America.

See also **Cabral, Pedro Álvares; Indigenous Peoples; Jesuits; Mining: Colonial Brazil; Slave Trade; Tavares, Antônio Rapôso.**

BIBLIOGRAPHY

Charles R. Boxer, *Salvador de Sá and the Struggle for Brazil and Angola, 1602–1686* (1952), *The Dutch in Brazil, 1624–1654* (1957), and *The Golden Age of Brazil, 1695–1750* (1962).

Gilberto Freyre, *The Masters and the Slaves: A Study in the Development of Brazilian Civilization*, translated by Samuel Putnam, rev. ed. (1963).

Caio Prado, Jr., *The Colonial Background of Modern Brazil*, translated by Suzette Macedo (1967).

Dauril Alden, *Royal Government in Colonial Brazil with Special Reference to the Administration of the Marquis of Lavradio, Viceroy 1769–1779* (1968).

A. J. R. Russell-Wood, *Fidalgos and Philanthropists: The Santa Casa da Misericórdia of Bahia, 1550–1755* (1968).

Kenneth R. Maxwell, *Conflicts and Conspiracies: Brazil and Portugal, 1750–1808* (1973).

Stuart B. Schwartz, *Sovereignty and Society in Colonial Brazil: The High Court of Bahia and Its Judges, 1609–1751* (1973).

A. J. R. Russell-Wood, ed., *From Colony to Nation: Essays on the Independence of Brazil* (1975).

John Hemming, *Red Gold: The Conquest of the Brazilian Indians* (1978).

James Lang, *Portuguese Brazil: The King's Plantation* (1979).

A. J. R. Russell-Wood, *The Black Man in Slavery and Freedom in Colonial Brazil* (1982).

Stuart B. Schwartz, *Sugar Plantations in the Formation of Brazilian Society: Bahia, 1550–1835* (1985).

Leslie Bethell, ed., *Colonial Brazil* (1987).

John Hemming, *Amazon Frontier: The Defeat of the Brazilian Indians* (1987).

Alida C. Metcalf, *Family and Frontier in Colonial Brazil: Santana de Parnaíba, 1580–1822* (1991).

Muriel Nazzari, *Disappearance of the Dowry: Women, Families, and Social Change in São Paulo, Brazil (1600–1900)* (1991).

A. J. R. Russell-Wood, *Society and Government in Colonial Brazil, 1500–1822* (1992).

Stuart B. Schwartz, *Slaves, Peasants, and Rebels: Reconsidering Brazilian Slavery* (1992).

Additional Bibliography

Abreu, João Capistrano de. *Chapters of Brazil's Colonial History, 1500-1800.* Trans. Arthur Brakel. New York: Oxford University Press, 1997.

Bueno, Eduardo. *Náufragos, traficantes e degredados: As primeiras expedições ao Brasil, 1500–1531.* Rio de Janeiro: Objetiva, 1998.

Del Priore, Mary. *Festas e utopias no Brasil colonial.* São Paulo: Editora Brasiliense, 1994.

Goldschmidt, Eliana M.R. *Convivendo com o pecado na sociedade colonial paulista, 1719–1822.* São Paulo: Annablume, 1998.

Higgins, Kathleen. *"Licentious Liberty" in a Brazilian Gold-Mining Region: Slavery, Gender, and Social Control in Eighteenth-Century Sabara, Minas Gerais.* University Park: Pennsylvania State University Press, 1999.

Kiddy, Elizabeth W. *Blacks of the Rosary: Memory and History in Minas Gerais, Brazil.* University Park: Pennsylvania State University Press, 2005.

Langfur, Hal. *The Forbidden Lands: Colonial Identity, Frontier Violence, and the Persistence of Brazil's Eastern Indians, 1750–1830.* Stanford, CA: Stanford University Press, 2006.

Metcalf, Alida C. *Family and Frontier in Colonial Brazil: Santana de Parnaíba, 1580–1822.* Austin: University of Texas Press, 2005.

Silva, Maria Beatriz Nizza da. *História da família no Brasil colonial.* Rio de Janeiro: Editora Nova Fronteira, 1998.

Souza, Laura de Mello e. *The Devil and the Land of the Holy Cross: Witchcraft, Slavery, and Popular Religion in Colonial Brazil.* Trans. Diane Grosklaus Whitty. Austin: University of Texas Press, Teresa Lozano Long Institute of Latin American Studies, 2003.

Vainfas, Ronaldo. *A heresia dos índios: Catolicismo e rebeldia no Brasil colonial.* São Paulo: Companhia das Letras, 1995.

A. J. R. RUSSELL-WOOD

1808-1889

FROM COLONY TO INDEPENDENCE

Brazil's nineteenth-century political trajectory was unique in the Western Hemisphere in that it became and remained a monarchy for eighty-one years. This was largely due to a single peculiar event: when Napoleon's armies invaded the Iberian Peninsula in 1807, ostensibly to punish the Portuguese for violations of his continental policy, the prince regent, João, the future João VI, decided to retreat to his dominions in South America. Escorted by the British navy, he arrived in Rio de Janeiro with all his court and the royal treasury to begin what became a fourteen-year sojourn. His arrival represented the first step toward independence, since the king immediately opened the ports of Brazil to foreign shipping and turned the colonial capital into the seat of government.

To this end, João installed novelties that until then had been forbidden to the colonials: among them printing presses, schools of higher learning, iron mills, and a gunpowder factory. He established a botanical garden to acclimatize plants that might diversify the economy and contracted numerous foreign scientists and technicians to stimulate mining, metallurgy, and the fine arts. Unfortunately, his reign also intensified most of the policies that had made the colony a hellish place for most of its inhabitants: he permitted the renewal of attacks on native tribal peoples, he condoned the continuation of the slave trade even while signing a treaty to restrict it, he accelerated the bestowal of vast land grants upon courtiers and local notables, he persisted in expansionism in the Río de la Plata, where patriots were seeking to establish republics independent of Spain, and he resisted forcefully the spread among his subjects of the liberal and democratic ideals of the North American and French Revolutions. Dependent on the British for help in regaining his kingdom, João agreed in 1810 to reduce tariffs on British goods and granted British merchants extraterritoriality, a humiliating concession.

João remained in Rio de Janeiro even after the fall of Napoleon. In 1815, Brazil was declared a kingdom, coequal with Portugal, partly to cast a larger shadow among the diplomats assembled at the Congress of Vienna. João's tropical idyll was finally brought to an end by liberal revolutionaries in Lisbon, who in 1820 called together a parliament and demanded his return. Fearing the loss of his European throne, he complied, leaving his son Pedro behind as regent. Soon after, Brazilian delegates to the Portuguese parliament withdrew, incensed at mercantilist proposals that would have returned them to a colonial status.

INDEPENDENCE

The drift toward separation accelerated as Pedro gave evidence of his willingness to lead such a movement. For the rich, monarchy offered the prospect of legitimacy and, therefore, stability, qualities frighteningly lacking among the new Spanish American republics but essential in a state that would contain a majority of slaves and their descendants. Independence was declared, by the prince regent himself, on 7 September 1822. The Portuguese garrisons were cut off by sea and nearly all were persuaded to evacuate peacefully, so that the costs of war were small. Brazil was declared an empire, to emphasize again to the Europeans the vast potential of a territory grander than any of theirs, even the czar of Russia's. Pedro's marriage to an Austrian princess, Leopoldina, had already established an impressive dynastic linkage.

Great Britain, which saw an advantage in the establishment of a strong monarchical, liberal state in South America, acted as broker in the delicate issue of recognition. Although the United States quickly recognized Brazil, none of the European monarchies would do so until Portugal had been reconciled to its loss. This was at last accomplished when Brazil accepted responsibility for a part of the Portuguese national debt—even though João had taken the whole of the treasury from Rio de Janeiro when he returned to Lisbon. Brazil, under duress, also renewed the trade treaty with Britain, including its disastrous provisions of low tariffs and extraterritoriality.

THE EMPIRE

Pedro convened an assembly to frame a constitution but, displeased with the result, sent soldiers to close the assembly down and wrote one of his own that reserved the Crown's right not only to executive but also to so-called moderative powers, including those of dismissing cabinets and legislatures and of naming a council of state and the senate. Participation in political life was limited by indirect elections and income qualifications for office holding and voting. The abolition of slavery was proposed by the savant José Bonifácio de Andrada E Silva, Pedro's closest adviser, but it was not given serious consideration, nor did Brazil honor renewed commitments to the British to restrict the slave trade. The legislature abolished royal land grants but could not agree on an alternate means of alienating frontier land; consequently, land began to be usurped on a vast scale, in a contest that excluded prospective farmers of modest means.

Pedro soon wore away his popularity among the Brazilian elite. His bestowed constitution caused a sizable rebellion in the Northeast. He leaned too much on emigré Portuguese cronies of questionable repute. His public affair with a married woman, D. Domitila de Castro, whom he ennobled, scandalized them, and when his wife died, as it was said of a broken heart, he had to settle for a much less advantageous second marriage to Princess Amélia, a niece of the king of Bavaria. Pedro's foreign adventures were even more damaging. He persisted in the campaign to incorporate Uruguay into his realm, but, faced with military defeats, rising deficits, and inflationary pressures, he was forced to recognize its independence, again with the good offices of the British. Finally, after the death of his father João, Pedro used state resources to try to put his daughter Maria on the throne of Portugal, an ambition that looked toward eventual reunification. In 1831, angered by bottle-throwing anti-Portuguese rioters in the capital and seething disloyalty in the army, Pedro abdicated and departed for Portugal.

THE REGENCY

Left behind was his son, Pedro II, who was too young to take the throne. A regency was formed, at first a triumvirate. Its agenda was decidedly liberal and decentralizing, a reaction to the authoritarian emperor. New laws were passed or old ones newly enforced to create provincial assemblies, to turn much of the administration of justice to locally elected or nominated judges, and to guarantee jury trials and habeas corpus. The Council of State, considered too much an arbitrary instrument of monarchical power, was abolished. Entailed estates (of which there had been few) were abolished. None of these measures could have any effect, however, upon the informal institutions of elite power, the ties of kinship, loyalties, and connections that underlay party membership and penetrated the bureaucracy. Arranged marriages, dowries, godparenthood, nepotism, and clientelism all stood as respected social bulwarks against the penetration of individualism, competition, and social mobility.

The regency carried out similarly ineffectual forays against the institution of slavery. Indian slavery was abolished and the African slave trade declared illegal. Unfortunately, many of the semisedentary tribes that might have served the purpose of steady labor had already disappeared. Along the frontier settlers thereafter followed their own policy of extermination of tribal peoples who chose resistance over retreat. The regency took no effective measures to enforce its ban on the African trade, which only intensified under the threat of the new law.

The interim government's greatest threat, however, was that of regionalism, unacknowledged during the first reign. Support for the throne waned the greater the distance from Rio de Janeiro. Despite the Additional Act of 1834, the central government appointed the provincial presidents and judges and controlled most sources of tax revenue. In the southernmost province of Rio Grande do Sul, the policy of low tariffs ruined beef jerky producers, who could not compete in the domestic market with those of Buenos Aires. This conflict, and continued cross-border involvement in the affairs of Uruguay, led to the Farroupilha Revolt (1835–1845). In the north,

the bloodiest rebellion, the Cabanagem revolt (1834–1840), broke out in Pará province, where struggles between political factions led finally to an uprising by the enslaved Indian and African masses. Indeed, the threat of social revolution everywhere forced the liberal regency to reimpose central authority, accompanied by ferocious reprisals against lower-class participants.

THE SECOND REIGN

These troubles were a mirror of those of the former Spanish viceroyalties, which fragmented further during this period. It is remarkable that Brazil weathered this storm and remained intact. At court, the more conservative faction sought to put a stop to the decentralization and liberalizing tendencies of the regency—policies which it supposed would eventuate in a republican revolution—by bringing Pedro II to the throne before the age of constitutional majority. The precocious Pedro himself agreed to this measure, a veiled sort of coup d'état, and took the throne in 1840.

Pedro II turned out to be an ideal monarch for balancing his country's political and economic forces. He favored the most gradual of reforms, so that, until the end of his reign, he appeared to their proponents, including the slaves, to favor them, and to those opposed to reform, including the slave owners, to protect them from the reformers. Two law schools, founded in 1831 in Recife and São Paulo, provided the empire a class of loyal bureaucrats who staffed the state administration. The factions of the regency evolved into Liberal and Conservative parties, which Pedro balanced against each other through the use of the moderating power. The army's senior general, the duke of Caxias, Luís Alves de Lima E Silva, was a close friend of the emperor, and the leading officers associated themselves with one party or another, which guaranteed their advancement as ministries succeeded each other. The emperor used his power to appoint councillors and senators and to bestow honors and lifetime peerages to reward service and loyalty within the established order. The ministry came to be directed by a prime minister, responsible to his party, so that for all the world the second empire resembled Westminster.

The empire interfered very little in the rights of citizens: freedom of speech, the press, and association were openly exercised. But the legislature did not end income requirements on the right to vote, and indirect elections and the lifetime senate were preserved. Unhappily, elections were an entire fraud, engineered by whichever ministry had been called to power. Local party leaders, furthermore, frequently resorted to election-time violence.

The reign of Pedro II, given these arrangements, could not be entirely tranquil. Regional rebellions, however, did come to an end. Liberals rose up in 1842 and 1848, briefly and unsuccessfully. The mass of the population, however, remained entirely alienated from government and its decisions. The squatters' rights of frontier dwellers were continually ignored, those among the poor who had not sworn fealty to an elite family risked impressment into the army—the equivalent of a death sentence—and everywhere intermittent unrest and flight among the slaves demanded much of the attention of the police and militia. On occasions these outrages caused open rebellion.

The government nevertheless was much fortified by the appearance of a profitable export to replace the decadent gold mines—coffee. Conveniently for taxation purposes, coffee was produced in the region surrounding the capital of Rio de Janeiro. Coffee was well suited to local soils and climate and in demand by the rapidly growing urban markets of the industrialized countries, especially Germany and the United States. Coffee was the salvation of a moribund plantation system. Sugar had gone into decline as more fertile areas came into production and Europeans began growing beet sugar.

It is remarkable that this vast subcontinent was unable to produce any significant amount of any other commodity for world trade. For a brief period during and after civil war in the United States, cotton became an important export, fostered by British agents. In the final years of the empire, rubber, gathered from wild trees in the Amazon basin under conditions differing only superficially from slavery, grew rapidly in value and volume. Unfortunately, it was destined to be cultivated as an exotic in southeast Asia, just as coffee had been transferred to Brazil. Coffee profits made possible the replacement of mule trails, which had been the nearly exclusive means of transport, with railways, at least in the southeast, beginning in 1867. The first steamboat braved the currents of the Amazon in

1853, and Brazil was connected with Europe by telegraph cable in 1874.

The second reign increased the empire's range of economic independence when, upon the lapse of its commercial treaty with Great Britain, it refused to renew on the same terms. Brazil soon began to increase its tariffs, achieving protection for a number of locally manufactured products, including Rio Grande do Sul's jerky. In retaliation, the British began to press much harder for the abolition of the slave trade, a business that now was entirely in the hands of local or emigré merchants, well connected at court. When the British squadron went so far as to sail into Brazilian harbors to capture slavers, however, the government decided in 1850 to enforce the law of 7 November 1831 that abolished the African slave trade rather than admit its inability to defend its waters against superior forces.

REFORMS

At mid-century a reform ministry undertook a number of measures designed to overcome the country's more and more evident backwardness relative to the industrializing countries. A commercial code based on the British model was implemented to foster foreign trade. Increased banking activities were authorized, as well as guarantees of interest on railroad bonds. The anomalous lack of a law on the alienation of public lands was at last resolved with passage of the Land Law of 1850: In the future they were to be sold in lots, the better to stimulate smallholding. Unfortunately, the law also permitted the legalization of past usurpations of crown lands, which, because surveyors were not contracted to demarcate remaining crown lands, stimulated continued usurpations. The government failed to recognize Indian rights to tribal lands excepting those bestowed upon them by its own acts. These were limited to missionary villages—the empire turned over to Italian Capuchin Friars the task of acculturating tribal peoples on the frontier. Even these grants were nearly always encroached upon and extinguished.

Also during this period slaves on a few plantations were experimentally replaced with wage workers. Since native-born Brazilian country people were accustomed to squat on free frontier land or to receive customary rights of tenure on the lands of estate owners in return for minor responsibilities, they were not expected to take up wage work, nor were slaves expected to remain on the plantations once freed. Planters, therefore, desired European immigrants, who were preferred because they were white. Unfortunately, a group of Swiss and German plantation laborers imported in the mid-1850s proved intractable, principally because the immigrants were saddled with the cost of passage and because the landowners were unable to deal with workers who insisted on equal social treatment. There were, however, a few colonization projects that offered European immigrants smallholdings on frontier lands. Although abandoned to their own devices, these pioneers managed to survive and multiply in Rio Grande do Sul, Santa Catarina, and Espírito Santo provinces.

The empire resolved several border disputes, but at considerable cost in blood. In 1852, having invaded Uruguay and put a puppet in charge, the empire, then in league with Argentine rebels, gained a major victory over the dictator Juan Manuel de Rosas. In 1864, it again invaded Uruguay, provoking the Paraguayan dictator, Francisco Solano López, who feared for the survival of his own country, to invade both Argentine and Brazilian territory. The ensuing War of the Triple Alliance (Uruguay, again under Brazilian control, joined the allies) lasted five years, killing off much of the male population of Paraguay. The slices of territory gained from Uruguay and Paraguay also cost the empire its stability. The war had been fought largely by troops of mixed race, some of them slaves recruited with the promise of freedom, who, in Argentina and Paraguay, had encountered societies free of the taint of slavery; it had been extremely expensive, making necessary a large increase in the foreign debt; and the officer class had grown and become a formidable and potentially challenging political force.

A postwar Conservative cabinet undertook to carry out further structural reforms in response to the weaknesses revealed by the wartime crisis. A census was carried out for the first time: 10 million inhabitants were counted, an increase of 7 million over the estimates of the turn of the century. The budgets of scientific and educational institutions were much increased. Obstacles to the organization of corporations were partially removed. Most important, the government at last sought to transform the aging slave labor force, which had

declined to 1.5 million in 1872. (Some slaves had children, but most were single African males.) Pressed by foreign opinion, the threat of slave rebellion, and the realization that wage labor had to be gradually introduced, the legislature passed a law in 1871 (the Free Birth Law), freeing the children of slave mothers. This was a very gradual measure, since the children were obliged to work for their keep until age twenty-one. Coffee plantation owners, meanwhile, had been trying to stave off inevitable collapse by importing young male slaves from the economically stagnant Northeast.

DECLINE AND FALL

In 1868, the emperor expelled the Liberals from power. Although this action was constitutional, some Liberals interpreted it as a coup d'état, and they reacted by forming, in 1870, the Republican Party. In its principles it was decidedly ideological, a clear alternative to liberalism, and most of its leading members were inspired by Comtian positivism, secularism, and social Darwinism. Unlike that of other Liberals, their position on slavery was muted, but they were greatly concerned with the question of decentralization, or federalism. Their insistence on devolution of powers and revenues to the provinces (to be called states when the republic was at last formed) was an expression of the annoyance of the southeastern and southern provinces at the overrepresentation of the economically decadent and traditional Northeast, a circumstance that caused them a net loss of tax revenues. Republicanism also appealed to opportunism, as the more prosperous and politically ambitious foresaw a decline of a dynasty that lacked a male heir. Even so, it won few local or provincial elections during the 1870s and 1880s, and only in São Paulo, Minas Gerais, and Rio Grande do Sul did its candidates gain enough votes to represent a margin of victory in its coalitions with the major parliamentary parties.

One of the more contradictory aspects of the monarchy was its relation to the Catholic Church. Catholicism remained the official religion, and the empire retained powers over it that the Portuguese crown had gained centuries before. Close church-state ties proved to be a hindrance to the residence and immigration of Protestants and Jews. Only tardily did the legislature act to reduce the disabilities that non-Catholic citizens suffered. In 1874, Pedro exercised his constitutional power to forbid the application of the pope's condemnation of the Masons. He then jailed two bishops who refused to obey this order. Curiously, his intent was to defend the right of free association of influential members of the elite, some of whom were priests, but he employed an archaic prerogative to do so. The case embarrassed the throne, while failing to gain the sympathy of Liberals and Republicans who favored the separation of church and state.

The movement toward abolition of slavery was only briefly turned aside by the 1871 Free Birth Law. Adherents multiplied among middle-class townspeople and especially among the free working class, which consisted largely of persons of color, many of them former slaves. Brazilian slavery had permitted manumission, and freedom through flight was becoming easier to achieve. In São Paulo, coffee planters contemplated final abolition as they observed that their slaves were willing to accept labor contracts and as the evident truth finally struck them that European immigration could be achieved only after slavery had been done away with. In 1885, sexagenarian slaves were freed, and finally, in 1888, Brazil became the last country in the Western world to abolish slavery entirely.

Had the franchise been in the meantime extended, and its free exercise guaranteed, this act would have granted the empire many more years of existence. The act was signed by Princess Isabela, daughter of the emperor, acting as regent while her father was ill. She immediately became the idol of the freedmen and freedwomen. The empire, furthermore, while far from colorblind, had permitted the rise of many persons of color in the ranks of the bureaucracy. As it happened, the franchise had been further restricted by "reform" in 1881 and the empire was doomed. The instrument of its overthrow was the army. The inevitable cuts in its budget after the war had caused great anguish, which was exacerbated by Pedro's inability to deal tactfully with an officer class that prided itself on its pridefulness. Unfortunately, the duke of Caxias, upon whom the emperor had depended for this chore, had died in 1880. The Republican Party used every opportunity to heighten these tensions, and some of its leaders called openly for an army coup to bring about the downfall of the empire.

Many among the ruling elite did not expect the empire to deal effectively with the very rapid social and economic changes of the 1880s: urban growth (the city of Rio de Janeiro reached half a million by 1890), the beginning of mass immigration, the enlargement of the free population of color, and the increase in factory production. While these underlying forces may have been influential, it was an army general of limited political and economic awareness who, on 15 November 1889, packed the imperial family off into exile. The republican era had begun.

See also **Agriculture; Cities and Urbanization; Economic Development; Military Dictatorships: 1821-1945; Slavery: Brazil; Tenentismo.**

BIBLIOGRAPHY

Alan K. Manchester, *British Preeminence in Brazil: Its Rise and Decline* (1933).

Stanley Stein, *Vassouras: A Brazilian Coffee Country, 1850–1900* (1957).

Clarence H. Haring, *Empire in Brazil: A New World Experiment with Monarchy* (1958).

Anyda Marchant, *Viscount Mauá and the Empire of Brazil* (1965).

Richard Graham, *Britain and the Onset of Modernization in Brazil, 1850–1914* (1968).

Leslie Bethell, *The Abolition of the Brazilian Slave Trade* (1970).

Robert Brent Toplin, *The Abolition of Slavery in Brazil* (1972).

Peter L. Eisenberg, *The Sugar Industry in Pernambuco: Modernization Without Change, 1840–1910* (1974).

Victor Nunes Leal, *Coronelismo: The Municipality and Representative Government in Brazil*, translated by June Henfrey (1977).

Thomas Flory, *Judge and Jury in Imperial Brazil, 1808–1871* (1981).

Nathaniel H. Leff, *Underdevelopment and Development in Brazil*, 2 vols. (1982).

Robert Conrad, *Children of God's Fire: A Documentary History of Black Slavery in Brazil* (1983).

Barbara Weinstein, *The Amazon Rubber Boom, 1850–1920* (1983).

Ron Seckinger, *The Brazilian Monarchy and the South American Republics, 1822–1831: Diplomacy and State Building* (1984).

Emilia Viotti Da Costa, *The Brazilian Empire: Myths and Histories* (1985).

Warren Dean, *Brazil and the Struggle for Rubber* (1987).

Neill Macaulay, *Dom Pedro: The Struggle for Liberty in Brazil and Portugal* (1986).

Mary C. Karasch, *Slave Life in Rio de Janeiro, 1808–1850* (1987).

Joseph Sweigart, *Coffee Factorage and the Emergence of a Brazilian Capital Market* (1987).

Roderick Barman, *Brazil: The Forging of a Nation, 1798–1852* (1988).

Leslie Bethell, *Brazil: Empire and Republic, 1822–1930* (1989).

Richard Graham, *Patronage and Politics in Nineteenth-Century Brazil* (1990).

Additional Bibliography

Baer, Werner. *Brazilian Economy: Growth and Deveopment.* Boulder, CO: L. Rienner Publishers, 2007.

Barman, Roderick. *Citizen Emperor: Pedro II and the Making of Brazil, 1825–1891.* Stanford, CA: Stanford University Press, 1999.

Cronologia de história do Brasil monárquico, 1808–1889. São Paulo: Humanitas, FFLCH/USP: Departamento de História, FFLCH-USP, 2000.

Malerba, Jurandir. *O Brasil Imperial, 1808–1889: Panorama da história do Brasil no século XIX.* Maringá, Brazil: EDUEM, 1999.

Naro, Nancy Priscilla, ed. *Blacks, Coloureds and National Identity in Nineteenth-century Latin America.* London: Institute of Latin American Studies, 2003.

Riviére, Peter. *Absent-minded Imperialism: Britain and the Expansion of Empire in Nineteenth-century Brazil.* London; New York: Tauris Academic Studies; St. Martin's Press, 1995.

Tosto, Milton. *The Meaning of Liberalism in Brazil.* Lanham, MD: Lexington Books, 2005.

Viotti da Costa, Emilia. *The Brazilian Empire: Myths and Histories.* Chapel Hill: University of North Carolina Press, 2000.

WARREN DEAN

SINCE 1889

The year 1889 is traditionally considered a turning point in Brazilian history. The abolition of slavery in 1888 resulted in an important increase in immigration and in-migration from the countryside to urban centers, the weakening of the old Rio de Janeiro coffee planters' oligarchy, and the emergence of a military in alliance with the middle sectors—the preconditions for the proclamation of the republic in 1889. Rather than accepting a strictly causal relationship between abolition and the downfall of the Brazilian monarchy, many historians have come to accept that both abolition and the rise of the republic were part of a larger movement towards a modern Brazilian state. This overall change included issues of military discontent, church-state conflicts, and the continued lack of sufficient European immigration to both replace the dwindling enslaved population and to help "whiten" Brazil's mixed-race population.

PROCLAMATION OF THE REPUBLIC

On November 15, 1889, a military coup, supported by small groups of civilian conspirators, resulted in the establishment of the Republic. The army officers had lost political power after the War of the Triple Alliance against Paraguay and were influenced by positivism, whereas the bishops were disaffected because of the refusal of the state to accept the authority of the Catholic Church regarding Freemasonry. Royal patronage of the church also caused friction, stemming mainly from its reduction in size, the closing of monastic orders, and the limiting of resources available to clerical institutions.

However, the military and the church did not act alone in bringing down the monarchy. The Brazilian economy relied on agricultural exports, and the land-owning elite played an important role in the establishment of the Brazilian Republic. During the nineteenth century Brazil's economic center shifted from the traditional sugar production of the Northeast to the coffee plantations of the South centered around São Paulo. With this transition Brazil's reliance on slavery as the primary source of labor clashed with the notion of "progress" at the heart of the positivism embraced by the military elite. In contrast to the traditional sugar *fazendeiro* (plantation owner), the new coffee elite embraced modern agricultural technology, and could thus accept a paid labor force rather than relying on the centuries-old tradition of slavery. During the second half of the nineteenth century Brazilian abolition became inevitable: The importation of African slaves ended in 1850; the Law of the Free Womb of 1871 eventually freed slaves born after its passage; the 1884 Saraiva-Cotegipe Law (also known as the Sexagenarian Law) freed slaves over the age of sixty; and Princess Isabel (1846–1921) signed the Golden Law granting final abolition in 1888. Rather than fighting those changes, the southern land-owning elite positioned

themselves to both profit and retain their political control following the end of slavery. White immigrants (mostly Italian) were drawn to the growing economy of São Paulo. In the face of the growing acceptance of "scientific racism" in Europe and the United States, the growth of a white working class offered the Brazilian elite the means to displace the descendents of the millions of Africans brought to Brazil during the centuries-long Atlantic slave trade—to "whiten" the nation. Because European immigrants refused to come to Brazil to work alongside slaves before abolition, choosing instead to go to the United States or Argentina, some of the wealthiest plantation owners in São Paulo supported unconditional abolition as a necessary step towards a modern Brazilian state.

Brazil

Population:	190,010,647 (2007 est.)
Area:	3,286,488 sq mi
Official language:	Portuguese
Languages:	Portuguese, Spanish, English, French
National currency:	Real
Principal religions:	Roman Catholic, 73.6%; Protestant, 15.4%
Ethnicity:	white, 53.7%; mulatto, 38.5%; black, 6.2%
Capital:	Brasília
Other urban centers:	Belém, Belo Horizonte, Campinas, Curitiba, Fortaleza, Goiânia, Manaus, Porto Alegre, Recife, Río de Janiero, Salvador, Santos, São Paulo
Annual rainfall:	Up to 300 inches annually in the Amazon basin; heavy to moderate in most of the rest of the country; periodic droughts in the northeast.
Principal geographical features:	*Mountains:* The Brazilian Highlands, Great Escarpment, and Guiana Highlands, later includes Pico de Neblina (9,888 ft) *Rivers:* The Amazon and its many tributaries, including the Negro and Tocantins; Paraguay, Paraná, São Francisco, Uruguay *Lakes:* Lagoa dos Patos, Furnas, Itaipú, Sobradinho, Tucuruí *Islands:* Fernando de Noronha, Marajó *Other:* The rainforests in the Amazon basin are the largest in the world.
Economy:	*GDP per capita:* $8,800 (2006 est.)
Principal products and exports:	*Agricultural:* cocoa, coffee, corn, meat, rice, soybeans, sugar, wheat *Manufacturing:* aircraft, cement, chemicals, footwear, lumber, machinery, motor vehicles, textiles, steel *Mining:* iron, tin
Government:	Gained independence from Portugal in 1822. It is a federal republic with a bicameral National Congress consisting of an 81-seat Senate and a 513-seat Chamberof Deputies. Members of congress are elected through proportional representation. The chief of state and head of government is an elected president.
Armed forces:	*Army:* 189,000 *Navy:* 48,600 *Air force:* 69,309 *Paramilitary:* 385,600 *Reserves:* 1,340,000
Transportation:	*Rail:* 18,230 mi *Ports:* Gebig, Itaqui, Rio de Janeiro, Rio Grande, San Sebasttiao, Santos, Sepetiba Terminal, Tubarao, Vitoria *Roads:* 59,871 mi paved; 1,028,689 mi unpaved *Airports:* 718 paved runway airports, over 5,000 unpaved airports, and 16 heliports
Media:	Over 100 daily newspapers, including *Estado de São Paulo, Globo, Folha de São Paulo, Jornal o Dia*, and *Zero Hora*; 1,365 AM and 296 FM radio stations; 138 television stations.
Literacy and education:	*Total literacy rate:* 88.6% Public education is free at all levels. Most children complete 8 years of primary school and roughly 75% receive secondary schooling. There are over 9 universities, including at least one in each state.

Various historians favor different interpretations. Thomas E. Skidmore examines how the elite perceptions of race and nation affected the transition from monarchy to republic. Edgard Carone ascribes the fall of the empire to a betrayal of the aristocracy, which was not hereditary and traditional and thus had no organic link to the monarchy. Another author, João Cruz Costa, sees an important role for the middle class in the proclamation of the republic, although he attributes more significance to the antagonism of the military and clergy toward the empire. José Murilo de Carvalho denies that the people were indifferent and apathetic to the proclamation of the republic, as claimed by Aristides Lobo. In Murilo de Carvalho's opinion, people were active in religious brotherhoods, popular festivities, and mutual help organizations. This activity involved communal behavior and was devoid of individualistic attitudes inspired by bourgeois values, which were weak in Brazilian cities, where administrative and political functions prevailed. He also emphasizes the distance between formal and real life due in part to the pervading influence of slavery. In his view, people were not apathetic but cynical about the proclamation of the republic. George Reid Andrews examines how Afro-Brazilians competed with white immigrants during the period following abolition, and the state's role in excluding black workers from the better jobs during the decades of the First Republic. José Luiz Werneck da Silva calls attention to the fact, generally unacknowledged, that people demonstrated in the streets on the day of the proclamation of the republic and invaded the capital's municipal chamber, thus deposing the monarchy before Marshal Manuel Deodoro da Fonseca led a parade elsewhere and officially proclaimed the republic. Emilia Viotti da Costa weighs several aspects of the above arguments in her examination of the late Brazilian Empire and the rise of a republic: slavery; liberalism; land policies; and elite landowners.

At the time there were several currents of republican thought. Silva Jardim developed a concept of a republic based on the social contract of Jean Jacques Rousseau, whereas a significant segment of the officers supported Auguste Comte's positivism. The military also aspired to vote and claimed a full citizen's status, with the right to be elected, hold free meetings, publicly express their opinions, and have greater weight in the decision-making process of the state. Raul Pompéia argued that the army was indeed made up of the common man. Republicans excluded labor from the political system mainly because of illiteracy, the presence of many immigrants in its ranks, and fear of anarchist ideology.

CONSOLIDATION OF THE REPUBLIC: 1889–1894

An elected constituent assembly met in 1890 to draft the first republican constitution. It was based on a committee proposal subsequently revised by Rui Barbosa De Oliveira, who tried to conciliate the authoritarian state defended by positivists against the federalism favored by political leaders.

The Constitution of 1891 reflected the ideal of restricted democracy supported by liberals. The constitution embodied the principle that political rights are granted by society to those deemed deserving of them. And so the vote was to be direct but not to include the illiterate (some 83% of the population), minors (under twenty-one years), common soldiers, clergy, and women. (In the first direct election for president in 1894, only about 2 percent of the total population voted.) Deleted from an early version of the Constitution was the obligation of the state to provide education, which had figured in the empire's charter. The republic maintained the prohibition against the foundation of new monastic orders, the exclusion of the Jesuits, and the ban on religious teaching in public schools.

Additional features of the Brazilian charter were the establishment of three separate and independent powers: judicial, legislative (Chamber of Deputies and Senate), and executive; a presidential regime; federalism; separation of church and state; and the rights to freedom of thought, assembly, profession, and property. During the operation of this constitution (1894–1930), the executive was supported by the wealthiest states— São Paulo and Minas Gerais— which formed a coalition with Rio Grande do Sul, Rio de Janeiro, and Pernambuco; this regionalism hampered the formation of national parties. In São Paulo, politics were controlled by coffee plantation owners and export-import commercial concerns.

The Constituent Assembly elected the first president and vice president, Deodoro da Fonseca and Floriano Peixoto, respectively. Fonseca, who had been ruling since the fall of the empire, was supported by part of the army. Peixoto was backed by a substantial part of the army and by urban industrial and service sectors. During Fonseca's rule (1889–1891), the country was disturbed by economic and political crises. The old coffee plantations of the state of Rio de Janeiro declined due to the abolition of slavery, soil exhaustion, and plant disease. To fight the depression, Finance Minister Rui Barbosa launched a policy of economic recovery based upon an increase of currency emissions and credit. He attempted to redirect the economy toward activities other than agriculture for export. The policies of Rui Barbosa that led to the Encilhamento, a period of feverish, speculative economic activity, are a matter of controversy. Public credit that had been restricted to coffee production and export was thenceforth extended to industry and other activities. The devaluation of currency and the imposition of tariffs to be paid in gold produced an increase in custom duties and deterred the importation of competitive manufactured goods. At the same time, special measures ensured the entry of capital goods and raw materials. Industrial expansion was further favored by declines in energy prices. Labor costs also fell due to a surplus of labor; this, however, sparked workers' strikes and conflict between labor and the federal government. Negative aspects of the Encilhamento included a high rate of inflation, increased speculation, formation of fictitious enterprises to gain favorable credits, corruption, and bankruptcies.

Bankruptcies were frequent but mostly related to fake or small, weak enterprises, whereas the major industrial concerns acquired capital in spite of inflation and increased production. Nevertheless, popular discontent exploded as food prices and rent rose, salaries and wages remained low, and unemployment became extensive. The executive, which lost the support of Congress, was closed by President Deodoro, who decreed a state of siege and announced new elections. Opponents sought support from the navy, which revolted under the command of Admiral Custódio de Melo. To avoid civil war, Deodoro resigned in 1891 and Vice President Peixoto took over (1891–1894). He reversed the policy of enlarging the currency, suspended the state of siege, and deposed state governors who had supported the former president. In 1892 an unsuccessful uprising at two fortresses in Rio de Janeiro sought immediate presidential elections.

In 1893, with the support of Admiral Luís Filipe Saldanha Da Gama, a monarchist who claimed that Floriano Peixoto's government was unconstitutional, the navy, under the leadership of Custódio de Melo revolted once again. In the same year, federalists in Rio Grande do Sul rebelled against the authoritarian local government and, after joining forces, dominated the south of the country. The decisive victory of federal forces in 1894 ended a period of troubled consolidation of the republic, although the hopeless resistance of Saldanha da Gama lasted until August 1895. The main urban centers were also disturbed by conflicts between the National Guard, police, and army and between Brazilians and Portuguese.

DEVELOPMENT OF THE REPUBLIC: 1894–1930
The recovery and expansion of coffee plantations, employing free, mostly immigrant labor in São Paulo, was responsible for the victory of Prudente José de Morais (1894–1898) as presidential candidate and the return to power of the coffee oligarchy. Morais pacified Rio Grande do Sul, but during his rule a rural movement sprang up in the interior of Bahia, where in 1893 Antônio Vicente Mendes Maciel, a messianic religious leader called the Counselor by his followers, settled the village of Canudos. An economically self-sufficient peasant community, it served as a refuge for the poor and unemployed, refused to pay taxes, and led a revolt that lasted until 1897.

Despite the fact that the Morais government made no attempt to promote it, industry, with the help of exports and the inflow of foreign capital and immigrants, developed. Nevertheless, in the early decades after the founding of the republic, the country's economy remained massively agricultural, essentially dominated by coffee produced for export. The pattern of land ownership varied widely. Prosperous coffee plantations prevailed in São Paulo, declining coffee plantations prevailed in Rio, and deteriorating sugar plantations characterized the Northeast. Sharecroppers and salaried field hands replaced slaves. Blacks and people of color were dominant, but great numbers of European immigrants were brought in to work on São Paulo plantations. In declining gold-mining areas (Minas Gerais, Goiás, Mato Grosso) and in the Northeast backlands, extensive cattle raising and agriculture developed. The Indian population was still important in the central plateau. The Amazon basin—typified by communal and tribal subsistence agriculture and gathering, fishing, and hunting—was largely unexploited and sparsely populated. Rubber was the only important export from the area.

The main urban industrial centers were Rio de Janeiro (the capital), São Paulo, Recife, Salvador, Belo Horizonte, and Pôrto Alegre. The pattern of urban development did not center around one primary city, as was the case in some Latin American countries.

After the efforts of Rui Barbosa, the federal government had no industrialization policy. From 1895 to 1904, investments in import machinery for textile mills diminished because of the fall of coffee prices beginning in 1896, a policy of deflation, reduction of tariffs, and a bank panic in 1900 at a time of intensive gold speculation. The government negotiated a funding loan with the Rothschild group to stabilize currency. In 1903 a general strike occurred in Rio de Janeiro to protest low salaries, unemployment, and poor health and housing conditions. In the early twentieth century, competition in the international coffee market caused prices to fall further. In 1906 valorization agreement among the main coffee-producing states to limit exports led to an increase in prices from 1909 to 1912 and helped to stabilize currency and expand the importation of capital goods. In the period from 1915 to 1919, imports of equipment dwindled due to World War I, while industrial production increased at different rates in various regions due to full employment of industries to attend the increased market.

In 1912 strikes reached a peak. A general strike in São Paulo during World War I marked the height of anarchist influence and the beginning of its decline. From 1920 onward the unions won recognition, several laws protecting labor were enacted, and security for laborers injured in work-related accidents began to be developed. Founded in 1922, the Communist Party tended to supersede anarchism.

In 1922, Modern Art Week, organized by São Paulo intellectuals, questioned Brazil's traditional European-inspired elite culture. The movement encompassed all forms of art, sought the Brazilian popular roots of national culture, and had strong political overtones. The 1920s also witnessed protests against the old republican order—the manipulation of votes, the absence of electoral fairness, the coalition among the larger states, and the exclusion of the majority from the political process through the literacy requirement for voting. Also criticized were the distorted structure of land ownership, in which inefficiently exploited large estates stood alongside landholdings too small to support a family, the abuses against sharecroppers, the absence of labor laws to protect field hands, and the dominance of foreign capital in the economy.

The *tenentes* (lieutenant) revolts of 1922 and 1924–1925 voiced some of these qualms as well as aspirations for the reform of federalism, restoration of balance between the three branches of government, the secret ballot, individual rights, and nationalism. The *tenentes* movement is variously interpreted as military intervention to uphold legitimacy or as an expression of middle-class discontent with the corrupt democratic system of the 1920s. The military body known as the Prestes Column wandered through the interior for several years without fighting a decisive battle with the regular military forces. Its leader, Captain Luís Carlos Prestes, became a mythic figure called the Cavalier of Hope. The degree of popular support for the *tenentes* column is a matter of debate.

The states' policy of supporting coffee prices could not cope with the plummeting prices resulting from the Great Depression of 1929. The problem was reinforced by the credit restriction imposed by the last president of the Old Republic period,

Washington Luís, who aimed at restoring convertibility of the currency through a funding loan.

THE 1930 REVOLUTION AND ITS AFTERMATH

The Revolution of 1930 that brought Getúlio Vargas to power has been regarded as a movement of the industrial bourgeoisie seeking to overthrow a state dominated by the coffee landlords and the commercial complexes linked to them. Nevertheless, the associations of entrepreneurs in São Paulo, Brazil's main industrial center, supported President Washington Luís, and two years after the victory of Vargas, they revolted against his rule. Furthermore, the industrial bourgeoisie was too weak to form a national movement of its own, depending as it did upon foreign capital and state support. Also, industry stood to benefit from a policy aimed at avoiding the collapse of the coffee economy.

Another interpretation of the period views the revolution as a result of conflict that pitted the middle classes (public and commercial employees, liberal professionals, and small commerical, industrial, and financial entrepreneurs) with low political consciousness against the oligarchies. The weak middle classes might have found political expression in the *tenentes* movements, but the latter were unable to establish common ground with the civilian middle classes, whose goals were different. When the *tenentes* reached power in 1930, they did not represent middle-class interests. The Depression and cancellation of coffee price supports led to a diversification of production (coffee represented 70 percent of total exports), which in turn weakened the coffee oligarchy.

The Aliança Liberal (Liberal Alliance), organized in 1930, was a coalition of dissident oligarchies from Minas Gerais, Rio Grande do Sul, and Paraíba that supported Vargas in his 1930 bid for the presidency against Júlio Prestes, the candidate favored by Washington Luís. Vargas lost the possibly fraudulent election. Revolt broke out after João Pessoa, Vargas's vice-presidential candidate, was assassinated in Recife. A joint civilian-military movement quickly swept Vargas into power as provisional president in October 1930.

Francisco Weffort observed a political void in 1930 stemming from the weakness of the industrial bourgeoisie, the crisis of hegemony of the coffee bourgeoisie (plantation owners, export-import concerns), the lack of cohesion and limited consciousness of the middle sectors, and the diffuse thinking of the popular masses, who favored the formation of a state of compromise above class interests. Into this void stepped the coalition that brought Vargas to power. It included regional interest groups harmed by São Paulo's dominance, *tenentes* discontented with the republic's lack of authenticity, and urban middle sectors negatively affected by the Depression. The senior officers in the army were divided. At the heart of the coalition were elements of the bourgeoisie (commercial, industrial, financial) and part of the middle classes, with the latter in a subordinate position. Labor was excluded from power.

Vargas's rule reflected this coalition when in 1931 he established the Conselho Nacional do Café (renamed Departamento Nacional do Café in 1933), which from 1931 to 1944 was in charge of buying coffee and burning it, thus forcing coffee planters to restrict their fields and crops. Further encouraging this process, the government transferred resources from coffee plantations to industries and to other types of agriculture. In 1933 the planters' debts to banks had reduced by 50 percent. The coffee policy diminished unemployment, ensured a certain level of income for the growers, maintained the internal market, and resulted in an effective antidepression policy. Brazil showed signs of economic recovery in 1932, much earlier than other nations. Yet in spite of these measures, a 1932 revolt in São Paulo called for the return to constitutional rule. Afterward, the *tenentes* were excluded from the governments of some states.

The Ministry of Labor, Industry, and Commerce, founded in 1930, was in charge of implementing the new regime's philosophy of cooperation between capital and labor. Labor laws, later codified, aimed at forcing workers into government-regulated unions. Entrepreneurs were also pressed to join unions. Conflicts between labor and capital were to be decided by labor courts. The government collected a mandatory tax on unions to whom it later dispensed these resources. Unions were discouraged from delving into politics. Their role was to promote culture. The right to strike was restricted. Nevertheless, workers formed factory commissions to resist government control.

Vargas's rule (1930–1945) was characterized by nationalism, economic self-sufficiency, restri-

ction of immigration and foreign capital, and state regulation and direct participation in the economy. Vargas returned Brazil to democratic rule, reestablishing in 1933 the National Constituent Assembly, comprising representatives of employee and emp-loyer unions. The Constitution of 1934, Brazil's third, was based on the corporatist ideas of Germany's Weimar Republic. It incorporated Vargas's labor and electoral laws (women's suffrage, the right to vote at age eighteen). The state regulated the ownership and exploitation of underground resources and water, established free and mandatory primary education, and created the regional minimum wage.

In 1933 the Brazilian Integralist Action Party (Ação Integralista Brasileira—AIB) was founded. With fascist leanings, the party supported a centralized and strong federal state, powerful municipal chambers, indirect elections, and representatives from employer and employee unions. The patriarchical Catholic family would be the cell of society. Plinio Salgado, its leader and founder, had belonged to the Modern Art Week movement. Most of the supporters of this party were professionals and members of the navy.

Opposed to the AIB was the National Liberating Alliance (Aliança Nacional Libertadora—ANL), a loose coalition of liberals and Communists. In 1935 it acquired a stronger Communist overtone when Luís Carlos Prestes became its honorary leader. Its program was land reform, nationalization of foreign enterprises, suspension of foreign debt payments, and establishment of a democratic bourgeois government as a step toward larger popular participation. In November 1935 the ANL, supported by some military sectors, attempted to take power in Rio de Janeiro, Recife, and Natal but failed for lack of popular support. The government then "found" the Cohen Plan, a forgery that contained a blueprint for Communist terrorism. It was used as a justification for launching a coup d'état in 1937 that established the lengthy dictatorship of Vargas, known as the Estado Nôvo. From that time both followers of the AIB and the Communists were repressed.

THE ESTADO NÔVO (NEW STATE): 1937–1945
It is almost impossible to summarize the many interpretations of the Estado Nôvo and their views as to whether it was authoritarian or totalitarian and fascist in nature. The army was not monolithic, giving

"March of the Family with God for Freedom" (Marcha da Família com Deus Pela Liberdade) demonstration, São Paulo, March 19, 1964. Hundreds of thousands demonstrated in the "March of the Family with God for Freedom," organized partly in response to President Goulart's program of reforms. Political conflict, economic trouble, and perceived communist threat contributed to the Brazilian military's coup d'état in late March 1964. BETTMANN/CORBIS

Vargas room to play one faction against the other and remain somewhat independent. Corporatism had some impact, but it was mostly a matter of rhetoric. For some the Estado Nôvo was a decisive moment in state building for its creation of a rational-legal bureaucracy that promoted industrialization.

Ruling without parties under the new Constitution of 1937, Vargas's government favored national integration, import substitution, industrialization, and urban over rural interests, policies that profoundly transformed Brazil in the war years. His government also realigned Brazil from neutrality to an anti-Axis stance in January 1942, thereby enabling the country to obtain U.S. credit for the construction of the Volta Redonda steel mill. The sinking of Brazilian ships in March 1942 led to a declaration of war on the Axis powers five months later and Brazilian participation in the Italian campaign. Returning from Europe, officers in the Brazilian Expeditionary Force would play a key role in the downfall of Vargas in October 1945. The removal of Vargas was linked to the defeat of the Axis powers, the quelling of political discontent through repressive labor

practices, and the refusal to adopt rural labor laws. In 1945 workers, through urban labor strikes organized by factory commissions, supported a return to democracy. Pressure for the end of the dictatorship also came from political parties such as the National Democratic Union (União Democrática Nacional—UDN), representing urban bourgeois liberalism; the Social Democratic Party (Partido Social Democrático—PSD), the party of traditional landed interests; and the Brazilian Labor Party (Partido Trabalhista Brasileiro—PTB), based on the official bureaucracy of the unions and organized by Vargas himself. Finally democracy was restored, and General Eurico Dutra won the presidential election with the support of Vargas, the PTB, and the PSD.

DEMOCRACY: 1945 TO 1964

From an economic standpoint, the 1945–1964 period was one of installing and developing the import-substitution industrialization model to its limits. This model implied the need for direct state intervention in the economy. The Dutra government (1946–1951) tried briefly to reestablish free trade, but the quick loss of foreign money reserves earned by Brazil during World War II led to a policy of selected noncompetitive imports. In spite of democracy's return, labor unions suspected of Communist leanings were closed and the Communist Party itself was outlawed.

The return of Vargas as president (1951–1954) meant continuation of state enterprises in strategic sectors (water, power, electricity, steel, petroleum), economic planning, and co-option of urban labor, which had been repressed under Dutra's conservative rule. Opposition to these policies as well as nationalism, eventually led the army to try to overthrow the president. After an attempt on the life of journalist Carlos Lacerda that killed an air force major, the generals demanded Vargas's resignation. Instead, he committed suicide in 1954. In November 1955 the vice president who had taken over, João Café Filho (1954–1955), was replaced by the president of the Chamber of Deputies, Carlos Luz, allegedly because of an illness of the former. But during the same year, Luz and leading supporters fled for fear of an army takeover. Also in 1955, Juscelino Kubitschek was elected president, and War Minister Henrique Lott ensured his taking office despite maneuvers to keep him out. A transitional government headed by Nereu Ramos (speaker of the Senate), chosen by the Chamber of Deputies, ruled from November 1955 to the end of January 1956, when Kubitschek assumed power.

The Kubitschek government (1956–1961) adopted an economic planning policy inspired by U.S. economist Walt W. Rostow's theory of take-off. It concentrated investments in an area (Minas Gerais, São Paulo, and Rio de Janeiro) where the preconditions for self-sustained growth existed. The plan of targets (1958) provided for government investment in that area to unclog bottlenecks for industrial growth—for example, power, transportation (mainly shipyards and cars), roads, and chemical industries. The government also sought private and foreign investments for the region. Planners assumed that as the area developed, it would carry in its wake the growth of the other regions so that industry would bring change to the backward rural areas. Kubitschek diverged from Vargas by fostering foreign investment. The march to the west and the establishment of the capital in Brasília (1960) would, he believed, redistribute the

population, which was concentrated along the coast, and integrate the country. Between 1955 and 1961, industrial production grew 80 percent in constant prices. From 1957 to 1961, the real rate of growth was 7 percent per year and nearly 4 percent per capita. Brazil had achieved virtual self-sufficiency in light consumer goods by the mid-1950s.

Kubitschek has been criticized, however, for reinforcing regional differences, neglecting backward states, depressing the standard of living of urban workers, and promoting inflation through the construction of Brasília at a time of declining export earnings. Furthermore, some have asserted that the option for roads and an automobile industry instead of trains was a mistake in a country that imported petroleum. Finally, education and agriculture were the forgotten goals. Foreign indebtedness reached higher levels that were difficult to reduce.

In the 1945–1964 period, the Social Democratic Party and the Brazilian Labor Party formed a dominant political alliance that implied the exclusion of rural workers and cooptive populist policies toward urban workers. The economic policies of the alliance broadened the gap between rural and urban areas and caused heavy migration from countryside to cities (mainly from the Northeast to São Paulo), which resulted in the growth of tenements and shacks and mass unemployment. The 1946 constitution (Brazil's fifth), adopted the Vargas labor code.

The government of Jânio Quadros, who succeeded Kubitschek in 1961, made a frustrated attempt to reestablish a market economy, follow an independent foreign policy, and impose an authoritarian regime combating corruption and administrative inefficiency. After eight months, Quadros suddenly resigned, hoping to return with increased authority, but the interference of the military prevented that maneuver from succeeding.

Popular and labor mobilization and division within the military made it possible for Vice President João Goulart to complete the term (beginning in September 1961) but within a parliamentary system. Goulart, former labor minister of Vargas and PTB leader, fought for the return of presidential government in 1962 and won a January 1963 plebiscite on that issue. To gain labor support, Goulart departed from the traditional PSD-PTB policy of demobilizing workers, which helped to break the power of the bureaucracy in the government-controlled unions. The plan of basic structural reforms sponsored by Goulart, including land and tax reforms, antagonized landowners. Educational and housing reforms were less controversial, but industrialists felt aggrieved by the revived workers' movement and increases in wages.

From the beginning of Goulart's term until his overthrow by the military in April 1964, inflation worsened while the split between leftist-nationalists and anti-Communists within labor became wider. A general radicalization of mass movements took place, and leftist unions became more powerful, independent, and better coordinated on the national level, particularly in the General Command of Workers (Comando Geral do Trabalho). Unions pressed for higher wages and joined the movement for basic reforms. Rural workers were organized both locally and nationally, and literacy campaigns, involving an effort to promote political awareness, were launched. The students' movement, led by the National Students Union (UNE), coordinated its activities with workers' protests. A segment of the Catholic clergy supported reform, whereas some members were outright revolutionary. Several popular fronts were formed, while the PSD, UDN, PTB, and PCB suffered splits. In the last case, dissidents formed the Labor Policy (Política Operária—POLOP), which revised the Marxist analysis and strategies of the PCB.

The discontent with structural inequalities was reinforced by the declining growth rate of industrial production due to international market conditions and exhaustion of the import-substitution model. Through domestic production, the country had replaced a large number of imported goods until most imports (e.g., petroleum), could not be substituted for. Also, regional differences of income, as well as class differences, had deepened.

The 1964 military coup against Goulart had the support of the great majority of the military and part of the industrial and the landed elites. It could count on the immediate recognition of the new regime by the United States. The supposed threat of the so-called unions' republic, the basic reforms of Goulart, a law restricting the repatriation of profits by foreign enterprises, and the high rate of inflation were factors behind the coup,

particularly because some of the army leaders no longer supported civilian rule and had a nationalistic ideology.

THE MILITARY REGIME AND THE RETURN TO DEMOCRACY: 1964–1994

After the 1964 coup Congress lost its power, becoming a mere rubber stamp. Opponents of the new regime lost their political rights. Under the regime's First Institutional Act, Marshal Humberto Castelo Branco, the coup's leader, was selected as president by the military leaders and given automatic approval by Congress. The CGT, Peasant Leagues, and UNE and its affiliates were dissolved. Labor unions were purged, and some state governors were removed. Strict censorship was established, and the secret police gained new power. In 1969 university professors were dismissed, the number of social science classes was reduced, and a mandatory course on moral and civic education was imposed. The Second Institutional Act established indirect elections for the presidency, denied illiterates the vote, extinguished old political parties, and organized two new ones, the Brazilian Democratic Movement (Movimento Democrático Brasileiro—MDB) as the opposition and the National Renovating Alliance (Aliança Renovadora Nacional—ARENA) as the pro-government organization. The same act gave the president the right to suspend Congress, to expel members of parliament, to suspend political rights for ten years, and to decree a state of siege. In 1966 the federal legislature was suspended; subsequently it was this demoralized Congress that elected General Artur da Costa E Silva president and approved Brazil's sixth constitution in 1967 (drafted by a committee of jurists close to the regime), which incorporated the institutional acts. Under this charter the executive could enact laws by decree, suspend political rights of members of Congress, and extend the jurisdiction of the military courts to civilians committing political crimes. In 1969 extensive amendments to the Constitution further centralized power in the federal government and further weakened Congress in relation to the president.

During the rule of Castelo Branco (1964–1967), Costa e Silva (1967–1969), and the military junta that briefly replaced the latter when he became ill, the economic depression deepened partly because of deflationary austerity measures. Opposition was forced underground, assuming the form of urban and rural guerrilla activity. Part of the Catholic clergy remained the last open resistance to the military regime; some clerics supported rural unionism and other organizations of the poor as they worked for a humanized capitalism preached by Father Bastos d'ávila. Anti-Communist organizations were supported by a segment of the industrial bourgeoisie. The Superior War College defended an all-encompassing concept of national security including government repression of dissidents by imprisonment without due process, torture, murder, and secret burial under a false or no name.

Whereas the Left deemed that the national economic crisis could be resolved only by a radical redistribution of wealth, the Right believed that growth and modernization could be achieved through a pattern of income concentration. The military government emphasized the expansion of manufactured and agricultural exports and a process of modernization. During the rule of Emílio Garrastazú Médici (1969–1974), important sectors of business and finance were restructured, inflation was reduced to 20 percent in 1971 (it had been 80 percent in 1963), exports grew from $2.7 billion in 1968 to $6.2 billion in 1973, exchange reserves reached $1 billion, and foreign capital once again entered the country. Before 1964 the country had achieved self-sufficiency in most durable goods. The goals of the plan of 1970–1973 were the development of capital goods production and nuclear power and the massive absorption of technology.

For many the so-called Brazilian Miracle legitimized the military regime. By the same token, the decline of the economy after 1974, resulting in part from higher petroleum prices, promoted a democratization process. President Ernesto Geisel (1974–1979), under the pressure of large strikes and public opinion, started a gradual return to democracy with the constitutional amendment of 1978 that revoked the institutional acts, restored local elections, and allowed the formation of new political parties. João Baptista Figueiredo (1979–1985) granted political amnesty in 1979 and made it easier to organize parties. Remodeled and new parties, the Catholic Church, and class organizations participated in a huge campaign for direct and immediate presidential elections in which the masses would participate. Instead, indirect elections were

held on January 15, 1985, with Tancredo Neves and José Sarney chosen as president and vice president, respectively. The latter assumed office in 1985 due to the illness and death of the former.

Between 1950 and 1980 the country underwent deep changes. In 1950, 64 percent of the total population was rural and 36 percent urban. In 1980 the figures were, respectively, 33 percent and 67 percent. In 1980 Greater São Paulo reached more than 12.5 million inhabitants—more than 10 percent of the total population. The number of workers grew 500 percent between 1950 and 1980, when they represented 32.7 percent of the population, and 52.1 percent of labor was concentrated in the production of capital goods. In 1980 the primary sector of the economy incorporated 29.9 percent, the secondary 24.4 percent, and the tertiary 45.7 percent. The participation in elections broadened from 15 percent of the population in 1945 to 48 percent in 1982.

During the military regime, the malnourished increased from 27 million in 1961–1963 (38 percent of the population) to 72 million in 1974–1975 (67 percent); the percentage dropped slightly in 1984 to 65 percent. In the 1980s, the richest 1 percent of the population increased its share of the national income from 13 percent to 17.3 percent, whereas the poorer 50 percent suffered a decline from 13.4 percent to 10.4 percent. In 1989, 18.9 percent of the population age fifteen or more (17.2 million people, concentrated mainly in the Northeast) were illiterate. More than 44 percent of all families earned less than twice the minimum wage, and only 3.5 percent of the members of these families went to college (1989). Poverty and lack of proper sanitary conditions were responsible for the persistence of epidemic diseases such as malaria, and for the reappearance of cholera in 1989, with 1.1 million cases.

The relationship between the volume of foreign debt and the internal gross production deteriorated from 18.9 in 1980 to 46.3 in 1984. Conspicuous consumption by the government, extensive investments in nuclear programs, and military expenditures represented a drawback. The breakdown of democracy weakened parties and reinforced populist, authoritarian, and clientele practices. The problem of maldistribution of infrastructure, income, and land remained; the number of landless rural workers increased whereas the number of sharecroppers dwindled and that of migrant salaried field hands grew.

Two years after the drafting of Brazil's seventh constitution in 1988, Fernando Collor de Mello became the first president elected by direct popular vote since 1961. Collor ran for the presidency on an anticorruption platform, promising to sweep out government corruption and remove inefficient state employees who collected inflated salaries. Ironically, his presidency is best remembered for its high level of personal corruption, which led to massive anti-Collor demonstrations and formal impeachment proceedings. Collor also implemented an unorthodox and highly unpopular economic "shock" policy by abandoning wage and price indexing and freezing all funds held in personal bank accounts for eighteen months. His goal was to control inflation, which reached nearly 80 percent per month during his presidency, but his policy failed to slow those rates. Collor's commitment to neoliberal reform through privatization of government-owned industry also marked a change in Brazilian economic policy. In 1992 he became the first Brazilian president to face removal from office through an impeachment trial before the Brazilian senate; at the opening of the trial in December he resigned his office. His vice president, Itamar Franco, completed Collor's term, taking office in December 1992 and serving through 1994.

Under Franco, in May 1993, Fernando Henrique Cardoso, a senator and former minister of foreign affairs, was appointed minister of finance. In that position he implemented the Plan Real, which successfully controlled Brazil's hyperinflation. The Plan Real was implemented in three stages. The first stage, put into action in December 1993, enabled the federal government to balance the budget through tighter control of both taxes and transactions between the central government and the various municipalities. Once the budget was balanced, the second stage, introduced in March 1994, indexed the currency, controlling salaries through daily adjustments. The final stage of the plan took effect in July 1994 with the introduction of the new Brazilian currency, the real, which was introduced at a 1:1 ratio with the U.S. dollar. The economic stability gained by Cardoso's plan easily swept him into the presidency in January 1995, with 54 percent of the vote in the first round.

Cardoso, who had been a distinguished sociologist best known as a Left-leaning dependency theorist, spent his two presidential terms pushing through an agenda of privatization and liberalization of the Brazilian economy. Even in the face of well-defined opposition from the Left, Cardoso managed to build a large majority of supporters in Congress to implement most of his desired reforms, several of which required a three-fifths majority from both houses of Congress. One hard-fought constitutional amendment allowed for the reelection of the president for a second term. Based on that amendment, Cardoso was able to run again in the 1998 election, which he again won in the first round, with 53 percent of the popular vote. Cardoso continued his push for privatization and liberal reform, but growing unemployment and slow economic growth cost him much of the popularity he had enjoyed early in his presidency.

In 2002 Luiz Inácio Lula da Silva, better known in Brazil as Lula, ran for the presidency of Brazil for the fourth time—having lost in 1989, 1994, and 1998. This time, for the first time, he led in the polls. Lula is an anomaly in Brazilian politics, because in stark contrast to the Brazilian political elite, he has a working-class background. He has little formal education, having dropped out of school after the fourth grade. He was a union activist in São Paulo in the 1960s and 1970s, and in 1975 he was elected president of the metalworkers union. In 1980 he was a founding member of the Workers' Party (Partido dos Trabalharores, or PT), the first major political party to espouse a socialist agenda following the military coup of 1964.

With the first round of the presidential election on October 6, 2002, Lula won a plurality of 46.4 percent, but the Brazilian constitution requires a majority; in the October 28 runoff, Lula won 61.3 percent of the overall vote. Both during the campaign and in his two presidential terms Lula has sought compromise, balancing the expectations of his well-established Leftist backers in the PT while at the same time trying to appease the fears of the middle class and the economic elite.

Following the election, Lula was cautious in setting his agenda and forming his government. He surrounded himself with diverse advisers and ministers, including two Afro-Brazilians and one indigenous Brazilian in his cabinet. He also sent a message by selecting a very moderate minister of finance. During his first term he disappointed his traditional supporters from the PT Left who were clamoring for social reform, increased minimum wages, and a break from Cardoso's neoliberal policies. Although Lula did halt privatization by retaining several hydroelectric companies and the national oil monopoly (Petrobras), his economic policy was a strict continuation of Cardoso's. Lula's commitment to the previous liberal policies was not enough to immediately appease the fears of foreign investors, who pulled most of their dollars out of Brazil early in his presidency.

During Lula's first presidential term Brazilian exports grew rapidly, and the nation had a growing trade surplus (expanding from $13.1 billion in 2002 to $33.3 billion in 2004), allowing Brazil to pay off portions of its sizable international debts ahead of schedule. By 2004 international investments came back into the country. In terms of social reforms, Lula introduced an antipoverty plan called Fome Zero (Zero Hunger), but due to overall underfunding and poor administration it was later replaced by the Bolsa da Familia (Family Allowance), which gave subsidies to poor families who kept their children in school. He also passed a 26 percent increase in the minimum wage in 2006.

Lula and his PT were hurt by several corruption scandals during his first presidential term, and even in the face of expanding trade, economic growth lagged behind expectations. Nonetheless, he won his second Brazilian presidential election in two rounds in October 2006. In his victory speech he promised to "give attention to the most needy," suggesting that he would use his second term to address more of the social needs that he had overlooked while consolidating power in his first term.

See also **Barbosa de Oliveira, Rui; Brazil, Constitutions; Brazil, Political Parties: Brazilian Communist Party (PCB); Brazil, Political Parties: Integralist Action (AIB); Brazil, Political Parties: Liberal Alliance; Brazil, Political Parties: National Democratic Union of Brazil (UDN); Brazil, Political Parties: Workers Party (PT); Café Filho, João; Cardoso, Fernando Henrique; Collor de Mello, Fernando Affonso; Dutra, Eurico Gaspar; Figueiredo, João Baptista de Oliveira; Fonseca, Manoel Deodoro da; Geisel, Ernesto; Goulart, João Belchior Marques; Isabel, Princess of Brazil; Kubitschek de Oliveira, Juscelino;** **Lacerda, Carlos Frederico Werneck de; Médici, Emílio Garrastazú; Modern Art Week; Morais Barros, Prudente José de; Peixoto, Floriano Vieira; Positivism; Prestes Column; Silva, Luis Inácio Lula da; Tenentismo; Vargas, Getúlio Dornelles.**

BIBLIOGRAPHY

Basbaum, Leonico. *Historia sincera da República*, 4 vols. São Paulo: Editora Alfa-Omega, 1968–1976.

Bello, José Maria. *História da República*. Rio de Janeiro: Civilização Brasileira, 1940.

Burns, E. Bradford. *A History of Brazil*, 3rd edition. New York: Columbia University Press, 1993.

Carone, Edgard. *A Primeira República, 1889–1930*. (1969).

Carone, Edgard. *A Segunda República, 1930–1937*. São Paulo: DIFEL, 1973.

Carone, Edgard. *A Terceira República, 1937–1945*. São Paulo: DIFEL, 1976.

Cruz Costa, João. *Pequena historia da república*, 3rd edition. São Paulo: Brasiliense, 1989.

da Silva, José Luiz Werneck, ed. *O feixe e o prisma: O autoritarismo como questão teórica e historiográfica*. Rio de Janeiro: Jorge Zahar, 1991.

Filgueiras, Luíz. *História do Plano Real*. São Paulo: Boitempo Editorial, 2000.

Levine, Robert M. *The Vargas Regime: The Critical Years, 1934–1938*. New York: Columbia University Press, 1970.

Mauricio de Albuquerque, Maneol. *Pequena história da formação social brasileira*. Rio de Janeiro: Editora Graal, 1981

Murilo de Carvalho, José. *Os Bestializados: O Rio de Janeiro e a república que não foi*. São Paulo: Companhia das Letras, 1987.

Pena, Lincoln de Abreu. *Uma história da República*, 2nd edition. Rio de Janeiro: Nova Fronteira, 1999.

Schneider, Ronald M. *The Political System of Brazil: Emergence of a "Modernizing" Authoritarian Regime, 1964–1970*. New York: Columbia University Press, 1971.

Schneider, Ronald M. *"Order and Progress": A Political History of Brazil*. Boulder, CO: Westview Press, 1991.

Silva, Hélio. *O ciclo de Vargas*, 12 vols. Rio de Janeiro: Civilizacao Brasileira, 1964–1974.

Silva, Hélio. *1889: A República não esperou o amanhecer*. Rio de Janeiro: Editora Civilizacao Brasileira, 1972.

Skidmore, Thomas E. *Politics in Brazil, 1930–1964: An Experiment in Democracy*. New York and London: Oxford University Press, 1967.

Skidmore, Thomas E. *Black into White.* Durham, NC: Duke University Press, 1993.

Telles, Edward E. *Race in Another America.* Princeton, NJ: Princeton University Press, 2004.

Versiani, Flavio Rabelo, and José Roberto Mendoça de Barros, eds. *Formação econômica do Brasil.* São Paulo: Saraiva, 1977.

Vidal Luna, Francisco, and Herbert S. Klein. *Brazil since 1980.* Cambridge, U.K.: Cambridge University Press, 2006.

Viotti da Costa, Emilia. *The Brazilian Empire.* Chapel Hill: University of North Carolina Press, 2000.

EULALIA MARIA LAHMEYER LOBO
ZACHARY R. MORGAN

BRAZIL, AMNESTY ACT (1979). The Amnesty Act (1979), a bill passed by the Brazilian Congress on 22 August 1979 to provide amnesty to most Brazilian political prisoners and exiles. While benefiting approximately 4,500 people, the act excluded any persons found guilty of murder, kidnapping, or terrorist activities and classified them as common criminals. Sixty-nine amendments were added to the bill, including one that allowed families of missing people to petition for a certificate of presumed death and another that guaranteed normal benefits to families of those political prisoners who had died while in custody. The amendments also allowed exonerated former government employees to petition for reinstatement at their previous grade. By allowing the return of opposition leaders from exile, the Amnesty Act was an important step toward the return of free elections in Brazil.

See also **Human Rights.**

BIBLIOGRAPHY

Marti Harden, ed., *Latin American Index* (1979), pp. 44, 48, 60, 62.

Maria Helena Moreira Alves, *State and Opposition in Military Brazil* (1985), pp. 211–212.

Thomas E. Skidmore, *The Politics of Military Rule in Brazil, 1964–85* (1988), pp. 218–219.

Additional Bibliography

Ferreira, Elizabeth F. Xavier. *Mulheres, militância e memória: Histórias de vida, histórias de sobrevivência.* Rio de Janeiro: Fundação Getulio Vargas Editora, 1996.

Gilberto, João Deputado, Guaraciara Barros Leal, and Sérgio Lima. *Anistia, 20 anos.* Brasília, Brazil: Instituto Teotônio Vilela, 2000.

Martins, Roberto Ribeiro, and Luís Antônio Palmeira. *Liberdade para os brasileiros: anistia ontem e hoje.* Rio de Janeiro: Civilização Brasileira, 1978.

Souza, Daniel, and Gilmar Chaves. *Nossa paixão era inventar um novo tempo.* Rio de Janeiro: Editora Rosa dos Tempos, 1999.

MICHAEL J. BROYLES

BRAZIL, CIVIL CODE. Following four unsuccessful attempts during the nineteenth century to codify Brazilian civil law, the Brazilian Civil Code (Codigo Civil Brasileiro), drafted by Clóvis Bevilaqua, was approved by Congress (Law 3,071 of January 1, 1916) and took effect on January 1, 1917. Corrections ordered by Law 3,725 of January 15, 1919 were promulgated on July 13, 1919. The Civil Code superseded the Ordinações Filipinas, compiled in Portugal in 1603, and as of 2007 remains in effect, although it has been altered significantly by subsequent laws.

Widely praised at the time for its scientific and practical nature, the Civil Code is divided into two parts. The general part deals with persons, property, and legal acts; the special part treats the rights of family, rights of things, laws of obligations, and rights of succession. The Civil Code is a conservative document that reinforces capitalist and patriarchal social relations. Especially concerned with relations within the family, it declares the husband the legal head of household and leaves married women legally incapacitated. A wife can assume *patria poder* only in the case of the legal absence of her husband. The husband has the right to administer the wife's property, and she has to secure his authorization to pursue a profession as well as to accept or relinquish an inheritance. The Civil Code originally permitted annulment of marriage (under restrictive circumstances) and legal separation (*desquite*) only; divorce was legalized in 1977 (Law 6,515 of 26 December 1977), but only once in any person's lifetime.

Proposals to update Brazil's Civil Code commenced in the mid-1970s, and in January 2003 the country's new Civil Code (Law 10.406/2002) went into effect. In part, the reform aimed to consolidate related laws and decrees and make the code conform to the Constitution of 1988. Yet in replacing paternal power with family power, it took new steps in recognizing women's equality. Moreover, the new Civil Code eased divorce proceedings and eliminated distinctions between legitimate and illegitimate children. The new code also included changes affecting business and contract law.

See also **Marriage and Divorce; Ordenações do Reino.**

BIBLIOGRAPHY

A useful early edition of the Civil Code, which includes a historical and descriptive introduction and an index, is *Código civil brasileira*, edited by Paulo de Lacerda (1916). A later compilation of modifications of the Civil Code is *Código civil e legislação complementar*, edited by Geraldo Magela Alves (1989). An older English translation is *The Civil Code of Brazil*, translated by Joseph Wheless (St. Louis, Thomas Law Book Company, 1920).

Additional Bibliography

Barretto Ferreira da Silva, Ricardo, ed. *Doing Business in Brazil*. Chicago: Section of International Law and Practice, American Bar Association, 2002.

Caulfield, Sueann. *In Defense of Honor: Sexual Morality, Modernity, and Nation in Early-Twentieth-Century Brazil*. Durham, DC: Duke University Press, 2000.

Htun, Mala. *Sex and the State: Abortion, Divorce, and the Family under Latin American Dictatorships and Democracies*. Cambridge, U.K.; New York: Cambridge University Press, 2003.

SUSAN K. BESSE

BRAZIL, CONSTITUTIONS.

Since proclaiming independence in 1822, Brazil has had eight constitutions, well below the Latin American per-country average of thirteen. None has worked very well. It is not clear, however, to what extent the problems should be attributed to the constitutional rules and to what extent to the individuals governing under and around these rules. Until Brazil can resolve some of its most pressing economic, social, and political problems, it is doubtful that any constitution will work well.

THE 1824 CONSTITUTION

Brazil's first constitution was its most enduring, lasting sixty-five years with only one amendment.

Modeled upon the French Constitution of 1814, it established a hereditary Catholic monarchy, headed by the emperor Dom Pedro I. This document, containing 172 articles, inaugurated Brazil's tradition of complex and lengthy constitutions. It established a centralized, unitary system of government. Although it divided the country into provinces and counties (*municípios*), these territorial units had little independent authority. The central government was divided into four powers: legislative, executive, judicial, and moderating.

Legislative power was exercised by a bicameral General Assembly with a Chamber of Deputies, whose members were chosen for four-year terms, and a Senate, whose members were chosen for life. The number of deputies per province depended upon population, and each province had half as many senators as deputies. Both houses were selected indirectly by provincial electors chosen by parish assemblies, but the emperor selected senators from lists of three nominated by provincial electors. The government's manipulation of the electoral process, however, destroyed even the limited representative nature of the assembly. The assembly both enacted and interpreted the laws. It had the power to choose a new dynasty if the royal family became extinct and to elect a regent if the emperor was a minor. The deputies could impeach all officials except the emperor, who was legally inviolable.

The emperor exercised both the executive and moderating powers. The moderating power was designed to resolve conflicts among the other powers of government. The executive had extensive powers, including appointments, foreign relations, security, execution of the laws, appropriations, and veto of ecclesiastical decrees. The moderating power included selecting senators, calling extraordinary legislative sessions, approving or vetoing legislation, dissolving the Chamber of Deputies and calling new elections, nominating or dismissing ministers of state, suspending judges, and granting pardons and amnesties. The emperor also appointed for life a Council of State that advised him and resolved administrative law disputes.

The judiciary consisted of a Supreme Tribunal of Justice, Provincial Tribunals (*Relações*), law-trained judges, and elected justices of the peace. Lay jurors determined the facts in both civil and criminal cases. Judges had life tenure, but they could be transferred or suspended by the emperor.

This was in many ways a progressive constitution. It guaranteed many individual rights, protected freedom of thought and expression, and abolished many cruel penalties inherited from Portugal. Equal protection of the laws was guaranteed to citizens. Even though Catholicism was the state religion and only Catholics could become deputies, it provided for religious tolerance. At the same time, however, it permitted slavery and failed to create procedural devices to protect basic rights.

THE 1891 CONSTITUTION

In 1889 the monarchy was overthrown by the military, whose first act, drafted by Rui Barbosa, abolished the Constitution of 1824 and proclaimed the Republic of the United States of Brazil. Heavily influenced by the U.S. Constitution, the 1891 Constitution was Brazil's shortest, containing only ninety-one articles and eight transitional provisions. It changed Brazil into a republican federation and converted the former provinces into twenty sovereign states. It also extended the franchise to all literate adult males.

The government was reduced to three branches: executive, legislative, and judicial. The bicameral legislature consisted of a Chamber of Deputies and a Senate. Each state and the federal district elected three senators; deputies were apportioned by population, each state having at least four. Senators were elected for nine years; deputies for three years. In contradistinction to the United States, where such subjects are primarily governed by state legislation, the 1891 Constitution specifically authorized the National Congress to enact federal codes of civil, commercial and criminal law.

The executive was headed by a president elected by direct vote for a four-year term and ineligible for immediate reelection. His powers included administration of the armed forces, conducting foreign affairs, vetoing or approving legislation, granting pardons, and calling extraordinary congressional sessions. With Senate approval, the president could appoint members of the Supreme Court and the diplomatic corps. He appointed inferior federal judges from lists submitted by the Supreme Court.

As in the United States, the Constitution created the highest court, the Supreme Federal Tribunal, and authorized the legislature to establish the inferior federal courts. Unlike the United States, Brazil's Constitution expressly conferred the power to determine the constitutionality of legislation upon the judiciary. The jury system was retained. Guarantees of judicial independence were taken directly from Article III of the U.S. Constitution: life tenure and nondiminution of salaries.

Basic constitutional rights, such as liberty and property, which previously had been assured only to Brazilian citizens, were extended to foreign residents. Habeas corpus, which had merely a statutory basis under the empire, was made a constitutional right. The penalties of death, banishment, and galley service were abolished.

This U.S.-inspired Constitution worked poorly. The period during which it was in force, known as the Old Republic, was marked by continual political instability and widespread electoral fraud. In 1926 a constitutional amendment greatly expanded the power of the federal government to intervene in the states, limited state autonomy, cut back habeas corpus, and modified congressional powers.

THE 1934 CONSTITUTION

Even as amended, the 1891 Constitution never conformed to Brazilian political reality. It perished in 1930, a casualty of a military revolt that brought to power Getúlio Vargas, whose provisional government promptly modified the 1891 Constitution to assume dictatorial powers. An unsuccessful São Paulo revolt against the dictatorship eventually led to restoration of constitutional government. In 1934 a new constitution, modeled upon the German Weimar Constitution of 1919 and the Spanish Constitution of 1931, was adopted. This was even longer than prior constitutions, containing 187 articles and 26 transitional provisions.

Federalism and the tripartite division of powers were retained, but the powers of the federal government were enhanced at the expense of the states. Legislative power was actually controlled by the Chamber of Deputies, with the Senate assuming the role of a fourth power, similar to the moderating power of the emperor. The deputies, apportioned by population, were elected for four-year terms. Five-sixths were chosen by universal direct vote of the people in each state, while one-sixth were chosen by indirect vote of professional associations, divided between employers and employees. The executive power was exercised by the president and his cabinet. There was no vice president.

The Constitution created two new court systems, the electoral and labor courts. The former represented a reaction to the electoral fraud that had characterized the Old Republic, whereas the latter reflected Vargas's concern with protection of the working class.

The 1934 Constitution made several other important innovations. It was the first to extend the franchise to all literate Brazilians over the age of eighteen, regardless of sex. Voting, which had been optional during the Old Republic, was made obligatory for all males and for female civil servants. It created the writ of security (*mandado de segurança*), a summary procedure to protect clear and summarily ascertainable constitutional rights unprotected by habeas corpus. It also began the process of nationalization of certain sectors of the economy, such as navigation, newspapers, advertising agencies, mining, and insurance.

THE 1937 CONSTITUTION
In 1937, the year before his presidential term was to expire, Vargas staged a coup d'état and proclaimed the *Estado Nôvo*, the "new state." Vargas replaced the 1934 Constitution with a constitution that enabled him to exercise dictatorial powers. This was a shadow constitution for two reasons. First, article 187 required that the constitution be ratified by a plebiscite, which was never held. Second, Vargas ignored its basic provisions, dissolving all political parties and holding no elections. Article 180 authorized the president to legislate by decree-law until Congress met. Congress never met, and Vargas issued more than 8,000 decree-laws between 1937 and 1945.

During the entire period of the 1937 Constitution, individual rights were suspended by a continual state of emergency. A number of rights protected in prior constitutions remained unprotected in the 1937 Constitution. The state of emergency lasted until 30 November 1945, a month after Vargas was overthrown by the military.

THE 1946 CONSTITUTION
The Constitution of 1946 was even longer than its predecessors, containing 218 articles and 36 transitional provisions. Like the 1891 Constitution, it reflected the influence of the U.S. Constitution, particularly with respect to federalism. In structure and in protection of socioeconomic rights, it reflected the Weimar Constitution. As a reaction to the Vargas dictatorship, it denied the executive the power to issue decree-laws. The legislature resembled that of prior constitutions but functioned very inefficiently, resulting in the growth of administrative decrees as a substitute for legislation. The judiciary recovered its autonomy as well as the power of judicial review. Article 125 provided for creation of the Public Ministry, a civil-law institution that performed prosecutorial functions and defended the interests of law and society before the courts. Individual rights were generously protected, and exclusion from judicial consideration of any injury to an individual right was expressly prohibited.

The demise of the 1946 Constitution began in 1961, when President Jânio Quadros resigned, claiming that Brazil was ungovernable under the existing constitutional regime. Vice President João Goulart was permitted to assume the presidency only after a constitutional amendment created a parliamentary regime. Thus restructured, the new government functioned poorly, and a 1963 constitutional amendment restored presidential powers. Miscalculating the depth of his political support, Goulart tried moving the country to the left and was overthrown by the military in 1964.

The 1946 Constitution remained in force, as modified by a series of "institutional acts" issued by the military high command, functioning as a self-designated ambulatory constituent assembly. The military quickly selected General Humberto Castello Branco as the new president, removed opposition legislators, and deprived opponents of political and civil rights for ten years. The president packed the Supreme Court, increasing its size from eleven to sixteen justices. The president was empowered to issue decree-laws in matters involving national security, finances, and administration.

THE 1967 CONSTITUTION
The 1967 Constitution, formally ratified by a Congress from which most political opposition had been purged, centralized power in the executive and in the federal government. The president was elected by an electoral college, but in practice only a military leader could be a candidate. The legislative provisions

resembled those of the 1946 Constitution except for the authority of the president to enact decree-laws even when the legislature was in session. The Constitution guaranteed an impressive array of individual rights, but the guarantees were seldom in force.

A period of constant crisis followed promulgation of the Constitution, due to widespread opposition to military government. The military responded by issuing an additional dozen institutional acts. Act 5 of 13 December 1968 removed virtually all restraints on presidential power. The president suspended all legislative bodies and exercised total legislative power himself. The president not only compulsorily retired three unduly independent Supreme Court members and many lower-court judges, but also suspended habeas corpus for crimes against national security.

In August 1969 President Artur da Costa e Silva suffered a stroke. Rather than permit the civilian vice president to replace him, a military junta assumed the presidency. The junta also issued Constitutional Amendment 1, rewriting the entire text of the 1967 Constitution.

THE 1969 CONSTITUTION

Whether the 1969 Constitution should be regarded as a new constitution or merely an amendment is an unsettled issue. This Constitution further strengthened executive powers, expanding the presidential term to five years and authorizing the president to issue decree-laws not only with respect to national security, but also taxation, creation of public employment, and public salaries. The greatest expansion of presidential power came from granting the president the power to submit "short-fused" bills on any subject. Each house had forty-five days to consider such bills; if labeled urgent, both houses had only forty days for joint consideration. Bills not considered during these periods were deemed automatically approved.

The protection previously accorded to individual rights was badly diluted. Moreover, such rights were suspended until 1 January 1979, when Institutional Act 5 finally expired. In January 1985 Brazil elected, albeit indirectly, its first civilian president since 1960. Restoration of democracy led to the adoption of a new constitution in 1988.

THE 1988 CONSTITUTION

The 1988 Constitution is a lengthy, detailed, and convoluted document, originally containing 245 articles and 70 transitory provisions. Some of these articles run on for more than five pages, such as Article 5, which has 78 sections, many with multiple subsections. As of 22 May 2007, fifty-nine amendments have been enacted, many of which have made extensive changes to the original text. The Constitution at this writing contains 250 articles and 94 transitory provisions. This count is misleading, however, because certain new articles have been inserted interstitially, such as Arts. 29-A, 103-A and 103-B, whereas some articles have been totally or partly revoked. Moreover, many provisions of amendments have never been inserted either into the constitutional text or into the transitory provisions.

Heavily influenced by the 1976 Portuguese Constitution, the text contains a plethora of detailed rules normally found in ordinary legislation. Paradoxically, despite the great detail with which many subjects have been regulated, some 285 ordinary statutes and 41 complementary laws were required to effectuate its provisions. Thus far, Congress has failed to enact all the necessary implementing legislation.

The Constitution is a hodgepodge of progressive, conservative, liberal, radical, and moderate provisions. This is partly because it was drafted from scratch by the entire 559 members of Congress and partly because the initial drafts contemplated a parliamentary system. At the last minute, Congress switched to presidentialism but left numerous parliamentary provisions in the text.

The 1988 Constitution weakens the executive and strengthens the legislature. It makes the president accountable to Congress, which can impeach, as it did Fernando Collor de Mello, Brazil's first popularly elected president since Quadros. Congress has exclusive power to control rulemaking by administrative agencies. All acts of the executive, including acts of indirect administration, are theoretically subject to control by one or both houses of Congress.

The drafters refused to grant the president the power to issue decree-laws. Instead, they granted him the powers to issue delegated laws and provisional measures. Except for a few reserved subjects,

Congress may delegate to the president the power to enact legislation, a power that has been relatively unimportant. On the other hand, the power to issue provisional measures, which was borrowed from Italy's parliamentary Constitution, has been important and much abused in Brazil's presidential system. Prior to 2001, by simply alleging relevance and urgency, Brazilian presidents were able to issue provisional measures with the force of law on virtually any subject. While in theory provisional measures lost their efficacy *ab initio* unless converted into law within thirty days, presidents routinely reissued provisional measures not specifically rejected by Congress, some as many as eighty times, until they were either finally adopted or rejected by Congress.

Amendment 32 of 11 September 2001 curbed the egregious abuses of the provisional measure. Presidents are now prohibited from issuing provisional measures on many subjects. Provisional measures are valid for sixty rather than thirty days, and they may be extended only once if Congress fails to act upon them within sixty days. Provisional measures that lapse because of passage of time are no longer void *ab initio*; any legal relations constituted under them are to be regulated by legislative decrees.

The 1988 Constitution considerably strengthens the powers of the judiciary. Courts have much greater financial independence and substantially greater power to declare statutes unconstitutional. Amendment 45 of 8 December 2004, the long-delayed Judicial Reform Amendment, attempts to make Brazil's notoriously lethargic judiciary more rapid, efficient, and transparent. It creates a National Council of Justice with the power to control the judiciary's finances and administration, as well as to discipline judges and their staffs. It relieves some of the overcrowded docket of the Supreme Federal Tribunal by transferring its exclusive jurisdiction to recognize foreign judgments and to grant letters rogatory to the Superior Tribunal of Justice, and by limiting its hearing of extraordinary appeals to those presenting constitutional issues with general repercussions. The Amendment also enables the Supreme Federal Tribunal to make constitutional decisions approved by a two-thirds majority into binding precedents.

Among the most impressive achievements of the new Constitution are its procedural innovations in the protection of constitutional and legal rights. Substantive guarantees of individual rights are also impressive, protecting virtually every human right. Unfortunately, this is an area where the gap between the Constitution on paper and the Constitution in practice looms largest. The Constitution also protects a vast array of socioeconomic rights. Education, health, labor, leisure, security, social security, protection of maternity and infancy, and assistance of the unprotected are declared to be social rights. Article 7 contains numerous sections and subsections that read like a miniature progressive labor code.

A number of provisions in the original version of the Constitution made little or no sense, and some posed serious obstacles to the country's governability and economic development. For example, a provision declared that charging an annual real rate of interest in excess of 12 percent constituted the crime of usury. Had it been enforced, this provision might have destroyed the Brazilian financial system. Fortunately, it was never implemented and was revoked by of 29 May 2003. Major obstacles to reducing the bloated bureaucracy were provisions that granted tenure to irregularly hired civil servants with five years of public service and made it exceedingly difficult to fire a tenured civil servant. Amendment 19 of 4 June 1998 made it easier to fire tenured civil servants, restricted tenure to those who passed public competitive entrance examinations, and prohibited any civil servant from earning more than the salary of a Supreme Court justice. Amendments 5 to 9, 13, and 36 eliminated most of the Constitution's nationalistic provisions that discouraged or discriminated against foreign investment.

The 1988 Constitution was intended to endure for only five years. It mandated that a plebiscite be held in 1993 to determine whether Brazil should remain a republic or become a constitutional monarchy, and whether it should retain a presidential system or adopt a parliamentary system. In the plebiscite, a majority voted to retain both republicanism and presidentialism. Another provision mandated that the constitutional text be revised by a vote of an absolute majority of the member of the National Congress in 1993. A scandal involving corruption in the congressional budget process delayed this revision until March 1994. More than 17,000 amendments to the Constitution were proposed, but only six were ultimately adopted. The only significant constitutional amendment passed by Congress was Amendment of Revision 1 of 1 March 1994, which created the Emergency Social Fund. This amendment changed the revenue-sharing rules of the 1988 Constitution, transferring an estimated $9 billion from state and local governments to the federal government, but only for fiscal years 1994–1995. The revenue-sharing rules, which transferred substantial portions of federal tax revenues, but not corresponding governmental obligations, to state and local governments, were partially to blame for Brazil's quadruple-digit inflation rates that followed adoption of the 1988 Constitution. These revenue sharing rules have been relaxed by a series of constitutional amendments. Several new federal revenue sources have been created by constitutional amendments, including a very important tax on all bank checks, thereby making it possible for Brazil to continue its successful economic stabilization program.

Despite its many flaws, Brazil's current Constitution actually works. Democratic elections, without complaints of fraud, are regularly held in accordance with its provisions. It has survived triple-digit inflation, a presidential impeachment, election of a populist leftist president, and a long series of governmental corruption scandals. Brazilians no longer express the fear that the Constitution will be overturned by yet another military coup d'ètat. There is little support in Brazil for convening another constituent assembly to draft a new Constitution, but amending the existing Constitution has become the favorite sport of Congress.

See also **Democracy.**

BIBLIOGRAPHY

Agra, Walber de Moura. *Curso de Direito Constitucional,* Rio de Janeiro: Editora Forense, 2006.

Senado Federal. *Constituições do Brasil; DE 1824, 1891, 1934, 1937, 1946 E 1967 e Suas Alterações.* 2 VOLS. Brasília: Senado Federal, Subsecretaria de Edições Técnicas, 1986.

Alves, Francisco de Assis. "Constituições do Brasil." *Revista de Direito Constitucional e Ciência Política* Special Number (1987), 1–72.

Barbosa Sobrinho, Osório Silva. *Constituição Federal Vista Pelo STF.* 3a. ed. São Paulo: Editora Juarez De Oliveira, 2001.

Barroso, Luís Roberto. *Constituição da República Federativa do Brasil: Anotada.* 5a. ed., reformulada. São Paulo: Editora Saraiva, 2006.

Barroso, Luís Roberto. *O Controle de Constitucionalidade no Direito Brasileiro: Exposição Sistemática da Doutrina e Análise Crítica da Jurisprudência,* rev. e actualizada. São Paulo: Editora Saraiva, 2006.

Bastos, Celso Ribeiro. *Curso de Direito Constitucional.* 16a. ed. São Paulo: Celso Basdtos Editora, 2002

Camargo, Margarida Maria Lacombe, ed. *1988–1998: Uma Decada de Constituição.* Rio de Janeiro: Renovar, 1999.

D'Ávila, Luiz F. C., ed. *Constituições Brasileiras: Análise Histórica e Propostas de Mudança.* São Paulo: Editora Brasiliense, 1993.

de Oliveira, Rodrigo M. Carneiro. *As Constituições Brasileiras: Uma Análise Histórica Para a Revisão Constitucional de 1993.* Pamphlet. São Paulo: Pinheiro Neto, Advogados, 1993.

Ferreira Filho, Manoel Gonçalves. "Fundamental Aspects of the 1988 Constitutionalism for a Transitional Society." In *A Panorama of Brazilian Law,* edited by Jacob Dolinger and Keith S. Rosenn. Coral Gables, FL: North-South Center and Editora Esplanada Ltda., 1992.

James, Herman G. *The Constitutional System of Brazil.* Washington, DC: Carnegie Institution of Washington, 1923.

Junqueira Filho, Manoel Octaviano. "Constituições do Brasil (Evolução Histórica)." In *Enciclopédia Saraiva do Direito.* Vol. 18. Coord. R. Limongi França. São Paulo: Saraiva, 1977.

Martínez-Lara, Javier. *Building Democracy in Brazil: The Politics of Constitutional Change, 1985–95.* New York: St. Martin's Press, 1996.

Moraes, Alexandre de. *Constituição do Brasil Interpretada e Legislação Constitucional,* São Paulo: Editora Atlas, 2002.

Nery, Nelson, Jr., and Rosa Maria de Andrade Nery. *Constituição Federal Comentada e Legislação Constitucional.* São Paulo: Editora Revista dos Tribunais, 2006.

Presidência da República. "Constituições." (Continually updated Portuguese version of the constitutional text and amendments, as well as all state constitutions and prior Brazilian constitutions.) Available from http://www.presidencia.gov.br/legislacao/constituicao.

Reich, Gary M. "The 1988 Constitution a Decade Later: Ugly Compromises Reconsidered." *Journal of Inter-American Studies and World Affairs* 40 (Winter 1998), 5–24.

Rosenn, Keith S. "Brazil's New Constitution: An Exercise in Transient Constitutionalism for a Transitional Society." *American Journal of Comparative Law* 38 (1990), 773–802.

Rosenn, Keith S. "The Federative Republic of Brazil [An Annotated Translation]." In *Constitutions of the Countries of the World.* Vol. 3., Release 2006-4, edited by Rüdiger Wolfrum and Rainer Grote. Dobbs Ferry, NY: Oceana Publications, 2006.

Zimmermann, Augusto. *Curso de Direito Constitucional.* 3a ed. Rio de Janeiro: Editora Lumen Juris, 2002.

KEITH S. ROSENN

BRAZIL, COUNCIL OF STATE.

The Council of State, an institution that advised the Brazilian crown on the use of the moderate power, matters of state, general measures of public administration, declarations of war, and treaties with foreign nations. Formed in 1824, its members were party leaders who were appointed for life and who frequently were appointed to cabinet posts. During the First Empire the constitution required the crown to consult the council, whose perception as a tool of Pedro I made it increasingly unpopular.

The council was abolished during the Regency and reinstated in 1841 with modifications: Imperial consultation became optional except on the exercise of the moderate power, its membership was increased from ten to twelve permanent members, and it became a court of appeals for administrative justice. It was divided into a plenary council and four sections: empire, finances, foreign relations and justice, and war and navy. The plenary council advised the emperor, and the four sections advised the respective ministries on administrative matters. Although consultation was now optional, there developed a de facto system of decision making in which its advice was required, making the council an unofficial legislative body that influenced all areas of administration. In 1889 it was abolished by the republic.

See also **Brazil: 1808–1889; Pedro I of Brazil.**

BIBLIOGRAPHY

José Honório Rodrigues, *O Conselho de estado, o quinto poder?* (1978).

Additional Bibliography

Fundação, Alexandre de Gusmão, and Centro de História e Documentação Diplomática. *O Conselho de Estado e a política externa do Império: Consultas da Seção dos Negocios Estrangeiros, 1858–1862.* Rio de Janeiro: FUNAG, 2005.

LYDIA M. GARNER

BRAZIL, ECONOMIC MIRACLE (1968–1974).

The Economic Miracle (1968–1974) was a period of prosperity that was marked by high annual rates of economic growth, an expanded number of public and private development projects, and an increase in the volume and the diversity of exports. The miracle resulted from the economic policies adopted by military leaders following the 1964 coup against João Goulart. These policies were designed to favor business and encourage foreign and domestic investment. The economy stagnated in the first few years after the coup, but beginning in 1968 improved dramatically, and continued to grow for the next six years. Between 1968 and 1974 the annual real gross domestic product rose by an average of 11 percent, compared to the average 3.7 percent in the preceding five years.

The industrial sector expanded at an annual average rate of 12.6 percent as basic industries substantially increased production. Steel output rose from 2.8 million tons in 1964 to 9.2 million tons in 1976, and passenger car production soared from 184,000 vehicles in 1964 to 986,000 in 1976. Increased manufacturing capacity helped diversify exports. Coffee accounted for 42 percent of exports in the mid-1960s, but only 12.6 percent in 1974; manufacturing jumped from 7.2 percent of exports to 27.7 percent. To create and maintain this growth, the military regimes sharply augmented spending for development projects and improved conditions for business. When President Artur da Costa e Silva closed the National Congress in December 1968, he revised tax policy to reduce the constitutionally mandated amount of tax revenue the national government shared with the states, from 20 percent to 12 percent. This shift allowed the government to undertake massive economic development projects, such as the Transamazon Highway. Besides shifting resources to development projects, the military maintained relatively low tax rates and checked labor costs by cracking down on strikes and labor turmoil. As a result, foreign investors infused large amounts of capital.

The economic boom helped generate public support for military rule and justify that rule to critics abroad. Although federal spending and foreign capital further developed the industrial infrastructure of Brazil, the "economic miracle" failed to address some basic problems. Wealth was unevenly distributed, with only 20 percent of the population owning 63 percent of the country's wealth. By increasing federal spending and manipulating the financial system, the military regimes created the conditions for the inflation that followed. Moreover, the overreliance on foreign capital led to the massive external debt of the 1980s.

See also **Economic Development.**

BIBLIOGRAPHY

Thomas Skidmore, *The Politics of Military Rule in Brazil* (1988).

Werner Baer, *The Brazilian Economy* (1989).

Additional Bibliography

Chafee, Wilber A. *Desenvolvimento: Politics and Economy in Brazil.* Boulder: L. Rienner Publishers, 1998.

Coes, Donald V. *Macroeconomic Crises, Policies, and Growth in Brazil, 1964-90.* Washington, DC: World Bank, 1995.

Oliveira, Fabrício Augusto de. *Autoritarismo e crise fiscal no Brasil, 1964-1984.* São Paulo: Editora Hucitec, 1995.

Smith, Joseph, and Francisco Luiz Teixeira Vinhosa. *History of Brazil, 1500-2000: Politics, Economy, Society, Diplomacy.* New York: Longman, 2002.

ROSS WILKINSON

BRAZIL, ELECTORAL REFORM LEGISLATION.

Brazil's Electoral Code, Law 4.737 (July 15, 1965), and Organic Law on Political Parties, Law 5.682 (July 21, 1971), date back to the period of the military dictatorship. Although some of their provisions have been revoked or modified by constitutional reforms or subsequent legislation, they remain in force as basic legislation on the electoral rules.

The restoration of democracy in 1985 produced basic changes in the electoral rules. These changes were mandated by Constitutional Amendment 25 (May 15, 1985), which reinstituted direct elections for the president and vice president and for municipal offices, permitted reorganization of banned political parties, enfranchised illiterates, and eliminated a constitutional provision that required loss of mandate for a senator or deputy who failed to follow his or her political party.

The right to vote was further expanded by the 1988 Constitution. Article 14 provides that "popular sovereignty shall be exercised by universal suffrage through direct and secret vote, with equal value for all." Illiterates and juveniles as young as sixteen may vote in all elections, but literacy is required in order to be eligible to run for public office. Voting is mandatory for all literate persons between the ages of eighteen and seventy. Suffrage is, however, not universal, for conscripts are disfranchised during their period of obligatory military service.

Supervision of elections and political parties, as well as the resolution of election disputes, is committed to the Electoral Courts. The Superior Electoral Tribunal (TSE) is made up of three members of the Supreme Court (STF), two members of the Superior Tribunal of Justice (STJ), and two distinguished lawyers, all of whom serve two-year terms that can be renewed only once. The Electoral Code sets out in great detail the rules for the operation of the Electoral Tribunals, whose jurisdiction is defined by the 1988 Constitution. It also sets out in great detail rules for the registration of voters and the conduct of elections, including measures such as secret ballots, transportation to the polls, and processing of returns. Candidates must be registered by parties. The Code provides methods for supervision of the balloting process and for nullifying contested ballots. It also defines a series of electoral crimes, triable before the Electoral Tribunals. Finally, the Code regulates electoral propaganda. Supervision of this propaganda by the Electoral Courts was eliminated by Law 7.332 (July 1, 1985).

The 1988 Constitution reformed prior practice to require runoff elections between the top two candidates for the president, governors, and mayors of cities with at least 200,000 voters if no candidate attains an absolute majority on the first ballot. Elections for senators and mayors of cities with fewer than 200,000 voters may be decided a plurality. Federal and state deputies and city council members are chosen by proportional elections. The constitution also confers a right to free radio and television time on political parties.

Complimentary Law 78 of 1993 provides that each state have a minimum of eight federal deputies and a maximum of sixty, a system that gives the less populous states gross overrepresentation in the federal congress.

In 1993 Brazil's legislature passed a law requiring all candidates to report their campaign contributions on a register known as the *prestação de contas*. The Organic Law of Political Parties, passed in 1995, intended to reduce party switching, among other goals. It also imposed tougher restrictions for establishing new political parties. Quotas for women candidates at the level of city council were added the following year.

Constitutional Amendment 16 of 1997 permits reelection of the president, governors, and mayors for one subsequent term and reduces the presidential mandate from a five- to a four-year term. Law 9504 of 1997 requires each party to reserve a minimum of thirty percent and a maximum of seventy percent of their candidacies for persons of each sex, a curious form of gender quota. This law also provides for electronic voting and regulation of electoral propaganda. Constitutional Amendment 52 of 2006 assures political parties that there be no requirement of linkage among national, state, district, or county candidates.

See also **Brazil, Constitutions.**

BIBLIOGRAPHY

The Electoral Code and the Organic Law of Political Parties with subsequent amendments are published in Juarez De Oliveira, ed., *Código Eleitoral: Lei orgánica dos partidos políticos; Legislação correlata e Súmulas do Tribunal Superior Eleitoral,* 10th ed. (1993). A useful historical perspective on Brazilian electoral reform can be found in Toshio Mukai, "Sistemas eleitorais no Brasil," *Revista de Direito Constitucional e Ciência Política* (Special number, 1987): 307–348.

Additional Bibliography

Krause, Silvana, and Rogério Schmitt. *Partidos e coligações eleitorais no Brasil.* Rio de Janeiro: Konrad Adenauer Stiftung; São Paulo, Brazil: Editora Unesp, 2005.

Mainwaring, Scott P. *Rethinking Party Systems in the Third Wave of Democratization: The Case of Brazil.* Stanford, CA: Stanford University Press, 1999.

Martínez-Lara, Javier. *Building Democracy in Brazil: The Politics of Constitutional Change, 1985–95.* New York: St. Martin's Press, 1996.

Nicolau, Jairo Marconi. *História do voto no Brasil.* Rio de Janeiro: Jorge Zahar Editor, 2002.

Trindade, Hélgio, ed. *Reforma eleitoral e representação política: Brasil anos 90.* Porto Alegre, Brazil: Editora da Universidade, Universidade Federal do Rio Grande do Sul, 1992.

KEITH S. ROSENN

BRAZIL, THE EMPIRE (FIRST). The First Empire (1822–1831) was a period of consolidation of Brazilian independence and of struggle between the crown and the elites. Territorial unification of the empire, foreign recognition of its independence, and the enactment of a constitution were the major achievements of the period. The convergence of the conflicting ideologies of centralism and federalism, an opposition to monarchical absolutism and centralized power, and the fear of reunification with Portugal led to continual conflict between the crown and the General Assembly for control of political power, and eventually paralyzed the government. A number of royal actions irrevocably alienated the Chamber of Deputies; among them Pedro I's dissolution of the constituent assembly and his subsequent granting of a centralizing constitution, the disclosure of secret conventions in the treaty with Portugal, and the Anglo-Brazilian treaty to end the slave trade, which was signed and ratified by the emperor without the General Assembly's knowledge. Pedro's inheritance of the Portuguese throne in 1827 fueled anti-Portuguese tendencies and reawakened fears of reunification and the suspicion that Pedro's interests were with Portugal.

Despite the adversarial climate of the First Empire, a supreme court of justice, a postal service, and a criminal code were established. During this period several separatist insurrections were suppressed with various degrees of success. In 1824 the Confederation of the Equator was defeated, but the revolt in the Cisplatine province led to a protracted war and ultimately to the creation of Uruguay. Economic progress was scant: measures to promote immigration failed, coffee exports tripled but the prices for other exports fell due to international competition, inflation was high, public and foreign debt rose, the exchange rate declined, the equalization of duties did not allow for increases of revenues, and the Bank of Brazil was liquidated. The continual political and institutional crises led to the abdication of Pedro I in 1831.

See also **Pedro I of Brazil.**

BIBLIOGRAPHY

John Armitage, *A History of Brazil*, 2 vols., (repr. 1970).

Emilia Viotti Da Costa, *The Brazilian Empire: Myths and Histories* (1985), pp. 1–77.

Neill Macaulay, *Dom Pedro: The Struggle for Liberty in Brazil and Portugal, 1798–1834* (1986), pp. 87–253.

Leslie Bethell, ed., *Brazil Empire and Republic, 1822–1930* (1989).

Additional Bibliography

Costa, Emília Viotti da. *The Brazilian Empire: Myths & Histories.* Rev. ed. Chapel Hill: University of North Carolina Press, 2000.

Lustosa, Isabel. *Insultos impressos: A guerra dos jornalistas na Independência, 1821-1823.* São Paulo: Companhia das Letras, 2000.

Morel, Marco. *As transformações dos espaços públicos: Imprensa, atores políticos e sociabilidades na cidade imperial, 1820-1840.* São Paulo: Hucitec, 2005.

Schultz, Kirsten. *Tropical Versailles: Empire, Monarchy, and the Portuguese Royal Court in Rio de Janeiro, 1808-1821.* New York: Routledge, 2001.

Seckinger, Ron. *The Brazilian Monarchy and the South American Republics, 1822-1831: Diplomacy and State Building.* Baton Rouge: Louisiana State University, 1984.

LYDIA M. GARNER

BRAZIL, THE EMPIRE (SECOND).

The reign of Pedro II (1840–1889) was a period of recentralization, restoration of order and legitimate authority, state building, and economic development, especially in the years 1845–1870. Consensus among parties and the elite on fundamental issues promoted political unity and a liberal and stable regime. Federalism receded, and the cycle of revolts ended. Institutionalized control over the provinces was established as was crown authority over the executive and legislative branches. The Council of State was reinstated, and reform of the Criminal Procedures Code gave the executive control over the police and judiciary.

Empiricism and gradualism guided the government on legislation. Freedom of the press, a two-party system, and parliamentarism were institutionalized and electoral reforms were implemented. The banking, diplomatic, and administrative systems were organized, civil laws were consolidated, and a commercial code was compiled. The economy grew as Brazil became the leading exporter of coffee, as imports and exports increased, and as the tariff reform of 1844 strengthened finances. The quickening of the economy fostered railway building, introduction of steam navigation, construction of public works, incorporation of joint-stock companies, development of public utilities, increasing urbanization, and some industrial growth. Under British pressure the slave trade had ended, and in 1867 the government began to plan the gradual abolition of slavery. Beyond Brazil's borders progressive involvement in the Plata region helped to defeat Juan Manuel de Rosas of Argentina, but the War of the Triple Alliance (1865–1870) proved a costly victory for the empire. The last two decades of the monarchy brought impressive growth in population, immigration, wage labor, capital accumulation, and economic prosperity, as well as measures for administrative decentralization. It was also a time of ferment. The centralization that had provided stability was seen now as an impediment to progress. Divergent views and interests among elite groups broke the unity of the social and political pact. Positivism influenced the younger generation, especially that in the army, which developed a messianic view and contempt for civilian politicians. Old issues resurfaced. In the early 1870s, state control of the church on temporal matters led to the Religious Question, which only reinforced the perception of a powerful and unbending state. The law of the Free Womb (Free Birth Law) and the concept of gradual abolition of slavery were attacked as inadequate, and the abolitionist movement increasingly gained strength. Republican propaganda grew in its advocacy of federalism and changes in the moderative power and the Council of State.

The increasing unrest was only slightly checked by a complacent political elite, which was certain of the strength and solid foundations of the political system. In reality, the lack of mechanisms to handle and accommodate the compounding political and social changes occurring in society paralyzed the system, ensuring its demise. In 1888 Princess

Isabel abolished slavery by bypassing the traditional system of decision making. Unrest in the army, manipulated by a small group of civilians, led to the easy overthrow of the monarchy in 1889.

See also **Isabel, Princess of Brazil; Pedro II of Brazil; Slavery: Brazil.**

BIBLIOGRAPHY

Richard Graham, *Britain and the Onset of Modernization in Brazil, 1850–1914* (1968).

Robert Conrad, *The Destruction of Brazilian Slavery, 1850–1888,* 2d ed. (1972).

Emilia Viotti Da Costa, *The Brazilian Empire: Myths and Histories* (1985).

Leslie Bethell, ed., *Brazil Empire and Republic, 1822–1930* (1989).

Additional Bibliography

Barman, Roderick J. *Citizen Emperor: Pedro II and the Making of Brazil, 1825-1891.* Stanford: Stanford University Press, 1999.

Barman, Roderick J. *Princess Isabel of Brazil: Gender and Power in the Nineteenth Century.* Wilmington: SR Books, 2002.

Costa, Emília Viotti da. *The Brazilian Empire: Myths & Histories.* Rev. ed. Chapel Hill: University of North Carolina Press, 2000.

Costa, Wilma Peres. *A espada de Dâmocles: O exército, a Guerra do Paraguai e a crise do Império.* São Paulo: Editora Hucitec: Editora da UNICAMP, 1996.

Dolhnikoff, Miriam. *O pacto imperial: Origens do federalismo no Brasil.* São Paulo: Editora Globo, 2005.

Graham, Richard. *Patronage and Politics in Nineteenth-Century Brazil.* Stanford: Stanford University Press, 1990.

Grinberg, Keila. *O fiador dos brasileiros: Cidadania, escravidão e direito civil no tempo de Antonio Pereira Rebouças.* Rio de Janeiro: Civilização Brasileira, 2002.

Needell, Jeffrey D. *The Party of Order: The Conservatives, the State, and Slavery in the Brazilian Monarchy, 1831-1871.* Stanford: Stanford University Press, 2006.

Santos, Luís Cláudio Villafañe Gomes. *O império e as repúblicas do Pacífico: As relações do Brasil com Chile, Bolívia, Peru, Equador y Colômbia.* Curitiba: Editora UFPR, 2002.

LYDIA M. GARNER

BRAZIL, GEOGRAPHY. Brazil is characterized by diversity and marked regional contrasts. This variety reflects its size (3.3 million square miles), making it the world's fifth largest country. As the largest country in South America, it occupies almost half of the continent and is more than 2,700 miles in extent from north to south and from east to west. It is also essentially tropical, extending from 5 N to 33 S, with only 6 percent of its territory south of the Tropic of Capricorn. Bounded on the east by the Atlantic Ocean, it has frontiers with all the countries of South America except Chile and Ecuador. The lack of a Pacific seaboard may have inhibited notions of "manifest destiny," but the political boundaries, empty lands, and resource potential foster an active interest in Amazonia. The population is a mélange of Amerindians, Portuguese, Africans, south and east Europeans, and Asians, with a profound contrast in distribution between the coastlands and the still empty interior.

PHYSICAL ENVIRONMENT

Lowland areas (below 650 feet) are limited to the Amazon basin, the far south, the Pantanal of Mato Grosso, and a narrow coastal plain. Much of the country consists of upland, the Brazilian highlands south of the Amazon and the Guyana highlands to the north. These are formed by geologically ancient crystalline rocks, partially overlain by limestone and sandstone sediments, and in the south by basaltic lavas. The terrain is generally of gently rounded hills, with occasional resistant residuals on the crystalline areas and more angular tablelands in the sediments and basalts. Highest points are the Pico da Neblina (9,885 feet) on the Venezuelan border and the Pico de Bandeira (9,479 feet) in the southeast. The uplands closely abut the shore from Salvador to Pôrto Alegre as complex ranges or a single escarpment in excess of 2,500 feet.

This barrier is cut by few rivers, posing a major obstacle to colonial and contemporary access to the interior. The rivers are generally broken by falls and rapids, limiting their navigability. Those of the center form tributaries of the Amazon; the Paraná-Paraguay-Uruguay system debouches into the Río de la Plata, and the São Francisco parallels the coast for 750 miles before tumbling over the 275-foot Paulo Afonso Falls to reach the sea.

A humid tropical climate gives average temperatures above 68 F and rainfall above 47 inches, both of which vary with increasing altitude and latitude. Rainfall seasonality and temperature range increase away from the equator, and the interior Sertão (hinterland) of the northeast experiences low and markedly seasonal rainfall and occasional drought. Southern Brazil has a temperate climate, subject to frost hazard, which fosters a different agriculture.

The climax vegetation is mainly woodland, though varying from evergreen equatorial forest in Amazonia to tropical forest on the coastal uplands and the Araucária pine forest in the south. There are patches of grassland savanna in northern Amazonia, and the central highlands are covered by shrub grassland called *cerrado*. The semiarid Sertão sustains only poor *caatinga* thorn scrub, and southern Rio Grande do Sul has an extension of the pampas grassland.

The thick forests engendered notions of fertility, but most soils are fragile, leached, and of low productivity. Significant exceptions are the *massapé* soils of coastal Pernambuco and Bahia and *terra roxa* of the basalt plateaus.

Brazil is, however, evidently rich in other natural resources and these have exerted considerable influence on the pattern of occupation. Between 1500 and 1930 the development process can be described as the assembling of a loose jigsaw, as various resources were identified and exploited, prompting the settlement of different areas. These include dyewood along the coast before 1550, sugar on the *massapé* soils in the sixteenth and seventeenth centuries, gold in Minas Gerais, Goiás, and Mato Grosso (1690–1750), and coffee in Rio de Janeiro and São Paulo (1830–1930). Gathering of spices and later rubber fostered slight and largely ephemeral exploitation of Amazonia before 1910, and the *caatinga* and pampas supported pastoralism, which provided meat, hides, and draft animals for other regions. More recently base metals such as iron, manganese, and bauxite; abundant hydroelectricity; and, since 1970, offshore oil, have provided major resources for industrialization.

POPULATION

There has been rapid demographic growth in the twentieth century. From an estimated 3.8 million inhabitants at the end of the colonial period, Brazil's population rose to 17.4 million in 1900 and 51.9 million in 1950. By 1991, Brazil was the world's sixth most populous country with over 147 million inhabitants and by 2007 the number reached over 188 million. Between 1950 and 1980 the annual rate of increase often exceeded 2.2 percent, and consequently almost two-thirds of Brazilians were below twenty-five years of age. Brazil's yearly population growth rate has since fallen, and is estimated at just over one percent (2007).

The precolonial population has been calculated at about 2 million, but this was diminished by disease, warfare, miscegenation, and acculturation, and surviving Amerindians are mainly confined to Amazonia. Colonial immigration from Portugal was limited, possibly to around 1 million people, and an estimated 2.5 to 3 million African slaves imported between 1538 and 1850 provided much of the labor force. Following emancipation in 1888, there was substantial immigration from Iberia, Italy, Germany, and eastern Europe, and between 1908 and 1935 from Japan, to São Paulo and the south. Total foreign immigration between 1884 and 1933 was almost 4 million people. As a result of miscegenation Brazil's population is ethnically heterogeneous, but with significant regional variations in the admixture.

Overall population density is low, less than six persons per square mile, but there is a distinct contrast between the coastal states from Ceará to Rio Grande do Sul, with densities generally above twelve per square mile, and the interior of Amazonia and the center-west, where it is below two. Since 1950 the population has become increasingly urbanized, and in the twenty-first century it is estimated that more than 80 percent of Brazilians are now defined as urban dwellers. This urbanization has been fueled by migration from the countryside to the larger cities. More than 36 million people live in ten metropolitan regions, of which São Paulo, Rio de Janeiro, Belo Horizonte, Salvador, Recife, and Pôrto Alegre are the largest.

ECONOMY

Urban-based manufacturing and services dominate the gross domestic product and provide two-thirds of employment. The Brazilian economy ranks as the world's eleventh largest, and recent investments by the government and multinational corporations have given it the status of Newly Industrializing Country, with significant metal, engineering, and vehicle industries. The agricultural sector encompasses small-scale subsistence, traditional plantation crops such as sugar and coffee, pastoralism, and innovative production of soybeans, citrus, and vegetables.

As a consequence of economic development, profound spatial inequities exist, within the cities between skyscrapers and *favelas,* between the towns and the countryside, and regionally. Most of the stimuli of modernization have concentrated in the southeast and south and their principal cities. The northeast, particularly the *sertão,* remains impoverished, while the interior is still undeveloped, despite the construction of Brasília and major penetrative highways and the exploitation of minerals, timber, and land.

BIBLIOGRAPHY

Preston E. James, *Latin America,* 4th ed. (1969), pp. 683–897.

John Dickenson, *Brazil* (1982).

Instituto Brasileiro De Geografia E Estatística, *Geografia do Brasil,* 5 vols. (1989).

Instituto Brasileiro De Geografia E Estatística, *Anuário estatístico do Brasil, 1990* (1990).

Neil Mac Donald, *Brazil: A Mask Called Progress* (1991).

Additional Bibliography

Gallup, John Luke, Alejandro Gaviria, and Eduardo Lora. *Is Geography Destiny?: Lessons from Latin America.* Palo Alto: Stanford University Press; Washington, DC: World Bank, 2003.

Magnoli, Demétrio. *O corpo da pátria: Imaginação geográfica e política externa no Brasil, 1808-1912.* São Paulo: Editora UNESP Fundação: Editora Moderna, 1997.

Moraes, Antonio Carlos Robert. *Território e história no Brasil.* São Paulo: Editora Hucitec: Annablume, 2002.

Ross, Jurandyr L Sanches. *Geografia do Brasil.* São Paulo: Edusp: Fundação para o Desenvolvimento da Educação, 1996.

Vincent, Jon S. *Culture and Customs of Brazil.* Westport, CT: Greenwood Press, 2003.

JOHN P. DICKENSON

BRAZILIAN ACADEMY OF LETTERS.

Brazilian Academy of Letters, a Brazilian equivalent of the French Academy, founded in 1897. The academy's rules and rites reflected the centrality of French models for almost all formal cultural expression in nineteenth-century Brazil after the French Artistic Mission (1816). Its purpose was to celebrate earlier Brazilian literature and to promote present literary effort and literati as respectable and necessary constituents of society at a time when Brazil was perceived to be undergoing national regeneration. Founders of the academy included leading figures in the abolition movement (1888) and militants of the Republic (1889). Many were veterans of the era's new, mass-circulation periodicals; many, like other members of the social and political elites, were liberal professionals who cultivated belles lettres in their youth and leisure.

Unlike Joaquim Nabuco, better known as a celebrated abolitionist, most founders were contemporary literati who have since fallen into relative obscurity: like Coelho Neto, Olavo Bilac, José Veríssimo, Silvio Romero, and the Viscount de Taunay. However, there is one significant exception. The Forty Immortals were presided over by Machado De Assis, Brazil's preeminent novelist, who devoted his last years to the academy's survival. Early on, the ideal of literary integrity was challenged by the desire to cultivate public support through the inclusion of key public figures, a tendency that triumphed in that first generation. The goal of securing a place in the nation's establishment was thus satisfied, although many continue to despair at the cost.

See also **Literature: Brazil.**

BIBLIOGRAPHY

Josué Montello, *O presidente Machado de Assis* (1961).

João Alexandre Barbosa, *A tradição do impasse* (1974).

Nicolau Sevcenko, *Literatura como missão* (1983).

Jeffrey D. Needell, *A Tropical Belle Époque,* chap. 6 (1987).

Additional Bibliography

Graham, Richard. *Machado de Assis: Reflections on a Brazilian Master Writer.* Austin: University of Texas Press, 1999.

Trigo, Luciano and Aldo Arantes. *O viajante imóvel: Machado de Assis e o Rio de Janeiro de seu tempo.* Rio de Janeiro: Editora Record, 2001.

JEFFREY D. NEEDELL

BRAZILIAN EXPEDITIONARY FORCE (FEB).

Brazilian Expeditionary Force (FEB), a unit that served in Italy with U.S. General Mark Clark's Fifth Army from August 1944 to May 1945 in the Allied campaign against the German Nazis and Italian Fascists. Led by General João Batista Mascarenhas de Morais, the Força Expedicionária Brasileira, as the unit was known in its home country, was comprised of 25,334 officers and men, of whom some fifteen hundred were casualties. On 15 September 1944, the Sixth Regimental Combat Team (São Paulo) entered the line north of Pisa near the Serchio Valley and advanced northward as the Germans withdrew to the Gothic Line. By October only the First Division remained after two others were canceled by President Getúlio Vargas. The First Infantry, Sampaio (Rio de Janeiro), Eleventh Infantry (Minas Gerais), Divisional Artillery (Rio and São Paulo), Ninth Engineering Battalion (Mato Grosso), Second Motorized Reconnaissance Squadron (Rio), and First Medical Battalion (Rio and São Paulo) were deployed south of Bologna, in the Reno Valley, ahead of which lay Monte Castelo, a key position in the Gothic Line. The FEB launched four unsuccessful assaults on Monte Castelo between 24 November and 12 December 1944. After ten more cold, grueling weeks a fifth attack, on 21 February 1945, succeeded. The FEB pushed forward with the U.S. Tenth Mountain Division and by April received the surrender of three Italian divisions and the 148th German Grenadier Division. The Brazilians then pushed into the Po Valley and on to the French frontier.

Distrustful of this truly national, combat-tested force, Vargas disbanded it upon its return to Brazil in July 1945 and ignored General Mascarenhas. Chief of Staff Colonel Floriano de Lima Brayner was shipped back to Italy to care for the Brazilian cemetery at Pistóia, and the junior officers were posted to isolated interior garrisons. Nevertheless, many of the staff and line officers (henceforth called *Febianos*) later achieved prominence, especially during the 1964 revolution against President João Goulart, after which Chief of Operations Humberto Castello Branco served as president (1964–1967). Supporters of the uprising included Chief of Intelligence Amaury Kruel, who commanded the powerful Second Army (São Paulo), and Staff Liaison Officer Carlos de Meira Matos, who led the Minas Gerais column against Brasília. Brazilian-based FEB interior officer Henrique Batista Duffles Teixeira Lott served as minister of war (1954–1960) and was a presidential candidate (1960), and coconspirator Artur da Costa e Silva actually served as president (1967–1969).

Line officers João Segadas Vianna and Jurandir Mamede founded the Anti-Communist Crusade. Legalist infantry colonel Nélson de Melo served as minister of war (1961–1962) but later broke with Goulart and joined the conspiracy. Raimundo Ferreira de Souza led his Sampaio regiment against the Goulart government. Ernesto Geisel became president (1974–1979). On 29 October 1945 FEB Artillery Commander Oswaldo Cordeiro de Farias delivered the military's ultimatum to Vargas, provoking his resignation. The Febianos Cordeiro de Farias and César Obino were also instrumental in founding the Escola Superior Da Guerra (Superior War College), in 1949. Many Febianos made fast friends with U.S. liaison officer Vernon A. Walters, later the U.S. defense attaché to Brazil (1962–1967). Thus, the friendships forged on World War II Italian battlefields affected Brazil from 1945 on.

See also **Armed Forces; World War II.**

BIBLIOGRAPHY

João Batista Mascarenhas De Morais, *A FEB pelo seu comandante* (1947).

Joel Silveira, *As duas guerras da FEB* (1965).

Floriano De Lima Brayner, *A verdade sobre a FEB* (1968).

Raymond Estep, *The Military in Brazilian Politics, 1821–1970* (1971).

Lewis A. Tambs, "Five Times Against the System," in *Perspectives on Armed Politics in Brazil,* edited by Henry H. Keith and Robert A. Hayes (1976), pp. 177–206.

Vernon A. Walters, *Silent Missions* (1978).

Additional Bibliography

Ferraz, Francisco César Alves. *Os brasileiros e a Segunda Guerra Mundial.* Rio de Janeiro: Jorge Zahar, 2005.

Gonçalves, José and Cesar Campiani Maximiano. *Irmãos de armas: Um pelotão da FEB na II Guerra Mundial.* São Paulo: Códex, 2005.

LEWIS A. TAMBS

BRAZILIAN HIGHLANDS.

Brazilian Highlands (also, *Planalto central* or, less frequently, *Planalto Brasileiro*), a plateau region of southeastern Brazil located chiefly in the states of Minas Gerais and São Paulo. The climate is temperate. Elevations of the low mountains, hilly uplands, and tabular plateaus characteristic of the highlands average 1,970–2,950 feet above sea level and are generally highest near the Atlantic coast. The highlands meet the Atlantic coast in a steep slope called "the Great Escarpment," which stretches from the city of Salvador, Bahia, to Pôrto Alegre, Rio Grande do Sul. Three major river systems—the Amazon, the Paraná and the São Francisco—drain the region.

See also **Brazil, Geography.**

BIBLIOGRAPHY

Additional Bibliography

Thomas E. Skidmore, *Brazil: Five Centuries of Change* (1999).

CARA SHELLY

BRAZIL, INDEPENDENCE MOVEMENTS.

Unlike Spanish America, which experienced a long and at times bloody struggle for independence from Spain, Portuguese America was emancipated from European domination in three distinct steps: (1) in 1808 the prince regent and his court were established in Rio de Janeiro, and the ports of Brazil were formally opened to international commerce, ending the old mercantilist system; (2) in 1815 the United Kingdom of Portugal and Brazil was proclaimed; and (3) in 1822 the heir to the Portuguese throne, Dom Pedro I, declared Brazil's independence and became the first emperor of a new world monarchy. Much institutional and dynastic continuity was thus preserved in Brazil, and while there were separatist revolts (most significantly in Pernambuco in 1817), the transition from colonial to national status was considerably less traumatic than it was elsewhere in the hemisphere.

This outcome was partly the result of international circumstances and the particular relationship that the Portuguese Empire had with respect to the great naval power of the period, Great Britain. Yet the failure of a series of nationalist plots in Brazil in the last two decades of the eighteenth century also played a significant role. The most important of these conspiracies were in Minas (1788–1789) and Bahia (1798). Each was very different in composition, objectives, and consequences. The Minas conspiracy was republican in inspiration and looked to the newly established United States as a model. Involved in this plot were leading members of the regional oligarchy, including magistrates, priests, landowners, and businessmen, as well as the commanding officer of the local professional military and members of the officer corps, including the Alferes Joaquim José da Silva Xavier (Tiradentes). The Minas plotters wanted independence for Brazil but they equivocated over changes in Brazilian society and were divided in their attitudes toward slavery. The Bahian plot involved shopkeepers, soldiers, and even slaves, who, unlike the white elite members of the Minas group, were in the main African Brazilians and *pardos* (in colonial terminology, persons of mixed racial origins, originally applied to the offspring of African women and European men, but by the late eighteenth century this group encompassed almost a quarter of the population in many areas). The Bahian conspirators wished to see a revolution in social relationships and the elimination of discrimination based on skin color. They were more concerned with social reform than with independence and took as their model the revolution in France. But like the Minas plotters they were uncovered and imprisoned before they were able to act. The Portuguese authorities dealt with both plots harshly. Tiradentes was hanged and quartered and his co-conspirators exiled. The Bahian plotters were executed or abandoned along the African coast.

Enlightened members of the Portuguese government, however, used the failure of the two plots to co-opt leading younger Brazilian intellectuals by granting them access to government patronage and exploiting Brazilian elite fears of racial upheaval (something well demonstrated by the slave revolt in Haiti). Thus, young Brazilians like José Bonifácio de Andrada e Silva received a government scholarship for study and travel in Europe, high positions in the administration in Portugal, and membership in the Lisbon Academy of Sciences. Men like Andrada e Silva would later play key roles in the emergence of an independent Brazil, ruled by monarchical institutions and led by the Bragança dynasty.

See also **Inconfidência dos Alfaiates; Inconfidência Mineira.**

BIBLIOGRAPHY

Kenneth R. Maxwell, *Conflicts and Conspiracies: Brazil and Portugal, 1750–1808* (1973).

A. J. R. Russell-Wood, *From Colony to Nation: Essays on the Independence of Brazil* (1975).

Neill Macaulay, *Dom Pedro: The Struggle for Liberty in Brazil and Portugal, 1798–1834* (1986).

Additional Bibliography

Barman, Roderick. *Brazil: The Forging of a Nation, 1798–1852.* Stanford: Stanford University Press, 1988.

Barman, Roderick. *Citizen Emperor: Pedro II and the Making of Brazil, 1825–91.* Stanford: Stanford University Press, 1999.

Costa, Emilia Viotti da. *The Braziliam Empire: Myths and Histories.* Chapel Hill: University of North Carolina Press, 2000.

Graham, Richard. *Patronage and Politics in Nineteenth-century Brazil.* Stanford: Stanford University Press, 1990.

Janscó, István. *Independencia: Historia e historiografia.* São Paulo: Editora Hucitec, 2005.

Malerba, Jurandir. *As independencia brasileira: Novas dimensões.* Rio de Janeiro: FGV Editora, 2006.

Maxwell, Kenneth. *Naked Tropics: Essays on Empire and other Rogues.* New York: Routledge, 2003.

Maxwell, Kenneth. *Why Was Brazil Different? The Contexts of Independence.* Cambridge, MA: David Rockefeller Center for Latin American Studies, Harvard University, 2000.

Schultz, Kirsten. *Tropical Versailles: Empire, Monarchy, and the Portuguese Royal Court in Rio de Janeiro, 1808–1821.* New York: Routledge, 2001.

KENNETH MAXWELL

BRAZIL, LIBERAL MOVEMENTS.

Liberal movements during the monarchy (1822–1889) varied considerably between partisan developments and inchoate reform mobilizations. Responding to the absolutism and Portuguese interests associated with Pedro I, political and socioeconomic elite members and (often urban, middle-sector) radical ideologues joined in opposition. Although repressed in the Constituent Assembly of 1823 and the secessionist Confederation of the Equator (1824), they were successful in parliamentary obstruction after 1826. That, and the associated street violence and military insubordination, unexpectedly led the emperor to abdicate (1831).

Though colored by lusophobia, this movement emphasized the native elite's control of the state and their aspiration to more decentralized rule and revenue sharing at the local and provincial levels. These issues drove elite members to spurn the radicals (Exaltados) and form the Moderado Party, which dominated Parliament, elected the regents, nearly rewrote the Constitution of 1824, and did, in fact, reform it in the Additional Act of 1834. The Moderados hoped ideally to create a progressive nation; more pragmatically, they hoped to eliminate the possibilities of absolutist restoration and to secure political support in the face of rightist and leftist pressure. By 1835, certain elite groups held the decentralizing reforms responsible for uprisings that threatened social revolution and national dismemberment. Representatives of these groups left the Moderados, joined the reactionaries in parliament, and formed the Conservative Party, which soon dominated the state and began the legislative reversal of the reforms (1836–1841). The more liberal minority joined the *exaltados* to form the Liberal Party, and broke the Conservatives' control of the state by successfully conspiring to bring Pedro II to power in 1840. They correctly anticipated that he would call them to form his first cabinet. Their excesses, however, led the emperor's advisers to bring a more conservative cabinet to power (1841), which completed the legislative reaction and drove the Liberals of São Paulo and Minas Gerais to revolt (1842). Their military defeat crowned the success of the reactionaries and the creation of a highly centralized, authoritarian regime.

Ephemeral Liberal administrations and one failed revolt in the 1840s confirmed the subsequent era (1842–1862) as one in which reactionary triumph abruptly shifted to a kind of halting, conservative reformism in 1853. That year the emperor tapped the Conservative chieftain, the marquês de Paraná, to bring about partisan conciliation and electoral reform. After Paraná, the Conservatives' moderate wing reached out to the Liberals and led them toward the gradualist reformism of the Progressive League (ca. 1862–1868) and its cabinets (1862, 1864–1868).

The last such cabinet, beset by the purists of both parties, was undermined by the emperor, who then called in the reactionary cabinet of 1868. The Liberal response (ranging from the dramatic reforms of the Liberal Manifesto of 1869 to the 1870 formation of the Republican Party) reflected the florescence of 1860s criticism associated with such figures as Teofilo Ottoni and Aureliano Cándido Tavares Bastos. Critics called for the Abolition of Slavery, direct elections, separation of church and state, the reform or eradication of the crown's role, and decentralization. However, they lacked organizational or ideological unity. The Liberals, occasionally in power after 1878, divided over the choice and extent of reforms; the Republicans did not officially endorse abolition; and abolition had adherents in the two traditional parties.

However divided, such liberal reformism, often associated with the Generation of 1870 or the Recife School, suggests vague coherence and a general movement in opposition to the status quo (although positivism's increasing influence complicates the use of "liberal"). As such, it retains importance in understanding the milieu and mobilization that informed both the abolitionist movement (1879–1888) and the monarchy's political crisis, culminating in the Republic of 1889.

See also **Brazil: 1808-1889; Brazil, Political Parties: Liberal Party: Liberalism.**

BIBLIOGRAPHY

Joaquim Nabuco, *Um estadista do império*, 3 vols. (1898–1899).

Emilia Viotti Da Costa, *The Brazilian Empire* (1985).

Ilmar Rohloff De Mattos, *O tempo saquarema* (1987).

Roderick J. Barman, *Brazil: The Forging of a Nation* (1988).

Leslie Bethell, ed., *Brazil: Empire and Republic* (1989).

Richard Graham, *Patronage and Politics in Nineteenth-Century Brazil* (1990).

Additional Bibliography

Paim, Antônio. *História do liberalismo brasileiro.* São Paulo, Brazil: Editora Mandarim, 1998.

Silva, Ana Rosa Cloclet da. *Construçao da nação e escravidão no pensamento de José Bonifácio, 1783–1823.* Campinas, Brazil: Editora de Unicamp, Centro de Memória, 1999.

Tosto, Milton. *The Meaning of Liberalism in Brazil.* Lanham, MD: Lexington Books, 2005.

JEFFREY D. NEEDELL

BRAZIL, NATIONAL SECURITY DOCTRINE.

The National Security Doctrine was a set of principles and beliefs that evolved out of the Brazilian officer corps' participation in the dismantling of the empire in 1889. Out of that experience came the belief that the military was directly responsible for the well-being of the nation.

In the first quarter of the twentieth century, the officer corps, especially the army, considered the military as the only force capable of both building a national consciousness that superseded regional differences and solving the problems of the country. This view colored the military's vision of its mission and its role in society, and influenced its actions. Though the doctrine of national security grew out of early experiences, it was refined from 1949 to 1964 at the Escola Superior de Guerra (ESG, or Higher War School) and the Escola de Comando e Estado Maior do Exército (ECEME, or Army Command and General Staff School). The doctrine offered the rationale for the 1964 military coup that overthrew President João Goulart and provided the justification for repressive actions of the subsequent military governments. According to the doctrine, national security and economic development were possible only if Brazil's economic, political, and social structures were altered, and civilian elites lacked both the will and ability to make changes. Inherent in national security ideology was adherence to the capitalist development model, with government intervention, and anticommunism as espoused by the United States.

Courses studied at the ESG and ECEME, which included classes on inflation, banking reform, Land Tenure, voting systems, transportation, education, and conventional and guerrilla warfare, gave Brazilian officers the confidence that they had the ideology, trained personnel, and institutional will to maintain internal order while developing the country. That belief led the officer corps, many of whom helped formulate the national security doctrine as instructors or students at the ESG and ECEME, to overthrow the Goulart government and install a series of military presidents who attempted to implement the doctrine's precepts.

The economic policies of the various military governments attacked inflation and promoted rapid growth, which led to the so-called economic miracle.

Rapid development allowed the military governments to claim legitimacy on the basis of seemingly successful economic policies. Ironically, the "miracle" coincided with the period of the greatest political repression. Using the national security doctrine as justification, the military governments imposed censorship, eliminated popular participation in politics, controlled labor unions and political organizations, and curtailed civil and human rights. Political rights were denied opponents of the regimes, and arbitrary arrests, exile, torture, and murder with methods used in the name of national security through statutes such as the SNI Law, the National Security Law, AI-5, and the 1969 Constitution.

Use of the doctrine to justify government actions began to lose force with the relaxation of the system in the late 1970s and early 1980s, and seemed to disappear with the return to civilian rule in 1985. The officer corps now concentrates on preparation for external threats, and the development of technical expertise and institutional discipline; it generally takes a nonpolitical stance. Still, underlying military thinking is the concept that economic and social progress occurs when internal order is maintained.

See also **Brazil, National Security Law.**

BIBLIOGRAPHY

Numerous works speak of the national security doctrine but the most comprehensive is Antônio Arruda, *ESG História de sua doutrina* (1980). Alfred Stepan, ed., *Authoritarian Brazil: Origins, Policies, and Future* (1973), provides an excellent analysis in the chapter "Professionalism of Internal Order and Military Role Expansion." Formulation and implementation of the doctrine is sprinkled throughout Thomas E. Skidmore, *The Politics of Military Rule in Brazil, 1964–1985* (1988), and Ronald Schneider, *Order and Progress: A Political History of Brazil* (1991).

Additional Bibliography

Carvalho, José Murilo de. *Forças armadas e política no Brasil*. Rio de Janeiro: Jorge Zahar Editor, 2005.

Couto, Ronaldo Costa. *História indiscreta da ditadura e da abertura: Brasil: 1964-1985*. Rio de Janeiro: Editora Record, 1998.

SONNY B. DAVIS

BRAZIL, NATIONAL SECURITY LAW.

The National Security Law was a legal justification for the Brazilian military junta's crackdown on political opposition. Established on 29 September 1969, the law gave the government vast discretion in defining crimes against national security and allowed detention for up to twenty days without charge. Prohibited conduct included fomenting class struggle, distributing subversive propaganda, engaging in public strikes, and inciting collective disobedience. Criminal sanctions prevented journalists and editors from reporting events or opinions that violated the national security law. The numerous arrests under this law, frequently accompanied by torture, created a climate of fear that sustained the power of Brazil's authoritarian regime for over a decade.

See also **Brazil, National Security Doctrine.**

BIBLIOGRAPHY

Peter Flynn, *Brazil: A Political Analysis* (1972).

Maria Helena Moreia Alves, *State and Opposition in Military Brazil* (1985).

Thomas E. Skidmore, *The Politics of Military Rule in Brazil, 1964–85* (1988).

Additional Bibliography

Pereira, Anthony W. *Political (In)Justice: Authoritarianism and the Rule of Law in Brazil, Chile, and Argentina*. Pittsburgh, PA: University of Pittsburgh Press, 2005.

Reznik, Luís. *Democracia e segurança nacional: A polícia política no pós-guerra*. Rio de Janeiro: FGV, 2004.

MICHAEL A. POLL

BRAZIL, NEW REPUBLIC.

The New Republic, a term denoting both the period in Brazilian politics and the governmental system that began on 15 March 1985, when civilians regained control of the federal government after twenty-one years of authoritarian military rule. The transition to democratic civilian rule was the culmination of Abertura, a lengthy process of political liberalization that began in the late 1970s under military president João Baptista Figueiredo. Initially, Brazilians hoped that the New Republic would restore political freedoms and achieve economic growth under democratic procedures. The widespread social and political mobilization against military rule seemed to promise a period of more inclusive politics, incorporating grass-roots organizations, church-based social movements, and unionized labor into the more traditional political establishment. This optimism, however, has been marred by incessant political gridlock, economic stagnation, high inflation, scandal, and deteriorating social conditions, which plagued Brazil during the 1980s and 1990s.

The New Republic began under unexpectedly tense circumstances when illness prevented President-elect Tancredo Neves from assuming the presidency and Vice President–elect José Sarney was sworn in as "acting president." Sarney assumed full presidential powers the week before Neves's death in April 1985. Sarney's coalition government was an immediate victim of the widespread grief and disappointment surrounding Neves's death, as well as its own numerous political missteps. During his five-year presidency, Sarney was generally unsuccessful at effective leadership of the executive branch. The executive was unable to form a lasting coalition with the legislative branch to overhaul Brazil's political system. The Constituent Assembly, convened in late 1986 to write a new federal constitution, also proved ineffective in implementing most major reforms of the national political system. Although democratic procedures, most notably open elections and the lack of direct military intervention in politics, were consolidated and expanded during Sarney's presidency, a party system weakened by extreme factionalism and corruption undermined much of the program of political reform. Economic reform packages such as the Cruzado Plan (1986) and the Verão Plan (1989), which included currency devaluation, price controls, wage freezes, and debt renegotiations, provided only temporary respites from high inflation and economic instability.

Hopes for true change in national political and economic life were renewed during the 1990 presidential race, the first direct presidential elections in Brazil since 1960. In the November runoff election, former metalworker Luiz Inácio Lula da Silva, a candidate of the Workers Party (PT), faced the conservative governor of the state of Alagoas, Fernando Collor De Mello. Collor defeated Silva and immediately after assuming the presidency enacted a radical economic reform package that included strict price controls, the seizure of private assets, and the aggressive downsizing of the federal bureaucracy and state-owned enterprises. Like its predecessors, this economic stabilization package functioned briefly and drastically reduced inflation. The Collor administration crumbled when a 1992 congressional committee uncovered massive corruption within the executive branch. Collor was impeached and resigned in December 1992, and Vice President Itamar Franco became president. The Brazilian republican system continues to strain under the weight of a bloated federal bureaucracy, recurring economic recessions, and abysmal social disparities. The New Republic consolidated the end to active military presence in national politics, but not to the socioeconomic distortions of the authoritarian period. The economic stabilization package and political reforms introduced during the early months of Fernando Henrique Cardoso's presidency, which began in January 1995, were a continuation of the Plano Real he enacted in 1993 while he was serving as Brazil's Minister of Finance. Cardoso's successor was Luiz Inácio Lula da Silva, who won the presidency in 2002. Silva befriended both Venezuelan President Hugo Chávez and U.S. President George W. Bush in an effort to expand Brazil's presence in the international marketplace and to strengthen the country's economic position. Domestically, Silva enacted social programs to tackle what he saw as the country's most pressing needs: eliminating hunger, poverty, and child labor, and increasing education.

See also **Brazil: Since 1889.**

BIBLIOGRAPHY

John Wirth et al., eds., *State and Society in Brazil: Continuity and Change* (1987).

Thomas Skidmore, *The Politics of Military Rule in Brazil, 1964–85* (1988), pp. 256–310.

Alfred Stepan, ed., *Democratizing Brazil: Problems of Transition and Consolidation* (1989).

Sonia Alvarez, *Engendering Democracy in Brazil: Women's Movements in Transition Politics* (1990).

Miguel Reale, *De Tancredo a Collor* (1992).

Pedro Collor, *Passando a limpo: A trajetória de um farsante* (1993).

Additional Bibliography

Hagopian, Frances. *Traditional Politics and Regime Change in Brazil*. Cambridge, U.K.: Cambridge University Press, 1996.

Martínez-Lara, Javier. *Building Democracy in Brazil: The Politics of Constitutional Change, 1985–1995*. New York: St. Martin's Press, 1996.

Santos, Theotonio dos. *Evolução histórica do Brasil: Da colônia à crise da Nova República*. Petrópolis, Brazil: Vozes, 1995.

DARYLE WILLIAMS

BRAZILNUT INDUSTRY. The *castanha do Pará* (Pará chestnut) grows on black, Amazonian rain-forest giants (*castanheiras*) that tower 150 feet in the air and have a girth of 20 feet. Gatherers wait until the grapefruit-sized *ouriço* (outer casing) falls to the ground before collecting the fifteen to twenty nutritious nuts (17% protein) found inside the hard casing. One tree produces between 250 and 500 pounds of nuts in a good season. The nuts are so important to the Amazonian economy that the Brazilian government passed a law in 1965 making it illegal to cut down *castanheiras*.

In January, gatherers, who often double as *seringueiros* (rubber gatherers), begin harvesting the nuts. They break open the shells with machete-type knives (*terçados*), leaving the heavy, bulky *ouriços* on the forest floor. Some *seringueiros* collect more than three tons of Brazilnuts in one rainy season. They take their harvest to the trading center (*barracão*), where in 1989 they were paid three or four cents a pound for unshelled Brazilnuts. Shelling plants process the nuts, which are soaked for twenty-four hours, placed in boiling water for a few minutes, then shelled with a hand-operated machine. The majority of shelling plants are located in Pará and Bélem.

Before World War II, most Brazilnuts were exported to Europe; afterwards, the United States received most of them; and by 1990, the United States imported $16 million worth of Pará chestnuts annually. In 2007, Brazil shipped approximately 27,000 tons of Brazilnuts abroad. Bolivia has also entered the market, becoming a major competitor for Brazil. The nuts became such an important part of the extractive reserve program begun in the 1980s that manufacturers soon produced and marketed other Brazilnut products, such as hair conditioners, based on its oil, to appeal to environmentally conscious consumers. Many environmental groups promote Brazilnuts because gathering them harms the rain forest far less than other types of agricultural development.

See also **Extractive Reserves; Seringueiros.**

BIBLIOGRAPHY

Benjamin H. Hunnicutt, *Brazil: World Frontier* (1969).

Andrew Revkin, *The Burning Season* (1990).

Additional Bibliography

Homma, Alfredo Kingo Oyama. *História da agricultura na Amazônia, da era pré-colombiana ao terceiro milênio*. Brasília: Embrapa Informação Tecnológica, 2003.

Kainer, Karen A. "Enrichment Prospects for Extractive Reserves in a Nutshell: Brazil Nut Germination and Seedling Autecology in the Brazilian Amazon." Ph.D. diss., University of Florida, 1997.

Wood, Charles W., and Roberto Porro. *Deforestation and Land Use in the Amazon*. Gainesville: University Press of Florida, 2002.

CAROLYN JOSTOCK

BRAZIL, ORGANIZATIONS

This entry includes the following articles:

NATIONAL STUDENTS UNION (UNE)

PASTORAL LAND COMMISSION (CPT)

PEASANT LEAGUES

SUPERINTENDENCY FOR THE DEVELOPMENT OF AMAZONIA (SUDAM)

SUPERINTENDENCY OF AGRARIAN REFORM (SUPRA)

SUPERIOR MILITARY TRIBUNAL

UNION OF FARMERS AND AGRICULTURAL LABORERS OF BRAZIL (ULTAB)

UNION OF INDIGENOUS NATIONS (UNI)

ADVANCED INSTITUTE OF BRAZILIAN STUDIES (ISEB)

Created by Decree 37608 on 14 July 1955, the ISEB was devoted to the study of Brazilian development problems. Part of the Ministry of Education and Culture, ISEB had its roots in the private Brazilian Institute of Economics, Sociology, and Politics (IBESP). The ISEB was designed as a vehicle through which leading academics could address issues of development and industrialization by pursuing research and providing training courses to Brazilian government officials. From its beginning at the start of the Juscelino Kubitschek presidency, the ISEB supported the nationalist-developmentalist policies of the administration. The ISEB included among its scholars Hélio Jaguaribe, Cândido Mendes de Almeida, Roberto Campos, Nélson Werneck Sodré, and Roland Corbisier. Plagued by internal divisions and political disputes, the ISEB was reorganized in 1959 and many of its members resigned. The institute became increasingly nationalistic in its views on development and foreign investment, and broadened the political scope of its activities to establish ties to student groups, syndicalists, the Communist Party (PCB), and various nationalist groups. The military government that seized power in 1964 closed the ISEB and opened an investigation into the activities of its members and the political leaders who had supported it.

See also **Campos, Roberto (de Oliveira); Kubitschek de Oliveira, Juscelino.**

BIBLIOGRAPHY

Thomas E. Skidmore, *Politics in Brazil* (1967).

Israel Beloch and Alzira Alves De Abreu, eds., *Dicionário histórico-biográfico brasileiro, 1930–1983* (1984).

Additional Bibliography

Sodré, Nelson Werneck. *A ofensiva reacionária*. Rio de Janeiro: Bertrand Brasil, 1992.

Toledo, Caio Navarro de. *Intelectuais e política no Brasil: A experiência do ISEB*. Rio de Janeiro: Editora Revan, 2005.

William Summerhill

BRAZILIAN BAR ASSOCIATION (OAB)

The Brazilian Bar Association (Ordem dos Avogados do Brasil—OAB) is authorized by the Brazilian government to regulate entry to the bar and to uphold professional conduct among lawyers. Its predecessor was the Instituto da Ordem dos Advogados Brasileiros, founded in 1843, when statutes were approved by the emperor, Dom Pedro II. The OAB was effectively organized in 1931, with government approval of the statutes coming in December of that year. As of the early 2000s the OAB's organization stems from 1963 legislation that recognizes it as an organ working in the public interest and that mandates a federated structure. In each state capital there is a section of the OAB, with councilors who serve as members of the Federal Council of Lawyers. Also serving as members of the council are all its former presidents. The presidencies of the Federal Council and of the OAB are coextensive and are customarily occupied by well-known and highly reputable lawyers. The OAB has regularly published a law journal and a newsletter. The OAB has often been at the forefront in defending human and civil rights and in upholding democratic institutions, whether in the twenty-first century, during the period of redemocratization, or at earlier turbulent periods of Brazilian history.

See also **Brazil, National Security Law.**

BIBLIOGRAPHY

Coelho, Fernando. *A OAB e o regime militar, 1964–1986*. Recife, Brazil: Ordem dos Advogados do Brasil, Secção de Pernambuco, 1996.

Machado, Rubens Approbato, and Hermann Assis Baeta. *História da Ordem dos Advogados do Brasil*. 4 vols. Brasília: OAB, Conselho Federal, 2003.

Skidmore, Thomas E. *Politics in Brazil, 1930–1964: An Experiment in Democracy*. New York: Oxford University Press, 1967.

Skidmore, Thomas E. *The Politics of Military Rule in Brazil, 1964–1985*. New York: Oxford University Press, 1988.

Stepan, Alfred, ed. *Democratizing Brazil: Problems of Transition and Consolidation.* Oxford, U.K.: Oxford University Press, 1989.

OLAVO BRASIL DE LIMA JÚNIOR
DOUGLAS COLE LIBBY

Presidência da república, secretaria do meio ambiente, instituto brasileiro do meio ambiente e dos recursos naturais renovaacute;veis— IBAMA, *Coletânea da legislação federal de meio ambiente* (1992).

LAURA JARNAGIN

BRAZILIAN INSTITUTE OF THE ENVIRONMENT AND RENEWABLE NATURAL RESOURCES (IBAMA)

The Brazilian Institute of the Environment and Renewable Natural Resources (Instituto Brasileiro do Meio Ambiente e dos Recursos Naturais Renováveis—IBAMA) enforces federal environmental laws and international treaties with environmental content to which Brazil is a signatory. Created in 1988 under President José Sarney, the institute initially suffered a severe lack of human and financial resources. Sarney's successor, Fernando Collor de Mello, accorded the environment a higher priority in his administration and elevated IBAMA to the status of an autonomous ministry. Resource allocation to IBAMA then improved, but chronic insufficiencies remained the norm.

In Brazil's decentralized postmilitary political system, a significant amount of environmental protection is being implemented by state agencies, not IBAMA. Its most visible activities tend to be in the Amazon, where, with all nine states that comprise Legal Amazonia, IBAMA has made accords to interact with their law enforcement agencies in the protection of flora and fauna. Endeavors to reduce deforestation are utilizing satellite technology to identify sites of illegal burning, with mixed results; a decrease in deforestation in one year has been followed by an increase the next, perhaps due as much to climatic factors (wet versus dry years) as to IBAMA's enforcement efforts.

See also **Environmental Movements.**

BIBLIOGRAPHY

Bibliography

Schmink, Marianne, and Charles H. Wood. *Contested Frontiers in Amazonia* (1992).

"International Network Formed to Map Tropical Deforestation by Satellite," *International Environment Reporter: Current Report* 13, no. 2 (14 February 1990): 65–66.

"Brazil Beefs Up Efforts Aimed at Slowing Amazon Deforestation," *International Environment Reporter: Current Report* 13, no. 14 (21 November 1990): 485–486.

BRAZILIAN LABOR CONFEDERATION (COB)

As an increasing number of artisans and tradesmen organized mutual aid societies and unions in the first years of the twentieth century, anarchist and socialist leaders in Rio and São Paulo saw the need for a central labor organization. Rio labor leaders formed a regional labor federation in 1903, and in 1906 they sponsored Brazil's first national labor congress. These labor leaders formed the Confederação Operária Brasileira (COB) in 1908 to help coordinate national labor policies.

The COB represented some fifty unions throughout Brazil, but more than half of them were located in the cities of Rio and São Paulo. The Confederação published a national labor newspaper, the pro-anarchist *A Voz do Trabalhador,* which sought to coordinate union and leftist politics. As an umbrella organization, the COB was only as effective as the unions it represented. COB activists sponsored the Second National Labor Congress in 1913 to establish a set of national policies for Brazilian workers. The participants protested the federal government's antilabor practices, especially its use of a 1907 deportation law to expel foreign-born anarchists.

The COB not only had to contend with government repression, it also presided over a weak and divided labor movement. Divisions by ethnicity, race, and gender plagued Brazil's nascent labor movement in the first two decades of the twentieth century. Union and leftist groups also conducted ideological debates. Many anarchists concentrated on cultural and educational programs for the working class and did little to organize among the rank and file. With the advent of World War I, many of them articulated antiwar positions while ignoring such issues as the increasing cost of living and the intensification of work regimes on the shop floor. The persistent weakness of local unions undermined the effectiveness of the COB. The Confederação faded during the 1910s, but many of its leaders went on to participate in the Third National Labor Congress in 1920 and continued to coordinate anarchist activities throughout Brazil in the 1920s and early 1930s.

See also **Labor Movements; World War I.**

BIBLIOGRAPHY

One of the most complete studies of the early labor movement is John W. F. Dulles, *Anarchists and Communists in Brazil, 1900–1935* (1973). The most complete single volume on workers and labor in these years is Boris Fausto, *Trabalho urbano e conflito social* (1976). For an analysis of the rise and fall of the anarchist movement, see Sheldon L. Maram, "Labor and the Left in Brazil, 1890–1921: A Movement Aborted," in *Hispanic American Historical Review* 57 (1977): 254–272. For analyses of the divisions within the labor movement in São Paulo, see George Reid Andrews, "Black and White Workers: São Paulo, Brazil, 1888–1928," in *Hispanic American Historical Review* 68 (1988): 491–524, and Joel Wolfe, "Anarchist Ideology, Worker Practice: The 1917 General Strike and the Formation of São Paulo's Working Class," in *Hispanic American Historical Review* 71 (1991): 809–846.

Additional Bibliography

Alexander, Robert Jackson, and Eldon M. Parker. *A History of Organized Labor in Brazil.* Westport, CT: Praeger, 2003.

Alves, Paulo. *Anarquismo e anarcosindicalismo: Teoria e prática no movimento operário brasileiro, 1906–1922.* Curitiba: Aos Quatro Ventos, 2002.

Aurélio Santana, Marco. *Homens partidos: Comunistas e sindicatos no Brasil.* Rio de Janeiro: Universidade do Rio de Janeiro; São Paulo: Boitempo Editorial, 2001.

Batalha, Claudio H. M. *O movimento operário na Primeira República.* Rio de Janeiro: Jorge Zahar Editor, 2000.

Caira Gitahy, Maria Lucia. *Ventos do mar: Trabalhadores do porto, movimento operário e cultura urbana em Santos, 1889–1914.* São Paulo: Editora UNESP, Fundação para o Desenvolvimento da UNESP; Cidade de Santos: Prefeitura Municipal de Santos, 1992.

Wolfe, Joel. *Working Women, Working Men: São Paulo and the Rise of Brazil's Industrial Working Class, 1900–1955.* Durham, NC: Duke University Press, 1993.

JOEL WOLFE

DEMOCRATIC RURAL UNION (UDR)

The Democratic Rural Union (União Democrática Ruralista—UDR) was formed in Brazil in 1985 to represent the interests of large landowners and cattle ranchers in the debate over agrarian reform that accompanied the transition from military to civilian rule. Started in the prairie lands of central Brazil, the UDR soon became a national presence, due in part to its provocative founding president, the Goiás-based physician and rancher Ronaldo Ramos Caiado.

The UDR developed a reputation as the most reactionary of landowner groups, the shock troop at the front of the battle against land reform. Raising money through widely publicized cattle auctions, the UDR organized mass rallies in the nation's capital and enhanced its political power through campaign contributions and running its own candidates. The UDR took credit for the absence of land distribution measures in the October 1985 agrarian reform law and tried, unsuccessfully, to exclude the issue from the 1988 national constitution.

In 1989, Caiado ran for president as the UDR candidate, receiving a small percentage of votes. Thereafter, the UDR pursued two characteristic strategies: It continued to lobby government to slow the agrarian reform process and it threatened violence to prevent landless peasants from occupying disputed lands. In various cases, UDR members were implicated as the alleged sponsors of gunmen who killed peasant and rural labor activists.

While the UDR could take credit for frustrating agrarian reform, the very existence of the organization raised questions about the strength of Brazil's rural elite and showed how far the country had come from the days when the rural oligarchy could take its influence for granted.

See also **Agrarian Reform; Agriculture.**

BIBLIOGRAPHY

Chico Mendes, *Fight for the Forest* (1989).

Biorn Maybury-Lewis, *The Debate Over Agrarian Reform in Brazil* (Papers on Latin America, no. 14, Columbia University, 1990); and "UDR cria milícia armada contra sem-terra," in *Folha de São Paulo* (30 June 1994): p. 9.

Additional Bibliography

Bruno, Regina. *Senhores da terra, senhores da guerra: A nova face política das elites agroindustriais no Brasil.* Rio de Janeiro: Forense Universitária: Editora Universidade Rural, 1997.

Payne, Leigh A. *Uncivil Movements: The Armed Right Wing and Democracy in Latin America.* Baltimore, MD: Johns Hopkins University Press, 2000.

CLIFF WELCH

DEVELOPMENT SUPERINTENDENCY OF THE NORTHEAST (SUDENE)

The Development Superintendency of the Northeast (SUperintendência do DEsenvolvimento do NordEste—SUDENE) was a Brazilian government agency concerned with the economic development of the country's northeastern coastal and Sertão regions. Established in 1959 under President Juscelino Kubitschek, the agency attempted to address the growing economic unrest that prevailed in the impoverished Northeast by means of creating tax breaks for producers and exporters. The Brazilian Congress allocated the necessary funds and gave SUDENE the authority to control and coordinate the activities of other federal agencies in the Northeast so as to incorporate northeastern Brazil into the country's industrializing economy and reduce the region's dependence upon agriculture.

The Brazilian economist Celso Furtado, a renowned economic structuralist and colleague of Raúl Prebish at the Economic Commission for Latin America and the Caribbean (ECLA), directed SUDENE between 1959 and 1964. He drafted ambitious policy programs for attracting industries to the Northeast, which used fiscal incentives as lures. Participating firms received a tax credit that allowed them to reduce their income tax liabilities and invest the tax savings in SUDENE projects. In 1961 President John F. Kennedy extolled the program, which led to significant U.S. funding through USAID and continued funds put forth by the Brazilian government. The military-controlled government that dominated state and national politics between 1964 and 1985, however, hampered SUDENE projects and debated the merits of the political and social aspects of SUDENE's modernization plan, causing SUDENE to fall short of many of its goals. The importance of the Northeast's agrarian structure prevailed, and attempts to combat unemployment through industrialization generated relatively few jobs in the wider region because most firms were located in the cities of Recife and Salvador. SUDENE, nevertheless, is a significant example of Brazilian industrial development policy. The program encouraged private investment by local and foreign investors to promote regional development. Remnants of the program continued into the beginning of 2001, in the form of tax concessions.

See also **Economic Commission for Latin America and the Caribbean (ECLAC); Furtado, Celso; Kubitschek de Oliveira, Juscelino.**

BIBLIOGRAPHY

Alexander, Robert J. *Juscelino Kubitschek and the Development of Brazil.* Athens: Ohio University Center for International Studies, 1991.

Baer, Werner. *The Brazilian Economy: Growth and Development,* 6th edition. Boulder, CO: L. Rienner, 2007.

Borello, José Antonio. "Una evaluación del programa de industrialización de la SUDENE: El caso de Pernambuco, Brasil, 1960–1975." *Revista Geográfica* (January–June 1989): 157–165.

Martins, Mônica Dias, and Laurence Hallewell. "Globalization and Development in Brazil." *Latin American Perspectives* 29, no. 6 (2002): 94–99.

Roett, Riordan. *The Politics of Foreign Aid in the Brazilian Northeast.* Nashville, TN: Vanderbilt University Press, 1972.

Santana, Jorge Fernando de. "O planejamento regional do Nordeste brasileiro e o papel da SUDENE." *Revista Brasileira de Geografia* 51, no. 2 (1989): 5–15.

CHARLENE VAN DIJK

ESCOLA SUPERIOR DA GUERRA (ESG)

Brazil's Superior War College. Following the failure of two short-lived military institutions in the 1890s and 1930s, the ESG was founded in 1949 on the recommendation of a commission of the General Staff (now the General Staff of the Combined Armed Forces), which, after surveying the post–World War II political and strategic scene, concluded that Brazil possessed all the geopolitical prerequisites to become a world power but lacked a political elite prepared to lead the nation to prosperity and international prestige. The commission thus favored the founding of an institution to prepare promising civilian and military personnel with the potential to rise to the highest levels of political, economic, social, and strategic leadership.

The ESG was initially commanded by General Oswaldo Cordeiro de Farias, a veteran of the Revolution of 1930 and of the Brazilian Expeditionary Force (FEB) of 1944–1945. From this early association with the military reformers (*Tenentes*) and the World War II veterans (*Febianos*), who had been trained by the French Military Mission of 1919–1940, these military intellectuals and civilian technocrats came to prominence after the coup of 1964 and were referred to as the Sorbonne Group.

The curriculum of the ESG centers on the *curso superior,* a study of development, strategy, and internal and international policies. It is open to officers of all three services above the rank of lieutenant colonel or its equivalent, as well as selected civilians—academics, government functionaries, and businessmen—who are generally in the majority. The final phase of the program consists of teams engaged in simulated strategic planning on various issues.

The ESG also offers courses on the General Staff of the Combined Armed Forces as well as on national mobilization. Seminars on current topics are scheduled all year. The motto of the ESG, "Security and Development" (a modern version of Comtian "Order and Progress"), is disseminated by the ESG's Alumni Association, which is active throughout Brazil.

See also **Brazilian Expeditionary Force (FEB).**

BIBLIOGRAPHY

Thomas E. Skidmore, *Politics in Brazil: 1930–1964* (1967).

Raymond Estep, *The Military in Brazilian Politics, 1821–1970* (1971).

Henry H. Keith and Robert A. Hayes, eds., *Perspectives on Armed Politics in Brazil* (1976).

José Osvaldo de Meira Penna, *O Dinossauro* (1988).

Additional Bibliography

Ferraz, Francisco César Alves. *A sombra dos carvalhos: Escola Superior de Guerra e política no Brasil, 1948–1955.* Londrina: Editora UEL, 1997.

LEWIS A. TAMBS

FRENTE AGRÁRIA (FA)

In 1962, the Brazilian Catholic Church established the Frente Agrária to promote the interests of rural workers through the formation of labor unions. Begun in the South, the Frente was preceded in the Northeast by the church's Rural Assistance Service (SAR; founded 1949) and Rural Orientation Service of Pernambuco (SORPE: founded 1961). New church teachings promulgated by the peasant-born Pope John XXIII inspired the young priests who led the organization. Although the Church wanted them to combat communism and Peasant League influences in the countryside, some of the Frente's radical clergy eventually worked together with Communists in the Superintendency of Agrarian Reform (SUPRA). The 1964 mili-

tary coup d'état suppressed the front and jailed its leaders.

See also **Agrarian Reform; Catholic Church: The Modern Period.**

BIBLIOGRAPHY

Emanuel de Kadt, *Catholic Radicals in Brazil* (1970).

Thomas C. Bruneau, *The Political Transformation of the Brazilian Catholic Church* (1974).

Additional Bibliography

Bandeira, Marina. *A Igreja Católica na virada da questão social (1930–1964): Anotações para uma história da Igreja no Brasil: (ensaio de interpretação).* Rio de Janeiro: Editora Vozes: Educam: Centro Alceu Amoroso Lima para a Liberdade, 2000.

Stédile, João Pedro, and Douglas Estevam. *A questão agrária no Brasil.* 2nd ed. São Paulo: Editora Expressão Popular, 2005.

CLIFF WELCH

GENERAL LABOR COMMAND (CGT)

As Brazil's first functioning national trade union confederation, the General Labor Command (Comando Geral dos Trabalhadores—CGT) spoke for an insurgent labor movement that demonstrated organizational sophistication and an unprecedented capacity for mass mobilization during the early 1960s. The creation of a unified national labor organization, banned by law, had been heatedly debated in 1960 at the Third National Union Congress in Rio de Janeiro. After ousting conservatives from the National Confederation of Industrial Workers (CNTI) the next year, the proponents of a more aggressive and independent union movement formed a coordinating body during an August 1961 strike in support of João "Jango" Goulart's accession to the presidency following the resignation of Jânio Quadros. This General Strike Command was renamed the General Labor Command during the Fourth National Union Congress held in São Paulo in August 1962. The CGT was to be an "organ of orientation, coordination, and direction" linking legally recognized unions, federations, and confederations throughout Brazil.

Although never legally recognized, the CGT nonetheless played a prominent role in political and economic affairs in the last years of the Populist Republic. Led by a new generation of Communist, nationalist, and *trabalhista* (laborite) trade unionists, the CGT experimented with the use of general strikes that involved hundreds of thousands of workers. In 1962 the CGT organized Brazil's first politically motivated strikes that could credibly claim to be national in scope.

With the CGT's top leaders increasingly elected to local, state, and national legislative bodies, organized labor fought boldly for a program of change inspired by the *reformas de base* (basic reforms) of Goulart and his Brazilian Labor Party (PTB). Although the CGT's power was exaggerated, it won a number of important victories including the thirteenth salary (a legally mandated Christmas bonus) and the legalization of rural trade unionism. In March 1964, however, Goulart and his supporters proved too weak to prevent the right-wing military coup that outlawed the CGT and persecuted its leaders and supporters.

See also **Communism; Labor Movements.**

BIBLIOGRAPHY

On the CGT, see Lucília de Almeida Neves Delgado, *O Comando Geral dos Trabalhadores no Brasil 1961–1964* (1981) and Sérgio Amad Costa, *O C.G.T. e as lutas sindicais Brasileiras (1960–1964)* (1981). For more general treatments, see Kenneth P. Erickson, *The Brazilian Corporative State and Working-Class Politics* (1977); and Jover Telles, *O movimento sindical no Brasil* (1962; repr. 1981). On two key CGT leaders and their base in Rio de Janeiro, see Hércules Corrêa, *A Classe Operária e seu Partido* (1980); and issue #3 of *Memoria e Historia* (1987) on Roberto Morena.

Additional Bibliography

Gouveia, Oserias. *Os descaminhos da utopia: Glória e derrocada do comunismo na memória política de militantes dos anos sessenta.* Recife: Editoria Universitária UFPE, 2004.

Kushnir, Beatriz. *Perfis cruzados: Trajetórias e militância política no Brasil.* Rio de Janeiro: Imago, 2002.

Penna, Lincoln de Abreu. *Roberto Morena, o militante.* São Paulo: Editora Expressão Popular, 2006.

Souza, Donaldo Bello de., Marco Aurélio Santana, and Neise Deluiz. *Trabalho e educação: Centrais sindicais e reestruturação produtiva no Brasil.* Rio de Janeiro: Quartet, 1999.

JOHN D. FRENCH

GETÚLIO VARGAS FOUNDATION (FGV)

A quasi-governmental but politically independent research and education center, the Getúlio Vargas Foundation (Fundação Getúlio Vargas—FGV) was created in 1944 by Luís Simões Lopes, the head of the Departamento Administrativo do Serviço Público (DASP), during the Estado Nôvo as part of an effort to make the bureaucracy more efficient and professional. The FGV studies administrative problems and trains future administrators.

In the early 2000s, FGV is a vast complex of institutes, schools, centers, and a press that provides scholarly impetus in economics, public administration, accounting, education, human resources, political science, contemporary history, and documentation. FGV economists established the Instituto Brasileiro de Economia (IBRE) and the publications *Revista Brasileira de Economia* and *Conjuntura Econômica*, as well as a graduate school in economics. They have provided three finance ministers, a minister of planning, a president of the Central Bank, and a president of the National Development Bank (BNDE). In public administration, the FGV created two graduate schools and a research center (Rio de Janeiro and São Paulo) and two journals, *Revista de Administração Pública* and *Revista de Administração de Empresas*. Similar leadership has been exercised in political science with the Instituto de Direito Público e Ciência Política (INDIPO), which offers graduate courses and publishes the *Revista de Ciência Política*. Linked to INDIPO is perhaps the best-organized archive in Latin America, the Centro de Pesquisa e Documentação de História Contemporanea (CPDOC). CPDOC focuses on post-1930 Brazilian political history and has the personal papers of most of the men who shaped the 1930–1964 period.

See also **Brazil, Organizations: National Bank for Economic Development (BNDE).**

BIBLIOGRAPHY

Robert T. Daland, ed., *Perspectives of Brazilian Public Administration* (1963).

Israel Beloch and Alzira Alves De Abreu, eds., *Dicionário histórico-biográfico brasileiro, 1930–1983*, vol. 2 (1984), 1407–1408.

W. Michael Weis, "The Fundação Getúlio Vargas and the New Getúlio," in *Luso-Brazilian Review*, 24, no. 2 (1987): 49–60.

Additional Bibliography

Lamounier, Bolivar, Dionísio Dias Carneiro Netto, and Marcelo de Paiva Abreu. *50 Years of Brazil: 50 Years of Getulio Vargas Foundation.* Rio de Janeiro: Fundação Getulio Vargas, Editoraa, 1995.

W. MICHAEL WEIS

INDIAN PROTECTION SERVICE (SPI)

Originally known as the Service for the Protection of Indians (Serviço de Proteção ao Indio) and the Settlement of National Workers (SPILTN), the SPI was the first Brazilian federal agency charged with protecting Indian peoples against acts of frontier violence, persecution, and extermination. In the wake of the first public international accusations of indigenous genocide (XVI Congress of Americanists in Vienna, 1908) and in the midst of a period of intense national debate concerning the rights of indigenous peoples, President Nilo Peçanha, on 20 June 1910, signed Decree no. 8.072, the legislation mandating the formation of the SPI under the directorship of General Cândido Mariano da Silva Rondon. Reflecting the positivist ideals of Rondon and his supporters, this legislation recognized the rights of indigenous peoples to the lands they traditionally inhabited, as well as to their traditional customs, and provided for the demarcation of lands for which indigenous peoples would have exclusive usufructory rights. The SPI was charged with ensuring implementation of this legislation and also for facilitating the establishment of new settlements in areas previously unoccupied by peoples of European descent.

To mediate against the possibility of violent interethnic conflicts, Rondon adopted a strategy, known as pacification, for establishing friendly relations with previously uncontacted indigenous peoples. In a country as vast as Brazil and with a consistently small operating budget, the SPI had difficulty carrying out its responsibilities. From the 1920s until its dissolution, the SPI was fraught with scandal and corruption. It was replaced by the National Indian Foundation (funai) in 1967.

See also **Indigenous Peoples; Peçanha, Nilo Procópio.**

BIBLIOGRAPHY

Shelton H. Davis, *Victims of the Miracle: Development and the Indians of Brazil* (1977), pp. 1–18.

Manuela Carneiro Da Cunha, *Os direitos do índio: Ensaios e documentos* (1987), pp. 78–82.

Greg Urban and Joel Sherzer, eds., *Nation-States and Indians in Latin America* (1991), esp. pp. 218–222, 236–258.

Additional Bibliography

Diacon, Todd. *Stringing Together a Nation: Candido Mariano da Silva Rondon and the Construction of a Modern Brazil, 1906–1930.* Durham, NC: Duke University Press, 2004.

LAURA GRAHAM

INDIGENIST MISSIONARY COUNCIL (CIMI)

Indigenist Missionary Council (Conselho Indigenista Missionário—CIMI) was founded in 1972 by the Catholic bishops of Brazil to defend the rights of Brazilian Indians. In a reversal of the former view of how missionary effort should be directed, CIMI has seen as its primary duty not the conversion of Indians to Christianity but the conversion of the wider society to a recognition of the Indians' right to self-determination. The council has worked in support of the Indians' cultural distinctiveness, and has aided their efforts to regain and secure traditional lands. CIMI has denounced acts of violence against and economic exploitation of Indians, and has assisted Indian leaders in setting up their own organizations and in defining common problems and strategies.

See also **Catholic Church: The Modern Period; Indian Policy, Brazil; Missions: Brazil.**

BIBLIOGRAPHY

Thomas C. Bruneau and W. E. Hewett, "Catholicism and Political Action in Brazil: Limitations and Prospects," in *Conflict and Competition: The Latin American Church in a Changing Society,* edited by Edward R. Cleary and Hannah Stewart-Gambino (1992), pp. 45–62.

Judith R. Shapiro, "Ideologies and Catholic Missionary Practice in a Post-Colonial Era," in *Comparative Studies in Society and History,* vol. 23, no. 1 (1981), pp. 130–149, and "From Tupã to the Land Without Evil: The Christianization of Tupi-Guarani Cosmology," in *American Ethnologist* 14 (1987): 125–133.

Additional Bibliography

Luz, Lídia. *Outros 500: Construindo uma nova história.* São Paulo: Editoria Salesiana, 2001.

NANCY M. FLOWERS

MOVIMENTO SEM TERRA

In January 1984 some one hundred peasants, priests, labor union leaders, and intellectuals founded the Movimento dos Trabalhadores Rurais Sem Terra (MST; Landless Rural Workers Movement) in Cascavel, Paraná. It united peasants struggling to preserve their farms as well as those who had already lost either their land or livelihoods as a result of rampant capitalist agricultural development policies promoted by transnational corporations and Brazil's military regime. Advocating an aggressive agrarian reform, the MST used direct occupations of land to force its redistribution, helping more than two million people settle in farm communities by 2004. Tithing, political independence, participatory democracy, and cultural activities designed to fortify a common peasant identity secured both organizational vitality and loyalty. Its successes inspired dozens of copycat organizations, but none achieved the institutional durability that has enabled the MST to establish a place as one of the world's most successful social movements.

See also **Agrarian Reform; Land Tenure, Brazil.**

BIBLIOGRAPHY

Branford, Sue, and Jan Rocha. *Cutting the Wire: The Story of the Landless Movement in Brazil.* London: Latin American Bureau, 2002.

Fernandes, Bernardo Mançano. *A formação do MST no Brasil.* Petrópolis, Brazil: Editora Vozes, 2000.

CLIFF WELCH

NATIONAL BANK FOR ECONOMIC DEVELOPMENT (BNDE)

Created in 1952 by the Joint Brazil–United States Economic Commission (1951–1953), the National Bank for Economic Development (Banco Nacional de Desenvolvimento Econômico e Social—BNDES; originally the BNDE) has been the major source of long-term financing of capital investment in Brazil since its creation. The scope of its operations was somewhat limited in the 1950s. The Bank Reform Act (Law 4595 of 1964), however, expanded its functions and programs by creating a group of special funds designed to serve different sectors of the economy, the most important of which was the Special Agency of Industrial Financing (FINAME). The BNDES's funds stem from two forced savings funds: the Program of Social Integration (PIS) and the Public Employees Financial Reserve Fund (PASEP, originally at the Bank of Brazil). The BNDE carried out a selective credit policy according to the norms determined by the National Monetary Council (CMN) through the network of public and private development banks set up with the 1964–1966 reforms.

The main publicly owned development banks subordinate to the BNDES are the Bank of the Northeast (BNB, 1952), the Bank of Amazonia (BASA, 1966), the National Bank of Cooperative Credit (BNCC, 1966), the Regional Development Bank of the Extreme South (BRDE, 1962), and the state development banks, which are owned and operated by the various states. The BNDES also owns its own participation corporation, BNDES Participações (BNDESPAR), to spur equity financing in addition to the BNDES system's role as a minority shareholder.

The divestiture (privatization) of enterprises held by the BNDES, started in late 1991, should decrease the BNDES's role in direct ownership of the Brazilian corporate structure. However, the BNDES should still have an important role in financing basic infrastructure investment.

See also **Banking: Since 1990; Economic Development.**

BIBLIOGRAPHY

John H. Welch, *Capital Markets in the Development Process: The Case of Brazil* (1993).

Additional Bibliography

Bacha, Edmar Lisboa and Luiz Chrysostomo de Oliveira Filho. *Mercado de capitais e crescimento econômico: Lições internacionais, desafios brasileiros.* Rio de Janeiro: Contra Capa Livraria: ANBID: IEPE, CdG, 2005.

Love, Joseph LeRoy. *Crafting the Third World: Theorizing Underdevelopment in Rumania and Brazil.* Stanford, CA: Stanford University Press, 1996.

JOHN H. WELCH

NATIONAL CONFERENCE OF BRAZILIAN BISHOPS (CNBB)

Created in 1952, the National Conference of Brazilian Bishops (Confêrencia Nacional dos Bispos do Brasil—CNBB) has become the most important organization within the Brazilian Catholic Church. It was one of the first national episcopal conferences in the world and the first one in Latin America. Although the CNBB and other national episcopal conferences have circumscribed authority according to canon law, the CNBB has been of fundamental importance, for it has given the Brazilian church a centralized structure and a voice on behalf of the country's bishops.

Between 1952 and 1964, the CNBB supported ecclesiastical innovation and many reformist measures promoted by Brazil's governments. During this period, Bishop Hélder Câmara, the prime mover behind the CNBB's creation, served as secretary-general. In 1964, however, support grew within the Brazilian hierarchy for more conservative positions, and shortly after the military coup, the CNBB issued a statement that praised the armed forces for their intervention. Known for their progressive orientations, Câmara and his supporters were defeated by a conservative slate in CNBB elections in October 1964.

In 1968, Bishop Aloísio Lorscheider was elected secretary-general and began a new period of CNBB activism. During the 1970s, the CNBB became known for its criticisms of human rights violations, its calls for more attention to the plight of the poor, and its support for ecclesiastical innovations, especially Christian Base Communities. It also became a more organized institution that presented official church reactions to major public issues; by 1968 it was the only legitimate national voice for the Brazilian Catholic Church. In the 1980s, reflecting worldwide trends in the Roman Catholic Church as well as a period of democratization in Brazil, the CNBB retreated from the more visible political role it had assumed in the 1970s. Representing about 370 bishops, it is one of the three largest national bishops' conferences in the world.

See also **Catholic Church: The Modern Period; Liberation Theology.**

BIBLIOGRAPHY

Thomas Bruneau, *The Political Transformation of the Brazilian Catholic Church* (1974), esp. pp. 107–126.

Gervásio Fernandes De Queiroga, *Conferência Nacional dos Bispos do Brasil: Comunhão e corresponsabilidade* (1977).

Additional Bibliography

Catholic Church, The. *Pronunciamentos da CNBB: 1997–2003.* 2nd ed. São Paulo: Edições Paulinas, 2004.

Félix, Loiva Otero, Daniela Oliveira Silveira, and Maria A. Ghisleni. *Escrevam porque as ditaduras não duram para sempre.* Passo Fundo: Universidade de Passo Fundo, 2004.

Guider, Margaret Eletta. *Daughters of Rahab: Prostitution and the Church of Liberation in Brazil.* Minneapolis, MN: Fortress Press, 1995.

Mainwaring, Scott. *The Catholic Church and Politics in Brazil, 1916–1985.* Stanford, CA: Stanford University Press, 1986.

SCOTT MAINWARING

NATIONAL GUARD

The part-time civilian militia in Brazil that was established on 18 August 1831 during the politically tumultuous period following Brazilian independence from Portugal. In its founding charter the militia was pledged to defend the Constitution of 1824 and to maintain internal order. The new government hoped that the force would counterbalance the army, which still harbored Portuguese officers whose loyalties were suspect. Though it persisted into the twentieth century, when it became a mere reserve force of the army (as determined by the Constitution of 1934), the National Guard played its most significant role during the forty years following its formation.

Participation in the National Guard was mandatory for free men between the ages of eighteen and sixty who were not already serving in another military force and who possessed the minimum annual income required for voting. Guard units were organized by county, and most members were artisans, modest farmers, or petty businessmen—in short, a group which stood several notches above the poorest men, who were often forcibly recruited into the army. Although men of color were admitted from the beginning, their chance to become officers narrowed in the 1830s, when reform measures in many provinces deprived the rank and file of the right to elect local officers and placed provincial governments in charge of the appointments. This change precipitated the Guard's slide into the mire of electoral fraud, as officer positions were bestowed on those who could swing the vote in the right direction. The process was accelerated between 1850 and 1871, during which time local units often became the personal armies of the rural colonels who commanded them.

Although the National Guard drew praise for its performance in the War of the Triple Alliance (1864–1870), its past could not be erased, and the state finally curtailed its functions in 1873. From that point on, the Guard lost its policing powers and would be called into action only during times of extreme crisis.

See also **War of the Triple Alliance.**

BIBLIOGRAPHY

Sources in English are limited, though a good discussion is found in Fernando Uricoechea, *The Patrimonial Foundations of the Brazilian Bureaucratic State* (1980). See also Jeanne Berrance De Castro, *A milícia cidadã: A Guarda Nacional de 1831 a 1850* (1977).

Additional Bibliography

Ribeiro, José Iran. *Quando o serviço os chamava: Milicianos e guardas nacionais no Rio Grande do Sul (1825–1845)*. Santa Maria: Editora UFSM, 2005.

JUDITH L. ALLEN

NATIONAL HOUSING BANK (BNH)

Created as part of the financial market reforms of Humberto Castelo Branco's administration by Law 4380 of 1964, the National Housing Bank (Banco Nacional de Habitação—BNH) served as the center of the Housing Finance System (Sistema Financeira de Habitação—SFH). The reformers designed the system to create a supply of mortgage funds for lower-income groups, to be financed through the creation of inflation-indexed passbook savings deposits. The BNH supervised the activities of three sets of institutions: the state and federal savings banks (*caixas econômicas estaduais e federais*), the housing credit societies (*sociedades de crédito imobiliário*), and savings and loan associations (*associações de poupança e emprestimo*). Like many thrift systems throughout the world, the Brazilian thrift system has suffered from significant nonperforming loans and difficulties competing with other parts of the financial system. Any improvement in the Brazilian government's fiscal situation and the efficiency of the financial system was anticipated to depend upon the improvement in financial status of these institutions. As a first step to this adjustment, the government dissolved the BNH in the reforms of 1987–1989.

See also **Banking: Since 1990; Economic Development.**

BIBLIOGRAPHY

John H. Welch, *Capital Markets in the Development Process: The Case of Brazil* (1993).

Additional Bibliography

Banco Nacional da Habitação. *Plano nacional da habitação popular*. Rio de Janeiro: Secretaria de Divulgação do BNH, 1973.

Faro, Clóvis de. *Vinte anos de BNH: A evolução dos planos básicos de financiamento para aquisição da casa própria do Banco Nacional de Habitação, 1964–84*. Niterói: Editora Universitária, Universidade Federal Fluminense; Rio de Janeiro, RJ: Editora da Fundação Getulio Vargas, 1992.

JOHN H. WELCH

NATIONAL INDIAN FOUNDATION (FUNAI)

Successor to the Indian Protection Service (or SPI), the National Indian Foundation (Fundação Nacional ao Índio—FUNAI) is the governmental agency charged with the protection of the rights of indigenous peoples and the demarcation of their lands. The agency was established in 1967 at the urging of the minister of the interior, General Albuquerque Lima, in response to allegations of administrative corruption among officials of the SPI and findings of an investigative commission led by Attorney General Jader Figueiredo (Figueiredo Report [1968]). Although founded to rectify the corruption and misdeeds of the SPI, FUNAI itself has had a checkered history, with instances of corruption, neglect of its responsibility to demarcate indigenous lands, failure to protect the interests of those whom the agency is purported to defend, and economic exploitation. For example, since its establishment, the agency has been involved in numerous scandals invoking illegal mineral and timber extraction. One reason for these problems is that, prior to the Constitution of 1988, FUNAI was subordinate to the Ministry of the Interior, an administrative status that often conflicted with the agency's legal objectives. To repair the agency's ambiguous structural position, the new constitution transferred its supervision to the Ministry of Justice.

In 1986, following a period of administrative chaos during which FUNAI had five different presidents in a one-year period, the agency underwent reorganization. Its form as a centrally administered agency with headquarters in Brasilía and multiple regional *delegacias*, was decentralized such that greater regional administrative power was localized in five *superintendencias* (Curitiba, Cuiabá, Recife, Belém, Manaus)—a change that enabled regional political and economic interests to have greater sway in questions related to indigenous peoples. Moreover, because it provided a space for local economic interests to reassert themselves in decisions related to indigenous peoples, such as use of land, decentralization effectively offset the benefits of FUNAI's changed administrative status within the Ministry of Justice under the new constitution. In addition FUNAI was made responsible for coordinating services provided by other ministries (for example, Education, Health, and Welfare) rather than for offering these services itself, as previously.

The first decade of the twenty-first century has been marked by tenuous relations between Indigenous groups and FUNAI, especially after the Foundation's president, Mércio Pereira Gomes, announced to the press in January 2006 that indigenous people have too much land in Brazil, suggesting that Supreme Court needed to define limits.

See also **Brazil, Organizations: Indian Protection Service (IPS); Indigenous Peoples.**

BIBLIOGRAPHY

Shelton H. Davis, *Victims of the Miracle: Development and the Indians of Brazil* (1977).

Centro De Documentação E Informação, *Povos indígenas no Brasil—85/86.* Aconteceu Especial 17.

LAURA GRAHAM

NATIONAL INSTITUTE OF COLONIZATION AND AGRARIAN REFORM

National Institute of Colonization and Agrarian Reform (Instituto Nacional de Colonização e Reforma Agrária; INCRA) was founded in 1970 during General Emílio Garrastazu Médici's presidency. It was one of several agencies created under the 1964–1985 military-technocratic authoritarian regime to develop the Amazon Region. Its four main tasks were: to alleviate conflict over land tenure; to resettle thousands of landless peasants, especially from the northeast of Brazil; to establish peasant cooperatives to provide economic support; and to standardize and modernize existing legal forms of large-scale ownership so as to increase production and hence government revenues. In the twenty-first century, sustainable development and diversification aiming to reduce rural-to-urban migration has risen in the agency's priorities. Programs designed to register rural workers and their families have also been implemented. Particularly in the northeast, INCRA continues to expropriate unproductive areas for resettlement.

INCRA's dual role of simultaneously supporting both colonization projects and large land sales to various capitalist enterprises was inherently too contradictory for the agency to do both well. By the mid-1970s, INCRA was acquiescing to political and economic pressures from business groups, usually to the detriment of colonization projects, which were expensive undertakings under the best of conditions. As a result, original settlement goals never came close to being met, and many settlements were later abandoned.

After the establishment of Brazil's new democracy in the mid-1980s, INCRA's mandate emphasized agrarian reform, support to settlements, and clarification of property titles for lands held in abeyance since José Sarney's administration. INCRA reported to the minister of agriculture and agrarian reform until 2000, when the Institute came under the supervision of the newly created Ministry of Agrarian Development (Ministério do Desenvolvimento Agrário).

See also **Land Tenure, Brazil; Médici, Emílio Garrastazú.**

BIBLIOGRAPHY

Scholarly treatments of INCRA are usually subsumed in broader works treating agrarian reform or development of the Amazon in general, or have been the subject of doctoral dissertations. One of the best and most comprehensive studies of INCRA in English is found in Stephen G. Bunker, *Underdeveloping the Amazon: Extraction, Unequal Exchange, and the Failure of the Modern State* (1985). See also Otávio Guilherme Velho, *Capitalismo autoritário e campesinato: Um estudo comparativo a partir da fronteira em movimento* (1976).

Peter Flynn, *Brazil: A Political Analysis* (1978); esp. pp. 451–454.

Thomas E. Skidmore, *The Politics of Military Rule in Brazil, 1964–1985* (1988), esp. pp. 298–302.

Additional Bibliography

Abramovay, Ricardo, and Milton Silvestro. *Juventude e agricultura familiar: Desafios dos novos padrões sucessórios.* Brasília: Edições UNESCO, 1998.

Almedia, Anna Luiza Ozorio de. *The Colonization of the Amazon.* Austin: University of Texas Press, 1992.

Alston, Lee J., Gary D. Libecap, and Bernardo Mueller. *Titles, Conflict, and Land Use: The Development of Property Rights and Land Reform on the Brazilian Amazon Frontier.* Ann Arbor: University of Michigan Press, 1999.

Arruda, Hélio Palma de. *Desenvolvimento rural, atuação do INCRA: Palestra.* Brasília: Ministério da Agricultura,

Instituto Nacional de Colonização e Reforma Agrária (INCRA), Departamento de Projetos e Operações, 1974.

Fico, Carlos. *Reinventando o otimismo: Ditadura, propaganda e imaginário social no Brasil.* Rio de Janeiro: Fundação Getúlio Vargas, Editora, 1997.

Graziano Neto, Francisco. *O carma da terra no Brasil.* São Paulo: A Girafa, 2004.

Martins, José de Souza. *A militarização da questão agrária no Brasil: Terra e poder, o problema da terra na crise política.* Petrópolis, Brazil: Vozes, 1984.

Medeiros, Leonilde Sérvolo de, ed. *Assentamentos rurais: Uma visão multidisciplinar.* São Paulo: Editora Unesp, Fundação para o Desenvolvimento da UNESP, 1995.

LAURA GRAHAM

NATIONAL STUDENTS UNION (UNE)

The National Students Union (União Nacional dos Estudantes—UNE) emerged from the Second National Students Conference, held in Rio de Janeiro in 1938. Formally recognized by presidential decree in 1942 as the representative entity of Brazil's university students, the UNE initially devoted itself to creating branches throughout the states. The UNE's organization inspired similar efforts at the level of Brazilian secondary schools, giving rise to the Secondary Students Union of Brazil (UBES). The UNE soon devoted itself to political issues beyond the universities, working during 1940–1941 to secure Brazil's entry into World War II on the side of the Allies. It also participated in campaigns against the "fifth column" and provided domestic support to the Brazilian Expeditionary Force. Later in the 1940s and 1950s the UNE led political campaigns in defense of the state petroleum monopoly, in opposition to the rising cost of living, and in support of an independent foreign policy. In the early 1960s the UNE pursued university reforms, leading a strike in 1962 that shut down almost all of Brazilian higher education for three months. In 1967–1968 the UNE staged protests against the dictatorship in major Brazilian cities. Government repression and imprisonment of student leaders in the late 1960s made it difficult for the organization to maintain its bases of support and level of activity. The UNE returned to the public arena only with the lessening of repression in the second half of the 1970s. University and high school students in 1992 actively participated in the protests against the corruption of President Fernando Collor. In contrast to the organized strikes of the 1960s, this manifestation was more spontaneous and less aligned with student organizations.

See also **World War II.**

BIBLIOGRAPHY

Thomas E. Skidmore, *Politics in Brazil, 1930–1964* (1967).

Israel Beloch and Alzira Alves De Abreu, eds., *Dicionário histórico-biográfico brasileiro, 1930–1983* (1984).

Additional Bibliography

Barcellos, Jalusa. *CPC da UNE: Uma história de paixão e consciência.* Rio de Janeiro: Editora Nova Fronteira; IBAC/MINC, 1994.

Fávero, Maria de Lourdes de A. *UNE em tempos de autoritarismo.* Rio de Janeiro: Editora UFRJ, 1995.

Saldanha, Alberto. *A UNE e o mito do poder jovem.* Maceió, Brazil: UFAL, 2005.

WILLIAM SUMMERHILL

PASTORAL LAND COMMISSION (CPT)

The Pastoral Land Commission (Comissão Pastoral da Terra—CPT) is an organ of the Brazilian Catholic Church that deals with the problems of the poor in rural areas. Linked to the progressive sectors of the church, it was officially created in its present form in 1975; its precursor dates back to 1972. The CPT was created in response to a need felt by radical pastoral agents, who sought an end to the widespread violence of landowners and the state against the rural poor during the period of military rule (1964–1985), especially in the Amazon region. It offers legal services, encourages the creation of rural unions, denounces the use of violence against the rural poor, and offers courses in faith and politics.

Since its creation, the CPT has been highly controversial. It regularly clashed with the military government and large landowners, which saw the CPT as obstructionist and even subversive. It has also come under fire from conservative bishops, who believe that the CPT is excessively involved in politics, that it has at times incited peasants to seize land, that it is too close to the Workers' Party, and that it reduces the Bible's message to a political one.

See also **Catholic Church: The Modern Period; Liberation Theology.**

BIBLIOGRAPHY

Commissão Pastoral da Terra, *CPT: Pastoral e compromisso* (1983).

Vanilda Paiva, ed., *Igreja e questão agrária* (1985), esp. pp. 129–136, 248–273.

Additional Bibliography

Adriance, Madeleine. *Promised Land: Base Christian Communities and the Struggle for the Amazon.* Albany, NY: State University of New York Press, 1995.

Poletto, Ivo, and Antônio Canuto. *Nas pegadas do povo da terra: 25 anos da Comissão Pastoral da Terra.* São Paulo: Edições Loyola, 2002.

SCOTT MAINWARING

PEASANT LEAGUES

Various *ligas camponensas* were formed after World War II to defend the interests of tenant and small farmers and rural laborers. There were two distinct phases of league activity, one (1945–1947) led by the Brazilian Communist Party (PCB), and the other (1955–1964) led by peasants, students, and politicians from the Northeast. By the time they were suppressed, the Peasant Leagues had attained both national and international notoriety.

With political liberalization in 1945, the PCB established leagues throughout Brazil and used them to register new voters. By enfranchising thousands of peasants, many Communists won electoral office. In 1947, the government suppressed the PCB and its leagues were disbanded. In 1955, a former PCB militant organized the Agricultural Society of Farmers and Ranchers (SAPP) at the Galiléia plantation in Pernambuco State. To red-bait SAPP, landowners called it a "peasant league," but their plan backfired and dozens of Peasant Leagues formed throughout the state and region.

The leagues, headed by Francisco Julião, achieved national recognition in 1960, when they forced the state government to divide Galiléia lands among peasants. Dedicated to a policy of confiscating land without compensating owners in cash, the Peasant Leagues' call for agrarian reform "by law or by force" became predominant in the rural labor movement. In 1962, the leagues expanded into thirteen of Brazil's twenty-two states and started a weekly newspaper, *Liga.* Numerous groups of students, women, and soldiers imitated the peasants by naming their organizations "*ligas.*"

The leagues' growth peaked in 1963 when internal squabbles fractured the organization. A decentralized structure enabled some local leaders to emphasize land seizures, others union organizing, and still others armed rebellion. When news of league guerrilla bands reached the United States, the Kennedy administration made the Northeast a test case for Alliance for Progress programs designed to thwart revolution. The PCB and Catholic Church also challenged the leagues. Isolated, they were repressed by the military in 1964.

See also **Brazil, Political Parties: Brazilian Communist Party (PCB); Julião Arruda de Paula, Francisco.**

BIBLIOGRAPHY

Shepard Forman, *The Brazilian Peasantry* (1975).

Florencia Mallon, "Peasants and Rural Laborers in Pernambuco, 1955–1964," in *Latin American Perspectives* 5, no. 4 (1978):49–70.

Elide Rugai Bastos, *As ligas camponesas* (1984).

Additional Bibliography

Aued, Bernardete Wrublevski. *A vitória dos vencidos: Partido Comunista Brasileiro—PCB—e ligas camponesas, 1955–64.* Florianópolis: Editora da UFSC, 1986.

Bombardi, Larissa Mies. *O bairro reforma agrária e o processo de territorialização camponesa.* São Paulo: Annablume, 2004.

Pereira, Anthony W. *The End of the Peasantry: The Rural Labor Movement in Northeast Brazil, 1961–1988.* Pittsburgh, PA: University of Pittsburgh Press, 1997.

Santiago, Vandeck. *Francisco Julião, as Ligas e o golpe militar de 64.* Recife: Comunigraf Editora, 2004.

Welch, Cliff. *The Seed Was Planted: The Saõ Paulo Roots of Brazil's Rural Labor Movement, 1924–1964.* University Park: Pennsylvania State University Press, 1999.

CLIFF WELCH

SUPERINTENDENCY FOR THE DEVELOPMENT OF AMAZONIA (SUDAM)

Superintendency for the Development of Amazonia (Superintendencia do Desenvolvimento da Amazonia—SUDAM) was a Brazilian government agency that administered developmental projects in Amazonia—a vast 2-million-square-mile area of northern Brazil, with a 2005 population of 6-7 million. Created in 1966, SUDAM was headquartered in Belém, Pará. The agency oversaw the Fiscal Incentive Law of October 1966, which granted tax exemptions and deductions for certain investments within the region. The agency emphasized projects that called for territorial occupation for the extraction of regional resources by regional labor.

In 1970 disputes over land ownership between SUDAM-supported ranchers and indigenous Indians and rural peasants led to violence. By 1973 the upheaval caused a shift in government policy from supporting homesteads to promoting large agribusiness interests, whose purpose was to lay the groundwork for the expansion of large domestic and multinational agribusinesses into the Amazon Basin and to increase the export agricultural capacity of the Brazilian economy. These new goals threatened the territorial integrity of indigenous and peasant populations, increasing the disparities between land-poor and land-rich inhabitants, while creating a class of exploited agricultural workers. This decreased the food supply in the domestic market, which worsened the severe pattern of hunger and malnourishment already present.

Into the twenty-first century, SUDAM's primary mission remained the development of the Amazon Basin. Yet in the face of deforestation, continuing violence, lawlessness, and a massive corruption scandal involving high-ranking politicians, the Brazilian government closed the agency in 2002.

See also **Brazil, Geography; Indigenous Peoples.**

BIBLIOGRAPHY

Stefan H. Robock, *Brazil: A Study in Development Progress* (1975).

Shelton H. Davis, *Victims of the Miracle* (1977).

Lawrence S. Graham and Robert H. Wilson, *The Political Economy of Brazil: Public Policies in an Era of Transition* (1990).

Additional Bibliography

Little, Paul E. *Amazonia: Territorial Struggles on Perennial Frontiers.* Baltimore, MD: Johns Hopkins University Press, 2001.

Posey, Darrell Addison, and Michael J. Balick, eds. *Human Impacts on Amazonia: The Role of Traditional Ecological Knowledge in Conservation and Development.* New York: Columbia University Press, 2006.

Schmink, Marianne, and Charles H. Wood. *Contested Frontiers in Amazonia.* New York: Columbia University Press, 1992.

MICHAEL J. BROYLES

SUPERINTENDENCY OF AGRARIAN REFORM (SUPRA)

SUPRA, established in October 1962, was an executive-branch agency charged with implementing the rural policies of President João Goulart, including land and labor reforms. SUPRA distributed some land to landless peasants and started a campaign to form 2,000 unions, establish 500 labor courts, and register 3 million new voters by 1965. To do this, SUPRA opened dozens of regional offices and contracted experienced Communist and Catholic labor organizers. The effort was to regiment the fractious rural labor movement and thereby weaken the rural oligarchy. Hundreds of new unions had been established by April 1964, when the military coup d'état outlawed SUPRA and persecuted its agents for subversion.

See also **Goulart, João Belchior Marques.**

BIBLIOGRAPHY

John W. F. Dulles, *Unrest in Brazil: Political and Military Crises, 1955–1964* (1970), pp. 220–275.

Aspásia de Alcântara Camargo, "A questão agrária: Crise de poder e reforma de base," in *História de civilização brasileira,* no. 10, tomo 3, *O Brasil republicano,* vol. 3, *Sociedade e politica* (1930–1964), edited by Boris Fausto, 3d ed. (1986), pp. 121–224.

Additional Bibliography

Pereira, Anthony W. *The End of the Peasantry: The Rural Labor Movement in Northeast Brazil, 1961–1988.* Pittsburgh, PA: University of Pittsburgh Press, 1997.

Stédile, João Pedro, and Douglas Estevam. *A questão agrária no Brasil.* 2nd ed. São Paulo: Editora Expressão Popular, 2005.

Welch, Cliff. *The Seed Was Planted: The São Paulo Roots of Brazil's Rural Labor Movement, 1924–1964.* University Park: Pennsylvania State University Press, 1999.

CLIFF WELCH

SUPERIOR MILITARY TRIBUNAL

The Superior Military Tribunal is Brazil's military supreme court. This judicial body came to prominence in national life after the 1964 military coup. Under a variety of institutional acts and the Constitution of 1967, civilians charged with crimes relating to national security were removed from the jurisdiction of the civilian courts and put under the jurisdiction of this military court. The power of the Superior Military Tribunal even extended to the governors of Brazil's constituent states, who no longer had special forums in which to be tried. This judicial body also was empowered to silence and punish military officers who were critical of the regime.

The use of the military tribunal for trying individuals charged with political crimes was the result of pressure from conservative hardliners angered over the ability of individuals to appeal to civilian courts after being tried by Military Police Investigation panels. Extending the jurisdiction of the Superior Military Tribunal enabled the military regime to toss aside a variety of legal guarantees, especially the right of habeas corpus, and made it much easier for the regime to ignore the rights of political prisoners. A wide variety of regime critics were tried by the Superior Military Tribunal, including intellectuals, labor leaders, politicians, and military officers. The jurisdiction of the tribunal effectively ended in 1978 with a reform package that restored some individual legal safeguards and independence to the nation's judicial system.

See also **Brazil, Revolutions: Revolution of 1964.**

BIBLIOGRAPHY

Ronald M. Schneider, *The Political System of Brazil: Emergence of a "Modernizing" Authoritarian Regime, 1964–1970* (1971).

Peter Flynn, *Brazil: A Political Analysis* (1978).

Maria Helena Moreira Alves, *State and Opposition in Military Brazil* (1985).

Additional Bibliography

Gaspari, Elio. *A ditadura envergonhada*. São Paulo: Companhia das Letras, 2002.

Lemos, Renato. *Justiça fardada: O General Peri Bevilaqua no superior tribunal military (1965–1969)*. Rio de Janeiro: Bom Texto, 2004.

Skidmore, Thomas E. *The Politics of Military Rule in Brazil, 1964–1985*. New York: Oxford University Press, 1988.

SONNY B. DAVIS

UNION OF FARMERS AND AGRICULTURAL LABORERS OF BRAZIL (ULTAB)

Founded in 1954, Union of Farmers and Agricultural Laborers of Brazil (Uniãodos Lavradores e Trabalhadores Agrícolas do Brasil—ULTAB) helped the Brazilian Communist Party (PCB) coordinate and control the national rural labor movement. Although non-Communists participated in ULTAB, the party paid the salaries of top directors such as Lindolfo Silva and Heros Trench and financed ULTAB's monthly journal, *Terra Livre*. Active in nearly every state, ULTAB enabled the PCB to overwhelm rivals like the Peasant Leagues and Frente Agrária.

With headquarters in São Paulo's state capital, ULTAB sought to weaken the influence of the state's powerful coffee- and sugar-growers' lobby by unionizing sugarcane and coffee harvesters. While providing a welcome challenge to growers, ULTAB has been criticized for neglecting the immediate needs of workers by favoring political over economic solutions to their problems. On numerous occasions, ULTAB squelched labor protests in order to demonstrate the PCB's authority over rural workers to enhance its image among bureaucrats and politicians with whom the party hoped to ally in backing agrarian reform laws.

When the government-sanctioned National Confederation of Agricultural Laborers (CONTAG) formed in November 1963, the semiclandestine ULTAB disbanded and its militants joined the new organization. A third of CONTAG's elected officers, including its president, responded to party discipline.

See also **Brazil, Political Parties: Brazilian Communist Party (PCB).**

BIBLIOGRAPHY

Robert E. Price, "Rural Unionization in Brazil," Land Tenure Center, University of Wisconsin, Madison (1964).

Verena Stolcke, *Coffee Planters, Workers, and Wives: Class Conflict and Gender Relations on São Paulo Plantations, 1850–1980* (1988), pp. 100–108.

Additional Bibliography

Athos Magno Costa e Silva. *O estado e o campo no Brazil, 1930-1964: Revolução conservadora das elites e luta pela terra na retaguarda do país*. Goiânia: UCG Editora, 2001.

Bombardi, Larissa Mies. *O bairro reforma agrária e o processo de territorialização camponesa*. São Paulo: Annablume, 2004.

Linhares, Maria Yedda Leite, and Carlos Teixeira Silva. *Terra prometida: Uma história da questão agrária no Brasil*. Rio de Janeiro: Editora Campus, 1999.

Silva, Lyndolpho, and Paulo Ribeiro da Cunha. *O camponês e a história: A construção da Ultab e a fundação da Contag nas memórias de Lyndolpho Silva*. São Paulo: Instituto Astrojildo Pereira (IAP), 2004.

Stédile, João Pedro, and Douglas Estevam. *A questão agrária no Brasil*. 2nd ed. São Paulo: Editora Expressão Popular, 2005.

CLIFF WELCH

UNION OF INDIGENOUS NATIONS (UNI)

The Union of Indigenous Nations (União das Nações Indígenas—UNI), founded in June 1980, was the first independent organization of Brazilian indigenous peoples. Although never formally recognized by the government, it had immense symbolic significance for the development of political consciousness during the 1980s. Created and led by indigenous peoples, UNI was intended to give voice to the concerns of the people; to assist them in their struggles to secure rights to land, self-determination, and autonomy; and to help them develop cultural and community projects. From the time of its founding until the beginning of the 1990s, UNI representatives were involved in drafting the sections of Brazil's new constitution that deal with indigenous peoples, establishing alliances between members of Brazil's approximately 180 indigenous groups, and promoting recognition of strategies common to indigenous peoples and other oppressed sectors of the Brazilian population. For example, UNI was active in the formation of the Alliance of the Peoples of the Forest (March 1989), an organization comprised of indigenous peoples, rubber tappers, and river dwellers who recognized their common struggles, renounced old animosities, and pledged to promote their common interests. It also founded, in 1987, the Center for Indigenous Research (Centro de Pesquisa Indígena) in Goiânia. The Terena leader Domingos Verissimo Marcos (Marcos Terena) served briefly as UNI's first president; he was succeeded by Ailton Krenak.

In the early 1990s indigenous peoples started to become more organized at community and regional levels, and independent indigenous organizations began to proliferate throughout Brazil. As a result, UNI eventually disbanded as a national organization and the political configuration of indigenous organizations entered into a process of redefinition. By the mid-1990s, approximately 100 independent indigenous organizations were active in Brazil. Among these was the Center for Indigenous Culture in São Paulo (Nucleo de Cultura Indígena—NCI), founded by Krenak. No single entity had yet developed that claimed to represent the interests of all of Brazil's diverse indigenous peoples.

See also **Indigenous Peoples.**

BIBLIOGRAPHY

Ismaelillo Wright and Robin Wright, *Native Peoples in Struggle: Cases from the Fourth Russell Tribunal and Other International Forums* (1982), p. 66.

LAURA GRAHAM

BRAZIL, POLITICAL PARTIES

This entry includes the following articles:
BRAZILIAN COMMUNIST PARTY (PCB)
BRAZILIAN DEMOCRATIC MOVEMENT (MDB)
BRAZILIAN DEMOCRATIC MOVEMENT PARTY (PMDB)
BRAZILIAN LABOR PARTY (PTB)
CONSERVATIVE PARTY
INTEGRALIST ACTION (AIB)
LIBERAL ALLIANCE
LIBERAL PARTY
MODERADOS
NATIONAL DEMOCRATIC UNION OF BRAZIL (UDN)
NATIONAL RENOVATING ALLIANCE (ARENA)
PARTY OF BRAZILIAN SOCIAL DEMOCRACY (PSDB)
POPULAR ACTION (AP)
REPUBLICAN PARTY (PR)
WORKERS PARTY (PT)

BRAZILIAN COMMUNIST PARTY (PCB)

In March 1922 a group of former anarchist activists met in Rio de Janeiro to found Brazil's Communist Party. Led by journalist Astrogildo Pereira, this group of male artisans were breaking ranks with Brazil's anarchists. Their main goals were to create a national proletarian movement that could coordinate its activities throughout Brazil and to tie this movement to the Soviet Union's new Third International. The party sought to establish centralized control of all labor and left-wing movements. In turn the PCB became a component of the international structure of Communist parties (the Comintern) centered in Moscow.

Unlike the anarchists, who had eschewed participation in the political system, the Communists relied on a two-track program to gain power. At Moscow's behest, they both participated in elections and planned military coups. In 1930 the party leadership even relinquished power to a military man, the former Tenente Luís Carlos Prestes, in accordance with the Comintern's directives. Rather than organizing among the nation's urban and rural laborers, Prestes and his followers launched a revolt in Brazil's Northeast (far from the industrial centers of São Paulo and Rio) in November 1935. The coup's failure ushered in almost a decade of intense government repression of the PCB as well as labor and left-ist groups that had had little contact with the Communists.

During the period of nominally open politics from 1945 to 1964, the PCB reemerged. With Prestes still controlling the party, it again followed policies prescribed by the Soviet Union. By participating in elections, Prestes and other party members gained seats in both national and state legislatures in the mid-1940s, only to lose their positions when the federal government of Eurico Gaspar Dutra (1946–1951) followed the lead of the United States by declaring the PCB an illegal political party.

An important generational and ideological division developed within the PCB at this time. Younger members who worked in factories and on large plantations began to organize among the rank and file. Although formally Communists, many of these younger members openly defied the PCB's national politics, which often called for making alliances with industrialists and other elites. These young activists managed, for the first time, to spread the PCB's influence within the urban and rural trade union movements from the mid-1940s through the mid-1960s.

By 1962 there had emerged within the party a pro-Chinese splinter group, which in that year formed the Communist Party of Brazil (Partido Comunista do Brasil—PC do B). Prestes and other Communists clandestinely maintained the party during the 1964–1985 military dictatorship and emerged as participants in the broad-based opposition Brazilian Democratic Movement Party (PMDB) coalition. At first the PCB openly opposed many programs of the newly formed Workers Party (PT). But in the late 1980s, the PCB leadership formally admitted it did not have the allegiance of Brazil's working people and ceded that responsibility to the PT.

See also **Brazil, Revolutions: Communist Revolts of 1935; Dutra, Eurico Gaspar; Prestes, Luís Carlos.**

BIBLIOGRAPHY

Two volumes by John W. F. Dulles, *Anarchists and Communists in Brazil, 1900–1935* (1973), and *Brazilian Communism, 1935–1945: Repression during World Upheaval* (1983), detail the founding and operation of the PCB. An excellent institutional history of the party is provided in Ronald H. Chilcote, *The Brazilian Communist Party: Conflict and Integration, 1922–1972* (1974). On the often conflict-laden relationship between the PCB and rank-and-file workers, see Joel Wolfe, *Working Women, Working Men: São Paulo and the Rise of Brazil's Industrial Working Class, 1900–1955* (1993).

Additional Bibliography

Brandão, Gildo Marçal. *A esquerda positiva: As duas almas do Partido Comunista, 1920–1964.* São Paulo: Editora Hucitec, 1997.

Ferreira, Jorge Luiz. *Prisioneiros do mito: Cultura e imaginário político dos comunistas no Brasil (1930–1956).* Niterói: EdUFF, Editora da Universidade Federal Fluminense; Rio de Janeiro: Mauad, 2002.

Mazzeo, Antonio Carlos, Maria Izabel Lagoa, and Aldo Agosti. *Corações vermelhos: Os comunistas brasileiros no século XX.* São Paulo: Cortez Editora, 2003.

JOEL WOLFE

BRAZILIAN DEMOCRATIC MOVEMENT (MDB)

The Brazilian Democratic Movement (Movimento Democrático Brasilero—MDB) was founded in 1966, after the two-year-old military regime decreed that Brazilian politics be restructured as a two-party system. Under the new two-party system, the MDB was the official opposition party and the more conservative National Renovating Alliance (ARENA) was the official pro-regime party. Following the relegalization of a multiparty system in 1979, the MDB was dissolved. The bulk of the MDB party structure and leadership subsequently formed the Brazilian Democratic Movement Party (PMDB).

The MDB initially drew its membership from parties such as the Brazilian Labor Party (PTB) and Social Democratic Party (PSD), which had formerly occupied the center-left end of the political spectrum before the military government purged the Congress and executive of leftist party members. As the only legal opposition party, the MDB maintained a critical stance towards the military regime's authoritarian policies, which stimulated rapid economic expansion while clamping down on political dissent and social unrest. However, the legal restrictions placed on individual and party activism circumscribed the MDB's abilities to challenge authoritarian rule.

Throughout its existence, the MDB maintained minority representation in federal and state legislatures, with the greatest party representation found in the urban, industrialized states of the Southeast and South. Although the party rarely exercised political supremacy at the federal or state levels, several of the party's most prominent members, including Ulysses Guimarães and Tancredo Neves, played crucial roles in the political re-democratization process known as *abertura* (1979–1985). As of 2006, the PMDB was the largest party in the Chamber of Deputies and the third largest in the Senate.

See also **Guimarães, Ulysses Silveira; Neves, Tancredo de Almeida.**

BIBLIOGRAPHY

"Movimento Democrático Brasileiro," in *Dicionário histórico-biográfico brasileiro, 1930–1983,* vol. 3, edited by Israel Beloch and Alzira Alves de Abreu (1984), pp. 2,322–2,324.

Maria Helena Moreira Alves, *State and Opposition in Military Brazil* (1985).

Maria D'Alva Gil Kinzo, *Legal Opposition Politics Under Authoritarian Rule in Brazil* (1988).

Additional Bibliography

Brandão, Gildo Marçal. *A esquerda positiva: As duas almas do Partido Comunista, 1920–1964.* São Paulo: Editora Hucitec, 1997.

Mattos, Marco Aurélio Vannucchi Leme de and Walter Cruz Swensson, Jr. *Contra os inimigos da ordem: A repressão política do regime militar brasileiro, 1964–1985.* Rio de Janeiro: DP & A Editora, 2003.

Mazzeo, Antonio Carlos, Maria Izabel Lagoa, and Aldo Agosti, eds. *Corações vermelhos: Os comunistas brasileiros no século XX.* São Paulo: Cortez Editora, 2003.

DARYLE WILLIAMS

BRAZILIAN DEMOCRATIC MOVEMENT PARTY (PMDB)

The Brazilian Democratic Movement Party (Partido do Movimento Democrático Brasileiro—PMDB) is one of the few Brazilian parties to have maintained a political profile consistent with that which it had at the time of its founding in the 1970s. When, in 1965, the military regime banned existing parties,

a diversified group of opposition forces formed the Brazilian Democratic Movement (MDB). The Brazilian Democratic Movement Party formally came into being when the 1979 reform reinstated the multiparty system, and it has remained the country's largest party, albeit in a context of extreme and continuing political fragmentation. During the process of Distensão (gradual liberalization) carried out by the military government in the 1970s, PMDB's widest support generally came from the urban and industrialized centers of south central Brazil, but it became a progressively national party owing to local municipal organizational efforts throughout the country. Largely because of its organizational power and its identification with resistance to military government, the PMDB was well prepared to garner popular support once redemocratization began in earnest.

The party's historical trajectory can be outlined as follows: First, in the context of the restrictions imposed by the authoritarian regime, it firmly established itself as the party of resistance and won widespread popular support in elections held in the late 1970s. Second, during the 1980s it continued its strategy as a catchall party, but given the multiplication of parties and the resulting dispersion of the federal and state parliaments into numerous factions, its dimensions were substantially reduced. Finally, as of 2007, it continues as a party linked to popular interests.

The PMDB's greatest victory came in the general elections of 1986 and can be attributed to the momentary, preelection success of President José Sarney's economic plan, which included wage and price freezes. Since then, two events have contributed to the party's loss of electoral support: a 1988 internal rift in which the left wing abandoned ship to form its own party—the Brazilian Social Democratic Party—and the first post-authoritarian presidential elections, in 1989, when none of the larger parties, PMDB included, were able to capture the votes of the electorate. As of 2006, the PMDB was the largest party in the Chamber of Deputies and the third largest in the Senate.

See also **Brazil, Political Parties: Brazilian Democratic Movement (MDB).**

BIBLIOGRAPHY

Olavo Brasil de Lima Júnior, "Electoral Participation in Brazil (1945–1978): The Legislation, the Party

System, and Electoral Turnouts," *Luso-Brazilian Review* 20, no. 1 (1983): 65–92.

Maria d'Alva Gil Kinzo, *Oposição e autoritarianismo: Gênese e trajetória do MDB* (1988).

Thomas E. Skidmore, *The Politics of Military Rule in Brazil, 1964–1985* (1988).

Alfred Stepan, ed., *Democratizing Brazil: Problems of Transition and Consolidation* (1989).

Olavo Brasil de Lima Júnior, *Democracia e instituições políticas no Brasil dos anos 80* (1993).

Additional Bibliography

Ferreira, Denise Paiva. *PFL x PMDB: Marchas e contra-marchas (1982–2000).* Goiânia, Brazil: Editora Alternativa, 2002.

Friedman, Sofia. *Brazil, 1960–1990: Structures of Power and Processes of Change.* Lanham, MD: University Press of America, 2003.

Luna, Francisco Vidal, and Herbert S Klein. *Brazil Since 1980.* Cambridge, U.K., and New York: Cambridge University Press, 2006.

Melhem, Celia Soibelmann. *Política de botinas amarelas: O MDB-PMDB paulista de 1965 a 1988.* São Paulo: Editora Hucitec; Departamento de Ciência Política, USP, 1998.

OLAVO BRASIL DE LIMA JÚNIOR
DOUGLAS COLE LIBBY

BRAZILIAN LABOR PARTY (PTB)

Getúlio Vargas created the Brazilian Labor Party (Partido Trabalhista Brasileiro—PTB) along with the Social Democratic Party (Partido Social Democrático—PSD) in early 1945. The two political parties sought to represent Vargas's constituencies in the electoral politics that followed the Estado Nôvo dictatorship. The PTB was to be a non-Communist alternative for the country's recently enfranchised industrial workers. Vargas hoped that the PTB would mirror the British Labour Party by marshaling union support. The PTB never achieved such status. Rather than becoming the institutional representative of Brazilian workers, the party served as the home base for a series of populist politicians, beginning with Vargas himself.

Vargas and his allies closely controlled the PTB's affairs, and by doing so failed to build ties to either unionized or nonunionized workers. The party was particularly weak in the state of São Paulo, Brazil's industrial heartland. From its founding in 1945 to Vargas's suicide in 1954, the PTB served as an electoral vehicle for the former dictator, who refashioned himself as a pro-worker populist. Vargas was elected president in 1950 running as a PTB candidate.

With Vargas's death, control of the party fell to his former minister of labor and fellow Gaúcho, João (Jângo) Goulart. From the mid-1950s through the early 1960s, government labor bureaucrats and left-wing populists fought for control of the PTB. Jângo's elevation to the presidency in 1961 intensified this conflict. In the early 1960s, Goulart's brother-in-law, Leonel Brizola, controlled the radical wing of the PTB that effectively pushed Jângo to adopt policies favoring urban and rural labor. This turn to the left hastened the military coup of 1964.

During the late 1970s and early 1980s, Brizola sought to lead a reconstituted PTB that would continue in the spirit of Vargas and Goulart. Brizola lost access to the party's name and so formed the Democratic Labor Party (Partido Democrático Trabalhista—PDT). The reconstituted PTB became a home base for conservative unionists who opposed the new unionism of the Workers Party (Partido dos Trabalhadores—PT). Yet, as of 2006, the PTB held 22 seats in the Chamber of Deputies and participated in a coalition in support of President Luiz Inácio Lula da Silva of the PT.

See also **Goulart, João Belchior Marques; Vargas, Getúlio Dornelles.**

BIBLIOGRAPHY

For a detailed analysis of the PTB's role in national politics, see Thomas E. Skidmore, *Politics in Brazil, 1930–1964: An Experiment in Democracy* (1967). Case studies of the PTB are provided in Maria Andréa Loyola, *Os sindicatos e o PTB; Estudo de um caso em Minas Gerais* (1980), and Maria Victoria Benevides, *O PTB e o trabalhismo em São Paulo, 1945–1964* (1989). On the origins of the PTB, see Angela Castro Gomes, *A invenção do trabalhismo* (1988).

Additional Bibliography

Ferreira, Jorge Luiz. *O imaginário trabalhista: Getulismo, PTB e cultura política popular, 1945–1964.* Rio de Janeiro: Civilização Brasileira, 2005.

Kingstone, Peter R. and Timothy J. Power, eds. *Democratic Brazil: Actors, Institutions, and Processes.* Pittsburgh, PA: University of Pittsburgh Press, 2000.

Lavaud, Jean-Pierre. *El embrollo boliviano: Turbulencias sociales y desplazamientos políticos, 1952–1982.* Lima: IEFA; La Paz: Hisbol, 1998.

JOEL WOLFE

CONSERVATIVE PARTY

The Conservative Party was the most important of the Brazilian monarchy. Founded in 1837 by reactionaries among the liberal Moderados, the party dominated the last years of the Regency (1831–1840) and the seminal beginnings of the Second Reign (1840–1889). Indeed, its leaders figured in the most important initiatives of the period, for example, the *conciliação* (1853–1857), which ended the initial partisan struggles between Conservatives and Liberals; foreign policy in the Río de la Plata area (1848–1870); far-reaching reformism in the early 1870s; and the final abolition of slavery in 1888. From 1837 to the monarchy's fall in 1889, there were forty cabinets; Conservatives controlled more than half of the cabinets over more than thirty-two years in power. Moreover, nine of the ten longest administrations had Conservative leadership, including the three longest and most decisive: that of the Marquês de Olinda and Viscount de Monte Alegre (1848–1852), that of Marquês de Paraná (1853–1857), and that of Viscount do Rio Branco (1871–1875).

The party was born of the reaction against Regency decentralization and democratization, which were perceived to be the cause of the secessionist popular revolts of the era. The most dynamic party element, called the Saquaremas, dominated the party during the period when these issues remained unresolved, ca. 1837–1852. Generally trained magistrates, Saquaremas were identified with the slaveholding planter and merchant interests of Rio de Janeiro, allied to similar elements of Bahia and Pernambuco, and emphasized an authoritarian, constitutional state as the only secure guarantor of social order and national integrity. Eusébio de Queirós, Paulino José Soares de Sousa (later Viscount do Uruguai), and Joaquim José Rodrigues Tôrres (later Viscount de Itaboraí), the Saquarema "trinity," organized the Conservative majority in the Chamber and, working closely with Bernardo Pereira de Vasconcelos and Honório Hermeto Carneiro Leão (later Marquês de Paraná), led the parliamentary *Regresso*, or reaction, which, by 1841, reversed the liberal reforms of 1831–1834. As ministers, senators, and councilors of state, they later figured in the repression of the last Liberal revolts of 1842 and 1848 and oversaw the ministry of 1848–1853, which consolidated the Monarchy as the preeminent force in national politics and in the international relations of the Río de la Plata.

With the maturity of Pedro II by the 1850s, a movement against Saquarema hegemony and partisan strife triumphed, associated with the Marquês de Paraná's opening to Liberals and electoral reforms. By the 1860s, key moderate Conservatives, such as José Tomás Nabuco De Araújo, shifted over to the Liberals, and the Conservative Party itself was increasingly dominated by Paraná's protege, the one-time Liberal, José Maria Paranhos de Silva (later Viscount do Rio Branco). The latter was able to defeat the Saquaremas' heirs in the struggle over gradual abolition of slavery in 1871, thus fatally dividing the party. By 1888, the party's reformist wing successfully presided over slavery's complete abolition. The ideological incoherence this suggests points to the party's increasing demoralization and disarray, central to the context for the military's republican coup of 1889.

See also **Brazil, The Empire (First); Brazil, The Empire (Second).**

BIBLIOGRAPHY

Joaquim Nabuco, *Um estadista do impérro* (1898–1899).

José Antonio Soares De Sousa, *A vida do visconde do Uruguai* (1944).

Ilmar Rohloff De Mattos, *O tempo saquarema* (1987).

Roderick Barman, *Brazil: The Forging of a Nation, 1798–1852* (1988).

José Murilo De Carvalho, *Teatro de sombras* (1988).

Emília Viotti Da Costa, *The Brazilian Empire* (1988).

Richard Graham, *Patronage and Politics in Nineteenth-Century Brazil* (1990).

Jeffrey D. Needell, "Brasilien 1830–1889," in Raymond Buve and John Fisher, eds., *Handbuch der Geschichte Lateinamericas,* vol. 2 (1992).

Additional Bibliography

Needell, Jeffrey D. *The Party of Order: The Conservatives, the State, and Slavery in the Brazilian Monarchy, 1831–1871.* Stanford, CA: Stanford University Press, 2006.

JEFFREY D. NEEDELL

INTEGRALIST ACTION (AIB)

The Integralist Action (Ação Integralista Brasileira—AIB; commonly known as Integralismo) was the first Brazilian fascist movement to gain national prominence. Formed in 1932 and headed by Plínio Salgado, the AIB was primarily modeled after the Italian and Portuguese fascist movements, although it did use Nazi-influenced trappings such as green shirts to distinguish its members and the swastika-like Greek sigma as a party sign. Its nationalistic goal was an integral state with a single authoritarian leader.

The AIB, whose motto was "God, Country, and Family," took the nationalism, Catholicism, and antiforeign nature of the Revolution of 1930 to an extreme. As Brazil's urban middle class became increasingly poorer during the worldwide Great Depression, the AIB attacked liberals, Communists, foreigners, and Masons, but never clearly articulated a positive political platform. Gustavo Barroso, president of Brazil's Academy of Letters and the AIB's chief ideologue, was a rabid anti-Semite whose Jew-baiting dominated the AIB's public discourse even though the Jewish population of Brazil was small.

In 1937 Salgado was one of three candidates in the presidential election and may have been strong enough to play power broker in a close election. When Getúlio Vargas declared the Estado Novo dictatorship in 1937, the presidential election was canceled and all political parties, including the AIB, were banned. When a group of Integralists attacked the Presidential Palace in 1938, most AIB leaders were arrested and Salgado was exiled to Portugal. Many important members of Estado Novo, however, including Justice Minister Francisco Campos and Federal Chief of Police Fillinto Müller, remained tied to both Salgado and the Integralist platform. Later the Integralist party was legally reconstituted in a number of Brazilian states, although its membership was tiny.

See also **Fascism; Salgado, Plinio.**

BIBLIOGRAPHY

Robert Levine, *The Vargas Regime: The Critical Years, 1934–1938* (1970), esp. pp. 81–99, 159–175.

Helgio Trindade, *Integralismo: O fascismo brasileiro na década de 30* (1979).

Stanley Hilton, *Hitler's Secret War in South America, 1939–1945* (1981), esp. pp. 82–93.

René Gertz, *O fascismo no sul do Brasil: Germanismo, nazismo, integralismo* (1987).

Additional Bibliography

Calil, Gilberto Grassi. *O integralismo no pós-guerra: A formação do PRP, 1945–1950.* Porto Alegre, Brazil: EDIPUCRS, 2001.

Cavalari, Rosa Maria Feiteiro. *Integralismo: Ideologia e organização de um partido de massa no Brasil, 1932–1937.* Bauru, Brazil: Editora da Universidade do Sagrado Coração, 1999.

Deutsch, Sandra McGee. *Las Derechas: The Extreme Right in Argentina, Brazil, and Chile, 1890–1939.* Stanford, CA: Stanford University Press, 1999.

JEFFREY LESSER

LIBERAL ALLIANCE

Founded in August 1929 by political leaders in Minas Gerais and Rio Grande do Sul, this opposition party supported Getúlio Vargas as president and João Pessoa as vice president in the 1930 elections. The Liberal Alliance (Alianca Liberal—AL) was formed when President Washington Luiz, a representative of São Paulo's large landowners, announced that he had decided to break the tradition of alternating politicians from São Paulo and Minas Gerais in the presidency and intended to support São Paulo state president Júlio Prestes as his successor.

The AL was composed of a number of groups whose power was not based on coffee wealth and who looked to modernize Brazil's economy. It represented an emerging middle class increasingly disenfranchised by the central government's policy of favoring the interests of the major plantation owners. The AL platform was based on national political reform, including a secret vote and popular representation, freedom of the press, educational reform, and the adoption of protectionist policies for export products other than coffee.

After a campaign marked by violence, the Vargas-Pessoa ticket was defeated amid accusations of widespread fraud. After Pessoa's assassination in July, some members of the AL called for an armed rebellion. In October the Revolution of 1930 began, putting Vargas in power for the next fifteen years.

See also **Vargas, Getúlio Dornelles.**

BIBLIOGRAPHY

John W. F. Dulles, *Vargas of Brazil: A Political Biography* (1967), esp. pp. 49–67.

Boris Fausto, *A revolução de 1930: Historiografia e história* (1986).

Additional Bibliography

Levine, Robert M. *Father of the Poor? Vargas and His Era.* Cambridge, U.K.: Cambridge University Press, 1998.

Williams, Daryle. *Culture Wars in Brazil: The First Vargas Regime, 1930–1945.* Durham, NC: Duke University Press, 2001.

JEFFREY LESSER

LIBERAL PARTY

The Liberal Party (Partido Liberal), one of the two great parties of the monarchy (1822–1889), formed (c. 1837) in opposition to the Conservative Party's reactionary, authoritarian regime. A minority party, the Liberals circumvented Conservative hegemony by an 1840 coup (the *Majoridade,* bringing the adolescent emperor to power early in return for cabinet control). When the emperor's advisers engineered their fall (1841), the Liberals revolted (1842) in São Paulo and Minas Gerais and were pitilessly repressed. This failure, and that of Pernambuco's Praieira Revolt (1848), confirmed the Conservatives' goal: state power was to be preeminent and exercised indirectly by the Crown through cabinet control of patronage, elections, and legislation.

In order to defend and increase their partisans, the Liberal cabinets of the mid-1840s refused to reverse such control. This pragmatism caused a rift between purists and the party's leadership. Indeed, pragmatists from both parties joined to form the Conciliation cabinets (1853–1857) and some successors, culminating in the Progressive League (1862).

This league was a parliamentary coalition in which moderate Conservative dissidents led the Liberals against the Conservative Party (despite divisions over reforms and marked internal suspicion) and presided over cabinets in 1862 and 1864–1868. The league's gradual reformism and crown support were undermined in parliament, where the purists of both parties attacked them as either going too far or attempting too little.

In 1868, the emperor brought the Conservatives to power (partly to support the Conservative general leading imperial forces in the War of the Triple Alliance); they held it exclusively until 1878. This monopoly led to Liberal radicalization. The Progressive League leaders and the old Liberal purists united to refound the Liberal Party and called for dramatic reforms in the Liberal Manifesto of 1869. A radical faction called for even more dramatic reform, and others went still further, deciding to form the Republican Party (1870).

The Liberals used reformism to critique the Conservative cabinets until 1879; afterward several Liberal cabinets, increasingly divided, failed to effect such programs themselves: abolition of slavery, reform of the emperor's prerogatives, decentralization, separation of church and state. By 1889, the last prime minister, a Liberal, led a party so badly splintered that his refurbished radical proposals (designed to save the monarchy) failed to secure support in the Chamber of Deputies, thereby adding to the postabolitionist milieu of political crisis.

See also **Brazil, Liberal Movements; Conciliação.**

BIBLIOGRAPHY

Joaquim Nabuco, *Um estadista do império,* 3 vols. (1898–1899).

Emilia Viotti Da Costa, *The Brazilian Empire* (1985).

Ilmar Rohloff De Mattos, *O tempo saquarema* (1987).

Roderick J. Barman, *Brazil: The Forging of a Nation* (1988).

Leslie Bethell, ed., *Brazil: Empire and Republic* (1989), chaps. 2–4.

Richard Graham, *Patronage and Politics in Nineteenth-Century Brazil* (1990).

Additional Bibliography

Needell, Jeffrey D. *The Party of Order: The Conservatives, the State, and Slavery in the Brazilian Monarchy, 1831–1871.* Stanford, CA: Stanford University Press, 2006.

Peixoto, Antonio Carlos, Lucia Maria Paschoal Guimarães, and Maria Emília Prado. *O liberalismo no Brasil imperial: Origens, conceitos e prática.* Rio de Janeiro: Editora Revan, 2001.

JEFFREY D. NEEDELL

MODERADOS

This Brazilian political party that initially dominated the Regency (1831–1840), imposing decentralization and a limited monarchy. Liberal monarchists had joined more radical elements to oppose Pedro I's pretensions and Portuguese interests during the First Reign (1822–1831). They sought to force Pedro I to accept greater parliamentary participation and more freedom for men of property to direct affairs in their provinces. When Pedro's abdication brought them to power, they elected the three regents who governed for the emperor's child heir, Pedro II. Class prejudice, monarchism, and provincial revolts soon forced them to break with the radicals (1831–1832) and elect Diogo Antônio Feijó (1784–1843) as sole regent in 1835. Simultaneously, they reformed the Constitution of 1824 with the Additional Act (1834), which curbed the crown and devolved power to parliament and provincial electors.

Personal resentment of Feijó and unchecked threats of provincial secession and social revolt soon disenchanted the *moderados'* right wing. They made a reactionary parliamentary alliance with former supporters of Pedro I, and they founded the Conservative Party in 1837. Feijó resigned, and the Conservative majority elected Pedro de Araújo Lima, later Marqués de Olinda, sole regent in 1837. The minority *moderado* left wing, known as the *progressistas,* joined the old radicals in support of the 1834 reforms and Feijó, thus forming the Liberal Party.

See also **Brazil, The Regency; Pedro I of Brazil.**

BIBLIOGRAPHY

Octávio Tarqüinio De Sousa, *Bernardo Pereira de Vasconcellos e seu tempo* (1937), *Historia de dois golpes de estado* (1939), and *Diogo Antônio Feijó* (1942).

Roderick Barman, *Brazil: The Forging of a Nation, 1798–1852* (1988).

Additional Bibliography

Dolhnikoff, Miriam. *O pacto imperial: Origens do federalismo no Brasil.* São Paulo: Editora Globo, 2005.

Needell, Jeffrey D. *The Party of Order: The Conservatives, the State, and Slavery in the Brazilian Monarchy, 1831–1871.* Stanford, CA: Stanford University Press, 2006.

Peixoto, Antonio Carlos, Lucia Maria Paschoal Guimarães, and Maria Emília Prado. *O liberalismo no Brasil imperial: Origens, conceitos e prática.* Rio de Janeiro: Editora Revan, 2001.

JEFFREY D. NEEDELL

NATIONAL DEMOCRATIC UNION OF BRAZIL (UDN)

Founded in April 1945 as a coalition of groups opposed to the Estado Novo, an authoritarian regime headed by Getúlio Vargas, the National Democratic Union (União Democrática Nacional—UDN) maintained a prominent role in Brazilian politics until the party was disbanded in 1965. During its existence, party membership and party platforms were in constant tension between moderates and hard-liners. In general the party tended to represent moderate-to-conservative, middle-class interests, supporting basic democratic processes, morality in public life, and state nonintervention in the economy. The UDN sharply opposed the populist, nationalist elements of the presidencies of Getúlio Vargas (1951–1954), Juscelino Kubitschek (1956–1961), and João Goulart (1961–1964). In 1964 the UDN supported military intervention to restore economic stability and combat alleged communist infiltration of Brazilian politics and society. After disbandment in 1965, most party members joined the pro-government National Renovating Alliance (Aliança de Renovação Nacional—ARENA).

The party fielded four presidential candidates: Eduardo Gomes (defeated in 1945 and 1950), Juarez Távora (defeated in 1955), and Jânio Quadros (victorious in 1960). The UDN enjoyed greater electoral success in national legislative races, winning enough seats to become the principal opposition party from 1945 to 1960, and in state elections, particularly in the Northeast, Minas Gerais, and Rio de Janeiro. The UDN consistently experienced difficulties in reconciling its heterogeneous bases of support, which ranged from staunch anticommunists who often called for military intervention to moderates who advocated stable political and economic development through democratic measures.

See also **Estado Novo; Vargas, Getúlio Dornelles.**

BIBLIOGRAPHY

Thomas Skidmore, *Politics in Brazil, 1930–1964: An Experiment in Democracy* (1967).

Maria Vitória Benevides, *A UDN e o udenismo* (1981).

Maria Vitória Benevides, "União Democrático Nacional," in *Dicionário históricobiográfico brasileiro* (1984), pp. 3396–3403.

Otávio Soares Dulci, *A UDN e o anti-populismo no Brasil* (1986).

Additional Bibliography

Fernandes, Clever Luiz, and Reginaldo Lima de Arquino. *A UDN e o PSD goianos: Ensaio de história política (1945–1966).* Goiania, Brazil: Kelps, 2005.

Johnson, Ollie A. *Brazilian Party Politics and the Coup of 1964.* Gainesville: University Press of Florida, 2001.

DARYLE WILLIAMS

NATIONAL RENOVATING ALLIANCE (ARENA)

In an effort to reduce the number of political parties, considered a root cause of Brazil's problems, and to instill discipline in the political system, the military regime of Humberto Castello Branco issued the Second Institutional Act on 27 October 1965 and the Complementary Act No. 4 on 30 November 1965. The former act dissolved all existing political parties in Brazil, while the latter act allowed the formation of political organizations only if such bodies were endorsed by at least 120 congressmen and 20 senators. The result was the formation of two parties: National Renovating Alliance (Aliança Renovardora Nacional—ARENA) and the Brazilian Democratic Movement (Movimento Democratico Brasileiro—MDB), an opposition party.

Despite appearances, the various military administrations in Brazil maintained tight control of ARENA and the political system. The president of the republic was head of the party and selected all its candidates. ARENA politicians were in the majority in both houses of Congress and in all the state assemblies, and they also held most of the governorships and mayoral offices. However, the 1974 congressional and state assembly elections, held during the period of political relaxation, indicated the growing strength of the MDB opponents. As opposition to the military government grew, ARENA politicians gradually attempted to distance themselves from identification with the military regime.

In an effort to strengthen the weakened government party by splitting the opposition or by forming coalitions with more conservative elements of the opposition, the government of João Baptista de Figueiredo dissolved the two-party system and allowed the creation of multiple parties. By the end of 1979 ARENA had re-formed as the Social Democratic Party (Partido Democrático Social—PDS). The PDS was defeated soundly in the 1985 presidential election that returned Brazil to civilian rule.

See also **Castello Branco, Humberto de Alencar.**

BIBLIOGRAPHY

Peter Flynn, *Brazil: A Political Analysis* (1978).

Ronald M. Schneider, *The Political System of Brazil: Emergence of a "Modernizing" Authoritarian Regime, 1964–1970* (1971).

Riordon Roett, *Brazil: Politics in a Partrimonial Society* (1978).

Maria Helena Moreira Alves, *State and Opposition in Military Brazil* (1985).

Thomas E. Skidmore, *The Politics of Military Rule in Brazil, 1964–1985* (1988).

Additional Bibliography

Friedman, Sofia. *Brazil, 1960–1990: Structures of Power and Processes of Change.* Lanham, MD: University Press of America, 2003.

Luna, Francisco Vidal, and Herbert S. Klein. *Brazil Since 1980.* New York: Cambridge University Press, 2006.

Mattos, Marco Aurélio Vannucchi Leme de, and Walter Cruz Swensson. *Contra os inimigos da ordem: A repressão política do regime militar brasileiro (1964–1985).* Rio de Janeiro: DP & A Editora, 2003.

SONNY B. DAVIS

PARTY OF BRAZILIAN SOCIAL DEMOCRACY (PSDB)

The Party of Brazilian Social Democracy (Partido da Social Democracia Brasileira; PSDB), one of Brazil's largest political parties, was founded on June 24, 1988, seventy-two hours after the proclamation of the 1988 constitution. The party's founders, almost all of whom were members of the Brazilian Democratic Movement Party (PMDB), were leaders of the democracy movement that had mobilized and managed Brazil's transition from military dictatorship and had helped craft the constitution. Once a democratic framework was established, the PSDB founders left the PMDB because they felt it had lost its focus on political and social reform in a scramble for political office and patronage. The key leaders in the founding of the party were Franco Montoro, the PMDB governor of the state of São Paulo; Fernando Henrique Cardoso, leader of the PMDB in the federal senate; and Mário Covas, a PMDB senator and former mayor of the city of São Paulo. Other members of the nucleus that founded the party were José Serra, Pimenta da Viega, José Richa, Euclides Scalco, and Artur da Távola. The party is known by the nickname *tucanos* (toucans).

With its strong base in the state of São Paulo, and its large number of well-known national leaders, the party grew steadily. In the 1990 elections it elected 38 federal deputies and 67 state deputies in 19 states, but it lost important campaigns for the governorships of the states of São Paulo, Paraná, and Minas Gerais. The party's greatest triumph was the election of Fernando Henrique Cardoso—who as finance minister in the previous government had ended the hyperinflation that had plagued Brazil for decades—as president with 54.3 percent of the vote in 1994, against 27.1 percent for Workers Party candidate Luiz Inácio Lula da Silva. He was reelected with 53.1 percent of the vote against Lula da Silva's 31.7 percent in 1998. PSDB candidate Mário Covas won the governorship of São Paulo in 1994 and was reelected in 1998, but the party lost governorship elections in Minas Gerais, Rio de Janeiro, and Rio Grande do Sul.

In the 2002 presidential elections, PSDB candidate José Serra received 23.2 percent of the vote in the first round, against 46.4 percent for Lula da Silva, who won in the runoff. However, the PSDB won seven governorships in that year, including the most populous states of São Paulo and Minas Gerais, while the Workers Party won only three smaller states.

See also **Cardoso, Fernando Henrique; Silva, Luis Inácio Lula da.**

BIBLIOGRAPHY

Goertzel, Ted G. *Fernando Henrique Cardoso: Reinventing Democracy in Brazil.* Boulder, CO: Lynne Rienner, 1999.

Nascisdo para mudar o Brasil—A história do PSDB. Available from PSDB, http://www.psdb.org.br/opartido/ahistoria.asp.

Serra, José, as interviewed by Teodomiro Braga. *O Sonhador que Faz: A vida, a trajetória política e as idéias de José Serra.* Rio de Janeiro: Editora Record, 2002.

TED GOERTZEL

POPULAR ACTION (AP)

Created in 1962 by a contingent of young Brazilian radicals, Popular Action (Ação Popular—AP) was a small (no more than 3,000 members) yet influential movement that sought to transform Brazilian society. Its members engaged in grass-roots political work with the poor, encouraging popular organization and mobilization, with the ultimate objective of realizing socialism. AP was an important part of the burgeoning Left in Brazilian politics between 1962 and 1964. Most of the founding members had previously been active in progressive Catholic circles, and this religious genesis strongly marked the movement

until after the 1964 military coup. Nevertheless, AP was independent of the church.

After the 1964 coup, AP underwent a rapid process of radicalization, embracing Marxism, Maoism, and eventually armed struggle. Like the other small guerrilla groups that stippled the Brazilian political scene after 1964, AP had a tragic postcoup fate; many activists were imprisoned and tortured. By 1973, the military government had vanquished the guerrilla left. Reduced to a small Maoist party with several dozen members, AP decided in 1973 to join forces with the Communist Party of Brazil.

See also **Communism.**

BIBLIOGRAPHY

Luíz Gonzaga De Souza Lima, *Evolução política dos católicos e da igreja no Brasil* (1979), esp. pp. 43–51.

Haroldo Lima and Aldo Arantes, *História da Ação Popular* (1984).

Additional Bibliography

Dias, Reginaldo Benedito. *Sob o signo da revolução Brasileira: A experiêncie Da Ação Popular no Paraná.* Maringá, Brazil: EDUEM, 2003.

Johnson, Ollie A. *Brazilian Party Politics and the Coup of 1964.* Gainesville: University Press of Florida, 2001.

Mattos, Marco Aurélio Vannucchi Leme de, and Walter Cruz Swensson. *Contra os inimigos da ordem: A repressão política do regime militar brasileiro (1964–1985).* Rio de Janeiro: DP & A Editora, 2003.

SCOTT MAINWARING

REPUBLICAN PARTY (PR)

The Republican Party (Partido Republicano—PR) emerged in Brazil with the founding of the first Republican Club in Rio de Janeiro on 3 November 1870. One month later, the Republican Manifesto enunciated the party's principles, calling for an end to the monarchy and the creation of a federal republic. Republican sentiment had surfaced as early as 1789 in Brazil with the Inconfidência Mineira, and had been important in separatist movements during the 1810s, 1820s, and 1830s. The turmoil of the 1830s, however, when Brazilians experimented with federalism, caused republican sentiment to subside, and by mid-century politically active Brazilians had come to appreciate the stability of their monarchy. The potential for political discontent, nonetheless, had been retained in the divisions between the

Liberal and Conservative parties. The fall of the Liberal cabinet in 1868 caused disgruntled members to seek radical redress by supporting the republican cause. Other political and economic forces also contributed to the appeal of republicanism in 1870. The War of the Triple Alliance (1865–1870), which cast Brazilian soldiers into closer contact with their Argentine and Uruguayan allies, heightened the appreciation for republican government elsewhere. The growth of cities brought with it the increased importance of educated, professional groups sympathetic to republican ideals. Furthermore, after 1850 economic power transferred from the Paraíba Valley to the rich coffee lands of São Paulo province. Since political influence did not immediately follow, Paulista planters tended to support republicanism. In 1884, São Paulo elected three Republican representatives to the national Chamber of Deputies, the first Republicans to sit in Parliament. With the return of the Liberals to national power in 1878, however, many Republicans had deserted their new party and returned to the Liberal fold. In 1886–1887 the Republican Party reemerged under a leadership more heavily influenced by the positivist vision of a dictatorial republic and supported by important sectors of the military. On 15 November 1889 the military deposed Emperor Pedro II and ushered in a republican form of government.

See also **Pedro II of Brazil.**

BIBLIOGRAPHY

Francisco José De Oliveira Viana, *O ocaso do império*, 3d ed. (1959).

Heitor Lyra, *História da queda do império*, 2 vols. (1964).

E. Bradford Burns, *A History of Brazil*, 2d ed. (1980), esp. pp. 224–225.

Emilia Viotti Da Costa, *The Brazilian Empire* (1985), esp. pp. 202–233.

Additional Bibliography

Barman, Roderick J. *Citizen Emperor: Pedro II and the Making of Brazil, 1825–91.* Stanford, CA: Stanford University Press, 1999.

Dolhnikoff, Miriam. *O pacto imperial: Origens do federalismo no Brasil.* São Paulo: Editora Globo, 2005.

Peixoto, Antonio Carlos, Lucia Maria Paschoal Guimarães, and Maria Emília Prado. *O liberalismo no Brasil imperial: Origens, conceitos e prática.* Rio de Janeiro: Editora Revan, 2001.

JOAN MEZNAR

WORKERS PARTY (PT)

During the late 1970s, while Brazil was still under military rule, workers in the metallurgical industries (especially in automobile factories) located in São Paulo's industrial suburb of São Bernardo do Campo organized through factory commissions to push for increased wages and improved working conditions. The strike waves that these workers launched in 1978 and 1979 (in 1979 alone, more than 3 million workers were involved in 113 strikes in fifteen states) ushered in a form of organizing known as the new unionism and eventually led to the founding of the Brazilian Workers Party (Partido dos Trabalhadores—PT) in 1979 and 1980.

These workers founded their own party—under new political guidelines set out in 1979 by the dictatorship— because they saw the main opposition party (the Brazilian Democratic Movement [MDB], later the Brazilian Democratic Movement Party [PMDB]), the reconstituted Brazilian Labor Party (PTB), and the Brazilian Communist Party (PCB) as too alienated from the concerns of rank-and-file workers. Thus, on May Day 1979, a group of labor leaders from the metalworkers' unions (who referred to themselves as labor's "authentic" leaders) issued a set of goals. They sought: (1) direct negotiations between workers and employers and, therefore, an end to the state-run industrial-relations system; (2) the formal acceptance by employers and the state of factory commissions and the recognition of union delegates on the shop floors as the primary bargaining agents for workers; (3) complete autonomy from the federal government's Ministry of Labor; and (4) the unrestricted right to strike.

The "authentics," led by Luís Inácio da Silva (popularly known as Lula), formed the Central Workers' Union (CUT) in 1983 to coordinate national labor practices for the unions associated with the PT. The CUT opposed the more conservative unions associated with the PMDB and PCB that organized into the General Confederation of Workers (CGT), which modeled itself on the AFL-CIO of the United States.

The PT is really Brazil's first national political party. It is not simply a vehicle for a single politician, and it has a well-defined structure that is rooted not only in the factory commissions, but also in Christian Base Communities and rural workers' movements. Indeed, the PT has organized throughout Brazil to push for improved conditions not only for industrial workers, but also for rural proletarians and the poor, who do not have access to steady employment. The PT has been successful in electing big-city mayors, state governors, and state and federal representatives and senators. The party's leader, Lula, finished second in the 1989 presidential election.

Lula again competed in the 1994 presidential election. While he initially led in the polls, moderate and right parties worked together to help elect Fernando Henrique Cardoso. However, Lula won the 2002 presidential race. Businessmen and foreign investors feared that Lula was planning to implement detrimental economic policies, but in general he has maintained the policies of his conserative predecessor, Cardoso. These conservative economic policies caused some more radical party members to leave the PT. In 2005, the PT was also accused of paying members of congress to vote with it. This crisis, known as the Mensalão scandal, forced several of Lula's key advisors to resign. Despite the notoriety of this corruption, Lula was re-elected president in 2006.

See also **Brazil, Political Parties: Brazilian Communist Party (PCB); Labor Movements; Liberation Theology; Silva, Luis Inácio Lula da.**

BIBLIOGRAPHY

The single best study of the PT is Margaret E. Keck, *The Workers Party and Democratization in Brazil* (1992). A good work on the party's origins is Isabel Ribeiro De Oliveira Gómez De Souza, *Trabalho e política: As origens do Partido dos Trabalhadores* (1988). An informative study that provides a good analysis of the PT's organizing in the rural sector as well as a detailed description of the 1989 presidential campaign is Emir Sader and Ken Silverstein, *Without Fear of Being Happy: Lula, the Workers Party, and Brazil* (1991). For an analysis of the relationship of the PT to Brazil's increasingly important feminist groups, see Sonia E. álvarez, *Engendering Democracy in Brazil: Women's Movements in Transition Politics* (1990).

Additional Bibliography

Borba, Angela, Nalu Faria, and Tatau Godinho, eds. *Mulher e política: Gênero e feminismo no Partido dos Trabalhadores.* São Paulo: Editora Fundação Perseu Abramo, 1998.

Demier, Felipe, ed. *As transformações do PT e os rumos da esquerda no Brasil.* Rio de Janeiro: Bom Texto, 2003.

Luna, Francisco Vidal and Herbert S Klein. *Brazil since 1980.* Cambridge, U.K., and New York: Cambridge University Press, 2006.

Munakata, Kazumi, Maria Alice Vieira, and Alexandre Fortes. *Partido dos Trabalhadores: Trajetórias.* 2nd ed. São Paulo: Editora Fundação Perseu Abramo, 2003.

JOEL WOLFE

BRAZIL, POPULIST REPUBLIC, 1945–1964. The so-called Populist Republic in Brazil was characterized by an unstable balance of alliances among unequal social classes and political forces, within a relatively democratic institutional framework. One of the main challenges was to reconcile different quarreling factions and interest groups in an increasingly complex society.

From 1945 to 1964, Brazil turned into something quite different from what it had been just a few years before. Extraordinary urban and industrial growth, the arrival of new players on the political scene, strong government intervention in the economy, some respect for the formal rules of democracy, unprecedented mobilization of the working class, and growing politicization of social movements shaped and defined these years.

The economy diversified considerably with rapid industrialization in the capital goods sector and most notably the automotive industry that started in the mid-1950s. The strong nationalism that pervaded policies in which the state intervened in the economy did not preclude incentives for private enterprise, or the entry of foreign technology and capital. From the mid-1930s to 1964 the real average annual growth rate was roughly 8 percent, an extremely fast pace compared to the world economy at that time (Oliveira 1997, p. 25).

The population grew from 30 million in 1920 to 41 million in 1940 and 52 million in 1950. In the 1950s Brazil had 3 million industrial workers. Urban growth turned São Paulo into a city with few peers anywhere in the world, through intense migration of workers from rural areas, particularly the northeast of the country, significantly modifying the social composition of the working class. Over the course of that decade, nearly 1 million people moved to the city, accounting for nearly 60 percent of its population growth (Fontes, 2002).

The postwar transition to democracy brought a wider range of people into the political process.

The number of voters in Brazil jumped from 1 million in 1930 to 7.5 million in 1945, half of whom were women (Levine 2001, p. 113). Mass voter participation was an unprecedented, and for the first time, decisive phenomenon in the country's politics. Winning an election through patronage-based deals under the control of local oligarchies did not disappear, but it was no longer the political system's sole defining mechanism. A result of this change was the appearance of nationally organized political parties.

Within this context, it became more and more difficult to govern without taking into account urban workers and their interests. Yet, as both the economy and democracy expanded, other growing social groups entered the political stage, including civil servants, service-industry workers, low-ranking members of the armed forces, and an educated middle class with considerable influence in the public sphere.

THE FORMATION OF CORPORATISM

The structure of a populist political system began to emerge at the end of World War II. Brazil's entry into the war provided the backdrop for tensions that defined both the internal conflicts and pressure from workers and groups opposed to the *Estado Novo* (New State) dictatorship (1937–1945). President Getúlio Vargas (1930–1945) gradually loosened the regime's authoritarian grip, but he sought to control the road to democracy and to ensure a smooth transition. In early 1945 he scheduled elections for the end of the year, legalized the Partido Comunista Brasileiro (PCB, Communist Party of Brazil), and granted amnesty to political prisoners. His strategy of reaching out to workers included the establishment of the Partido Trabalhista Brasileiro (PTB, Brazilian Labor Party), and the strengthening of trade unionism (Gomes 1988).

Unlike the case in other countries, as in England, in Brazil what became known as "Laborism" (*trabalhismo* in Portuguese, from the name of the PTB), meaning that part of the Labor Movement allied with Vargas and his political heirs, did not originate autonomously from the working class. The PTB represented a proposal aimed at urban workers. It sought to use union as a base on which to build its structure and militancy, touting Vargas as a protector of the working class and competing with the PCB to represent workers both in politics and at work (D'Araujo, 1996; Delgado 1989).

Laborism had close ties to the project aimed at preserving corporatist trade unionism during the transition to democracy. Since 1931, unions had been associated with the Ministry of Labor and defined as support agencies that collaborated with the public authorities. There were bans on political and ideological activities, any meaningful type of labor action in the workplace, and in any given city or county, only one labor union was allowed per sector or type of business. Rights had to be ensured through labor laws and official channels, creating an institutional framework that, for the most part, still remains intact (Hall 2002).

Social and labor policies undoubtedly played an important role in legitimizing Vargas's power and legacy. Welfare agencies offered public health, housing, retirement, and pension services. The labor court did not invariably side with big business, but its judgments sometimes went against employers even in economic circumstances not always favorable to workers (Pacheco 1996; Silva 1995). Yet justice was not achieved without a fight for rights. The laws and labor court system were an arena for legitimately demanding and securing broader rights brought about by workers' actions against their employers' arbitrary power, little by little modifying the original meaning of corporatism and of the control and cooptation of the working class. Institutional channels only really worked when there was mobilization, collective organization, and pressure from the working class (French 2004; Fortes 1999).

Indeed, in 1945 many workers saw Getúlio Vargas as a guarantor of their rights and one choice among other quarreling options. The Queremist movement (i.e., the "We Want" movement, short for "We Want a Constituent Assembly with Getúlio") began in mid-1945. It marked the PTB's first large political demonstration and its first broad mobilization of the people. The goal was to install a constituent assembly that included Vargas, so that elections could later be held with Vargas as a candidate for president of the republic.

REDEMOCRATIZATION AND THE LABOR MOVEMENT

Political tensions, however, were worsening, and the opposition believed that Vargas was taking steps to preserve the status quo. In October 1945 Getúlio Vargas was deposed in a coup led by his minister of war, Eurico Dutra. But the presidential election in December had surprising results. Brigadier Eduardo Gomes was the candidate from the União Democrática Nacional (UDN, National Democratic Union), a liberal-conservative party opposed to Vargas. Both the UDN and the growing prestige of the PCB among workers posed threats to Dutra's candidacy under the banner of the Partido Social Democrata (PSD, Social Democratic Party), another party that Vargas had established. Then, a branch of the PTB decided to support Dutra, and convinced Vargas to do the same.

Dutra was elected, and his government (1946–1950) did not follow the strategy of wooing workers; instead, it governed in alliance with the UDN. When Dutra took office, his administration soon faced an unprecedented mobilization of workers. There were numerous strikes, most of them called by committees that carried along with union leaders usually opposed to labor actions. Many groups negotiated directly with management, ignoring or running roughshod over the corporatist institutions that were retained in the 1946 constitution.

During the brief period when the PCB was legal, its candidates won significant victories in elections, mostly in cities with large working-class populations. In December 1945 fifteen Communists were elected as federal legislators, nine of whom were laborers themselves. Despite its policy of national unity, PCB militants participated actively in organizing and mobilizing workers (Costa 1995). But this momentum did not survive the repressive crackdown. In May 1947 the PCB was outlawed, its militants were jailed, and several labor unions came under government control. In January 1948 Communist legislators' terms of office were summarily ended. This repression showed how fragile democracy could be, though Dutra's government did not have a monopoly on repression. Throughout this period, the political police worked with business owners to keep mechanisms in place to monitor and control workers, both in and out of the workplace (Negro and Fontes 2001).

THE SECOND VARGAS ADMINISTRATION (1951–1954)

In 1950 support was clearly strong for Vargas and Laborism. Vargas returned to the presidency as a

PTB candidate with significant political capital among workers, but he created and faced serious contradictions as he tried to form a coalition government (D'Araujo 2004). He formed alliances with politicians from the PSD, UDN, and the Partido Social Progress (PSP, Social Progress Party), whose leading figure was Adhemar de Barros (1901–1969), a populist governor of São Paulo. But these politicians questioned the sincerity of Vargas's intentions. Though he said he wanted to revitalize Laborism, he kept only the Ministry of Labor in the hands of the PTB. The nationalist wing of the armed forces lost face as a consequence of the government's military pacts with the United States. The nationalization of key industries and restrictions on sending profits abroad made foreign support less likely. Shrinking wages and the government's inflationary policies magnified workers' discontent and led to an explosion of massive strikes in 1953, such as the Rio de Janeiro seafarers' strike, and the "strike of the 300,000" in São Paulo, which united wage earners from a broad range of occupations.

Increasingly isolated, Vargas went on to court the working-class vote by naming João Belchior Marques Goulart ("Jango," 1918–1976) minister of labor. Jango launched a new era in the relationship with union officials, bringing them closer to the ministry through his informal and personal style. His short-lived administration implemented more flexible policies: For instance, it suspended government intervention in unions, halted the persecution of Communists, loosened laws governing strikes, and defended a nationalist project of social reforms. His boldest initiative was a decree doubling the minimum wage, which led to his removal as minister and stirred up opposition to the Vargas administration (Ferreira 2005).

In August, in the midst of a serious institutional crisis, the civilian and military oposition, led by the UDN, demanded the president's removal. On 24, August Vargas picked up a gun and committed suicide. Members of the opposition barely had time to celebrate before they were besieged with mass demonstrations (including rioting, fires, and uprisings) blaming them for the president's drastic act. The fiercely anti-Vargas UDN had lost its main rallying point: Vargas himself (Benevides 1981). It was Vargas's death that saved the statist, nationalist, and populist political tradition associated with Vargas, known as *Getulismo*, avoided a

Troops on patrol outside the War Ministry, Rio de Janeiro, Brazil, April 1, 1964. Dissatisfaction among Brazil's military and political elites led to the 1964 coup d'état of President João Goulart's leftist government and the beginning of a twenty-one-year-long military dictatorship. © BETTMANN/CORBIS

planned coup, and preserved the constitutional rule of law that eventually led to the victory of Juscelino Kubitschek (JK) in the 1955 elections.

LABORISM WITHOUT VARGAS

Over time, Laborism revolved less and less around the figure of Vargas. The party opened itself up to a social-reform approach and formed closer ties to labor organizers who were involved in unions and who defended autonomous development of the national economy. Laborism was even taken up by other rising regional populist leaders, such as Adhemar de Barros and Jânio da Silva Quadros (1917–1992) in São Paulo, and Leonel Brizola (1922–2004) in Rio Grande do Sul. The success of these politicians hinged less on Laborism and unions and more on addressing public demand for urban infrastructure (Fontes 2002).

JK's administration (1955–1960) retained a nationalist rhetoric and a policy of nationalization. However, it strengthened the state bureaucratic machinery and invested heavily in the iron and steel industry, power, and major highways to attract a large influx of foreign capital and technology. In doing so, his administration furthered capitalism associated with multinational interests, especially in the automotive industry.

The Left's focus on working with national business interests and supporting the "nationalist face" of JK's government did not keep the Left from playing an active role in labor unions with ties to local industries or participating in large-scale actions, such as the October 1957 "strike of the 400,000" in São Paulo. The democratic climate was very favorable to organizing workers (Negro 2004).

THE RISE AND FALL OF LABOR IN THE 1960S

The early 1960s were the golden age of the nationalist labor movement. The first trial by fire came after Jânio Quadros resigned as president of the republic in August 1961. The Left threw itself full throttle behind the cause of constitutional rule of law, given a threatened coup against the installation of Jânio's vice president, João Goulart, as president. A far-reaching, five-day work stoppage by 300,000 workers occurred in September, after which the victory of constitutional law was celebrated.

Communists and Laborists supported Jango and pressured him to impose a nationalist, reformist orientation on his administration, acting independently and seeking to structure a national workers' movement. In 1962 nearly 600 labor organizations joined together to create the Confederação Geral dos Trabalhadores (CGT, General Confederation of Workers), a national union confederation established outside the law. Beyond demanding better living and working conditions, the CGT launched a campaign for structural reforms (such as agrarian, welfare, banking, urban, and university reforms). The union movement fought for participation in the country's government and eventually managed to influence the choice of government ministers who were committed to their causes (Delgado 1986). Impressive growth even occurred in the struggle for rural workers' rights, leading to the formation of a strong confederation of rural workers in 1963.

The PTB became the second-largest party in Congress and achieved a majority in the Nationalist Parliamentary Front, an organization that stood up for structural reforms and also acted outside Congress, working with business people, students, and intellectuals.

The swift, remarkable growth of social movements under the Jango administration stirred up the opposition, which decried the Cubanization of the country and the Labor Union Republic. The government was accused of protecting and promoting nationalist groups within the unions, Congress, and the armed forces. "Enough!" cried the newspaper headlines. On April 1, 1964, a civilian and military coup brought down João Goulart. The new government took control of unions, deposing leaders, arresting militants (some of whom were eventually tortured and killed), and launching a long-term stringent control over workers.

The coup put an end to the unstable balance among diffuse alliances that characterized populism and that sought to incorporate workers into a multiclass political project. From 1945 to 1964 a network of institutions (parliament, unions, political parties, press, and so on) transcended the supposed direct relationship between leaders and the masses. Populist political maneuvering was open to negotiations and conflicts, whose twists and turns depended more on correlations of power at specific historical moments than simply on the will or style of specific politicians (French 1995; Silva and Costa 2001). The civil-military takeover in 1964 blocked that dynamic out of a belief that it would be possible to govern without the involvement of workers in the political process.

See also **Vargas, Getúlio Dornelles.**

BIBLIOGRAPHY

Benevides, Maria Victoria. *A UDN e o udenismo. Ambiguidades do liberalismo brasileiro (1945–1065)*. São Paulo: Paz e Terra, 1981.

Costa, Hélio da. *Em busca da memória: Comissão de fábrica, partido e sindicato no pós-guerra*. São Paulo: Scritta, 1995.

D'Araujo, Maria Celina. *Sindicatos, carisma e poder. O PTB de 1945–1965*. Rio de Janeiro: Editora Fundação Getúlio Vargas, 1996.

D'Araujo, Maria Celina. "A volta de Vargas ao poder e a polarização das forças políticas e sociais." In *Getúlio Vargas & a economia nacional*, ed. Tamás Szmrecsányi and Rui Granziera. São Paulo: Hucitec, 2004.

Delgado, Lucília Neves de A. *O Comando Geral dos Trabalhadores no Brasil: 1961–1964*. Petrópolis, Brazil: Vozes, 1986.

Delgado, Lucília Neves de A. *PTB: do getulismo ao reformismo (1945–1964)*. São Paulo: Marco Zero, 1989.

Ferreira, Jorge. *O imaginário trabalhista: getulismo, PTB e cultura política popular, 1945–1964*. Rio de Janeiro: Civilização Brasileira, 2005.

Fontes, Paulo. *Comunidade operária, migração nordestina e lutas sociais: São Miguel Paulista (1945–1966)*. Campinas, Brazil: Editora da Unicamp, 2002.

Fontes, Paulo. "Migração nordestina e experiência operárias." In *Culturas de classe: identidade e diversidade na formação do operariado*, ed. Cláudio Batalha et al. Campinas, Brazil: Editora da Unicamp, 2004.

Fortes, Alexandre. "Revendo a legalização dos sindicatos: metalúrgicos de Porto Alegre (1931–1945)." In *Na luta por direitos. Estudos recentes em história social do trabalho*, ed. Alexandre Fortes et al. Campinas, Brazil: Editora da Unicamp, 1999.

Fortes, Alexandre. *Nós do quarto distrito: a classe trabalhadora portoalegrense e a Era Vargas.* Rio de Janeiro: Garamond, 2004.

French, John D. *O ABC dos operários: Conflitos e alianças de classe em São Paulo, 1900–1950.* São Paulo: Hucitec, 1995.

French, John D. *Drowning in Laws: Labor Law and Brazilian Political Culture.* Chapel Hill: University of North Carolina Press, 2004.

Gomes, Ângela de Castro. *A invenção do trabalhismo.* Rio de Janeiro: Vértice/IUPERJ, 1988.

Hall, Michael M. "Corporativismo e fascismo: As origens das leis trabalhistas brasileiras." In *Do corporativismo ao neoliberalismo: Estado e trabalhadores no Brasil e na Inglaterra,* ed. Ângela Araújo. São Paulo: Boitempo, 2002.

Levine, Robert M. *Pai dos pobres? O Brasil e a Era Vargas.* São Paulo: Companhia das Letras, 2001.

Negro, Antonio Luigi. *Linhas de montagem: O industrialismo nacional-desenvolvimentista e a sindicalização dos trabalhadores.* São Paulo: Boitempo, 2004.

Negro, Antonio L., and Paulo Fontes. "Trabalhadores em São Paulo: ainda um caso de polícia. O acervo do Deops paulista e o movimento sindical." In *No coração das trevas: O Deops–SP visto por dentro,* ed. Maria A. Aquino et al. São Paulo: Arquivo do Estado de São Paulo/Imprensa Oficial, 2001.

Oliveira, Francisco de. "Dilemas e perspectivas da economia brasileira no pré-1964." In *1964: Visões críticas do golpe,* ed. Caio Navarro de Toledo. Campinas, Brazil: Ed. Unicamp, 1997.

Pacheco, Jairo Queiroz. "Guerra na fábrica: Cotidiano operário fabril durante a segunda guerra, o caso de Juiz de Fora." M.A. diss., Universidade de São Paulo, 1996.

Silva, Fernando Teixeira da. *A carga e a culpa. Os operários das Docas de Santos: Direitos e Cultura de Solidariedade—1937–1968.* São Paulo: Hucitec, 1995.

Silva, Fernando Teixeira da, and Hélio da Costa. "Trabalhadores urbanos e populismo: Um balanço dos estudos recentes." In *O Populismo e sua história: Debate e crítica,* ed. Jorge Ferreira. Rio de Janeiro: Civilização Brasileira, 2001.

FERNANDO TEIXEIRA DA SILVA

BRAZIL, THE REGENCY. The period in Brazilian history following the 1831 abdication of Pedro I was a time of sweeping reform and chaos. In the absence of a ruling monarch, the General Assembly appointed a three-man regency to govern until Dom Pedro's son reached the age of eighteen. Its tenure was characterized by a political and constitutional vacuum, unstable governments, subordination of the executive to the legislative, transference of central power to provincial assemblies, and Liberal measures to create a federalist form of government. Reforms enacted in 1834 curtailed the power of the executive and of the emperor, and decentralized the government. The regents lost some prerogatives of the executive and of the moderative powers, including the ability to dissolve the Chamber of Deputies and to confer titles of nobility, and became subordinate to the legislative. The Additional Act (1834) transferred to the provinces powers heretofore belonging to the central government, abolished the Council of State and entailed estates, and created elected provincial assemblies. The National Guard was created to counterbalance the army.

The reforms rendered the central government a shadow, eliminated the center of authority and legitimacy, and encouraged regionalist centrifugal forces. A number of revolts and uprisings ensued, among them: Cabanos—Pernambuco and Alagoas (1835–1836); Cabanagem—Pará (1831–1833, 1835–1837); Balaiada (1838–1840); Sabinada—Bahia (1838–1840); and Farroupilha—Rio Grande do Sul (1835–1845).

The threat of anarchy resulting from Liberal policies caused a realignment of political forces bent on restoring order and the authority of the central government. The retrogression began in 1837, during the regency of the conservative leader Pedro de Araújo Lima, viscount of Olinda, with passage in May 1840 of the Law of Interpretation, which took away some prerogatives of provincial governments, and of a project to amend the Criminal Procedure Code to return to central control the police and judicial appointments. The crisis of political legitimacy continued, however, and in 1839 the country was near chaos and in danger of political dissolution. Luís Alves de Lima E Silva, duke of Caxias, utilized a core of loyal officers (the Sacred Battalion) at the head of the newly created National Guard to put down the rebellions. The success of the guard notwithstanding, the early accession of Pedro II was seen as the only solution to restore order and legitimacy. Although the Liberals initiated the movement for his majority for their own reasons, public support ultimately swayed the conservatives. In 1841,

Pedro II assumed the throne at age 15, thereby ending the Regency.

See also **Brazil: 1808-1889.**

BIBLIOGRAPHY

Thomas W. Palmer, Jr., "A Momentous Decade in Brazilian Administrative History, 1831–1840," in *Hispanic American Historical Review* 30, no. 2 (May 1950): 209–217.

João Pandiá Calogeras, *A History of Brazil,* translated and edited by Percy Alvin Martin (1939; repr. 1963), pp. 119–140.

Sérgio Buarque De Hollanda, *Historia geral da civilização brasileira,* vol. 6, no. 2 (1964), pp. 9–60.

E. Bradford Burns, *A History of Brazil,* 2d ed. (1980), pp. 170–176.

Roderick J. Barman, *Brazil: The Forging of a Nation, 1798–1852* (1988), pp. 189–209.

Additional Bibliography

Needell, Jeffrey D. *The Party of Order: The Conservatives, the State, and Slavery in the Brazilian Monarchy, 1831–1871.* Stanford, CA: Stanford University Press, 2006.

LYDIA M. GARNER
ROBERT A. HAYES

BRAZIL, REVOLUTIONS

This entry includes the following articles:
COMMUNIST REVOLTS OF 1935
CONSTITUTIONALIST REVOLT (SÃO PAULO)
FEDERALIST REVOLT OF 1893
LIBERAL REVOLUTION OF 1842
REVOLTS OF 1923–1924
REVOLUTION OF 1930
REVOLUTION OF 1964

COMMUNIST REVOLTS OF 1935

In 1934 and 1935, the Brazilian Communist Party (PCB) initiated a two-track policy in its attempt to gain power. On the one hand, it participated in a popular front–inspired strategy of making alliances with progressive political groups for an eventual electoral movement. This policy led to the creation in March 1935 of the National Liberation Alliance (ANL). On the other hand, Luís Carlos Prestes and other party leaders planned to stage a coup d'état with disaffected military men. The Comintern in Moscow initiated both strategies, in keeping with its own foreign-policy objectives. The popular front sought to limit the growing influence of fascism, and the coup was an attempt to undermine the smooth functioning of the U.S. and British colonial networks, formal and informal. Moreover, Comintern planners, including Brazilian exiles, looked to the experience of China—another large agrarian country—as their guide for formulating policies for Brazil.

Conceived in Moscow as part of the Soviet Union's offensive against Brazil as a U.S. client, the November 1935 putsch attempt (also known as the *intentona*) was a complete failure that adversely affected any group that had had ties to the ANL but had played no role in the uprising. A group of noncommissioned army men initiated the revolt on the evening of 23 November 1935 in the city of Natal, Rio Grande do Norte. Another group of men rebelled in Recife, Pernambuco. As the federal and state governments moved to crush this small-scale military uprising, Prestes and other PCB leaders initiated a similar uprising in Rio de Janeiro. Loyal troops quickly beat back the rebels.

In just four days, the PCB's quixotic putsch attempt not only failed but also ushered in a decade of state-sponsored repression of all left-wing and labor groups, even though they had not participated in the failed uprising. Getúlio Vargas's police arrested politicians of various leanings associated with the ANL, and the federal government purged labor union leaders throughout Brazil. The failed coup gave Vargas and his allies the political pretext for instituting a state of siege and eventually establishing the Estado Nôvo dictatorship in 1937.

See also **Communism; Soviet-Latin American Relations.**

BIBLIOGRAPHY

The standard work on politics in the mid-1930s, which includes analyses of the ANL and the *intentona*, is Robert M. Levine, *The Vargas Regime: The Critical Years, 1934–1938* (1970). Specific studies of the 1935 uprising include Thomas E. Skidmore, "Failure in Brazil: From Popular Front to Armed Revolt," in *Journal of Contemporary History* 5 (1970): 137–157, and Stanley E. Hilton, *Brazil and the Soviet Challenge, 1917–1947* (1991).

Additional Bibliography

Brown, Diana. *Umbanda: Religion and Politics in Urban Brazil.* New York: Columbia University Press, 1994.

Levine, Robert M. *Father of the Poor? Vargas and his Era.* Cambridge, U.K.: Cambridge University Press, 1998.

Oliveira Filho, Moacyr de. *Praxede, um operario no poder: a insurreiçao comunista de 1935 vista por dentro.* São Paulo: Editora Alfa-Omega, 1985.

Williams, Daryle. *Culture Wars in Brazil: The First Vargas Regime, 1930–1945.* Durham, NC: Duke University Press, 2001.

JOEL WOLFE

CONSTITUTIONALIST REVOLT (SÃO PAULO)

In 1932 the Brazilian state of São Paulo rebelled against the central government. The seeds of this uprising were sown right after the Revolution of 1930, when the Democratic Party (PD) expected to run the state by replacing the São Paulo Republican Party (PRP). President Getúlio Vargas, however, put *tenentes* (army lieutenants) in control of the state and agreed with their objections to a speedy reconstitutionalization of Brazil. Leaders of São Paulo, a state accustomed to a dominant national role, became so alienated by Vargas that the PD and PRP formed the anti-Vargas, pro-constitution Frente Única Paulista (FUP), which plotted with the Rio Grande do Sul Frente Única Riograndense (FUR) to overthrow Vargas. In May 1932 Vargas promised a constitutional assembly election in 1933, and São Paulo achieved its cherished FUP state government. But in July, General Bertoldo Klinger, chosen by the plotters in April to lead the revolt, was dismissed by Vargas from his troop command in Mato Grosso, a development that, according to a FUP–FUR agreement, called for revolt. Paulistas, incited by pro-constitution, anti-Vargas oratory, were determined to overthrow Vargas and thus regain their state's dominant nationale role. So they sent troops to battle and were disappointed when the other states, especially Rio Grande do Sul and Minas Gerais, did not join the rebellion. In September, after the Paulistas retreated before superior federal forces, their state troops surrendered, to the surprise of their politicians. Vargas exiled São Paulo's leaders to Portugal, but he treated the people of São Paulo generously and implemented his plans for a constitution.

See also **Brazil, Revolutions: Revolution of 1930.**

BIBLIOGRAPHY

Euclydes Figueiredo, *Contribuição para a história da Revolução Constitucionalista de 1932* (1954).

Paulo Nogueira Filho, *A guerra cívica, 1932,* 4 vols. (1965–1967, 1981).

John W. F. Dulles, *Vargas of Brazil* (1967).

Additional Bibliography

Aggio, Alberto, Agnaldo de Sousa Barbosa, and Hercídia Mara Facuri Coelho Lambert. *Política e sociedade no Brasil, 1930–1964.* São Paulo, SP, Brasil: Annablume, 2002.

Levine, Robert M. *Father of the Poor? Vargas and His Era.* Cambridge, U.K.: Cambridge University Press, 1998.

Williams, Daryle. *Culture Wars in Brazil: The First Vargas Regime, 1930–1945.* Durham, NC: Duke University Press, 2001.

JOHN W. F. DULLES

FEDERALIST REVOLT OF 1893

In the state of Rio Grande do Sul, a challenge to Governor Júlio de Castilhos arose in 1893. Rebels joined forces with the naval rebellion of Admiral Custódio de Melo to oppose the republican regime of Floriano Vieira Peixoto, convulsing Rio Grande do Sul in a civil war that took 10,000 casualties before its end in August 1895. Led by Gaspar Silveira Martins, Federalists ranged from monarchists to dissident Republicans, united by hatred of Castilhos and resentment of his Republican Party's monopoly on power. They called for his ouster, abrogation of his authoritarian, positivist 1891 state constitution, and Brazil's conversion to a parliamentary regime. Support from Peixoto and the army gave Castilhos military superiority. Rebels raided north into Santa Catarina in November 1893, linking up with naval rebels who had taken that state's capital, and into Paraná, to take Curitiba on 20 January 1894, before turning back. The death of leading rebel general Gumercindo Saraiva, assumption of the presidency by Prudente de Morais, and defeat of Admiral Luís Felipe Saldanha Da Gama's invasion of Rio Grande in April 1895, led to the revolt's demise.

Two and a half years of fighting, with mass atrocities on both sides, bred hatreds that deeply divided Rio Grande for three decades. These years also confirmed the Castilhista machine's control of the state and laid the foundations for future Riograndense strength in national politics.

See also **Castilhos, Júlio de.**

BIBLIOGRAPHY

Joseph L. Love, *Rio Grande do Sul and Brazilian Regionalism, 1882–1930* (1971).

Silvio do Duncan Baretta, "Political Violence and Regime Change: A Study of the 1893 Civil War in Southern Brazil" (Ph.D. diss., Univ. of Pittsburgh, 1985).

Additional Bibliography

Campos, Maria da Carmo and Martha Geralda Alves d'Azevedo. *Protasio Alves e o seu tempo, 1859–1933*. Porto Alegre: Já Editores, 2006.

Ferreira, Mariluci Melo. *Tramas de poder: A política no Rio Grande do Sul, século XIX*. Passo Fundo: Universidade do Passo Fundo, 2003.

Kraay, Hendrik. *Race, State, and Armed Forces in Independence-era Brazil: Bahia, 17902s–1840s*. Stanford, CA: Stanford University Press, 2004.

Needell, Jeffrey D. *The Party of Order: Conservatives, the State, and Slavery in the Brazilian Monarchy, 1831–1871*. Stanford, CA: Stanford University Press, 2001.

Summerhill, William Roderick. *Order against Progress: Government, Foreign Investment, and Railroads in Brazil, 1854–1913*. Stanford, CA: Stanford University Press, 2003.

JOAN BAK

LIBERAL REVOLUTION OF 1842

In 1841 there was a revolt in the Brazilian provinces of Minas Gerais and São Paulo against the measures taken by the Conservative cabinet. The dismissal of several Liberal provincial presidents, the dissolution of the Chamber of Deputies, the reform of the Criminal Procedure Code, and the reinstatement of the Council of State were acts strongly opposed by Liberals since they weakened provincial authority and strengthened the central government. The conspirators aimed at bringing down the Conservative cabinet and reversing the changes, but the revolt was poorly planned and miscalculated. The national uprising, which was expected to follow events in São Paulo and Minas Gerais, never materialized, and the rebellious military forces were few, disorganized, and plagued by desertion. The central government, in turn, acted swiftly with a military campaign led by Luís Alves de Lima E Silva, the baron of Caxias, which brought the revolt to an end in August 1842.

As the first major challenge to the reign of Pedro II, the revolt was especially threatening to the central government because of the political and social status of its leaders and the geographical location of the provinces involved. Its defeat accelerated the pace of political and administrative centralization. In 1844 amnesty was granted to all participants.

See also **Pedro II of Brazil.**

BIBLIOGRAPHY

Roderick J. Barman, *Brazil: The Forging of a Nation, 1798–1852* (1988), pp. 212–216.

Additional Bibliography

Chamone, Carla Simone. *Festejos imperiais: Festas cívias em Minas Gerais, 1815–1845*. Bragança Paulista: Centro de Documentaçao e Apoio a Pesquisa em Historia da Educaçao, 2002.

Graça Filho, Afonso de Alencastro. *A princesa do oeste e o mito da decadencia de Minas Gerais: São João del Rei, 1831–1888*. São Paulo: Annablume, 2002.

Kiddy, Elizabeth W. *Blacks of the Rosary: Memory and History in Minas Gerais, Brazil*. University Park: Pennsylvania State University Press, 2005.

Langfur, Hal. *The Forbidden Lands: Colonial Identity, Frontier Violence, and the Persistence of Brazil's Eastern Indians, 1750–1830*. Stanford, CA: Stanford University Press, 2006.

Marinho, José Antonio. *Historia do movimiento politico que no anno de 1842 teve lugar na provinca de Minas Geraes*. Rio de Janeiro: Typographia Alameida, 1939.

LYDIA M. GARNER

REVOLTS OF 1923–1924

Political and economic unrest sparked revolts in Rio Grande do Sul and São Paulo in 1923 and 1924. When the governor of Rio Grande do Sul, Antônio Augusto Borges de Medeiros, ran for a fifth consecutive term, his opponents united in the Liberation Alliance to support the candidacy of Joaquim Francisco de Assis Brasil. Borges apparently garnered the requisite three-quarters of the popular vote, but the Libertadores claimed fraud, and on inauguration day (25 January 1923), uprisings erupted throughout the state. The unrest was resolved in December 1923 with the Pact of Pedras Altas, a compromise that maintained Borges's right to the governorship while granting some concessions to the opposition. Discontent continued to simmer, nonetheless, especially in the state's outlying areas.

On 5 July 1924, the second anniversary of the Tenentes' Revolt, military officers who remained unhappy with the political preeminence of Brazil's coffee elite represented by President Artur da Silva Bernardes rebelled in several states. They were most successful in São Paulo, where they captured and held the state capital for almost three weeks before fleeing into the interior. By late 1924 the rebel forces, under the leadership of Isidoro Dias Lopes, had moved into the state of Paraná, where they controlled the towns of Guaíra, Foz do Iguaçu, and Catanduvas. Meanwhile, rebellion erupted once again in Rio Grande do Sul, this time in army garrisons of the Missões district. The Paulistas found support for their movement in Luis Carlos Prestes, a young captain at the time, who linked Rio Grande's revolt to that of São Paulo. Many gaucho rebels, when forced into flight by government forces, joined Isidoro Dias Lopes's troops in Paraná. Following the fall of Catanduvas, the center of the rebellion, on 27 March 1925, leaders agreed to carry the struggle to overthrow Bernardes to the more remote interior. Thus began the three-year march of the Prestes Column through the backlands of Brazil.

See also **Tenentismo.**

BIBLIOGRAPHY

E. Bradford Burns, *A History of Brazil* (1970).

Joseph L. Love, *Rio Grande do Sul and Brazilian Regionalism, 1882–1930* (1971).

Edgard Carone, *Revoluções do Brasil contemporâneo, 1922–1938* (1975).

Ronald M. Schneider, *"Order and Progress": A Political History of Brazil* (1991).

Additional Bibliography

Antonacci, Maria Antoneta. *RS, as oposições & a Revolução de 1923*. Porto Alegre: Mercado Aberto, 1981.

Caldas, Pedro Henrique. *Zeca Netto & a conquista de Pelotas*. Porto Alegre: Ediições EST, 1995.

Cunha, José Antonio Flores da. *A campanha de 1923*. Brasília: Senado Federal, 1979.

Franco, Sergio da Costa. *A pacifacação de 1923: As negociações de Bagé*. Porto Alegre: Editora da Universidade Federal do Rio Grande do Sul, 1996.

Lago, Luis A. Correa do. *Oswaldo Aranha, o Rio Grande e a Revoluçao de 1930: Um político gaucho na República Velha*. Rio de Janeiro: Editora Noval Fronteira, 1995.

JOAN E. MEZNAR

REVOLUTION OF 1930

Unsuccessful in the presidential race of 1930, Getúlio Vargas, governor of Rio Grande do Sul, led a military uprising that overturned the government of Brazil. The revolt began in Porto Alegre, capital of Rio Grande do Sul, the southernmost state of Brazil. There was little bloodshed.

The "revolution" stemmed in part from the domination of Brazil by the state of São Paulo since the fall of the monarchy in 1889, and in part from the fact that the incumbent president, Washington Luís Pereira De Sousa of São Paulo misjudged the mood of the nation when he imposed another paulista as the official candidate for the presidential election of March 1930 after an earlier promise that the new chief executive would come from Minas Gerais. Minas Gerais politicians felt betrayed by this action and broke the traditional alliance of the two states. Led by Antônio Carlos de Andrada, they threw their support to a reluctant presidential opposition candidate, Getúlio Vargas, in the 1930 presidential race. Minas Gerais and Rio Grande do Sul formed a political alliance with the tiny northeastern state of Paraíba to oppose the official paulista candidate, Júlio Prestes. This new political group, called the Liberal Alliance, opposed the traditional Republican Party of Brazil, which controlled the seventeen other states. Vargas, an astute political realist, doubted the voting power of the three-state Liberal Alliance.

The presidential campaign was traditional, and though Brazil was in an economic crisis, Vargas did not mount a populist crusade. He campaigned in a low-keyed manner against political corruption, favored amnesty for the 1922 and 1924 military rebels, and pushed for a reorganization of the federal Justice and Education departments. He privately assured President Luís that if he, Vargas, lost the race he would support the victor unconditionally.

During the campaign the world market price of coffee dropped to less than five cents a pound (from its high of twenty-three cents in 1928). This change profoundly affected the financial structure of the nation, as the president spent great sums of federal funds to support the coffee export price and prevent the collapse of the paulista coffee economy.

The election, held 1 March 1930, came out as predicted by Vargas. Although he was very popular, the franchise was extremely limited, and Prestes won with just over 1 million votes to Vargas's 750,000. In Rio Grande do Sul, one of Vargas's closest advisers,

Oswaldo Aranha, claimed that Prestes's victory had been obtained fraudulently and declared that the time had come for an armed rebellion.

Active revolutionary plotting began in Rio Grande do Sul and soon spread through the rest of Brazil as economic conditions continued to deteriorate. Military dissidents—most notably the group of *tenentes* who had led rebellions against political corruption in 1922 and 1924—were contacted. The revolution broke on 3 October, and by 24 October the country was securely in the rebels' hands. Luís and Prestes went into exile, and the Vargas forces took over.

In the fifteen years the Vargas forces remained in control of the nation, they temporarily shifted economic and political power away from São Paulo and Minas Gerais. The new wave of politicians also increased the role of the government in the nation's economic life.

See also **Vargas, Getúlio Dornelles.**

BIBLIOGRAPHY

Thomas E. Skidmore, *Politics in Brazil, 1930–1964* (1967).

Jordan M. Young, *The Brazilian Revolution of 1930 and the Aftermath* (1967).

Boris Fausto, *A revolução de 1930* (1970).

Peter Flynn, *Brazil: A Political Analysis* (1978).

Additional Bibliography

Dulles, John W.F. *Sobral Pinto, "the Conscience of Brazil": Leading the Attack against Vargas (1930–1945.)* Austin: University of Texas, 2002.

Hentschke, Jens R. *Vargas and Brazil: New Perspectives.* New York: Palgrave Macmillan, 2006.

Meade, Theresa. *A Brief History of Brazil.* New York: Facts on File, 2003.

Prestes, Anita Leocádia. *Da insurreiçao armada, 1935 a união nacional, 1938–1945: A virada táctica na política do PCB.* São Paulo: Paz e Terra, 2001.

Ribeiro, José Augusto. *A era Vargas.* Rio de Janeiro: Casa Jorge, 2001.

Rose, R.S. *One of the Forgotten Things: Getúlio Vargas and Brazilian Social Control, 1930–1954.* Westport, CT: Greenwood Press, 2000.

Williams, Daryle. *Culture Wars in Brazil: The First Vargas Regime, 1930–1945.* Durham, NC: Duke University Press, 2001.

JORDAN M. YOUNG

REVOLUTION OF 1964

In a military coup (31 March–2 April 1964) the Brazilian armed forces overthrew the democratically elected government of President João Goulart and went on to rule Brazil for the next twenty-one years. Believing Goulart to be a radical leftist, the military high command and the political Right had long opposed him. The candidate of the Brazilian Labor Party (PTB), Goulart was elected vice president in 1960. When President Jânio Quadros resigned in August 1961, the military vehemently opposed Goulart's inauguration. Only after the congress created a quasi-parliamentary system, stripping the president of many of his powers, was he allowed to be sworn in. In January 1963, a national plebiscite abolished the compromise solution and reinstated Goulart's full presidential powers.

Goulart inherited major economic problems from previous administrations. His mishandling of the economy aggravated these problems and along with a move to the left, contributed to the crisis leading to the coup. After drawn-out negotiations with the International Monetary Fund, the government abandoned any effort to formulate an economic austerity plan and to resolve a balance of payments and external debt crisis. By early 1964 the annual inflation rate approached 100 percent. When Goulart staged a series of mass rallies calling for such basic reforms as nationalization of foreign corporations, the franchise for illiterates, and agrarian reform, the military high command made plans for a coup d'état.

As peasants organized unions in the countryside and leftist labor leaders mobilized workers in the cities, many Brazilians believed the country was moving toward a leftist revolution. Opponents on the Right increasingly called for a military coup and mobilized resources to check the government. The U.S. government, also fearing a leftist revolution, supported the conspirators and the coup. By 1964, the political Center was rapidly disappearing as both the Right and the Left promoted political polarization.

Goulart's intervention into the military chain of command provided the spark for the coup. His mishandling of a naval mutiny infuriated the high command. In a nationally televised speech to a group of sergeants on 30 March, he essentially called for them to disobey their superiors should they feel their orders were not in the best interest of the nation. Incensed by the speech, the commander of the First Army in Minas Gerais, General Olímpio Mourão Filho, ordered his troops to move on Rio de Janeiro on the morning of 31 March, thus setting the coup into action. Within hours other army commanders joined the coup led by General Humberto Castello Branco. Goulart fled into exile in Uruguay, and the military took control in a virtually bloodless coup d'état.

See also **Goulart, João Belchior Marques; Military Dictatorships: Since 1945.**

BIBLIOGRAPHY

Thomas E. Skidmore, *Politics in Brazil, 1930–1964* (1967).

Alfred Stepan, "The Breakdown of Democratic Regimes: Brazil," in *The Breakdown of Democratic Regimes: Latin America,* edited by Juan J. Linz and Alfred Stepan (1978).

René Armand Dreifuss, *1964: A conquista do estado* (1981).

Wanderley Guilherme dos Santos, *Sessenta e quatro: Anatomia da crise* (1986).

Additional Bibliography

Borges, Maruo. *O golpe em Goiás: História de uma grande traição.* Goiás: Editora Viera, 2006.

Johnson, Ollie A. *Brazilian Party Politics and the Coup of 1964.* Gainesville: University Press of Florida, 2001.

Lattman-Wetlman, Fernando, and Alfonso Arinos de Melo Franco. *A política domesticada: Afonso Arinos e o colapso de democracia em 1964.* Rio de Janeiro: Editora FGV, 2005.

Leacock, Ruth. *Requiem for Revolution: The United States and Brazil, 1961–1969.* Kent, OH: Kent State University Press, 1990.

Silva, Marcos A. *Brasil, 1964–1968: A ditadura já era ditadura.* São Paulo: LCTE Editora, 2006.

MARSHALL C. EAKIN

BRAZILIAN TRUTH COMMISSION.

Beginning in 1979, the Archbishop of São Paulo and the World Council of Churches sponsored a clandestine nongovernmental investigation of human rights abuses by the military since the 1964 coup that had overthrown Brazilian democracy. Lawyers connected to the Catholic Church checked out documents,

which they were legally authorized to do, related to more than 700 cases before military courts and photocopied more than a million pages of records (which they immediately had microfilmed, with copies sent abroad for safekeeping). In August 1985 the São Paulo diocese published *Brasil: Nunca Mais,* a collection of allegations of torture and murder by government forces since the military takeover. It became an instant bestseller and ensured that past human rights abuses remained in the public eye during the transition back to democratic government (Pereira). In the ten weeks after its publication, *Brasil: Nunca Mais* sold more than 100,000 copies (at the time, the latest novel by Brazil's most popular writer, Jorge Amado, took nearly a year to sell 200,000 copies) (Pereira). Interest in the past was not uniform across Brazilian society, however: Few Brazilians over age forty, for example, purchased *Brasil: Nunca Mais* (Hamber). The project also leaked the names of perpetrators, but there were few repercussions for them. No prosecutions took place and many continued to hold prominent positions in the armed forces and the police.

See also **Brazil: Since 1889; Brazil, Revolutions: Revolution of 1964; Truth Commissions.**

BIBLIOGRAPHY

Catholic Church, Archdiocese of São Paulo. *Torture in Brazil: A Report* (English translation of *Brasil: Nunca Mais*). Translated by Jaime Wright. New York: Vintage Books, 1986.

Hamber, Brandon. "Living with the Legacy of Impunity: Lessons for South Africa about Truth, Justice and Crime in Brazil." *Latin American Report* 13: 2, 4–16.

Pereira, Anthony. "An Ugly Democracy? State Violence and the Rule of Law in Brazil." In *Democratic Brazil: Actors, Institutions, and Processes,* edited by Peter R. Kingstone and Timothy J. Power. Pittsburgh, PA: University of Pittsburgh Press, 2000.

Weschler, Lawrence. *A Miracle, a Universe: Settling Accounts with Torturers.* New York: Pantheon Books, 1990.

ERIC BRAHM

BRAZIL, VICEROYS OF.

The viceroy was the highest royal official in Brazil. Usually military men of noble birth, viceroys in Brazil occupied the office of governor-general of Bahia from 1549 to

1720. They were the highest appointed royal officials in colonial Brazil. Like the other governors, the viceroys represented the king and embodied royal authority. Called the "shadows of the King," they were similar to but not as powerful as the Spanish American viceroys. They were royal commissioners who enforced the king's justice in his domain in colonial Brazil. In theory the captains-general or governors were subordinate to the viceroy, but in practice the viceroy's authority was limited to his own captaincy. As the supreme commander of all the armed forces in his district, he was responsible primarily for defending his captaincy from Indian attacks and foreign interlopers.

After 1720 the governors-general of Brazil used the title of viceroy. The early governors-general centralized governmental administration and consolidated royal control over Brazil. They dispensed royal justice, collected taxes, founded towns, oversaw the work of the church, and appointed judges. The viceroys of Brazil sat on the High Court (*Relação*) and presided over the meetings of the town councils in Salvador da Bahia and Rio de Janeiro. Colonial Brazilians complained that the viceroys and governors-general interfered in local affairs. In the eighteenth century their power increased to the point where the viceroys could recall a disobedient governor and recommend a successor, but they had no coercive powers to remove a stubborn captain-general. The eighteenth-century captain-general Gomes Freire de Andrade (1685–1763) exercised more power and governed a larger domain in Rio de Janeiro, Minas Gerais, and São Paulo than did the viceroys. By the eighteenth century the captains-general reported directly to the king rather than to the viceroy. The viceroys of the eighteenth century were stronger than their predecessors and more effective administrators.

The viceroy in Brazil ordinarily served a term of six and one-half years in the sixteenth century, three and one-half years in the seventeenth century, and six years in the eighteenth century. As appointed royal representatives, the viceroys tried to be independent of local interests. Their authority increased in times of war and foreign attacks, since their military powers were great. Among the outstanding viceroys were the count of Sabugosa (1720–1735), the marquis of Lavradio (1769–1779), and Luís de Vasconcelos e Sousa (1778–1790). Under close local and royal scrutiny, the viceroys were subject to an inspection at the end of their term (*residencia*). As chiefs of state and official royal representatives, the viceroys tried to keep Brazil unified and loyal to the crown while defending the domain from foreign interlopers.

Governors-General and Viceroys of Brazil (1549–1769).

Tomé de Sousa (1549–1553)

Duarte da Costa (1553–1556)

Mem de Sá (1556–1570)

D. Luís de Brito e Almeida—North (1570–1572)

D. Antônio de Salema—South (1570–1572)

D. Luís de Brito e Almeida—North (1572–1577)

Lourenço da Veiga (1577–1581)

Cosme Rangel (1581–1583)

Manuel Teles Barreto (1583–1587)

Junta do Governo: D. Antônio de Barreiros and Cristóvão de Barros (1587–1591)

D. Francisco de Sousa (1591–1602)

D. Diogo Botelho (1602–1608)

D. Diogo de Meneses e Siqueira—North and South (1608–1612)

D. Gaspar de Sousa (1612–1617)

D. Luís de Sousa (1617–1621)

D. Diogo de Mendonça Furtado (1621–1624)

Matias de Albuquerque (1624)

D. Francisco Nunes Marinho d'Eça (1624–1626)

D. Francisco de Moura Rolim (1624–1626)

Diogo Luís de Oliveira (1626–1635)

D. Pedro da Silva (1635–1639)

D. Fernando Mascarenhas, count of Torre (1639)

D. Vasco Mascarenhas, count of Óbidos (1639–1640)

D. Jorge Mascarenhas, marquis of Montalvão, considered the first viceroy of Brazil (1640–1641)

Junta do Governo: Bishop D. Pedro, Luís Barbalho, and Provedor-Mor Lourenço Brito Correia, who assumed office upon the death of his predecessor (1641–1642)

Antônio Teles da Silva (1642–1647)

Antônio Teles de Meneses, count of Vila Pouca de Aguiar (1647–1650)

João Rodrigues de Vasconcelos e Sousa, count of Castelo Melhor (1650–1654)

D. Jerônimo de Ataíde, count of Atouguia (1654–1657)

Francisco Barreto (1657–1663)

D. Vasco de Mascarenhas, count of Óbidos, considered the second viceroy of Brazil (1663–1667)

Alexandre e Sousa Freire (1667–1671)

Francisco Correia da Silva (declined the appointment)

Afonso Furtado de Castro do Rio de Mendonça, viscount of Barbacena (1671–1675)

Junta do Governo: Desembargador Agostinho de Azevedo Monteiro, Álvaro de Azevedo, and Antônio Guedes de Brito, who assumed office on the death of his predecessor (1675–1678)

Roque da Costa Barreto (1678–1682)

Antônio de Sousa de Meneses, the Braço de Prata (1682–1684)

Antônio Luís de Sousa, marquis of Minas (1684–1687)

Matias da Cunha (1687–1688)

D. Frei Manuel da Ressurreição (1688–1690)

Antônio Luís Gonçalves da Câmara Coutinho (1690–1694)

D. João de Lencastre (1694–1702)

D. Rodrigo da Costa (1702–1708)

D. Luís César de Meneses (1708–1710)

D. Lourenço de Almada (1710–1711)

D. Pedro de Vasconcelos e Sousa (1711–1714)

D. Pedro de Noronha, count of Vila Verde and marquis of Angeja, third viceroy of Brazil (1714–1718)

D. Sancho de Faro e Sousa, count of Vimieiro (1718–1719)

Interim government of the Archbishop: Dom Sebastião Monteiro da Vide, chancellor of the High Court, Caetano de Brito de Figueredo, and Master of the Field João de Araujo e Azevedo (1719–1720)

Vasco Fernandes César de Meneses, count of Sabugosa, fourth viceroy of Brazil (1720–1735)

André de Mello e Castro, count of Galveas, fifth viceroy of Brazil (1735–1749)

D. Luís Pedro Peregrino de Carvalho Meneses e Ataíde, tenth count of Atouquia (1749–1754)

Interim government of the Archbishop: Dom José Botelho de Mattos, chancellor of the High Court, Manuel Antônio da Cunha Sotto Maior, and Colonel Lourenço Monteiro (1755)

D. Marcos de Noronha e Brito, sixth count of Arcos (1755–1760)

D. Antônio de Almeida Soares e Portugal, first marquis of Lavradio, third count of Arintes (1760)

Interim government of the Archbishop: Tomás Rubi de Barros Barreto, José Carvalho de Andrade, and Barrose Alvim (1760–1763)

D. Antônio Alvares da Cunha, count of Cunha (1763–1767)

D. Antônio Rolim de Moura, count of Azambuja (1767–1769)

Governors-General of Rio de Janeiro (1769–1808).

D. Luis de Almeida, Portugal Soares d'Eça Alarcao e Melo Silva e Mascarenhas, second marquis of Lavradio (1769–1779)

D. Luís de Vasconcelos e Sousa, count of Figueiro (1778–1790)

D. José Luís de Castro, second count of Rezende (1790–1801)

Fernando José de Portugal e Castro, count of Resende (1801–1806)

Marcos de Noronha e Brito, eighth count of Arcos (1806–1808)

See also **Brazil: The Colonial Era, 1500-1808; Viceroyalty, Viceroy.**

BIBLIOGRAPHY

Dauril Alden, *Royal Government in Colonial Brazil with Special Reference to the Administration of the Marquis of Lavradio, Viceroy 1769–1779* (1968).

Helio Vianna, *Dicionário da história do Brasil: Moral e civismo* 4th ed. (1976), pp. 265, 266, 552, 553.

Additional Bibliography

Monteiro, Rodrigo Bentes. *O rei no espelho. A monarquia portuguesa e a. colonização da América: 1640–1720.* São Paulo: Editora Hucitec, 2002.

PATRICIA MULVEY

BRAZILWOOD. Brazilwood, a dyewood from various tropical trees (especially genus *Caesalpinia*) whose extracts yield shades of red and purple.

Caesalpinia enchinata, Brazil's first important export, lured French and Portuguese traders to the coast in the early 1500s; its similarity to *Caesalpinia brasiliensis,* a species indigenous to the Near East and long familiar to Europeans, gave Brazil its name.

Although Brazil's earliest permanent settlements sprang from brazilwood trading forts and factories, participants in the trade did not intend to settle the region. In the 1530s, however, Portugal's increased interest in colonization stemmed in part from the crown's desire to establish control of the dyewood trade in the face of French competition.

European traders depended on indigenous peoples to fell the dyewood trees and transport the wood to collection points. The Portuguese employed a factory system: the Indians brought the wood to forts on the coast, where ships later called for it. The French, on the other hand, collected cargoes by anchoring offshore and sending crewmen to arrange an exchange with local tribes.

Initially, the brazilwood trade was based on peaceful barter between Europeans and Indians, but these arrangements soon degenerated into coercion of indigenous peoples.

Bow makers prefer brazilwood because of its quality. However, since the eighteenth century, brazilwood has been in decline as a result of over-harvesting. The World Conservation Union in 2007 declared brazilwood an endangered species.

See also **Portuguese Trade and International Relations.**

BIBLIOGRAPHY

Alexander Marchant, *From Barter to Slavery: The Economic Relations of Portuguese and Indians in the Settlement of Brazil, 1500–1580* (1942).

John Hemming, *Red Gold: The Conquest of the Brazilian Indians* (1978).

Additional Bibliography

Cunha, Manuela Carneiro da, and Francisco M. Salzano. *História dos índios no Brasil.* São Paulo: Fundação de Amparo à Pesquisa do Estado de São Paulo: Companhia das Letras: Secretaria Municipal de Cultura, 1992.

Metcalf, Alida C. *Go-Betweens and the Colonization of Brazil, 1500–1600.* Austin: University of Texas Press, 2005.

Smith, Nigel J. H. *The Amazon River Forest: A Natural History of Plants, Animals, and People.* New York: Oxford University Press, 1999.

Wood, Charles H., and Roberto Porro. *Deforestation and Land Use in the Amazon.* Gainesville: University Press of Florida, 2002.

CARA SHELLY

BRECHERET, VÍTOR (1894–1955).

Vítor Brecheret (*b.* 22 February 1894; *d.* 17 December 1955), Brazilian sculptor. Born in Italy, Brecheret moved to Brazil with his sister in 1913 and began his formal artistic education at the Liceu de Artes e Ofícios de São Paulo in 1912. For the next six years he studied art in Europe, where he came to greatly appreciate the work of the French sculptor Auguste Rodin. While in Rome, he won first place in Rome's International Exhibition of Fine Arts for his *Despertar.*

When Brecheret returned to São Paulo in 1919, he set up a studio, and by January 1920 he had met fellow artists Di Cavalcanti, Hélios Seelinger, Menotti des Picchia, and Oswald de Andrade, who recognized his importance for modernism. That same year he was selected to submit plans for a monument commemorating the participation of the bandeira in Brazil's early history. In 1921, after his *Eva* was acquired by the prefecture of São Paulo, Brecheret obtained a government stipend to finance a second trip to Europe. Before leaving for France, however, he selected twelve of his sculptures for exhibition during São Paulo's Modern Art Week in 1922.

Between his return to Brazil in 1930 and his death in 1955, Brecheret realized numerous exhibitions and founded the Sociedade Pró-Arte Moderna (1932). He received the French Legion of Honor and won the National Prize for Sculpture in the 1951 São Paulo Biennial. He also did several commemorative public monuments.

See also **Art: The Twentieth Century.**

BIBLIOGRAPHY

Mário Da Silva Brito, *História do modernismo brasileiro* (1978), esp. pp. 104–134.

Aracy Amaral, *Artes plásticas na Semana de 22: Subsídios para uma história da renovação das artes no Brasil,* 4th ed. (1979), esp. pp. 240–242.

Additional Bibliography

Alvarado, Daisy V. M. Peccinini de. *Brecheret: A linguagem das formas.* São Paulo: Instituto Vitor Brecheret, 2004.

Camargos, Marcia. *Semana de 22: Entre vaias e aplausos.* São Paulo: Boitempo, 2002.

CAREN A. MEGHREBLIAN

BRENNER, ANITA

BRENNER, ANITA (1905–1974). Anita Brenner (*b.* 13 August 1905; *d.* 1 December 1974), journalist, author, and editor who lived in Mexico. Born of American Jewish parents in Aguascalientes, Mexico, Brenner matured in Mexican, Jewish, and North American cultures. She was a member of the cosmopolitan intellectual community in Mexico City in the 1920s and did key archival research for Ernest Gruening's *Mexico and Its Heritage* (1928). Her first book, *Idols behind Altars* (1929), emphasized the Indian component of Mexican art and culture. In the 1930s Brenner worked as a journalist and completed a doctorate in anthropology at Columbia University. She wrote the text to accompany George Leighton's photographs for *The Wind that Swept Mexico* (1943), an overview of the Mexican Revolution. From 1955 to 1971 she was editor of *Mexico This Month,* an English-language magazine based in Mexico.

See also **Journalism in Mexico.**

BIBLIOGRAPHY

Anita Brenner, *Idols behind Altars* (1929) and *The Wind that Swept Mexico* (1943). See also Ernest Gruening, *Mexico and Its Heritage* (1928), esp. pp. 393–493, in which Brenner's research appeared.

Additional Bibliography

Glusker, Susannah Joel. *Anita Brenner: A Mind of Her Own.* Austin: University of Texas Press, 1998.

JOHN A. BRITTON

BRESSER PEREIRA, LUIZ CARLOS

BRESSER PEREIRA, LUIZ CARLOS (1934–). Luiz Carlos Bresser Pereira (*b.* 30 June 1934), Brazilian economist. Born in São Paulo,

Bresser Pereira received a law degree from the University of São Paulo (USP) in 1957. After joining the faculty of the Getúlio Vargas Foundation in São Paulo (FGV-SP) in 1959, he went to Michigan State University, where he earned an M.B.A. in 1961. Returning to Brazil, he continued his academic career at FGV-SP, becoming a full professor in 1972, the same year in which he earned a Ph.D. in economics from USP. A prolific writer, he has written more than fifteen books and hundreds of articles covering a broad array of subjects. Sometimes characterized as a neo-structuralist, he took the role of the state in the process of economic development as a major theme of research. In the early 1980s, together with Yoshiaki Nakano, he wrote seminal contributions to the formulation of the theory of inertial inflation. He also had a successful career in the private sector (as administrative director of a major Brazilian supermarket chain) and was politically active (as one of the leading economists of the Brazilian Democratic Movement Party (PMDB)—the main opposition party to the military regime).

In 1983, Bresser Pereira was appointed president of the state-owned bank of São Paulo (BANESPA), and from March 1985 to April 1987 he served both the Montoro and the Quércia administrations as state secretary. Appointed by President José Sarney, Bresser Pereira replaced Dilson Funaro on 29 April 1987 as Brazil's finance minister after the collapse of the Cruzado Plan. His stabilization program (the Bresser Plan) relied on a temporary price freeze and on measures of fiscal austerity. When the resistance of President Sarney to fiscal austerity became evident, Bresser Pereira resigned on 18 December 1987. He is also known for his attempts to persuade foreign creditors of the necessity for debt relief in developing countries.

See also **Brazil, Political Parties: Brazilian Democratic Movement Party (PMDB); Sarney, José.**

BIBLIOGRAPHY

Oxhorn, Phillip. *What Kind of Democracy? What Kind of Market? Latin America in the Age of Neoliberalism.* University Park, PA: Pennsylvania State University Press, 1998.

Pereira, Luis Carlos Bresser. *Economic Crisis and State Reform in Brazil: Toward a New Interpretation of Latin America.* Boulder, CO: L. Reinner, 1996.

Pereira, Luis Carlos Bresser. *Economic Reforms in New Democracies: A Social-Democratic Approach*. Cambridge, U.K.: Cambridge University Press, 1993.

Williamson, John. *The Political Economy of Policy Reform*. Washington, DC: Institute for International Economics, 1994.

CARLOS ALBERTO PRIMO BRAGA

BRIERRE, JEAN-FERNAND (1909–1992).

Jean-Fernand Brierre (pseud. Jean-François; b. 28 September 1909; d. 24 December 1992). Haitian writer and government official in Haiti and Senegal. In 1932, after serving as secretary to the Haitian Embassy in Paris (1929–1930), Brierre founded the opposition newspaper *La Bataille*. The paper was suspended and Brierre was imprisoned. After an appointment as inspector of schools in Jérémie, Brierre finally became ambassador to Argentina under President Paul Magloire. Imprisoned again by President François Duvalier in 1961, Brierre left for Jamaica. He settled in Dakar when Senegalese President Léopold Sédar Senghor offered him a position in the ministry of culture.

Brierre's writing has been characterized by a celebration of the suffering and the triumphs of black people, especially Haitians. Addressing both slaves and his contemporaries in "Black Soul," Brierre wrote that "the black serpent of pain ripples through the contortions of your body." A current of Christian ideology informs even his more erotic poetry. Brierre published copiously from his early twenties into his seventies in Haiti, Argentina, Paris, and Dakar. His name has been associated variously with the Haitian Indigenist poets as well as with the negritude poets.

Works by Jean-Fernand Brierre include: *Le drapeau de demain* (play, 1931); *Chansons secrètes* (poetry, 1933); *Nous garderons le dieu* (poetry, 1945); *Les aïeules* (drama, 1945); *Black Soul* (poetry, 1947); *Belle* (drama, 1948); *Dessalines nous parle* (poetry, 1953); *Au milieu des flammes* (drama, 1953); *Les horizons sans ciel* (novel, 1953); *Pétion et Bolivar*, avec *Adieu à la Marseillaise* (poetry, 1955); *La Source* (poetry, 1956); *La Nuit* (poetry, 1957); *Hommage au Maître Occilius Jeanty* (poetry, 1960); *Cantique à trois voix pour une poupée d'ébène* (poetry, 1960); *Or, uranium, cuivre, radium* (poetry, 1961); *Découvertes* (poetry, 1966); *Un autre monde* (essay, 1973); *Images d'argile*

et d'or (poetry, 1977); *Un Noël pour Gorée* (poetry, 1980); and *Sculptures de proue* (poetry, 1983).

See also **Literature: Spanish America.**

BIBLIOGRAPHY

Naomi M. Garret, *The Renaissance of Haitian Poetry* (1963), pp. 148–158.

Maurice A. Lubin, "Jean-F. Brierre and His Work," in *Black World* 22, no. 3 (1973): 36–48.

F. Raphaël Berrou and Pradel Pompilus, *Histoire de la littérature haïtienne illustrée par les textes*, vol. 3 (1977), pp. 190–237.

Max Dominique, *L'Arme de la critique littéraire: Littérature et idéologie en Haïti* (1988), pp. 173–203.

Additional Bibliography

Pierre-Louis, Ulysse. *L'univers poétique de Jean F. Rrierre [sic]: Une obsédante quête d'identité*. Port-au-Prince, Haiti: Editions Christophe, 1997.

CARROL F. COATES

BRIÓN, LUIS (1782–1821).

Luis Brión (b. 1782; d. 27 September 1821), Venezuelan naval commander. The son of a successful Flemish Jewish merchant of Curaçao, Brión became commander of Simón Bolívar's Venezuela squadron in 1813 and his most trusted naval adviser. He played a major role in the assault on Spanish maritime interests in the Caribbean during the Wars of Independence, bringing British arms to Bolívar's support and thwarting the reconquest campaign of General Pablo Morillo. His commercial connections in the Caribbean, especially with Maxwell Hyslop at Jamaica, also helped secure credit for Bolívar's forces. Brión's bitter rivalry with French privateer Louis-Michael Aury undermined the pat-riot naval effort when Aury refused to serve under Brión's command in 1816, but Brión's fleet, operating out of Margarita Island, continued to harass the Spaniards. In 1820 Brión took charge of the transition from a privateer fleet to a more formal Venezuelan navy, but when he became ill in the spring of 1821, his command was transferred to Lino de Clemente.

See also **Bolívar, Simón.**

BIBLIOGRAPHY

Stanley Faye, "Commodore Aury," in *Louisiana Historical Quarterly* 24, no. 3 (1941): 611–697.

Enrique Ortega Ricaurte, *Luis Brión de la Orden de Libertadores: Primer Almirante de la República de Colombia y General en jefe de sus ejércitos 1782–1828* (1953).

Jane Lucas De Grummond, *Renato Beluche: Smuggler, Privateer, and Patriot, 1780–1860* (1983).

Jaime Duarte French, *Los tres Luises del Caribe: ¿Corsarios o libertadores?* (1988).

Additional Bibliography

Díax Ugueto, Manuel. *Luis Brion: Almirante de la libertad.* Caracas: Fundación Ricardo Zuloaga: Fundación Mendoza: Fundación Vollmer: Libros de El Nacional, 2002.

RALPH LEE WOODWARD JR.

BRITISH HONDURAS. *See* Belize.

BRITISH IN ARGENTINA.

Just before the advent of Juan D. Perón in 1943, the British in Argentina numbered about 40,000. Compared with Italians, Spaniards, or even Jews, this figure appears small. Nevertheless, the British community in Argentina was the largest outside the empire and commanded formidable assets in Argentina. British railways there were not far short of the network in Britain, while port installations, meat-packing plants, grain elevators, banking, and even retailing exhibited remarkably high British participation. However, with the substantial dismantling of the Anglo-Argentine connection between 1946 and 1955, numbers dwindled to 16,000 British residents, becoming a community less distinct within the country's population at large.

The Anglo-Argentine connection began with the British penetration of the South Atlantic in the seventeenth century and intensified with the commercial association of London and Buenos Aires in the 1820s. The restricted market in Britain for Argentine products, however, prevented Argentina from keeping up debt service on British capital investment. By contrast, British export trade to Argentina remained the weakest element of the economic trilogy—foodstuffs, manufactures, and capital. By 1914, British exports were worth only half of Argentina's exports to the United Kingdom. Henceforward, the British persistently sought opportunities to compel the Argentines to reject foreign manufactures even though Britain was a proponent of free trade. Although World War I afforded Britain the opportunity to uproot German business through the use of blacklisting and shipping controls, the United States took advantage of the opening. By the 1920s the Anglo–United States trade rivalry in Argentina was so great that war seemed imminent. During this period Argentine railroad workers came into increasing conflict with the British-owned railroad companies. Consequently, the Argentine government began to regulate the industry to placate labor in this critical sector.

The D'Abernon trade mission in 1929 would have diverted enough Argentine purchases to Britain to enforce a balance of trade, but the agreement remained unsigned when Hipólito Irigoyen's government was overthrown by General José Evaristo Uriburu. The Roca–Runciman Pact (1933), however, turned the tide in Britain's favor. It harnessed the Argentines to obsolete British manufacturing by threatening Argentina's meat industry with the diversion of British import trade to her colonies.

In reality, the treaty led directly to the dissolution of the very Anglo-Argentine connection it was intended to shore up. It was a political gift to incipient Peronism, which made it a byword for the collaboration of the ruling oligarchy with British imperialism. In June 1943 Peronists overthrew the "vendepatria" elite. Three years later Perón became president and ordered the buying up of British assets and the diversification of Argentina's commerce and industry.

The Falkland Islands were the focus of the last major dispute between Britain and Argentina. With a population descended from nineteenth-Century Scottish immigrants, the Falklands (in Argentina known as the Islas Malvinas) lie off the coast of Argentina and are under British rule. In 1982 Argentina laid claim to this territory, invading the islands and thus provoking war with the United Kingdom; after holding the islands for ten weeks, Argentina lost to Britain. Britain and Argentina resumed diplomatic relations in 1990, but a permanent agreement as of 2007 had not been reached on the status of the islands.

See also **British-Latin American Relations; Falklands/Malvinas War.**

BIBLIOGRAPHY

Henry S. Ferns, *Britain and Argentina in the Nineteenth Century* (1960).

Andrew Graham-Yooll, *The Forgotten Colony: A History of the English-Speaking Communities in Argentina* (1981).

Roger Gravil, *The Anglo-Argentine Connection, 1900–1939* (1985).

Additional Bibliography

Gallo, Klaus. *Great Britain and Argentina: From Invasion to Recognition, 1806–1826.* New York: Palgrave, 2001.

Gúber, Rosana. *Por qué Malvinas?: De la causa nacional a la guerra absurda.* Buenos Aires: Fondo de Cultura Económica, 2001.

Lynch, John. *Massacre in the Pampas, 1872: Britain and Argentina in the Age of Migration.* Norman: University of Oklahoma Press, 1998.

McLean, David. *War, Diplomacy and Informal Empire: Britain and the Republics of La Plata, 1836–1853.* London and New York: British Academic Press, 1995.

ROGER GRAVIL

BRITISH INVASIONS, RÍO DE LA PLATA.

Efforts by a British expeditionary force (1806–1807) to take Buenos Aires from Spain are known as the Río de la Plata British Invasions. In 1804 Spain aligned with Napoleonic France, only to have its navy devastated at Trafalgar in 1805. British trade with the Río de la Plata had been flourishing since the 1780s, and fueled by the Venezuelan patriot Francisco de Miranda's promises of Spanish American sympathy for direct relations with Britain, some British sectors advocated open support for independence struggles. Commodore Sir Home Popham, a seasoned veteran of the Napoleonic Wars, attracted by commercial possibilities in South America, ordered 1,600 troops to invade Buenos Aires, which they did in June 1806. Faced with an invasion led by General William Carr Beresford, the viceroy, Fernando Rafael de Sobremonte, fled with the Spanish garrison and the treasury, leaving the city to civilians. The British were welcomed at first. However, when the British imposed free-trade policies, they lost support of local business leaders and civilians soon turned on them. After two months a ragtag militia, organized in Montevideo and led by a French officer in the imperial employ, Captain Santiago de Liniers, captured Beresford and his troops. A coalition emerged of Spanish merchants, led by Martín de Álzaga, creole merchants (led by Juan Martín de Peuyrredón), and lesser imperial officers.

Popham ordered General John Whitelocke to lead a second expedition to retake the viceregal capital. After seizing Montevideo in May 1807, Whitelocke fought his way to Buenos Aires with 7,000 soldiers but was mowed down by civilians and militia armed with cannon and muskets captured from Beresford. Whitelocke proved himself profoundly incompetent, leading his forces down narrow streets, where bullets rained down from the rooftops. He surrendered unconditionally on 7 July 1807.

The British invasions shattered the legitimacy of the viceroy, who had left his capital with threadbare defenses. Liniers became the interim viceroy but was much more attuned to the interests of creoles than of peninsular concerns, thereby opening a power struggle between pro-Spanish (led by Álzaga) and patriotic factions. Each side squared off in armed confrontation between various factions of the militia. The creole majority of the militia soon defeated Álzaga's followers. The municipal Cabildo also had become a battlefield for internecine bickering. Peninsular sympathizers eventually convinced Charles IV to replace Liniers with Balthasar de Cisneros. He proved to be as incompetent as Sobremonte; therefore the creoles, supported by the militia, declared open defiance on 25 May 1810. The British invasions instigated a sequence of events leading to independence in the Río de la Plata and to the militarization of local politics. Eventually, in 1825, the British recognized the independence of the Río de la Plata.

See also **British in Argentina; British-Latin American Relations.**

BIBLIOGRAPHY

Henry Stanley Ferns, *Britain and Argentina in the Nineteenth Century* (1960), esp. pp. 18–47.

Tulio Halperín Donghi, *Politics, Economics, and Society in Argentina in the Revolutionary Period* (1975), esp. pp. 133–139.

Additional Bibliography

Gallo, Klaus. *Las invasiones inglesas.* Buenos Aires: Editorial Universitaria de Buenos Aires, 2004.

Luzuriaga, J. C. *Una gesta heroica: Las invasiones inglesas y la defensa del Plata.* Montevideo, Uruguay: Torre del Vigía Ediciones, 2004.

JEREMY ADELMAN

BRITISH–LATIN AMERICAN RELATIONS.

Commercial interaction has been the mainspring of British–Latin American relations, with the English goal being commercial ascendancy and the means varying with historical circumstances. England began a continuous and expanding role in Latin America by challenging Spain's efforts to monopolize the wealth of the new lands discovered by Columbus. An assortment of corsairs based in the Old World, among them Francis Drake and John Hawkins, preyed on Spanish shipping and plundered the American coasts during the Elizabethan Age. In the seventeenth century, England established enclaves in several small islands in the Lesser Antilles, in neighboring Guiana, in the Bahamas and Bermuda, in what is now Belize and along the Mosquito Coast of Central America, and gained strategic advantage by seizing Jamaica in 1655. Privateering and piracy now blended with contraband trade, dyewood and mahogany lumbering, and colonizing ventures as the English expanded their efforts to breach the Spanish monopoly. An era of plunder left a trail of carnage and wreckage over a wide expanse of the Caribbean.

As Spanish power waned in the eighteenth century, England was able to wring commercial concessions from Spain in the Americas. By mid-century England had become the major market for the raw materials of Spanish America and the principal source for its manufactured goods, with Spanish merchants in Cádiz and Seville serving more as intermediaries in this trade. During the prolonged wars of the French Revolution, Spain's interaction with her colonies was often interrupted, enabling England to make further commercial inroads. The long Napoleonic struggle disrupted traditional trading patterns, and England compensated by expanding commercial ties with Spain's overseas colonies.

Spanish resistance to Napoleon's occupation of the Iberian Peninsula in 1808 prompted Creole leaders overseas to vie with royal officials to resist French pretensions by governing in the name of the deposed Spanish king, Ferdinand VII. The ambiguous situation allowed England, now an ally of Spain, to further her commercial penetration of the Spanish Empire. The defeat of Napoleon and the restoration of Ferdinand VII were followed at first by a hesitant and later by a mushrooming independence movement in Spain's colonies. England was in a quandary. An independent Latin America would provide England with commercial access on an unprecedented scale, but as the ally of Spain, England could not officially support Spanish American independence. By insisting that the independence movement was a domestic uprising involving only Spain and her colonies, England dissuaded the other European monarchs from assisting Ferdinand VII.

The English correctly concluded that without outside assistance Ferdinand would be unable to recover his mainland colonies, and one by one, they won their independence. Brazilians were further indebted to the English for their evacuation of the Portuguese court to Rio de Janeiro to escape capture by Napoleon. Brazilian independence, being more a family matter, did not necessitate any juggling of British policy. The United States also supported Latin American independence and, well aware of England's position, used the Monroe Doctrine to warn the European powers not to interfere in New World affairs. The new Latin American nations viewed England not only as the major supporter of their independence but also as their principal partner for achieving anticipated prosperity.

In the post-Napoleonic world England emerged as the international hub of commerce. To expand global commerce England led the way in replacing the restrictive policies of mercantilism with freer trade, and preached the comparative advantage of international specialization. Competing for the lion's share of global trade became the focus of the British government during the relatively peaceful nineteenth century, and the tenets of economic liberalism provided the cutting edge. England was confident that in the long run she could not be overtaken by other nations because of the natural advantages she derived from an unrivaled superiority in industry, commerce, and finance. Latin America was a prime target for British commercial expansion, and for the next century England enjoyed an overwhelming preeminence in Latin America that was not seriously challenged until the twentieth century.

Initially, opportunities in independent Latin America were greeted enthusiastically in England, but after the speculative investment bubble of 1824–1826 burst, investors became more wary. Political instability and internecine wars in Latin

America during the age of the *caudillos* (1825–1870) had a sobering effect and dimmed the vision of Latin America as a new El Dorado for quick wealth. Absorbing whatever trade existed, the British were unwilling to incur risks by trying to expand it, given the political climate.

As political order and stability were imposed by a new generation of authoritarian leaders after 1870, prospects for commercial expansion in Latin America brightened. The British responded with mounting investment to develop the export sectors of the more promising countries, especially in Argentina, Brazil, and Mexico. Brazil was an early target because the constitutional monarchy was seen as providing a continuity and stability lacking in Spanish America. Later, British commercial interests revolutionized the meat industry in Argentina, developed the mining economies in Chile and Mexico, expanded the petroleum industry in Venezuela and Mexico, and made similar incursions into most other Latin American countries. Railroad construction was launched on a major scale, with the heaviest British commitment in Argentina. Enjoying a dramatic advantage in capital and credit, the British established commanding control in railroads, communications, utilities, port installations, banking, technology, shipping, insurance, government bonds, and trade.

Latin America experienced a degree of prosperity and growth, but its economy tended to become an appendage to that of Great Britain; any benefits that accrued to Latin America were the by-product of prosperity overseas. Latin America emerged as part of the peripheral world serving the major industrial powers, principally England. The heavy British imprint in Latin America eventually generated a reaction against what was perceived as economic imperialism in the twentieth century, especially in Argentina, which was viewed as almost a British dominion. The first major challenge to British preeminence appeared in the Caribbean with the sudden emergence of the United States as a global industrial power after 1900. New interpretations of the Monroe Doctrine encouraged U.S. business and banking interests to supersede their British counterparts in areas essential to U.S. security.

British ascendancy continued unabated up to World War I and carried into the 1920s, but it encountered more competition from the United States and more resistance within various Latin American nations, a trend that became more apparent between the wars. The Great Depression undercut British–Latin U.S. economic ties. Relations were further strained by anti-imperialist nationalism demanding more autonomy, a trend most evident with Getúlio Vargas in Brazil, Lázaro, Cardenas in Mexico, and later Juan Perón in Argentina.

World War II marked the end of an era in British-Latin American relations. The postwar realignment witnessed a serious eclipse of British influence both in the world in general and in Latin America in particular. Faced with diminishing assets, Great Britain had to rearrange priorities in an increasingly polarized world. Independence was granted to her tiny Caribbean colonies as the empire was dismantled. Investment and trade with Latin America slowly eroded and passed overwhelmingly to the United States. Military collaboration and economic aid underwrote the new U.S. preeminence. The United States rapidly displaced Great Britain in Latin America as Britain had once displaced Spain.

In 1982 Argentina's military government invaded the British-controlled Falkland Islands (in Argentina known as the Islas Malvinas) off the coast of Argentina, provoking war with the United Kingdom. Argentina lost, and the British reestablished sovereignty, with diplomatic relations between the countries restored in 1990. A permanent agreement still has not been reached on the status of the islands.

See also **Buccaneers and Privateers; Falklands/Malvinas War.**

BIBLIOGRAPHY

Alan K. Manchester, *British Preëminence in Brazil: Its Rise and Decline* (1933).

Philip A. Means, *The Spanish Main: Focus of Envy, 1492–1700* (1935).

Richard Pares, *War and Trade in the West Indies, 1739–1763* (1936).

Simon G. Hanson, *Argentine Meat and the British Market* (1938).

Charles W. Centner, *Great Britain and Chile, 1810–1914* (1944).

William W. Kaufmann, *British Policy and the Independence of Latin America 1804–1828* (1951).

J. Fred Rippy, *British Investments in Latin America, 1822–1949* (1959).

Henry S. Ferns, *Britain and Argentina in the Nineteenth Century* (1960, repr. 1977).

Robert A. Naylor, "The British Role in Central America Prior to the Clayton-Bulwer Treaty of 1850," in *Hispanic American Historical Review* 40 (1960): 361–382.

Alfred Tischendorf, *Great Britain and Mexico in the Era of Porfirio Díaz* (1961).

Alec G. Ford, *The Gold Standard, 1880–1914: Britain and Argentina* (1962).

Richard Graham, *Britain and the Onset of Modernization in Brazil, 1850–1914* (1968).

Robert A. Naylor, *Influencia británica en el comercio centroamericano durante las primeras décadas de la independencia: 1821–1851* (1988).

Additional Bibliography

Jayne, Catherine E. *Oil, War, and Anglo-American Relations: American and British Reactions to Mexico's Expropriation of Foreign Oil Properties, 1937–1941.* Westport, CT: Greenwood Press, 2001.

Marshall, Oliver, ed. *English-Speaking Communities in Latin America.* New York: St. Martin's, 2000.

Mayo, John K. "The Development of British Interests in Chile's Norte Chico in the Early Nineteenth Century." *The Americas* 57, no. 3 (2001): 363–394.

Miller, Rory. *Britain and Latin America in the Nineteenth and Twentieth Centuries.* London and New York: Longman, 1993.

Villegas Revueltas, Silvestre. *Deuda y diplomacia: La relación México-Gran Bretaña, 1824–1884.* Mexico: Universidad Nacional Autónoma de México, 2005.

ROBERT A. NAYLOR

BRIZOLA, LEONEL (1922–2004). Leonel Brizola (*b.* 22 January 1922; *d.* 21 June 2004), governor of Rio Grande do Sul (1959–1963) and Rio de Janeiro, Brazil (1983–1987, 1991–1995). Born into a poor family in rural Rio Grande do Sul, Leonel Brizola was raised by his mother. He worked hard to complete his education, moving to Pôrto Alegre at age fourteen. By taking different jobs, he managed to complete his engineering degree.

In 1945, as a recruiter for the Brazilian Labor Party (PTB), Brizola cultivated the working-class and socialist identity that helped him win election to the state legislature. His association with João Goulart led to his marriage to the latter's sister and to closer ties to Getúlio Vargas. After several state posts, Brizola won election as federal deputy in 1954.

In 1955 Brizola's promises to improve the lives of the workers won him the mayoralty of Porto Alegre. For three years he developed his reputation as an engineer with a social conscience, speaking on the radio, writing newspaper columns, meeting with civic groups, and overseeing projects.

His success as mayor led to his victory in the 1958 gubernatorial election. Two controversial nationalizations—the American-owned electric power and telephone companies—projected Brizola onto the national scene. Moreover, he mobilized civilian and military forces in Rio Grande to compel the succession of Goulart to the presidency in 1961. A year later Brizola heightened his national prominence when he was elected Guanabara's federal deputy by the most votes ever cast. From his new political base he pressured Goulart and Congress to carry out major reforms, such as land distribution, rent control, and nationalization of utilities. Although popular among workers, Brizola's campaign alienated businessmen, the upper middle class, the U.S. government, and the military. His tendency to polarize issues contributed to the crisis of 1964.

After the 1964 coup, Brizola fled in exile to Uruguay, where he organized guerrilla resistance and participated in various conspiracies; eventually he settled down and conducted business there. Deported in 1977, he traveled in the United States and Europe, making contacts and developing a democratic socialist image.

In 1979 he returned to Brazil under the amnesty and founded the Democratic Labor Party (PDT), with which he won election as governor of Rio in 1982. He was notable for founding integrated school centers for children, curbing police abuses, and pressuring Congress to hold direct elections for president in 1984–1985. Having run unsuccessfully for president in 1989, he was elected governor of Rio the following year. After a successful term as governor, he again ran an unsuccessful race for president in 1994. In May 2004, he announced his intention to run again for the presidency in 2006, but he died of heart failure on June 21, 2004.

See also **Brazil: Since 1889.**

BIBLIOGRAPHY

John W. F. Dulles, *Unrest in Brazil* (1970).

Guita Grin Debert, *Ideologia e populismo* (1979).

Luís Alberto Moniz Bandeira, *Brizola e o trabalhismo* (1979).

Israel Beloch and Alzira Alves De Abreu, comps., *Dicionário histórico-biográfico brasileiro, 1930–1983* (1984).

Additional Bibliography

Aguiar, Ricardo Osman G. *Leonel Brizola: Uma trajetoría política*. Rio de Janeiro: Editora Record, 1991.

Basilio de Olivera. *Brizola e o estado brazileiro perante a história*. Rio de Janiero: Liber Juris, 1989.

Kuhn, Dione. *Brizola: Da legalidad ao exílio*. Porto Alegre: RBS Publicacãoes, 2004.

Quadros, Claudemir de. *As brizoletos cobrindo o Rio Grande: A educacão pública no Rio Grande do Sul durante o governo de Leonel Brizola, 1959-1963*. Santa Maria, Brazil: Editora UFSM, 2003.

MICHAEL L. CONNIFF

BRIZUELA, FRANCISCO (1879–1947).

Francisco Brizuela (*b.* 17 February 1879; *d.* 14 August 1947), Paraguayan soldier in the Chaco War and civil war of 1947. Born in Carapeguá, Brizuela entered the armed forces at an early age and participated in several of Paraguay's minor civil wars of the 1900–1920 period. Having advanced to the rank of major, he acted as chief of police for Asunción between June 1918 and September 1919.

Brizuela made little secret of his own political ambitions and therefore spent most of the 1920s out of uniform. At the end of the decade, however, he was called out of retirement to command a Paraguayan infantry division in the early stages of the Chaco War. The energetic defense he prepared at Fort Nanawa in 1933 prevented the Bolivians from advancing southward toward Asunción. Soon afterward, they began their long retreat to the Altiplano.

Brizuela later participated in the 1947 civil war. While attempting to fly munitions to rebel forces in Paraguay, he was killed in an airplane accident outside Montevideo.

See also **Chaco War.**

BIBLIOGRAPHY

Carlos Zubizarreta, *Cien vidas paraguayas* (1985), pp. 311–313.

R. Andrew Nickson, *Historical Dictionary of Paraguay* (1993), p. 82.

Additional Bibliography

Farcau, Bruce W. *The Chaco War: Bolivia and Paraguay, 1932-1935*. Westport, CT: Praeger, 1996.

THOMAS L. WHIGHAM

BROQUA, ALFONSO (1876–1946).

Alfonso Broqua (*b.* 11 September 1876; *d.* 24 November 1946), Uruguayan composer. Broqua was born in Montevideo, where he began his music studies. In 1894 he went to Paris and entered the Schola Cantorum, where he studied composition under Vincent d'Indy for six years. After spending some time in Brussels with Eduardo Fabini, he returned to Montevideo in 1904. His first nationalist work, *Tabaré*, based on a poem by Juan Zorrilla De San Martín, premiered in 1910. Broqua set out to create a new musical aesthetic based on the use of vocal themes and dance forms and rhythms from Uruguayan folk music. *Tabaré*, a lyric poem for soprano, female chorus, and orchestra, was considered a major event at Montevideo. It was performed at the Teatro Solís on 30 June 1910 and conducted by the composer. That same year the National Orchestra presented his version of *El poema de las lomas*, originally a major piano triptych premiered by Ernest Drangosh in 1909. Two other works from this period are *Quinteto en sol menor* and *La cruz del Sud*, a never performed opera.

In terms of musical form and aesthetics, the Piano Quintet in G minor is the best written of his works; its last movement, *Variaciones sobre temas regionales*, shows a clear influence of the new nationalist style, which he, Fabini, and Luis Cluzeau-Mortet helped to inaugurate. In 1922 Broqua settled in Paris, where he continued composing. His other major works include *Impresiones sinfónicas* (1912) for orchestra, *Preludios pampeanos* (1938) for guitar, *Evocaciones criollas, Estudios criollos*, and *Preludios* (1929), as well as three suites for guitar and numerous pieces for solo piano and for voice, piano, and guitar. He died in Paris.

See also **Music: Art Music.**

BIBLIOGRAPHY

Composers of the Americas, vol. 16 (1970), p. 59; *New Grove Dictionary of Music and Musicians,* vol. 3 (1980).

S. Salgado, *Breve historia de la música culta en el Uruguay,* 2d ed. (1980).

Additional Bibliography

Salgado, Susana. *The Teatro Solis: 150 Years of Opera, Concert, and Ballet in Montevideo.* Middletown, CT: Wesleyan University Press, 2003.

SUSANA SALGADO

BROTHERHOODS. Originating in the Iberian Middle Ages when they were usually formed by the memberships of individual guilds, lay brotherhoods (*confrarias* and *irmandades*) were organized throughout colonial Brazil on the basis of noncraft-oriented social groupings within the local community. Brotherhoods were dedicated to more than fifty patron saints, whose life histories represented an ideal shared by the various social groupings associated with a particular one. These lay sodalities contributed to social cohesion by providing social services, alms, dowries, and burials, according to members' needs, as well as by by promoting religious observances. The diversity of brotherhoods reflected the relative complexity of colonial society. Thus, the elite almost invariably belonged to the Order of Saint Francis of Assisi; slaves and free blacks normally were members of the Brotherhood of Our Lady of the Rosary; while intermediate social and racial groupings formed the dozens of other lay associations.

Historians have tended to emphasize the mutual assistance that characterized the brotherhoods, their role in upholding practices of the Catholic faith, as well as their contribution to the construction and maintenance of churches. Recent studies, however, have pointed to the associative spirit of brotherhoods as presenting a potential challenge to overbearing colonial authority.

BIBLIOGRAPHY

Lay brotherhoods are highlighted in Stuart B. Schwartz, "Plantation and Peripheries, *c.* 1580–*c.* 1750," in *Colonial Brazil,* edited by Leslie Bethell (1987), esp. pp. 133–139. An important study of the racial demarcations of orders is found in A. J. R. Russell-Wood, "Black and Mulatto Brotherhoods in Colonial Brazil: A Study in Collective Behavior," in *Hispanic American Historical Review* 54, no. 4 (1974). A recent major analysis of the role of brotherhoods is contained in Caio César Boschi, *Os leigos e o poder* (1986).

Additional Bibliography

Amaral, R. Joviano. *Os pretos do Rosário de São Paulo: Subsidios histories.* 2nd ed. São Paulo: J. Scortecci Editora, 1992.

Braga, Júlio Santana. *Sociedade Protetora dos Desvalidos: Uma irmandade de cor.* Salvador: Ianamá, 1987.

Kiddy, Elizabeth W. *Blacks of the Rosary: Memory and History in Minas Gerais, Brazil.* University Park: Pennsylvania State University Press, 2005.

MacCord, Marcelo. *O rosário de D. Antônio: Irmandades negras, alianças e conflitos na história social do Recife, 1848-1872.* Recife: Editora Universitária da UFPE, 2005.

Mulvey, Patricia Ann. "The Black Lay Brotherhoods of Colonial Brazil, a History." Ph.d. diss., City University of New York, 1976.

DOUGLAS COLE LIBBY

BROUWER, LEO (1939–). Leo Brouwer (*b.* 1 March 1939), Cuban composer and guitarist. A student of Stefan Wolpe and Vincent Persichetti at the Julliard School of Music, Brouwer also studied at the Hartt College of Music under Isadore Freed. He was a music assistant with Radio Havana (1960–1961) and director of the music department at the Institute of the Film Industry and Art (IAIC) in 1960–1962. He taught theory and composition at the National Conservatory in Havana (1961–1967) and in 1969 he became director of the experimental branch of the IAIC. A guitarist of international recognition, he has made many recordings of classical and contemporary music. He has achieved similar success as a composer of orchestral and chamber music and has written music for film and for the theater. Brouwer used conventional styles at the beginning of his career. For example, in the more than fifty compositions he wrote from 1956 to 1962 he used mostly folkloric elements within a nationalistic and rather conventional style. Having had contacts in the 1960s with contemporary composers like Boguslaw Schäffer and Henyrk Górecki and also with Luigi Nono and Hans Werner Henze, Brouwer turned toward the avant-garde, chance, and experimental music. He has explored contemporary techniques and is probably among the first Cuban composers to successfully utilize the open forms and aleatoric techniques, frequently including graphic and proportional notation in his scores. He has also collaborated with pop artists and mass-media productions.

Among his more important works are *Danzas concertantes* for guitar and string orchestra (1958); *Variantes* for percussion (1962); *Sonograma I* for prepared piano (1963); *Sonograma II* for orchestra (1964); *2 Conceptos del tiempo* for ten players (1965); *Homage to Mingus* for jazz combo and orchestra (1965); *Tropos* for orchestra (1967); *Sonograma III* for two pianos (1968); *5 Epigrams* for cello and piano (1968); *Conmutaciones* for prepared piano and two percussionists (1966); *El reino de esto mundo* for woodwind quintet (1968); *Rem tene verba sequentur* for string quartet (1969); *Cantigas del tiempo nuevo* for actors, children's choir, piano, harp, and percussion (1969); *Exaedros,* for six players or multiples of six (1969–1970); *Anima Latina* (Madrigali guerrieri ed amorosi) for orchestra (1977); and *Es el amor quién ve,* for voice and chamber ensemble (1972). He has written for guitar *Canticum* (1972); *La espiral eterna* (1970); *Tarantos* (1977); *Per sonare a due* (1973); and *El decamerón negro* (1981). In 1992, he oversaw the founding, and is the emeritus director, of the Orquesta de Córdoba in Spain. He is Honoris Causa Professor of Art at the Instituto Superior de Arte de Cuba. He has received the highest honor given by the Cuban state in recognition of cultural achievements, the Orden Félix Varela.

See also **Music: Popular Music and Dance.**

BIBLIOGRAPHY

John Vinton, ed. *Dictionary of Contemporary Music* (1974); *Primero Festival Latinoamericano de Música Contemporánea "Ciudad de Maracaibo"* (1977), p. 34.

Gérard Béhague, *Music in Latin America: An Introduction* (1979); *New Grove Dictionary of Music and Musicians* (1980).

Additional Bibliography

Brouwer, Leo. *Gajes del oficio.* Havana: Letras Cubanas, 2004.

Hdez (Hernández), Isabelle. *Leo Brouwer.* Havana: Editora Musical de Cuba, 2000.

Reiss, Timothy J., ed. *Music, Writing, and Cultural Unity in the Caribbean.* Trenton, NJ: Africa World, 2005.

ALCIDES LANZA

BROWN, WILLIAM (1777–1857). William Brown (Guillermo Brown; *b.* 22 June 1777; *d.* 3 March 1857), Irish privateer in the service of Buenos Aires during the Wars for Independence. Born in Foxford, Ireland, Brown came to Philadelphia at age nine. He soon signed on a merchant ship and had become a captain before reaching age twenty. In 1809 he arrived in the Río de la Plata, where he played a major role in the Buenos Aires campaign against Montevideo and became one of the principal captains in the Buenos Aires privateering fleet. In 1815 Brown led a privateering expedition into the Pacific in support of Chilean independence, and was joined by the squadron of another notable Buenos Aires privateer, Hipólito Bouchard. This expedition harassed Spanish commerce along the Peruvian and Chilean coasts. Following independence, Admiral Brown was a leading officer in the Buenos Aires navy and led Argentine naval forces in the war against Uruguay (1825–1828) and, later, during the administration of Juan Manuel de Rosas, against the French and British blockades.

See also **Piracy.**

BIBLIOGRAPHY

Lewis Bealer, *Los corsarios de Buenos Aires, sus actividades en las guerras hispano-americanas de la independencia, 1815–1821* (1937). *Documentos del almirante Brown,* 2 vols. (1958–1959).

Felipe Bosch, *Historia naval argentina* (1962).

Donald E. Worcester, *Sea Power and Chilean Independence* (1962), pp. 11–16.

Additional Bibliography

Ireland, John de Courcy. *The Admiral from Mayo: A Life of Almirante William Brown, Father of the Argentine Way.* Dublin: E. Burke, 1995.

RALPH LEE WOODWARD JR.

BRULL, MARIANO (1891–1956). Mariano Brull (*b.* 24 February 1891; *d.* 6 August 1956), Cuban poet. Brull was born in Camagüey Province but spent his childhood in Spain. He returned to Cuba as an adolescent and began publishing his early poems. In 1913 he received a law degree from the University of Havana and worked as a lawyer until 1917, when he obtained a diplomatic post in Washington, D.C. He later served in Cuba's embassies in Peru, Belgium, Spain, Switzerland, France, Italy, Canada, and Uruguay. Brull was published in several key literary magazines, including *Clavileño* and the legendary *Orígenes,* founded by José Lezama Lima. One of the most influential poets of the first decades of this century, he is well known for his *jitanjáforas,* poems constructed with words invented for the beauty of their sound and their rhythm, as the term *jitanjáfora* itself, the title of one of those poems. Well-known poets and critics of his time acclaimed Brull's poetry, among them Paul Valéry, Alfonso Reyes, Gastón Baquero, Pedro Henríquez Ureña, and Cintio Vitier, and he exerted great influence upon the following generation of Cuban poets. Among his works are *La casa del silencio: Antología de su obra, 1916–1954* (1976) and *Una antología de poesía cubana* (1984).

See also **Literature: Spanish America.**

BIBLIOGRAPHY

Additional Bibliography

Larraga, Ricardo. *Mariano Brull y la poesía pura en Cuba.* Miami: Ediciones Universal, 1994.

Saínz, Enrique. *Indagaciones.* La Habana: Editorial Letras Cubanas, 1998.

ROBERTO VALERO

BRUM, BALTASAR (1883–1933). Baltasar Brum (*b.* 18 June 1883; *d.* 31 March 1933), president of Uruguay (1919–1923). Brum was one of the most prominent politicians in the country from 1913 to 1933. As well as president of Uruguay, he was president of the National Council of Administration from 1929 to 1931 and served as minister of public education (1913–1915) and of foreign affairs (1914–1915).

The son of landowners of Brazilian origin, he subscribed to the beliefs of Batllism, specifically to its reformist tendencies. He began his political career young and by the age of thirty was minister of education. He was the first president to govern under the system of a collegial executive branch consisting of the president and the National Council of Administration, which had been approved in 1917. During his administration legislation for the benefit of the working class was promoted on issues such as a minimum wage for rural laborers, social security, workplace safety, weekly time off, and an attempt at regulating labor practices regarding women and children.

Brum's administration was followed by Riverista leaders who represented the conservative wing of the Colorado Party. Batllism regained the presidency in 1931 with the election of Gabriel Terra, although he was more conservative than the original Batllistas. Brum belonged to the National Council of Administration, which confronted the president on more than one occasion. When Terra assumed dictatorial powers in 1933, Brum committed suicide in public as a symbolic gesture, even though his personal liberty was not at stake.

BIBLIOGRAPHY

Juan Carlos Welker, *Baltasar Brum: Verbo y acción* (1945).

Gerardo Caetano and Raúl Jacob, *El nacimiento del terrismo,* vol. 3 (1991).

Additional Bibliography

Filartigas, Juan M. *Baltasar Brum, el colegialista.* Montevideo: s.n., 1954.

Laddaga, Reinaldo. *La euforia de Baltasar Brum.* Buenos Aires: Tusquets Editores, 1999.

Manini Ríos, Carlos. *Una nave en la tormenta: Una etapa de transición, 1919-1923.* Montevideo: s.n., 1972.

FERNANDO FILGUEIRA

BRUNET, MARTA (1897–1967). Marta Brunet (*b.* 9 August 1897; *d.* 10 August 1967), Chilean feminist writer. Brunet was born in Chillán and raised in southern Chile but spent most of her life in other countries, living first in Europe (1911–1914) and later working as cultural attaché to the Chilean Embassy in Argentina (1939–1952), Brazil (1962–1963), and Uruguay (1963–1967). She wrote nine novels and ten collections of short stories. Her most important fictional works are *Montaña adentro* (1923; Deep into the Mountains), "Soledad de la sangre" (1943; "The Solitude of the Blood"),

Humo hacia el sur (1946; Smoke Towards the South), *María Nadie* (1957; Maria Nobody), and *Amasijo* (1962; Dough for Baking). Her *Obras completas* were published in Chile in 1963.

Although Brunet initially followed the *criollista* tendency in fiction that was prevalent in Chile through the 1930s, she soon went beyond its nativist parameters to present universal concerns through the psychological and existential conflicts of her characters. Based primarily on the world of women, her work characterizes female desire for self-actualization. By means of the opposition between reality and dream, Brunet focuses at once on a woman's submission to the patriarchal forces of family and community and her possibility for spiritual empowerment through the realm of fantasy. In 1961 she became the second woman to receive the National Prize for literature. She died in Montevideo.

See also **Literature: Spanish America; Philosophy: Feminist.**

BIBLIOGRAPHY

Esther Melón De Díaz, *La narrativa de Marta Brunet* (1975).

Gabriela Mora, "Una lectura de *Soledad de la sangre* de Marta Brunet," *Estudios Filológicos* 19 (1984): 81–90.

Mary Berg, "The Short Stories of Marta Brunet," in *Monographic Review/Revista Monográfica* 4 (1988): 195–206.

Additional Bibliography

Balart Carmona, Carmen. *Narrativa feminina chilena: Marta Brunet*. Santiago de Chile: Santillana, 1999.

Orozco Vera, Ma Jesús. *La narrative feminina chilena, 1923-1980: Escritura y enajenación*. Zaragoza: Anubar Ediciones, 1995.

                                                    J. A. EPPLE

BRYAN-CHAMORRO TREATY (1914).

Bryan-Chamorro Treaty (1914), a treaty between the United States and Nicaragua providing for the construction of a canal across Nicaragua. The proposed route followed the nineteenth-century proposal for a waterway using the San Juan River (which forms a part of the Costa Rican–Nicaraguan boundary), Lake Nicaragua, and Lake Managua, and with a possible outlet at the Gulf of Fonseca, which borders on El Salvador, Honduras, and Nicaragua on the Pacific coast of Central America.

The treaty came about because of the breakdown in President William Howard Taft's plan to create a financial protectorate in Nicaragua. In 1907, the Theodore Roosevelt administration had lent its support to Central American treaties providing for the peaceful settlement of isthmian disputes. But two years later, despite its professions that U.S. policy would be conducted with "dollars and not bullets," Taft began an intervention in Nicaragua that overthrew President José Santos Zelaya and culminated in a large-scale military intervention in 1912. General Emiliano Chamorro aided the U.S. military in this intervention; and when the country was pacified, President Adolfo Díaz seemed secure.

In the aftermath, however, Nicaragua's efforts to secure a badly needed loan to create a national bank and reform the currency were frustrated when the U.S. Senate rejected the loan convention. Nicaragua proposed the canal concession, which ceded (for $3 million) construction rights for a canal across Nicaraguan territory and naval bases on Great and Little Corn islands (on the Caribbean side) and in the Gulf of Fonseca (on the Pacific side). Incoming President Woodrow Wilson and Secretary of State William Jennings Bryan tried to use the proposal to create a protectorate over Nicaragua, but the Senate again balked, and the treaty was not ratified until 1916. Nonetheless, Costa Rica and El Salvador protested that the concession violated existing treaties, and took their case to the Central American Court of Justice. The Court declared in their favor but said that it was unable to enforce the decision against Nicaragua. The Court dissolved shortly afterward.

See also **Central American Court of Justice; United States–Latin American Relations.**

BIBLIOGRAPHY

Dana G. Munro. *Intervention and Dollar Diplomacy in the Caribbean, 1900–1921*. Princeton, NJ: Princeton University Press, 1964.

Walter La Feber. *Inevitable Revolutions: The United States in Central America*. 2d ed. New York: W.W. Norton & Company, 1993.

Ralph Lee Woodward. *Central America: A Nation Divided*. 3d ed. New York: Oxford University Press, 1999.

Lester D. Langley. *The United States and the Caribbean in the Twentieth Century,* 4th ed. Athens: University of Georgia Press, 1989.

Additional Bibliography

Michel Gobat. *Confronting the American Dream: Nicaragua Under U.S. Imperial Rule.* Durham, NC: Duke University Press, 2005.

LESTER D. LANGLEY

Bryce Echenique, Alfredo. *Permiso para vivir: Antimemorias.* Barcelona: Anagrama, 1993.

Kohut, Karl, and José Morales Saravia. *Literatura peruana hoy: Crisis y creación.* Madrid: Iberoamericana, 1988.

Schwartz, Marcy E. *Writing Paris: Urban Topographies of Desire in Contemporary Latin American Fiction.* Albany: SUNY Press, 1999.

JESÚS DÍAZ CABALLERO

BRYCE ECHENIQUE, ALFREDO

(1939–). Alfredo Bryce Echenique (*b.* 19 February 1939), Peruvian novelist, short-story writer, and journalist. Bryce Echenique was born in Lima to an aristocratic family. He studied literature and law at the University of San Marcos in Lima, receiving a Ph.D. in 1964. He then studied at the Sorbonne in Paris. Beginning in 1968 he taught at the universities of Nanterre, Sorbonne, and Vincennes. In 1980 he relocated to Montpellier and taught literature at Paul Valéry University. In 1986 he moved to Spain.

An original combination of the oral tradition, memory, and humor is the basic feature of Bryce Echenique's entire body of literary work. *Un mundo para Julius* (1970; *A World for Julius,* 1992) was his first novel and one of his most successful ones. It depicts a sector of the Lima oligarchy with authenticity, humor, and irony. In 1998, he was awarded the prestigious Premio Nacional de Narrativa prize in Spain.

In his novels *Tantas veces Pedro* (1977), *La vida exagerada de Martín Romaña* (1981), *El hombre que hablaba de Octavia de Cádiz* (1985), and *La última mudanza de Felipe Carrillo* (1988), Bryce Echenique narrates the cycle of apprenticeship and maturity in the erotic experience of one Latin American character, of oligarchic origin, in Europe in the 1960s and 1970s. He has also published several short-story collections: *Huerto cerrado* (1968), *La felicidad ja, ja* (1974), *Cuentos completos* (1981), and *Crónicas personales* (1988). His journalistic work is equally extensive in magazines and newspapers.

See also **Literature: Spanish America.**

BIBLIOGRAPHY

Bryce Echenique, Alfredo. *Antología personal.* San Juan, PR: Editorial de la Universidad de Puerto Rico, 1995.

BUARQUE, CHICO

(1944–). Chico Buarque (Francisco Buarque de Holanda; *b.* 19 July 1944), Brazilian singer, songwriter, and writer. The son of historian Sérgio Buarque de Holanda, Buarque has distinguished himself as an insightful artist in the field of entertainment. He studied in Rio and São Paulo but abandoned architecture to dedicate himself to music in the mid-1960s. His involvement in drama began in 1966 with the musical settings for a stage version of João Cabral de Melo Neto's verse play *Morte e vida severina* (Death and Life of Severina). Through the historic songwriters' festivals of the late 1960s, Buarque gained national attention as an incomparable songsmith of both traditional vocal samba and bossa nova. Also known for the social criticism in his lyrics, he went into voluntary exile in Italy in 1969 to escape the military regime, which censored an appreciable portion of his work in the 1970s.

The composer's battles with government censors comprise a major chapter of the history of institutional intervention in the arts during that decade. His most controversial play, *Calabar,* a musical collaboration with Ruy Guerra, reexamined a Brazilian figure accused of treason during the Dutch occupation in the early seventeenth century. In 1974, Buarque published a novel, *Fazenda modelo: Novela pecuária* (Model Farm: A Bovine Novel), an allegorical sociohistorical critique inspired by George Orwell. He also wrote some children's literature. On a cultural mission in 1978, Buarque made his first of several visits to Cuba and introduced some new Cuban music to the Brazilian public. In the 1970s and 1980s, in addition to crafted sentimental songs and numerous masterpiece sambas of social observation, Buarque wrote many songs for films (e.g., *Bye Bye Brazil*) and for his own stage productions, including *Ópera do malandro* (Hustler's Opera), which later was adapted for film. Buarque is respected as one of the leading performing songwriters in the history of the nation and as one of her most perspicacious artists.

See also **Literature: Spanish America; Melo Neto, João Cabral de; Music: Popular Music and Dance; Theater.**

BIBLIOGRAPHY

Charles A. Perrone, "Dissonance and Dissent: The Musical Dramatics of Chico Buarque," in *Latin American Theatre Review* 22, no. 2 (1989): 81–94; *Masters of Contemporary Brazilian Song: MPB, 1965–1985* (1989).

Additional Bibliography

Meneses, Adélia Bezerra de. *Figuras do femenino na canção de Chico Buarque.* Sao Pãulo: Biotempo Editorial, 2000.

Werneck, Humberto. *Chico Buarque: Letra é musica.* São Paulo: Companhia das Letras, 1989.

Woodall, James. *A Simple Brazilian Song: Journeys through the Rio Sound.* London: Little, Brown, 1997.

Zappa, Regina. *Chico Buarque: Para todos.* Rio de Janeiro: Relume Dumaraá, 1999.

CHARLES A. PERRONE

BUCARAM, ABDALÁ (1952–). Abdalá Bucaram's political career, which began with a brief tenure as major of Guayaquil in the early 1980s, coincides with the phase of democratic regimes in Ecuador that began in 1979 and continues into the twenty-first century. He participated in the 1988, 1992, and 1996 elections, becoming president in July 1996. Through humor and mockery he transformed politics into his own flamboyant show, challenging the elite's power and privileges and portraying white and mestizo upper classes as the source of all ills and the poor as the incarnation of authentic national values.

During his time as president Bucaram recorded a CD titled *El Loco que Ama* ("the crazy one who loves") and presented it on national television, became president of Guayaquil's most important soccer team, and auctioned off his mustache for a million dollars for charities. Lorena Bobbitt, the Ecuadorian woman who became notorious for cutting off her abusive American husband's penis in 1993, was his honorary guest. In the midst of this populist spectacle, Bucaram's neoliberal policies resulted in an increase in the prices of basic services. He alienated entrepreneurs, who were fearful of corruption; he angered the armed forces by making gestures of peace toward Peru; and he provoked the leadership of social movements, who staged massive demonstrations. After six months in office, he faced charges of embezzlement. Forced out of office by congress on grounds of "mental incapacity," he fled to Panama.

In March 2005 President Lucio Gutiérrez appointed one of Bucaram's close friends president of the Supreme Court, who proceeded to absolve Bucaram of corruption charges. Bucaram's brief return to Ecuador from Panama was one of the main reasons for Gutiérrez's removal from office. When charges against Bucaram were reinstated, he went back to Panama.

See also **Arteaga, Rosalía; Ecuador: Since 1830.**

BIBLIOGRAPHY

Bucaram, Abdalá. *Golpe de Estado.* Guayaquil: Prediciones, 1998.

Cornejo, Diego, ed. *¡Que se vaya! Crónica el bucaramato.* Quito: Edimpres-Hoy, 1997.

Freidenberg, Flavia. *Jama, caleta y camello: Las estrategias de Abdalá Bucaram y el PRE para ganar elecciones.* Quito: Corporación Editora Nacional, 2003.

Torre, Carlos de la. *¡Un sólo toque! Populismo y cultura política en Ecuador.* Quito: CAAP, 1996.

Torre, Carlos de la. *Populist Seduction in Latin America: The Ecuadorian Experience.* Athens: Ohio University Center for International Studies, 2000.

CARLOS DE LA TORRE

BUCARAM ELMHALIN, ASAAD (1916–1981). Asaad Bucaram Elmhalin (*b.* 24 December 1916; *d.* 5 November 1981), leader of the populist Concentración de Fuerzas Populares (1962–1981) in Ecuador. Born in Ambato to Lebanese parents and self-taught, Bucaram assumed leadership of the Concentration of Popular Forces (Concentración de Fuerzas Populares—CFP) after the resignation of Carlos Guevara Moreno. Elected mayor of Guayaquil (1962–1963) during a period of economic prosperity, he earned a reputation for personal honesty and administrative ability. He was deposed, jailed, and deported by the military government in 1963, when he attempted to mobilize the CFP to defend the government of Carlos Julio Arosemena Monroy (1963).

After returning to Ecuador, Bucaram headed the CFP delegation to the 1966 constituent assembly and was elected vice president of the assembly. Reelected as mayor of Guayaquil in 1967, he brought his party into the Front of the Democratic Left (Frente de la Izquierda Democrática—FID), which supported the candidacy of Andrés F. Córdova Nieto in the 1968 presidential election. Elected prefect of Guayas Province in 1970, he was subsequently exiled, a second time, by Velasco Ibarra.

Bucaram was the leading candidate for president in 1972, but the military coup of 15 February 1972 prevented his election and exiled him a third time. Prior to the restoration of constitutional government in 1979, the military government disqualified his candidacy. Bucaram then selected Guayaquil lawyer Jaime Roldós Aguilera to run as the candidate of the CFP. Prior to the election of Roldós, however, relations between the two CFP leaders began to deteriorate, and the party subsequently divided into two factions. The conflict was ideological as well as personal. Bucaram was a populist whose power base was primarily regional. Thus, he favored government expenditures that provided patronage for his supporters and coastal public works projects at the expense of fiscal responsibility and projects selected on the basis of national criteria. Bucaram was unsuccessful in his bid to prevent Roldós from taking office but cemented an agreement with the conservatives that allowed him to become president of the Chamber of Deputies, a position he used to obstruct presidential initiatives until his death.

See also **Ecuador, Political Parties: Concentration of Popular Forces (CFP).**

BIBLIOGRAPHY

Marco Proaño Maya, *Bucaram: Historia de una lucha* (1981).

John D. Martz, "Populist Leadership and the Party Caudillo: Ecuador and the CFP, 1962–1981," in *Studies in Comparative International Development* 18 (1983): 22–49; and *Politics and Petroleum in Ecuador* (1987), esp. pp. 84–90, 247–269.

Additional Bibliography

Guerrero Burgos, Rafael. *Regionalismo y democracia social en los orígenes del "CFP."* Quito: CAAP, 1994.

LINDA ALEXANDER RODRÍGUEZ

BUCARELI CONFERENCES. Bucareli Conferences, a series of meetings between representatives of Mexico and the United States in 1923 that reduced tensions between the two nations through largely tentative agreements. Named for the street in Mexico City where they took place, these conferences addressed the impact of Article 27 of the Mexican Constitution of 1917 on property ownership. U.S. owners of Mexican agricultural and petroleum lands feared their loss. The meetings also had an urgency for Mexican President Álvaro Obregón. The United States had not extended diplomatic recognition to his three-year-old regime, which undercut its legitimacy internationally and limited its ability to handle domestic opposition.

The results of these meetings were ambiguous. Obregón reaffirmed the basic intent of Article 27, but the United States extracted two concessions in return for the opening of diplomatic relations: Mexico could take large estates for the purpose of land reform only if the owners received immediate compensation at market value, and oil concessions would not be affected by Article 27 if the owner had taken positive acts to develop this resource before 1917. Most important, these arrangements were not formal treaties. Enforcement depended on the goodwill of both nations.

The meetings also produced two official treaties. One involved claims against the Mexican government as a result of disruptions of the revolution from 1910 to 1920. The other concerned civil disputes between nationals of the two countries since 1868. The treaties set up two claims commissions to settle these cases.

BIBLIOGRAPHY

Robert Freeman Smith, *The United States and Revolutionary Nationalism in Mexico, 1916–1932* (1972), esp. pp. 213–223.

Josefina Zoraida Vázquez and Lorenzo Meyer, *The United States and Mexico* (1985), esp. pp. 126–132.

Additional Bibliography

Spenser, Daniela. *The Impossible Triangle: Mexico, Soviet Russia, and the United States in the 1920s.* Durham: Duke University Press, 1999.

Zebadúa, Emilio. *Banqueros y revolucionarios: La soberanía financiera de México.* México, D.F.: Colegio de México: Fideicomiso Historia de las Américas: Fondo de Cultura Económica, 1994.

JOHN A. BRITTON

BUCARELI Y URSÚA, ANTONIO MARÍA (1717–1779).

Antonio María Bucareli y Ursúa (*b.* 24 January 1717; *d.* 9 April 1779), captain-general of Cuba (1766–1771) and viceroy of New Spain (1771–1779). Born in Seville, Spain, to a noble family, Bucareli joined the Spanish army as a cadet and served in campaigns in Italy and Portugal. He achieved the rank of lieutenant general and was inspector general of cavalry and inspector of coastal fortifications of the Kingdom of Granada. In 1766, he was named governor and captain-general of Cuba, a difficult post that he occupied with distinction. Although Bucareli wished to return to Spain following his Cuban assignment, the crown wanted an experienced administrator in the Mexican viceregency who could deal with the reforms proposed by Visitor General José de Gálvez.

Bucareli was conservative in his approach to change and, where possible, tended to support traditional solutions. He reorganized the militia units, rebuilt coastal fortifications, and oversaw the construction of the fortress of Perote, which was designed to prevent an enemy invasion inland. In the north of New Spain, Bucareli dealt with growing Indian depredations against frontier presidios and problems related to the exploration and settlement of Alta California. To verify the possibility of Russian penetration on the North American coast, Bucareli dispatched the maritime expedition of Juan Pérez, the first in a series of voyages that carried Spanish exploration into Alaskan waters.

As a colonial administrator, Bucareli rejected many of the reforms proposed by Gálvez. He criticized schemes for territorial reorganization and doubted the possible benefits of introducing a system of powerful provincial intendants. A zealous and capable bureaucrat, Bucareli was able to get the best results out of the cumbersome colonial regime. He is recognized as one of the best eighteenth-century viceroys of New Spain. Bucareli died in office, and his remains were interred at the shrine of the Virgin of Guadalupe.

BIBLIOGRAPHY

Rómulo Velasco Ceballos, *La administración de D. Frey Antonio María de Bucareli y Ursúa, cuadragésimo sexto virrey de México,* 2 vols. (1936).

Bernard E. Bobb, *The Viceregency of Antonio María Bucareli in New Spain, 1771–1779* (1962).

David A. Brading, *Miners and Merchants in Bourbon Mexico, 1763–1810* (1971).

Additional Bibliography

Martin, Cheryl English. *Governance and Society in Colonial Mexico: Chihuahua in the Eighteenth-Century.* Stanford, CA: Stanford University Press, 1996.

Río, Ignacio del. *La aplicación regional de las reformas borbónicas en Nueva España: Sonora y Sinaloa, 1768–1787.* Mexico: Universidad Nacional Autónoma de México, Instituto de Investigaciones Históricas, 1995.

CHRISTON I. ARCHER

BUCARELI Y URSÚA, FRANCISCO DE PAULA (?–1770).

Francisco de Paula Bucareli y Ursúa (*d.* after 1770), governor of Buenos Aires (1766–1770), brother of Antonio María Bucareli, viceroy of New Spain. Bucareli, probably born in Seville, Spain, was a career army officer imbued with the ideas of the Spanish version of the Enlightenment. In 1776 he assumed the post of governor of Buenos Aires, where he immediately became involved in expelling the Portuguese from Rio Grande do Sul in May of 1767. In the same year he directed the expulsion of 345 Jesuits from the twelve colleges, residences, and missions of the Río de la Plata. As a result, over fifty estates with thousands of head of cattle, slaves, and real estate were auctioned and sold. In 1770 Bucareli ousted English settlers from Port Egmond in the Falkland Islands, reclaiming the islands for Spain. Soon afterward he returned to Spain, where he died.

See also **Río de la Plata.**

BIBLIOGRAPHY

Additional Bibliography

Alterach, Miguel Angel. *La expulsión de los jesuitas: Misión Bucareli y Ursúa y "Memoria histórica" de Doblas para Felix de Azara.* Buenos Aires: s.nn, 2000.

NICHOLAS P. CUSHNER

BUCCANEERS AND PRIVATEERS.

Although the term "buccaneer" is sometimes used to refer generally to maritime freebooters, in Latin American history it refers specifically to a group that arose in the Caribbean between about 1630 and 1670 to attack Spanish commerce and settlements. The buccaneers of the seventeenth century were in many ways the debased successors of the French corsairs, English sea dogs, and Dutch sea beggars. Unlike these earlier privateers, however, they had New World bases from which to operate. They also differ from later pirates in two important respects: They generally were allowed to use the ports of Spain's rivals in the region, and they often operated with the approval, either overt or tacit, of government authorities. The buccaneers ventured all over the world, but the Caribbean remained their favorite haunt until 1674, when the British enlisted the Welsh Henry Morgan to help curtail their activities.

Buccaneering communities emerged in Jamaica and western Hispaniola, especially at Old Providence, Tortuga Island, and the Bay Islands of the Gulf of Honduras, as well as the islands of the eastern Caribbean. Many of the early buccaneers were struggling French, British, and Dutch colonists who were increasingly squeezed out as sugar production replaced tobacco in the non-Spanish islands. By 1640 tobacco production exceeded demand, causing a tobacco depression that contributed to a bifurcation in land and labor to large-scale sugar plantations. This manifested itself in the Caribbean with the transition to fewer but larger landholdings and the replacement of European farm labor with African slaves.

Some of the displaced turned to a life outside the law or moved into regions abandoned by the Spanish, especially the north coast of Hispaniola, where they lived by hunting and killing wild cattle the Spaniards left behind. The term buccaneer originated with Frenchmen in the area who roasted meat in smoke shacks called boucans and thus were called boucaniers. They often sold their meat and hides to passing ships.

PRIVATEERS

The idea of employing desperadoes, most of whom were English or French, as commercial raiders in time of war probably occurred first to the French governor of Saint Christopher, L. de Poincy, in the 1630s. To legitimize and direct the actions of these groups the French, as well as the British, issued letters of marque, essentially authorizing raids against the ships of the wartime enemy. Privateers, who held such letters of marque, were provided sovereign sanction for their raids; in exchange, the French and British governments enlisted cheap naval muscle that was effective in interrupting commerce and, according to the letters of marque, received a portion of the bounty recovered. In the ensuing decades the legitimacy of the buccaneers', or privateers', activities depended on the state of relations and policies between the governments of England, France, and Spain.

The practice of privateering took place during the era of the buccaneers, and parsing the difference between a privateer raid and a buccaneer raid is often a point of historical interpretation (especially with regard to William Kidd) given the dubious legality of many expeditions and the fact that the privateer ranks were almost exclusively filled by buccaneers; moreover, the gray area created by enlisting privateers was, at least at first, of benefit to the French and English governments. Most famous among those issued letters of marque were Francis Drake, Henry Morgan, and William Kidd.

In practice, the role of privateers ventured far beyond that of interrupting commerce. The French and English governments could not always control or stop the buccaneers once peace was restored. Furthermore, even when they did not openly encourage the buccaneers, the marauders found friendly ports in the non-Spanish Caribbean and along the North American coast as far north as Boston. Their tactics were violent; calculated terror became one of their most important weapons as they created a climate of fear among the Spanish colonists. Promising to spare the lives of those who did not resist, they typically fulfilled their promises to torture and murder those who did.

THE ENGLISH BUCCANEERS

The English buccaneers operating from Port Royal, Jamaica, flourished between 1650 and 1680. Between 1655 and 1661 alone, Henry Morgan's privateers instigated a reign of terror by pillaging eighteen cities, four towns, and nearly forty villages. Following major raids on Cuba in 1665-1666, the leadership of the Port Royal privateers fell to Morgan, a brilliant tactician who launched several successful but brutal enterprises against strategic transit routes in Panama and Nicaragua. His reputation climaxed when he led an expedition in 1668 to Portobelo, Panama, surprising the garrison there by entering from a swampy, forested area at night. He pillaged the town and killed most of its inhabitants. After going to Maracaibo, Venezuela, but discovering little booty there, Morgan still managed to take three Spanish ships loaded with silver. His final and largest expedition, in 1670, was an assault on Santa Marta, Rio Hacha, Portobelo, and Panama City, which he burned to the ground.

When the Treaty of Madrid (1670) established peace between Spain and England, England no longer needed privateers. Governor Sir Thomas Lynch of Jamaica attempted to stifle the buccaneering enterprise altogether. When his lack of sufficient armed forces made this difficult, two of his successors, Lord John Vaughan and the earl of Carlisle, employed Henry Morgan as lieutenant governor of Jamaica and specifically instructed him to suppress buccaneering. Although his efforts were at first only somewhat successful, as demonstrated by major buccaneer raids on Santa Marta in 1677 and on the Honduran coast in 1678, after 1685 the rise of public opposition and arrival of a new frigate squadron led to the decline of buccaneering. Many buccaneers spread outside the Caribbean, and their activities degenerated into piracy.

THE FRENCH BUCCANEERS

Throughout this period the French island of Tortuga remained an unmolested harbor for buccaneers. The French, not having signed a treaty with Spain, continued to allow buccaneers to use their Caribbean ports. With the encouragement of Governor d'Ogeron of Tortuga, beginning in 1665 the great buccaneers Francois L'Ollonai (Jean-David Nau) and Michel le Basque carried out extensive plundering of the Caribbean even as d'Ogeron attempted to establish a more respectable colony on the coast of Haiti.

The Tortuga buccaneers played a large part in the Caribbean theater of the third Anglo-Dutch War (1672–1678). Still, like the English, the French buccaneers preferred to attack Spanish ships and settlements, which was a more lucrative activity than participating in war. The Tortuga buccaneers achieved great success between 1678 and 1685, gaining a reputation for savagery. The names of Van Horn, de Graaf, de Grammont, and the Marquis de Maintenor stand out among the raiders of Venezuela, Trinidad, San Juan de Ulua (Veracruz), and the Yucatan coast. Eventually, however, the French government also felt compelled to combat the atrocities of the buccaneers.

As had the Dutch in the Treaty of the Hague (1673) and the English in the treaties of Windsor and Madrid, France promised Spain in the Truce of Ratison (1684) to stop supporting privateers and buccaneers. The actual end to buccaneering took longer to achieve, of course. Some buccaneers were bribed into royal service, as in the case of Governor du Casse of Saint Domingue (now the Dominican Republic), who was eventually able to pay off and disband most of the buccaneers. His forces helped halt further raids, and after Saint Domingue was ceded to France in 1697 by the Treaty of Ryswyck, du Casse persuaded the remaining buccaneers on Tortuga to abandon their activities and settle on the newly recognized French territory to the south. The era of buccaneering thus concluded at the turn of the seventeenth century; in 1697 France agreed to end its buccaneer raids in exchange for recognition of its authority over Saint Domingue, although some continued their activities as pirates. Perhaps more symbolically, in 1701 William Kidd was tried for piracy in England and hanged.

See also **Morgan, Henry; Piracy.**

BIBLIOGRAPHY

Burney, James. *History of the Buccaneers of America*. London, Unit Library, 1902. Reprint of 1816 edition.

Exquemelin, Alexander D. *The Buccaneers of America*. London: Folio Society, 1972 (originally published in 1864).

Haring, C. H. *The Buccaneers in the West Indies in the XVII Century*. New York: E. P. Dutton and Company, 1910.

Newton, Arthur Percival. *Colonising Activities of the English Puritans*. New Haven, CT: Yale University Press, 1914.

Parry, J. H. *A Short History of the West Indies*, 4th ed. New York: Macmillan, 1987.

Père P-F-X. Charlevoix, *Histoire de l'Isle Espagnole ou de S. Domingue*, 2 vols. Paris, 1731; repr. New York, 1943.

BLAKE D. PATTRIDGE

BUDDHISM. Most Latin American Buddhists are of Japanese ancestry and live in Brazil, which has about 175,000 Buddhists. (Brazil has 491,000 persons of Japanese ancestry, Peru has 45,000, and Bolivia has 10,000.) From 1900 until the 1970s approximately 250,000 Japanese immigrants entered Brazil, mostly as agricultural laborers on coffee plantations. After several years they often were able to save enough money to purchase their own farms. Over the years Japanese immigrants and their descendants increasingly adopted Catholicism. By the 1958 census 42.8 percent of Japanese Brazilians had converted to Catholicism, while 44.5 percent remained Buddhists.

Suzuki, who analyzed census data from the 1950s on Japanese Brazilians, determined that adherents of Buddhism and other "Japanese religions" comprised 76.6 percent of the immigrant *issei*, 32.5 percent of the second-generation *nisei*, and 21.4 percent of third- and fourth-generation *sansei* and *yonsei*. Among both immigrants and their descendants, older people were approximately twice as likely as younger people to follow Japanese religions. Individuals with more schooling in Japan practiced a Japanese religion more often than those with more schooling in Brazil. In rural areas more Japanese Brazilians followed Japanese religions (54.8 percent) than in urban areas (41.7 percent). There was no significant difference between men and women in their commitment to Japanese religions.

Mizuki offers a variety of reasons for the declining numbers of Buddhists. Japanese Brazilians had their children baptized as Catholics to help their children get ahead through the Compadresco (godparent) relationship. Catholic teachers suggested that their Japanese students be baptized to avoid teasing by their peers about being sinners. Also, during World War II, Japanese-language schools and newspapers were shut down and speaking Japanese in public was forbidden. Japanese Brazilians had to learn more Portuguese, consequently developing a broader knowledge about Brazilian culture, including Catholicism.

In recent years Japanese-language newspapers, magazines, radio stations, and schools have emerged, especially in São Paulo, where 75 percent of Japanese Brazilians live. While there are few Japanese immigrants today, there is a large contingent of overseas Japanese businessmen and their families in São Paulo.

See also **Japanese-Latin American Relations.**

BIBLIOGRAPHY

Teiiti Suzuki, *The Japanese Immigrant in Brazil*, vol. 2 (1969), esp. pp. 121–131.

Thomas E. Weil, et al., *Area Handbook for Brazil*, 3d ed. (1975).

John Mizuki, *The Growth of Japanese Churches in Brazil* (1978), esp. pp. 16–19.

Hiroki Kanazawa and Leo Loveday, "The Japanese Immigrant Community in Brazil: Language Contact and Shift," in *Journal of Multilingual and Multicultural Development* 9 (1988): 423–435.

Additional Bibliography

Albuquerque, Leila Marrach Basto de. *Seicho-no-Ie do Brasil: Agradecimento, obediência e salvação*. São Paulo: FAPESP: Annablume, 1999.

Fujiwara, Eiko. *El Zen y su desarrollo en México*. Ecatepec: CEAPAC; México, D.F.: Plaza y Valdés Editores, 1998.

Fukumoto Sato, Mary Nancy. *Hacia un nuevo sol: Japoneses y sus descendientes en el Perú: Historia, cultura e identidad*. Perú: Asociación Peruano Japonesa del Perú, 1997.

Irie, Toraji, and Toru Yano. *Hojin kaigai hattenshi*. 2 v. 2nd ed. Tokyo: Hara Shobo, 1981.

Lesser, Jeff. *Searching for Home Abroad: Japanese Brazilians and Transnationalism*. Durham: Duke University Press, 2003.

Masterson, Daniel M., and Sayaka Funada-Classen. *The Japanese in Latin America*. Urbana: University of Illinois Press, 2004.

Morimoto, Amelia. *Los japoneses y sus descendientes en el Perú*. Lima, Peru: Fondo Editorial del Congreso del Perú, 1999.

Nakamaki, Hirochika. *Japanese Religions at Home and Abroad: Anthropological Perspectives.* New York: Routledge Curzon, 2003.

Ozaki, André Masao. *As religiões japonesas no Brasil.* Brazil: Missão Japonesa no Brasil; São Paulo: Edições Loyola, 1990.

Rocha, Cristina. *Zen in Brazil: The Quest for Cosmopolitan Modernity.* Honolulu: University of Hawai'i Press, 2006.

ESTHER J. PRESSEL

BUENAVENTURA. Buenaventura, Colombia's most important port. Buenaventura (1985 population of nearly 200,000) serves as the outlet to the Pacific Ocean for the agricultural and industrial produce of the Cauca Valley region. Established in 1539 amid hostility from the Noanamaes, the port's only passage through the western cordillera to the fertile Cauca Valley was provided by the treacherous Dagua River. It remained isolated and impoverished until the second half of the nineteenth century, when it began to grow as a point of export for sugar and coffee, which helped stimulate demands for the construction of the Pacific railroad to Cali. The completion of the railroad in 1915, along with the construction of the Panama Canal, defined the town's twentieth-century economic function. Although Buenaventura has a poorly developed infrastructure, it has the best port facilities in the country, through which one-half of Colombia's exports and most of its coffee travel.

See also **Coffee Industry; Sugar Industry.**

BIBLIOGRAPHY

Hernán Horna, *Transport Modernization and Entrepreneurship in Nineteenth Century Colombia: Cisneros and Friends* (1992).

David Bushnell, *The Making of Modern Colombia: A Nation in Spite of Itself* (1993).

Additional Bibliography

Poveda Ramos, Gabriel. *Historia económica de Colombia en el siglo XX.* Medellín: Universidad Pontificia Bolivariana, 2005.

DAVID SOWELL

BUENA VISTA, BATTLE OF. Battle of Buena Vista, also known as the battle of La Angostura, an indecisive engagement between the Mexican and U.S. armies that took place on 22–23 February 1847 southwest of Monterrey, with both sides claiming victory. Following the conquest of northern old Mexico, Upper California, and New Mexico, the United States sought to bring the Mexican-American War to an end by invading the central valley and capturing Mexico City. Antonio López de Santa Anna, at that time rebuilding the Mexican Army at San Luis Potosí, intercepted a message between generals Winfield Scott and Zachary Taylor outlining a plan whereby all of Taylor's regulars (the better half of his army) were to be transferred to Scott for the assault on Veracruz. Santa Anna decided to strike at Taylor's weakened army. In the dead of winter, Santa Anna marched his poorly equipped 18,000-man army north across 200 miles of inhospitable desert. Some 4,000 died or deserted.

Although President James Polk had ordered Taylor to remain on the defensive, Taylor had disobeyed and captured Saltillo on 11 November 1846. It was here that Taylor learned of Santa Anna's advance, so he fell back to a narrow ravine through which the road passed near a ranch named Buena Vista. Mexican scouts came upon American supplies which had not been burned due to the haste of the retreat. Santa Anna apparently concluded that the American army was in flight and ordered his exhausted army to make a forced march over the remaining distances separating the two armies.

By now Taylor held a strong defensive position. The Mexicans attacked on 22 February and pushed back the American left. The Mexican troops held their position throughout the night without camp fires or food. The next day the Mexicans renewed the attack. The fighting became so intense that Taylor was forced to commit his reserves to prevent his left from collapsing. The Mexicans sustained heavy casualties, particularly from the American horse-drawn "flying artillery" and the rifle-armed First Mississippi volunteers led by Colonel Jefferson Davis.

Unexpectedly, Santa Anna ordered his army to fall back, abandoning hundreds of wounded. He ordered his exhausted army on a disastrous march back across the desert to San Luis Potosí, arriving on 9 March. The Mexican Army sustained more than 10,000 casualties, and throughout the campaign, including the long marches across the desert in the winter, the United States suffered 290 dead and missing, plus 500 wounded. The Battle of Buena Vista concluded the fighting in northern Mexico. Zachary Taylor returned to the United States and entered politics. With a war-hero reputation, Taylor won the U.S. presidency in 1848.

See also **Mexico, Wars and Revolutions: Mexican-American War; Santa Anna, Antonio López de.**

BIBLIOGRAPHY

Nathaniel W. Stephenson, *Texas and the Mexican War* (1921).

Wilfrid Hardy Callcott, *Santa Anna: The Story of an Enigma Who Once Was Mexico* (1936).

Carlos María De Bustamante, *El nuevo Bernal Díaz del Castillo; o sea, Historia de la invasión de los anglo-americanos en México*, 2 vols. (1949).

Additional Bibliography

Heidler, David S., and Jeanne T. Heidler. *The Mexican War*. Westport, CT: Greenwood Press, 2006.

Vázquez, Josefina Zoraida, ed. *México al tiempo de su guerra con Estados Unidos, 1846–1848*. México: Secretaría de Exteriores, El Colegio de México, Fondo de Cultura Económica, 1997.

ROBERT SCHEINA

BUENA VISTA SOCIAL CLUB.

The Buena Vista Social Club was a black members-only club in eastern Havana that became a hotspot for musicians to meet, play together and experiment, which reached its zenith in the 1940s. The name has become an umbrella term referring to the frenzy of musical output that marked Cuba's "golden age of music" from the 1930s through the 1950s. Its fame owes much to the revival of the 1990s, when Cuban musician Juan de Marcos González teamed with American guitarist Ry Cooder and several musicians from the original club's heyday to produce the album *Buena Vista Social Club* in 1997.

The album enjoyed both international popularity and critical acclaim for its revival of traditional Cuban rhythms; in 2003, the American magazine *Rolling Stone* deemed the album no. 260 of the "500 Greatest Albums of All Time." Soon after the release of the album the group was invited to play at Carnegie Hall in New York City, where German film director Wim Wenders began to create a documentary film also entitled *Buena Vista Social Club*. The film, which traced the history of the group and featured extensive interviews with band members, garnered critical acclaim and was nominated for an Academy Award for Best Documentary Feature in 2000. The film reportedly grossed over $23 million, a huge sum for a documentary, and was praised not just for the music but for the spotlight it placed on the musicians who played only for enjoyment, without prospects for financial reward.

The success of the BVSC projects, with their focus on the skill and originality of Cuban musicians of a previous era, allowed some of the original members belated recognition of their talents. Vocalist Ibrahim Ferrer, pianist Rubén González, and guitarist and vocalist Compay Segundo, who lived to be 95, were able to enjoy the renewal of interest in their passion before passing away.

See also **Compay Segundo; Music: Popular Music and Dance.**

BIBLIOGRAPHY

Buena Vista Social Club (recording, 1997).

Buena Vista Social Club (documentary film, 2000, and other information). Online at http://www.pbs.org/buenavista/.

SEAN H. GOFORTH

BUENOS AIRES.

The city of Buenos Aires was first settled in 1536 by the explorer Pedro de Mendoza, whose attempt to establish a permanent outpost of the Spanish colonial empire on the banks of the Río de la Plata estuary failed after five difficult years. It was not until 1580 that an expedition from Asunción, Paraguay, led by Juan de Garay, succeeded in permanently settling the city of Buenos Aires (whose name means "good airs or winds" after a popular patron saint of navigators, Nuestra Señora Santa María de Buen Aire). From humble beginnings the city grew to become one of the most important urban centers in the world. Moreover, it came to dominate the rest of the Argentine republic in a manner that has few parallels.

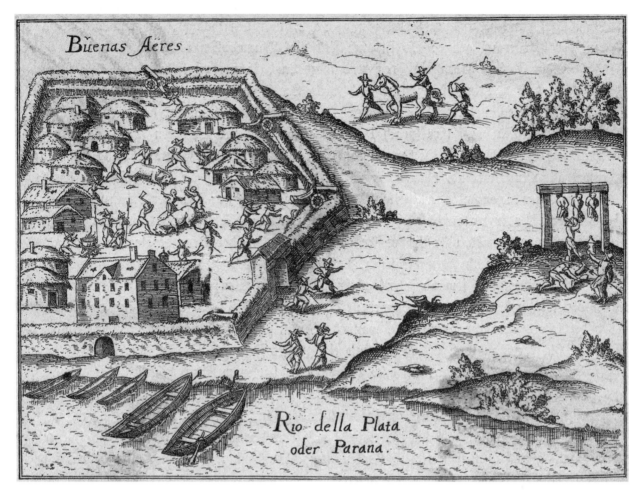

An illustration of Buenos Aires as an early European settlement on the Rio de la Plata, 16th century. © BETTMANN/ CORBIS

THE CITY

During the Spanish colonial period (1580–1810), the city of Buenos Aires served primarily as an administrative and commercial center. Despite crown restrictions that limited trading activities, the city's strategic location as the principal outlet to the Atlantic for the growing agricultural production of its immensely fertile hinterland led inevitably to its increasing importance within the Spanish realm. In 1618 it became the seat of an imperial governorship and in 1776 was named the fourth viceregal capital of the Americas. At that time, its administrative authority extended through most of southern South America. The population of the city dominated by bureaucrats and merchants increased from some 14,000 people in 1750 to 40,000 by 1800.

The movement for Argentine independence from Spanish control began in the city of Buenos Aires on May 25, 1810, with the convocation of a *cabildo abierto* (open town meeting) and the replacement of the peninsular viceroy with a creole-dominated junta. Over the next decade the city served as the main center of revolutionary activity as a variety of governing bodies, or triumvirates, sought to lead the break from Spain while retaining the territorial integrity of the viceroyalty. During this period a major split occurred among the creole leadership between Unitarios, those who favored a strong centralized government located in Buenos Aires, and Federales, who championed provincial autonomy. Independence was officially declared in 1816 and confirmed with military victories in the early 1820s.

Independence ended the administrative control the city had once enjoyed over its viceregal dominions, but at the same time it set in motion forces and events that assured Buenos Aires's dominance over the emerging nation it was destined to lead. The elimination of restrictions on trade that came with independence enabled the city to flourish economically. At the same time, the disappearance of the crown protection that had favored certain cities in the interior produced in them a corresponding decline, which led to their subordination to the nation's main port, whose inhabitants became known as *porteños*. Serving as the capital both of the province of Buenos Aires and of the nation, except for minor interruptions, the city developed a predominance in the nineteenth century that resulted in frequent wars and antagonisms with the rest of the republic. These clashes were resolved to some degree in 1880 with the establishment of a separate federal capital district.

The population growth of Buenos Aires paralleled the city's economic and political expansion. By 1860 the number of porteños had more than doubled since the turn of the century, reaching almost 100,000 in that year. This expansion paled, however, in comparison with that which followed. Between 1869 and 1914 the city's population exploded from 177,000 to 1,577,000, making Buenos Aires one of the world's ten largest cities. By 1914 one in five Argentines lived in the city, and when the surrounding provincial cities of what was called Greater Buenos Aires were included, the proportion reached one in four.

Massive foreign immigration fueled this demographic explosion. Beginning slowly in the mid-nineteenth century and gaining increasing momentum until the outbreak of World War I, waves of immigration brought hundreds of thousands of foreigners to settle in Argentina. The federal capital absorbed many of these: By 1914 one of every two porteños was of foreign birth. About 80 percent of these new arrivals were from Italy and Spain. Also significant within the city was a sizable Jewish community, mostly from Russia, and smaller but important groups from Britain, France, Germany, and the Ottoman Empire.

Rapid economic growth in the country as a whole, which was based primarily on agricultural exports and foreign investment, accompanied the immigration and demographic expansion. This economic growth in turn spurred the modernization of the city. Between 1870 and 1910 Buenos Aires was transformed from an overgrown riverside town to an imposing cosmopolitan metropolis and the major capital city of Latin America. During this period there were extensive public improvements in transportation, sanitation, street paving, and services such as gas, water, and electricity. The city was also the main terminus for Latin America's most extensive railroad system and the site of major new port facilities. Widespread civic beautification programs led some to call Buenos Aires the Paris of South America. Even with its growth and change, however, the capital retained the bureaucratic-commercial character that had marked it since the colonial period.

The modernization and beautification of Buenos Aires continued throughout the twentieth century. By the 1940s the city boasted a public transportation system that included Latin America's first major subway as well as streetcars, buses, and taxis. To accommodate these new conveyances, the colonial grid pattern of narrow, congested streets was broken by the construction of broad new avenues to open up the capital's downtown and link it with the rapidly growing suburban districts. At the same time, imposing multistory residential and commercial buildings appeared in the center and near north side, complementing the horizontal growth of the capital.

Another factor in the growth of Buenos Aires in the twentieth century was industrialization. Between 1914 and 1964, for example, the number of industrial establishments in the metropolitan area grew from 17,000 to 73,000 and the number of people employed in them increased from 308,000 to 726,000. Through the twentieth century, Buenos Aires and its surrounding suburbs contained 40 percent of all Argentine industry and more than 50 percent of those who toiled in industrial occupations.

This growth of industry has had important demographic consequences. Opportunities for employment in the expanding manufacturing sector of Buenos Aires encouraged native-born Argentines from the interior to relocate to the capital and its environs. Beginning in earnest in the 1930s, hundreds of thousands of *provincianos* undertook the trek to the capital, largely compensating for the decline in foreign immigration following the Great Depression. Settling primarily in the suburban areas surrounding the capital, they contributed significantly to the rapid growth of Greater Buenos

Shantytown outside Buenos Aires, Argentina, 2001. Despite a thriving downtown business district and exclusive residential areas, Buenos Aires continued to struggle with infrastructure and housing deficiencies at the beginning of the twenty-first century. © REUTERS/CORBIS

Aires, which by the early twenty-first century contained more than three times as many inhabitants (10,000,000) as the capital (3,000,000). The continuing flow into the metropolitan area maintained its demographic predominance: It is now home to one in three Argentines.

The pattern of growth and settlement in Buenos Aires has been from the central core outward. Foreign-born immigrants and native-born migrants alike have gravitated toward the more open and accessible outlying districts of the city and its suburbs, which have grown at phenomenal rates. Despite this outward expansion, the central historical core has remained the vital heart of the city and, in many respects, of the country, as the principal location of the nation's main governmental, com-

mercial, and financial buildings, and as the site of its most important social and cultural institutions.

A coalition of national and local leaders has directed the growth of Buenos Aires. As the seat of national administration, the city has been officially under the jurisdiction of federal authorities who retain ultimate control over its governance and provide such essential services as fire and police protection and education. From 1880 to 1996, local administration was under the direction of an *intendente* (intendant) appointed by the national government, who served in conjunction with an elected *concejo deliberante* (city council). Since 1996 the intendant has been popularly elected, a change meant to give local government greater autonomy and authority.

Containing from 10 to 15 percent of the nation's population, Buenos Aires has been a valued prize for political parties competing in national elections. The capital has also been the locale for most of the principal political developments in the nation's history. These events have ranged from the street rallies and demonstrations of democratic election campaigns, to the frequent military takeovers that marked the nation between 1930 and 1976, to the popular protests related to the "Dirty War" of the 1970s and 1980s, to the economic crisis of 2001–2002.

During the 1990s the city underwent some major transformations, driven by private-sector investment. These included the renovation of the port area, Puerto Madero, into a complex of swank restaurants, apartments, and bars and the refurbishing of the centrally-located Mercado de Abasto (Provisions Market) into an upscale shopping center, accompanied by a process of gentrification that led to the removal of low-cost housing and its inhabitants from the surrounding area. At the same time, United States-style shopping malls proliferated to the point that by the late 1990s Buenos Aires boasted one-third of the national total (with less than 10 percent of the population) and the metropolitan area half the country's megastores. In addition, in the downtown area and to the north so-called "smart" multistory office buildings designed for up-to-date computer use began to dominate the cityscape along with numerous international hotels. In well-to-do neighborhoods such as the *Barrio Norte* (Northern Neighborhood) and Belgrano, exclusive self-contained torre (garden tower) high-rise condominiums, offering modern amenities and, through controlled access, personal security, became increasingly popular for those who could afford them. In the northern suburbs, connected to the center of the city by a growing network of superhighways, gated residential communities offered similar security and comfort for those who preferred not to live in the capital itself.

By the beginning of the twenty-first century, Buenos Aires and its surrounding region, representing the tenth largest urban agglomeration in the world, aspired to "global city" status. While size and continued modernization underpinned these aspirations, problems of infrastructure and environmental issues clouded the city's prospects. Moreover, development remained uneven. Whereas the downtown held its own and the northern neighborhoods and suburbs flourished, the southern part of the city and many of the suburbs to the south and west, where most of the metropolitan area's *villas miserias* (shantytowns) were located, languished. Indeed, this historical division was accentuated both by the growth of exclusive residences and suburban enclaves and a severe economic crisis in the first years of the new century. It seemed likely, therefore, that aspirations to "global city" status would not be fully realized while these obstacles and inequalities persisted.

THE PROVINCE

The city of Buenos Aires has historically had a close and significant relationship with the surrounding province of the same name. Since independence, the province has been Argentina's largest, wealthiest, and most influential. Much of this influence derives from the fact that it contains the heart of the grassy plain known as the Pampa, the principal location and source of Argentina's great agricultural wealth. Almost half of the nation's sheep and cattle are raised in the province, which also produces much of the country's wheat, corn, oats, and barley. For much of its history, the land was controlled by a small group of owners called *estancieros*, whose family-owned estates (*estancias*) were passed down from generation to generation. For much of the period after independence it was the estancieros who dominated both provincial and national political life.

The province of Buenos Aires has experienced many of the same socioeconomic changes as has the city. Foreign immigration had a great impact, dramatically changing the province's social and demographic composition. Overall, between 1857 and 1941 the province received the greatest number of immigrants of any area in the country, slightly more than two million people, mostly from Italy and Spain. By 1914 foreigners represented more than one in three of the province's inhabitants. Beginning in the 1930s, however, the province witnessed a massive internal migration, especially to the suburban counties (*partidos*) of Greater Buenos Aires. In 1914, these counties contained a total population of 458,000 persons (22 percent of the provincial total); by 2000 that number had skyrocketed to 10,000,000 (80 percent of the provincial total). This population growth contributed to a significant urbanization of the province as a whole, especially in Greater Buenos Aires but also in such cities as Bahía Blanca, La Plata (the provincial capital), Mar del Plata, and Tandil. Much of the major industrial growth of the post-1930 era has also taken place within the province, especially in Greater Buenos Aires and along the coastal area in general.

Being the country's largest province in terms of population with 30 to 35 percent of the national total has meant a corresponding political importance. With the single largest concentration of the country's voters, this rich electoral bounty has often made the province the scene of some of the country's fiercest—and occasionally most violent—political struggles. Underscoring the electoral importance of the province is the fact that in only one instance (1916) has an Argentine captured the nation's presidency without also carrying the province. Ironically, no governor or other major political figure of the province has been able to win the presidency in an open election despite the enormous electoral advantages that control of the provincial administration provides.

See also **Porteño; Argentina: The Nineteenth Century; Argentina: The Twentieth Century; Bahía Blanca; Dirty War; Garay, Juan de; La Plata; Mar del Plata; Mendoza, Pedro de; Unitario.**

BIBLIOGRAPHY

Keeling, David J. *Buenos Aires: Global Dreams, Local Crises.* Chichester, U.K., and New York: Wiley, 1996.

Romero, José Luis, and Luis Alberto Romero, eds. *Buenos Aires: Historia de cuatro siglos.* 2 vols. Buenos Aires, Editorial Abril, 1983.

Ross, Stanley R., and Thomas F. McGann, eds. *Buenos Aires, 400 Years.* Austin: University of Texas Press, 1982.

Scobie, James R. *Buenos Aires: Plaza to Suburb, 1870–1910.* New York: Oxford University Press, 1974.

Welch Guerra, Max, ed. *Buenos Aires a la deriva: Transformaciones urbanas recientes.* Buenos Aires: Biblos, 2005.

RICHARD J. WALTER

BUENOS AIRES CONFERENCES. *See* **Pan-American Conferences: Buenos Aires Conference (1936).**

BULAS CUADRAGESIMALES. Bulas Cuadragesimales, new ecclesiastical indulgences introduced into the Spanish Indies in 1794. Because these *bulas cuadragesimales* allowed the grantee to eat meat up to four days a week during Lent, except for the first four days and Holy Week, they took on the label "meat bulls" (*bulas de carne*). Calculated to raise crown revenues during the severe fiscal crisis of the 1790s, income from these indulgences never approached revenues produced from the long-standing Bulas De Santa Cruzada. In 1800 in the Viceroyalty of Peru, net revenues from *bulas cuadragesimales* amounted to 5,000 pesos, whereas income from bulls of the Holy Crusade approached 80,000 pesos.

See also **Catholic Church: The Colonial Period.**

BIBLIOGRAPHY

Additional Bibliography

Hernández, Francisco Javier. *Colección de bulas, breves y otros documentos relativos a la iglesia de América y Filipinas.* 2 v. Vaduz, Kraus Reprint, 1964.

JOHN JAY TEPASKE

BULAS DE SANTA CRUZADA. Bulas de Santa Cruzada, ecclesiastical indulgences or remissions of temporal or purgatorial punishment dispensed for payment of a fee or donation. In 1509 Pope Julius II awarded the Spanish crown the right to collect fees for the *bulas de santa cruzada* (Bulls of the Holy Crusade) in Spain, which, on 5 September 1578, Pope Gregory XIII extended to the Spanish Indies. By agreement with the pope, royal income generated by indulgences was reserved exclusively for fighting the heathens, heretics, schismatics, and enemies of the Catholic faith and for building religious edifices such as Saint Peter's in Rome and San Lorenzo del Escorial in Spain. Spanish monarchs, however, used the steady revenues from the *bulas* for their own purposes and in the late eighteenth century to meet financial exigencies throughout the Indies. In 1800 net income from these indulgences amounted to approximately 250,000 pesos annually in Mexico and 80,000 pesos in Peru.

See also **Catholic Church: The Colonial Period.**

BIBLIOGRAPHY

Recipilación de leyes de los reynos de las Indias, 4 vols. (1681; repr. 1973), libro I, título XX.

Gabriel Martínez Reyes, *Finanzas de las 44 diócesis de Indias, 1515–1816* (1980).

Additional Bibliography

Hernández, Francisco Javier. *Colección de bulas, breves y otros documentos relativos a la iglesia de América y Filipinas.* 2 v. Vaduz, Kraus Reprint, 1964.

JOHN JAY TEPASKE

BULLFIGHTING. Bullfighting, a colorful spectacle combining ritualized drama, big business, and life-and-death ballet, is considered the national fiesta of Spain. Along with Catholicism and the Spanish language, the conquistadores brought to the New World the age-old Iberian custom of playing with the bull and evading its charges. Spain has always been the center of the bullfighting world, but parts of Latin America have an extensive and passionate bullfighting history. Mexico and Venezuela have produced important matadors who have played a key role in the history of the spectacle.

Professional bullfighting on foot dates from the 1770s. Long before that, however, New World Spaniards, especially noblemen on horseback, enjoyed challenging charging bulls. The forces of Hernán Cortés conquered the Aztecs of Tenochtitlán (Mexico City) in 1521, and by 1529 the town council had mandated bullfights for every August 13 to honor Saint Hipólito and celebrate the conquest of the city.

The first ranch in the New World to raise fighting bulls was established by the conquistador Juan Gutiérrez Altamirano, a cousin of Cortés, who in 1527 received the town of Calimaya from the crown. He subsequently acquired other lands in the Toluca Valley and formed the Atenco hacienda, importing twelve pairs of fighting bulls and one hundred cows from Navarre (the cradle of bullfighting in Spain). Thus was established the renowned Atenco Bull Ranch, which survives as the Mexicapán Ranch.

Mexico's first major matador was Rodolfo Gaona (1888–1975). Gaona became a full matador in Spain in May 1908, and he performed successfully there and in Latin America from 1908 to 1920 and in Mexico from 1921 to his retirement in 1925.

Another notable Mexican contribution to world tauromachy was Carlos Arruza (1920–1966). He took the *alternativa* (ceremony to become a full matador) in Mexico City in 1940 and began performing in Spain in 1944, where he was an immediate success. He had extraordinary courage and good technique and was excellent at placing the *banderillas* (barbed, decorated sticks) into the bull. At the top of his form in 1945, he appeared in 108 bullfights in Spain and France (more than any other matador). Retiring in 1953, he returned as a *rejoneador* (bullfighter on horseback) in 1956.

Although Peru has a long history of bullfights (dating back to 1540) and the oldest permanent bullring still in use in Latin America (the Plaza de Acho, from 1768), Venezuelan matadors have played a much more significant role in the international bullfighting world in the twentieth century. On four occasions Venezuelan matadors have placed at the top of the list of the number of *corridas* fought during the year in Spain: César Girón in 1954 and 1956 and Curro Girón, his younger brother, in 1959 and 1961. Mexican matadors have accomplished this only twice.

César Girón (1933–1971) was the oldest of six brothers, all of whom became professional bullfighters. He took the *alternativa* in Barcelona, Spain, in 1952, with Carlos Arruza as his godfather. (Ironically, Arruza and Girón, after extensive and illustrious careers facing death at the horns of a bull, both died in auto accidents.) He met with great success from then until the end of 1958 (his first "retirement"). Girón was respected for his strong will to succeed, his technical facility, his expertise in placing the *banderillas*, and his aplomb before the bulls.

The ritualized procedures of the bullfight have a universal sameness. Latin American bullfights and bullfighters, however, share some superficial differences from those of Spain. New World matadors tend to exhibit more variety, utilizing an extensive repertoire of passes. Almost all are skilled in the placing of the *banderillas*. The fighting bull is usually somewhat smaller and lighter than the Spanish animal, giving it more mobility and speed.

For many years no Latin American matador was at the top of the bullfighting world. At the 1991 Fair of San Isidro in Madrid, however, César Rincón, a Colombian, was declared the "absolute best," and he set a record by being carried out of the bullring on his admirers' shoulders on two consecutive days.

See also **Sports.**

BIBLIOGRAPHY

Castoreño, Pepe. *Historia de los toros en Cali: Segunda época, 1940–1964.* Cali, Colombia: Feriva, 1965.

De Cossío, José María. "Toros en Méjico." In *Los toros: Tratado técnico e histórico,* vol. 4. Madrid: Espasa-Calpe, 1961.

De Cossío, José María. "Toros en el Perú." In *Los toros: Tratado técnico e histórico,* vol. 6. Madrid: Espasa-Calpe, 1981.

Díaz, Carlos F. *La historia de los toros en Ecuador.* Quito: Dino Producciones, 1997?

Garland, Antonio. *Lima y el toreo: Prólogo de Raúl de Mugaburu.* Lima: Librería Internacional del Perú, 1948.

Landaeta Rosales, Manuel. *Los toros en Caracas desde 1560 hasta.* Caracas: Peña Taurina Eleazar Sananes, 1971.

Miller, Ann D. *Matadors of Mexico.* Globe, AZ: D. S. King, 1961.

Mitchell, Timothy. *Blood Sport: A Social History of Spanish Bullfighting.* Philadelphia: University of Pennsylvania Press, 1991.

ROSARIO CAMBRIA

BULNES, FRANCISCO (1847–1924).

Francisco Bulnes (*b.* 4 October 1847; *d.* 22 September 1924), Mexican political writer. Bulnes, a native of Mexico City, received a civil and mining engineering degree from the National School of Mines. After 1874 he turned to politics, journalism, and economic affairs. He was periodically a national deputy and senator for thirty years, and in 1893 and 1903 led in the effort of the Científico group to limit presidential power. He served on numerous committees devoted to banking, mining, and financial legislation, and in 1885 he wrote on the British debt.

Bulnes won notoriety for his polemical works attacking Benito Juárez and the doctrinaire liberal (Jacobin) tradition in Mexican politics, including *El verdadero Juárez* (1904) and *Juárez y las revoluciones de Ayutla y de reforma* (1905). He later defended the regime of Porfirio Díaz in *El verdadero Díaz y la revolución* (1920). His intellectual orientation was positivist, and as a writer he was influenced by Hippolyte Taine. His critical insights have attracted many modern scholars to his work.

See also **Científicos.**

BIBLIOGRAPHY

George Lemus, *Francisco Bulnes: Su vida y sus obras* (1965).

Additional Bibliography

Jiménez Marce, Rogelio. *La pasión por la polémica: El debate sobre la historia en la época de Francisco Bulnes.* Mexico, D.F.: Instituto de Investigaciones Dr. José María Luis Mora, 2003.

CHARLES A. HALE

BULNES PINTO, GONZALO (1851–1936).

The Chilean historian Gonzalo Bulnes Pinto, son of President Manuel Bulnes Prieto (1841–1851), was educated at the Padres Franceses school and at the Instituto Nacional in Santiago, continuing his education in Europe between 1871 and 1874. Back in Chile, he established his reputation as a historian with his *Historia de la campaña del Perú en 1838* (1878), a book that did much to advance a Chilean sense of national identity. As did other historians of the period, Bulnes combined politics and scholarship, first becoming a congressman in 1882, then Intendant of Tarapacá Province in 1883, senator in 1912, and Chilean ambassador to Germany, Italy, and Argentina from the 1890s to the 1920s. He sided with Congressional forces against President José Manuel Balmaceda in 1891, and was an opponent of President Arturo Alessandri in the 1920s. Although active as a politician and diplomat, it is his work as a historian that endures. In addition to monographs on the independence period, his best known and in some respects still unsurpassed work is *La Guerra del Pacífico* (three volumes, 1911–1919), a massively researched book on the War of the Pacific (1879–1883) that creatively combined the use of traditional primary sources with innovative oral history. This highly readable book generated much criticism from military historians for asserting that Chilean victory was due to civilian leadership. Toward the end of his life Bulnes returned to the themes of independence with his *Nacimiento de las repúblicas americanas* (Birth of the American Republics, 1927), and his unfinished study of José Miguel Carrera.

See also **Alessandri Palma, Arturo; Balmaceda Fernández, José Manuel; Bulnes Prieto, Manuel; Carrera, José Miguel; Chile, Revolutions: Revolution of 1891; Chile: The Nineteenth Century; War of the Pacific.**

BIBLIOGRAPHY

Bulnes Pinto, Gonzalo. *Historia de la campaña del Perú en 1838.* Santiago de Chile: Los Tiempos, 1878.

Bulnes Pinto, Gonzalo. *Nacimiento de las repúblicas americanas.* Buenos Aires: J. Roldán, 1927.

Bulnes Pinto, Gonzalo. *La guerra del Pacífico.* 3 vols., 4th ed. Santiago de Chile: Editorial del Pacifico, 1979.

Gazmuri R., Cristián. *La historiografia chilena, 1842–1970.* Santiago de Chile: Taurus, 2006.

Ossa Santa Cruz, Juan Luis. "Gonzalo Bulnes y su Historia de la campaña del Perú en 1838." *Seminario Simon Collier,* Santiago: Instituto de Historia, Pontificia Universidad Catolica de Chile (2005): 195–222.

IVAN JAKSIC

BULNES PRIETO, MANUEL (1799–1866).

Manuel Bulnes Prieto (*b.* 25 December 1799; *d.* 19 October 1866), president of Chile (1841–1851). Born in Concepción, Bulnes became a soldier at the age of twelve. He distinguished himself in the Wars of Independence and he fought at the battle of Maipú (5 April 1818). Promoted to general in 1831, he was placed in command of the second Chilean expedition to Peru during the war against the Peru-Bolivian Confederation, and won the decisive battle of Yungay (20 January 1839). On the strength of his popularity as a war hero, he was chosen to succeed Joaquín Prieto (1831–1841) as Chile's president.

A bluff, amiable man with an enormous appetite, Bulnes served two consecutive terms; he displayed great tolerance in tranquil periods but used a firm hand at times of political agitation (1845–1846 and 1850–1851). He was the first Chilean president to use the late-colonial Casa de la Moneda as the presidential palace.

When he finished his second term in September 1851, Bulnes took charge of an army to quell a major revolt in the southern provinces, which was led by his cousin, General José María de la Cruz (1799–1875). Bulnes defeated Cruz in the bloody battle of Loncomilla (8 December 1851). In 1866, opponents of the reelection of President José Joaquín Pérez (1851–1871) proclaimed Bulnes a presidential candidate; had he won, he would have served only one month.

See also **Peru-Bolivia Confederation; Prieto Vial, Joaquín; Wars of Independence, South America.**

BIBLIOGRAPHY

Diego Barros Arana, *Un decenio de la historia de Chile: 1841–1851,* 2 vols. (1905).

Additional Bibliography

Garfias Villarreal, Jorge. *Manuel Bulnes Prieto: General del ejército de Chile, gran mariscal de Ancash y presidente de la república.* Santiago, Chile: del Instituto Geográfico Militar de Chile. 1986.

SIMON COLLIER

BUMBA-MEU-BOI.

Bumba-Meu-Boi, Brazil's richest, best-loved folk pageant, depicting the death and resurrection of an ox, its central figure. A slave, named Pai Francisco or Mateus, kills his owner's prize ox, in most versions at the request of his pregnant wife, Mãe Catarina, who craves ox tongue. Pai Francisco is captured, but because the bull is resuscitated he escapes punishment. The pageant includes drama, dance, pantomime, music, and song, the lyrics of which are composed annually and feature commentary on current events. Although the first performance was recorded in 1840 near Recife, Pernambuco, the pageant probably originated in the seventeenth and eighteenth centuries on northeastern coastal plantations as a satirical adaptation of an Iberian folk tradition by African slaves. In the Northeast, where it is most expressive, it is known as *bumba-meu-boi* (Maranhão, Piauí), *bumba* or *boi calemba* (Pernambuco), *três pedaços* (Alagoas), *boi, boi-surubi,* or *boi de careta* (Ceará), and *boizinho* (Bahia). Variants include *boi-bumbá* (Pará, Amazonas), *boi de mamão* or *melão* (Santa Catarina), *boi de chita* (Minas Gerais), and *reis de boi* (Rio de Janeiro).

The pageant is presented in most of Brazil from mid-November through Epiphany (6 January). In Maranhão and Pará, however, it appears during the June festivals (which honor saints John, Anthony, Peter, and Marsalius), often as a personal religious obligation. *Bumba-meu-boi* in Maranhão reaches heights unmatched elsewhere. African, indigenous, and, more recently, European styles of performance have evolved, each with its distinctive choreography, music, instruments, story-line variations, and apparel. The velvet, hand-beaded ox costumes and massive beaded, feathered, and ribboned hats worn by the performers rival those of Carnival in Rio.

See also **Carnival; MPB: Música Popular Brasileira.**

BIBLIOGRAPHY

Luís Da Câmara Cascudo, *Dicionário do folclore Brasileiro,* 3d ed. (1972).

Américo Azevedo Neto, *Bumba-meu-boi no Maranhão* (1983).

Jomar Da Silva Moraes, "Feasts and Festivals: Maranhão's Bumba-Meu-Bullfest!" in *Companhia do Vale do Rio Doce Annual Report 1990* (1991).

Additional Bibliography

Farias, Julio Cesar. *De Parintins para o mundo ouvir: Na cadência das toadas dos bois-bumbás Caprichoso e Garantido.* Rio de Janeiro: Litteris, 2005.

Mukuna, Kazadi wa. *An Interdisciplinary Study of the Ox and the Slave (Bumba-meu-Boi): A Satirical Music Drama in Brazil.* Lewiston, NY: E. Mellen Press, 2003.

Murphy, John P. *Music in Brazil: Experiencing Music, Expressing Culture.* New York: Oxford University Press, 2006.

GAYLE WAGGONER LOPES

BUNAU-VARILLA, PHILIPPE JEAN

(1859–1940). Philippe Jean Bunau-Varilla (*b.* 26 July 1859; *d.* 20 May 1940), French engineer and promoter of the Panama Canal. Philippe Bunau-Varilla was apparently an illegitimate child from a modest Protestant background whose mother managed to send him to the École Polytechnique on a scholarship. He attended the École des Ponts et Chaussés, where he was spellbound by a lecture of Ferdinand Márie de Lesseps. After graduation in 1884, he headed for Panama, fortunately on the same ship as Charles Dingler, the head engineer of the French Panama Canal project. When Bunau-Varilla arrived in Panama, he was assigned to head the engineering section of the Culebra and Pacific division. After the Panama Canal Company went bankrupt in 1889, he helped organize and manage the New Interoceanic Canal Company from 1894 to 1902.

Bunau-Varilla arranged the sale of the company to the U.S. government in 1902 for $40 million and then lobbied and schemed to have the Panamanians revolt so that the U.S. government could acquire a canal treaty from an independent Panamanian government. He reportedly earned several million dollars from the sale of his canal company stock when the United States acquired the rights. He maintained an intermediary role between a Panamanian revolutionary group formed around Dr. Manuel Amador Guerrero and the U.S. government. Bunau-Varilla met frequently with U.S. Assistant Secretary of State Francis Loomis and occasionally with Professor John Bassett Moore, Secretary of State John Hay, and President Theodore Roosevelt. During a meeting with Roosevelt on 29 October 1903, Bunau-Varilla was given the signal that the U.S. government would intervene to prevent Colombian soldiers from landing to combat the revolutionary forces. This signal prompted him to leave the meeting hastily and telegraph Amador that the planned revolt could proceed. While serving as Panama's minister, he quickly negotiated a canal treaty with the U.S. government in November 1903—the Hay-Bunau-Varilla Treaty—which conceded the United States all the terms it wished for in a canal government.

After the de Lesseps canal company failed, Bunau-Varilla returned to France to enter the publishing business. He acquired a share of *Le Matin,* which he managed for several decades. He was personally involved in exposing as forgeries the documents of the Austrian major C. F. Walsin-Esterhazy, which had suggested that the Jewish officer Alfred Dreyfus was guilty of treason. *Le Matin* also served as a vehicle to combat opposition to the New Interoceanic Canal Company and to promote Bunau-Varilla's views of the New World and transit affairs.

Bunau-Varilla volunteered for military service in World War I. During the war, he lobbied for chlorination of water as a means of reducing disease and illness among the French troops and after the war continued to urge the chlorination of city water supplies. He died during the German invasion of France in World War II.

See also **Hay-Bunau-Varilla Treaty (1903); Panama Canal.**

BIBLIOGRAPHY

Philippe Bunau-Varilla, *Panama: The Creation, Destruction, and Resurrection* (1913), and *From Panama to Verdun: My Fight for France* (1940).

Charles D. Ameringer, "The Panama Canal Lobby of Philippe Bunau-Varilla and William Nelson Cromwell," in *American Historical Review* 68 (January 1963): 346–363, and "Philippe Bunau-Varilla: New Light on the Panama Canal Treaty," in *Hispanic American Historical Review* 46, no. 1 (1966): 28–52.

William Spence Robertson, "Hay–Bunau-Varilla Treaty," in *Dictionary of American History,* rev. ed. (1976), p. 265.

David McCullough, *The Path Between the Seas: The Creation of the Panama Canal 1870–1914* (1977).

Gustave Anguizola, *Philippe Bunau-Varilla: The Man Behind the Panama Canal* (1980).

Additional Bibliography

Bonilla, Heraclio, and Gustavo Montañez. *Colombia y Panamá: La metamorfosis de la nación en el siglo XX.* Bogotá: Universidad Nacional de Colombia, 2004.

Perigault Sánchez, Bolívar. *Cronología complementada del Canal de Panamá, 1492–2000.* Panamá: Editorial Universitaria, 1998.

THOMAS SCHOONOVER

BUNGE, ALEJANDRO (1880–1943). The Argentine economist and statesman Alejandro Bunge was born on January 8, 1880, into a wealthy and public-spirited family of German extraction. Bunge studied engineering in Germany, graduating from the Royal University of Saxony in 1903. There he discovered the work of the economist Friedrich List, whose emphasis on industrialization influenced Bunge's subsequent career as statesman, writer, and teacher.

After practicing his profession for several years in Spain, Bunge returned to Buenos Aires around 1909. He set about organizing Argentina's labor statistics during the period 1913–1915, and then served as the director of national statistics 1915–1920 and 1923–1925. He made the first estimates of Argentina's gross national product, and frequently served as an adviser to Argentina's National Bank and the Ministry of Finance. Meanwhile he taught economics at the University of Buenos Aires, where among his students were the future economist Raúl Prebisch and Federico Pinedo, a future minister of finance.

In 1918 Bunge founded the *Revista Económica Argentina*, which played a leading role in economic policy debates during the next three decades. Bunge conceived of the world economy as organized around the large industrial countries—the *astro* (star) states—that prescribed free trade and economic specialization, according to the doctrine of comparative advantage. But Bunge believed that only those countries producing manufactured goods prospered. Thus he opposed Argentina's policy of agricultural specialization, which he believed led to slower economic growth and to financial and economic dependence on the astro states. He died on May 24, 1943.

See also **Argentina: The Twentieth Century; Pinedo, Federico; Prebisch, Raúl.**

BIBLIOGRAPHY

Bunge, Alejandro. *La economía argentina,* 4 vols. Buenos Aires: Agencia General de Librerías, 1928, 1930.

Bunge, Alejandro. *Una nueva Argentina.* Buenos Aires: Kraft, 1940.

Llach, Juan José. *La Argentina que no fué,* Vol. 1. Buenos Aires: IDES, 1985.

JOSEPH LOVE

BUNGE, AUGUSTO (1877–1948). Augusto Bunge (*b.* 25 April 1877; *d.* 1 August 1948), Argentine hygienist and politician. After graduating with honors from the Medical School of the University of Buenos Aires in 1900, Bunge specialized in public health and in 1906 was sent to Europe by the national government to study the organization of public health and safety measures in factories and workshops. He was put in charge of the Industrial and Public Health Section of the National Department of Public Health, where he launched a campaign for the improvement of working conditions in local industries, as can be seen in his *Las conquistas de la higiene social* (1910–1911). He was a founder and member of the Independent Socialist Party (PSI) and was elected to Congress for five consecutive terms in 1916, 1920, 1924, 1928, and 1932. In Congress, he actively promoted social and labor legislation, drafting in 1917 a detailed system of social insurance based on the German and British models.

Bunge's thought was representative of the fusion of biological and social ideas with a strong racialist component that characterized much of the intellectual life of turn-of-the-century Latin America. In several works he argued for a biological foundation of human ethics, and he was a firm believer in the anthropological and moral inferiority of nonwhite races to Caucasians, as stated in his book *El culto de la vida* (1915).

See also **Argentina, Political Parties: Independent Socialist Party; Public Health.**

BIBLIOGRAPHY

On Bunge's activities as a socialist leader, see Richard J. Walter, *The Socialist Party of Argentina, 1890–1930* (1977) and Horacio Sanguinetti, *Los Socialistas Independientes* (1981). On Bunge's work in public health, see Héctor Recalde, *La higiene y el trabajo,* 2 vols. (1988); on the intellectual background, see Eduardo A. Zimmermann, "Racial Ideas and Social Reform: Argentina, 1890–1916," in *Hispanic American Historical Review* 72, no. 1 (February 1992): 23–46.

Additional Bibliography

Barrancos, Dora. *La escena iluminada: Ciencias para trabajadores, 1890–1930.* Buenos Aires: Plus Ultra, 1996.

EDUARDO A. ZIMMERMANN

BUNGE, CARLOS OCTAVIO (1875–1918).

Carlos Octavio Bunge, Argentine author, educator, and positivist social critic, was born January 19, 1875, in Buenos Aires. Bunge studied law at the University of Buenos Aires and later joined the faculty there. He was the author of numerous works; among the most important are *El espíritu de la educación* (1901), *Nuestra América* (1903), and a biography of Domingo Faustino Sarmiento. While critical of tyrants, such as Juan Manuel de Rosas (ruled 1829–1852), he appreciated such modernizing authoritarian states as the Porfiriato (1876–1910) in México, which promoted order and progress. In his work he criticized the Spanish, American, and African elements of Latin American culture and society. For him, the mixture of indigenous peoples, Africans and Spaniards, which he referred to as *hibridación degenerativa* (degenerative hybridization), was the main "problem" of Latin American societies. He used this intellectual framework to explain how the process of modernization, accelerated because of the arrival of thousands of European immigrants, would affect Latin American societies. Influenced by biological social theories, but also by the nascent study of crowd psychology, he legitimated the role of the socioeconomic elite as the only group that could enhance the process of modernization. Reflecting on his own country in *Nuestra América*, he asserted that European immigration would facilitate Argentina's efforts to become one of the world's leading nations. In these respects, he was typical of many Latin American intellectuals of his generation who echoed the Eurocentric ideals of Social Darwinism and positivism. Bunge died May 22, 1918.

See also **Argentina: The Twentieth Century; Porfiriato; Positivism; Rosas, Juan Manuel de; Sarmiento, Domingo Faustino.**

BIBLIOGRAPHY

Bunge, Carlos O. *El espíritu de la educación.* Buenos Aires: Taller Tip. de la Penitenciaria Nacional, 1901.

Bunge, Carlos O. *Nuestra América: Ensayo de psicología social,* 6th ed. Buenos Aires: Vaccaro, 1918.

Bunge, Carlos O. *Sarmiento: estudio biográfico y crítico.* Madrid: Espasa-Calpe, 1926.

Romero, José Luis. *El desarrollo de las ideas en la sociedad argentina del siglo XX.* Mexico City: Fondo de Cultura Económica, 1965.

Terán, Oscar. *Vida intelectual en el Buenos Aires fin-de-siglo (1880–1910): Derivas de la "cultura científica."* Mexico City and Buenos Aires: Fondo de Cultura Económica, 2000.

DANIEL LEWIS
VICENTE PALERMO

BUÑUEL, LUIS (1900–1983).

Luis Buñuel (*b.* 22 February 1900; *d.* 29 July 1983), surrealist film director and naturalized Mexican citizen. Born in Calanda, Spain, Buñuel studied at the University of Madrid, where his friends included Salvador Dalí and Federico García Lorca. Interested in film from a very young age, Buñuel moved to Paris in 1923 and worked as assistant to the film director Jean Epstein. Buñuel's first film, *Un chien andalou* (1928), a collaborative effort with Dalí, created a scandal and made both of them famous. Their second film, *L'âge d'or* (1930), attracted praise from literary figures, but the "respectable" press was deeply shocked. Fascist thugs took their criticism to the streets, viciously attacking theaters and moviegoers. The Paris prefect of police, believing surrealism to be more dangerous than fascism, banned the film. Buñuel returned to Spain for his third film, *Las hurdes—tierra sin pan* (1932), a documentary about rural misery.

Working for the Republican government of Spain during the Civil War, he produced documentaries and was sent on a diplomatic mission to Hollywood in 1938. After Franco's victory, Buñuel remained in the United States, working on anti-Nazi projects for the Museum of Modern Art in New York, and the U.S. Army during World War II. After the war, Buñuel worked in Hollywood (1944–1946) before moving to Mexico, where he began his most prolific period, directing twenty-one films (including nineteen in Mexico) between 1947 and 1962. His *Los olvidados* (1950) won the prize for the best direction and the International Critics' Prize at the Cannes Festival in 1951, reestablishing Buñuel's international reputation. The film combined elements of a neorealist study of juvenile delinquency and social protest with dream sequences and surrealistic violence that linked *Los olvidados* to his earlier work. Among the outstanding films Buñuel directed in this period are *Subida al cielo* (1951); *El bruto* (1952); *Él* (1952); *La ilusión viaja en tranvía* (1953); *Ensayo de un crimen* (1955); *Nazarín* (1958); *La fièvre monte à El Pao* (1959); *Viridiana* (1961); and *El ángel exterminador* (1962).

Making his first three films outside the film industry afforded Buñuel greater control over his work than he had while working as director for less imaginative producers during this middle period. Nevertheless, Buñuel was able to infuse these projects with his own style while appealing simultaneously to the uneducated audiences and the aesthetically sophisticated. In the words of Raymond Durgnat, Buñuel's films "have thrills galore at a lowbrow level, and a subtler meaning on a highbrow level, and a great deal of human meaning on all levels. But their sorts of aesthetic refinement, philosophical interest, and particularly, moral issues, tend to puzzle the bourgeois middlebrow, to leave him dissatisfied and perhaps a little contemptuous" (p. 13).

Commercial success permitted Buñuel greater artistic control over his French-made films in the late 1960s and early 1970s, including *La voie lactée* (1969), *Le charme discret de la bourgeoisie* (1972), and *Le fantôme de la liberté* (1974). Buñuel sought to portray social reality while undermining conventional ideas and destroying the illusion of the inevitability of the bourgeois world. He died in Mexico City.

See also **Cinema: From the Silent Film to 1990.**

BIBLIOGRAPHY

Ado Kyrou, *Luis Buñuel: An Introduction,* translated by Adrienne Foulke (1963).

J. Francisco Aranda, *Luis Buñuel: A Critical Biography,* translated and edited by David Robinson (1976).

Raymond Durgnat, *Luis Buñuel,* new and enl. ed. (1977).

Luis Buñuel, *My Last Sigh,* translated by Abigail Israel (1983).

Paul Sandro, *Diversions of Pleasure: Luis Buñuel and the Crises of Desire* (1987).

Additional Bibliography

Buñuel, Luis. *An Unspeakable Betrayal: The Writings of Luis Buñuel.* Berkeley: University of California Press, 2000.

Evans, Peter Williams. *The Films of Luis Buñuel: Subjectivity and Desire.* Oxford: Clarendon Press, 1995.

Kinder, Marsha. *Luis Buñuel's The Discreet Charm of the Bourgeoisie.* Cambridge: Cambridge University Press, 1999.

Paranaguá, Paulo Antonio. *Mexican Cinema.* London: British Film Institute, 1995.

D. F. STEVENS

BURGOS, JULIA DE (1914–1953). Julia de Burgos (*b.* 17 February 1914?; *d.* 6 July 1953), Puerto Rican poet. Born to a poor family in Carolina, Puerto Rico, Julia Constanza Burgos García studied at the University of Puerto Rico's High School and Normal School. She taught at a small rural school while continuing her university studies. Her first work, a small typewritten edition of *Poemas exactos a mí misma* (Poems exactly like myself, 1937), was followed by *Poemas en veinte surcos* (Poems in twenty furrows, 1938) and *Canción de la verdad sencilla* (Songs of simple truth, 1939), honored by the Institute of Puerto Rican Literature. In 1940 Burgos left Puerto Rico for New York, where she lived a bohemian life. Later that year she moved to Cuba, where she remained until 1942. A failed love affair brought her back to New York, where she suffered from ill health and the alcoholism that eventually caused her death. Two poems, "Welfare Island," written in English, and "Dadme mi número" (Give me my number) foreshadowed her death, alone and anonymous, in New York. Her body was later brought to Puerto Rico and buried near the Río

Grande de Loíza, which she had glorified in one of her most famous poems.

Burgos's poems are about love, death, the passing of time, Puerto Rico, freedom, and justice. Images of rivers and the sea permeate her poetry, especially in *El mar y tú* (The sea and you), published posthumously in 1954.

See also **Literature: Spanish America.**

BIBLIOGRAPHY

Ivette Jiménez De Báez, *Julia de Burgos, vida y poesía* (1966).

Sherezada Vicioso, *Julia de Burgos, la nuestra* (1987).

Additional Bibliography

López, Ivette. *Julia de Burgos: La canción y el silencio*. San Juan, PR: Fundación Puertorriqueña de las Humanidades, 2002.

Vázquez, Lourdes. *Hablar sobre Julia: Julia de Burgos: bibliografía 1934-2002*. Austin, TX: SALALM Secretariat, 2006.

ESTELLE IRIZARRY

BURGOS, LAWS OF.

Laws of Burgos, early Spanish response to reports of abuse of the native Caribbean population. The Laws of Burgos were the response to growing complaints, especially by Dominican friars, that the colonists on Hispaniola were treating the rapidly declining native population cruelly and inhumanely. The Dominican Antonio de Montesinos stated in a sermon delivered in Hispaniola in 1511, "For with the excessive work you demand of them they fall ill and die, or rather you kill them with your desire to extract and acquire gold every day."

The Laws of Burgos, promulgated on 27 December 1512, constituted the first comprehensive legislation devoted to regulating the relationship between the Spaniards and the native population. They outlined *encomenderos'* responsibilities toward the natives they held in encomienda: bringing the natives together in new villages built near the Spaniards, ensuring that the natives received religious instruction, and providing them with food and clothing. Although at least a third of the natives would continue to labor in the gold mines, their working conditions were carefully specified and numerous abuses, such as

beating natives with whips or calling a native a "dog," were explicitly prohibited. While the laws allowed natives to be exploited, their intention was to make the exploitation "just." Despite good intentions, in practice the laws led to no improvement in the natives' living and working conditions.

See also **Indigenous Peoples.**

BIBLIOGRAPHY

Lewis Hanke, *The Spanish Struggle for Justice in the Conquest of America* (1949), pp. 17, 23–24.

Charles Gibson, ed., *The Spanish Tradition in America* (1968), pp. 61–82.

Additional Bibliography

Rivera Pagán, Luis. *A Violent Evangelism: The Political and Religious Conquest of the Americas*. Louisville, KY: Westminster/John Knox Press, 1992.

Simpson, Lesley Byrd. *The Laws of Burgos of 1512–1513: Royal Ordinances for the Good Government and Treatment of the Indians*. San Francisco: J. Howell, 1960.

MARK A. BURKHOLDER

BURLE MARX, ROBERTO (1909–1994).

Roberto Burle Marx (*b.* 1909; *d.* 4 June 1994), foremost landscape architect in Brazil. Roberto Burle Marx was born to a German businessman and his wife, a Brazilian pianist. Although he shared his mother's interest in gardening, Burle Marx originally intended to become a painter. It was while studying art in Berlin in 1928 that he discovered the beauty of Brazil's native plants, which were often neglected in the gardens of his own country.

Returning to Brazil, Burle Marx took up painting as his career and gardening as a hobby. One of his gardens attracted the attention of Lucio Costa, an architect and longtime friend, who asked Burle Marx to design a garden for a private residence. This garden, containing a variety of Brazilian plants, as opposed to the formal, European-style gardens that had been the custom, was an immediate success and the first of many commissions. Among his many award-winning projects are Flamengo Park and the plant-lined mosaic sidewalks that run along Copacabana Beach in Rio. Not limiting himself to Brazil, he designed gardens for the UNESCO headquarters in Paris, public parks in Venezuela, a waterfront renovation project in Key Biscayne, Florida, and private gardens on three continents and numerous islands.

Burle Marx planned his gardens with a painter's eye. Sharp contrasts in color and shape characterize his style. "The garden must be linked to nature," appears to be his prevailing philosophy. Other Burle Marx hallmarks are his use of stone and water plants, which grace many of his gardens.

Working so intimately with plants, Burle Marx became an advocate for the preservation of Brazil's natural environment and frequently spoke out against the threat that development poses to his beloved plants. He, himself, discovered several of the country's native plants, some of which are named after him.

See also **Architecture: Modern Architecture; Environmental Movements.**

BIBLIOGRAPHY

Geri Smith, "Thumbs Up," in *Americas* 40 (September–October 1988): 26–31.

Michael Parfit, "A Brazilian Master Who Finds the Art in Nature's Bounty, in *Smithsonian* 21 (July 1990): 96–107.

Additional Bibliography

Berrizbeitia, Anita. *Roberto Burle Marx in Caracas: Parque del Este, 1956-1961.* Philadelphia: University of Pennsylvania, 2005.

Cals, Soraia. *Roberto Burle Marx: Uma fotobiografia.* Rio de Janeiro: s.n., 1995.

Montero, Marta Iris. *Roberto Burle Marx: The Lyrical Landscape.* Berkeley: University of California Press, 2001.

SHEILA L. HOOKER

BURNHAM, LINDEN FORBES SAMPSON

(1923–1985). Born in Kitty, British Guiana in 1923, Linden Forbes Sampson Burnham was prime minister of Guyana (which until 1966 was British Guiana) between 1964 and 1980, and president between 1980 and 1985.

After receiving his law degree from the University of London, in 1949 Burnham returned to Guyana, where he joined a Marxist-Leninist party founded by Cheddi Jagan (1918–1997), the People's Progressive Party (PPP). When the PPP won the 1953 elections, Britain worried about the socialist leaning of the party-suspended the nation's constitution and reinstated colonial rule. Burnham left the PPP and in 1955 created the more moderate People's National Congress (PNC).

After the United Kingdom in 1964 introduced a new electoral system based on proportional representation, Burnham established a coalition with a right-wing party, United Force, and became the first prime minister of the nation. He pursued moderate policies until 1970, but in the 1970s, despite the anticommunist platform on which he became prime minister, Burnham established close relations with Cuba, the Soviet Union, and other socialist countries. In 1971 Burnham began a process of nationalization of foreign-owned bauxite mines, sugar plantations, and refineries. In 1973 he introduced the principle of the "paramountcy of the party," by which the three branches of government and all organizations and institutions in Guyana were subordinated to the PNC.

Burnham was reelected several times; allegations of electoral fraud had an impact on the perceived legitimacy of his administration. In 1980 the promulgation of a new constitution established the Co-operative Republic of Guyana, a process of transition from capitalism to socialism, and the position of an executive president with extensive powers (a job that Burnham filled).

He died in office, in Georgetown, Guyana in 1985, while undergoing a throat operation, and was succeeded by his vice president, Desmond Hoyte.

See also **Guyana.**

BIBLIOGRAPHY

Brotherson, Festus Jr. "The Foreign Policy of Guyana, 1970–1985: Forbes Burnham's Search for Legitimacy." *Journal of Interamerican Studies and World Affairs* 31, no. 3 (Autumn 1989): 9-35.

Economist Intelligence Unit. *Country Profile: Guyana, 1997.* London: Author, 1997.

Economist Intelligence Unit. *Country Profile: Guyana, 2007.* London: Author, 2007.

Griffith, Ivelaw L. "Political Change, Democracy, and Human Rights in Guyana." *Third World Quarterly* 18, no. 2 (June 1997): 270.

MARIANA MCLOUGHLIN

BUSCH BECERRA, GERMÁN (1903–1939).

Germán Busch Becerra (*b.* 23 March 1903; *d.* 23 August 1939), president of Bolivia (July 1937–August 1939). Busch was born in Trinidad, in the eastern department of El Beni. His father was an eccentric German medical doctor, and his mother, Raquel Becerra, was a native of Trinidad. In his early youth Busch joined the army as a cadet. He became noted for his daring, physical fitness, and hot temper—characteristics that served him well in the Chaco War.

After participating in the overthrow of presidents Daniel Salamanca, José Luis Tejada Sorzano, and David Toro, in July 1937 he assumed the presidency in the belief that all three previous presidents had been inept in their handling of the war. On 27 May 1938 Busch was elected constitutional president for the period 1938 to 1942. On 24 April 1939 he declared himself a dictator, proclaiming "military socialism" and undertaking radical reforms that included the nationalization of the Standard Oil holdings. He condemned the German-born tin magnate Mauricio Hochschild to death and nationalized the tin mines. Prevented by his cabinet from executing the sentence, in a fit of rage, Busch committed suicide in front of his aides, saying it "is best to terminate my life" to convince the Bolivian nation of the righteousness of his action. Although the suicide is an accepted historical fact, there has been some talk of assassination. Just before Busch's death a permanent peace treaty with Paraguay went into effect, although hostilities had long since ended. Busch, considered a forerunner of Bolivia's great reforms of the next three decades, has become virtually a legendary figure in Bolivian history.

See also **Chaco War; Germans in Latin America; Military Dictatorships: 1821–1945.**

BIBLIOGRAPHY

Moïsés Alcázar, *Sangre en la historia* (1956).

Augusto Céspedes, *El dictator suicida* (1956).

Porfirio Díaz Machicao, *Historia de Bolivia*. Vol. 4, *Toro, Busch, Quintanilla* (1957), pp. 59–119.

Additional Bibliography

Durán S., Juan Carlos. *Germán Busch y los orígenes de la revolución nacional: Fragmentos para una biografía*. La Paz: Honorable Senado Nacional, 1997.

Farcau, Bruce W. *The Chaco War: Bolivia and Paraguay, 1932–1935*. Westport, CT: Praeger, 1996.

Charles W. Arnade

BUSTAMANTE, ANASTASIO (1780–1853).

Anastasio Bustamante (*b.* 17 July 1780; *d.* 1853), Mexican military man and politician. Born in Jiquilpán, Michoacán, Bustamante studied medicine in Mexico City. During the struggle for independence, he joined the royal army, distinguishing himself in combat. Nevertheless, he supported Agustín de Iturbide (later emperor) in 1821. After the fall of the empire, he allied himself with the Escoceses (Scottish rite Masons), was elected vice president in 1829, and overthrew the government in January 1830. His administration (1830–1832) was noted for its conservatism, political repression, and the execution of President Vicente Guerrero. Subsequently ousted and exiled, Bustamante returned to office as president in 1837–1839, 1840, and 1841, becoming one of the most important politicians of the early republic. He also served as senator and participated in various military campaigns, the last of which was the pacification of the Sierra Gorda insurrection in 1848.

See also **Escoceses; Mexico: 1810–1910.**

BIBLIOGRAPHY

Carlos María De Bustamante, *Continuación del cuadro histórico*, 4 vols. (1953–1963).

Michael P. Costeloe, "The Triangular Revolt in Mexico and the Fall of Anastasio Bustamante," in *Journal of Latin American Studies* 20, pt. 2 (November 1988): 337–360.

Michael Costeloe, "A Pronunciamiento in Nineteenth-Century Mexico, '15 de julio de 1840,'" in *Mexican Studies/Estudios Mexicanos* 4, pt. 2 (Summer 1988): 245–264.

Jaime E. Rodríguez O., "The Origins of the 1832 Revolt," in his *Patterns of Contention in Mexican History* (1992).

Additional Bibliography

Archer, Christon I. *The Birth of Modern Mexico, 1780–1824*. Wilmington, DE: Scholarly Resources Inc., 2003.

Jaime E. Rodríguez O.

BUSTAMANTE, CARLOS MARÍA DE

(1774–1848). Carlos María de Bustamante (*b.* 4 November 1774; *d.* 21 September 1848), Mexican patriot, politician, and writer. Born in Oaxaca, Bustamante studied theology and law. He distinguished himself early as a champion of the poor, and during the Wars of Independence became defense counsel for various conspirators. One of the founders of the *Diario de Méjico* in 1805, he became famous in 1812 as the editor of the anti-government *El Jugetillo* (The Small Toy) and was chosen "elector" of the city of Mexico that year. Later he became an adviser to José María Morelos and was instrumental in convincing the insurgents to hold a congress in Apatzingán and in writing the Constitution of Apatzingán (1814). After independence he served in nearly every congress from 1822 until his death.

A strong centralist, Bustamante grew increasingly conservative as the country he loved fell into anarchy. He was extremely influential as a journalist and a pamphleteer; over his lifetime he published many newspapers and hundreds of pamphlets. Following his intellectual mentor, Father Mier Noriega y Guerra, in recovering pre-Columbian and colonial manuscripts and in creating the political myth of the ancient "Mexican Empire," Bustamante also helped to create the "official history" of independence that persists to the present day. In addition, he was one of the principal chroniclers of the period, having written Mexico's history from independence until the U.S. invasion, an event that left him "sick of soul and body" and coincided with his death.

Bustamante's most important historical works are *Cuadro histórico de la revolución de la América mexicana* 3 (1823–1832), and *Continuación del cuadro histórico de la revolución mexicana* 4 (1953–1963). Perhaps the most significant of all his contributions was his personal diary, "Diario histórico de México," forty-eight volumes, which records the events of the period 1822–1848.

See also **Journalism in Mexico; Mexico, Wars and Revolutions: War of Independence.**

BIBLIOGRAPHY

Juan Ortega y Medina, *El historiador D. C. M. de Bustamante ante la conciencia histórica mexicana* (1963).

Edmundo O'Gorman, ed., *Guía bibliográfica de Carlos María de Bustamante* (1967).

Virginia Guedea, "Las primeras elecciones populares en la ciudad de México, 1812–1813," in *Mexican Studies/Estudios Mexicanos* 7, pt. 1 (Winter 1991): 1–28, and her "Los procesos electorales insurgentes," in *Estudios de historia novohispana* 11 (1992).

Jaime E. Rodríguez O., "The Struggle for the Nation: The First Centralist-Federalist Conflict in Mexico," in *The Americas* 49 (July 1992): 1–22.

Additional Bibliography

Castelán Rueda, Roberto. *La fuerza de la palabra impresa: Carlos María Bustamente y el discurso de la modernidad, 1805-1827.* Mexico: Fondo de Cultura Económica/Universidad de Guadalajara, 1997.

López Betancourt, Raúl Eduardo. *Carlos María de Bustamante: Legislador, 1822–1824.* Mexico: Porrúa, 2003.

López Betancourt, Raúl Eduardo. *El antifederalismo de Carlos María de Bustamante.* Mexico: Universidad Nacional Autonóma de México, 1997.

JAIME E. RODRÍGUEZ O.

BUSTAMANTE, WILLIAM ALEXANDER

(1884–1977). Born to an Irish Catholic farmer and an indigenous mother, William Alexander Bustamante became a tireless advocate of workers' rights and, eventually, the first prime minister of Jamaica. In his youth he lived in Cuba, Panama, and the United States; when he returned home, his passions were stirred by the ubiquitous poverty in Jamaica. Throughout the 1930s Bustamante spearheaded protests and workers' rallies, wrote extensively about social inequalities in Jamaica, fought for universal suffrage, and was imprisoned repeatedly for his protest activities. In 1938 he founded Jamaica's first trade union, the Bustamante Industrial Trade Union. In the 1940s he joined forces with his cousin Norman W. Manley (1893–1969), a lawyer who was forming the People's National Party (PNP). Bustamante split with the PNP in 1942, forming the Jamaica Labour Party (JLP). The JLP acquired significant clout in the 1940s and 1950s. The split between Bustamante and Manley widened over the issue of federation with other British West Indian islands, which Bustamante opposed. When the JLP won 26 of 45 seats in a general election on 10 April 1962, Bustamante was appointed premier, moving Jamaica toward independence. On 6 August 1962, the island gained its independence, and with it Bustamante became the first prime minister of Jamaica. Illness truncated his agenda two years later, and he officially retired in 1967. He died on 6 August 1977, the fifteenth anniversary of Jamaica's independence.

See also **Jamaica.**

BIBLIOGRAPHY

Hurwitz, Samuel J. "The Federation of the West Indies: A Study in Nationalism." *Journal of British Studies* 6, no. 1 (November 1966): 139-168.

Jamaican Ministry of Education, Youth and Culture. "Jamaica's National Heroes: William Alexander Bustamante." Available from http://www.moec.gov.jm/heroes/ bustamante.htm.

SEAN H. GOFORTH

BUSTAMANTE Y GUERRA, JOSÉ

(1759–1825). José Bustamante y Guerra (*b.* 1759; *d.* 1825), Spanish naval officer who served as captain-general and governor of Uruguay (1795–1810) and Guatemala (1811–1818). Bustamante distinguished himself in Spain's North African campaign in 1774 and was a member of the Malespina expedition that circumnavigated the globe between 1784 and 1791. He became governor of Uruguay in 1795 and later commanded Spanish naval forces in the Río de la Plata. He was transferred to Guatemala in 1811, where he served as captain-general until 1818. Unsympathetic to the Cádiz Constitution of 1812, Bustamante delayed implementing its reforms in Guatemala and concentrated instead on insulating Central America from the revolutionary events occurring in Mexico. He became notorious in Central American history for authoritarian rule, especially after the restoration of Ferdinand VII of Spain in 1814.

Although Bustamante subdued several revolts and maintained the loyalty of Central America when much of the rest of the Spanish Empire was in rebellion, his draconian policies stimulated animosities among the creoles and sentiment for independence, which erupted soon after his departure. He became director-general of the Spanish Navy in 1819 and died six years later in a shipwreck en route to Buenos Aires.

See also **Captain-General: Spanish America.**

BIBLIOGRAPHY

Eduardo Cárdenas, *20,000 biografías breves* (1963).

Mario Rodríguez, *The Cádiz Experiment in Central America, 1808 to 1826* (1978).

Additional Bibliography

Hawkins, Timothy. *José de Bustamante and Central American Independence: Colonial Administration in an Age of Imperial Crisis.* Tuscaloosa: University of Alabama Press, 2004.

SUE DAWN MCGRADY

BUSTAMANTE Y RIVERO, JOSÉ LUIS

(1894–1990). José Luis Bustamante y Rivero (*b.* 1894; *d.* 1990), democratically elected president of Peru (1945) who was ousted in 1948 by a military coup led by General Manuel Odría. Bustamante y Rivero, born in Arequipa, was educated as a lawyer at the universities of Arequipa and Cuzco. During his early political activities he expressed southern regionalist interests influenced by the local version of *pierolismo* (after the civilian caudillo Nicolás de Piérola). He opposed President Augusto B. Leguía's failed policies toward the provinces. In 1930, as political secretary of the Revolutionary Junta in Arequipa, Bustamante supported the military coup led by Colonel Luis M. Sánchez Cerro. Between 1934 and 1945 he held diplomatic posts in Bolivia, Paraguay, and Uruguay.

In 1945, a group of middle-class leaders of moderate populist ideology, supported by the illegal Aprista movement and the Communist Party, formed the National Democratic Front (FDN) in Arequipa. With the consent of the army, the FDN announced Bustamante's candidacy in the 1945 elections, in which he successfully defeated the right.

In several ways the Bustamante administration continued and enhanced protectionist measures introduced by the previous president, Manuel Prado. These measures included exchange and price control and import quotas. As a result, the moderate inflation that had begun to rise under the Prado administration increased substantially under Bustamante. The floating internal debt also increased, contributing to inflation. President Bustamante was under the political pressure of the well-organized Aprista Party, which was strongly represented in the parliament. A failed Aprista armed uprising in 1948 precipitated the coup by Odría, who, with the help of U.S. financial advisers, reintroduced liberal economic measures. He died in Lima.

See also **Peru, Political Parties: National Democratic Front.**

BIBLIOGRAPHY

See his *Tres años de lucha por la democracia en el Perú* (1949); Gonzalo Portocarrero Maisch, *De Bustamante a Odría* (1983).

Additional Bibliography

Díaz Orihuela, Javier. *El triunvirato de la libertad.* Lima: Gráfica Israel, 2003.

Ortiz Caballero, René. *José Luis Bustamante y Rivero.* Lima: Editorial Brasa, 1995.

Rávago Bustamante, Enrique de. *4 juristas y 1 soldado jurista: Vicente Morales Duárez, Manuel Lorenzo de Vidaurre y Encalada, Francisco García Calderón, José Luis Bustamante y Rivero, Ramón Castilla y Marquesado.* Lima: s.n., 2005.

ALFONSO W. QUIROZ

BUSTOS, HERMENEGILDO (1832–1907).

Hermenegildo Bustos (*b.* 1832; *d.* 1907), Mexican painter. Bustos lived his entire life in the town of Purísima del Rincón, Guanajuato. The diverse types of jobs he held—ice vendor, sacristan, carpenter, maguey planter, and musician—allowed him to bring to his canvases a variety of themes, which were combined with the freshness of a small-town painter who worked by assignment.

The great majority of his work consists of ex-votos, a form of religious expression popularized in the eighteenth and nineteenth centuries. These small works, painted in lamina, depict tragic scenes from which the subjects felt they had been saved by the miraculous intercession of a saint, to whom the ex-voto was dedicated. The ex-votos of Bustos are distinguished by the individuality he gave to his subjects. His talent as a portraitist enabled him to capture with a rural flavor the features of his

subjects—whom we know by name, thanks to an inscription on the ex-voto.

Bustos did more than paint models; he instilled his subjects with a character that went beyond physical features. Two of his dining-room paintings are outstanding for their iconography and extraordinary pictorial quality, recalling the botanical illustrations of the eighteenth century. The paintings must have been highly prized by Bustos, since they remained in his home until his death.

See also **Art: The Nineteenth Century; Retablos and Ex-Votos.**

BIBLIOGRAPHY

Pascual Aceves Barajas, *Hermenegildo Bustos; su vida y su obra* (1956).

Raquel Tibol, *Hermenegildo Bustos; Pintor del Pueblo,* 2d ed. (1992).

Additional Bibliography

Ortiz Angulo, Ana. *La pintura mexicana independiente de la Academia en el siglo XIX.* Mexico, D.F.: Instituto Nacional de Antropología e Historia, 1995.

ESTHER ACEVEDO

BUSTOS, JUAN BAUTISTA (1779–1830).

Bustos, an Argentinean military man and politician, was a central figure in the Rio Plata revolutionary armies during the wars of independence and the civil wars of the first half of the nineteenth century. Born in Santa María de Punilla on 29 August 1779, he played an important role in the wars of independence. He served in the military campaigns of the Peruvian highlands under the command of General Manuel Belgrano, and as the head of the Northern Army High Command, he rose up against the central government of the United Provinces in Arequito in January 1820. At that time he went to the province of Córdoba and in March had himself appointed governor, a position he held until 1829, when he was defeated by the troops of José María Paz in the Battle of San Roque in April and in La Tablada in June. Shortly after his defeat, he withdrew to Santa Fe, where he died two years later, on 18 September 1930. The role he played in these events has led historians to consider him a classic example of *caudillismo* (leadership by a strong charismatic leader) in the Rio Plata region in the first half of the nineteenth century. However, it is also worth emphasizing the importance of his legislative work, which includes the creation of the School Protection Board, reforms made to the university course of studies, the reorganization of border militias, and the legal ordering of trade and commerce.

See also **Caudillismo, Caudillo; Wars of Independence, South America.**

PABLO BUCHBINDER

BUTANTÃ INSTITUTE.

The Butantã Institute is a center for the study and development of snakebite serum. Founded by Dr. Vital Brazil in 1888, the institute was established not only to prevent deaths by snakebite, but also to find a vaccine for bubonic plague. In the early twenty-first century Butantã functions as a distributor of antivenom throughout Brazil and is also a research and production center for a variety of vaccines for diseases such as diphtheria, rabies, and tetanus. Among several biotechnological projects in the 1980s, the institute founded a blood bank. The institute is attached to Butantã Snake Farm, the largest in Latin America. Along with the farm and the institute is a museum that houses poisonous snakes and spiders. The museum, which is a popular tourist attraction, has displays that explain the functions of the institute and describe the correct treatment for snakebite. Butantã is located in Pinheiros, a suburb of São Paulo, on the grounds of the Cidade Universitária, under the control of the Ministry of Health. The university itself was built on the former Fazenda Butantã (Butantã Farm).

See also **Medicine: The Modern Era.**

BIBLIOGRAPHY

Benchimol, Jaime Larry, and Luiz Antonio Teixeira. *Cobras, lagartos and outros bichos: Uma história comparada dos institutos Oswaldo Cruz e Butantan.* Rio de Janeiro: Editora UFRJ, 1993.

Gualtieri, Regina Cândida Ellero. *Ciência e serviço: O Instituto Butantã e a saúde pública (Sao Paulo, 1901–1927).* Sao Paulo, 1994.

Marques, Otávio A. V., André Eterovic, and Ivan Sazima. *Serpentes da Mata Atlântica: Guia ilustrado para a Serra do Mar.* Ribeirão Preto, Brazil: Holos, 2001.

Schwartzman, Simon. *A Space for Science: The Development of the Scientific Community in Brazil.* University Park: Pennsylvania State University Press, 1991.

Vital Brazil, Oswaldo. *Vital Brazil e o Instituto Butantan.* Campinas, Brazil: Editora da Unicamp, 1996.

SHEILA L. HOOKER

BUTLER, SMEDLEY DARLINGTON

(1881–1940). Smedley Darlington Butler (*b.* 30 July 1881; *d.* 21 June 1940), an American marine officer popularly known as "Old Gimlet Eye." Following his commission in 1898, Butler served during the Spanish-American War and in China during the Boxer Rebellion of 1900. In 1912, Butler led marine battalions in Nicaragua that helped suppress its civil war and in 1914 at Veracruz, where U.S. forces prevented armaments from reaching Mexico's warring factions. His dominant role during the Haitian intervention in 1915 earned Butler the Congressional Medal of Honor. He was awarded the Distinguished Service Medal for his service in World War I. Butler retired as major general in 1931.

See also **Spanish-American War.**

BIBLIOGRAPHY

Lowell Thomas, *Old Gimlet Eye* (1933).

Robert E. Quirk, *An Affair of Honor: Woodrow Wilson and the Occupation of Vera Cruz* (1962).

Lester D. Langley, *The Banana Wars: An Inner History of American Empire, 1900–1934* (1983).

Additional Bibliography

Butler, Smedley D. *War Is a Racket: The Antiwar Classic by America's Most Decorated General, Two Other Anti-Interventionist Tracts, and Photographs from the "Horror of It."* Los Angeles: Feral House, 2003.

Langley, Lester D., and Thomas David Schoonover. *The Banana Men: American Mercenaries and Entrepreneurs in Central America, 1880–1930.* Lexington: University Press of Kentucky, 1995.

O'Brien, Thomas F. *The Revolutionary Mission: American Enterprise in Latin America, 1900–1945.* Cambridge, U.K.: Cambridge University Press, 1996.

THOMAS M. LEONARD

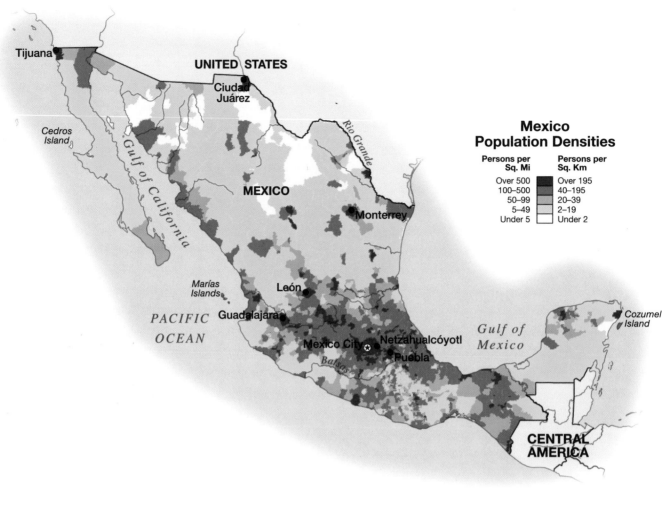

Mexico Population Densities

Persons per Sq. Mi	Persons per Sq. Km
Over 500	Over 195
100–500	40–195
50–99	20–39
5–49	2–19
Under 5	Under 2

Tijuana
UNITED STATES
Ciudad Juárez
Cedros Island
Gulf of California
MEXICO
Rio Grande
Monterrey
Marías Islands
León
PACIFIC OCEAN
Guadalajara
Gulf of Mexico
Cozumel Island
Mexico City
Netzahualcóyotl
Puebla
Balsas
CENTRAL AMERICA

Central America and the Caribbean Population Densities

Persons per Sq. Mi	Persons per Sq. Km
Over 500	Over 195
100–500	40–195
50–99	20–39
5–49	2–19
Under 5	Under 2

Grand Bahama
UNITED STATES
BAHAMAS
Gulf of Mexico
Nassau
ATLANTIC OCEAN
Andros
Havana
CUBA
Turks and Caicos Islands (U.K.)
Isla de la Juventud
Cayman Islands (U.K.)
Virgin Islands (U.S.)
Virgin Islands (U.K.)
Anguilla (U.K.)
ANTIGUA AND BARBUDA
HAITI
DOMINICAN REPUBLIC
Puerto Rico (U.S.)
MEXICO
Port-au-Prince
Santo Domingo
San Juan
Basseterre
St. John's
JAMAICA
Kingston
Hispaniola
ST. KITTS AND NEVIS
Montserrat (U.K.)
Belmopan
Guadeloupe (Fr.)
DOMINICA
BELIZE
Roseau
Martinique (Fr.)
Caribbean Sea
GUATEMALA
Castries
ST. LUCIA
Guatemala City
HONDURAS
Netherlands Antilles (Neth.)
Kingstown
Bridgetown
San Salvador
Tegucigalpa
Aruba (Neth.)
ST. VINCENT AND THE GRENADINES
BARBADOS
EL SALVADOR
Grande
NICARAGUA
St. George's
GRENADA
Managua
TRINIDAD AND TOBAGO
San José
Port-of-Spain
COSTA RICA
PANAMA
Panama City
Coiba Island
SOUTH AMERICA